2012
Poet's
MARKET®

Includes a 1-year online subscription to **Poet's Market** on

WritersMarket.com
Where & How to Sell What You Write

THE ULTIMATE MARKET RESEARCH TOOL FOR WRITERS

To register your *2012 Poet's Market* and **start your 1-year online poetry subscription**, scratch off the block below to reveal your activation code, then go to WritersMarket.com. Click on "Sign Up Now" and enter your contact information and activation code. It's that easy!

WITHDRAWN

UPDATED MARKET LISTINGS FOR YOUR INTEREST AREA
EASY-TO-USE SEARCHABLE DATABASE • RECORD-KEEPING TOOLS
PROFESSIONAL TIPS & ADVICE • INDUSTRY NEWS

Your purchase of *Poet's Market* gives you access to updated
(valid through 12/31/12). For just $9.99, you can upgrade your su
all of our best-selling Market books. Visit **WritersMark**

D1402835

25TH ANNUAL EDITION

2012 Poet's MARKET

Robert Lee Brewer, Editor

WRITER'S DIGEST
BOOKS

WritersDigest.com
Cincinnati, Ohio

Publisher & Community Leader: Phil Sexton
Managing Editor: Adria Haley

Writer's Market website: www.writersmarket.com
Writer's Digest website: www.writersdigest.com
Writer's Digest Bookstore: www.writersdigestshop.com

Distributed in Canada by Fraser Direct
100 Armstrong Avenue
Georgetown, Ontario, Canada L7G 5S4
Tel: (905) 877-4411

Distributed in the U.K and Europe by F&W Media International
Brunel House, Newton Abbot, Devon, TQ12 4PU, England
Tel: (+44) 1626-323200, Fax: (+44) 1626-323319
E-mail: postmaster@davidandcharles.co.uk

Distributed in Australia by Capricorn Link
P.O. Box 704, Windsor, NSW 2756 Australia
Tel: (02) 4577-3555

ISSN: 0883-5470
ISBN-13: 9781599632308
ISBN-10: 1599632306

Attention Booksellers: This is an annual directory of F+W Media, Inc. Return deadline for this edition is December 31, 2012.

Edited by: Robert Lee Brewer
Cover designed by: Jessica Boonstra

Interior designed by: Claudean Wheeler
Page layout by: Terri Woesner
Production coordinated by: Greg Nock
Cover illustration by: Emily Keafer

CONTENTS

CRAFT OF POETRY

INTERVIEWS OF POETS

FROM THE EDITOR

This past April, I published my first collection of poems. It was a self-published chapbook of 21 poems that I released as a limited edition. It sold out before reaching the month of May. How did it sell out so fast? I have my theories.

First, I spent more than 17 years writing poetry before putting together this collection. A lot of effort went into improving (notice that I didn't use the term perfecting) my craft. Second, I built an audience through years of blogging, online social networking, and public speaking. Third, I took care of the business end of things.

In this edition of *Poet's Market*, I hope to provide poets with all the information they need to achieve the same type of success I had in April, whether they go the self-publishing or traditional publishing route.

The sections in this book include Business of Poetry, Promotion of Poetry, Craft of Poetry, and Interviews of Poets. The business section provides poets with the nuts and bolts information to manage submissions and consider various publishing options. The promotion section guides poets through the process of audience building. Of course, the craft section looks at the actual poeming itself. The interviews section allows poets to learn from other poets and find inspiration. Hopefully, this combination of information (along with the hundreds of poetry publishing opportunities) will help poets have an amazing 2012.

Until next time, keep poeming!

Robert Lee Brewer
Senior Content Editor
Poet's Market
http://blog.writersdigest.com/poeticasides
http://twitter.com/robertleebrewer

HOW TO USE
POET'S MARKET

Delving into the pages of *Poet's Market* indicates a commitment—you've decided to take that big step and begin submitting your poems for publication. How do you *really* begin, though? Here are eight quick tips to help make sense of the marketing/submission process:

1. BE AN AVID READER. The best way to hone your writing skills (besides writing) is to immerse yourself in poetry of all kinds. It's essential to study the masters; however, from a marketing standpoint, it's equally vital to read what your contemporaries are writing and publishing. Read journals and magazines, chapbooks and collections, anthologies for a variety of voices; scope out the many poetry sites on the Internet. Develop an eye for quality, and then use that eye to assess your own work. Don't rush to publish until you know you're writing the best poetry you're capable of producing.

2. KNOW WHAT YOU LIKE TO WRITE—AND WHAT YOU WRITE BEST. Ideally, you should be experimenting with all kinds of poetic forms, from free verse to villanelles. However, there's sure to be a certain style with which you feel most comfortable, that conveys your true "voice." Whether you favor more formal, traditional verse or avant-garde poetry that breaks all the rules, you should identify which markets publish work similar to yours. Those are the magazines and presses you should target to give your submissions the best chance of being read favorably—and accepted. (See the Subject Index to observe how some magazines and presses specify their needs.)

3. LEARN THE "BUSINESS" OF POETRY PUBLISHING. Poetry may not be a high-paying writing market, but there's still a right way to go about the "business" of submitting and publishing poems. Learn all you can by reading writing-related books and magazines. Read the articles and interviews in this book for plenty of helpful advice. Surf the Internet for a wealth of sites filled with writing advice, market news and informative links. (See Additional Resources for some leads.)

4. RESEARCH THE MARKETS. Study the listings in *Poet's Market* thoroughly; these present submission guidelines, editorial preferences and editors' comments as well as contact information (names, postal and e-mail addresses, website URLs). In addition, the indexes in the back of this book provide insights into what an editor or publisher may be looking for.

However, studying market listings alone won't cut it. The best way to gauge the kinds of poetry a market publishes is to read several issues of a magazine/journal or several of a press's books to get a feel for the style and content of each. If the market has a website, log on and take a look. Web sites may include poetry samples, reviews, archives of past issues, exclusive content, and especially submission guidelines. (If the market is an online publication, the current issue will be available in its entirety.) If the market has no online presence, send for guidelines and sample copies (include a SASE—self-addressed stamped envelope—for guidelines; include appropriate cost for sample copy).

Submission guidelines are pure gold for the specific information they provide. However you acquire them—by SASE or e-mail, online, or in a magazine itself—make them an integral part of your market research.

✚	market new to this edition
⊘	market does not accept unsolicited submissions
♻	Canadian market
➲	market located outside of the U.S. and Canada
◑	online opportunity
⑤	market pays
☛	tips to break into a specific market
○	market welcomes submissions from beginning poets
◑	market prefers submissions from skilled, experienced poets; will consider work from beginning poets
●	market prefers submissions from poets with a high degree of skill and experience
◉	market has a specialized focus

5. START SLOWLY. It may be tempting to send your work directly to *The New Yorker* or *Poetry*, but try to adopt a more modest approach if you're just starting out. Most listings in this book display symbols that reflect the level of writing a magazine or publisher prefers to receive. The ○ symbol indicates a market that welcomes submissions from beginning or unpublished poets. As you gain confidence and experience (and increased skill in your writing), you can move on to markets coded with the ◑ symbol. Later, when you've built a publication history, submit to the more prestigious magazines and presses (the markets). Although it may tax your patience, slow and steady progress is a proven route to success.

6. BE PROFESSIONAL. Professionalism is not something you should "work up to." Make it show in your first submission, from the way you prepare your manuscript to the attitude you project in your communications with editors.

Follow those guidelines. Submit a polished manuscript. (See "Frequently Asked Questions" for details on manuscript formatting and preparation.) Choose poems carefully with the editor's needs in mind. *Always* include a SASE with any submission or inquiry. Such practices show respect for the editor, the publication and the process; and they reflect *your* self-respect and the fact that you take your work seriously. Editors love that; and even if your work is rejected, you've made a good first impression that could help your chances with your next submission.

7. KEEP TRACK OF YOUR SUBMISSIONS. First, do *not* send out the only copies of your work. There are no guarantees your submission won't get lost in the mail, misplaced in a busy editorial office, or vanish into a black hole if the publication or press closes down. Create a special file folder for poems you're submitting. Even if you use a word processing program and store your manuscripts on disk, keep a hard copy file as well (and be sure to back up your electronic files).

Second, establish a tracking system so you always know which poems are where. This can be extremely simple: index cards, a chart created with word processing or database software, or even a simple notebook used as a log. (You can enlarge and photocopy the Submission Tracker or use it as a model to design your own version.) Note the titles of the poems submitted (or the title of the collection if you're submitting a book/chapbook manuscript); the name of the publication, press, or contest; date sent; estimated response time; and date returned *or* date accepted. Additional information you may want to log: the name of the editor/contact, date the accepted piece is published and/or issue number of the magazine, type/amount of pay received, rights acquired by the publication or press, and any pertinent comments.

Without a tracking system, you risk forgetting where and when manuscripts were submitted. This is even more problematic if you simultaneously send the same manuscripts to different magazines, presses or contests. And if you learn of an acceptance by one magazine or publisher, you *must* notify the others that the poem or collection you sent them is no longer available. You run a bigger chance of overlooking someone without an organized approach. This causes hard feelings among editors you may have inconvenienced, hurting your chances with these markets in the future.

8. DON'T FEAR REJECTION. LEARN FROM IT. No one enjoys rejection, but every writer faces it. The best way to turn a negative into a positive is to learn as much as you can from your rejections. Don't let them get you down. A rejection slip isn't a permission slip to doubt yourself, condemn your poetry or give up.

Look over the rejection. Did the editor provide any comments about your work or reasons why your poems were rejected? Probably he or she didn't. Editors are extremely busy and don't necessarily have time to comment on rejections. If that's the case, move on to the next magazine or publisher you've targeted and send your work out again.

SUBMISSION TRACKER

Poem Title	Publication Contest	Editor/Contact	Date Sent	Date Returned	Date Accepted	Date Published	Pay Recieved	Comments

If, however, the editor *has* commented on your work, pay attention. It counts for something that the editor took the time and trouble to say anything, however brief, good or bad. And consider any remark or suggestion with an open mind. You don't have to agree, but you shouldn't automatically disregard the feedback, either. Tell your ego to sit down and be quiet, then use the editor's comments to review your work from a new perspective. You might be surprised by how much you'll learn from a single scribbled word in the margin; or how encouraged you'll feel from a simple "Try again!" written on the rejection slip.

Note on your free webinar: To take advantage of your free webinar, type the following url into your browser: http://www.WritersMarket.com/2012PM.

GUIDE TO LISTING FEATURES

Below is an example of a Magazines/Journal listing (Book/Chapbook Publishers listings follow a similar format). Note the callouts that identify various format features of the listing. A key to the symbols displayed at the beginning of each listing is located on the inside cover of this book.

EASY-TO-USE REFERENCE ICONS

E-MAIL ADDRESSES AND WEBSITES

SPECIFIC CONTACT NAMES

TYPES OF POETRY CONSIDERED

DETAILED SUBMISSION GUIDELINES

EDITOR'S COMMENTS

❶❸ ALASKA QUARTERLY REVIEW

ESB 208, University of Alaska-Anchorage, 3211 Providence Dr., Anchorage AK 99508. (907)786-6916. E-mail: aqr@uaa.alaska.edu. Website: www.uaa.alaska.edu/aqr. **Contact:** Ronald Spatz. "*AQR* publishes fiction, poetry, literary nonfiction and short plays in traditional and experimental styles."

- *Alaska Quarterly* reports they are always looking for freelance material and new writers.

MAGAZINES NEEDS *Alaska Quarterly Review*, published in 2 double issues/year, is "devoted to contemporary literary art. We publish both traditional and experimental fiction, poetry, literary nonfiction, and short plays." Wants all styles and forms of poetry, "with the most emphasis perhaps on voice and content that displays 'risk,' or intriguing ideas or situations." Has published poetry by Maxine Kumin, Jane Hirshfield, David Lehman, Pattiann Rogers, Albert Goldbarth, David Wagoner, Robert Pinsky, Linda Pastan, Ted Kooser, Kay Ryan, W. S. Merwin, Sharon Olds and Billy Collins. *Alaska Quarterly Review* is 224-300 pages, digest-sized, professionally printed, perfect-bound, with card cover with color or b&w photo. Receives up to 6,000 submissions/year, accepts 40-90. Subscription: $18. Sample: $6. Pays $10-50 subject to availability of funds; pays in contributor's copies and subscriptions when funding is limited.

HOW TO CONTACT No fax or e-mail submissions. Reads submissions mid-August to mid-May; manuscripts are *not* read May 15-August 15. Responds in up to 5 months, "sometimes longer during peak periods in late winter."

ADDITIONAL INFORMATION Guest poetry editors have included Stuart Dybek, Jane Hirshfield, Stuart Dischell, Maxine Kumin, Pattiann Rogers, Dorianne Laux, Peggy Shumaker, Olena Kalytiak Davis, Nancy Eimers, Michael Ryan, and Billy Collins.

TIPS "All sections are open to freelancers. We rely almost exclusively on unsolicited manuscripts. *AQR* is a nonprofit literary magazine and does not always have funds to pay authors."

FREQUENTLY ASKED QUESTIONS

The following FAQ (Frequently Asked Questions) section provides the expert knowledge you need to submit your poetry in a professional manner. Answers to most basic questions, such as "How many poems should I send?," "How long should I wait for a reply?" and "Are simultaneous submissions okay?" can be found by simply reading the listings in the Magazines/Journals and Book/Chapbook Publishers sections. See the introduction to each section for an explanation of the information contained in the listings. Also, see the Glossary of Listing terms.

Is it okay to submit handwritten poems?

Usually, no. Now and then a publisher or editor makes an exception and accepts handwritten manuscripts. However, check the preferences stated in each listing. If no mention is made of handwritten submissions, assume your poetry should be typed or computer-generated.

How should I format my poems for submission to magazines and journals?

If you're submitting poems by regular mail (also referred to as *land mail*, *postal mail* or *snail mail*), follow this format:

Poems should be typed or computer-printed on white 8½×11 paper of at least 20 lb. weight. Left, right and bottom margins should be at least one inch. Starting ½ inch from the top of the page, type your name, address, telephone number, e-mail address (if you have one) and number of lines in the poem in the *upper right* corner, in individual lines, single-spaced. Space down about six lines and type the poem title, either centered or flush left. The title may appear in all caps or in upper and lower case. Space down another two lines (at least) and begin to type your poem. Poems are usually single-spaced,

MAILED SUBMISSION FORMAT

S.T. Coleridge
1796 Ancient Way
Mariner Heights OH 45007 **②**
(852) 555-5555
albatross@strophe.vv.cy
54 lines

③

KUBLA KHAN **④**

⑤ In Xanadu did Kubla Khan
a stately pleasure dome decree:
where Alph, the sacred river, ran
through caverns measureless to man
down to a sunless sea.
So twice five miles of furtile ground
with walls and towers were girdled round:
and there were gardens bright with sinuous rills,
where blossomed many an incense-bearing tree;
and here were forests ancient as the hills,
enfolding sunny spots of greenery.

⑥ But oh! that deep romantic chasm which slanted
down the green hill athwart a cedarn cover!
A savage place! as holy and enchanted
as e'er beneath a waning moon was haunted
by woman wailing for her demon lover!
And from this chasm, with ceaseless turmoil seething,
as if this earth in fast thick pants were breathing, **⑦**
a mighty fountain momentarily was forced:
amid whose swift half-intermitted burst
huge fragments vaulted like rebounding hail,
or chaffy grain beneath the thresher's flail;
And 'mid these dancing rocks at once and ever
it flung up momently the sacred river.

① DO leave ½" margin on top, at least 1" on sides and bottom. **②** DO list contact information and number of lines in upper right corner. **③** DO space down about 6 lines. **④** DO type title in all caps or upper/lower case. Type flush with left margin. **⑤** DON'T type a byline but DO space down at least 2 lines. **⑥** DO double-space between spaces. **⑦** DO type poems single-space unless guidelines specify double spacing. **⑧** For multi-page poems, DO show your name, keyword(s) from title, page number, and "continue stanza" or "new stanza." **⑨** DO space down at least 3 lines before resuming poem.

S.T. Coleridge
KUBLA KAHN, Page 2, continued stanza.

Five miles meandering with a mazy motion
through wood and dale the sacred river ran,
then reached the caverns measureless to man,
and sank in tumult to a lifeless ocean:
and 'mid this tumult Kubla heard from afar
ancestral voices prophesying war!

The shadow of the dome of pleasure
floated midway on the waves;
where was heard the mingled measure
from the fountain and the caves.
It was a miracle of rare device,
a sunny pleasure dome with caves of ice!

A damsel with a dulcimer
in a vision once I saw:
It was an Abyssinian maid,

although some magazines may request double-spaced submissions. (Be alert to each market's preferences.) Double-space between stanzas. Type one poem to a page. For poems longer than one page, type your name in the *upper left* corner; on the next line type a key word from the title of your poem, the page number, and indicate whether the stanza begins or is continued on the new page (i.e., MOTHMAN, Page 2, continue stanza *or* begin new stanza).

If you're submitting poems by e-mail:

First, make sure the publication accepts e-mail submissions. This information, when available, is included in all *Poet's Market* listings. In most cases, editors will request that poems be pasted within the body of your e-mail, *not* sent as attachments. Many editors prefer this format because of the danger of viruses, the possibility of software incompatibility, and other concerns associated with e-mail attachments. Editors who consider e-mail attachments taboo may even delete the message without opening the attachment.

Of course, other editors do accept, and even prefer e-mail submissions as attachments. This information should be clearly stated in the market listing. If it's not, you're probably safer submitting your poems in the body of the e-mail. (All the more reason to pay close attention to details given in the listings.)

Note, too, the number of poems the editor recommends including in the e-mail submission. If no quantity is given specifically for e-mails, go with the number of poems an editor recommends submitting in general. Identify your submission with a notation in the subject line. While some editors simply want the words "Poetry Submission," others want poem titles. Check the market listing for preferences. **Note:** Because of spam, filters and other concerns, some editors are strict about what must be printed in the subject line and how. If you're uncertain about any aspect of e-mail submission formats, double-check the website (if available) for information or contact the publication for directions.

What is a chapbook? How is it different from a regular poetry book?

A chapbook is a booklet, averaging 24-50 pages in length (some are shorter), usually digest-sized (5½×8½, although chapbooks can come in all sizes, even published within the pages of a magazine). Typically, a chapbook is saddle-stapled with a soft cover (card or special paper); chapbooks can also be produced with a plain paper cover the same weight as the pages, especially if the booklet is photocopied.

A chapbook is a much smaller collection of poetry than a full-length book (which runs anywhere from 50 pages to well over 100 pages, longer for "best of" collections and retrospectives). There are probably more poetry chapbooks being published than full-length books, and that's an important point to consider. Don't think of the chapbook as a poor relation to the full-length collection. While it's true a chapbook won't attract big

E-MAIL SUBMISSION FORMAT

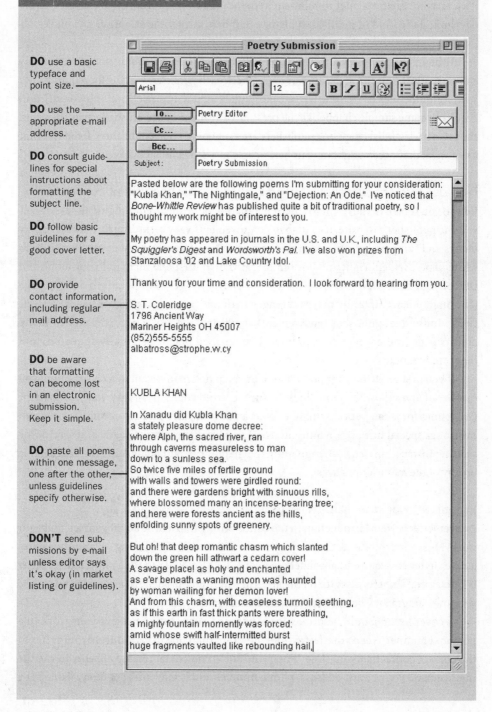

DO use a basic typeface and point size.

DO use the appropriate e-mail address.

DO consult guidelines for special instructions about formatting the subject line.

DO follow basic guidelines for a good cover letter.

DO provide contact information, including regular mail address.

DO be aware that formatting can become lost in an electronic submission. Keep it simple.

DO paste all poems within one message, one after the other, unless guidelines specify otherwise.

DON'T send submissions by e-mail unless editor says it's okay (in market listing or guidelines).

Poetry Submission

Arial 12 **B** / U

To... Poetry Editor
Cc...
Bcc...
Subject: Poetry Submission

Pasted below are the following poems I'm submitting for your consideration: "Kubla Khan," "The Nightingale," and "Dejection: An Ode." I've noticed that *Bone-Whittle Review* has published quite a bit of traditional poetry, so I thought my work might be of interest to you.

My poetry has appeared in journals in the U.S. and U.K., including *The Squiggler's Digest* and *Wordsworth's Pal*. I've also won prizes from Stanzaloosa '02 and Lake Country Idol.

Thank you for your time and consideration. I look forward to hearing from you.

S. T. Coleridge
1796 Ancient Way
Mariner Heights OH 45007
(852)555-5555
albatross@strophe.w.cy

KUBLA KHAN

In Xanadu did Kubla Khan
a stately pleasure dome decree:
where Alph, the sacred river, ran
through caverns measureless to man
down to a sunless sea.
So twice five miles of fertile ground
with walls and towers were girdled round:
and there were gardens bright with sinuous rills,
where blossomed many an incense-bearing tree;
and here were forests ancient as the hills,
enfolding sunny spots of greenery.

But oh! that deep romantic chasm which slanted
down the green hill athwart a cedarn cover!
A savage place! as holy and enchanted
as e'er beneath a waning moon was haunted
by woman wailing for her demon lover!
And from this chasm, with ceaseless turmoil seething,
as if this earth in fast thick pants were breathing,
a mighty fountain momently was forced:
amid whose swift half-intermitted burst
huge fragments vaulted like rebounding hail,

reviews, qualify for major prizes or find national distribution through chain bookstores, it's a terrific way for a poet to build an audience (and reputation) in increments, while developing the kind of publishing history that may attract the attention of a book publisher one day.

Although some presses consider chapbooks through a regular submission process, many choose manuscripts through competitions. Check each publisher's listing for requirements, send for guidelines or visit the website (absolutely vital if a competition is involved), and check out some sample chapbooks the press has already produced (usually available from the press itself). Most chapbook publishers are as choosy as book publishers about the quality of work they accept. Submit your best poems in a professional manner.

How do I format a collection of poems to submit to a book/chapbook publisher?

Before you send a manuscript to a book/chapbook publisher, request guidelines (or consult the publisher's website, if available). Requirements vary regarding formatting, query letters and samples, length, and other considerations. Usually you will use 8½×11, 20 lb. white paper; set left, right and bottom margins of at least one inch; put your name and title of your collection in the top left corner of every page; limit poems to one per page (although poems certainly may run longer than one page); and number pages consecutively. Individual publisher requirements might include a title page, table of contents, credits page (indicating where previously published poems originally appeared) and biographical note.

If you're submitting your poetry book or chapbook manuscript to a competition, you *must* read and follow the guidelines. Failure to do so could disqualify your manuscript. Guidelines for a competition might call for an official entry form to accompany the submission, a special title page, a minimum and maximum number of pages, and specific formatting instructions (such as paginating the manuscript and not putting the poet's name on any of the manuscript pages).

What is a cover letter? Do I have to send one? What should it say?

A cover letter is your introduction to the editor, telling him a little about yourself and your work. Most editors indicate their cover letter preferences in their listings. If an editor states a cover letter is "required," absolutely send one! It's also better to send one if a cover letter is "preferred." Experts disagree on the necessity and appropriateness of cover letters, so use your own judgment when preferences aren't clear in the listing.

A cover letter should be professional but also allow you to present your work in a personal manner. Keep your letter brief, no more than one page. Address your letter to the correct contact person. (Use "Poetry Editor" if no contact name appears in the listing.) Include your name, address, phone number and e-mail address (if available). If a

PREPARING YOUR COVER LETTER

Perry Lineskanner **1**
1954 Eastern Blvd.
Pentameter OH 45007
(852) 555-5555
soneteer@trochee.vv.cy

April 24, 2009

Spack Saddlestaple, Editor
The Squiggler's Digest **2**
Double-Toe Press
P.O. Box 54X
Submission Junction AZ 85009

Dear Mr. Saddlestaple:

3   Enclosed are three poems for your consideration for The Squiggler's Digest: "The Diamond Queen," "The Boy Who Was Gromit," and "The Maker of Everything."

4   Although this is my first submission to your journal, I'm a long-time reader of The Squiggler's Digest and enjoy the scope of narrative poetry you feature. I especially enjoyed Sydney Dogwood's poetry cycle in Issue 4.

My own poetry has appeared recently in The Bone-Whittle Review, Bumper-Car Reverie, and Stock Still.

Thank you for considering my manuscript. I look forward to hearing from you.

Sincerely,

Perry Lineskanner

> **1** DO type on one side of 8½ × 11 20lb. paper. **2** DO use a standard 12-point typeface (like Times New Roman). **3** DO list the poems you're submitting for consideration. **4** DO mention something about the magazine and about yourself.

biographical note is requested, include 2-3 lines about your background, interests, why you write poetry, etc. Avoid praising yourself or your poems in your letter (your submission should speak for itself). Include titles (or first lines) of the poems you're submitting. You may list a few of your most recent publishing credits, but no more than five; and keep in mind that some editors find publishing credits tiresome—they're more interested in the quality of the work you're submitting to *them*.

> Use a business-style format for a professional appearance and proofread carefully; typos, misspellings and other errors make a poor first impression.

Show your familiarity with the magazine to which you're submitting: comment on a poem the magazine published, tell the editor why you chose to submit to her magazine, mention poets the magazine has published. Use a business-style format for a professional appearance and proofread carefully; typos, misspellings and other errors make a poor first impression. Remember that editors are people, too. Respect, professionalism and kindness go a long way in poet/editor relationships.

What is a SASE? An IRC (with SAE)?

A SASE is a self-addressed, stamped envelope—and you should never send a submission by regular mail without one. Also include a SASE if you send an inquiry to an editor. If your submission is too large for an envelope (for instance, a bulky book-length collection of poems), use a box and include a self-addressed mailing label with adequate return postage paper-clipped to it.

An IRC is an International Reply Coupon, enclosed with a self-addressed envelope for manuscripts submitted to foreign markets. Each coupon is equivalent in value to the minimum postage rate for an unregistered airmail letter. IRCs may be exchanged for postage stamps at post offices in all foreign countries that are members of the Universal Postal Union (UPU). When you provide the adequate number of IRCs and a self-addressed envelope (SAE), you give a foreign editor financial means to return your submission (U.S. postage stamps cannot be used to send mail *to* the United States from outside the country). Purchase price is $2 per coupon. Call your local post office to check for availability (sometimes only larger post offices sell them).

IMPORTANT NOTE ABOUT IRCS: Foreign editors sometimes find the IRCs have been stamped incorrectly by the U.S. post office when purchased. This voids the IRCs and makes it impossible for the foreign editor to exchange the coupons for return postage for your manuscript. When buying IRCs, make sure yours have been stamped correctly before you leave the counter. (The Postal Service clerk must place a postmark in the block with the heading *control stamp of the country of origin*.) More information about International Reply Coupons is available on the USPS website (www.usps.com).

To save time and money, poets sometimes send disposable manuscripts to foreign markets and inform the editor to discard the manuscript after it's been read. Some enclose an IRC and SAE for reply only; others establish a deadline after which they will withdraw the manuscript from consideration and market it elsewhere.

How much postage does my submission need?

As much as it takes—you do *not* want your manuscript to arrive postage due. Purchase a postage scale or take your manuscript to the post office for weighing. Remember, you'll need postage on two envelopes: the one containing your submission and SASE, and the return envelope itself. Submissions without SASEs usually will not be returned (and possibly may not even be read).

Note: New postage rates went into effect on May 12, 2008. There is now a new fee structure for First-Class Postage. For letters and cards (including business-size envelopes), the First-Class rate is 42 cents for the first ounce, and 17 cents per additional ounce up to and including 3.5 ounces. **Letter-sized mail that weighs more than 3.5 ounces is charged the "flats" rate** ("flats" include any envelope large enough to mail an 8½×11 manuscript page unfolded) of 83 cents for the first ounce, and 17 cents for each additional ounce up to and including 13 ounces. This means if you send a large envelope that weighs only one ounce, it costs 83 cents at the First-Class flats rate instead of the 42 cents charged for First-Class letters and cards. (See the charts on page 14 for First-Class rates for letters and flats, or go to www.usps.com for complete information on all rates questions.)

The USPS also offers its Click-N-Ship® program, which allows a customer to print domestic and international shipping labels with postage, buy insurance and pay for postage by credit card. See the USPS website for a one-time software download, to check system requirements and to register for an account.

The website is also your source for ordering supplies (such as postage scale and labels), reviewing postal regulations, calculating postage and more. Canada Post information and services are available at www.canadapost.com.

POSTAGE INFORMATION

First Class Mail Rates: Letters & Cards

1 ounce	$0.44	3 ounces	$0.78
2 ounces	$0.61	3.5 ounces	$0.95
Postcard	$0.28		

First Class Mail Rates: Flats

Weight not over (ounces)	Rate	Weight not over (ounces)	Rate
1	$0.88	8	$2.07
2	$1.05	9	$2.24
3	$1.22	10	$2.41
4	$1.39	11	$2.58
5	$1.56	12	$2.75
6	$1.73	13	$2.92
7	$1.90		

Source: Website of the United States Postal Service (www.usps.com)

U.S. Postal Codes

AL	Alabama	KY	Kentucky	OK	Oklahoma
AK	Alaska	LA	Louisiana	OR	Oregon
AZ	Arizona	ME	Maine	PA	Pennsylvania
AR	Arkansas	MD	Maryland	PR	Puerto Rico
CA	California	MA	Massachusetts	RI	Rhode Island
CO	Colorado	MI	Michigan	SC	South Carolina
CT	Connecticut	MN	Minnesota	SD	South Dakota
DE	Delaware	MS	Mississippi	TN	Tennessee
DC	District of Columbia	MO	Missouri	TX	Texas
FL	Florida	NE	Montana	UT	Utah
GA	Georgia	NV	Nevada	VT	Vermont
GU	Guam	NH	New Hampshire	VI	Virgin Islands
HI	Hawaii	NJ	New Jersey	VA	Virginia
ID	Idaho	NM	New Mexico	WA	Washington
IL	Illinois	NY	New York	WV	West Virginia
IN	Indiana	NC	North Carolina	WI	Wisconsin
IA	Iowa	ND	North Dakota	WY	Wyoming
KS	Kansas	OH	Ohio		

Canadian Postal Codes

AB	Alberta	NS	Nova Scotia	QC	Quebec
BC	British Columbia	NT	Northwest Territories	SK	Saskatchewan
MB	Manitoba	NU	Nunavut	YT	Yukon
NB	New Brunswick	ON	Ontario		
NL	Newfoundland & Labrador	PE	Prince Edward Island		

What does it mean when an editor says "no previously published" poems? Does this include poems that have appeared in anthologies? What if one of my poems appeared online through a group or forum?

If your poem appears *anywhere* in print for a public audience, it's considered "previously" published. That includes magazines, anthologies, websites and online journals, and even printed programs (say for a church service, wedding, etc.). See the explanation for rights below, especially *second serial (reprint) rights* and *all rights* for additional concerns about previously published material.

One exception to the above guidelines is if your poem appears online in a *private* poetry forum, critique group, etc. As long as the site is private (i.e., a password is required to view and participate), your poem isn't considered "published." However, if your poem is printed on an online forum or bulletin board that's available for public viewing, even if you must use a password to post the poem or to comment, then your poem is considered "published" as far as rights are concerned.

What rights should I offer for my poems? What do these different rights mean?

Editors usually indicate in their listings what rights they acquire. Most journals and magazines license *first rights* (a.k.a. *first serial rights*), which means the poet offers the right to publish the poem for the first time in any periodical. All other rights to the material remain with the poet. (Note that some editors state that rights to poems "revert to poets upon publication" when first rights are acquired.) When poems are excerpted from a book prior to publication and printed in a magazine/journal, this is also called *first serial rights*. The addition of *North American* indicates the editor is the first to publish a poem in a U.S. or Canadian periodical. The poem may still be submitted to editors outside of North America or to those who acquire reprint rights.

When a magazine/journal licenses *one-time rights* to a poem (also known as *simultaneous rights*), the editor has *nonexclusive* rights to publish the poem once. The poet may submit that same poem to other publications at the same time (usually markets that don't have overlapping audiences).

Editors/publishers open to submission of work already published elsewhere seek *second serial (reprint) rights*. The poet is obliged to inform them where and when the poem previously appeared so they can give proper credit to the original publication. In essence, chapbook or book collections license reprint rights, listing the magazines in which poems previously appeared somewhere in the book (usually on the copyright page or separate credits page).

If a publisher or editor requires you to relinquish *all rights*, be aware that you're giving up ownership of that poem or group of poems. You cannot resubmit the work elsewhere, nor can you include it in a poetry collection without permission or by negotiating for reprint rights to be returned to you. Before you agree to this type of arrangement, ask the editor first if he or she is willing to acquire first rights instead of all rights. If you receive a refusal and you don't want to relinquish all rights, simply write a letter withdrawing your work from consideration. Some editors will reassign rights to a writer after a given amount of time, such as one year.

With the growth in Internet publishing opportunities, *electronic rights* have become very important. These cover a broad range of electronic media, including online magazines, CD recordings of poetry readings and CD-ROM editions of magazines. When submitting to an electronic market of any kind, find out what rights the market acquires upfront (many online magazines also stipulate the right to archive poetry they've published so it's continually available on their websites).

What is a copyright? Should I have my poems copyrighted before I submit them for publication?

Copyright is a proprietary right that gives you the power to control your work's reproduction, distribution and public display or performance, as well as its adaptation to other forms. In other words, you have the legal right to the exclusive publication, sale or distribution of your poetry. What's more, your "original works of authorship" are protected as soon as they are "fixed in a tangible form of expression," i.e., written down or recorded. Since March 1989, copyright notices are no longer required to secure protection, so it's not necessary to include them on your poetry manuscript. Also, in many editors' minds, copyright notices signal the work of amateurs who are distrustful and paranoid about having work stolen.

If you still want to indicate copyright, use the © symbol or the word *copyright*, your name and the year. If you wish, you can register your copyright with the Copyright Office for a $45 fee, using Form TX (directions and form available for download from www.copyright.gov). Since paying $45 per poem is costly and impractical, you may prefer to copyright a group of unpublished poems for that single fee. Further information is available from the U.S. Copyright Office, Library of Congress, 101 Independence Ave. S.E., Washington DC 20559-6000; by download from www.copyright.gov; or by calling (202)707-3000 between 8:30 a.m. and 5:00 p.m. (EST) weekdays.

SPECIAL NOTE REGARDING COPYRIGHT OFFICE MAIL DELIVERY: The "effective date of registration" for copyright applications is usually the day the Copyright Office actually receives all elements of an application (application form, fee and copies of work being registered). Because of security concerns, all USPS and private-carrier mail is screened off-site prior to arrival at the Copyright Office. This can add 3-5 days to delivery time and could, therefore, impact the effective date of registration. See the website for details about proper packaging, special handling and other related information.

OUT OF THE SLUSH AND INTO PRINT

....

by Kelly Davio

So you've written some poems. You've shared them with friends you trust for candid feedback, and they genuinely enjoy the poetry. Better still, your writing group, teachers or workshop compatriots think the work is strong enough to send to literary journals. You've done your homework by identifying venues that print poems like yours, and because you're a good literary citizen, you've subscribed to some of your favorite journals. Having identified the strongest three to five poems in your repertoire, you bundle your poems up, stamp the envelopes, rub said envelopes against your dog's head for luck, and say a little prayer as you pop them into the mail.

A few weeks or months pass, a rejection slip or two filtering in as you wait, but you don't worry that "your work does not meet our editorial needs at this time." You keep the faith. Then a few more slips find their way into your mailbox. When the very last journal rejects your work as well, you begin to wonder what's going wrong.

MY WRITING IS STRONG, SO WHY CAN'T I SEEM TO PUBLISH?

If you're asking this question, you're in good company with many other poets. Let's be clear: the odds of having work selected for publication are never in your favor. Consider the numbers of poems editors read: for each issue of *The Los Angeles Review*, for example, we consider more than 1,000 poems, eventually accepting about 40 or so. Many journals have room to showcase only half as many pieces. Not only are your poems pitted against many others, but in some cases, they also have to fight their way past early readers. At many journals, particularly those run by universities, undergraduate students of creative writing make initial calls on poems in the "slush pile" (the unsolicited manuscripts considered by journals) and determine whether an editor will even lay eyes on your work.

Depressed yet? Cheer up! There are a number of ways to increase the likelihood that your poetry will make it out of the slush, onto the editor's desk, and into print.

FIRST IMPRESSIONS

Think of your submission as a blind date with an editor. She doesn't know you, but she's hoping she finds that elusive spark with your work; you want to show her that your poetry is worth her time. When she opens your envelope or e-mail, the first thing she sees is your cover letter. Just as you would dress nicely to meet a possible romantic interest, your cover letter should show that you're competent, classy, and professional.

Start your date well by addressing the editor by name, not as "Sir or Madam," "To Whom it May Concern," or, worst of all, "Friend." Taking a few moments to find an editor's name on a journal's website, rather than dashing off a form letter, shows the editor you care about your submission.

> Taking the time to follow simple instructions will get you places with an editor or reader.

Now that you're off to a good start, keep that cover letter strong by following all guidelines. It baffles editors that many—even most—writers who want to publish don't bother to read or follow guidelines. If an editor asks for three to five poems stapled to a cover letter, don't send six with a paperclip. If the editor asks for the titles of your submitted poems in the cover letter, don't omit them. Taking the time to follow simple instructions will get you places with an editor or reader; when I open that rare submission that is correctly formatted, is addressed to me, and—for the win—spells my name correctly, I automatically want to give more time and attention to that poet's work than to the poems of a writer who sent sloppy slush.

THE RIGHT KIND OF ATTENTION

Now that you've followed the journal's guidelines, the next step in presenting your work well includes telling a little about yourself. Your cover letter gives an editor a sense of you as a person and as a poet. By including information about where you went to school, what you do for a living, and how you heard about the publication in one, brief paragraph, you'll help the editor warm up to your work. It's also great to remind the editor that you met at a conference or reading, or that you are a loyal subscriber to the magazine (I shouldn't have to tell you it's a bad idea to make these claims if they're untrue). Showing that you're a friendly, engaged person puts an editor in a receptive frame of mind.

There is, however, such a thing as showing too much personality. Sure, using a quirky font, adding glitter to your envelope, or attaching photos of yourself in beachwear will get an editor's attention, but it's the wrong sort of attention. At literary journals, editors develop relationships with writers. If your submission suggests you might not be a person an editor would want to engage—let's say you include a sketch of yourself with your collection of medieval torture devices—she'll be understandably skittish about entering a working relationship with you. Making bold assertions about the importance or innovative nature of the enclosed poetry is a similarly bad idea; however much you may want to explain your work in detail, allow your poetry to speak for itself. As a rule, if you're in doubt as to whether any part of your submission is inappropriate or puts you in a bad light, take it out.

SECOND DATES

Every poet—fledgling or established—receives rejection. Sometimes rejection slips come as tiny scraps of paper that appear to have been cut by a toddler. Other times, a writer might be lucky enough to receive a whole sheet of paper on actual letterhead. And every now and then, an editor may put ink to paper or cursor to screen to give a writer some constructive feedback or request to see more work.

Let's be clear: being invited to resubmit is like being asked on a second date. There's no commitment at this stage, but there's genuine interest on the editor's part. She likes your poems, and now that you have her attention, you've got a chance to really impress her with the full range of your charms. You may be excited to have a second shot, but follow the rules of playing it cool: don't e-mail a group of poems five minutes after an editor has asked for them, and don't pop a new batch of work into the mail the same day as you receive a rejection. Just as calling your date moments after you've left the restaurant would smack of desperation, don't run the risk of turning your editor off with enthusiasm that resembles stalking. You needn't worry that the editor will forget you; if she's taken the time to ask for a resubmission, it's because she likes the work and finds it memorable. When you do resubmit, after having taken the time to consider what poems might be better suited to the journal's needs, you can jog the editor's memory by mentioning her offer to consider more work.

IT'S NOT PERSONAL UNLESS YOU MAKE IT PERSONAL

So let's say your second date doesn't go well, or that you never got to the second date at all. Maybe an editor flatly rejected your best poem, your magnum opus. You feel sure that the editor's taste is sorely lacking. While the editor may, in fact, be missing out, there are a number of reasons a journal might not be able to accept your work. The editor might be looking for variety, and your work may feel too similar to poems already accepted. Perhaps your poems do not fit the theme of the issue. Maybe the editor has already filled her allotted pages, and just can't squeeze another piece in the issue. A rejection of a poem isn't a rejection of a person.

However, some poets, in moments of frustration, have been known to dash off angry missives to editors, questioning levels of taste or qualification for the editorial position. When personal attacks are leveled, it discourages those editors who spend great swaths of their free time working to promote the craft and appreciation of poetry. In an industry that runs less on money than it does on good will, hostility will only breed a bad reputation. Spare yourself from becoming the pariah in the inbox by taking setbacks graciously.

PERSISTENCE PAYS ... IN CONTRIBUTOR'S COPIES

The longer you write and continue to send out work, the more you will find success in publishing. Given the vast number of publications in the Western world, there is undoubtedly a journal for every writer. And as you begin to see your poems come out in print, it will likely be a point of pride for you to see your collection of contributor's copies—copies given in payment for the use of the poet's work—grow to overfill your bookshelf.

But if you have visions of your bank account growing to such seam-bursting proportions, skim back up to the line about the literary world running on good vibes, not on hard cash. Placing poems in journals doesn't pay much, if anything. From time to time, a journal may be able to offer a poet a small honorarium, but publications can generally afford only to give complimentary or discounted copies.

So why put yourself through the rigmarole of writing, submitting, finding rejection and, somewhere down the line, getting some copies of magazines? Hopefully it's because you're genuinely in love with language and with poetry, and it brings you joy to share that love with others. As you go forward in your writing career, remember: be friendly, be courteous, be kind and, by all means, keep going.

KELLY DAVIO currently serves as the Managing Editor/Poetry Editor at the *Los Angeles Review*, and reads poetry for *Fifth Wednesday Journal*. Her work can be found in *Women's Review of Books*, *Cincinnati Review*, and *Best New Poets 2009*, among others. Her poetry collection, *Burn This House*, is forthcoming from Red Hen Press, and she is currently working on a novel in verse.

WHY PUBLISHING A CHAPBOOK MAKES SENSE

by Jeannine Hall Gailey

Maybe you've published some poems in good literary journals, you've started giving readings around town, and you're ready for the next step. You have a lot of poems in your repertoire, but aren't sure exactly how to get your work into the hands of the public. Now is the time to consider putting together a chapbook. This article describes the benefits of publishing chapbooks and how to go about it, including advice from chapbook publishers and writers with successful chapbooks.

WHAT IS A POETRY CHAPBOOK?

Definitions abound (one is even included in the FAQ section at the beginning of *Poet's Market,*) but today's chapbooks are primarily defined by length (usually fewer than 30 pages) and production (usually limited edition, sometimes handmade.) While some are beautiful book-arts products, perfect bound with high-quality covers, like those published by Washington State Chapbook Press, Floating Bridge or Tupelo Press, a chapbook can also be a stapled-together affair produced at the local copy shop.

As for the means of production, there are many chapbook presses out there (New Michigan Press, Concrete Wolf, Floating Bridge, Finishing Line Press, Pudding House Press…). But you can also self-publish a chapbook to sell at readings.

Chapbooks used to be mainly an emerging poet's way of getting their work out to the public, but these days, presses like Sarabande Press have created in-demand chapbooks for well-known authors such as Louise Glück and James Tate as well. Dorianne Laux, for instance, recently published a chapbook, "Superman," with Red Dragonfly Press.

WHY A POETRY CHAPBOOK?

The benefits are multiple. First, the task of putting together a chapbook collection of poems—thinking about organization, which poems to include or exclude, polishing up poems you meant to revise but never got around to—is great training for putting together a full-length book. Second, learning to market and sell your own work—getting over the embarrassment of asking bookstores to carry your chapbook, or telling friends about your chapbook publication—is essential for any poet, because the usual marketing machinery of publishing (talk shows, end-caps at Barnes & Nobles, advertising campaigns) doesn't really exist in the poetry publishing world, which is run on slim margins by a very few overworked but dedicated people.

Kelli Russell Agodon, whose sold-out chapbook, "Geography," was one of Floating Bridge Press' best sellers, talked about how the experience of having a chapbook had benefited her. "Having a chapbook has helped me by opening new doors. It has allowed me to have opportunities such as teaching or reading at poetry festivals and conferences that may not have been open to me if I didn't have a book. It also helped me understand the publishing process a little better before my full-length collection. Also, crafting the chapbook really allowed me to focus on one particular subject."

Chapbooks provide an opportunity for authors to produce tightly woven or themed collections.

Lana Ayers, editor and publisher at Concrete Wolf, a chapbook publisher, details further benefits. "Chapbooks provide an opportunity for authors to produce tightly woven or themed collections. And since most chapbooks, are less expensive than full-length collections, it is easier to convince a reader to take the plunge. Also, the shorter length of the collection can be less intimidating for readers new to poetry. So chapbooks are an all-around great opportunity for both poets and readers to get acquainted."

Kristy Bowen, editor and publisher at Dancing Girl Press, talks about why she started publishing chapbooks. "I also have a love for the chapbook itself as form, a small morsel of poetry that can be devoured in one sitting. Also, they are an affordable way to get new work into the hands of readers with very little fuss. I'm interested as well in how to expand the traditional notion of chapbooks further into the realm of book arts."

Writers have different motivations for publishing chapbooks—fascination with the form, building a relationship with an audience, or finding a home for a particular set of poems. Dorianne Laux described her decision to publish a chapbook after several highly successful full-length collections.

"I met Scott King, of Red Dragonfly Press, while I was at the Anderson Center for the Arts for a writing residency and he was producing letterpress broadsides. He later asked if I'd like to do a chapbook. At the time, I wasn't sure if I had enough poems on a theme to make a book, but said yes anyway, not wanting to miss a chance to work with Scott. It took me about a year to come up with the poems in "Superman," which are all loosely based around pop culture figures, icons and objects of the 20th century. I wasn't yet ready for a fifth book of poems and so a chapbook seemed a great way to have something in the interim. But more important was my desire to have a beautiful book, hand set on gorgeous paper and sewn together, something that would be a small, elegant gift I could give to friends. It was also a way to bring attention to this small press and its poet/editor, Scott King, who had taught me so much about the quality of labor that went into reproducing a page of words before the invention of carbon paper, mimeo and xerox machines, computers and desktop printers. It was exacting, dangerous and dirty work, performed amidst smoke, sparks and fire by some anonymous typesetter bent over in a greasy smock, delicately choosing the next stately letter with the deafening clatter of the molten lead foundry pounding against the drums in his ears. It's also wonderfully ironic to have a book about 20th century characters like Cher and The Beatles produced using a 16th-century technology!"

So now you're intrigued. But how, exactly, do you put together a chapbook?

WHAT DOES PUTTING TOGETHER A CHAPBOOK ENTAIL?

The good news is that it's a lot like putting together a book, but a more compact, and perhaps, more tightly themed collection. Usually, writers have obsessions, and those obsessions manifest themselves over time. You'll find 20 poems on superheroes, for instance, or on abandoned gas stations in the Midwest. Or you'll find 20 poems that tell their own story.

Kelli Russell Agodon's advice for someone putting together a chapbook for the first time? "My advice would be to focus your chapbook on one subject, theme, or story. The best chapbooks look deeply at a topic, but also make new discoveries in their poems throughout the book. I suggest choosing only your strongest poems for your chapbook, then determine if there are certain poems you need to write to make the chapbook stronger and more complete."

Kristy Bowen adds that "sometimes, especially poets at the beginning of their career see a chapbook as a stepping stone to the first book, which it usually is, but I suspect they sometimes see the chapbook merely as a shorter volume sort of tossed together without any real feel of cohesion in the chapbook itself. So what you get is an odd mismatch of the poems they consider best, but without any sort of thematic or formal binding." So what is Dancing Girl Press' editor looking for? "We particularly look for work that has a strong sense of image and music, cohesiveness as a manuscript, interesting and surprising, sometimes unusual, use of language. We love humor when done well, strangeness, wackiness. Hybridity, collage, inter-textuality. Manuscripts that create their own worlds."

This brings us to the next subject—how to get your chapbook published.

HOW ARE CHAPBOOKS PUBLISHED?

You've got your manuscript of 15-30 pages of thematically engaged, tightly edited poetry together, so now what? Well, many chapbook publishers, just like poetry book publishers, decide what they are going to publish through a contest system. Presses like this include Tupelo Press, Concrete Wolf, Pudding House, and New Michigan Press. If you go this route, you should research the publisher by obtaining at least one of their previous publications, checking out the production and writing quality, and decide if it's a good fit for you. If it is, then you send off your manuscript with a cover letter, a check (usually $10-15), and a SASE, and hope for the best. Some presses publish runners-up and finalists as well as winners. Be sure to read the guidelines thoroughly, and follow them to the letter.

Some chapbook publishers, like Sarabande Press, only publish through solicitation—that is, they contact the person they want to publish directly—so unless you get a call, you won't be getting your chapbook published through them. Some chapbook publishers will read "open submissions," for a few months a year, like Dancing Girl Press, but these are few and far between.

Of course, there's always self-publishing, and this is an easier (and more affordable) feat if you're attempting a saddle-stitched chapbook than a perfect bound book. You could even put it all up—your poems, the cover art, your table of contents and acknowledgements—on your own computer, using basic publishing software, print it out on your own laser printer, and staple it at your kitchen table. If you Google "make your own saddle-stitched chapbook" you can find a couple of sets of instructions, or if you're lucky enough to have a book arts center near you, sign up for a class.

MARKETING A POETRY CHAPBOOK

Marketing a chapbook is, admittedly, more difficult to market than a poetry book. Many bookstores won't carry them because they are difficult to store and display. Your best bet is to talk an independent bookstore into carrying a copy or two on consignment. Most re-view outlets don't take chapbook reviews, and chapbooks are not usually eligible for major book awards.

But chapbooks are by nature ephemeral, and that can be an advantage. A limited run means an especially beautiful or well-written chapbook might later become a collector's item, and no writer keeps too many chapbooks on hand—though, unlike books, they don't take up too much space to store. Many people see chapbooks as a more intimate way to get to know a poet's work, and value the fact that the chapbooks may only be around for a short amount of time. Chapbooks are easy to sell at poetry readings, where the buyer is more likely to want a souvenir of that experience, and on poet's websites, where the buyers are already familiar with the poet and their work. If you have friends with blogs, send them a review copy of your chapbook and ask them to say a few words.

So, remember this—give readings. Be an interesting, enthusiastic reader who has actually organized their work and practiced it a few times. This will increase the odds that audience members might want to buy your chapbook! And, make sure you have a personal website or blog that your fans can come to and find out how to buy your chapbook—whether it's directly from you or from a link to your publisher or even Amazon. Don't make them hunt for it!

WHY SHOULD YOU CONSIDER PUBLISHING A CHAPBOOK?

A chapbook gives you a way to connect with your reader. It gives your reader a physical reminder of your work, and sometimes it's a beautiful artifact, sometimes a humble set of copies, folded over and stapled. Creating a chapbook helps you practice organizing your work into a coherent collection. Selling your chapbook orients you in the world of marketing poetry, and, if you do it yourself or watch it being produced, a way to understand the physical work of book publishing.

> Creating a chapbook helps you practice organizing your work into a cohereent collection.

Because of these benefits, it's more than just a step towards a full-length poetry collection—it's a way for you to build an audience, to put your work out into the world in a considered, deliberate way. Take a look at the chapbook publishers listed in *Poet's Market*, and order some samples to get an idea of the diversity of the production and content of chapbooks available as well as figure out which publisher might be right for you. Before you know it, you'll have something in hand to share at readings and with friends and family.

JEANNINE HALL GAILEY is a San Diego writer whose first book of poetry, *Becoming the Villainess*, was published by Steel Toe Books. She was awarded a 2007 Dorothy Sargent Rosenberg Prize for Poetry and a 2007 Washington State Artist Trust GAP grant. Her poems have appeared in several publications, including *The Iowa Review*, *The Columbia Poetry Review*, and *Smartish Pace*. She currently teaches at the MFA program at National University.

MISTAKES POETS MAKE

In putting together listings for *Poet's Market*, we ask editors for any words of advice they want to share with our readers. Often the editors' responses include comments about what poets should and shouldn't do when submitting work—the same comments, over and over. That means a lot of poets are repeating similar mistakes when they send out their poems for consideration.

The following list includes the most common of those mistakes—the ones poets should work hardest to avoid.

NOT READING A PUBLICATION BEFORE SUBMITTING WORK

Researching a publication is essential before submitting your poetry. Try to buy a sample copy of a magazine (by mail, if necessary) or at least see if an issue is available at the library. It may not be economically feasible for poets to purchase a copy of every magazine they target, especially if they send out a lot of poems. However, there are additional ways to familiarize yourself with a publication.

Read the market listing thoroughly. If guidelines are available, send for them by e-mail or regular mail, or check for them online. A publication's website often presents valuable information, including sample poems, magazine covers—and guidelines.

SUBMITTING INAPPROPRIATE WORK

Make good use of your research so you're sure you understand what a magazine publishes. Don't rationalize that a journal favoring free verse might jump at the chance to consider your long epic poem in heroic couplets. Don't convince yourself your experimental style will be a good fit for the traditional journal filled with rhyming poetry. Don't go into denial about whether a certain journal and your poetry are made for each other. It's counterproductive and ultimately wastes postage (not to mention time—yours and the editor's).

SUBMITTING AN UNREASONABLE NUMBER OF POEMS

If an editor recommends sending three to five poems (a typical range), don't send six. Don't send a dozen poems and tell the editor to pick the five she wants to consider. If the editor doesn't specify a number (or the listing says "no limit"), don't take that as an invitation to mail off 20 poems. The editors and staff of literary magazines are busy enough as it is, and they may decide they don't have time to cope with you. (When submitting book or chapbook manuscripts to publishers, make sure your page count falls within the range they state.)

Don't go to the other extreme and send only one poem, unless an editor says it's okay (which is rare). One poem doesn't give an editor much of a perspective on your work, and it doesn't give you very good odds on getting the piece accepted.

IGNORING THE EDITOR'S PREFERENCES REGARDING FORMATS

If an editor makes a point of describing a preferred manuscript format, follow it, even if that format seems to contradict the standard. (Standard format includes using 8½ × 11 white paper and conventional typeface and point size; avoid special graphics, colors or type flourishes; put your name and address on every page.) Don't devise your own format to make your submission stand out. Keep everything clean, crisp and easy to read (and professional).

Be alert to e-mail submission formats. Follow directions regarding what the editor wants printed in the subject line, how many poems to include in a single e-mail, whether to use attachments or paste work in the body of the message, and other elements. Editors have good reasons for outlining their preferences; ignoring them could mean having your e-mail deleted before your poems are even read.

OMITTING A SELF-ADDRESSED STAMPED ENVELOPE (SASE)

Why do editors continuously say "include a SASE with your submission?" Because so many poets don't do it. Here's a simple rule: Unless the editor gives alternate instructions, include a #10 SASE, whether submitting poems or sending an inquiry.

WRITING BAD COVER LETTERS (OR OMITTING THEM COMPLETELY)

Cover letters have become an established part of the submission process. There are editors who remain indifferent about the necessity of a cover letter, but many consider it rude to be sent a submission without any other communication from the poet.

Unless the editor says otherwise, send a cover letter. Keep it short and direct, a polite introduction of you and your work. (See "Frequently Asked Questions" for more tips on cover letters, and an example.)

Here are a few important Don'ts:

- **DON'T** list all the magazines where your work has appeared; limit yourself to five magazine titles. The work you're submitting has to stand on its own.
- **DON'T** tell the editor what a good poet you are—or how good someone else thinks you are.
- **DON'T** tell the editor how to edit, lay out or print your poem. Some of those decisions are up to the editor, assuming she decides to accept your poem in the first place.
- **DON'T** point out the poem is copyrighted in your name or include the copyright symbol. All poems are automatically copyrighted in the poet's name as soon as they're "fixed" (i.e., written down), and editors know this.

NOT MAINTAINING GOOD EDITOR/POET RELATIONS

Most editors are hard-working poetry lovers dedicated to finding and promoting good work. They aspire to turn submissions around as quickly as possible and to treat all poets with respect. They don't want to steal your work. Often they aren't paid for their labor and may even have to dip into their own pockets just to keep their magazines going.

Poets should finesse their communications with editors regarding problems, especially in initial letters and e-mail. Editors (and their magazines and presses) aren't service-oriented businesses, like the phone company. Getting huffy with an editor as if arguing with your cable provider about an overcharge is inappropriate. Attitude isn't going to get you anywhere; in fact, it could create additional obstacles.

That's not to say poets shouldn't feel exasperated when they're inconvenienced or ill-treated. None of us likes to see our creations vanish, or to pay good money for something we're never going to receive (like a subscription or sample copy). However, exasperated is one thing; outraged is another. Too often poets go on the offensive with editors and make matters worse. Experts on how to complain effectively recommend you keep your cool and stay professional, no matter what kind of problem you're trying to work out.

For additional advice on editor/poet relations, see "Dealing With Problem Editors."

DEALING WITH PROBLEM EDITORS

There *are* problem editors out there, and we've all encountered them at one time or another. Some rip people off, prey on poets' desires to be published, or treat poets and their work with flagrant disregard. Fortunately, such editors are very much in the minority.

Now and then you may discover the disorganized editor or the overwhelmed editor; these two cause heartache (and heartburn) by closing up shop without returning manuscripts, or failing to honor paid requests for subscriptions and sample copies. More often than not, their transgressions are rooted in chaos and irresponsibility, not malicious intent. Frustrating as such editors are, they're not out to get you.

There are many instances, too, where larger circumstances are beyond an editor's control. For example, a college-oriented journal may be student-staffed, with editors changing each academic year. Funds for the journal may be cut unexpectedly by administration belt-tightening, or a grant could be cancelled. The editorial office may be moved to another part of the university. An exam schedule could impact a publishing schedule. All of these things cause problems and delays.

Then again, a literary journal may be a one-person, home-based operation. The editor may get sick or have an illness in the family. Her regular job may suddenly demand lots of overtime. There may be divorce or death with which the editor has to cope. A computer could crash. Or the editor may need to scramble for money before the magazine can go to the printer. Emergencies happen, and they take their toll on deadlines. The last thing the editor wants is to inconvenience poets and readers, but sometimes life gets in the way.

Usually, difficulties with these kinds of "problem" editors can be resolved satisfactorily through communication and patience. There are always exceptions, though. Here are a few typical situations with problem editors and how to handle them:

AN EDITOR IS RUDE.

If it's a matter of bad attitude, take it with a grain of salt. Maybe he's having a rotten day. If there's abusive language and excessive profanity involved, let us know about it. (See the complaint procedure .)

COMPLAINT PROCEDURE

If you feel you have not been treated fairly by a market listed in *Poet's Market*, we advise you to take the following steps:

- First, try to contact the market. Sometimes one phone call, letter, or e-mail can quickly clear up the matter. Document all your communications with the market.
- When you contact us with a complaint, provide the details of your submission, the date of your first contact with the market and the nature of your subsequent communication.
- We will file a record of your complaint and further investigate the market.
- The number and severity of complaints will be considered when deciding whether or not to delete a market from the next edition of *Poet's Market*.

AN EDITOR HARSHLY CRITICIZES YOUR POEM.

If an editor takes time to comment on your poetry, even if the feedback seems overly critical, consider the suggestions with an open mind and try to find something valid and useful in them. If, after you've given the matter fair consideration, you think the editor was out of line, don't rush to defend your poetry or wave your bruised ego in the editor's face. Allow that the editor has a right to her opinion (which you're not obligated to take as the final word on the quality of your work), forget about it and move on.

AN EDITOR IS SLOW TO RESPOND TO A SUBMISSION.

As explained above, there may be many reasons why an editor's response takes longer than the time stated in the market listing or guidelines. Allow a few more weeks to pass beyond the deadline, then write a polite inquiry to the editor about the status of your manuscript. (Include a SASE if sending by regular mail.) Understand an editor may not be able to read your letter right away if deadlines are pressing or if he's embroiled in a personal crisis. Try to be patient. If you haven't received a reply to your inquiry after a month or so, however, it's time for further action.

AN EDITOR WON'T RETURN YOUR MANUSCRIPT.

Decide whether you want to invest any more time in this journal or publisher. If you conclude you've been patient long enough, write a firm but professional letter to the editor withdrawing your manuscript from consideration. Request that the manuscript be returned; but know, too, a truly indifferent editor probably won't bother to send it back or reply in any way. Keep a copy of your withdrawal letter for your files, make a new copy of your manuscript and look for a better market.

Also, contact *Poet's Market* by letter or e-mail with details of your experience. We always look into problems with editors, although we don't withdraw a listing on the basis of a single complaint unless we discover further evidence of consistent misbehavior. We do, however, keep complaints on file and watch for patterns of unacceptable behavior from any specific market.

AN EDITOR TAKES YOUR MONEY.

If you sent a check for a subscription or sample copy and you haven't received anything, review your bank statement to see if the check has been cashed. If it has, send the editor a query. Politely point out the editor has cashed your check, but you haven't yet received the material you were expecting. Give the editor the benefit of the doubt: An upcoming issue of a magazine could be running late, your subscription could have been overlooked by mistake, or your copy could have been lost in transit or sent in error to the wrong address.

If your check has *not* been cashed, query the editor to see if your order was ever received. It may have been lost (in the mail or on the editor's desk), the editor may be holding several checks to cash at one time, or the editor may be waiting to cash checks until a tardy issue is finally published.

If you get an unsatisfactory response from the editor (or no response at all), wait a few weeks and try again. If the matter still isn't resolved, let us know about it. We're especially interested in publishers who take money from poets but don't deliver the goods. Be sure to send us all the details of the transaction, plus copies of any correspondence (yours and the editor's). We can't pursue your situation in any legal way or act as mediator, but we can ban an unscrupulous publisher from *Poet's Market* and keep the information as a resource in case we get later complaints.

Should you continue trying to get your money back from such editors? That's your decision. If your loss is under $10 (say, for a subscription or sample copy), it might cost you less in the long run to let the matter go. And the fee for a "stop payment" order on a check can be hefty—possibly more than the amount you sent the editor in the first place. Yes, it's infuriating to be cheated, but sometimes fighting on principle costs more than it's worth.

If your monetary loss is significant (for instance, you shelled out a couple hundred dollars in a subsidy publishing agreement), consider contacting your state attorney general's office for advice about small claims court, filing a complaint and other actions you can take.

WHEN TO GO SMALL

How to Decide if You Should Target a Micropress

....

by Jeannine Hall Gailey

Tired of the book-contest merry-go-round, tired of sending your $25 (and up—ouch!) check and manuscript off and hoping for the best against discouraging odds? Tired of knocking on the doors of the big publishing houses and hearing nothing in return? If you feel like there must be a better way to get your book of poetry published—you might be right!

If you have a book of poetry that is slightly experimental, slightly odd, or outside the mainstream, you might want to consider an independent small press or "micropress." Approaching these publishers means writing a query or sending in your manuscript—after you've done your homework. Small presses and micropresses often have specific niches that they fill—speculative work, experimental work, a particular style or genre. It's your job to do the research and find out which press might be a good fit for you.

WHAT IS A MICROPRESS?

For the purposes of this article, a micropress is a smaller version of an independent small press. An independent small press is one that doesn't rely on a university or a large corporation to bankroll its operations. Often, these presses deliver quality literature that might have slipped through the cracks of a publishing behemoth only interested in the bottom line, and they do it with more care and attention than a big press might have time to give. A micropress might be run by only or two people, and might only have the resources to produce one or two books a year. *Poet's Market* lists more than 100 poetry presses in its pages, so it's your job to try and target the right market for you. A micropress or independent small press might not charge a fee, but might ask you to buy one of their books during an open reading period, which seems like a much better deal for the writer; you get to support a press and you receive something in return, a book that will help you know the press (and their particular editorial tastes) better.

FINDING THE RIGHT PRESS FOR YOU

One of the best ways to figure out the right press for your book of poetry is to look at the presses that publish the books you adore. If you've never bought a book of poetry that wasn't published by a giant press like Norton or even a large University press like Wesleyan, now is the time to start looking critically at the books that independent small presses are putting out. Every year there is such a diverse and appealing multitude that it is easy to feel over-whelmed. Local book fairs or writers conferences (or academic conferences like the AWP Conference) offer a great opportunity for you to look at the books from different publishers and actually have conversations with the people behind the presses.

If you really love the poetry a press publishes, chances are, they might be a good fit for you. But it's a little like matchmaking—trying to figure out the best press for your book can be difficult. You'll want to think hard about what you write—whether you're experimental or avant-garde, confessional, nature-oriented, feminist, etc.—and whether the presses you are looking at publish in that same vein. Don't waste your time sending your sonnet series on Orpheus to an avant-garde publisher that prefers poems of urban grit.

Adam Deutch, Editor of Cooper Dillon Books, illustrates how book-buying decisions can help make you a part of a larger poetry community: "I buy books directly from presses (either online or at AWP) for the same reason I go to the local brewery for beer: it gives me re-lief to know exactly where my money is going, the poems (and beer) are fresher, I make con-nections with like-minded people in the process, and know I'm engaged in my community. If you aspire to be published by one of these presses, that's something to keep in mind."

WHAT ARE SMALLER PRESSES LOOKING FOR?

I've interviewed the editors of a few small independent presses to find out more about how they work, what they like, and what advice they have for poets considering the option of querying or sending to open submission at a small independent or micropress. Adam Deutch of Cooper Dillon suggests "Know why you want to have a book *with that press.* Do your research—read the books they publish, follow them on the Internet, and attend their events if they're in your town. Also, respect the guidelines; we've designed guidelines to make a manageable workflow for ourselves, and also to make a system that is easy for you to work with.

3 SMALL PRESSES OPEN TO QUERIES OR SUBMISSIONS

KITSUNE BOOKS

PUBLISHES: Poetry, fiction, nonfiction, memoir.

LOCATION: Crawfordville, FL

PRESS SIZE: 4 full-time staff, plus several contractors and volunteers.

DISTRIBUTION: Locally by Bella Distribution; Nationally and in the U.K. through Ingram. Also available at Barnes & Noble and Amazon.

ESTHETIC: Eclectic, broad-minded, intelligent, fun, literary, unusual, irreverent, thought-provoking.

SEEKING: Mature collections from authors with depth of subject or experience and pitch-perfect ear for language.

QUOTE: "We seek to publish books that bewitch and beguile, that provoke thought and evoke emotions, that produce laughter, invite play, and even shock on occasion."

CONNECT: www.kitsunebooks.com, Twitter, Blog, and Facebook

COOPER DILLON

PUBLISHES: Poetry.

LOCATION: San Diego, CA

PRESS SIZE: 2 full-time staff, plus a contract art director.

DISTRIBUTION: Self-distributed via the website.

ESTHETIC: "The process of discovery—of surrendering and transcending the limits of our aesthetic preferences—is too good to squash with a statement of style or genre preference."

MISSION: "To promote and maintain the values which make poems timeless, books with joy, beauty, honesty and intimacy—poetry that transcends."

CONNECT: cooperdillon.com, Blog, Twitter, and Facebook

SMALL DESK PRESS

PUBLISHES: Poetry, fiction, non-fiction, memoir.

LOCATION: San Francisco, CA

PRESS SIZE: 6 staff, full and part-time.

DISTRIBUTION: Small Press Distribution (SPD), on the website, and locally in selected SF bookstores.

ESTHETIC: Bold, badass, hilarious, and heartbreaking.

SEEKING: Work that pushes boundaries in terms of form as well as content, that is fairly accessible, and that doesn't shy away from using emotional content in a bold and subversive way.

> **QUOTE:** "Small Desk is unique because we seek out work that's challenging and innovative, and that also might have an emotionally raw quality or employ taboo subject matter in a way that might scare away more mainstream presses."
> **CONNECT:** www.smalldeskpress.com, blog, and Facebook

WHAT ARE THE BENEFITS OF GOING SMALLER?

The benefits of working with a small press, some of which I know firsthand, include not getting lost in the shuffle, enjoying an actual relationship with your editor—the kind where they might stop over for supper, or at the very least, offer some comments on your manuscript before you go to press, and the feeling of being a participant in a more independent and quirky artistic world.

As a writer, my sense is that you'll get a more dedicated editor, and a point of contact you can trust to always be upfront with you about your book.

Lynn Holschuh, an editor at Kitsune Books, points out that "smaller publishing companies allow for more individualized interaction between author and publisher. Kitsune Books, in particular, goes the extra mile to assure the final product both looks stunning and is a quality piece of writing that author and editors are proud of." Adam of Cooper Dillon Books adds: "As a reader, you'll find something from each press you won't find coming from a university press, or a major house. As a writer, my sense is that you'll get a more dedicated editor, and a point of contact you can trust to always be upfront with you about your book." Marissa Crawford, an editor at Small Desk Press, says that the advantages also include "working with a great group of literary advocates who support and promote your work and your vision, without wanting to change it to appeal to a mass market."

POTENTIAL DOWNSIDES OF GOING SMALLER

But, you may be asking, what are the downsides of going with a smaller press? A big press's books may have better distribution and they have more of a budget for promotion, although the likelihood is, for a new poet, the distribution and promotion for a book of poetry is going to be modest no matter what size press you work with. Expect in advance to participate in setting up readings to promote your book, contacting people about doing reviews, and helping get the word out about your book through your website. These days, because Amazon and e-books take a big slice out of traditional book sales, a small press that distributes through Amazon and makes e-books available might be surprisingly competitive in terms of book sales.

Lynne of Kitsune Books advises, "Distribution/promotional opportunities are greater with the larger houses, but any size company these days will expect the author to take an active role in promoting and publicizing their work." Crawford from Small Desk Press adds that "since most small presses are volunteer-based endeavors run by people who also have full-time jobs and often artistic pursuits of their own, I think it's really important for a poet/author to be proactive in promoting their own book. Small presses simply don't have the resources to promote their books as much as they'd like to, so an author who's excited about setting up readings, being active in the literary community and networking with other writers can be so important for making a book successful."

Small presses simply don't have the resources to promote their books as much as they'd like to, so an author who's excited about setting up readings, being active in the literary community and networking with other writers can be so important for making a book successful.

Of course everyone wants the widest distribution and the biggest promotional efforts for their books. But in the poetry world, where a fairly successful book usually only sells a few thousand copies, the differences between efforts of a larger or smaller press may be relatively minor.

RESOURCES

There are a few resources for people researching small presses that accept queries and open submissions. Besides *Poet's Market*, which should get you started, there is Rachel Dacus's website (www.dacushome.com) listing "Non-Contest Poetry Publishers."

Dacus says her list "is intended as a service, and the more poets who hear about it, the more suggestions I get to add to the list. Most poets should consider their options, and going with a traditional small press, rather than the contest route, is a great way to go, if you connect with a press good for your needs. A contest win isn't the only way to get the word out about a book! Though it's a nice way to be briefly featured, it probably doesn't sell books any more than doing readings, networking online, etc. If we all bought more books from independent presses, we could have more alternatives to contests. And poets should read voraciously!! (Okay, stepping off my soapbox now.)"

Another is Steven Schroeder's list of poetry presses with open reading periods: http://steveschroeder.info/open-reading-periods/

Since a lot of presses keep up a blog, a Twitter account, or a Facebook page, I recommend signing up to find out more about the poetry publishers you like. I actually found the publisher of my latest book through new media research. Kitsune Books has a Twitter account, a Facebook page, as well as a blog that I followed, and I found the more I read about them, the more I liked their aesthetic. The editors twittered about the anime they liked and the music they listened to, even their editorial processes, and from that, I thought that my manuscript would be a good fit for them.

Deciding if you want to try going smaller with your book of poetry means becoming more aware of the poetry presses behind the books on the shelves. There's always a benefit to being more educated and aware of what the small independent poetry presses are doing, because that's often where the most exciting poetry is found. Take a look around you, read up, and use the Web to find out more.

BE CREATIVE IN YOUR CAREER:

Offer Private Writing Workshops

....

by Chloe Yelena Miller

There is no single way to earn an income as a poet. I didn't realize that at first. After finishing an MFA program, I went the common route of teaching required composition writing classes at local colleges. On the side, I tutored Italian and English. I was at the whim of my many employers. I needed to take some of the creativity from my craft and put it into my career planning.

A few years later, I gave a workshop on just that—creativity—at a writing conference. An attendee asked me if I knew a private writing coach. I smiled and my eyebrows shot up. I realized I hadn't been using the right label to prompt me to lead private workshops. I answered a resounding, "Yes! I am one!" and my career shifted into gear.

Writing coaching was, in fact, exactly the work I had been doing all along in my day and moonlighting jobs. Are you in a similar situation?

WHY TEACH PRIVATELY?

Working as a private writing and workshop coach has been wonderful. I have the opportunity to set my own schedule and focus on topics I'm passionate about. I work with students who are motivated by interest instead of a university requirement. I make my own course and day-to-day schedule. The final reward is not only keeping 100% of the net profits, but also spending my days doing something I believe in. All of this ultimately nourishes my writing.

Writers teach because we love to discuss writing and encourage others as we've been encouraged. A private writing coach can continue talking about writing while organizing private workshops and earning enough to make it worthwhile. This is unlike the adjunct route that often leads to little money, running from campus to campus, and then committing to a program before discovering your class was cancelled.

That's not to say that you should abandon adjuncting. Teaching at a local university can help you gain authority in the eyes of potential private clients. Similarly, the experience of running successful private workshops might make you more attractive to a hiring committee for a better paying teaching position at a university. The two career paths can work in tandem.

STARTING YOUR OWN BUSINESS

Running your own business takes work to create, organize and maintain, not to mention to help it grow. Yes, writers can run businesses like the best entrepreneurs. If, like most writers, you freelance or juggle a number of part-time jobs, then you have already honed the right skills.

A private writing workshop can be as short as an hour or as long as an ongoing semester-length program. The workshop instructor must dedicate time not only to teaching and developing stimulating syllabi, but also to advertising, collecting and keeping track of fees paid, and finding new students while maintaining the current ones. It can be a balancing act, but one that pays off in the end on many levels.

To get started, think about your skills. Are you more knowledgeable in one topic or do you have particular fields of interest? For example, do you know a lot about both poetry and architecture? You could lead a subject-specific or themed creative writing workshop which will distinguish you from other courses.

Be sure to teach a topic that you not only know, but that interests you.

Start with a working title and course description of the first workshop. Be sure to teach a topic that you not only know, but that interests you. I run primarily free-verse poetry and creative nonfiction memoir workshops organized around food and memoir.

As you grow your business, you'll meet others who do similar work. As with any career, networking is necessary and you want to be a good colleague. If a potential student contacts you who might not be a good fit with your background, recommend a colleague. You will find that others will return the favor and recommend clients to you.

WHERE TO MEET?

The next step is to choose a venue. I've given readings and led talks in obvious venues, as well as train stations and lingerie stores (don't ask). When you consider a venue, think widely. Of course, some will work better than others.

The most successful creative writing workshops that I've led have been at an urban library, an upscale community center, a small town continuing education program and through school programs. The key to developing your business and class location is to think creatively.

Consider your connections in the community; walk around the town and think about spaces from a writing teacher's point of view. What organization's space might benefit from additional foot traffic? Which space has enough room, is accessible, has parking or access to mass transportation and enough light?

First, consider the obvious: a library, bookstore or community center. Then, think more widely: yoga studio, natural foods store, paper store, art gallery, bar, etc. You might also consider paying to rent out a space. Think about how long you'll need the space, how regularly, any costs involved, if the venue will help with advertising, if you'll be responsible for cleaning, any restrictions (food, moving furniture), if you'll need to bring chairs, lights or something to write on, surrounding noise level, etc.

You might also decide to teach solely online or combine online and in-person workshops. In these cases, you might be targeting different populations. When you choose dates, think about religious, local and state holidays, as well as the seasons. I currently run mainly online workshops around my in-person commitments.

LET POTENTIAL STUDENTS KNOW: ADVERTISE!

Now it is time to make an advertising plan. Think about the classes you've enjoyed taking, from a short workshop at a library to an MFA course. How did you hear about them? What about the title and course description drew you in? You, in the beginning of your career, were the market you are looking at now.

Think widely about your advertising plan. For example, I teach memoir writing and have blogged and written guest blogs and newspaper articles on related topics. This is a great way to connect with a related community who might be interested in creative writing. You definitely want to research similar businesses both in your area and elsewhere. Look at these businesses as models and see what you can do to make your services unique.

One great way to advertise is to offer donations. Perhaps there is an upcoming charity auction for an organization that you believe in. You could donate one hour, one workshop or a discount coupon. This is a win-win situation: potential clients will learn about you and the charity will benefit.

You might also consider contacting your alumni organizations and offering a workshop with one of those groups. Perhaps you could offer your services as a team-building exercise through a forwarding-thinking HR department of a nonprofit business?

You'll develop an e-mail mailing list by asking people who contact you if you may add them to the mailing list. Be sure to keep your communications brief and only when necessary to avoid the spam folder.

You don't want to be hard to find. Invite these folks to follow your blog and/or join a Facebook group. Be sure to regularly update your blog and Facebook page. As you read books, attend conferences, hear about submission opportunities, etc., share that information with your readers. Keep in touch every way that you promise.

LOOK THE PART

To run a business, you need to look like a business. This means a website and/or blog, business cards, social networking presence on sites like Facebook and perhaps even brochures. Use your blog or other social networking as a means to attract possible clients. You might want to guest blog on related blogs in order to gain readership. You can leave business cards and/or pamphlets in local coffee shops or bookstores.

You can set up most of your business for free. Your online presence takes time, but not money. As you get used to it, you'll work more quickly. You might, however, need to pay for space, computer equipment and business cards.

From the business side of things, you'll want to register your business. Check with the local town or city government and see what steps need to be taken. Unless you register and run your business as a not-for-profit, your services are for-profit.

MONEY DOESN'T HAVE TO BE A TABOO SUBJECT

Now for the potentially daunting question: What to charge? You don't have the overhead of a large school, but you want to make a profit. Consider the amount of time that you'll spend advertising, planning and actually running a class. Look around and see what local programs and individual writing coaches cost in your metro-area. Then, set a price that seems both fair and worth the time and effort that you'll put into your business.

Write a business plan and speak with an experienced professional for advice.

You might consider offering repeat students discounts and running the occasional special. To make your services available to a wider range of clients, offer a scholarship.

Regarding your income and net costs, you probably want to discuss possible deductions with a tax accountant. Write a business plan and speak with an experienced professional for advice.

Until your literary work is widely published, you'll be teaching mostly beginner to intermediate students. Therefore, you'll want to discuss poetry in an accessible and practical fashion. Learn more about the students before you start. See how much experience they've had in workshops and proceed accordingly. As your earlier teachers did, set ground rules in the workshop. Explain to the students who to best offer feedback in a workshop setting.

You should explain in your course descriptions how much experience the students are expected to have. Decide if there will be an application process to join the class. For example, will students be submitting work before being accepted to the class or will it be first come, first serve?

> You should explain in your course descriptions how much experience the students are expected to have.

You might be asking why writers should pay you instead of working with you in a graduate-style workshop group free of charge? I've organized peer writing workshops and the difference is just that: we are peers and we all offer and receive feedback. In classes, I might share something I've written as a part of a lecture, but I don't expect the students to offer feedback.

If a potential client seems to be on the same level as you, perhaps you'll have less to offer that person. Chances are, however, that your students will mostly be beginning-level students. I find that most of my clients consider graduate school after our classes or are taking the class to see if they want to seriously pursue graduate school. If it seems that someone has moved beyond your skill set, she will appreciate your suggesting a higher-level coach or university class.

AVOID THE PITFALLS

There are possible reasons not to offer private writing workshops. All of the steps above can be time consuming, especially at the beginning of the learning curve. If it seems daunting, start small. Don't quit your day-job, but rather slowly build the necessary network. I have doubled my income each year that I've been doing this. I started off quite slowly as I was learning the ropes and meeting people.

Always check in regularly with the students. It is easy enough to tweak the curriculum to fit their needs. You might even send out a questionnaire before the class starts. This careful attention will help them to meet their goals and enjoy the class before sharing news about it with other people. Gather positive comments and ask the students if you can use these testimonials on your website.

Of course, there are always students who are less happy. Follow-up with them and ask questions. Sometimes it is a simple misunderstanding or perhaps the student had impossible expectations. Regardless of the reason, you can learn from this feedback. Your business will grow and change as you learn from your experiences.

I know that my students enjoy the workshops not only because they repeat classes, but because they keep in touch. If you teach in other settings, you know that teaching can be quite rewarding as you develop relationships and witness the long-term effects of your teaching.

Teaching writing keeps us honest as we continue to not only practice our craft, but examine it closely. Instead of working for someone else, work for yourself.

CHLOE YELENA MILLER is a poet, essayist and writing teacher in Washington, DC. She has work forthcoming or published in the *Cortland Review*, *Alimentum* and *Narrative*, among others. Her manuscript was a finalist for the Philip Levine Prize in Poetry. She teaches at George Mason University, Fairleigh Dickinson University and privately. Chloe blogs about writing at http://chloeyelenamiller. blogspot.com.

FROM A JUDGE'S PERSPECTIVE:

On Poetry Contests and Competitions

···

by Nancy Susanna Breen

Ever since I first helped judge a poetry contest 25 years ago, I've believed every poet could benefit from seeing the contest process from the other side. If you could read a stack of entries and weigh one poem against the other, you'd see competitions in a whole new light.

I used to enter poetry contests all the time, usually those sponsored by state poetry societies or literary magazines. Now I seem to participate more as a judge than an entrant. I've served as a screening, final, or sole judge for the National Federation of State Poetry Societies, small literary magazines, writers' groups, arts festivals, and *Writer's Digest*, among others.

I've learned a lot; and I'd like to share a few observations I hope will help you improve your next contest experience.

FOLLOW THE GUIDELINES

Guidelines are rules. Assume your work will be eliminated if you don't follow them. You wouldn't participate in a poker tournament or even a baking contest at the county fair without knowing the rules, would you? (Please say no.) Then do *not* enter a poetry contest without reading and following the guidelines to the letter.

LINE LIMITS. I toss out too many contest entries because they exceed the stated line limit. Sometimes the poet simply wasn't paying attention. Alarmingly, too many poets don't know how to break and count lines in a poem. In a few instances, the poet deliberately tries to fudge the line limit.

Example: Long prose poems often turn out to be rhymed; or line breaks have been removed so the poem appears to be several paragraphs of dense text. This is a sneaky way the poet can try to enter, say, a 64-line poem when the contest limit is 32 lines. My approach to such entries is to count the end rhymes within the paragraphs. If the poem, properly formatted, would have run over the line limit, out it goes.

FORMAT CORRECTLY. Depending on the contest, guidelines may state a variety of formatting requirements: standard 8½ × 11 white paper, certain margins, basic fonts (that means no italics or flowery typefaces), personal information in a specific area of the page or no personal information at all. The National Federation of State Poetry Societies (NFSPS) and its related groups have contest formatting rules that involve duplicate copies, how and where categories are listed on the page, and more. Contests that accept e-mail entries can be even stricter about formatting, such as requiring what must appear in the subject line of the e-mail. Know what's required before you prepare your entry.

NOTE THE DEADLINE. Pay attention to that date and whether it's a postmark or received-by deadline. Find out what happens to late entries. Your poems and fee may be returned or they might go right into the trash.

PROOFREAD

Review every line of your poetry carefully. I wouldn't eliminate an entry because of a typographical error, but that may not be true of other judges. What about a misspelled word? It would depend. Sometimes a word isn't misspelled; the poet used the wrong version of the word. I hate that (and yes, I've made that mistake). I also bristle if there's more than one error in a poem. That's just plain sloppy, and a judge questions how serious the poet is about his work.

I ignore punctuation if the poem is good, but I know from experience judges can be really unfair and sometimes old-fashioned about usage.

Punctuation is harder to pin down. Standards change according to the reference source and what the reader thinks is correct, plus there's that little matter of "poetic license." I ignore punctuation if the poem is good, but I know from experience judges can be really unfair and sometimes old-fashioned about usage. Don't get hung up on whether to use serial commas or dashes versus semicolons. Shoot for clarity. Really erratic punctuation or none at all may have an impact; you'll have to decide if that's a risk you want to take, but do what you feel is best for your poem.

HOW TO PICK A CONTEST

There are many reasons to enter a contest: prestige, publication, and even money. However, there are so many contests and most of them have entry fees. So it makes sense to figure out which contests are winners for your goals.

- **ENTER CONTESTS THAT OFFER PUBLICATION.** Most poets want validation, and there's no greater validation than publication.

- **ENTER CONTESTS THAT OFFER PAYMENT.** Did I say publication was the greatest validation? I meant money, because money and poetry usually mix about as well as running and scissors.

- **ENTER CONTESTS THAT ARE WELL-KNOWN.** Sure, it's nice to win contests, but it's even nicer if someone has heard of it before.

- **ENTER CONTESTS THAT PROVIDE A PREMIUM.** For instance, enter a contest that provides a subscription to the magazine or the winning collection as part of the entry fee. That way, you know you'll get something out of the experience.

—*Robert Lee Brewer*

CONTENT AND STYLE

AVOID THE "SAME OLD, SAME OLD." Often clichés and tired imagery turn up in poems because the poet is lazy. In other cases, the poet is overwriting. Seriously, say "she cried" instead of "the tears ran down her face." By the time a judge has seen the twentieth poem where tears are cascading like Niagara down someone's cheeks, she's ready to wet a few tissues herself. In fact, watch out for "tears" in general: rain falling like tears, wax dripping like tears...trust me, it's been done.

As an exercise, read some bad poetry. Come on, you know the Internet is full of it. Print some out and circle all the clichés and worn-out images. Make a list, if you like, and memorize it so you can avoid such lapses in your own work.

THINK TWICE ABOUT LOVE POEMS. One kind of love poem that doesn't win prizes resembles what a teenager might write to or about a new crush. Another kind emulates Elizabeth Barrett Browning ("How do I love thee..."), including the antiquated language. Many are heartfelt but simply don't distinguish themselves. They read as if they were written as private messages to the beloved, without any attempt at craft, and many have a taint of desperation. To a disinterested reader, they're usually pretty dull. Unless your love poetry has at least the snap and originality of boxed valentines for kids, don't enter it in contests.

THE NATURE OF NATURE IMAGES. Nature poems seem to be a breeding ground for stock images poets can't resist using over and over. Leaves, usually rust-colored or fiery, rain down in autumn. Snow always blankets the landscape in winter. Spring is all about bursting buds and renewal. In summer, the sun blazes and storm clouds gather on the horizon.

You're a poet! If you turn to such bland imagery, you're writing half-asleep. Okay, use these images as placeholders in the heat of composition; but when you revise your poem, stretch your imagination as you describe that snowy field, November forest, re-awakening garden, or hot summer day.

GETTING RELIGIOUS. Religious contest poems tend to resemble the prayers or hymns of the poet's faith. Consequently, the poems all sound the same, without much of the poets' individual thoughts, fervor or perspectives. If you want to enter a religious poem in a general contest, make it yours, not a paraphrase of the "Our Father" or the lyrics of "A Mighty Fortress is Our God." Nobody said religious poems must sound a certain way. If you don't believe me, track down some good contemporary religious poetry and see how well-crafted and exciting it can be.

ABOUT RHYMING, METERED POEMS

Judging a contest of all-rhyming poetry usually makes my brain swell. Logic suggests the extra effort of writing in meter and rhyme would dissuade poets from even trying. Far from it! A well-publicized contest for rhyming poetry brings in a deluge of entries, many of them really bad. No one's reading poetry, yet everyone thinks he or she can write it if it rhymes.

Here are some tips to make your rhymed, metered poems stand out in competition:

- Keep *oo* and *ay* rhymes to a minimum. They're monotonous and contribute to your poem sounding the same as everyone else's.
- Avoid writing in rhymed couplets, especially iambic verse in lines shorter than five feet. Since it's the easiest, most familiar poetic style, the number of such entries overwhelms contests. Again, your poems fade into the crowd. Also, it's too easy to create that sing-song effect that destroys a poem.
- Shakespearean sonnets are very popular with entrants. Unfortunately, without finesse, these can come across as lightweight, especially if the closing couplet is too clever or on the nose. Go for individuality and try another sonnet form, or even another poetic form entirely.
- Always read your poem out loud. Better yet, have someone read it to you cold. You'll find out if you forced the meter in places, if the rhythm is rocky or awkward, or if you were so exacting your lines sound as if a metronome is ticking.
- If you think your poem would make a lovely greeting card, don't enter it.

- Understand that humorous or juvenile poems don't stand up well against serious entries. This is doubly true in a contest that welcomes all kinds of poetry. Save whimsy and cleverness for contests that call specifically for light verse or children's poetry.
- You live in the 21st century. Don't you dare use "thee," "thou," "whilst," or insert apostrophes for letters ("ne'er," "'tis," "enter'd").

FINAL THOUGHTS

Remember, judges are human and often poets themselves. They're supposed to remain objective, but their preferences regarding style and craft probably are going to influence their choices. I have my own ideas and prejudices—this article reflects some of them. I look for quality above all other considerations. In the end, though, I can't help the innate reasons I respond more favorably to one poem over another, especially when it comes to ranking the top poems.

That's why not winning is different from failure. Another judge may have chosen your work over that of the prizewinners, so move on to another contest.

Best of luck on your next poetry competition! I hope someday I get to choose *your* work for a prize.

NANCY SUSANNA BREEN is a published poet, contest judge, and former editor of *Poet's Market*. Her chapbooks include *Rites and Observances* (Finishing Line Press) and *How Time Got Away* (Pudding House Publications). She founded and maintains the writing website Nudged to Write (www.nudged2write.com).

PHOTO: Joshua Bodenstein

IS IT A 'CON'?

Think Before You Trust

What is a "con?" Con is short for "confidence," an adjective defined by *Webster's* as "of, relating to, or adept at swindling by false promise," as in "confidence man" or "confidence game." While the publishing world is full of legitimate opportunities for poets to gain honor and exposure for their work, there are also plenty of "cons." How can you tell the difference? The following are some of the most common situations that cost poets disappointment, frustration—and cash. Learn to spot them before submitting your work, and don't let your vanity be your guide.

ANTHOLOGIES

Has this happened to you? You see an ad in a perfectly respectable publication announcing a poetry contest with big cash prizes. You enter, and later you receive a glowing letter congratulating you on your exceptional poem, which the contest sponsor wants to include in his deluxe hardbound anthology of the best poetry submitted to the contest. The anthology costs only, say, $65. You don't have to buy it—they'll still publish your poem—but wouldn't you be proud to own one? And wouldn't it be nice to buy additional copies to give to family and friends? And for an extra charge you can include a biographical note. And so on . . .

Of course, when the anthology arrives, the quality of the poetry may not be what you were expecting, with several poems crammed unattractively onto a page. Apparently everyone who entered the contest was invited to be published; you basically paid cash to see your poem appear in a phone-book-like volume with no literary merit whatsoever.

Were you conned? Depends on how you look at it. If you bought into the flattery and believed you were being published in an exclusive, high-quality publication, no doubt you feel duped. On the other hand, if all you were after was seeing your poem in print, even knowing you'd have to pay for the privilege, then you got what you wanted. (Unless you've deceived yourself into believing you've truly won an honor and now have a worthy publishing credit; you don't.)

HELPFUL WEBSITES

The following websites include specific information about questionable poetry publishers and awards. For more websites of value to poets, see Additional Resources.

- An Incomplete Guide to Print On Demand Publishers offers articles on POD publishing, comparisons of POD publishers (contracts, distribution, fees, etc.) and an online forum: http://booksandtales.com/pod/index.php
- Answers to frequently asked questions about poetry awards from the Academy of American Poets: www.poets.org/page.php/prmID/116
- Poets will find warnings and other valuable publishing information on the Preditors & Editors website: www.anotherealm.com/prededitors/
- Writer Beware tracks contests, publishers and literary agents: www.sfwa.org/beware
- Literary Contest Caution at http://windpub.com/literary.scams

---

If you don't want to add insult to injury, resist additional spiels, like having your poem printed on coffee mugs and T-shirts (you can do this yourself through print shops or online services like www.cafepress.com) or spending large sums on awards banquets and conferences. And, before you submit a single line of poetry, find out what rights the contest sponsor acquires. You may be relinquishing all rights to your poem simply by mailing it in or submitting it through a website. If the poem no longer belongs to you, the publisher can do whatever he wishes with it. Don't let your vanity propel you into a situation you'll always regret.

READING AND CONTEST FEES

Suppose you notice a promising market for your poetry, but the editor requires a set fee just to consider your work. Or you see a contest that interests you, but you have to pay the sponsor a fee just to enter. Are you being conned?

In the case of reading fees, keep these points in mind: Is the market so exceptional that you feel it's worth risking the cost of the reading fee to have your work considered? What makes it so much better than markets that do not charge fees? Has the market been around awhile, with an established publishing schedule? What are you paid if your work is accepted? Are reasonably priced samples available so you can judge the production values and quality of the writing?

Reading fees don't necessarily signal a suspicious market. In fact, they're increasingly popular as editors struggle with the costs of publishing books and magazines, including the man-hours required to read loads of (often bad) submissions. However, fees represent an additional financial burden on poets, who often don't receive any monetary reward for their poems to begin with. It's really up to individual poets to decide whether paying a fee is beneficial to their publishing efforts. Think long and hard about fee-charging markets that are new and untried, don't pay poets for their work (at the very least a print publication should offer a contributor's copy), charge high prices for sample copies or set fees that seem unreasonable.

Entry fees for contests often fund prizes, judges' fees, honorariums and expenses of running and promoting the contest (including publishing a "prize" collection or issue of a magazine). Other kinds of contests charge entry fees, from Irish dancing competitions to bake-offs at a county fair. Why not poetry contests?

....

Watch out for contests that charge higher than average fees, especially if the fees are out of proportion to the amount of money being given.

....

That's not to say you shouldn't be cautious. Watch out for contests that charge higher-than-average fees, especially if the fees are out of proportion to the amount of prize money being given. (Look through the Contests & Awards section to get a sense of what most competitions charge.) Find out how long the contest has been around, and verify whether prizes have been awarded each year and to whom. In the case of book and chapbook contests, send for one of the winning publications to confirm that the publisher puts out a quality product. Regard with skepticism any contest that tells you you've won something, then demands payment for an anthology, trophy or other item. (It's okay if a group offers an anthology for a modest price without providing winners with free copies. Most state poetry societies have to do this; but they also present cash awards in each category of the contest, and their entry fees are low.)

SUBSIDY PUBLISHERS, PRINT-ON-DEMAND

Poetry books are a hard sell to the book-buying public. Few of the big publishers handle these books, and those that do feature the "name" poets (i.e., the major prize winners and contemporary masters with breathtaking reputations). Even the small presses publish only so many books per year—far less than the number of poets writing.

No wonder so many poets decide to pay to have their poetry collections published. While some may self-publish (i.e., take full control of their book, working directly with a printer), others turn to subsidy publishers (also called "vanity publishers") and print-on-demand (POD) publishers.

There are many differences between subsidy publishing and POD publishing, as well as similarities (having to pay to get published is a big one). Whether or not you get conned is entirely up to you. You have to take responsibility for asking questions, doing research on presses, and reading the fine print on the contract to make sure you know exactly what you're paying for. There are landmines in dealing with subsidy and POD publishers, and you have to investigate thoroughly and intelligently to avoid damage.

Some questions to keep in mind: Are fees inflated compared to the product and services you'll be receiving? Will you still own the rights to your book? Does the publisher put out a quality product that's attractive and cleanly printed? (Get a sample copy and find out.) How many copies of the book will you receive? How much will you have to pay for additional copies? How will your book be sold and distributed? (Don't count on seeing your volume in bookstores.)

Will you receive royalties? How much? Does the publisher offer any kind of promotional assistance or is it all up to you? Will those promotion efforts be realistic and results-oriented? (Sometimes "promotion" means sending out review copies, which is a waste—such volumes are rarely reviewed.) Don't wait until *after* you've signed a contract (and a check) to raise these issues. Do your homework first.

Obviously, poets who don't stay on their toes may find themselves preyed upon. And a questionable publishing opportunity doesn't have to be an out-and-out rip-off for you to feel cheated. In every situation, you have a choice *not* to participate. Exercise that choice, or at least develop a healthy sense of skepticism before you fling yourself and your poetry at the first smooth talker who compliments your work. Poets get burned because they're much too impatient to see their work in print. Calm your ego, slow down and devote that time, energy and money toward reading other poets and improving your own writing. You'll find that getting published will eventually take care of itself.

FINDING READERS:

How to Get Your Poetry Into Their Hands

....

by Diane Lockward

Poets who are fortunate enough to have a full-length collection from a large publishing house receive the services of a marketing department with a budget that covers advertising and a book tour. But if you, like most of us, get your book from a small press, you will find that your publisher has little or no budget for promotion. There are a number of benefits to working with a small press publisher, for example, more involvement in the design of the book and a personal relationship with your publisher. However, if you want your book to find its way into the hands of readers, you are going to have to work to make that happen.

SPREADING THE WORD

The work of promoting your book begins before the book is even out. Most small press publishers have found that ads are not cost effective, but they will design a press release and do a snail mailing for you. While you wait for your book to get published, compile an up-to-date snail mail list. Since mailings are expensive, include only your best prospects, not everyone you've ever met. Many publishers also do an e-mail blitz, so prepare a list of e-mail addresses. Your publisher will most likely send the press release and a review copy to journals that have published your work. Assemble a list of the names and addresses of those journals, but only the ones that run reviews.

After your book is published, supplement your publisher's mailings with your own. Many publishers provide postcards for this purpose, but if yours doesn't, you can design your own inexpensively at an online service such as vistaprint.com. Upload your cover image onto one side and add ordering information on the other, leaving space for the name and address of the recipient. In your e-mail notes include your cover image, but do not add an attachment as many people will not open it. It doesn't matter if people receive more than one notice about your book. Janet Holmes, publisher of Ahsahta Books, says, "Sometimes a reader needs to see the title of a book multiple times before it sinks in as something to acquire." Many recipients will appreciate—and act upon—the reminder.

Ask your publisher to provide you with the press release via attachment. Save it on your computer and include it with any additional review copies you mail out. Send the press release to your college alumni newsletter. Put one up on the bulletin board where you work. Fire off some to local libraries and bookstores. Send another with a fact sheet to your local newspaper. Request an article and offer to go in for an interview. My local paper interviewed me and ran an article for each of my books. That would not have happened if I hadn't asked.

LINING UP READINGS

Tom Hunley, director of Steel Toe Books, says, "Readings are far and away the #1 way for poets to sell books." Let your first reading be a book launch party. Invite your relatives, friends, and poet pals. Have food. This reading may well be your best sales event. If you have a friend with a book coming out around the same time, consider joining forces. Publisher Joan Cusack Handler celebrates each new CavanKerry Press book with a literary salon held in someone's home. Poet Claire Keyes (*The Question of Rapture*, Mayapple Press, 2008) had house readings held by friends. She and her hosts collaborated on the guest list and shared expenses.

After the initial round of readings, you need to get proactive. Poet Kate Greenstreet (*case sensitive*, Ahsahta Books, 2006) warns that "if you won't ask—and people aren't already inviting you—obviously, you won't be reading." To get readings, you need to compose a query letter. Keep it informative and succinct. I send most of mine by e-mail with links to my website and online sites where my work is available. Make a list of venues in your area. Try bookstores, libraries, art galleries, coffeehouses—all the usual places. Then get creative. I have friends who've read in chocolate stores, wine bars, and hip jewelry stores. Contact local book clubs and suggest that your book be a selection. Offer to present a reading and discussion for the group. Senior citizens' residences and nursing homes are often looking for social programs. Offer your services for a reading. If you have friends who teach, offer to do a reading, a Q & A, and a workshop. Apply to conferences, festivals, and book fairs.

Target audiences that might likely have an interest in your work and in poetry. For example, I'm a former high school English teacher. One of my most successful readings was for a district-wide English department meeting. I read 10 poems and offered 10 teaching tips. The supervisor purchased a copy of my book for each department member—all 40 of them. Plus, that presentation led to an offer to teach a six-hour workshop for a small group of teachers.

Also target groups that don't ordinarily attend readings but are somehow connected to your subject matter. Are your poems about flowers? Query nearby garden clubs and suggest a reading at one of their upcoming meetings. Do your poems deal with woman-related topics? Contact area women's clubs. Marion Haddad (*Somewhere Between Mexico and a River Called Home*, Pecan Grove Press, 2004) is the American-born daughter of Syrian immigrants and for 35 years lived a few minutes from the Mexican border, so she often seeks readings at Arab-American gatherings and border studies events. Richard Jeffrey Newman, whose *The Silence of Men* (CavanKerry, 2006) deals with gender, sexuality, and recovery from child sexual abuse, solicited and received an invitation to read at the 2008 Wellness and Writing Connections Conference. One of my favorite readings was at New York Life Investment Management, certainly an unlikely place for poetry, but the woman who heads Human Resources runs special programs for women employees. I proposed a reading entitled "Poetry and the Lives of Women." My host pre-ordered six of my books and had a drawing for them, a great alternative when reading at an event where selling books might not be appropriate.

Remember that the farther you cast your net, the fewer responses you're likely to get.

Eventually you will need to seek readings outside of your own area. Remember that the farther you cast your net, the fewer responses you're likely to get. Cast it anyhow because you will get some responses. To find out where readings are held, map out the distance you're willing to travel. Then do a Google search, for example, "poetry venues in New Jersey" or "poetry readings in Boston." That should bring up some listings. If there's contact information, send off your query letter. Check out reading schedules on other poets' websites. Visit online calendars, for example, those at The Academy of American Poets' and Poets & Writers' websites. Use these to suggest possible venues to query. When you get readings, publicize them as widely as possible. List them in online calendars and send out e-mail notices to people you know in the area of the reading. Do not rely solely on the venue host to drum up an audience for you.

Regardless of where you're reading, remember that you're promoting your book, so be prepared to read poems from the book. Greg Kosmicki, of The Backwaters Press, advises poets that while they may get tired of reading the same poems, the audience will be hearing them for the first time. Your listeners will be more inclined to buy your book if you hold it and read from it. Remember, too, that not everyone who attends your reading will buy your book. My own publisher, Charlie Hughes of Wind Publications, suggests that often the "value in a reading or personal appearance is not in the number of books sold at the event, but in getting the writer's name in the newspaper announcing the event—building name recognition." I usually bring along oversized postcards with my cover image on one side and a poem and ordering information on the other. I give these away and like to think that some of the recipients might make a later purchase. I also always carry some business cards with me, cover image on one side, contact information on the other.

USING THE INTERNET

The Internet is one of your best resources for promoting your book. If you don't already have a website, get one. Even if your publisher has a page for your book at the press' website, you should have your own website. You can get a domain name very inexpensively. Since this is your website's address, use your own name so people can easily locate your website. If you design your own website, you will pay only for the hosting. If you use a free hosting site, be sure it's ad-free. A website with ads looks awful and unprofessional. If you use a web designer's services, you will, of course, pay more, but don't go wild. Your site should include a bio, an image of your book cover, purchase information, sample poems, links to other poems, links to online reviews and interviews, a calendar of your readings, and contact information. Be sure your website is attractive and up to date. A website that is not maintained does not make a good impression.

A blog takes some time, but it's a great place to establish contacts with other poets and another place to display your book cover and list readings.

Consider keeping a blog. There's a big community now of poet bloggers. A blog takes some time, but it's a great place to establish contacts with other poets and another place to display your book cover and list readings. You can add podcasts and videos, thus creating long-distance readings for potential fans who might not otherwise be able to get to a reading. Kate Greenstreet kept a blog for two years. She used it to do a series of more than 100 first-book interviews and undoubtedly earned many friends. As much as she gave to the poetry community, she got back in support when her own book came out.

Join an Internet social network such as Facebook, MySpace, or Red Room. These are hot gathering places for poets, and all are free. I'm on Facebook where I create event listings for my readings and send out invitations to "friends" who live in the area of an upcoming reading. Without this resource, I would not know these people's names or how to contact them. I've learned about venues and booked readings through Facebook contacts, gotten an online interview, and participated in a college student's poetry course project. Richard

Jeffrey Newman received an invitation from a Facebook contact to go to Chile as part of Chile Poesia, an international poetry festival. A poetry listserv will also put you among poets and offer opportunities for sales and readings.

A final suggestion for your internet use, this one fast and easy. Use your e-mail signature to good advantage. Set your e-mail program to automatically add a link to your website at the bottom of each new message you write. If you like, you can add a link to your blog or anything special you have online such as a poem feature. Think of the signature area as free billboard space. You'll be amazed how many people will click on those links and go visiting.

KEEPING EXPECTATIONS REALISTIC

Promoting your book is the business of poetry, but don't expect to make money. As Kate Greenstreet says, "When we're talking about selling poetry books, we're talking about doing business, but it isn't conventional business even if you work really hard at it." Richard Jeffrey Newman reminds us that books of poetry "find their audience one reader at a time, slowly, over time." If you want your book to find those readers, you need to be industrious, adventurous, persistent and patient.

DIANE LOCKWARD'S second collection, *What Feeds Us* (Wind Publications), received the 2006 Quentin R. Howard Poetry Prize. Her poems appear in Garrison Keillor's *Good Poems for Hard Times* and in such journals as *Harvard Review, Spoon River Poetry Review,* and *Prairie Schooner.* (www.dianelockward.com)

10 TIPS FOR THE PERFECT READING

....

by Taylor Mali

The extent of the advice given to poets for how to present their work aloud at poetry readings usually boils down to reading slower, louder, and clearer. And while those are important improvements to almost anyone's style of recitation (albeit extremely difficult to make yourself do, especially at the same time), there are several other factors to keep in mind if you want your audience to appreciate your skills as a writer and perhaps even buy your book after the reading.

1. **TRY TO MAKE THE FIRST THING OUT OF YOUR MOUTH POETRY.** What else could be more important than immediately giving the audience an example of what they came to the reading to hear? Insipid chatter between poems is bad enough, but introductory insipid chatter is even worse and tends to go on and on. Sometimes it will be five minutes before a poet even gets to the first poem! Everything you think you need to say—thank yous, shout outs, announcements about journals in which your poetry will be forthcoming, or plugs for your books and next appearances— all of this can be mentioned after the first poem. Or maybe not at all (except for the thank yous).

2. **KNOW WHAT POEMS YOU WILL READ AND HAVE THEM CLOSE AT HAND.** Don't burden the audience with having to watch you flip through your own book or resort to looking at the table of contents while you make a self-deprecating joke only to realize finally that the poem you wanted to read is actually in your other book. Have your poems picked out in advance as well as the order in which you will read them. All of your fussing between poems counts toward the time you have been given to read.

3. **DON'T BE THE POET WHO READS FOREVER!** Time limits do not only apply to bad poets; they apply to brilliant poets like you as well. Unfortunately, it's usually the bad poets who have no concept of time. Before the reading, rehearse your set (with a stopwatch if possible) and do not go over the time you've been allotted. Losing track of how long you've been reading is no excuse for going over. Don't ask the organizer to give you a signal when you have five minutes left or periodically look up and ask, "How am I doing on time?" It's your responsibility to know how you are "doing on time." If anything, be a little under time and leave your audience wanting more.

4. **KEEP YOUR CHATTER BETWEEN POEMS TO A MINIMUM.** Most of what poets say between poems comes from nervousness and not any real need to explicate the poem.

5. **PERFORM ONE POEM BY SOMEONE ELSE.** Depending on how much time you have been given, it's a nice idea to celebrate the work of someone else beside yourself. Introduce your audience to one of your favorite poems by one of your favorite poets. Tell them where they can find this particular poem and two things you love about it. Then, at the end of your reading of the poem, say the author's name one last time.

6. **PERFORM AT LEAST ONE OF YOUR POEMS FROM MEMORY.** Once you experience the freedom of being able to make constant eye contact while having your hands completely free to gesture or hang naturally at your sides (which doesn't feel natural at all but looks perfectly normal), you will want to memorize more of your work. And you should! The roots of poetry are bardic, not literary, so it is entirely fitting to work on making the recitation of your poem a better performance. Work at memorizing more and more poetry every day. The mind is a muscle; the more you use it, the stronger it gets.

7. **LET THE AUDIENCE CLAP IF THEY WANT TO CLAP.** If one definition of a "performance" poem is that after it's over, the audience not only wants to applaud but knows that applause is appropriate, then you could say that one definition of an "academic" poem is that after it's over—assuming you know when that is—the audience doesn't even know if they are supposed to clap. Poets with limited performance skills will often request that audiences not applaud between poems because they are uncomfortable with the awkward silence that fills the room when they finish each poem. In fact, sometimes the only clue that such poets have finished a poem is when they say, "The next poem I'd like to read." Certainly don't telegraph the end of your poem by speeding up or trailing off or both. Rather build toward it, perhaps nodding your head ever so slightly at the end.

8. **MAKE EYE CONTACT.** Real eye contact. Look at different parts of the room as you glance up from your text every now and then. Poets who look at the exact same spot as they methodically lift their heads every seven seconds to pretend they are looking at the same person (whose chair is apparently attached to one of the lighting fixtures) aren't fooling anyone. It is better never to look up at all than to do so perfunctorily to mask your nervousness.

9. **IF THERE IS A MICROPHONE, USE IT.** Granted, when the microphone is attached to a podium, you won't have much choice but to use it. But faced with a solitary mic stand and the possibly awkward task of having to adjust it for your height while somehow also managing a bottle of water and the text from which you are about to read, you might decide you don't need a microphone at all. Not a good decision, even if you have a big, boomy voice. Without a microphone, you cannot get quiet when the poem invites it, or else no one will hear you when you do. Unless the system sounds like crap and has for the whole night, use the microphone, even if it takes a few extra seconds at the outset to adjust it.

10. **ENJOY YOURSELF.** This seems obvious, but audiences love to see people who love what they do, especially when they do it well. Smile a lot. Try reciting an entire poem while smiling. Let people suspect you are having the time of your life. And whatever you do, don't ever suggest that your reading is a kind of torture you are inflicting on the audience ("Don't worry. You only have to listen to three more!"). You are a genius, and your words are the proof. Knock 'em dead!

WHAT IS A PRESS KIT?

And Why Would You Want One?

....

by Kerry Dexter

//

A press kit, or media kit, is a tool that helps you tell your story—the story of your poetry, your work, and your ideas—succinctly and powerfully, to those who will help you share your work: writers and editors for print and web publications, people who organize readings, those who are looking for people to teach workshops and people to speak to their groups, and others you'll think of who'll help you spread the word, as well

If you're feeling a bit hesitant about promoting yourself and your work, Minnesota-based poet Susan Budig knows where you're coming from. "Try to look at the task from another angle," she advises. "Why do you want to share your poetry? Look at your work as something of value that you want to give to others."

HOW TO BUILD A MEDIA KIT

Your media kit needs to include four basic elements: a biography, information about your books, workshops, and other experience and credits, a short example of your work, and your contact information. There are a number of things you may want to add, and a few you'll want to stay away from, too. First, though, a look at what you need to know to put together the the basic four, from the easiest to prepare to the most challenging. Point to remember: every element is about telling your story.

Contact information is the easiest element: your name, and whatever way you choose for people to get in touch with you—e-mail address, physical address, website, telephone number—should be on each page of your media kit. That's true for physical copies as well as for pages you set up for Web use. You'd like to make it easy for people who want to know more about your work to get in touch.

Choose a short sample of your work, something characteristic, up beat if that suits your natural style, and, yes, short. Even if you specialize in epic poetry, choose an 10- or 12-line excerpt to represent your work.

Brief information about your books, workshops, and other publication credits and media appearances. In choosing these and writing about them, think about how this helps you tell your story. What if you do not have any such credits? A short narrative about your work, descrptions of workshops you'll offer even it you have not done so yet, topics of talks you could give would all work here.

Here is the way musician, poet, and writer Carrie Newcomer describes a workshop she teaches:

"In Writing Mindfully: Exploring The Sacred Ordinary, songwriters, poetry, and prose writers of all experience levels are welcome to explore writing in this workshop. It focuses on the power, value, and healing in telling our stories from our authentic voices and everyday experiences. Carrie has presented this workshop in spiritual and secular settings throughout the United States. This class is presented in a safe, and nurturing context."

This brief description gives an idea of who might come to such a workshop, and a bit about Newcomer's personality as an artist and as a teacher. Notice that it says something distinctive about the workshop, and it helps tell her story as a musician interested in spiritual values and healing who is comfortable in religious and non-religious situations, and who welcomes students in both settings.

Your biography will likely be the part of your media kit that requires the most time and thought. As you are preparing it, take some time and give that thought to the story you wish to tell. Did your love of writing sonnets come from your background as a Shakespearean actor? Is your current writing focused on family memories of Christmas in New England? Do you teach poetry to at-risk youth? What is it you do, and why do you do it?

Then, the idea is to take what you learn from this and create a narrative that will represent you professionally, and one that you'll be happy to see excerpted, quoted, and used to explain you and your work. What you want is a narrative biography, written in the third person. It is not your life story, and it's not your resume. It is a short piece that gives the reader a distinct impression of your voice, your style, and what your work is about. It's a short piece that a busy journalist can use as is to tell your story.

Here is the beginning of a bio I wrote to go along with bluegrass musician Dale Ann Bradley's release of her album "Catch Tomorrow:"

"A mountain murder ballad, a haunting tale of the Underground Railroad, a trip on a moonshine run, a walk in the mists of Ireland, a wild ride with Bobby McGee: whatever Dale Ann Bradley sings, people believe her. That's because she's the real deal, a Primitive Baptist preacher's daughter raised in the rural southeastern Kentucky crossroads of Williams Branch, where family and faith came first."

You come away from that with an impression of the project, and of the artist. Your own work and your own experiences are filled with equally vivid points. For the bio for your media kit, you are looking to distill them in a way that represents you and your work, and intrigues readers to find out more .

Here's another example:

"Melanie McMinn is an artist in fibre. Her creations include wall hangings and free-standing pieces whose gentle colours draw from the New Zealand landscape, sculptures of whimsical creatures of fantasy, custom portraits of household pets, and on occasion, hand-bags and hats. 'Wool is the most versatile medium imaginable. I can sculpt fine art objects, make vessels, bags, clothing, shoes, scarves, blankets, rugs, and I could even make my own shelter by felting a yurt, if I had to do so. What other medium has that range of applica-tion?' McMinn says, pointing out that she also loves sharing the ideas of warmth and con-nection that wool suggests.

McMinn has been drawn to art and craft since her childhood growing up in the Ameri-can South, where she learned needlework as a young child in a family where creating with one's hands was valued. As an older child she took up oil paints, and while at university sup-ported herself working as a mendhi (henna) temporary body art artist. She has also worked (and still does) creating with words, as a freelance copywriter.

Her wool and felt creations may be serious and thoughtful. They are equally likely to show her sense of humor and playfulness. Both these qualities stood McMinn in good stead when she had a stroke at age 36. Looking for ways to create as she recovered, she turned to felting and working in wool. and found there ways to draw together her creative gifts, her interests in nature and landscape, and her sense of whimsy."

Every sentence here could strand alone as a story about McMinn's work, and the whole works together to show her personality as well as what her work is like. Any sentence could be used, too, by a busy writer looking for quick information, or a gallery owner writing copy for a catalogue. McMinn's bio is about 250 words. That's a good length to aim for. You may also consider adding shorter and longer biographies, once you have the basic one in hand.

Guideposts to use when preparing your bio: keep it short, make it vivid, tell the story of your ideas not your life story, think about what you want people to know and remember about you as a poet.

There's an approach you don't want to take, too. Sandra Beckwith, New York based former publicist who publishes the free newsletter Build Book Buzz, points out that an over-the-top style favored by product marketers is showing up more and more in media kits, and that's not the right way to go. "When a poet's bio is presented in this format, the writer has to work hard to separate fact from hyperbole and will eventually give up. When the reporter can't find the necessary information quickly and easily, the poet risks losing the media opportunity," she says.

You might be wondering: Should I write my bio myself? Yes and no. Writing a biography is a challenge, and it is often hard to get the right perspective and tone when enwriting about yourself and your work, too.

Begin by writing out notes and ideas based on thinking about the guidelines above. If you are struggling with the idea or you think what you came up with could be better, enlist the help of another writer. One way to find someone is to check out the bylines on stories, profiles, and reviews you like online and in print, and approach these writers to see if one of them will help you, and what they might charge.

BEYOND THE BASICS

With the four basics in hand, it's time to think about what else you may want to add to your media kit, and why.

If you have quotes from reviews and/or comments from colleagues and students, you may want to have a sheet or a Web page with a few well-chosen selections. You may also or instead choose to include one or two of these on your basics pages. As you're choosing what to include (and what not to) remember the idea of story: an enthusiastic endorsement from a workshop organizer could go along with your description of your workshops, for example, and a line or two from a good review could accompany your bio.

Sandra Beckwith suggests creating "a fact sheet that educates about the poetry you write. Do you specialize in haiku? Create a fact sheet that uses bullets to educate the journalist about this art form. Or, develop a fact sheet that enlightens the reader about poems and poetry."

You may also want to include a professionally done head shot of yourself, copies of reviews of your work, and information about upcoming appearances or classes you'll be teaching. If you've appeared on radio or television or read your work at festivals or reading series, a sheet with information about these, as well as testimonials from the hosts and presenters, may be useful. How do you get these quotes and testimonials? Ask. If people are happy with your work, they will most likely be equally happy to do this.

What's next?

Now that you've got your media kit set up, online and in hard copy, what are things you might do with it?

Write a news or press release about your latest publication credit, about a reading you are doing, something that relates to your poetry, and send it out in hard copy or online with a link to your media kit.

Take a copy or two with you when you do readings or give talks, or teach—you never know when someone who is listening might step up to offer you another opportunity to share your work. Joyce Stohl, who organizes a reading series at Scarritt Bennett Center in Nashville, listened to one poet's recommendations and "From there I made contact with several of those she recommended. Sometimes people come to a reading, introduce themselves and ask to be considered. I talk to them then if I can and follow up with an e-mail conversation," in which she wants to know the sort of information included in the media kit basics.

Alisa Bowman, a non fiction writer who is based in Pennsylvania, put together a six page media kit for the latest book, *Project: Happily Ever After*. She include the press kit basics along with a question-and-answer article, and testimonials from media appearances. As Bowman's book has to do with saving her marriage, she was presenting herself, and was often interviewed and booked as, a marriage expert rather than solely as a nonfiction writer. How could you apply that subject matter approach to your poetry?

It took a lot of work, but it paid off for Bowman, in more ways than one. "I put my media kit online and I created hard copies, too," she says. "I included one with every review copy of the book I sent to the media. I linked to it when asking bloggers if they wanted to join the *Project: Happily Ever After* virtual tour. I made it easy to find on my blog, too." It helped her get booked for dozens of radio interviews, and helped her sign up high-profile bloggers for a virtual tour where she was interviewed by writers across the country. Creating her press kit, and using it wisely, allowed Bowman to create opportunities to share her work, and to respond to them.

"But, most important," she says, "it made my life easier. It saved me a tremendous amount of time—time that I could then devote to what I do and love the most—writing."

WHY POETS NEED PLATFORMS:

And How to Create One

....

by Sage Cohen

If you want your poetry to be read, people need to know who you are, what you write, and where to find it. A viable platform can take you there. The good news is that anyone who wants to establish a poetry platform can take the necessary steps to build one over time. No matter what your level of writing, publishing and social media savvy, you can have more fun end enjoy more success as you take small steps over time to cultivate your poetry platform. This article will tell you how.

WHAT A PLATFORM IS

Platform is the turf you name and claim as your area of writing expertise, and it's everything you do to make that expertise visible. Just as a thesis is the foundation of a term paper around which its argument is built, a platform is an organizing principle around which a poet's many expressions of work revolve. A platform says to both the poet and the world, "I am an expert in [fill in the blanks with your specialty]!"

Platform is both the destination and the path. Think of your platform as your portfolio of accomplishments (publications, leadership roles, Web presence, public appearances, classes) that demonstrate your authority on a given topic. You build it as you go. It keeps you moving forward, tells you where forward is, and is the measure against which you decide if you're getting there.

HOW A PLATFORM CAN HELP YOU

Every poet can benefit from having a platform—even you. Following are the primary advantages of platform consciousness:

- **POETIC PROWESS.** The more focused you are on taking your poetry forward, the more likely you will stay engaged in honing your craft, polishing drafts, completing poems and identifying organizing principles or themes in your growing collection of work.

- **PUBLISHING.** As you gain experience researching literary journals and sending out your work, your knowledge about the publications best suited (and most receptive) to your work will grow. Over time, you will develop relationships, insight and a publishing track record that may significantly increase your chances of publishing (both individual poems and collections of poems).

- **FUNDRAISING.** Platform gives success an opportunity to snowball. With each publication, award, recognition or other notch on your belt, you'll improve the odds of winning prizes and receiving grants and residencies if this is of interest to you.

- **AUTHORITY.** The more experience you have writing and publishing poetry (and potentially educating/exciting others about their own poetic process), the more you and others will trust in your authority.

- **OPPORTUNITY.** Once you have earned a reputable name among your poetic peers, requests for interviews, articles, speaking engagements, teaching, and more are likely to start rolling in. But more importantly, you will have paved the way to go after exactly what you want to create in your writing life, buoyed by the confidence that comes from proven expertise.

NAMING AND CLAIMING YOUR PLATFORM

Not sure what your platform is or what you want it to be? It may be as simple as "Poetry." Or you could name what you believe your poetry is serving or striving for—if this is relevant to your work. Several years ago I named my platform "Writing the Life Poetic," which quickly led to me authoring a nonfiction book by this name. One thing is certain: naming and claiming your area of expertise is going to give you a new sense of clarity and purpose. And you may be surprised at how quickly this clarity magnetizes new, relevant opportunities to you.

If you'd like to explore some of the possibilities for your poetic platform, the following exercise can help. I encourage you to map out your own Platform at a Glance using the example below as a starting place. It's OK if you don't have all the answers yet. Having a record of what you're aspiring to today can help you learn about where you're headed over time.

PLATFORM AT A GLANCE

PLATFORM BUILDING BLOCKS	INSIGHTS
Theme, topic, genre, or area of expertise	Poetry for the people: with a goal of encouraging writers of all levels to write, read, and enjoy poetry.
Audience(s) you serve	• People who feel afraid, unwelcome, or unsure of how to start writing poetry. • People already writing poetry who want to write more, improve their craft, and have more fun. • Writers of all stripes wanting to invigorate their relationship with language. • People who love poetry and read poems.
Needs, desires, and preferences of your audience(s)	• People who feel afraid: Want to be invited in to poetry and assured that they are welcome/can do it. • People already writing poetry: Seeking tools, techniques, and tips to help improve their craft. • Writers of all stripes: Seeking a poetic lens through which to better appreciate and apply language in anything and everything they write. • People who love reading poems: Want to find poems that connect, move them, reveal something new.
Value you bring to each different type of reader	• People who feel afraid: Friendly encouragement and useful information. • People already writing poetry: Vast selection of tips, tools, strategies, and examples. • Writers of all stripes: A way into—and an enjoyable exploration of—the life poetic. • People who love reading poems: Poems I've written that they can embrace and enjoy.

PLATFORM NAME	WRITING THE LIFE POETIC
Why you are the ideal person to develop this platform over time	I have more than 20 years of experience cultivating a poetic way of life. I have an advanced degree in creative writing, a great deal of teaching experience, and a well-established career of writing and publishing poetry.
Why you are passionate about doing so	Poetry matters—not just as a literary form, but as a way of life. I know from my own experience that a relationship with poetry can significantly expand a person's sense of possibility, delight, and camaraderie with one's self, universal human truths, and life itself. I want to make this gift available to anyone who's interested in receiving it—as a teacher, author and poet.

MULTIPLE PATHS TO PLATFORM DEVELOPMENT

Publishing is certainly a significant way to establish and build your platform. But it is one of many. The good news is that while you're waiting for your latest batch of poems to make a safe landing in just the right literary journal(s), there are many ways to grow your visibility as an expert in your field that are available to you right now. Let's consider a few:

- **GO PUBLIC.** Read your work publicly as much as possible—either as a featured reader through a reading series or special event or at an open mic reading. (Open mics are far more widely accessible and encourage everyone to participate. They're a good way to establish a community of writers if you attend and share work regularly. Over time, people will start to recognize you and your work. This will help you learn who your audience is and what it is about your poems that appeals to them.

- **TEACH WHAT YOU KNOW.** If you are passionate about poetry and have been schooling yourself in the craft (either through formal education or self-study), chances are good that you have something to offer other poets. From tenured academic positions to workshops you've organized and publicized yourself, you can choose the forum that fits your experience and temperament—then bring people together to learn about what's possible in poetry.

- **GIVE SERVICE.** There are endless ways to give service to poets—both paid and volunteer. You could become active in an online community—or start your own—that writes or contemplates poetry. Depending on your level of expertise, you could offer coaching, consulting, or editing. If you enjoy working with people of certain ages or circumstances (such as students, prisoners, elders), you could find ways to share poetry in your community through religious, educational or civic organizations.

- **PUBLISH.** Most poets are likely to experience multiple types and stages of publishing throughout their career. Because publishing individual poems can be slow and full collections even slower, you may want to explore other ways of sharing your knowledge of poetry along the way by publishing how-to articles, interviews or essays about the life poetic. You can query print and online magazines, share free content with organizations or online communities that serve poets and writers and/or create Squidoo lenses on any number of craft or publishing issues. If self-publishing is of interest to you, you could write and sell instructional e-books or publish print-on-demand collections of your poems (only if you are not seeking "mainstream" publication for this work.)

- **GO SOCIAL.** Social media gives poets instantaneous access to a virtually limitless community that can help your poetry and your platform evolve over time. When you want to exchange ideas, inspiration, poems, encouragement, tips and resources, book reviews, links, or professional recommendations, you can do so using any number of social media outlets. Facebook, Twitter, GoodReads and LinkedIn are just a few of the most popular places to do so. Choose one or two online forums in which to start; spend some time investigating how others are using these; decide what kind of information exchange best reflects your platform; and then pace yourself as you become a relevant contributor to the online conversation.

- **BECOME YOUR OWN MEDIA CHANNEL.** With a wide range of simple and inexpensive interactive media available today, you have numerous options for getting your message out. First, consider your platform aspirations. Then, decide what kind of information you'd like to share—and whether your goal is to inspire, collaborate, teach, build community or some combination of these. Depending on your goals, you might consider employing interactive media such as: webinars, teleclasses, e-zines, podcasts, and specialized online communities such as Ning. Try one and commit to it for at least six months; then evaluate, refine and expand as you go.

COHERENCE AND YOUR POETIC SOUL

These days, readers expect to have a personal connection with the poets they enjoy through their websites, blogs, teaching and live appearances. Plus, with the widespread use of social media bridging the space between writer and reader, anyone who has admired your work can tap into your moment-by-moment publicized thinking through the social media communities you frequent.

Therefore, who you are (or more accurately, how you present yourself publicly) and what you write are often one continuous experience for readers. A writing life that grows out of and reflects who you authentically are is going to be the most grounded and sustainable path to success.

My friend Dan Raphael is an example of someone who has built a writing empire on the foundation of his wildly entertaining and unusual command of language and life. On the back of one of Dan's books is a quote that says:

She: Do you think he's ever taken acid?

He: Taken it? I think he wears a patch.

Dan delivers on this very engaging and entertaining promise. He is a transcendent force of nature and engaging linguistic acrobatics on stage when delivering his poems and behind the scenes, when sending e-mail to friends.

I have another friend who is a widely sought photographer who has recently been recognized in several national magazines. This photographer has a parallel platform as a poet; and a good number of her poems explore the socioeconomic dynamics of being a person providing a service for the elite and the wealthy. This presents a bit of a platform pretzel, as she has no desire to alienate valued clients with her poetry. The expert photographer/poet is very delicately navigating how to hold these two parts of her life with integrity and authenticity as she quickly becomes more visible and respected in both chosen fields.

How is your life in alignment or out of whack with your platform(s) today? Is there anything you need to reconcile to create a greater coherence between what you write and how you live?

HAVE PLATFORM, WILL PROSPER

With a clear platform as the organizing principle in your life poetic, you can take the steps that will make your poems and your life poetic more visible in the communities and publications that matter to you. As you become increasingly effective at creating the writing results you want, over time you will attract more readers, expand your sphere of influence and generate far more opportunities to share your love of poetry.

 **SAGE COHEN** is the author of *Writing the Life Poetic: An Invitation to Read and Write Poetry* and *The Productive Writer: Tips & Tools to Help You Write More, Stress Less & Create Success*, both from Writer's Digest Books, and the poetry collection *Like the Heart, the World*. She holds an MFA from New York University and a BA from Brown University. A few notches in her platform belt include: winning first place in the Ghost Road Poetry contest, nomination for a Pushcart Prize and publication of multiple articles in *Writer's Digest* magazine. She writes about the poetic and productive writing life at pathofpossibility.com where she also offers online classes ranging from poetry to productivity to business writing.

BLOGGING BASICS:

Get the Most Out of Your Blog

....

by Robert Lee Brewer

In these days of publishing and media change, writers have to build platforms and learn how to connect to audiences if they want to improve their chances of publication and over-all success. There are many methods of audience connection available to writers, but one of the most important is through blogging.

Since I've spent several years successfully blogging—both personally and professionally—I figure I've got a few nuggets of wisdom to pass on to writers who are curious about blog-ging or who already are.

Here's my quick list of tips:

1. **START BLOGGING TODAY.** If you don't have a blog, use Blogger, WordPress, or some other blogging software to start your blog today. It's free, and you can start off with your very personal "Here I am, world" post.

2. **START SMALL.** Blogs are essentially very simple, but they can get very complicated (for people who like complications). However, I advise bloggers to start small and evolve over time.

3. **USE YOUR NAME IN YOUR URL.** This will make it easier for search engines to find you when your audience eventually starts seeking you out by name. For instance, my url is http://robertleebrewer.blogspot.com. If you try Googling "Robert Lee Brewer," you'll notice that My Name Is Not Bob is one of the top 5 search results (behind my other blog: Poetic Asides).

4. **UNLESS YOU HAVE A REASON, USE YOUR NAME AS THE TITLE OF YOUR BLOG.** Again, this helps with search engine results. My Poetic Asides blog includes my name in

the title, and it ranks higher than My Name Is Not Bob. However, I felt the play on my name was worth the trade off.

5. **FIGURE OUT YOUR BLOGGING GOALS.** You should return to this step every couple months, because it's natural for your blogging goals to evolve over time. Initially, your blogging goals may be to make a post a week about what you have written, submitted, etc. Over time, you may incorporate guests posts, contests, tips, etc.

6. **BE YOURSELF.** I'm a big supporter of the idea that your image should match your identity. It gets too confusing trying to maintain a million personas. Know who you are and be that on your blog, whether that means you're sincere, funny, sarcastic, etc.

7. **POST AT LEAST ONCE A WEEK.** This is for starters. Eventually, you may find it better to post once a day or multiple times per day. But remember: Start small and evolve over time.

8. **POST RELEVANT CONTENT.** This means that you post things that your readers might actually care to know.

....

Don't spend a week writing each post. Try to keep it to an hour or two tops and then post.

....

9. **USEFUL AND HELPFUL POSTS WILL ATTRACT MORE VISITORS.** Talking about yourself is all fine and great. I do it myself. But if you share truly helpful advice, your readers will share it with others, and visitors will find you on search engines.

10. **TITLE YOUR POSTS IN A WAY THAT GETS YOU FOUND IN SEARCH ENGINES.** The more specific you can get the better. For instance, the title "Blogging Tips" will most likely get lost in search results. However, the title "Blogging Tips for Writers" specifies which audience I'm targeting and increases the chances of being found on the first page of search results.

11. **LINK TO POSTS IN OTHER MEDIA.** If you have an e-mail newsletter, link to your blog posts in your newsletter. If you have social media accounts, link to your blog posts there. If you have a helpful post, link to it in relevant forums and on message boards.

12. **WRITE WELL, BUT BE CONCISE.** At the end of the day, you're writing blog posts, not literary manifestos. Don't spend a week writing each post. Try to keep it to an hour

or two tops and then post. Make sure your spelling and grammar are good, but don't stress yourself out too much.

13. **FIND LIKE-MINDED BLOGGERS.** Comment on their blogs regularly and link to them from yours. Eventually, they may do the same. Keep in mind that blogging is a form of social media, so the more you communicate with your peers the more you'll get out of the process.

14. **RESPOND TO COMMENTS ON YOUR BLOG.** Even if it's just a simple "Thanks," respond to your readers if they comment on your blog. After all, you want your readers to be engaged with your blog, and you want them to know that you care they took time to comment.

15. **EXPERIMENT.** Start small, but don't get complacent. Every so often, try something new. For instance, the biggest draw to my Poetic Asides blog are the poetry prompts and challenges I issue to poets. Initially, that was an experiment—one that worked very well. I've tried other experiments that haven't panned out, and that's fine. It's all part of a process.

SEO TIPS FOR WRITERS

Most writers may already know what SEO is. If not, SEO stands for *search engine optimization*. Basically, a site or blog that practices good SEO habits should improve its rankings in search engines, such as Google and Bing. Most huge corporations have realized the importance of SEO and spend enormous sums of time, energy and money on perfecting their SEO practices. However, writers can improve their SEO without going to those same extremes.

In this section, I will use the terms of *site pages* and *blog posts* interchangeably. In both cases, you should be practicing the same SEO strategies (when it makes sense).

Here are my top tips on ways to improve your SEO starting today:

1. **USE APPROPRIATE KEYWORDS.** Make sure that your page displays your main keyword(s) in the page title, content, URL, title tags, page header, image names and tags (if you're including images). All of this is easy to do, but if you feel overwhelmed, just remember to use your keyword(s) in your page title and content (especially in the first and last 50 words of your page).

2. **USE KEYWORDS NATURALLY.** Don't kill your content and make yourself look like a spammer to search engines by overloading your page with your keyword(s). You don't get SEO points for quantity but for quality. Plus, one of the main ways to improve your page rankings is when you...

3. **DELIVER QUALITY CONTENT.** The best way to improve your SEO is by providing content that readers want to share with others by linking to your pages. Some of the top results in search engines can be years old, because the content is so good that people keep coming back. So, incorporate your keywords in a smart way, but make sure it works organically with your content.

4. **UPDATE CONTENT REGULARLY.** If your site looks dead to visitors, then it'll appear that way to search engines too. So update your content regularly. This should be very easy for writers who have blogs. For writers who have sites, incorporate your blog into your site. This will make it easier for visitors to your blog to discover more about you on your site (through your site navigation tools).

> If you interview someone on your blog, don't title your post with an interesting quotation. While that strategy may help get readers in the print world, it doesn't help with SEO at all.

5. **LINK BACK TO YOUR OWN CONTENT.** If I have a post on Blogging Tips for Writers, for instance, I'll link back to it if I have a Platform Building post, because the two complement each other. This also helps clicks on my blog, which helps SEO. The one caveat is that you don't go crazy with your linking and that you make sure your links are relevant. Otherwise, you'll kill your traffic, which is not good for your page rankings.

6. **LINK TO OTHERS YOU CONSIDER HELPFUL.** Back in 2000, I remember being ordered by my boss at the time (who didn't last too much longer afterward) to ignore any competitive or complementary websites—no matter how helpful their content—because they were our competitors. You can try basing your online strategy on these principles, but I'm nearly 100% confident you'll fail. It's helpful for other sites and your own to link to other great resources. I shine a light on others to help them out (if I find their content truly helpful) in the hopes that they'll do the same if ever they find my content truly helpful for their audience.

7. **GET SPECIFIC WITH YOUR HEADLINES.** If you interview someone on your blog, don't title your post with an interesting quotation. While that strategy may help get readers in the print world, it doesn't help with SEO at all. Instead, title your post as "Interview With (insert name here)." If you have a way to identify the person further, include that in the title too. For instance, when I interview poets on my Poetic Asides blog, I'll title those posts like this: Interview With Poet Erika Meitner. Erika's name is a keyword, but so are the terms *poet* and *interview*.

8. **USE IMAGES.** Many expert sources state that the use of images can improve SEO, because it shows search engines that the person creating the page is spending a little extra time and effort on the page than a common spammer. However, I'd caution anyone using images to make sure those images are somehow complementary to the content. Don't just throw up a lot of images that have no relevance to anything. At the same time...

9. **OPTIMIZE IMAGES THROUGH STRATEGIC LABELING.** Writers can do this by making sure the image file is labeled using your keyword(s) for the post. Using the Erika Meitner example above (which does include images), I would label the file "Erika Meitner headshot.jpg"—or whatever the image file type happens to be. Writers can also improve image SEO through the use of captions and ALT tagging. Of course, at the same time, writers should always ask themselves if it's worth going through all that trouble for each image or not. Each writer has to answer that question for him (or her) self.

10. **USE YOUR SOCIAL MEDIA PLATFORM TO SPREAD THE WORD.** Whenever you do something new on your site or blog, you should share that information on your other social media sites, such as Twitter, Facebook, LinkedIn, online forums, etc. This lets your social media connections know that something new is on your site/blog. If it's relevant and/or valuable, they'll let others know. And that's a great way to build your SEO.

Programmers and marketers could get even more involved in the dynamics of SEO optimization, but I think these tips will help most writers out immediately and effectively while still allowing plenty of time and energy for the actual work of writing.

BLOG DESIGN TIPS FOR WRITERS

Design is an important element to any blog's success. But how can you improve your blog's design if you're not a designer? I'm just an editor with an English Lit degree and no formal training in design. However, I've worked in media for more than a decade now and can share some very fundamental and easy tricks to improve the design of your blog.

Here are my seven blog design tips for writers:

1. **USE LISTS.** Whether they're numbered or bullet points, use lists when possible. Lists break up the text and make it easy for readers to follow what you're blogging.

2. **BOLD MAIN POINTS IN LISTS.** Again, this helps break up the text while also highlighting the important points of your post.

3. **USE HEADINGS.** If your posts are longer than 300 words and you don't use lists, then please break up the text by using basic headings.

4. **USE A READABLE FONT.** Avoid using fonts that are too large or too small. Avoid using cursive or weird fonts. Times New Roman or Arial works, but if you want to get "creative," use something similar to those.

5. **LEFT ALIGN.** English-speaking readers are trained to read left to right. If you want to make your blog easier to read, avoid centering or right aligning your text (unless you're purposefully calling out the text).

6. **USE SMALL PARAGRAPHS.** A good rule of thumb is to try and avoid paragraphs that drone on longer than five sentences. I usually try to keep paragraphs to around three sentences myself.

7. **ADD RELEVANT IMAGES.** Personally, I shy away from using too many images. My reason is that I only like to use them if they're relevant. However, images are very powerful on blogs, so please use them—just make sure they're relevant to your blog post.

If you're already doing everything on my list, keep it up! If you're not, then you might want to re-think your design strategy on your blog. Simply adding a header here and a list there can easily improve the design of a blog post.

GUEST POSTING TIPS FOR WRITERS

Recently, I've broken into guest posting as both a guest poster and as a host of guest posts (over at my Poetic Asides blog). So far, I'm pretty pleased with both sides of the guest posting process. As a writer, it gives me access to an engaged audience I may not usually reach. As a blogger, it provides me with fresh and valuable content I don't have to create. Guest blogging is a rare win-win scenario.

That said, writers could benefit from a few tips on the process of guest posting:

1. **PITCH GUEST POSTS LIKE ONE WOULD PITCH ARTICLES TO A MAGAZINE.** Include what your hook is for the post, what you plan to cover, and a little about who you are. Remember: Your post should somehow benefit the audience of the blog you'd like to guest post.

2. **OFFER PROMOTIONAL COPY OF BOOK (OR OTHER GIVEAWAYS) AS PART OF YOUR GUEST POST.** Having a random giveaway for people who comment on a blog post can help spur conversation and interest in your guest post, which is a great way to get the most mileage out of your guest appearance.

3. **CATER POSTS TO AUDIENCE.** As the editor of *Writer's Market* and *Poet's Market*, I have great range in the topics I can cover. However, if I'm writing a guest post for a fiction blog, I'll write about things of interest to a novelist—not a poet.

4. **MAKE IT PERSONAL, BUT PROVIDE NUGGET.** Guest posts are a great opportunity for you to really show your stuff to a new audience. You could write a very helpful and impersonal post, but that won't connect with readers the same way as if you write a very helpful and personal post that makes them want to learn more about you (and your blog, your book, your Twitter account, etc.). Speaking of which...

5. **SHARE LINKS TO YOUR WEBSITE, BLOG, SOCIAL NETWORKS, ETC.** After all, you need to make it easy for readers who enjoyed your guest post to learn more about you and your projects. Start the conversation in your guest post and keep it going on your own sites, profiles, etc. And related to that...

6. **PROMOTE YOUR GUEST POST THROUGH YOUR NORMAL CHANNELS ONCE THE POST GOES LIVE.** Your normal audience will want to know where you've been and what you've been doing. Plus, guest posts lend a little extra "street cred" to your projects. But don't stop there...

7. **CHECK FOR COMMENTS ON YOUR GUEST POST AND RESPOND IN A TIMELY MANNER.** Sometimes the comments are the most interesting part of a guest post (no offense). This is where readers can ask more in-depth or related questions, and it's also where you can show your expertise on the subject by being as helpful as possible. And guiding all seven of these tips is this one:

8. **PUT SOME EFFORT INTO YOUR GUEST POST.** Part of the benefit to guest posting is the opportunity to connect with a new audience. Make sure you bring your A-game, because you need to make a good impression if you want this exposure to actually help grow your audience. Don't stress yourself out, but put a little thought into what you submit.

ONE ADDITIONAL TIP: Have fun with it. Passion is what really drives the popularity of blogs. Share your passion and enthusiasm, and readers are sure to be impressed.

ROBERT LEE BREWER is Senior Content Editor for the Writer's Digest Writing Community and edits *Writer's Market* and WritersMarket.com among other responsibilities. He manages the Poetic Asides (http://blog.writersdigest.com/poeticasides) and My Name Is Not Bob (http://robertleebrewer.blogspot.com) blogs, which is where most of this article originated.

TWITTER CHEAT SHEET FOR WRITERS

....

by Robert Lee Brewer

With the publishing (and/or media) industry changing at the speed of light, so are the roles of writers (or content providers), editors (or content managers), agents (or content strategists), etc. One big change for writers (even in fiction, poetry, and other fields) is that they are expected to take an active role in building their own platforms via online and real world networking and exposure. One great tool for this online is Twitter.

It's easy (and free) enough to create a Twitter account, but how can writers take advantage of this social networking tool? What can they logically expect to gain from using it? What is a hashtag anyway? Well, hopefully, this cheat sheet will help.

First, let's look at some basic terminology:

- **TWEET** = Any message sent out to everyone on Twitter. Unless you direct message (DM) someone, everything on Twitter is a Tweet and viewable by anyone.

- **RT** = Retweet. Twitter created a RT-ing tool that makes for easy retweets, but the standard convention is to put an RT and cite the source before reposting something funny or useful that someone else has shared. For example, if I tweeted "Nouns are verbs waiting to happen," you could RT me this way: RT @robertleebrewer Nouns are verbs waiting to happen.

- **DM** = Direct message. These are private and only between people who DM each other.

- **# = HASHTAG.** These are used in front of a word (or set of letters) to allow people to easily communicate on a specific topic. For instance, I tweet poetry with other poets on Twitter by using the hashtag #poettalk. Poets can click on the "poettalk" after the hashtag (no space) or they can search on the term "poettalk" in Twitter (right-hand toolbar).

- **#FF** = Follow Friday. This is a nice way to show support for other tweeters on Twitter. On Friday.

Second, here are 10 things you can do to optimize your use of Twitter:

1. **USE YOUR REAL NAME IF POSSIBLE.** Make it easy for people you know or meet to find you on Twitter.

2. **ADD A PROFILE PICTURE.** Preferably this will be a picture of you. People connect better with other people, not cartoons, book covers, logos, etc.

3. **LINK TO A WEBSITE.** Hopefully, you have a blog or website you can link to in your profile. If you don't have a website or blog, make one. Now. And then, link to it from your Twitter profile.

4. **WRITE YOUR BIO.** Make this memorable in some way. You don't have to be funny or cute, but more power to you if you can do this and still make it relevant to who you are.

5. **TWEET REGULARLY.** It doesn't matter if you have only 2 followers (and one is your mom); you still need to tweet daily (or nearly daily) for Twitter to be effective. And remember: If you don't have anything original to add, you can always RT something funny or useful from someone else.

6. **TWEET RELEVANT INFORMATION.** Don't be the person who tweets like this: "I am making a salad;" "I am eating a salad;" "That salad was good;" "I wonder what I'm going to eat next;" etc. These tweets are not interesting or relevant. However, if your salad eating experience rocked your world in a unique way, feel free to share: "Just ate the best salad ever. Now, I'm ready to write a novel."

7. **LINK AND DON'T LINK.** It's good to link to other places and share things you're doing or that you've found elsewhere. At the same time, if all you do is link, people may think you're just trying to sell them stuff all the time.

8. **HAVE A PERSONALITY.** Be yourself. You don't have to be overly cute, funny, smart, etc. Just be yourself and remember that Twitter is all about connecting people. So be a person.

9. **FOLLOW THOSE WORTH FOLLOWING.** Just because you're being followed you don't have to return the follow. For instance, if some local restaurant starts following

me, I'm not going to follow them back, because they aren't relevant to me or to my audience.

10. **COMMUNICATE WITH OTHERS.** I once heard someone refer to Twitter as one big cocktail party, and it's true. Twitter is all about communication. If people talk to you or RT you, make sure you talk back and/or thank them. (*Here's a secret: People like to feel involved and acknowledged. I like it; you like it; and so does everyone else.*)

And, of course, if you're not already, please follow me on Twitter @robetleebrewer (http://twitter.com/robertleebrewer).

HERE ARE SOME EXTRA RESOURCES:

- **TwitterGrader.com** (http://twittergrader.com) This site allows you to enter your profile at any given time and find out how you're doing (according to them) in using Twitter effectively. Of course, the grade you receive is bound to not be perfect, but it is a good measuring stick.

- **What the Hashtag?** (http://wthashtag.com) This site allows you to search for hashtags, run reports on them, get transcripts between specific time periods, and more.

- **Hootsuite** (http://hootsuite.com) This is one of many tools that give the ability to Tweet and track your account without even going to Twitter. Many (maybe even most) people use these. There are others, such as TweetDeck, Seesmic, etc. Find one that you like and let it make your social networking life easier to manage.

- **bit.ly** (http://bit.ly) This is one of many URL shortening services out there, which is very helpful when tweeting URL links, since they can easily eat into your 140-character limit on Twitter. This particular one makes it easy for you to track clicks, though I'm sure that's fairly standard.

FACEBOOK VS. LINKEDIN:

Tips for Using Two Social Networking Sites

by Robert Lee Brewer

Many writers ask why start a LinkedIn account if they already have a Facebook, or conversely, why start a Facebook if they already have a LinkedIn? That's a fair question, but the answer is simple: Both these sites cater to different audiences, and both of these audiences are important to writers.

LinkedIn is the more professional site of the two. Many professionals use it to make meaningful connections with other like-minded professionals. HR departments use the site to find potential job candidates, and potential job candidates use their LinkedIn profiles as their resumes.

Facebook is a lot less professional, but smart writers treat this site as an important piece to their marketing puzzle. In fact, it's natural for writers to have more fun with their Facebook profiles, but they should still remember that editors, agents, writers, and other professionals may be interested in linking up on Facebook.

FACEBOOK TIPS FOR WRITERS

As of the writing of this article, Facebook is the most popular website on the Internet. Chances are good that you already have a profile on this social networking site. (If you don't have a Facebook profile, then you should create one now, since they're free.) However, you may or may not be optimizing your Facebook use.

Here are some tips for writers who are either new to Facebook or who aren't sure if they're using it the correct way:

1. **COMPLETE YOUR PROFILE.** You don't have to include EVERYTHING, but I'd suggest at least covering these bases: Current City, Birthday (you don't have to include the year), Bio, Education and Work, Contact Information.

2. **MAKE EVERYTHING PUBLIC.** As a writer, you should be using sites like Facebook and Twitter to connect with other writers, editors, agents, and your audience. So make it easy for them to find you and learn more about you by making everything available to the public. That said...

3. **THINK ABOUT YOUR AUDIENCE, FRIENDS, FAMILY, BOSS, FORMER TEACHERS, ETC., IN EVERYTHING YOU DO ON FACEBOOK.** Like it or not, you have to understand that if you are completely public on Facebook (and you should be if you want to connect with your audience) that you need to think about what you do on Facebook before you do it. Because Facebook isn't like Vegas: What happens on Facebook could easily go viral. But don't get paranoid; just use common sense.

··

Even though it's virtual, you want your profile to be as human as possible so that you can connect with others.

··

4. **INCLUDE A PROFILE PICTURE OF YOURSELF.** Don't use a picture of a cute animal, house pet, your children, an animated character, a famous celebrity, a model, etc. Just a nice pic of yourself. Even though it's virtual, you want your profile to be as human as possible so that you can connect with others.

5. **UPDATE YOUR STATUS REGULARLY.** You shouldn't update your status every hour, but once a day is a good pace. This just lets others on Facebook know that you are actively using the site.

6. **COMMUNICATE WITH FRIENDS ON FACEBOOK.** Don't stalk your friends; communicate with them. If you like a friend's status update, comment on it—or at the very least, click the Like button (to acknowledge that you liked their update). Speaking of friends...

7. **BE SELECTIVE ABOUT FRIENDS YOU ADD.** Don't blindly accept every friend request, because some may be bogus, and others may be from serial frienders (people who are trying to hit their friend limits). You want quality friends who share your interests or who you know from the "real world."

8. **BE SELECTIVE ABOUT ADDING APPS.** I'm not a huge fan of apps, because they are a distraction and time killer on Facebook. But there are some that could be useful.

However, don't waste a month of your life playing Farmville or Mafia Wars; you'd be better off completing a crossword or sudoku puzzle.

9. **JOIN RELEVANT GROUPS.** For writers, there are an abundance of groups you could join, from professional organizations to those based around magazines, publishers and literary events. These are great places to connect with other writers. On that same note...

10. **FOLLOW RELEVANT FAN PAGES.** There are many who once had groups that migrated over to using fan pages, so there are fan pages for writing organizations, magazines, publishers, literary events, and more. (I even have a fan page on Facebook; just search for Robert Lee Brewer.)

BONUS TIP: If you have a blog, you can feed your Facebook profile automatically by using the Notes function. All you have to do is go to Notes, click the "Edit import settings" link, and enter your blog url in the correct field. (Note: I had to enter my full url, including the forward slash at the end, before the Notes function accepted my url.)

OTHER SOCIAL NETWORKING SITES

This book contains articles on Twitter, Facebook, and LinkedIn, but there are many other powerful social networking sites on the Internet. Here's a list of some of them:

- **Bebo** (http://bebo.com)
- **Classmates** (http://classmates.com)
- **Digg** (http://digg.com)
- **Flickr** (http://flickr.com)
- **Friendster** (http://friendster.com)
- **Habbo** (http://habbo.com)
- **Hi5** (http://hi5.com)
- **MeetUp** (http://meetup.com)
- **MySpace** (http://myspace.com)
- **Ning** (http://ning.com)
- **Orkut** (http://orkut.com)
- **StumbleUpon** (http://stumbleupon.com)
- **Tagged** (http://tagged.com)
- **Yelp** (http://yelp.com)
- **YouTube** (http://youtube.com)
- **Zorpia** (http://zorpia.com)

LINKEDIN TIPS FOR WRITERS

If Twitter and Facebook are the social networks where writers can just "hang out," then LinkedIn is the one where writers can "network" and make meaningful connections. Some writers may even be able to make connections with editors (like myself) and agents.

Many writers may not use LinkedIn anywhere near as much as they use Facebook or Twitter, but I believe in making yourself easy to find. Having a completed and optimized LinkedIn profile could lead to connections with editors, event coordinators, and other writers.

Here are a few tips I've picked up over time on how to use LinkedIn:

1. **USE YOUR OWN HEAD SHOT FOR YOUR AVATAR. I** recommend this on all social networks, because people want to make "real" connections on these sites. It's hard to take a picture of a family pet or cartoon character seriously.

2. **COMPLETE YOUR PROFILE.** There are many steps to completing your profile, including completing your resume and getting a few recommendations from connections, which leads to the next tip...

3. **GIVE THOUGHTFUL RECOMMENDATIONS TO RECEIVE THEM.** Give if you wish to receive. The recommendations you write will make you feel and look better, but the recommendations you receive in return will truly rock your solar system. Of course, to make and receive recommendations, you'll need to...

4. **SEARCH FOR CONNECTIONS YOU ALREADY HAVE.** These could be "real world" connections and/or connections from other social networks. The ones who are (or have been) most valuable to you are the best to make at first. Then...

5. **MAKE MEANINGFUL CONNECTIONS WITH OTHERS.** Search for other writers, editors, agents, or whoever you think might benefit your writing career. But don't ever spam. Look for meaningful connections and include a note about why you're contacting them through LinkedIn. Remember: Social networking is about *who* you know, not *how many*.

6. **ACCEPT INVITATIONS.** While I think it's a good rule of thumb to be selective about who you invite to connect with you, I also don't see any harm in accepting invitations with abandon—unless they are obviously not a good fit. My reasoning here is that you never know why someone is contacting you. Of course, you can always kill the connection later if it's not working.

7. **MAKE YOUR PROFILE EASY TO FIND.** If possible, put your name in your LinkedIn url. For instance, you can view my LinkedIn profile at http://www.linkedin.com/

in/robertleebrewer. Also, connect to your profile in blog posts and on other social networks.

8. **TAILOR YOUR PROFILE TO THE VISITOR.** It's easy to make me-centric profiles on social networks, because they're asking questions about you. However, remember that these descriptions are more beneficial to you if you're filling them out for the prospective connections you can make on social networking sites. Make it easy for them to figure out who you are, what you do, and how you might improve their lives. As such...

9. **UPDATE YOUR PROFILE REGULARLY WITH USEFUL CONTENT.** You can feed blog posts into your profile easily, and that will keep your profile active. You can also update your status by feeding in tweets or Facebook updates, but I refrain from doing that myself. My reasoning is that my updates are slightly different for each place. However, I can make meaningful tweets and LinkedIn status updates simultaneously by simply adding an #in hashtag to the tweet in question.

10. **JOIN (AND PARTICIPATE) IN GROUPS.** Heck, start your own group if you feel so inclined. Of course, participating in groups will require an extra level of engagement with the site, so this last tip is more of an extra credit assignment for those who want to unlock the full potential of LinkedIn.

POETRY CALENDAR

The best way for writers to achieve success is by setting goals. Goals are usually met by writers who give themselves or are given deadlines. Something about having an actual date to hit helps create a sense of urgency in most writers (and editors for that matter). This writing calendar is a great place to keep your important deadlines.

Also, this writing calendar is a good tool for recording upcoming writing events you'd like to attend or contests you'd like to enter. Or use this calendar to block out time for yourself—to just write.

Of course, you can use this calendar to record other special events, especially if you have a habit of remembering to write but of forgetting birthdays or anniversaries. After all, this calendar is now yours. Do with it what you will.

AUGUST 2011

SUN	MON	TUE	WED	THURS	FRI	SAT
	1	2	3	4	5	6
7	8	9	10	11	12	13
14	15	16	17	18	19	20
21	22	23	24	25	26	27
28	29	30	31			

Start a blog and make at least one post per week.

SEPTEMBER 2011

SUN	MON	TUE	WED	THU	FRI	SAT
				1	2	3
4	5	6	7	8	9	10
11	12	13	14	15	16	17
18	19	20	21	22	23	24
25	26	27	28	29	30	

Try sending out one submission package per week this month.

OCTOBER 2011

SUN	MON	TUE	WED	THU	FRI	SAT
						1
2	3	4	5	6	7	8
9	10	11	12	13	14	15
16	17	18	19	20	21	22
23	24	25	26	27	28	29
30	31					

Are you on Twitter? Try leaving a meaningful tweet daily.

NOVEMBER 2011

SUN	MON	TUE	WED	THU	FRI	SAT
		1	2	3	4	5
6	7	8	9	10	11	12
13	14	15	16	17	18	19
20	21	22	23	24	25	26
27	28	29	30			

Participate in the Poetic Asides 2011 November Poem-A-Day Chapbook Challenge!

_____

_____

_____

_____

_____

DECEMBER 2011

SUN	MON	TUE	WED	THU	FRI	SAT
				1	2	3
4	5	6	7	8	9	10
11	12	13	14	15	16	17
18	19	20	21	22	23	24
25	26	27	28	29	30	31

Evaluate your 2011 accomplishments and make 2012 goals.

_____

_____

_____

_____

_____

JANUARY 2012

SUN	MON	TUE	WED	THU	FRI	SAT
1	2	3	4	5	6	7
8	9	10	11	12	13	14
15	16	17	18	19	20	21
22	23	24	25	26	27	28
29	30	31				

Make 2012 your best year poeming yet!

FEBRUARY 2012

SUN	MON	TUE	WED	THU	FRI	SAT
			1	2	3	4
5	6	7	8	9	10	11
12	13	14	15	16	17	18
19	20	21	22	23	24	25
26	27	28	29			

Use the extra day in February to submit more poems.

_____

_____

_____

_____

_____

MARCH 2012

SUN	MON	TUE	WED	THU	FRI	SAT
				1	2	3
4	5	6	7	8	9	10
11	12	13	14	15	16	17
18	19	20	21	22	23	24
25	26	27	28	29	30	31

Put a chapbook together.

_____

_____

_____

_____

_____

APRIL 2012

SUN	MON	TUE	WED	THU	FRI	SAT
1	2	3	4	5	6	7
8	9	10	11	12	13	14
15	16	17	18	19	20	21
22	23	24	25	26	27	28
29	30					

Write a poem a day for National Poetry Month.

_____

_____

_____

_____

_____

MAY 2012

SUN	MON	TUE	WED	THU	FRI	SAT
		1	2	3	4	5
6	7	8	9	10	11	12
13	14	15	16	17	18	19
20	21	22	23	24	25	26
27	28	29	30	31		

Plan to attend a writing conference this summer.

JUNE 2012

SUN	MON	TUE	WED	THU	FRI	SAT
					1	2
3	4	5	6	7	8	9
10	11	12	13	14	15	16
17	18	19	20	21	22	23
24	25	26	27	28	29	30

Revise one poem each week.

JULY 2012

SUN	MON	TUE	WED	THU	FRI	SAT
1	2	3	4	5	6	7
8	9	10	11	12	13	14
15	16	17	18	19	20	21
22	23	24	25	26	27	28
29	30	31				

Try reading a new poetry collection each week.

AUGUST 2012

SUN	MON	TUE	WED	THU	FRI	SAT
			1	2	3	4
5	6	7	8	9	10	11
12	13	14	15	16	17	18
19	20	21	22	23	24	25
26	27	28	29	30	31	

Try tackling a new poetic form to help you grow as a poet.

_____

_____

_____

_____

_____

SEPTEMBER 2012

SUN	MON	TUE	WED	THU	FRI	SAT
						1
2	3	4	5	6	7	8
9	10	11	12	13	14	15
16	17	18	19	20	21	22
23	24	25	26	27	28	29
30						

Read a poetry blog and leave a comment each day.

_____

_____

_____

_____

_____

OCTOBER 2012

SUN	MON	TUE	WED	THU	FRI	SAT
	1	2	3	4	5	6
7	8	9	10	11	12	13
14	15	16	17	18	19	20
21	22	23	24	25	26	27
28	29	30	31			

Remember to hit the save button when you're writing.

NOVEMBER 2012

SUN	MON	TUE	WED	THU	FRI	SAT
				1	2	3
4	5	6	7	8	9	10
11	12	13	14	15	16	17
18	19	20	21	22	23	24
25	26	27	28	29	30	

Participate in the Poetic Asides 2012 November Poem-A-Day Chapbook Challenge!

DECEMBER 2012

SUN	MON	TUE	WED	THU	FRI	SAT
						1
2	3	4	5	6	7	8
9	10	11	12	13	14	15
16	17	18	19	20	21	22
23	24	25	26	27	28	29
30	31					

If you don't have it yet, find a copy of *2013 Poet's Market*.

TRUTH AND CONSEQUENCES IN POETRY

....

by Collin Kelley

One of the questions I'm invariably asked after a reading is whether or not my poetry is "true"? Did a certain incident really happen? Is a person I mentioned by name a real person? My answer, more often than not, is yes. I am, unashamedly, a confessional poet. I cut my teeth on Robert Lowell, Anne Sexton, Sylvia Plath, Sharon Olds, Stan Rice and Margaret Atwood. Pastoral "little birdies flying past the window" poetry bores me, unless it's Frost. I want poetry that bleeds, and I don't want it to be fake blood.

My mother believes that poetry inhabits the same realm as fiction. When she's read one of my poems that contain references to her, she refuses to believe the "I" is me and the "she" is her. When I call ex lovers, friends, and enemies by name in my poems, their names have not been changed to protect the innocent or guilty. It seems inauthentic, as if I am covering something up when my goal as a poet is to mine the truth.

Confessional or truthful poetry has been criticized as didactic, diary evacuation, naïve, lacking in lyricism and a host of other marginalizing words I don't subscribe to. Those criticisms are easily dismissed by reading Sexton's poetry about her battle with mental illness, Rice's heartbreaking poems about the death of his young daughter from cancer or Atwood's loving poems about her father's deterioration from Alzheimer's disease.

My chapbook, *Slow To Burn*, includes a poem about a close friend's suicidal tendencies in the 1980s, using her first name and detailing conversations we'd had. Although I hadn't spoken to Aimee in nearly 20 years, I received an e-mail from her both chastising me for writing about the subject and thanking me for getting the facts straight. I never second-guessed writing the poem and including it in the book. The poem, "Double Fantasy," was as much about me as it was Aimee. She had made me part of her dramatic scenario. As a poet I had to decide whether I would censor my emotions and memories to avoid a possibly unpleasant confrontation later.

When writing confessional poetry, where do you draw the line? Personally, I haven't found the line yet; my taboo threshold has yet to be breached. Other poets handle their "truth" differently.

Denise Duhamel altered the poet's identity in her poem "Sex With a Famous Poet" because she didn't want to "embarrass a stranger" (a stinging rebuke to the poet and herself), yet it's undeniable that the indiscretion is true. Without the self-effacing nature of the poem, the metaphor of sleeping with her arm "around his belly, which lifted up and down all night, gently like lake water" the poem would lose its immediacy and power.

Award-winning poet Mary Karr's controversial essay "Against Decoration" calls for more emotion, clarity and precise poetry rather than "foggy" poems that rely on imperceptible metaphor and "yards of adjectives" that short-change the reader. Karr's call for honesty in poetry came shortly before the publication of her bestselling memoir, *The Liar's Club*, delving into her troubled childhood.

There is a new generation of poets who are exploding the notion that truth is only found in tragedy. Cecilia Woloch's playful, loving recollections of her parents in her collections *Late* and *Carpathia* have the immediacy of memoir, but retain a musicality and lyricism that is important to poetry. Mark Doty writes about mortality – his own, that of a late partner and his dogs—with an elegance and clarity that transcends tragedy. Sometimes personal travail can illuminate, such as in Tania Rochelle's collection *The World's Last Bone*, where she lays the groundwork to rebuild a relationship with her estranged daughter.

There is a new generation of poets who are exploring the notion that truth is only found in tragedy.

The coining of Language poetry in the '70s and New Formalism in the '80s arose as backlash to the confessional movement, a desire to blur the line between poet and narrator and return to metrical and rhymed verse. Poet and former chairman of the National Endowment for the Arts Dana Gioia decried the "bankruptcy" of confessional poetry in his 1987 essay "Notes on New Formalism."

There's plenty of empty rhetoric about the corruption of the art by confessional poets, but perhaps the best marriage of formalism and truth is Marilyn Hacker's *Love, Death and The Changing of the Seasons*, a chronicle of her affair with a poetry student written in sonnets and villanelles. It's one of the finest examples of how confessional context can be wrangled into traditional verse with stunning results. It's also refreshingly sexual, another taboo that many poets are loath to write about with realism and frank language.

My first collection, *Better To Travel*, was written in second person with gender lines blurred to offer easy access to the work about first love and heartbreak without what I considered at the time to be the baggage of sexuality. While those poems are truthful, when I read them now I feel there's an emotional dishonesty. Moving forward, I challenged myself to write about my experience as a gay man and still write poems about passion, desire and sex that would resonate with men and women, regardless of their sexual orientation.

In the same vein, writing about politics is also considered by many poets to be verboten. *After the Poison*, my chapbook about the legacy of Reagan, George W. Bush, Hurricane Katrina and race relations, was criticized for being "ranty" and time locked, since the subject matter has a sell-by date. I disagree.

Some of the finest political poetry, such as those written by Wilfred Owen and Seigfried Sassoon about the horrors of World War I, has withstood the test of time. Owen said, "All a poet can do today is warn. That is why true poets must be truthful." If you are moved to write about politics—whether you lean left or right—don't worry about what other poets think is appropriate. Always, write for you first. That should be the tenet of every poet.

Kim Addonizio asks in her poem "The Numbers," *How many days / are left of my life, how much does it matter if I manage to say / one true thing about it…"* To me, it matters greatly. If my poetry manages to survive and is read by future generations, I want the take-away to be that I wrote honestly and accessibly about the world and myself.

PHOTO: Krystyna FitzGerald-Morris

COLLIN KELLEY is a published poet, novelist and playwright living in Atlanta, Georgia. His debut poetry collection, *Better to Travel*, was nominated for the 2003 Georgia Author of the Year Award, Kate Tufts Discovery Award and Lambda Literary Award. His other collections include *After the Poison* and *Slow to Burn*. Learn more at http://collinkelley.blogspot.com.

A DIFFERENT TAKE ON TRUTH & POETRY

....

by Sandra Beasley

"As any poet can tell you, one often sees better
with eyes closed than with eyes wide open."

—CHARLES SIMIC, *The New York Review of Books blog*

There are many variations in the way a poet relates to truth. For some, truth is the soil from which poems grow organically. The poet acts as gardener, tending the small shoots of inspiration, cultivating revelations from the ground of everyday life.

For others, truth is an ingredient—part of a larger recipe, added in the same way salt is dashed for flavor, or citrus for acidity. These chef-poets use elements from observed life (a playground game, an aunt's way of shaping pie crusts, a style of kiss) to give an authentic texture to imagined circumstances.

Then there are poets like me. I love to lie. And even when I'm telling the truth, I'd rather you assumed I was lying.

I am part of a third group, I suppose—those who would argue that evaluating a poem's "truths" is a mistake, albeit a seductive one. With every word choice and editorial turn, we move away from the diffuse and inspiring truth and toward the narrow, focused art. We take things out of context. We omit. We collage. That's because we're poets; we're not diarists, not historians, not anthropologists. And we need not apologize for that.

My first book of poems, *Theories of Falling*, is frankly autobiographical. It's hard to deny the relevance of a real-life medical condition when you include a sequence titled "Allergy Girl." I examined infidelities. I celebrated the desire to be bitten. I called a former boyfriend out by name.

Do I regret that? No. I don't advocate protecting yourself by avoiding the truth in poems. What I do I regret is allowing the critical conversation in interviews and in the classroom to so often wallow in the particularities of *what* was true, what was edited to seem more truthful on the page, and what was satire. (Note to self: Best not to title your take on war criminals "The General" if your father is, in fact, an Army General.)

In conceptualizing my second collection, *I Was the Jukebox,* I pushed away from the biographical. Many of the poems are in the third or second person, or—if indulging in an "I"—they occupy the perspective of mythological or inanimate characters. I discovered the brazen pleasure and freedom of stretching beyond the self. When my earlier poems were published, I feared what my mother would say. In contrast, in "The Minotaur Speaks," "My mother / gave me the apple of her breast, / and I bit it off."

I have still been amazed by the way readers dig for glimmers of truth amidst the obvious fictions. After sharing "Another Failed Poem about the Greeks" with one undergraduate class, a student asked if I'd grown up in northern Virginia.

"Yes," I said, surprised. "What makes you guess that?"

"You mention the Log Flume"—an amusement park ride, one of several listed in the poem—"and that's at Kings Dominion, right?"

"Well…yes."

"Awesome. I knew I'd caught that." This poem's surrealist premise involved the appearance of a dead Greek warrior on a girl's suburban doorstep, and the date that follows. Given the exoticisms of severed Gorgon's heads and hippogriffs, what caught his attention instead was the chance to divine a small, banal fact about me, the author.

....

Sometimes I wish poets were more like painters, who are reminded of the artificiality of their materials every time they prime a canvas or mix a palette.

....

If we want our readers' expectations to change, we must change the way we talk about poems. Sometimes I wish poets were more like painters, who are reminded of the artificiality of their materials every time they prime a canvas or mix a palette. To paint in blood-red is not the same as to render in blood, no matter how nuanced your balance of sulfur and mercury. We don't ask whether Mark Rothko's abstract expressionist blocks of color are "true" as they float in the un-horizoned space. We do not judge Amedeo Modigliani a fraud if the friends whose portraits he painted didn't *really* have such catlike eyes and elongated necks.

Lie! Don't mimic. Don't reflect. Exaggerate. Heighten. The art world would be impoverished if it contained nothing but still lifes and anatomical drawings. Though Pablo Picasso's women might have preferred a prettier, non-Cubist version of their faces, what they got instead will be seen for generations. When it comes to painting, we accept disconnecting from reality as part of the process. We must give ourselves permission to pursue the same on the page.

The next time you catch yourself praising someone's "sincere" voice in workshop, stop and ask yourself: What's so great about being sincere?

Many American poets under the age of 35 would list Sharon Olds among their patron saints of the Confessional instinct. In her seminal works (*The Living and The Dead, The Father, The Gold Cell*) Olds cut a memorable path with poems that seem as remarkable for their hard truths as their craft. So I find it telling that in an interview with *Salon*, Olds is careful to preserve the divide between poet and speaker:

> *"I do sometimes make an effort to use the word 'I' as little as possible. I would not have chosen to have that word appear so much in my poems....Not that anyone else wrote them. But we know that only people who are really close to us care about our personal experience. Art is something else. It has something to do with wanting to be accurate about what we think and feel. To me the difference between the paper world and the flesh world is so great that I don't think we could put ourselves in our poems even if we wanted to."*

I became a better poet when I stopped congratulating myself for being honest; when I stopped casting my heart's shadow on the page and calling it a poem. There are great poems of witness out there, and meaningful confrontations of personal trauma. But what makes those poems great is that their authors took the truth as a starting point, not as a goal. Honor the powers of your craft. At the end of the day, we have only one face. But the masks we can wear are infinite.

SANDRA BEASLEY is the author of *I Was the Jukebox*, winner of the 2009 Barnard Women Poets Prize, and *Theories of Falling*, winner of the 2007 New Issues Poetry Prize. Other honors include inclusion in the *2010 Best American Poetry*, the University of Mississippi Summer Poet in Residence position, a DCCAH Individual Artist Fellowship, the Friends of Literature Prize from the Poetry Foundation, and the Maureen Egen Exchange Award from *Poets & Writers*. She lives in Washington, D.C.

PHOTO: Matthew Worden

AN APOLOGY FOR FREE VERSE:

or Let My Verse Go!

....

by Nate Pritts

I've never much liked the term "free verse" for three reasons – though I'll likely think of a few more, and maybe even a few reasons why I do like the term. But, for starters:

1) It implies something *cheap* while the adjectiveless term VERSE sounds somehow stronger or purer (or costly?). Free verse thus seems particularly open to attacks disparaging anything labeled "free" as being "not worth it."

2) It is a label and labels are by their very nature static, an already existent condition, something that has stopped breathing and can be pinned down and labeled in a museum.

3) It sounds like a label cooked up by suits, by pie charts and textbooks. In short, it's not in any way descriptive nomenclature and is thus empty.

I'd like to invent a new term—like FREED VERSE, which imagines verse sprung loose and soaring on fire! Or, alternatively, I'd like to turn the term into an injunction, the kind you might find on a protestor's sign "FREE VERSE!" I'm imagining Poets everywhere picketing the Nonce Form factory where verse is being held captive without explanation!

Let my verse go!

Part of the problem stems from all the invectives aimed at free verse. We have prominent poets like Robert Frost famously declaring that "writing free verse is like playing tennis with the net down," and the respected, initialed, W.H. Auden equating the writing of free verse with an aversion to discipline, saying "But I can't understand—strictly from a hedonistic point of view—how one can enjoy writing with no form at all. If one plays a game, one needs rules, otherwise there is no fun. The wildest poem has to have a firm basis in common sense, and this, I think, is the advantage of formal verse."

This, I think, is the hole in the argument against free verse. The dangerous assumption underneath these attacks is that FORMAL verse is CONTROLLED while FREE verse is not only UNCONTROLED but also UNCONTROLLABLE. The truth is far more subtle, and far more empowering for the creative intellects that chose to write free verse. What Auden and Frost are assuming is that (to borrow their conceit) writing poetry is a game, and every game needs a set of objectives and parameters. But writers of free verse are not simply playing a game with no rules. We are—flagrantly! enthusiastically!—rejecting following *someone else's* rules! We are—unabashedly! belligerently!—playing by our own rules!

Many types of formal poetry are well-known and terrifying—the elegant and precise sonnet, the obsessive sestina, the smothery-sounding pantoum. They scare people off, partly, because in their awkward fusion of math and words, a writer might feel as if something outside of her own impulses may be guiding her utterance—sapping strength from her own volition and control as a writer. While this isn't entirely true, it foregrounds the fact that one of the qualities most prized by a writer is, in fact, control.

Formal poetry is constructed by a creative consciousness working in tandem with a scaffold of controlling mechanisms that are applied externally. Free verse is built as a record of a writer's attempts at control—their failures and successes at managing their own creative impulses.

Isn't it grand to have choices? Isn't it nice to have options?

I would assert that neither camp is right or wrong, neither is inherently more honorable or dishonorable. It's a matter of taste, preference, and (luckily) they are both always available to employ whenever! Isn't it grand to have choices? Isn't it nice to have options?

Also, I would submit that while end rhyme and syllable count and numerical repetition patterns make for interesting and generative parameters for a writer, isn't it also true that the writer of free verse is developing and deploying her own pressure-of-form in order to shape her utterance—to make a *different* urn, instead of shattering the well-wrought one?

Many writers end up creating their own forms and while these may not be as widely known or employed as the sonnet, they are still valid and interesting and wildly varied. Dancing to someone else's beat requires a rare precision and grace, and can force a dancer through contortions she might never have imagined on her own. But creating your own beat requires a scrappy and resilient sensibility, and the drive to see it through to its (hopefully) transcendent and transformative end.

Further, even when a writer doesn't create a form to follow there are myriad devices and strategies to be employed, sometimes intuitively and sometimes with patient consideration.

It's a long list of effects; grab any handy poetry textbook or toolbox and you'll find a hundred possibilities and then a hundred more.

So it might be helpful to end with a declaration, a consummation, a new manifesto (with caveats) of free verse:

1) Free verse joyfully and energetically relishes in the creative power of the writer to say whatever she wants to say, however she wants to say it! (so long as she remembers that without the pressure of craft and care and consideration, her words may be nothing more than an inarticulate cry…)

2) Free verse exists benignly alongside Formal verse, two siblings charged with facilitating expression. Write and let write! (though if either side attacks the other, or tries to assert that it is better than the other, an obfuscating cloud might descend making it impossible to write poems at all…)

3) Free verse exists for all of us—the yous and the mes, the grandly ambitious who seek to declaim their writings from the highest peak of immortality and those who seek to pass their writings quietly from row to row in class while the teacher's back is turned, and yes even the Audens and the Frosts!

Free verse is for all of us, for any of us—those with feelings, those with forms, those with formal feelings and those who are feeling formal. When we attempt to put our intellectual, emotional and physical experiences into words that take shape as lines and stanzas, we are engaging in a dizzying and humbling and human endeavor. We must not lose sight of the importance of writing verse, whether free or formal. And we must not let its importance intimidate us or keep us from doing it, often, however we please!

PHOTO: used with permission

NATE PRITTS is the author of four full-length books of poems, most recently *Big Bright Sun* (BlazeVOX) and *The Wonderfull Yeare* (Cooper Dillon Books). His poetry and prose have been published widely, both online and in print, in journals such as *The Southern Review*, *Black Warrior Review*, *Columbia Poetry Review*, *DIAGRAM*, and *Gulf Coast* among many others. He is the founder and principal editor of *H_NGM_N* and H_NGM_N BKS. Learn more at www.natepritts.com.

WRITING EXPERIMENTAL POETRY

by Geof Huth

Poetry can be broken down into myriad categories, each of which might tell you something about the structure of the poem (the size and shape of a sonnet, for instance, is set exactly in place) but little about the actual content, the spark of life, the surprise of the poem itself. This gap between the definition of a kind of poem and an understanding of the poem is greatest, probably, when discussing experimental poetry, which covers such a huge area of writing that the term provides little guidance at all.

People write experimental poetry out of a desire to do something different, to avoid the mundane, and to eschew the overused practices of the past. That description doesn't quite demonstrate what an experimental poem might be, so here are a few concrete examples. A common type of poetry these days is visual poetry, which can be poetry whose visual presentation is essential to this meaning. Collage poetry that combines scraps of found text with visual images would be an example of this, because the poem just isn't the same thing if the words are extracted from the poem and presented in nice neat lines. Visual poetry also includes wordless textual designs made to give the reader a visual yet textual panorama to view and consider.

The poet Christian Bök has been working for years to write a poem that he can encode into the genome of a bacterium so that the body of that animal will manufacture a protein that will itself be another decodable poem. In this way, he hopes to preserve his poem in the only way that can outlast geological eras: within the genetic code of living things. The poet Vanessa Place, who is also a lawyer, has created poems that reuse legal briefs and depositions she creates as a part of her work as a lawyer. Sound poets create very musical poems, some with written scores, some created extemporaneously, made out of nothing but nonsense sounds. Still other experimental poems are experimental in milder ways, by combining dramatically different styles of writing in one poem or by writing poems in which each sentence of the poem seems unrelated to the other sentences in the piece. Because of these and many other examples, some people consider experimental poems not to be poems at all, questioning how poetic these literary forms are, just as experimental poets tend to question that value of a poem that does little more than tell a small piece of an individual poet's life.

Poetry, at its core, is a dramatic experiment with language. More than in any other form of writing, the poem is where the writer tries to create a transformative experience, one that changes the reader or the reader's perspective on the world, one that allows a little eureka to awaken within the person. Experimental poems do this sometimes very beautifully. The harshly fragmented writing of Leslie Scalapino's later years of life has a sweet aloofness to them, but they are made beautiful by their strange coldness and the way they are broken into bits of syntax that don't always cleave cleanly to one another. The late F.A. Nettebeck's great book *Bug Death* is filled with scraps of urban ugliness that don't cohere into a single narrative, but which hold together thematically. The result is a book that is deeply human and moving, and one that is also frightening and, finally, beautiful for all that it does. So an experimental poem is not necessarily anything ugly. It is still a little beast of words straining towards beauty. It is merely that the experimental poem allows for a broader definition of beauty.

And the reason for this is that the experimental poem is intent on the new. The experimental poem usually rejects the ways of the past (meter, rhyme, figurative language) and tries to find new paths towards poetic experience. Although the new is never perfectly possible, this striving for the new forces the experimental poet to question everything that might be written. The poet is required to find a new experience, find a new way to write a poem, a new form for the poem to take. So the poem might be a sequence of sounds spoken into the air or a found object encrusted with words. The experimental poem might require the reader to decrypt its message just to see what its actual words are. Digital poets even create poems where the experience of the poem changes with every viewing, based on what words the poem collects from the Internet and on how the reader interacts with the poem to make it move. Experimental poetry is about possibility and often combines separate kinds of experience (poetry and music, poetry and visual art) into one experience.

Experimental poets are an interesting band of poets, also, because they tend to be more connected to each other internationally than more traditional poets. One reason for this is that many of these poets have shared traditions of their own that bring them together—for instance, an interest in the Dadaists, the more experimental of the Modernists, or the concrete poets of the mid-twentieth century. This is why the vibrant band of visual poets in Turkey is well known across the world of visual poetry: this and the fact that they're talented visual poets. They have the same interests as the visual poets of the United States or Canada or Belgium.

It is difficult to define what an experimental poet is and what that poet does, because exactly what these might be changes with each experimental poet. These poets are scientists of sorts. They work hard to create forms of poetry that have not lived before, to breathe life into an idea that no one has ever had before, and to make a poetry of continuous surprise and enchantment. Sometimes, though, their ideas about enchantment are about disturbing our sometimes too-comfortable sense of what a poem is and should be.

The scope of **GEOF HUTH**'s poetic production includes handdrawn and computer-generated visual poems (some of them wordsless), one-word poems, and poems performed in a language that doesn't exist with melodies created on the spot. He writes almost daily on visual poetry and other poetry at his blog, dbqp: visualizing poetics. His latest book is *ntst: the collected pwoermds of geof huth*, a book of 775 one-word poems.

WHY PROSE POEMS?

....

by Nin Andrews

I always love it when other poets ask me, *Why prose poems?* It's the way they ask the question I particularly appreciate, as if prose poems are somehow defective. I am reminded of how Episcopalians spoke of Baptists when I was a girl. *He's not a Baptist?* my grandmother would ask of a boyfriend, her nose in the air. No wonder I used to shirk this definition of myself, pretend I wasn't *really* a prose poet. After all, I write verse poems and stories on occasion. But I'd have to admit to myself that I do have a deep love for the prose poem. I love both writing and reading them. So why shouldn't I accept the label? Who knows? Maybe it fits.

After years of being asked this question, I've decided I need to invent an answer. Never mind that I don't really have one, that I don't think there is a good definition of a prose poem out there, though Russell Edson's comparison of a prose poem to an airplane comes to mind. *A prose poem is a cast iron aeroplane that can actually fly, mainly because it's pilot does not care if it does or not.* Like Edson I do believe that prose poems fly, at least as well as any other form of writing. The best prose poems give me a sensation of lifting off, defying gravity or the very weight of form, logic, and tradition. They move me beyond the familiar, the expected, and suggest the possibilities for bliss or insight, not easily defined. It's no wonder certain critics suspect and even despise prose poetry. After all, it's often the definition of the thing, rather than the thing itself, that inspires a critic.

But it's the very definition of things that makes me laugh, especially in this era. I sometimes feel as if I am living in a world that resembles a surreal prose poem, if not a science fiction novel. Language, as we use it, often seems stranger than Gertrude Stein's poetry. Instead of describing reality it attempts to mask it. I am thinking of the names our government uses for military terminology. Names that are designed to hide death, bloodshed, accidents, and mass destruction associated with war. Names like special operations, smart bombs, friendly fire, collateral damage, peace-keeping missiles, and absolute duds. An absolute dud, for example, is a nuclear weapon that fails to explode. So one man's dud is another's absolute blessing. I am also thinking of how our culture treats death as if it were something we have a moral duty to put off forever. As a result, I have signed a piece of paper called a living will, which certifies I am willing to die. And it's hard not to think of all the millions of dollars made from products that promise eternal youth, extra-large penises, unblemished skin, infinite bliss and instant success. The printed words that are all around me in catalogs, newspapers, billboards and on the air provide an endless source of entertainment, wonder, and inspiration for prose poetry.

For me, the extreme pleasure of prose poetry is derived from the extent to which the form not only incorporates but also mocks and mimics other forms of writing. My favorite prose poems are like Houdinis or shape-shifters, slipping in and out of other forms. Amy Gerstler, for example, has written one prose poem that looks like a page of singles ads, another which looks like a page from a name-your-baby book, and another, which is a parody of a fan letter. Greg Boyd, Morton Marcus, and David Shumate have written prose poems which are parables, myths and fairy tales or perhaps anti-parables, anti-fairy tales and anti-myths, well-suited to our times.

To me it makes no difference what someone calls a prose poem. ... I am simply happy they exist, in whatever shapes and forms and under whatever titles or labels they might occur.

In her new and stunning book, *Coronology*, Claire Bateman takes off on the form of a dictionary, and in her novel, *The Widening*, Carol Maldow writes what she calls a short novel in which each page, or chapter, is a prose poem. In my book, *The Book of Orgasms*, one poem is an interview with an orgasm, another an ad, and another a glossary of selected terms. In *Supernatural Overtones*, a book of prose poems by Ron Padgett and Clark Coolidge, it appears that Coolidge wrote language poems, and Padgett interpreted them as if they were old sci-fi movies. Then there are the darkly humorous and magical prose poems of Charles Simic, Russell Edson, Peter Johnson, and Maxine Chernoff. And I would be remiss if I left out the LANGUAGE poets who challenge the very nature and structure of meaning and language itself. Three of my favorite language poets are Gertrude Stein, Rosemary Waldrop, and Lyn Hejinian.

Some of the more traditional poets and writers who have written prose poems deny they have ever done so. They might call their prose poems something else—perhaps paragraphs or mini-stories with lyrical qualities. Other poets say they have simply found a prose poem, more or less, while looking at a billboard or reading the newspaper or listening to the radio or their neighbors. Others call prose poems flash fiction, and others ask, *What is the difference between flash fiction and prose poetry?* Still others spend their time trying to determine the exact line where prose poetry ends and flash fiction begins. To me it makes no difference what someone calls a prose poem. A poem in a paragraph, a paragraph in a poem. A story like a poem, a poem like a story. Nor does it matter where the poems come from, the gutter or the sky. I am simply happy they exist, in whatever shapes and forms, under whatever titles or labels they might occur.

PHOTO: Alan Doe

NIN ANDREWS is the author of several poetry collections, including *The Book of Orgasms, Spontaneous Breasts, Why They Grow Wings, Midlife Crisis With Dick and Jane, Sleeping With Houdini,* and *Dear Professor, Do You Live in a Vacuum?* She also edited *Someone Wants to Steal My Name,* a book of translations of the French poet, Henri Michaux.

POETIC FORMS

....

by Robert Lee Brewer

Not every poet likes the idea of writing in poetic forms, but for many poets—including myself—poetic forms are a sort of fun challenge. Whether playing with a sestina or working haiku, I find that attempting poetic forms often forces me into corners that make me think differently than if I'm just writing in free verse.

If you don't have any—or much—experience with poetic forms, I encourage you to peruse the following list and try them. If you are very familiar with poetic forms, I hope the following list can act as a reference for when you're unsure of the rhyme scheme for a triolet versus a kyrielle—or shadorma.

Have fun poeming!

Abstract poetry

Apparently, *abstract* was a term used by Dame Edith Sitwell to describe poems in her book *Facade*. Abstract (or sound) poetry is more about how sounds, rhythms, and textures evoke emotions than about the actual meanings of words.

Acrostic poetry

Acrostic poetry is very easy and fun. The most basic form spells words out on the left-hand side of the page using the first letter of each line. For instance,

> *I like to write*
> *Acrostic poems*
> *Mostly because*
> *Reading them*
> *Out loud is*
> *Bound to be fun.*

If you notice, the first letter of every line makes the simple sentence, "I am Rob." It's very simple, and you can make it as difficult as you want—where the fun part begins.

The brave at heart can even try double acrostics—that is, spelling things out using the first and last letter of each line.

Alphabet poetry

There are many different ways to write an alphabet poem. You can write a poem in which the first letter of each word is a different letter of the alphabet. A tactic for writing this poem is to write out the alphabet ahead of time so that you can pay attention to which letters have been used and which letters are still up for grabs. Of course, you can also do this consecutively through the alphabet.

Another method for alphabet poems is to go through the alphabet using the first letter of the first word for each line.

Poets can always flip the alphabet, too. That is, instead of going A to Z, write alphabet poems from Z to A. It's all about having fun and stretching your mind. Kind of like school.

Anagrammatic Poetry

In Christian Bok's comments about his poem "Vowels" in *The Best American Poetry 2007*, he writes, "'Vowels' is an anagrammatic text, permuting the fixed array of letters found only in the title. 'Vowels' appears in my book *Eunoia*, a lipogrammatic suite of stories, in which each vowel appears by itself in its own chapter." So an anagrammatic poem uses only the letters used in the title.

For instance, if I titled a poem "Spread," it could use only words like red, dresses, drape, spare, pear, pressed, etc.

The real challenge with this kind of poem is first picking a word that has at least a couple vowels and a good mix of consonants. Then, brainstorm all the words you can think of using only those letters (as many times as you wish, of course).

The Blitz Poem

The blitz poem was created by Robert Keim and is a 50-line poem of short phrases and images.

Here are the rules:

- Line 1 should be one short phrase or image (like "build a boat")
- Line 2 should be another short phrase or image using the same first word as the first word in Line 1 (something like "build a house")
- Lines 3 and 4 should be short phrases or images using the last word of Line 2 as their first words (so Line 3 might be "house for sale" and Line 4 might be "house for rent")

- Lines 5 and 6 should be short phrases or images using the last word of Line 4 as their first words, and so on until you've made it through 48 lines
- Line 49 should be the last word of Line 48
- Line 50 should be the last word of Line 47
- The title of the poem should be three words long and follow this format: (first word of Line 3) (preposition or conjunction) (first word of line 47)
- There should be no punctuation

There are a lot of rules, but it's a pretty simple and fun poem to write once you get the hang of it.

The Bop

The Bop is a poetic form that was developed by poet Afaa Michael Weaver at a Cave Canem summer retreat. Here are the basic rules:

- 3 stanzas
- Each stanza is followed by a refrain
- First stanza is 6 lines long and presents a problem
- Second stanza is 8 lines long and explores or expands the problem
- Third stanza is 6 lines long and either presents a solution or documents the failed attempt to resolve the problem

Cascade Poem

The cascade poem was a form invented by Udit Bhatia. For the cascade poem, a poet takes each line from the first stanza of a poem and makes those the final lines of each stanza afterward. Beyond that, there are no additional rules for rhyming, meter, etc.

So to help this make sense, here's what a cascade poem with a tercet would look like:

A
B
C

a
b
A

c
d
B

e
f
C

A quatrain cascade would look so:

A
B
C
D

a
b
c
A

d
e
f
B

g
h
i
C

j
k
l
D

And, of course, you can make this even more involved if you want.

Concrete poetry

Concrete poetry is one of the more experimental poetic forms available to poets. Concrete poems use space and sound to communicate the meanings of the words. Words can cover other words; and the poem has trouble standing without the structure. Concrete poetry is more visual than other poetic forms.

Of course, concrete poetry has plenty of detractors because of the weight structure has on the words, but as much thought goes into concrete poetry as any other form.

Elegy

An elegy is a song of sorrow or mourning—often for someone who has died. However, poets being an especially creative and contrary group have also written elegies for the ends of things, whether a life, a love affair, a great era, a football season, etc.

While there are such things as elegiac couplets and elegiac stanzas, form does not rule an elegy; content *is* king (or queen) when writing elegies.

Epitaphs

The epitaph is a note meant to appear on a tombstone. From the Greek, epitaph means "upon a tomb." Since it has to fit on a tombstone, this note is usually brief and often rhymes. Some epitaphs are funny; most are serious. Most try to get the reader thinking about the subject of the tombstone.

The Fib

Fibonacci poetry was founded by Gregory K. Pincus as a 6-line poem that follows the Fibonacci sequence for syllable count per line.

For the 6-line poem that means:

- 1 syllable for first line
- 1 syllable for second line
- 2 syllables for third
- 3 syllables for fourth
- 5 syllables for fifth
- 8 syllables for sixth

There are variations where the Fibonacci expands even further with each line, but to understand how to accomplish this, you need to understand the Fibonacci math sequence of starting with 0 and 1 and then adding the last two numbers together to add to infinity.

$$0+1=1$$
$$1+1=2$$
$$1+2=3$$
$$2+3=5$$
$$3+5=8$$
$$5+8=13$$
$$8+13=21$$
$$13+21=34$$

and so on and so forth...

Anyway, those lines can easily get more and more unwieldy the more you let them expand. So, there's another variation that has taken flight in making Fibonacci poems that ascend and descend in syllables. For poets who also like mathematics, this is definitely an interesting form to get your mind working.

Found Poems

Found poetry is all about taking words not originally meant to be a poem (as they originally appeared) and turning those words into a poem anyway. You can use newspaper articles, bits of conversation, instructions, recipes, letters, e-mails, direct mail and even spam e-mail.

With found poetry, you do not alter the original words, but you can make line breaks and cut out excess before and/or after the poem you've "found." The power of found poetry is how words not intended as poetry can take on new and profound meanings as found poems.

Ghazal

The ghazal (pronounced "guzzle") is a Persian poetic form. The original form was very simple: five to 15 couplets using the same rhyme with the poet's name in the final couplet. The main themes were usually love or drinking wine.

Contemporary ghazals have abandoned the rhymes and insertion of the poet's name in the final couplet. In fact, even the themes of love and drinking wine are no longer mandatory—as the poem now just needs the couplets which are complete thoughts on their own but also all work together to explore a common theme (whatever that might be).

If you wish to stay traditional though, here's the rhyme scheme you would follow:

a

a

b

a

c

a

and so on to the final stanza (depending upon how many you include).

Many traditional ghazals will also incorporate a refrain at the end of each couplet that could be one word or a phrase.

Haiku

Haiku is descended from the Japanese *renga* form, which was often a collaborative poem comprised of many short stanzas. The opening stanza of the renga was called *hokku*. Eventually, haiku evolved from the leftover and most interesting hokku that were not used in renga.

Most haiku deal with natural topics. They avoid metaphor and simile. While most poets agree that haiku have three short lines, there is some disagreement on how long those lines are. For instance, some traditional haiku poets insist on 17 syllables in lines of 5/7/5. Other contemporary haiku poets feel that the first and third lines can be any length as long as they're shorter than the middle line.

Haiku do not have to include complete sentences or thoughts. They do not have titles. The best haiku contain some shift in the final line.

Hay(na)ku

Hay(na)ku is a very simple poetic form created in 2003 by poet Eileen Tabios. Hay(na)ku is a 3-line poem with one word in the first line, two words in the second, and three in the third. There are no restrictions beyond this.

There are already some variations of this new poetic form. For instance, a reverse hay(na)ku has lines of three, two, and one word(s) for lines one, two, and three respectively. Also, multiple hay(na)ku can be chained together to form longer poems.

Insult poetry

There are no hard and fast rules to the insult poem, but it's usually done in a joking (all in good fun) fashion as opposed to seriously trying to annoy anyone. Many insult poems also have a repetitive form or recurring method of delivering the insults. The insult poem is a good way to show just how clever you are (or think you are). But beware writing them! Once you attack someone (even in jest), you are suddenly fair game to receive an insult poem in retaliation.

Kyrielle

The kyrielle is a French four-line stanza form—with 8 syllables per line—that has a refrain in the fourth line. Often, there is a rhyme scheme in the poem consisting of the following possibilities:

- aabb
- abab
- aaab
- abcb

The poem can be as long as you wish and as short as two stanzas (otherwise, the refrain is not really a refrain, is it?), and, as with many French forms, it is very nice for stretching your poetic muscles.

Limericks

The origin of the limerick is shrouded in some mystery, but most sources seem to point to the early 18th century—one theory being that soldiers returning from France to the Irish town of Limerick started the form, the other theory pointing to the 1719 publication of *Mother Goose Melodies for Children*. Either way, Edward Lear popularized the form in the mid-19th century.

Basically, the limerick is a five-line poem consisting of a tercet split by a couplet. That is, lines 1, 2, and 5 are a bit longer and rhyme, while the shorter lines of 3 and 4 rhyme. After studying many effective limericks, there is not a precise syllable count per line, but the norm is about 8-10 syllables in the longer lines and around 6 syllables in the shorter lines.

List Poems

A list poem (also known as a catalog poem) is a poem that lists things, whether names, places, actions, thoughts, images, etc. Even a grocery list could turn into a poem with this form.

Lune

The lune is also known as the American Haiku. It was first created by the poet Robert Kelly and was a result of Kelly's frustration with English haiku. After much experimentation, he settled on a 13-syllable, self-contained poem that has 5 syllables in the first line, 3 syllables in the second line and 5 syllables in the final line.

Unlike haiku, there are no other rules. No need for a cutting word. Rhymes are fine; subject matter is open. While there are fewer syllables to use, this form has a little more freedom.

There is also a variant lune created by the poet Jack Collom. His form is also a self-contained tercet, but it's word-based (not syllable-based) and has the structure of 3 words in the first line, 5 words in the second line and 3 words in the final line.

Monotetra

The monotetra is a poetic form developed by Michael Walker. Here are the basic rules:

- Comprised of quatrains (four-line stanzas) in tetrameter (four metrical feet) for a total of 8 syllables per line
- Each quatrain consists of mono-rhymed lines (so each line in the first stanza has the same type of rhyme, as does each line in the second stanza, etc.)
- The final line of each stanza repeats the same four syllables
- This poem can be as short as one quatrain and as long as a poet wishes

Personally, I like the rhyme scheme and the repetitive final line of each stanza. I also appreciate the flexibility of this form in terms of how long or short the poem can be.

Occasional Poems

There are no specific guidelines for occasional poems except that they mark a specific occasion. The poems can be long or short, serious or humorous, good or bad—just as long as they mark the occasion. Good occasions for poems include birthdays, weddings and holidays.

Odes

The ode is a poetic form formed for flattery. There are three types of odes: the Horation; the Pindaric; and the Irregular.

The Horation ode (named for the Latin poet, Horace) contains one stanza pattern that repeats throughout the poem—usually 2 or 4 lines in length.

The Pindaric ode (named for the Greek poet, Pindar) is made up of a pattern of three stanzas called triads. This type of ode can be composed of several triads, but the first (the strophe) and the second (antistrophe) should be identical metrically with the third (epode) wandering off on its own metrical path.

The irregular ode (named for no one in particular) does away with formalities and focuses on the praising aspect of the ode.

Palindrome poetry

The palindrome seems like a simple enough form—until you actually try to write a good one. The rules are simple enough:

1. You must use the same words in the first half of the poem as the second half, but
2. Reverse the order for the second half, and
3. Use a word in the middle as a bridge from the first half to the second half of the poem.

At first, the simplicity of the rules made me feel like this would be easy enough to do, but I ran into problems almost immediately. For instance, you can't start the poem with the word "the" unless you plan to end the poem on the word "the." And just because something makes sense in the first half doesn't guarantee it'll pass the same test on the way back.

Pantoum

The **pantoum** is a poetic form originating in Malay where poets write quatrains (4-line stanzas) with an *abab* rhyme scheme and repeat lines 2 and 4 in the previous stanza as lines 1 and 3 in the next stanza.

Poets differ on how to treat the final quatrain: Some poets repeat lines 1 and 3 of the original quatrain as lines 2 and 4 in the final quatrain; other poets invert lines 1 and 3 so that the beginning line of the poem is also the final line of the poem.

Also, the pantoum can be as long or as short as you wish it to be, though mathematically it does require at least 4 lines.

Paradelle

The paradelle is a poetic form that Billy Collins originally introduced as "one of the more demanding French forms," though eventually Collins fessed up that he created it as a joke.

However, Collins was not kidding about the demanding rules of the paradelle. Here they are:

- The paradelle is a 4-stanza poem.
- Each stanza consists of 6 lines.

- For the first 3 stanzas, the 1st and 2nd lines should be the same; the 3rd and 4th lines should also be the same; and the 5th and 6th lines should be composed of all the words from the 1st and 3rd lines and only the words from the 1st and 3rd lines.
- The final stanza should be composed of all the words in the 5th and 6th lines of the first three stanzas and only the words from the 5th and 6th lines of the first three stanzas.

Parody Poems

A parody poem is one that pokes fun at another poem or poet. For instance, I recently read a parody of "We Real Cool," by Gwendolyn Brooks, in an online version of *Coe Review* called "We Real White." The best parodies are those that are easily recognizable—and funny, of course.

Rondeau

The rondeau is a form that has a refrain and rhymes—two elements I love in many French poems. The traditional rondeau is a poem consisting of 3 stanzas, 13 original lines, and 2 refrains (of the first line of the poem) with 8 to 10 syllables per line and an A/B rhyme scheme.

The skeleton of the traditional rondeau looks like this:

A(R)
A
B
B
A

A
A
B
A(R)

A
A
B
B
A
A(R)

There are variations of the rondeau, including the rondeau redouble, rondel, rondel double, rondelet, roundel, and roundelay. Of course, poets tend to break the rules on each of these as well, which is what poets like to do.

Sestina

The sestina is one of my favorite forms. You pick 6 words, rotate them as the end words in 6 stanzas and then include 2 of the end words per line in your final stanza.

Let's pick 6 random words: bears, carving, dynamite, hunters, mothers, blessing.

Here's how the end words would go:

Stanza 1

Line 1-bears (A)
Line 2-carving (B)
Line 3-dynamite (C)
Line 4-hunters (D)
Line 5-mothers (E)
Line 6-blessing (F)

Stanza 2

Line 7-blessing (F)
Line 8-bears (A)
Line 9-mothers (E)
Line 10-carving (B)
Line 11-hunters (D)
Line 12-dynamite (C)

Stanza 3

Line 13-dynamite (C)
Line 14-blessing (F)
Line 15-hunters (D)
Line 16-bears (A)
Line 17-carving (B)
Line 18-mothers (E)

Stanza 4

Line 19-mothers (E)
Line 20-dynamite (C)
Line 21-carving (B)
Line 22-blessing (F)
Line 23-bears (A)
Line 24-hunters (D)

Stanza 5

Line 25-hunters (D)

Line 26-mothers (E)
Line 27-bears (A)
Line 28-dynamite (C)
Line 29-blessing (F)
Line 30-carving (B)

Stanza 6

Line 31-carving (B)
Line 32-hunters (D)
Line 33-blessing (F)
Line 34-mothers (E)
Line 35-dynamite (C)
Line 36-bears (A)

Stanza 7

Line 37-bears (A), carving (B)
Line 38-dynamite (C), hunters (D)
Line 39-mothers (E), blessing (F)

While many poets try to write sestinas in iambic pentameter, that is not a requirement. Also, when choosing your six end words, it does help to choose words that can be altered if needed to help keep the flow of the poem going.

Sevenling

The sevenling was created by Roddy Lumsden. Here are the rules:

- The sevenling is a 7-line poem (clever, huh?) split into three stanzas.
- The first three lines should contain an element of three. It could be three connected or contrasting statements, a list of three details or names, or something else along these lines. The three things can take up all three lines or be contained anywhere within the stanza.
- The second three lines should also contain an element of three. Same deal as the first stanza, but the two stanzas do not need to relate to each other directly.
- The final line/stanza should act as either narrative summary, punchline, or unusual juxtaposition.
- Titles are not required. But when titles are present, they should be titled Sevenling followed by the first few words in parentheses.
- Tone should be mysterious, offbeat or disturbing.
- Poem should have ambience which invites guesswork from the reader.

Shadorma

Shadorma is a Spanish 6-line syllabic poem of 3/5/3/3/7/5 syllable lines respectively. Simple as that.

Skeltonic poetry

Skeltonic verse is named after the poet John Skelton (1460-1529), who wrote short rhyming lines that just sort of go on from one rhyme to the next for however long a poet wishes to take it. Most skeltonic poems average less than six words a line, but keeping the short rhymes moving down the page is the real key to this form.

Sonnet

The sonnet is a 14-line poem that usually rhymes and is often written in iambic pentameter, though not always. Over time, this Italian poem has been pushed to its limits and some contemporary sonnets abandon many of the general guidelines.

The two most famous forms of the sonnet are the *Shakespearean Sonnet* (named after William Shakespeare) and the *Petrarcan Sonnet* (named after Francesco Petrarca).

The rhyme scheme for a Shakespearean Sonnet is:

a
b
a
b

c
d
c
d

e
f
e
f

g
g

The rhyme scheme for the Petrarcan Sonnet is a little more complicated. The first eight lines (or octave) are always rhymed abbaabba. But the final six lines (or sestet) can be rhymed any number of ways: cdcdcd, cdedce, ccdccd, cdecde, or cddcee. Of course, this offers a little more flexibility near the end of the poem.

But sonnets don't necessarily need to be Shakespearean or Petrarcan to be considered sonnets. In fact, there are any number of other sonnet varieties.

A few extra notes about the sonnet:

- A crown of sonnets is made by seven sonnets. The last line of each sonnet must be used as the first line of the next until the seventh sonnet. The last line of that seventh sonnet must be the first line of the first sonnet.
- A sonnet redouble is a sequence of 15 sonnets. Each line from the first sonnet is used (in order) as the the last line of the following 14 sonnets.

Tanka

If a haiku is usually (mistakenly) thought of as a 3-line, 5-7-5 syllable poem, then the tanka would be a 5-line, 5-7-5-7-7 syllable poem. However, as with haiku, it's better to think of a tanka as a 5-line poem with 3 short lines (lines 2, 4, 5) and 2 very short lines (lines 1 and 3).

While imagery is still important in tanka, the form is a little more conversational than haiku at times. It also allows for the use of poetic devices such as metaphor and personification (2 big haiku no-no's).

Like haiku, tanka is a Japanese poetic form.

Triolet

The triolet (TREE-o-LAY) has 13th-century French roots linked to the rondeau or "round" poem. Like other French forms, the triolet is great for repetition, because the first line of the poem is used three times and the second line is used twice. If you do the math on this 8-line poem, you'll realize there are only three other lines to write: two of those lines rhyme with the first line, the other rhymes with the second line.

A diagram of the triolet would look like this:

A (first line)
B (second line)
a (rhymes with first line)
A (repeat first line)
a (rhymes with first line)
b (rhymes with second line)
A (repeat first line)
B (repeat second line)

Villanelle

The villanelle, like the other French forms, does have many of the same properties: plenty of rhyme and repetition. This French form was actually adapted from Italian folk songs (villanella) about rural life. One of the more famous contemporary villanelles is "Do Not Go Gentle Into That Good Night," by Dylan Thomas.

The villanelle consists of five tercets and a quatrain with line lengths of 8-10 syllables. The first and third lines of the first stanza become refrains that repeat throughout the poem. It looks like this:

A(1)
b
A(2)

a
b
A(1)

a
b
A(2)

a
b
A(1)

a
b
A(2)

a
b
A(1)
A(2)

1 0 1 POETRY PROMPTS

....

by Robert Lee Brewer

ON MY POETIC ASIDES BLOG, I LEAD POEM-A-DAY CHALLENGES DURING THE MONTHS OF APRIL AND NOVEMBER. For these challenges, I share a prompt and my own attempt at the prompt each morning; then, other poets from around the world write their own poems and share them in the comments of that day's post. During the other 10 months of the year, I share a poetry prompt each week on Wednesday. Here are 101 poetry prompts for you to try throughout the year. To join in the fun on Poetic Asides, visit http://blog.writersdigest. com/poeticasides.

WRITE A POEM ABOUT A FIRST OR SERIES OF FIRSTS. This first could be a first love, first job, first funeral, first marriage, or first poem.

PUT YOURSELF IN SOMEONE (OR SOMETHING) ELSE'S SKIN AND WRITE A POEM ABOUT THE EX-PERIENCE. WHO (OR WHAT) EVER YOU BECOME, MAKE THAT THE TITLE OF THE POEM. If you're Buddy Holly, your poem should be titled "Buddy Holly."

WRITE A WORRY POEM. Anything that causes you worry can be used to help you write this poem. Are you worried about paying the bills? Asking a friend on a date? Circus clowns?

RECORD ALL THE DETAILS OF YOUR DAY AND GENERATE A POEM FROM THAT MATERIAL. To make the poem interesting, you probably do NOT want to just list out everything from the beginning of the day to the end. But then again, maybe you could prove me wrong on that assumption.

WRITE A RAMBLE POEM. That is, write a poem in which you just start rambling without worrying about where you're headed. Very interesting things can happen in these poems. Then, go back through and revise.

PICK A WORD (ANY WORD) AND WRITE A POEM ABOUT IT. If you wish, you can make that word the title of your poem. Look up the definition. Think about how the word is used by people and in what situations. Then, write.

WRITE A LOCATION POEM. This poem could be about a room, a city, a country or some other specific place. The location you choose could be a place you've actually visited, or just one you'd like to see someday—or that you've created in your imagination.

WRITE AN APOLOGY POEM. If you're not the type of poet who apologizes for anything, then pretend that someone is apologizing to you in the poem.

LISTEN TO A SONG (OR TWO) AND WRITE A POEM IN RESPONSE. Your poem can take the song to another level, or it can level an argument against the lyrics. Or your poem can spring into a completely new direction.

TAKE THE PHRASE "HOW (BLANK) BEHAVES," REPLACE THE BLANK WITH A WORD OR PHRASE, MAKE THE NEW PHRASE THE TITLE OF YOUR POEM, AND THEN, WRITE YOUR POEM. Sample titles might include: "How My Poem Behaves," "How Robert Lee Brewer Behaves," or "How Children Behave." Don't be afraid to misbehave with this prompt.

Take the phrase "I'm so over (blank)," replace the blank with a word or phrase, make the new phrase the title of your poem, and then, write the poem. Example titles include: "I'm so over time sheets," "I'm so over bad poetry," or "I'm so over rainy days."

WRITE AN INSULT POEM. If you get along with everyone you meet, this might be a tough one to write. However, if you can find something to criticize in everyone you know, then this prompt alone could give an entire collection worth of material.

GIVE YOUR POEM A TWIST ENDING. The easiest way to accomplish a twist ending might be to write a narrative poem that takes a left when the reader was expecting a right. But it might also be a twist in rhyme scheme, form, or something else completely unexpected.

WRITE A POEM ABOUT A MEMORY OF YOU THAT YOU DON'T PERSONALLY REMEMBER. Maybe a friend or family member remembers something when you were small or a little too intoxicated or asleep. Write about this memory that you've had to hear through another.

FIND A LINE THAT YOU REALLY ENJOY AND USE IT AS THE FIRST LINE OF YOUR POEM. Be sure to give credit to the source that provided you with the first line.

WRITE A LOVE POEM. That's simple enough, isn't it?

PICK AN IMAGE AND WRITE A POEM ABOUT IT. The image could be a painting, a photograph, graffiti, or something else. If you pick a famous image, you may want to identify it in the title of your poem.

WRITE A SNOOPING (OR EAVESDROPPING) POEM. Pay attention to conversations from the next table or room. Watch people from a balcony or behind a bush. Just don't do anything to get yourself arrested or hit with a restraining order.

WRITE A POEM ABOUT GETTING OLDER. It doesn't matter how old you are, you're aging by the minute. The longer you wait to write this poem the older you'll be when you finally get around to it. So poem.

WRITE A NATURE POEM. This poem can celebrate trees, creeks, birds, and clouds. Or it can dive into the psychological natures of people. Or it can attack the nature of writing poetry.

TAKE THE PHRASE "I'M SO OVER (BLANK)," REPLACE THE BLANK WITH A WORD OR PHRASE, MAKE THE NEW PHRASE THE TITLE OF YOUR POEM, AND THEN, WRITE THE POEM. Example titles include: "I'm so over time sheets," "I'm so over bad poetry," or "I'm so over rainy days."

WRITE AN OCCUPATIONAL POEM. Are you a lawyer or paralegal? Write about working in the law field. Do you bus tables or wait on hungry customers? Write about working in a restaurant. Or imagine what it's like to have a job that you don't have.

WRITE A POEM THAT IS ONLY ONE SIDE OF A TWO-SIDED CONVERSATION. Leave the other half of the conversation to the imagination. To help you achieve this poem, you could write both sides of the conversation and then edit out one of the voices.

PICK AN ANIMAL AND WRITE A POEM ABOUT IT. In fact, make the animal the title of your poem so that readers know your subject.

WRITE AN EXERCISE POEM. Either you love it or you hate it, but anyone can write a poem about the act of working out. Plus, there are so many ways to exercise from hitting the gym to stretching or from running around a lake to swimming in a pool.

VISIT A LANDMARK AND WRITE A POEM ABOUT IT. If you're not able to get out of the house, then visit the landmark through a book or the Internet. There are many ways to experience landmarks these days.

WRITE AN ORIGIN POEM. This poem could be about the origin of a superhero or just a regular person. It could be about the origin of a problem or a solution.

THINK ABOUT SOMETHING THAT'S MISSING AND WRITE A POEM ABOUT IT. The missing something might be a physical object (like your keys or a sock) or something more abstract (like an emotion or an idea).

Think about a routine you have and write a poem about it. Or write about the routines of other people (or animals). The tricky part is to make the poem anything but routine.

WRITE AN OUTSIDER POEM. The outsider in the poem could be yourself or someone else. You could even write a poem about an animal or plant that is considered an outsider.

WRITE A CLEAN POEM. This poem could be about cleaning something or something that's clean. Or it could just be a poem that uses clean language. For extra credit, write a dirty poem.

TAKE THE PHRASE "THE PROBLEM WITH (BLANK)," REPLACE THE BLANK WITH A WORD OR PHRASE, MAKE THE NEW PHRASE THE TITLE OF YOUR POEM, AND THEN, WRITE YOUR POEM. Example titles include: "The Problem With Poets," "The Problem With Money," or "The Problem With Love."

WRITE A POEM WITH AN INTERACTION. The interaction could be verbal, physical or emotional. For instance, an interaction could be as simple as two people making eye contact and then looking away from each other.

THINK ABOUT A ROUTINE YOU HAVE AND WRITE A POEM ABOUT IT. Or write about the routines of other people (or animals). The tricky part is to make the poem anything but routine.

WRITE AN ANGRY POEM. Even the most mild-mannered poets surely get upset from time to time. Unleash the fury with a poem.

PICK A DAY OF THE WEEK AND WRITE A POEM ABOUT IT. Or write a short seven-poem collection titled Days of the Week. Explore how a Friday poem might be different from a Tuesday or Sunday poem.

WRITE A REBIRTH POEM. This poem could tackle the rebirth of a person's identity or the changing of a season. There are many ways in which animals, people, plants and ideas are reborn.

SELECT AN OBJECT AND WRITE A POEM ABOUT IT. Think of William Carlos Williams' "The Red Wheelbarrow." Of course, pick your own object and do it in your own style.

WRITE A POEM OF REGRET. Think of something you wish you'd done differently. Write about someone else's regrets. This might be a perfect opportunity to write a blues poem, but a hopeful poem with regret may make it even more interesting.

INCORPORATE A HOBBY INTO A POEM. There aren't enough poems about collecting stamps and bird spotting. Write an ode to collecting baseball cards or dolls.

WRITE A POSTCARD POEM. In about the same confined space you would have to scribble a message on a postcard, write a poem. To make it even more realistic, address your poem directly to a reader.

TAKE THE PHRASE "NEVER (BLANK)," REPLACE THE BLANK WITH A WORD OR PHRASE, MAKE THE NEW PHRASE THE TITLE OF YOUR POEM, AND THEN, WRITE THE POEM. Example titles include: "Never Say Never," "Never Leave Home Without a Pen," or "Never Again."

WRITE A MISCOMMUNICATION POEM. Poems are a form of communication between the poet and the reader. However, good poetry can come from the miscommunication between one character and another.

LOOK AT SOMETHING FAMILIAR IN A NEW WAY OR FROM A DIFFERENT ANGLE AND WRITE A POEM ABOUT YOUR NEW PERSPECTIVE. The something familiar could be a physical object (like a statue or building) or it could be something more abstract (like a relationship or daily routine). Just look for something new in the familiar.

WRITE A POEM OF LONGING. IN THIS POEM, HAVE THE NARRATOR OR A CHARACTER PINING AWAY FOR SOMEONE (OR SOMETHING) ELSE. Some might mistake this for a love poem, but people could be longing for a vacation on a tropical island or a bowl of chocolate ice cream.

PICK A COLOR, MAKE THAT THE TITLE OF YOUR POEM, AND WRITE THE POEM. Your color-titled poem can directly investigate the color itself, or the color could suggest a mood that sets the scene for whatever happens in your poem.

WRITE A POSITIVE POEM. Pulling off an effective happy poem may seem difficult for some, but positive poems are often very refreshing for readers. However, if you want an extra challenge, write a negative poem too.

WRITE A SLOW POEM. This is the perfect opportunity to write about turtles and snails or the slow drip of syrup. Or rush hour traffic.

WRITE A GROWTH POEM. This poem could be about physical growth (like growing a few inches or growing hair) or emotional growth. It could even be about a normal-sized person who comes into contact with radiation and turns into the 50-foot Poet. Or something along those lines.

PICK AN INVENTION AND WRITE A POEM ABOUT IT. The invention could be something real, such as an airplane or food processor. The invention could also be something not so real, such as a time travel machine or teleportation device.

WRITE A SLIPPERY POEM. Maybe the subject matter of this poem is on a slippery slope. Or maybe the poem is about slipping on banana peels or black ice.

TAKE THE PHRASE "IF ONLY (BLANK)," REPLACE THE BLANK WITH A WORD OR PHRASE, MAKE THE NEW PHRASE THE TITLE OF YOUR POEM, AND THEN, WRITE THE POEM. Possible titles include: "If Only It Didn't Snow," "If Only We Remembered to Change the Oil," or "If Only This Poem Were Easier to Revise."

WRITE A POEM ABOUT A MEMORY. Sound familiar? Earlier, I had you write about a memory that you did not remember. However, I want you to write about something you do remember for this memory poem.

CHOOSE A SHAPE AND WRITE A POEM ABOUT IT. For instance, you could write a poem about a crescent moon or box kite. There are a lot of simple and complex shapes out there, and some of them can even be used to describe other people or objects.

WRITE A CONSTRUCTION POEM. It's your choice whether you want to write about building construction, road construction or construction paper.

PICK A PLANT AND WRITE ABOUT IT. There are so many plant species on this planet that you're bound to find one that's never been tackled before or on which you can put a new spin.

WRITE A POEM INVOLVING LINES. I know, I know, all poems have lines. Well, you could write about poetic lines, sure, but I also encourage you to write about lines drawn in the sand, lines used in architecture, lines used in sports, or lines used in a sports bar.

CONSIDER SOMETHING THAT WILL ALWAYS STICK WITH YOU AND WRITE A POEM ABOUT IT. Maybe it's something that happened to you when you were young. Maybe it's a good thing or a bad thing. Maybe it's just a random thing that someone said that has always stuck with you and even played an important role in decisions you've made afterward.

WRITE A HANGING POEM. There are a lot of things that can hang. Pick one (or more) and write about it.

WRITE AN EMERGENCY POEM. Emergencies can sometimes be a subjective thing, so the possibility for creating tension between two people in a poem is ripe in an emergency poem. Of course, there are other emergencies that put everyone on edge, and those can be engaging too.

WRITE AN ATTACHMENT POEM. People make all manner of attachments—physical, mental and emotional. Pick one (or two) and write about them.

Write a poem filled with noise. The noise could be loud, but also soft. Noise could be something mechanical or sounds that build in nature. (Note: I do not advise writing a poem about whether trees falling along in the forest make a sound, but that doesn't mean you can't go that route anyway.)

TAKE THE PHRASE "EVERYBODY SAYS (BLANK)," REPLACE THE BLANK WITH A WORD OR PHRASE, MAKE THE NEW PHRASE THE TITLE OF YOUR POEM, AND THEN, WRITE THE POEM. Example titles include: "Everybody Says the Same Thing," "Everybody Says I Should Quit," or "Everybody Says Things in a Foreign Language." For an alternate option, do the same thing with the phrase "Nobody Says (blank)."

WRITE AN EXPLOSION POEM. Write a poem about fireworks or having an explosion of emotion. For extra credit, write an implosion poem.

WRITE A LONELY POEM. The narrator can be lonely or another character, but there should definitely be some loneliness in the poem.

WRITE A POEM FILLED WITH NOISE. The noise could be loud, but also soft. Noise could be something mechanical or sounds that build in nature. (Note: I do not advise writing a poem about whether trees falling along in the forest make a sound, but that doesn't mean you can't go that route anyway.)

THINK ABOUT HISTORY AND WRITE A POEM ABOUT IT. The history could be ancient history, national history or personal history. The poem could be about big concepts or a very particular snapshot in time.

WRITE A TOO MUCH INFORMATION POEM. This poem could be one in which the narrator shares a little too much personal information, or it could tackle the information overload of the Internet, social media, and smart phones.

WRITE A DEADLINE POEM. Poems and deadlines don't usually go together, which is why this prompt may deliver some good poems. If you want to put some pressure on your poeming, give this poem a deadline to be written, revised and published.

PICK AN EVENT, MAKE THAT THE TITLE OF YOUR POEM, AND THEN, WRITE THE POEM. The event could be a national celebration or a parade. It could be a local festival, an annual gathering, or even something as mundane as a weekly department meeting.

WRITE A FAREWELL POEM. This poem could be about a person leaving a group or situation, or it could be directed to a specific reader or audience.

THINK SCARY AND WRITE A HORROR POEM. Relate an urban legend. Give a new slant on timeless terror.

TAKE THE PHRASE "PARTLY (BLANK)," REPLACE THE BLANK WITH A WORD OR PHRASE, MAKE THE NEW PHRASE THE TITLE OF YOUR POEM, AND THEN, WRITE THE POEM. Example titles include: "Partly Cloudy," "Partly Insane," or "Partly Poetic."

WRITE A WATER POEM. Water can be a main feature of the poem, or it can just factor into the poem in an indirect way, such as a character standing next to a water fountain or a poem that takes place on a yacht.

Write a self-portrait poem. Of course, it's up to every poet whether to airbrush out the blemishes or be excessively harsh (or somewhere in between), but I'd really be missing a poetic goldmine if I didn't mention that you can write about yourself.

WRITE A DEATH POEM. You could write about a specific death or consider death in general.

PICK A CITY, MAKE THAT THE TITLE OF YOUR POEM, AND THEN, WRITE THE POEM. Choose your own city, one that you've visited, or one you'd like to visit.

WRITE A SCIENCE POEM. Science encompasses a lot. In fact, science either touches or rubs up against about everything that poetry does.

SELECT A PERSON AND WRITE A POEM ABOUT HIM OR HER. The person could be a famous historical figure, such as Emily Dickinson or Abraham Lincoln, or someone from your own sphere of influence. The person could even be someone you don't personally know, but who you've mythologized over time.

WRITE A LOOKING BACK POEM. There are a couple ways to attack this poem. The narrator could be looking over past events or literally looking over his or her shoulder.

WRITE AN EVENING POEM. Pretty simple—just write a poem that takes place at night.

PICK A TOOL, MAKE THAT THE TITLE OF YOUR POEM, AND THEN, WRITE THE POEM. Tools are everywhere—from writing implements to computers and from hammers to sporks. So while there is plenty of inspiration in the workshop, tools can be found elsewhere too.

Write an agreement poem. In this poem, there could be an agreement made between two parties, or the narrator could be agreeing with a statement. Or the poet could lay out a contractual agreement between himself and the reader.

WRITE A SELF-PORTRAIT POEM. Of course, it's up to every poet whether to airbrush out the blemishes or be excessively harsh (or somewhere in between), but I'd really be missing a poetic goldmine if I didn't mention that you can write about yourself.

TAKE THE PHRASE "LOOKING FOR (BLANK)," REPLACE THE BLANK WITH A WORD OR PHRASE, MAKE THE NEW PHRASE THE TITLE OF YOUR POEM, AND THEN, WRITE THE POEM. Example titles include: "Looking for Reasons to Write a Poem," "Looking for the North Pole," or "Looking for the Answer to This Question."

WRITE A HOPEFUL POEM. The poem can present a hopeful vision, or the poem can follow someone who is filled with hope. As an alternative, write a hopeless poem.

LET GO OF SOMETHING AND WRITE A POEM ABOUT IT. Let go of junk. Let go of resentments. Let go of self-loathing. Write a poem (or two) that releases something.

WRITE A CONTAINMENT POEM. The poem could cover containers like plastic baggies and cardboard boxes or containers like jails and prisons. There are also more abstract containers, such as our minds and computers.

WRITE A METAMORPHOSIS POEM. This poem is one in which the original subject changes into something else—maybe even multiple times during the poem.

TAKE A STAND ON AN ISSUE AND WRITE A POEM ABOUT IT. Maybe you can take a stand on form poems or pick a side on the political spectrum. Maybe you support public transportation—write a poem that expresses your position.

WRITE AN AGREEMENT POEM. In this poem, there could be an agreement made between two parties, or the narrator could be agreeing with a statement. Or the poet could lay out a contractual agreement between himself and the reader.

WRITE A CROSSROADS POEM. This could be a poem about a physical, mental or emotional crossroads.

THINK OF A QUESTION, MAKE THAT THE TITLE OF YOUR POEM, AND THEN, WRITE THE POEM. The poem could continue asking more questions, or it could attempt to answer the question that was posed in the title. Or it could describe a scene that is heightened by the question in the title.

WRITE A LOST AND FOUND POEM. You could focus on the actual losing and finding. Or your poem might examine how things change after something is lost—or how things change after something is found.

Pick a type of person and write about him or her. Your person could be a firefighter, police officer, pedestrian, mountain biker, or any number of other people.

TAKE THE PHRASE "BLAME THE (BLANK)," REPLACE THE BLANK WITH A WORD OR PHRASE, MAKE THE NEW WORD PHRASE THE TITLE OF YOUR POEM, AND THEN, WRITE THE POEM. Example titles include: "Blame the Prompt," "Blame the Barry White Music," or "Blame the Scientists."

WRITE A SPACES POEM. The spaces could be physical spaces, such as an open field or a confined closet. Or the spaces could be spaces in time or logic.

PICK A NUMBER, MAKE THAT NUMBER THE TITLE OF YOUR POEM, AND THEN, WRITE YOUR POEM. Personally, I like the numbers eight and 23, but there are any number of numbers from which to choose. Sorry, I couldn't resist.

WRITE A LESSONS LEARNED POEM. Usually, you can only learn your lesson after you've made a mistake, so keep that in mind. For an alternate prompt, write a poem in which a character never learns.

IMAGINE THE WORLD WITHOUT YOU AND WRITE A POEM ABOUT IT. If this seems too self-centered to you, then you can always imagine the world without someone else and write a poem about that.

WRITE A GOOFY POEM. Who says poetry always has to be serious? It doesn't. However, if you have trouble getting silly with your verse, write a serious poem. Make it deadly serious even.

WRITE A POEM THAT REMEMBERS AN OLD RELATIONSHIP. The poem could be about a romantic relationship, but also about a long lost friend or an estranged or distant family member.

PICK A TYPE OF PERSON AND WRITE ABOUT HIM OR HER. Your person could be a firefighter, police officer, pedestrian, mountain biker, or any number of other people.

THINK ABOUT THE BIG PICTURE AND WRITE A POEM ABOUT IT. This is your chance to write a poem about what's really important in life—or what's unimportant in the big scheme of things.

WRITE A NEXT STEPS POEM. Think about what you're going to do after you write this poem, after you leave this room, after you wake up tomorrow morning.

TAKE THE PHRASE "THE LAST (BLANK)," REPLACE THE BLANK WITH A WORD OR PHRASE, MAKE THE NEW PHRASE THE TITLE OF YOUR POEM, AND THEN, WRITE YOUR POEM. Example titles include: "The Last Poem," "The Last Reader," or "The Last Cupcake."

WRITE A POEM ABOUT ENDINGS OR FINISHES. This poem could be about ending a relationship or finishing a poem. If you've finished this list of prompts, I challenge you to start creating your own.

JESSIE CARTY:

A Regional Blogging Poet

....

by Robert Lee Brewer

Poet and blogger Jessie Carty, who is one of the harder working poets I know. Based in North Carolina, Carty makes multiple submissions weekly, networks with other poets (online and off), teaches, and still finds time to maintain an excellent poetry blog: http://jessiecarty.com/blog.

In 2010, Folded Word Press released Carty's collection *Paper House* (which actually briefly made the poetry bestseller list). The poems in the collection are narrative poems that often surprise and delight, and I'm pleased that she recently took some time out of her busy schedule for this interview.

What are you up to?

The first word that comes to mind is: trouble. But, I doubt I'm actually up to much of that. Mostly, I'm trying to learn how to balance teaching (I just started adjunct teaching at RCCC in Concord, NC), blogging, housework and that other thing—what is it again? Oh! The actual poetry part of being a poet.

What do you try to accomplish with your blog?

I started my blog so I could talk about my MFA experience. I went back to school just a year into a return to writing after a five-year gap, so I wanted to try and wrap my brain around being a full-time worker and a student/writer. The blog, however, has evolved into a place that people actually visit! Each week I share poems in progress, speak about the process of trying to obtain publication and just in general speak about what it is like to be a writer and reader. I like connecting and helping writers who are all at different stages in their careers/journeys as writers.

Is there anything you'd like to try with your blog that you're not currently doing?
I asked around about having guest bloggers, but no one has taken me up on that yet!

....

When I was writing poetry as an undergrad back in the 90s, I did so in a sort of vacuum.

....

Blogging and social networking is one way to build a community of poets; reading poetry at live events is another way to build community. What are your thoughts on poetry community and building an audience for your poetry?
When I was writing poetry as an undergrad back in the 90s, I did so in a sort of vacuum. There were a few people with whom I shared my writing, but the number was very, very small. I enjoyed the creative writing classes I took, but building a community of writers wasn't really emphasized at that level. I think it is the biggest reason I stopped writing in my late 20s.

When I came back to writing after a 5-year gap, I quickly found myself seeking out other writers at local events and online. Finding these other fantastic writers has kept me going. If I have a chance to teach creative writing at the college level, even for undergrads, I want to make a point of fostering community.

And I do see it more as community building. Sure, most of us, want readership, but I generally see myself as a teacher first. I want to help other writers because I learn so much from the act of teaching.

You are the founder and editor of Referential Magazine. Could you explain the magazine, including how it works, what writers should know before submitting, etc.?
I had been toying with the idea for *Referential* for quite a while, but I wasn't sure logistically how it would work. When the magazine started back in January, I made a call for poetry, fiction, nonfiction and art. I weeded through all the e-mails and selected Scott Owens' poem "13 Ways of Angels" as the first featured piece. I also picked other poems, stories and art that would appear on the website.

Once these initial items were up, authors could then pick a poem, story, piece of art (or an individual word or line in a piece) from which to "refer" their own work. Every few months I send out another call for new featured work that does not refer from anything on the site.

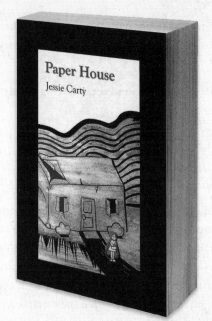

Paper House is Jessie Carty's first full-length collection of poems.

Back in June I added editors for each genre which has helped with the workload but has increased the response time. You still should have a response, in most cases, within 30 days. The only thing I hate about running the magazine is the number of submissions we receive that do not refer to one of the published pieces as is stated in the guidelines. That is a red flag that you didn't even take the time to skim that one page, let alone actually read a poem or two!

For an example, Helen Losse's poem "Concerning Apple Pie" referred from Scott Owens' original poem. Helen's poem has then inspired an art referral as well as a photographic notation.

Folded Word Press released your first poetry collection Paper House earlier this year. How did you go about getting that first collection published?

Paper House is a revised version of my MFA thesis. I sent it out for about 6 months—to contests and open reading periods—before I started getting tired of it. I just wasn't sure if I had it in me to go back through it for more revisions.

At about the same time the new managing editor of Folded Word (I actually had started the press name when I had my YouTube journal, but I had transferred ownership several months before that to my assistant), contacted me and said she wanted to see my manuscript. I was shocked! She accepted the manuscript, and we spent several months fine tuning it into the collection it is now. (See what networking can do for you?)

The only thing I hate about running the magazine is the number of submissions we receive that do not refer to one of the published pieces as is stated in the guidelines. That is a red flag that you didn't even take the time to skim that one page, let alone actually read a poem or two!

Were there any surprises during or after publication of the collection?

I was a bit surprised by how hard it was to schedule events at bookstores and such. I know part of the difficulty came because I was working with a new small press, but also because poetry, in general, has a harder time finding a home on the shelves of stores. Thank goodness my publisher did go with one of the national distributors, or I'd have had no luck at all getting into stores!

Also, I was surprised by how helpful it was to have an editor work with you. I eyed some of the big publishers and prizes but having an editor go through the book poem by poem with me (challenging me) made the book much better. I don't think I would have been able to produce a collection that I liked so well if I had just continued working on my own.

Once a week I go through the poems I've recently revised, the ones that feel "done," and I group them up to send out.

It always seems like you're submitting and publishing poems. Do you have a writing and submission routine?

Every year I try to update my whole submission strategy, but this year I started with a list of places I wanted to submit to. I made the list from journals that I read: subscriptions, online, found in *Best American Poetry* and *Poet's Market* that interest me along with journals that had previously sent me comments. I try to send to those places first.

As the year goes on, and I hear of new journals (or new to me), I add them to the list so I always have a few places that I can send work to. Once a week I go through the poems I've recently revised, the ones that feel "done," and I group them up to send out.

I used to send out less than once a month but taking a few hours to just do it once a week keeps me from feeling overwhelmed. I feel, at times, I write and revise a bit too much. But after years of not writing, I fear gaps when I don't write!

Who (or what) are you currently reading?

I'm, as always, probably reading too much! I just finished Maureen Sherbondy's chapbook "Praying at Coffee Shops." I'm in the midst of *Best American Poetry 2010* as well as the *NC Literary Review*. I also read a lot of fiction and nonfiction, but I wanted to catch up on a back log of lit mags and poetry books I had purchased (or been given) over the last year. Each day I also read quite a few blogs and online literary magazines. As I type this, I'm scanning through some of "ken*again," "Ragazine," "The Dead Mule" and "Pedestal." Can you ever read too much?

If you could pass on only one piece of advice for other poets, what would it be?

Can I cheat and say two?

First and foremost is to read. Read poetry. Read blogs. Read graphic novels. Read literary magazines. Read whatever interests you but read and read often.

The second would be, when revising, read (there is that word again) your work out loud to yourself. Even if you aren't a performance poet, hearing the sound of your words out loud makes a huge difference!

AARON BELZ:

Making Poems Social

....

by Robert Lee Brewer

In 2010, Aaron Belz's second collection of poetry—*Lovely, Raspberry*—was released by Persea Books. Before that, there was the *The Bird Hoverer,* which *Boston Review* called "masterfully strange."

There are a few qualities I enjoy with Belz's poetry. The first is that he employs humor successfully. The second is that he's not afraid to tackle contemporary culture. The third is that he doesn't get lazy when he's using humor or making pop culture references.

Belz is an English professor at Providence Christian College (in Pasadena, California). Plus, he's a very welcoming and friendly poet who founded the Observable Poetry reading series in St. Louis. He now lives in the Los Angeles area with his wife and three children.

Around the beginning of 2011, Belz took out some time from teaching and writing poetry to answer a few questions.

What are you currently up to?

Hey Robert, first let me say thank you for your important role in connecting the American poetry community and keeping us informed and ambitious. You're one of our great optimists and hardest workers. I hope you keep it up.

What I'm currently up to is sitting in a ranch-style house in Arcadia, California. My family (better half Becca and three kids, Elijah, Natalie, and Amelia) and I moved out here in the summer of 2008 to help start a new school, Providence Christian College. It's a non-profit, non-denominational liberal arts college with 60+ students, and I am its sole English professor. I know—poor students!

I'm also writing poems, of course, and giving readings and stuff as much as possible. I've got three poetry jags in the next three months: to the Midwest in late January, New York in late February, and central California in mid-March. Right now I'm between my second book, *Lovely, Raspberry*, which came out last summer, and a hopeful third, the manuscript for which, as chance would have it, I mailed to my publisher today.

Your website has a really nice design, and so does your blog. Did you design these yourself?

That's good to hear, because in December I hired a former student to combine the two and do a total redesign—then un-hired him because it would take too much time, money, and attention to make it cooler, and I just don't have the resources right now.

The current design of Belz.net is more than 10 years old. I created it with the help of my former partners at Schwa Digital Design, especially Derek Odegard, who's now an interface engineer at OpenSky. We did meaningless.com at the same time. They both hold up, don't they? Kudos to Derek. The blog is nothing special, one of Wordpress's themes called "What as Milk." I chose it for its simplicity.

The laughter response is a laugh of recognition. The stuff I write sounds like things readers and listeners have said themselves—or read on the internet, or on text messages or e-mails. I think there's some release in it.

As a follow-up question, do you employ any sort of Web strategy for connecting with readers?

My Web strategy is not really a strategy. I use belz.net as a home base to link to information about me and my writings. My blog is the most current but also most transient, and a lot of stuff I put up there eventually goes away—it's junky and experimental. And meaningless.com is a portfolio of my poems. It has perhaps the most potential for good use, but I update it very infrequently. Four years ago a European company offered quite a bit of money for it, but I kept haggling, and they eventually lost interest.

I was just about to brag that I don't use Facebook or Twitter *at all*, on principle, but then I realized that I'm still incredibly dependent on social media: Goodreads, LinkedIn, Booktour, Google Buzz, Flickr, Academia.edu. Gosh, I'm all over the map. And I'm even more of a hypocrite, because I like it when other people post stuff about me on Twitter and Facebook. But my life is simpler not having to think about those things. My fear of missing out (FOMO) factor is practically nil.

My wife and I found ourselves reading poems to each other from Lovely, Raspberry. When I told you this, you said you get this a lot and then made a remark that maybe the poems are "social poems." This got me wondering, how social do you think poets (and perhaps their poems) should be?

Well *my* wife reads and edits all my poems, though she used to be completely outside the process. These days she has ultimate veto power on anything that I might want to publish. I couldn't be happier to have a partner in this bizarre business.

We had a discussion recently about the nature and/or purpose of my poems and concluded that they use relationship rhetoric in a way that people like. This is why people like to hear them read, and why couples like to read them to each other (which, as I said earlier, I've heard at least a half-dozen times). The laughter response is a laugh of recognition. The stuff I write sounds like things readers and listeners have said themselves—or read on the Internet, or on text messages or e-mails. I think there's some release in it.

I think poems should be social. Writing is social by nature. As a poet, you're creating a relationship with a reader or audience via the poem. In Comp 101, we call this the "rhetorical bridge." In romantic love, the same paradigm is mirrored in sex; in theological terms, it's incarnation and communion. A poem is a pact, a treaty. In other words, I think social is everything. That doesn't mean the content is public, though. What I've found is that people like to be private together—nerds en masse.

Your poems incorporate a lot of pop culture references. For instance, Lovely, Raspberry references Count Chocula, Al Gore and Katherine Hepburn (not all in the same poem), in addition to others; there's even a poem about Alberto VO5 Extra Body Shampoo. What do you feel are the benefits to using pop culture references in your poems?

These are touchstones. The words themselves are important to people. People appreciate the particularity of them and that the words they see every day are rescued from the ephemeral and put in a holy place, the poem space. It also makes them laugh, sometimes because it's unexpected.

By the way, I don't mean the pop references in my poetry to be cute or camp. I think our imaginations are shaped by products and proper nouns. The odyssey of our lives is walking down the aisles of Wal-Mart, sitting in an AMC theater watching previews, driving down the interstate deciding where to stop for fast food. Sad but true. And not so sad, actually—this is what we've got. It's our blessing.

You currently teach English and creative writing at Providence Christian College. Do you feel teaching helps with your writing?

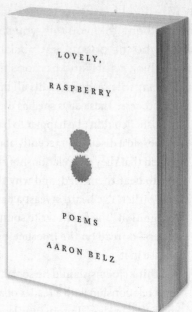

Lovely, Raspberry is Aaron Belz's second full-length collection of poems. *Boston Review* called his first collection, The Bird Hoverer, "masterfully strange."

For example, yellow leaves in October argue that yellow leaves in October ought to exist. They are also other things, such as a symbol of time passing, but they are at least that.

The boundary between teaching and writing overlaps. The lowest common denominator, I suppose, is that I am telling people things I believe to be true and hoping they'll agree with me. In both cases, there is a burden on me to be articulate and resourceful. Both are exercises in community and persuasion.

As we learn in the Intro to Lit Theory course I teach, every text makes a case. Every thing, simply by existing, makes an implicit case for its own existence. For example, yellow leaves in October argue that yellow leaves in October ought to exist. They are also other things, such as a symbol of time passing, but they are at least that.

As a poet and writer, I'm inherently an advocate for my kind, and that affects everything I do.

You've written and reviewed multiple collections of poetry. What do you feel makes for a good collection of poems?

Poetry, like stand-up comedy, succeeds when it strikes a balance between fulfilling its audience's sense of what it ought to be and seeming totally ignorant of what it is. The worst mistake a comedian can make is to appear to be trying to make his or her audience laugh. Anxiety about laughter leads to stage death. But a comedian does need to be comedian-ish or the audience won't have that necessary context, which is deeply satisfying to them.

Poets err in the same two directions. Either they pander to the reader or they are too obscure and "innovative." Readers do expect poems to seem like poems and poets to seem like poets. That has to be okay. At the same time, readers expect something totally new. So a poet must fulfill the preconceived notions the audience holds about what a poet is, and does, while at the same time seeming almost completely unaware of his status as a poet. You know, I think a poet like Carl Phillips does this really well. He makes it look effortless, which is the mark of a master.

There's also a role for a poet's-poet, whose technical skill is extremely high but who has trouble relating to other people. I think most Modernists and quite a few Postmodernists fit this bill, while natural-born entertainers like Robert Burns and Bob Dylan have had more direct value as poets in their respective societies.

....

One thing I wish I could magically change is the sing-songy way many poets read their poems. Maybe we can't go back to the driving monotone of Frost or Yeats, or the pitch-perfect tenor of Dylan Thomas, but the current poetry inflection, which has been in vogue since the late 80s really ought to end.

....

You spent years curating a poetry reading series in St. Louis. Could you share a poetry reading tip or two?

At a live reading, poets should speak directly into the microphone, or, if there isn't one, raise their voices. Poets tend to be rather sheepish, or they get weird and embarrass themselves (and their host!). One thing I wish I could magically change is the sing-songy way many poets read their poems. Maybe we can't go back to the driving monotone of Frost or Yeats, or the pitch-perfect tenor of Dylan Thomas, but the current poetry inflection, which has been in vogue since the late 80s really ought to end. Just say the poem naturally. Say it directly, smartly, and let the language's natural rhythm carry you.

Finally, poets should not be shy about selling their books or advocating their own work. It's hard to be a poet in a world that's watching Justin Bieber and "Jersey Shore."

What (or who) are you currently reading?

When school's in session, I'm reading what I'm teaching. Right now, that means the entire oeuvre of Mark Twain, among many other things. Also, generally, I'm reading what I'm reviewing. Right now, I'm not reviewing anything. For fun, I'm reading Dietrich Bonhoeffer's *Life Together*.

If you could pass on only one piece of advice to other poets, what would it be?

The first thing I'd tell new or young poets is not to get caught up in the whirlwind of stuff in the poetry world. Prizes, books, MFAs, writers colonies, networking opportunities—there are thousands upon thousands of poets in America who've been through the system and come out the other side not much better as poets. Remember that most English-speaking people, your presumed audience, don't know or care about the pecking orders within the American poetry system. The key for you is to find your own way of talking and try it out often with some sort of audience. Write poems on a blog, e-mail poems to honest friends, and then listen to what sorts of reactions you get.

The second thing I'd say is you must read old stuff. Dante, Herrick, Donne, Pope, Dickinson...Gertrude Stein, William Carlos Williams, Marianne Moore. Read voraciously! And read aloud.

COLLIN KELLEY:

Blogging, Vlogging and Tweeting

....

by Robert Lee Brewer

I first discovered Collin Kelley through my wife, who loves his blog: Modern Confessional (http://collinkelley.blogspot.com). Over time, I've been lucky enough to meet him a few times in person, but I still love reading his blog, which has a lot of personality. But Collin is more than just a blogger, he's a great poet and writer of both fiction and nonfiction. Plus, he's a key poetry advocate in the Atlanta, Georgia, area through his involvement with Poetry Atlanta events.

Collin's debut novel *Conquering Venus* has been garnering a lot of praise, and he's currently working on another. He self-published his first collection of poetry *Better to Travel*, which was nominated for the 2003 Georgia Author of the Year Award, Kate Tufts Discovery Award and Lambda Literary Award. Collin has also had two other chapbooks of poetry published: *Slow to Burn* (originally released by MetroMania Press—and will be re-released in 2011 as part of the ReBound Series from Seven Kitchens Press) and *After the Poison* (Finishing Line Press).

What are you currently up to?

I'm finishing my second novel, which will probably be out in early 2012. It's a follow-up to *Conquering Venus*, but also a stand-alone story. This one has a more mystery/thriller vibe. I also have a full-length collection of poetry I plan to start sending out to presses early in the year. It's been sitting in my file cabinet for nearly two years, so time to dust it off and get it out there.

What do you try to accomplish with your blog Modern Confessional?

It's just me talking about what's on my mind, really. I never set out to give the blog an agenda or focus. I review books, I recap *American Idol*, I get into heated debates over politics and poetry, I post music videos. I post whatever I feel like posting. I don't want to drone on about poetry and literature every single day. I want people to get to know me and, by extension, my writing.

Those who say they don't "get" Twitter just aren't trying.

Is there anything that you'd like to try with your blog that you're currently not doing?

I want to start vlogging. I've never made a video blog before, but I plan to in January. I think I've under-utilized video and YouTube, so it's time to explore. I just hate having to put on clothes and fix my hair.

You're very active on Twitter. Do you think other poets could benefit from being on Twitter?

I do. Twitter has been very good to me as a poet. I was asked to edit an issue of *OCHO* magazine by Didi Menendez because of Twitter. I've found out about contests and calls for submissions there, and I've found a community of poets who are happy to share links and knowledge with others. Those who say they don't "get" Twitter just aren't trying. It's the easiest type of social media to use and requires the least amount of effort. If you can sit on Facebook playing Farmville for hours on end while trying to come up with that next great line of poetry, you can send out a few tweets each day.

You're involved in the Atlanta poetry scene, especially through your work with Poetry Atlanta. What are the various roles you play to help promote poetry in the Atlanta area?

I've been hosting a reading series or open mic in Atlanta now for seven years. The latest incarnation is the great partnership Poetry Atlanta with Georgia Center for the Book. It's a quarterly series and we bring in two or three poets each time to read from their new work. I try to get someone from out of town and pair them with a local poet—poetry stew. Many poets are embarrassed to promote themselves or their work, but since I'm a publicity whore, I have no qualms about it. When there's a book out by a poet I love or a great reading about to happen, I promote it relentlessly. E-mails, Facebook, Twitter, blogging—I try to put it everywhere. Calling myself a cheerleader for poetry in Atlanta is cliche, but I guess I am.

Collin Kelley is known for his great poetry, but also for the way he helps other poets online and in person at events.

Most small presses are going to require you to do all your own publicity, send books out for review and set up your own readings. If you're going to have to do all that, you might as well self-pub, put together a good marketing campaign and keep all the profits.

I know your first collection of poetry was self-published. Could you give your take on whether poets should consider self-publishing as an option for their own poetry?

I think there's no shame in self-publishing, although many highfalutin poets make the sign of the cross at the mere suggestion. There's been a bit of revisionism in poetry. It was quite all right when Whitman, Pound, Eliot and cummings were doing it, but they're "famous" poets now. Canon. It seems that the statute of limitations ran out on self-publishing beign the norm and became useless "vanity" poetry instead. That is, until the last 10 years or so when self-publishing has made a big, big comeback. There are some fine self-published poetry collections out there—Jilly Dybka and Reb Livingston come instantly to mind.

If you want complete control of the book, do it yourself and be prepared to promote the hell out of it. Shamelessly. Most small presses are going to require you to do all your own publicity, send books out for review and set up your own readings. If you're going to have to do all that, you might as well self-pub, put together a good marketing campaign and keep all the profits. The biggest piece of advice I can give is that you should make sure your poetry is ready to be published. Let others read it, comment, critique and listen to them. Self-pubbing gets a bad rap because people aren't careful about editing their work.

Where are the craziest places you've done poetry readings? And how did you end up reading there?

I read at a beauty salon once, which was cool, but not the craziest place. The craziest was at this junk shop over in Douglas County back in the 90s. I mean, stuff stacked to the ceiling—soft-drink crates, broken ovens, lamps from every era. But the owner had carved out this "salon" of ratty old sofas and chairs in the middle of the shop and you followed this maze of junk to get to it. I read there a couple times and it was very womb-like.

What (or who) are you currently reading?

I am still buzzing over two collections—Jackie Sheeler's *Earthquake Came to Harlem*, which just came out from NYC Quarterly Books, and Steven Reigns' *Inheritance* from Lethe Press. The two best books of poetry I've read all year. Both books are deep and dark recollections of abuse, and they will leave you scarred but hopeful, too. And I'm still telling everyone I know about Karen Head's *Sassing* from WordTech Editions. Karen and I are very simpatico in our writing. We both draw on deep wells of family history, pop culture, love of travel and a little bit of Southern snark to make our poetry work.

Do you have any favorite poetry blogs that you regularly read?

I just checked my Google Reader, and I have 281 blogs listed there, the majority of which are about poetry. I try to drop in on them a few times a month when I can. The ones I simply cannot miss are C. Dale Young's Avoiding the Muse, Charles Jensen's Kinemapoetics, January O'Neil's Poet Mom and Kelli Russell Agodon's Book of Kells.

If you could only share one piece of advice with fellow poets, what would it be?

Don't let anyone tell you that your poetry has to appear in "important" journals or your collections published by "reputable" presses to be good poetry. Get the work out there by any means possible and to the largest audience you can find. The truth is, poetry doesn't pay the rent, so let it enrich you artistically, emotionally and spiritually instead.

ANNIE FINCH:

The Importance of Form

....

by Robert Lee Brewer

Annie Finch is the author of four books of poetry, including *Eve, Calendars, The Encyclopedia of Scotland,* and *Among the Goddesses: An Epic and Libretto.* Her book of poetry *Calendars* was short-listed for the Foreword Book of the Year Award and in 2009 she was awarded the Robert Fitzgerald Award. Finch has performed poetry across the U.S. and in England, France, Greece, Ireland, and Spain, and she lives in Maine, where she directs Stonecoast, the low-residency MFA program in creative writing at the University of Southern Maine.

Red Hen Press released *Among the Goddesses: An Epic and Libretto* in 2010. The book weaves together an epic poem with an opera libretto. In addition to everything else Finch does for poetry, she also posts about poetry at her American Witch blog (www.americanwitch.net). Plus, she has contributed more than 40 guest posts for the Poetry Foundation's Harriet blog.

What are you currently up to?

I've got three projects on the front burner right now, one each in poetry, prose, and drama. I'm putting together a *New and Selected Poems* for Wesleyan University Press; working hard on *American Witch,* a prose memoir about my spiritual and poetic life; and about to start rehearsals for a poetic theater piece, "Wolf Song." In the poetics department, I'm about to read proofs for my new poetry-writing textbooks, *A Poet's Craft* and *A Poet's Ear.* In the editing department, I'm working on *Poetry in Rhythm: An Anthology* with Alexandra Oliver and finishing up *The Book of Villanelles* with Marie-Elizabeth Mali.

Annie Finch is a formal poet. In *Among the Goddesses*, she weaves together an epic poem with an opera libretto.

When I'm revising, I usually reorder parts quite a bit; I use arrows and numbers to keep track of the order I want. I read aloud a lot, and carry the poem everywhere with me.

Your first book of poetry appeared in part as a self-published chapbook in 1982. Could you speak a little about why and how you went about self-publishing back then?

I self-published because I was completely unknown, and I wanted copies to sell at my musical performance of the poem. Producing the book was very exciting. I was working at the American Museum of Natural History, and I typed the whole manuscript on an IBM Selectric after-hours in the editorial offices of *Natural History* magazine. Alix Baer Bacon made the woodcut illustrations, and I brought the camera-ready sheets to the printer. It ended up looking exactly how I wanted.

How much attention do you pay to form and meter when composing your poems?

A lot. I often think about formal issues as a way of entering into writing the poem. And then I read them aloud constantly as I write. Sometimes a poem takes years to finish, and then I realize the problem was that it was in the wrong meter all along, so I adjust that and it works out on the other levels as well.

Do you have any sort of method to revising your poems?

Some poems I revise exhaustively, for years or even decades. Others arrive finished and need virtually no revision. When I'm revising, I usually reorder parts quite a bit; I use arrows and numbers to keep track of the order I want. I read aloud a lot, and carry the poem everywhere with me. When I get stuck, I try to change something rather than trying the same strategies over and over. Sometimes the changes are physical: I will pace back and forth contemplating a line, or dance, or shout, or run around the block, or lie on the floor with my eyes closed.

My own preference is always to use the original form, meter, and rhyme scheme, since form is the one part of the poem it is possible to replicate exactly.

While you've obviously been writing poetry since at least the 70s, it appears most of your poetry collections and honors have come in the past 10 years or so. What (if anything) do you think has changed since the mid- to late-90s?

There's more room for emotion in poetry than there was a decade ago, and more room for experimentation and irrational uses of syntax and image, and to some extent more room for poetic form. Case in point: one of my favorite poets who exemplifies all of these tendencies, Hart Crane, is finally back in fashion. The poems I wrote in the late 1980s and called the "lost poems," which combine experimental and formal elements, are finally finding publishers. Five of them appear in the most recent issue of *Smartish Pace*. Overall, I'd say there's a bit more room for poetic language to be poetic than there used to be.

You are the Director of the Stonecoast MFA program. What are your responsibilities as the Director of an MFA program?

It's a low-residency MFA program so a lot of my job is over e-mail, except during our semiannual residencies. I oversee everything about the program, from publicity to curriculum to facilities to staff, but in particular I focus on the academic aspects of the program: classes, students, and faculty. It's a fantastic community and an extremely gratifying job.

In another interview, you mentioned that when you teach contemporary poetry you divide it into four tendencies: Formalist, Oral Tradition-Performance, Mainstream Free Verse, and Experimental. Two questions: Do you still feel this way, and is there a tendency you prefer?

Yes, I still do feel this way, though I would now call it "anecdotal" or "narrative" free verse. My poetry tends more towards the Formalist point of the compass, but it is clearly influenced by all four.

You've worked as a translator. Do you feel translation has helped you as a poet?

Translation has helped me grow as a poet, has helped me to stretch in exciting directions and practice different voices, personae, and techniques. After translating Louise Labe, my poetry became more explicitly sensual; after translating Akhmatova's amphibrachic verse, I was much more comfortable using that meter.

Could you share some advice for poets who are interested in breaking into poetry translation?

Become familiar with every other translation of your poet; immerse yourself in your poet's world; work with native speakers or experts if you are not familiar with the language; and don't be shy in asking a scholar of the language to check it over. My own preference is *always* to use the original form, meter, and rhyme scheme, since form is the one part of the poem it is possible to replicate exactly. If you don't know how to write in that meter, this is a great reason to learn how.

Who (or what) are you currently reading?

For poetry, I'm reading a lot of poetry in non-iambic meter for the *Poetry in Rhythm* book, including Paul Laurence Dunbar and the Fireside Poets. I'm also revisiting some 18th century poets including my namesake Anne Finch, and reading Ben Mazer's wonderful brand-new edition of Frederick Goddard Tuckerman. I try to keep up with contemporary poets and read journals including *Fulcrum* and *Prairie Schooner*. I just finished Patti Smith's memoir *Just Kids*. Lately, I read a lot of mythology, psychology, and spirituality; I'm currently reading *Thou Shalt Not Be Aware* by the psychologist Alice Miller and *Sacred Contracts* and *Anatomy of the Spirit* by the healer Caroline Myss, and an amazing book on relationships, *Intimacy and Desire* by David Schnarch.

If you could only share one piece of advice with fellow poets, what would it be?

Listen!

ERIKA MEITNER:

Don't Edit Out the Ugly

....

by Robert Lee Brewer

In 2010, Harper Perennial released Erika Meitner's *Ideal Cities*, which has already received praise from poets such as Paul Guest, Nikki Giovanni and Denise Duhamel. And you can go ahead and throw me on the bandwagon too, because I really enjoyed the way *Ideal Cities* dealt with both location and family.

In addition to *Ideal Cities*, Meitner is the author of *Inventory at the All-night Drugstore* (winner of the 2002 Anhinga Prize for Poetry). Her poems have been anthologized widely and have appeared in several publications, including *The New Republic, Virginia Quarterly Review*, and on Slate. com. She is an assistant professor of English at Virginia Tech, and is also completing her doctorate in religious studies at the University of Virginia.

Recently, Meitner took time out of her writing and teaching schedule for this interview.

What are you currently up to?

At this moment I'm sitting at my dining room table, surrounded by piles of unopened junk mail, desperately hoping my son doesn't start yelling "mama! Mama! MaMa! MAMA! I have to poop!" so I can finish typing out the answers to your fantastic questions. He's totally potty trained except when it comes to pooping—he asks for a diaper, I oblige, he poops in it, I change him. He's three and a half years old, and I'm hoping we don't have to send him to college in Depends.

If you mean what I'm currently up to poetry-wise, I've been traveling around a lot to do readings from *Ideal Cities*. I've been to Indiana, various parts of Ohio and Virginia, and New York so far this fall, and I'm headed to Mississippi next week, and multiple parts of North

PHOTO: Steve Trost

Carolina the week after that. I'm also teaching an undergraduate poetry workshop, and a literary editing class. Virginia Tech just inherited *The Minnesota Review,* so my MFA students have been selecting the poetry and fiction for the next issue. (We realize, incidentally, that we're not in Minnesota, but the name came with it.) It's been hard to get a substantial amount of writing done with so much on-the-road time this semester, but I'm chipping away at two poetic projects slowly—one involves writing poems that all include Walmart in some way; the other is a project that has to do with writing documentary poems about Detroit. My fourth manuscript, tentatively titled *Copia* (after Brian Ulrich's series of photos of ghost box stores and dead malls), has to do with consumerism, place, and memory.

In Ideal Cities, there are quite a few poems dealing with location. In fact, the book is divided into two sections: Rental Towns and Ideal Cities. Have you traveled a lot? And depending on your answer, how have your experiences helped shape your sense of location in your poems?

I don't know that I've traveled a lot compared to other friends that I have who are real globetrotters, but I've definitely moved a lot. Being in academia is like being in the domestic foreign service. From the year I graduated college (1996) through 2007, when I got my job at Virginia Tech, I've moved every single year. I've lived in New Hampshire, Jerusalem, Brooklyn, Charlottesville (VA), Santa Cruz (CA), Wisconsin, Washington, DC, and now I live in Blacksburg, which is rural Appalachian Virginia, close to the West Virginia border. I boomeranged quite a bit, back and forth from Charlottesville, as I kept getting one-year fellowships and jobs, and then would head back to my PhD program in Religious Studies at UVA, so many of the poems in *Ideal Cities* deal with that cyclical shiftiness and homecoming.

I do think I try to write my way back home a lot through my poems, but moving a lot also makes me a bit of an outsider wherever I go, and heightens my observational abilities. I'm always sort of anthropological about my surroundings, and I feel like I'm very adaptable because of that. I find every place I've lived fascinating in its own way. Here, when you call your doctor to make an appointment, and you tell him what's wrong, the receptionist will always unfailingly say, "Bless your heart." They also have Bibles in all the doctors' waiting rooms here. I think both these things are strange and amazing, since I'm a Jew from New York. Details like that are what provide a sense of place, a texture of place, in poems, and why would you ever notice them if they're commonplace and not weird to you?

Many other poems I love from Ideal Cities deal with pregnancy and motherhood. How do you go about writing sincere parenting poems that don't dissolve into abstractions or sentimentality?

I think the first reason the poems aren't sentimental is that in order to be sentimental about an experience, you need distance from it. I wrote *Ideal Cities* while I was in the middle of what, in retrospect, was the most difficult phase of parenting so far for me (and my husband)—early babyhood. I wasn't sleeping, our kid was sick a lot, he cried a lot, he had tones of trouble nursing, and we had no family near us as backup caregivers. I was also quite ill with an infection that I picked up in the hospital, which hung on for over a year, and made everything twice as hard as it might have been otherwise. And I was negotiating for my job at Virginia Tech while I was in labor (literally), and then started this big new job when my son was four months old. Those first months were often hellish, because of the convergence of parenthood, radical change, and illness. I think the poems in the book reflect some of that hardship, ambivalence, fear, and loneliness, which undercut the preciousness of that experience of first-time parenthood for me.

....

I'm partial to poetry that resists the 'transcendent' ending— where everything breaks into light and all is redeemed at the end of the poem.

....

In my poems, I've also been working for a long time with what I've slap-dashedly nicknamed 'the resistant ending.' Many of my poems are narrative-ish, and there aren't really that many ways to end a narrative poem. I'm partial to poetry that resists the 'transcendent' ending—where everything breaks into light and all is redeemed at the end of the poem. (In my head I call this the "fruit and light" ending after Louise Gluck's poem "Winter Morning"—"And suddenly it is summer, all puzzling fruit and light.") Joel Brouwer does resistant endings. Carrie Fountain, in her new book *Burn Lake* does resistant endings. Mark Doty's amazing book, *My Alexandria*, uses transcendent endings to great effect, but those endings are balanced out by the subject material he tackles in there: homelessness, AIDS, urban blight, poverty. If I tried to put a transcendent ending on a parenting poem, I'd risk moving into cloying or sentimental territory.

I think, with parenting, as with other life experiences that I write about, I'm more into realism. Rather than raising the reader or the subject material up in a poem via transcendent language, I instead ask the reader to look at the things depicted in the poem closely, to make their own connections between accumulated images and statements. It's sort of the Bishop vs. Whitman schools of contemporary American poetry—Bishop blesses things just by bestowing attention on them, whereas Whitman uses a lot of elevated rhetoric and flourishes to get to a similar place of praise. I fall into the 'look closely' category, but I don't have the patience of Bishop—I move through my subject material much faster. If the poems in *Ideal Cities* were an event, they would be those contests people win where they get to go into a store for five minutes and toss anything they can into their shopping carts. There's a lot of stuff in my cart, but it all has a pattern—a reason I put it in there; I'm just usually not going to tell you what that reason is outright.

National Poetry Series Selected by Paul Guest

idEAL CiTiES

Erika Meitner

poems

"These poems are so generous, so bright and sharp, so funny and winning, they feel immense."
—Paul Guest

Ideal Cities is Erika Meitner's second full-length collection of poetry. Her first collection, *Inventory at the All-night Drugstore,* won the 2002 Anhinga Prize for Poetry.

Canzones are also amazing—like sestinas on crack.

Do you have a favorite poetic form?

I love sestinas! They have the potential to be such a wickedly funny form, and the repetition lends itself to everyday speech. Some of my favorites are Denise Duhamel's "On Delta Flight 659 with Sean Penn," and Catherine Bowman's "Mr. X." The McSweeney's archives, from back when Dan Nester was editing their all-sestina poetry section, have some really imaginative ones: www.mcsweeneys.net/links/sestinas. Canzones are also amazing—like sestinas on crack. Sean Thomas Dougherty writes fantastic canzones, as does Paisley Rekdal.

In your acknowledgments, you give shout outs to Blue Mountain Center and the Virginia Center for the Creative Arts. Could you explain how these centers assisted in the completion of Ideal Cities?

I spent a month at Blue Mountain Center when I was about five months pregnant, and a few of the very early seeds of *Ideal Cities* got started there. They had assigned me to a room in a little house there, and the woman who had the studio next to me on one side was the musician Basya Schecter, from the band Pharaoh's Daughter, and she was working on a project where she was setting Abraham Joshua Heschel's Yiddish poetry to music. An entire super-long lyric poem from *Ideal Cities* called (shockingly) "Pharaoh's Daughter" comes from my interactions and late-night conversations with Basya. Also, I'd take these epic walks in the woods while I was there, and those led to "North Country Canzone." VCCA is the closest artist colony to my house, and they've been wonderful in letting me have really short week-long residencies that I could use to work on the book in various ways. Now that I have a kid, it's hard on him if I'm gone longer than a week. I've been going to VCCA on and off for the last 10 years, and it's the only place where I can tack up an entire book manuscript on the walls of a studio and really dig in to a project as a whole. I can write individual poems at home, but clearing out the head-space and physical space to put together an entire manuscript is something I feel like I can only do at a colony.

....

I had just moved, I was starting a new job, I was sick, I had a new baby. But I decided that even if I got a little writing done, it would prove that I could write through anything.

....

In your acknowledgments, you also mention your virtual NaPoWriMo group, which includes poets Sandra Beasley, Mary Biddinger, Oliver de la Paz and Aimee Nezhukumatathil. Could you explain how you connected with these poets and how your group virtually workshops poems?

We actually don't workshop poems at all—we just write them at the same time, then post them online for a form of group accountability! The group started because Sandra Beasley spearheaded a movement to get together a group of poets (this was back in August of 2007, when I had just moved to Blacksburg) to do a NaPoWriMo together virtually. The NaPoWriMo idea originally came from Maureen Thorson as a creative response to National Poetry Month in April—poets would gather virtually, and write a poem a day for the month of April. But Sandra decided to gather a bunch of us together and implement it in August, which was the busiest month I could possibly imagine—I had just moved, I was starting a new job, I was sick, I had a new baby. But I decided that even if I got a little writing done, it would prove that I could write through anything. I mostly wrote late at night—I would start at 11 p.m. or midnight, and then wait up until my son woke up for his night feeding. And I wrote most of *Ideal Cities* through various NaPoWriMo sessions; I really needed that indirect push from the more faithful members of the group. Oliver's a poetry machine! We still keep meeting two or three times a year, sometimes for a month, and sometimes for shorter two-week stints, where we all try to produce a poem a day, sometimes with prompts and sometimes without.

And the membership fluctuates too—usually we have others that come on for a session, and then drop off.

I think of those poets, the first one I met was Aimee, back in 2001-ish. I went to visit Madison, Wisconsin, to apartment-hunt—I had just found out I had won the Diane Middlebrook Poetry Fellowship from the Wisconsin Institute for Creative Writing—and I ended up having dinner with a bunch of the current fellows that year, and Aimee was among them. Something about our shared love of Hello Kitty, and the fact that we both had new books out around the same time and were Wisconsin Fellowship alums drew us together, and kept us connected throughout the years. It's great to have someone who, at certain points, has a similar career trajectory to you, but is a little ahead of you too, I think. Aimee was always an invaluable resource for publishing and fellowship and colony advice for me, and just such a source of sunniness and light. I met Oliver and Mary via Aimee—and actually, I had been in the virtual writing group with both of them for a few years before I met either of them in person. And Sandra and I connected when I moved to DC in 2006. I had known her in passing when she was an undergraduate at UVA, but when I moved to DC, we became friends in person, as the poetry community in DC is quite close-knit.

You're currently an Assistant Professor of English at Virginia Tech, but you've previously worked as a dating columnist, a Hebrew school instructor, a computer consultant, a lifeguard, a documentary film production assistant, and a middle school teacher in the New York City public school system. Of all your previous jobs, which one did you enjoy the most and why?

I loved working on documentary films, and I feel, really, like my poems are an extension of that early interest in telling true stories, and being aware of the interplay of image and sound. I worked for a tiny documentary film production company while I was still in college, and right after I graduated (called Tatge-Lasseur Productions), that did a lot of contract work for PBS and the American Masters series. This meant that for the most part, I got to watch master artists at work, which was pretty life-changing. I was a production assistant on so many different gigs—I watched ballerinas like Maria Tallchief and Merrill Ashley recreate all of George Balanchine's dances for his archives; I worked on the film version of Bill T. Jones' "Still/Here"; I sat in on the taping of Bill Moyers' "Book of Genesis" series, which was actually one of the reasons I went back to graduate school in religion. I researched a program for FR3 (French public broadcasting) on Philip Roth, so I had to read all of his collected works. And I can still tell you how much it cost in 1994 to move a Jimmy Jib (giant camera crane) from Arizona to NYC.

Following up on the varied occupations, do you feel having a diverse job history has passed on any benefits for your writing?

I definitely think that my diverse job history has made me more functional as both a writer, and a human being in general. My job as a computer consultant meant that I could support myself financially through my MFA program without going into debt. We got funding at UVA, but at that time, in the late 90s, it wasn't very much. Our first year it was about $4,000 above tuition. I also designed and still maintain my own website with the skills I learned at Andersen Consulting (now Accenture). Being a New York City public school teacher (and a Hebrew school teacher) gave me a thick skin—something that was critical for me when I started in MFA workshops, and also began to send my work out to publish. My work in film also taught me not to take no for an answer—if that crane had to get to New York, we would find a way to do it. Being a poet most of the time seems like a similar feat of not taking no for an answer. I mean, what a ludicrous career path, to be a poet! I always think of this Nike ad that I had tacked to my wall in college: "All your life they will tell you no, quite firmly and very quickly. AND YOU WILL TELL THEM YES."

I mean, what a ludicrous career path, to be a poet!

Who (or what) are you currently reading?

Right now I'm reading a few different things: I'm right in the middle of *The Origins of the Urban Crisis: Race and Inequality in Postwar Detroit*, by Thomas Sugrue, as part of the research for the Detroit project I'm working on. I'm also an avid reader of *The New Yorker*, and I take great pride in being up-to-date on each issue (so that I don't get the dreaded '*New Yorker* guilt' when the issues pile up). I'm generally working my way too, at any given time, through multiple books of poems, reading and re-reading. Right now, I have Sarah Vap's newest, *Faulkner's Rosary*, on my bedside table, piled up along with Julie Carr's *100 Notes on Violence*, Claudia Rankine's *Don't Let Me be Lonely* (a re-read), and the manuscript for a new book due out in the spring from Persea that I'm reading to blurb—*Sightseer*, by Cynthia Marie Hoffman, which is snappy and excellent. With poetry books, I tend to pick them up and put them down a lot, and read three or four at once.

If you could pass on only one piece of advice to fellow poets, what would it be?

Go live abroad, travel around the US too, road-trip and fall in love, work weird and mundane jobs—live a little, and grow a thick skin, and collect your images and snippets and bring them with you wherever you land. And most of all, don't edit out the ugly.

MAGAZINES/ JOURNALS

Literary magazines and journals usually provide a poet's first publishing success. In fact, you shouldn't be thinking about book/chapbook publication until your poems have appeared in a variety of magazines, journals and zines (both print and online). This is the preferred way to develop an audience, build publishing credits and learn the ins and outs of the publishing process.

In this section you'll find hundreds of magazines and journals that publish poetry. They range from small black-and-white booklets produced on home computers to major periodicals with high production values and important reputations. To help you sort through these markets and direct your submissions most effectively, we've organized information in each listing according to a basic format.

HOW LISTINGS ARE FORMATTED

Content of each market listing was provided or verified by a representative of the publication (editor, poetry editor, managing editor, etc.). Here is how that content is arranged within the listing:

ICONS. Icons at the beginning of each listing offer visual signposts to specific information about the publication: ⊕ this market is recently established and new to *Poet's Market*; ◐ this market publishes primarily online (although it may also produce an annual print version or a "best of" anthology); ☺ this market is located in Canada or ◓ outside the U.S. and Canada; ⊛ this market pays a monetary amount (as opposed to contributor's copies); ○ this market welcomes submissions from beginning poets; ◑ this market prefers submissions from skilled, experienced poets, will consider work from beginning poets; ● this market prefers submissions from poets with a high degree of skill and experience; ⊙ this market has a specialized focus (listed in parentheses after magazine/journal title); ⊘ this market does not consider unsolicited submissions. (Keys to these icons are listed on the inside cover of this book.)

CONTACT INFORMATION. Depending on what was provided by each editor, contact information includes: magazine/journal title (in bold) with areas of specialization noted in parentheses where appropriate; regular mail address; telephone number; fax number; e-mail address; website address; year the publication was established; the name of the person to contact (or an editorial title); and membership in small press/publishing organizations. (Note: If a magazine/journal publishes only online and/or wants submissions by e-mail exclusively, no street address may be given.)

MAGAZINE NEEDS. It's important to study this section as you research potential markets. Here you'll find such helpful information as the editor's overview of the publication, with individual poetry needs and preferences; a list of recently published poets; production information (number of pages, printing/binding details, type of cover); the number of poetry submissions the publication receives vs. the number accepted; and press run, distribution and price information.

HOW TO SUBMIT. This section focuses on the specific details of submitting work: how many poems to send; minimum/maximum number of lines per poem; whether previously published poems or simultaneous submissions are considered; submission format preferences (including whether to submit by e-mail, and how); response times; payment; rights acquired and more.

ADDITIONAL INFORMATION. Editors may use this section to explain other publishing activities, elaborate on some aspect of the magazine/journal, suggest future plans—anything beyond the basic details that readers may find of interest.

CONTEST/AWARD OFFERINGS. This section discusses prizes and competitions associated with the publication, with either brief guidelines or a cross-reference to a separate listing in the Contests & Awards section.

ALSO OFFERS. Describes additional offerings associated with this publication (i.e., sponsored readings, website activities such as blogs and forums, related poetry groups, etc.).

TIPS. Provides direct quotes from editors about everything from pet peeves to tips on writing to perspectives on the state of poetry today.

GETTING STARTED, FINDING MARKETS

If you don't have a certain magazine or journal in mind, read randomly through the listings, making notes as you go. (Don't hesitate to write in the margins, underline, use highlighters; it also helps to flag markets that interest you with Post-It Notes). Browsing the listings is an effective way to familiarize yourself with the kind of information presented and the publishing opportunities that are available at various skill levels.

If you have a specific market in mind, however, begin with the General Index. Here all the book's listings are alphabetized along with additional references that may be buried within a listing (such as a press name or competition title).

REFINE YOUR SEARCH

To supplement the General Index, we provide the following indexes to help you refine your marketing plan for submitting your poems to publications. Not every listing appears in one of these indexes, so use them only to reinforce your other research efforts:

Geographic Index sorts magazines and journals by state or by countries outside the U.S. Some markets are more open to poets from their respective regions, so this index is helpful when pinpointing local opportunities.

Subject Index groups markets according to areas of special focus. These include all specialized markets as well as broader categories such as online markets, poetry for children, markets that consider translations and others. When you want to submit a poem that features a certain topic or theme, is written in a specific form or style or addresses a unique audience, check this index first.

THE NEXT STEP

Once you know how to interpret the listings in this section and identify markets for your work, the next step is to start submitting your poems. See "How to Use Poet's Market" and "Frequently Asked Questions" for advice, guidelines for preparing your manuscript and proper submissions procedures.

◐◑ 2 RIVER VIEW

7474 Drexel Dr., University City MO 63130. E-mail: long@2River.org. E-mail: submissions@2river.org. Website: www.2River.org. **Contact:** Richard Long. *2River View*, published quarterly online, restricts each issue to ten poets.

MAGAZINES NEEDS *2River View*, published quarterly online, restricts each issue to ten poets. "We prefer poems with these qualities: image, subtlety, and point of view; a surface of worldly exactitude, as well as a depth of semantic ambiguity; and a voice that negotiates with its body of predecessors." Robert Creeley, R. Virgil Davis, Tony Colella, David Appelbaum, Michelle Askin, Rebecca Givens. Accepts 1-5% of unsolicited submissions.

HOW TO CONTACT Submit up to 5 poems once per reading period. No previously published poems or simultaneous submissions. Accepts e-mail submissions pasted into the body of the e-mail; no fax or disk submissions. Reads submissions year round (see website for reading period for each issue). Time between acceptance and publication is 3 months. Guidelines on website.

◐ 5 AM

Box 205, Spring Church PA 15686. (715)284-0328. Website: www.5ampoetry.com. **Contact:** Ed Ochester and Judith Vollmer.

MAGAZINES NEEDS *5 AM*, published twice/year, is a poetry publication open in regard to form, length, subject matter, and style. Does not want religious poetry or "naive rhymers." Has published poetry by Virgil Suaárez, Nin Andrews, Alicia Ostriker, Edward Field, Billy Collins, and Denise Duhamel. *5 AM* is 24-pages, tabloid size, offset-printed. Receives about 5,000 poems/year, accepts about 2%. Press run is 1,200. Subscription: $12 for 2 issues (one year), $20 for 4 issues (two years). Sample: $5.

HOW TO CONTACT P.O. Box 205, Spring Church PA 15686. Website: www.5ampoetry.com. Established 1987. **Contact:** Ed Ochester and Judith Vollmer, editors. No previously published poems or simultaneous submissions. Seldom comments on rejected poems. Responds within 6 weeks. Pays 2 contributor's copies. Acquires first rights.

TIPS "We read all year. Manuscripts cannot be returned without SASE with sufficient postage."

◑◑ 10TH MUSE

33 Hartington Rd., Southampton SO14 0EW, UK. E-mail: a.jordan@surfree.co.uk. Website: www.nonism. org.uk/muse.html. **Contact:** Andrew Jordan, editor.

MAGAZINES NEEDS *10th Muse* "includes poetry and reviews, as well as short prose and graphics." Has published poetry by Richard Caddel, Stephen M. Dickey, Andrew Duncan, Carrie Etter, Becky Gould Gibson, and Bill Griffiths. *10th Muse* is 48-72 pages, A5, photocopied, saddle-stapled, with card cover. Press run is 200. Single copy: £3.50 (UK); subscription: £9 for 3 issues (UK). Make checks payable to *10th Muse*. "U.S. subscribers: Send $10 in bills for single copy (including postage)."

HOW TO CONTACT Submit up to 6 poems at a time. No e-mail submissions. Include SASE (or SAE with IRCs). Responds in 3 months. Pays one contributor's copy. Staff reviews books of poetry. Send materials for review consideration.

◐◑ THE 13TH WARRIOR REVIEW

P.O. Box 5122, Seabrook NJ 08302-3511. E-mail: theeditor@asteriusonline.com. Website: www.asteriusonline.com/13thWR/. **Contact:** John C. Erianne, editor.

MAGAZINES NEEDS *The 13th Warrior Review*, published 2-2 times annually online, seeks "excellent literary-quality poetry as well as fiction, essays, and reviews. All excellent poetry will be given serious consideration." Has published poetry by P.Q. Perron, Cindy Rosmus, B.Z Niditch, Genine Hanns, John Sweet, and Corey Ginsberg.

HOW TO CONTACT Submit no more than 5 poems at a time. Considers simultaneous submissions, but "not encouraged"; no previously published poems. Accepts e-mail submissions only, pasted as text into body of message—no attachments. "Use 'submission' as the subject header. Any submission that comes as a file attachment will be deleted without reply." Cover letter is preferred; "should be brief and to the point." Include SASE for postal submissions. Time between acceptance and publication is up to 6 months. Seldom comments on rejected poems. Guidelines available on website. No payment. Acquires first rights, first electronic rights, and non-exclusive anthology rights.

⊕ ◑ ◐ 34TH PARALLEL

P.O. Box 4823, Irvine CA 92623. E-mail: tracesherida n@34thParallel.net. Website: www.34thparallel.net/ submit.html. Member: CLMP.

MAGAZINES NEEDS *34th Parallel*, published quarterly in print and online, seeks "to promote and publish the exceptional writing of new and emerging writers overlooked by large commercial publishing houses and mainstream presses. Wants work that experiments with and tests boundaries. Anything that communicates a sense of wonder, reality, tragedy, fantasy, and/or brilliance. Does not want historical romance, science fiction, erotica, Gothic horror, book reviews, or nonfiction." Single copy: $11; subscription: $36.

HOW TO CONTACT "In the subject heading of your e-mail, type in 'story submissions' or 'poetry submission' or 'image submission'. Will discard as spam those submissions that do not contain one of these subject headings. Submit 1 poem only. Considers simultaneous submissions; no previously published poems. Accepts electronic submissions. Cover letter is required, containing a short bio about your life, your writing, and where we can see some of your other work online. Reads submissions year round. Often comments on rejected poems. Guidelines on website. Pays one contributor's copy in PDF format. Magazine is copyrighted, but the rights to all contributions remain with the owners."

⊕ ◐ ⑤ AASRA PUNJABI ENGLISH MAGAZINE

P.O. Box 5716, Kent WA 98064. E-mail: aasra@q.com. **Contact:** Sarab Singh, editor. Submit 1-2 small poems at a time. Cover letter is required. Include SASE, name, address, telephone number, and e-mail address with age and sex on cover letter. Include a short bio. "If interested we can print 'About the Poet' also along with the poem. Aasra Punjabi English Magazine, published bimonthly, features current events mainly Indian, but have featured others, too, of interest. Also features interviews, yogAnd other articles, and poetry. The magazine is distributed free in the Seattle area and available through other libraries. We charge postage for a copy to be mailed. Please include $3 to allow us to send you the copy of the magazine. $2 per copy if more than 10 copies are purchased." Reads submissions year round. Sometimes comments on rejected poems. Sometimes published theme issues.

Guidelines in magazine. Rights revert to poet upon publication. Best Poem of the Year is awarded one-year free subscription.

MAGAZINES NEEDS "Aasra Punjabi English Magazine, in print only, published bimonthly, features current events mainly Indian, but have featured others, too, of interest. Also features interviews, yogAnd other articles, and poetry." Has published poetry by Joan Robers, Elizabeth Tallmadge, Carmen Arhiveleta. Page count varies. Measures approximately 81/2x11, press printed, staple bound, includes ads. Single copy cost $3 (postage); subscription: $20/year.

HOW TO CONTACT Submit 1-2 small poems at a time. Does not consider previously published poems or simultaneous submissions. Cover letter is required. Include SASE, name, address, telephone number, and e-mail address with age and sex on cover letter. Include a short bio. (If interested we can print 'About the Poet' also along with the poem). "The magazine is distributed free in the Seattle area and available through other libraries. We charge postage for a copy to be mailed. Please include $3 to allow us to send you the copy of the magazine. $2 per copy if more than 10 copies are purchased." Reads submissions year round. Time between acceptance and publication is 2 months. Sometimes comments on rejected poems. Sometimes published theme issues. Guidelines in magazine. Acquires one-time rights. Rights revert to poet upon publication.

CONTEST/AWARD OFFERINGS Best Poem of the Year is awarded one-year free subscription.

◑ ABBEY

5360 Fallriver Row Court, Columbia MD 21044. E-mail: greisman@aol.com. **Contact:** David Greisman, editor.

MAGAZINES NEEDS *Abbey* is "a more-or-less informal zine looking for poetry that does for the mind what the first sip of Molson Ale does for the palate." Does not want "pornography or politics." Has published poetry by Richard Peabody, Ruth Moon Kempher, Carol Hamilton, Harry Calhoun, Kyle Laws, Joel Poudrier, Wayne Hogan, and Edmund Conti. *Abbey* is usually 20-26 pages, magazine-sized, photocopied, and held together with 1 low-alloy metal staple in the top left corner. Receives about 1,000 poems/year, accepts about 150. Press run is 200. Subscription: $2. Sample: 50¢.

HOW TO CONTACT Responds in 1 month "except during baseball season." Pays 1-2 contributor's copies.

ADDITIONAL INFORMATION Abbey Cheapochapbooks come out once or twice every 5 years, averaging 10-15 pages. For chapbook consideration, query with 4-6 sample poems, bio, and list of publications. Responds in 2 months "including baseball season." Pays 25-50 author's copies.

ABLE MUSE

467 Saratoga Ave., #602, San Jose CA 95129-1326. (267)224-7478. Fax: (267)224-7478. Website: www.ablemuse.com. **Contact:** Alex Pepple, editor. Subscription: $22/1 year.

MAGAZINES NEEDS *Able Muse: a review of metrical poetry* published 3 times/year, "spotlights formal poetry via an online presentation, in the supportive environment of art, photography, essays, interviews, book reviews, fiction, and a literary forum. Also includes electronic books of poetry. *Able Muse* exclusively publishes formal poetry. We are looking for well-crafted poems of any length or subject that employ skillful and imaginative use of meter, or meter and rhyme, executed in contemporary idiom, that reads as naturally as your free-verse poems." Does not want "free-verse, greeting card verse, or poems in forms with no regard to meter (such as a free verse pantoum, sestina, etc.)." Considers poetry by teens. "High levels of craft still required even for teen writers." Has published poetry by Mark Jarman, A.E. Stallings, Annie Finch, Rhina P. Espaillat, Rachel Hadas, and R.S. Gwynn. Receives about 1,500 poems/year, accepts about 5%.

HOW TO CONTACT Submit 1-5 poems and short bio. No previously published poems or simultaneous submissions. Submit using e-mail and online submission manager. "The e-mail submission method is being phased out. We strongly encourage using the online submission method." Will not accept postal submissions. Time between acceptance and publication is 3 months. Sometimes comments on rejected poems. Sometimes publishes theme issues. Responds in 4 months. Sometimes sends prepublication galleys. Acquires first rights. Reviews books of poetry. Send materials for review consideration.

ABRAMELIN, THE JOURNAL OF POETRY AND MAGICK

E-mail: nessaralindaran@aol.com. Website: www.abramelin.net. **Contact:** Vanessa Kittle, editor.

MAGAZINES NEEDS *Abramelin, the Journal of Poetry and Magick*, published biannually online and a yearly best of edition each December, offers "literary poetry and essays concerning the western esoteric traditions." Wants "poetry that shows rather than tells. Poems that make me jealous of the writer. Poems that are inspired with wonderful language and imagery. In short—literature. Poetry submissions needn\rquote t be about magick at all. I feel that real poetry is magick. In fact, poetry that is literally magickal in theme has to be twice as good." Does not want "rhyming poems. Very short fiction. But beware, I learned from the best." Considers poetry by teens. Has published poetry by Simon Perchik, Rich Kostelanetz, and Lyn Lifshin. *Abramelin* receives about 1,000 poems/year, accepts about 5%. Distributed free online. Number of unique visitors: 3,000/issue.

HOW TO CONTACT Submit 1-5 poems at a time. Lines/poem: no minimum/maximum. Considers previously published poems and simultaneous submissions (with notification). Accepts e-mail (pasted into body of message). Cover letter is preferred. Reads submissions year round. Submit seasonal poems 2 months in advance. Time between acceptance and publication is 1-3 months. Often comments on rejected poems. Sometimes publishes theme issues. Upcoming themes available in magazine or on website. Guidelines available by e-mail or on website. Responds in 1 month. Pays 1 contributor's copy. Acquires one-time rights, with option to include in a yearly print anthology. Rights revert to poets upon publication.

ABRAXAS

P.O. Box 260113, Madison WI 53726-0113. E-mail: abraxaspress@hotmail.com. Website: www.abraxaspressinc.com/Welcome.html. **Contact:** Ingrid Swanberg, Editor/Publisher. P.O. Box 260113, Madison, WI 53726-0113. E-mail: abraxaspress@hotmail.com. Website: www.abraxaspressinc.com/Welcome.html. New format: presenting larger selections of the work of fewer poets in every issue. "We are interested in poetry that attends to language, rhythm, and music, and have a particular interest in the lyric mode. However, we are open to all forms." *ABRAXAS*' primary commitment is to contemporary American poetry, presenting work by both established and lesser-known writers. Has published poetry by Ivan Arguüelles, Denise Levertov, Ceésar Vallejo, d.a. levy, T.L. Kryss, and Andrea Moorhead. *ABRAXAS* is up to 80 pages, digest-sized, litho-offset-printed, flat-spined, with matte or glossy card cover with original art and photography. Press run is 700. Subscription: $16 (4 issues). Sample: $4 USD plus $1.90 s&h.

MAGAZINES NEEDS *ABRAXAS*, published "irregularly; 9- to 12-month intervals or much longer," is interested in poetry that's "contemporary lyric, experimental, and poetry in translation. When submitting translations, please include poems in the original language. *ABRAXAS'* new format features longer selections of fewer contributors." Does not want "political posing; academic regurgitations." Has published poetry by Ivan Argüelles, Denise Levertov, Ceésar Vallejo, d.a. levy, T.L. Kryss, and Andrea Moorhead. *ABRAXAS* is up to 80 pages, digest-sized, litho-offset-printed, flat-spined, with matte or glossy card cover with original art and photography. Press run is 700. Subscription: $16 (4 issues). Sample: $4 USD plus $1.90 s&h.

HOW TO CONTACT Submit 7-10 poems along with SASE. No electronic submissions. Payment is contributer's copy and 40% discount on additional copies.

ABZ

P.O. Box 2746, Huntington WV 25727. E-mail: editorial@abzpress.com. Website: www.abzpress.com.

MAGAZINES NEEDS *ABZ*, published annually, wants poetry using interesting and exciting language. Sample copies and subscriptions: $8.

HOW TO CONTACT Submit 1 to 6 poems at a time. Reading period is September 1-December 1. Guidelines on website. "Contributors receive a small stipend and two copies of the magazine."

☾ ACM (ANOTHER CHICAGO MAGAZINE)

P.O. Box 408439, Chicago IL 60640. Website: www.anotherchicagomagazine.net. Jennifer Moore, poetry editor. **Contact:** Jacob S. Knabb, editor-in-chief. "*Another Chicago Magazine* is a literary magazine that publishes work by both new and established writers. We look for work that goes beyond the artistic and academic to include and address the larger world. The editors read submissions in Fiction, Poetry, Creative Nonfiction, and Et Al. year round. We often publish special theme issues and sections. We will post upcoming themes on our website. Fiction: Short stories and novel excerpts of 15-20 pages or less. Poetry: Usu-

ally no more than 4 pages. Creative Nonfiction: Usually no more than 20 pages. Et Al.: Work that doesn't quite fit into the other genres such as Word & Image Texts, Satire, and Interviews."

○ Work published in *ACM* has been included frequently in *The Best American Poetry* and *The Pushcart Prize*.

HOW TO CONTACT "Please include the following contact information in your cover letter and on your ms: Byline (name as you want it to appear if published), mailing address, phone number, and e-mail. Include a self-addressed stamped envelope (SASE). If a SASE is not enclosed, you will only hear from us if we are interested in your work. Include the genre (e.g., fiction, et al.) of your work in the address."

TIPS "Support literary publishing by subscribing to at least one literary journal—if not ours, another. Get used to rejection slips, and don't get discouraged. Keep introductory letters short. Make sure manuscript has name and address on every page, and that it is clean, neat and proofread. We are looking for stories with freshness and originality in subject angle and style, and work that encounters the world."

○○ A COMPANION IN ZEOR

1622 Swallow Crest Dr., Apt. B, Edgewood MD 21040-1751. Website: www.simegen.com/sgfandom/rimonslibrary/cz/. **Contact:** Karen MacLeod, Editor.

MAGAZINES NEEDS *A Companion in Zeor*, published irregularly online, is a science fiction/fantasy fanzine. "Material used is now limited to creations based solely on works (universes) of Jacqueline Lichtenberg and Jean Lorrah. No other submission types considered. Prefer nothing obscene. Homosexuality not acceptable unless very relevant to the piece. Prefer a 'clean' publication image." Considers poetry written by young writers over 13; "copyright release form (on the web) available for all submissions."

HOW TO CONTACT Accepts fax, e-mail (pasted into body of message), and disk submissions. For regular mail submissions, "note whether to return or dispose of rejected mss." Cover letter is preferred. Guidelines available for SASE, by fax, e-mail, or on website. Sometimes sends prepublication galleys. Acquires first rights. "Always willing to work with authors or poets to help in improving their work." Reviews books of poetry. Poets may send material for review consideration.

⦿ ACUMEN MAGAZINE

Ember Press, 6 The Mount, Higher Furzeham, Brixham, South Devon TQ5 8QY, UK. E-mail: patricia-oxley6@gmail.com. Website: www.acumen-poetry.co.uk. **Contact:** Patricia Oxley, Poetry Editor. Acumen is published three times a year (January, May and September), A5 perfect bound, with at least 120pp per issue. Looking for poetry which is not trivial, not obvious, doesn't use outworn images or diction, and which works at many levels simultaneously. Receives around 10,000- 15,000; publishes 150. Subscription: £13/1 year individual; £15/1 year institution. *Acumen*, published 3 times/year in January, May, and September, is "a general literary magazine with emphasis on good poetry." Wants "well-crafted, high-quality, imaginative poems showing a sense of form." Does not want "experimental verse of an obscene type." Has published poetry by Ruth Padel, William Oxley, Hugo Williams, Peter Porter, Danielle Hope, and Leah Fritz. *Acumen* is 120 pages, A5, perfect-bound. Receives about 12,000 poems, accepts about 120. Press run is 650. Subscription: $45 surface/$50 air. Sample: $15.

HOW TO CONTACT All submissions should be accompanied by SASE. Include name and address on each separate sheet. Postal submissions only. Doesn't accept e-mail submissions, but will send rejections, acceptances, proofs and other communications via email overseas to dispense with IRCs and other international postage. Any poem that may have chance of publication is shortlisted and from list final poems are chosen. All other poems returned within 2 months.

TIPS "Read *Acumen* carefully to see what kind of poetry we publish. Also, read widely in many poetry magazines, and don't forget the poets of the past—they can still teach us a great deal."

⦿ THE ADIRONDACK REVIEW

E-mail: editors@theadirondackreview.com; angela@blacklawrencepress.com. Website: www.adirondackreview.homestead.com. **Contact:** Angela Leroux-Lindsey, Kara Christenson, Diane Goettel, editor. *The Adirondack Review*, published quarterly online, is a literary journal dedicated to quality free verse poetry and short fiction as well as book and film reviews, art, photography, and interviews. "We are open to both new and established writers. Our only requirement is excellence. We would like to publish more French

and German poetry translations as well as original poems in these languages. We publish an eclectic mix of voices and styles, but all poems should show attention to craft. We are open to beginners who demonstrate talent, as well as established voices. The work should speak for itself."

MAGAZINES NEEDS "Well-crafted, thoughtful writing full of imagery." Does not want "religious, overly sentimental, horror/gothic, rhyming, greeting card, pet-related, humor, or science fiction poetry." Has published poetry by Bob Hicok, Timothy Liu, Lola Haskins, D.C. Berry, David Rigsbee, and Paul Guest. Accepts about 3-5% of poems submitted.

HOW TO CONTACT Submit 2-7 poems at a time. Considers simultaneous submissions (with notification); no previously published poems. Accepts e-mail submissions only. "All submissions should be pasted into the body of an e-mail (no attached files, please). We no longer accept postal submissions. All postal submissions will be discarded unread." Cover letter is preferred. Reads submissions year round. Submit seasonal poems 3 months in advance. Time between acceptance and publication is 1-3 months. Seldom comments on rejected poems. Guidelines available on website. Responds in 1 week to 4 months. Acquires first or one-time rights. Rights revert to poet upon publication. "We reserve the right to reprint the work in the event of a print-based anthology at a later date." Reviews books of poetry. Send materials for review consideration.

CONTEST/AWARD OFFERINGS With Black Lawrence Press, offers The 46er Prize for Poetry (see separate listing in Contests & Awards).

⦿ ADVOCATE, PKA'S PUBLICATION

1881 Little Westkill Rd., Prattsville NY 12468. (518)299-3103. E-mail: advoad@localnet.com. Website: http://Advocatepka.weebly.com or www.facebook.com/pages/Advocate-PKAs-Publication/111826035499969. **Contact:** Patricia Keller, publisher. "PKA's *Advocate*, published bimonthly, is an advertiser-supported tabloid, publishing original, previously unpublished poetry, short stories, art and photos on many subjects. The publication has a strong horse orientation."

⦿ Gaited Horse Association newsletter is included in this publication. Horse-oriented stories, poetry, art and photos are currently needed.

MAGAZINES NEEDS "Please, no work that has appeared on the Internet." Submissions may be typed or legibly handwritten. "Send a SASE with your submission; no postcards, please." Time between acceptance and publication is up to 6 months.

TIPS "Please, no simultaneous submissions, work that has appeared on the Internet, pornography, overt religiousity, anti-environmentalism or gratuitous violence. Artists and photographers should keep in mind that we are a b&w paper. Please do not send postcards. Use envelope with SASE." " Please, no simultaneous submissions, work that has appeared on the Internet, pornography, overt religiousity, anti-environmentalism or gratuitous violence. Artists and photographers should keep in mind that we are a b&w paper. Please do not send postcards. Use envelope with SASE."

AFRICAN VOICES

270 W. 96th St., New York NY 10025. (212)865-2982. Fax: (212)316-3335. E-mail: africanvoices@aol.com. Website: www.africanvoices.com. "*African Voices*, published quarterly, is dedicated to highlighting the art, literature, and history of people of color."*African Voices*, published quarterly, is an "art and literary magazine that highlights the work of people of color. We publish ethnic literature and poetry on any subject. We also consider all themes and styles: avant-garde, free verse, haiku, light verse, and traditional. We do not wish to limit the reader or author." Considers poetry written by children. Has published poetry by Reg E. Gaines, Maya Angelou, Jessica Care Moore, Asha Bandele, Tony MedinAnd Louis Reyes Rivera. *African Voices* is about 48 pages, magazine-sized, professionally printed, saddle-stapled, with paper cover. Receives about 100 submissions/year, accepts about 30%. Press run is 20,000. Single copy: $4; subscription: $12.

HOW TO CONTACT Submit no more than 2 poems at any one time. Accepts previously published poems and simultaneous submissions. Accepts submissions by e-mail (in text box), by fax, and by postal mail. Cover letter and SASE required. Seldom comments on rejected poems. Guidelines available for SASE or on website. Responds in 3 months. Pays 2 copies. Acquires first or one-time rights.

TIPS (Specialized: ethnic, people of color) "A manuscript stands out if it is neatly typed with a well-written and interesting story line or plot. Originality is encouraged. We are interested in more horror, erotic and drama pieces. *AV* wants to highlight the diversity in our culture. Stories must touch the humanity

in us all." "We strongly encourage new writers/poets to send in their work. Accepted contributors are encouraged to subscribe."

AGNI

(617)353-7135. Fax: (617)353-7134. E-mail: agni@bu.edu. Website: www.agnimagazine.org. **Contact:** Sven Birkerts, editor. "Eclectic literary magazine publishing first-rate poems, essays, translations, and stories."

Reading period September 1-May 31 only. "Online magazine carries original content not found in print edition. All submissions are considered for both." Founding editor Askold Melnyczuk won the 2001 Nora Magid Award for Magazine Editing. Work from *AGNI* has been included and cited regularly in the *Pushcart Prize* and *Best American* anthologies.

MAGAZINES NEEDS *AGNI*, published semiannually, prints poetry, fiction, and essays "by both emerging and established writers. We publish quite a bit of poetry in forms as well as 'language'poetry, but we don't begin to try and place parameters on the 'kind of work' that *AGNI* selects." Wants readable, intelligent poetry—mostly lyric free verse (with some narrative and dramatic)—that somehow communicates tension or risk. Has published poetry by Patricia Goedicke, Stephen Dunn, Kim Addonizio, Kate Northrop, Matt Donovan, and Seamus Heaney. *AGNI* is typeset, offset-printed, perfect-bound. Circulation is 3,000 for subscriptions, mail orders, and bookstore sales. Subscription: $20. Sample: $10.

HOW TO CONTACT Submit no more than 5 poems at a time. Considers simultaneous submissions; no previously published poems. No e-mail submissions. Cover letter is required ("brief, sincere"). "No fancy fonts, gimmicks. Include SASE or e-mail address; no preformatted reply cards." Reads submissions September 1-May 31. Pays $20/page ($150 maximum), a 1-year subscription, and for print publication: 2 contributor's copies and 4 gift copies. Acquires first serial rights.

TIPS "We're also looking for extraordinary translations from little-translated languages. It is important to read work published in *AGNI* before submitting, to see if your own might be compatible."

AGNIESZKA'S DOWRY (AGD)

A Small Garlic Press (ASGP), 5445 Sheridan Rd., #3003, Chicago IL 60640. E-mail: marek@enteract.

com; ketzle@ketzle.net. Website: http://asgp.org. **Contact:** Marek Lugowski and Katrina Grace Craig, Co-Editors.

MAGAZINES NEEDS *Agnieszka's Dowry (AgD)* is "a magazine published both in print and as a permanent Internet installation of poems and graphics, letters to Agnieszka. The print version consists of professionally crafted chapbooks. The online version comprises fast-loading pages employing an intuitive, if uncanny, navigation in an interesting space, all conducive to fast and comfortable reading. No restrictions on form or type. We use contextual and juxtapositional tie-ins with other material in making choices, so visiting the online AgD or reading a chapbook of an AgD issue is required of anyone making a submission." Single copy: $3 plus $5 shipping, if ordered from website by an individual. Make checks payable to A Small Garlic Press.

HOW TO CONTACT Submit 5-10 poems at a time. Accepts e-mail submissions only (NOTE: pasted into body of message in plain text, sent to both editors simultaneously; no attachments). "We ask you to read well into *Agnieszka's Dowry*, and to fit your submissions to the partially filled content of its open issues." Responds by e-mail or SASE, usually within 2 months. Pays 1 contributor's copy. Acquires one-time rights where applicable.

ADDITIONAL INFORMATION A Small Garlic Press (ASGP) publishes up to 3 chapbooks of poetry/year. Query with a full online ms, ASCII (plain text) only.

◑◉ ALASKA QUARTERLY REVIEW

ESB 208, University of Alaska-Anchorage, 3211 Providence Dr., Anchorage AK 99508. (907)786-6916. E-mail: aqr@uaa.alaska.edu. Website: www.uaa.alaska.edu/aqr. **Contact:** Ronald Spatz. "*AQR* publishes fiction, poetry, literary nonfiction and short plays in traditional and experimental styles."

◔ *Alaska Quarterly* reports they are always looking for freelance material and new writers.

MAGAZINES NEEDS *Alaska Quarterly Review*, published in 2 double issues/year, is "devoted to contemporary literary art. We publish both traditional and experimental fiction, poetry, literary nonfiction, and short plays." Wants all styles and forms of poetry, "with the most emphasis perhaps on voice and content that displays 'risk,' or intriguing ideas or situations." Has published poetry by Has published poetry by Maxine Kumin, Jane Hirshfield, David Lehman, Pattiann Rogers, Albert Goldbarth, David Wagoner, Robert Pinsky, Linda Pastan, Ted Kooser, Kay Ryan, W. S. Merwin, Sharon Olds and Billy Collins. *Alaska Quarterly Review* is 224-300 pages, digest-sized, professionally printed, perfect-bound, with card cover with color or b&w photo. Receives up to 6,000 submissions/year, accepts 40-90. Subscription: $18. Sample: $6. Pays $10-50 subject to availability of funds; pays in contributor's copies and subscriptions when funding is limited.

HOW TO CONTACT No fax or e-mail submissions. Reads submissions mid-August to mid-May; manuscripts are *not* read May 15-August 15. Responds in up to 5 months, "sometimes longer during peak periods in late winter."

ADDITIONAL INFORMATION Guest poetry editors have included Stuart Dybek, Jane Hirshfield, Stuart Dischell, Maxine Kumin, Pattiann Rogers, Dorianne Laux, Peggy Shumaker, Olena Kalytiak Davis, Nancy Eimers, Michael Ryan, and Billy Collins.

TIPS "All sections are open to freelancers. We rely almost exclusively on unsolicited manuscripts. *AQR* is a nonprofit literary magazine and does not always have funds to pay authors."

◑ ALBATROSS

The Anabiosis Press, 2 South New St., Bradford MA 01835. (978)469-7085. E-mail: rsmyth@anabiosispress.org. Website: www.anabiosispress.org. **Contact:** Richard Smyth, editor.

MAGAZINES NEEDS *Albatross*, published "as soon as we have accepted enough quality poems to publish an issue—about 1 per year," considers the albatross "to be a metaphor for the environment. The journal's title is drawn from Coleridge's *The Rime of the Ancient Mariner* and is intended to invoke the allegorical implications of that poem. This is not to say that we publish only environmental or nature poetry, but that we are biased toward such subject matter. We publish mostly free verse, and we prefer a narrative style." Wants "poetry written in a strong, mature voice that conveys a deeply felt experience or makes a powerful statement." Does not want "rhyming poetry, prose poetry, or haiku." Has published poetry by Don Thompson, Joan Colby, Temple Cone, Fredrick Zydeck and Don Russ. *Albatross* is 28 pages, digest-sized, laser-typeset, with linen cover. Subscription: $8 for 2 issues. Sample: $5.

HOW TO CONTACT Submit 3-5 poems at a time. Lines/poem: 200 maximum. No simultaneous submissions. Accepts e-mail submissions if included in body of message (but is "often quicker at returning mailed submissions"). Name and address must accompany e-mail submissions. Cover letter is not required. "We do, however, need bio notes and SASE for return or response. Poems should be typed single-spaced, with name, address, and phone number in upper left corner." Time between acceptance and publication is up to 6 months to a year. Guidelines available for SASE or on website. Responds in 2-3 months. Pays 1 contributor's copy. Acquires all rights. Returns rights provided that "previous publication in *Albatross* is mentioned in all subsequent reprintings."

CONTEST/AWARD OFFERINGS The Anabiosis Press Chapbook Contest (see separate listing Contests & Awards).

① ALIMENTUM, THE LITERATURE OF FOOD

P.O. Box 210028, Nashville TN 37221, Nashville TN 37221. E-mail: submissions@alimentumjournal. com. Website: www.alimentumjournal.com. **Contact:** Cortney Davis, Poetry Editor. (Specialized: poems about/referencing food; menupoems; recipe poems)"We're seeking fiction, creative nonfiction, and poetry all around the subject of food or drink. We do not read year-round. Check website for reading periods."

MAGAZINES NEEDS *Alimentum, The Literature of Food*, published semiannually in winter and summer, is "the only literary journal all about food." Wants "fiction, creative nonfiction, and poetry all around the subject of food." Has published poetry by Dick Allen, Stephen Gibson, Carly Sachs, Jen Karetnik, Virginia Chase Sutton. *Alimentum* is 128 pages, 6x7.5, perfect-bound, with matte coated cover with 4-color art, interior b&w illustration includes ads. Receives about 2,000 poems/year, accepts about 30-40. Press run is 2,000-3,000. Single copy: $10 ($18 Canada/foreign); subscription: $18 for 1 year ($30 Canada/foreign). Make checks payable to *Alimentum* (payment available online through credit card or PayPal).

HOW TO CONTACT Submit no more than 5 poems at a time. Lines/poem: no minimum or maximum. Considers simultaneous submissions; no previously published poems. No e-mail submissions; postal submissions only. Include SASE. Check website for reading periods which vary from year to year. Guidelines available on website. Responds 1-3 months. Pays contributor's copy. Acquires First North American Serial rights. Rights revert to poets upon publication.

ALSO OFFERS Publishes an annual broadside of "menupoems" for restaurants during National Poetry Month in April. "While food is our subject, we like poems to be about more than just the food. As in the stories we publish, the poems should also carry a personal element, even a story, not just a list of ingredients. Some special poem categories that we look for are menupoems and recipe poems."

TIPS "No email submissions, only snail mail. Mark outside envelope to the attention of Poetry, Fiction, or Nonfiction Editor."

① ⑤ ALIVE NOW

1908 Grand Ave., P.O. Box 340004, Nashville TN 37203-0004. E-mail: alivenow@upperroom.org. Website: www.alivenow.org; www.upperroom.org. **Contact:** Beth A. Richardson, Editor. 1908 Grand Ave., P.O. Box 340004, Nashville, TN 37203-0004. (615)-340-7254. Fax: (615)340-7267. E-mail: alivenow@ upperroom.org. Website: www.alivenow.org; www. upperroom.org. *Alive Now* is a thematic, bi-monthly magazine that seeks to nourish people who are hungry for a sacred way of living. This 4-color, 48-page publication of The Upper Room speaks to the opportunities and challenges of following Christ in the modern world. Scripture and prayer are two foundational cornerstones of content. "We accept freelance theme-based writing that is submitted either by mail or electronically and strive to represent the widest possible diversity (theological, geographical, denominational, racial, cultural) among our writers."

MAGAZINES NEEDS *Alive Now*, published bimonthly, is a devotional magazine that invites readers to enter an ever-deepening relationship with God. "*Alive Now* seeks to nourish people who are hungry for a sacred way of living. Submissions should invite readers to see God in the midst of daily life by exploring how contemporary issues impact their faith lives. Each word must be vivid and dynamic and contribute to the whole. We make selections based on a list of upcoming themes. Manuscripts which do not fit a theme will be returned." Considers avant-garde and free verse. *Alive Now* is 64 pages. Accepts

20 poems/year. Circulation is 70,000. Subscription: $17.95/year (6 issues); $26.95 for 2 years (12 issues). Additional subscription information, including foreign rates, available on website.

HOW TO CONTACT Submissions should invite readers to seek God in the midst of daily life by exploring how contemporary issues impact their faith lives. If ms does not fit a theme, it will not be considered. Themes can be found on website. Prefers electronic submissions, pasted into body of e-mail or attached as Word document. Postal submissions should include SASE. Include name, address, theme on each sheet. Payment will be made at the time of acceptance for publication. "We will notify contributors of manuscript status when we make final decisions for an issue, approximately two months before the issue date." Pays $35 or more on acceptance. Purchases newspaper, periodical, and electronic rights; may purchase one-time use.

❶❸ AMAZE: THE CINQUAIN JOURNAL

Website: www.amaze-cinquain.com. (Specialized: American cinquain)10529 Olive St., Temple City CA 91780. E-mail: cinquains@hotmail.com. Website: www.amaze-cinquain.com. Established 2002. **Contact:** Deborah P. Kolodji, editor. Webmaster: Lisa Janice Cohen.

MAGAZINES NEEDS *AMAZE: The Cinquain Journal*, published bianually online, is a literary Webzine devoted to the cinquain poetry form. Wants American cinquains as invented by Adelaide Crapsey (5 lines with a 2-4-6-8-2 syllable pattern) and cinquain variations (mirror cinquains, crown cinquains, cinquain sequences, etc.). Does not want any poetry not based upon the American cinquain, nor "grammar-lesson" cinquains based upon parts of speech; nothing hateful, racist, or sexually explicit. Considers poetry by teens (16 and older). Has published poetry by an'yAnn K. Schwader, Michael McClintock, naiAnd Denis Garrison. Receives about 1,500 poems/year, accepts about 100.

HOW TO CONTACT Submit 1-5 poems at a time. Lines/poem: 5. Considers previously published poems; no simultaneous submissions. Accepts e-mail submissions; no disk submissioins. "E-mail submissions preferred, with poems in the body of the e-mail. Do not send attachments." Include SASE with postal mail submissions. "Poems are evaluated on quality, form, and content." Often comments on rejected poems. Guidelines available for SASE or on website. Responds in up to 6 weeks. Acquires one-time rights and reprint rights for annual print anthology.

❾❶❸ AMBIT

17 Priory Gardens, Highgate, London N6 5QY, England. E-mail: info@ambitmagazine.co.uk. Website: www.ambitmagazine.co.uk. **Contact:** Edwin Brock, Carol Ann Duffy, and Henry Graham, Poetry Editors. 17 Priory Gardens, Highgate, London N6 5QY UK. (44)(020)8340 3566. E-mail: info@ambitmagazine. co.uk. Website: www.ambitmagazine.co.uk. *Ambit* magazine is a literary and artwork quarterly created in London, published in the UK, and read internationally. *Ambit* is put together entirely from unsolicited, previously unpublished poetry and short fiction submissions. Does not want "indiscriminately centre-justified poems; jazzy fonts; poems all in italics for the sake of it." Subscription: £28/1 year. (NOTE: online subcriptions renew automatically unless canceled.) Single Issue: £9. *Ambit*, published quarterly, is a 96-page quarterly of avant-garde, contemporary, and experimental work. *Ambit* is perfect-bound, with 2-color cover with artwork. Accepts about 3% of submissions received. Subscription: £28 UK, £30/€44 rest of Europe, £32/$64 everywhere else. Sample: £7 UK, £9/€15 rest of Europe, £10/$20 overseas.

HOW TO CONTACT Submit 5-6 poems. Postal mail only; does not accept e-mail submissions. Enclose SASE with UK stamps, or with IRCs. Include e-mail address on your cover letter. Responds in 3-4 months. Pays 2 contributor's copies and discount on further copies.

TIPS "Read a copy of the magazine before submitting!"

❶ THE AMERICAN DISSIDENT: A JOURNAL OF LITERATURE, DEMOCRACY & DISSIDENCE

217 Commerce Rd., Barnstable MA 02630. E-mail: todslone@yahoo.com. Website: www.TheAmerican-Dissident.org. **Contact:** G. Tod Slone, editor. Journal published 2 times/year. Almost always comments on rejected poems. Pays 1 contributor's copy. Reviews books/chapbooks of poetry and other magazines in 250 words, single-book format. Send materials for review consideration.

MAGAZINES NEEDS *The American Dissident*, 217 Commerce Rd., Barnstable, MA 02630, e-mail: todslone@yahoo.com. Contact: G. Tod Slone, editor. Published 2 times/year, provides "a forum for, amongst other things, criticism of the academic/literary established order, which clearly discourages vigorous debate, cornerstone of democracy, to the evident detriment of American Literature. The Journal seeks rare poets daring to risk going against that established-order grain." Wants "poetry, reviews, artwork, and short (1,000 words) essays in English, French, or Spanish, written on the edge with a dash of personal risk and stemming from personal experience, conflict with power, and/or involvement." Submissions should be "iconoclastic and parrhesiastic in nature." *The American Dissident* is 56-64 pages, digest-sized, offset-printed, perfect-bound, with card cover. Press run is 200. Single copy: $9; subscriptions: individuals, $18; institutions $20.

HOW TO CONTACT Submit 3 poems at a time. Considers simultaneous submissions; no previously published poems. E-mail submissions from subscribers only. "Far too many poets submit without even reading the guidelines. Include SASE and cover letter containing not credits, but rather personal dissident information, as well as incidents that provoked you to 'go upright and vital, and speak the rude truth in all ways' (Emerson)." Time between acceptance and publication is up to 2 months. Almost always comments on rejected poems. Guidelines available for SASE. Responds in 1 month. Pays 1 contributor's copy. Acquires first North American serial rights. Reviews books/chapbooks of poetry and other magazines in 250 words, single-book format. Send materials for review consideration.

AMERICAN LITERARY REVIEW

University of North Texas, P.O. Box 311307, Denton TX 76203-1307. (940)565-2755. E-mail: americanliteraryreview@gmail.com; bond@unt.edu. Website: www.engl.unt.edu/alr/. "The *American Literary Review* welcomes submissions of previously unpublished poems, short stories, and creative non-fiction. We also accept submissions for cover art. Please include an SASE and cover letter with your submission. Also include enough postage to return your work. Please mark envelopes and cover letters "Fiction", "Poetry", or "Nonfiction". Simultaneous submissions are acceptable if noted in your cover letter. For any questions not covered in this section, please refer to our "Frequently Asked Questions" page. Our reading period extends from October 1 to May 1. Unsolicited manuscripts received outside this reading period will be returned

unread. Currently, we do not accept submissions via email. Submissions should be directed to the appropriate editor (Fiction, Poetry, Nonfiction, or Art)."

HOW TO CONTACT No fax or e-mail submissions. Cover letter is required. Include author's name, address, phone number, and poem titles. Reads mss October 1-May 1. Guidelines available on website. Responds in up to 3 months. Pays 2 contributor's copies. Considers simultaneous submissions.

CONTEST/AWARD OFFERINGS Check website for contest details.

TIPS "We encourage writers and artists to examine our journal. The *American Literary Review* publishes semi-annually. If you would like to subscribe to our journal, subscription rates run $14 for a 1 year subscription, $26 for a 2 year subscription, and $36 for a 3 year subscription. You may also obtain a sample copy of the American Literary Review for $7 plus $1 per issue for shipping and handling in the U.S. and Canada ($2 for postage elsewhere)."

THE AMERICAN POETRY JOURNAL

P. O. Box 2080, Aptos CA 95001-2080. E-mail: editor@americanpoetryjournal.com. Website: www.americanpoetryjournal.com. *The APJ* seeks to publish work using **poetic device**, favoring **image**, **metaphor** and good **sound**. "We like alliteration, extended metaphors, image, movement." An awareness of poetics, wide exposure to a variety of poets' work, and an appreciation of craft contribute to a well-written piece. Subscriptions: $20/1 issue, $37/2 issues. Make checks payable to "Dream Horse Press." *The American Poetry Journal*, published annually (July), seeks "to publish work using poetic device, favoring image, metaphor, and good sound. We like alliteration, extended metaphors, image, movement, and poems that can pass the 'so what' test. *The American Poetry Journal* has in mind the reader who delights in discovering what a poem can do to the tongue and what the poem paints on the cave of the mind." Wants poems "that exhibit strong, fresh imagery, metaphor, and good sound." Does not want "narratives about family, simplistic verse, annoying word hodge-podges." Has published poetry by C.J. Sage, Natasha Sage, Lola Haskins, Dorianne Laux, and Sarah J. Sloat. *The American Poetry Journal* is 100 pages, 6X9, perfect-bound. Accepts about 1% of poems submitted. Single copy: $12; subscription: $12. Make checks payable to Dream Horse Press.

HOW TO CONTACT Submit no more than 5 original, unpublished poems. Cover letter preferred. Include name, address, phone, e-mail address on each page. ONLY accepts submissions through submission manager on website. Simultaneous submissions accepted with notice of such. Pays 1 contributor's copy. Reads between February 1 and May 31.

TIPS "Know the magazine you are submitting to, before you commit your work and yourself. It's not that difficult, but it helps your odds when the editor can tell that you get what the magazine is about. Reading an issue is the easiest way to do this."

⊕ THE AMERICAN POETRY REVIEW

1700 Sansom St., Suite 800, Philadelphia, PA 19103. E-mail: sberg@aprweb.org. Website: www.aprweb.org. **Contact:** Stephen Berg, Editor. *APR* is dedicated to reaching a worldwide audience with a diverse array of the best contemporary poetry and literary prose. Subscription information available online.

MAGAZINES NEEDS *The American Poetry Review*, published bimonthly, "contains some of the best contemporary poetry and prose from a diverse ray of authors. Over the last 35 years, *APR* has helped to make poetry a more public art form without compromising the art of poetry." Circ. 6,000-10,000.

HOW TO CONTACT Submit up to 5 poems at a time on 8.5 X 11" paper. Only accepts postal submissions, no e-mail or fax submissions. No previously published poems or simultaneous submissions. Include SASE. Guidelines available on website. Responds in 3 months. First serial rights.

CONTEST/AWARD OFFERINGS "The Jerome J. Shestack Poetry Prizes of $1000 are awarded annually to each of 2 poets whose work has appeared in APR during the preceding calendar year."

◑ AMERICAN TANKA

(Specialized: English-language tanka). E-mail: laura@lauramaffei.com. Website: www.americantanka.com. Estab. 1996. **Contact:** Laura Maffei, Editor. *American Tanka* seeks to present the best and most well-crafted English-language tanka being written today, in a visually calm space that allows the reader's eye to focus on the single poem and linger in the moment it evokes.

MAGAZINES NEEDS *American Tanka* is devoted to single English-language tanka. Wants "concise and vivid language, good crafting, and echo of the original Japanese form, but with unique and contemporary

content." Does not want "anything that's not tanka. No sequences or titled groupings." Has published poetry by Sanford Goldstein, Marianne Bluger, Jeanne Emrich, Tom Hartman, Larry Kimmel, Pamela Miller Ness, and George Swede.

HOW TO CONTACT Submit up to 5 poems. No previously published poems or simultaneous submissions. Accepts submissions by online submission form found on website or by e-mail (pasted into body). Responds in 3 months. Acquires first North American serial rights. Welcomes submissions from anyone who has been writing tanka: experienced tanka poets, experienced poets in other forms, and novices. Seeks concise, well-crafted, five-line tanka that evoke a specific moment in time.

◑⑤ ANCIENT PATHS

P.O. Box 7505, Fairfax Station VA 22039. E-mail: SS-Burris@msn.com. Website: www.editorskylar.com. **Contact:** Skylar H. Burris, Editor. *Ancient Paths*, published biennially in odd-numbered years, provides "a forum for quality Christian poetry." Wants "traditional rhymed/metrical forms and free verse; subtle Christian themes. I seek poetry that makes the reader both think and feel." Does not want 'preachy' poetry, inconsistent meter, or forced rhyme; no stream of conscious or avant-garde work; no esoteric academic poetry. Has published poetry by Nicholas Samaras, Paul David Adkins, Ida Fasel, and Donna Farley. *Ancient Paths* is 60+ pages, digest-sized, printed, perfect-bound, with glossy cover. Issue 17 will feature the work of multiple poets. Receives about 600 queries/year, accepts 10-20 poets. Press run to be determined. Single copy: $10. Make checks payable to Skylar Burris.*Ancient Paths*, published biennially in odd-numbered years, provides "a forum for quality Christian poetry."

HOW TO CONTACT Query with 3-6 of your best poems. Lines/poem: 8 minimum, no maximum. Considers previously published poems and simultaneous submissions. Accepts e-mail submissions. Submissions should be pasted directly into the message, single-spaced, 1 poem per message, using a small or normal font size, with name and address at the top of each submission. Use subject heading: ANCIENT PATHS SUBMISSION, followed by your title." For postal submissions, poems should be single-spaced; "always include name, address, and line count on first page of all submissions, and note if the poem is previously published and what rights (if any) were purchased." Check website for reading period and submission details for Issue 17. Time between acceptance and publication is up to one year. Sometimes comments on rejected poems. Guidelines available for SASE or on website. Responds in 3-4 weeks "if rejected, longer if being seriously considered." Pays $5 for the first poem and $2 for each additional poem published plus one contributor's copy. Acquires one-time or reprint rights.

TIPS "Read the great religious poets: John Donne, George Herbert, T.S. Eliot, Lord Tennyson. Remember not to preach. This is a literary magazine, not a pulpit. This does not mean you do not communicate morals or celebrate God. It means you are not overbearing or simplistic when you do so."

THE ANTIGONISH REVIEW

(902)867-3962. Fax: (902)867-5563. E-mail: tar@stfx.ca. Website: www.antigonishreview.com. **Contact:** Bonnie McIsaac, office manager. *The Antigonish Review* is 144 pages, digest-sized, offset-printed, flat-spined, with glossy card cover with art. Receives 2,500 submissions/year, accepts about 10%. Press run is 1,000. Subscription: $24 CAD, $30 US, International $40. Sample: $7. TAR is open to poetry on any subject written from any point of view and in any form. However, writers should expect their work to be considered within the full context of old and new poetry in English and other languages. No more than 6-8 poems should be submitted at any one time. A preferable submission would be from 3-4 poemsLiterary magazine for educated and creative readers.

MAGAZINES NEEDS TAR is open to poetry on any subject written from any point of view and in any form. However, writers should expect their work to be considered within the full context of old and new poetry in English and other languages. No more than 6-8 poems should be submitted at any one time. A preferable submission would be from 3-4 poems

HOW TO CONTACT P.O. Box 5000, Antigonish NSB2G 2W5, Canada. (902)867-396. Faz: (902)867-5563. E-mail: tar@stfx.ca. Website: www.antigonishreview.com. Accepts fax submissions; e-mail submissions accepted from overseas only. Include SASE (SAE and IRCs if outside Canada; "we cannot use U.S. postage") or we can respond by e-mail. Time between acceptance and publication is up to 8 months. Sometimes comments on rejected poems.

Guidelines available for SASE, by e-mail, or on website. Responds in up to 6 months.

TIPS "Send for guidelines and/or sample copy. Send ms with cover letter and SASE with submission."

ANTIOCH REVIEW

P.O. Box 148, Yellow Springs OH 45387-0148. E-mail: mkeyes@antiochreview.org. Website: http://antioch-college.org/antioch_review/. Judith Hall, poetry editor. **Contact:** Muriel Keyes. Guidelines available on website. Responds in 8-10 weeks. Pays $15/published page plus 2 contributor's copies; additional copies available at 40% discount. Poetry submissions are not accepted between between May 1 and September 1.Literary and cultural review of contemporary issues, and literature for general readership.

   Work published in *The Antioch Review* has been included frequently in *The Best American Poetry, The Best New Poets* and *The Pushcart Prize.*

HOW TO CONTACT P.O. Box 148 Yellow Springs, OH 45387-0148. (937)769-1365. E-mail: mkeyes@antiochreview.org. Website: http://antiochcollege.org/antioch_review/. Submit 3-6 poems at a time. No previously published poems or simultaneous submissions. Include SASE with all submissions.

AOIFE'S KISS

The Speculative Fiction Foundation, P.O. Box 782, Cedar Rapids IA 52406-0782. E-mail: aoifeskiss@yahoo.com. Website: www.samsdotpublishing.com. **Contact:** Tyree Campbell, Managing Editor. (Specialized: fantasy; science fiction) Member: The Speculative Literature Foundation (http://SpeculativeLiterature.org)."Aoife's Kiss is a print and online magazine of fantasy, science fiction, horror, sword & sorcery, and slipstream, published quarterly in March, June, September, and December. Aoife's Kiss publishes short stories, poems, illustrations, articles, and movie/book/chapbook reviews, and interviews with noted individuals in those genres."

MAGAZINES NEEDS *Aoife's Kiss*, published quarterly, prints "fantasy, science fiction, sword and sorcery, alternate history, dark fantasy short stories, poems, illustrations, and movie and book reviews." Wants "fantasy, science fiction, spooky horror, and speculative poetry with minimal angst." Considers poetry by children and teens. Has published poetry by Bruce Boston, Karen A. Romanko, Mike Allen, Corrine De Winter, Julie Shiel, and Marge B. Simon.

Aoife's Kiss (print version) is 54 pages, magazine-sized, offset-printed, saddle-stapled, perfect-bound, with color paper cover, includes ads. Receives about 300 poems/year, accepts about 50 (17%). Press run is 150; 5 distributed free to reviewers. Single copy: $7; subscription: $22/year, $40 for 2 years. Make checks payable to Sam's Dot Publishing.

HOW TO CONTACT Submit up to 5 poems at a time. Lines/poem: prefers less than 100. Considers previously published poems; no simultaneous submissions. Accepts e-mail submissions (pasted into body of message); no disk submissions. "Submission should include snail mail address and a short (1-2 lines) bio." Reads submissions year round. Submit seasonal poems 6 months in advance. Time between acceptance and publication is 2-5 months. Often comments on rejected poems. Guidelines available on website. Responds in 4-6 weeks. Pays $5/poem, $3/reprint, $1 for scifaiku and related forms, and 1 contributor's copy. Acquires first North American serial rights. Reviews books/chapbooks of poetry. Send materials for review consideration to Tyree Campbell.

◑ APALACHEE REVIEW

Apalachee Press, P.O. Box 10469, Tallahassee FL 32302. (850)644-9114. E-mail: arsubmissions@hotmail.com (for queries outside of the U.S.). Website: http://apalacheereview.org/index.html. **Contact:** Michael Trammell, editor; Mary Jane Ryals, fiction editor.

◑ APPARATUS MAGAZINE

E-mail: submissions@apparatusmagazine.com; editor@apparatusmagazine.com. Website: www.apparatusmagazine.com. **Contact:** Adam W. Hart, publisher/editor."*Apparatus Magazine* strives to bring readers poetry and fiction from around the world that explores the mythos of 'man (or woman) vs. machine,' that conjures up words from the inner machine, and more. Each issue features work from around the world, bringing the reader literary updates from the *internal machine.*"

⊘ Online monthly magazine which "strives to bring readers poetry and fiction from around the world that explores the mythos of "man (or woman) vs. machine," that conjures up words from the inner machine, and more. Each issue of apparatus magazine features work from around the world, bringing the reader liter-ary updates from the internal machine. Fiction consists of short fiction/flash fiction (500 words or less), and each issue of the magazine has a specific theme.

MAGAZINES NEEDS Wants "shorter poetry, free verse. Attention given to poems with a strong, natural voice. apparatus magazine accepts poetry on general themes, but does feature monthly thematic issues." Does not want overtly inspirational poetry, poetry aimed at children, or confessional poetry. Avoid "work that is overtly racist, sexist, violent, homophobic, discriminatory, pornographic, or otherwise in questionable taste." Has published poetry by Rayne Arroyo, Anne Brooke, Lesley Dame, Gregg Shapiro, Inara Cedrins, and Chanming Yuan.

HOW TO CONTACT Submit 3-5 poems at a time, 2 pages maximum/poem. Accepts submissions by e-mail pasted into body of e-mail message. Cover letter is required. "Please include list of submitted poems, as well as a (maximum) 3-line bio listing other publications/journals in which poet has published his/her work." Reads submissions year round. Submit seasonal poems 2-3 months in advance. Time between acceptance and publication is 1-3 months. Often comments on rejected poems. Regularly publishes theme issues. Upcoming themes available in magazine, by e-mail, and on website. Guidelines available in magazine, by e-mail, and on website. Acquires first North American serial rights, electronic rights, option with poet's permission to reprint accepted work in yearly anthology. Rights rever to poet upon publication.

CONTEST/AWARD OFFERINGS The Apparatus Award is offered annually for best poem published in *Apparatus Magazine* during the publication year (June to May). Award: $100. Guidelines available in magazine, on website, by e-mail.

TIPS "Be sure to read the guidelines as posted. Themes for each issue are typically posted 3 months (or more) in advance. Include cover letter and bio with e-maill submissions. Submit more than just one poem, so I can get a feel for your work. Be sure to read back issues of the magazine. The journal tends to select work that focuses on specific themes, and usually tries to pick work that will compliment/contrast with other pieces selected for the issue. Send your best work and don't be afraid of trying again. I often suggest other publications/markets if a piece is not a good match for the journal."

○●● APPLE VALLEY REVIEW: A JOURNAL OF CONTEMPORARY LITERATURE

E-mail: editor@leahbrowning.net. Website: www.applevalleyreview.com. **Contact:** Leah Browning, editor. E-mail: editor@leahbrowning.net. Website: www.applevalleyreview.com. *Apple Valley Review: A Journal of Contemporary Literature*, published semiannually online, features "beautifully crafted poetry, short fiction, and essays."

MAGAZINES NEEDS *Apple Valley Review: A Journal of Contemporary Literature*, published semiannually online, features "beautifully crafted poetry, short fiction, and essays." Wants "work that has both mainstream and literary appeal. All work must be original, previously unpublished, and in English. Translations are welcome if permission has been granted. Preference is given to short (under 2 pages), non-rhyming poetry." Does not want "erotica, work containing explicit language or violence, or work that is scholarly, critical, inspirational, or intended for children." Considers poetry by children and teens; "all work is considered regardless of the author's age." Has published poetry by Vince Corvaia, Michael Lauchlan, Jin Cordaro, Gregory Lawless, Anna Evans, and Keetje Kuipers. Receives about 5,000+ poems/year, accepts less than 1%.

HOW TO CONTACT Submit 2-6 poems at a time. Lines/poem: "no limit, though we prefer short poems (under 2 pages)." No previously published poems or simultaneous submissions. Accepts e-mail submissions (pasted into body of message, with "poetry" in subject line); no disk submissions. Reads submissions year round. Time between acceptance and publication is 2 months. Sometimes comments on rejected poems. Guidelines available by e-mail or on website. Acquires first rights and first serial rights and retains the right to archive the work online for an indefinite period of time. "As appropriate, we may also choose to nominate published work for awards or recognition. Author retains all other rights."

CONTEST/AWARD OFFERINGS Offers the annual *Apple Valley Review* Editor's Prize. Award varies. "From 2006-2009, the prize was $100 and a book of poetry or fiction." Submit 2-6 poems. **Entry fee:** none. **Deadline:** rolling; all submissions to the *Apple Valley Review*, and all work published during a given calendar year will be considered for the prize.

⊕ A PUBLIC SPACE

323 Dean St., Brooklyn NY 11217. (718)858-8067. E-mail: general@apublicspace.org. Website: www.apublicspace.org. **Contact:** Brigid Hughes, editor.

◑ *A Public Space*, published quarterly, "is an independent magazine of literature and culture. In an era that has relegated literature to the margins, we plan to make fiction and poetry the stars of a new conversation. We believe that stories are how we make sense of our lives and how we learn about other lives. We believe that stories matter." Single copy: $15; subscription: $36/year or $60/2 years.

HOW TO CONTACT Submit up to 4 poems at a time. Considers simultaneous submissions; no previously published poems. Prefers submissions through online process; accepts mail. Include SASE. See website for submission dates and guidelines.

○⊖ THE APUTAMKON REVIEW: VOICES FROM DOWNEAST MAINE AND THE CANADIAN MARITIMES (OR THEREABOUTS)

the WordShed, LLC, P.O. Box 190, Jonesboro ME 04648. E-mail: thewordshed@tds.net. Website: http://thewordshed.com. Send complete ms with cover letter. Accepts submissions in the body of an e-mail, on disk via USPS. Submission period is 12 months a year; reading January 1 through March 31. Responds only between Jan. 31 and April 31. Include age if under 18, and a bio will be requested upon acceptance of work. Responds to queries or submissions in 2-8 weeks. Send SASE (or IRC) for return of ms or a disposable copy of ms and #10 SASE for reply only. Considers simultaneous submissions, multiple submissions. Sample copy available for $12.85 US plus $2.75 US s/h. Guidelines available for SASE, via e-mail, via fax. Submissions receive $10-35 depending on medium, plus one copy. Pays on acceptance. Acquires first North American serial rights. Publication is copyrighted. All rights revert back to the contributors upon publication." The Aputamkon Review will present a mismash of truths, half truths and outright lies, including but not limited to short fiction, tall tales, creative non-fiction, essays, (some) poetry, haiku, b&w visual arts, interviews, lyrics and music, quips, quirks, quotes that should be famous, witticisms, follies, comic strips, cartoons, jokes, riddles, recipes, puzzles, games. Stretch your imagination. Practically anything goes." Annual. Estab. 2006. Circ. 500. Member Maine Writers and Publishers Alliance.

TIPS "Be colorful, heartfelt not mainstream. Write what you want and then submit."

○○⊙ ARC POETRY MAGAZINE

P.O. Box 81060, Ottawa ON K1P 1B1, Canada. E-mail: editor@arcpoetry.ca. Website: www.arcpoetry.ca. **Contact:** Pauline Conley, managing editor.

MAGAZINES NEEDS *Arc Poetry Magazine*, published semiannually, prints poetry, poetry-related articles, interviews, and book reviews. "Tastes are eclectic. International submissions are welcome and encouraged." Has published poetry by Don Coles, Karen Solie, Carmine Starnino, David O'Meara, Elizabeth Bachinsky, George Elliott Clarke, Daryl Hine, Michael Ondaatje, Stephanie Bolster, and Don Domanski. *Arc Poetry Magazine* is 130-160 pages, perfect-bound, printed on matte white stock "with a crisp, engaging design and a striking visual art portfolio in each issue." Receives about 1,000 submissions/year, accepts about 40-50 poems. Press run is 1,500. Single copy: $12.50 CAD; subscription: 1 year — $30 CAD (in Canada), 2 years — $60 CAD (in Canada). Online ordering available for subscriptions and single copies (with occasional promotions).

HOW TO CONTACT No previously published poems or simultaneous submissions. Doesn't accept ms over 5 pages. No e-mail submissions. Cover letter is required. Submissions should be single-spaced, with name and address on each page. Guidelines available for SAE and IRC or on website. Accepts submissions using submission manager on website. "Only one ms per poet will be accepted during each calendar year." Responds in 4-6 months. Pays $40 CAD/page plus 2 contributor's copies. Acquires first Canadian serial rights.

CONTEST/AWARD OFFERINGS The Confederation Poets Prize is an annual award of $250 for the best poem published in *Arc* that year. *Arc* also sponsors an international Poem of the Year Contest: 1st Prize: $1,500 CAD; 2nd Prize: $1,000 CAD; 3rd Prize: $750 CAD. Guidelines available on website. **Entry fee:** $23 CAD for 4 poems. **Deadline:** February 1. Other awards include the Lampman-Scott Award for Poetry, Critic's Desk Award, and the Diana Brebner Prize for Poetry.

ARDENT!

Poetry in the Arts, Inc., 302 Cripple Creek, Cedar Park TX 78613. E-mail: rimer777@gmail.com. Website: www.poetryinarts.org/publishing/ardent.html. **Contact:** Dillon McKinsey, executive editor. Subscription: $5.50/issue (2 issues/year). Back issue: $5.

MAGAZINES NEEDS *Ardent!*, published semiannually, is a journal of poetry and art. All forms and styles are considered. *Ardent!* is perfect-bound.

HOW TO CONTACT E-mail up to 3 poems (pasted in body of e-mail). "Include a statement giving Poetry in the Arts, Inc. your permission to use your work." Provide brief biography. Accepts attachments in e-mails. Strongly prefers e-mail submissions but will accept postal submissions. See website for guidelines.

◐ ARIES: A JOURNAL OF CREATIVE EXPRESSION

Dept. of Languages and Literature, 1201 Wesleyan St., Fort Worth TX 76105-1536. (817)531-4907. E-mail: sneeley@txwes.edu. Website: www.department.txwes.edu/aries/Aries.Htm. **Contact:** Stacia Dunn Neeley, General Editor. Press run is 300. Single copy: $7; back issues: $6.

MAGAZINES NEEDS *Aries: A Journal of Creative Expression*, published annually in summer, prints quality poetry, b&w photography/art, fiction, creative non-fiction, essays, and short plays. Poetry 3 to 50 lines. Original poetry in languages other than English welcome if submitted with English translation as companion. Has published poetry by Virgil Suárez, Richard Robbins, Susan Smith Nash, Gerald Zipper, and Lynn Veach Sadler. *Aries* is 70-100 pages, digest-sized, offset-printed, perfect-bound, with slick cover. Receives about 800 poems/year, accepts about 10%. Press run is 300. Single copy: $7; back issues: $6.

HOW TO CONTACT Send 5 submissions maximum per year. Lines/poem: 3 minimum, 50 maximum. Considers simultaneous submissions with notification; no previously published poems. Cover letter required. Include titles of submissions and 100-word bio required; no names allowed on submissions themselves. Accepts submissions September 1-January 31 only. "At least 3 reviewers read every submission via blind review." Guidelines available in magazine, for SASE or by e-mail. Responds by May. Acquires first rights.

○ ARKANSAS REVIEW

(870) 972-3043; (870)972-3674. Fax: (870)972-3045. E-mail: arkansasreview@astate.edu. E-mail: jcollins@astate.edu; arkansasreview@astate.edu. Website: http://altweb.astate.edu/arkreview/. Tom Williams. **Contact:** Dr. Janelle Collins, general editor/Associate Professor of English. *Arkansas Review* is 92 pages, magazine-sized, photo offset-printed, saddle-stapled, with 4-color cover. Receives about 500 poems/year, accepts about 5%. Press run is 600; 50 distributed free to contributors. Subscription: $20. Sample: $7.50. Make checks payable to ASU Foundation. Submit any number of poems at a time. No previously published poems or simultaneous submissions."All material, creative and scholarly, published in the *Arkansas Review*, must evoke or respond to the natural and/or cultural experience of the Mississippi River Delta region."

HOW TO CONTACT Accepts e-mail and disk submissions. Cover letter is preferred. Include SASE. Time between acceptance and publication is about 6 months. Occasionally publishes theme issues. Guidelines available for SASE or by e-mail. Responds in 4 months. Pays 3 contributor's copies. Acquires first rights. Staff reviews books/chapbooks of poetry "that are relevant to the Delta" in 500 words, single- and multi-book format. Send materials for review consideration to Janelle Collins ("inquire in advance").

TIPS Submit via mail. E-mails are more likely to be overlooked or lost. Submit a cover letter, but don't try to impress us with credentials or explanations of the submission. Immerse yourself in the literature of the Delta, but provide us with a fresh and original take on its land, its people, its culture. Surprise us. Amuse us. Recognize what makes this region particular as well as universal, and take risks. Help us shape a new Delta literature.

○ ART:MAG

Limited Editions Press, P.O. Box 70896, Las Vegas NV 89170. (702)734-8121. E-mail: magman@iopener.net. Established 1982. **Contact:** Peter Magliocco, editor.

MAGAZINES NEEDS *ART:MAG*, published 1-2 times/year, has "become, due to economic and other factors, more limited to a select audience of poets as well as readers. We seek to expel the superficiality of our factitious culture, in all its drive-thru, junk-food-brain, commercial-ridden extravagance—and stylize a magazine of hard-line aesthetics, where truth and beauty meet on a vector not shallowly drawn. Conforming to this outlook is an operational policy of seeking poetry from solicited poets primarily, though unsolicited submissions will be read, considered, and perhaps used infrequently. Sought from the chosen is a creative use of poetic styles, systems, and emotional morphologies other than banally constricting." Has published poetry by Neal Wilgus, Lorraine Tolliver, Kenneth Di Maggio, Dave Church, and Paul Joseph Notarianni. *ART:MAG* is published in large issues of 100 copies, limited to a few poets. Subscription: $8 for 2 issues. Sample: $3 or more. Make checks payable to Peter Magliocco.

HOW TO CONTACT Submit 5 poems at a time. Considers simultaneous submissions; sometimes previously published poems. No e-mail submissions. Cover letter is optional. SASE required. "Submissions should be neat and use consistent style format (except experimental work)." Sometimes comments on rejected poems. Publishes theme issues. Guidelines available for SASE. Responds within 3 months. Pays one contributor's copy. Acquires first rights. Staff occasionally reviews books of poetry. Send materials for review consideration.

ADDITIONAL INFORMATION Limited Editions Press recently published *Under the Oak* by Bill Chown. Query the editor before submitting any ms.

○ ⑤ ARTFUL DODGE

Website: www.wooster.edu/artfuldodge/. Dept. of English, College of Wooster, Wooster OH 44691. E-mail: artfuldodge@wooster.edu. Website: www.wooster.edu/artfuldodge/. Established 1979. **Contact:** Daniel Bourne, poetry editor.

MAGAZINES NEEDS *Artful Dodge*, published annually, takes "a strong interest in poets who are continually testing what they can get away with successfully in regard to subject, perspective, language, etc.—but who also show mastery of current American poetic techniques, its varied textures and its achievement in the illumination of the particular. Poems can be on any subject, of any length, from any perspective, in any voice." Wants poems "that utilize stylistic persuasions both old and new to good effect. We're not afraid of poems that try to deal with large social, political, historical, and even philosophical questions—especially if the poem emerges from one's own life experience and is not the result of armchair pontificating." Encourages translations, "but we ask for original text and statement from translator that he/she has copyright clearance and permission of author." Has published poetry by Gregory Orr, Julia Kasdorf, Denise Duhamel, Tess Gallagher, and William Heyen. *Artful Dodge* is digest-sized, professionally printed, perfect-bound, with glossy cover, includes ads. Receives at least 2,000 poems/year, accepts about 60. Press run is 1,000. Single copy: $7; subscription: $7/year, $14 for 2 years, $25 for 4 years. Sample: $5 (back issue).

HOW TO CONTACT Submit 6 poems at a time. Lines/poem: long poems may be of any length, but send only one at a time. Considers simultaneous submissions "if we are informed of acceptance elsewhere." Responds in up to six months. Send materials for review consideration; however, "there is no guarantee we can review them or respond! In fact, our reviews almost invariably involve books published by past contributors to the magazine."

ⓞⓢ ARTS & LETTERS JOURNAL OF CONTEMPORARY CULTURE

Campus Box 89, Georgia College & State University, Milledgeville GA 31061. (478)445-1289. E-mail: al.journal@gcsu.edu. Website: http://al.gcsu.edu. Established 1999. **Contact:** Laura Newbern, poetry editor. Editor: Martin Lammon.

◯ Work published in *Arts & Letters Journal* has received the Pushcart Prize.

MAGAZINES NEEDS *Arts & Letters Journal of Contemporary Culture*, published semiannually, is devoted to contemporary arts and literature, featuring ongoing series such as The World Poetry Translation Series and The Mentors Interview Series. Wants work that is of the highest literary and artistic quality. Does not want genre fiction, light verse. Has published poetry by Margaret Gibson, Marilyn Nelson, Stuart Lishan, R.T. Smith, Laurie Lamon, and Miller Williams. *Arts & Letters Journal of Contemporary Culture* is 180 pages, offset-printed, perfect-bound, with glossy cover with varied artwork, includes ads. Receives about 4,000 poems/year, accepts about .5%. Press run is 1,500. Single copy: $8 plus $1 postage for current issue; subscription: $15 for 2 issues (one year). Sample: $5 plus $1 postage for back issue. Make checks payable to Georgia College & State University.

HOW TO CONTACT Submit 4-6 poems at a time. Considers simultaneous submissions "if notified immediately of publication elsewhere"; no previously published poems. Submit via online submission manager found on website or postal submission. Cover letter is preferred. Include SASE. Reads submissions August 1-January 31. "Poems are screened, discussed by group of readers, then if approved, submitted to poetry editor for final approval." Seldom comments on rejected poems. Guidelines available in magazine, for SASE, by e-mail, or on website. Responds in 1-2 months. Always sends prepublication galleys. Pays $10/published page ($50 minimum), a contributor's copy and one-year subscription. Acquires one-time rights. Reviews books of poetry in 500 words, single-book format. Query first to Martin Lammon.

CONTEST/AWARD OFFERINGS Offers the annual Arts & Letters/Rumi Prize for Poets (see separate listing in Contests & Awards).

ⓞⓢ ART TIMES

A Literary Journal and Resource for All the Arts, P.O. Box 730, Mount Marion NY 12456-0730. (845)246-6944. Fax: (845)246-6944. E-mail: info@ArtTimesJournal.com. Website: www.arttimesjournal.com. **Contact:** Raymond J. Steiner. "*Art Times* covers the art fields and is distributed in locations most frequented by those enjoying the arts. Our copies are distributed throughout the lower part of the northeast as well as metropolitan New York area; locations include theaters, galleries, museums, schools, art clubs, cultural centers and the like. Our readers are mostly over 40, affluent, art-conscious and sophisticated. Subscribers are located across US and abroad (Italy, France, Germany, Greece, Russia, etc.)."

TIPS "Competition is greater (more submissions received), but keep trying. We print new as well as published writers." "Be advised that we are presently on an approximate 3-year lead for short stories, 2-year lead for poetry. We are now receiving 300-400 poems and 40-50 short stories per month. Be familiar with *Art Times* and its special audience."

ⓞ◯ ASCENT ASPIRATIONS

1560 Arbutus Dr., Nanoose Bay BC C9P 9C8, Canada. E-mail: ascentaspirations@shaw.ca. Website: www.ascentaspirations.ca. **Contact:** David Fraser, Editor. *Ascent Aspirations Magazine*, publishes monthly online and publishes one anthology in print as a separate themed title in spring, specializes in poetry, short fiction, essays, and visual art. "A quality electronic and print publication, *Ascent* is dedicated to encouraging aspiring poets and fiction writers. We accept all forms of poetry on any theme. Poetry needs to be unique and touch the reader emotionally with relevant human, social, and philosophical imagery." Does not want poetry "that focuses on mainstream overtly religious verse." Considers poetry by children and teens. Has published poetry by Janet Buck and Taylor Graham. Work is considered for the print *The Yearly Anthology* through contests (see below). Receives about 1,500 poems/year, accepts about 15%. Submit 1-5 poems at a time. Considers previously published poems and simultaneous submissions. Prefers e-mail submissions (pasted into body of message or as attachment in Word); no disk submissions. "If you must submit by postal mail because it is your only avenue, provide a SASE with IRCs or Canadian stamps." Reads submissions on a regular basis year round. Time between acceptance and publication is 3 months or sooner. Editor makes decisions on all poems. Seldom comments on rejected poems. Occasionally publishes theme issues. Upcoming themes available on website. Responds in 3 months. Acquires one-time rights.To fund the printing of the1 annual anthology, *Ascent* offers a contest for poetry and fiction. 1st Prize: $100 CAD; 2nd Prize: $75 CAD; 3rd Prize: $50 CAD; 4th Prize: $25 CAD; 5 Honorable Mentions: $10 CAD each. All winners and honorable mentions receive 1-2 copies of anthology; all other entrants published in anthology receive 1 free copy. Guidelines available for SASE, by e-mail, or on website. **Entry fee:** $5 CAD/poem or $10 CAD/3 poems. **Deadlines:** "these vary for each contest." **NOTE: "Fee, awards, and the number of copies for winners of contests can change. Refer always to the website for the most up-to-date information."** Address: 1560 Arbutus Dr., Nanoose Bay BCC 9P 9C8 Canada. Email: ascentaspirations@shaw.ca. Website: www.ascentaspirations.ca. Contact: David Fraser, Editor.

TIPS "Short fiction should, first of all tell, a good story, take the reader to new and interesting imaginary or real places. Short fiction should use language lyrically and effectively, be experimental in either form or content and take the reader into realms where they can analyze and think about the human condition. Write with passion for your material, be concise and economical and let the reader work to unravel your story. In terms of editing, always proofread to the point where what you submit is the best it possibly can be. Never be discouraged if your work is not ac-cepted; it may just not be the right fit for a current publication."

ASHEVILLE POETRY REVIEW

P.O. Box 7086, Asheville NC 28802. (828)649-0217. Website: www.ashevillereview.com. **Contact:** Keith Flynn, founder/managing editor.

MAGAZINES NEEDS *Asheville Poetry Review*, published annually, prints "the best regional, national, and international poems we can find. We publish translations, interviews, essays, historical perspectives, and book reviews as well." Wants "quality work with well-crafted ideas married to a dynamic style. Any subject matter is fit to be considered so long as the language is vivid with a clear sense of rhythm. We subscribe to the Borges dictum that great poetry is a combination of 'algebra and fire.'" Has published poetry by Sherman Alexie, Eavan Boland, Gary Snyder, Colette Inez, Robert Bly, and Fred Chappell. *Asheville Poetry Review* is 160-300 pages, digest-sized, perfect-bound, laminated, with full-color cover. Receives about 8,000 submissions/year, accepts about 5%. Press run is 3,000. Subscription: $22.50 for 2 years, $43.50 for 4 years. Sample: $13. **"We prefer poets purchase a sample copy prior to submitting."** Time between acceptance and publication is up to one year. Poems are circulated to an editorial board. Seldom comments on rejected poems. Occasionally publishes theme issues. Guidelines available for SASE or on website. Responds in up to 7 months. Pays 1 contributor's copy. Rights revert back to author upon publication. Reviews books/chapbooks of poetry. Send materials for review consideration.

HOW TO CONTACT Submit 3-5 poems at a time. No previously published poems or simultaneous submissions. No e-mail submissions. Cover letter is required. Include comprehensive bio, recent publishing credits, and SASE. Reads submissions January 15-July 15.

ASININE POETRY

E-mail: editor@asininepoetry.com. Website: www.asininepoetry.com. **Contact:** R. Narvaez, editor. Founded in 2000, AsininePoetry.com is an online literary journal featuring silly, salacious, satirical, and/or sick prose and poetry. *asinine poetry and prose*, published monthly online, "features 10-12 new works each month. We specialize in poetry that does not take itself too seriously." Wants "any form of poetry, but for us the poetry must be in a humorous, parodic, or satirical style. We prefer well-crafted poems that may contain serious elements or cover serious subjects—but which are also amusing, absurd, or hilarious." Does not want serious, straightforward poems. **MAGAZINES NEEDS** *asinine poetry and prose*, published monthly online, "features 10-12 new works each month. We specialize in poetry that does not take itself too seriously." Wants "any form of poetry, but for us the poetry must be in a humorous, parodic, or satirical style. We prefer well-crafted poems that may contain serious elements or cover serious subjects—but which are also amusing, absurd, or hilarious." Does not want serious, straightforward poems. Has published poetry by Hal Sirowitz, William Trowbridge, Elizabeth Swados, Daniel Thomas Moran, and Colonel Drunky Bob. Receives about 1,000 poems/year, accepts about 10%.

HOW TO CONTACT Submit 3-4 poems at a time. Lines/poem: 50 maximum. Considers previously published poems and simultaneous submissions. Accepts e-mail (pasted into body of message).

CONTEST/AWARD OFFERINGS Sponsors 1 contest/year. Guidelines available on website.

ASSENT

11 Orkney Close, Stenson Fields, Derbyshire DE24 3LW, England. E-mail: nottposoc@btinternet.com. Website: nottinghampoetrysociety.co.uk. **Contact:** Adrian Buckner, editor.

MAGAZINES NEEDS *Assent*, formerly *Poetry Nottingham*, published 3 times/year, features articles and reviews in addition to poetry. Open to submissions from UK and overseas. Has published poetry from Europe, Australasia, the U.S., and Japan. *Assent* is 6x8, perfect-bound, professionally printed. Receives about 2,000 submissions/year, accepts about 120. Press run is 250. Single copy: £4; subscription: £12 UK, £20 overseas. Checks payable to Poetry Nottingham Publications. Subscribers who wish to pay in U.S. dollars please send check for $25, payable to Karen Crosbie, to 1036 Menlo Avenue, Apt 103, Los Angeles, CA, 90006. Single copy $7.

HOW TO CONTACT Submit up to 6 poems at a time. No previously published poems. Cover letter is required. "Send SAE and 3 IRCs for stamps. No need to query." Responds in 2 months. Pays 1 contributor's copy. Staff reviews books of poetry, usually confined to UK publications.

CONTEST/AWARD OFFERINGS The Nottingham Open Poetry Competition offers cash prizes, annual subscriptions, and publication in *Assent*. Open to all. Guidelines available on website.

ATLANTA REVIEW

P.O. Box 8248, Atlanta GA 31106. E-mail: atlrev@yahoo.com. Website: www.atlantareview.com. **Contact:** Dan Veach, Editor/Publisher.

Work published in *Atlanta Review* has been included in *The Best American Poetry* and *The Pushcart Prize*.

MAGAZINES NEEDS *Atlanta Review*, published semiannually, is devoted primarily to poetry, but occasionally features interviews and b&w artwork. Wants "quality poetry of genuine human appeal." Has published poetry by Seamus Heaney, Billy Collins, Derek Walcott, Maxine Kumin, Alicia Stallings, Gunter Grass, Eugenio Montale, and Thomas Lux. Atlanta Review is 128 pages, digest-sized, professionally printed on acid-free paper, flat-spined, with glossy color cover. Receives about 10,000 poems/year, accepts about 1%. Press run is 2,500. Single copy: $6; subscription: $10. Sample: $5.

HOW TO CONTACT Submit no more than 5 poems at a time. No previously published poems. No e-mail submissions from within the U.S.; postal submissions only. Include SASE for reply. "Authors living outside the United States and Canada may submit work via e-mail." Cover letter is preferred. Include brief bio. Put name and address on each poem. Reads submissions according to the following deadlines: June 1 for Fall; December 1 for Spring. "While we do read year round, response time may be slower during summer and the winter holidays." Time between acceptance and publication is 6 months. Seldom comments on rejected poems. Guidelines available for SASE, by e-mail, or on website. Responds in 1 month. Pays 2 contributor's copies, author's discounts on additional copies. Acquires first North American serial rights.

CONTEST/AWARD OFFERINGS *Atlanta Review* sponsors the Poetry 2012 International Poetry Competition (see separate listing in Contests & Awards).

THE ATLANTIC MONTHLY

The Watergate, 600 New Hampshire Ave, NW, Washington DC 20037. (202)266-6000. Website: www.theatlantic.com. **Contact:** C. Michael Curtis, fiction editor. Editorial Office, The Watergate, 600 New Hampshire Ave. NW, Washington, DC 20037. (202)266-6000. Fax: (202)266-6001. E-mail: dbarber@theatlantic.com. Website: www.theatlantic.com. "Interest is in the broadest possible range of work: traditional forms and free verse, the meditative lyric and the "light" or comic poem, the work of the famous and the work of the unknown. We have long been committed to the discovery of new poets. Our one limitation is length; we are unable to publish very long poems."General magazine for an educated readership with broad cultural and public-affairs interests. "The Atlantic considers unsolicited manuscripts, either fiction or nonfiction. A general familiarity with what we have published in the past is the best guide to our needs and preferences. Manuscripts must be typewritten and double-spaced. Receipt of manuscripts will be acknowledged if accompanied by a self-addressed stamped envelope. Manuscripts will not be returned. **At this time, the print magazine does not read submissions sent via fax or e-mail.** TheAtlantic.com no longer accepts unsolicited submissions."

MAGAZINES NEEDS Wants "the broadest possible range of work: traditional forms and free verse, the meditative lyric and the 'light' or comic poem, the work of the famous and the work of the unknown."

HOW TO CONTACT Submit 2-6 poems at a time. No previously published poems or simultaneous submissions. No e-mail or disk submissions; postal submissions only. SASE required. Responds in 4-6 weeks. Pays upon acceptance. Always sends prepublication galleys. Acquires first North American serial rights only.

TIPS "Writers should be aware that this is not a market for beginner's work (nonfiction and fiction), nor is it truly for intermediate work. Study this magazine before sending only your best, most professional work. When making first contact, cover letters are sometimes helpful, particularly if they cite prior publications or involvement in writing programs. Common mistakes: melodrama, inconclusiveness, lack of development, unpersuasive characters and/or dialogue."

⊕○⊜ ATLANTIC PACIFIC PRESS

The Wale Inn Publishing House, P.O. Box 4394, Danbury CT 06813. (508)994-7869. Fax: (774) 263 2839. E-mail: lyric_songs@yahoo.com. Website: atlanticpacificpress.com. **Contact:** Christine Walen, editor. P.O. Box 4394, Danbury, CT 06813. (508)994-7869; (774) 263 2839. E-mail: lyric_songs@yahoo.com. Website:

atlanticpacificpress.com. Quarterly. Has published poetry by D. Davis Phillips, Michael Foster, Lynn Veach Sadler, James Hoggard, Mediha F. Saliba, Sheryl L. Nelms, Marjorie Bixler, Sheila Golburgh Johnson, James Fowler, Claudia Barnett. APP is digest sized, 90+ pages, saddle stapled. Guidelines: send for with a SASE. Deadlines: Spg/Feb 20, Sum/May 20, Fall/Aug 20, Win/Nov 20. Single: $10 Subscription: $30/year.Atlantic Pacific Press is a quarterly journal of fiction, drama, poetry, prose poetry, flash fiction, lyrics, cartoons, sci-fi, fantasy, veterans/military, romance, mystery, horror, westerns, family life, children's stories, nonfiction, art, and photography. No porn.

CONTEST/AWARD OFFERINGS Guidelines: send for with a SASE. Pays contributor copy. Deadlines: Spg/Feb 1, Sum/May 1, Fall/Aug 1, Win/Nov 1.

ALSO OFFERS Offers annual drama contest. Deadline January 30. Send for guidelines with a SASE.

TIPS "Consider taking a writing class or workshop. Read your mss to someone before sending."

◑ AUTUMN SKY POETRY

5263 Arctic Circle, Emmaus PA 18049, USA. E-mail: autumnskypoetryeditor@gmail.com. Website: www.autumnskypoetry.com. **Contact:** Christine Klocek-Lim, editor.

MAGAZINES NEEDS Wants formal verse, free verse, prose poetry. "I'm open to everything, but each poem must intrigue me within the first 4-6 lines. I want to be surprised, moved, interested, impressed." Does not want badly rhymed poems, overemphasis on -ing words, too many adjectives, poems that are all emotion, no craft or all craft and no emotion. Technical skill and voice should balance within the poem. Has published poetry by David McAleavey, Anna Evans, Carolyn Kreiter-Foronda, David Landrum.

HOW TO CONTACT Submit up to 4 poems at a time, 70 lines maximum. Considers previously published and simultaneous submissions. Accepts e-mail submissions only, pasted into body of message. No cover letter necessary. Include a bio with poems, use standard 12 pt font in e-mail. Accepts poems year round, read the last two weeks before issue is released. Submit seasonal poems 3 months in advance. Time between acceptance and publication is 1 week. Sometimes comments on rejected poems. Sometimes publishes theme issues. Themes and guidelines available on website. Responds in 1 week to 3 months. Always sends e-mail receipt of submission. Always sends prepublication galleys. Acquires First Electronic Rights upon acceptance of poems. Rights return to author upon publication. Reserves right to archive poem indefinitely online, but will remove at request of author.

⦿ AVOCET, A JOURNAL OF NATURE POEMS

P.O. Box 1717, Southold NY 11971. Website: www.avocetreview.com. **Contact:** Peter C. Leverich, Editor. P.O. Box 1717, Southold, NY 11971. E-mail: peter@avocetreview.com. Website: www.avocetreview.com. **MAGAZINES NEEDS** *Avocet, A Journal of Nature Poems*, published quarterly, is "devoted to poets who find meaning in their lives from the natural world." Wants "imagist/transcendental poetry that explores the beauty and divinity in nature." Does not want "poems that have rhyme, cliché, or abstraction." Has published poetry by Louis Daniel Brodsky, Gary Every, Ruth Goring, Gayle Elen Harvey, Lyn Lifshin, Holly Rose Diane Shaw, and Kristin Camitta Zimet. *Avocet* is 30-36 pages, 4 1/4x5 1/2, professionally printed, saddle-stapled, with card cover. Single copy: $6; subscription: $24. Make checks payable to Peter C. Leverich.

HOW TO CONTACT Submit 3-5 poems at a time. Considers previously published poems, if acknowledged. Cover letter with e-mail address is helpful. Include SASE for reply only; mss will not be returned. Time between acceptance and publication is up to 3 months. Responds in up to 2 months.

⦿⦿ BABEL: THE MULTILINGUAL, MULTICULTURAL ONLINE JOURNAL AND COMMUNITY OF ARTS AND IDEAS

E-mail: submissions@towerofbabel.com. Website: http://towerofbabel.com. **Contact:** Malcolm Lawrence, Editor-in-Chief. "Babel is an electronic zine recognized by the UN as one of the most important social and human sciences online periodicals. Writers whose work discriminates against the opposite sex, different cultures, or belief systems will not be considered." Time between acceptance and publication vis usually no more than 2 months." Seldom comments on rejected poems. Guidelines available on website. Responds in 2-4 weeks. Reviews books/chapbooks of poetry and other magazines, single- and multi-book format. Open to unsolicited reviews. Publishes regional reports from international stringers all over the planet, as well as features, round table discussions, fiction, columns, poetry, erotica, travelogues, and reviews of all the arts and editorials. We're interested in fiction, non-fiction and poetry from all over the world, including multicultural or multilingual work, as well as poetry that has been translated from or into another language, as long as it is also in English. We also appreciate gay/lesbian and bisexual poetry. Cover letter is required. Reviews books/chapbooks of poetry and other magazines, single- and multi-book format. Open to unsolicited reviews. Send materials for review consideration.

⦿ Babel: The multilingual, multicultural online journal and community of arts and ideas. E-mail: submissions@towerofbabel.com. Website: http://towerofbabel.com. (Specialized: bilingual/foreign language) Acquisitions: Malcolm Lawrence, editor-in-chief. Estab. 1995. *Babel* is recognized by the UN as one of the most important Social and Human Sciences Online Periodicals. We are currently looking for WordPress bloggers in the following languages: Arabic, Bulgarian, Bengali, Catalan, Czech, Welsh, Danish, German, English, Esperanto, Spanish, Persian, Finnish, Faroese, French, Hebrew, Croatian, Indonesian, Italian, Japanese, Korean, Latvian, Malay, Dutch, Polish, Portuguese, Russian, Albanian, Serbian, Swedish, Tamil, Thai, Ukrainian, Urdu, Uzbek, Vietnamese and Chinese. Our bloggers include James Schwartz, the first out gay poet raised in the Old Order Amish community in Southwestern Michigan and author of the book *The Literary Party*; Susanna Zaraysky, author of the book *Language Is Music: Making People Multilingual*; James RovirAssistant Professor of English and Program Chair of Humanities at Tiffin University and author of the book *Blake & Kierkegaard: Creation and Anxiety*; and Paul B. Miller, Assistant Professor Dept. of French and Italian at Vanderbilt Univ. Publishes regional reports from international stringers all over the planet, as well as features, round table discussions, fiction, columns, poetry, erotica, travelogues, and reviews of all the arts and editorials. We're interested in fiction, non-fiction and poetry from all over the world, including multicultural or multilingual work, as well as poetry that has been translated from or into another language, as long as it is also in English. We also appreciate gay/lesbian and bisexual poetry. Cover letter is required. Seldom comments on rejected poems. Reviews books/chapbooks of poetry and other magazines, single- and multi-book format. Open to unsolicited reviews.

MAGAZINES NEEDS WordPress bloggers in the following languages: Arabic, Bulgarian, Bengali, Catalan, Czech, Welsh, Danish, German, English, Esperanto, Spanish, Persian, Finnish, Faroese, French, Hebrew, Croatian, Indonesian, Italian, Japanese, Korean, Latvian, Malay, Dutch, Polish, Portuguese, Russian, Albanian, Serbian, Swedish, Tamil, Thai, Ukrainian, Urdu, Uzbek, Vietnamese and Chinese.

HOW TO CONTACT Submit no more than 10 poems at a time. Considers previously published poems and simultaneous submissions. Accepts e-mail submissions only. Cover letter is required. "Please send submissions with a résumé or bio as a Microsoft Word or RTF document attached to e-mail."

ADDITIONAL INFORMATION Our bloggers include James Schwartz, the first out gay poet raised in the Old Order Amish community in Southwestern Michigan and author of the book *The Literary Party*; Susanna Zaraysky, author of the book *Language Is Music: Making People Multilingual*; James RovirAssistant Professor of English and Program Chair of Humanities at Tiffin University and author of the book *Blake & Kierkegaard: Creation and Anxiety*; and Paul B. Miller, Assistant Professor Department of French and Italian at Vanderbilt University.

TIPS "We would like to see more fiction with first-person male characters written by female authors, as well as more fiction first-person female characters written by male authors. We would also like to see that dynamic in action when it comes to other languages, cultures, races, classes, sexual orientations and ages. Know what you are writing about and write passionately about it."

BABEL FRUIT

E-mail: babelfruit@live.com. Website: http://web.mac.com/renkat/BABEL_FRUIT/BabelFruit.html. BA de OliveirAssoc. Editor. **Contact:** Ren Powell, Founding Editor; Cati Porter, Assoc. Editor. "Ezine that publishes literature of exile, expatriation, repatriation, integration and exploration. We want to read poetry 'under the influence of 'the other.' Travel, look around

or reach within to wherever you see the other." Invites submissions from new and established poets. Send 4 poems max (or 5 pages, whichever comes first) with cover letter. Accepts simultaneous and previously published submissions; see guidelines online. Does not pay.

"Ezine that publishes literature of exile, expatriation, repatriation, integration and exploration. We want to read poetry 'under the influence of 'the other.' Travel, look around or reach within. Wherever you see the other."

HOW TO CONTACT Send email to: babelfruit@live.com

ADDITIONAL INFORMATION "Published biannually and nominates contributors for the Pushcart and other awards."

TIPS "If you use an attachment to submit, use: babel-fruit.submission.doc and put your name in the subject line. We invite new and established writers."

BABYBUG

Carus Publishing, 70 East Lake St., Chicago IL 60601. E-mail: babybug@caruspub.com. Website: http://www.cricketmag.com. **Contact:** Marianne Carus, editor-in-chief. *BABYBUG Magazine*, published 9 times/year, is a read-aloud magazine for ages 6 months to 2 years. Wants "rhythmic, rhyming" short poems. *BABYBUG* is 24 pages, $6^1\!_4$x7, printed on cardstock with nontoxic glued spine. Subscription: $33.95/year (9 issues). Sample: $5; sample pages available on website.

HOW TO CONTACT Submit no more than 5 poems at a time. Lines/poem: 8 lines maximum. Considers previously published poems. Include SASE. Guidelines available for SASE or on website. Responds in 6 months.

TIPS "*Babybug* would like to reach as many children's authors and artists as possible for original contributions, but our standards are very high, and we will accept only top-quality material. Before attempting to write for *Babybug*, be sure to familiarize yourself with this age child. Imagine having to read your story or poem—out loud—50 times or more! That's what parents will have to do. Babies and toddlers demand, 'Read it again!' Your material must hold up under repetition. And humor is much appreciated by all."

BABYSUE®

babysue ATTN: LMNOP aka dONW7, P.O. Box 15749, Chattanooga TN 373415. E-mail: LMNOP@babysue.

com. Website: www.babysue.com; www.LMNOP.com. **Contact:** Don W. Seven, Editor/Publisher. *babysue* is an ongoing online magazine featuring continually updated cartoons, poems, literature and reviews. Single issue: $5.

MAGAZINES NEEDS *babysue*, published twice/year, offers obtuse humor for the extremely open-minded. "We are open to all styles, but prefer short poems." No restrictions. Has published poetry by Edward Mycue, Susan Andrews, and Barry Bishop. *babysue* is 32 pages, offset-printed. "We print prose, poems, and cartoons. We usually accept about 5% of what we receive." Sample: $5. Payment may be made in either cash, check, or money order payable to M. Fievet.

HOW TO CONTACT Considers previously published poems and simultaneous submissions. Seldom comments on rejected poems. Responds "immediately, if we are interested." Pays 1 contributor's copy. "We do occasionally review other magazines."

● BACKSTREET

P.O. Box 1377, Berthoud CO 80513. E-mail: clarkreview@earthlink.net. **Contact:** Ray Foreman, Editor. P.O. Box 1377 Berthoud CO 80513. (970)669-5175. E-mail: clarkreview@earthlink.net.

MAGAZINES NEEDS *Backstreet*, published 6 times/year, wants "strong, clear narrative poems relevant to the times and the human condition, and appropriate for a readership of experienced poets. We are a 'poet's magazine for poets' whose purpose is keeping them writing by providing an easy and regular publishing outlet. Has published poetry by Anselm Brocki, Charles Ries, Laurel Speer, Arthur Gotlieb, and Steven Levi. *Backstreet* "has a special layout that has the equivalent content of a 36-page magazine," laser-printed, stapled, with paper cover. Receives about 600 poems/year, accepts about 200. Press run is 150. Single copy: $2; subscription: $10 for 10 issues. Make checks payable to R. Foreman.

HOW TO CONTACT Submit 3 poems at a time. Lines/poem: 15 minimum, 50 maximum. "Maximum width is 65 characters per line." Considers previously published poems and simultaneous submissions. No e-mail or disk submissions. "SASE for first submission only. No cover letter, bio, or credits list. No graphic layout. Flush left, preferably in Times Roman or Garamond. No long skinnys. Disposable sharp hard copies. Your work speaks for you." Reads submissions year round. Time between acceptance

and publication is 3 months. Sometimes comments on rejected poems. Responds in one week to one month. Acquires one-time rights. Rights revert to poet upon publication.

◑ THE BALTIMORE REVIEW

P.O. Box 36418, Towson MD 21286. Website: www.baltimorereview.org. **Contact:** Susan Muaddi Darraj, managing editor. *The Baltimore Review* is 144 pages, 6x9, offset-lithograph-printed, perfect-bound, with 10-pt. CS1 cover. Subscription: $15/year, $28 for 2 years. Sample: $10 (includes $2 p&h). Make checks payable to *The Baltimore Review*. Reads submissions year round. Time between acceptance and publication is up to 4-6 months. "Poems are circulated to at least two reviewers." Sometimes comments on rejected poems. Guidelines available on website. Responds in up to 4 months. Submit between 1-4 poems. No previously published work. Payment is in copies."The Baltimore Review publishes poetry, fiction, and creative nonfiction from Baltimore and beyond."

○ "We publish work of high literary quality from established and new writers. No specific preferences regarding theme or style, and all are considered."

HOW TO CONTACT Submit 1-4 poems at a time. Considers simultaneous submissions, "but notify us immediately if your work is accepted elsewhere"; no previously published poems. Accepts submissions only via online submissions system at website (www.baltimorereview.org/submissions/). Cover letter is preferred.

CONTEST/AWARD OFFERINGS Sponsors an annual poetry contest. Offers 1st Prize: $300 plus publication in *The Baltimore Review*; 2nd Prize: $150; 3rd Prize: $50. Submit 1-4 poems (no more than 5 pages total). All forms and styles accepted, including prose poems. Guidelines available on website. **Entry fee:** $12 (includes copy of issue in which 1st-Prize winner is published) or $20 (includes one-year subscription).

TIPS "Please read what is being published in other literary journals, including our own. As in any other profession, writers must know what the trends and the major issues are in the field." ,"We look for compelling stories and a masterful use of the English language. We want to feel that we have never heard this story, or this voice, before. Read the kinds of publications you want your work to appear in. Make your reader believe and care."

BARBARIC YAWP

Boneworld Publishing, 3700 County Rt. 24, Russell NY 13684. **Established 1996. Contact:** John and Nancy Berbrich, editors.

MAGAZINES NEEDS *Barbaric Yawp*, published quarterly, prints "the best fiction, poetry, and essays available." Encourages beginning writers. "We are not preachers of any particular poetic or literary school. We publish any type of quality material appropriate for our intelligent and wide-awake audience; all types considered: blank, free, found, concrete, traditional rhymed and metered forms." Does not want "any pornography, gratuitous violence, or any whining, pissing, or moaning." Considers poetry by teens. Has published poetry by Nancy Henry, Mark Spitzer, and Jeff Grimshaw. *Barbaric Yawp* is a 60-page booklet, stapled, with 67 lb. cover. Receives 2,000 poems/year, accepts about 5%. Press run is 150. Single copy: $4; subscription: $15/year (4 issues). Make checks payable to John Berbrich.

HOW TO CONTACT Submit up to 5 poems at a time. Lines/poem: 50 maximum. Considers previously published poems and simultaneous submissions. Cover letter is preferred (1 page). Include a short publication history (if available) and a brief bio. Include SASE. Reads submissions year round. Time between acceptance and publication is up to 6 months. Often comments on rejected poems. Guidelines available for SASE. Responds in up to 2 months. Pays 1 contributor's copy. Acquires one-time rights.

BARROW STREET

Website: www.barrowstreet.org. P.O. Box 1831, New York NY 10156. E-mail: infobarrow@gmail.com. Website: www.barrowstreet.org. Established 1998. **Contact:** Lorna Blake, Patricia Carlin, Peter Covino, and Melissa Hotchkiss, editors.

Poetry published in *Barrow Street* is often selected for *The Best American Poetry*.

MAGAZINES NEEDS *Barrow Street,* published annually, "is dedicated to publishing new and established poets." Wants "poetry of the highest quality; open to all styles and forms." Has published poetry by Molly Peacock, Lyn Hejinian, Carl Phillips, Marie Ponsot, Charles Bernstein, and Stephen Burt. *Barrow Street* is 96-120 pages, digest-sized, professionally printed, perfect-bound, with glossy cardstock cover with color or b&w photography. Receives about 3,000 poems/year, accepts about 3%. Press run is 1,000. Subscription: $18 for 2years, $25 for 3 years. Sample: $10.

HOW TO CONTACT Submit up to 5 poems at a time. Considers simultaneous submissions (when notified); no previously published poems. Cover letter is preferred. Include brief bio. Must have name, address, e-mail, and phone on each page submitted or submission will not be considered. Reads submissions October 1 - March 31. Poems circulated to an editorial board. Guidelines available on website. Responds 2-9 months. Does not return or respond to submissions made outside the reading period. Always sends prepublication galleys. Pays 2 contributor's copies. Acquires first rights.

CONTEST/AWARD OFFERINGS The Barrow Street Press Book Contest (see separate listing in Contests & Awards).

BATEAU

P.O. Box 1584, Northampton MA 01061. (413)586-2494. E-mail: info@bateaupress.org. Website: www.bateaupress.org. **Contact:** James Grinwis, editor. "*Bateau* subscribes to no trend but serves to represent as wide a cross-section of contemporary writing as possible. For this reason, readers will most likely love and hate at least something in each issue. We consider this a good thing. To us, it means Bateau is eclectic, open-ended, and not mired in a particular strain."

MAGAZINES NEEDS "*Bateau*, published semiannually, subscribes to no trend but serves to represent as wide a cross-section of contemporary writing as possible. For this reason, readers will most likely love and hate at least something in each issue. We consider this a good thing. To us, it means Bateau is eclectic, open-ended, and not mired in a particular strain." Has published poetry by Tomaz Salamun, John Olsen, Michael Burkhardt, Joshua Marie Wilkinson, Allison Titus, Allan Peterson, Dean Young. *Bateau* is around 80 pages, digest-sized, offset print, perfect-bound, with a 100% recycled letterpress cover. Receives about 5,000 poems/year, accepts about 60. Press run is 250. Single copy: $12; subscription $24. Make checks payable to Bateau Press.

HOW TO CONTACT Submit 5 poems at a time, up to 2 pages. Considers simultaneous submissions, no previously published poems or work concurrently available online. Work should only be submitted via our online submission upload system or the postal system. Thanks! Reads submissions year round. Time between acceptance and publication is 3-8 months. Poems are circulated to an editorial board. Often comments on rejected poems. Sometimes publishes theme issues. Upcoming themes available on website; guidelines availalbe for SASE or on website. Responds in 3-6 months. Sometimes sends prepublication galleries. Pays 2 contributor's copies. Acquires first North American serial rights, electronic rights. "We reserve the right to display work on internet for promotional, advertising, and to store, transmit, and distribute electronic copies of the work as required to facilitate the printing and distribution process of *Bateau*." Rights revert to poet upon publication.

BATEAU PRESS

E-mail: info@bateaupress.org; ashley@bateaupress.org; submit@bateaupress.org. Website: www.bateaupress.org. **Contact:** Ashley Schaffer, managing editor. "*Bateau*, published semiannually, subscribes to no trend but serves to represent as wide a cross-section of contemporary writing as possible. For this reason, readers will most likely love and hate at least something in each issue. We consider this a good thing. To us, it means Bateau is eclectic, open-ended, and not mired in a particular strain." Has published poetry by Tomaz Salamun, John Olsen, Michael Burkhardt, Joshua Marie Wilkinson, Allison Titus, Allan Peterson. *Bateau* is around 80 pages, digest-sized, offset print, perfect-bound, with a 100% recycled letterpress cover. Receives about 5,000 poems/year, accepts about 50. Press run is 250. Single copy: $10; subscription $18. Make checks payable to Bateau Press. Submit 5 poems at a time, up to 2 pages. Considers simultaneous submissions, no previously published poems or work concurrently available online. Reads submissions year round. Time between acceptance and publication is 3-8 months. Poems are circulated to an editorial board. Often comments on rejected poems. Sometimes publishes theme issues. Upcoming themes available on website; guidelines availalbe for SASE or on website. Responds in 3-6 months. Sometimes sends prepublication galleries. Pays 2 contributor's copies. Acquires first North American serial rights, electronic rights. "We reserve the right to display work on internet for promotional, advertising, and to store, transmit, and distribute electronic copies of the work as required

to facilitate the printing and distribution process of *Bateau*." Rights revert to poet upon publication.

"*Bateau* subscribes to no trend but serves to represent as wide a cross-section of contemporary writing as possible. For this reason, readers will most likely love and hate at least something in each issue. We consider this a good thing. To us, it means Bateau is eclectic, open-ended, and not mired in a particular strain."

HOW TO CONTACT Submit up to five poems electronically and by mail. Work should only be submitted via our online submission upload system or the postal system. Accepts simultaneous submissions; no previously published poetry.

TIPS "We recommend ordering a copy to better understand our aesthetics. It will save you and us a lot of time and resources."

BAYOU

English Dept. University of New Orleans, 2000 Lakeshore Dr., New Orleans LA 70148. (504)280-5423. E-mail: bayou@uno.edu. Website: http://137.30.242.125/cww/bayou/index.cfm. Accepts material written in a variety of styles and about a broad range of topics. *Bayou* is packed with a range of material from established, award-winning authors as well as new voices on the rise. Recent contributors include Eric Trethewey,Virgil Suarez, Marilyn Hacker, Sean Beaudoin, Tom Whalen, Mark Doty, Philip Cioffari, Lyn Lifshin, Timothy Liu and Gaylord Brewer. And in one issue every year, *Bayou* features the winner of the annual Tennessee Williams/New Orleans Literary Festival One-Act Play Competition. Subscription: $15. Single Issue: $8. Sample: $7."A non-profit journal for the arts, each issue of *Bayou Magazine* contains beautiful fiction, nonfiction and poetry. From quirky shorts to more traditional stories, we are committed to publishing solid work. Regardless of style, at *Bayou* we are always interested first in a well-told tale. Our poetry and prose are filled with memorable characters observing their world, acknowledging both the mundane and the sublime, often at once, and always with an eye toward beauty. *Bayou* is packed with a range of material from established, award-winning authors as well as new voices on the rise. Recent contributors include Eric Trethewey, Virgil Suarez, Marilyn Hacker, Sean Beaudoin, Tom Whalen, Mark Doty, Philip Cioffari, Lyn Lifshin, Timothy Liu and Gaylord Brewer. And in one issue every year, *Bayou* features the winner of the annual Tennessee Williams/New Orleans Literary Festival One-Act Play Competition."

HOW TO CONTACT Submit no more than 5 poems at a time. No e-mail or disk submissions. "A brief cover letter is necessary, but don't tell us your life story, explain your poems, or tell us how wonderful your poems are. Do give us your contact information." Reads submissions year round. Responds in 4-6 months. After publication in *Bayou*, all rights revert to the author. Payment is 2 contributor's copies plus a year's subscription to the magazine. All work published in Bayou is considered for the annual O. Henry Awards and the Pushcart Prize as well as Best American Essays.

ADDITIONAL INFORMATION Reads submissions year round, "but we tend to slow down in the summer months." Time between acceptance and publication varies "but we give the author a general idea when the work is accepted." Poems are circulated to an editorial board. Never comments on rejected poems. Guidelines available in magazine, for SASE, or by e-mail. Responds in 4 months.

TIPS "Do not submit in more than one genre at a time. Don't send a second submission until you receive a response to the first."

◑ BEAR CREEK HAIKU

P.O. Box 3787, Boulder CO 80307. **Contact:** Ayaz Daryl Nielsen, Editor. Small publication (3 x 11) published irregularly; 6-7/year recently. Has published poetry by Quinn Rennerfeldt, Carl Mayfield, HeyokAnd Sean Perkins. *bear creek haiku* is 24 pages, photocopied on legal-sized blue paper cut in thirds lengthwise, stacked 3-high, folded, and stapled. Receives about 6,000 poems/year, accepts about 5%. Press run is about 200/issue. Single copy: free for SASE; subscription: $5. Make checks payable to Daryl Nielsen. **Subscriptions:** One year $5, renewed for free yearly if subscriber asks. Send SASE for a sample issue. **Submissions:** *Bear Creek Haiku* accepts haiku and poetry of 11 lines or less at any time via postal mail (include SASE with all submissions). Reply time and time between acceptance and publication vary. Published poet receives two copies if a 24-page issue, one copy if a 36-page issue (size affects postage rate)."

◔ Reads submissions year round.

MAGAZINES NEEDS *bear creek haiku* prints haiku/senryu and any form/style less than 15 lines.

HOW TO CONTACT Submit 5-20 poems at a time. Considers previously published or unpublished poems, translations, and simultaneous submissions. "Include name, address, and several poems on each page. Keep your postage expenses at two first-class stamps, one of which is on the SASE." Pays 2 contributor's copies.

◐◑ THE BEATNIK COWBOY

Box 603 Mail Box ETC, 221/19 M.5.T. Nakleay, A. Banglamung Chonburi , Thailand. E-mail: randall_ro@yahoo.com; beatnik_cowboy@yahoo.com.au. **Contact:** David Soloman, assistant editor.

MAGAZINES NEEDS *The Beatnik Cowboy*, published quarterly, wants " Beat-influenced poetry from all poets. We are a young and vibrant magazine, seeking to publish the best of the best poets of the world." Have published poetry by Steve Dalchinsky, David Pointer, Susan Maurer, Randall Rogers, and Joe Speer.

HOW TO CONTACT Submit 5 poems at a time. Shorter poems preferred. Considers previously published poems and simultaneous submissions. Accepts e-mail (as attachment) and disk submissions. Either post poems in the body of the text or as Word attachment. SAE with IRCs required for return of poems. Reads submissions year round. Submit seasonal poems 2 months in advance. Time between acceptance and publication is 3 months. "At times if we like your stuff we will encourage you to send in more." Sometimes comments on rejected poems. Guidelines available in the magazine, by SASE, or by e-mail request. Responds in 2 months. Acquires one-time rights.

◔◑ BELLEVUE LITERARY REVIEW

NYU Langone Medical Center, Department of Medicine, 550 First Ave., OBV-A612, New York NY 10016. (212)263-3973. E-mail: info@BLReview.org. E-mail: stacy.bodziak@nyumc.org. Website: www.blreview.org. **Contact:** Stacy Bodziak, managing editor. *Bellevue Literary Review*, published semiannually, prints "works of fiction, nonfiction, and poetry that touch upon relationships to the human body, illness, health, and healing." Has published poetry by Rafael Campo, Sharon Olds, James Tate, David Wagoner, John Stone, and Floyd Skloot.(Specialized: humanity, health, and healing) Member: CLMP.

◔ Work published in *Bellevue Literary Review* has appeared in *The Pushcart Prize*.

MAGAZINES NEEDS *Bellevue Literary Review* is 160 pages, digest-sized, perfect-bound, includes ads. Receives about 1,800 poems/year, accepts about 3%. Press run is 5,000; distributed free to lit mag conferences, promotions, and other contacts. Single copy: $9; subscription: $15/year, $35 for 3 years (plus $5/year postage to Canada, $8/year postage foreign). Make checks payable to *Bellevue Literary Review*.

HOW TO CONTACT Submit up to 3 poems at a time. Lines/poem: prefers poems of one page or less. Considers simultaneous submissions. No previously published poems; work published on personal blogs or Web sites will be considered on a case-by-case basis. No e-mail or disk submissions. "We accept poems via regular mail and through our website; when submitting via regular mail, please include SASE." Cover letter is preferred. Reads submissions year round. Time between acceptance and publication is about 6-7 months. "Poems are reviewed by two independent readers, then sent to an editor." Sometimes comments on rejected poems. Sometimes publishes theme issues. Upcoming themes available on website. Guidelines available for SASE or on website. Responds in 3-5 months. Always sends prepublication galleys.

CONTEST/AWARD OFFERINGS The annual *Bellevue Literary Review* Prize for Poetry (see separate listing in Contests & Awards).

BELLINGHAM REVIEW

Mail Stop 9053, Western Washington University, Bellingham WA 98225. (360)650-4863. E-mail: bhreview@wwu.edu. Website: www.wwu.edu/bhreview. Brenda Miller, editor-in-chief. **Contact:** Christopher Carlson, managing editor. *Bellingham Review* is digest-sized, perfect-bound, with matte cover. Subscription: $12/year, $20 for 2 years, $20/year for libraries and institutions. Sample: $12. Make checks payable to *Bellingham Review*. Considers simultaneous submissions with notification. Guidelines available with SASE or on website. Acquires first North American serial rights. Annual nonprofit magazine published once a year in the Spring. Seeks "Literature of palpable quality: poems stories and essays so beguiling they invite us to touch their essence. The *Bellingham Review* hungers for a kind of writing that nudges the limits of form, or executes traditional forms exquisitely."

The editors are actively seeking submissions of creative nonfiction, as well as stories that push the boundaries of the form. The Tobias Wolff Award in Fiction Contest runs December 1-March 15; see website for guidelines or send SASE.

HOW TO CONTACT No e-mail submissions; accepts submissions by postal mail only. Include SASE. Reads submissions September 15-February 1 only (submissions must be postmarked within this reading period). Responds in 2 months.

CONTEST/AWARD OFFERINGS The 49th Parallel Poetry Award (see separate listing in Contests & Awards).

TIPS "Open submission period is from Sept. 15-Dec. 15. Manuscripts arriving between December 16 and September 14 will be returned unread. The *Bellingham Review* holds 3 annual contests: the 49th Parallel Poetry Award, the Annie Dillard Award in Nonfiction, and the Tobias Wolff Award in Fiction. Submissions: December 1 - March 15. See the individual listings for these contests under Contests & Awards for full details."

BELLOWING ARK

P.O. Box 55564, Shoreline WA 98155. E-mail: bellowingark@bellowingark.org. Website: www.bellowingark.org. **Contact:** Robert R. Ward, editor. *Bellowing Ark* is 32 pages, tabloid-sized, printed on electrobright stock. Press run is 1,000. Subscription: $20/year. Sample: $4. No e-mail submissions; accepts postal submissions only. Guidelines available for SASE or on website. Responds in up to 3 months; publishes accepted work within the next 2 issues." We have published serialized novels, plays, short stories, poems, long-poems, epic poems (Nelson Bentley's *Tracking the Transcendental Moose*"—in 14 books, serialized over two years—ran to 20,000 lines) essays, memoirs, drawings, photographs, all forms of self expression, in fact, that we consider to meet our single, and sufficient criterion: everything that we publish demonstrates, to our satisfaction, that life is both meaningful and worth living. We are biased toward the narrative, both in poetry and fiction; that is, stories should have a plot, characterization, a beginning, a middle, and an end. We have not, in our years of publication, ever published *a fiction*, nor anything pointlessly minimalist or surrealist; it seems to us that practitioners of those elegantly academic art forms have deliberately cut themselves off from an audience. We are interested in audience; we believe that art must be shared, to be art."

○ Work from *Bellowing Ark* appeared in the *Pushcart Prize* anthology. Work from *Bellowing Ark* appeared in the *Pushcart Prize* anthology.

CONTEST/AWARD OFFERINGS Three cash awards: The Lois and Marine Robert Warden (poetry), The Lucas Doolin (fiction), and The Michael L. Newell (black and white line art), are given.

ALSO OFFERS Occasionally comments on rejected poems if they "seem to display potential to become the kind of work we want." Sometimes sends prepublication galleys. Reviews books of poetry. Send materials for review consideration.

TIPS "*Bellowing Ark* began as (and remains) an alternative to the despair and negativity of the workshop/ academic literary scene; we believe that life has meaning and is worth living—the work we publish reflects that belief. Learn how to tell a story before submitting. Avoid 'trick' endings; they have all been done before and better. *Bellowing Ark* is interested in publishing writers who will develop with the magazine, as in an extended community. We find good writers and stick with them. This is why the magazine has grown from 12 to 32 pages."

◑ BELL'S LETTERS POET

P.O. Box 14319 N. Swan Rd., Gulfport MS 39503. E-mail: jimbelpoet@aol.com. **Contact:** Jim Bell, editor/publisher. *Bell's Letters Poet*, published quarterly, **must be purchased by contributors before they can be published.** Wants "clean writing in good taste; no vulgarity, no artsy vulgarity." Has published poetry by Betty Wallace, C. David Hay, Mary L. Ports, and Tgrai Warden. *Bell's Letters Poet* is about 60 pages, digest-sized, photocopied on plain bond paper (including cover), saddle-stapled. Single copy: $7; subscription: $28. Sample: $5. Considers previously published poems "if cleared by author with prior publisher"; no simultaneous submissions. Accepts submissions by postal mail or e-mail. Submission deadline is 2 months prior to publication. Accepted poems by subscribers are published immediately in the next issue. Guidelines available online or for SASE. Reviews chapbooks of poetry by subscribers.

HOW TO CONTACT "Send a poem (20 lines or under, in good taste) with your sample order, and we will publish it in our next issue." Submit 4 poems at a time. Lines/poem: 4-20. Address: 14319 N. Swan Rd., Gulfport MS 39503. E-mail: jimbelpoet@aol.com.

ADDITIONAL INFORMATION No payment for accepted poetry, but "many patrons send cash awards to the poets whose work they especially like."

TIPS "The Ratings" is a competition in each issue. Readers are asked to vote on their favorite poems, and the "Top 40" are announced in the next issue, along with awards sent to the poets by patrons. News releases are then sent to subscriber's hometown newspaper. Bell's Letters Poet also features a telephone and e-mail exchange among poets, a birth-date listing, and a profile of its poets." Tired of seeing no bylines this year? Subscription guarantees a byline in each issue."

◑ BELOIT POETRY JOURNAL

P.O. Box 151, Farmington, ME 04938. (207)778-0020. E-mail: bpj@bpj.org. Website: www.bpj.org. *Beloit Poetry Journal* is about 48 pages, digest-sized, saddle-stapled, attractively printed, with "beautiful" 4-color covers. Circulation is 1,250. Subscription: $18/year, $48 for 3 years (individuals); $23/year, $65 for 3 years (institutions). Check website for international subscription rates. Sample: $5. No previously published poems or simultaneous submissions. Manuscripts under active consideration we keep for up to 4 months, circulating them among our readers, and continuing to winnow. At the quarterly meetings of the Editorial Board, we read aloud all the surviving poems and put together an issue of the best we have." Open to a wide range of forms and styles in contemporary poetry. Complete guidelines available on website. Acquires first serial rights." The *BPJ* is open to a wide range of forms and styles. We are always watching for new poets, quickened language and poems that offer a new purchase on the political or social landscape. The Chad Walsh Poetry Prize ($3,000 in 2010) is awarded to the author of the poem or group of poems the editorial board judges to be outstanding among those we published during the previous year."

HOW TO CONTACT Submissions accepted by mail or submission manager found on website. "Limit submissions to five pages, unless it is a long poem." Cover note not necessary.

ADDITIONAL INFORMATION Please send no more than two manuscripts within a six-month period. Put no more than one poem on a page, single-spaced. Include your name and address (postal and email) on every sheet. No cover note is necessary.

CONTEST/AWARD OFFERINGS Awards the Chad Walsh Poetry Prize ($3,000 in 2010) to a poem or group of poems published in the calendar year. "Every poem we publish will be considered for the 2011 prize."

ALSO OFFERS Reviews books by and about poets. Send books for review consideration. "To diversify our offerings, we occasionally publish chapbooks (for example, our 60th Anniversary Chapbook of Chad Walsh prize-winning poets). These are never the work of a single poet."

TIPS "We seek only unpublished poems or translations of poems not already available in English. Poems may be submitted electronically on our website Submission Manager, or by postal mail. Before submitting, please buy a sample issue or browse our website archive."

BEYOND CENTAURI

P.O. Box 782, Cedar Rapids IA 52406-0782. E-mail: beyondcentauri@yahoo.com. Website: www.samsdotpublishing.com. Established 2003. **Contact:** Tyree Campbell, managing editor. Member: The Speculative Literature Foundation. Single copy: $6; subscription: $20/year, $37 for 2 years. Make checks payable to Tyree Campbell/Sam's Dot Publishing. (Specialized: fantasy, science fiction, & mild horror for older children and teens)

MAGAZINES NEEDS *Beyond Centauri*, published quarterly, contains "fantasy, science fiction, sword and sorcery, very mild horror short stories, poetry, and illustrations for readers ages 10 and up. " Wants "fantasy, science fiction, spooky horror, and speculative poetry for younger readers." Does not want "horror with excessive blood and gore." Considers poetry by children and teens. Has published poetry by Bruce Boston, Bobbi Sinha-Morey, Debbie Feo, Dorothy Imm, CytherAnd Terrie Leigh Relf. *Beyond Centauri* is 44 pages, magazine-sized, offset printed, perfect bound, with paper cover for color art, includes ads. Receives about 200 poems/year, accepts about 50 (25%). Press run is 100; 5 distributed free to reviewers. Single copy: $6; subscription: $20/year, $37 for 2 years. Make checks payable to Tyree Campbell/Sam's Dot Publishing.

HOW TO CONTACT Submit up to 5 poems at a time. Lines/poem: prefers less than 50. Considers previously published poems; no simultaneous submissions. Accepts e-mail submissions (pasted into body of message); no disk submissions. "Submission should include snail mail address and a short (1-2 lines) bio." Reads submissions year round. Submit seasonal poems 6 months in advance. Time between acceptance and publication is 1-2 months. Often comments on rejected poems. Guidelines available on website. Responds in 4-6 weeks. Pays $2/original poem, plus 1 contributor's copy. Acquires first North American serial rights. Reviews books/chapbooks of poetry. Send materials for review consideration to Tyree Campbell.

BIBLE ADVOCATE

(303)452-7973. E-mail: bibleadvocate@cog7.org. Website: www.cog7.org/publications/ba/; www.cog7.org/ba. **Contact:** Sherri Langton, Associate Editor. "Our purpose is to advocate the Bible and represent the Church of God (Seventh Day) to a Christian audience."

MAGAZINES NEEDS Free verse, some traditional, with Christian/Bible themes. Does not want avant-garde poetry.

HOW TO CONTACT Prefers e-mail submissions. Cover letter is preferred. "No handwritten submissions, please." Time between acceptance and publication is up to 1 year. "I read them first and reject those that won't work for us. I send good ones to editor for approval." Seldom comments on rejected poems.

TIPS "Be fresh, not preachy! We're trying to reach a younger audience now, so think how you can cover contemporary and biblical topics with this audience in mind. Articles must be in keeping with the doctrinal understanding of the Church of God (Seventh Day). Therefore, the writer should become familiar with what the Church generally accepts as truth as set forth in its doctrinal beliefs. We reserve the right to edit manuscripts to fit our space requirements, doctrinal stands and church terminology. Significant changes are referred to writers for approval. No fax or handwritten submissions, please."

BLACKBIRD

Virginia Commonwealth University Department of English, P.O. Box 843082, Richmond VA 23284. (804)827-4729. E-mail: blackbird@vcu.edu. Website: www.blackbird.vcu.edu. **Contact:** Mary Flinn, Gregory Donovan, senior editors.

HOW TO CONTACT Send complete ms online at www.blackbirdsubmissions.vcu.edu. Include cover letter, name, address, telephone number, brief biographical comment. Responds in 6 months to mss.

Accepts simultaneous submissions. Sample copy online. Writer's guidelines online. Pays $200 for fiction, $40 for poetry. Pays on publication for first North American serial rights. Does not read from April 15-November 1. Publishes ms 3-6 months after acceptance. **Publishes 1-2 new writers/year.**

TIPS "We like a story that invites us into its world, that engages our senses, soul and mind."

BLACK WARRIOR REVIEW

P.O. Box 862936, Tuscaloosa AL 35486. (205)348-4518. E-mail: bwr@ua.edu; blackwarriorreview@gmail.com. Website: www.bwr.ua.edu. **Contact:** Jenny Gropp Hess, editor. "We publish contemporary fiction, poetry, reviews, essays, and art for a literary audience. We publish the freshest work we can find."

Work that appeared in the *Black Warrior Review* has been included in the *Pushcart Prize* anthology, *Harper's Magazine*, *Best American Short Stories*, *Best American Poetry* and *New Stories from the South*. Work that appeared in the *Black Warrior Review* has been included in the *Pushcart Prize* anthology, *Harper's Magazine*, *Best American Short Stories*, *Best American Poetry* and *New Stories from the South*.

HOW TO CONTACT Submit up to 7 poems at a time. Considers simultaneous submissions if noted. No e-mail or disk submissions. Online submission system: http://bwrsubmissions.ua.edu. Responds in up to 5 months. Pays up to $75 and one-year subscription. Acquires first rights. Reviews books of poetry in single- or multi-book format. Send materials for review consideration.

TIPS "We look for attention to language, freshness, honesty, a convincing and sharp voice. Send us a clean, well-printed, proofread manuscript. Become familiar with the magazine prior to submission."

BLOOD LOTUS

E-mail: bloodlotusjournal@gmail.com. Website: www.bloodlotusjournal.com. **Contact:** Stacia M. Fleegal, managing editor.

MAGAZINES NEEDS *Blood Lotus*, published quarterly online, publishes "poetry, fiction, and anything in between!" Wants "fresh language, memorable characters, strong images, and vivid artwork."

HOW TO CONTACT View submission guidelines at http://www.bloodlotusjournal.com/p/submit.

html. Considers simultaneous submissions; no previously published work. Will not open attachments. Reads submissions year round. Guidelines on website. Acquires first North American rights, electronic archival rights.

BLOOD ORANGE REVIEW

E-mail: admin@bloodorangereview.com. Website: www.bloodorangereview.com. **Contact:** H.K. Hummel, Stephanie Lenox, Bryan Fry. Estab. 2005. *Blood Orange Review* publishes fiction, poetry, and nonfiction in an online quarterly. The *Review* is committed to cultivating an audience for exciting literary voices and promoting its writers. *Blood Orange Review* publishes fiction, poetry, and nonfiction in an online quarterly. The *Review* is committed to cultivating an audience for exciting literary voices and promoting its writers.

MAGAZINES NEEDS *Blood Orange Review*, published online quarterly, is "looking for more than an interesting story or a descriptive image. The pieces we publish are the ones that we remember days or even weeks afterward for their compelling characters, believable voices, or sharp revelations. We're not afraid of anything, but if we bristle or stop having fun, we figure there is a good chance our readers will too. In a word, write deftly. Leave us desiring more."

HOW TO CONTACT Submit 3-5 poems through online submission manager in one document. Accepts simultaneous submissions; no previously published poems. Responds in 8 weeks. Reads submissions year round. Additional guidelines can be found on website.

BLUE COLLAR REVIEW

Partisan Press, P.O. Box 11417, Norfolk VA 23517. E-mail: red-ink@earthlink.net. Website: www.partisan-press.org. **Contact:** A. Markowitz, editor, and Mary Franke, co-editor.

MAGAZINES NEEDS *Blue Collar Review (Journal of Progressive Working Class Literature)*, published quarterly, contains poetry, short stories, and illustrations "reflecting the working class experience—a broad range from the personal to the societal. Our purpose is to promote and expand working class literature and an awareness of the connections between workers of all occupations and the social context in which we live. Also to inspire the creativity and latent talent in 'common' working people." Has published poetry by Simon Perchik, Jim Daniels,

Mary McAnally, Marge Piercy, Alan Catlin, and Rob Whitbeck. *Blue Collar Review* is 60 pages, digest-sized, offset-printed, saddle-stapled, with colored card cover, includes ads. Receives hundreds of poems/year, accepts about 15%. Press run is 500. Subscription: $15/year, $25 for 2 years. Sample: $5. Make checks payable to Partisan Press.

HOW TO CONTACT Send no more than 5 poems. Include name and address on each page. Cover letter is helpful though not required. Include SASE for response. Does not accept simultaneous submissions.

ADDITIONAL INFORMATION Partisan Press looks for "poetry of power that reflects a working class consciousness and moves us forward as a society. Must be good writing reflecting social realism including but not limited to political issues." Publishes about 3 chapbooks/year; not presently open to unsolicited submissions. "Submissions are requested from among the poets published in the *Blue Collar Review*." Has published *A Possible Explanation* by Peggy Safire and *American Sounds* by Robert Edwards. Chapbooks are usually 20-60 pages, digest-sized, offset-printed, saddle-stapled or flat-spined, with card or glossy covers. Sample chapbooks are $7 and listed on website.

CONTEST/AWARD OFFERINGS Sponsors the annual Working People's Poetry Competition (see separate listing in Contests & Awards).

ⓞ BLUELINE

120 Morey Hall, Dept. of English and Communication, Postdam NY 13676. (315)267-2043. E-mail: blueline@potsdam.edu. Website: www2.potsdam.edu/blueline. **Contact:** Donald McNutt, editor. *Blueline* is 200 pages, digest-sized. Press run is 600."Blueline seeks poems, stories, and essays relating to the Adirondacks and regions similar in geography and spirit, or focusing on the shaping influence of nature. Payment in copies. Submission period is July through November. *Blueline* welcomes electronic submissions, either in the body of an e-mail message or in Word or html formatted files. Please avoid using compression software."

Ⓠ Proofread all submissions. It is difficult for our editors to get excited about work containing typographical and syntactic errors.

HOW TO CONTACT Submit 3 poems at a time. Lines/poem: 75 maximum; "occasionally we publish longer poems." No simultaneous submissions.

Submit September 1-November 30 only. Include short bio. Poems are circulated to an editorial board. Sometimes comments on rejected poems.

ADDITIONAL INFORMATION "We are interested in both beginning and established poets whose poems evoke universal themes in nature and show human interaction with the natural world. We look for thoughtful craftsmanship rather than stylistic trickery."

TIPS "We look for concise, clear, concrete prose that tells a story and touches upon a universal theme or situation. We prefer realism to romanticism but will consider nostalgia if well done. Pay attention to grammar and syntax. Avoid murky language, sentimentality, cuteness or folkiness. We would like to see more good fiction related to the Adirondacks and more literary fiction and prose poems. If manuscript has potential, we work with author to improve and reconsider for publication. Our readers prefer fiction to poetry (in general) or reviews. Write from your own experience, be specific and factual (within the bounds of your story) and if you write about universal features such as love, death, change, etc., write about them in a fresh way. Triteness and mediocrity are the hallmarks of the majority of stories seen today."

ⓞ BLUE UNICORN, A TRI-QUARTERLY OF POETRY

Website: www.blueunicorn.org. 22 Avon Rd., Kensington CA 94707. (510)526-8439. Website: www.blueunicorn.org. Established 1977. **Contact:** Ruth G. Iodice, John Hart, and Fred Ostrander, editors.

MAGAZINES NEEDS *Blue Unicorn, A Tri-Quarterly of Poetry*, published in October, February, and June, is "distinguished by its fastidious editing, both with regard to contents and format." Wants "well-crafted poetry of all kinds, in form or free verse, as well as expert translations on any subject matter. We shun the trite or inane, the soft-centered, the contrived poem. Shorter poems have more chance with us because of limited space." *Blue Unicorn* is 56 pages, narrow digest-sized, finely printed, saddle-stapled. Receives more than 2,000 submissions/year, accepts about 150. Single copy: $7 (foreign add $3); subscription: $18 for 3 issues (foreign add $6).

HOW TO CONTACT Submit 3-5 poems at a time. No previously published poems or simultaneous submissions. Cover letter is "OK, but will not affect our selection." Submit poems typed on $8\frac{1}{2}$x11 paper.

Sometimes comments on rejected poems. Guidelines available for SASE. Responds in up to 3 months (generally within 6 weeks). Pays one contributor's copy.

CONTEST/AWARD OFFERINGS Sponsors an annual (spring) contest with prizes of $150, $75, $50, and sometimes special awards; distinguished poets as judges; publication of top 3 poems and 6 honorable mentions in the magazine. Guidelines available for SASE. **Entry fee:** $6 for first poem, $3 for each additional poem.

ⓘ BOGG: A JOURNAL OF CONTEMPORARY WRITING

Bogg Publications, 422 N. Cleveland St., Arlington VA 22201-1424. **Contact:** John Elsberg, Poetry Editor. Bogg Publications, 422 N. Cleveland St., Arlington VA 22201-1424. *"Bogg: A Journal of Contemporary Writing,* is a journal of contemporary writing. Its goal is to combine memorable and innovative American work with a healthy leavening of writing from England and the Commonwealth. It contains poetry (to include prose poems, experimental/visual poems, and haiku and tanka), very short fiction, occasional interviews, reviews, and line art. It is published in America and distributed in the U.S., England, CanadAustraliAnd New Zealand." Has published work by Ann Menebroker, Guy Beining, Miriam Sagan, Hugh Fox, Lyn Lifshin, Robert Peters, Laurel Speer, Charles Bukowski, Joan Payne Kincaid, John M. Bennett, Richard Peabody, Todd Moore, Kyle Laws, Gary Blankenburg, A.D. Winans, Marcia Arrieta, Dan Lenihan, David Hilton, Kathy Ernst and more. Subscription: $15/3 issues. *Bogg: A Journal of Contemporary Writing,* combines "innovative American work with a range of writing from England and the Commonwealth. It features poetry (including haiku and tanka, prose poems, and experimental/visual poems), very short experimental or satirical/wry fiction, interviews, essays on the small press scene, reviews, review essays, and line art. We also publish occasional free-for-postage pamphlets." Uses a great deal of poetry in each issue (with featured poets). Wants "poetry in all styles, with a healthy leavening of shorts (under 10 lines). *Bogg* seeks original voices." Considers all subject matter. "Some have even found the magazine's sense of play offensive. Overt religious and political poems have to have strong poetical merits—statement alone is not sufficient." *Bogg* started in England and

in 1975 began including a supplement of American work; it is now published in the U.S. and mixes U.S., Canadian, Australian, and UK work with reviews of small press publications from all of those areas. *Bogg* is 56 pages, digest-sized, typeset, saddle-stapled, in a format "that leaves enough white space to let each poem stand and breathe alone." Receives more than 10,000 American poems/year, accepts about 100-150. Press run is 850. Single copy: $6; subscription: $15 for 3 issues. Sample: $4.

HOW TO CONTACT Submit 6 poems at a time. Considers previously published poems "occasionally, but with a credit line to the previous publisher"; no simultaneous submissions. Cover letter is preferred ("it can help us get a 'feel' for the writer's intentions/slant"). SASE required or material will be discarded ("no exceptions"). Prefers hard copy mss. with author's name and address on each sheet. Guidelines available for SASE. Responds in 1 week. Pays 2 contributor's copies.

TIPS "Become familiar with a magazine before submitting to it. Long lists of previous credits irritate us. Short notes about how the writer has heard about *Bogg* or what he or she finds interesting or annoying in the magazine are welcome."

ⓘ BOMBAY GIN

Writing and Poetics Dept., Naropa University, 2130 Arapahoe Ave., Boulder CO 80302. (303)546-3540. Fax: (303)546-5297. E-mail: bgin@naropa.edu. Established 1974. **Contact:** Amy Catanzano.

MAGAZINES NEEDS *Bombay Gin,* published annually in Fall and Spring, is the literary journal of the Jack Kerouac School of Disembodied Poetics at Naropa University. "Produced and edited by MFA students, *Bombay Gin* publishes established writers alongside unpublished and emerging writers. It has a special interest in works that push conventional literary boundaries. Submissions of poetry, prose, visual art, translation, and works involving hybrid forms and cross-genre exploration are encouraged. Translations are also considered. Guidelines are the same as for original work. Translators are responsible for obtaining any necessary permissions." Has published poetry by Amiri Baraka, Joanne Kyger, Jerome Rothenberg, Lawrence Ferlinghetti, Edwin Torres, and Edward Sanders. *Bombay Gin* is 150-200 pages, digest-sized, professionally printed, perfect-bound, with color card cover. Receives about 300 poems/year, accepts about 5%. Press run is 250; 100 distributed free to contributors. Single copy: $12.

HOW TO CONTACT Submit up to 8 pages of poetry at a time. No previously published poems or simultaneous submissions. Accepts e-mail (as attachment) and disk (PC format) submissions. Cover letter is preferred. **Contact info should not appear anywhere on the ms (only on cover letter).** Poems should be typed/computer-generated in 12-pt. Times New Roman. SASE required for reply. Submissions are accepted September 1-March 1 only. Notification of acceptance/rejection: March 15. Guidelines available for SASE, by e-mail, or on website. Pays 2 contributor's copies. Acquires one-time rights.

BOMB MAGAZINE

(718)636-9100. Fax: (718)636-9200. E-mail: firstproof@bombsite.com; generalinquiries@bombsite.com. Website: www.bombsite.com. **Contact:** Monica de la Torre.

MAGAZINES NEEDS *BOMB Magazine* accepts unsolicited poetry and prose submissions for our literary pull-out *First Proof* by mail from January 1- August 31. Submissions sent outside these dates will be returned unread."Written, edited and produced by industry professionals and funded by those interested in the arts. Publishes work which is unconventional and contains an edge, whether it be in style or subject matter."

HOW TO CONTACT Send completed ms with SASE. Manuscripts should be typed, double-spaced (prose only), proofread, and should be final drafts, not exceeding 20 pages in length." Accepts simultaneous submissions. Include SASE. Responds in 4-6 months to queries. Responds in 3-5 months to mss. Accepts multiple submissions. Sample copy for $10 plus $2.50 for Media Mail shipment, or $5.00 for Priority Mail shipment. Writer's guidelines on website: http://bombsite.com/issues/0/articles/3406 or by email. Accepts submissions from January 1 to August 31; mss sent "outside those dates will be returned unread. We cannot report on ms status, nor offer editorial feedback."

TIPS "Mss should be typed, double-spaced, proofread and should be final drafts. Purchase a sample issue before submitting work."

BORDERLANDS: TEXAS POETRY REVIEW

P.O. Box 33096, Austin TX 78764. Website: www.borderlands.org. **Contact:** Editor. Email: borderlandspoetry@sbcglobal.net. Website: www.borderlands.org. Editor: Deb Akers. *Borderlands* is 100-150 pages, digest-sized, offset-printed, perfect-bound, with 4-color cover. Receives about 2,000 poems/year, accepts about 120. Press run is 1,000. Sample: $12.*Borderlands: Texas Poetry Review*, published semiannually, prints "high-quality, outward-looking poetry by new and established poets, as well as brief reviews of poetry books and critical essays. Cosmopolitan in content, but particularly welcomes Texas and Southwest writers." Wants "outward-looking poems that exhibit social, political, geographical, historical, feminist, or spiritual awareness coupled with concise artistry. Does not want "introspective work about the speaker's psyche, childhood, or intimate relationships." Has published poetry by Walter McDonald, Naomi Shihab Nye, Mario Susko, Wendy Barker, Larry D. Thomas, Reza Shirazi, and Scott Hightower. *Borderlands* is 100-150 pages, digest-sized, offset-printed, perfect-bound, with 4-color cover. Receives about 2,000 poems/year, accepts about 120. Press run is 1,000. Sample: $12.

BORDERLINES

Nant Y Brithyll, Llangynyw, Powys SY21 0JS Wales. Established 1977. **Contact:** Kevin Bamford, co-editor.

MAGAZINES NEEDS *Borderlines*, published semiannually in June and December, aims to encourage the reading and writing of poetry. "We try to be open-minded and look at anything. We do not normally publish very long poems. Most poems fit on one page." Does not want "poems about poems; unshaped recitals of thoughts and/or feelings." Has published poetry by Peter Abbs, Mike Jenkins, and Vuyelwa Carlin. *Borderlines* is 40-48 pages, digest-sized, neatly printed, saddle-stapled, with light card cover with art. Receives about 600 poems/year, accepts about 16%. Press run is 200. Single copy: £2.50 UK, £3.50 other EU countries, £4.50 non-EU countries; subscription: £5 UK, £7 other EU countries, £9 non-EU countries (payment in sterling only). Make checks payable to Anglo-Welsh Poetry Society.

HOW TO CONTACT Cover letter is preferred. "Please write name and address on each page of poetry." Time between acceptance and publication is up to 6 months. Seldom comments on rejected poems. Guidelines available for SASE (or SAE and IRC). Responds in 6 weeks. Sometimes sends prepublication galleys. Pays one contributor's copy.

ALSO OFFERS "The Anglo-Welsh Poetry Society is a group of people interested in the reading, writing, and promotion of poetry, particularly in the Marches— the Anglo-Welsh border country. It is based in the border counties of Shropshire and Montgomeryshire, though there are members all over the country. A core group of members meets on the first Tuesday of the month at the Loggerheads pub in Shrewsbury. Other meetings such as readings, workshops, and poetry parties are arranged at intervals over the course of the year. A monthly newsletter gives information of interest to members on events, publications, competitions, and other news of the poetry world." Levels of membership/dues: £10/year.

ⓞⓞⓢ BOSTON REVIEW

(617)324-1360. Fax: (617)452-3356. E-mail: review@ bostonreview.net. Website: www.bostonreview.net. Timothy Donnelly. **Contact:** Dept. Editor. "The editors are committed to a society and culture that foster human diversity and a democracy in which we seek common grounds of principle amidst our many differences. In the hope of advancing these ideals, the *Review* acts as a forum that seeks to enrich the language of public debate."

○ *Boston Review* is a recipient of the Pushcart Prize in Poetry.

HOW TO CONTACT Submit 5-6 poems at a time through online submissions system. Does not accept faxed or e-mailed submissions. Include brief bio. Time between acceptance and publication is 6 months to one year.

CONTEST/AWARD OFFERINGS The *Boston Review* Annual Poetry Contest (see separate listing in Contests & Awards).

TIPS The best way to get a sense of the kind of material *Boston Review* is looking for is to read the magazine. (Sample copies are available for $6.95 plus shipping.) We do not consider previously published material. Simultaneous submissions are fine as long as we are notified of the fact. We accept submissions through our **online submissions system**. We strongly encourage online submission, however, if you must use postal mail, our address is *Boston Review*, PO Box 425786, Cambridge, MA 02142. We do not accept faxed or

emailed submissions. Payment varies. Response time is generally 2-4 months. A SASE must accompany all postal submissions.

ⓞⓞⓢ BOULEVARD

Opojaz, Inc., 6614 Clayton Rd., Box 325, Richmond Heights MO 63117. (314)862-2643. Fax: (314)862- 2982. E-mail: kellyleavitt@boulevardmagazine.org; richardburgin@att.net; richardburgin@netzero.net. E-mail: http://boulevard.submishmash.com/submit. Website: www.boulevardmagazine.org. Kelly Leavitt, managing editor. **Contact:** Richard Burgin, editor. "*Boulevard* is a diverse literary magazine presenting original creative work by well-known authors, as well as by writers of exciting promise."

○ "*Boulevard* has been called 'one of the half-dozen best literary journals' by Poet Laureate Daniel Hoffman in *The Philadelphia Inquirer*. We strive to publish the finest in poetry, fiction and non-fiction."

HOW TO CONTACT No e-mail submissions. All submissions must include SASE. Author's name and address must appear on each submission, with author's first and last name on each page. Cover letter is encouraged ("but not required"). Reads submissions October 1-April 30 only. Sometimes comments on rejected poems.

CONTEST/AWARD OFFERINGS The *Boulevard* Emerging Poets Contest (see separate listing in Contests & Awards).

TIPS "Read the magazine first. The work *Boulevard* publishes is generally recognized as among the finest in the country. We continue to seek more good literary or cultural essays. Send only your best work."

ⓞⓢ BOYDS MILLS PRESS

Website: www.boydsmillspress.com. (Specialized: picture books, novels, poetry, fiction, nonfiction, and various activity books for children and teen) Boyds Mills Press, 815 Church St., Honesdale PA 18431. (800)490- 5111. E-mail: admin@boydsmillspress.com. Website: www.boydsmillspress.com. Established 1990.

ⓞ THE BREAD OF LIFE MAGAZINE

P.O. Box 127, Burlington ON L7R 3X5, Canada. E-mail: info@thebreadoflife.ca. Website: www.thebreadoflife.ca. Established 1977. **Contact:** Fr. Peter Coughlin, editor.

MAGAZINE NEEDS *The Bread of Life*, published semimonthly, is "a Catholic charismatic magazine designed to encourage spiritual growth in areas of renewal in the Catholic Church today." Includes feature articles, poetry, regular columns, quizzes and photography. "It's good if contributors are members of The Bread of Life Renewal Centre, a nonprofit, charitable organization. All of our contributors do so in humble service to our Lord on a volunteer basis." *The Bread of Life* is 48 pages, digest-sized, professionally printed, saddle-stapled, with glossy paper cover. Receives about 50-60 poems/year, accepts about 25%. Press run is 1,700. Membership: $35/year (includes magazine subscription).R, TConsiders previously published poems and simultaneous submissions. Cover letter is preferred. Publishes theme issues. Guidelines available for SAE with IRC.

THE BREAKTHROUGH INTERCESSOR

(Specialized: intercessory prayer), Breakthrough, Inc., P.O. Box 121, Lincoln VA 20160. (540)338-4131. Fax: (540)338-1934. E-mail: breakthrough@intercessors. org. Website: http://intercessors.org. Established 1980. **Contact:** Andrea Doudera, editor.

MAGAZINES NEEDS Articles and Poetry *The Breakthrough Intercessor*, published quarterly, focuses on "encouraging people in prayer and faith; preparing and equipping those who pray." Accpets multiple articles per issue: 600-1,000 word true stories on prayer; **poetry very rarely due to space limitations.** Has published poetry by Norman Vincent Peale. *The Breakthrough Intercessor* is 36 pages, magazine-sized, professionally printed, saddle-stapled with self cover, includes art/graphics. Press run is 4,000. Subscription: $18. Make checks payable to Breakthrough, Inc.

HOW TO CONTACT Considers previously published articles and poems. Accepts fax, e-mail (pasted into body of message or attachment), and mailed hard copy. Time between acceptance and publication varies. Articles and poems are circulated to an editorial board.

THE BRIAR CLIFF REVIEW

3303 Rebecca St., Sioux City IA 51104-0100. (712)279-5477. E-mail: curranst@briarcliff.edu. E-mail: jeanne. emmons@briarcliff.edu (poetry). Website: www.briarcliff.edu/bcreview. **Contact:** Phil Hey or Tricia Currans-Sheehan, fiction editors.

MAGAZINES NEEDS *The Briar Cliff Review* is 100 pages, magazine-sized, professionally printed on 100 lb. Altima Satin text paper, perfect-bound, with 4-color cover on dull stock. Receives about 1,000 poems/

year, accepts about 30. Member: CLMP; American Humanities Index; EBSCO/Humanities International Complete. Considers simultaneous submissions, but expects prompt notification of acceptance elsewhere. No e-mail submissions. Cover letter is required. "Include short bio. Submissions should be typewritten or letter quality, with author's name and address on each page. No mss returned without SASE." Reads submissions August 1-November 1 only. Needs quality poetry with strong imagery and tight, well-wrought language; especially interested in, but not limited to, regional, Midwestern content.

HOW TO CONTACT Considers simultaneous submissions, but expects prompt notification of acceptance elsewhere; no previously published poems. No e-mail submissions; postal submissions only. Cover letter is required. "Include short bio. Submissions should be typewritten or letter quality, with author's name and address on each page. No manuscripts returned without SASE." Reads submissions August 1-November 1 only. Time between acceptance and publication is up to 6 months. Seldom comments on rejected poems. Guidelines available on website. Responds in 6-8 months.

CONTEST/AWARD OFFERINGS The *Briar Cliff Review* Annual Fiction, Poetry and Creative Nonfiction Contest (see separate listing in Contests & Awards).

TIPS "So many stories are just telling. We want some action. It has to move. We prefer stories in which there is no gimmick, no mechanical turn of events, no moral except the one we would draw privately."

BRYANT LITERARY REVIEW

Faculty Suite F, Bryant University, 1150 Douglas Pike, Smithfield RI 02917. E-mail: blr@bryant.edu. Website: http://web.bryant.edu/~blr. **Contact:** Tom Chandler, Editor. "We expect readers of the *Bryant Literary Review* to be sophisticated, educated, and familiar with the conventions of contemporary literature. We see our purpose to be the cultivation of an active and growing connection between our community and the larger literary culture. Our production values are of the highest caliber, and our roster of published authors includes major award and fellowship winners. The *BLR* provides a respected venue for creative writing of every kind from around the world. Our only standard is quality."*Bryant Literary Review* is an international magazine of poetry and fiction published annually in May. Features poetry, fiction, photography, and art. "Our only standard is quality." Has published poetry by Michael S. Harper, Mary Crow, Denise Duhamel, and Baron Wormser. Bryant Literary Review is 125 pages, digest-sized, offset-printed, perfect-bound, with 4-color cover with art or photo. Receives about 3,000 poems/year, accepts about 1%. Press run is 2,500. Single copy: $8; subscription: $8. For more information, contact blr@bryant.edu. To submit work, please review the submission guidelines on our website.

HOW TO CONTACT Submit up to 5 poems through postal mail only. Will not accept e-mail submissions. Doesn't accept previously published work. All mss must include SASE. Reads submissions September 1-December 31. Pays contributor's copies. Copyright reverts to author upon publication. Additional copies are $10.00.

TIPS "No abstract expressionist poems, please. We prefer accessible work of depth and quality."

● ❸ BUTTON

P.O. Box 77, Westminster, MA 01473. E-mail: sally@moonsigns.net. Website: www.moonsigns.net. E-mail: sally@moonsigns.net. Website: www.moonsigns.net. Has published poetry by Amanda Powell, Brendan Galvin, Jean Monahan, Mary Campbell, Kevin McGrath, and Ed Conti. *Button* is 30 pages, 4¼x5½, saddle-stapled, with cardstock offset cover with illustrations that incorporate 1 or more buttons. Press run is 1,200. Subscription: $5/4 issues. "We don't take email submissions, unless you're living overseas, in which case we respond electronically. But we *strongly* suggest you request writers' guidelines (send an SASE). Better still, look over our online issue or order a sample copy for $2.50, which includes postage. *Button* is New England's tiniest magazine of poetry, fiction, and gracious living, published once a year. As 'gracious living' is on the cover, we like wit, brevity, cleverly-conceived essay/recipe, poetry that isn't sentimental or song lyrics. I started *Button* so that a century from now, when people read it in landfils or, preferably, libraries, they'll say, 'Gee, what a great time to have lived. I wish I lived back then.' Submit only between April 1 and September 30 please."

MAGAZINES NEEDS Quality poetry; "poetry that incises a perfect figure eight on the ice, but also cuts beneath that mirrored surface. Minimal use of vertical pronoun." Does not want "sentiment; no

'musing' on who or what done ya wrong."

HOW TO CONTACT "Do not submit more than twice in one year." No previously published poems. Cover letter is required. Time between acceptance and publication is up to 6 months. "Our reading period is April 1-September 30. Work sent at other times will be discarded." Poems are circulated to an editorial board. Often comments on rejected poems. Guidelines available by e-mail. Responds within 4 months.

TIPS "*Button* writers have been widely published elsewhere, in virtually all the major national magazines. They include, Ralph Lombreglia, Lawrence Millman, They Might Be Giants, Combustible Edison, Sven Birkerts, Stephen McCauley, Amanda Powell, Wayne Wilson, David Barber, Romayne Dawnay, Brendan Galvin, and Diana DerHovanessian. It's $2.50 for a sample, which seems reasonable. Follow the guidelines, make sure you read your work aloud, and don't inflate or deflate your publications and experience. We've published plenty of new folks, but on the merits of the work."

● CALIFORNIA QUARTERLY

P.O. Box 7126, Orange CA 92863-7126. E-mail: pearlk@covad.net. Julian Palley, Co-Editor. **Contact:** The Editors. The California State Poetry Society "is dedicated to the adventure of poetry and its dissemination. Although located in California, its members are from all over the U.S. and abroad." Levels of membership/dues: $30/year. Benefits include membership in the National Federation of State Poetry Societies (NFSPS); 4 issues of California Quarterly (see separate listing in Magazines/Journals), *Newsbriefs*, and *The Poetry Letter*. Sponsors monthly and annual contests. Additional information available for SASE.

MAGAZINES NEEDS Wants poetry on any subject. "No geographical limitations. Quality is all that matters." *California Quarterly* is 64 pages, digest-sized, offset-printed, perfect-bound with cover art. Receives 3,000-4,000 poems/year, accepts about 5%. Press run is 500. Membership in CSPS is $30/year and includes a subscription to *California Quarterly*. Sample: $7 (includes guidelines).

HOW TO CONTACT Submit up to 6 poems at a time. Lines/poem: 60 maximum. No previously published poems. Accepts submissions by postal mail only; no e-mail submissions. Put name and address on each sheet, include SASE. Acquires first rights. Rights revert to poet after publication.

CALLALOO: A JOURNAL OF AFRICAN DIASPORA ARTS & LETTERS

Dept. of English, Texas A&M University, 4212 TAMU, College Station TX 77843-4227. (979)458-3108. Fax: (979)458-3275. E-mail: callaloo@tamu.edu. Website: http://callaloo.tamu.edu. Established 1976. **Contact:** Charles H. Rowell, editor. Poetry published in *Callaloo* has been included frequently in volumes of The Best American Poetry. Subscription: $50/1 year electronic access; $50/1 year (4 print issues).

MAGAZINES NEEDS *Callaloo: A Journal of African Diaspora Arts & Letters*, published quarterly, is devoted to poetry dealing with the African Diaspora, including North America, Europe, Africa, Latin and Central America, South AmericAnd the Caribbean. Has published poetry by Aimeé Ceésaire, Lucille Clifton, Rita Dove, Yusef Komunyakaa, Natasha Tretheway, and Carl Phillips. Features about 15-20 poems (all forms and styles) in each issue along with short fiction, interviews, literary criticism, and concise critical book reviews. Circulation is 1,600 subscribers of which half are libraries. Subscription: $39, $107 for institutions.

HOW TO CONTACT Submit no more than 5 poems at a time; no more than 10 per calendar year. Submit using online ms tracking system only. Responds in 6 months.

CALYX

Calyx, Inc., P.O. Box B, Corvallis OR 97339. (541)753-9384. Fax: (541)753-0515. E-mail: editor@calyxpress. org. Website: www.calyxpress.org. **Contact:** The Editor. *CALYX* is 6x8, handsomely printed on heavy paper, flat-spined, with glossy color cover. Single copy: $10 plus $4 shipping; subscription: $23/volume (3 issues), $41 for 2 volumes (6 issues). Sample: $14. See website for foreign and institutional rates. Guidelines available for SASE, by e-mail, or on website. Responds in 4-9 months. Send materials for review consideration. "*Calyx* exists to publish fine literature and art by women and is committed to publishing the work of all women, including women of color, older women, working class women and other voices that need to be heard. We are committed to discovering and nurturing developing writers."

"Annual open submission period is October 1-December 31. Mss received when not open will be returned. Electronic submissions are accepted only from overseas. E-mail for guidelines only."

MAGAZINES NEEDS "Excellently crafted poetry that also has excellent content."

HOW TO CONTACT Send up to 6 poems at a time. Considers previously published poems "occasionally" and simultaneous submissions "if kept up-to-date on publication." No fax or e-mail submissions except from overseas. Include SASE and short bio. Prose and poetry should be submitted separately with separate SASEs for each submission category. "We accept copies in good condition and clearly readable. *CALYX* is edited by a collective editorial board." Reads submissions postmarked October 1-December 31 only. **Manuscripts received outside of reading period will be returned unread.**

CONTEST/AWARD OFFERINGS The annual Lois Cranston Memorial Poetry Prize and the new Sarah Lantz Memorial Poetry Book Prize (see separate listing in Contests & Awards).

ALSO OFFERS CALYX Books publishes one book of poetry/year. All work published is by women. Has published *Storytelling in Cambodia* by Willa Schneberg and *Black Candle: Poems about Women from India, Pakistan, and Bangladesh* by Chitra Banerjee Divakaruni. **Closed to submissions until further notice.**

TIPS "Most mss are rejected because the writers are not familiar with *Calyx*—writers should read *Calyx* and be familar with the publication. We look for good writing, imagination and important/interesting subject matter."

CANADIAN WRITER'S JOURNAL

Website: www.cwj.ca. (Specialized: writing)White Mountain Publications, Box 1178, New Liskeard ON P0J 1P0 Canada. (705)647-5424. Fax: (705)647-8366. E-mail: editor@cwj.ca. Website: www.cwj.ca.

MAGAZINES NEEDS *Canadian Writer's Journal*, published bimonthly, uses a few "short poems or portions thereof as part of 'how-to' articles relating to the writing of poetry, and occasional short poems with tie-in to the writing theme. We try for 90% Canadian content." *Canadian Writer's Journal* is digest-sized. Subscription "prices are under review as publishing schedule is changing." Sample: $9.

HOW TO CONTACT Submit up to 5 poems at a time. No previously published poems. Accepts e-mail submissions (pasted into body of message, with 'Submission' in the subject line). Include SASE with postal submissions. "U.S. postage accepted; do not affix to envelope. Poems should be titled. Hard copy and SASE required if accepted." Responds in 3-6 months. Pays $2-5/poem and 1 contributor's copy.

⊙⓪ CANDELABRUM
POETRY MAGAZINE

c/o 77 Homegrove House, Grove Rd. N., Southsea PO5 1HW, UK. Website: www.members.tripod.com/redcandlepress. Contact: M.L. McCarthy. *Candelabrum Poetry Magazine* appears semianually, in April and October. "Now well established as Britain's longest standing traditionalist poetry magazine, attracting poets and poetry-lovers internationally, it has subscribers in Britain, the United States, Canada, New Zealand and Australia. The editor specially welcomes metrical work, particularly with rhyme, but good quality free verse, and formal haiku and waka (tanka), are also considered." Subscription $12. Single issue: $6. *Candelabrum*, published twice/year in April and October, prints "good-quality metrical verse." Wants "rhymed verse especially. Elegantly cadenced free verse is acceptable. Accepts 5-7-5 haiku. Any subject, including eroticism (but not porn)—satire, love poems, nature lyrics, philosophical." Does not want "weak stuff (moons and Junes, loves and doves, etc.). No chopped-up prose pretending to be free verse. Nothing racist, ageist, or sexist." Has published poetry by Pam Russell, Ryan Underwood, David Britton, Alice Evans, Jack Harvey, and Nick Spargo. Receives about 2,000 submissions/year, accepts about 10% (usually holds poems for the next year). Press run is 900. Sample: $6 (in U.S. bills only; non-sterling checks not accepted).

HOW TO CONTACT Submit 3-6 poems through postal mail, include SASE. Does not accept submissions via e-mail. "Poems are accepted on condition that they be not offered to any British, US or Canadian magazine in the two years following publication in Candelabrum."

TIPS "Formalist poetry is much more popular here in Britain, and we think also in the United States, now than it was in 1970, when we established *Candelabrum*. We always welcome new poets, especially formalists, and we like to hear from the U.S. as well as from here at home. General tip: Study the various outlets at the library, or buy a copy of *Candelabrum*,

or borrow a copy from a subscriber, before you go to the expense of submitting your work. The Red Candle Press regrets that, because of bank charges, it is unable to accept dollar cheques. However, it is always happy to accept U.S. dollar bills."

⊙⊙⊙ THE CAPILANO REVIEW

2055 Purcell Way, North Vancouver BC V7J 3H5, Canada. (604)984-1712. E-mail: contact@thecapilanoreview.ca; tcr@capilanou.ca. Website: www.thecapilanoreview.ca. **Contact:** Tamara Lee, managing editor.

MAGAZINES NEEDS *The Capilano Review*, published 3 times/year, is a literary and visual arts review. *The Capilano Review* is 100-120 pages, digest-sized, finely printed, perfect-bound, with glossy full-color card cover. Circulation is 800. Sample: $15 CAD prepaid. Tri-annual visual and literary arts magazine that "publishes only what the editors consider to be the very best fiction, poetry, drama, or visual art being produced. *TCR* editors are interested in fresh, original work that stimulates and challenges readers. Over the years, the magazine has developed a reputation for pushing beyond the boundaries of traditional art and writing. We are interested in work that is new in concept and in execution."

HOW TO CONTACT No simultaneous submissions. No e-mail or disk submissions. Cover letter is required. Include SAE with IRCs; "submissions with U.S. postage will not be considered." Responds in up to 4 months.

⊙ THE CARIBBEAN WRITER

University of the Virgin Islands, RR 1, P.O. Box 10,000, Kingshill, St. Croix USVI 00850. (340)692-4152. Fax: (340)692-4026. E-mail: info@thecaribbeanwriter.org. E-mail: submit@thecaribbeanwriter.org. Website: www.TheCaribbeanWriter.org. **Contact:** Erika J. Waters, founding editor.

⊙ Poetry published in *The Caribbean Writer* has appeared in The Pushcart Prize.

MAGAZINES NEEDS *The Caribbean Writer*, published annually, is a literary anthology with a Caribbean focus (Caribbean must be central to the literary work, or the work must reflect a Caribbean heritage, experience, or perspective). "*The Caribbean Writer* features new and exciting voices from the region, and beyond that explore the diverse and multi-ethnic culture in poetry, short fiction, personal essays, creative non-fiction, and plays. Social, cultural, economic and sometimes controversial issues are also explored, employing a wide array of literary devices." Has published poetry by Edwidge Danticat, Geoffrey Philp, and Thomas Reiter. *The Caribbean Writer* is 300+ pages, digest-sized, handsomely printed on heavy stock, perfect-bound, with glossy card cover. Press run is 1,200. Single copy: $10; subscription: $25/2 years.

HOW TO CONTACT Submit up to 5 poems at a time. Considers simultaneous submissions; no previously published poems. Accepts e-mail as attachment; no fax submissions. Name, address, phone number, e-mail address, and title of ms should appear in cover letter along with brief bio. Title only on ms. Guidelines available in magazine, for SASE, by e-mail, or on website. Pays 2 contributor's copies. Acquires first North American serial rights. Reviews books of poetry and fiction in 1,000 words. Send materials for review consideration.

CONTEST/AWARD OFFERINGS All submissions are eligible for the Daily News Prize ($300) for poetry, The Marguerite Cobb McKay Prize to a Virgin Island author ($200), the David Hough Literary Prize to a Caribbean author ($500), the Canute A. Brodhurst Prize for Fiction ($400), and the Charlotte and Isidor Paiewonsky Prize ($200) for first-time publication.

◑ THE CAROLINA QUARTERLY

CB #3520 Greenlaw Hall, University of North Carolina, Chapel Hill NC 27599-3520. (919)962-0244. E-mail: carolina.quarterly@gmail.com. Website: www.thecarolinaquarterly.com.

MAGAZINES NEEDS *The Carolina Quarterly*, published 3 times/year, prints fiction, poetry, reviews, nonfiction, and graphic art. No specifications regarding form, length, subject matter, or style of poetry. Considers translations of work originally written in languages other than English. Has published poetry by Denise Levertov, Richard Wilbur, Robert Morgan, Ha Jin, and Charles Wright. *The Carolina Quarterly* is about 100 pages, digest-sized, professionally printed, perfect-bound, with glossy cover, includes ads. Receives about 6,000 poems/year, accepts about 1%. Press run is 900. Subscription: $24 for individuals, $30 for institutions. Sample: $9.

HOW TO CONTACT Submit 1-6 poems at a time. No previously published poems or simultaneous submissions. No e-mail submissions. SASE required. Electronic submissions accepted, see website for majority consensus. "Manuscripts that make it to the meeting of the full poetry staff are discussed by all. Poems are accepted by majority consensus." Seldom comments on rejected poems. Responds in 4-6 months. "Poets are welcome to write or e-mail regarding their submission's status, but please wait about four months before doing so." Pays 2 contributor's copies. Acquires first rights. Reviews books of poetry. Send materials for review consideration (attn: Editor).

CONTEST/AWARD OFFERINGS The Charles B. Wood Award for Distinguished Writing is given to the author of the best poem or short story published in each volume of *The Carolina Quarterly*. Only those writers without major publications are considered, and the winner receives a cash award.

◐ CAVEAT LECTOR

400 Hyde St., Apt. 606, San Francisco CA 94109-7445. (415)928-7431. Fax: (415)928-7431. E-mail: editors@caveat-lector.org. Website: www.caveat-lector.org. **Contact:** Christopher Bernard, Co-Editor.

MAGAZINES NEEDS *Caveat Lector*, published 2 times/year, "is devoted to the arts and cultural and philosophical commentary. As well as literary work, we publish art, photography, music, streaming audio of selected literary pieces, and short films. Our website includes an art gallery and a multimedia section, including links to websites we think might be of interest to our readers." Wants poems "on any subject, in any style, as long as the work is authentic in feeling and appropriately crafted. We are looking for accomplished poems, something that resonates in the mind long after the reader has laid the poem aside. We want work that has authenticity of emotion and high craft; poems that, whether raw or polished, ring true—and if humorous, are actually funny, or at least witty. Classical to experimental. Note: We sometimes request authors for audio of work we publish to post on our website." Has published poetry by Joanne Lowery, Simon Perchik, Les Murray, Alfred Robinson, and Ernest Hilbert. *Caveat Lector* is 32-48 pages, 11X4¼, photocopied, saddle-stapled, with b&w cover. Receives 200-600 poems/year, accepts about 2%. Press run is 250.

HOW TO CONTACT Submit poetry through postal mail only. Send brief bio and SASE with submission. Accepts submissions between February 1 and June

30. Pays contributor's copies. Acquires first publication rights.

CC&D/CHILDREN, CHURCHES AND DADDIES

Scars Publications, 829 Brian Court, Gurnee IL 60031. E-mail: ccandd96@scars.tv. Website: http://scars.tv. **Contact:** Janet Kuypers, editor/publisher. All copies found electronically on website.

MAGAZINES NEEDS *CC&D/Children, Churches and Daddies (The Unreligious, Non-Family-Oriented Literary Magazine)*, published monthly, contains poetry, prose, art, and essays. "Also run electronic issues and collection books. We accept poetry of almost any genre, but no rhyme or religious poems (look at our current issue for a better idea of what we're like). We are okay with gay/lesbian/bisexual, nature/rural/ecology, political/social issues, women/feminism." Does not want "racist, sexist (therefore we're not into pornography, either), or homophobic stuff." Has published poetry by Mel Waldman, Pat Dixon, Angeline Hawkes-Craig, Cheryl Townsend, Kenneth DiMaggio. *CC&D/Children, Churches and Daddies* is 84 pages, perfect-bound. Receives hundreds of poems/year, accepts about 40%. Sample: $6 (print for pre-2010 issues); free electronic sample online. 2010 copies can be ordered from our printer. See website for more information. Make checks payable to Janet Kuypers.

HOW TO CONTACT Submit "as much work as you want at a time" via e-mail only. Lines/poem: accepts longer works, "within 2 pages for an individual poem is appreciated." Considers previously published poems and simultaneous submissions. Accepts e-mail submissions (preferred, pasted into body of message or as attachment in Microsoft Word .doc file) or disk submissions. Does not accept PDF attachments. "When submitting via e-mail in body of message, explain in preceding paragraph that it is a submission; for disk submissions, mail floppy disk with ASCII text, or Macintosh disk." Comments on rejected poems "if asked." Guidelines available for SASE, by e-mail, or on website. Responds in 2 weeks.

CONTEST/AWARD OFFERINGS Scars Publications sometimes sponsors a contest "where writing appears in an annual book." Write or e-mail (editor@scars.tv) for information.

ALSO OFFERS Also able to publish electronic chapbooks. Additional information available by e-mail or on website.

CENTER: A JOURNAL OF THE LITERARY ARTS

202 Tate Hall, University of Missouri-Columbia, Columbia MO 65211-1500. Fax: (573)884-3122. E-mail: cla@missouri.edu. Website: center.missouri.edu. **Contact:** Managing Editor.

MAGAZINES NEEDS *Center: A Journal of the Literary Arts*, publishes "poetry, fiction, creative nonfiction, and, on occasion, translations. Center publishes from a broad range of aesthetic categories and privileges work that is deliberately crafted, engaging, and accessible." Has published poetry by Kim Chinquee, Mark Conway, Debra Anne Davis, William Eisner, Kathy Fagan, Kathleen Flenniken, and more. *Center: A Journal* is 100+ pages, digest-sized, perfect-bound, with 4-color card cover, includes ads for literary journals. Receives about 1,000 poems/year, accepts about 30. Press run is 500. Single copy: $7 (current issue). Sample: $3.50 (back issue). Make checks payable to *Center: A Journal.*

HOW TO CONTACT Submit 3-6 poems each time via postal mail. Considers simultaneous submissions with notification; no previously published poems. Cover letter is preferred. Reads submissions July 1-December 1. "Submissions received outside of the reading period will be returned unread." Guidelines available on website. Responds in 3-5 months. Acquires first North American serial rights. Rights revert to poets upon publication.

CEREMONY, A JOURNAL OF POETRY AND OTHER ARTS

Website: www.danceofmyhands.com. Dance of My Hands Publishing, 120 Vista Dr., Warminster PA 18974. E-mail: danceofmyhands@aol.com. Website: www.danceofmyhands.com. **Contact:** Melanie M. Eyth, editor.

MAGAZINES NEEDS *Ceremony, a Journal of Poetry and Other Arts*, published biannually, encourages "all expression and articism. Beginning poets are especially encouraged." Wants poetry, short pieces of prose, photography and other printable arts. Considers poetry by teens. *Ceremony* is small, home-printed on 20 lb. recycled paper, and single staple-bound. Receives about 200 submissions/year, accepts 50%. Single copy: $3.

HOW TO CONTACT Submit up to 6 poems at a time. Poems of shorter length preferred. Considers previously published poems and simultaneous submissions. Accepts e-mail submissions only. Reads submissions year round. Time between acceptance and publication is 1-2 years. Sometimes comments on rejected poems. Sometimes publishes theme issues. Guidelines available on website under 'Contact.' Pays 1 contributor's copy. Rights revert to poet upon publication.

◐ ◑ CERISE PRESS

P.O. Box 241187, Omaha NE 68124. E-mail: editors@cerisepress.com; submissions@cerisepress.com. Website: www.cerisepress.com. **Contact:** Karen Rigby, Fiona Sze-Lorrain, Sally Molini, editors.

MAGAZINES NEEDS *Cerise Press*, published 3 times/year, is an "international, online journal of literature, arts, and culture (with a forthcoming print anthology) based in the US and France, offering poetry, nonfiction, translations, fiction, artwork, and photography." Has published Mahmoud Darwish, Auxeméry, Tess Gallagher, Yusef Komunyakaa, Eleanor Wilner, Pierre-Albert Jourdan, Abdelwahab Meddeb, Pura López-Colomé, Dorianne Laux, Ray Gonzalez, Victoria Chang.

HOW TO CONTACT Submit via e-mail. Considers simultaneous submissions. Cover letter is required. "Please let us know if work is accepted elsewhere. Do not query until three months from the date of submission." Reads submissions year round. Never comments on rejected poems. Guidelines on website. Responds in 2-3 months. Acquires first North American serial rights. Rights revert to poet upon publication. Reviews books and chapbooks of poetry, fiction, critical essays, biographies, photography, and more.

◐ CHAFFIN JOURNAL

English Department, Eastern Kentucky University, C, Richmond KY 40475-3102. (859)622-3080. E-mail: robert.witt@eku.edu. Website: www.english.edu/chaffin_journal. **Contact:** Robert Witt, editor. *The Chaffin Journal* is 120 pages, digest-sized, offset-printed, perfect-bound, with plain cover with title only. Receives about 500 poems/year, accepts about 10%. Press run is 300; 40-50 distributed free to contributors. Single copy: $6; subscription: $6/year. Sample (back issue): $6. Make checks payable to *The Chaffin Journal*. Reads submissions June 1-October 1. Time between acceptance and publication is 6 months. Poems are reviewed by the general editor and 2 poetry editors.

Never comments on rejected poems. Guidelines available in magazine or on website. Responds in 3 months. Acquires one-time rights."We publish fiction on any subject; our only consideration is the quality." Annual. Ethnic/multicultural, historical, humor/satire, literary, mainstream, regional (Appalachia). "No erotica, fantasy." Receives 20 unsolicited mss/month. Accepts 6-8 mss/year. Does not read mss October 1 through May 31. **Publishes 2-3 new writers/year.** Recently published work by Meridith Sue Willis, Marie Manilla, Raymond Abbott, Marjorie Bixler, Chris Helvey. Length: 10,000 words per submission period; average length: 5,000 words. Send SASE for return of ms. Accepts simultaneous, multiple submissions. Pays 1 contributor's copy; additional copies $6. Pays on publication for one-time rights.

HOW TO CONTACT Submit 5 poems per submission period. Considers simultaneous submissions (although not preferred); no previously published poems. No e-mail or disk submissions. Cover letter is preferred. "Submit typed pages with only one poem per page. Enclose SASE."

TIPS "All manuscripts submitted are considered."

◐ ◑ CHALLENGER INTERNATIONAL

E-mail: lukivdan@hotmail.com. Website: http://challengerinternational.20m.com/index.html.

MAGAZINES NEEDS *Challenger international*, published annually, contains "poetry and (on occasion) short fiction." Wants "any type of work, especially by teenagers (our mandate: to encourage young writers, and to publish their work alongside established writers), providing it is not pornographic, profane, or overly abstract." Has published poetry from Canada, the continental U.S., Hawaii, Switzerland, Russia, Malta, Italy, Slovenia, Ireland, England, Korea, Pakistan, Australia, Zimbabwe, Argentin And Columbia. *Challenger international* is generally 20-50 pages, magazine-sized, laser-printed, side-stapled. Press run is 50. *Challenger international* is distributed free to McNaughton Centre Secondary Alternate School sudents.

HOW TO CONTACT Considers previously published poems and simultaneous submissions. Cover letter is required. Include list of credits, if any. Accepts e-mail submissions only; no postal submissions. "Sometimes we edit to save the poet rejection." Responds in 6 months. Payment is 1 e-copy (sent as an e-mail attachment) of the issue in which the author's work appears. Poet retains rights.

ADDITIONAL INFORMATION Island Scholastic Press publishes chapbooks by authors featured in *Challenger international*. Pays 3 author's copies. Copyright remains with author. Distribution of free copies through McNaughton Centre.

⬤$ CHAMPAGNE SHIVERS

E-mail: ChampagneShivers@hotmail.com. Website: http://samsdotpublishing.com/vineyard/Champagne%20Shivers.htm. **Contact:** Cathy Buburuz, Editor. *Champagne Shivers* is published annually as a print magazine "designed to showcase the work of poets, fiction writers, non fiction writers, cartoonists, photographers and artists with the ability to inspire shivers in readers. The most significant challenge for potential contributors is to inspire those chills with work done in good taste." Wants scary stuff, "but I don't want anything that falls short of eloquent and poetic language." *Champagne Shivers* is "a classy horror magazine. This is not the place to submit offensive language. We prefer poetic, well-written horror." Wants "horror poetry only. We prefer poems that do not rhyme, but all verse will be considered. Poems 20-30 lines stand the best chance for acceptance, especially if they're scary and entertaining." Does not want "anything that isn't horror related, and always proof and edit before you send your submission. If your work does not have high entertainment or high impact, do not send it here." Has published poetry by Lee Clark Zumpe, Nancy Bennett, Steve Vernon, Kurt Newton, W.B. Vogel III, and Keith W. Sikora. *Champagne Shivers* is more than 60 pages, 8 1/2x11, professionally printed and perfect-bound, with full color cover art depicting a chilling, yet beautiful female. Receives about 1,000 poems/year, accepts 15 poems/issue. Press run and subscriber base vary; the only free copies go to reviewers and contributors. Single copy: $12 U.S. and Canada. Sample: $10 U.S. and Canada. ("Foreign countries, please inquire about costs.") Make checks payable to Tyree Campbell, Sam's Dot Publishing, P.O. Box 782, Cedar Rapids IA 52406-0782 (for subscriptions and sample copies only; DO NOT SEND SUBMISSIONS TO THIS ADDRESS).

> ○ "I want scary stuff, but I don't want anything that falls short of eloquent and poetic language.. To me, the word "Champagne" sig-

nifies quality and good taste, thus the title "Champagne Shivers."

HOW TO CONTACT Submit 20-30 line poems pasted in body of an email. "Shorter or longer work will not be considered." Submit "as often as you'd like but send just one poem (with bio) per email." Will not accept e-mails with attachments. Unpublished horror poems only. "Always let the editor know which rights you're offering. Your byline should always appear under your submission's title. At the end of your submission, include a fascinating bio of four or five sentences (written in the third person) that tells me something about yourself, other than where you've been published. Include your snail mail address if you want payment for your work. Score points with the editor by submitting in Times Roman 11 or 12. Type CS and the title of your submission in the subject line." Pays 10 cents per line and one contributor's copy.

TIPS "Submit horror poems only. I love psychological horror poetry, horror poetry about the Old West, horror poems about asylums, or anything that's just plain scary. I do not want poems about werewolves, vampires, ghosts, or traditional monsters. I want to read poetry that's fresh and exciting. Most of all, send me something that's high in entertainment, that's never been done before. Send poems that will give me and my audience the shivers." Sam's Dot Publishing offers The James Award (Trophy) annually. The editor selects one poem per year from the pages of Champagne Shivers to nominate for the award. **Entry fee:** "None—it's free." **Deadline:** August. Guidelines available on website. "Never send snail mail submissions; always submit in the body of an e-mail after reading the information under How to Submit."

⬤$ CHANTARELLE'S NOTEBOOK

E-mail: chantarellesnotebook@yahoo.com. Website: www.chantarellesnotebook.com. **Contact:** Kendall A. Bell and Christinia Bell, editors. *"Chantarelle's Notebook* will publish a 'best of' print journal that will cull poems from each of the previous 4 quarterly issues in the past year. The authors of the poems chosen will receive 1 contributor's copy and can buy additional copies at half price."

MAGAZINES NEEDS *Chantarelle's Notebook*, published quarterly online, seeks "quality work from undiscovered poets. We enjoy poems that speak to us—poems with great sonics and visuals." Wants "all styles of poetry, as long as it's quality work." Does not want "infantile rants, juvenile confessionals, greeting card-styled verse, political posturing, or religious outpourings." Considers poetry by children and teens. "There are no age restrictions, but submissions from younger people will be held to the same guidelines and standards as those from adults." Has published poetry by Donna Vorreyer, Heather Cadenhead, Taylor Copeland, Taylor Graham, Stacey Balkun, and Bill Roberts. Receives about 500 poems/year, accepts about 20%. Sample: see website for latest issue.

HOW TO CONTACT Submit 3-5 poems at a time. Lines/poem: "shorter poems have a better chance, but long poems are fine." Considers previously published poems; no simultaneous submissions. Accepts e-mail submissions (pasted into body of message; "we will not open any attachments—they will be deleted"). Cover letter is required. "Please include a short bio of no more than 75 words, should we decide to accept your work." Reads submissions year round. Submit seasonal poems 2-3 months in advance. "The editors will review all submissions and make a decision within a week's time." Never comments on rejected poems. Guidelines available on website. "Please follow the guidelines—all the information is there!" Responds in 4-6 weeks. Acquires one-time rights. Rights revert to poets upon publication. *Chantarelle's Notebook* is also accepting photo submissions. Please visit the website for guidelines on how to submit your photos to us."

ADDITIONAL INFORMATION The deadline for Issue #23 submissions is April 10, 2011. Any submissions after that date will be considered for Issue #24 in July 2011.

ALSO OFFERS "*Chantarelle's Notebook* will publish a 'best of' print journal that will cull poems from each of the previous 4 quarterly issues in the past year. The authors of the poems chosen will receive 1 contributor's copy and can buy additional copies at half price."

THE CHARITON REVIEW

Truman State University Press, The Chariton Review, Truman State Univ., 100 E Normal Ave, Kirksville MO 63501. (800)916-6802. E-mail: chariton@truman.edu; bsm@truman.edu. Website: tsup.truman.edu; http://tsup.truman.edu/aboutChariton.asp. **Contact:** Barbara Smith-Mandell, acquisitions editor. "Please include your name and contact informa-

tion on the first page of your printout. Include a self-addressed stamped envelope for response only if you do not provide an email address. Printouts will not be returned.""Truman State University Press (TSUP) publishes peer-reviewed research in the humanities for the scholarly community and the broader public, and publishes creative literary works. TSUP is a resource to the Truman campus community, where students explore their publishing interests and scholars seek publishing advice." TSUP is now publishing The Chariton Review, an international literary journal.

CONTEST/AWARD OFFERINGS T. S. Eliot Prize for Poetry

THE CHATTAHOOCHEE REVIEW

Website: www.chattahoochee-review.org. Georgia Perimeter College, 2101 Womack Rd., Dunwoody GA 30338. (770)274-5479. E-mail: gpccr@gpc.edu. Website: www.chattahoochee-review.org. Established 1980. **Contact:** Anna Schachner, editor-in-chief.

MAGAZINES NEEDS *The Chattahoochee Review*, published quarterly, prints poetry, short fiction, essays, reviews, and interviews. "We publish a number of Southern writers, but *The Chattahoochee Review* is not by design a regional magazine. All themes, forms, and styles are considered as long as they impact the whole person: heart, mind, intuition, and imagination." Has recently published work by George Garrett, Jim Daniels, Jack Pendarvis, Ignacio PadillAnd Kevin Canty. *The Chattahoochee Review* is 160 pages, digest-sized, professionally printed, flat-spined, with four-color silk-matte card cover. Press run is 1,250; 300 are complimentary copies sent to editors and "miscellaneous VIPs." Subscription: $20/year. Sample: $6.

HOW TO CONTACT Submit 3-5 poems at a time. Submit one piece of fiction and/or nonfiction, up to 6,000 words, at a time. No previously published work. Simultaneous submissions okay only if we are told. No e-mail or disk submissions. Cover letter is "encouraged, but not required." Include bio material when sending cover letter. Poems and prose should be typed on one side of page with poet's name clearly visible. No reply without SASE. Time between acceptance and publication is up to 6 months. Publishes theme issues. Guidelines available for SASE or on website. Responds in 1 week to 6 months. Pays $50/poem and 2 contributor's copies; pays $25/page for fiction and 2 contributor's copies. Acquires first rights. Staff reviews books of poetry and short fiction in 1,500 words, single- or multi-book format. Send materials for review consideration.

◑ CHAUTAUQUA LITERARY JOURNAL CHAUTAUQUA

Department of Creative Writing, 601 S. College Rd., Wilmington NC 28403. Website: http://writers.ciweb. org. **Contact:** Jill Gerard, editor.

○ Poetry published in *Chautauqua Literary Journal Chautauqua* has been included in *The Pushcart Prize* anthology.

MAGAZINES NEEDS *Chautauqua Literary Journal Chautauqua*, published annually in June, prints poetry, short fiction, and creative nonfiction. "The editors actively solicit writing that expresses the values of Chautauqua Institution broadly construed: A sense of inquiry into questions of personal, social, political, spiritual, and aesthetic importance, regardless of genre. We consider the work of any writer, whether or not affiliated with Chautauqua institution. The qualities we seek include a mastery of craft, attention to vivid and accurate language, a true lyric 'ear,' an original and compelling vision, and strong narrative instinct. Above all, we value work that is intensely personal, yet somehow implicitly comments on larger public concerns—work that answers every reader's most urgent question: Why are you telling me this?" Has published poetry by Robert Cording, Lucille Clifton, Carl Dennis, George Looney, Michael McFee, and many more. *Chautauqua Literary Journal Chautauqua* is approximately 230 pages, digest-sized, offset-printed, with notch adhesive binding and matte cover with original artwork. Receives about 4,000 poems/year, publishes about 30 poems per year. Press run is 1,500; 300 distributed free to contributors and others. Single copy: $14.95. Make checks payable to *Chautauqua Literary Journal*.

HOW TO CONTACT Submit 3 poems maximum at a time. Considers simultaneous submissions (if notified); no previously published poems. Prefers writers submit via www.manuscripthub.com. Cover letter is preferred. "We prefer single-spaced manuscripts in 12 pt. font. Cover letters should be brief and mention recent publications (if any). SASE is mandatory." Reads submissions February 15-April 15 and August 15-November 15. Time between acceptance and publication is up to 1 year. "The editor is the sole arbiter, but we do have advisory editors who make rec-

ommendations." Sometimes comments on rejected poems. Guidelines available on website. Responds in 3 months or less. Always sends prepublication galleys. Pays 2 contributor's copies. Acquires first rights "plus one-time non-exclusive rights to reprint accepted work in an anniversary issue."

◐ CHEST

3300 Dundee Rd, Northbrook IL 60062. 800-343-2222. E-mail: poetrychest@aol.com. Website: www. chestjournal.org. **Contact:** Michael Zack, M.D., poetry editor.

MAGAZINES NEEDS *Chest*, published monthly, "is the official medical journal of the American College of Chest Physicians, the world's largest medical journal for pulmonologists, sleep, and critical care specialists, with over 30,000 subscribers." Wants "poetry with themes of medical relevance." *Chest* is approximately 300 pages, magazine-sized, perfect-bound, with a glossy cover, and includes ads. Press run is 22,000. Number of unique visitors: 400,000 to website. Subscription: $276. Make checks payable to American College Chest Physicians.

HOW TO CONTACT Submit up to 1 poem at a time, between 10 and 80 lines. Only accepts e-mail submissions (as attachment or in body of e-mail); no fax or disk submissions. Brief cover letter preferred. Reads submissions year round. Poems are circulated to an editorial board. Sometimes comments on rejected poems. Never publishes theme issues. Guidelines available in magazine and on website. Responds in 2 months; always sends prepublication galleys. Retains all rights.

◑ CHIRON REVIEW

522 E. South Ave., St. John KS 67576-2212. (620)786-4955. E-mail: editor@chironreview.com. Website: http://chironreview.com. **Contact:** Gerald and Zachary Locklin, poetry editors.

MAGAZINES NEEDS *Chiron Review*, published quarterly, presents the widest possible range of contemporary creative writing — fiction and non-fiction, traditional and off-beat — in an attractive, professional tabloid format, including artwork and photographs of featured writers.No taboos. Has published poetry by Quentin Crisp, Felice Picano, Edward Field, Wanda Coleman, and Marge Piercy. Press run is about 1,000. Subscription: $20/year (4 issues). Single issue: $7.

HOW TO CONTACT Submit up to 5 poems or 1 long poem at a time. Only submit 4 times a year. Accepts e-mail and postal mail submissions. "Send all poems in ONE MS Word or translatable attachment. Complete postal address must accompany every single submission regardless of how many times you have submitted in the past. It helps if you put your name and genre of submission in subject line." Include SASE via postal mail. Does not accept simultaneous or previously published submissions. Guidelines available for SASE or on website. Responds in 2-6 weeks. Pays 1 contributor's copy. Acquires first-time rights. Reviews books of poetry in 500-700 words.

ADDITIONAL INFORMATION Will also publish occasional chapbooks; see website for details.

○❶◒⑤ CHIZINE: TREATMENT OF LIGHT AND SHADE IN WORDS

"Subtle, sophisticated dark fiction with a literary bent." Quarterly. Experimental, fantasy, horror (dark fantasy, futuristic, psychological, supernatural), literary, mystery, science fiction (soft/sociological). Does not want "tropes of vampires, werewolves, mummies, monsters, or anything that's been done to death." Receives 100 mss/month. Accepts 3-4 mss/issue; 12-16 mss/year. Does not read June, July and August due to Chizine Short Story Contest. Length: 4,000 words (max). Publishes short shorts. Average length of short shorts: 500 words. Also publishes poetry. Send to savory@rogers.com to query. Always comments on/critiques rejected mss.

○ Received Bram Stoker Award for Other Media in 2000.

CHRISTIAN COMMUNICATOR

(847)296-3964. Fax: (847)296-0754. E-mail: ljohnson@wordprocommunications.com. Website: acwriters.com. **Contact:** Lin Johnson, managing editor.

TIPS "We primarily use 'how to' articles and personality features on experienced writers and editors. However, we're willing to look at any other pieces geared to the writing life."

❶ CHRISTIANITY AND LITERATURE

Humanities Division, Pepperdine University, 24255 Pacific Coast Highway, Malibu CA 90263. Website: www.pepperdine.edu/sponsored/ccl/journal. **Contact:** Julia S. Kasdorf, poetry editor (Pennsylvania State University, English Dept., 114 Burrows Bldg, University Park, PA 16802).

MAGAZINES NEEDS "*Christianity & Literature* is devoted to the scholarly exploration of how literature engages Christian thought, experience, and practice. The journal presupposes no particular theological orientation but respects an orthodox understanding of Christianity as a historically defined faith. Contributions appropriate for submission should demonstrate a keen awareness of the author's own critical assumptions in addressing significant issues of literary history, interpretation, and theory." Subscription: $25/1 year; $45/2 years. Back issues: $10. *Christianity and Literature*, a quarterly scholarly journal, publishes about 4-6 poems/issue. Press run is 1,100. Single copy: $10; subscription: $25/year, $45 for 2 years. Make checks payable to CCL.

HOW TO CONTACT Submit hard copies only to Poetry Editor. Include contact information and SASE. Wants poems that are clear and surprising. "They should have a compelling sense of voice, formal sophistication (though not necessarily rhyme and meter), and the ability to reveal the spiritual through concrete images." Julia S. Kasdorf, Pennsylvania State University, English Dept., 114 Burrows Bldg., University Park, PA 16802.

TIPS "We look for poems that are clear and surprising. They should have a compelling sense of voice, formal sophistication (though not necessarily rhyme and meter), and the ability to reveal the spiritual through concrete images. We cannot return submissions that are not accompanied by SASE."

❶⑤ CHRYSALIS READER

1745 Gravel Hill Rd., Dillwyn VA 23936. (434)983-3021. E-mail: editor@swedenborg.com; rlawson@sover.net. E-mail: chrysalis@hovac.com. Website: www.swedenborg.com/chrysalis. **Contact:** Robert F. Lawson, editor. *Chrysalis Reader* is 208 pages, 7x10, professionally printed on archival paper, perfect-bound, with coated coverstock. Receives about 1,000 submissions/year, accepts about 16 poems. Press run is 3,500. Sample: $10. (Sample poems available on website. Regularly publishes theme issues (the 2010 issue theme is "The Marketplace"). Themes and guidelines available with SASE or on website. Responds in 3 months. Always sends prepublication galleys. Pays $25 and 3 contributor's copies. Acquires first-time rights. "We expect to be credited for reprints after permission is given." *The Chrysalis Reader* is a contemporary journal of spiritual discovery published in honor of Emanuel Swedenborg. Each issue focuses on a meaningful theme that inspires current writings and artwork that address today's questions on spirituality. Essays, fiction, poetry, and artwork give fresh and diverse perspectives from many traditions, personal experiences, and fields of study. As Swedenborg says, 'the essence of a thing cannot come into being unless it unites with a means that can express it." *The Chrysalis Reader* is published annually in the fall. Content of fiction, articles, poetry, etc. should be focused on that issue's theme and directed to the intellectual reader.

○ "This journal explores contemporary questions of spirituality from a Swedenborgian multifaith perspective."

MAGAZINES NEEDS *Chrysalis Reader*, published annually in September by the Swedenborg Foundation, is a "contribution to the search for spiritual wisdom, a book series that challenges inquiring minds through the use of literate and scholarly fiction, essays, and poetry." Wants "poetry that surprises, that pushes the language, gets our attention." Has published work by Robert Bly, Linda Pastan, Wesley McNair, Wyn Cooper, William Kloefkorn, and Virgil Suárez.

HOW TO CONTACT Submit no more than 5-6 poems at a time. Considers simultaneous submissions "if notified immediately when work is accepted elsewhere"; no previously published poems. Include SASE. Reads submissions year round. Time between acceptance and publication is typically 18 months.

CONTEST/AWARD OFFERINGS "The Bailey Prize (see separate listing in Contests & Awards).

CICADA MAGAZINE

(312)701-1720. Fax: (312)701-1728. E-mail: dvetter@caruspub.com. Website: www.cicadamag.com. **Contact:** Deborah Vetter, executive editor; John Sandford, art director. *CICADA Magazine*, published semi-monthly, is "the groundbreaking teen literary magazine that raises the issues that today's young adults find most important; a high-quality literary magazine for ages 14 and up." Wants "serious or humorous poetry; rhymed or free verse." Considers poetry by teens. *CICADA* is 128 pages, digest-sized, perfect-bound, with full-color cover. Receives more than 1,200 submissions/month, accept 25-30. Circulation is 10,000. Subscription: $35.97/year (6 issues). Sample: $8.50;

sample pages available online. Guidelines available on website. Responds in 2 months. Acquires North American publication rights for previously published poems; rights vary for unpublished poems.Bimonthly literary magazine for ages 14 and up. Publishes original short stories, poems, and first-person essays written for teens and young adults.

HOW TO CONTACT Submit no more than 5 poems at a time electronically. Considers previously published poems. Show line count on each poem submitted.

ALSO OFFERS "The Slam," is an online writing forum "for young writers who want the world to see what they can do with words."

TIPS "Quality writing, good literary style, genuine teen sensibility, depth, humor, good character development, avoidance of stereotypes. Read several issues to familarize yourself with our style."

① CIDER PRESS REVIEW

777 Braddock Lane, Halifax PA 17032. E-mail: editor@ciderpressreview.com. Website: http://ciderpressreview.com. **Contact:** Caron Andregg, editor-in-chief; Ruth Foley, associate poetry editor.

MAGAZINES NEEDS *Cider Press Review*, published annually, features "the best new work from contemporary poets." Wants "thoughtful, well-crafted poems with vivid language and strong images. We prefer poems that have something to say. We would like to see more well-written humor. We also encourage translations." Does not want "didactic, inspirational, greeting card verse, empty word play, therapy, or religious doggerel." Also welcomes reviews in not more than 500 words of current full-length books of poetry. Has published poetry by Robert Arroyo, Jr., Virgil Suaárez, Linda Pastan, Kathleen Flenniken, Tim Seibles, Joanne Lowery, Thomas Lux, and Mark Cox. *Cider Press Review* is 128 pages, digest-sized, offset-printed, perfect-bound, with 4-color coated card cover. Receives about 2,500 poems/year, accepts about 3%. Press run is 500. Single copy: $13.95; subscription: $24 for 2 issues (1 journal, 1 book from the *Cider Press Review* Book Award). Sample: $12 (journal).

HOW TO CONTACT Submit up to 5 poems at a time. No previously published poems or simultaneous submissions. Submit by postal mail or through online submission form at website. "International authors or special needs, please query via e-mail.

Do not send unsolicited disk or e-mail submissions." Cover letter is preferred. Include short bio (25 words maximum). SASE required for reply. Reads submissions April 1-August 31 only. Time between acceptance and publication is 6-9 months. Poems are circulated to an editorial board. Guidelines available for SASE or on website. Responds in 1-4 months. Always sends prepublication galleys. Pays 1 contributor's copy. Acquires first North American serial rights.

CONTEST/AWARD OFFERINGS *The Cider Press Review* Book Award (see separate listing in Contests & Awards). Our reading period is from Apr. 1 - Aug. 31 each year, and full mss. (in conjunction with the CPR Annual Book Award) between Sept. 1 - Nov. 30 each year. Prize is $1,500 and publication for a full length book of poetry and 25 copies.

◑ CIMARRON REVIEW

English Dept., Oklahoma State Univ., 205 Morrill Hall, Stillwater, OK 74078. E-mail: cimarronreview@okstate. edu. Website: http://cimarronreview.okstate.edu. **Contact:** Toni Graham, fiction editor. *Cimarron Review* is 100-150 pages, digest-sized, perfect-bound, with color cover. Press run is 600. Single copy: $7; subscription: $24/year ($28 Canada), $42 for 2 years ($48 Canada), $65 for 3 years ($72 Canada)."We want strong literary writing. We are partial to fiction in the modern realist tradition and distinctive poetry—lyrical, narrative, etc."

HOW TO CONTACT Considers simultaneous submissions. No e-mail submissions; accepts postal submissions only. "Writers outside North America may query by e-mail." No response without SASE. Guidelines available on website. Responds in up to 6 months. Submit 3-6 poems at a time. Include cover letter.

ADDITIONAL INFORMATION Reviews books of poetry in 500-900 words, single-book format, occasionally multi-book.

TIPS "All work must come with SASE. A cover letter is encouraged. No email submissions from authors living in North America. Query first and follow guidelines.", "In order to get a feel for the kind of work we publish, please read an issue or two before submitting."

● CLARK STREET REVIEW

P.O. Box 1377, Berthoud CO 80513. E-mail: clarkreview@earthlink.net. **Contact:** Ray Foreman, Editor. P.O. Box 1377, Berthoud, CO 80513. *Clark Street Re-*

view is a national bi-monthly small literary magazine. Focus is more on communicable content that is interesting, entertaining and informative than on literature.

MAGAZINES NEEDS *Clark Street Review*, published 6 times/year, uses narrative poetry and short shorts. Tries "to give writers and poets cause to keep writing by publishing their best work." Wants "narrative poetry under 100 lines that reaches readers who are mostly published poets and writers. Subjects are open." Does not want "obscure or formalist work." Has published poetry by Charles Ries, Anselm Brocki, Ed Galling, Ellaraine Lockie, and J. Glenn Evans. *Clark Street Review* is 20 pages, digest-sized, photocopied, saddle-stapled, with paper cover. Receives about 1,000 poems/year, accepts about 10%. Press run is 200. Single copy: $2; subscription: $10 for 10 issues postpaid for writers only. Make checks payable to R. Foreman.

HOW TO CONTACT Submit narrative poems only. Maximum 65 characters in width. Flush left. Considers previously published poems and simultaneous submissions. Send "disposable sharp hard copies. Include SASE for reply. No cover letter." No limit on submissions. Time between acceptance and publication is 4 months. "Editor reads everything with a critical eye of 30 years of experience in writing and publishing small press work." Guidelines available for SASE or by e-mail. Responds in 3 weeks. Acquires one-time rights.

○ COAL CITY REVIEW

Coal City Press, University of Kansas, Lawrence KS 66045. E-mail: coalcity@sunflower.com. E-mail: briandal@ku.edu. Website: www.coalcityreview.com. Brian Daldorph, poetry editor. **Contact:** Mary Wharff, fiction editor.

MAGAZINES NEEDS *Coal City Review* is 100 pages, digest-sized, professionally printed on recycled paper, perfect-bound, with colored card cover. Accepts about 5% of material received. Press run is 200. Subscription: $10. Sample: $6. Seldom comments on rejected poems. Guidelines available for SASE. Responds in up to 3 months.

HOW TO CONTACT Submit 6 poems at a time. Considers previously published poems "occasionally"; no simultaneous submissions. No e-mail submissions. "Please do not send list of prior publications." Include name and address on each page.

Reviews books of poetry in 300-1,000 words, mostly single-book format. Send materials for review consideration.

ADDITIONAL INFORMATION *Coal City Review* also publishes occasional books and chapbooks as issues of the magazine, but **does not accept unsolicited book/chapbook submissions**. Most recent book is *Douglas County Jail Blues,* poetry from inmates at Douglas County Correctional Facility, Lawrence, Kansas (2001-2010).

TIPS "We are looking for artful stories—with great language and great heart. Please do not send work that has not been thoughtfully and carefully revised or edited."

◐⊜ C/OASIS

P.O. Box 626, Largo FL 33779-0626. (727)345-8505. E-mail: oasislit@aol.com. Website: http://www.sunoasis.com/sunoasisopinion.html. **Contact:** David Eide, Editor. "C/Oasis has been dedicated to bringing, to the Net, the best short story writing and poetry writing available."

○ "C/Oasis is published by Sunoasis Publishing. It has published some of the finest poets and short story writers around, as well as essayists. Almost all the work published in C/Oasis is freelance. It usually buys one-time rights. The readers of C/Oasis are a varied bunch. Some are what could be defined as literary writers, even, teachers and professors. Others are students in liberal arts colleges. More than a few are writers themselves, although not necessarily literary writers. The editors are dedicated to bringing the best literature possible to C/Oasis. We are respectful of the variety of styles and regions in the present world. We have published writers from India, Brazil, Costa RicAustralia, GhanAs well as America. We are looking for innovative writing that takes the art seriously. We are looking for impassioned arguments or fantastic voyages. We are looking for several distinctive types of writing. Literary work: Mostly poems and stories since those are the appropriate forms for the web. Any work sent to Oasis will be respected. The editors respond to artful poems that have some consciousness of the poetry written in the 20th century. For short stories, interesting twists are more valuable than character analysis. Personal Essays: Evocative, personalist, complex, wise observations etc. Think Thoreau. Writing for writers: Articles that deal with problems writers encounter in the electronic publishing age. Commentary: Take on something in the real world and deal with it, enhance it with resources, and keep it under 2,000 words. We do publish writing resource articles only if they are written with a slant we haven't seen anywhere. We will look carefully at any article that says something intelligent about electronic publishing."

ADDITIONAL INFORMATION Estab. 1992. Poetry Oasis is a quarterly forum for high quality literary prose and poetry written almost exclusively by freelancers. Usually contains 6 prose pieces and the work of 4-5 poets. Wants "to see poetry of stylistic beauty. Prefer free verse with a distinct, subtle music. No superficial sentimentality, old-fashioned rhymes or rhythms." Has published poetry by Carolyn Stoloff and Simon Perchik. Oasis is about 75 pages, 7ï¿½10, attractively printed on heavy book paper, perfect-bound with medium-weight card cover, no art. Receives about 2,000 poems/year. Press run is 300 (90 subscribers, 5 libraries). Subscription: $20/year. Sample: $7.50. Submit any number of poems. Accepts simultaneous submissions; rarely accepts previously published poems. Accepts e-mail submissions (include in body of message). Cover letter preferred. Time between acceptance and publication is usually 4 months. Seldom comments on rejected poems. Guidelines available for SASE. Responds "the same or following day more than 99% of the time." Sends prepublication galleys on request. Pays $5/poem and 1 contributor's copy. Acquires first or ne-time rights.

COBBLESTONE

Cobblestone Publishing, 30 Grove Street, Suite C, Peterborough NH 03458. (800)821-0115. Fax: (603)924-7380. E-mail: customerservice@caruspub.com. Website: www.cobblestonepub.com. *COBBLESTONE Magazine*, published 9 times/year, is a magazine of American history for children ages 9-14. "All material must relate to the theme of a specific upcoming issue in order to be considered.""We are interested in articles of historical accuracy and lively, original approaches to the subject at hand. Our magazine is aimed at youths from ages 9 to 14. Writers are encouraged to study recent COBBLESTONE back issues for content and style. (Sample issues are available for $6.95 plus $2.00 shipping and handling. Sample issues will not be sent without prepayment.) All material must relate to the theme of a specific upcoming issue in order to be considered. To be considered, a query must accompany each individual idea (however, you can mail them all together) and must include the following: a brief cover letter stating the subject and word length of the proposed article, a detailed one-page outline explaining the information to be presented in the article, an extensive bibliography of materials the author intends to use in preparing the article, a SASE. Authors are urged to use primary resources and up-to-date scholarly resources in their bibliography. Writers new to COBBLESTONE' should send a writing sample with the query. If you would like to know if your query has been received, please also include a stamped postcard that requests acknowledgment of receipt. In all correspondence, please include your complete address as well as a telephone number where you can be reached. A writer may send as many queries for one issue as he or she wishes, but each query must have a separate cover letter, outline, bibliography, and SASE. All queries must be typed. **Please do not send unsolicited manuscripts - queries only!** Prefers to work with published/established writers. Each issue presents a particular theme, making it exciting as well as informative. Half of all subscriptions are for schools. All material must relate to monthly theme."

○ "Cobblestone stands apart from other children's magazines by offering a solid look at one subject and stressing strong editorial content, color photographs throughout, and original illustrations." *Cobblestone* themes and deadline are available on website or with SASE.

MAGAZINES NEEDS Wants "clear, objective imagery. Serious and light verse considered. Must relate to theme."

HOW TO CONTACT Query first. Lines/poem: up to 100. No e-mail submissions or queries. Include SASE. Reads submissions according to deadlines for queries (see website for schedule and details).

ADDITIONAL INFORMATION Subscription: $33.95/year (9 issues). Sample: $5.95 plus $2.00 s&h (include 10x13 SASE); sample pages available on website. Always publishes theme issue. Guidelines available on website.

TIPS "Review theme lists and past issues to see what we're looking for."

COLD MOUNTAIN REVIEW

English Dept., Appalachian State University, ASU Box 32052, Boone, NC 28608. (828)262-7108. E-mail: coldmountain@appstate.edu (inquiries only). Website: www.coldmountain.appstate.edu. **Contact:** Betty Miller Conway, managing editor. Subscription: $15. Sample copies: $8.

MAGAZINES NEEDS *Cold Mountain Review*, published twice/year (Spring and Fall), features poetry, interviews with poets, poetry book reviews, and b&w graphic art. Has published poetry by Sarah Kennedy, Robert Morgan, Susan Ludvigson, Aleida Rodriíguez, R.T. Smith, and Virgil Suaárez. *Cold Mountain Review* is about 72 pages, digest-sized, neatly printed with one poem/page (or 2-page spread), perfect-bound, with light cardstock cover. Publishes only 10-12 poems/issue; "hence, we are extremely competitive: send only your best."

HOW TO CONTACT Submit up to 5 poems at a time. No previously published poems or simultaneous submissions. No e-mail submissions; postal submissions only. Cover letter is required. Include short bio and SASE. "Please include name, address, phone number, and (if available) e-mail address on each poem. Poems should be single-spaced on one side of the page." Reads submissions August-May. Strongly suggest subscribing to magazing before submitting work. Guidelines available for SASE. Responds in up to 3 months. Pays 2 contributor's copies.

COLUMBIA: A JOURNAL OF LITERATURE AND ART

Columbia University, New York, NY 10027. E-mail: columbia.editor@gmail.com. Website: www.columbia.edu/cu/arts/journal.

MAGAZINES NEEDS *Columbia: A Journal of Literature and Art*, published annually, will consider "any poem that is eclectic and spans from traditional to experimental genres." Has published poetry by Louise Gluck, James Tate, Eamon Grennan, Mary Jo Salter, and Yuse Komunyakaa. *Columbia* is 176 pages, digest-sized, offset-printed, notch-bound, with glossy cover, includes ads. Receives about 2,000 poems/year, accepts about 2%. Press run is 2,000. Subscription: $10/year, $17/2 years.

HOW TO CONTACT Submit up to 5 poems at a time. Submit using online submission manager only. Considers simultaneous submissions when noted; no previously published poems. Accepts submissions through website only. Cover letter is preferred. Reads submissions year round. Poems are circulated to an editorial board. Guidelines available in magazine or on website. Responds in 3-4 months. Pays 2 contributor's copies. Acquires first North American serial rights.

CONTEST/AWARD OFFERINGS Sponsors annual contest with an award of $500. Submit no more than 5 poems/entry or 20 double-spaced pages for fiction and nonfiction submissions. **Entry fee:** $12. **Deadline:** see website or recent journal issue. All entrants receive a copy of the issue publishing the winners.

COMMON GROUND REVIEW

E-5309, Western New England College, 1215 Wilbraham Rd., Springfield MA 01119. E-mail: editors@cgreview.org. Website: http://cgreview.org. **Contact:** Janet Bowdan, Editor. *Common Ground Review*, published semiannually (Spring/Summer, Fall/Winter), prints poetry and original artwork by the art editor Alice Ahrens Williams. Has published poetry by James Doyle, Martin Galvin, CB Follett, Kathryn Howd Machan, and Sheryl L. Nelms. Single issue: $10; back issue: $5."We want poems with a fresh message, that instill a sense of wonder. This is the official poetry journal of Western New England College."

MAGAZINES NEEDS Poetry with strong imagery; well-written free or traditional forms.

HOW TO CONTACT Submit up to 3 poems under 61 lines. No previously published poems. Simultaneous submissions are allowed; see website for details. Cover letter and biography is required. "Poems should be single-spaced indicating stanza breaks; include name, address, phone number, e-mail address, brief biography, and SASE (submissions without SASE will not be notified)." Reads submissions year round, but deadlines for non-contest submissions are August 31 and March 1. Submit seasonal poems 6 months in advance. Time between acceptance and publication is 4-6 months. "Editor reads and culls submissions. Final decisions made by editorial board." Seldom comments on rejected poems. Guidelines available in magazine or on website. Responds in 2 months.

CONTEST/AWARD OFFERINGS Sponsors an annual poetry contest. Offers 1st Prize: $500; 2nd Prize: $200; 3rd Prize: $100; Honorable Mentions. **Entry fee:** $15 for 1-3 unpublished poems. **Deadline:** February 28 for contest submissions only. All contest submissions are considered for publication in *Common Ground Review*.

TIPS "For poems, use a few good images. Run-on, convoluted imagery may derail the reader. Poems should be condensed and concise, free from words that do not contribute. The subject matter should be worthy of the reader's time and appeal to a wide range of readers. Sometimes the editors may suggest possible revisions."

COMMON THREADS

3510 North High Street, Columbus OH 43214. (614)268-5094. E-mail: Team@ohiopoetryassn.org. Website: ohiopoetryassn.com. (Specialized: submissions by members only)

MAGAZINES NEEDS *Common Threads*, published semiannually in April and October, is the Ohio Poetry Association's member poetry magazine. **Only members of OPA may submit poems.** We use beginners' poetry, but like it to be good, tight, revised. In short, not first drafts. We like poems to make us think as well as feel something. Short poems 32 lines or under are treasured. We Do not want to see poetry that is highly sentimental, overly morbid, religiously coercive, or pornographic. Poetry by teens will be considered equally as members and prioritized if the teen poet is a high school contest winner. Poetry by Bill Reyer, Michael Bugeja, Timothy Russell, Yvonne Hardenbrook, Dalene Stull & other well published artists. Common Threads is 52 pages, digest-sized, computer-typeset, with matte card cover. Common Threads is a forum for OPA members, with reprints done so new members can see what is going well in more general magazines. Subscription: annual OPA dues, including 2 issues of Common Threads are $18; $15 for seniors (over age 65). Single copy: $2; $8 for students (through college).

HOW TO CONTACT Lines/poem: Nothing over 40 lines published (unless exceptional). Previously published poems are considered, if author notes when and where the work was previously published. Currently submissions are accepted by postal mail only. Submissions are accepted and read year round. Guidelines available for SASE. All rights revert to poet after publication.

COMMONWEAL

(212)662-4200. Fax: (212)662-4183. E-mail: editors@commonwealmagazine.org. Website: www.commonwealmagazine.org. **Contact:** Paul Baumann, editor. (Specialized: Catholic) Subscription: $59.

MAGAZINES NEEDS Serious, witty, well-written poems. Reviews books of poetry in 750-1,000 words, single- or multi-book format.

HOW TO CONTACT No simultaneous submissions. Only accepts hardcopy submissions with an SASE. Reads submissions September 1-June 30 only.

TIPS "Articles should be written for a general but well-educated audience. While religious articles are always topical, we are less interested in devotional and churchy pieces than in articles which examine the links between 'worldly' concerns and religious beliefs."

ⓘ THE COMSTOCK REVIEW

4956 St. John Dr., Syracuse, NY 13215. (315)488-8077. E-mail: poetry@comstockreview.org. Website: www.comstockreview.org.

MAGAZINES NEEDS "*Comstock Review* enters its 25th year of publication in 2011. We accept poetry strictly on the basis of quality, not reputation. We publish both noted and mid-career poets as well as those who are new to publishing. It is the quality of the poem that is the decisive factor. We do not accept overly sexual material, sentimental or "greeting card" verse, and very few haiku." approximately 100 pages, digest-sized, professionally printed, perfect-bound. Press run is 500. Subscription: $20/year, $36/2 years. Samples issues available for $12.

HOW TO CONTACT Submit 3-5 poems, one submission per reading period. No previously published poems or simultaneous submissions accepted. "Average poem published is one page in length. Please also consider our 65 character line width when submitting." Postal submissions only; no e-mail. Cover letter is optional, three line bio preferred. Include three line bio. Put name, address, phone number, and e-mail address on each page. Reads submissions January 1-March 15 only. Acceptances mailed out 8-12 weeks after close of reading period. Editorial comments and suggestions sometimes given. Guidelines available in magazine, for SASE, or on website. Pays 1 contributor's copy. Acquires first North American serial rights.

CONTEST/AWARD OFFERINGS The annual Muriel Craft Bailey Memorial Award and the biennial Jesse Bryce Niles Memorial Chapbook Award (see separate listings in Contests & Awards).

CONFRONTATION MAGAZINE

Confrontation Press, English Dept., C. W. Post Campus Long Island University, 720 Northern Blvd., Brookville NY 11548-1300. (516)299-2720. Fax: (516)299-2735. E-mail: confrontation@liu.edu; martin.tucker@liu.edu. Website: www.liu.edu/confrontation. **Contact:** Jonna Semeiks, editor. *Confrontation* is about 300 pages, digest-sized, professionally printed, flat-spined. Receives about l,200 submissions/year, accepts about 150. Circulation is 2,000. Subscription: $15/year. Sample: $3." We are eclectic in our taste. Excellence of style is our dominant concern. We bring new talent to light. We are open to all submissions, each issue contains original work by famous and lesser-known writers and also contains a thematic supplement that 'confront' a topic; the ensuing confrontation is an attempt to see the many sides of an issue rather than a formed conclusion." - Martin Tucker, director Confrontation Publications

○ *Confrontation* has garnered a long list of awards and honors, including the Editor's Award for Distinguished Achievement from CCLP (to Martin Tucker) and NEA grants. Work from the magazine has appeared in numerous anthologies including the *Pushcart Prize, Best Short Stories* and *The O. Henry Prize Stories. Confrontation* does not read mss during June, July, or August and will be returned unread unless commissioned or requested.

MAGAZINES NEEDS Prefers lyric poems. Considers poetry by children and teens.

HOW TO CONTACT Submit no more than 10 pages of poetry at a time. "Prefer single submissions. Clear copy." No e-mail submissions; postal submissions only. Reads submissions September-May. "Do not submit mss June through August." Publishes theme issues. Upcoming themes available for SASE. Guidelines available on website. Responds in 2 months. Sometimes sends prepublication galleys.

ADDITIONAL INFORMATION Staff reviews books of poetry. Send materials for review consideration. Occasionally publishes "book" issues or "anthologies." Most recent book is *Plenty of Exits: New and Selected Poems* by Martin Tucker, a collection of narrative, lyrical, and humorous poems.

TIPS Most open to fiction and poetry. Prizes are offered for The Sarah Tucker Award for fiction and The

John V. Gurry Drama Award. "We look for literary merit. Keep trying."

⊕ ⊙ ⊙ CONNECTICUT REVIEW

Connecticut Review, Connecticut State University System, 39 Woodland Street, Hartford, CT 06105-2337. (860)493-0095. Fax: (860)493-0120. E-mail: ct-review@southernct.edu. Website: www.ctstateu.edu/ctreview/index.html. JP Briggs, Jian-Zhong Lin, Mary Collins. **Contact:** Vivian Shipley, editor. Connecticut Review is published twice each year by the Connecticut State University System as a public service contribution to the national literary and intellectual discourse. Each issue of the journal is 200-212 pages in perfect bound 6 x 9 format and contains poetry, fiction, short essays, scholarly articles and fine artwork. The journal publishes the best in contemporary literature and essays. The selection process focuses on bringing to general readers cutting edge work that is both thought provoking and accessible."*Connecticut Review* is a high-quality literary magazine. We take both traditional literary pieces and those on the cutting edge of their genres. We are looking for poetry, fiction, short-shorts, creative essays, and scholarly articles accessible to a general audience. Each issue features an 8-page color fine art section with statements from the painters or photographers featured."

> ⊙ Poetry published in *Connecticut Review* has been included in *The Best American Poetry* and *The Pushcart Prize* anthologies; has received special recognition for Literary Excellence from Public Radio's series *The Poet and the Poem*; and has won the Phoenix Award for Significant Editorial Achievement from the Council of Editors of Learned Journals (CELJ).

MAGAZINES NEEDS Essays, poetry, articles, fiction, b&w photographs, and color artwork

HOW TO CONTACT Submit 3-5 typed poems at a time. Accepts submissions by postal mail only. Name, address, and phone number in the upper left corner of each page. Include SASE for reply only. Guidelines available for SASE. Pays 2 contributor's copies. Acquires first or one-time rights.

TIPS "We read manuscripts blind—stripping off the cover letter—but the biographical information should be there. Be patient. Our editors are spread over 4 campuses and it takes a while to move the manuscripts around."

⊙ THE CONNECTICUT RIVER REVIEW

53 Pearl St, New Haven CT 06511. E-mail: connpoetry@comcast.net. Website: www.ct-poetry-society.org/publications.htm. **Contact:** Lisa Siedlarz, editor. **MAGAZINES NEEDS** *Connecticut River Review*, published annually in July or August by the Connecticut Poetry Society, prints "original, honest, diverse, vital, well-crafted poetry." Wants "any form, any subject. Translations and long poems welcome." Has published poetry by Marilyn Nelson, Jack Bedell, Maria Mazziotti Gillan, and Vivian Shipley. *Connecticut River Review* is digest-sized, attractively printed, perfect-bound. Receives about 2,000 submissions/year, accepts about 100. Press run is about 300. Membership in the CT poetry society is $25 per year and includes *Connecticut River Review* and *Long River Run*, a members-only magazine.

HOW TO CONTACT Submit no more than 3-5 poems at a time. Considers simultaneous submissions if notified of acceptance elsewhere; no previously published poems. Cover letter is preferred. Include bio. "Complete contact information typed in upper right corner; SASE required." Reads submissions October 1-April 15. Guidelines available for SASE or on website. Responds in up to 8 weeks. Pays 1 contributor's copy. "Poet retains copyright."

⊙ ⊙ CONTE, AN ONLINE JOURNAL OF NARRATIVE WRITING

E-mail: poetry@conteonline.net. E-mail: prose@conteonline.net. Website: http://www.conteonline.net. **Contact:** Adam Tavel, poetry editor. *Conte, an Online Journal of Narrative Writing*, published biannually online, prints "narrative writing of the highest quality. Writing that displays some degree of familiarity with our journal is likely to attract our attention, so make sure your work has a narrative bent." Has published poetry by William Hathaway, Jim Daniels, E. Ethelbert Miller, Erika Meitner, and Roger Weingarten, among others. Receives about 2,000 poems/year, accepts about 24. Number of unique visitors: approximately 1,000/month."We publish short stories, chapter-length excerpts from novels and novel mss. and pieces of creative nonfiction. Mention previous publications in your letter and share how you heard about *Conte*. We read year-round. Query with an excerpt for longer pieces."

MAGAZINES NEEDS Cover letters are optional for some magazines, but we like to know a little about our submitters. "The type of things you should probably include are: 1) how you learned about our journal; 2) a few places you have been published previously, if at all; and 3) whether or not you are sending a simultaneous submission." Reads submissions year-round. Time between acceptance and publication is typically 2-4 months. Since *Conte* is a small journal, it is truly a labor of love for our 3 editors. While we occasionally share work with one another during the screening process, primarily we rely on our respective expertise in poetry and prose when making editorial selections. "Ultimately, a good poem is fresh and engaging from its very first line, so the chief responsibility for any poetry editor is to sift through clichés and mediocrity to share the best submitted work with the world." Sometimes comments on rejected poems. Does not publish theme issues. Guidelines available on website. Responds in 3-5 months. Sometimes sends prepublication galleys. Acquires one-time rights. Rights revert to poets upon publication. Publication not copyrighted.

HOW TO CONTACT Submit up to 3 poems at a time. Query before sending poems over 100 lines in length. Considers simultaneous submissions; "please state clearly in your cover letter that your work is under consideration elsewhere and notify us immediately if it is accepted by another publication"; does not accept previously published poems (considers poetry posted on a public website/blog/forum and poetry posted on a private, password-protected forum as published). Accepts e-mail submissions (pasted into body of message); no fax or disk submissions. Cover letter is preferred.

TIPS "Submit poems in the body of an email to: poetry@conteonline.net, with subject line 'Poetry Submission' followed by the title. We are averse to rhyme schemes and attachments. Submit prose to: prose@conteonline.net, with subject line 'Prose Submission' followed by title. Rich Text (.rtf) attachments are preferred but submissions in the body of an email are acceptable."

●●⑤ CONTEMPORARY HAIBUN

P.O. Box 2461, Winchester VA 22604-1661. (540)722-2156. E-mail: jim.kacian@comcast.net; ray@raysweb.net. Website: www.contemporaryhaibunonline.com; www.redmoonpress.com. **Contact:** Jim Kacian, Editor/Publisher.

MAGAZINES NEEDS *contemporary haibun*, published annually in April, is the first Western journal dedicated to haibun. Considers poetry by children and teens. Has published poetry by Fran Masat, Carol Pearce-Worthington, Ray Rasmussen, and Jeff Winke. *contemporary haibun* is 128 pages, digest-sized, offset-printed on quality paper, with 4-color heavy-stock cover. Receives several hundred submissions/year, accepts about 5%. Print run is 1,000. Subscription: $17 plus $5 p&h. Sample available for SASE or by e-mail.

HOW TO CONTACT Submit up to 3 haibun at a time. Considers previously published poems. Accepts e-mail submissions. "Subject line should contain cho, your name, your haibun title(s) and the date." Include SASE for postal submissions. Time between acceptance and publication varies according to time of submission. Poems are circulated to an editorial board. "Only haibun and haiga will be considered. Guidelines available in magazine, for SASE, by e-mail, or on website. Pays $1/page. Acquires first North American serial rights.

ALSO OFFERS Publishes *The Red Moon Anthology*, "an annual volume of the finest English-language haiku and related work published anywhere in the world." (See separate listing in this section.)

●●⑤ CONTRARY

3133 S. Emerald Ave., Chicago IL 60616-3299. E-mail: chicago@contrarymagazine.com (no submissions). Website: www.contrarymagazine.com. **Contact:** Jeff McMahon, editor.

MAGAZINES NEEDS "Fiction, poetry, literary commentary, and prefers work that combines the virtues of all those categories"

HOW TO CONTACT No mail or e-mail submissions; submit work via the website. Considers simultaneous submissions; no previously published poems. Accepts submissions through online form only.

ADDITIONAL INFORMATION "We like work that is not only contrary in content, but contrary in its evasion of the expectations established by its genre. Our fiction defies traditional story form. For example, a story may bring us to closure without ever delivering an ending. And we value fiction as poetic as any poem. We look especially for plurality or meaning, for dual reverberation or beauty and concern. *Contrary's* poetry in particular often mimics the effects of fiction or commentary. We find ourselves enamored of prose poems because they are naturally ambiguous about form — they tug overtly on the forces of narrative — but prose poems remain the minority of all the poetic forms we publish."

TIPS "Beautiful writing catches our eye first. If we realize we're in the presence of unanticipated meaning, that's what clinches the deal. Also, we're not fond of expository fiction. We prefer to be seduced by beauty, profundity and mystery than to be presented with the obvious. We look for fiction that entrances, that stays the reader's finger above the mouse button. That is, in part, why we favor microfiction, flash fiction and short-shorts. Also, we hope writers will remember that most editors are looking for very particular species of work. We try to describe our particular species in our mission statement and our submission guidelines, but those descriptions don't always convey nuance. That's why many editors urge writers to read the publication itself; in the hope that they will intuit an understanding of its particularities. If you happen to write that particular species of work we favor, your submission may find a happy home with us. If you don't, it does not necessarily reflect on your quality or your ability. It usually just means that your work has a happier home somewhere else."

◑ CONVERGENCE: AN ONLINE JOURNAL OF POETRY AND ART

E-mail: clinville@csus.edu. E-mail: clinville@csus.edu. Website: www.convergence-journal.com. **Contact:** Cynthia Linville, managing editor. "We look for well-crafted work with fresh images and a strong voice. Work from a series or with a common theme has a greater chance of being accepted. Seasonally-themed work is appreciated (spring and summer for the January deadline, fall and winter for the June deadline). Please include a 75-word bio with your work (bios may be edited for length and clarity). A cover letter is not needed. Absolutely no simultaneous or previously published submissions."

C Deadlines are January 5 and June 5.

MAGAZINES NEEDS New interpretations of the written word by pairing poems and flash fiction with complementary art. "We are open to many different styles, but we do not often publish formal verse. Read a couple of issues to get a sense of what we like; namely, well-crafted work with fresh images and a strong voice."

HOW TO CONTACT No simultaneous or previously published submissions. Accepts e-mail submissions only. Reads submissions year round. Time between acceptance and publication is 1-2 months. Poems are circulated to an editorial board. Responds in 6 months. Acquires first rights.

TIPS "We look for freshness and originality and a mastery of the craft of flash fiction. Working with a common theme has a greater chance of being accepted."

◐ COTTONWOOD

1301 Jayhawk Blvd., Room 400, Kansas Union, University of Kansas, Lawrence, KS 66045. E-mail: pwedge@ku.edu. Website: www.cottonwoodmagazine.org/read. **Contact:** Phil Wedge, poetry editor.

MAGAZINES NEEDS *Cottonwood*, published semiannually, emphasizes the Midwest "but publishes the best poetry received regardless of region." Wants poems "on daily experience, perception; strong narrative or sensory impact, non-derivative." Does not want "'literary,' not 'academic.'" Has published poetry by Rita Dove, Virgil Suárez, Walt McDonald, Oliver Rice, and Luci Tapahonso. *Cottonwood* is 112 pages, digest-sized, printed from computer offset, flat-spined. Receives about 3,000 submissions/year, accepts about 20. Press run is 500-600. Single copy: $8.00. Sample: $5.

HOW TO CONTACT Submit up to 5 pages of poetry at a time with SASE. Lines/poem: 60 maximum. No simultaneous or e-mailed submissions. Sometimes comments on rejected poems. Responds in up to 5 months. Pays 1 contributor's copy.

ADDITIONAL INFORMATION Cottonwood Press "is auxiliary to *Cottonwood Magazine* and publishes material by authors in the region. **Material is usually solicited.**" Has published *Violence and Grace* by Michael L. Johnson and *Midwestern Buildings* by Victor Contoski.

TIPS "We're looking for depth and/or originality of subject matter, engaging voice and style, emotional honesty, command of the material and the structure. *Cottonwood* publishes high quality literary fiction, but we are very open to the work of talented new writers. Write something honest and that you care about and write it as well as you can. Don't hesitate to keep trying us. We sometimes take a piece from a writer we've rejected a number of times. We generally don't like clever, gimmicky writing. The style should be engaging but not claim all the the attention itself."

● THE COUNTRY DOG REVIEW

E-mail: countrydogreview@gmail.com. Website: www.countrydogreview.org. **Contact:** Danielle Sellers, editor.

MAGAZINES NEEDS *The Country Dog Review*, published semiannually online, publishes "poetry, book reviews, and interviews with poets."Wants "poetry of the highest quality, not limited to style or region. Also accepts book reviews and interviews. Query first." Does not want "translations, fiction, nonfiction." Receives about 400 poems/year, accepts about 10%.

HOW TO CONTACT Submit 3-5 poems at a time. No previously published poems or simultaneous submissions. Only accepts e-mail submissions with attachment; no fax or disk submissions. Subject of e-mail should read: last name, date, poetry. Bio is required. Reads submissions year round. Submit seasonal poems 6 months in advance. "Please submit no more than twice a submission period." Time between acceptance and publication is 1-4 months. Never comments on rejected poems. Sometimes publishes theme issues. Upcoming themes and guidelines available by e-mail and on website. Responds in 1-2 months. Sometimes sends prepublication galleys. Acquires first North American serial rights. Reviews books of poetry in 500 words, single-book format.

CRAB CREEK REVIEW

7315 34th Ave. NW, Seattle WA 98117. E-mail: crabcreekreview@gmail.com. Website: www.crabcreekreview.org.

 "Nominates for the Pushcart Prize and offers annual Crab Creek Review editors' prize of $100 for the best poem, essay, or short story published in the previous year."

MAGAZINES NEEDS *Crab Creek Review*, published biannually, is seeking "poetry, short fiction, and creative non-fiction that takes us somewhere unexpected, keeps us engaged, and stays with us beyond the initial reading. We appreciate lyrical and narrative forms of poetry, with a slight bias toward free verse. Translations are welcome—please submit with a copy of the poem in its original language, if possible." Has published poetry by Oliver de la Paz, Dorianne Laux, Greg Nicholl, and translations by Ilya

Kaminsky and Matthew Zapruder. Fiction by karen Heuler and Daniel Homan. *Crab Creek Review* is an 80- to 120-page, perfect-bound paperback. Subscription: $15/year, $28/2 year. Sample: $6.

HOW TO CONTACT Send up to 5 poems between September 1 and April 30, to "Poetry Editor." No e-mail submissions. Cover letter is preferred. Include cover letter and SASE for reply only. "Without one we will not consider your work." Responds in up to 6 months. Pays 1 contributor copy.

CONTEST/AWARD OFFERINGS Offers annual poetry contest with deadline of May 31st. Entry fee: $10. Submit up to 5 poems. All entries will be considered for publication. See website for more information.

TIPS "We currently welcome submissions of poetry, short fiction, and creative nonfiction."

CRAB ORCHARD REVIEW

(618)453-6833. Fax: (618)453-8224. Website: www.siu.edu/~crborchd. We are a general interest literary journal published twice/year. We strive to be a journal that writers admire and readers enjoy. We publish fiction, poetry, creative nonfiction, fiction translations, interviews and reviews.

MAGAZINES NEEDS *Crab Orchard Review*, published semiannually in March and September, prints poetry, fiction, creative nonfiction, interviews, book reviews, and novel excerpts. Wants all styles and forms from traditional to experimental. Does not want greeting card verse; literary poetry only. Has published poetry by Luisa A. Igloria, Erinn Batykefer, Jim Daniels, Bryan Tso Jones. *Crab Orchard Review* is 256-280 pages, digest-sized, professionally printed, perfect-bound, with (usually) glossy card cover with color photos. Receives about 12,000 poems/year, accepts about 1%. Press run is 3,500; 100 exchanged with other journals; remainder in shelf sales. Subscription: $20. Sample: $12.

HOW TO CONTACT Submit up to 5 poems at a time. Considers simultaneous submissions with notification; no previously published poems. Postal submissions only. Cover letter is preferred. "Indicate stanza breaks on poems of more than 1 page." Reads submissions April-November for Summer/Fall special theme issue, February-April for regular, non-thematic Winter/Spring issue. Time between acceptance and publication is 6 months to a year. "Poems that are under serious consideration are discussed and decided on by the managing editor and poetry editor." Seldom comments on rejected poems. Publishes theme issues. Upcoming themes available in magazine, for SASE, or on website. Guidelines available for SASE or on website. Responds in up to 9 months. Pays $20/page ($50 minimum), 2 contributor's copies, and 1 year's subscription. Acquires first North American serial rights. Staff reviews books of poetry in 500-700 words, single-book format. Send materials for review consideration to Jon C. Tribble, Managing Editor.

CONTEST/AWARD OFFERINGS The Crab Orchard Series in Poetry Open Competition Awards, The Crab Orchard Series in Poetry First Book Award, and The Richard Peterson Poetry Prize (see separate listings in Contests & Awards).

TIPS We publish two issues per volume—one has a theme (we read from May to November for the theme issue), the other doesn't (we read from January through April for the nonthematic issue). Consult our website for information about our upcoming themes.

CRAZYHORSE

College of Charleston, Dept. of English, 66 George St., Charleston SC 29424. (843)953-7740. E-mail: crazyhorse@cofc.edu. Website: www.crazyhorsejournal. org. See website for e-book and print subscriptions. We like to print a mix of writing regardless of its form, genre, school, or politics. We're especially on the lookout for original writing that doesn't fit the categories and that engages in the work of honest communication.

MAGAZINES NEEDS *Crazyhorse*, published semiannually, prints fine fiction, poetry, and essays. "Send your best words our way. We like to print a mix of writing regardless of its form, genre, school, or politics. We're especially on the lookout for writing that doesn't fit the categories. Before sending, ask 'What's reckoned with that's important for other people to read?'" Has published poetry by David Wojahn, Mary Ruefle, Nance Van Winkle, Dean Young, Marvin Bell, and A.V. Christie.

HOW TO CONTACT Submit 3-5 poems at a time. Considers simultaneous submissions; no previously published poems. No fax, e-mail, or disk submissions. Cover letter is preferred. Reads submissions year round. "We read slower in summer." Time between acceptance and publication is 6 months. Seldom comments on rejected poems. Guidelines available in magazine, for SASE, by e-mail, or on website. Responds in 3 months. Sometimes sends prepublication galleys. Pays $20-35/page, 2 contributor's copies, and one-year subscription (2 issues). Acquires first North American serial rights.

CONTEST/AWARD OFFERINGS The annual Lynda Hull Memorial Poetry Prize (see separate listing in Contests & Awards).

TIPS Write to explore subjects you care about. The subject should be one in which something is at stake. Before sending, ask 'What's reckoned with that's important for other people to read?'

CRICKET MAGAZINE

Website: www.cricketmag.com. (Specialized: for young reades ages 9-14) Carus Publishing, 70 E. Lake St., Suite 300, Chicago IL 60601. Website: www.cricketmag.com. Established 1973. **Contact:** Submissions Editor.

MAGAZINES NEEDS *CRICKET* Magazine, published monthly, is a literary magazine for young readers ages 9-14. Wants "serious and humorous poetry, nonsense rhymes." Does not want "forced or trite rhyming or imagery that doesn't hang together to create a unified whole." *CRICKET* is 64 pages, 8x10, saddle-stapled, with color cover. Circulation is 73,000. Subscription: $33.95/year (12 issues). Sample: $6.95; sample pages available on website.

HOW TO CONTACT Submit no more than 5 poems at a time. Lines/poem: 50 (2 pages) maximum. Considers previously published poems. Put line count on each poem submitted. Include SASE. Guidelines available for SASE or on website. Responds in 6 months. Payment is up to $3/line on publication. Acquires North American publication rights for previously published poems; rights vary for unpublished poems.

CONTEST/AWARD OFFERINGS Sponsors poetry contests for readers.

CURRENT ACCOUNTS

Current Accounts, Apt. 2D, Bradshaw Hall, Hardcastle Gardens, Bolton BL2 4NZ, UK. E-mail: bswscribe@gmail.com; fjameshartnell@aol.com. Website: http://bankstreetwriters.webs.com/currentaccounts.htm. **Contact:** FJ Hartnell. Published semiannually. Doesn't want rhyming poetry. "Travel or tourist poetry needs to be more than just exotic names and places. Titles need care. Poetry should be poetic in some form. Experimental work is welcome. As a writer you are expected to be able to spell." Welcomes submissions from any writers or any age. Subscription: $15/3 issues.*Current Accounts*, published semiannually, prints poetry, fiction, and nonfiction by members of Bank Street Writers, and other contributors. Open to all types of poetry. "No requirements, although some space is reserved for members." Considers poetry by children and teens. Has published poetry by Pat Winslow, M.R. Peacocke, and Gerald England. *Current Accounts* is 52 pages, A5, photocopied, saddle-stapled, with card cover with b&w or color photo or artwork. Receives about 300 poems/year, accepts about 5%. Press run is 80; 8 distributed free to competition winners. Subscription: £6. Sample: £3. Make checks payable to Bank Street Writers (sterling checks only).

HOW TO CONTACT Submit up to 4 poems, no more than 40 lines each. Accepts postal and e-mail submissions. Postal submissions should include SASE or IRC. E-mail submissions should be pasted in body, not attached. All submissions must include name, address, post code and e-mail address. "We cannot publish anonymous work nor reply to same." Reads year round. "You should contact us again if you have heard nothing after a month." Does not accept previously published poems. Pays one contributor's copy. See website for detailed guidelines.

TIPS Bank Street Writers meets once/month and offers workshops, guest speakers, and other activities. Write for details."We like originality of ideas, images, and use of language. No inspirational or religious verse unless it's also good in poetic terms."

○ CURRICULUM VITAE

Simpson Publications, P.O. Box 1082, Franklin PA 16323. E-mail: simpub@hotmail.com. **Contact:** Amy Dittman, managing editor.

MAGAZINES NEEDS *Curriculum Vitae*, published semiannually in January and July, is "a zine where quality work is always welcome. We'd like to see more metrical work, especially more translations, and well-crafted narrative free verse is always welcome. We do not want to see rambling Bukowski-esque free verse or poetry that overly relies on sentimentality." *Curriculum Vitae* is 40 pages, digest-sized, photocopied, saddle-stapled, with 2-color cardstock cover. Receives about 500 poems/year, accepts about 75. Press run is 1,000. Subscription: $6 for 4 issues.

Sample: $4.

HOW TO CONTACT Submit 3 poems at a time. Considers previously published poems and simultaneous submissions. Cover letter is preferred ("to give us an idea of who you are"). "Submissions without a SASE cannot be acknowledged due to postage costs." Time between acceptance and publication is 8 months. Poetry is circulated among 3 board members. Often comments on rejected poems. Publishes theme issues. Guidelines available for SASE or by e-mail. Responds within 1 month. Pays 2 contributor's copies plus one-year subscription.

ADDITIONAL INFORMATION "We're also interested in expanding our list of innovative side projects, books, graphic novels, chapbooks like *The Iowa Monster*, and the CV Poetry Postcard Project." Simpson Publications publishes about 5 chapbooks/year. Query with full manuscripts or well-thought-out plans with clips. Include SASE.

ALSO OFFERS "We are currently looking for poets who would like to be part of our Poetry Postcard series."

◐ CUTBANK

Website: www.cutbankonline.org. **Contact:** Kate Rutledge Jaffe, Editor-in-Chief. English Dept. LA 133, University of Montana, Missoula MT 59812. (406)243-6156. E-mail: cutbank@umontana.edu. Website: www.cutbankonline.org. Established 1973.

MAGAZINES NEEDS *CutBank*, published semiannually, prints regional, national, and international poetry, prose, interviews, and artwork. Has published poetry by Richard Hugo, Carl Phillips, Sandra Alcosser, and Virgil Suarez. Press run is 1000. Single copy: $10; subscription: $15/1 year. Sample: $8.

HOW TO CONTACT Submit up to 5 poems at a time. Considers simultaneous submissions ("discouraged, but accepted with notification"). Poems should be single-spaced; include SASE. Should include name, address, phone number, and e-mail address on the first page of each poem. Reads submissions October 1-February 15 only. Responds in up to 4 months. Pays 2 contributor's copies. All rights return to author upon publication.

TIPS "Familiarity with the magazine is essential. *Cutbank* is very open to new voices—we have a legacy of publishing acclaimed writers early in their careers—but we will consider only your best work."

◑ CUTTHROAT, A JOURNAL OF THE ARTS

P.O. Box 2414, Durango CO 81302. (970) 903-7914. E-mail: cutthroatmag@gmail.com. Website: www. cutthroatmag.com. **Contact:** William Luvaas, fiction editor.

MAGAZINES NEEDS Literary magazine/journal and "one separate online edition of poetry, translations, short fiction, and book reviews yearly. 6×9, 180+ pages, fine cream paper, slick cover. Includes photographs. "We publish only high quality fiction and poetry. We are looking for the cutting edge, the endangered word, fiction with wit, heart, soul and meaning." Annual. Estab. 2005. Member CCLMP.

HOW TO CONTACT Submit 3-5 poems attn: William Pitt Root, poetry editor. International submissions can be electronic. Reading periods for online editions are March 15-June 1; for print editions, July 15-October 10. Please include cover letter and SASE for response only; ms are recycled.

TIPS "Read our magazine and see what types of stories we've published. The piece must have heart and soul, excellence in craft. "

◎◑ DALHOUSIE REVIEW

Dalhousie University, Halifax, NS, B3H 4R2 Canada. (902)494-2541. E-mail: dalhousie.review@dal. ca. Website: http://dalhousiereview.dal.ca. Anthony Stewart, editor. **Contact:** Poetry editor. "Beyond our spelling preferences being those of *The Canadian Oxford Dictionary*, writers of creative non-fiction, fiction and poetry are encouraged to follow whatever canons of usage might govern the particular work in question, and to be inventive with language, ideas and form." Subscription: $30/1 year (3 issues); $75/3 years (9 issues).*Dalhousie Review*, published 3 times/year, is a journal of criticism publishing poetry and fiction. Considers poetry from both new and established writers. *Dalhousie Review* is 144 pages, digest-sized. Accepts about 5% of poems received. Press run is 500. Single copy: $15 CAD; subscription: $22.50 CAD, $28 USD. Make checks payable to *Dalhousie Review*.

HOW TO CONTACT Submit up to 5 poems, no more than 40 lines each. Does not accept simultaneous submissions or previously published submissions. Accepts postal submissions only, include e-mail address on submission. Reads year round. Responds in 3-9 months. Pays 2 contributor's copies and 10 offprints.

DARKLING MAGAZINE

Darkling Publications, 28780 318th Avenue, Colome SD 57528. (605)455-2892. E-mail: darkling@mitchelltelecom.net. **Contact:** James C. Van Oort, editor in chief. (Specialized: poetry of a dark nature)

MAGAZINES NEEDS *Darkling Magazine*, published annually in late summer, is "primarily interested in poetry. All submissions should be dark in nature and should help expose the darker side of man. Dark nature does not mean whiny or overly murderous, and being depressed does not make an artist's work dark. Pornography will not be considered and will merit no response. Profanity that is meritless or does not support the subject of any piece is unacceptable. Has published poems by Robert Cooperman, Kenneth DiMaggio, Arthur Gottlieb, Simon Perchik, Cathy Porter and Susanna Rich, among others. Subscription: $10 with s&h. Sample copies are $10.00. Make checks payable to Darkling Publications.

HOW TO CONTACT Submit up to 8 poems at a time. Lines/poem: any length is acceptable, but "Epic poems must be of exceptional quality. Considers simultaneous submissions but please no previously published poems. Will accept e-mail submissions; no disk submissions. Cover letter is required. Reads submissions June or July. Time between acceptance and publication is varies. Poems are circulated to an editorial board. Sometimes comments on rejected poems. Guidelines available in magazine. Announces rejections and acceptance in May or June. Pays 1 contributor's copy. All rights revert to author upon publication.

CONTEST/AWARD OFFERINGS Submit approximately 30 pages of poetry for the Darkling Magazine Annual Chapbook Contest. No theme is necessary. Dark poetry is preferred but excellent poetry of any type will be considered. Again no pornography or excessive profanity will be printed. The editors reserve the right to determine which poems and in which order the poems shall be printed and thus the final publication may deviate from the original manuscript sent in by the contestant. A reading fee of $20.00 is required. Checks should be made out to Darkling Publications. Open for chapbook submissions from January 1 thru May 15. Winner will be notified in July and expected publication will be in November. Each entrant will receive 1 copy of the winning chapbook. The winner will receive 10 copies of the chapbook and a 20% discount on any additional copies they may wish to purchase. Editors may offer comments on chapbooks submitted.

⊕ ◑ ◐ DEAD MULE SCHOOL OF SOUTHERN LITERATURE

E-mail: deadmule.poetry@gmail.com. Website: www. deadmule.com. **Contact:** Helen Losse, poetry editor.

MAGAZINES NEEDS "*The Dead Mule School of Southern Literature* wants stories. Good ones. Your writing? Hmmmmm. Write about sweat-dripping, Bible-thumping, pick-up driving, beer drinking rednecks. Chauvinistic, Mama-loving, hounddog-owning porch sitters - stereotypes we love to hate or hate to love. Heroes who drink sweet tea, eat Moon Pies, grits, and collards, frying in lard… lard pie, lard eggs, lard sandwiches. Lard. Mule skinners and mud runners. The esoteric, the strange, the truly captivating story will make it onto our pages. Be it about folks who are uncouth, semi-literate, tobacco chewing adolescents, or PhDs, Scholars, Scientists, Artists, Inventors, and Entrepreneurs. Write about brilliant, kind, thoughtful folks who will help you in your time of need or spit on your grandma. The South contains them all. There's no New South, there is only The South."

HOW TO CONTACT Submit 1-4 Poems at a time. No previously published poems or simultaneous submissions. Submit by e-mail, "along with Southern Legitimacy Statement with your submission. *The Dead Mule* does not publish standard bios." Reads submissions year round. Guidelines found on website. "Submission to and acceptance by *Dead Mule* grants us first electronic and indefinite archive rights. All other rights revert to the author upon publication. Please credit *Dead Mule* as the first publisher if you reprint elsewhere; we like seeing our name in print, too." Accepts submissions through online submission manager.

● ◯ DENVER QUARTERLY

University of Denver, 2000 E. Asbury, Denver CO 80208. (303)871-2892. Website: www.denverquarterly.com. **Contact:** Bill Ramke. Magazine: 6×9; 144-160 pages; occasional illustrations. . Estab. 1996. Circ. 2,000. Subscription: $20/1 year, $37/2 years. Sample: $10."We publish fiction, articles and poetry for a generally well-educated audience, primarily interested in literature and the literary experience. They read DQ to find something a little different from a stictly academic quarterly or a creative writing outlet."

Quarterly. Pays $5/page for fiction and poetry and 2 contributor's copies. Acquires first North American serial rights.

○ *Denver Quarterly* received an Honorable Mention for Content from the American Literary Magazine Awards and selections have been anthologized in the *Pushcart Prize* anthologies. *Denver Quarterly*. received an Honorable Mention for Content from the American Literary Magazine Awards and selections have been anthologized in the *Pushcart Prize* anthologies.

HOW TO CONTACT Submit 3-5 poems. Accompany each ms with SASE. Postal submissions only. Reads between September 15 and May 15.

TIPS "We look for serious, realistic and experimental fiction; stories which appeal to intelligent, demanding readers who are not themselves fiction writers. Nothing so quickly disqualifies a manuscript as sloppy proofreading and mechanics. Read the magazine before submitting to it. We try to remain eclectic, but the odds for beginners are bound to be small considering the fact that we receive nearly 10,000 mss per year and publish only about ten short stories."

◐ DESCANT: FORT WORTH'S JOURNAL OF POETRY AND FICTION

English Dept., Texas Christian University, Box 297270, Fort Worth TX 76129. Fax: (817)257-6239. E-mail: descant@tcu.edu. Website: www.descant.tcu.edu. **Contact:** Dave Kuhne, Editor. For fifty years, *descant*, the literary journal of Texas Christian University, has been publishing outstanding poetry and fiction, and, over the course of five decades, *descant* has become Fort Worth's journal of poetry and fiction. A forum for fiction and poetry, *descant* seeks high-quality work in either innovative or traditional forms. Subscription: $12 ($18 outside U.S.). Sample: $10.

MAGAZINES NEEDS *descant: Fort Worth's Journal of Poetry and Fiction*, published annually during the summer, seeks "well-crafted poems of interest. No restrictions as to subject matter or form." *descant* is 100+ pages, digest-sized, professionally printed and bound, with matte card cover. Receives about 3,000 poems/year. Press run is 500. Subscription: $12 ($18 outside U.S.). Sample: $10.

HOW TO CONTACT Submit no more than 5 poems at a time. Lines/poem: 60 or fewer, "but sometimes longer." Accepts simultaneous submissions. Include

SASE. No fax or e-mail submissions. Reads submissions September 1-April 1 only. Responds in 6 weeks. Pays 2 contributor's copies.

CONTEST/AWARD OFFERINGS Sponsors the annual Betsy Colquitt Award for Poetry, offering $500 to the best poem or series of poems by a single author in a volume. *descant* also offers a $250 award for an outstanding poem in an issue. No application process or reading fee; all published submissions are eligible for consideration.

DEVIL BLOSSOMS

Asterius Press, P.O. Box 5122, Seabrook NJ 08302-3511. Website: www.asteriuspress.com. **Contact:** John C. Erianne, Editor. Asterius Press P.O. Box 5122, Seabrook, NJ 08302-3511. E-mail: theeditor@asteriuspress.com. Website: www.asteriuspress.com. Needs: Dark, edgy poetry and prose. Literary, erotic, noir, satirical, absurdist, sick, twisted, maniacal, strange, psychological, Kafkaesque horror, sf, hard-boiled. Single issue: $5. Subscription: $14/3 issues; $25/6 issues. Back issues: $3. *Devil Blossoms*, published irregularly 1-2 times/year, seeks "poetry in which the words show the scars of real life. Sensual poetry that's occasionally ugly. I'd rather read a poem that makes me sick than a poem without meaning." Wants poetry that is "darkly comical, ironic, visceral, horrific; or any tidbit of human experience that moves me." Does not want "religious greetings, 'I'm-so-happy-to-be-alive' tree poetry." Has published poetry by Marie Kazalia, Stephanie Savage, Mitchell Metz, Normal, John Sweet, and Alison Daniel. *Devil Blossoms* is 32 pages, 7½x10, saddle-stapled, with matte card cover with ink drawings. Receives about 10,000 poems/year, accepts about 1%. Press run is 750. Single copy: $5; subscription: $14. Make checks payable to John C. Erianne.

HOW TO CONTACT Submit 3-5 poems by e-mail only. Must have "Submission" in subject line. Accepts simultaneous submissions. Doesn't accept previously published submissions.

TIPS "Write from love; don't expect love in return, don't take rejection personally, and don't let anyone stop you."

DEVOZINE

1908 Grand Ave., P.O. Box 340004, Nashville TN 37203-0004. E-mail: smiller@upperroom.org. Website: www.devozine.org. **Contact:** Sandi Miller, Editor.

MAGAZINES NEEDS *devozine*, published bimonthly, is a 64-page devotional magazine for youth (ages 12-19) and adults who care about youth. Offers meditations, scripture, prayers, poems, stories, songs, and feature articles to "aid youth in their prayer life, introduce them to spiritual disciplines, help them shape their concept of God, and encourage them in the life of discipleship." Considers poetry by teens.

HOW TO CONTACT Lines/poem: 10-20. No e-mail submissions; submit by regular mail with SASE or use online submmission form. Include name, age/birth date (if younger than 25), mailing address, e-mail address, phone number, and fax number (if available). Always publishes theme issues (focuses on nine themes/issue, one for each week). Indicate theme you are writing for. Guidelines available for SASE or on website. Pays $25.

DIAGRAM

E-mail: editor@thediagram.com. Website: www.the-diagram.com. "*Diagram* is an electronic journal of text and art, found and created. We're interested in representations, naming, indicating, schematics, labeling and taxonomy of things; in poems that masquerade as stories; in stories that disguise themselves as indices or obituaries."

"We sponsor yearly contests for unpublished hybrid essays and innovative fiction. Guidelines on website."

MAGAZINES NEEDS *DIAGRAM*, published semimonthly online, prints "poetry, prose, and schematic (found or created), plus nonfiction, art, and sound. We're especially interested in unusual forms and structures, and work that blurs genre boundaries." Does not want light verse. Has published poetry by Arielle Greenberg, Jason Bredle, Lia Purpura, GC Waldrep. Receives about 1,000 poems/year, accepts about 5%. Number of unique visitors:1,500/day.

HOW TO CONTACT Submit 3-6 poems at a time. Lines/poem: no limit. Considers simultaneous submissions; no previously published poems. Electronic submissions accepted through submissions manager; no e-mail, disk, or fax submissions. Electronic submissions MUCH preferred; print submissions must include SASE if response is expected." Cover letter is preferred. Reads submissions year round. Time between acceptance and publication is 1-10 months. Poems are circulated to an editorial board. Sometimes comments on rejected poems. Sometimes publishes theme issues. Guidelines available on website. Responds in 1-3 months. Always sends prepublication galleys. Acquires first rights and first North American serial rights. Rights revert to poet upon publication. Reviews books/chapbooks of poetry in 500-1,500 words, single- or multi-book format. Send materials for review consideration to Pablo Peschiera, reviews editor. Info on website **ADDITIONAL INFORMATION** *DIAGRAM* also publishes periodic perfect-bound print anthologies. **CONTEST/AWARD OFFERINGS** Sponsors the annual *DIAGRAM*/Michigan Press Chapbook Contest (see separate listing in Contests & Awards). **TIPS** "Submit interesting text, images, sound and new media. We value the insides of things, vivisection, urgency, risk, elegance, flamboyance, work that moves us, language that does something new, or does something old - well. We like iteration and reiteration. Ruins and ghosts. Mechanical, moving parts, balloons, and frenzy. We want art and writing that demonstrates/interaction; the processes of things; how functions are accomplished; how things become or expire, move or stand. We'll consider anything. We do not consider email submissions, but encourage electronic submissions via our submissions manager software. Look at the journal and submissions guidelines before submitting."

● JAMES DICKEY NEWSLETTER

(Specialized: life & works of James Dickey), Dept. of English, University of South Carolina, Columbia SC 29208. (803)777-4203. Fax: (803)777-9064. E-mail: tcompton@mailbox.sc.edu. Website: www.james-dickey.org. Established 1984 (newsletter), 1990 (society). **Contact:** Thorne Compton, editor.
MAGAZINES NEEDS *James Dickey Newsletter*, published semiannually in the spring and fall by the James Dickey Society, is "devoted to critical articles/studies of James Dickey's works/biography and bibliography." Publishes "a few poems of high quality. No poems lacking form, meter, or grammatical correctness." Has published poetry by Henry Taylor, Fred Chappell, George Garrett, and Dave Smith.
HOW TO CONTACT Accepts fax and e-mail (pasted into body of message/as attachment) submissions. "However, if poet wants written comments/suggestions line by line, send manuscript by postal mail with SASE." Cover letter is required. "Contributors should follow MLA style and standard manuscript format, sending one copy, double-spaced." Guide-

lines available in magazine or on website. Pays 2 contributor's copies. Acquires first rights. Reviews "only works on Dickey or that include Dickey."
ALSO OFFERS The James Dickey Society is devoted to discussions, dissemination, and interpretive scholarship and research concerning the works of James Dickey. Additional information available on website.

DIG MAGAZINE

(603)924-7209. Fax: (603)924-7380. Website: www.digonsite.com. **Contact:** Rosalie Baker, editor.
MAGAZINES NEEDS *DIG Magazine*, published 9 times/year in partnership with *Archeology* magazine, features archeology and exploration for children ages 9-14. "All material must relate to the theme of a specific upcoming issue in order to be considered." Wants "clear, objective imagery. Serious and light verse considered. Must relate to theme." Subscription: $32.97/year (9 issues). Sample: $5.95 plus $2.00 s&h (include 10X13 SASE); sample pages available on website.
HOW TO CONTACT Query first. Lines/poem: up to 100. No e-mail submissions or queries. Include SASE. Reads submissions according to deadlines for queries (see website for schedule and details). Always publishes theme issue. Themes and guidelines available on website. Pays varied rates. Acquires all rights.
TIPS "Please remember that this is a children's magazine for kids ages 9-14 so the tone is as kid-friendly as possible given the scholarship involved in researching and describing a site or a find."

●●● DIODE POETRY JOURNAL

Virginia Commonwealth University in Qatar, Doha Qatar, Qatar. +9744134812. Fax: +9744920332. E-mail: ppaine@qatar.vcu.edu. Website: diodepoetry.com. **Contact:** Patty Paine, editor. "Diode is looking for 'electropositive' poetry. What is electropositive poetry? It's poetry that excites and energizes. It's poetry that uses language that crackles and sparks. We're looking for poetry from all points on the arc, from formal to experimental."
MAGAZINES NEEDS Does not want "light verse, erotic." Has published poetry by Bob Hicok, Beckian Fritz Golberg, G.C. Waldrep, Dorianne Laux, Ada Limon, Joshua Maries Wilkinson. Receives about 4000 poems/year, accepts about 3%.

HOW TO CONTACT Submit 3-5 poems at a time. Considers simultaneous submissions, no previously published poetry. Accepts submissions by e-mail; attach document. Cover letter is required. Reads submissions year round. Time between acceptance and publication is 3-5 weeks. Sometimes comments on rejected poems. Guidelines available on website, by e-mail, in magazine. Responds in 3-5 weeks. Always sends prepublication galleys. Acquires one-time rights. Rights rever to poet upon publication. Reviews books and chapbooks of poetry in 2,000-4,000 words, single and multi-book format. Send review materials to Patty Paine.

◐◑ THE DIRTY NAPKIN

E-mail: thedirtynapkin@thedirtynapkin.com. Website: thedirtynapkin.com. **Contact:** J. Argyl Plath, Managing Director.

MAGAZINES NEEDS "Have you ever felt the urgency to write while you were out, at a restaurant, say, and scribbled a thought down on a napkin or the closest thing you could find? Have you ever told your friends to 'hang on a sec' until you finished that thought? As writers, we do not know when the muse will slap us silly. Luckily, there are many napkins filling the world waiting for us to dirty them. Luckily, there are many napkins filling the world waiting for us to dirty them. We believe writing cannot be separated from the voice, breath, and personality of the author. Further, we feel that if a piece of writing is separated from this literal voice, much power is lost. Therefore, we seek to include this voice by providing recordings of each author reading their work." Our mission is to create an active community of exceptional writers via an online literary journal. We believe that writing cannot be separated from the voice, breath, and personality of the author. Further, we feel that if a piece of writing is separated from this literal voice much power is lost. Therefore, we seek to include this voice by providing recordings of each author reading their work." Has published poetry by Alicia Ostriker, Jane Mead, F.D. Reeve, Sarah J. Sloat, Jacqueline Garlitos, and Doug Ramspeck. Single copy: $10-40 for POD (varies based on page count), subscription $16 (includes access to all author recordings and discounts on merchandise).

HOW TO CONTACT Submit 3 poems at a time. Accepts electronic submissions (through online form only); no fax or disk submissions. Cover letter is preferred. Reads submissions year round. Time be-

tween acceptance and publication is 2-3 months. Poems are circulated to an editorial board. Sometimes comments on rejected poems. Guidelines on website. Responds in 1-2 months. Acquires first North American serial and electronic rights. Rights revert to poets upon publication.

ALSO OFFERS "Each issue will feature one writer on its cover. The winner will be determined by the staff from the pool of accepted submissions. There are no entry fees or application procedures other than the regular submission of your work. If you are selected to win the cover prize we will ask that you handwrite your work on a napkin of your choosing. Your work will also appear inside the magazine as usual."

◐ DISLOCATE

University of Minnesota English Department, the Edelstein-Keller Endowment, and Adam Lerner of the Lerner Publishing Group., Dept. of English, University of Minnesota, 1 Lind Hall, 207 Church St. SE, Minneapolis MN 55455. Website: http://dislocate. umn.edu. *dislocate* is a print and online literary journal dedicated to publishing the literature that pushes the traditional boundaries of form and genre. We like work that operates in the gray areas, that resists categorization, that ignores the limits; we like work that plays with the relationship between form and content. We publish fiction, nonfiction, and poetry, but we don't mind if we can't tell which one we're dealing with. In addition to our more "literary" content, dislocate also publishes articles and columns of interest to readers, writers, and other aesthetically curious individuals.

⭕ *Reading period currently closed.*

ADDITIONAL INFORMATION "We are now using Submishmash for all submissions. (Submissions will become available when the reading period begins.) We will not consider or respond to submissions or by post or email."

CONTEST/AWARD OFFERINGS dislocate.umn.edu also runs a monthly Short Forms Contest; winners are published on the website and awarded prizes that vary from month to month. See contest submission guidelines and prize details.

TIPS "Looking for excellent writing that rearranges the world."

DMQ REVIEW

E-mail: editors@dmqreview.com. Website: www. dmqreview.com. **Contact:** Sally Ashton, editor-in-chief. We seek work that represents the diversity of contemporary poetry and demonstrates literary excellence, whether it be lyric, free verse, prose, or experimental form.

MAGAZINES NEEDS *DMQ Review*, published quarterly online, is "a quality magazine of poetry presented with visual art." Wants "finely crafted poetry that represents the diversity of contemporary poetry." Has published poetry by David Lehman, Ellen Bass, Amy Gerstler, Bob Hicok, Ilya Kaminsky, and Jane Hirshfield. Receives about 3,000-5,000 poems/year, accepts about 1%.

HOW TO CONTACT Submit up to 3 poems at a time ("no more than once per quarter"). Considers simultaneous submissions (with notifications only); no previously published poems. Accepts e-mail submissions (pasted into body of message; no attachments will be read) only. "Please read and follow complete submission guidelines on our website." Reads submissions year round. Time between acceptance and publication is 1-3 months. Poems are circulated to an editorial board. Never comments on rejected poems. Responds within 3 months. Acquires first rights.

ADDITIONAL INFORMATION Nominates for the Pushcart Prize. "We also consider submissions of visual art, which we publish with the poems in the magazine, with links to the artists' Web sites."

TIPS Check our current and past issues and read and follow submission guidelines closely. Important: Copy and include the permission statement with your submission (it's in our guidelines online). For Visual Art submissions: Type 'Art Submission' followed by your name in your email. Send a working URL where we may view samples of your work.

DOWN IN THE DIRT

829 Brian Court, Gurnee IL 60031-3155. (847)281-9070. E-mail: alexrand@scars.tv. Website: scars.tv. **Contact:** Alexandria Rand, editor.

MAGAZINES NEEDS *Down in the Dirt*, published monthly online, prints "good work that makes you think, that makes you feel like you've lived through a scene instead of merely read it." Also can consider poems. Does not want smut, rhyming poetry, or religious writing. Has published work by I.B. Rad, Pat Dixon, Mel Waldman, and Ken Dean. *Down in the Dirt* is published "electronically as well as in print, either on the Web or in e-book form (PDF file)."

Sample: available on website.

HOW TO CONTACT Lines/poem: any length is appreciated. Considers previously published poems and simultaneous submissions. Accepts e-mail submissions (vastly preferred to snail mail; pasted into body of message or as Microsoft Word .doc file attachment) and disk submissions (formatted for Macintosh). Guidelines available for SASE, by e-mail, or on website. No payment. "Currently, accepted writings get their own web page in the "writings" section at http://scars.tv, and samples of accepted writings are placed into an annual collection book Scars Publications produces."

ADDITIONAL INFORMATION Also able to publish electronic chapbooks. Write for more information.

CONTEST/AWARD OFFERINGS Scars Publications sponsors a contest "where accepted writing appears in a collection book. Write or e-mail (editor@scars.tv) for information."

DROWN IN MY OWN FEARS

E-mail: drowninmyownfears@yahoo.com. Website: http://drowninmyownfears.angelfire.com. **Contact:** Chantal Hejduk, Alla Kozak and Kaia Braeburn, editors.

MAGAZINES NEEDS *Drown In My Own Fears*, published quarterly online, "is a poetry journal about the human condition, therefore, we want poems reflecting that. Poems submitted should be about love, hate, pain, sorrow, etc. We don't want maudlin sentimentality, we want the depths of your very being. We want well-written, deeply conceived pieces of work. Anything that isn't about the human condition really isn\rquote t for us." Wants "all styles of poetry, as long as it's your best work." Does not want "syrupy sweet, gooey nonsense, religious rants, political grandstandings." Considers poetry by teens. Has published poetry by Kendall A. Bell, April Michelle Bratten, Natalie Carpentieri, MK Chavez, James H. Duncan and Taylor Graham. Receives about 300 poems/year, accepts about 10%.

HOW TO CONTACT Submit 3-5 poems at a time. "We prefer short poems, but long ones are ok." Considers previously published poems; no simultaneous submissions. Accepts e-mail submissions (pasted into body of e-mail message); no fax or disk submissions. Cover letter is rquired. Include a brief bio with your submission. Reads submissions year round. Submit seasonal poems 3 months in advance. Time between acceptance and publication is 1-2 months. Never comments on rejected poems. Sometimes publishes theme issues. Upcoming themes and guidelines available on website. Responds in 2-4 weeks. Acquires first rights. Rights revert to poets upon publication.

DRUNKEN BOAT

119 Main St., Chester, CT 06412. E-mail: editor@ drunkenboat.com. Website: www.drunkenboat. com.

MAGAZINES NEEDS *Drunken Boat*, published twice yearly online, is a multimedia publication reaching an international audience with an extremely broad aesthetic. Considers poetry by teens. "We judge by quality, not age. However, most poetry we publish is written by published poets with training in creative writing. "Has published more than 500 poets, including Heather McHugh, Jane Hirshfield, Alfred Corn, Alice Fulton, Ron Silliman, and Roseanna Warren. Received about 3,000 poems/year, accepts about 5%.

HOW TO CONTACT Submit up to 3 poems at a time. Considers simultaneous submissions. Accepts submissions through online submissions system on website only. Cover letter is preferred. "Due to the high number of poetry submissions, we limit submissions to 3 poems, in .doc or .rtf format. "Reads submissions year round. Time between acceptance and publication is 2-4 months. "Readers have MFAs in poetry, pass work to assistant poetry editor, who passes to poetry editor. "Sometimes comments on rejected poems. Sometimes publishes theme issues. Guidelines on website. Responds in 4-12 weeks. Always sends prepublication galleys. Acquires one-time rights. "Unless reprinted something already published, *Drunken Boat* has exclusive electronic rights of the work in question. Work that appears in print needs to acknowledge prior publication in *Drunken Boat*. Also, *Drunken Boat* reserves the right to republish work in print or DVD format with the permission of author/artist. "Reviews books, chapbooks of poetry. Will consider reviews of any length. Send materials for review consideration to editor@drunkenboat.com.

TIPS "Submissions should be submitted in Word & rtf format only. (This does not apply to audio, visual & web work.) Accepts chapbooks. See our submissions manager system."

✚ ◑ DUCTS

P.O. Box 3203, Grand Central Station, New York NY 10163. E-mail: fiction@ducts.org; essays@ducts.org. Website: http://ducts.org. **Contact:** Jonathan Kravetz. poDUCTS is a webzine of personal stories, fiction, essays, memoirs, poetry, humor, profiles, reviews and art. "DUCTS was founded in 1999 with the intent of giving emerging writers a venue to regularly publish their compelling, personal stories. The site has been expanded to include art and creative works of all genres. We believe that these genres must and do overlap. DUCTS publishes the best, most compelling stories and we hope to attract readers who are drawn to work that rises above." Semi-annual.

HOW TO CONTACT Reading period is January 1 through August 31. Send complete ms to poetry@ ducts.org. Accepts submissions by e-mail to appropriate departments. Responds in 1-4 weeks to queries; 1-6 months to mss. Accepts simultaneous and reprints submissions. Writer's guidelines on ducts.org.

TIPS "We prefer writing that tells a compelling story with a strong narrative drive."

◑ ◐ EARTHSHINE

PO Box 245, Hummelstown PA 17036. E-mail: poetry@ruminations.us. Website: www.ruminations. us. **Contact:** Sally Zaino and Julie Moffitt, poetry editors.

MAGAZINES NEEDS *Earthshine*, published irregularly in print, and online, features poetry and 1-2 pieces of cover art per volume. "When the online journal is full, a printed volume is produced and offered for sale. Subscriptions will be available as the publication becomes regular. The voice of *Earthshine* is one of illumination, compassion, humanity, and reason. Please see submission guidelines Web page for updated information. Poems are the ultimate rumination, and if the world is to be saved, the poets will be needed; they are who see the connections between all things, and the patterns shared. We seek poetry of high literary quality which will generate its own light for our readers." Has published poetry by Rachel Barroso, Fredrik Zydek, Steven Klepetar, Mario Susko.

HOW TO CONTACT Considers previously published poems; no simultaneous submissions. (Considers poetry posted on a public website/blog/forum and poetry posted on a private, password-protected forum as published.) Accepts e-mail submissions (pasted into body of message); no fax or disk submissions. Cover letter is preferred. "Please let us know where you heard about *Earthshine*. If submitting by mail, please include a SASE for reply only. Please do not send the only copy of your work." Reads submissions year round. Submit seasonal poems 1 month in advance. Time between acceptance and publication is: "online publication is almost immediate, printed publication TBD." Sometimes comments on rejected poems. Never publishes theme issues. Guidelines available in magazine, for SASE, and on website. Responds in 1-2 months. Pays 2 contributor's copies. Acquires first rights, one-time rights, electronic rights. Archive rights negotiated separately. Rights revert to poets upon publication.

ALSO OFFERS "The parent of *Earthshine* is also at Ruminations.us, and offers full editing and review services for a fee."

ECLECTICA

E-mail: editors@eclectica.org. E-mail: submissions@eclectica.org. Website: www.eclectica.org. Online magazine. "Eclectica is a quarterly World Wide Web journal devoted to showcasing the best writing on the Web, regardless of genre or subject matter. 'Literary' and 'genre' work appear side-by-side in each issue, along with pieces that blur the distinctions between such categories. Pushcart Prize, National Poetry Series, and Pulitzer Prize winners, as well as Nebula Award nominees, have shared issues with previously unpublished authors." Magazine seeks outstanding poetry, fiction, nonfiction, opinion, and reviews."A sterling quality literary magazine on the World Wide Web. Not bound by formula or genre, harnessing technology to further the reading experience and dynamic and interesting in content."

MAGAZINES NEEDS Magazine seeks outstanding poetry, fiction, nonfiction, opinion, and reviews.

HOW TO CONTACT Accepts submissions by e-mail. E-mail: submissions@eclectica.org. Must be plain text, no attachments. Poetry submissions should be limited to 5 works per author. "While we will consider simultaneous submissions, please be sure to let us know that they are simultaneous and keep us updated on their publication status." Guidelines available on website. Acquires first North American serial rights, electronic rights.

TIPS "Works which cross genres—or create new ones—are encouraged. This includes prose poems,

'heavy' opinion, works combining visual art and writing, electronic multimedia, hypertext/html, and types we have yet to imagine. No length restrictions. We will consider long stories and novel excerpts, and serialization of long pieces. Include short cover letter."

⊙● THE ECLECTIC MUSE

Suite 307, 6311 Gilbert Rd., Richmond BC V7C 3V7, Canada. (604)447-0979. E-mail: jrmbooks@hotmail.com. Website: mbooksofbc.com; thehypertexts.com. **Contact:** Joe M. Ruggier, publisher.

MAGAZINES NEEDS *The Eclectic Muse*, published annually at Christmas, is devoted "to publishing all kinds of poetry (eclectic in style and taste) but specializing in rhyme- and neo-classicist revival." Does not want "bad work (stylistically bad or thematically offensive)." Has published poetry by Mary Keelan Meisel, John Laycock, Philip Higson, Roy Harrison, Michael Burch, and Ralph O. Cunningham. *The Eclectic Muse* is magazine-sized, digitally copied, saddle-stapled, with paper cover. The number of pages varies from year to year (32 minimum to 56 maximum). Receives about 300 poems/year, accepts about 15%. Press run is 200; distributed free to all contributing authors plus selected gift subscription recipients. Single copy: $8; subscription: $25. Make checks payable to Joe M. Ruggier.

HOW TO CONTACT Submit no more than 5 poems at a time. Lines/poem: 60 maximum; "please consult if longer." Considers previously published poems and simultaneous submissions. Accepts e-mail submissions (preferred, as a single .doc or .rtf attachment containing all 5 poems) and disk submissions. "Send your submission by regular mail only if you have no access to a computer or you are computer illiterate. Typeset everything in Times New Roman 12 point. If your poetry features indents and special line spacing, please make sure you reproduce these features yourself in your data entry since it will not be possible for the editor to determine your intentions." Cover letter is preferred. "Include brief bio (100 words maximum) with your name, credentials (degrees, etc.), occupation and marital status, your most major publication credits only, and any hobbies or interests." Provide SASE plus clear e-mail and postal addresses for communication and for sending contributor's copy. Reads submissions year round. Time between acceptance and publication is 1 year. Poems are circulated to an editorial board. Sometimes comments on rejected poems. **"If authors wish to have a manuscript carefully assessed and edited, the fee is $250 USD; will respond within 8 weeks."** Guidelines available in magazine or on website. Responds in 2 months. Pays 2 contributor's copies. Reviews books/chapbooks of poetry and other magazines/journals in 900 words. Send materials for review consideration to Joe M. Ruggier, managing editor.

ALSO OFFERS "Look us up on www.thehypertexts. com, where myself and my services are listed (featured) permanently. The host of this splendid poetry website is my U.S. associate, Mr. Michael Burch. He features, on this site, most of the leading names in contemporary North America."

ECOTONE

(910)962-2547. Fax: (910)962-7461. E-mail: info@ ecotonejournal.com. Website: www.ecotonejournal. com.

MAGAZINES NEEDS "*Ecotone* is a literary journal of place that seeks to publish creative works about the environment and the natural world while avoiding the hushed tones and cliches of much of so-called nature writing. Reading period is August 15-April 15."

TIPS "www.ecotonejournal.com/submissions.html."

◔ EKPHRASIS

Frith Press, P.O. Box 161236, Sacramento CA 95816-1236. E-mail: frithpress@aol.com. Website: ekphrasisjournal.com. **Contact:** Laverne Frith and Carol Frith, Editors.

◑ Poems from *Ekphrasis* have been featured on *Poetry Daily*. Nominates for Pushcart Prize.

MAGAZINES NEEDS *Ekphrasis*, published semiannually in March and September, is an "outlet for the growing body of poetry focusing on individual works from any artistic genre." Wants "poetry mainly based on individual works from any artistic genre. Poetry should transcend mere description. Open to all forms." Does not want "poetry without ekphrastic focus. No poorly crafted work. No archaic language." Has published poetry by Jeffrey Levine, Peter Meinke, David Hamilton, Barbara Lefcowitz, Molly McQuade, and Annie Boutelle. *Ekphrasis* is 35-50 pages, digest-sized, photocopied, saddle-stapled. Subscription: $12/year. Sample: $6. Make checks payable, in U.S. funds, to Laverne Frith.

HOW TO CONTACT Submit 3-5 poems at a time. Considers previously published poems "infrequently, must be credited"; no simultaneous submissions. Accepts submissions by postal mail only. Cover letter is required, including short bio with representative credits and phone number. Include SASE. Time between acceptance and publication is up to 1 year. Seldom comments on rejected poems. Guidelines available for SASE or on website. Responds in 4 months. Pays 1 contributor's copy. Nominates for Pushcart Prize. Acquires first North American serial or one-time rights.

ADDITIONAL INFORMATION Until further notice, Frith Press will publish **occasional chapbooks by invitation only**.

CONTEST/AWARD OFFERINGS The Ekphrasis Prize, a $500 award, "is now being presented to the best poem published in Ekphrasis in each calendar year, as determined by the editors of the journal. There will be no contest. No reading fees will be required. The 2010 prize was awarded to Diana Pinckney for "The Kiss of Water."

◑◔◉ ELLERY QUEEN'S MYSTERY MAGAZINE

Dell Magazines Fiction Group, 267 Broadway, 4th Floor, New York NY 10017. (212)686-7188. Fax: (212)686-7414. E-mail: elleryqueenmm@dellmagazines.com. Website: www.themysteryplace.com/eqmm. (Specialized: mystery/suspense)"*Ellery Queen's Mystery Magazine* welcomes submissions from both new and established writers. We publish every kind of mystery short story: the psychological suspense tale, the deductive puzzle, the private eye case—the gamut of crime and detection from the realistic (including the policeman's lot and stories of police procedure) to the more imaginative (including 'locked rooms' and 'impossible crimes'). We look for strong writing, an original and exciting plot, and professional craftsmanship. We encourage writers whose work meets these general criteria to read an issue of *EQMM* before making a submission."

◑ "EQMM uses an online submission system (http://eqmm.magazinesubmissions.com) that has been designed to streamline our process and improve communication with authors. We ask that all submissions be made electronically, using this system, rather than on paper. All stories should be in standard manuscript format and submitted in .DOC format. We cannot accept .DOCX, .RTF, or .TXT files at this time. For detailed submission instructions, see http://eqmm.magazinesubmissions.com or our writers guidelines page (http://www.themysteryplace.com/eqmm/guidelines)."

MAGAZINES NEEDS *Ellery Queen's Mystery Magazine*, published 10 times/year, uses primarily short stories of mystery, crime, or suspense—little poetry. *Ellery Queen's Mystery Magazine* is 112 pages (double-issue, published twice/year, is 192 pages), digest-sized, professionally printed on newsprint, flat-spined, with glossy paper cover. Single copy: $5.50 by check to publisher, available for $4.99 on newsstands; subscription: $55.90.

HOW TO CONTACT Considers simultaneous submissions; no previously published poems. Guidelines available on website. Responds in 3 months. Pays $15-65 and 3 contributor's copies. "EQMM uses an online submission system (http://eqmm.magazinesubmissions.com) that has been designed to streamline our process and improve communication with authors. We ask that all submissions be made electronically, using this system, rather than on paper. All stories should be in standard ms format and submitted in .DOC format. We cannot accept .DOCX, .RTF, or .TXT files at this time. For detailed submission instructions, see http://eqmm.magazinesubmissions.com or our writers guidelines page (http://www.themysteryplace.com/eqmm/guidelines)."

TIPS "We have a Department of First Stories to encourage writers whose fiction has never before been in print. We publish an average of 10 first stories every year. Mark subject line Attn: Dept. of First Stories."

⦿⑨ ELLIPSIS MAGAZINE

(801)832-2321. E-mail: ellipsis@westminstercollege.edu. Website: www.westminstercollege.edu/ellipsis. Submit 3-5 poems at a time. Considers simultaneous submissions if notified of acceptance elsewhere; no previously published poems. Reads submissions August 1 - November 1. Responds in up to 8 months. Pays $10/poem, plus two contributor's copies.

C Reads submissions August 1 to November 1.

HOW TO CONTACT No fax or e-mail submissions; postal submissions only. One poem per page, with name and contact information on every page. Include SASE and brief bio.

CONTEST/AWARD OFFERINGS All accepted poems are eligible for the *Ellipsis* Award which includes a $100 prize. Past judges have included Jorie Graham, Sandra Cisneros, and Stanley Plumly.

⦿ ENGLISH JOURNAL

Interdisciplinary Studies in Curriculum & Instruction, National-Louis University, Tampa FL 33609. (941)629-0541. E-mail: asullivan@nl.edu (inquiries). E-mail: ejpoetry@nl.edu. Website: www.ncte.org/journals/EJ. Ken Lindblom. **Contact:** Anne McCrary Sullivan, poetry editor. Current theme: Students Reading and Writing for Their Own Purposes. Deadline: March 15, 2011.Published 6 times annually. Submit poems that reflect in some way the thematic concerns announced for each issue. The poetry editor is free to interpret these themes broadly. Upcoming themes, deadlines and details appear in each issue of EJ and at the NCTE website. "General Interest" poems are not considered. Poems may be in any form or style, serious or humorous, and do not have to specifically address teaching or classrooms." English Journal accepts fewer than 10% of submissions. Seldom comments on rejected poems. Responds in 2-4 months after deadline.

MAGAZINES NEEDS *English Journal*, established 1912, published 6 times annually by The National Council of Teachers of English, is a professional education journal, circulation over 20,000. "Poetry submissions that respond to announced themes, either implicitly or explicitly, are encouraged. Themes are announced in every issue and at the NCTE. Poems may be in any form or style, serious or humorous, and do not have to specifically address teaching or classrooms." English Journal accepts fewer than 10% of submissions.

HOW TO CONTACT Submissions are accepted electronically only via website. "Send by email attachment, for blind review, up to 5 poems with only phone number and initials on the page. In your accompanying message, include 50-60 word biographical statement. In subject line, indicate theme for which you are submitting. If you have already submitted without indicating a theme, it's okay to resubmit. Type "Resubmit" in the subject line along with the theme." No previously published poems or simultaneous submissions. Seldom comments on rejected poems. Responds in 2-4 months after deadline.

● EPICENTER: A LITERARY MAGAZINE

P.O. Box 367, Riverside CA 92502. E-mail: submissions@epicentermagazine.org. Website: www.epicentermagazine.org. **Contact:** Rowena Silver, Editor. P.O. Box 367, Riverside CA 92502. E-mail: submissions@epicentermagazine.org. Website: www.epicentermagazine.org.

MAGAZINES NEEDS *Epicenter: A Literary Magazine* is a literary periodical based in Riverside, California. *Epicenter* began publishing in 1994 from Riverside California. Publishes poetry, short-stories, essays, and artwork. Open to a wide variety of styles and subjects. Has published work by Ilya Kaminsky, Virgil Suarez, Stephen Pyle, Guy R Beining, Zdravka Evtimova, Egon H. E. Lass, B.Z. Niditch, Roibeard Ui-Neill, Buzzsaw, Alexander Chertok, and Randy Koch. Subscription: $28. Single issue: $9. Back issue: $7. *Epicenter: A Literary Magazine* published semiannually, is open to all styles. "*Epicenter* is looking for poetry, essays, short stories, creative nonfiction, and artwork. We publish new and established writers." Considers translations. Does not want "angst-ridden, sentimental, or earthquake poetry. We are not adverse to graphic images as long as the work contains literary merit." Has published poetry by Virgil Suarez, Alba Cruz-Hacher, B.Z. Niditch, Egon Lass, and Zdravka Evtimova. *Epicenter* is 100 pages, perfect-bound. Receives about 2,000 submissions/year, accepts about 5%. Press run is 800. Single copy: $7. Make checks payable to *Epicenter: A Literary Magazine.*

HOW TO CONTACT Submit up to 5 poems at a time. Send poetry with vivid imagery and fresh ideas. Accepts any style of poetry. Submit through postal mail or e-mail. "Due to the volume of e-mail submissions, we do not respond unless we wish to use a piece." Include SASE with postal mail. Pays 1 contributor's copy.

EPOCH

(607)255-3385. Fax: (607)255-6661. "Well-written literary fiction, poetry, personal essays. Newcomers always welcome. Open to mainstream and avant-garde writing."

MAGAZINES NEEDS *Epoch*, published 3 times/year, has a distinguished and long record of publishing exceptionally fine poetry and fiction. Has published poetry by Kevin Prufer, Peter Dale Scott, Martin Walls, Maxine Kumin, Heather McHugh, and D. James Smith. *Epoch* is 128 pages, digest-sized, professionally printed, perfect-bound, with glossy color cover. Accepts less than 1% of the many submissions received each year. Has 1,000 subscribers. Subscription: $11/year domestic, $15/year foreign. Sample: $5.

HOW TO CONTACT No simultaneous submissions. Manuscripts not accompanied by SASE will be discarded unread. Reads submissions September 15-April 15. Responds in up to 10 weeks. Occasionally provides criticism on mss. Pays 3 contributor's copies and at least $10/page. "We pay more when we have more!" Acquires first serial rights.

TIPS "Tell your story, speak your poem, straight from the heart. We are attracted to language and to good writing, but we are most interested in what the good writing leads us to, or where."

➕ ● ESSAYS & FICTIONS

209 Cascadilla St., Ithaca NY 14850. (914)572-7351. E-mail: essaysandfictions@gmail.com. Website: http://essaysandfictions.com. **Contact:** David Pollock and Danielle Winterton, co-founding editors. Publishes literary essays, literary criticism, and poetry, and reviews. Literary magazine.

MAGAZINES NEEDS Essays & Fictions is an online journal of literature and criticism.

HOW TO CONTACT Send complete ms with cover letter. Accepts submissions by e-mail. Responds to mss in 1-3 months. Accepts multiple submissions; no simultaneous or previously published submissions. Guidelines available by e-mail or on website. Acquires first and electronic rights. Publication is copyrighted. Sends prepublication galleys to author. See website or e-mail for more information. Sample copy: $15.

TIPS "We look for confident work that uses form/structure and voice in interesting ways without sounding overly self-conscious or deliberate. We encourage rigorous excellence of complex craft in our submissions and discourage bland reproductions of reality. Read the journal. Be familiar with the *Essays & Fictions* aesthetic. We are particularly interested in writers who read theory and/or have multiple intellectual and artistic interests, and who set high intellectual standards for themselves and their work."

● ● EUROPEAN JUDAISM

LBC, The Sternberg Centre, 80 East End Rd., London N3 2SY, England. E-mail: european.judaism@lbc.ac.uk. Website: www.berghahnbooks.com/journals/ej. **Contact:** Managing Editor. LBC, The Sternberg Centre, 80 East End Rd., London N3 2SY England. E-mail: european.judaism@lbc.ac.uk. Website: www.berghahnbooks.com/journals/ej. *European Judaism* offers literary exchange as a unique exploration of ideas from leading Jewish writers, poets, scholars, and intellectuals with a variety of documentation, poetry, and book reviews section; and book reviews covering a wide range of international publications. Subscription: $56 (USA); £32 (UK). Sample: Free.*European Judaism*, published twice/year, is a "glossy, elegant magazine with emphasis on European Jewish theology/philosophy/literature/history, with some poetry in every issue. Poems should (preferably) be short and have some relevance to matters of Jewish interest." Has published poetry by Linda Pastan, Elaine Feinstein, Daniel Weissbort, and Dannie Abse. *European Judaism* is 110 pages, digest-sized, flat-spined. Press run is 950 (about 500 subscribers, over 100 libraries). Subscription: $45 individual, $20 student, $162 institution.

HOW TO CONTACT Submit through postal mail. "Any material submitted for publication should be supplied on disk, accompanied by one double-spaced hard copy, and a brief biographical note on the author."

◐⊗ EVANGEL

Free Methodist Publishing House, P.O. Box 535002, Indianapolis IN 46253-5002. (317)244-3660. **Contact:** Julie Innes, Editor.

MAGAZINES NEEDS *Evangel*, published quarterly, is an adult Sunday school paper. "Devotional in nature, it lifts up Christ as the source of salvation and hope. The mission of *Evangel* is to increase the reader's understanding of the nature and character of God and the nature of a life lived for Christ. Material that fits this mission and isn't longer than one page will be considered." Does not want rhyming work. *Evangel* is 8 pages, $5\frac{1}{2} \times 8\frac{1}{2}$, printed in 4-color, unbound. Accepts about 5% of poetry received. Press run is about 10,000. Subscription: $2.59/quarter (13 weeks). Sample: free for #10 SASE.

HOW TO CONTACT Submit no more than 5 poems at a time. Considers simultaneous submissions. Cover letter is preferred. "Poetry must be typed on $8\frac{1}{2}$x11 white paper. In the upper left-hand corner of each page, include your name, address, phone number, and social security number. In the upper right-hand corner of cover page, specify what rights you are offering. One-eighth of the way down the page, give the title. All subsequent material must be double-spaced, with one-inch margins." Submit seasonal poems 1 year in advance. Seldom comments on rejected poems. Guidelines available for #10 SASE. "Write 'guidelines request' on your envelope so we can sort it from the submissions." Responds in up to 2 months. Pays $10 plus 2 contributor's copies. Acquires one-time rights.

TIPS "Desire, concise, tight writing that supports a solid thesis and fits the mission expressed in the quidelines."

◑ EVANSVILLE REVIEW

University of Evansville English Dept., 1800 Lincoln Ave., Evansville IN 47722. (812)488-1402. E-mail: evansvillereview@evansville.edu. Website: http://evansvillereview.evansville.edu. **Contact:** Poetry editor. *The Evansville Review*, published annually in April, prints "prose, poems, and drama of literary merit." Wants "anything of quality." No excessively experimental work; no erotica. Has published poetry by Joseph Brodsky, J.L. Borges, John Updike, Willis Barnstone, Rita Dove, and Vivian Shipley. *The Evansville Review* is 140-200 pages, digest-sized, perfect-bound, with art on cover. Receives about 2,000 poems/year, accepts about 2%. Press run is 1,500. Sample: $5.

HOW TO CONTACT Submit 3-5 poems at a time. Considers previously published poems and simultaneous submissions. No fax or e-mail submissions; postal submissions only. Cover letter is required. Include brief bio. Manuscripts not returned without SASE. Reads submissions September 1-December 1 only. Time between acceptance and publication is 3 months. Poems are circulated to an editorial board. Seldom comments on rejected poems. Guidelines available for SASE or on website. Responds within 3 months of the deadline. Pays 2 contributor's copies. Rights remain with poet.

CONTEST/AWARD OFFERINGS The Willis Barnstone Translation Prize (see separate listing in Contests & Awards).

TIPS "Because editorial staff rolls over every 1-2 years, the journal always has a new flavor."

EXIT 13

P.O. Box 423, Fanwood NJ 07023-1162. E-mail: exit-13magazine@yahoo.com. **Contact:** Tom Plante Editor.

MAGAZINES NEEDS *Exit 13*, published annually, uses poetry that is "short, to the point, with a sense of geography. It features poets of all ages, writing styles and degrees of experience, focusing on where and how we live and what's going on around us. The emphasis is on geography, travel, adventure and the fertile ground of the imagination. It's a travelogue in poetry, a reflection of the world we see, and a chronicle of the people we meet along the way." Has published poetry by Paul Brooke, Ruth Moon Kempher, Sandy McCord, Sander Zulauf, Paul Sohar, and Charles Rammelkamp. *Exit 13* is about 76 pages. Press run is 300. Sample: $8.

HOW TO CONTACT Submit through postal mail or e-mail. Paste in body of e-mail. Considers simultaneous submissions and previously published poems. Guidelines available in magazine or for SASE. Responds in 4 months. Pays 1 contributor's copy. Acquires one-time and possible anthology rights.

➕ ◖ EYE ON LIFE ONLINE MAGAZINE

E-mail: eyeonlife.ezine@gmail.com. Website: http://eyeonlifemag.com. **Contact:** Tom Rubenoff, senior poetry editor.

MAGAZINES NEEDS *Eye on Life* published weekly online, wants poems with striking and original imagery. "We like to see poems in which meaning exceeds form." Does not want "forced rhyming, poems stuffed into forms into which they do not fit." Accepts poetry by teens, but "please let us know if you are under 21 years old. Has published poetry by Donal Mahoney and Eileen Carney Hulme. Receives about 500 poems/year, accepts about 150.

HOW TO CONTACT Submit 5 poems at a time by e-mail, no more than one page in length. No attachments, please. Does not considers simultaneous submissions. Reads submissions year round. Submit seasonal poems one month in advance. Time between acceptance and publication is 2 weeks. Poems are circulated to an editorial board. Comments on rejected poems in exchange for $5 donation to Eye On Life Poetry Travel Fund. Guidelines and upcoming themes available on website. Responds in 2 weeks. Acquires one-time rights. Rights revert to poets upon publication.

CONTEST/AWARD OFFERINGS Eyes on Life Poetry Contest first prize $100 second prize $50. Submit up to 5 poems. Entry fee: $1/poem; deadline: January 31st. Guidelines available on website after November 1.

❸ FACES MAGAZINE

(Specialized: theme-specific; world cultures; children/teens ages 9-14), Editorial Dept., Cobblestone Publishing, 30 Grove Street, Suite C, Peterborough NH 03458. E-mail: facesmag@yahoo.com. Website: www.cricketmag.com.

MAGAZINES NEEDS *FACES Magazine*, published 9 times/year, features cultures from around the globe for children ages 9-14. "Readers learn how other kids live around the world and about the important inventions and ideas that a particular culture has given to the world. All material must relate to the theme of a specific upcoming issue in order to be considered." Wants "clear, objective imagery. Serious and light verse considered. Must relate to theme." Subscription: $33.95/year (9 issues). Sample pages available on website.

HOW TO CONTACT Query first. Lines/poem: up to 100. Accepts e-mail queries. Include SASE for postal submissions and queries. Reads submissions according to deadlines for queries (see website for schedule and details). Always publishes theme issue. Themes and guidelines available on website. Pays varied rates. Acquires all rights.

❸ ◖ FAILBETTER.COM

2022 Grove Ave., Richmond VA 23220. E-mail: editor@failbetter.com. E-mail: submissions@failbetter.com. Website: www.failbetter.com. Thom Didato, Andrew Day, Publisher. Member: CLMP. **Contact:** Poetry Editors: Mary Donnelly, Christina Kallery. *failbetter.com*, published online, seeks "that which is at once original and personal. When choosing work to submit, be certain that what you have created could only have come from you." Publishes translations and interviews with such poets as Paul Muldoon, Marie Ponsot, Mary Jo Salter, and Billy Collins. Has published poetry by J. Allyn Rosser, Terrance Hayes, Mary Donnely, and Thaddeus Rutkowski. Receives about 2,000 poetry submissions/year, accepts about 9-12. Publishes 3-4 poets/issue.

○ Works published in *failbetter* have received recognition in various award anthologies including *Best American Poetry*, *The Pushcart Prize* and *Best of the Net*.

TIPS "With a readership of more than 60,000 per issue, *failbetter* is one of the Web's widely read literary magazines, offering exposure of poets' works to a much broader, worldwide audience than the typical print journal. For both established and emerging poets our advice remains the same: We strongly recommend that you not only read the previous issue, but also sign up on our e-mail list (subscribe@failbetter.com) to be notified of future publications."

◐ FAT TUESDAY

E-mail: FrankCotolo@yahoo.com. Website: http://groups.yahoo.com/group/FatTuesday. **Contact:** FM Cotolo. E-mail: FrankCotolo@yahoo.com. Website: http://groups.yahoo.com/group/FatTuesday. "For two decades, *Fat Tuesday* has pushed the boundaries of small-press literati. Bring your poetry, prose, lyrics and scribblings to this special group of readers and writers through the internet. Co-founder, editor-in-chief and publisher FM Cotolo moderates this free e-mail "magazine" in the spirit of the publication known the world over. Post your words or forever hold your piece.""For two decades, "Fat Tuesday" has pushed the boundaries of small-press literati. Bring your poetry, prose, lyrics and scribblings to this special group of readers and writers through the internet. Co-founder, editor-in-chief and publisher FM Cotolo moderates this free e-mail "magazine" in the spirit of the publication known the world over. Post your words or forever hold your piece."

HOW TO CONTACT Submit via Yahoo! group website page. Make a post, type poem in body. Accepts all poems. No limit on length.

TIPS "In 1998, *Fat Tuesday* was presented in a different format with the production of a stereo audio cassette edition. *Fat Tuesday*'s Cool Noise features readings, music, collage, and songs, all in the spirit of *Fat's* printed versions. *Fat Tuesday* has released other audio projects. In-print magazines will still be produced as planned when funds are available.""Support the magazine that publishes your work!"

FAULTLINE

Dept. of English and Comparative Literature, University of California at Irvine, Irvine CA 92697-2650. E-mail: faultline@uci.edu. Website: www.humanities.uci.edu/faultline.

◌ Reading period is September 15-February 15. Submissions sent at any other time will not be read.

MAGAZINES NEEDS *Faultline*, published annually each spring, features new poetry, fiction, and translation. Has published poetry by C.K. Williams, Larissa Szporluk, Yusef KomunyakaAmy Gerstler,

and Killarney Clary. *Faultline* is about 200 pages, digest-sized, professionally printed on 60 lb. paper, perfect-bound, with 80 lb. coverstock. Receives about 5,000 poems/year, accepts less than 1%. Press run is 1,000. Single copy: $10. Sample: $5.

HOW TO CONTACT Submit up to 5 poems at a time. Considers simultaneous submissions, "but please note in cover letter that the manuscript is being considered elsewhere." No fax or e-mail submissions. Cover letter is required. Include name, postal and e-mail addresses, and titles of work submitted; do not put name and address on ms pages themselves. SASE required. Reads submissions September 15-February 15 only. Poems are selected by a board of up to 6 readers. Seldom comments on rejected poems. Guidelines available for SASE or on website. Responds in 3 months. Pays 2 contributor's copies. Acquires first or one-time serial rights.

◐ FEELINGS OF THE HEART

Website: www.freewebs.com/feelingsoftheheartliteraryjournal. E-mail: allie.harnisch@yahoo.com. Website: www.freewebs.com/feelingsoftheheartliteraryjournal. Established 1999. **Contact:** Alice M. Harnisch, editor/publisher/founder/poetess. *Feelings of the Heart*, published online, seeks "poetry from the heart." Considers poetry by children and teens. Has published poetry by Mark Hurley, Jerry S. Reynolds, and Sharon Kroenlein.

MAGAZINES NEEDS *Feelings of the Heart*, published online, seeks "poetry from the heart." Considers poetry by children and teens. Has published poetry by Mark Hurley, Jerry S. Reynolds, and Sharon Kroenlein.

HOW TO CONTACT Accepts all poems, all lengths. Considers previously published poems and simultaneous submissions. Accepts e-mail (pasted into body of message or as attachment in Word). Poems "are read by me, the editor, and decided by the poetic intent of poetry submitted." Often comments on rejected poems. "If asked why rejected, you will receive an answer."

CONTEST/AWARD OFFERINGS Holds annual contests for cash prizes. Guidelines available on website.

ALSO OFFERS Prints poetry chapbooks for those interested **in being self-published**. E-mail for details.

◑ FICKLE MUSES

E-mail: fiction2@ficklemuses.com. Website: www.
ficklemuses.com. (Specialized: myth and legend). E-
mail: editor@ficklemuses.com. Website: www.fickl-
emuses.com. Established 2006. **Contact:** Sari Kros-
insky, editor.

MAGAZINES NEEDS *Fickle Muses*, published
weekly online, is a journal of myth and legend
printing poetry, fiction and art. Open to all styles
and forms. Has published poetry by J.V. Foerster, Ray
Hinman, Maureen Seaton, Kenneth P. Gurney, Doug
Ramspeck. Accepts about 10% of poems received.
Number of unique visitors: 160/week.

HOW TO CONTACT Submit up to 5 poems at a
time. Lines/poem: no limits on length. Considers
previously published poems and simultaneous submissions. Accepts e-mail submissions (pasted into
body of message preferred, unless special formatting requires an attachment); no disk submissions.
Cover letter is preferred. Reads submissions year
round. Time between acceptance and publication is
up to 3 months. Never comments on rejected poems.
Guidelines available on website. Responds in up to
3 months. Acquires one-time and archival rights.
Rights revert to poets upon publication. Reviews
books/chapbooks of poetry and other magazines/
journals in 500 words, single-book format. For review consideration, query by e-mail.

TIPS "Originality. An innovative look at an old story. I'm looking to be swept away. Get a feel for our
website."

♲◑⑤ THE FIDDLEHEAD

University of New Brunswick, Campus House, 11
Garland Court, Box 4400, Fredericton NB E3B 5A3,
Canada. (506)453-3501. Fax: (506) 453-5069. E-mail:
fiddlehd@unb.ca; scl@unb.ca. Website: www.thefid-
dlehead.ca. Mark Anthony Jarman or Gerard Beirne,
Fiction Editors. **Contact:** Kathryn Taglia, Managing
Editor. Literary. Receives 100-150 unsolicited mss/
month. Accepts 4-5 mss/issue; 20-40 mss/year. Publishes ms within 1 year after acceptance. Agented fiction: small percentage. **Publishes high percentage of
new writers/year.** Send SASE and *Canadian* stamps
or IRCs for return of mss. Responds in 6 months to
mss. No email submissions. Simultaneous submissions only if stated on cover letter; must contact immediately if accepted elsewhere. Sample copy for $15
(US). Pays up to $40 (Canadian)/published page and

2 contributor's copies. Pays on publication for first or
one-time serial rights."Canada's longest living literary journal, *The Fiddlehead* is published four times
a year at the University of New Brunswick, with the
generous assistance of the University of New Brunswick, the Canada Council for the Arts, and the Province of New Brunswick. It is experienced; wise enough
to recognize excellence; always looking for freshness
and surprise. *The Fiddlehead* publishes short stories,
poems, book reviews, and a small number of personal
essays. Our full-colour covers have become collectors'
items, and feature work by New Brunswick artists and
from New Brunswick museums and art galleries. *The
Fiddlehead* also sponsors an annual writing contest."

CONTEST/AWARD OFFERINGS Sponsors poetry
contest.

TIPS "If you are serious about submitting to *The Fiddlehead*, you should subscribe or read an issue or two
to get a sense of the journal. Contact us if you would to
order sample back issues ($10-$15 plus postage)."

FIELD: CONTEMPORARY POETRY & POETICS

Oberlin College Press, 50 N. Professor St., Oberlin
OH 44074-1091. (440)775-8408. Fax: (440)775-8124.
E-mail: oc.press@oberlin.edu. Website: www.oberlin.
edu/ocpress. **Contact:** Linda Slocum, man. editor.
C "See electronic submission guidelines."

MAGAZINES NEEDS contemporary, prose poems,
free verse, traditional. *FIELD: Contemporary Poetry
and Poetics*, published semiannually in April and
October, is a literary journal with "emphasis on poetry,
translations, and essays by poets." Has published
poetry by Michelle Glazer, Tom Lux, Carl Phillips,
Betsy Sholl, Charles Simic, Jean Valentine and
translations by Marilyn Hacker and Stuart Friebert.
FIELD is 100 pages, digest-sized, printed on rag stock,
flat-spined, with glossy color card cover. Subscription:
$16/year, $28 for 2 years. Sample: $8 postpaid.

HOW TO CONTACT Submit up to 5 poems at a time.
No previously published poems or simultaneous
submissions. No e-mail submissions. Include cover
letter and SASE. Reads submissions year round. Seldom comments on rejected poems. Guidelines available for SASE, by e-mail, or on website. Responds
in 6-8 weeks. Always sends prepublication galleys.
Pays $15/page and 2 contributor's copies. Staff re-
views books of poetry. Send materials for review
consideration.

ADDITIONAL INFORMATION Oberlin College Press publishes books of translations in the FIELD Translation Series. Books are usually flat-spined paperbacks averaging 150 pages. Query regarding translations. Also publishes books of poetry in the FIELD Poetry Series, **by invitation only.** Has published *Tryst* by Angie Estes; *Kurosawa's Dog* by Dennis Hinrichsen; *He and I,* by Emmanuel Moses, translated by Marilyn Hacker; *The Sleep Hotel* by Amy Newlove Schroeder. Write for catalog or visit website to buy sample books.

CONTEST/AWARD OFFERINGS Sponsors the annual FIELD Poetry Prize for a book-length collection of poems (see separate listing in Contests & Awards). Entries accepted during May ONLY.

TIPS "Submit 3-5 of your best poems with a cover letter and SASE. No simultaneous submissions. Keep trying! Submissions are read year-round."

◯◖◗⑤ THE FIFTH DI...

Tyree Campbell, attn: Sam's Dot Publishing, PO Box 782, Cedar Rapids IO 52406-0782. Website: www.samsdotpublishing.com/fifth/fifth.htm. PO Box 782, Cedar Rapids IO 52406-0782. E-mail: jerwine@samsdotpublishing.com; fifth@samsdotpublishing.com. Website: www.samsdotpublishing.com/fifth/fifth.htm. *The Fifth Di..,* published quarterly online, features fiction and poetry from the science fiction and fantasy genres. Open to most forms, but all poems must be science fiction or fantasy. Does not want horror, or anything that is not science fiction or fantasy. Considers poetry by children and teens. Has published poetry by Bruce Boston, Cathy Buburuz, Marge Simon, Aurelio Rico Lopez III, Terrie Relf, and John Bushore. Receives about 200 poems/year, accepts about 20. Free E-Zine.*The Fifth Di..,* published quarterly online, features fiction and poetry from the science fiction and fantasy genres. Open to most forms, but all poems must be science fiction or fantasy. Does not want horror, or anything that is not science fiction or fantasy. Considers poetry by children and teens. Has published poetry by Bruce Boston, Cathy Buburuz, Marge Simon, Aurelio Rico Lopez III, Terrie Relf, and John Bushore. Receives about 200 poems/year, accepts about 20.

▢ Honored by Preditors & Editors as Best Fiction Zine.

HOW TO CONTACT Submit through e-mail. Attachments as rtf only, must include "Submission" in subject line. Prefers attachments but will accept poems pasted into body of e-mail. Include name, by-line, address, page number on submission. Include bio written in third person. Poems must fall into the science fiction or fantasy genres. **NO HORROR.** Will not accept reprints or simultaneous submissions. Prefers longer poems. "Haiku and other short forms aren't likely to get picked up here." Response time is 2 months. Pays $5 per poem.

◯● FILLING STATION

Website: www.fillingstation.ca. **Contact:** Laurie Fuhr, general editor. P.O. Box 22135, Bankers Hall, Calgary AB T2P 4J5 Canada. (403)999-2566. E-mail: mgmt@fillingstation.ca; poetry@fillingstation.ca; poetry.fs@gmail.com. Website: www.fillingstation.ca. *filling Station Magazine,* published 3 times/year, is a literary and arts magazine publishing innovative poetry, fiction, non-fiction (creative non-fiction, reviews, articles, interviews, live event reviews, photo essays, etc), and presenting a featured visual artist each issue. "At *filling Station*, more original or innovative submissions tend to be favoured for publication." Subscription: $15/3 issues. Single issue: $8.*filling Station*, published 3 times/year, prints contemporary poetry, fiction, visual art, interviews, reviews, and articles. "We are looking for all forms of contemporary writing, but especially that which is original and/or experimental." Has published poetry by Fred Wah, Larissa Lai, Margaret Christakos, Robert Kroetsch, Ron Silliman, Susan Holbrook, and many more. *filling Station* is 80-100 pages, 8½×11, perfect-bound, with card cover, includes photos and artwork. Receives about 100 submissions for each issue, accepts approximately 10%. Press run is 700. Subscription: $22/year, $38 for 2 years. Sample: $8.

HOW TO CONTACT Submit up to 6 pages by e-mail. Include name, address, e-mail address and bio. Attach work as a Word document. No previously published material. Accepts simultaneous submissions. Pays 3 issue subscription and discount on future renewals and subscriptions.

TIPS "We favour work on the innovative cutting-edge. Please read our magazine before submitting."

● FIRST CLASS

P.O. Box 86, Friendship IN 47021. E-mail: christopherm@four-sep.com. Website: www.four-sep.com. **Contact:** Christopher M, editor. Four-Sep Publications, P.O. Box 86, Friendship IN 47021. E-mail: christopherm@four-sep.com. Website: www.four-sep.com. Established 1994. **Contact:** Christopher M., editor.

MAGAZINES NEEDS *First Class*, published in May and November, prints "excellent/odd writing for intelligent/creative readers." Does not want "traditional work." Has published poetry by Bennett, Locklin, Every, Ui-Neill, Catlin, and Huffstickler. *First Class* is 48-56 pages, $4\frac{1}{4}$x11, printed, saddle-stapled, with colored cover. Receives about 1,500 poems/year, accepts about 30. Press run is 300-400. Sample: $6 (includes guidelines). Make checks payable to Christopher M.

HOW TO CONTACT Submit 5 poems at a time. Considers previously published poems and simultaneous submissions. No fax or e-mail submissions. Cover letter is preferred. "Manuscripts will not be returned." Time between acceptance and publication is 2-4 months. Often comments on rejected poems. Guidelines available in magazine, or on website. Responds in 4-8 weeks. Pays 1 contributor's copy. Acquires one-time rights. Reviews books of poetry and fiction. Send materials for review consideration.

ADDITIONAL INFORMATION Chapbook production available.

TIPS "Don't bore me with puppy dogs and the morose/sappy feeling you have about death. Belt out a good, short, thought-provoking, graphic, uncommon piece."

◑ FLINT HILLS REVIEW

Dept. of English, Box 4019, Emporia State University, Emporia KS 66801-5087. Website: www.emporia.edu/fhr/. **Contact:** Editors.

MAGAZINES NEEDS Department of English, Box 4019, Emporia State University, Emporia, KS 66801-5087. E-mail: webbamy@emporia.edu. Website: www.emporia.edu/fhr/. *Flint Hills Review*, published annually in late summer, is "a regionally focused journal presenting writers of national distinction alongside new authors." Wants all forms of poetry except rhyming. Does not want sentimental or gratuitous verse. Has published poetry by E. Ethelbert Miller, Elizabeth Dodd, Walt McDonald, and Gwendolyn Brooks. *Flint Hills Review* is about 100 pages, digest-sized, offset-printed, perfect-bound, with glossy card cover with b&w photo. Receives about 2,000 poems/year, accepts about 5%. Single copy: $7.

HOW TO CONTACT Submit 3-5 poems at a time. Considers simultaneous submissions; no previously published poems. Accepts submissions by fax or e-mail (pasted into body of message). Cover letter is required. Include SASE. Reads submissions January-March only. Time between acceptance and publication is about one year. Seldom comments on rejected poems. Occasionally publishes theme issues. Guidelines available for SASE or on website. Pays 1 contributor's copy. Acquires first rights.

CONTEST/AWARD OFFERINGS FHR hosts an annual nonfiction contest. **Entry Fee:** $10. **Deadline:** March 15.

TIPS "Strong imagery and voice, writing that is informed by place or region, writing of literary quality with depth of character development. Hone the language down to the most literary depiction that is possible in the shortest space that still provides depth of development without excess length."

⊕ FLOYD COUNTY MOONSHINE

720 Christiansburg Pike, Floyd VA 24091. (540)745-5150. E-mail: floydshine@gmail.com. Website: www.floydcountymoonshine.com. **Contact:** Aaron Moore, editor-in-chief. 720 Christiansburg Pike, Floyd VA 24091. E-mail: floydshine@gmail.com. Website: www.floydcountymoonshine.com. *Floyd County Moonshine*, published quarterly, is a "literary and arts magazine in Floyd, Virginia and the New River Valley. We accept poetry, short stories, and essays addressing all manner of themes; however, preference is given to those works of a rural or Southern/Appalachian nature. We welcome cutting-edge and innovative fiction and poetry in particular." Wants "rustic innovation." Has published poetry by Steve Kistulentz, Louis Gallo, Ernie Wormwood, Rodney Smith, Chelsea Adams, and Justin Askins. Single copy: $8; subscription: $20/1 year, $38/2 years.

MAGAZINES NEEDS *Floyd County Moonshine*, published quarterly, is a "literary and arts magazine in Floyd, Virginia and the New River Valley. We accept poetry, short stories, and essays addressing all manner of themes; however, preference is given to those works of a rural or Southern/Appalachian nature. We welcome cutting-edge and innovative fiction and poetry in particular." Wants "rustic innovation." Has published poetry by Steve Kistulentz, Louis Gallo, Ernie Wormwood, Rodney Smith, Chelsea Adams, and Justin Askins. Single copy: $8; subscription: $20/1 year, $38/2 years.

HOW TO CONTACT Accepts e-mail submissions only. Submit a Word document as attachment. Accepts previously published poems and simultaneous submissions. Cover letter is unnecessary. Include brief bio. Reads submissions year round.

◐ FLYWAY

Iowa State University, 206 Ross Hall, Ames IA 50011. Website: www.flyway.org. *Flyway* is 120 pages, digest-sized, professionally printed, perfect-bound, with matte card cover with color. Press run is 500. Subscription: $24. Sample: $8. Submit 4-6 poems at a time. Cover letter is preferred. "We do not read mss between the first of May and the end of August." Responds in 6 weeks (often sooner).10-12 poetry mss/issue. Reads mss September 1-May 1. Publishes ms 6-8 months after acceptance. Accepts 10/12 poetry mss/issue. **Publishes 7-10 new writers/year.** Pays 2 contributor's copies. Acquires first rights.*Flyway, A Journal of Writing and Environment*, published 3 times/year, "is one of the best literary magazines for the money. It's packed with some of the most readable poems being published today—all styles, forms, lengths, and subjects. We publish quality fiction, creative nonfiction, and poetry with a particular interest in place as a component of 'story,' or with an 'environmental' sensibility. Accepted works are accompanied by brief commentaries by their authors, the sort of thing a writer might say introducing a piece at a reading." Biannual.

CONTEST/AWARD OFFERINGS Sponsors an annual award for poetry, fiction, and nonfiction. Details available for SASE or on website.

TIPS "Quality, originality, voice, drama, tension. Make it as strong as you can."

◐◐ THE FOLIATE OAK ONLINE

University of Arkansas, Arts and Humanities, Monticello AK 71656. (870)460-1247. E-mail: foliateoak@uamont.edu. Website: www.foliateoak.uamont.edu. **Contact:** John Ragsdale.

MAGAZINES NEEDS *The Foliate Oak Online*, published monthly online, prints prose, poetry, and artwork reviewed by college students, edited and added to the website. Wants all genres and forms of poetry are accepted. Does not want: "We're not interested in homophobic, religious rants, or pornographic, violent stories. Please avoid using offensive language." Considers poetry by teens. Has published poetry by

Tony Hoagland, Richard Fein, and FJ Bergmann. Receives about 300 poems/year, accepts about 100. Number of unique visitors: 500 monthly.

HOW TO CONTACT Submit no more than 5 poems at a time, maximum 30 lines. Does not accept previously published poems (considers poetry posted on a public website/blog/forum and poetry posted on a private, password-protected forum as published). Submit using online submission manager found on website. Cover letter is unnecessary. See website for guidelines; Word documents are preferred, submit a third person bio. Reads submissions August 1-April 24. Submit seasonal poems 1 months in advance. Time between acceptance and publication is 2-3 weeks. Poems are circulated to an editorial board. Guidelines available on website. Responds in 1 month. Acquires one-time rights. Reviews other magazines/journals.

ADDITIONAL INFORMATION "We are accepting submissions at this time! If accepted, the work will be posted in our monthly magazine for a minimum of 4 weeks. Send us what you have via e-mail."

◐ FOLIO, A LITERARY JOURNAL AT AMERICAN UNIVERSITY

Website: www.american.edu/cas/literature/folio/. Jenny Dunnington; Abdul Ali, Poetry Editors. Dept. of Literature, American University, Washington, DC 20016. (202)885-2971. Fax: (202)885-2938. E-mail: folio.editors@gmail.com. Website: www.american.edu/cas/literature/folio. *Folio*, published 2 times/year, Since 1984, we have published original creative work by both new and established authors. Past issues have included work by Michael Reid Busk, Billy Collins, William Stafford, and Bruce Weigl, and interviews with Michael Cunningham, Charles Baxter, Amy Bloom, Ann Beattie, and Walter Kirn. We look for well-crafted poetry and prose that is bold and memorable. *Folio* is 80 pages, digest-sized, with matte cover with graphic art. Receives about 1,000 poems/year, accepts about 25. Press run is 400; 50-60 distributed free to the American University community and contributors. Single copy: $6; subscription: $12/year. Make checks payable to "*Folio* at American University."

MAGAZINES NEEDS *Folio*, published 2 times/year, Since 1984, we have published original creative work by both new and established authors. Past issues have included work by Michael Reid Busk, Billy Collins, William Stafford, and Bruce Weigl, and interviews with Michael Cunningham, Charles Baxter, Amy Bloom, Ann Beattie, and Walter Kirn. We look for well-crafted poetry and prose that is bold and memorable. *Folio* is 80 pages, digest-sized, with matte cover with graphic art. Receives about 1,000 poems/year, accepts about 25. Press run is 400; 50-60 distributed free to the American University community and contributors. Single copy: $6; subscription: $12/year. Make checks payable to "*Folio* at American University."

HOW TO CONTACT Submit up to 5 poems or one prose piece at a time. Considers simultaneous submissions "with notice." No fax, e-mail, or disk submissions. Cover letter is preferred. Include name, address, e-mail address, brief brio and phone number. "SASE required for notification only; manuscripts are not returned." Reads submissions August 1-February 14. Time between acceptance and publication is 2 months. "Poems and prose are reviewed by editorial staff and senior editors." Seldom comments on rejected poems. Occasionally publishes theme issues. Guidelines available on website. Pays 2 contributor's copies. Acquires first North American serial rights.

FORPOETRY.COM

E-mail: sub@ForPoetry.com. Website: www.forpoetry.com. **Contact:** Jackie Marcus, editor. E-mail: sub@ForPoetry.com. Website: www.forpoetry.com. *ForPoetry.Com*, published online with daily updates, wants "lyric poetry, vivid imagery, open form, natural landscape, philosophical themes—but not at the expense of honesty and passion." Does not want "city punk, corny sentimental fluff, or academic workshop imitations." Has published poetry by Sherod Santos, John Koethe, Robert Hass, Kim Addonizio, and Brenda Hillman.

MAGAZINES NEEDS *ForPoetry.Com*, published online with daily updates, wants "lyric poetry, vivid imagery, open form, natural landscape, philosophical themes—but not at the expense of honesty and passion." Does not want "city punk, corny sentimental fluff, or academic workshop imitations." Has published poetry by Sherod Santos, John Koethe, Robert Hass, Kim Addonizio, and Brenda Hillman.

HOW TO CONTACT Submit no more than 2 poems at a time. Considers simultaneous submissions; no previously published poems. Accepts e-mail submissions only (pasted into body of message; no attachments). Cover letter is preferred. Reads sub-

missions September-May only. Guidelines available on website. Responds in 2 weeks. "If you do not hear back from us within two weeks, then your poems were not accepted. Rejection of poems may have more to do with a back-log; i.e., there are periods when we cannot read new submissions." Reviews books/chapbooks of poetry and other magazines in 800 words.

FOURTEEN HILLS

Dept. of Creative Writing, San Francisco State Univ., 1600 Holloway Ave., San Francisco CA 94132-1722. E-mail: hills@sfsu.edu. Website: www.14hills.net. "Always send prepublication galleys. Pays 2 contributor copies. Submit 3-5 unpublished, unsolicited poems. 1 Prose ms, max of 25 pages; visual art, experimental and cross-genre literature also accepted; see website for guidelines. Writers may submit once per submission period. The submission periods are: Sept. 1 - Jan. 1 for inclusion in the spring issue (released in May) Feb. 1 - July 1 for inclusion in the winter issue (released in Dec.). Response times vary from 4-9 months, depending on where your submission falls in the reading period, but we will usually respond within 5 months. Mss and artwork should be mailed and addressed to the proper genre editor, and MUST be accompanied by a sase for notification, in addition to an e-mail and telephone contact. Due to the volume of submissions, mss CANNOT BE RETURNED so please, do not send any originals. We accept simultaneous submissions; however, please be sure to notify us immediately by email should you need to withdraw submissions due to publication elsewhere. Please note that we do not accept electronic submissions at this time in the form of an email or otherwise. However, check website for changes in submission policies."

TIPS "Please read an isssue of *Fourteen Hills* before submitting."

THE FOURTH RIVER

E-mail: 4thriver@gmail.com. Website: http://fourthriver.chatham.edu. **Contact:** Sheryl St. Germain, executive editor. Chatham College, Woodland Rd., Pittsburgh, PA 15232. E-mail: 4thriver@gmail.com. Website: http://fourthriver.chatham.edu. *The Fourth River*, an annual publication of the MFA program at Chatham University, features "literature that engages and explores the relationship between humans and their environments." Wants "writings that are richly situated at the confluence of place, space, and identity, or that reflect upon or make use of landscape and place in new ways." *The Fourth River* is digest-sized, perfect-bound, with full-color cover by various artists. Accepts about 30-40 poems/year. Press run is 500. Single copy: $10 (or 1 year); subscription: $16 for 2 years. Back issues: $5. Make checks payable to Chatham University."Biannual magazine interested in literature that engages and explores the relationship between humans and their environments through writing that is thoughtful, daring, and richly situated at the confluence of place, space, and identity."

MAGAZINES NEEDS *The Fourth River,* an annual publication of the MFA program at Chatham University, features "literature that engages and explores the relationship between humans and their environments." Wants "writings that are richly situated at the confluence of place, space, and identity, or that reflect upon or make use of landscape and place in new ways." *The Fourth River* is digest-sized, perfect-bound, with full-color cover by various artists. Accepts about 30-40 poems/year. Press run is 500. Single copy: $10; subscription: $16 for 2 years. Back issues: $5. Make checks payable to Chatham University.

HOW TO CONTACT Chatham College, Woodland Rd., Pittsburgh, PA 15232. Submit 7 poems at a time. Lines/poem: submit 25 pages maximum. No previously published poems. No e-mail submissions. Postal submissions only. Cover letter is preferred. "SASE is required for response." Reads submissions September 1-February 15. Time between acceptance and publication is 5-8 months. Poems are circulated to an editorial board. Sometimes comments on rejected poems. Sometimes publishes theme issues. Guidelines available on website. Responds in 3-5 months. Acquires first North American serial rights.

✪⊙ FREEFALL MAGAZINE

Freefall Literary Society of Calgary, 922 Ninth Ave. SE, Calgary AB T2G 0S4, Canada. E-mail: freefallmagazine@yahoo.com. Website: www.freefallmagazine.ca. **Contact:** Lynn S. Fraser, managing editor. Freefall, 922 Ninth Ave. SE, Calgary AB T2G 0S4 Canada. (403)264-4730. Website: www.freefallmagazine.ca. Established 1990. Pays $25 per poem and one copy of the issue poems appeaer in. Wants prose of all types, up to 3,000 words; pays $10/page to a maximum of $100 per piece and one copy of issue piece

appears in."Magazine published biannually containing fiction, poetry, creative nonfiction, essays on writing, interviews, and reviews. Submit up to 5 poems at once. Pays $25 per poem and one copy of the issue poems appeaer in. Wants prose of all types, up to 3,000 words; pays $10/page to a maximum of $100 per piece and one copy of issue piece appears in. We are looking for exquisite writing with a strong narrative."

ADDITIONAL INFORMATION See website for information about the Freefall Literary Society of Calgary activities and services, and for additional information about *FreeFall Magazine.*

CONTEST/AWARD OFFERINGS Hosts an annual fiction and poetry contest. **Deadline:** December 31. Guidelines available by e-mail or on website.

TIPS "We look for thoughtful word usage, craftmanship, strong voice and unique expression coupled with clarity and narrative structure. Professional, clean presentation of work is essential. Carefully read *FreeFall* guidelines before submitting. Do not fold manuscript, and submit 9×11 envelope. Include SASE/IRC for reply and/or return of manuscript. You may contact us by e-mail after initial hardcopy submission. For accepted pieces a request is made for disk or e-mail copy. Strong Web presence attracts submissions from writers all over the world."

✪⊙ FREEXPRESSION

P.O. Box 4, West Hoxton NSW 2171, Australia. E-mail: peter@freexpression.net. Website: www.freexpression.com.au. **Contact:** Peter F. Pike, Managing Editor.

MAGAZINES NEEDS *FreeXpresSion,* published monthly, contains "creative writing, how-to articles, short stories, and poetry including cinquain, haiku, etc., and bush verse." Open to all forms. "Christian themes OK. Humorous material welcome. No gratuitous sex; bad language OK. We don't want to see anything degrading." Has published poetry by Ron Stevens, Ellis Campbell, John Ryan, and Ken Dean. *FreeXpresSion* is 28 pages, magazine-sized, offset-printed, saddle-stapled, with paper cover. Receives about 2,500 poems/year, accepts about 30%. Subscription: $15 AUS/3 months, $25 AUS/6 months, $42 AUS/1 year.

HOW TO CONTACT Submit 3-4 poems at a time. Lines/poem: "very long poems are not desired but would be considered." Considers previously published poems and simultaneous submissions. Accepts e-mail (pasted into body of message) and disk submissions. Cover letter is preferred. Time between acceptance and publication is 2 months. Guidelines available in magazine, for SAE and IRC, or by fax or e-mail. Responds in 2 months. Sometimes sends prepublication galleys. Acquires first Australian rights only. Reviews books of poetry in 500 words. Send materials for review consideration.

ADDITIONAL INFORMATION *FreeXpresSion* also publishes books up to 200 pages **through subsidy arrangements with authors.** "Some poems published throughout the year are used in *Yearbooks* (annual anthologies)."

CONTEST/AWARD OFFERINGS Sponsors an annual contest with 3 categories for poetry: blank verse (up to 60 lines); traditional verse (up to 80 lines), and haiku. 1st Prize in blank verse: $200 AUS; 2nd Prize: $100 AUS; 1st Prize in traditional rhyming poetry: $250 AUS; 2nd Prize: $150 AUS; 3rd Prize: $100 AUS. Haiku, one prize $100 AUS. Guidelines and entry form available by e-mail.

🐸● THE FROGMORE PAPERS

Website: www.frogmorepress.co.uk. 21 Mildmay Road, Lewes, East Sussex BN71PJ, England. Website: www.frogmorepress.co.uk. Established 1983. **Contact:** Jeremy Page, poetry editor.

MAGAZINES NEEDS *The Frogmore Papers*, published semiannually, is a literary magazine with emphasis on new poetry and short stories. "Quality is generally the only criterion, although pressure of space means very long work (over 100 lines) is unlikely to be published." Has published poetry by Marita Over, Brian Aldiss, Carole Satyamurti, John Mole, Linda France, and Tobias Hill. *The Frogmore Papers* is 46 pages, photocopied in photo-reduced typescript, saddle-stapled, with matte card cover. Accepts 2% of poetry received. Press run is 500. Subscription: £10/1 year (2 issues); £15/2 years (4 issues).

HOW TO CONTACT Submit 4-6 poems at a time. Lines/poem: prefers 20-80 lines. Considers simultaneous submissions. Rarely comments on rejected poems. Responds in 6 months. Pays 1 contributor's copy. Staff reviews books of poetry in 2-3 sentences, single-book format.

CONTEST/AWARD OFFERINGS Sponsors the annual Frogmore Poetry Prize. Write for information.

FROGPOND: JOURNAL OF THE HAIKU SOCIETY OF AMERICA

Haiku Society of America, P.O. Box 31, Nassau NY 12123. E-mail: gswede@ryerson.ca. Website: www.hsa-haiku.org/frogpond/index.html. **Contact:** George Swede, Editor.

MAGAZINES NEEDS *Frogpond*, published triannually, is the international journal of the Haiku Society of AmericAn affiliate of the American Literature Association. Its primary function is to publish the best in contemporary English-language haiku and senryu, linked forms including sequences, renku, rengay, and haibun, essays and articles on these forms, and book reviews. Subscription: $33/year. Single issue: $12.

HOW TO CONTACT Submissions by e-mail preferred. No simultaneous submissions. Include SASE with postal submissions. Guidelines available for SASE or on website. Detailed instructions on website. Responds at the end of each submission period (June 1-August 1; September 15-November 15; February 15-April 15). Reviews books of poetry, usually in 1,000 words or less.

ADDITIONAL INFORMATION Also accepts articles, 1,000-4,000 words, that are properly referenced according to 1 of the 3 style guides: MLAPA, Chicago Manual.

CONTEST/AWARD OFFERINGS The "best of issue" prize of 4100 is awarded to a poem from each issue of *Frogpond* through a gift from the Museum of Haiku Literature, located in Tokyo. The Haiku Society of America also sponsors a number of other contests, most of which have cash prizes: The Harold G. Henderson Haiku Award Contest, the Gerald Brady Senryu Award Contest, the Bernard Lionel Einbond Memorial Renku Contest, the Nicholas A. Virgilio Memorial Haiku Competition for High School Students, the Mildred Kanterman Merit Book Awards for outstanding books in the haiku field. Guidelines available on website.

🅞🅖⑤ FUGUE LITERARY MAGAZINE

200 Brink Hall, University of Idaho P.O. Box 44110, Moscow ID 83844-1102. E-mail: fugue@uidaho.edu. Website: http://www.uiweb.uidaho.edu/fugue/. **Contact:** Jennifer Yeatts, Managing Editor. Biannual literary magazine. See website for details. Submissions of poetry, essays, and short stories are accepted Sept. 1 through May 1 (online submissions only). All mate-

rial received outside of this period will be unread. See website for submission instructions. at: www.uiweb. uidho.edu/fugure/submit.html.

○ Work published in *Fugue* has won the Pushcart Prize and has been cited in *Best American Essays*. Work published in *Fugue* has won the Pushcart Prize and has been cited in *Best American Essays*.

MAGAZINES NEEDS *Fugue*, published semiannually in summer and winter, is a literary magazine of the University of Idaho. "There are no restrictions on type of poetry; however, we are not interested in trite or quaint verse." Has published poetry by Sonia Sanchez, Simon Perchik, Denise Duhamel, Dean Young, and W.S. Merwin. *Fugue* is up to 200 pages, perfect-bound. Receives about 400 poems/semester, accepts only 15-20 poems/issue. Press run is 250. There is also an online version. Sample: $8.

HOW TO CONTACT Submit 3-5 poems at a time (10 pages maximum). No previously published poems. Considers simultaneous submissions "with the explicit provision that the writer inform us immediately if the work is accepted for publication elsewhere." E-mail submissions only. Include brief cover letter in body of e-mail with name, address, e-mail, phone number, poem titles, and a brief bio citing any awards/publications. Paste poems in body of e-mail and include one attached file which includes all poems in .pdf, .rtf, or .doc format. Reads submissions September 1-May 1 only. Time between acceptance and publication is up to 1 year. "Submissions are reviewed by staff members and chosen with consensus by the editorial board. No major changes are made to a manuscript without authorial approval." Publishes theme issues. Guidelines available for SASE or on website. Responds in up to 5 months. Pays at least 1 contributor's copy plus an honorarium (up to $25 as funds allow). Acquires first North American serial rights.

CONTEST/AWARD OFFERINGS "For information regarding our annual spring poetry contest, please visit our website."

TIPS "The best way, of course, to determine what we're looking for is to read the journal. As the name *Fugue* indicates, our goal is to present a wide range of literary perspectives. We like stories that satisfy us both intellectually and emotionally, with fresh language and characters so captivating that they stick with us and invite a second reading. We are also seeking creative literary criticism which illuminates a piece of literature or a specific writer by examining that writer's personal experience."

○ **FULLOSIA PRESS**

P.O. Box 280, Ronkonkoma NY 11779. E-mail: deanofrpps@aol.com. Website: rpps_fullosia_press.tripod. com. **Contact:** J.D. Collins, editor; Geoff Jackson, associate editor.

MAGAZINES NEEDS *Fullosia Press*, published monthly online, presents news, information, satire, and right/conservative perspective. Wants any style of poetry. "If you have something to say, say it. We consider many different points of view." Does not want "anti-American, anti-Christian." Considers poetry by children with parental consent. Has published poetry by Awesome David Lawrence, John Grey, Peter Vetrano, Michael Levy, and Taylor Graham. Receives about 50 poems/year, accepts about 40%. Single copy: $15 and SASE (free online); subscription: $25/year (free online). Make checks payable to RPPS-Fullosia Press.

HOW TO CONTACT Accepts e-mail (pasted into body of message) and disk submissions. "E-mail preferred. Final submission by disk or e-mail only." Cover letter is required. Reads submissions when received. Submit seasonal poems 1 month in advance. Time between acceptance and publication varies. "I review all poems: 1) Do they say something?; 2) Is there some thought behind it?; 3) Is it more than words strung together?" Always comments on rejected poems. Publishes theme issues. Guidelines available for SASE, by e-mail, or on website. Responds in 1 month. Acquires one-time rights. Reviews books/chapbooks of poetry and other magazines/journals. Send materials for review consideration to RPPS-Fullosia Press.

TIPS "Make your point quickly. If you haven't done so, after five pages, everybody hates you and your characters."

○ **THE FURNACE REVIEW**

E-mail: editor@thefurnacereview.com. E-mail: submissions@thefurnacereview.com. Website: http://thefurnacereview.com. **Contact:** Ciara LaVelle, editor.

MAGAZINES NEEDS *The Furnace Review*, published quarterly online, is "dedicated to new writers and unique or groundbreaking work." Wants "all forms, from haiku to sonnets to free verse to totally experimental. Just make it interesting." Has published poetry by Carolynn Kingyens, Charles Geoghegan-

Clements, Curtis Evans, and Richard Matthes. Receives about 1,500 pieces/year, accepts about 30.

HOW TO CONTACT Submit up to 5 poems at a time. Lines/poem: 75 maximum. Considers simultaneous submissions; no previously published poems. Accepts e-mail submissions; no disk submissions. Cover letter is preferred. "Include a short biography with all submissions." Reads submissions year round. Time between acceptance and publication is 3 months. Poems are circulated to an editorial board. Sometimes comments on rejected poems. Guidelines available on website. Responds in 6 months. Acquires first North American serial rights.

GARGOYLE

Paycock Press, 3819 N. 13th St., Arlington VA 22201. (703)525-9296. E-mail: hedgehog2@erols.com. Website: www.gargoylemagazine.com. **Contact:** Richard Peabody, co-editor, Lucinda Ebersole, co-editor. *Gargoyle Magazine*, published annually, has always been a scallywag magazine, a maverick magazine, a bit too academic for the underground and way too underground for the academics. We generally run short, one-page poems. We like wit, imagery, killer lines." Has published poetry by Nin Andrews, Kim Chinquee, Kate Braverman, Laura Chester, Thaisa Frank, Thylias Moss, Patricia Smith, Elizabeth Swados, and Paul West. *Gargoyle* is about 500 pages, digest-sized, offset-printed, perfectbound, with color cover, includes ads. Accepts about 10% of the poems received each year. Press run is 2,000. Subscription: $30 for 2 issues (individuals); $40 (institutions). Sample: $10. Reads submissions "all summer—June, July, and August." Time between acceptance and publication is 12 months. "The 2 editors make some concessions but generally concur." Often comments on rejected poems. Responds in 3 months. Always sends prepublication galleys. Pays 1 contributor's copy and offers 50% discount on additional copies.

MAGAZINES NEEDS Not looking for poetry volumes for 2012.

HOW TO CONTACT Query by email. Submit 5 poems at a time. Considers simultaneous submissions. Submit electronically.

TIPS "We have to fall in love with a particular fiction."

GEORGETOWN REVIEW

Box 227, 400 East College St., Georgetown KY 40324. (502)863-8308. Fax: (502)868-8888. E-mail: gtownre-

view@georgetowncollege.edu. Website: http://georgetownreview.georgetowncollege.edu. **Contact:** Steven Carter, editor.

MAGAZINES NEEDS *Georgetown Review*, published annually in May, is a literary journal of poetry, fiction, and creative nonfiction. "We have no specific guidelines concerning form or content of poetry, but are always eager to see poetry that is insightful, rooted in reality, and human." Does not want "work that is merely sentimental, political, or inspirational." Considers poetry by children and teens. Has published poetry by Denise Duhamel, X.J. Kennedy, Fred Chappell, Frederick Smock, Mark Halperin, David Citino, William Greenway, James Harms, and Margarita Engle. *Georgetown Review* is 192 pages, digest-sized, offset-printed, perfect-bound, with 60 lb. glossy 4-color cover with art/graphics, includes ads. Receives about 1,000 poems/year, accepts about 50-60. Press run is 1,000. Single copy: $7; subscription: $. Make checks payable to *Georgetown Review*.

HOW TO CONTACT Submit 1-10 poems at a time. Lines/poem: open. Considers simultaneous submissions; no previously published poems. No fax, e-mail, or disk submissions. Cover letter is preferred. "In cover letter, please include short bio and a list of publications. Also, must include SASE for reply." Reads submissions September 1-March 15. Submit seasonal poems 1 year in advance. Time between acceptance and publication is 6-12 months. Poems are circulated to an editorial board. "The first reader passes the poem along to the poetry editor, and then a final decision is made by the poetry editor and the head editor." Seldom comments on rejected poems. Guidelines available for SASE, by e-mail, or on website. Responds in 1-3 months. Pays 2 contributor's copies. Acquires first North American serial rights. Reviews books/chapbooks of poetry in 1,000 words, multi-book format.

CONTEST/AWARD OFFERINGS Sponsors annual contest, offering $1,000 prize and publication; runners-up also receive publication. Guidelines available for SASE, by e-mail, or on website. **Entry fee:** $10/poem, $5 for each additional poem.

TIPS "We look for fiction that is well written and that has a story line that keeps our interest. Don't send a first draft, and even if we don't take your first, second, or third submission, keep trying."

THE GEORGIA REVIEW

The University of GeorgiAthens GA 30602-9009. (706)542-3481. Fax: (706)542-0047. E-mail: garev@uga.edu. Website: www.uga.edu/garev. **Contact:** Stephen Corey, editor. *The Georgia Review*, published quarterly, seeks "the very best work we can find, whether by Nobel laureates and Pulitzer Prize-winners or by little-known (or even previously unpublished) writers. All manuscripts receive serious, careful attention. We have featured first-ever publications by many new voices over the years, but encourage all potential contributors to become familiar with past offerings before submitting." Has published poetry by Rita Dove, Stephen Dunn, Margaret Gibson, Albert Goldbarth, and Lola Haskins. *The Georgia Review* is180-200 pages, 7x10, professionally printed, flat-spined, with glossy card cover. Publishes 60-70 poems/year, less than .5% of those received. Press run is 4,500. Subscription: $35/year. Single: $15.Our readers are educated, inquisitive people who read a lot of work in the areas we feature, so they expect only the best in our pages. All work submitted should show evidence that the writer is at least as well-educated and well-read as our readers. Essays should be authoritative but accessible to a range of readers.

C No simultaneous or electronic submissions.

TIPS "Unsolicited manuscripts will not be considered from May 15-August 15 (annually); all such submissions received during that period will be returned unread. Check website for submission guidelines."

◑ GERTRUDE

E-mail: editor@gertrudepress.org. Website: www.gertrudepress.org. PO Box 83948, Portland OR 97283. E-mail: poetry@gertrudepress.org. Website:www.gertrudepress.org. **Contact:** Steven Rydman, poetry editor. (Specialized: gay, lesbian, bisexual, transgendered, queer-identified & allied)

MAGAZINES NEEDS *Gertrude*, published semiannually, is the literary publication of Gertrude Press (see separate listing in Books/Chapbooks), "a nonprofit 501(c)(3) organization showcasing and developing the creative talents of lesbian, gay, bisexual, trans, queer-identified, and allied individuals." Has published poetry by Judith Barrington, Deanna Kern Ludwin, Casey Charles, Michael Montlack, Megan Kruse, and Noah Tysick. *Gertrude* is 64-112 pages, digest-sized, offset-printed, perfect-bound, with glossy 4-color cardstock cover with art. Receives about 500 poems/year, accepts about 6-8%. Press run is 300; 50 distributed free. Single copy: $8.25; subscription: $15/year, $27 for 2 years. Sample: $6.25. Make checks payable to Gertrude Press.

HOW TO CONTACT Submit via online submission form on website. Submit 6 poems at a time. Lines/poem: open. Considers simultaneous submissions; no previously published poems. Accepts e-mail submissions via the website only; no disk submissions. Cover letter is preferred. Include short bio and SASE. Reads submissions year round. Time between acceptance and publication is 3-6 months. Poems are circulated to an editorial board. Sometimes comments on rejected poems. Guidelines available in magazine, by e-mail, or on website. Responds in 3 months. Sometimes sends prepublication galleys. Pays 1 contributor's copy plus discount on additional copies/subscriptions. Acquires one-time rights. Rights revert to poets upon publication.

CONTEST/AWARD OFFERINGS The Gertrude Press Poetry Chapbook Contest (see separate listing in Contests & Awards).

TIPS "We look for strong characterization, imagery and new, unique ways of writing about universal experiences. Follow the construction of your work until the ending. Many stories start out with zest, then flipper and die. Show us, don't tell us."

THE GETTYSBURG REVIEW

(717)337-6770. Fax: (717)337-6775. Website: www.gettysburgreview.com. *The Gettysburg Review*, published quarterly, considers "well-written poems of all kinds." Has published poetry by Rita Dove, Alice Friman, Philip Schultz, Michelle, Boisseau, Bob Hicok, Linda Pastan, and G.C. Waldrep. Accepts 1-2% of submissions received. Press run is 4,500. Subscription: $28/year. Sample: $10."Our concern is quality. Manuscripts submitted here should be extremely well written. Reading period September-May."

HOW TO CONTACT Submit 3-5 poems at a time. Considers simultaneous submissions; no previously published poems. Cover letter is preferred. Include SASE. Reads submissions September-May only. Occasionally publishes theme issues. "Response time can be slow during heavy submission periods, especially in the late fall." Pays $2.50/line, one-year subscription, and 1 contributor's copy. Essay-reviews are featured in most issues. Send materials for review consideration.

GLASS: A JOURNAL OF POETRY

E-mail: glasspoetry@yahoo.com. Website: www. glass-poetry.com. **Contact:** Holly Burnside, Editor. "We are not bound by any specific aesthetic; our mission is to present high quality writing. Easy rhyme and 'light' verse are less likely to inspire us. We want to see poetry that enacts the artistic and creative purity of glass."

C Submissions must follow our guidelines.

TIPS "Accepts submissions from Sept. - May. We like poems that show a careful understanding of language, sound, passion and creativity and poems that surprise us. Include brief cover letter and biography. Include your email address."

○○**⑤** GRAIN

P.O. Box 67, Saskatoon SK S7K 3K1, Canada. (306)244-2828. Fax: (306)244-0255. E-mail: grainmag@sasktel. net. Website: www.grainmagazine.ca. **Contact:** Sylvia Legris, Editor.

MAGAZINES NEEDS *Grain, The Journal Of Eclectic writing*, is a literary quarterly that publishes engaging, diverse, and challenging writing and art by some of the best Canadian and international writers and artists. Every issue features superb new writing from both developing and established writers. Each issue also highlights the unique artwork of a different visual artist. Grain has garnered national and international recognition for its distinctive, cutting-edge content and design. Has published poetry by Lorna Crozier, Don Domanski, Cornelia Haeussler, Patrick Lane, Karen Solie, and Monty Reid. *Grain* is 112-128 pages, digest-sized, professionally printed. Press run is 1,100. Receives about 3,000 submissions/year. Subscription: $35 CAD/year, $55 CAD for 2 years. Sample: $13 CAD. (See website for U.S. and foreign postage fees.)

HOW TO CONTACT Submit up to 12 pages of poetry, typed in readable font on one side only. No previously published poems or simultaneous submissions. No fax or e-mail submissions; postal submissions only. Cover letter with all contact information, title(s), and genre of work is required. "No staples. Your name and address must be on every page. Pieces of more than one page must be numbered. Please only submit work in one genre at one time." Reads submissions September-May only. "Manuscripts postmarked between June 1 and August 31 will not be read." Guidelines available by SASE (or SAE and IRC), e-mail, or on website. Typically responds in 3-

6 months. Pays $50-225 CAD (depending on number of pages) and 2 contributor's copies. Acquires first Canadian serial rights only. Copyright remains with the author.

◑ THE GREAT AMERICAN POETRY SHOW

The Muse Media, P.O. Box 69506, West Hollywood CA 90069. (323)969-4905. E-mail: info@tgaps.net. Website: www.tgaps.net. **Contact:** Larry Ziman, Editor/Publisher. Submit any number of poems at a time. Considers previously published poems and simultaneous submissions. Accepts e-mail submissions in body of email or as attachment. Cover letter is optional. Include SASE. "If we reject a submission of your work, please send us another group to go through. We have 3 editors who can handle a lot of submissions." Pays 1 contributor's copy.

MAGAZINES NEEDS *The Great American Poetry Show*, published about every 3 years, is an $8\frac{1}{2}$x11 hardcover serial poetry anthology. Wants poems on any subject, in any style, of any length. Has published poetry by Carol Carpenter, Philip Wexler, Fredrick Zydek, Patrick Polak, Steve de Frances, Lois Swann, Alan Catlin, and Julie M. Tate. *The Great American Poetry Show* is 150 pages, sheet-fed offset-printed, perfect-bound, with cloth cover with art/graphics. "For Volume 1, we read over 8,000 poems from about 1,400 poets and accepted only 113 poems from 83 poets. For Volume 2 we read over 15,000 poems and accepted 134 poems from 92 poets." Press run is 1,000. Single copy: $35 (print), $.99 (e-book, download only).

HOW TO CONTACT Submit any number of poems at a time. Considers previously published poems and simultaneous submissions. Accepts e-mail submissions in body of email or as attachment. Cover letter is optional. Include SASE. "If we reject a submission of your work, please send us another group to go through. We have 3 editors who can handle a lot of submissions." Responds within a week or two usually ("depends on how busy we are"). Pays 1 contributor's copy.

ALSO OFFERS "Please visit our message boards where anyone can have us post poetry news, reviews, essays, articles, and recommended books." Please visit our website where you can link to over 10,000 literary subjects such as articles, essays, interviews, reviews, publishers, and blogs.

GREEN HILLS LITERARY LANTERN

McClain Hall, Truman State University, Kirksville MO 63501. (660)785-4513. E-mail: jbeneven@truman.edu. Website: http://ll.truman.edu/ghllweb/. **Contact:** Joe Benevento, Poetry Editor.

MAGAZINES NEEDS *Green Hills Literary Lantern*, published annually online in June, is "an open-access journal of short fiction and poetry of exceptional quality." Wants "the best poetry, in any style, preferably understandable. There are no restrictions on subject matter. Both free and formal verse forms are fine, though we publish more free verse overall." Does not want "haiku, limericks, or anything over 2 pages. Pornography and gratuitous violence will not be accepted. Obscurity for its own sake is also frowned upon." Has published poetry by Jim Thomas, David Lawrence, Mark Belair, Louis Philips, Francine Tolf, and Julie Lechevsky. Sample: $7 (back issue).

HOW TO CONTACT Submit 3-7 poems at a time. Considers simultaneous submissions, "but not preferred"; no previously published poems. No e-mail submissions. Cover letter is preferred. Include list of publication credits. Type poems one/page. Often comments on rejected poems. Guidelines available for SASE, by e-mail, or on website. Responds within 4 months. Always sends prepublication galleys. Acquires one-time rights.

GREEN MOUNTAINS REVIEW

Johnson State College, Johnson VT 05656. (802)635-1350. Fax: (802)635-1210. E-mail: gmr@jsc.edu. Website: http://greenmountainsreview.jsc.vsc.edu. **Contact:** Elizabeth Powell, Poetry Editor. Established 1975.

MAGAZINES NEEDS *Green Mountains Review*, published twice/year, includes poetry (and other writing) by well-known authors and promising newcomers. Has published poetry by Carol Frost, Sharon Olds, Carl Phillips, David St. John, and David Wojahn. *Green Mountains Review* is 150-200 pages, digest-sized, flat-spined. Receives about 5,000 submissions/year, publishes 60 authors. Press run is 1,550. Subscription: $16.50/1 year, $24/2 years. Sample issue: $7.

HOW TO CONTACT Submit no more than 5 poems at a time. Considers simultaneous submissions. No e-mail submissions. Reads submissions September 1-March 1 only. Sometimes comments rejected poems. Publishes theme issues. Guidelines available for

SASE. Responds in up to 6 months. Pays 2 contributor's copies plus one-year subscription. Acquires first North American serial rights. Send materials for review consideration.

TIPS We encourage you to order some of our back issues to acquaint yourself with what has been accepted in the past. Unsolicited mss. are read from Sept. 1 - Mar. 1.

THE GREENSBORO REVIEW

MFA Writing Program, 3302 HHRA Building, UNC Greensboro, Greensboro NC 27402-6170. (336)334-5459. E-mail: jlclark@uncg.edu. Website: www.greensbororeview.org. **Contact:** Jim Clark, editor.

MAGAZINES NEEDS *The Greensboro Review*, published twice/year, showcases well-made verse in all styles and forms, though shorter poems (under 50 lines) are preferred. Has published poetry by Carl Dennis, Jack Gilbert, Linda Gregg, Tung-Hui Hu, A. Van Jordan, and Natasha Tretheway. *The Greensboro Review* is 144 pages, digest-sized, professionally printed, flat-spined, with colored matte cover. Subscription: $14/year, $24 for 2 years, and $30 for 3 years. Sample: $8.

> Stories for *The Greensboro Review* have been included in *Best American Short Stories, The O. Henry Awards Prize Stories, New Stories from The South* and *Pushcart Prize*.

HOW TO CONTACT Submit no more than 5 poems at a time. Lines/poem: under 50 lines preferred. No previously published poems. Simultaneous submissions accepted. No fax or e-mail submissions. Cover letter is preferred. Include number of poems submitted. Provide SASE for reply; manuscripts arriving after those dates will be held for consideration for the next issue. Reads submissions according to the following deadlines: mss must arrive by September 15 to be considered for the Spring issue (acceptances in December), or February 15 to be considered for the Fall issue (acceptances in May). "Manuscripts arriving after those dates will be held for consideration for the next issue." Guidelines available in magazine, for SASE, or on website. Responds in 4 months. Always sends prepublication galleys. Pays 3 contributor's copies. Acquires first North American serial rights. Submit by regular mail or submission form on website.

TIPS "We want to see the best being written regardless of theme, subject or style."

◐ ⊕ GUERNICA

A Magazine of Art and Politics, Attn: Michael Archer, 165 Bennett Ave., 4C, New York NY 10040. E-mail: editors@guernicamag.com; art@guernicamag.com (art/photography); poetry@guernicamag.com; publisher@guernicamag.com. Website: www.guernicamag.com. **Contact:** Erica Wright, poetry; Dan Eckstein, art/photography. "*Guernica*, published biweekly, is one of the web's most acclaimed new magazines. 2009: Guernica is called a "great online literary magazine" by *Esquire*. *Guernica* contributors come from dozens of countries and write in nearly as many languages."

> ◯ Received Caine Prize for African Writing, Best of the Net, cited by Esquire as a "great literary magazine."

MAGAZINES NEEDS In subject line (please follow this format exactly): "poetry submission." Submit up to five poems, any length to poetry@guernicamag.com.

TIPS "Please read the magazine first before submitting. Most stories that are rejected simply do not fit our approach. Submission guidelines available online."

⊕ GULF COAST: A JOURNAL OF LITERATURE AND FINE ARTS

University of Houston, Dept. of English, University of Houston, Houston TX 77204-3013. (713)743-3223. E-mail: editors@gulfcoastmag.org. Website: www.gulfcoastmag.org. Christine Ha, Eric Howerton, Edward Porter, fiction editors. **Contact:** The Editors. Buys 5-10 ms/year. Receives 300 unsolicited mss/month. Accepts 4-8 mss/issue; 12-16 mss/year. Agented fiction 5%. **Publishes 2-8 new writers/year.** Recently published work by Matt Bell, Megan Mayhew Bergman, Sarah Shun-Lien Bynum, Jenine Capot Crucet, Benjamin Percy, John Weir. Publishes short shorts. Sometimes comments on rejected mss.

MAGAZINES NEEDS *Gulf Coast: A Journal of Literature and Fine Arts*, published twice/year in April and October, includes poetry, fiction, essays, interviews, and color reproductions of work by artists from across the nation. While the journal features work by a number of established poets, editors are also interested in "providing a forum for new and emerging writers who are producing well-crafted work that takes risks." Has published poetry by Anne Carson, Carl Dennis, Terrance Hayes, Bob Hicok, Alice Notley, Srikanth Reddy, Karen Volkman, and Dean Young. *Gulf Coast* is 270 pages, 7x9, offset-printed, perfect-bound. Single copy: $10; subscription: $16/year, $28 for 2 years. Sample: $8.

HOW TO CONTACT Submit up to 5 poems at a time. Considers simultaneous submissions with notification; no previously published poems. Cover letter is required. List previous publications and include a brief bio. Reads submissions September-April. Guidelines available for SASE or on website. Responds within 4-6 months. Pays $50/poem and 2 contributor's copies. Returns all rights (except electronic) upon publication.

CONTEST/AWARD OFFERINGS The 2011 Gulf Coast Contests, awarding publication and $1,000 each in Poetry, Fiction, and Nonfiction, are now open. Honorable mentions in each category will receive a $250 second prize. Ilya Kaminsky will judge the contest in poetry, Frederick Reiken will judge in fiction, and John D'Agata will judge in nonfiction. Postmark/Online Entry deadline: March 15, 2011. Winners and Honorable Mentions will be announced in May. **Entry fee:** $20 (includes one-year subscription). Make checks payable to *Gulf Coast*. Guidelines available on website.

TIPS "Submit only previously unpublished works. Include a cover letter. Online submissions are strongly preferred. Stories or essays should be typed, double-spaced, and paginated with your name, address, and phone number on the 1st page, title on subsequent pages. Poems should have your name, address, and phone number on the 1st page of each." The 2011 Gulf Coast Contests, awarding publication and $1,000 each in Poetry, Fiction, and Nonfiction, are now open. Honorable mentions in each category will receive a $250 second prize. Ilya Kaminsky will judge the contest in poetry, Frederick Reiken will judge in fiction, and John D'Agata will judge in nonfiction. Postmark/Online Entry deadline: March 15, 2011. Winners and Honorable Mentions will be announced in May. Entry fee: $20 (includes one-year subscription). Make checks payable to *Gulf Coast*. Guidelines available on website.

◐ GULF STREAM MAGAZINE

Florida International Univ., English Dept., N. Miami FL 33181-3000. E-mail: gulfstreamfiu@yahoo.com. Website: www.gulfstreamlitmag.com.

○ "Submit online only. Please read guidelines on website in full. Submissions that do not conform to our guidelines will be discarded. We do not accept emailed or mailed submissions. We read from Sept 15- Dec 15; Jan 15 - Mar 15." Does not pay writers' expenses.

MAGAZINES NEEDS *Gulf Stream*, published semiannually, is associated with the Creative Writing program at Florida International University. Wants "poetry of any style and subject matter as long as it's of high literary quality." Has published poetry by Robert Wrigley, Jan Beatty, Jill Bialosky, and Catherine Bowman. *Gulf Stream* is 124 pages, digest-sized, flat-spined, printed on quality stock, with matte card cover. Accepts less than 10% of poetry received. Print back-issue sample: $5.

HOW TO CONTACT Submit no more than 5 poems at a time. Considers simultaneous submissions with notification. Accepts electronic online submissions only; no snail mail/hard copy or e-mail submissions. "See website for details." Cover letter is required. Reads submissions September 15-December 15; January 15-March 15 only. Publishes theme issue every other issue. Guidelines available in magazine or on website. Responds in 3 weeks to 3 months. Acquires first North American serial rights.

TIPS "Looks for fresh, original writing—well plotted stories with unforgettable characters, fresh poetry and experimental writing. Usually longer stories do not get accepted. There are exceptions, however."

① HAIGHT ASHBURY LITERARY JOURNAL

558 Joost Ave., San Francisco CA 94127. (415)584-8264. E-mail: haljeditor@gmail.com; poetship@comcast.net. Website: http://haightashburyliterary-journal.wordpress.com/; www.facebook.com/pages/Haight-Ashbury-Literary-Journal/365542018331. **Contact:** Alice Rogoff, Taylor Landry.

MAGAZINES NEEDS *Haight Ashbury Literary Journal*, publishes "well-written poetry and fiction. HALJ's voices are often of people who have been marginalized, oppressed, or abused. HALJ strives to bring literary arts to the general public, to the San Francisco community of writers, to the Haight Ashbury neighborhood, and to people of varying ages, genders, ethnicities, and sexual preferences. The Journal is produced as a tabloid to maintain an accessible price for low-income people." Has

published poetry by Dan O'Connell, Diane Frank, Dancing Bear, Lee Herrick, Al Young, and Laura Beausoleil. *Haight Ashbury* is 16 pages, includes ads. Includes fiction under 20 pages, one story/issue, and b&w drawings. Press run is 2,500. Subscription: $8/ 2 issues, $16 for 4 issues; $50 for a lifetime subscription. Sample: $3.

HOW TO CONTACT Submit up to 6 poems at a time. Submit only once/6 months. No e-mail submissions; postal submissions only. "Please type 1 poem to a page, put name and address on every page, and include SASE. No bio." Sometimes publishes theme issues (each issue changes its theme and emphasis). Guidelines available for SASE. Responds in 4 months. Rights revert to author.

ADDITIONAL INFORMATION An anthology of past issues, *This Far Together*, is available for $12.

●○ HANDSHAKE

(Specialized: science fiction; fantasy; horror)5 Cross Farm, Station Rd. N., Fearnhead, Warrington, Cheshire WA2 0QG England. Established 1992. **Contact:** J.F. Haines.

MAGAZINES NEEDS *Handshake*, published irregularly, "is a newsletter for science fiction poets." Wants "science fiction/fantasy poetry of all styles. Prefer short poems." Does not want "epics or foul language." Has published poetry by Cardinal Cox, Neil K. Henderson, Andrew Dallington, Peter Day, Steve Sneyd, John Light, and Joanne Tolson. *Handshake* is 1 sheet of A4 paper, photocopied, includes ads. "It has evolved into being 1 side of news and information and 1 side of poetry."

HOW TO CONTACT Submit 2-3 poems. No previously published poems or simultaneous submissions. Cover letter is preferred. Poems must be typed and camera-ready. Time between acceptance and publication varies. Editor selects "whatever takes my fancy and is of suitable length." Responds ASAP. Pays 1 contributor's copy. Acquires first rights. Reviews books/chapbooks of poetry or other magazines/journals of very short length. Send material for review consideration. Time-sensitive material may not be accepted unless received well in advance.

ALSO OFFERS *Handshake* is also the newsletter for The Eight Hand Gang, an organization for British science fiction poets established in 1991. Currently has 100 members. Information about the organization available in *Handshake*.

⊙ ⑤ HANGING LOOSE

Hanging Loose Press, 231 Wyckoff St., Brooklyn NY 11217. E-mail: editor@hangingloosepress.com. Website: www.hangingloosepress.com. **Contact:** Robert Hershon, Dick Lourie, and Mark Pawlak, poetry editors. Hanging Loose Press, 231 Wyckoff St., Brooklyn NY 11217. (347)529-4738. Fax: (347)227-8215. E-mail: editor@hangingloosepress.com. Website: www. hangingloosepress.com. *Hanging Loose*, published in April and October, "concentrates on the work of new writers." Wants "excellent, energetic" poems. Considers poetry by teens ("one section contains poems by high-school-age poets"). Has published poetry by Sherman Alexie, Paul Violi, Donna Brook, Kimiko Hahn, Harvey Shapiro, and Ha Jin. *Hanging Loose* is 120 pages, offset-printed on heavy stock, flat-spined, with 4-color glossy card cover. Sample: $12.

MAGAZINES NEEDS *Hanging Loose*, published in April and October, "concentrates on the work of new writers." Wants "excellent, energetic" poems. Considers poetry by teens ("one section contains poems by high-school-age poets"). Has published poetry by Sherman Alexie, Paul Violi, Donna Brook, Kimiko Hahn, Harvey Shapiro, and Ha Jin. *Hanging Loose* is 120 pages, offset-printed on heavy stock, flat-spined, with 4-color glossy card cover. Sample: $12.

HOW TO CONTACT Submit up to 6 poems at a time. No fax or e-mail submissions; postal submissions only. No simultaneous submissions. "Would-be contributors should read the magazine first." Responds in 3 months. Pays small fee and 2 contributor's copies.

ADDITIONAL INFORMATION Hanging Loose Press does not consider unsolicited book mss or artwork.

HARPUR PALATE

English Department, P.O. Box 6000, Binghamton University, Binghamton, NY 13902-6000. (607)355-4761. Fax: (607)777-2408. E-mail: harpur.palate@gmail.com. Website: http://harpurpalate.blogspot.com. **Contact:** Barrett Bowlin, managing editor. "We have no restrictions on subject matter or form. Quite simply, send us your highest-quality fiction and poetry."

MAGAZINES NEEDS *Harpur Palate*, published biannually, is "dedicated to publishing the best poetry and prose, regardless of style, form, or genre." Has published poetry by Sherman Alexie, Tess Gallagher,

Alex Lemon, Marvin Bell, Ryan G. Van Cleave, Sascha Feinstein, Allison Joseph, Neil Shepard, and Ruth Stone. *Harpur Palate* is 180-220 pages, digest-sized, offset-printed, perfect-bound, with matte or glossy cover. Receives about 1,000 poems/year, accepts about 50. Press run is 800. Single copy: $10; subscription: $16/year (2 issues). Sample: $5. Make checks payable to *Harpur Palate*.

HOW TO CONTACT Submit 3-5 poems at a time. Lines/poem: "No restrictions; entire submission must be 10 pages or fewer." Considers simultaneous submissions, "but we must be notified immediately if the piece is taken somewhere else"; no previously published poems. No e-mail submissions. Accepts postal submissions. Cover letter and SASE is required. Reads submissions year round. Time between acceptance and publication is 2 months. Poems are circulated to an editorial board. Seldom comments on rejected poems. Guidelines available in magazine, for SASE, or on website. Responds in up to 8 months. Pays 2 contributor's copies. Acquires first North American serial rights.

CONTEST/AWARD OFFERINGS The Milton Kessler Memorial Prize for Poetry (see separate listing).

TIPS "*Harpur Palate* now accepts submissions all year; deadline for Winter issue is November 15, for Summer issue is April 15. We also sponsor a fiction contest for the Summer issue and a poetry contest for the Winter issue. We do not accept submissions via e-mail. We are interested in high quality writing of all genres, but especially literary poetry and fiction."

HARTWORKS

Website: www.dccww.org. D.C. Creative Writing Workshop, 601 Mississippi Ave. SE, Washington DC 20032. (202)445-4280. E-mail: info@dccww.org. Website: www.dccww.org. Established 2000. **Contact:** Nancy Schwalb, artistic director.

○ Although this journal doesn't accept submissions from the general public, it's included here as an outstanding example of what a literary journal can be (for anyone of any age).

MAGAZINES NEEDS *hArtworks* appears 3 times/year. "We publish the poetry of Hart Middle School students (as far as we know, Hart may be the only public middle school in the U.S. with its own poetry magazine) and the writing of guest writers such as Nikki Giovanni, Alan Cheuse, Arnost Lustig, Henry Taylor, Mark Craver, and Cornelius Eady, along with interviews between the kids and the grown-up pros. We also publish work by our writers-in-residence, who teach workshops at Hart, and provide trips to readings, slams, museums, and plays." Wants "vivid, precise, imaginative language that communicates from the heart as well as the head." Does not want "poetry that only 'sounds' good; it also needs to say something meaningful." Has published poetry by Maryum Abdullah, Myron Jones, Nichell Kee, Kiana Murphy, James Tindle, and Sequan Wilson. *hArtworks* is 92 pages, magazine-sized, professionally printed, perfect bound, with card cover. Receives about 1,000 poems/year, accepts about 20%. Press run is 500; 100 distributed free to writers, teachers. Single copy: $12; subscription: $30. Make checks payable to D.C. Creative Writing Workshop.

HOW TO CONTACT "Writers-in-residence solicit most submissions from their classes, and then a committee of student editors makes the final selections. Each year, our second issue is devoted to responses to the Holocaust."

HAWAI'I PACIFIC REVIEW

1060 Bishop St., Honolulu HI 96813. (808)544-1108. Fax: (808)544-0862. E-mail: pwilson@hpu.edu. E-mail: hprsubmissions@hpu.edu. Website: www.hpu.edu/hpr. **Contact:** Patrice M. Wilson, editor. 1060 Bishop St., Honolulu, HI 96813. (808)544-1108. Fax: (808)544-0862. E-mail: pwilson@hpu.edu; hprsubmissions@hpu.edu. Website: www.hpu.edu/hpr. **Contact:** Dr. Patrice M. Wilson, editor. Establ. 1987. *Hawai'i Pacific Review*, published annually in September by Hawai'i Pacific University, prints "quality poetry, short fiction, and personal essays from writers worldwide. Our journal seeks to promote a world view that celebrates a variety of cultural themes, beliefs, values, and viewpoints. We wish to further the growth of artistic vision and talent by encouraging sophisticated and innovative poetic and narrative techniques." Has published poetry by Wendy Bishop, Rick Bursky, Virgil Suárez, Bob Hikok, Daniel Gutstein, and Linda Bierds. *Hawai'i Pacific Review* is 80-120 pages, digest-sized, professionally printed on quality paper, perfect-bound, with coated card cover. Receives 800-1,000 poems/year, accepts up to 30-40. Press run is about 500 (100 shelf sales). Single copy: $8.95. Sample: $5.

HOW TO CONTACT Submit up to 5 poems at a time. Lines/poem: 100 maximum. No previously published poems or simultaneous submissions. No fax or e-mail submissions. Cover letter is required. Include 5-line professional bio including prior publications. SASE required. "One submission per issue. No handwritten manuscripts. Include name on all pages." Reads submissions September 1-December 31 annually. Seldom comments on rejected poems. Guidelines available for SASE, by e-mail, or on website. Responds within 3 months. Pays 2 contributor's copies. Acquires first North American serial rights. Rights revert to poet upon publication. "Must acknowledge *Hawai'i Pacific Review* as first publisher."

TIPS "We look for the unusual or original plot; prose with the texture and nuance of poetry. Character development or portrayal must be unusual/original; humanity shown in an original insightful way (or characters); sense of humor where applicable. Be sure it's a draft that has gone through substantial changes, with supervision from a more experienced writer, if you're a beginner. Write about intense emotion and feeling, not just about someone's divorce or shaky relationship. No soap-opera-like fiction."

HAYDEN'S FERRY REVIEW

c/o Virginia G. Piper Center for Creative Writing, Arizona State University, P.O. Box 875002, Tempe AZ 85287-5002. (480)965-1337. E-mail: HFR@asu.edu. Website: www.haydensferryreview.org. **Contact:** Beth Staples, managing editor. *Hayden's Ferry* is a handsome literary magazine appearing in November and April. Has published poetry by Dennis Schmitz, Raymond Carver, Maura Stanton, Ai, and David St. John. *Hayden's Ferry Review* is 120 pages, digest-sized, flat-spined, with glossy card cover. Press run is 1,300 (400 subscribers, 100 libraries, 400 shelf sales). Accepts about 1% of 12,000 submissions annually. Subscription: $22. Sample: $13. Word length open."*Hayden's Ferry Review* publishes the best quality fiction, poetry, and creative nonfiction from new, emerging, and established writers."

Work from *Hayden's Ferry Review* has been selected for inclusion in *Pushcart Prize* anthologies and *Best Creative Nonfiction*. Work from *Hayden's Ferry Review* has been selected for inclusion in *Pushcart Prize* anthologies, Best of the West, and *Best Creative Nonfiction*.

HOW TO CONTACT "No specifications other than limit in number (6)." Now accepting submissions online. Submissions are circulated to two poetry editors. Editors comment on submissions "sometimes". See guidelines online. Sends contributor's page proofs. Pays $50 per contributor, one year subscription, and 2 contributor's copies.

HIGHLIGHTS FOR CHILDREN

803 Church St., Honesdale PA 18431-1824. (570)253-1080. Fax: (570)251-7847. Website: www.Highlights.com. Christine French Clark, editor-in-chief; Cindy Faber Smith, art director. **Contact:** Manuscript Coordinator. "This book of wholesome fun is dedicated to helping children grow in basic skills and knowledge, in creativeness, in ability to think and reason, in sensitivity to others, in high ideals, and worthy ways of living—for children are the world's most important people. We publish stories for beginning and advanced readers. Up to 500 words for beginners (ages 3-7), up to 800 words for advanced (ages 8-12)."

TIPS "We are pleased that many authors of children's literature report that their first published work was in the pages of *Highlights*. It is not our policy to consider fiction on the strength of the reputation of the author. We judge each submission on its own merits. With factual material, however, we do prefer that writers be authorities in their field or people with first-hand experience. In this manner we can avoid the encyclopedic article that merely restates information readily available elsewhere. We don't make assignments. Query with simple letter to establish whether the nonfiction subject is likely to be of interest. A beginning writer should first become familiar with the type of material that *Highlights* publishes. Include special qualifications, if any, of author. Write for the child, not the editor. Write in a voice that children understand and relate to. Speak to today's kids, avoiding didactic, overt messages. Even though our general principles haven't changed over the years, we are contemporary in our approach to issues. Avoid worn themes."

◐ HIRAM POETRY REVIEW

P.O. Box 162, Hiram OH 44234. (330)569-5331. E-mail: poetryreview@hiram.edu. Website: http://hirampoetryreview.wordpress.com/. **Contact:** Willard Greenwood, poetry editor.

MAGAZINES NEEDS *Hiram Poetry Review*, published annually in spring, features "distinctive, beautiful, and heroic poetry." Wants "works of high and low art. We tend to favor poems that are pockets of resistance in the undeclared war against 'plain speech,'

but we're interested in any work of high quality." Press run is 400 (300 subscribers, 150 libraries). Subscription: $9/year; $23/3 years.

HOW TO CONTACT Send 3-5 poems at a time. Lines/poem: under 50 (3 single-spaced pages or less). Considers simultaneous submissions. No e-mail submissions unless international. Cover letter is required. Include brief bio. Reads submissions year round. Responds in up to 6 months. Pays 2 contributor's copies. Acquires first North American serial rights. Rights return to poets upon publication.

THE HOLLINS CRITIC

E-mail: acockrell@hollins.edu. Website: www.hollins.edu/academics/critic. **Contact:** Cathryn Hankla. C No e-mail submissions.

MAGAZINES NEEDS *The Hollins Critic*, published 5 times/year, prints critical essays, poetry, and book reviews. Uses a few short poems in each issue, interesting in form, content, or both. Has published poetry by William Miller, R.T. Smith, David Huddle, Margaret Gibson, and Julia Johnson. *The Hollins Critic* is 24 pages, magazine-sized. Press run is 500. Subscription: $10/year ($15 outside U.S.). Sample: $3.

HOW TO CONTACT Submit up to 5 poems at a time using the online submission form at www.hollinscriticsubmissions.com, available from September 1-December 15. Submissions received at other times will be returned unread. Responds in 6 weeks. Pays $25/poem plus 5 contributor's copies.

TIPS We accept unsolicited poetry submissions; all other content is by prearrangement.

◐◌ HOME PLANET NEWS

P.O. Box 455, High Falls NY 12440. (845)687-4084. E-mail: homeplanetnews@yahoo.com. Website: www.homeplanetnews.org. **Contact:** Donald Lev, editor. P.O. Box 455, High Falls, NY 12440. (845)687-4084. E-mail: homeplanetnews@yahoo.com. Website: www.homeplanetnews.org. **Contact:** Donald Lev, editor. *Home Planet News*, published 3 times/year, aims "to publish lively and eclectic poetry, from a wide range of sensibilities, and to provide news of the small press and poetry scenes, thereby fostering a sense of community among contributors and readers." Wants "honest, well-crafted poems, open or closed form, on any subject." Does not want "any work which seems to us to be racist, sexist, ageist, anti-Semitic, or imposes limitations on the human spirit." Considers poetry by children and teens. Has published poetry by

Enid Dame, Antler, Lyn Lifshin, Gerald Locklin, Hal Sirowitz, and Janine Pommy Vega. *Home Planet News* is 24 pages, tabloid, Web offset-printed, includes ads. Receives about 1,000 poems/year, accepts up to 3%. Press run is 1,000 (300 subscribers). Single copy: $5; subscription: $12/3 issues, $18/6 issues.

○ *HPN* has received a small grant from the Puffin Foundation for its focus on AIDS issues.

HOW TO CONTACT Submit 3-6 poems at a time. Lines/poem: no limit on length, "but shorter poems (under 30 lines) stand a better chance." No previously published poems or simultaneous submissions. Cover letter is preferred. "SASE is a must." Time between acceptance and publication is 1 year. Seldom comments on rejected poems. Occasionally publishes theme issues. Upcoming themes available in magazine. Guidelines available for SASE or on website; "however, it is usually best to simply send work." Responds in 4 months. Pays one-year gift subscription plus 3 contributor's copies. Acquires first rights. Rights revert to poet upon publication. Reviews books/chapbooks of poetry and other magazines in 1,200 words, single- and multi-book format. Send materials for review consideration to Donald Lev. "Note: we do have guidelines for book reviewers; please write for them or check website. Magazines are reviewed by a staff member."

TIPS "We use very little fiction, and a story we accept just has to grab us. We need short pieces of some complexity, stories about complex people facing situations which resist simple resolutions."

❶ HOMESTEAD REVIEW

Box A-5, 156 Homestead Ave., Hartnell College, Salinas CA 93901. (831)755-6943. Fax: (831)755-6751. E-mail: mgteutsch@gmail.com. Website: www.hartnell.cc.ca.us/homestead_review. Established 1985. **Contact:** Maria Garcia Teutsch, editor. *Homestead Review*, published annually in April, seeks "avant-garde poetry as well as fixed form styles of remarkable quality and originality." Does not want "Hallmark-style writing or first drafts." Considers poetry written by children and teens. Has published poetry by Sally Van Doren, Kathryn Kirkpatrick, Laura Le Hew, Allison Joseph, and Hal Sirowitz. Receives about 1,000 poems/year, accepts about 15%. Press run is 500 (300 subscribers/libraries); 200 are distributed free to poets, writers, bookstores. Single copy: $10; subscrip-tion: $10/year. Make checks payable to *Homestead Review*.

MAGAZINES NEEDS *Homestead Review*, published annually in April, seeks "avant-garde poetry as well as fixed form styles of remarkable quality and originality." Does not want "Hallmark-style writing or first drafts." Considers poetry written by children and teens. Has published poetry by Sally Van Doren, Kathryn Kirkpatrick, Laura Le Hew, Allison Joseph, and Hal Sirowitz. Receives about 1,000 poems/year, accepts about 15%. Press run is 500 (300 subscribers/libraries); 200 are distributed free to poets, writers, bookstores. Single copy: $10; subscription: $10/year. Make checks payable to *Homestead Review*.

HOW TO CONTACT Submit 3 poems at a time. No previously published poems or simultaneous submissions. Postal submissions preferred. Cover letter is required. "A brief bio should be included in the cover letter." Reads submissions year round. Deleted. Time between acceptance and publication is up to 6 months. "Manuscripts are read by the staff and discussed. Poems/fiction accepted by majority consensus." Often comments on rejected poems. Guidelines available for SASE. Responds in 5 months. Pays 1 contributor's copy. Acquires one-time rights.

CONTEST/AWARD OFFERINGS Contest with categories for poetry and fiction. Offers 1st Prize: $250 plus publication in *Homestead Review*. All entries will be considered for publication in *Homestead Review*. Guidelines available on website. **Entry fee:** $15 for 3 poems. **Deadline:** see website for current dates.

❶❷❸ HOSPITAL DRIVE

Hospital Drive, PO Box 800793, Charlottesville VA 22908-0761. E-mail: hospitaldrive@virginia.edu. Website: http://hospitaldrive.med.virginia.edu. **Contact:** Dr. Daniel Becker, Editor. Hospital Drive PO Box 800793, Charlottesville VA 22908-0761. 434-924-5118. E-mail: hospitaldrive@virginia.edu. http://hospital-drive.med.virginia.edu. *Hospital Drive* is the on-line literary and humanities journal of the University of Virginia School of Medicine. The journal publishes original literature and art on themes of health, illness, and healing. *Hospital Drive*, published irregularly, "encourages original creative work that examines themes of health, illness, and healing. Submissions will be accepted from anyone, but preference is given to those involved in providing, teaching, studying, or researching patient care. All work will be judged anonymously by reviewers and the editorial board. Poems, short fiction, personal essays, reviews, photography, and visual art (painting, drawing, sculpture, mixed media) will be considered. Issues will be released at least once/year, and include invited work." Please review our web site thoroughly, and direct any additional questions to: query@hospitaldrive.med. virginia.edu.

HOW TO CONTACT Submit no more than 5 poems, 10 pages in length. Accepts e-mail submissions only. Attach submission as Word document. Include contact information and title for each poem. "The editorial board and outside reviewers will judge each submission anonymously."

HOTEL AMERIKA

Columbia College Chicago, English Dept., 600 S. Michigan Ave., Chicago IL 60605-1996. (312)344-8101. E-mail: editors@HotelAmerika.net. Website: www.hotelamerika.net. Established 2002. **Contact:** David Lazar, editor.

Work published in *Hotel Amerika* has been included in *The Pushcart Prize* and *The Best American Poetry* and featured on *Poetry Daily*.

MAGAZINES NEEDS *Hotel Amerika*, published semiannually, is open to all genres and schools of writing, "from the most formalistic to the most avant-garde." Has published poetry by Antler, Denise Duhamel, Maureen Seaton, Mark Irwin, Simon Perchik, and Lisa Samuels. *Hotel Amerika* is about 110 pages, magazine-sized, offset-printed, perfect-bound, with cardstock cover with artwork, sometimes includes ads. Receives about 1,500 poems/year, accepts about 100. Press run is 2,000. Single copy: $10; subscription: $18/1 year, $34/2 years; back issues: $6. Make checks payable to Columbia College Chicago.

HOW TO CONTACT Submit 3-6 poems at a time. No previously published poems or simultaneous submissions. No e-mail or disk submissions. Cover letter is preferred. "Please include titles of poems in the cover letter, and include a SASE for our response." Reads submissions September 1-May 1. Manuscripts received outside of the reading period will be returned unread. "A pool of readers and an assistant editor read the poetry submissions and pass their recommendations on to David Lazar, who makes all final decisions." Seldom comments on rejected

poems. Guidelines available for SASE or on website. Responds in up to 3 months. Pays 1-2 contributor's copies. Acquires first North American serial rights. Rights revert to poets upon publication.

HQ POETRY MAGAZINE (THE HAIKU QUARTERLY)

Website: http://volecentral.co.uk/hq/. 39 Exmouth St., Kingshill, Swindon, Wiltshire SN1 3PU England. Website: http://volecentral.co.uk/hq/. Established 1990. **Contact:** Kevin Bailey, editor.

MAGAZINES NEEDS *HQ Poetry Magazine*, published quarterly, is "a platform from which new and established poets can speak and have the opportunity to experiment with new forms and ideas." Wants "any poetry of good quality." Considers poetry by children and teens. Has published poetry by Al Alvarez, D.M. Thomas, James Kirkup, Cid Corman, Brian Patten, and Penelope Shuttle. *HQ Poetry Magazine* is 48-64 pages, A5, perfect-bound, includes ads. Accepts about 5% of poetry received. Press run is 500-600. Subscription: (4 issues) £10 UK, £13 foreign. Sample: £2.80.

HOW TO CONTACT No previously published poems or simultaneous submissions. Cover letter is required. Must include SASE (or SAE and IRCs). Time between acceptance and publication is 3-6 months. Often comments on rejected poems. Responds "as time allows." Pays 1 contributor's copy. Reviews books of poetry in about 1,000 words, single-book format. Send materials for review consideration.

ALSO OFFERS Sponsors "Piccadilly Poets" in London, and "Live Poet's Society" based in Bath, Somerset, England. Also acts as "advisor to Poetry on the Lake Annual Poetry Festival in Orta, Italy."

HUBBUB

5344 SE 38th Ave., Portland OR 97202. E-mail: lisa. steinman@reed.edu. Website: http://www.reed.edu/ hubbub/. J. Shugrue, Co-Editor. **Contact:** Lisa M. Steinman. *Hubbub*, published once/year in the spring, is designed "to feature a multitude of voices from interesting contemporary American poets." Wants "poems that are well-crafted, with something to say. We have no single style, subject, or length requirement and, in particular, will consider long poems." Does not want light verse. Has published poetry by Madeline DeFrees, Cecil Giscombe, Carolyn Kizer, Primus St. John, Shara McCallum, and Alice Fulton. *Hubbub* is 50-70 pages, digest-sized, offset-printed, perfect-bound, with cover art. Receives about 1,200 submissions/year, accepts up to 2%. Press run is 350. Subscription: $7/year. Sample: $3.35 (back issues), $7 (current issue).

TIPS Outside judges choose poems from each volume for 3 awards: Vi Gale Award ($200), Stout Award ($75), and Kenneth O. Hanson Award ($100). There are no special submission procedures or entry fees involved.

●●⑤ THE HUDSON REVIEW

Website: www.hudsonreview.com. 684 Park Ave., New York NY 10021. Website: www.hudsonreview. com.

Work published in *The Hudson Review* has been included in *The Best American Poetry*.

MAGAZINES NEEDS *The Hudson Review*, published quarterly, is considered one of the most prestigious and influential journals in the nation. Editors welcome all styles and forms; however, competition is extraordinarily keen. Has published poetry by Marilyn Nelson, Hayden Carruth, Louis Simpson, and Dana Gioia. *The Hudson Review* is 176 pages, flat-spined. Subscription: $36/year ($44 foreign), institutions $44/year. Sample: $10.

HOW TO CONTACT Submit no more than seven poems at a time. No previously published poems or simultaneous submissions. Reads unsolicited mss. April 1-June 30 only. "Manuscripts submitted by subscribers who so identify themselves will be read throughout the year." Guidelines available in magazine, for SASE, or on website. Responds in 3 months. Always sends prepublication galleys. Pays 50¢/line and 2 contributor's copies.

⑤⑤ HUNGER MOUNTAIN

Vermont College of Fine Arts, Vermont College of Fine Arts, 36 College St., Montpelier VT 05602. (802)828-8517. E-mail: hungermtn@vermontcollege. edu. Website: www.hungermtn.org. Member: CLMPAccepts high quality work from unknown, emerging, or successful writers and artists. No genre fiction, drama, or academic articles, please.

MAGAZINES NEEDS *Hunger Mountain, The Vermont College Journal of Arts & Letters*, published semiannually, prints "high-quality poetry, prose, and artwork selected by guest editors from the Vermont College MFA in Writing Program." Wants poems "ready for publication." Does not want entire mss, or children's or young adult poetry. Has published

poetry by Hayden Carruth, Mark Doty, Carol Muske-Dukes, Maxine Kumin, Charles Simic, and Ruth Stone. *Hunger Mountain* is about 200 pages, 7x10, professionally printed, perfect-bound, with full-bleed color artwork on cover, includes ads (only in back). Receives about 600 poems/year, accepts about 5%. Press run is 1,500 (700 subscribers, 50 libraries, 200 shelf sales); 100 distributed free to writing centers, book fairs, and other journals. Single copy: $10; subscription: $17/year, $32 for 2 years, $60 for 4 years. Make checks payable to *Hunger Mountain*.

HOW TO CONTACT Submit 3-10 poems at a time. Considers simultaneous submissions; no previously published poems. No fax, e-mail, or disk submissions; please use online submissions manager. Cover letter is preferred. "*Include double copies of everything*, including cover letter." Reads submissions year round. Time between acceptance and publication is 6 months. Poems are circulated to an editorial board. Occasionally comments on rejected poems. Guidelines available for SASE, by fax, e-mail, or on website. Responds in 4 months. Always sends prepublication galleys. Pays $5/page (minimum $30) and 2 contributor's copies. Acquires first North American serial rights.

CONTEST/AWARD OFFERINGS The annual Ruth Stone Prize in Poetry (see separate listing in Contests & Awards).

TIPS "We want high quality work! Submit in duplicate. Manuscripts must be typed, prose double-spaced. Poets submit at least 3 poems. No multiple genre submissions. We need more b&w photography and short shorts. Fresh viewpoints and human interest are very important, as is originality. We are committed to publishing an outstanding journal of arts & letters. Do not send entire novels, manuscripts, or short story collections. Do not send previously published work. See website for *Hunger Mountain*-sponsored literary prizes."

◐⑤ HUNGUR MAGAZINE

P.O. Box 782, Cedar Rapids IA 52406-0782. E-mail: hungurmagazine@yahoo.com. Website: www.samsdotpublishing.com. **Contact:** Terrie Leigh Relf, editor. P.O. Box 782 Cedar Rapids IA 52406. E-mail: hungurmagazine@yahoo.com. Website: www.samsdotpublishing.com. *Hungur Magazine*, published bi-annually, features "stories and poems about vampires, and especially about vampires on other worlds." Prefers a "decadent literary style." *Hungur Magazine* is 32 pages, magazine-sized, offset-printed, saddle-stapled, with paper cover with color art, includes ads. Receives about 200 poems/year, accepts about 20 (10%). Press run is 100/issue. Subscription: $13/year. $23/2 years. Make checks payable to Tyree Campbell/Sam's Dot Publishing. Member: The Speculative Literature Foundation (http://SpeculativeLiterature.org).

MAGAZINES NEEDS *Hungur Magazine*, published bi-annually, features "stories and poems about vampires, and especially about vampires on other worlds." Prefers a "decadent literary style." *Hungur Magazine* is 32 pages, magazine-sized, offset-printed, saddle-stapled, with paper cover with color art, includes ads. Receives about 200 poems/year, accepts about 20 (10%). Press run is 100/issue. Subscription: $13/year. $23/2 years. Make checks payable to Tyree Campbell/Sam's Dot Publishing.

HOW TO CONTACT Submit up to 5 poems at a time. Lines/poem: prefers less than 100. No previously published poems or simultaneous submissions. Accepts e-mail submissions (pasted into body of message); no disk submissions. Reads submissions year round. Submit seasonal poems 6 months in advance. Time between acceptance and publication is 3-4 months. Editor: Terrie Leigh Relf. Often comments on rejected poems. Guidelines available on website. Responds in 4-6 weeks. Pays $4/poem and 1 contributor's copy. Acquires first North American serial rights. Reviews books and chapbooks of poetry. Send materials for review consideration to Tyree Campbell.

THE HYCO REVIEW

P.O. Box 1197, Roxboro NC 27573. E-mail: langled@piedmontcc.edu; reflect@piedmontcc.edu. Website: http://www2.piedmontcc.edu/hycoreview/index.html. **Contact:** Dawn Langley, Editor. The Hyco Review, an online arts and literary magazine, published by Piedmont Community College, proudly announces the publication of its first online version. The magazine, originally titled Reflections and published in the traditional manner (paper), focuses on showcasing the works of artists and writers from Person and Caswell counties, North CarolinAs well as of alumni from the College. We publish annually and welcome quality submissions in any of the formats listed on our submission page. **Accepts submissions from NC authors only (residents or natives).** "If time and space

permit, we'll consider submissions from southeastern U.S. authors and from authors we've previously published." Has published poetry by Robert Cooperman, Fredrick Zydek, Bruce Bennett, Fred Chappell, Shari O'Brien, and Daniel Green.

HOW TO CONTACT Submit 5 poems maximum at a time. Lines/poem: no longer than 1 page (single-spaced). Considers previously published poems and simultaneous submissions (if notified). Accepts e-mail submissions (pasted into body of message or as attachment in MS Word). "Include a 25-word bio with submission. Include 2 copies of each poem—1 with name and address, 1 without. Affix adequate postage to SAE for return of manuscript if desired, or use First-Class stamps on SAE for notification. Poems are read by an 8- to 12-member editorial board who rank submissions through 'blind' readings. Board members refrain from ranking their own submissions." Sometimes comments on rejected poems. Guidelines available in magazine, for SASE, or by e-mail. Responds in up to 9 months (in March or April). Pays 1 contributor's copy. Acquires first North American serial rights (if poem is unpublished) or one-time rights (if poem is previously published).

IBBETSON ST. PRESS

Website: http://ibbetsonpress.com. 25 School St., Somerville MA 02143-1721. (617)628-2313. E-mail: dougholder@post.harvard.edu. Website: http://ibbetsonpress.com. Established 1998. **Contact:** Doug Holder, editors; submissions editor: Mary Rice, Harris Gardner; copy editor: Dorian Brooks. Consulting Editor: Robert K. Johnson; Designer: Steve Glines.

MAGAZINES NEEDS *Ibbetson St. Press*, published semiannually in June and November, prints "'down to earth' poetry that is well-written; has clean, crisp images; with a sense of irony and humor." Wants "mostly free verse, but are open to rhyme." Does not want "maudlin, trite, overly political, vulgar for vulgar's sake work." Has published poetry by Miriam Goodman, Elizabeth Swados, Sarah Hannah, Gloria Mindock, Harris Gardner, Diana-der Hovanessian, Robert K. Johnson, Gary Metras, and others. *Ibbetson St. Press* is 50 pages, magazine-sized, desktop-published, with glossy white cover, includes ads. Receives about 1,000 poems/year, accepts up to 10%. Press run is 200. Also archived at Harvard, Brown, University of Wisconsin, Poets House-NYC, Endicott

College and Buffalo University Libraries. Single copy: $8; subscription: $13. Make checks payable to *Ibbetson St. Press*.

HOW TO CONTACT Submit 3-5 poems at a time. Considers previously published poems; no simultaneous submissions. No e-mail submissions; postal submissions only. Cover letter is required. Time between acceptance and publication is up to 6 months. "3 editors comment on submissions." Guidelines available for SASE. Responds in 2 months or more. Pays 1 contributor's copy. Acquires one-time rights. Reviews books/chapbooks of poetry and other magazines in 250-500 words. Send materials for review consideration.

ADDITIONAL INFORMATION Does not accept unsolicited chapbook mss. Has published *King of the Jungle*, by Zvi Sesling; *Steerage*, by Bert Stern; *From the Paris of New England*, by Doug Holder; *Ti and Blood Soaked*; *East of the Moon,* by Ruth Kramer Baden; and *Lousia Solano: The Grolier Poetry Book Shop*, edited by Steve Glines and Doug Holder. Responds to queries in 1 month.

ⓘ IDEALS MAGAZINE

2630 Elm Hill Pike., Suite 100, Nashville TN 37214. (615)333-0478. Fax: (888)815-2759. Website: www.idealsbooks.com. **Contact:** Melinda Rathjen Rumbaugh, editor.

TIPS "For submissions, target our needs as far as style is concerned, but show representative subject matter. Artists are strongly advised to be familiar with our magazine before submitting samples of work."

⚫ⓞ IDIOM 23

Central Queensland University, Idiom 23 Literary Magazine, Rockhampton QLD 4702, Australia. E-mail: idiom@cqu.edu.au; l.huf@cqu.edu.au; l.hawryluk@cqu.edu.au. Website: http://idiom23.cqu.edu.au/FCW Viewer/view.do?site=191. **Contact:** Dr. Lynda Hawryluk, Editorial Board.

MAGAZINES NEEDS *Idiom 23*, published annually, is "named for the Tropic of Capricorn and is dedicated to developing the literary arts throughout the Central Queensland region. Submissions of original short stories, poems, articles, and black-and-white drawings and photographs are welcomed by the editorial collective. *Idiom 23* is not limited to a particular viewpoint but, on the contrary, hopes to encourage and publish a broad spectrum of writing. The collective seeks out creative work from community groups with as varied backgrounds as possible. The magazine hopes to reflect and contest idiomatic fictional representations of marginalized or non-privileged positions and values." Considers poetry written by children and teens (10 years of age and older). *Idiom 23* is about 140 pages, 7³₄ X 10, professionally printed, perfect-bound, with 4-color cover, includes ads. Single copy: $15.

HOW TO CONTACT Considers previously published poems. Cover letter is required. Poems are circulated to an editorial board. Reviews books of poetry in single-book format. Send materials for review consideration to Dr. Lynda Hawryluk.

ILLUMEN

Sam's Dot Publishing, P.O. Box 782, Cedar Rapids IA 52406-0782. E-mail: illumensdp@yahoo.com. Website: www.samsdotpublishing.com/aoife/cover.htm. **Contact:** Karen L. Newman, ed. "*Illumen* publishes speculative poetry and articles about speculative poetry, and reviews of poetry and collections."

MAGAZINES NEEDS *Illumen*, published biannually, contains speculative poetry and articles about speculative poetry. "Speculative poetry includes, but is not limited to, fantasy, science fiction, sword and sorcery, alternate history, and horror." Wants "fantasy, science fiction, spooky horror, and speculative poetry with minimal angst." Does not want "horror with excessive blood and gore." Considers poetry by children and teens. Has published poetry by Ian Watson, Bruce Boston, Sonya Taaffe, Mike Allen, Marge B. Simon, and David C. Kopaska-Merkel. *Illumen* is 50 pages, digest-sized, offset-printed, perfect-bound, with color cover with color art, includes ads. Receives about 200 poems/year, accepts about 50 (25%). Press run is 100/issue (20 subscribers, 50 shelf sales); 5 distributed free to reviewers. Single copy: $9; subscription: $15/year. Make checks payable to Tyree Campbell/Sam's Dot Publishing.

HOW TO CONTACT Submit up to 5 poems at a time. Lines/poem: prefers less than 200. Considers previously published poems; no simultaneous submissions. Accepts e-mail submissions (pasted into body of message); no disk submissions. "Submission should include snail mail address and a short (1-2 lines) bio." Reads submissions year round. Submit seasonal poems 6 months in advance. Time between acceptance and publication is 1-2 months. Often comments on rejected poems. Guidelines available on website. Responds in 4-6 weeks. Pays 2 cents/word (minimum: $3) for original poems and 1 contributor's copy. Acquires first North American serial rights. Reviews books/chapbooks of poetry. Send materials for review consideration to Tyree Campbell.

TIPS *"Illumen* publishes beginning writers, as well as seasoned veterans. Be sure to read and follow the guidelines before submitting your work. The best advice for beginning writers is to send your best effort, not your first draft."

ⓘ ILLUMINATIONS

Dept. of English, College of Charleston, 66 George St., Charleston SC 29424-0001. (843)953-1920. Fax: (843)953-3180. E-mail: lewiss@cofc.edu. Website: www.cofc.edu/illuminations. **Contact:** Simon Lewis, editor. Dept. of English, College of Charleston, 66 George St., Charleston, SC 29424-0001. (843)953-1920. Fax: (843)953-3180. E-mail: lewiss@cofc.edu. Website:www.cofc.edu/illuminations. **Contact:** Simon Lewis, editor. *Illuminations: An International Magazine of Contemporary Writing*, published annually, provides "a forum for new writers alongside already established ones." Open as to form and style, and to translations. Does not want to see anything "bland or formally clunky." Has published poetry by Brenda Marie Osbey, Geri Doran, Dennis Brutus, and Carole Satyamurti. *Illuminations* is 64-88 pages, digest-sized, offset-printed, perfect-bound, with 2-color card cover. Receives about 1,500 poems/year, accepts up to 5%. Press run is 400. Subscription: $15/2 issues. Sample: $10.

MAGAZINES NEEDS Open as to form and style, and to translations. Does not want to see anything "bland or formally clunky." Has published poetry by Brenda Marie Osbey, Geri Doran, Dennis Brutus, and Carole Satyamurti. *Illuminations* is 64-88 pages, digest-sized, offset-printed, perfect-bound, with 2-color card cover. Receives about 1,500 poems/year, accepts up to 5%. Press run is 400. Subscription: $15/2 issues. Sample: $10.

HOW TO CONTACT Submit up to 6 poems at a time. No previously published poems or simultaneous submissions. Accepts fax, e-mail (pasted into body of message, no attachments), and mail. Cover letter is preferred (brief). Time between acceptance and publication "depends on when received. Can be up to a year." Occasionally publishes theme issues.

Guidelines available by e-mail or on website. Responds within 2 months. Pays 2 contributor's copies plus 1 subsequent issue. Acquires all rights. Returns rights on request.

● ⑤ IMAGE: ART, FAITH, MYSTERY

3307 3rd Ave. W., Seattle WA 98119. E-mail: image@imagejournal.org. Website: www.imagejournal.org. (Specialized: religious faith; Judeo-Christian)3307 3rd Ave. W., Seattle WA 98119. E-mail: image@imagejournal.org. Website: www.imagejournal.org. Established 1989. **Contact:** Gregory Wolfe, publisher. *Image: Art, Faith, Mystery*, published quarterly, "explores and illustrates the relationship between faith and art through world-class fiction, poetry, essays, visual art, and other arts." Wants "poems that grapple with religious faith, usually Judeo-Christian." Has published work from Philip Levine, Scott Cairns, Annie Dillard, Mary Oliver, Mark Jarman, and Kathleen Norris. *Image* is 136 pages, 10x7, printed on acid-free paper, perfect-bound, with glossy 4-color cover, includes ads. Receives about 800 poems/year, accepts up to 3%. Has 5,000 subscribers (100 are libraries). Subscription: $39.95. Sample: $16 postpaid. Submit up to 4 poems at a time. No previously published poems. No e-mail submissions. Cover letter is preferred. Guidelines available on website. Always sends prepublication galleys. Pays 4 contributor's copies plus $2/line ($150 maximum). Reviews books of poetry in 2,000 words, single- or multi-book format. Send materials for review consideration.

MAGAZINES NEEDS *Image: Art, Faith, Mystery*, published quarterly, "explores and illustrates the relationship between faith and art through world-class fiction, poetry, essays, visual art, and other arts." Wants "poems that grapple with religious faith, usually Judeo-Christian." Has published work by Philip Levine, Scott Cairns, Annie Dillard, Mary Oliver, Mark Jarman, and Kathleen Norris. *Image* is 136 pages, 10x7, printed on acid-free paper, perfect-bound, with glossy 4-color cover, includes ads. Receives about 800 poems/year, accepts up to 3%. Has 5,000 subscribers (100 are libraries). Subscription: $39.95. Sample: $16 postpaid.

HOW TO CONTACT Submit up to 4 poems at a time. No previously published poems. No e-mail submissions. Cover letter is preferred. Time between acceptance and publication is 1 year. Guidelines available on website. Responds in 3 months. Always sends prepublication galleys. Pays 4 contributor's copies plus $2/line ($150 maximum). Acquires first North American serial rights. Reviews books of poetry in 2,000 words, single- or multi-book format. Send materials for review consideration.

◐ INDEFINITE SPACE

Website: http://www.indefinitespace.net/indefinitespace09.htm. P.O. Box 40101, Pasadena CA 91114. E-mail: indefinitespace@yahoo.com. Website: www.indefinitespace.net/indefinitespace09.htm. "From minimalist to avant-garde, open to innovative, imagistic, philosophical, experimental creations- poetry, drawings, collage, photography." Has published work by Charlie Malone, Michael Gause, Ingrid Swanberg, Felino Soriano, Jeffrey Pethybridge, Betzi Richardson, Brian Foley, Stuart Jay Silverman, Kristen Orser, William Garvin, Mark Young, Hugh Fox and more. Subscription: $12. Single issue: $7."Published annually. From minimalist to avant-garde—-open to innovative, imagistic, philosophical, experimental creations—-poetry drawings, collage photography; reads year round. Guidelines do not exist. Contributors receive one copy. Has published poetry by Marthe Reed, Anne Blonstein, Kevin Magee, Petra Backonja, Peter Layton, and Jill Magi. *Indefinite Space* is 48 pages, digest-sized. Single copy: $7; subscription: $12 for 2 issues. Make checks payable to Marcia Arrieta. Seldom comments on rejected poems."

HOW TO CONTACT "Guidelines do not exist." Reads year round. Pays one contributor's copy.

◐◑◒ INDIANA REVIEW

Ballantine Hall 465, 1020 E. Kirkwood, Indiana University, Bloomington IN 47405-7103. (812)855-3439. E-mail: inreview@indiana.edu. Website: www.indiana.edu/~inreview. "*Indiana Review*, a nonprofit organization run by IU graduate students, is a journal of previously unpublished poetry and fiction. Literary interviews and essays are also considered. We publish innovative fiction, nonfiction, and poetry. We're interested in energy, originality, and careful attention to craft. While we publish many well-known writers, we also welcome new and emerging poets and fiction writers."

○ Work published in *Indiana Review* received a Pushcart Prize (2001) and was included in *Best New American Voices* (2001). *IR* also received an Indiana Arts Council Grant and a NEA grant. Work published in *Indiana Re-*

view received a Pushcart Prize (2001) and was included in *Best New American Voices* (2001). *IR* also received an Indiana Arts Council Grant and a NEA grant.

MAGAZINES NEEDS *Indiana Review*, published semiannually, includes prose, poetry, creative nonfiction, book reviews, and visual art. "We look for an intelligent sense of form and language, and admire poems of risk, ambition, and scope." Wants "all types of poems—free verse, traditional, experimental. Reading a sample issue is the best way to determine if *Indiana Review* is a potential home for your work. Any subject matter is acceptable if it is written well. Translations are welcome." Has published poetry by Denise Duhamel, Sherman Alexie, Marilyn Chin, Julianna Baggott, and Alberto Rios. *Indiana Review* is 160 pages, digest-sized, professionally printed, flat-spined, with color matte cover. Receives more than 9,000 submissions/year, accepts up to 60. Has 2,000 subscribers. Subscription: $17/year, $28 for 2 years. Sample: $9.

HOW TO CONTACT Submit 4-6 poems at a time. Lines/poem: "do not send more than 10 pages of poetry per submission." Considers simultaneous submissions with notification; no previously published poems. Cover letter with brief bio is desired. SASE is mandatory for response. Guidelines available on website. "We try to respond to manuscripts in 3-4 months. Reading time is often slower during summer and holiday months." Pays $5/page ($10 minimum), 2 contributor's copies, and remainder of year's subscription. Acquires first North American serial rights only. Reviews books of poetry. Send materials for review consideration.

CONTEST/AWARD OFFERINGS Holds yearly poetry and prose-poem contests. Guidelines available for SASE or on website.

TIPS "We're always looking for nonfiction essays that go beyond merely autobiographical revelation and utilize sophisticated organization and slightly radical narrative strategies. We want essays that are both lyrical and analytical where confession does not mean nostalgia. Read us before you submit. Often reading is slower in summer and holiday months. Only submit work to journals you would proudly subscribe to, then subscribe to a few. Take care to read the latest 2 issues and specifically mention work you identify with and why. Submit work that 'stacks up' with the work we've published. Offers annual poetry, fiction, short-short/prose-poem prizes. See website for full guidelines."

○ INKWELL

(914)323-7239. Fax: (914)323-3122. E-mail: inkwell@mville.edu. Website: www.inkwelljournal.org. *Inkwell*, published semiannually, features "emerging writers, high quality poems and short stories, creative nonfiction, artwork, literary essays, memoir and interviews on writing by established figures, and yearly compeitions in poetry and fiction." Wants "serious work—very well made verse, any form, any genre." Does not want "doggerel, light or humorous verse." Please review archives online or send for sample copy. *Inkwell* is 150 pages, digest-sized, press-printed, perfect-bound, with cover with illustration/photography. Receives about 2,500 poems/year, accepts about 30. Press run is 700. Single copy: $10; subscription: $18/year. Sample: $6 (back issue). Make checks payable to Manhattanville College—*Inkwell*.

○ *Inkwell* is produced in affiliation with the Master of Arts in Writing program at Manhattanville College, and is staffed by faculty and graduate students of the program.

HOW TO CONTACT Submit up to 5 poems at a time. Lines/poem: 70 maximum. Considers simultaneous submissions; no previously published poems. ("Previously published" work includes poetry posted on a public website/blog/forum, but not on a private, password-protected forum.) No fax, e-mail, or disk submissions. Cover letter is required. Include SASE. Reads submissions August 1-November 30. Time between acceptance and publication is 6 months. Poems are circulated to an editorial board. Never comments on rejected poems. Guidelines available for SASE or on website. Responds in 4 months. Pays $10/page and 2 contributor's copies. Acquires first North American serial rights. Rights revert to poets upon publication.

CONTEST/AWARD OFFERINGS The Inkwell Annual Poetry Competition (see separate listing in Contests & Awards).

TIPS "We cannot accept electronic submissions."

INNISFREE POETRY JOURNAL

E-mail: editor@innisfreepoetry.org. Website: www.innisfreepoetry.org. **Contact:** Greg McBride.

HOW TO CONTACT Submit up to 5 poems by e-mail; single Word attachment. Include your name, as you would like it to appear in Innisfree, in the subject line of your submission. Format all poems flush with the left margin—no indents other than any within the poem itself. Simultaneous submissions are welcome. "If a poem is accepted elsewhere, however, please be sure to notify us immediately." Does not accept previously published poetry.

ADDITIONAL INFORMATION Acquires first publication rights, including the right to publish it online and maintain it there as part of the issue in which it appears, to make it available in a printer-friendly format, to make the issue of *Innisfree* in which it appears downloadable as a PDF document and available as a printed volume. All other rights revert to the poet after online publication of the poem in *The Innisfree Poetry Journal*.

TIPS "Welcomes original previously unpublished poems year round. We accept poems only via email from both established and new writers whose work is excellent. We publish well-crafted poems, poems grounded in the specific which speak in fresh language and telling images. And we admire musicality. We welcome those who, like the late Lorenzo Thomas, 'write poems because I can't sing.'"

◑◐ IN OUR OWN WORDS

Burning Bush Publications, P.O. Box 4658, Santa Rosa CA 95402. Website: www.bbbooks.com. **Contact:** Amanda Majestie, editor. Burning Bush Publications P.O. Box 4658, Santa Rosa CA 95402. E-mail: pub@bbbooks.com. Website: www.bbbooks.com. *In Our Own Words*, published annually online, seeks poetry and prose poems for its literary e-zine. Wants "thought-provoking, creative, alternative writing. We choose work that inspires compassion, peace, and respect for diversity in original and unexpected ways." Does not want "manuscripts of full-length books." Sample: past issues available on website.

MAGAZINES NEEDS *In Our Own Words*, published annually online, seeks poetry and prose poems for its literary e-zine. Wants "thought-provoking, creative, alternative writing. We choose work that inspires compassion, peace, and respect for diversity in original and unexpected ways." Does not want "manuscripts of full-length books." Sample: past issues available on website.

HOW TO CONTACT Cover letter is required. "Send submissions to us by U.S. mail only. Include SASE. If you want us to reply your letter via e-mail, include your e-mail address! We will ask you for a digital file via e-mail, if we want to publish your submission." Reads submissions according to the following deadline: Annual Edition, June 1st. Guidelines available on website. Rights revert to poet upon publication. **CONTEST/AWARD OFFERINGS** The Burning Bush Poetry Prize (see separate listing in Contests & Awards).

🌑🌓 INTERPRETER'S HOUSE

9 Glenhurst Rd., Mannamead, Plymouth PL3 5LT, England. Website: www.interpretershouse.org.uk. **Contact:** Simon Curtis, Editor. 9 Glenhurst Rd. Mannamead Plymouth PL3 5LT England. Website: www.interpretershouse.org.uk. *Interpreter's House*, published 3 times/year in February, June, and October, prints short stories and poetry. Has published material by Elizabeth Bartlett, Ruth Bidgood, Alan Brownjohn, Toby Litt, Sheenagh Pugh, Carole Satyamurti, Penelope Shuttle, R.S. Thomas and more. Subscription: £12.00/3 issues. Single issue: £4.50.*Interpreter's House*, published 3 times/year in February, June, and October, prints short stories and poetry. Wants "good poetry, not too long." Does not want "Christmas-card verse or incomprehensible poetry." Has published poetry by Dannie Abse, Tony Curtis, Pauline Stainer, Alan Brownjohn, Peter Redgrove, and R.S. Thomas. *Interpreter's House* is 74 pages, A5, with attractive cover design. Receives about 1,000 poems/year, accepts up to 5%. Press run is 300 (200 subscribers). Single copy: £3 plus 55p. postage; subscription: £12 for 3 issues. Sample: £3.50.

🌑 Business correspondence (including subscriptions) should go to Matt Bright, Upper Flat, 251 Abingdon Rd., Oxford OX1 4TH England.

HOW TO CONTACT Submit up to 5 poems. Postal mail only. Include SASE. "All work is dealt with swiftly. Usually no more than one poem is accepted, and writers who have already appeared in the magazine are asked to wait for at least a year before submitting again."

TIPS Sponsors the Bedford Open Poetry Competition. Send SAE and IRC for details. The 2009/10 Bedford Open Poetry competition is now closed.

🌓 IN THE GROVE

Website: www.inthegrove.net. P.O. Box 16195 Fresno CA 93755. E-mail: leeherrick@hotmail.com. Website: www.inthegrove.net. *In the Grove*, published annually, publishes "short fiction, essays, and poetry by new and established writers currently living in the Central Valley and throughout California." Wants "poetry of all forms and subject matter. We seek the originality, distinct voice, and craft of a poem." Does not want "greeting card verse or forced rhyme. Be fresh. Take a risk." Has published poetry by Andres Montoya, Corrinne Clegg Hales, Daniel Chacon, Lawson Fusao InadAmy Uyematsu, and Charles Harper Webb.

MAGAZINES NEEDS *In the Grove*, published annually, publishes "short fiction, essays, and poetry by new and established writers currently living in the Central Valley and throughout California." Wants "poetry of all forms and subject matter. We seek the originality, distinct voice, and craft of a poem." Does not want "greeting card verse or forced rhyme. Be fresh. Take a risk." Has published poetry by Andres Montoya, Corrinne Clegg Hales, Daniel Chacon, Lawson Fusao InadAmy Uyematsu, and Charles Harper Webb.

HOW TO CONTACT Submit 3-5 poems at a time. Considers previously published poems ("on occasion") and simultaneous submissions ("with notice"). Cover letter is preferred. Time between acceptance and publication is up to 6 months. "Poetry editor reads all submissions and makes recommendations to editor, who makes final decisions." Reads September 1-December 1. Seldom comments on rejected poems. Guidelines available for SASE or on website. Responds in 3-6 months. Pays 1 contributor's copy. Acquires first or one-time rights as well as right to publish on website. Rights return to poets upon publication.

🌓 INVERTED-A HORN

Inverted-A, Inc., P.O. Box 267, Licking MO 65542. **Contact:** Nets Katz, and Aya Katz, editors.

MAGAZINES NEEDS *Inverted-A Horn*, published irregularly, welcomes political topics, social issues, and science fiction. Wants traditional poetry with meter and rhyme. Does not want to see anything "modern, formless, existentialist." *Inverted-A Horn* is usually 9 pages, magazine-sized, offset-printed. Press run is 300. Sample: SASE with postage for 2 ounces (subject to availability).

HOW TO CONTACT Considers simultaneous submissions. Accepts e-mail submissions (as attachment, ASCII). Responds in 4 months. Pays 1 contributor's copy; offers 40% discount on additional copies.

ADDITIONAL INFORMATION Inverted-A, Inc. is a very small press that evolved from publishing technical manuals for other products. "Our interests center on freedom, justice, and honor." Publishes 1 chapbook/year.

IODINE POETRY JOURNAL

P.O. Box 18548, Charlotte NC 28218-0548. (704)595-9526. E-mail: iodineopencut@aol.com. Website: www.iodinepoetryjournal.com. **Contact:** Jonathan K. Rice, editor/publisher.

○ Poetry published in *Iodine Poetry Journal* has been selected for inclusion in *The Best American Poetry.*

MAGAZINES NEEDS *Iodine Poetry Journal,* published semiannually, provides "a venue for both emerging and established poets." Wants "good poetry of almost any style, including form (e.g., pantoum and sestina) and experimental." Does not want rhyme, religion, or pornography. Has published poetry by Fred Chappell, Colette Inez, Ron Koertge, Dorianne Laux, and R.T. Smith. *Iodine Poetry Journal* is 84 pages, digest-sized, perfect-bound, with full-color laminated cover, includes ads. Receives about 2,000 poems/year, accepts about 75 poems/issue. Press run is 350. Single copy: $8; subscription: $14/year (2 issues) $26 for 2 years (4 issues). Sample: "Back issues vary in price." Make checks payable to *Iodine Poetry Journal.*

HOW TO CONTACT Submit 3-5 poems at a time. Lines/poem: 40 or less preferred, "but not totally averse to longer poems." No previously published poems or simultaneous submissions. Accepts e-mail submissions from international poets only; no disk submissions. Cover letter is preferred. "Always include SASE, and specify if SASE is for return of manuscript or reply only. I like a brief introduction of yourself in the cover letter." Reads submissions year round. Submit seasonal poems 6 months in advance. Time between acceptance and publication is 6 months to 1 year. Poems are circulated to an editorial board. "I occasionally have other readers assist in the selection process, but editor makes the final decision." Sometimes comments on rejected poems. Guidelines available in magazine, for SASE, or on website. Responds in 2-3 months. Sometimes sends prepublication galleys. Pays 1 contributor's copy and discounts extra copies of the issue in which work appears. Acquires first North American serial rights. Email: iodineopencut@aol.com. Website: www.iodinepoetryjournal.com. Contact: Jonathan K. Rice, editor/publisher.

ALSO OFFERS "We no longer publish our broadside, *Open Cut.*"

TIPS "We no longer publish our broadside, *Open Cut.*"

IOTA

P.O. Box 7721, Matlock, Derbyshire DE4 9DD England. E-mail: info@iotamagazine.co.uk. Website: www.iotapoetry.co.uk.

MAGAZINES NEEDS *iota,* published quarterly, considers "any style and subject; no specific limitations as to length." Has published poetry by Jane Kinninmont, John Robinson, Tony Petch, Chris Kinsey, Christopher James, and Michael Kriesel. *iota* is 56 pages, professionally printed, perfect-bound, with b&w photograph litho cover. Receives 6,000 poems/year, accepts about 300. Press run is 300. Single copy: £6.50 UK; subscription: £15 UK.

HOW TO CONTACT Submit up to 6 poems at a time. No previously published poems or simultaneous submissions. Cover letter is required. Prefers name and address on each poem, typed. "No SAE, no reply." Responds in 3 months (unless production of the next issue takes precedence). Pays 1 contributor's copy. Reviews books of poetry. Send materials for review consideration.

ADDITIONAL INFORMATION The editors also run Ragged Raven Press (www.raggedraven.co.uk), which publishes poetry collections, nonfiction, and an annual anthology of poetry linked to an international competition.

CONTEST/AWARD OFFERINGS Sponsors an annual poetry competition, offering 1st Prize: £200; 2nd and 3rd Prize: £25; publication in *iota* and on website. Guidelines available on website. **Entry fee**: free for up to 2 poems for subscribers, £2 for each subsequent poem; £2/poem for non-subscribers. **Deadline:** April 15.

THE IOWA REVIEW

308 EPB, The University of Iowa, Iowa City IA 52242. (319)335-0462. Website: iowareview.org. **Contact:** Russell Scott Valentino, editor. Stories, essays, and poems for a general readership interested in contemporary literature.

○ "This magazine uses the help of colleagues and graduate assistants. Its reading period for unsolicited work is September 1-December 1. From January through April, we read entries to our annual Iowa Awards competition. Check our website for further information."

MAGAZINES NEEDS *The Iowa Review,* published

3 times/year, prints fiction, poetry, essays, reviews, and, occasionally, interviews. "We simply look for poems that, at the time we read and choose, we find we admire. No specifications as to form, length, style, subject matter, or purpose. Though we print work from established writers, we're always delighted when we discover new talent." *The Iowa Review* is 192 pages, professionally printed, flat-spined. Receives about 5,000 submissions/year, accepts up to 100. Press run is 2,900; 1,500 distributed to stores. Subscription: $25. Sample: $9.

HOW TO CONTACT Submit 3-6 poems at a time. No e-mail submissions. Cover letter (with title of work and genre) is encouraged. SASE required. Reads submissions "only during the Fall semester, September through November, and then contest entries in the spring." Time between acceptance and publication is "around a year." Occasionally comments on rejected poems or offers suggestions on accepted poems. Responds in up to 4 months. Pays $1.50/line of poetry, $40 minimum. Acquires first North American serial rights, non-exclusive anthology rights, and non-exclusive electronic rights.

CONTEST/AWARD OFFERINGS *The Iowa Review* Award in Poetry, Fiction, and Essay (see separate listing in Contests & Awards).

TIPS "We publish essays, reviews, novel excerpts, stories, and poems, and would like for our essays not always to be works of academic criticism. We have no set guidelines as to content or length, but strongly recommend that writers read a sample issue before submitting. **Buys 65-80 unsolicited ms/year**. Submit complete ms with SASE. **Pays $25 for the first page and $15 for each subsequent page of poetry or prose**."

❶❸ THE IOWA REVIEW

308 EPB, University of Iowa, Iowa City IA 52242. (319)335-0462. E-mail: iowa-review@uiowa.edu. Website: www.iowareview.org. **Contact:** Russell Valentino, Editor.

 ◗ Poetry published in *The Iowa Review* has appeared often in *The Best American Poetry* and *The Pushcart Prize*.

MAGAZINES NEEDS *The Iowa Review*, published 3 times/year, prints fiction, poetry, essays, reviews, and, occasionally, interviews. "We simply look for poems that, at the time we read and choose, we find we admire. No specifications as to form, length, style, subject matter, or purpose. Though we print work from established writers, we're always delighted when we discover new talent." *The Iowa Review* is 192 pages, professionally printed, flat-spined. Receives about 5,000 submissions/year, accepts up to 100. Press run is 2,900; 1,500 distributed to stores. Subscription: $25. Sample: $9.

HOW TO CONTACT Submit up to 5 poems at a time. No e-mail submissions. Cover letter (with title of work and genre) is encouraged. SASE required. Reads submissions "only during the Fall semester, September through November, and then contest entries in the spring." Time between acceptance and publication is "around a year." Occasionally comments on rejected poems or offers suggestions on accepted poems. Responds in up to 4 months. Pays $1.50/line of poetry, $40 minimum. Acquires first North American serial rights, non-exclusive anthology rights, and non-exclusive electronic rights.

CONTEST/AWARD OFFERINGS *The Iowa Review* Award in Poetry, Fiction, and Essay (see separate listing in Contests & Awards).

❶ ITALIAN AMERICANA

80 Washington St., Providence RI 02903-1803. E-mail: itamericana@yahoo.com. Website: www.italianamericana.com. **Contact:** C.B. Albright, editor-in-chief.

MAGAZINES NEEDS *Italian Americana*, published twice/year, uses 16-20 poems of "no more than 3 pages." Does not want "trite nostalgia about grandparents." Has published poetry by Mary Jo Salter and Jay Parini. *Italian Americana* is 150-200 pages, digest-sized, professionally printed, flat-spined, with glossy card cover. Press run is 1,000. Singly copy: $10; subscription: $20/year, $35 for 2 years. Sample: $7.

HOW TO CONTACT Contact Michael Palma, poetry editor. Submit no more than 3 poems at a time. "Single copies of poems for submissions are sufficient." No previously published poems or simultaneous submissions. Cover letter is not required "but helpful." Name on first page of ms only. Occasionally comments on rejected poems. Responds in 6 weeks. Acquires first rights. Reviews books of poetry in 600 words, multi-book format. Send materials for review consideration to Prof. John Paul Russo, senior editor, English Dept., University of Miami, Coral Gables, FL 33124.

CONTEST/AWARD OFFERINGS Along with the National Italian American Foundation, *Italian*

Americana co-sponsors the annual $1,000 John Ciardi Award for Lifetime Contribution to Poetry. *Italian Americana* also presents $250 fiction or memoir award annually; and $1,500 in history prizes.

TIPS "Check out our new website supplement to the journal at www.italianamericana.com. Read *Wild Dreams: The Best of Italian Americana* (Fordham University Press), the best stories, poems and memoirs in the journal's 35-year history."

⊖ JACK AND JILL

Children's Better Health Institute, P.O. Box 567, Indianapolis IN 46206-0567. (317)636-8881. E-mail: j.goodman@cbhi.org. Website: www.jackandjillmag.org. "Material will not be returned unless accompanied by SASE with sufficient postage. No queries. May hold material being seriously considered for up to 1 year."

MAGAZINES NEEDS *Jack and Jill*, published bimonthly by The Children's Better Health Network, is a magazine for ages 8-12. Wants light-hearted poetry appropriate for the age group. Reviews submissions for possible use in all Children's Better Health Institute publications.

HOW TO CONTACT Manuscripts must be typewritten with poet's contact information in upper right-hand corner of each poem's page. SASE required. Submit seasonal material at least 8 months in advance. Guidelines available for SASE or on website. Responds in about 3 months. Pays $35 minimum for poetry.

TIPS "We are constantly looking for new writers who can tell good stories with interesting slants—stories that are not full of out-dated and time-worn expressions. We like to see stories about kids who are smart and capable, but not sarcastic or smug. Problem-solving skills, personal responsibility, and integrity are good topics for us. Obtain current issues of the magazine and study them to determine our present needs and editorial style."

⊖⊙ JERRY JAZZ MUSICIAN

2207 NE Broadway, Portland OR 97232. (503)287-5570. Fax: (801)749-9896. E-mail: jm@jerryjazz.com. Website: www.jerryjazz.com. (Specialized: mid-20th century America)

MAGAZINES NEEDS *Jerry Jazz Musician*, published monthly online, "celebrates mid-20th century America, with an emphasis on jazz, film, literature, art, civil rights history, and politics of the era. Open to all topics and poetic forms." Considers poetry by children and teens. Has published poetry by Pablo Neruda, Jim Harrison, Kenneth Rexroth, Golda Soloman, and Bunny M. Receives about 300 poems/year, accepts about 50. Has 4,000 subscribers; distributed free to 150,000 unique Internet visitors/month.

HOW TO CONTACT Submit 1-2 poems at a time. Lines/poem: 6-100. Considers previously published poems and simultaneous submissions. Accepts e-mail submissions. "Would prefer e-mail submissions pasted into message; however, if font and style are essential to the poem's success, will accept a Microsoft Word attachment." Cover letter is preferred. Reads submissions year round. Submit seasonal poems 4 months in advance. Time between acceptance and publication is 1 month. "Editor consults with a variety of readers, or may make choice on his own." Often comments on rejected poems. Guidelines available on website. Responds in 1 month. Poet retains all rights.

⊙ JEWISH CURRENTS

POB 111, Accord NY 12404. (845)626-2427. E-mail: info@jewishcurrents.org. Website: www.jewishcurrents.org. **Contact:** Lawrence Bush, editor. POB 111, Accord NY 12404. (845)626-2427. E-mail: info@jewishcurrents.org. Website: www.jewishcurrents.org. *Jewish Currents*, published 4 times/year, is a progressive Jewish bimonthly magazine that carries on the insurgent tradition of the Jewish left through independent journalism, political commentary, and a 'countercultural' approach to Jewish arts and literature. *Jewish Currents* is 48 pages, magazine-sized, offset-printed, saddle-stapled with a full-color arts section, "Jcultcha & Funny Pages." Press run is 700. Subscription: $25/year.

MAGAZINES NEEDS *Jewish Currents*, published 4 times/year, is a progressive Jewish bimonthly magazine that carries on the insurgent tradition of the Jewish left through independent journalism, political commentary, and a 'countercultural' approach to Jewish arts and literature. *Jewish Currents* is 48 pages, magazine-sized, offset-printed, saddle-stapled with a full-color arts section, "Jcultcha & Funny Pages." Press run is 700. Subscription: $25/year.

HOW TO CONTACT Submit 4 poems at a time with a cover letter. No previously published poems or simultaneous submissions. Cover letter is required.

"Include brief bio with author's publishing history." Poems should be typed, double-spaced; include SASE. Time between acceptance and publication is up to 2 years. Often comments on rejected poems. Responds within 3 months. Always sends prepublication galleys. Pays 3 contributor's copies. Reviews books of poetry.

◑⑤ JEWISH WOMEN'S LITERARY ANNUAL

NCJW Women New York Section, 820 Second Ave., New York NY 10017. (212)687-5030. E-mail: info@ncjwny.org. Website: www.ncjwny.org/services_annual.htm. NCJW Women New York, Section 820, Second Ave., New York NY 10017. (212)687-5030. Fax: (212)687-5032. E-mail: info@ncjwny.org. Website: www.ncjwny.org/services_annual.htm. "This collection provides examples of some of the best Jewish women's writing today: poetry, humor, fiction, memoirs, midrash- writing of high literary quality, by Jewish women, on almost any topic." Subscription: $18/3 issues. *Jewish Women's Literary Annual*, published in April, prints poetry and fiction by Jewish women. Wants "poems by Jewish women on any topic, but of the highest literary quality." Has published poetry by Linda Zisquit, Merle Feld, Helen Papell, Enid Dame, Marge Piercy, and Lesleéa Newman. *Jewish Women's Literary Annual* is 230 pages, digest-sized, perfect-bound, with laminated card cover. Receives about 1,500 poems/year, accepts about 10%. Press run is 1,500. Subscription: $18 for 3 issues. Sample: $7.50.

HOW TO CONTACT Submit previously unpublished poetry and prose written by Jewish women. Accepts any topic. Submit through postal mail only.

TIPS "Send only your very best. We are looking for humor, as well as other things, but nothing cutesy or smart-aleck. We do no politics; prefer topics other than 'Holocaust'."

◑◐ JONES AV.

OEL Press, 88 Dagmar Ave., Toronto ON M4M 1W1, Canada. E-mail: oel@interlog.com. Website: www.interlog.com/~oel. **Contact:** Pual Schwartz, Editor/Publisher. OEL Press, 88 Dagmar Ave., Toronto ON M4M 1W1 Canada. E-mail: oel@interlog.com. Website: www.interlog.com/~oel. *Jones Av.* published quarterly, contains "poems from the lyric to the ash can; starting poets and award winners." Wants poems "concise in thought and image. Prose poems sometimes. Rhymed poetry is very difficult to do well these days; it better be good." Has published poetry by Bert Almon, Michael Estabrook, John Grey, Bernice Lever, B.Z. Niditch, and Elana Wolff. *Jones Av.* is 24 pages, digest-sized, photocopied, saddle-stapled, with card cover. Receives about 300 poems/year, accepts 30-40%. Press run is 100. Subscription: $8. Sample: $2.

MAGAZINES NEEDS *Jones Av.* published quarterly, contains "poems from the lyric to the ash can; starting poets and award winners." Wants poems "concise in thought and image. Prose poems sometimes. Rhymed poetry is very difficult to do well these days; it better be good." Has published poetry by Bert Almon, Michael Estabrook, John Grey, Bernice Lever, B.Z. Niditch, and Elana Wolff. *Jones Av.* is 24 pages, digest-sized, photocopied, saddle-stapled, with card cover. Receives about 300 poems/year, accepts 30-40%. Press run is 100. Subscription: $8. Sample: $2. Make checks payable to Paul Schwartz .

HOW TO CONTACT Submit 3-5 poems at a time. Lines/poem: up to 30. No previously published poems or simultaneous submissions. Accepts e-mail submissions (pasted into body of message). Cover letter is required. Include bio and SASE (or SAE with IRCs). "Remember, U.S. stamps cannot be used in Canada." Time between acceptance and publication is up to 1 year. Often comments on rejected poems. Occasionally publishes theme issues. Upcoming themes available in magazine. Guidelines available for SASE or on website. Responds in 3 months. Pays 1 contributor's copy. Acquires first rights.

◑◐ THE JOURNAL

01900 812194. E-mail: smithsssj@aol.com. Website: thesamsmith.webs.com. 17 High St., Maryport, Cumbria CA15 6BQ, UK. E-mail: smithsssj@aol.com. Website: thesamsmith.webs.com. *The Journal*, published 3 times a year, features English poetry/translations, reviews, and articles. Wants "new poetry howsoever it comes; translations and original English-language poems." Does not want "staid, generalized, all form/no content." Has published poetry by David H. Grubb, Gary Allen, and Ozdemir Asaf. *The Journal* is 40 pages, A4, offset-printed, stapled. Receives about 1,000 poems/year, accepts about 5%. Press run is 100-150. Single copy: £4; subscription: £11 for 3 issues. Outside UK, single copy: £5; subscription: £13 for 3 issues. Make checks payable to Sam Smith or through PayPal. Back issues £2.

MAGAZINES NEEDS *The Journal*, published 3

times a year, features English poetry/translations, reviews, and articles. Wants "new poetry howsoever it comes; translations and original English-language poems." Does not want "staid, generalized, all form/no content." Has published poetry by David H. Grubb, Gary Allen, and Ozdemir Asaf. *The Journal* is 40 pages, A4, offset-printed, stapled. Receives about 1,000 poems/year, accepts about 5%. Press run is 100-150. Single copy: £4; subscription: £11 for 3 issues. Outside UK, single copy: £5; subscription: £14 for 3 issues. Make checks payable to Sam Smith or through PayPal. Back issues £2.

HOW TO CONTACT Submit up to 6 poems at a time. Considers previously published poems and simultaneous submissions. Accepts e-mail submissions. Cover letter is preferred. "Please send 2 IRCs with hard-copy submissions." Time between acceptance and publication is up to 1 year. Often comments on rejected poems. Guidelines available for SASE (or SAE and IRC). Responds in 1 month. Always sends prepublication galleys. Pays 1 contributor's copy.

ADDITIONAL INFORMATION Since 1997, Original Plus Press has been publishing collections of poetry. Has recently published books by Chris Hardy, Brian Daldorph, Siobhan Logan, Alice Lenkiewics and Helen Bunkingham. But from now will be publishing only chapbooks. Send SASE (or SAE and IRC) or e-mail for details.

TIPS "Send 6 poems; I'll soon let you know if it's not Journal material."

❸ JOURNAL OF ASIAN MARTIAL ARTS

Via Media Publishing Co., 941 Calle Mejia, #822, Santa Fe NM 87501. (505)983-1919. E-mail: info@goviamedia.com. Website: www.goviamedia.com.

MAGAZINES NEEDS *Journal of Asian Martial Arts*, published quarterly, is a "comprehensive journal on Asian martial arts with high standards and academic approach." Wants poetry about Asian martial arts and its history/culture. "No restrictions, provided the poet has a feel for, and good understanding of, the subject." Does not want poetry showing a narrow view. "We look for a variety of styles from an interdisciplinary approach." *Journal of Asian Martial Arts* is 124 pages, magazine-sized, professionally printed on coated stock, perfect-bound, with soft cover, includes ads. Press run is 12,000 (1,500 subscribers, 50 libraries, the rest mainly shelf sales). Single copy: $9.75; subscription: $32/year, $55/2 years. Sample: $10.

HOW TO CONTACT Considers previously published poems; no simultaneous submissions. Accepts e-mail submissions. Cover letter is required. Often comments on rejected poems. Guidelines available for SASE or by fax or e-mail. Responds in 2 months. Sometimes sends prepublication galleys. Pays $1-100 and/or 1-5 contributor's copies on publication. Buys first world and reprint rights. Reviews books of poetry "if they have some connection to Asian martial arts; length is open." Open to unsolicited reviews. Send materials for review consideration.

TIPS "Always query before sending a manuscript. We are open to varied types of articles; most however require a strong academic grasp of Asian culture. For those not having this background, we suggest trying a museum review, or interview, where authorities can be questioned, quoted, and provide supportive illustrations. We especially desire articles/reports from Asia, with photo illustrations, particularly of a martial art style, so readers can visually understand the unique attributes of that style, its applications, evolution, etc. Location and media reports are special areas that writers may consider, especially if they live in a location of martial art significance."

❶ JOURNAL OF THE AMERICAN MEDICAL ASSOCIATION (JAMA)

Website: www.jama.com. (Specialized: poetry related to a medical experience)515 N. State St., Chicago IL 60654. (312)464-2428. Fax: (312)464-5824. E-mail: jamams@jama-archives.org. Website: www.jama.com. Established 1883. **Contact:** Charlene Breedlove, associate editor. *Journal of the American Medical Association (JAMA)*, published weekly, includes a poetry and medicine column and publishes poetry "in some way related to a medical experience, whether from the point of view of a health care worker or patient, or simply an observer. No unskilled poetry." Has published poetry by Jack Coulehan, Floyd Skloot, and Walt McDonald. *JAMA* is magazine-sized, flat-spined, with glossy paper cover. Receives about 750 poems/year, accepts about 7%. Has 360,000 subscribers (369 libraries).

MAGAZINES NEEDS *Journal of the American Medical Association (JAMA)*, published weekly, includes a poetry and medicine column and publishes poetry "in some way related to a medical experience, whether from the point of view of a health care worker or patient, or simply an observer. No unskilled poetry."

Has published poetry by Jack Coulehan, Floyd Skloot, and Walt McDonald. *JAMA* is magazine-sized, flat-spined, with glossy paper cover. Receives about 750 poems/year, accepts about 7%. Has 360,000 subscribers (369 libraries). Subscription: $66. Sample: free, "no SASE needed."

HOW TO CONTACT No previously published poems or simultaneous submissions. Accepts submissions by fax or through *JAMA*'s Web-based submissions and review system at http://manuscripts.jama.com (or click the "Information for Authors/Reviewers" button on the www.jama.com home page). "I appreciate inclusion of a brief cover letter; mention of other publications and special biographical notes are always of interest." Publishes theme issues (i.e., in 2007: access to care; malaria; chronic diseases of children; violence/human rights; medical education; poverty and human development). "However, we would rather that poems relate obliquely to the theme." Guidelines available on website. Pays 1 contributor's copy, more by request. "We ask for a signed copyright release, but publication elsewhere is consistently granted."

● **KAIMANA: LITERARY ARTS HAWAI'I**

Hawai'i Literary Arts Council, P.O. Box 11213, Honolulu HI 96828. E-mail: reimersa001@hawaii.rr.com. Website: www.hawaii.edu/hlac. **Contact:** Poetry Editor. Hawai'i Literary Arts Council, P.O. Box 11213, Honolulu HI 96828. E-mail: reimersa001@hawaii.rr.com. Website: www.hawaii.edu/hlac. *KAIMANA* publishes annually. Wants poems with "some Pacific reference—Asia, Polynesia, Hawai'i—but not exclusively." Has published poetry by Kathryn Takara, Howard Nemerov, Anne Waldman, Reuel Denney, Haunani-Kay Trask, and Simon Perchik. Individual copies are free to HLAC members. *Kaimana: Literary Arts Hawai'i*, published annually, is the magazine of the Hawai'i Literary Arts Council. Wants poems with "some Pacific reference—Asia, Polynesia, Hawai'i—but not exclusively." Has published poetry by Kathryn Takara, Howard Nemerov, Anne Waldman, Reuel Denney, Haunani-Kay Trask, and Simon Perchik. *Kaimana* is 64-76 pages, 7$\frac{1}{2}$x10, saddle-stapled, with high-quality printing. Press run is 1,000. Subscription: $15, includes membership in HLAC. Sample: $10.

HOW TO CONTACT Submit through postal mail only. Include SASE. Doesn't accept e-mail submissions.

TIPS "Poets published in Kaimana have received the Pushcart Prize, the Hawaii Award for Literature, the Stefan Baciu Award, the Cades Award, and the John Unterecker Award."

●◐◑⑤ **KALEIDOSCOPE**

(330)762-9755. Fax: (330)762-0912. E-mail: mshiplett@udsakron.org. Website: www.udsakron.org/kaleidoscope.htm. **Contact:** Mildred Shiplett. "Subscribers include individuals, agencies, and organizations that assist people with disabilities and many university and public libraries. Appreciates work by established writers as well. Especially interested in work by writers with a disability, but features writers both with and without disabilities. Writers without a disability must limit themselves to our focus, while those with a disability may explore any topic (although we prefer original perspectives about experiences with disability)."

○ *Kaleidoscope* has received awards from the American Heart Association, the Great Lakes Awards Competition and Ohio Public Images. *Kaleidoscope* has received awards from the American Heart Association, the Great Lakes Awards Competition and Ohio Public Images.

MAGAZINES NEEDS *Kaleidoscope: Exploring the Experience of Disability through Literature and the Fine Arts*, published twice/year in January and July, is based at United Disability Services, a not-for-profit agency. Distributed by University of Akron Press. Poetry should deal with the experience of disability, but is not limited to that experience when the writer has a disability. Wants high-quality poetry with vivid, believable images and evocative language. Does not want "stereotyping, patronizing, or offending language about disability." Has published poetry by Gerald Wheeler, Jeff Worley, Barbara Crooker, and Sheryl L. Nelms. *Kaleidoscope* is 64 pages, magazine-sized, professionally printed, saddle-stapled, with 4-color semigloss card cover. Press run is 1,500 (for libraries, social service agencies, health care professionals, universities, and individual subscribers). Single copy: $7.50; subscription: $12.50 individual, $25 agency. Contact University of Akron Press at uapress@uakron.edu.

HOW TO CONTACT Submit up to 6 poems at a time. Considers previously published poems and simultaneous submissions "as long as we are notified in both instances." Accepts fax and e-mail submissions. Cover letter is required. Send photocopies with SASE for return of work. "All submissions must be accompanied by an autobiographical sketch and should be double-spaced, with pages numbered and author's name on each page." Reads submissions by March 1 and August 1 deadlines. Publishes theme issues. Upcoming themes available in magazine, for SASE, by fax, e-mail, or on website. Guidelines available for SASE, by fax, e-mail, and on website. Responds within 3 weeks; acceptance or rejection may take 6 months. Pays $10-25 plus 2 contributor's copies. Rights revert to author upon publication. Staff reviews books of poetry. Send materials for review consideration.

TIPS "Articles and personal experiences should be creative rather than journalistic and with some depth. Writers should use more than just the simple facts and chronology of an experience with disability. Inquire about future themes of upcoming issues. Sample copy very helpful. Works should not use stereotyping, patronizing, or offending language about disability. We seek fresh imagery and thought-provoking language. Please double-space work, number pages & include full name and address."

●●◎ KELSEY REVIEW

P.O. Box B, Liberal Arts Division, Trenton NJ 08690. E-mail: kelsey.review@mccc.edu. Website: www.mccc.edu/community_kelsey-review.shtml. **Contact:** Holly-Katharine Matthews. *Kelsey Review*, published annually in September by Mercer County Community College, serves as "an outlet for literary talent of people living and working in Mercer County, New Jersey only." Has no specifications as to form, length, subject matter, or style. Fiction: 4,000 word limit. Poetry: Not more than 6 pages. Non-Fiction: 2,500 word limit. Black and White art. Does not want to see poetry "about kittens and puppies." Has published poetry by Vida Chu, Carolyn Foote Edelmann, and Mary Mallery. *Kelsey Review* is about 90 glossy pages, 7x11, with paper cover. Receives 100+ submissions/year, accepts 10. Press run is 2,000; all distributed free to contributors, area libraries, bookstores, and schools.

MAGAZINES NEEDS *Kelsey Review*, published annually in September by Mercer County Community College, serves as "an outlet for literary talent of people living and working in Mercer County, New Jersey only." Has no specifications as to form, length,

subject matter, or style. Fiction: 4,000 word limit. Poetry: Not more than 6 pages. Non-Fiction: 2,500 word limit. Black and White art. Does not want to see poetry "about kittens and puppies." Has published poetry by Vida Chu, Carolyn Foote Edelmann, and Mary Mallery. *Kelsey Review* is about 90 glossy pages, 7x11, with paper cover. Receives 100+ submissions/year, accepts 10. Press run is 2,000; all distributed free to contributors, area libraries, bookstores, and schools.

HOW TO CONTACT Submit up to 6 poems at a time. No previously published poems or simultaneous submissions. No fax or e-mail submissions. Manuscripts must be typed. Submit poems by May 15 deadline. Send SASE for returns. Guidelines available by e-mail. Responds in August of each year. Pays 3 contributor's copies. All rights revert to authors.

TIPS Look for "quality, intellect, grace and guts. Avoid sentimentality, overwriting and self-indulgence. Work on clarity, depth and originality."

●●◎ THE KENYON REVIEW

Finn House, 102 W. Wiggin, Gambier OH 43022. (740)427-5208. Fax: (740)427-5417. E-mail: kenyonreview@kenyon.edu. Website: KenyonReview.org. **Contact:** Marlene Landefeld. "An international journal of literature, culture, and the arts dedicated to an inclusive representation of the best in new writing (fiction, poetry, essays, interviews, criticism) from established and emerging writers."

MAGAZINES NEEDS *The Kenyon Review*, published quarterly, contains poetry, fiction, essays, criticism, reviews, and memoirs. Features all styles, forms, lengths, and subject matters. Considers translations. Has published poetry by Billy Collins, Diane Ackerman, John Kinsella, Carol Muske-Dukes, Diane di PrimAnd Seamus Heaney. *The Kenyon Review* is 180 pages, digest-sized, flat-spined. Receives about 6,000 submissions/year. Press run is 6,000. Also now publishes *KR Online*, a separate and complementary literary magazine. Sample: $12 (includes postage).

HOW TO CONTACT Submit up to 6 poems at a time. No previously published poems or simultaneous submissions. Accepts submissions **through online registration only** at www.kenyon-review.org/submissions (group poems in a single document; do not submit poems individually). Reads submissions September 15-January 15. Guidelines available on website. Responds in up to 4 months. Payment for accepted work is made upon publication. Author retains rights and will receive a contract upon acceptance. Does not consider unsolicited reviews.

TIPS "We no longer accept mailed or e-mailed submissions. Work will only be read if it is submitted through our online program on our website. Reading period is September 15-January 15. We look for strong voice, unusual perspective, and power in the writing."

KOTAPRESS LOSS JOURNAL

(928)225-5416. E-mail: editor@kotapress.com. Website: www.kotapress.com; www.kotapress.blogspot.com. **Contact:** Kara L.C. Jones, editor. (928)225-5416. E-mail: editor@kotapress.com. Website: www.kotapress.com; www.kotapress.blogspot.com. *KotaPress Loss Journal*, published quarterly online with blogs almost daily, provides support "of the grief and healing process after the death of a child. We publish *only* non-fictional poetry that somehow relates to grief and healing in relation to the death of a child. Please do not make up poems about this kind of loss and send them just to get in the magazine; it is insulting to many of our readers who are living this reality. As always, our interest is more in the content and story rather than one's ability to write in form; more in the ideas of poetry therapy rather than the academic, critique, competitive ideas normally fostered in universities." Has published poetry by John Fox, Poppy Hullings, Patricia Wellingham-Jones, Carol Jo Horn, and Sarah Bain.

MAGAZINES NEEDS *KotaPress Loss Journal*, published quarterly online with blogs almost daily, provides support "of the grief and healing process after the death of a child. We publish *only* non-fictional poetry that somehow relates to grief and healing in relation to the death of a child. Please do not make up poems about this kind of loss and send them just to get in the magazine; it is insulting to many of our readers who are living this reality. As always, our interest is more in the content and story rather than one's ability to write in form; more in the ideas of poetry therapy rather than the academic, critique, competitive ideas normally fostered in universities." Has published poetry by John Fox, Poppy Hullings, Patricia Wellingham-Jones, Carol Jo Horn, and Sarah Bain.

HOW TO CONTACT "Please read the *Loss Journal* site and blog before sending anything. Then send a letter explaining your interest in contributing. We are interested in knowing how your personal experiences with death, dying, grief, and healing are playing out in the specific poems you are submitting. Include a bio. Send your letter, poems, and bio as text all in one e-mail. Submissions without letter explaining your interest will be ignored. Make sure the subject line of your e-mail says 'Loss Journal Submission'" Reads submissions year round on a rolling basis. Time between acceptance and publication is up to 6 months. Guidelines available on website. Responds in 2-6 months. Acquires one-time electronic rights and archive rights. "We do not remove works from our archives. Please see our website to find out more about us and about what we offer. We look forward to hearing from you and reading your poetry."

KRAX

63 Dixon Lane, Leeds, Yorkshire LS12 4RR, England. **Contact:** Andy Robson, Editor. 63 Dixon Lane, Leeds, Yorkshire LS12 4RR England. A light-hearted, whimsical poetry mag with some humour. Usually contains an interview with a writer or artist. Also a review selection of related books, CDs, magazines. Does not pay contributors other than by copy of magazine itself. 68 pages per issue. *Krax*, published annually in the summer, prints contemporary poetry from England and America. Wants "poetry that is light-hearted and witty; original ideas." All forms and styles considered. Does not want "haiku, religious, or topical politics." Has published poetry by Dean Blehert, Gail Holmes, and Salena Godden. *Krax* is 72 pages, digest-sized, offset-printed, saddle-stapled. Receives up to 700 submissions/year, accepts about 10%. Single copy: £3.50 ($7); subscription: £10 ($20). Sample: $1 (75p). Cheques payable to A. Robson.

HOW TO CONTACT Submit 6 poems maximum at a time. Lines/poem: 2,000 words maximum. No previously published poems or simultaneous submissions. No disk submissions. Cover letter is preferred. "Writer's name on same sheet as poem. SASE or SAE with IRC encouraged but not vital."

TIPS "Rewrite only to improve structure or format—unnecessary rewriting usually destroys the original spontaneity and rhythm."

❶❷❸ LADYBUG

(312)701-1720. Website: www.cricketmag.com. Suzanne Beck, man. art dir. **Contact:** Marianne Carus, editor-in-chief. "We look for quality literature and nonfiction."

MAGAZINES NEEDS *LADYBUG Magazine*, published monthly, is a reading and listening magazine for young children (ages 2-6). Wants poetry that is "rhythmic, rhyming; serious, humorous, active." *LADYBUG* is 40 pages, 8x10, staple-bound, with full color cover. Receives more than 1,200 submissions/month, accepts 25-30. Circulation is 120,000. Subscription: $35.97/year (12 issues). ample: $5; sample pages available on website.

HOW TO CONTACT Submit no more than 5 poems at a time. Lines/poem: up to 20. Considers previously published poems. Include SASE. Responds in 6 months. Guidelines available for SASE or on website. Pays $3/line ($25 minimum) on publication. Acquires North American publication rights for previously published poems; rights vary for unpublished poems.

TIPS "Reread ms before sending. Keep within specified word limits. Study back issues before submitting to learn about the types of material we're looking for. Writing style is paramount. We look for rich, evocative language and a sense of joy or wonder. Remember that you're writing for preschoolers—be age-appropriate, but not condescending or preachy. A story must hold enjoyment for both parent and child through repeated read-aloud sessions. Remember that people come in all colors, sizes, physical conditions, and have special needs. Be inclusive!"

❶❷❸ LA FOVEA

E-mail: editors@lafovea.org. Website: www.lafovea. org. **Contact:** Frank Giampietro, creator and senior editor. Estab.2006.

MAGAZINES NEEDS Published 20 times/year online. "Each Nerve editor (found on the main page of www.lafovea.org) is in charge of a nerve. The nerves are made up of poets who are invited to submit to La Fovea. Click on the editors name to see all the poets and poems in his or her nerve. The nerve editor asks a poet to submit two poems. After that poet has had his or her poems on La Fovea, he or she will ask another poet to submit poems. If the last poet on the nerve does not find a poet to submit poems for whatever reason, the nerve is dead. It's okay to have a dead nerve.

The most important thing is for the never editor to notice a nerve has died and begin a new nerve from their first page of poems."

HOW TO CONTACT Wants any poetry. "If a poet wants to submit to La Fovea but has not been invited, he or she may submit to La Fovea and choose the editor whom the poet believes most matches his or her family of aesthetic style. The editor of the never may choose to send these poems to the current nerve editor and ask if he or she wishes to publish the poet's work. If the poet does not wish to publish the work, than the work will be returned to the submitter." Has published poetry by Denise Duhamel, Campbell McGrath, Julianna Baggott. Submit 2 poems at a time and short bio. Considers simultaneous submissions, no previously published poetry. Reads submissions year round. Time between acceptance and publication is 1 month. Guidelines available on website. Responds in 1 month. Acquires one-time rights. Rights revert to poet upon publication.

❶ LAKE EFFECT: A JOURNAL OF THE LITERARY ARTS

School of Humanities & Social Sciences, Penn State Erie, 4951 College Dr., Erie PA 16563-1501. (814)898-6281. Fax: (814)898-6032. E-mail: gol1@psu.edu. Website: www.pserie.psu.edu/lakeeffect. **Contact:** George Looney, editor-in-chief. Member: CLMP.

MAGAZINES NEEDS *Lake Effect*, published annually in the spring, provides "an aesthetic venue for writing that uses language precisely to forge a genuine and rewarding experience for our readers. *Lake Effect* wishes to publish writing that rewards more than 1 reading, and to present side-by-side the voices of established and emerging writers." Has published poetry by Jim Daniels, Beckian Fritz Goldberg, David Kirby, Susan Ludvigson, Harry Humes, and Chase Twichell. *Lake Effect* is 180 pages, digest-sized, offset-printed, perfect-bound, with gloss-by-flat film lamination cover. Receives about 3,000 poems/year, accepts about 1%. Press run is 800 (300 shelf sales); 300 distributed free to contributors and writing programs. Single copy: $6; subscription: $6/1 year, $10/2 years. Make checks payable to The Pennsylvania State University.

HOW TO CONTACT Submit up to 4 poems at a time. Considers simultaneous submissions; no previously published poems. No fax, e-mail, or disk submissions. Cover letter is required. Reads submissions year round. Time between acceptance and publication is up to 4 months. "Want poems that demonstrate an original voice and that use multilayered, evocative images presented in a language shaped by an awareness of how words sound and mean. Each line should help to carry the poem." Guidelines available in magazine or on website. Responds in up to 4 months. Pays 2 contributor's copies. Acquires first North American serial rights.

● LANDFALL: NEW ZEALAND ARTS AND LETTERS

Otago University Press, P.O. Box 56, Dunedin , New Zealand. (64)(3)479-8807. Fax: (64)(3)479-8385. E-mail: landfall@otago.ac.nz. Website: www.otago.ac.nz/press/landfall. **Contact:** Richard Reeve, coordinator.

MAGAZINES NEEDS *Landfall: New Zealand Arts and Letters*, published twice/year in May and November, focuses "primarily on New Zealand literature and arts. It publishes new fiction, poetry, commentary, and interviews with New Zealand artists and writers, and reviews of New Zealand books." Single issue: $29.95 NZD; subscription: $49.95 NZD (2 issues) for New Zealand subscribers, $45 AUD for Australian subscribers, $42 USD for other overseas subscribers.

HOW TO CONTACT Submit no more than 10 poems. Prefers e-mail submissions. Accepts postal mail submissions, but must include SASE. Include contact information and brief bio. Publishes theme issues. Reads year round. Guidelines available for SASE. New Zealand poets should write for further information.

●● LANGUAGEANDCULTURE.NET

4000 Pimlico Dr., Suite 114-192, Pleasanton CA 94588. E-mail: review@languageandculture.net. Website: www.languageandculture.net. **Contact:** Liz Fortini, editor.

MAGAZINES NEEDS *Languageandculture.net*, published twice/year online, prints contemporary poetry in English. Also accepts translations of Spanish, French, German, Italian, and Russian; "other languages under review." No restrictions on form. Considers poetry by teens. Publishes 20-40 poems/issue.

HOW TO CONTACT Submit 3-5 poems at a time. Lines/poem: 70 maximum. Considers previously published poems and simultaneous submissions.

Accepts e-mail submissions; no disk submissions. "Return e-mail address must be included." Cover letter is preferred. Include brief bio. Reads submissions "yearly." Time between acceptance and publication "varies; no longer than 6-8 months." Poems are circulated to an editorial board. Rarely comments on rejected poems. No payment. Acquires one-time electronic rights.

●● LA PETITE ZINE

Website: www.lapetitezine.org. E-mail: lapetitezine@gmail.com. Website: www.lapetitezine.org. **Contact:** Melissa Broder and D.W. Lichtenberg, editors. Member: CLMP.

○ Work published in *La Petite Zine* has appeared in *The Best American Poetry*.

MAGAZINES NEEDS *La Petite Zine*, an online literary magazine publishes fierce poetry and petite prose pieces of 1000 words or less. LPZ is not affiliated with a particular literary school or movement; we like what we like. Above all else, LPZ seeks to be un-boring, a panacea for your emotional hangover. Has published work by Anne Boyer, Arielle Greenberg, Johannes Goransson, Joyelle McSweeney, Joshua Marie Wilkinson, and Jonah Winter. Receives about 3,000 poems/year, accepts about 150 (5%). Sample: free online; "there is no subscription, but readers are invited to sign up for e-mail notification of new issues at the submission address."

HOW TO CONTACT Submit up to 5 poems at a time ("please adhere to this guideline"). Considers simultaneous submissions, "but please notify us immediately if poems are accepted elsewhere"; no previously published poems. Only accepts submissions using submission manager on website. Cover letter is required. Include brief bio listing previous publications. Wait four months before submitting again. Reads year round. Time between acceptance and publication is up to 6 months. "Any deviation from our guidelines will result in the disposal of your submission." Responds in 2 weeks to 6 months. Always sends electronic prepublication galleys. No payment. Acquires first rights. Reviews books/chapbooks of poetry in 500 words, single- and multi-book format.

ALSO OFFERS *La Petite Zine*'s home page "indexes all authors for each specific issue and offers links to past issues, as well as information about the journal, its interests and editors, and links to other sites. Art and graphics are supplied by Web del Sol. Additionally, we publish graphic poems, excerpts from graphic novels, and the like."

⦿⑤ LEADING EDGE

E-mail: editor@leadingedgemagazine.com. Website: www.leadingedgemagazine.com. "*Leading Edge* is a magazine dedicated to new and upcoming talent in the field of science fiction and fantasy."
C Accepts unsolicited submissions.

MAGAZINES NEEDS *Leading Edge*, published biannually, is a journal of science fiction and fantasy. Wants "high-quality poetry reflecting both literary value and popular appeal. We accept traditional science fiction and fantasy poetry, but we like innovative stuff." Does not want "graphic sex, violence, or profanity." Considers poetry by children and teens. Has published poetry by Michael Collings, Tracy Ray, Susan Spilecki, and Bob Cook. *Leading Edge* is digest-sized. Receives about 60 poems/year, accepts about 6. Single copy: $5.95; subscription: $10 (2 issues), $20 (4 issues), $27.50 (6 issues).

HOW TO CONTACT Submit 1 or more poems at a time. No simultaneous submissions or previously published poems. No e-mail submissions. Cover letter is preferred. "Include name, address, phone number, length of poem, title, and type of poem at the top of each page. Please include SASE with every submission." Guidelines available in magazine, for SASE, or on website. Responds in 2-4 months. Always sends prepublication galleys. Pays $10 for the first 4 typeset pages, $1.50 for each additional page, plus 2 contributor's copies. Acquires first North American serial rights.

TIPS "Buy a sample issue to know what is currently selling in our magazine. Also, make sure to follow the writer's guidelines when submitting."

⦿ THE LEDGE MAGAZINE

40 Maple Ave., Bellport NY 11713-2011. E-mail: info@theledgemagazine.com. Website: www.theledgemagazine.com. **Contact:** Tim Monaghan, Editor-in-Chief. *The Ledge* is 300 pages, 6x9, typeset, perfect-bound, with glossy cover. Accepts 3% of poetry received. Press run is 1,000. Single copy: $10; subscription: $20 for 2 issues, $36 for 4 issues, $48 for 6 issues." The Ledge Magazine publishes cutting-edge contemporary fiction by emerging and established writers." Annual. Receives 120 mss/month. Accepts 9 mss/issue. Manuscript published 6 months after acceptance. Published Pia Chatterjee, Xujun Eberlein,

Clifford Garstang, Richard Jespers, William Luvaas, Michael Thompson. Also publishes poetry. Rarely comments on/critiques rejected mss. Send complete ms with cover letter. Include estimated word count, brief bio. Send SASE (or IRC) for return of ms. Sample copy available for $10. Subscription: $20 (2 issues), $36 (4 issues). Guidelines available for SASE. Writers receive 1 contributor's copy. Additional copies $6. Sends galleys to author. Publication is copyrighted.

HOW TO CONTACT Submit 3-5 poems at a time. Considers simultaneous submissions; no previously published poems. Include SASE. Reads submissions October-March. Responds in 4-6 months.

CONTEST/AWARD OFFERINGS *The Ledge* Poetry Awards Competition and *The Ledge* Poetry Chapbook Contest (see separate listings in Contests & Awards).

TIPS "We seek compelling stories that employ innovative language and complex characterization. We especially enjoy poignant stories with a sense of purpose. We dislike careless or hackneyed writing."

⦿ LEFT CURVE

P.O. Box 472, Oakland CA 94604-0472. (510)763-7193. E-mail: editor@leftcurve.org. Website: www.leftcurve.org. **Contact:** Csaba Polony, editor.

MAGAZINES NEEDS *Left Curve*, published "irregularly, about every 10 months," addresses the "problem(s) of cultural forms, emerging from the crisis of modernity, that strives to be independent from the control of dominant institutions, and free from the shackles of instrumental rationality." Wants poetry that is "critical culture, social, political, 'post-modern.' We will look at any form of poetry, from experimental to traditional." Does not want "purely formal, too self-centered, poetry that doesn't address in sufficient depth today's problems." Has published poetry by John Berger, Vincent Ferrini, Devorah Major, Jack Hirschman, and Lawrence Ferllinghetti. *Left Curve* is 144 pages, magazine-sized, offset-printed, perfect-bound, with 4-color Durosheen cover, includes ads. Press run is 2,000 (250 subscribers, 100 libraries, 1,600 shelf sales). Subscription: $35/3 issues (individuals), $50/3 issues (institutions). Sample: $12.

HOW TO CONTACT Submit up to 5 poems at a time. Lines/poem: "most of our published poetry is 1 page in length, though we have published longer poems of up to 8 pages." Accepts e-mail or disk submissions. Cover letter is required. "Explain why you are submitting." Publishes theme issues. Guidelines available for SASE, by e-mail, or on website. Responds in up to 6 months. Pays 2-3 contributor's copies. Send materials for review consideration.

TIPS "We look for continuity, adequate descriptive passages, endings that are not simply abandoned (in both meanings). Dig deep; no superficial personalisms, no corny satire. Be honest, realistic and gouge out the truth you wish to say. Understand yourself and the world. Have writing be a means to achieve or realize what is real."

LILITH MAGAZINE: INDEPENDENT, JEWISH & FRANKLY FEMINIST

250 W. 57th St., Suite 2432, New York NY 10107. (212)757-0818. Fax: (212)757-5705. E-mail: info@lilith.org. Website: www.lilith.org. Susan Weidman Schneider, editor-in-chief. **Contact:** Poetry Editor. *Lilith Magazine: Independent, Jewish & Frankly Feminist*, published quarterly, is "an independent magazine with a Jewish feminist perspective" that uses poetry by Jewish women "about the Jewish woman's experience." Does not want poetry on other subjects. "Generally we use short rather than long poems." Has published poetry by Irena Klepfisz, Lyn Lifshin, Marcia Falk, Adrienne Rich, and Muriel Rukeyser. *Lilith Magazine* is 48 pages, magazine-sized, with glossy color cover. Publishes about 4 poems/year. Press run is about 10,000 (about 6,000 subscribers). Subscription: $26/year. Sample: $7.

TIPS "Read a copy of the publication before you submit your work. Please be patient."

○ LINEBREAK

333 Kimpel Hall, University of Arkansas, Fayetteville, AR 72701. E-mail: editors@linebreak.org. Website: http://linebreak.org. **Contact:** Johnathon Williams, founding editor. "*Linebreak* is a weekly online magazine of original poetry. Each poem we publish is read and recorded by another working poet selected by the editors."

   ◑ Poems published on *Linebreak* have been selected for the Best New Poets anthology and nominated for the Pushcart Prize.

MAGAZINES NEEDS All styles. Has published Dorianne Laux, Bob Hicok, D.A. Powell, C. Dale Young, Richard Siken, Sandra Beasley. Receives about 2,200 poems/year; accepts about 52. Averages 3,000 unique visitors per month, with 220 additional subscribers to RSS feed, and 250 subscribers to weekly newsletter.

HOW TO CONTACT Submit up to 5 poems at a time through upload form on website. Considers simultaneous submissions. Reads submissions year round. Time between acceptance and publication is 2-16 weeks. Poems are circulated to an editorial board. Sometimes comments on rejected poems. Guidelines available on website. Responds in 6 weeks. Sometimes sends prepublication galleys. Acquires electronic rights: "We require the rights to publish and archive the work indefinitely on our website, and the right to create an audio recording of each poem, which is also archived indefinitely. Copyright remains with the author."

◑ LIPS

7002 Blvd. East, #2-26G, Guttenberg NJ 07093. (201)662-1303. E-mail: LBoss79270@aol.com. **Contact:** Laura Boss, Poetry Editor. Submit 6 pages maximum at a time. Poems should be typed. Reads submissions September-March only. Responds in 1 month (but has gotten backlogged at times). Sometimes sends prepublication galleys. Pays 1 contributor's copy.

MAGAZINES NEEDS *Lips*, published twice/year, takes pleasure "in publishing previously unpublished poets as well as the most established voices in contemporary poetry. We look for quality work: the strongest work of a poet; work that moves the reader; poems that take risks that work. We prefer clarity in the work rather than the abstract. Poems longer than 6 pages present a space problem." Has published poetry by Robert Bly, Allen Ginsberg, Michael Benedikt, Maria Gillan, Stanley Barkan, Lyn Lifshin, and Ishmael Reed. *Lips* is about 150 pages, digest-sized, flat-spined. Receives about 16,000 submissions/year, accepts about 1%. Press run is 1,000 (200 subscribers, 100 libraries). Sample: $10 plus $2 for postage.

HOW TO CONTACT Submit 6 pages maximum at a time. Poems should be typed. Reads submissions September-March only. Guidelines available for SASE. Responds in 1 month (but has gotten backlogged at times). Sometimes sends prepublication galleys. Pays 1 contributor's copy. Acquires first rights.

◑ THE LISTENING EYE

Kent State University Geauga Campus, 14111 Claridon-Troy Rd., Burton, OH 44021. (440)286-3840. E-mail:grace_butcher@msn.com. Websiste: http://reocities.com/Athens/3716/eye.htm. **Contact:** Grace Butcher, editor.

HOW TO CONTACT Submit up to 4 poems at a time. Lines/poem: "prefer shorter poems (less than 2 pages), but will consider longer if space allows." Accepts previously published poems "occasionally"; no simultaneous submissions. No e-mail submissions "unless from overseas." Cover letter is required. Poems should be typed, single-spaced, 1 poem/page—name, address, phone number, and e-mail address in upper left-hand corner of each page—with SASE for return of work. Reads submissions January 1-April 15 only: max four poems/ four pages. Time between acceptance and publication is up to 6 months. Poems are circulated to the editor and 2 assistant editors who read and evaluate work separately, then meet for final decisions. Occasionally comments on rejected poems. Guidelines available in magazine or for SASE. Responds in 3 months. Pays 2 contributor's copies. Acquires first or one-time rights. Awards $30 to the best sports poem in each issue.

TIPS "We look for powerful, unusual imagery, content and plot in our short stories. In poetry, we look for tight lines that don't sound like prose; unexpected images or juxtapositions; the unusual use of language; noticeable relationships of sounds; a twist in viewpoint; an ordinary idea in extraordinary language; an amazing and complex idea simply stated; play on words and with words; an obvious love of language. Poets need to read the 'Big 3'—Cummings, Thomas, Hopkins—to see the limits to which language can be taken. Then read the 'Big 2'—Dickinson to see how simultaneously tight, terse, and universal a poem can be, and Whitman to see how sprawling, cosmic, and personal. Then read everything you can find that's being published in literary magazines today, and see how your work compares to all of the above."

LITERAL LATTE

200 E. 10th St., Suite 240, New York NY 10003. (212)260-5532. E-mail: litlatte@aol.com. Website: www.literal-latte.com. 200 E. 10th St., Suite 240, New York, NY 10003. (212)260-5532. E-mail: litlatte@aol.com. Website: www.literal-latte.com. **Contact:** Jenine Gordon Bockman. "We want any poem that captures the magic of the form." *Literal Latté*, published continually online, is a literary journal of "pure prose, poetry, and art. Open to all styles of poetry—quality is the determining factor." Has published poetry by Allen Ginsberg, Carol Muske, Amy Holman, and John Updike. Receives about 3,000 poems/year, accepts 1%. Bimonthly online publication with an annual print anthology featuring the best of the website. "We want great writing in all styles and subjects. A feast is made of a variety of flavors."

HOW TO CONTACT Considers simultaneous submissions; no previously published poems. No e-mail submissions; postal submissions only. Cover letter is required. Include bio and e-mail address for response only. Time between acceptance and publication is within 1 year. Often comments on rejected poems. Guidelines available by e-mail or on website. Responds in 5 months.

ADDITIONAL INFORMATION "We will publish an anthology in book form at the end of each year, featuring the best of our Web magazine."

CONTEST/AWARD OFFERINGS *Literal Latté* Poetry Awards and *Literal Latté* Food Verse Awards (see separate listings in Contests & Awards).

TIPS "Keeping free thought free and challenging entertainment are not mutually exclusive. Words make a manuscript stand out, words beautifully woven together in striking and memorable patterns."

LITERARY MAMA

E-mail: lminfo@literarymama.com. Website: www.literarymama.com. Sharon Kraus, poetry editor. **Contact:** Caroline Grant, Editor-in-Chief. Departments include columns, creative nonfiction, fiction, Literary Reflections, poetry, Profiles & Reviews. We are interested in reading pieces that are long, complex, ambiguous, deep, raw, irreverent, ironic, body conscious.

MAGAZINES NEEDS *Literary Mama*, published monthly online, prints fiction, poetry, and creative nonfiction by writers of all ages who are "self-identified" mothers. "We also publish literary criticism, book reviews, and profiles about mother writers. *Literary Mama* is doing something for mama-centric literature that no one else is doing. The poetry, fiction, and creative nonfiction that may be too long, too complex, too ambiguous, too deep, too raw, too edgy, too irreverent, too ironic, too body-conscious, and too full of long words for the general reader will find a home with us. While there are plenty of online literary magazines that publish writing like this, none devote themselves exclusively to writing about motherhood." Wants poems of any form that are "extraordinary for their vision, craft, integrity, and originality; centered around parenting; written by writers who are also self-identified mothers: biological, non-biological, step, transgender, adoptive." Receives about 70 poems/month, accepts about 3%.

HOW TO CONTACT Maximum of four poems per submission. Please send submissions in the text of an email (please do not send attachments), and be sure to include full name and the word "Submission" in the subject line. Please expect a response within 2-6 months. No payment. Acquires first rights for previously unpublished work, non-exclusive one-time rights for reprints. Reviews books/chapbooks of poetry. Query via e-mail prior to sending materials for review consideration.

TIPS "We seek top-notch creative writing. We also look for quality literary criticism about mother-centric literature and profiles of mother writers. We publish writing with fresh voices, superior craft, vivid imagery. Please send submission (copied into e-mail) to appropriate departmental editors. Include a brief cover letter. We tend to like stark revelation (pathos, humor & joy), clarity, concrete details, strong narrative development; ambiguity, thoughtfulness, delicacy, irreverence, lyricism, sincerity; the elegant. We need the submissions 3 mos. before Oct.: Desiring Motherhood; May: Mother's Day Month; June: Father's Day Month."

● LOS

150 N. Catalina St., No. 2, Los Angeles CA 90004. E-mail: lospoesy@earthlink.net. Website: http://home.earthlink.net/~lospoesy.

MAGAZINES NEEDS 150 N. Catalina St., No. 2, Los Angeles, CA 90004. E-mail: lospoesy@earthlink.net. Website: http://home.earthlink.net/~lospoesy. **Contact:** The Editors. *Los*, published 4 times/year, features poetry. Has published poetry by John P. Campbell, Jean Esteve, Mary Kasimor, Bill Knott, Paul Lowe, and Charles Wuest. *Los* is digest-sized and saddle-stapled. Press run is 100.

HOW TO CONTACT Accepts e-mail submissions (pasted into body of message or as attachment). Time between acceptance and publication is up to 1 month. Guidelines available on website. Responds in 3 months. Pays 1 contributor's copy.

● LOUISIANA LITERATURE

SLU Box 10792, Southeastern Louisiana University, Hammond LA 70402. Website: www.louisianaliterature.org. **Contact:** Jack B. Bedell, editor. SLU Box 10792, Southeastern Louisiana University, Hammond,

LA 70402. E-mail: lalit@selu.edu; ngerman@selu.edu. Website:www.louisianaliterature.org. **Contact:** Jack B. Bedell, editor. *Louisiana Literature*, published twice/year, considers "creative work from anyone, though we strive to showcase our state's talent. We appreciate poetry that shows firm control and craft; is sophisticated yet accessible to a broad readership. We don't use highly experimental work." Has published poetry by Claire Bateman, Elton Glaser, Gray Jacobik, Vivian Shipley, D.C. Berry, and Judy Longley. *Louisiana Literature* is 150 pages, $6\frac{3}{4}$x$9\frac{3}{4}$, handsomely printed on heavy matte stock, flat-spined, with matte card cover. Single copy: $8 for individuals; subscription: $12 for individuals, $12.50 for institutions.

HOW TO CONTACT Submit 3-5 poems at a time. No simultaneous submissions. No fax or e-mail submissions. "Send cover letter, including bio to use in the event of acceptance. Enclose SASE and specify whether work is to be returned or discarded." Reads submissions year round, "although we work more slowly in summer." Publishes theme issues. Guidelines available for SASE or on website. Sometimes sends prepublication galleys. Pays 2 contributor's copies. Send materials for review consideration; include cover letter.

TIPS "Cut out everything that is not a functioning part of the story. Make sure your manuscript is professionally presented. Use relevant specific detail in every scene. We love detail, local color, voice and craft. Any professional manuscript stands out."

● THE LOUISIANA REVIEW

Division of Liberal Arts, Louisiana State University at Eunice, P.O. Box 1129, Eunice LA 70535. (337)550-1315. E-mail: bfonteno@lsue.edu. Website: web.lsue.edu/la-review. Dr. Michael Alleman, poetry editor. **Contact:** Dr. Billy Fontenot, editor.

MAGAZINES NEEDS *The Louisiana Review*, published annually during the fall or spring semester, offers "Louisiana poets, writers, and artists a place to showcase their most beautiful pieces. Others may submit Louisiana- or Southern-related poetry, stories, and b&w art, as well as interviews with Louisiana writers. We want to publish the highest-quality poetry, fiction, and art." Wants "strong imagery, metaphor, and evidence of craft." Does not want "sing-song rhymes, abstract, religious, or overly sentimental work." Has published poetry by Gary Snyder, Antler, David Cope, and Catfish McDaris. *The Louisiana*

Review is 100-200 pages, digest-sized, professionally printed, perfect-bound. Receives up to 2,000 poems/year, accepts 40-50. Press run is 300-600. Single copy: $5.

HOW TO CONTACT Submit up to 5 poems at a time. No previously published poems. No fax or e-mail submissions. "Include cover letter indicating your association with Louisiana, if any. Name and address should appear on each page." Reads submissions year round. Time between acceptance and publication is up to 2 years. Pays one contributor's copy. Poets retain all rights.

TIPS "We do like to have fiction play out visually as a film would rather than static and undramatized. Louisiana or Gulf Coast settings and themes preferred."

THE LOUISVILLE REVIEW

Spalding University, 851 S. Fourth St., Louisville KY 40203. (502)585-9911, ext. 2777. Fax: (502)992-2409. E-mail: louisvillereview@spalding.edu. Website: www.louisvillereview.org. **Contact:** Kathleen Driskell, associate editor.

MAGAZINES NEEDS *The Louisville Review*, published twice/year, prints all kinds of poetry. Has a section devoted to children's poetry (grades K-12) called The Children's Corner. Considers poetry by children and teens. Has published poetry by Wendy Bishop, Gary Fincke, Michael Burkard, and Sandra Kohler. *The Louisville Review* is 150 pages, digest-sized, flat-spined. Receives about 700 submissions/year, accepts about 10%. Single copy: $8; subscription: $14/year, $27/2 years, $40/3 years (foreign subscribers add $6/year for s&h). Sample: $5.

HOW TO CONTACT Considers simultaneous submissions; no previously published poems. Accepts submissions via online manager; please see website for more information. "Poetry by children must include permission of parent to publish if accepted. Address those submissions to The Children's Corner." Reads submissions year round. Time between acceptance and publication is up to 4 months. Submissions are read by 3 readers. Guidelines available on website. Responds in 4-6 months. Pays in contributor's copies.

LULLWATER REVIEW

Emory University, P.O. Box 122036, Emory University, Atlanta GA 30322. Fax: (404)727-7367. E-mail: lullwater@lullwaterreview.com. **Contact:** Arina Korneva, editor-in-chief. "We're a small, student-run literary magazine published out of Emory University in Atlanta, GA with two issues yearly—once in the fall and once in the spring. You can find us in the *Index of American Periodical Verse*, the *American Humanities Index* and as a member of the Council of Literary Magazines and Presses. We welcome work that brings a fresh perspective, whether through language or the visual arts."

MAGAZINES NEEDS *Lullwater Review*, published in May and December, prints poetry, short fiction, and artwork. Wants poetry of any genre with strong imagery, original voice, on any subject. Does not want profanity or pornographic material. Has published poetry by Amy Greenfield, Peter Serchuk, Katherine McCord, and Ha Jin. *Lullwater Review* is 60-80 pages, magazine-sized, with full-color cover, includes b&w and color pictures. Press run is 1,200. Subscription: $8 for individuals, $10 for institutions. Sample: $5.

HOW TO CONTACT Submit 6 or fewer poems at a time. Considers simultaneous submissions; no previously published poems. Cover letter is preferred. Prefers poems single-spaced with name and contact info on each page. "Poems longer than 1 page should include page numbers. We must have a SASE with which to reply." Reads submissions September 1-May 15 only. Time between acceptance and publication is up to 6 months. Poems are circulated to an editorial board. Seldom comments on rejected poems. Guidelines available for SASE. Responds in 5 months maximum. Pays 3 contributor's copies. Acquires first North American serial rights.

TIPS "We at the *Lullwater Review* look for clear cogent writing, strong character development and an engaging approach to the story in out fiction submissions. Stories with particularly strong voices and well-developed central themes are especially encouraged. Be sure that your manuscript is ready before mailing it off to us. Revise, revise, revise! Be original, honest, and of course, keep trying."

LUNGFULL!MAGAZINE

316 23rd St., Brooklyn NY 11215. E-mail: lungfull@rcn.com. Website: http://lungfull.org. **Contact:** Brendan Lorber, editor/publisher.

LUNGFULL! was the recipient of a grant from the New York State Council for the Arts.

MAGAZINES NEEDS *LUNGFULL!magazine*, published annually, prints "the rough draft of each poem, in addition to the final, so that the reader can see the creative process from start to finish. People who have not read the journal will be obvious and at a disadvantage." Wants "any style as long as it's urgent, immediate, playful, probing, showing great thought while remaining vivid and grounded. Poems should be as interesting as conversation." Does not want "empty poetic abstractions." Has published poetry by Alice Notley, Lorenzo Thomas, Tracie Morris, Hal Sirowitz, Eileen Myles, and John Ashbery. *LUNGFULL!* is 200 pages, $8\frac{1}{2}$X7, offset-printed, desktop-published, perfect-bound, with glossy waterproof 2-color cover, includes ads. Receives about 1,000 poems/year, accepts 3%. Press run is 3,000 (600 subscribers, 2300 shelf sales); 100 distributed free to contributors. Single copy: $9.95; subscription: $39.80 for 4 issues, $19.90 for 2 issues. Sample: $13.95. Make checks payable to Brendan Lorber, or order online.

HOW TO CONTACT Submit up to 6 poems at a time. Considers previously published poems and simultaneous submissions (with notification; "however, other material will be considered first and stands a much greater chance of publication"). Accepts e-mail submissions. "We prefer hard copy by USPS—but e-submissions can be made in the body of the e-mail itself; submissions with attachments will be deleted unread." Cover letter is preferred. Time between acceptance and publication is up to 8 months. "The editor looks at each piece for its own merit and for how well it will fit into the specific issue being planned based on other accepted work." Guidelines available by e-mail. Responds in 1 year. Pays 2 contributor's copies. "Read the magazine before submitting and mention why you want to be published in LUNGFULL! in your cover letter."

ALSO OFFERS "Each copy of *LUNGFULL!magazine* contains a Cultural Attache Sticker—they can be removed from the magazine and placed on any flat surface to make it a little less flat. Previous stickers contain statements like 'Together we can keep the poor poor' and 'You only live once—just not as long as in countries with free healthcare.'"

THE LUTHERAN DIGEST

The Lutheran Digest, Inc., 6160 Carmen Ave. E, Inver Grove Heights MN 55076. (952)933-2820. Fax: (952)933-5708. E-mail: editor@lutherandigest.com. Website: www.lutherandigest.com. David Tank, editor. **Contact:** Nicholas A. Skapyak, editor. "Articles frequently reflect a Lutheran Christian perspective, but are not intended to be sermonettes. Popular stories show how God has intervened in a person's life to help solve a problem."

MAGAZINES NEEDS *The Lutheran Digest* published quarterly, aims to "entertain and encourage believers and to subtly persuade non-believers to embrace the Lutheran-Christian faith. We publish short poems that will fit in a single column of the magazine. Most are inspirational, but that doesn't necessarily mean religious." Does not want "avant-garde poetry." Considers poetry by children and teens. Has published poetry by Kathleen A. Cain, William Beyer, Margaret Peterson, Florence Berg, and Erma Boetkher. *The Lutheran Digest* is 64 pages, digest-sized, offset-printed, saddle-stapled, with 4-color paper cover, includes local ads. Receives about 200 poems/year, accepts 10-20%. Press run is 60,000-65,000; most distributed free to Lutheran churches. Subscription: $16/year, $22/2 years. Sample: $3.50.

HOW TO CONTACT Submit 3 poems at a time. Lines/poem: 25 maximum. Considers previously published poems and simultaneous submissions. Accepts fax and e-mail (as attachment) submissions. Cover letter is preferred. "Include SASE if return is desired." Time between acceptance and publication is up to 9 months. "Poems are selected by editor and reviewed by publication panel." Guidelines available for SASE or on website. Responds in 3 months. Pays credit and 1 contributor's copy. Acquires one-time rights.

TIPS "Reading our writers' guidelines and sample articles online is encouraged and is the best way to get a 'feel' of the type of material we publish."

LYRIC POETRY REVIEW

P.O. Box 2494, Bloomington IN 47402. E-mail: lyric@lyricreview.org. Website: www.lyricreview.org. **Contact:** Nathaniel Perry, editor. P.O. Box 2494, Bloomington, IN 47402. E-mail: lyric@lyricreview.org. Website: www.lyricreview.org. **Contact:** Nathaniel Perry, editor. *Lyric Poetry Review*, published semiannually, presents "poetry by Americans and translations of both little-known and celebrated poets from around the world." Also publishes interviews and literary essays on poetry or poetics. Wants "poetry that has strong musicality and lyricism. We are open to all styles, including longer poems and lyrical narratives. We tend to publish more than 1 poem by any given author and try to find a group of poems that demonstrates both range and consistency of voice." Has published poetry by Marilyn Hacker, Maurice Manning, Czeslaw Milosz, Jean Valentine, Alicia Ostriker, and Gerald Stern. *Lyric Poetry Review* is 96 pages, digest-sized, perfect-bound, with full-color cover with original artwork. Receives about 2,500 poems/year, accepts about 5%. Press run is 1,000. Single copy: $16; subscription: $30/year (subscribers outside U.S. add $10/year, $15/2 years' postage). Make checks payable to *Lyric Poetry Review*. Poems published in *Lyric Poetry Review* have appeared in *The Best American Poetry* and *The Pushcart Prize* as well as on the Poetry Daily and Verse Daily Web sites. *We hope to begin reading again in Spring 2010 - Please check our website for updates.* In the meantime, keep an eye out for Lyric #12, due out soon, featuring long poems by Forrest Gander, Linda Zisquit, George Scarbrough and others. *Lyric Poetry Review*, published semiannually, presents "poetry by Americans and translations of both little-known and celebrated poets from around the world." Also publishes interviews and literary essays on poetry or poetics. Wants "poetry that has strong musicality and lyricism. We are open to all styles, including longer poems and lyrical narratives. We tend to publish more than 1 poem by any given author and try to find a group of poems that demonstrates both range and consistency of voice." Has published poetry by Marilyn Hacker, Maurice Manning, Czeslaw Milosz, Jean Valentine, Alicia Ostriker, and Gerald Stern. *Lyric Poetry Review* is 96 pages, digest-sized, perfect-bound, with full-color cover with original artwork. Receives about 2,500 poems/year, accepts about 5%. Press run is 1,000. Single copy: $16; subscription: $30/year (subscribers outside U.S. add $10/year, $15/2 years' postage). Make checks payable to *Lyric Poetry Review*.

O Poems published in *Lyric Poetry Review* have appeared in *The Best American Poetry* and *The Pushcart Prize* as well as on the Poetry Daily and Verse Daily Web sites.

HOW TO CONTACT Submit 3-6 poems at a time. Considers simultaneous submissions if notified; no previously published poems. No e-mail or disk submissions. Cover letter is required. Reads submissions year round. Response time may be considerably slower in the summer months. Time between acceptance and publication is up to 1 year. "We strongly advise that those submitting work read a recent issue first." Seldom comments on rejected poems. Occasionally publishes theme issues. Upcoming themes available by e-mail. Guidelines available in magazine, for SASE, or on website. Responds in up to 4 months. Always sends prepublication galleys. Pays 2 contributor's copies. Acquires first rights. Solicits reviews.

O THE MADISON REVIEW

University of Wisconsin, 600 N, Park St., 6193 Helen C. White Hall, Madison WI 53706. E-mail: madisonreview@gmail.com. Website: www.english.wisc.edu/madisonreview/. *The Madison Review* is a student-run literary magazine that looks to publish the best available fiction and poetry.

O "We do not publish unsolicited interviews or genre fiction."

MAGAZINES NEEDS *The Madison Review*, published semiannually in May and December, seeks poems that are "smart and tight, that fulfill their own propositions." Does not want "religious or patriotic dogma and light verse." Has published poetry by Simon Perchik, Amy Quan Barry, Mitch Raney, Erica Meitner, and Henry B. Stobbs. Selects 15-20 poems from a pool of 750. Subscription: $15/year, $25 for 2 years. Sample: $8.

HOW TO CONTACT Submit up to 5 poems at a time. No simultaneous submissions. No e-mail submissions. Cover letter is preferred. Include SASE. Submissions must be typed. Guidelines available in magazine, for SASE, by e-mail, or on website. Usually responds in 9 months. Pays 2 contributor's copies.

TIPS "Our editors have very ecclectic tastes, so don't specifically try to cater to us. Above all, we look for original, high quality work."

O$ THE MAGAZINE OF SPECULATIVE POETRY

P.O. Box 564, Beloit WI 53512. Website: www.sff.net/people/roger-dutcher/#mspgdln. **Contact:** Roger Dutcher, editor.

MAGAZINES NEEDS *The Magazine of Speculative Poetry*, published biannually, features "the best new speculative poetry. We are especially interested in narrative form, but open to any form, any length (within reason); interested in a variety of styles. We're looking for the best of the new poetry utilizing the ideas, imagery, and approaches developed by speculative fiction, and will welcome experimental techniques as well as the fresh employment of traditional forms." Has published poetry by Joanne Merriam, Jeannine Hall Gailey, Ann K. Schwader, and Kendall Evans. *The Magazine of Speculative Poetry* is 24-28 pages, digest-sized, offset-printed, saddle-stapled, with matte card cover. Receives about 500 poems/year, accepts less than 5%. Press run is 150-200. Subscription: $19 for 4 issues. Sample: $5.

HOW TO CONTACT Submit 3-5 poems at a time. Lines/poem: "Some poems run 2 or 3 pages, but rarely anything longer. We're a small magazine, we can't print epics." No previously published poems or simultaneous submissions. "We like cover letters, but they aren't necessary. We like to see where you heard of us; the names of the poems submitted; a statement if the poetry manuscript is disposable; a big enough SASE; and if you've been published, some recent places." Poems should be double-spaced. Comments on rejected poems "on occasion." Guidelines available for SASE. Responds in up to 2 months. Pays 3¢/word ($7 minimum, $25 maximum) and 1 contributor's copy. Acquires first North American serial rights. "All rights revert to author upon publication, except for permission to reprint in any 'Best of' or compilation volume. Payment will be made for such publication." Reviews books of speculative poetry. Query regarding unsolicited reviews, interviews, and articles. Send materials for review consideration.

🌀 MAGMA POETRY

23 Pine Walk, Carshalton Surrey SM5 4ES, United Kingdom. E-mail: contributions@magmapoetry.com. Website: www.magmapoetry.com. info@magmapoetry.com for general questions. **Contact:** Editor. 43 Keslake Rd., London NW6 6DH England. E-mail: contributions@magmapoetry.com; info@magmapoetry.com. Website: www.magmapoetry.com. **Contact:** David Boll, editorial secretary. *Magma* appears 3 times/year and contains "modern poetry, reviews and interviews with poets." Wants poetry that is "modern in idiom and shortish (2 pages maximum). Nothing sentimental or old fashioned." Has published poetry by Thomas Lynch, Thom Gunn, Michael Donaghy, John Burnside, Vicki Feaver, and Roddy Lumsden. *Magma* is 64 pages, 8×8, photocopied and stapled, includes b&w illustrations. Receives about 3,000 poems/year, accepts 4-5%. Press run is about 500. Single copy: £5.70 UK and Ireland, £6.15 rest of Europe, £7.50 airmail ROW. Subscription: £14.50 UK and Ire-

land, £18 rest of Europe, £20.50 airmail ROW. Make checks payable to *Magma*. For subscriptions, contact Helen Nicholson, distribution secretary, Flat 2, 86 St. James's Dr., London SW17 7RR England.

💬 "Triannual website covering the best in contemporary poetry and writing about poetry. We look for poems which give a direct sense of what it is to live today—honest about feelings, alert about the world, sometimes funny, always well crafted. We showcase a poet in each issue. A rotating editorship results in different emphasis. Many poems are from poets living abroad, including Ireland, USA, CanadAustralasia. Please submit in the body of an email rather than as an attachment or with our online form." Enter contest for the Troubadour International Poetry Prize. See website for details.

MAGAZINES NEEDS *Magma* appears 3 times/year and contains "modern poetry, reviews and interviews with poets." Wants poetry that is "modern in idiom and shortish (2 pages maximum). Nothing sentimental or old fashioned." Has published poetry by Thomas Lynch, Thom Gunn, Michael Donaghy, John Burnside, Vicki Feaver, and Roddy Lumsden. *Magma* is 64 pages, 8×8, photocopied and stapled, includes b&w illustrations. Receives about 3,000 poems/year, accepts 4-5%. Press run is about 500. Single copy: £5.70 UK and Ireland, £6.15 rest of Europe, £7.50 airmail ROW. Subscription: £14.50 UK and Ireland, £18 rest of Europe, £20.50 airmail ROW. Make checks payable to *Magma*. For subscriptions, contact Helen Nicholson, distribution secretary, Flat 2, 86 St. James's Dr., London SW17 7RR England.

HOW TO CONTACT Submit up to 6 poems at a time. Accepts simultaneous submissions. Accepts submissions by post (with SAE and IRCs) and by e-mail (preferably pasted into body of message; if attachment, only 1 file). Cover letter is preferred. Deadlines for submissions: end of February, mid-July, end of October. "Poems are considered for one issue only." Time between acceptance and publication is maximum 3 months. "Each issue has an editor who submits his/her selections to a board for final approval. Editor's selection very rarely changed." Occasionally publishes theme issues. Responds "as soon as a decision is made." Always sends prepublication galleys. Pays one contributor's copy.

ALSO OFFERS "We hold a public reading in London

three times/year, to coincide with each new issue, and poets in the issue are invited to read."

TIPS "See 'About Magma' and the contents of our website to gain an idea of the type of work we accept." Keep up with the latest news and comment from *Magma Poetry* by receiving free updates via email. Sign up online to receive the Magma Blog and/or the *Magma* newsletter.

☺O MAGNAPOETS

13300 Tecumseh Rd. E., Suite 226, Tecumseh ON N8N 4R8, Canada. E-mail: Magnapoets@gmail.com. Website: www.magnapoets.com. **Contact:** Aurora Antonovic, editor-in-chief. 13300 Tecumseh Rd. E., Suite 226, Tecumseh, ON N8N 4R8, Canada. E-mail: Magnapoets@gmail.com. Website: www.magnapoets.com. **Contact:** Aurora Antonovic, editor-in-chief. Estab. 2008. *Magnapoets*, published semiannually in January and July, prints "all forms of poetry, as well as short stories and articles." Wants all forms of poetry, including free verse, formal poetry, tanka, haiku, senryu. Does not want "anything hateful, racist, bigoted, or overtly partisan. Considers poetry by teens. Has published poetry by Robert Pinsky, Kirsty Karkow, Elisha Porat, Peggy Lyles Wills, Curtis Dunlap, an'ya. *Magnapoets* is 36-40 pages, magazine-sized, digital press print format, saddle-stitched, with a glossy cover with full-sized color photograph or art. Single copy: $5 CAN; subscription: $10 CAN. Make checks payable to Aurora Antonovic.

MAGAZINES NEEDS *Magnapoets*, published semiannually in January and July, prints "all forms of poetry, as well as short stories and articles." Wants all forms of poetry, including free verse, formal poetry, tanka, haiku, senryu. Does not want "anything hateful, racist, bigoted, or overtly partisan. Considers poetry by teens. Has published poetry by Robert Pinsky, Kirsty Karkow, Elisha Porat, Peggy Lyles Wills, Curtis Dunlap, an'ya. *Magnapoets* is 36-40 pages, magazine-sized, digital press print format, saddle-stitched, with a glossy cover with full-sized color photograph or art. Single copy: $5 CAN; subscription: $10 CAN. Make checks payable to Aurora Antonovic.

HOW TO CONTACT Follow submissions guidelines properly and be sure to submit to the appropriate editor and include "Magnapoets" in the subject line. E-mail submissions only. Submit up to 3 poems of free verse and formal poetry, maximum 48 lines including title, to Ursula Gibson at UrsulaTG1@aol.

com; for haiku and tanka, send up to 10 poems at a time, to Aurora Antonovic at Magnapoets@gmail.com; for short stories, submit ONE prose piece, Word length: 250 - 2,500 words to Marie Lecrivain at marie@poeticdiversity.org . Cover letter is preferred. Include a 25-word (or less) bio. Reads submissions in the months of May and October. Time between acceptance and publication is 2-3months. "Each editor edits his/her own section separately. Send submissions to each individual editor as specified. Currently, we have 5 editors: Ursula T. Gibson (free verse and form), Marie Lecrivain (short stories), David Herrle (special features), Guest Editor(haiku and senryu), Aurora Antonovic (tanka)." Never comments on rejected poems. Never publishes theme issues. Guidelines available in magazine and on website. Responds in 2 months. Pays 1 contributor's copy. Acquires first serial rights (magazine is distributed internationally). Rights revert to poets upon publication.

ADDITIONAL INFORMATION "We publish themed anthologies twice a year. For information, see the website."

O THE MAGNOLIA QUARTERLY

P.O. Box 10294, Gulfport MS 39506. E-mail: gcwriters@aol.com. Website: www.gcwriters.org. **Contact:** Phil Levin, editor; John Freeman, poetry editor. Publication of the Gulf Coast Writers Association. Estab. 1999.

MAGAZINES NEEDS *The Magnolia Quarterly* publishes poetry, fiction, nonfiction, reviews, and photography. **Membership required to submit to magazine** (exception: each issue features a non-member poet chosen by the poetry editor). Will consider all styles of poetry. Does not want "pornography, racial or sexist bigotry, far-left or far-right political poems." Has published poetry by Leonard Cirino, Catharine Savage Brosman, Angela Ball, Jack Bedell, and Larry Johnson. *The Magnolia Quarterly* is 40 pages, pocket-sized, stapled, with glossy cover, includes ads. Single copy: $5; subscription: included in $30 GCWA annual dues. Make checks payable to Gulf Coast Writers Association. Editing service offered on all prose.

HOW TO CONTACT Submit 1-5 poems at a time. Lines/poem: open. Considers previously published poems and simultaneous submissions. Prefers e-mail submissions. Cover letter is preferred. Reads submissions year round. Time between acceptance and publication varies. Guidelines available in magazine, for SASE, by e-mail, or on website. No payment. Returns rights to poet upon publication.

CONTEST/AWARD OFFERINGS "Let's Write" contest, with cash prizes for poetry and prose. Additional information available on website.

ALSO OFFERS The Gulf Coast Writers Association, "a nationally recognized organization dedicated to encouraging all writers."

◑ THE MAIN STREET RAG

P.O. Box 690100, Charlotte NC 28227-7001. (704)573-2516. E-mail: editor@mainstreetrag.com. Website: www.MainStreetRag.com. **Contact:** M. Scott Douglass, editor/publisher.

MAGAZINES NEEDS *The Main Street Rag*, published quarterly, prints "poetry, short fiction, essays, interviews, reviews, photos, art. We like publishing good material from people who are interested in more than notching another publishing credit, people who support small independent publishers like ourselves." Will consider "almost anything," but prefers "writing with an edge—either gritty or bitingly humorous. Contributors are advised to visit our website prior to submission to confirm current needs." Has published poetry by Silvia Curbelo, Sean Thomas Dougherty, Denise Duhamel, Cathy Essinger, Ishle Yi Park, and Dennis Must. *The Main Street Rag* is about 130 pages, digest-sized, perfect-bound, with 12-pt laminated color cover. Receives about 5,000 submissions/year; publishes 35-50 poems and 2-4 short stories per issue. Press run is about 600 (300 subscribers, 15 libraries). Single copy: $8; subscription: $24/year, $45 for 2 years.

HOW TO CONTACT Submit 6 pages of poetry at a time. No previously published poems or simultaneous submissions. Cover letter is preferred. "No bios or credits—let the work speak for itself." Time between acceptance and publication is up to 1 year. Guidelines available for SASE, by e-mail, or on website. Responds within 6 weeks. Pays 1 contributor's copy. Acquires first North American print rights.

CONTEST/AWARD OFFERINGS Main Street Rag's Annual Poetry Book Award and Main Street Rag's Annual Chapbook Contest (see separate listings in Contests & Awards).

◐◑◉ THE MALAHAT REVIEW

(250)721-8524. E-mail: malahat@uvic.ca (for queries only). Website: www.malahatreview.ca. **Contact:** John Barton, editor. "We try to achieve a balance of views and styles in each issue. We strive for a mix of the best writing by both established and new writers."

MAGAZINES NEEDS *The Malahat Review*, published quarterly, is "a high-quality, visually appealing literary journal that has earned the praise of notable literary figures throughout North America. Its purpose is to publish and promote poetry, and fiction, and creative nonfiction of a very high standard, both Canadian and international." Wants "various styles, lengths, and themes. The criterion is excellence." Has published poetry by Steven Heighton, George Elliot Clarke, Daryl Hine, and Jan Zwicky. Receives about 2,000 poems/year, accepts about 100. Subscription: $35 CAD for individuals, $50 USD for individuals in the United States, or $20CAD for online subscription, $50 CAD for institutions (or U.S. equivalent). Sample: $16.45 USD.

HOW TO CONTACT Submit 5-10 poems at a time. No previously published poems or simultaneous submissions. No e-mail submmissions; postal submissions only. Include SASE with Canadian stamps or IRC with each submission. Guidelines available for SASE (or SAE and IRC). Responds usually within 3 months. Pays $40 CAD per printed page, 2 contributor's copies, and 1 year's subscription. Acquires first world serial rights. Reviews Canadian books of poetry.

CONTEST/AWARD OFFERINGS Presents the P.K. Page Founders' Award for Poetry, a $1,000 prize to the author of the best poem or sequence of poems to be published in *The Malahat Review*'s quarterly issues during the previous calendar year. Also offers the Open Season Awards, biennial Long Poem Prize, and Far Horizons Award for Poetry (see separate listings in Contests & Awards).

TIPS "Please do not send more than 1 submission at a time: 4-8 poems, 1 piece of creative non-fiction, or 1 short story (do not mix poetry and prose in the same submission). See *The Malahat Review*'s Open Season Awards for poetry and short fiction, creative non-fiction, long poem, and novella contests in the Awards section of our website."

THE MANHATTAN REVIEW

440 Riverside Dr., #38, New York NY 10027. Website: http://themanhattanreview.com. 440 Riverside Dr., #38, New York, NY 10027. E-mail: phfried@earthlink. net. Website: http://themanhattanreview.com. **Contact:** Philip Fried, poetry editor. Estab. 1980.

MAGAZINES NEEDS *The Manhattan Review*, published annually "with ambitions to be semiannual," prints "American writers and foreign writers with something valuable to offer the American scene. We like to think of poetry as a powerful discipline engaged with many other fields." Wants to see "ambitious work. Interested in both lyric and narrative. We select high-quality work from a number of different countries, including the U.S." Does not want "mawkish, sentimental poetry." Has published poetry by Zbigniew Herbert, D. Nurkse, Baron Wormser, Penelope Shuttle, Marilyn Hacker, and Peter Redgrove. *The Manhattan Review* is 208 pages, digest-sized, professionally printed, with glossy card cover. Receives about 400 submissions/year, accepts few ("but I do read everything submitted carefully and with an open mind"). Press run is 500 (400 subscribers, 250 libraries). Single copy: $7.50; subscription: $15. Sample: $9 and 7×10 envelope.

HOW TO CONTACT Submit 3-5 pages of poetry at a time. Simultaneous submissions "discouraged; notification required." Cover letter is required. Include short bio and publication credits. Sometimes comments on poems, "but don't count on it." Responds in 3 months, if possible. Pays in contributor's copies. Staff reviews books of poetry. Send materials for review consideration.

MANOA

(808)956-3070. Fax: (808)956-3083. E-mail: mjournal-l@listserv.hawaii.edu. Website: manoajournal.hawaii. edu. **Contact:** Frank Stewart, Poetry Editor. "High quality literary fiction, poetry, essays, personal narrative. In general, each issue is devoted to new work from Pacific and Asian nations. Our audience is international. US writing need not be confined to Pacific settings or subjects. Please note that we seldom publish unsolicited work."

○ *Manoa* has received numerous awards, and work published in the magazine has been selected for prize anthologies. *Manoa* has received numerous awards, and work published in the magazine has been selected for prize an-

thologies. See website for recently published issues.

MAGAZINES NEEDS *Manoa*, published twice/year, is a general interest literary magazine that considers work "in many forms and styles, regardless of the author's publishing history. However, we are not for the beginning writer. It is best to look at a sample copy of the journal before submitting." Has published poetry by Arthur Sze, Ai, Linda Gregg, Jane Hirshfield, and Ha Jin. *Manoa* is 240 pages, 7x10, offset-printed, flat-spined. Receives about 1,000 poems/year, accepts 1%. Press run is more than 2,500 (several hundred subscribers, 130 libraries, 400 shelf sales). "In addition, *Manoa* is available through Project Muse to about 900 institutional subscribers throughout the world." Subscription: $22/year. Sample: $10.

TIPS "Not accepting unsolicited manuscripts at this time because of commitments to special projects. See website for more information."

THE MARLBORO REVIEW

E-mail: editor@marlbororeview.org. Website: www. marlbororeview.org. **Contact:** Ellen Dudley. The Marlboro Review Inc., P.O. Box 243, Marlboro VT 05344-0243. (802)254-4938. E-mail: editor@marlbororeview.com. Website: www.marlbororeview.com. **Contact:** Ellen Dudley, editor. Open to short fiction and poetry submissions. Include SASE with proper postage, otherwise your work will be discarded unread. Submissions received during the summer break will be returned unread. "Our only criterion for publication is strength of work." Semiannual. Estab. 1996. Circ. 1,000. Length: No line limits known. Check with publisher. Recent contributors include Stephen Dobyns, Joan Aleshire, Jean Valentine, Robert Hill Long, Carol Frost.

○ Open to short fiction and poetry submissions. Include SASE with proper postage, otherwise your work will be discarded unread. Submissions received during the summer break will be returned unread.

TIPS "Check Guidelines for details and restrictions. Open to most themes. We are particularly interested in translation, as well as cultural, scientific, and philosophical issues approached from a writer's sensibility. If you are overseas and must submit electronically, consult with Ellen Dudley before sending any files."

◑◐❸ THE MARTIAN WAVE

P.O. Box 782, Cedar Rapids IA 52406-0782. Website: www.samsdotpublishing.com. P.O. Box 782, Cedar Rapids IA 52406-0782. E-mail: tmwsubmissions@samsdotpublishing.com. Website: www.samsdotpublishing.com. **Contact:** J. Alan Erwine, editor. Estab. 1997. Member: The Speculative Literature Foundation (http://SpeculativeLiterature.org).

MAGAZINES NEEDS *The Martian Wave*, now a print zine, features "science fiction poetry and stories that are related in some way to the exploration and/or settlement of the Solar System." Does not want "anything other than science fiction." Considers poetry by children and teens. Has published poetry by Marge B. Simon, Kristine Ong Muslim, Christina Sng, Aurelio Rico Lopez III, s.c. virtes, and Tyree Campbell. Receives about 150 poems/year, accepts about 16 (12%).

HOW TO CONTACT Submit up to 5 poems at a time. Lines/poem: prefers less than 100. No previously published poems or simultaneous submissions. Accepts e-mail submissions (pasted into body of message); no disk submissions. "Submission should include snail mail address and a short (1-2 lines) bio." Reads submissions year round. Submit seasonal poems 6 months in advance. Time between acceptance and publication is 1-2 months. Sometimes comments on rejected poems. Guidelines available on website. Responds in 4-6 weeks. Pays $5/poem. Acquires first North American serial rights.

◑◐❸ THE MASSACHUSETTS REVIEW

South College, University of Massachusetts, Amherst MA 01003-9934. (413)545-2689. Fax: (413)577-0740. E-mail: massrev@external.umass.edu. Website: www.massreview.org.

MAGAZINES NEEDS *The Massachusetts Review*, published quarterly, prints "fiction, essays, artwork, and excellent poetry of all forms and styles." Has published poetry by Catherine Barnett, Billy Collins, and Dara Wier. *The Massachusetts Review* is digest-sized, offset-printed on bond paper, perfect-bound, with color card cover. Receives about 2,500 poems/year, accepts about 25. Press run is 1,600 (1,100-1,200 subscribers, 1,000 libraries, the rest for shelf sales). Subscription: $27/year U.S., $35 outside U.S., $37 for libraries. Sample: $9 U.S., $12 outside U.S.

HOW TO CONTACT No previously published poems or simultaneous submissions. Reads submissions October 1-May 31 only. "Guidelines are available online at our website, as is our new online submission manager." Responds in 2 months. Pays $25 plus 2 contributor's copies.

TIPS "No manuscripts are considered May-September. Electronic submission process on website. No fax or e-mail submissions. No simultaneous submissions. Shorter rather than longer stories preferred (up to 28-30 pages)." Looks for works that "stop us in our tracks." Manuscripts that stand out use "unexpected language, idiosyncrasy of outlook and are the opposite of ordinary."

◑❸ MATURE YEARS

(615)749-6292. Fax: (615)749-6512. E-mail: matureyears@umpublishing.org.

MAGAZINES NEEDS *Mature Years*, published quarterly, aims to "help persons understand and use the resources of Christian faith in dealing with specific opportunities and problems related to aging. Poems may or may not be overtly religious. Poems should not poke fun at older adults, but may take a humorous look at them." Does not want "sentimentality and saccharine. If using rhymes and meter, make sure they are accurate." *Mature Years* is 112 pages, magazine-sized, perfect-bound, with full-color glossy paper cover. Press run is 55,000. Sample: $6.

HOW TO CONTACT Lines/poem: 16 lines of up to 50 characters maximum. Accepts fax and e-mail submissions (e-mail preferred). Submit seasonal and nature poems for spring from December through February; for summer, March through May; for fall, June through August; and for winter, September through November. Time between acceptance and publication is up to 1 year. Guidelines available for SASE or by e-mail. Responds in 2 months. Pays $1/line upon acceptance.

TIPS "Practice writing dialogue! Listen to people talk; take notes; master dialogue writing! Not easy, but well worth it! Most inquiry letters are far too long. If you can't sell me an idea in a brief paragraph, you're not going to sell the reader on reading your finished article or story."

◑ MEASURE: A REVIEW OF FORMAL POETRY

Department of English, The University of Evansville, 1800 Lincoln Ave., Evansville, IN 47722. (812)488-2963. E-mail: measure@evansville.edu. Submissions:

http://measurepress.com. Website: http://measure.evansville.edu. **Contact:** The Editors. Estab. 2005.

MAGAZINES NEEDS *Measure: A Review of Formal Poetry* is "dedicated to publishing the best metrical, English-language verse from both the United States and abroad. In each issue we strive to bring you the best new poetry from both established and emerging writers, and we also reprint a small sampling of poems from the best books of metrical poetry published the previous year. Likewise, each issue includes interviews with some of our most important contemporary poets and offers short critical essays on the poetry that has helped to shape the craft." Wants "English-language metrical poetry with no particular stanza preference. See our website or a back issue for examples. *Measure* also reprints poems from books; send copy for consideration." Does not want "fixed forms written in free verse; syllabics; quantitative." Has published poetry by Timothy Steele, R.S. Gwynn, Philip Dacey, X.J. Kennedy, Rachel Hadas, and Charles Rafferty. *Measure* is 180 pages, digest-sized, perfect-bound, with glossy cover with color artwork. Receives about 1,500 poems/year, accepts about 10%. Press run is 1,000. Single copy: $10; subscription: $18 for one year, $34 for 2 years, $50 for 3 years. Make checks payable to *Measure.*

HOW TO CONTACT Submit 3-5 poems at a time at submissions website: measurepress.com. Lines/poem: no minimum or maximum. No previously published poems or simultaneous submissions. No e-mail or disk submissions. Cover letter is preferred. "All submissions should be typed. Each poem should include the poet's name and phone number. A self-addressed stamped envelope must accompany the submission." Reads submissions year round. Time between acceptance and publication "depends." Never comments on rejected poems. Guidelines available in magazine, for SASE, or on website. Responds in 3 months, longer in summer. Pays 2 contributor's copies. Acquires one-time rights. Rights revert to poet upon publication.

ADDITIONAL INFORMATION Prints the winners of the annual Howard Nemerov Sonnet Award (see separate listing in Contests & Awards).

THE MENNONITE

722 Main St., Newton KS 67114-1819. (866)866-2872 ext. 34398. Fax: (316)283-0454. E-mail: gordonh@themennonite.org. Website: www.themennonite.org. **Contact:** Gordon Houser, associate editor.

MAGAZINES NEEDS *The Mennonite*, published monthly, seeks "Christian poetry—usually free verse, not too long, with multiple layers of meaning." Does not want "sing-song rhymes or poems that merely describe or try to teach a lesson." Has published poetry by Jean Janzen and Julia Kasdorf. *The Mennonite* is 64 pages, magazine-sized, with full-color cover, includes ads. Receives about 200 poems/year, accepts about 5%. Press run is 10,000 (9,665 subscribers). Single copy: $3; subscription: $46 US. Sample: $3.

HOW TO CONTACT Submit up to 4 poems at a time. Considers previously published poems and simultaneous submissions. Accepts e-mail submissions (preferred). Cover letter is preferred. Time between acceptance and publication is up to 1 year. Seldom comments on rejected poems. Occasionally publishes theme issues. Guidelines available for SASE. Responds in 2 weeks. Pays 1 contributor copy. Acquires first or one-time rights; includes website archiving.

MERIDIAN

University of Virginia, P.O. Box 400145, Charlottesville VA 22904-4145. (434)982-5798. Fax: (434)924-1478. E-mail: MeridianUVA@yahoo.com; meridianpoetry@gmail.com. Website: www.readmeridian.org. **Contact:** Poetry Editor. Estab. 1998.

Work published in *Meridian* has appeared in *The Best American Poetry* and *The Pushcart Prize.*

MAGAZINES NEEDS *Meridian*, published semiannually, prints poetry, fiction, nonfiction, interviews, and reviews. Has published poetry by Joelle Biele, David Kirby, Larissa Szporluk, and Charles Wright. *Meridian* is 190 pages, digest-sized, offset-printed, perfect-bound, with color cover. Receives about 2,500 poems/year, accepts about 30 (less than 1%). Press run is 1,000 (750 subscribers, 15 libraries, 200 shelf sales); 150 distributed free to writing programs. Single copy: $7; subscription: $12/year. Make checks payable to *Meridian.*

HOW TO CONTACT Submit up to 4 poems at a time. Considers simultaneous submissions (with notification of acceptance elsewhere); no previously published poems. No e-mail or disk submissions; accepts postal and online submissions (**$2 upload fee for up to 4 poems**; no fee for postal submissions). Cover letter is preferred. Reads submissions September-May primarily (do not send submissions April 15-August 15; accepts online submissions year round). Time between acceptance and publication is 1-2 months. Seldom comments on rejected poems. Guidelines available on website. Responds in 1-4 months. Always sends prepublication galleys and author contracts. Pays 2 contributor's copies (additional copies available at discount). Reviews books of poetry.

CONTEST/AWARD OFFERINGS *Meridian* Editors' Prize Contest offers annual $1,000 award. Submit online only; see website for formatting details. **Entry fee:** $16, includes one-year subscription to *Meridian* for all US entries or one copy of the prize issue for all international entries. **Deadline:** December or January; see website for current deadline.

MERIDIAN ANTHOLOGY OF CONTEMPORARY POETRY

Attn: Marylin Krepf, 5068 Annunciation Cir., Unit 208, Immokalee FL 34142. E-mail: letarp@aol.com. Website: www.MeridianAnthology.com. **Contact:** Phyliss L. Geller, editor/publisher; Marylin Krepf, literary editor.

MAGAZINES NEEDS *Meridian Anthology of Contemporary Poetry*, next published Volume 7 in 2011, seeks "poetry that is contemporary, insightful, and illuminating; that touches the nerves. It should have color, content, and be deciphering of existence." Does not want vulgarity, clichés. Has published poetry by Elizabeth Swados, Ann McGovern, Gladys Justin Carr, Alan Britt, and Doug Ramspeck. Has reprinted poetry (with poet's permission) by Philip Levine, Jane Hirshfield, Dorianne Laux, Marie Howe, Thomas Lux and C.K. Williams. Sample copy $10, includes postage. Make checks payable to *Meridian Anthology of Contemporary Poetry*.

HOW TO CONTACT Submit 1-5 poems at a time. Lines/poem: 78 maximum. Considers previously published poems and simultaneous submissions. No e-mail or disk submissions. Cover letter is preferred. Must include SASE with sufficient postage if you want your poems returned. Reads submissions all year round. Time between acceptance and publication is up to one year. Seldom comments on rejected poems. Guidelines available for SASE or on website. Responds in 2-6 months, "depending on backlog."

Acquires one-time rights. Please include consent to publish, form is available on website.

ADDITIONAL INFORMATION "Volume 5, anniversary issue featured reprinted poems by Dorianne Laux, Jane Hirshfield, and Marie Howe. Volume 4 featured Jane Hirshfield, Volume 3 featured Philip Levine). Editing services available: please go to our website for information."

●◐⑤ MICHIGAN QUARTERLY REVIEW

(734)764-9265. E-mail: mqr@umich.edu. Website: www.umich.edu/~mqr. "An interdisciplinary journal which publishes mainly essays and reviews, with some high-quality fiction and poetry, for an intellectual, widely read audience."

○ "The Laurence Goldstein Award is a $1,000 annual award to the best poem published in the *Michigan Quarterly Review* during the previous year. The Lawrence Foundation Award is a $1,000 annual award to the best short story published in the *Michigan Quarterly Review* during the previous year."

MAGAZINES NEEDS *Michigan Quarterly Review* is "an interdisciplinary, general interest academic journal that publishes mainly essays and reviews on subjects of cultural and literary interest." Wants all kinds of poetry except light verse. No specifications as to form, length, style, subject matter, or purpose. Has published poetry by Susan Hahn, Campbell McGrath, Carl Phillips, and Cathy Song. *Michigan Quarterly Review* is 160 pages, digest-sized, professionally printed, flat-spined, with glossy card cover. Receives about 1,400 submissions/year, accepts about 30. Press run is 2,000 (1,200 subscribers, half are libraries). Single copy: $7; subscription: $25. Sample: $4.

HOW TO CONTACT No previously published poems or simultaneous submissions. No e-mail submissions. Cover letter is preferred. "It puts a human face on the manuscript. A few sentences of biography is all I want, nothing lengthy or defensive." Prefers typed mss. Publishes theme issues. Upcoming themes available in magazine and on website. Guidelines available for SASE or on website. Responds in 6 weeks. Always sends prepublication galleys. Pays $8-12/page. Acquires first rights only. Reviews books of poetry. "All reviews are commissioned."

CONTEST/AWARD OFFERINGS The Laurence Goldstein Poetry Award, an annual cash prize of $1,000, is given to the author of the best poem to appear in *Michigan Quarterly* during the calendar year. "Established in 2002, the prize is sponsored by the Office of the President of the University of Michigan."

TIPS "Read the journal and assess the range of contents and the level of writing. We have no guidelines to offer or set expectations; every manuscript is judged on its unique qualities. On essays—query with a very thorough description of the argument and a copy of the first page. Watch for announcements of special issues which are usually expanded issues and draw upon a lot of freelance writing. Be aware that this is a university quarterly that publishes a limited amount of fiction and poetry and that it is directed at an educated audience, one that has done a great deal of reading in all types of literature."

◑ ◔ MID-AMERICAN REVIEW

Bowling Green State University, Department of English, Box W, Bowling Green OH 43403. (419)372-2725. E-mail: mikeczy@bgsu.edu. Website: www.bgsu.edu/midamericanreview. **Contact:** Michael Czyzniejewski. "We try to put the best possible work in front of the biggest possible audience. We publish serious fiction and poetry, as well as critical studies in contemporary literature, translations and book reviews."

MAGAZINES NEEDS "Poems should emanate from textured, evocative images, use language with an awareness of how words sound and mean, and have a definite sense of voice. Each line should help carry the poem, and an individual vision must be evident. We encourage new as well as established writers. There is no length limit on individual poems, but please send no more than six poems."

HOW TO CONTACT Submit by mail with SASE or through online submissions form at website.

TIPS "We are seeking translations of contemporary authors from all languages into English; submissions must include the original and proof of permission to translate. We would also like to see more creative nonfiction."

◑ THE MIDWEST QUARTERLY

(620)235-4369; (620)235-4317. E-mail: midwestq@pittstate.edu; smeats@pittstate.edu. Website: www.pittstate.edu/department/english/midwest-quarterly. **Contact:** James B. M. Schick. English Department, Pittsburg State University, Pittsburg, Kansas 66762. (620)235-4689. Fax: (620)235-4686. E-mail: smeats@pittstate.edu. Website: www.pittstate.edu/department/english/midwest-quarterly. *The Midwest Quarterly* publishes "articles on any subject of contemporary interest, particularly literary criticism, political science, philosophy, education, biography, and sociology. Each issue contains a section of poetry usually 12 poems in length." Wants "well-crafted poems, traditional or untraditional, that use intense, vivid, concrete, and/or surrealistic images to explore the mysterious and surprising interactions of the natural and inner human worlds." Does not want "'nature poems,' per se, but if a poem doesn't engage nature in a significant way, as an integral part of the experience it is offering, I am unlikely to be interested in publishing it." Has published poetry by Peter Cooley, Jim Daniels, Naomi Shihab Nye, Jonathan Holden, William Kloefkorn, and Jeanne Murray Walker. *The Midwest Quarterly* is 130 pages, digest-sized, professionally printed, flat-spined, with matte cover. Press run is 650 (600 subscribers, 500 libraries). Receives about 3,500-4,000 poems/year, accepts about 60. Subscription: $15. Sample: $5. "We seek discussions of an analytical and speculative nature and well-crafted poems. Poems of interest to us use intense, vivid, concrete and/or surrealistic images to explore the mysterious and surprising interactions of the nature and inner human worlds."

◑ "For publication in MQ and eligibility for the annual Emmett Memorial Prize competition, the Editors invite submission of articles on any literary topic, but preferably on Victorian or Modern British Literature, Literary Criticism, or the Teaching of Literature. The winner receives an honorarium and invitation to deliver the annual Emmett Memorial Lecture. Contact Dr. Meats, Chairman, English Dept."

MAGAZINES NEEDS *The Midwest Quarterly* publishes "articles on any subject of contemporary interest, particularly literary criticism, political science, philosophy, education, biography, and sociology. Each issue contains a section of poetry usually 12 poems in length." Wants "well-crafted poems, traditional or untraditional, that use intense, vivid, concrete, and/or surrealistic images to explore the mysterious and surprising interactions of the natural and inner human worlds." Does not want "'nature poems,' per se, but if a poem doesn't engage nature in a significant way, as an integral part of the experience it is offering, I am unlikely to be interested in publishing it." Has published poetry by Peter

Cooley, Jim Daniels, Naomi Shihab Nye, Jonathan Holden, William Kloefkorn, and Jeanne Murray Walker. *The Midwest Quarterly* is 130 pages, digest-sized, professionally printed, flat-spined, with matte cover. Press run is 650 (600 subscribers, 500 libraries). Receives about 3,500-4,000 poems/year, accepts about 60. Subscription: $15. Sample: $5.

HOW TO CONTACT Submit no more than 5 poems at a time. Lines/poem: 60 maximum ("occasionally longer if exceptional"). Considers simultaneous submissions; no previously published poems. No fax or e-mail submissions. "Manuscripts should be typed with poet's name on each page. Submissions without SASE cannot be acknowledged." Comments on rejected poems "if the poet or poem seems particularly promising." Occasionally publishes theme issues or issues devoted to the work of a single poet. Guidelines available on website. Responds in 2 months. Pays 2 contributor's copies. Acquires first serial rights. Reviews books of poetry by *Midwest Quarterly*-published poets only.

TIPS "The quality and format of book reviews are of special importance to us. Their purpose is to evaluate the significance of new scholarly work: identify its contribution to knowledge and its deficiencies. See Guidelines before submitting."

MIDWIFERY TODAY

P.O Box 2672, Eugene OR 97402. (541)344-7438. Fax: (541)344-1422. E-mail: mgeditor@midwiferytoday. com. Website: www.midwiferytoday.com. **Contact:** Sarah Harwell, managing editor. (Specialized: childbirth) P.O. Box 2672, Eugene OR 97402-0223. (541)344-7438. Fax: (541)344-1422. E-mail: mgeditor@midwiferytoday.com. Website: www.midwifery-today.com. Established 1986. **Contact:** Sarah Harwell, managing editor. *Midwifery Today*, published quarterly, provides "a voice for midwives and childbirth educators. We are a midwifery magazine. Subject must be birth or birth profession related." *Midwifery Today* is 75 pages, magazine-sized, offset-printed, saddle-stapled, with glossy card cover with b&w photos and b&w artwork, includes ads. Press run is 5,000 (3,000 subscribers,1,000 shelf sales). Subscription: $50. Sample: $10. No previously published poems. Time between acceptance and publication is 1-2 years. Seldom comments on rejected poems. Publishes theme issues. Upcoming themes and deadlines available on

website. Guidelines available for SASE or on website. Responds in 6 months.

○ "Through networking and education, *Midwifery Today*'s mission is to return midwifery to its rightful position in the family; to make midwifery care the norm throughout the world; and to redefine midwifery as a vital partnership with women."

HOW TO CONTACT Accepts e-mail submissions (pasted into body of message or as attachment). Cover letter is required.

TIPS "Use Chicago Manual of Style formatting."

○ ⑤ MILLER'S POND

(570)376-3361. Fax: (570)376-2674. E-mail: mail@ handhpress.com (C.J. Houghtaling; inquiries only); mpwebeditor@yahoo.com (Julie Damerell). Website: www. millerspondpoetry.com. **Contact:** C.J. Houghtaling, publisher; Julie Damerell, editor. H&H Press, 980 Locey Creek Rd., Middlebury Center, PA 16935. (570)376-3361. Fax: (570)376-2674. E-mail: mail@handhpress.com (C.J. Houghtaling; inquiries only); mpwebeditor@yahoo.com (Julie Damerell). Website: www. millerspondpoetry.com. **Contacts:** C.J. Houghtaling, publisher; Julie Damerell, editor. Estab. 1987. *miller's pond*, published online, features contemporary poetry, interviews, reviews, and markets. Wants "contemporary poetry that is fresh, accessible, energetic, vivid, and flows with language and rhythm." Does not want "religious, horror, pornographic, vulgar, rhymed, preachy, lofty, trite, or overly sentimental work." Has published poetry by Vivian Shipley, Barbara Crooker, Philip Memmer, and Shoshauna Shy.

MAGAZINES NEEDS *miller's pond*, published online, features contemporary poetry, interviews, reviews, and markets. Wants "contemporary poetry that is fresh, accessible, energetic, vivid, and flows with language and rhythm." Does not want "religious, horror, pornographic, vulgar, rhymed, preachy, lofty, trite, or overly sentimental work." Has published poetry by Vivian Shipley, Barbara Crooker, Philip Memmer, and Shoshauna Shy.

HOW TO CONTACT *miller's pond* is exclusively an e-zine and does not publish in hard copy format. "All submissions must be sent electronically from our website. Mail sent through the post office will be returned. No payment for accepted poems or reviews. Current guidelines, updates, and changes are always available on our website. Check there first before submitting anything."

ADDITIONAL INFORMATION Books are available for sale via website, phone, or fax.

MINAS TIRITH EVENING-STAR: JOURNAL OF THE AMERICAN TOLKIEN SOCIETY

American Tolkien Society, P.O. Box 97, Highland MI 48357-0097. Website: www.americantolkiensociety. org. American Tolkien Society, P.O. Box 97, Highland MI 48357-0097. E-mail: editor@americantolkiensociety.org. Website: www.americantolkiensociety.org. **Contact:** Amalie A. Helms, editor. Estab. 1967. *Minas Tirith Evening-Star: Journal of the American Tolkien Society*, published quarterly, uses poetry of fantasy about Middle-Earth and Tolkien. Considers poetry by children and teens. Has published poetry by Thomas M. Egan, Anne Etkin, Nancy Pope, and Martha Benedict. *Minas Tirith Evening-Star* is digest-sized, offset-printed from typescript, with cartoon-like b&w graphics. Press run is 400. Single copy: $3.50; subscription: $12.50. Sample: $3. Make checks payable to American Tolkien Society.

MAGAZINES NEEDS *Minas Tirith Evening-Star: Journal of the American Tolkien Society*, published quarterly, uses poetry of fantasy about Middle-Earth and Tolkien. Considers poetry by children and teens. Has published poetry by Thomas M. Egan, Anne Etkin, Nancy Pope, and Martha Benedict. *Minas Tirith Evening-Star* is digest-sized, offset-printed from typescript, with cartoon-like b&w graphics. Press run is 400. Single copy: $3.50; subscription: $12.50. Sample: $3. Make checks payable to American Tolkien Society.

HOW TO CONTACT Considers previously published poems ("maybe"); no simultaneous submissions. Accepts e-mail and disk submissions. Cover letter is preferred. Sometimes comments on rejected poems. Occasionally publishes theme issues. Guidelines available for SASE or by e-mail. Responds in 2 weeks. Sometimes sends prepublication galleys. Pays 1 contributor's copy. Reviews related books of poetry; length depends on the volume ("a sentence to several pages"). Send materials for review consideration.

ADDITIONAL INFORMATION Under the imprint of W.W. Publications, publishes collections of poetry of fantasy about Middle-Earth and Tolkien. Books/chapbooks are 50-100 pages. Publishes 2 chapbooks/

year. For book or chapbook consideration, submit sample poems.

ALSO OFFERS Membership in the American Tolkien Society is open to all, regardless of country of residence, and entitles one to receive the quarterly journal. Dues are $12.50/year to addresses in U.S., $12.50 in CanadAnd $15 elsewhere. Sometimes sponsors contests.

THE MINNESOTA REVIEW

Virginia Tech, ASPECT, 202 Major Williams Hall (0192), Blacksburg VA 24061. E-mail: editors@theminnesotareview.org; submissions@theminnesotareview.org. Website: www.theminnesotareview.org. **Contact:** Janell Watson, editor.

MAGAZINES NEEDS *The Minnesota Review*, published biannually, features quality poetry, short fiction, and critical essays. Each issue is about 200 pages, digest-sized, flat-spined, with glossy card cover. Press run is 1,000 (400 subscribers). Also available online. Subscription: $30/2 years for individuals, $60/year for institutions. Sample: $15.

HOW TO CONTACT Submit up to 5 poems every 3 months online. Reads poetry August 1-November 1 and January 1-April 1. Payment is 2 contributor's copies.

M.I.P. COMPANY

Website: www.mipco.com. **Contact:** Michael Peltsman. (Specialized: Russian erotica) P.O. Box 27484, Minneapolis MN 55427. (763)544-5915. E-mail: mp@mipco.com. Website: www.mipco.com. Established in 1984. **Contact:** Michael Peltsman."The publisher of controversial Russian literature (erotic poetry)."
C Seldom comments on rejected poems.

HOW TO CONTACT Considers simultaneous submissions; no previously published poems. Responds to queries in one month. Seldom comments on rejected poems.

MISSISSIPPI REVIEW

Univ. of Southern Mississippi, 118 College Dr., #5144, Hattiesburg MS 39406-0001. (601)266-4321. Fax: (601)266-5757. E-mail: elizabeth@mississippireview.com. Website: www.mississippireview.com.

"We do not accept unsolicited manuscripts except under the rules and guidelines of the *Mississippi Review* Prize Competition. See website for guidelines."

HOW TO CONTACT "Literary publication for those interested in contemporary literature—writers, editors who read to be in touch with current modes. We do not accept unsolicited manuscripts except under the rules and guidelines of the *Mississippi Review* Prize Competition. See website for guidelines."

MOBIUS: THE JOURNAL OF SOCIAL CHANGE

Website: mobiusmagazine.com. (Specialized: Socially and politically relevant poetry and fiction) 505 Christianson St, Madison WI 53714.608-242-1009. E-mail: fmschep@charter.net. Website: mobiusmagazine.com. Established 1989 **Contact:** F.J. Bergmann, poetry editor or Fred Schepartz, general editor

MAGAZINES NEEDS *Mobius: The Journal of Social Change*, published quarterly, prints socially and politically relevant poetry and fiction and is distributed free in Madison, WI, and to libraries and subscribers. Wants any form of poetry on themes of social change. Does not want heavy-handed, transparent didacticism. Considers poetry by teens; however, the publication is not directed at children. Has published poetry by Rob Carney, Wade German, Michael Kriesel, Simon Perchik, Wendy Vardaman. *Mobius* is published quarterly online. Receives about 700 poems/year, accepts less than 30. Submit 3-5 poems at a time. Considers simultaneous submissions and poems previously published in print. Prefers e-mail submissions. Cover letter is unnecessary, but include short bio. Reads submissions year-round. Time between acceptance and publication is up to 6 months. Sometimes comments on rejected poems. Never publishes theme issues. Guidelines on website. Usually responds in 3 days; query if no response within one week. Acquires one-time electronic rights; rights revert to poets upon publication.

HOW TO CONTACT Submit 5 poems at a time. Considers previously published poems and simultaneous submissions. Accepts e-mail submissions (pasted into body of message); no fax or disk submissions. Cover letter is unnecessary. Include short bio and mailing address; postal submissions must include e-mail address or SASE. Reads submissions year round. Time between acceptance and publication is up to 6 months. Sometimes comments on rejected poems. Never publishes theme issues. Guidelines available by e-mail and on website. Responds in 3 months. Pays 2 contributor's copies. Acquires

one-time and electronic rights (reserves right to publish on website also). Rights revert to poets upon publication.

THE MOCCASIN

The League of Minnesota Poets, 427 N. Gorman St., Blue Earth MN 56013. (507)526-5321. Website: www. mnpoets.org. The League of Minnesota Poets, 427 N. Gorman St., Blue Earth, MN 56013. (507)526-5321. Website: www.mnpoets.org. **Contact:** Meredith R. Cook, editor. Estab. 1937. *he Moccasin*, published annually in October, is the literary magazine of The League of Minnesota Poets. **Membership is required to submit work.** Wants "all forms of poetry. Prefer strong short poems." Does not want "profanity or obscenity." Considers poetry by children and teens who are student members of The League of Minnesota Poets (write grade level on poems submitted). Has published poetry by Diane Glancy, Laurel Winter, Susan Stevens Chambers, Doris Stengel, Jeanette Hinds, and Charmaine Donovan. *The Moccasin* is 40 pages, digest-sized, offset-printed, stapled, with 80 lb. linen-finish text cover with drawing and poem. Receives about 190 poems/year, accepts about 170. Press run is 200. Single copy: $5.25; subscription: free with LOMP membership. *The Moccasin*, published annually in October, is the literary magazine of The League of Minnesota Poets. **Membership is required to submit work.** Wants "all forms of poetry. Prefer strong short poems." Does not want "profanity or obscenity." Considers poetry by children and teens who are student members of The League of Minnesota Poets (write grade level on poems submitted). Has published poetry by Diane Glancy, Laurel Winter, Susan Stevens Chambers, Doris Stengel, Jeanette Hinds, and Charmaine Donovan. *The Moccasin* is 40 pages, digest-sized, offset-printed, stapled, with 80 lb. linen-finish text cover with drawing and poem. Receives about 190 poems/year, accepts about 170. Press run is 200. Single copy: $5.25; subscription: free with LOMP membership.

HOW TO CONTACT Submit 6 or more poems at a time. Lines/poem: 24 maximum (unless poem has won a prize from the National Federation of State Poetry Societies in its annual competition). Considers previously published poems; no simultaneous submissions. No disk submissions. Cover letter is preferred. "No poems will be returned and no questions answered without a SASE." Reads submissions year round (deadline for each year's issue is mid-July). Sometimes comments on rejected poems. Guidelines available in magazine. No payment; poet receives contributor's copy as part of LOMP membership subscription. **Annual membership dues of $20.00 (Student membership dues $10.00) are payable by January 1** each year to Stash Hempeck, Membership Chair, P.O. Box 57, Hendrum, MN 56550. Acquires one-time rights.

ALSO OFFERS To become a member of The League of Minnesota Poets, send $20 ($10 if high school student or younger) to Angela Foster, LOMP Treasurer, 30036 St. Croix Rd, Pine City MN 55063. Make checks payable to LOMP. You do not have to live in Minnesota to become a member of LOMP. "Membership in LOMP automatically makes you a member of the National Federation of State Poetry Societies, which makes you eligible to enter its contests at a cheaper (members') rate."

⭕🌝 MODERN HAIKU

E-mail: trumbullc@comcast.net. Website: http://modernhaiku.org. "*Modern Haiku* publishes high quality material only. Haiku and related genres, articles on haiku, haiku book reviews, and translations comprise its contents. It has an international circulation; subscribers include many university, school, and public libraries."

MAGAZINES NEEDS *Modern Haiku*, published 3 times/year in February, June, and October, is "the foremost international journal of English-language haiku and criticism. We are devoted to publishing only the very best haiku. We also publish articles on haiku and have the most complete review section of haiku books." Wants "haiku in English (including translations into English) that incorporate the traditional aesthetics of the haiku genre, but which may be innovative as to subject matter, mode of approach or angle of perception, and form of expression. No tanka or renku. No special consideration given to work by children and teens." Has published haiku by Roberta Beary, Billy Collins, Lawrence Ferlinghetti, Carolyn Hall, Sharon Olds, Gary Snyder, John Stevenson, George Swede, and Cor van den Heuvel. *Modern Haiku* is 120 pages (average), digest-sized, printed on heavy quality stock, with full-color cover illustrations 4-page full-color art sections. Receives about 15,000-14,000 submissions/year, accepts about 1,000. Press run is 650. Subscription:

$30 ppd. Sample: $13 ppd in the U.S.

HOW TO CONTACT Submit "a maximum of 20 haiku on one or two letter-sized sheets." No e-mail submissions from North America. No previously published haiku or simultaneous submissions. Put name and address on each sheet. Include SASE. Guidelines available for SASE or on website. Responds in 4-6 weeks. Pays $1/haiku; no contributor's copies. Acquires first international serial rights. Reviews of books of haiku by staff and freelancers by invitation in 350-1,000 words, usually single-book format. Send materials for review consideration with complete ordering information.

CONTEST/AWARD OFFERINGS Sponsors the annual Robert Spiess Memorial Haiku Competition. Guidelines available for SASE or on website.

TIPS "Study the history of haiku, read books about haiku, learn the aesthetics of haiku and methods of composition. Write about your sense perceptions of the suchness of entities; avoid ego-centered interpretations."

⭕ MUDFISH

Box Turtle Press, 184 Franklin St., New York NY 10013. (212)219-9278. E-mail: mudfishmag@aol.com. Website: www.mudfish.org. **Contact:** Jill Hoffman, editor. Box Turtle Press, 184 Franklin St., New York, NY 10013. (212)219-9278. E-mail: mudfishmag@aol.com. Website: www.mudfish.org. **Contact:** Jill Hoffman, editor. *Mudfish*, published annually by Box Turtle Press, is an annual journal of poetry and art. Wants "free verse with energy, intensity, and originality of voice, mastery of style, the presence of passion." Has published poetry by Charles Simic, Jennifer Belle, Stephanie Dickinson, Ronald Wardall, Doug Dorph, and John Ashberry. Press run is 1,200. Single copy: $12 plus $3.50 subscription: $24 for 2 years (price includes s&h).

MAGAZINES NEEDS *Mudfish*, published annually by Box Turtle Press, is an annual journal of poetry and art. Wants "free verse with energy, intensity, and originality of voice, mastery of style, the presence of passion." Has published poetry by Charles Simic, Jennifer Belle, Stephanie Dickinson, Ronald Wardall, Doug Dorph, and John Ashberry. Press run is 1,200. Single copy: $12 plus $3.50 subscription: $24 for 2 years (price includes s&h).

HOW TO CONTACT Submit 4-6 poems at a time. No previously published poems or simultaneous submissions. No e-mail submissions; postal submissions only. Responds "immediately to three months." Pays one contributor's copy.

CONTEST/AWARD OFFERINGS Sponsors the Mudfish Poetry Prize Award of $1,000. **Entry fee:** $15 for up to 3 poems, $3 for each additional poem. **Deadline:** varies. Guidelines available for SASE.

ALSO OFFERS Also publishes Mudfish Individual Poet Series #6 marbles, by Mary Du Passage.

MUDLARK: AN ELECTRONIC JOURNAL OF POETRY & POETICS

Dept. of English, University of North Florida, Jacksonville FL 32224-2645. (904)620-2273. Fax: (904)620-3940. E-mail: mudlark@unf.edu. Website: www.unf.edu/mudlark. **Contact:** William Slaughter, editor.

MAGAZINES NEEDS *Mudlark: An Electronic Journal of Poetry & Poetics*, published online "irregularly, but frequently," offers 3 formats: issues of *Mudlark* "are the electronic equivalent of print chapbooks; posters are the electronic equivalent of print broadsides; and flash poems are poems that have news in them, poems that feel like current events. The poem is the thing at *Mudlark*, and the essay about it. As our full name suggests, we will consider accomplished work that locates itself anywhere on the spectrum of contemporary practice. We want poems, of course, but we want essays, too, that make us read poems (and write them?) differently somehow. Although we are not innocent, we do imagine ourselves capable of surprise. The work of hobbyists is not for *Mudlark*." Has published poetry by Sherman Alexie, Denise Duhamel, T. R. Hummer, Kurt Brown, Susan Kelly-DeWitt, and Michael Hettich. *Mudlark* is archived and permanently on view at www.unf.edu/mudlark.

HOW TO CONTACT Submit any number of poems at a time. "Prefers not to receive multiple submissions but will consider them if informed of the fact, up front, and if notified immediately when poems are accepted elsewhere. Considers previously published work only as part of a Mudlark issue, the electronic equivalent of a print chapbook, and only if the previous publication is acknowledged in a note that covers the sumbission. Only poems that have not been previously published will be considered for Mudlark posters, the electronic equivalent of print broadsides, or for Mudlark flashes." Accepts e-mail or USPS submissions with SASE; no fax submissions. Cover letter is optional. Time between acceptance

and publication is no more than 3 months. Seldom comments on rejected poems. Guidelines available for SASE, by e-mail, or on website. Responds in "1 day to 1 month, depending.." Always sends prepublication galleys "in the form of inviting the author to proof the work on a private website that *Mudlark* maintains for that purpose." No payment; however, "one of the things we can do at *Mudlark* to 'pay' our authors for their work is point to it here and there. We can tell our readers how to find it, how to subscribe to it, and how to buy it—if it is for sale. Toward that end, we maintain A-Notes on the authors we publish. We call attention to their work." Acquires one-time rights.

MYTHIC DELIRIUM

3514 Signal Hill Ave. NW, Roanoke VA 24017-5148. E-mail: mythicdelirium@gmail.com. Website: www.mythicdelirium.com. **Contact:** Mike Allen, editor. 3514 Signal Hill Ave. NW, Roanoke, VA 24017-5148. E-mail: mythicdelirium@gmail.com. Website: www.mythicdelirium.com. **Contact:** Mike Allen, editor. Estab. 1998.

MAGAZINES NEEDS *Mythic Delirium*, published biannually, is "a journal of speculative poetry for the new millennium. All forms considered. Must fit within the genres we consider, though we have published some mainstream verse." Does not want "forced rhyme, corny humor, jarringly gross sexual material, gratuitous obscenity, handwritten manuscripts." Has published poetry by Sonya Taaffe, Theodora Goss, Joe Haldeman, Ursula K. Le Guin, Ian Watson, and Jane Yolen. *Mythic Delirium* is 32 pages, digest-sized, saddle-stapled, with color cover art, includes house ads. Receives about 750 poems/year, accepts about 5%. Press run is 150. Subscription: $9/year, $16/2 years. Sample: $5. Make checks payable to Mike Allen. Member: Science Fiction Poetry Association, Science Fiction & Fantasy Writers of America.

HOW TO CONTACT Submit up to 6 poems at a time. No previously published poems or simultaneous submissions. Prefers electronic submissions; no disk submissions. Cover letter is preferred. Time between acceptance and publication is 9 months. Often comments on rejected poems. Guidelines available for SASE, by e-mail, or on website. Responds in 5 weeks. Pays $5/poem, plus 1 contributor's copy. Acquires first North American serial rights. **"Reading periods: March 1-May 1 for the Summer/Fall issue**

and August 1-October 1 for the Winter/Spring issue. Closed to submissions all other times."

TIPS "*Mythic Delirium* isn't easy to get into, but we publish newcomers in every issue. Show us how ambitious you can be, and don't give up."

ⓘ NASSAU REVIEW

Nassau Community College, English Dept. Y9, 1 Education Dr., Garden City NY 11530-6793. E-mail: christina.rau@ncc.edu. **Contact:** Christina Rau, editor. "The Nassau Review, published annually, welcomes submissions of many genres, preferring work that is innovative, captivating, well-crafted, and unique, work that crosses boundaries of genres and tradition. New and seasoned writers are both welcome. All work must be in English. Simultaneous submission accepted. No children's lit, fan fiction, or previously published work (online included). Full guidelines will be available at www.ncc.edu. Email submissions in the body of the email only with the subject line indicating genre and your full name. No attachments. No hard copies. Nassau Review is about 190 pages, digest-sized, flat-spined. Press run is 1,100. Sample: free. Contact: Christina M. Rau, editor. Email: christina.rau@ncc.edu. Submit 3-5 poems with 50 lines max each or 1 prose piece with 3,000 words max. Reading period: September 1—February 1. Responds in up to 4 months. Pays 2 contributor's copies. Sponsors an annual aitjprs awards contest with two $250 awards. Check the website for announcements."

TIPS "We look for narrative drive, perceptive characterization and professional competence. Write concretely. Does not want over-elaborate details, and avoid digressions."

●⊗ THE NATION

33 Irving Place, 8th Floor, New York NY 10003. Website: www.thenation.com. Steven Brower, art director. **Contact:** Jordan Davis, poetry editor. **Contact:** Jordan Davis, poetry editor. *The Nation*, published weekly, is a journal of left/liberal opinion, with arts coverage that includes poetry. The only requirement for poetry is "excellence." Has published poetry by W.S. Merwin, Maxine Kumin, James Merrill, May Swenson, Edward Hirsch, and Charles Simic. Submit up to 3 poems at a time, no more than 8 poems within the calendar year. No simultaneous submissions. No fax, e-mail, or disk submissions; send by first-class mail only. No reply without SASE. *The Nation*, published weekly, is a journal of left/liberal opinion, with arts

coverage that includes poetry. The only requirement for poetry is "excellence." Has published poetry by W.S. Merwin, Maxine Kumin, James Merrill, May Swenson, Edward Hirsch, and Charles Simic. Submit up to 3 poems at a time, no more than 8 poems within the calendar year. No simultaneous submissions. No fax, e-mail, or disk submissions; send by first-class mail only. No reply without SASE.

⊙ Poetry published by *The Nation* has been included in *The Best American Poetry*.

HOW TO CONTACT *The Nation* welcomes unsolicited poetry submissions. You may send up to three poems at a time, and no more than eight poems during a calendar year. Send poems by first-class mail, accompanied by a SASE. Does not reply to or return poems sent by fax or e-mail or submitted without an SASE. Submissions are not accepted from June 1 to September 15. Manuscripts may be mailed to: Jordan Davis, poetry editor.

● THE NATIONAL POETRY REVIEW

P.O. Box 2080, Aptos CA 95001-2080. E-mail: editor@nationalpoetryreview.com; nationalpoetryreview@yahoo.com. Website: www.nationalpoetryreview.com. **Contact:** C.J. Sage, Editor.

Ⓒ Poetry appearing in *The National Poetry Review* has also appeared in *The Pushcart Prize*.

MAGAZINES NEEDS *The National Poetry Review* seeks "distinction, innovation, and joie de vivre. We agree with Frost about delight and wisdom. We believe in rich sound. We believe in the beautiful— even if that beauty is not in the situation of the poem but simply the sounds of the poem, the images, or (and, ideally) the way the poem stays in the reader's mind long after it's been read." TNPR considers both experimental and 'mainstream' work." Does not want "overly self-centered or confessional poetry." Has published poetry by Bob Hicok, Jennifer Michael Hecht, Larissa Szplorluk, Margot Schilpp, Nance Van Winkel, and Ted Kooser. *The National Poetry Review* is 80 pages, perfect-bound, with full-color cover. Accepts less than 1% of submissions received. Single copy: $15; subscription: $15/year. Make checks payable to TNPR only.

HOW TO CONTACT Submit 3-5 poems at a time. Considers simultaneous submissions "with notification only." Submissions are accepted through e-mail only. Submit only between December 1 and February 28 unless you are a subscriber or benefactor. Put your name in the subject line of your e-mail and send to tnprsubmissions@yahoo.com." Bio is required. Subscribers and benefactors may submit any time during the year (please write 'subscriber' or 'benefactor' in the subject line). See website before submitting. Time between acceptance and publication is no more than 1 year. "The editor makes all publishing decisions." Sometimes comments on rejected poems. Guidelines available in magazine or on website. Usually responds in about 1-12 weeks. Pays 1 contributor's copy "and small honorarium if funds are available." Acquires first rights.

CONTEST/AWARD OFFERINGS The Finch Prize for Poetry, The Laureate Prize for Poetry, and *The National Poetry Review* Book Prize (see separate listings in Contests & Awards).

◑ NATURAL BRIDGE

Dept. of English, University of Missouri-St. Louis, One University Blvd., St. Louis MO 63121. (314)516-7327. Website: www.umsl.edu/~natural. **Contact:** Editor. Dept. of English, University of Missouri-St. Louis, One University Blvd., St. Louis, MO 63121. (314)516-7327. E-mail:natural@umsl.edu. Website: www.umsl.edu/~natural. **Contact:** Editor. Member: CLMP.

MAGAZINES NEEDS *Natural Bridge*, published biannually, seeks "fresh, innovative poetry, both free and formal, on any subject. We want poems that work on first and subsequent readings—poems that entertain and resonate and challenge our readers. *Natural Bridge* also publishes fiction, essays, and translations." Has published poetry by Ross Gay, Beckian Fritz Goldberg, Joy Harjo, Bob Hicok, Sandra Kohler, and Timothy Liu. *Natural Bridge* is 150-200 pages, digest-sized, printed on 60 lb. opaque recycled, acid-free paper, true binding, with 12 pt. coated glossy or matte cover. Receives about 1,200 poems/year, accepts about 1%. Press run is 1,000 (200 subscribers, 50 libraries). Single copy: $10; subscription: $15/year, $25/2 years. Make checks payable to *Natural Bridge*. Member: CLMP.

HOW TO CONTACT Submit 4-6 poems at a time. Lines/poem: no limit. Considers simultaneous submissions; no previously published poems. No e-mail or disk submissions. "Submissions should be typewritten, with name and address on each page. Do not staple manuscripts. Send SASE." Reads submissions July 1-August 31 and November 1-December 31. Time between acceptance and publication is 9

months. "Work is read and selected by the guest-editor and editor, along with editorial assistants made up of graduate students in our MFA program. We publish work by both established and new writers." Sometimes comments on rejected poems. Sometimes publishes theme issues. Upcoming themes available on website. Guidelines available in magazine or on website. Responds in 6 months after the close of the submission period. Sometimes sends prepublication galleys. Pays 2 contributor's copies plus one-year subscription. Rights revert to author upon publication.

TIPS "We look for fresh stories, extremely well written, on any subject. We publish mainstream literary fiction. We want stories that work on first and subsequent readings—stories, in other words, that both entertain and resonate. Study the journal. Read all of the fiction in it, especially in fiction-heavy issues like numbers 4 and 11."

NAUGATUCK RIVER REVIEW

P.O. Box 368, Westfield MA 01085. E-mail: naugatuckriver@aol.com. Website: http://naugatuckriverreview.wordpress.com/. **Contact:** Lori Desrosiers, Publisher.

MAGAZINES NEEDS The *Naugatuck River Review*, published semiannually, "is a literary journal for great narrative poetry looking for narrative poetry of high caliber, where the narrative is compressed with a strong emotional core." Considers poetry by teens. Has published poetry by Leslea Newman, Patricia Smith, Lyn Lifshin, Jeff Friedman, Pam Uschuk, Patricia Fargnoli. *Naugatuck River Review* is approx. 100 pages, digest-sized, perfect-bound with paper and artwork cover. Receives about 2,000 poems/year, accepts about 170. Press run is print-on-demand. Single copy: $15; Subscription (starting with next issue): $20/year. Make checks payable to *Naugatuck River Review*. Electronic submissions only go to website for guidelines.

HOW TO CONTACT Submit 3 poems at a time. Lines/poem: 50. Prefers unpublished poems but will consider simultaneous submissions. Accepts online submissions through submission manager; no fax or disk. Include a brief bio and mailing information. Reads submissions January 1-March 1 and July 1-September 1 for contest. Time between acceptance and publication is 2-3 months. "We have six poetry editors on staff and submissions are blind-read." Never comments on rejected poems. Sometimes publishes theme issues. Guidelines available in magazine and on website. Responds in 2-12 weeks. Always sends prepublication galleys. Pays 1 contributor's copy. Acquires first North American serial rights.

◐◑ NECROLOGY SHORTS

Isis International, P.O. Box 510232, Saint Louis MO 63151. E-mail: editor@necrologyshorts.com; submit@ necrologyshorts.com. Website: www.necrologyshorts. com. **Contact:** John Ferguson, editor. Consumer publication published online daily and through Amazon Kindle. Also offers an annual collection. *"Necrology Shorts* is an online publication which publishes fiction, articles, cartoons, artwork, and poetry daily. Embracing the Internet, e-book readers, and new technology, we aim to go beyond the long time standard of a regular publication to bringing our readers a daily flow of entertainment. We will also be publishing an annual collection for each year in print, e-book reader, and Adobe PDF format. Our main genre is suspense horror similar to H.P. Lovecraft and/or Robert E. Howard. We also publish science fiction and fantasy. We would love to see work continuing the Cthulhu Mythos, but we accept all horror. We also hold contests, judged by our readers, to select the top stories and artwork. Winners of contests receive various prizes, including cash."

MAGAZINES NEEDS *Necrology Shorts*, published online daily and through Amazon Kindle, is seeking avante-garde, free verse, haiku, light-verse, and traditional poetry in the genres of horror, fantasy, and science fiction. "We will also be publishing an annual collection for each year in print, e-book reader, and Adobe PDF format. Our main genre is suspense horror similar to H.P. Lovecraft and/or Robert E. Howard. We also publish science fiction and fantasy. We would love to see work continuing the Cthulhu Mythos, but we accept all horror." Buys 500 poems/year.

HOW TO CONTACT Submit up to 5 poems at one time. Length: 4-100 lines.

TIPS *"Necrology Shorts* is looking to break out of the traditional publication types to use the Internet, e-book readers, and other technology. We not only publish works of authors and artists, we let them use their published works to brand themselves and further their profits of their hard work. We love to see traditional short fiction and artwork, but we also look

forward to those that go beyond that to create multimedia works. The best way to get to us is to let your creative side run wild and not send us the typical fare. Don't forget that we publish horror, sci-fi, and fantasy. We expect deranged, warped, twisted, strange, sadistic, and things that question sanity and reality."

◑ NERVE COWBOY

Website: www.jwhagins.com/nervecowboy.html. **Contact:** Joseph Shields or Jerry Hagins. P.O. Box 4973, Austin, TX 78765. Website: www.jwhagins.com/ nervecowboy.html. *Nerve Cowboy*, published biannually, features contemporary poetry, short fiction, and b&w drawings. Editors will also consider color artwork for the front cover of an issue. "Open to all forms, styles, and subject matter, preferring writing that speaks directly and minimizes literary devices." Wants "poetry of experience and passion which can find that raw nerve and ride it. We are always looking for that rare writer who inherently knows what word comes next." Has published poetry by Mather Schneider, Suzanne Allen, Micki Myers, Charles Harper Webb, Karl Koweski, and David J. Thompson. *Nerve Cowboy* is 64 pages, 7x8$\frac{1}{2}$, attractively printed, saddle-stapled, with color artwork cover. Accepts about 5% of submissions received. Press run is 400. Subscription: $22 for 4 issues. Sample: $6."*Nerve Cowboy* publishes adventurous, comical, disturbing, thought-provoking, accessible poetry and fiction. We like to see work sensitive enough to make the hardest hard-ass cry, funny enough to make the most hopeless brooder laugh and disturbing enough to make us all glad we're not the author of the piece."

MAGAZINES NEEDS *Nerve Cowboy*, published biannually, features contemporary poetry, short fiction, and b&w drawings. Editors will also consider color artwork for the front cover of an issue. "Open to all forms, styles, and subject matter, preferring writing that speaks directly and minimizes literary devices." Wants "poetry of experience and passion which can find that raw nerve and ride it. We are always looking for that rare writer who inherently knows what word comes next." Has published poetry by Mather Schneider, Suzanne Allen, Micki Myers, Charles Harper Webb, Karl Koweski, and David J. Thompson. *Nerve Cowboy* is 64 pages, 7x8$\frac{1}{2}$, attractively printed, saddle-stapled, with color artwork cover. Accepts about 5% of submissions received. Press run is 400. Subscription: $22 for 4 issues. Sample: $6.

HOW TO CONTACT Submit 3-7 poems at a time. No e-mail submissions. Considers previously published poems with notification; no simultaneous submissions. Cover letter is preferred. Include bio and credits. Put name and mailing address on each page of ms. Seldom comments on rejected poems. Guidelines available for SASE or on website. Responds within 3 months. Pays 1 contributor's copy. Acquires first or one-time rights.

CONTEST/AWARD OFFERINGS The *Nerve Cowboy* Chapbook Contest (see separate listing Contests & Awards).

TIPS "We look for writing which is very direct and elicits a visceral reaction in the reader. Read magazines you submit to in order to get a feel for what the editors are looking for. Write simply and from the gut."

❶ NEW COLLAGE

New College of Florida, New College of Florida, c/o WRC, 5800 Bayshore Rd., Sarasota FL 34243. E-mail: newcollagemag@gmail.com. Website: newcollagemag. wordpress.com. **Contact:** Alexis Orgera, editor. "*New CollAge* accepts unsolicited submissions of previously unpublished poetry, short fiction (short shorts, fewer than 1,500/words), creative nonfiction, artwork (especially that of the collage-inspired variety), and hybrids thereof from August-May each year for both our print issue and web exclusives. Submissions received in June and July will not be read. Note that we publish primarily poetry."

> ❑ *New CollAge is not currently accepting submissions as we take two months to recalibrate and organize our online submission system. If you have sent us work within the past several months, please consider resending when we've reopened submissions.* (1-17-11)

MAGAZINES NEEDS *New CollAge*, published annually, is a "journal of new writing and visual art produced by a general editor alongside a staff of New College of Florida undergraduates who subscribe to the notion that a collage is an assemblage of different voices that merge to create new conversations."

HOW TO CONTACT E-mail no more than 1500 words in a single Word document. "Do not submit again until you've heard back." Note "submission" in the subject line, as well as the type of work you're submitting." Accepts simultaneous submissions. Reads September-May. Responds in 2-6 months.

ADDITIONAL INFORMATION Acquires first serial rights, print and online. All rights revert to author upon publication. Author receives 2 contributor copies.

TIPS "Our website includes online exclusives such as Artattack and (Editor)ials, featuring interviews from artists and editors. Also posts artwork from the magazine, contributor's notes and excerpts from the current issue."

❶❸ NEW ENGLAND REVIEW

Middlebury College, Middlebury VT 05753. (802)443-5075. E-mail: nereview@middlebury.edu. Website: go.middlebury.edu/nereview; www.nereview.com. Literary only. Reads September 1-May 31 (postmarked dates).

MAGAZINES NEEDS *New England Review*, published quarterly, is a prestigious, nationally distributed literary journal. Has published poetry by Carl Phillips, Lucia Perillo, Linda Gregerson, and Natasha Trethewey. *New England Review* is 200+ pages, 7x10, printed on heavy stock, flat-spined, with glossy cover with art. Receives 3,000-4,000 poetry submissions/year, accepts about 70-80 poems/year. Subscription: $30. Sample: $10. Overseas shipping fees add $25 for subscription, $12 for Canada; international shipping $5 for single issues.

HOW TO CONTACT Submit up to 6 poems at a time. No previously published poems or simultaneous submissions. Accepts submissions by postal mail only; accepts questions by e-mail. "Cover letters are useful." Address submissions to "Poetry Editor." Reads submissions postmarked September 1-May 31 only. Time between acceptance and publication is 3-6 months. Responds in up to 3 months. Always sends prepublication galleys. Pays $10/page ($20 minimum) plus 2 contributor's copies. Send materials for review consideration.

TIPS "We consider short fiction, including shortshorts, novellas, and self-contained extracts from novels in both traditional and experimental forms. In nonfiction, we consider a variety of general and literary, but not narrowly scholarly essays; we also publish long and short poems; ccreenplays; graphics; translations; critical reassessments; statements by artists working in various media; testimonies; and letters from abroad. We are committed to exploration of all forms of contemporary cultural expression in the US and abroad. With few exceptions, we print only work not published previously elsewhere."

THE NEW LAUREL REVIEW

828 Lesseps St., New Orleans LA 70117. Fax: (504)948-3834. Website: www.nathanielturner.com/newlaurelreview.htm. **Contact:** Lewis Schmidt, managing editor.

MAGAZINES NEEDS. *The New Laurel Review*, published annually, is "an independent nonprofit literary magazine dedicated to fine art. The magazine is meant to be eclectic, and we try to publish the best we receive, whether the submission is poem, translation, short story, essay, review, or interview. We have no domineering preferences regarding style, and we do consult with invited readers and writers for their opinions. We are seeking original work without hackneyed phrases, indulgent voices, or tired thinking. We love surprises and to see a writer or artist enliven our too often dull, editorial worlds." Has published poetry by Gerald Locklin, Roland John (British), Joyce Odam, Ryan G. Van Cleave, Robert Cooperman, and Jared Carter. *The New Laurel Review* is about 115-130 pages, 6×9, laser-printed, perfect-bound, with original art on laminated cover. Receives 400-600 submissions/year, accepts about 30-40 poems. Press run is about 500. Single copy: $12 for individuals, $14 for institutions. Sample (back issue): $5.

HOW TO CONTACT Submit 3-5 poems at a time. No simultaneous submissions. "Poems should be typed; no handwritten submissions will be read. Name and address should appear on each poem submitted. Include a brief biography of three or four typed lines, including previous publications. Do not send cover letters, which may or may not distract from the submission. Be sure to include SASE; manuscripts will not be returned otherwise. If you are submitting from outside the U.S., provide International Reply Coupons. Because we are totally independent from various funding agencies, we sometimes take an inordinate time to reply." Reads submissions September 1-May 30 only. Time between acceptance and publication "can be as long as a year from acceptance." Pays one contributor's copy. Acquires first rights, but will gladly grant permission for the writer to reprint.

TIPS "READ, READ, READ. And it is wise to obtain a copy of any magazine to which you plan to submit work. Also, you might remember that you cannot be cummings, Eliot, Faulkner, or Hemingway. One of the most disheartening aspects of editing is to receive a submission of poems with low caps, no punctuation, or words sprawled all over the page, under the pretense that the work is original and not pseudo-cummings or Yawping Whitman. Find your own voice and techniques."

NEW LETTERS

University of Missouri-Kansas City, University House, 5101 Rockhill Rd., Kansas City MO 64110-2499. (816)235-1168. Fax: (816)235-2611. E-mail: newletters@umkc.edu. Website: www.newletters.org. "*New Letters* is intended for the general literary reader. We publish literary fiction, nonfiction, essays, poetry. We also publish art."

Submissions are not read between May 1 and October 1.

MAGAZINES NEEDS *New Letters*, published quarterly, "is dedicated to publishing the best short fiction, contemporary poetry, literary articles, photography, and artwork by both established writers and new talents." Wants "fresh, new writing of all types. Short works are more likely to be accepted than very long ones." Has published poetry by Naomi Shihab Nye, Albert Goldbarth, Quincy Troupe, Ellen Bass, Joseph Millar, and Mia Leonin. *New Letters* is about 180 pages, digest-sized, professionally printed, flat-spined, with glossy 4-color cover with art. Press run is 3,600. Subscription: $22. Sample: $10.

HOW TO CONTACT Submit no more than 6 poems at a time. No previously published poems. No e-mail submissions. Short cover letter is preferred. Guidelines available on website.

CONTEST/AWARD OFFERINGS The annual *New Letters* Prize for Poetry (see separate listing in Contests & Awards).

TIPS "We aren't interested in essays that are footnoted, or essays usually described as scholarly or critical. Our preference is for creative nonfiction or personal essays. We prefer shorter stories and essays to longer ones (an average length is 3,500-4,000 words). We have no rigid preferences as to subject, style, or genre, although commercial efforts tend to put us off. Even so, our only fixed requirement is on good writing."

NEW MEXICO POETRY REVIEW

44 Via Punto Nuevo, Santa Fe NM 87508. E-mail: nmpr@live.com. Website: newmexicopoetryreview. com. **Contact:** Kathleen Johnson, editor.

MAGAZINES NEEDS *New Mexico Poetry Review*, published semiannually in April and October, is dedicated to publishing strong, imaginative, well-crafted poems by both new talents and established writers. Wants "poems, prose poems, poetry-related essays, and interviews." Does not want "dull or pretentious writing." *New Mexico Poetry Review* is 80-120 pages, digest-sized, professionally printed, perfect-bound, with a full-color glossy card with art, includes ads. Press run is 500. Single copy: $12; subscription: $22/year. Make checks payable to New Mexico Poetry Review.

HOW TO CONTACT Submit up to 5 poems at a time of no more than 70 lines. Does not consider simultaneous submissions; no previously published poems. Accepts e-mail submissions pasted into body of e-mail message; no fax or disk submissions. Cover letter is not required. Reads submissions year round. Time between acceptance and publication is 4-6 months. Sometimes comments on rejected poems. Sometimes publishes theme issues. Will publish New Mexico-themed poems for special New Mexico Centennial Edition in spring 2012. Guidelines available for SASE, by e-mail, or on website. Responds in 1-3 months. Sometimes sends prepublication galleys. Pays 1 contributor's copy. Acquires first North American serial rights. Reviews books and chapbooks of poetry by New Mexico poets in 500-700 words, single and multi-book format.

ADDITIONAL INFORMATION Publishes occasional books and chapbooks, but does not accept unsolicited book/chapbook submissions.

NEW OHIO REVIEW

English Department, 360 Ellis Hall, Ohio University, Athens OH 45701. (740)597-1360. E-mail: noreditors@ohio.edu. Website: www.ohiou.edu/nor. **Contact:** Jill Allyn Rosser, editor. *NOR*, published biannually in spring and fall, publishes fiction, nonfiction, and poetry. Wants "literary submissions in any genre. Translations are welcome if permission has been granted." Billy Collins, Stephen Dunn, Stuart Dybek, Eleanor Wilner, Yusef Komunyakaa, Kim Addonizio, William Olson. Single: $9; Subscription: $16. Member: CLMP.

NEW ORLEANS REVIEW

Box 195, Loyola University, New Orleans LA 70118. (504)865-2295. E-mail: noreview@loyno.edu. Website: neworleansreview.org. **Contact:** Christopher Chambers, editor. Biannual magazine publishing poetry, fiction, translations, photographs, and nonfiction on literature, art and film. Readership: those interested in contemporary literature and culture.

MAGAZINES NEEDS *New Orleans Review*, published twice/year, is an international journal of poetry, fiction, essays, book reviews, and interviews. Wants "dynamic writing that demonstrates attention to the language and a sense of the medium; writing that engages, surprises, moves us. We subscribe to the belief that in order to truly write well, one must first master the rudiments: grammar and syntax, punctuation, the sentence, the paragraph, the line, the stanza." Has published poetry by Chrisopher Howell, Martha Zweig, Lee Upton, Jeffrey Levine, Carlie Rosemurgy, and D.C. Berry. *New Orleans Review* is 200 pages, elegantly printed, perfect-bound, with glossy card cover. Receives about 3,000 mss/year. Press run is 1,500. Single copy: $10. Sample: $6.

HOW TO CONTACT Three to six poems or ten pages at a time only. No previously published work. Simultaneous submissions okay if we're notified immediately upon acceptance elsewhere. Guidelines available on website. Responds in 2-4 months. Pays 2 contributor's copies and honorarium. Acquires first North American serial rights.

TIPS "We're looking for dynamic writing that demonstrates attention to the language, and a sense of the medium, writing that engages, surprises, moves us. We're not looking for genre fiction, or academic articles. We subscribe to the belief that in order to truly write well, one must first master the rudiments: grammar and syntax, punctuation, the sentence, the paragraph, the line, the stanza. We receive about 3,000 manuscripts a year, and publish about 3% of them. Check out a recent issue, send us your best, proofread your work, be patient, be persistent."

THE NEW RENAISSANCE

26 Heath Rd. #11, Arlington MA 02474-3645. E-mail: tnrlitmag@earthlink.net. Website: www.tnrlitmag.org. 26 Heath Rd. #11, Arlington, MA 02474-3645. E-mail: tnrlitmag@earthlink.net. Website: www.tnrlitmag.org. **Contact:** Frank Finale, poetry editor. Estab. 1968.

MAGAZINES NEEDS *the new renaissance*, published spring and fall ("resources permitting"), is "intended for the 'renaissance' person—the generalist, not the specialist. We publish the best new writing and translations and offer a forum for articles on political, sociological topics; feature established as well as emerging visual artists and writers; highlight reviews of small press; and offer essays on a variety of topics from visual arts and literature to science. Open to a variety of styles, including traditional." Has published poetry by Anita Susan Brenner, Anne Struthers, Marc Widershien, Miguel Torga (trans. Alexis Levetin), Stephen Todd Booker, and Rabindranath Togore (trans. Wendy Barker and S. Togore). *the new renaissance* is 144-182 pages, digest-sized, professionally printed on heavy stock, flat-spined, with glossy color cover. Receives about 650 poetry submissions/year, accepts about 40. Press run is 1,500 (760 subscribers, 132 libraries). Single copy: $12.50 (current), $11.50 (recent), $7.50 (back issue); subscription: $30 for 3 issues in U.S., $35 in Canada, $38 all others. "All checks in U.S. dollars. A 3-issue subscription covers 18-22 months."

HOW TO CONTACT Submit 3-6 poems at a time, "unless a long poem—then 1." Considers simultaneous submissions, if notified; no previously published poems "unless magazine's circulation was under 250." Always include SASE or IRC. Accepts submissions by postal mail only; "when accepted, we ask if a disk is available, and we prefer accepted translations to be available in the original language on disk. **All poetry submissions are tied to our Awards Program for poetry published in a 3-issue volume; judged by independent judges.**" **Entry fee:** $16.50 for non-subscribers, $11.50 for subscribers, "for which they receive 2 back issues or a recent issue or an extension of their subscription. Submissions without entry fee are returned unread." Reads submissions January 2-June 30. Guidelines available for SASE. Responds in 5 months. Pays $21-40 (more for the occasional longer poem), plus 1 contributor's copy/poem. Acquires all rights but returns rights provided *the new renaissance* retains rights for any *the new renaissance* collection. Reviews books of poetry.

CONTEST/AWARD OFFERINGS The Awards Program offers 3 prizes of $250, $125, and $50, with 3-4 Honorable Mentions of $25 each; all submissions are tied to the Awards Program (see above for entry fee).

ⓘ NEW SOUTH

Campus Box 1894, Georgia State Univ., MSC 8R0322 Unit 8, Atlanta GA 30303-3083. (404)651-4804. Fax: (404)651-1710. E-mail: new_south@langate.gsu.edu. Website: www.review.gsu.edu. After more than 30 years *GSU Review* has become *New South*. Our role as George State University's journal of art & literature has not changed; however, it was time for a revision, a chance for a clearer mission.

MAGAZINES NEEDS *New South*, published semiannually, prints fiction, poetry, nonfiction, and visual art. Wants "original voices searching to rise above the ordinary. No subject or form biases." Does not want pornography or Hallmark verse. *New South* is 160+ pages. Press run is 2,000; 500 distributed free to students. Single copy: $5; subscription: $8/year; $14 for 2 issues. Single issue: $5. Sample: $3 (back issue).

HOW TO CONTACT Submit up to 3 poems at a time. Considers simultaneous submissions (with notification in cover letter); no previously published poems. No e-mail submissions. Name, address, and phone/e-mail must appear on each page of ms. Cover letter is required. Include "a 3-4 line bio, a list of the work(s) submitted in the order they appear, and your name, mailing address, phone number, and e-mail address." Include SASE for notification. New South is now accepting submissions through Tell It Slant, an online submission manager. For a small fee that's roughly the cost of printing and posting paper submissions, Tell it Slant will save time, reduce paper waste, and increase our efficiency. Time between acceptance and publication is 3-5 months. Seldom comments on rejected poems. Guidelines available for SASE, by e-mail, or on website. Pays 2 copies. Rights revert to poets upon publication.

CONTEST/AWARD OFFERINGS The *New South* Annual Writing Contest offers $1,000 for the best poem; copy of issue to all who submit. Submissions must be unpublished. Submit up to 3 poems on any subject or in any form. "Specify 'poetry' on outside envelope." Guidelines available for SASE, by e-mail, or on website. **Deadline:** March 4. Competition receives 200 entries. Past judges include Sharon Olds, Jane Hirschfield, Anthony Hecht, Phillip Levine and Jake Adam York. Winner will be announced in the Spring issue.

❾⓪◗ THE NEW VERSE NEWS

Jakarta International School, P.O. Box 1078JKS, Jakarta 12010, Indonesia. E-mail: nvneditor@yahoo.com; nvneditor@gmail.com. Website: www.newversenews.com. **Contact:** James Penha, Editor. *The New Verse News*, published online and updated "every day or 2," has "a clear liberal bias, but will consider various visions and views." Wants "poems, both serious and satirical, on current events and topical issues; will also consider prose poems and short-short stories and plays." Does not want "work unrelated to the news." Receives about 1,200 poems/year, accepts about 300.

❾◗ THE NEW WRITER

(44)(158)021-2626. E-mail: editor@thenewwriter.com. Website: www.thenewwriter.com. **Contact:** Sarah Jackson, poetry editor. "Contemporary writing magazine which publishes the best in fact, fiction and poetry."

MAGAZINES NEEDS *The New Writer*, published 6 times/year, is "aimed at writers with a serious intent, who want to develop their writing to meet the high expectations of today's editors. The team at *The New Writer* is committed to working with its readers to increase the chances of publication through masses of useful information and plenty of feedback. More than that, we let you know about the current state of the market with the best in contemporary fiction and cutting-edge poetry, backed up by searching articles and in-depth features." Wants "short and long unpublished poems, provided they are original and undeniably brilliant. No problems with length/form, but anything over 2 pages (150 lines) needs to be brilliant. Cutting edge shouldn't mean inaccessible. The poetry editor prefers poems which provide a good use of language, offering challenging imagery." *The New Writer* is 56 pages, A4, professionally printed, saddle-stapled, with paper cover. Press run is 1,500 (1,350 subscribers); 50 distributed free to publishers, agents. Single copy: £6.25 in U.S. (5 IRCs required); subscription: £37.50 in U.S. "We have a secure server for subscriptions and entry into the annual Prose and Poetry Prizes on the website. Monthly e-mail newsletter included free of charge in the subscription package."

HOW TO CONTACT Submit up to 3 poems at a time. Lines/poem: 150 maximum. Does not consider previously published poems. Accepts e-mail submissions (pasted into body of message). Time between acceptance and publication is up to 6 months. Often comments on rejected poems. Guidelines available for SASE (or SAE with IRC) or on website. Pays £3 voucher plus 1 contributor's copy. Acquires first British serial rights.

CONTEST/AWARD OFFERINGS Sponsors *The New Writer* Prose & Poetry Prizes annually. "All poets writing in the English language are invited to submit an original, previously unpublished poem or a collection of 6-10 poems. Up to 25 prizes will be presented, as well as publication for the prize-winning poets in an anthology, plus the chance for a further 10 shortlisted poets to see their work published in *The New Writer* during the year." Guidelines available by e-mail or on website.

TIPS "Hone it—always be prepared to improve the story. It's a competitive market."

❶❸ THE NEW YORKER

4 Times Square, New York NY 10036. (212) 286-5900. E-mail: beth_lusko@newyorker.com. E-mail: toon@cartoonbank.com. Website: www.newyorker.com; www.cartoonbank.com. David Remnick, editor-in-chief. **Contact:** Deborah Treisman, fiction editor. A quality weekly magazine of distinct news stories, articles, essays, and poems for a literate audience.

◖ *The New Yorker* receives approximately 4,000 submissions per month.

MAGAZINES NEEDS *The New Yorker*, published weekly, prints poetry of the highest quality (including translations). Subscription: $47/year (47 issues), $77 for 2 years (94 issues).

HOW TO CONTACT Submit no more than 6 poems at a time. No previously published poems or simultaneous submissions. Use online e-mail source and upload as pdf attachment. Include poet's name in the subject line and as the title of attached document. "We prefer to receive no more than two submissions per writer per year." Pays top rates.

TIPS "Be lively, original, not overly literary. Write what you want to write, not what you think the editor would like. Send poetry to Poetry Department."

◖ NEW YORK QUARTERLY

P.O. Box 2015, Old Chelsea Station, New York NY 10113. E-mail: info@nyquarterly.org. Website: www.nyquarterly.org. **Contact:** Raymond Hammond, editor.

MAGAZINES NEEDS *New York Quarterly*, published

3 times/year, seeks to print "a most eclectic cross-section of contemporary American poetry." Has published poetry by Charles Bukowski, James Dickey, Lola Haskins, Lyn Lifshin, Elisavietta Ritchie, and W.D. Snodgrass. *New York Quarterly* is digest-sized, elegantly printed, flat-spined, with glossy color cover. Subscription: $35.

HOW TO CONTACT Submit 3-5 poems at a time. No e-mail submissions, but accepts electronic submissions on website. Considers simultaneous submissions with notification. No previously published poems. Include your name and address on each page. "Include SASE; no international postage coupons." Guidelines available on website. Responds within 6 weeks. Pays in contributor's copies.

◐ NEXUS LITERARY JOURNAL

W104 Student Union, Wright State University, Dayton OH 45435. E-mail: bruce.15@wright.edu. Website: www.wsunexus.com. **Contact:** Logan Bruce, editor. **Contact:** Logan Bruce, editor. Estab. 1967. *Nexus Literary Journal*, published 3 times/year in fall, winter, and spring, is a student-operated magazine of mainstream and street poetry. Wants "truthful, direct poetry. Open to poets anywhere. We look for contemporary, imaginative work." *Nexus* is 80-96 pages. Receives about 1,000 submissions/year, accepts about 50-70. Circulation is 3,000. Sample: free for 10x15 SAE with 5 first-class stamps. *Nexus Literary Journal*, published 3 times/year in fall, winter, and spring, is a student-operated magazine of mainstream and street poetry. Wants "truthful, direct poetry. Open to poets anywhere. We look for contemporary, imaginative work." *Nexus* is 80-96 pages. Receives about 1,000 submissions/year, accepts about 50-70. Circulation is 3,000. Sample: free for 10x15 SAE with 5 first-class stamps.

HOW TO CONTACT Submit up to 5 poems at a time. Considers simultaneous submissions ("due to short response time, we want to be told it's a simultaneous submission"). Reads submissions year round. Sometimes comments on rejected poems. Upcoming themes and guidelines available in magazine, for SASE, or by e-mail. Responds in 5 months except during summer. Pays 2 contributor's copies. Acquires first rights. E-mail your prose/poetry to bruce.15@wright.edu with a subject line of "Short Story/Poetry/Other Submission" respective to your piece(s) you are submitting. Pieces should be at-tached to the e-mail as .doc, .docx, or .rtf files. The body of your e-mail should consist of a simple cover letter with your name, title of your piece, word count, what type of work it is, and contact information.

○ NIBBLE

1714 Franklin St., Suite 100-231, Oakland CA 94612. E-mail: nibblepoems@gmail.com. Website: http://nibblepoems.wordpress.com. **Contact:** Jeff Fleming, editor. Estab. 1995. *nibble*, published bimonthly, is a journal of poetry "focusing on short poems (less than 20 lines)." Does not want "inaccessible, self-important poems." *nibble* is 32 pages, digest-sized, laser-printed, side-stapled, with a cardstock, imaged cover. Receives about 1,500 poems/year, accepts about 250. Press run is 250; 50 distributed free to schools. Single copy: $6; Subscription: $24/6 issues. Make checks payable to Jeff Fleming. *nibble*, published bimonthly, is a journal of poetry "focusing on short poems (less than 20 lines)." Does not want "inaccessible, self-important poems." *nibble* is 32 pages, digest-sized, laser-printed, side-stapled, with a cardstock, imaged cover. Receives about 1,500 poems/year, accepts about 250. Press run is 250; 50 distributed free to schools. Single copy: $6; Subscription: $24/6 issues. Make checks payable to Jeff Fleming.

HOW TO CONTACT Prefers e-mail submissions. Submit 3-5 poems at a time. SASE required for mail submissions; cover letter is required. Reads submissions year round. Time between acceptance and publication is 2 months. Often comments on rejected poems. Sometimes publishes theme issues. Upcoming themes available by e-mail. Guidelines available for SASE, by e-mail, and online. Responds in 2-4 weeks. Pays 1 contributor's copy. Acquires one-time rights. Reviews books and chapbooks of poetry. Occasionally will publish chapbooks.

◐ NIMROD: INTERNATIONAL JOURNAL OF POETRY AND PROSE

University of Tulsa, 800 S. Tucker Dr., Tulsa OK 74104-3189. (918)631-3080. Fax: (918)631-3033. E-mail: nimrod@utulsa.edu. Website: www.utulsa.edu/nimrod. **Contact:** Lisa Ransom and Ann Stone, poetry editors; Susan Mase, fiction editor. Magazine: 6×9; 192 pages; 60 lb. white paper; illustrations; photos. "We publish one thematic issue and one awards issue each year. A recent theme was 'Crossing Borders,' a compilation of poetry and prose from all over the world. We seek vigorous, imaginative, quality writing. Our mission is to discover new writers and publish experimental writers who have not yet found a 'home' for their work." Semiannual. "We accept contemporary poetry and/or prose. May submit adventure, ethnic, experimental, prose poem or translations. No science fiction or romance." Receives 120 unsolicited mss/month. **Publishes 5-10 new writers/year.** Recently published work by Felicia Ward, Ellen Bass, Jeanette Turner Hospital, Kate Small. Also publishes poetry. SASE for return of ms. Accepts queries by e-mail. Does not accept submissions by e-mail unless the writer is living outside the U.S. Responds in 5 months to mss. Accepts multiple submissions. Pays 2 contributor's copies.

○ Poetry published in *Nimrod* has been included in *The Best American Poetry*.

MAGAZINES NEEDS *Nimrod: International Journal of Poetry and Prose*, published 2 times/year, is "an active 'little magazine,' part of the movement in American letters which has been essential to the development of modern literature." Publishes an awards issue in the fall, featuring the prizewinners of its national competition, and a thematic issue each spring. "Poems in non-award issues range from formal to freestyle with several translations." Wants "vigorous writing that is neither wholly of the academy nor the streets; typed manuscripts." Has published poetry by Diane Glancy, Judith Strasser, Steve Lautermilch, Virgil Suaárez, and Jen-Mark Sens. *Nimrod* is about 200 pages, digest-sized, professionally printed on coated stock, perfect-bound, with full-color glossy cover. Receives about 2,000 submissions/year, accepts 1%. Press run is 2,500. Subscription: $18.50/year U.S., $20 foreign. Sample: $11. "Specific back issues available. Please send check or money order."

HOW TO CONTACT Submit 5-10 poems at a time. No fax or e-mail submissions. Open to general submissions from January 1-November 30. Publishes theme issues. Guidelines available for SASE, by e-mail, or on website. Responds in up to 3 months. "During the months that the *Nimrod* Literary Awards competition is being conducted, reporting time on non-contest manuscripts will be longer." Pays 2 contributor's copies, plus reduced cost on additional copies.

CONTEST/AWARD OFFERINGS The annual *Nimrod* Literary Awards, including The Pablo Neruda Prize for Poetry (see separate listing in Contests & Awards).

ALSO OFFERS Sponsors the *Nimrod* workshop for readers and writers, a one-day workshop held annually in October. Cost is about $50. Send SASE for brochure and registration form.

●$ NINTH LETTER

Dept. of English, University of Illinois, 608 S. Wright St., Urbana IL 61801. (217)244-3145. E-mail: poetry@ninthletter.com. Website: www.ninthletter.com. Member: CLMP; CELJ. *Ninth Letter*, published semiannually, is "dedicated to the examination of literature as it intersects with various aspects of contemporary culture and intellectual life." Open to all forms of poetry. Wants "exceptional literary quality." Has published poetry by Paula Bohince, L.S. Asekoff, D.A. Powell, Bob Hicok, G.C. Waldrep, and Angie Estes. *Ninth Letter* is 176 pages, 7x10, offset-printed, perfect-bound, with 4-color cover with graphics. Receives about 9,000 poems/year, accepts about 40. Press run is 2,500 (500 subscribers, 1,000 shelf sales); 500 distributed free, 500 to contributors, mediAnd fundraising efforts. Single copy: $14.95; subscription: $21.95/year. Sample: $8.95 (back issue). Make checks payable to *Ninth Letter*.

○ *Ninth Letter* won Best New Literary Journal 2005 from the Council of Editors of Learned Journals (CELJ) and has had poetry selected for *The Pushcart Prize*, *Best New Poets*, and *The Year's Best Fantasy and Horror*.

● NITE-WRITER'S INTERNATIONAL LITERARY ARTS JOURNAL

158 Spencer Ave., Suite 100, Pittsburgh PA 15227. E-mail: nitewritersliteraryarts@gmail.com. Website: http://nitewritersinternational.webs.com. **Contact:** John Thompson. 158 Spencer Ave., Suite 100, Pittsburgh, PA 15227. (412)668-0691. E-mail: nitewritersliteraryarts@gmail.com. Website: http://nitewritersinternational.webs.com. **Contact:** John Thompson. *Nite-Writer's International Literary Arts Journal*, published quarterly, is open to beginners as well as professionals. "We are 'dedicated to the emotional intellectual' with a creative perception of life." Has published poetry by Lyn Lifshin, Rose Marie Hunold, Peter Vetrano, Carol Frances Brown, and Richard King Perkins II. 30-50 pages, magazine-sized, laser-printed, with stock cover with sleeve. Receives about 1,000 poems/year, accepts about 10-15%. Press run is about 100 (more than 60 subscribers, 10 libraries).

MAGAZINES NEEDS strong imagery and accepts free verse, avant-garde poetry, haiku, and senryu.

HOW TO CONTACT Considers previously published poems and simultaneous submissions. Cover letter is preferred. "Give brief bio, state where you heard of us, state if material has been previously published and where. Always enclose SASE if you seek reply and return of your material." Time between acceptance and publication is within one year. Always comments on rejected poems.

ADDITIONAL INFORMATION Single copy: $6; subscription: $20. Sample (when available): $4. Guidelines available for SASE. Responds in one month.

TIPS "Read a lot of what you write - study the market. Don't fear rejection, but use it as learning tool to strengthen your work before resubmitting."

ⓘⓢ NORTH AMERICAN REVIEW

University of Northern Iowa, 1222 West 27th St., Cedar Falls IA 50614-0516. (319)273-6455. Fax: (319)273-4326. E-mail: nar@uni.edu. Website: northamericanreview.org. **Contact:** Poetry Editor.

MAGAZINES NEEDS *North American Review*, published 4 times/year, is "the oldest literary magazine in America." Wants "poetry of the highest quality; poems that are passionate about subject, language, and image. Especially interested in work that addresses contemporary North American concerns and issues, particularly with the environment, race, ethnicity, gender, sexual orientation, and class." Has published poetry by Debra Marquart, Nick Carbó, Yusef Komunyakaa, Virgil Suaárez, Nance Van Winckel, and Dara Wier. *North American Review* is about 48 pages, magazine-sized, professionally printed, saddle-stapled, with glossy full-color paper cover. Receives about 10,000 poems/year, accepts 100. Press run is 2,500 (1,500 subscribers, 1,000 libraries). Subscription: $22 in U.S., $29 in Canada, $32 foreign. Sample: $5.

HOW TO CONTACT Submit 6 poems at a time. No previously published poems or simultaneous submissions. Electronic submission available through the website. No fax, e-mail, or disk submissions. Cover letter is preferred. Include brief bio and list poem titles. Include SASE. Time between acceptance and publication is up to 1 year. Guidelines available in magazine, for SASE, by e-mail, or on website. Responds in 4 months. Always sends prepub-

lication galleys. Pays $1/line ($20 minimum, $100 maximum) and 2 contributor's copies. Acquires first North American serial rights only. Rights revert to poets upon publication.

CONTEST/AWARD OFFERINGS The annual James Hearst Poetry Prize (see separate listing in Contest & Awards).

ⓢ NORTH CAROLINA LITERARY REVIEW

East Carolina University, ECU Mailstop 555 English, Greenville NC 27858-4353. (252)328-1537. Fax: (252)328-4889. E-mail: nclrsubmissions@ecu.edu; bauerm@ecu.edu. Website: www.nclr.ecu.edu. "Articles should have a North Carolina slant. First consideration is always for quality of work. Although we treat academic and scholarly subjects, we do not wish to see jargon-laden prose; our readers, we hope, are found as often in bookstores and libraries as in academia. We seek to combine the best elements of magazine for serious readers with best of scholarly journal."

MAGAZINES NEEDS *North Carolina Literary Review*, published annually in the summer, contains "articles and other works about North Carolina topics or by North Carolina authors." Wants "poetry by writers currently living in North Carolina, those who have lived in North Carolina, or those using North Carolina for subject matter." Has published poetry by Betty Adcock, James Applewhite, and A.R. Ammons. *North Carolina Literary Review* is 200 pages, magazine-sized. Receives about 100 submissions/year, accepts about 10%. Press run is 1,000 (350 subscribers, 100 libraries, 100 shelf sales); 100 distributed free to contributors. Subscription: $20 for 2 years, $36 for 4 years. Sample: $15.

HOW TO CONTACT Submit 3-5 poems at a time through online submission manager. Cover letter is required. Submit poetry September through April. "Because we do not read during the summer, submissions received during the summer will be sent through the review process after August 25th." Simultaneous submissions are permitted "as long as you notify *NCLR* immediately if accepted elsewhere." Time between acceptance and publication is up to 1 year. Often comments on rejected poems. Guidelines available for SASE, by e-mail, or on website. Responds in 3 months within reading period. Sometimes sends prepublication galleys. Pays 2-year subscription plus 1-2 contributor's copies. Acquires first or one-time rights. Reviews books of poetry by North Carolina poets in up to 2,000 words, multi-book format. Poets from North Carolina may send books for review consideration. Rarely reviews chapbooks.

TIPS "By far the easiest way to break in is with special issue sections. We are especially interested in reports on conferences, readings, meetings that involve North Carolina writers, and personal essays or short narratives with a strong sense of place. See back issues for other departments. Interviews are probably the other easiest place to break in; no discussions of poetics/theory, etc., except in reader-friendly (accessible) language; interviews should be personal, more like conversations, that explore connections between a writer's life and his/her work."

O NORTH CENTRAL REVIEW

North Central College, CM #235, 30 N. Brainard St., Naperville IL 60540. (630)637-5291. E-mail: nccreview@noctrl.edu. Website: http://orgs.noctrl.edu/review. **Contact:** The Editors.

MAGAZINES NEEDS *North Central Review*, published semiannually, considers "work in all literary genres, including occasional interviews, from undergraduate writers globally. The journal's goal is for college-level, emerging creative writers to share their work publicly and create a conversation with each other. ALL styles and forms are welcome as submissions. The readers tend to value attention to form (but not necessarily fixed form), voice, and detail. Very long poems or sequences (running more than 4 or 5 pages) may require particular excellence because of the journal's space and budget constraints." Does not want "overly sentimental language and hackneyed imagery. These are all-too-common weaknesses that readers see in submissions; we recommend revision and polishing before sending work." Considers poetry by teens (undergraduate writers only). *North Central Review* is 120 pages, digest-sized, perfect-bound, with cardstock cover with 4-color design. Press run is about 750, distributed free to contributors and publication reception attendees. Single copy: $5; subscription: $10. Make checks payable to North Central College.

HOW TO CONTACT Submit up to 5 poems at a time. Lines/poem: "no limit, but poems running more than 4-5 pages may undergo particular scrutiny." No previously published poems or simultaneous submissions. Accepts e-mail submissions (as

Word attachments only); no fax submissions. Cover letter is preferred. Include name, postal address, phone number, and e-mail address (.edu address as proof of student status). If necessary (i.e., .edu address not available), include a photocopy of student ID with number marked out as proof of undergraduate status. Reads submissions September-March, with deadlines of February 15 and October 15. Time between acceptance and publication is 1-4 months. Poems are circulated to an editorial board. "All submissions are read by at least 3 staff members, including an editor." Rarely comments on rejected poems. Guidelines available on website, in magazine, for SASE, or by e-mail. Responds in 1-4 months. Pays 2 contributor's copies. Acquires one-time rights. Rights revert to poet upon publication.

TIPS "Don't send anything you just finished moments ago—rethink, revise, and polish. Avoid sentimentality and abstraction. That said, the *North Central Review* publishes beginners, so don't hesitate to submit and, if rejected, submit again."

O O NORTH DAKOTA QUARTERLY

(701)777-3322. E-mail: ndq@und.edu. Website: www.und.nodak.edu/org/ndq. Merrifeild Hall Room 110, 276 Centennial Drive Stop 7209, Grand Forks, ND 58202-7209. (701)777-3322. E-mail:ndq@und.edu. Website: www.und.nodak.edu/org/ndq. **Contact:** Robert Lewis, editor.

MAGAZINES NEEDS *North Dakota Quarterly* is published by the University of North Dakota. Seeks material related to the arts and humanities—essays, fiction, interviews, poems, reviews, and visual art. Wants poetry "that reflects an understanding not only of the difficulties of the craft, but of the vitality and tact that each poem calls into play." Has published poetry by Maxine Kumin, Paul Muldoon, Robert Bagg, James Scully, Patricia Schneider, and Marianne Boruch. *North Dakota Quarterly* is about 200 pages, digest-sized, professionally designed and printed, perfect-bound, with full-color artwork on white card cover. Has 550 subscribers. Subscription: $25/year. Sample: $8.

○ Work published in *North Dakota Quarterly* was selected for inclusion in *The O. Henry Prize Stories, The Pushcart Prize Series*and *Best American Essays*. Work published in *North Dakota Quarterly* was selected for inclusion in

The O. Henry Prize Stories, The Pushcart Prize Series and *Best American Essays.*

HOW TO CONTACT Submit 5 poems at a time. No previously published poems or simultaneous submissions. No e-mail submissions; accepts only typed hard-copy submissions by postal mail. Time between acceptance and publication varies. Responds in up to 6 weeks. Always sends prepublication galleys. Pays 2 contributor's copies. Acquires first serial rights.

◑ NORTHWEST REVIEW

5243 University of Oregon, Eugene OR 97403-5243. (541)346-3957. Fax: (541)346-0537. E-mail: nweditor@uoregon.edu. Website: http://nwr.uoregon.edu. **Contact:** Geri Doran, general editor.

MAGAZINES NEEDS *Northwest Review*, published 2 times/year is "looking for smart, crisp writing about poetry and poetics. The only criterion for acceptance of material for publication is excellence." Has published poetry and essays by AI, Yusef Komunyakaa, Charles Wright, Brenda Hillman, Eavan Boland, and Marilyn Chin. *Northwest Review* is digest-sized, flat-spined. Receives about 3,500 submissions/year, accepts about 4%. Press run is 1,300. Single copy: $8-10; subscription: $20/year (two issues). Sample: $8-10.

> ◐ Poetry published by *Northwest Review* has been included in *The Best American Poetry*, *Poetry Daily*, and *Verse Daily*.

HOW TO CONTACT Send complete ms. Essays 4,000-8,000 words. No simultaneous submissions. No email submissions; postal submissions only. Include SASE. Send only clear, clean copies. Guidelines and reading periods available on website. Responds within 3 months. Acquires first North American serial rights. Pays 2 contributor's copies.

TIPS "Our advice is to persist."

◑◓◉ NOTRE DAME REVIEW

(574)631-6952. Fax: (574)631-4795. E-mail: english.ndreview.1@nd.edu. Website: www.nd.edu/~ndr/review.htm. The *Notre Dame Review* is an indepenent, noncommercial magazine of contemporary American and international fiction, poetry, criticism, and art. We are especially interested in work that takes on big issues by making the invisible seen, that gives voice to the voiceless. In addition to showcasing celebrated authors like Seamus Heaney and Czelaw Milosz, the *Notre Dame Review* introduces readers to authors they may have never encountered before, but who are doing innovative and important work. In conjunction with the *Notre Dame Review*, the online companion to the printed magazine, the *Notre Dame Re-view* engages readers as a community centered in literary rather than commercial concerns, a community we reach out to through critique and commentary as well as aesthetic experience.

MAGAZINES NEEDS *Notre Dame Review*, published semiannually, aims "to present a panoramic view of contemporary art and literature—no one style is advocated over another. We are especially interested in work that takes on big issues by making the invisible seen." Has published poetry by W.S. Merwin, R.T. Smith, Moira Egan, Michael Harper, Floyd Skloot, and Kevin Ducey. *Notre Dame Review* is 170 pages, magazine-sized, perfect-bound, with 4-color glossy cover, includes ads. Receives about 400 poems/year, accepts 10%. Press run is 2,000 (500 subscribers, 150 libraries, 1,000 shelf sales); 350 distributed free to contributors, assistants, etc. Single copy: $8; subscription: $15/year. Sample: $6 (back issue).T

HOW TO CONTACT Submit 3-5 poems at a time. Considers simultaneous submissions; no previously published poems. Cover letter is required. Reads submissions September-November and January-March only. Time between acceptance and publication is 3 months. Seldom comments on rejected poems. Publishes theme issues. Guidelines available on website. Responds in 3 months. Always sends prepublication galleys. Pays small gratuity on publication, plus 2 contributor's copies. Acquires first rights. Staff reviews books of poetry in 500 words, single- and multi-book format. Send materials for review consideration.

ADDITIONAL INFORMATION *nd[[re]]view* is the online companion to *Notre Dame Review*, offering "interviews, critique, and commentary on authors and artists showcased within the pages of the print magazine." See website for more details.

CONTEST/AWARD OFFERINGS The Ernest Sandeen Prize in Poetry (see separate listing in Contests & Awards).

TIPS "We're looking for high quality work that takes on big issues in a literary way. Please read our back issues before submitting."

◓◉◐ NTH POSITION

E-mail: val@nthposition.com. Website: www.nthposition.com. **Contact:** Rufo Quintavalle, Poetry

Editor. *nthposition*, published monthly online, is an eclectic, London-based journal dedicated to poetry, fiction, and nonfiction "with a weird or innovative edge." Wants "all kinds of poetry—from spoken word to new formalist to linguistically innovative. We also publish political poetry." Has published poetry by Charles Bernstein, George Szirtes, Stephanie Bolster, and Mimi Khalvati. Receives about 2,000 poems/year, accepts about 10%. E-mail: val@nthposition.com. Website: www.nthposition.com. Free ezine with politics and opinion, travel writing, fiction and poetry, art reviews and interviews, and some high weirdness.

C We can only notify people whose work we accept.

MAGAZINES NEEDS *nthposition*, published monthly online, is an eclectic, London-based journal dedicated to poetry, fiction, and nonfiction "with a weird or innovative edge." Wants "all kinds of poetry— from spoken word to new formalist to linguistically innovative. We also publish political poetry." Has published poetry by Charles Bernstein, George Szirtes, Stephanie Bolster, and Mimi Khalvati. Receives about 2,000 poems/year, accepts about 10%.

HOW TO CONTACT Submit 2-6 poems at a time. No previously published poems or simultaneous submissions. Accepts e-mail submissions only (pasted into body of message, no attachments). Cover letter is required. "Please include a brief (two sentences) biographical note." Reads submissions throughout the year. Time between acceptance and publication is 4 months. "Poems are read and selected by the poetry editor, who uses his own sense of what makes a poem work online to select." Never comments on rejected poems. Occasionally publishes theme issues. Guidelines available by e-mail or on website. Responds in 6 weeks. No payment. Does not request rights but expects proper acknowledgement if poems reprinted later.

ALSO OFFERS Publishes special theme e-books from time to time, such as *100 Poets Against the War*.

TIPS Submit as text in the body of an email, along with a brief bio note (2-3 sentences). If your work is accepted it will be archived into the British Library's permanent collection.

○ NUTHOUSE

Website: www.nthousemagazine.com. Twin Rivers Press, P.O. Box 119, Ellenton FL 34222. Website: www.nuthousemagazine.com. **Contact:** Dr. Ludwig

"Needles" Von Quirk, chief of staff. *Nuthouse*, published every 3 months, uses humor of all kinds, including homespun and political. Wants "humorous verse; virtually all genres considered." Has published poetry by Holly Day, Daveed Garstenstein-Ross, and Don Webb. *Nuthouse* is 12 pages, digest-sized, photocopied from desktop-published originals. Receives about 500 poems/year, accepts about 100. Press run is 100. Subscription: $5 for 4 issues. Sample: $1.50. Make checks payable to Twin Rivers Press.

MAGAZINES NEEDS *Nuthouse*, published every 3 months, uses humor of all kinds, including homespun and political. Wants "humorous verse; virtually all genres considered." Has published poetry by Holly Day, Daveed Garstenstein-Ross, and Don Webb. *Nuthouse* is 12 pages, digest-sized, photocopied from desktop-published originals. Receives about 500 poems/year, accepts about 100. Press run is 100. Subscription: $5 for 4 issues. Sample: $1.50. Make checks payable to Twin Rivers Press.

HOW TO CONTACT Considers previously published poems and simultaneous submissions. Time between acceptance and publication is 6 months to 1 year. Often comments on rejected poems. Responds within 1 month. Pays 1 contributor's copy/poem. Acquires one-time rights.

●○ OBSESSED WITH PIPEWORK

E-mail: cannula.dementia@virgin.net. *Obsessed with Pipework*, published quarterly, is "very keen to publish strong new voices—'new poems to surprise and delight' with somewhat of a high-wire aspect." Wants "original, exploratory poems—positive, authentic, oblique maybe—delighting in image and in the dance of words on the page." Does not want "the predictable, the unfresh, the rhyme-led, the clever, the didactic, the sure-of-itself. No formless outpourings, please." Has published poetry by David Hart, Jennifer Compton, Susan Wicks, Carol Burns, Lucille Gang Shulklapper, and Maria Jastrzebska. *Obsessed with Pipework* is 49-60 pages, A5, stapled, with card cover. Receives about 1,500 poems/year, accepts about 10%. Press run is 100. Single copy: £3.50; subscription: £12. Submit maximum of 6 poems at a time. Does not accept e-mail submissions. Cover letter is preferred. Often comments on rejected poems. Usually responds in 3 months. Pays 1 contributor's copy. Acquires first rights.

MAGAZINES NEEDS *Obsessed with Pipework*,

published quarterly, is "very keen to publish strong new voices—'new poems to surprise and delight' with somewhat of a high-wire aspect." Wants "original, exploratory poems—positive, authentic, oblique maybe—delighting in image and in the dance of words on the page." Does not want "the predictable, the unfresh, the rhyme-led, the clever, the didactic, the sure-of-itself. No formless outpourings, please." Has published poetry by David Hart, Jennifer Compton, Susan Wicks, Carol Burns, Lucille Gang Shulklapper, and Maria Jastrzebska. *Obsessed with Pipework* is 49-60 pages, A5, stapled, with hard cover. Receives about 1,500 poems/year, accepts about 10%. Press run is 100. Single copy: £3.50; subscription: £12. Sample: £2 if available. Make checks payable in pounds to Flarestack Publishing. Back issues are also available online at www.poetrymagazines.org.uk.

HOW TO CONTACT Submit maximum of 6 poems at a time. No previously published poems or simultaneous submissions. Does not accept e-mail submissions. Cover letter is preferred. Often comments on rejected poems. Guidelines available for SASE or by e-mail. Usually responds in 3 months. Pays 1 contributor's copy. Acquires first rights.

OFF THE COAST

Resolute Bear Press, P.O. Box 14, Robbinston ME 04671. (207)454-8026. E-mail: poetrylane2@gmail.com. E-mail: poetrylane2@gmail.com. Website: www.off-the-coast.com. Michael Brown, Editor & Publisher. **Contact:** Valerie Lawson, Editor & Publisher. Quarterly journal with deadlines of March, June, September and December 15. OTC is accepting submissions of poetry (any subject or style, e-mail submissions preferred, postal submissions OK with SASE), photography, graphics, and books for review (books only, no chapbooks). Subscriptions are $35. Single issue: $10. *Off the Coast*, prints all styles and forms of poetry. Considers poetry by children and teens. Has published poetry by Kate Barnes, Henry Braun, Wesley McNair, Baron Wormser, Betsy Sholl, and Robert Cording. *Off the Coast* is 80-100+ pages, perfect-bound, with stock cover with original art. Receives about 2,500 poems/year, accepts about 180. Press run is 300; occasional complimentary copies offered. Make checks payable to *Off the Coast*. Editorial decisions are not made until after the deadline for each issue. Notifications go out the first two weeks of the month following the deadline date eg: early April

for March 15 deadline. **For samples of poetry, art and reviews, visit our website.**"The Mission of *Off the Coast* is to become recognized around the world as Maine's international poetry journal, a publication that prizes quality, diversity and honesty in its publications and in its dealings with poets. *Off the Coast*, a quarterly journal, publishes poetry, artwork and reviews. Arranged much like an anthology, each issue bears a title drawn from a line or phrase from one of its poems."

"We continue to publish the work of youth poets and review a half dozen or more books in each issue." Send 1-3 previously unpublished poems, any subject or style cut-and-pasted in the body of an e-mail. If attaching poems, please also include in the body of the e-mail. Postal submissions with SASE with sufficient postage for return. Please include contact information and brief bio with submission. We accept simultaneous submissions, but please inform us if your work is accepted elsewhere. If sending both poems and artwork, please send in separate e-mails.

HOW TO CONTACT "Send 1-3 previously unpublished poems, any subject or style cut-and-pasted in the body of an e-mail. If attaching poems, please also include in the body of the e-mail. Postal submissions with SASE with sufficient postage for return. Please include contact information and brief bio with submission. We accept simultaneous submissions, but please inform us if your work is accepted elsewhere. If sending both poems and artwork, please send in separate e-mails. Lines/poem: prefers 32 maximum. Does not consider previously published poems. Reads submissions year-round. Time between acceptance and publication is 1-2 months. Sometimes comments on rejected poems. Guidelines available in magazine. Responds in 1-2 months. Pays one contributor's copy. "The rights to each individual poem and print are retained by each individual artist." For reviews, send a single copy of a newly published poetry book. Please send bound books only, we do not review chapbooks."

THE OLD RED KIMONO

Georgia Highlands College, 3175 Cedartown Highway SE, Rome GA 30161. E-mail: napplega@highlands.edu. Website: www.highlands.edu/ork/neworkweb/WELCOME.html. **Contact:** Dr. Nancy Applegate, professor of English. Georgia Highlands College, 3175 Cedartown Hwy. SE, Rome, GA 30161. E-mail: napplega@highlands.edu. Website: www.highlands.edu/ork/neworkweb/WELCOME.html. **Contact:** Dr. Nancy Applegate, professor of English. Estab. 1972. *The Old Red Kimono*, published annually, prints original, high-quality poetry and fiction. Has published poetry by Walter McDonald, Peter Huggins, Ruth Moon Kempher, John Cantey Knight, Kirsten Fox, and Al Braselton. *The Old Red Kimono* is 72 pages, magazine-sized, professionally printed on heavy stock, with colored matte cover with art. Receives about 500 submissions/year, accepts about 60-70. Sample: $3.

MAGAZINES NEEDS *The Old Red Kimono*, published annually, prints original, high-quality poetry and fiction. Has published poetry by Walter McDonald, Peter Huggins, Ruth Moon Kempher, John Cantey Knight, Kirsten Fox, and Al Braselton. *The Old Red Kimono* is 72 pages, magazine-sized, professionally printed on heavy stock, with colored matte cover with art. Receives about 500 submissions/year, accepts about 60-70. Sample: $3.

HOW TO CONTACT Submit 3-5 poems at a time. Accepts e-mail submissions. Reads submissions September 1-March 1 only. Guidelines available for SASE or on website for more submission information. Responds in 3 months. Pays 2 contributor's copies. Acquires first publication rights.

ON SPEC

P.O. Box 4727, Station South, Edmonton AB T6E 5G6, Canada. (780)413-0215. Fax: (780)413-1538. E-mail: onspec@onspec.ca. E-mail: onspecmag@gmail.com. Website: www.onspec.ca. "We publish speculative fiction and poetry by new and established writers, with a strong preference for Canadian authored works."

Submission deadlines are February 28, May 31, August 31, and November 30.

TIPS "We want to see stories with plausible characters, a well-constructed, consistent, and vividly described setting, a strong plot and believable emotions; characters must show us (not tell us) their emotional responses to each other and to the situation and/or challenge they face. Also: don't send us stories written for television. We don't like media tie-ins, so don't watch TV for inspiration! Read, instead! Absolutely no e-mailed or faxed submissions. Strong preference given to submissions by Canadians."

OPEN MINDS QUARTERLY

The Writer's Circle, 680 Kirkwood Dr., Building 1, Sudbury ON P3E 1X3, Canada. (705)675-9193, ext. 8286. E-mail: openminds@nisa.on.ca. Website: www.nisa.on.ca. **Contact:** Dinah Laprairie, editor.

MAGAZINES NEEDS *Open Minds Quarterly* provides a "venue for individuals who have experienced mental illness to express themselves via poetry, short fiction, essays, first-person accounts of living with mental illness, book/movie reviews." Wants "unique, well-written, provocative poetry." Does not want overly graphic or sexual violence. Considers poetry by children and teens. Has published poetry by Pamela MacBean, Sophie Soil, Alice Parris, and Kurt Sass. *Open Minds Quarterly* is 24 pages, magazine-sized, saddle-stapled, with 100 lb. stock cover with original artwork, includes ads. Receives about 300 poems/year, accepts about 30%. Press run is 750; 400 distributed free to potential subscribers, published writers, advertisers, and conferences and events. Single copy: $5.40 CAD, $5 USD; subscription: $35 CAD, $28.25 USD (special rates also available). Make checks payable to NISA/Northern Initiative for Social Action.

HOW TO CONTACT Submit 1-5 poems at a time. Considers previously published poems and simultaneous submissions. Accepts e-mail and disk submissions. Cover letter is required. "Info in cover letter: indication as to 'consumer/survivor' of the mental health system status." Reads submissions year round. Submit seasonal poems at least 8 months in advance. Time between acceptance and publication is 6-18 months. "Poems are first reviewed by poetry editor, then accepted/rejected by the editor. Sometimes, submissions are passed on to a third party for input or a third opinion." Seldom comments on rejected poems. Guidelines available for SASE, by fax, e-mail, or on website. Responds in up to 4 months. "Rarely" sends prepublication galleys. "All authors own their work—if another publisher seeks to reprint from our publication, we request they cite us as the source."

CONTEST/AWARD OFFERINGS "The Brainstorm Poetry Contest runs in first 2 months of each year. Contact the editor for information."

ALSO OFFERS "All material not accepted for our journal will be considered for The Writer's Circle Online, our Internet publication forum. Same guidelines apply. Same contact person."

● OPEN SPACES

PMB 134, 6327 C SW Capitol Hwy., Portland OR 97239-1937. (503)227-4361. Fax: (503)227-3401. E-mail: info@open-spaces.com. Website: www.open-spaces.com. **Contact:** Poetry Editor. Estab. 1997.

MAGAZINES NEEDS *Open Spaces*, published quarterly, "gives voice to the Northwest on issues that are regional, national, and international in scope. Our readership is thoughtful, intelligent, widely read, and appreciative of ideas and writing of the highest quality. With that in mind, we seek thoughtful, well-researched articles and insightful fiction, reviews, and poetry on a variety of subjects from a number of different viewpoints. Although we take ourselves seriously, we appreciate humor as well. Poetry is presented with care and respect." Has published poetry by Vern Rutsala, Pattiann Rogers, Lou Masson, and William Jolliff. *Open Spaces* is 64 pages, magazine-sized, sheet-fed-printed, with cover art. Press run is 5,000-10,000. Subscription: $25/year. Sample: $10. Make checks payable to Open Spaces Publications, Inc.

HOW TO CONTACT Submit 3-5 poems at a time. Considers simultaneous submissions. No fax or e-mail submissions; accepts submissions by postal mail only. Cover letter is required. Time between acceptance and publication is 2-3 months. Poems are circulated to an editorial board. Seldom comments on rejected poems. Guidelines available on website. Responds in up to 4 months. Payment varies. Reviews books/chapbooks of poetry.

●◑ OPEN WIDE MAGAZINE

40 Wingfield Road, Lakenheath, Brandon SK Ip27 9HR, UK. E-mail: contact@openwidemagazine.co.uk. Website: www.openwidemagazine.co.uk. **Contact:** Liz Roberts. Online literary magazine/journal: Quarterly. Open Wide Magazine has been publishing poetry, fiction, reviews and interviews. With our Feel Free Press imprint we published two print anthologies 'Poems Written Whilst Staring Death In The Face' and 'Destination Anywhere', 32 broadsides, a paperback poetry collection by K.M Dersley and chapbooks by Debbie Kirk, Luke Buckham, Shane Allison and Dan Provost. Also as Open Wide Books we published online chapbook collections from Ben Myers, Melissa Mann, Ben Barton, James D Quinton and Emily McPhillips. Receives 100 mss/month. Accepts 25 mss/issue. Publishes 30 new writers/year. Length: 500-4,000. Average length: 2,500. Publishes short shorts. Also publishes poetry, reviews (music, film, art) and interviews. Rarely comments on/critiques rejected mss. Include estimated word count, brief bio. Send either SASE (or IRC) for return of ms or disposable copy of ms and #10 SASE for reply only.

●○ ORBIS: AN INTERNATIONAL QUARTERLY OF POETRY AND PROSE

17 Greenhow Ave., West Kirby, Wirral CH48 5EL, England. E-mail: baldock.carole@googlemail.com. Website: www.kudoswritingcompetitions.com. **Contact:** Carole Baldock, editor.

MAGAZINES NEEDS *Orbis: An International Quarterly of Poetry and Prose* features "news, reviews, views, letters, prose, and quite a lot of poetry." Wants "more work from young people (this includes 20-somethings) and women writers." *Orbis* is 84 pages, digest-sized, professionally printed, flat-spined, with full-color glossy card cover. Receives "thousands" of submissions/year. Publishes 180. Single copy: £5 UK, £6 overseas (€10, $15 USD); subscription: £17 UK, £23 overseas (€30, $46 USD).

HOW TO CONTACT Submit up to 4 poems at a time. Accepts e-mail submissions "from outside UK only; Send press release in 1st instance to: Nessa O'Mahony, 5 Walnut View, Brookwood, Scholarstown Road, Rathfarnham, Dublin 16, Ireland. For postal submissions; enclose SASE (or SAE and 3 IRCs) with all correspondence." Response: 1-3 months. Reviews books and other magazines.

CONTEST/AWARD OFFERINGS Prizes in each issue: £50 for featured writer (3-4 poems); £50 Readers' Award for piece receiving the most votes; £50 split among 4 (or more) runners-up.

◑ OSIRIS

P.O. Box 297, Deerfield MA 01342-0297. E-mail: amoorhead@deerfield.edu. **Contact:** Andrea Moorhead, poetry editor. Estab. 1972.

MAGAZINES NEEDS *Osiris*, published semiannually, prints contemporary poetry in English, French, and Italian without translation, and in other languages with translation, including Polish, Danish, and German. Wants poetry that is "lyrical, non-narrative, multi-temporal, postmodern, well-crafted. Also looking for translations from non-IndoEuropean languages." Has published poetry by Abderrahmane Djelfaoui (Algeria), George Moore (USA), Flavio Ermini (Italy), Mylene Durand

(Quebec), Anne Blonstein (Switzerland), Astrid Cabral (Brazil), and Rob Cook (USA). *Osiris* is 48-56 pages, digest-sized, perfect-bound. Press run is 500 (50 subscription copies sent to college and university libraries, including foreign libraries). Receives 200-300 submissions/year, accepts about 12. Single copy: $10; subscription: $18. Sample: $6.

HOW TO CONTACT Submit 4-6 poems at a time. "Poems should be sent by postal mail. Include short bio and SASE with submission. Translators should include a letter of permission from the poet or publisher as well as copies of the original text." Responds in 1 month. Sometimes sends prepublication galleys. Pays 5 contributor's copies.

OVER THE TRANSOM

825 Bush St. #203, San Francisco CA 94108. (415)928-3965. E-mail: jsh619@earthlink.net. **Contact:** Jonathan Hayes, editor.

MAGAZINES NEEDS *Over The Transom*, published 2 times/year, is a free publication of poetry and prose. Open to all styles of poetry. "We look for the highest quality writing that best fits the issue." Considers poetry by children and teens. Has published poetry by Garrett Caples, Richard Lopez, Glen Chesnut, Daniel J. Langton. *Over The Transom* is 32 pages, magazine-sized, saddle-stapled, with cardstock cover. Receives about 1,000 poems/year, accepts about 5%. Press run is 300 (100 subscribers); 150 distributed free to cafes, bookstores, universities, and bars. Single copy: free. Sample: $3. Make checks payable to Jonathan Hayes.

HOW TO CONTACT Submit 5 poems at a time. Considers previously published poems and simultaneous submissions. Accepts e-mail submissions; no disk submissions. Must include a SASE with postal submissions. Reads submissions year round. Time between acceptance and publication is 2-6 months. Never comments on rejected poems. Occasionally publishes theme issues. Guidelines available for SASE or by e-mail. Responds in 2 months. Sometimes sends prepublication galleys. Pays 1 contributor's copy. Acquires first rights.

OXFORD MAGAZINE

356 Bachelor Hall, Miami University, Oxford OH 45056. (513)529-1274. E-mail: oxmagpoetryeditor@muohio.edu. Website: www.oxfordmagazine.org. **Contact:** Jonny Lohr, poetry editor. Estab. 1984.

Work published in *Oxford Magazine* has been included in the Pushcart Prize anthology.

MAGAZINES NEEDS *Oxford Magazine*, published annually in May online, is open in terms of form, content, and subject matter. "We have eclectic tastes, ranging from New Formalism to Language poetry to Nuyorican poetry." Has published poetry by Lisa Jarnot, Eve Shelnutt, Denise Duhamel, and Walter McDonald.

HOW TO CONTACT Submit 3-5 poems at a time. Considers simultaneous submissions; no previously published poems. Accepts e-mail (pasted into body of message or as MS Word attachment) and disk submissions. Cover letter is preferred. Reads submissions September 1-December 31. No payment. Acquires one-time rights.

OYEZ REVIEW

Roosevelt University, Dept. of Literature & Languages,, 430 S. Michigan Ave., Chicago IL 60605-1394. (312)341-3500. E-mail: oyezreview@roosevelt.edu. Website: legacy.roosevelt.edu/roosevelt.edu/oyezreview.

Reading period is August 1-October 1. Responds by mid-December.

MAGAZINES NEEDS *Oyez Review*, published annually in January by Roosevelt University's MFA Program in Creative Writing, receives "submissions from across the nation and around the world. We're open to poetic sequences and longer poems provided they hold the reader's attention. We welcome skilled and polished work from newcomers as well as poems from established authors. The quality of the individual poem is key, not the poet's reputation." Has published poetry by Gary Fincke, Moira Egan, Gaylord Brewer, Barbara De Cesare, Prairie Markussen, Gary Held. *Oyez Review* is 90 pages, digest-sized. Accepts 5% of poems received. Press run is 800. Single copy: $5.

HOW TO CONTACT Submit up to 5 poems, no more than 10 pages of poetry at a time. No simultaneous submissions. No fax, e-mail, or disk submissions. Cover letter is required. "Be sure to include a three- to five-sentence biography and complete contact information, including phone and e-mail." Reads submissions August 1-October 1 only. Time between acceptance and publication is 2 months. Guidelines available on website. Responds in 3 months. Pays 2 contributor's copies. Acquires first North American serial rights.

⬤ OYSTER BOY REVIEW

P.O. Box 1483, Pacifica CA 94044. E-mail: email_2010@oysterboyreview.com. Website: www.oysterboyreview.com. **Contact:** Damon Suave, editor/publisher. Electronic and print magazine. *Oyster Boy Review*, published 4 times a year, is interested in "the underrated, the ignored, the misunderstood, and the varietal. We'll make some mistakes. 'All styles are good except the boring kind'—Voltaire." Considers poetry by children and teens. Has published poetry by Jonathan Williams, Cid Corman, Lyn Lifshin, and Paul Dilsaver. *Oyster Boy Review* is 60 pages, 6½x11, Docutech printed, stapled, with paper cover, includes ads. Receives about 1,500 poems/year, accepts 2%. Press run is 200; 30 distributed free to editors, authors. Subscription: $20.

HOW TO CONTACT Submit up to 5 poems at a time. No previously published poems or simultaneous submissions. Accepts e-mail submissions if poems are included in body of message. Cover letter preferred. Postal submissions require SASE. Do not submit mss in late December. "Upon acceptance, authors asked to provide electronic version of work and a biographical statement." Time between acceptance and publication is 6 months. Seldom comments on rejected poems. Guidelines available by e-mail or on website. Responds in 3 months. Pays 2 copies. Reviews books/chapbooks of poetry in 250-500 words (first books only), in single or multi-book format. Send materials for review consideration.

ADDITIONAL INFORMATION Off the Cuff Books is not open to submissions or solicitations. Off the Cuff Books publishes "longer works on special projects of authors published in *Oyster Boy Review*."

TIPS "Keep writing, keep submitting, keep revising."

⬤☻ PACKINGTOWN REVIEW

The University of Illinois at Chicago, English Department, UH 2027 MC 162, University of Illinois at Chicago, 601 S. Morgan, Chicago IL 60607. (908)745-1547. E-mail: editors@packingtownreview.com. Website: www.packingtownreview.com. **Contact:** Editor. *Packingtown Review*, published annually in March, prints creative writing and critical prose by emerging and established writers. "We welcome submissions of poetry, scholarly articles, drama, creative nonfiction, fiction, and literary translation, as well as genre-bending pieces." Wants "well-crafted poetry. We are open to most styles and forms. We are also looking for poetry that takes risks and does so successfully. We will consider articles about poetry." Does not want "uninspired or unrevised work." *Packingtown Review* is 250 pages, magazine-sized. Press run is 500. Single copy: see website for prices.

HOW TO CONTACT Submit 3-5 poems at a time. Considers simultaneous submissions (with notification); no previously published poems (considers poems posted on a public website/blog/forum previously published, but not those posted on a private, password-protected forum). No e-mail or disk submissions. Cover letter is required. "Please include a SASE. If you have simultaneously submitted these poems, please indicate in the cover letter and let us know ASAP if a poem is accepted elsewhere." Reads submissions year round. Poems are circulated to an editorial board. Sometimes comments on rejected poems. Sometimes publishes theme issues. Guidelines available on website. Responds in 3 months. Always sends prepublication galleys. Pays 2 contributor's copies. Acquires first North American serial rights. Rights revert to poets upon publication. Review books/chapbooks of poetry and other magazines/journals. Send materials for review consideration to Lucas Johnson.

TIPS "We are looking for well-crafted prose. We are open to most styles and forms. We are also looking for prose that takes risks and does so successfully. We will consider articles about prose."

⬤⬤$ PAINTED BRIDE QUARTERLY

Drexel University, Dept. of English and Philosophy, 3141 Chestnut St., Philadelphia PA 19104. Website: http://webdelsol.com/pbq. Drexel University, Dept. of English and Philosophy, 3141 Chestnut St., Philadelphia, PA 19104. E-mail: pbq@drexel.edu. Website: http://webdelsol.com/pbq. *Painted Bride Quarterly*, published online, "aims to be a leader among little magazines published by and for independent poets and writers nationally. We have no specifications or restrictions. We'll look at anything." Has published poetry by Robert Bly, Charles Bukowski, S.J. Marks, and James Hazen. *Painted Bride Quarterly* is printed as one hardcopy anthology annually. Single copy: $15. *Painted Bride Quarterly* seeks literary fiction, experimental and traditional.

HOW TO CONTACT Submit up to 5 poems at a time. Lines/poem: any length. No previously published poems. No e-mail submissions. "Submissions must be original, typed, and should include a short bio." Time between acceptance and publication is 6-9 months. Seldom comments on rejected poems. Occasionally publishes theme issues. Guidelines available on website. Pays one-year subscription, one half-priced contributor's copy, and $5/accepted piece. Publishes reviews of poetry books.

CONTEST/AWARD OFFERINGS Sponsors an annual poetry contest and a chapbook competition. **Entry fee:** required for both. Guidelines available for SASE or on website.

TIPS "We look for freshness of idea incorporated with high-quality writing. We receive an awful lot of nicely written work with worn-out plots. We want quality in whatever—we hold experimental work to as strict standards as anything else. Many of our readers write fiction; most of them enjoy a good reading. We hope to be an outlet for quality. A good story gives, first, enjoyment to the reader. We've seen a good many of them lately, and we've published the best of them."

PARADOXISM

200 College Rd., Gallup NM 87301. Fax: (503)863-7532. E-mail: smarand@unm.edu. Website: www.gallup.unm.edu/~smarandache/a/paradoxism.htm. **Contact:** Dr. Florentin Smarandache.

MAGAZINES NEEDS *Paradoxism*, published annually, prints "avant-garde poetry, experiments, poems without verses, literature beyond the words, anti-language, non-literature and its literature, as well as the sense of the non-sense; revolutionary forms of poetry. Paradoxism, a 1980s movement of anti-totalitarian protest, is based on excessive use of antitheses, antinomies, contradictions, paradoxes in creation." Wants "avant-garde poetry, 1-2 pages, any subject, any style (lyrical experiments)." Does not want "classical, fixed forms." Has published poetry by Paul Georgelin, Mircea Monu, Ion Rotaru, Micheéle de LaPlante, and Claude LeRoy. *Paradoxism* is 52 pages, digest-sized, offset-printed, with soft cover. Press run is 500; distributed "to its collaborators, U.S. and Canadian university libraries, and the Library of Congress as well as European, Chinese, Indian, and Japanese libraries."

HOW TO CONTACT No previously published poems or simultaneous submissions. Do not submit during the summer. "We do not return published or unpublished poems or notify the author of date of publication." Responds in up to 3 weeks. Pays 1 contributor's copy.

ADDITIONAL INFORMATION Paradoxism Association also publishes 2 poetry paperbacks and 1-2 chapbooks/year, including translations. "The poems must be unpublished and must meet the requirements of the Paradoxism Association." Responds to queries in 2 months; to mss in up to 3 weeks. Pays 50 author's copies. Sample e-books available on website at www.gallup.unm.edu/~smarandache/eBooksLiterature.htm.

TIPS "We look for work that refers to the paradoxism or is written in the paradoxist style. The Basic Thesis of the paradoxism: everything has a meaning and a non-meaning in a harmony with each other. The Essence of the paradoxism: a) the sense has a non-sense, and reciprocally B) the non-sense has a sense. The Motto of the paradoxism: 'All is possible, the impossible too!' The Symbol of the paradoxism: a spiral—optic illusion, or vicious circle."

◐◉ THE PARIS REVIEW

62 White Street, New York NY 10013. (212)343-1333. E-mail: queries@theparisreview.org. Website: www.theparisreview.org. Nathaniel Rich, fiction editor. **Contact:** Philip Gourevitch, editor. "Fiction and poetry of superlative quality, whatever the genre, style or mode. Our contributors include prominent, as well as less well-known and previously unpublished writers. Writers at Work interview series includes important contemporary writers discussing their own work and the craft of writing."

◗ Address submissions to proper department. Do not make submissions via e-mail.

HOW TO CONTACT Submit no more than six poems at a time. Poetry can be sent to the Poetry Editor at the above address (please include a self-addressed, stamped envelope), or submitted online at http://www.theparisreview.org/poetry/. Pays $35 minimum varies according to length. Buys all rights, buys first English-language rights.

CONTEST/AWARD OFFERINGS Awards $1,000 in Bernard F. Conners Poetry Prize contest.

PARNASSUS: POETRY IN REVIEW

Poetry in Review Foundation, 205 W. 89th St., #8F, New York NY 10024. (212)362-3492. Fax: (212)875-0148. E-mail: parnew@aol.com. Website: www.parnassuspoetry.com. **Contact:** Herbert Leibowitz, editor & publisher. "We now publish one double issue a year."

TIPS "Be certain you have read the magazine and are aware of the editor's taste. Blind submissions are a waste of everybody's time. We'd like to see more poems that display intellectual acumen and curiosity about history, science, music, etc., and fewer trivial lyrical poems about the self, or critical prose that's academic and dull. Prose should sing."

PASSAGES NORTH

English Dept., Northern Michigan University, 1401 Presque Isle Ave., Marquette MI 49855. (906)227-1203. E-mail: passages@nmu.edu. Website: www.nmu.edu/passagesnorth. Established 1979. **Contact:** Austin Hummell, poetry editor.

MAGAZINES NEEDS *Passages North*, published annually in spring, prints poetry, short fiction, creative nonfiction, essays, and interviews. Publishes work by established and emerging writers. Has published poetry by Moira Egan, Frannie Lindsay, Ben Lerner, Bob Hicok, and Gabe Gudding. *Passages North* is 250 pages. Circulation is 1,500. Single copy: $13; subscription: $13/year, $23 for 2 years. Sample: $3 (back issue).

HOW TO CONTACT Submit up to 6 poems at a time. Considers simultaneous submissions. Time between acceptance and publication is 6 months. Reads submissions September-May only. Responds in 2 months. Pays 2 contributor's copies.

CONTEST/AWARD OFFERINGS Sponsors the Elinor Benedict Poetry Prize every other year. 1st Prize: $1,000, plus 2 Honorable Mentions. **Entry fee:** $10 for 1-3 poems (each entrant receives the contest issue of *Passages North*). Make checks payable to Northern Michigan University. **Deadline:** reads entries October 15-February 15. Guidelines available for SASE, by e-mail, or on website.

PASSION

Crescent Moon Publishing, P.O. Box 393, Maidstone Kent ME14 5XU, United Kingdom. (44)(162)272-9593. E-mail: cresmopub@yahoo.co.uk. Website: www.crescentmoon.org.uk. Crescent Moon Publishing, P.O. Box 393, Maidstone, Kent ME14 5XU United Kingdom. (44)(162)272-9593. E-mail: cresmopub@yahoo.co.uk. Website: www.crescentmoon.org.uk. Established 1988. **Contact:** Jeremy Robinson, editor. *Passion*, published quarterly, features poetry, fiction, reviews, and essays on feminism, art, philosophy,

and the media. Wants "thought-provoking, incisive, polemical, ironic, lyric, sensual, and hilarious work." Does not want "rubbish, trivia, party politics, sport, etc." Has published poetry by Jeremy Reed, Penelope Shuttle, Alan Bold, D.J. Enright, and Peter Redgrove. Single copy: £2.50 ($4 USD); subscription: £10 ($17 USD). Make checks payable to Crescent Moon Publishing. *Passion*, published quarterly, features poetry, fiction, reviews, and essays on feminism, art, philosophy, and the media. Wants "thought-provoking, incisive, polemical, ironic, lyric, sensual, and hilarious work." Does not want "rubbish, trivia, party politics, sport, etc." Has published poetry by Jeremy Reed, Penelope Shuttle, Alan Bold, D.J. Enright, and Peter Redgrove. Single copy: £2.50 ($4 USD); subscription: £10 ($17 USD). Make checks payable to Crescent Moon Publishing.

MAGAZINES NEEDS *Passion*, published quarterly, features poetry, fiction, reviews, and essays on feminism, art, philosophy, and the media. Wants "thought-provoking, incisive, polemical, ironic, lyric, sensual, and hilarious work." Does not want "rubbish, trivia, party politics, sport, etc." Has published poetry by Jeremy Reed, Penelope Shuttle, Alan Bold, D.J. Enright, and Peter Redgrove. Single copy: £2.50 ($4 USD); subscription: £10 ($17 USD). Make checks payable to Crescent Moon Publishing.

HOW TO CONTACT Submit 5-10 poems at a time. Cover letter is required. Include brief bio and publishing credits ("and please print your address in capitals"). Pays one contributor's copy.

ADDITIONAL INFORMATION Crescent Moon publishes about 25 books and chapbooks/year on arrangements **subsidized by the poet**. Wants "poetry that is passionate and authentic. Any form or length." Does not want "the trivial, insincere or derivative. We are also publishing two anthologies of new American poetry each year entitled *Pagan America*." Has also published studies of Rimbaud, Rilke, Cavafy, Shakespeare, Beckett, German Romantic poetry, and D.H. Lawrence. Books are usually about 76 pages, flat-spined, digest-sized. *Pagan America* available for £4.99 each ($8.95 USD) or £10 ($17 USD) for 2 issues.

THE PATERSON LITERARY REVIEW

Passaic County Community College, Cultural Affairs Dept., One College Blvd., Paterson NJ 07505-1179. (973)684-6555. Fax: (973)523-6085. E-mail: mGillan@pccc.edu. Website: www.pccc.edu/poetry. **Con-**

tact: Maria Mazziotti Gillan, editor/executive director. Passaic County Community College, One College Blvd., Paterson NJ 07505. (973) 684-6555. Fax: (973) 523-6085. E-mail: mGillan@pccc.edu. Website: www.pccc.edu/poetry. **Contact:** Maria Mazziotti Gillan, editor/executive director. *Paterson Literary Review*, published annually, is produced by the The Poetry Center at Passaic County Community College. Wants poetry of "high quality; clear, direct, powerful work." Has published poetry by Diane di Prima, Ruth Stone, Marge Piercy, and Laura Boss. *Paterson Literary Review* is 300-400 pages, magazine-sized, professionally printed, saddle-stapled, with glossy 4-color card cover. Press run is 2,500. Sample: $13.

○ Work for *PLR* has been included in the *Pushcart Prize* anthology and *Best American Poetry*. Work for *PLR* has been included in the *Pushcart Prize* anthology and *Best American Poetry*.

MAGAZINES NEEDS *Paterson Literary Review*, published annually, is produced by the The Poetry Center at Passaic County Community College. Wants poetry of "high quality; clear, direct, powerful work." Has published poetry by Diane di Prima, Ruth Stone, Marge Piercy, and Laura Boss. *Paterson Literary Review* is 300-400 pages, magazine-sized, professionally printed, saddle-stapled, with glossy 4-color card cover. Press run is 2,500. Sample: $13.

HOW TO CONTACT Submit up to 5 poems at a time. Lines/poem: 100 maximum. Considers simultaneous submissions. Reads submissions December 1-March 31 only. Responds within 1 year. Pays 1 contributor's copy. Acquires first rights.

CONTEST/AWARD OFFERINGS The Allen Ginsberg Poetry Awards and The Paterson Poetry Prize (see separate listings in Contests & Awards).

ALSO OFFERS Publishes *The New Jersey Poetry Resource Book* ($5 plus $1.50 p&h) and *The New Jersey Poetry Calendar*. The Distinguished Poets Series offers readings by poets of international, national, and regional reputation. Poetryworks/USA is a series of programs produced for UA Columbia-Cablevision. See website for details about these additional resources.

TIPS Looks for "clear, moving and specific work."

◐ PAVEMENT SAW

Pavement Saw Press, 321 Empire Street, Montpelier OH 43543. E-mail: info@pavementsaw.org. Website: http://pavementsaw.org. **Contact:** David Baratier, editor. Pavement Saw Press has been publishing steadily since the fall of 1993. Each year since 1999, we have published at least 4 full length paperback poetry collections, with some printed in library edition hard covers, one chapbook and a yearly literary journal anthology. We specialize in finding authors who have been widely published in literary journals but have not published a chapbook or full length book. *Pavement Saw*, published annually in August, wants "letters and short fiction, and poetry on any subject, especially work." Does not want "poems that tell; no work by a deceased writer, and no translations." Dedicates 15-20 pages of each issue to a featured writer. *Pavement Saw* is 88 pages, digest-sized, perfect-bound. Receives about 9,000 poems/year, accepts less than 1%. Press run is 550. Single copy: $8; subscription: $14. Sample: $7. Make checks payable to Pavement Saw Press. Sometimes sends prepublication galleys. Pays at least 2 contributor's copies.

MAGAZINES NEEDS *Pavement Saw*, published annually in August, wants "letters and short fiction, and poetry on any subject, especially work." Does not want "poems that tell; no work by a deceased writer, and no translations." Dedicates 15-20 pages of each issue to a featured writer. Has published poetry by Simon Perchik, Sofia Starnes, Alan Catlin, Adrianne Kalfopoulou, Jim Daniels, and Mary Weems. *Pavement Saw* is 88 pages, digest-sized, perfect-bound. Receives about 9,000 poems/year, accepts less than 1%. Press run is 550. Single copy: $8; subscription: $14. Sample: $7. Make checks payable to Pavement Saw Press.

HOW TO CONTACT Submit 5 poems at a time. Lines/poem: 1-2 pages. Considers simultaneous submissions, "as long as poet has not published a book with a press run of 1,000 or more"; no previously published poems. No e-mail submissions; postal submissions only. Cover letter is required. "No fancy typefaces." Seldom comments on rejected poems. Guidelines available in magazine or for SASE. Responds in 4 months. Sometimes sends prepublication galleys. Pays at least 2 contributor's copies. Acquires first rights.

ADDITIONAL INFORMATION Pavement Saw Press also publishes books of poetry. "Most are by authors who have been published in the journal." Published "7 titles in 2005 and 7 titles in 2006; 5 were full-length books ranging from 80 to 240 pages."

CONTEST/AWARD OFFERINGS Transcontinental Poetry Award and Pavement Saw Press Chapbook Award (see separate listings in Contests & Awards).

●○ PEACE & FREEDOM

Peace & Freedom Press, 17 Farrow Rd., Whaplode Drove, Spalding, Lincs PE12 0TS, England. Website: http://pande.booksmusicfilmstv.com/index.htm. Published semiannually; emphasizes social, humanitarian, and environmental issues. **Considers submissions from subscribers only.** "Those new to poetry are welcome. The poetry we publish is pro-animal rights/welfare, anti-war, environmental; poems reflecting love; erotic, but not obscene; humorous; spiritual, humanitarian; with or without rhyme/meter." Considers poetry by children and teens. Has published poetry by Dorothy Bell-Hall, Freda Moffatt, Andrew Bruce, Bernard Shough, Mona Miller, and Andrew Savage. *Peace & Freedom* has a varied format. Subscription: $20 U.S., £10 UK for 6 issues. Sample: $5 U.S., £1.75 UK. "Sample copies can be purchased only from the above address. Advisable to buy a sample copy before submitting. Banks charge the equivalent of $5 to cash foreign checks in the UK, so please only send bills, preferably by registered post."

HOW TO CONTACT Lines/poem: 32 maximum. No previously published poems or simultaneous submissions. Accepts e-mail submissions (pasted into body of message, no attachments; no more than 3 poems/e-mail); no fax submissions. Include bio. Reads submissions year round. Publishes theme issues. Upcoming themes available in magazine, for SAE with IRC, by e-mail, or on website. Responds to submissions in less than a month ("usually"), with SAE/IRC. "Work without correct postage will not be responded to or returned until proper postage is sent." Pays one contributor's copy. Reviews books of poetry.

CONTEST/AWARD OFFERINGS "*Peace & Freedom* holds regular poetry contests as does one of our other publications, *Eastern Rainbow*, which is a magazine concerning 20th-century popular culture using poetry up to 32 lines." Subscription: $20 U.S., £10 UK for 6 issues. Further details of competitions and publications available for SAE with IRC or on website.

ALSO OFFERS Publishes anthologies. Guidelines and details of upcoming anthologies available in magazine, for SAE with IRC, by e-mail, or on website.

TIPS "Too many writers have lost the personal touch that editors generally appreciate. It can make a difference when selecting work of equal merit."

● PEARL

3030 E. Second St., Long Beach CA 90803. (562)434-4523. E-mail: pearlmag@aol.com. Website: www.pearlmag.com. **Contact:** Joan Jobe Smith, Marilyn Johnson, and Barbara Hauk, poetry editors. 3030 E. Second St., Long Beach, CA 90803. (562)434-4523. E-mail: pearlmag@aol.com. Website: www.pearlmag.com. *Pearl*, published semiannually in May and November, is interested "in accessible, humanistic poetry that communicates and is related to real life. Humor and wit are welcome, along with the ironic and serious. No taboos, stylistically or subject-wise." Does not want "sentimental, obscure, predictable, abstract, or clicheé-ridden poetry. Our purpose is to provide a forum for lively, readable poetry that reflects a wide variety of contemporary voices, viewpoints, and experiences—that speaks to real people about real life in direct, living language, profane or sublime. Our Fall/Winter issue is devoted exclusively to poetry, with a 12- to 15-page section featuring the work of a single poet." Has published poetry by Christopher Buckley, Fred Voss, David Hernandez, Lisa Glatt, Jim Daniels, Nin Andrews, and Frank X. Gaspar. *Pearl* is 112-136 pages, digest-sized, offset-printed, perfect-bound, with glossy cover. Press run is 700. Subscription: $21/year (includes a copy of the Pearl Poetry Prize-winning book). Sample: $8."*Pearl* is an eclectic publication, a place for lively, readable poetry and prose that speaks to real people about real life in direct, living language, profane or sublime."

○ Submissions are accepted from Jan. - June only. Mss. received between July and Dec. will be returned unread. No email submissions, except from countries outside the U.S. See guidelines.

MAGAZINES NEEDS *Pearl*, published semiannually in May and November, is interested "in accessible, humanistic poetry that communicates and is related to real life. Humor and wit are welcome, along with the ironic and serious. No taboos, stylistically or subject-wise." Does not want "sentimental, obscure, predictable, abstract, or clicheé-ridden poetry. Our purpose is to provide a forum for lively, readable poetry that reflects a wide variety of contemporary voices, viewpoints, and experiences—that speaks to real people about real life in direct, living language, profane or sublime. Our Fall/Winter issue is devoted exclusively to poetry, with a 12- to 15-page section featuring the work of a single poet." Has published poetry by Christopher Buckley, Fred Voss, David Hernandez, Lisa Glatt, Jim Daniels, Nin Andrews, and Frank X. Gaspar. *Pearl* is 112-136 pages, digest-sized, offset-printed, perfect-bound, with glossy cover. Press run is 700. Subscription: $21/year (includes a copy of the Pearl Poetry Prize-winning book). Sample: $10.

HOW TO CONTACT Submit 3-5 poems at a time with cover letter and SASE. Lines/poem: no longer than 40 lines preferred, each line no more than 10-12 words, to accommodate page size and format. Considers simultaneous submissions ("must be acknowledged as such"); no previously published poems. NO e-mail submissions; postal submissions only. "Handwritten submissions and unreadable printouts are not acceptable." Reads submissions January-June only. Time between acceptance and publication is up to 1 year. Responds in 2 months. Sometimes sends prepublication galleys. Pays 1 contributor's copy. Acquires first serial rights.

ADDITIONAL INFORMATION Pearl Editions publishes the winner of the Pearl Poetry Prize only (see separate listing in Contests & Awards). All other books and chapbooks are by invitation only.

TIPS "We look for vivid, *dramatized* situations and characters, stories written in an original 'voice,' that make sense and follow a clear narrative line. What makes a manuscript stand out is more elusive, though—more to do with feeling and imagination than anything else."

⬤ PEBBLE LAKE REVIEW

Website: www.pebblelakereview.com. 15318 Pebble Lake Dr., Houston TX 77095. E-mail: submissions@pebblelakereview.com. Website: www.pebblelakereview.com. Established 2002. **Contact:** Amanda Auchter, editor.

⬤ Poems published in *Pebble Lake Review* have appeared on Verse Daily (www.versedaily.org) and were included in *Pushcart Prize XXXI: Best of the Small Presses.*

MAGAZINES NEEDS *Pebble Lake Review*, published twice a year in June and December, seeks "high-quality, image-rich poetry that demonstrates attention to language, form, and craft. Looking for

more experimental work." Does not want "anything clicheé, Hallmark-style, racist, or erotic." Has published poetry by Kim Addonizio, Oliver De ala Paz, Denise Duhamel, Bob Hicok, Ilya Kaminksy, David Kirby, Noelle Kocot, Timothy Liu, Charles Harper Webb, Franz Wright, and others. *Pebble Lake Review* is available online and includes an audio component. Receives about 5,000 poems/year, accepts less than 3%.

HOW TO CONTACT Submit September 1- February 1 annually, 3-5 poems at a time. Considers simultaneous submissions with notification; no previously published poems. Accepts e-mail submissions (pasted into body of message; attachments accepted if Word or RTF documents); no disk submissions. Cover letter is required. Time between acceptance and publication is 1-4 months. "Poems are circulated between the editors, and the decision is finalized by the editor-in-chief." Seldom comments on rejected poems. Guidelines available on website. Acquires one-time electronic rights; rights are returned to author upon publication. Reviews books/chapbooks of poetry in 500-1,000 words, single-book format. Send materials for review consideration.

ALSO OFFERS Selects poets to read work as part of the *Pebble Lake Review* Audio Project. E-mail the online editor at webmaster@pebblelakereview for details.

⬤⬤⬤ THE PEDESTAL MAGAZINE

6815 Honors Court, Charlotte NC 28210. (704)643-0244. E-mail: pedmagazine@carolina.rr.com. Website: www.thepedestalmagazine.com. **Contact:** Nathan Leslie, fiction editor; John Amen, editor-in-chief. Member: CLMP. "We are committed to promoting diversity and celebrating the voice of the individual."

MAGAZINES NEEDS *The Pedestal Magazine*, published bimonthly online, prints "12-15 poems per issue, as well as fiction, interviews, and book reviews. We are open to a wide variety of poetry, ranging from the highly experimental to the traditionally formal." Receives about 5,000 poems/year, accepts about 1%. "We have a readership of approximately 15,000 per month."

HOW TO CONTACT Submit up to 6 poems at a time. Lines/poem: open. Considers simultaneous submissions; no previously published poems. No e-mail or disk submissions. "Submissions are accepted via a submission form provided in the 'Submit' section of the website. Our submissions schedule is posted in the guidelines section." Time between acceptance and publication is 2-4 weeks. Poems are circulated to an editorial board. Sometimes comments on rejected poems. Sometimes publishes theme issues. Guidelines available on website. Responds in 4-6 weeks. Always sends prepublication galleys (by e-mail). Pays $40/poem. Acquires first rights. Reviews books/chapbooks of poetry in 850-1,000 words. "Please query via e-mail prior to sending books or related materials."

TIPS "If you send us your work, please wait for a response to your first submission before you submit again."

○ THE PEGASUS REVIEW

P.O. Box 88, Henderson MD 21640-0088. (410)482-6736. E-mail: pegasus.sgc.edu. Dr. William Webster, faculty adviser. P.O. Box 88, Henderson, MD 21640-0088. (410)482-6736. E-mail: pegasus.sgc.edu. **Contact:** Dr. William Webster, faculty adviser. Estab. 1980.

MAGAZINES NEEDS *The Pegasus Review*, now a quarterly, focuses on a specific theme for each issue and issued in calligraphic format. "Since themes might change it is advisable to contact editor about current themes. With us, brevity is the key. Themes may be submitted in the way of poetry, short-short fiction and essays." Has published work by Jane Stuart, Ed Galing, John Grey, and Burton R. Hoffman. Press run is 120 (100 subscribers, 2 libraries). Subscription: $12. Sample: $2.50, including shipping and handling. "We are currently accepting original poetry, prose, and artwork for consideration. Poetry and prose should be submitted electronically. Simply cut and paste it directly into an email sent to: pegasus@sgc.edu."

HOW TO CONTACT Submit 3-5 poems at a time. Lines/poem: 24 maximum. Considers previously published poems, "if there is no conflict or violation of rights agreement," and simultaneous submissions, "but author must notify proper parties once specific material is accepted." "Brief cover letter with specifics as they relate to one's writing background are welcome." Include name and address on each page. "The usual SASE would be appreciated, unless told to recycle material." Responds within 1 month, often with a personal response. Pays 2 contributor's copies and an occasional book award.

TIPS "Write and circulate your work. Constantly strive to improve your writing craft through local writers' groups and/or writing conferences. Remember: writers need readers, so offer to read your work before a group (schools, senior citizen centers, libraries).

◐◑ PENNINE INK MAGAZINE

1 Neptune St.,, Burnley BB11 1SF, England. E-mail: sheridansdandl@yahoo.co.uk. **Contact:** Laura Sheridan, Editor.

MAGAZINES NEEDS *Pennine Ink*, published annually in January, prints poems and short prose pieces. *Pennine Ink* is 48 pages, A5, with b&w illustrated cover. Receives about 400 poems/year, accepts about 40. Press run is 200. "Contributors wishing to purchase a copy of *Pennine Ink* should enclose £2 ($4 USD) per copy."

HOW TO CONTACT Submit up to 6 poems at a time. Lines/poem: 40 maximum; prose: no longer than 1,000 words. Considers previously published poems and simultaneous submissions. Accepts e-mail submissions. Seldom comments on rejected poems. Responds in 3 months. Pays 1 contributor's copy.

○ PENNSYLVANIA ENGLISH

Penn State DuBois, College Place, DuBois PA 15801-3199. (814)375-4785. Fax: (814)375-4785. E-mail: ajv2@psu.edu. Website: www.english.iup.edu/pcea. **Contact:** Antonio Vallone, editor.

MAGAZINES NEEDS *Pennsylvania English*, published annually, is "sponsored by the Pennsylvania College English Association." Wants poetry of "any length, any style." Has published poetry by Liz Rosenberg, Walt MacDonald, Amy Pence, Jennifer Richter, and Jeff Schiff. *Pennsylvania English* is up to 200 pages, digest-sized, perfect-bound, with full-color cover. Press run is 500. Subscription: $10/year.

HOW TO CONTACT Submit 3 or more poems at a time. Considers simultaneous submissions; no previously published poems. No e-mail submissions. Submissions must be typed. Include SASE. Guidelines available for SASE. Responds in 6 months. Pays 2 contributor's copies.

TIPS "Quality of the writing is our only measure. We're not impressed by long-winded cover letters detailing awards and publications we've never heard of. Beginners and professionals have the same chance with us. We receive stacks of competently written but boring fiction. For a story to rise out of the rejection pile, it takes more than the basic competence."

PENNY DREADFUL: TALES & POEMS OF FANTASTIC TERROR

E-mail: MMPENDRAGON@aol.com. Website: www.mpendragon.com. P.O. Box 719, Radio City Station, Hell's Kitchen NY 10101-0719. E-mail: MMPENDRAGON@aol.com. Website: www.mpendragon.com. **Contact:** Michael Pendragon, editor/publisher. Estab. 1996.

"Works appearing in *Penny Dreadful* have been reprinted in *The Year's Best Fantasy and Horror*." *Penny Dreadful* nominates best tales and poems for Pushcart Prizes.

MAGAZINES NEEDS *Penny Dreadful: Tales & Poems of Fanastic Terror*, published irregularly (about one/year), features goth-romantic poetry and prose. Publishes poetry, short stories, essays, letters, listings, reviews, and b&w artwork "which celebrate the darker aspects of Man, the World, and their Creator." Wants "literary horror in the tradition of Poe, M.R. James, Shelley, M.P. Shiel, and LeFanu—dark, disquieting tales and verses designed to challenge the reader's perception of human nature, morality, and man's place within the Darkness. Stories and poems should be set prior to 1910 and/or possess a timeless quality. Rhymed, metered verse preferred." Does not want "references to 20th- and 21st-century personages/events, graphic sex, strong language, excessive gore and shock elements." Has published poetry by Nancy Bennett, Michael R. Burch, Lee Clark, Louise Webster, K.S. Hardy, and Kevin N. Roberts. *Penny Dreadful* is about 170 pages, digest-sized, desktop-published, perfect-bound. Press run is 200. Subscription: $25/3 issues. Sample: $10. Make checks payable to Michael Pendragon.

HOW TO CONTACT Submit up to 12 poems at a time. Lines/poem: poems should not exceed 3 pages. Considers previously published poems and simultaneous submissions. "Due to the amount of submissions received, the editor cannot always respond. He encourages all contributors to submit work as simultaneous submissions." Accepts e-mail submissions (preferred; "include in body of message with a copy attached"). Put name and address on opening page, and name/title/page number on all following pages. SASE required with postal submissions. Reads submissions year round. Time between acceptance and publication is "indefinite." Poems are reviewed and chosen by editor. Guidelines available on website.

Always sends prepublication galleys. Pays one contributor's copy. Acquires one-time rights.

ADDITIONAL INFORMATION *Penny Dreadful* "includes market listings for, and reviews of, kindred magazines." Pendragon Publications also publishes *Songs of Innocence & Experience*.

THE PENWOOD REVIEW

P.O. Box 862, Los Alamitos CA 90720-0862. E-mail: lcameron65@verizon.net. E-mail: submissions@penwoodreview.com. Website: www.penwoodreview.com. **Contact:** Lori Cameron, editor. .

MAGAZINES NEEDS *The Penwood Review*, published semiannually, seeks "to explore the spiritual and sacred aspects of our existence and our relationship to God." Wants "disciplined, high-quality, well-crafted poetry on any subject. Rhyming poetry must be written in traditional forms (sonnets, tercets, villanelles, sestinas, etc.)." Has published poetry by Kathleen Spivack, Anne Babson, Hugh Fox, Anselm Brocki, Nina Tassi, and Gary Guinn. *The Penwood Review* is about 40 pages, magazine-sized, saddle-stapled, with heavy card cover. Press run is 50-100. Single copy: $8; subscription: $16.

HOW TO CONTACT Submit 3-5 poems at a time. Lines/poem: less than 2 pages preferred. No previously published poems or simultaneous submissions. Prefers e-mail submissions (pasted into body of message). Cover letter is optional. One poem to a page with the author's full name, address, and phone number in the upper right corner. Time between acceptance and publication is up to 1 year. "Submissions are circulated among an editorial staff for evaluations." Never comments on rejected poems. Responds in up to 4 months.

PEREGRINE

Amherst Writers & Artists Press, P.O. Box 1076, Amherst MA 01004. (413)253-3307. E-mail: peregrine@amherstwriters.com. Website: www.amherstwriters.com. **Contact:** Nancy Rose, editor. P.O. Box 1076, Amherst, MA 01004. (413)253-3307. Fax:(413)253-7764. E-mail: peregrine@amherstwriters.com. Website:www.amherstwriters.com. **Contact:** Nancy Rose, editor. *Peregrine*, published annually, features poetry and fiction. Open to all styles, forms, and subjects except greeting card verse. "*Peregrine* has provided a forum for national and international writers since 1983, and is committed to finding excellent work by emerging as well as established authors. We publish what we love, knowing that all editorial decisions are subjective." Has published poetry by Willie James King, Virgil Suaárez, Susan Terris, Myron Ernst, Pat Schneider, Edwina Trentham, Sacha Webley, Fred Yannantuono, and Ralph Hughes. *Peregrine* is 104 pages, digest-sized, professionally printed, perfect-bound, with glossy cover. Press run is 1,000. Single copy: $15. Sample: $12. Make checks payable to AWA Press.

HOW TO CONTACT Submit 3-5 poems at a time. Lines/poem: 60 maximum (including spaces). Considers simultaneous submissions; no previously published poems. No e-mail submissions. Include cover letter with bio, 40 words maximum; indicate line count for each poem. Enclose sufficiently stamped SASE for return of mss; if disposable copy, enclose #10 SASE for response. Reads submissions January 2-March 31 (postmark) only. Each ms read by several readers; final decisions made by the editor. Guidelines available for #10 SASE or on website. Pays 2 contributor's copies. Acquires first rights.

TIPS "Check guidelines before submitting your work. Familiarize yourself with Peregrine. We look for heart and soul as well as technical expertise. Trust your own voice."

◑ PERMAFROST: A LITERARY JOURNAL

c/o English Dept., Univ. of Alaska Fairbanks, P.O. Box 755720, Fairbanks AK 99775. Website: www.uaf.edu/english/permafrost. *Permafrost: A Literary Journal*, published in May/June, contains poems, short stories, creative nonfiction, b&w drawings, photographs, and prints. "We survive on both new and established writers, hoping and expecting to see the best work out there. We publish any style of poetry provided it is conceived, written, and revised with care. While we encourage submissions about Alaska and by Alaskans, we also welcome poems about anywhere, from anywhere. We have published work by E. Ethelbert Miller, W. Loran Smith, Peter Orlovsky, Jim Wayne Miller, Allen Ginsberg, and Andy Warhol." *Permafrost* is about 200 pages, digest-sized, professionally printed, flat-spined. Subscription: $9/year, $16/2 years, $22/3 years. Back-issues $5.

TIPS The Midnight Sun Poetry Chapbook Contest (formerly the Susan Blalock Contest; see separate listing)

◑ PHILADELPHIA STORIES

Fiction/Art/Poetry of the Delaware Valley, 93 Old York Road, Suite 1/#1-753, Jenkintown PA 19046.

(215) 551-5889. Fax: (215) 635-0195. E-mail: christine@philadelphiastories.org; info@philadelphiastories.org. Website: www.philadelphiastories.org. Carla Spataro, fiction editor/co-publisher. **Contact:** Christine Weiser, co-publisher/managing editor. Member: CLMP.

MAGAZINES NEEDS *Philadelphia Stories*, published quarterly, publishes "literary fiction, poetry, and art from Pennsylvania, New Jersey, and Delaware—and provide it to the general public free of charge." Wants "polished, well crafted poems." Does not want "first drafts." Considers poetry by teens. Has published poetry by Daniel Abdal-Hayy Moore, Scott Edward Anderson, Sandy Crimmins, Liz Dolan, Alison Hicks, and Margaret A. Robinson. *Philadelphia Stories* is 24 pages, magazine-sized, saddle-stapled, with 4-color cover with original art, includes ads. Receives about 600 poems/year, accepts about 15%. Press run is 12,000 per quarter, distributed free. Subscription: "we offer $20 memberships that include home delivery." Make checks payable to *Philadelphia Stories*.

HOW TO CONTACT Submit 3 poems at a time. Lines/poem: 36. Considers simultaneous submissions; no previously published poems. Accepts submissions through online submission form at www.philadelphiastories.org/submissions; no disk submissions. Cover letter is preferred. Reads submissions year round. Time between acceptance and publication is 3 months. Poems are circulated to an editorial board. "Each poem is reviewed by a preliminary board that decides on a final list; the entire board discusses this list and chooses the mutual favorites for print and Web." Guidelines available on website. Responds in 3 months. "We send a layout proof to check for print poems." Acquires one-time rights. Rights revert to poets upon publication. Reviews books of poetry.

TIPS "All work is screened by 3 editorial board members, who rank the work. These scores are processed at the end of the quarterly submission period, and then the board meets to decide which pieces will be published in print and online. We look for exceptional, polished prose, a controlled voice, strong characters and place, and interesting subjects. Follow guidelines. We cannot stress this enough. Read every guideline carefully and thoroughly before sending anything out. Send out only polished material. We reject many quality pieces for various reasons; try not to take rejection personally. Just because your piece isn't right for one publication doesn't mean it's bad. Selection is an extremely subjective process."

PHOEBE: A JOURNAL OF LITERATURE AND ART

MSN 2D6, George Mason Univ., 4400 University Dr., Fairfax VA 22030. E-mail: phoebe@gmu.edu. Website: www.phoebejournal.com. Kathy Goodkin, Editor. Phoebe Magazine: 9×6; 112-120 pages; 80 lb. paper; 0-5 illustrations; 0-10 photos. "We publish mainly fiction and poetry with some visual art." Biannual. "*Phoebe* prides itself on supporting up-and-coming writers, whose style, form, voice, and subject matter demostrate a vigorous appeal to the senses, intellect, and emotions of our readers. No romance, western, juvenile, or erotica." Receives 300 unsolicited mss/ month. Accepts 3-7 mss/issue. Does not read mss in summer. Publishes ms 3-6 months after acceptance. **Publishes 8-10 new writers/year.**

MAGAZINES NEEDS *Phoebe: A Journal of Literature and Art*, published semiannually in September and February, is interested in the uncanny, the assured— solid poetry. Has published poetry by C.D. Wright, Russell Edson, Yusef Komunyakaa, Rosemarie Waldrop, Charles Bernstein, and The Pines. Press run is 3,000, with 35-40 pages of poetry in each issue. Receives 4,000 submissions/year. Single copy: $6; subscription: $12/year.

HOW TO CONTACT Submit up to 5 poems at a time. No simultaneous submissions. No e-mail submissions; postal submissions only. Include SASE and a short bio. Reads submissions September 1-April 15 (postmark); mss postmarked April 16-August 31 will not be read. Guidelines available for SASE or on website. Responds in up to 3 months. Pays 2 contributor's copies or one-year subscription.

ADDITIONAL INFORMATION Check http:// phoebejournal.blogspot.com for additional information and commentary about *Phoebe*.

CONTEST/AWARD OFFERINGS The Greg Grummer Poetry Award (see separate listing in Contests & Awards).

PHOEBE: JOURNAL OF FEMINIST SCHOLARSHIP THEORY AND AESTHETICS

Women's & Gender Studies Dept., Suny-College at Oneonta, Oneonta NY 13820. E-mail: wesleym@ hartwick.edu. Website: www.oneonta.edu/academics/womens/phoebe_small.htm. Established 1989.

Contact: Marilyn Wesley, poetry editor. Editor: Kathleen O'Mara.

MAGAZINES NEEDS *Phoebe* is published semiannually. Wants "mostly poetry reflecting women's experiences; prefer 3 pages or less." Has published poetry by Barbara Crooker, Graham Duncan, and Patty Tana. *Phoebe* is 120 pages, digest-sized, offset-printed on coated paper and perfect-bound with glossy card cover, includes b&w art/ photos and "publishing swap" ads. Receives about 500 poems/year, accepts 8%. Press run is 500 (120 subscribers, 52 libraries). Single copy: $7.50; subscription: $15/year or $25/year institutional. Sample: $5.

HOW TO CONTACT No previously published poems. Accepts fax submissions. Cover letter preferred. Reads submissions October through January and May through July only. Time between acceptance and publication is 3 months. Seldom comments on rejected poems. Publishes theme issues occasionally. Guidelines available for SASE. Responds in up to 14 weeks. Sometimes sends prepublication galleys. Pays 1 contributor's copy. Staff reviews books and chapbooks of poetry in 500-1,000 words, single-book format. Send materials for review consideration.

PINYON

Mesa State College, Languages, Literature and Mass Communications, Mesa State College, 1100 North Ave., Grand Junction CO 81501-3122. E-mail: pinyonpoetry@hotmail.com. Website: www.mesastate.edu/ english/publications.html. **Contact:** Managing editor. *Pinyon*, published annually in June, prints "the best available contemporary American poetry and fiction. No restrictions other than excellence. We appreciate a strong voice." Does not want "inspirational, light verse, or sing-song poetry." Has published poetry by Mark Cox, Barry Spacks, Wendy Bishop, and Anne Ohman Youngs. *Pinyon* is about 120 pages, magazine-sized, perfect-bound. Receives about 4,000 poems/year, accepts 2%. Press run is 300; 100 distributed free to contributors, friends, etc. Subscription: $8/year. Sample: $5. Make checks payable to Pinyon, MSC.

HOW TO CONTACT Submit 3-5 poems at a time. No previously published poems or simultaneous submissions. Cover letter is preferred. "Name, address, e-mail, and phone number on each page. SASE required." Reads submissions August 1-December 1. "3 groups of assistant editors, led by an associate editor, make recommendations to the editor." Seldom comments on rejected poems. Guidelines available for SASE. Responds in February. Pays 2 contributor's copies. Acquires one-time rights.

TIPS "Ask yourself if the work is something you would like to read in a publication."

PIRENE'S FOUNTAIN

3616 Glenlake Dr, Glenview IL 60026. E-mail: pirenesfountain@gmail.com. Website: pirenesfountain.com. Editors: Oliver Lodge, Charles Morrison, Tony Walbran; Senior Editor: Lark Vernon; Publisher and Managing Editor: Ami Kaye. **Contact:** Submissions editor. "Poets whose work has been selected for publication in our journal during the past calendar year (with the exception of staff/featured poets) are automatically entered for the annual award. Our editors will each choose one poem from all of the selections. The 5 nominated poems will be sent "blind" to an outside editor/publisher for the final decision. The winning poet will be awarded a certificate and a $100 Amazon gift card via email. Pushcart and Best of the Net nominations: Editors select the best work published by PF during the year. This is open to all submitting and featured poets. Only previously unpublished poems will be considered; please indicate that in your submission. Nominated poets are notified after selections have been sent in."

MAGAZINES NEEDS *Pirene's Fountain* is published online 2 times per year in April and October. Has published work by Lisel Mueller, Linda Pastan, J.P. Dancing Bear, Alison Croggan, Dorianne Laux, Rebecca Seiferle, Joseph Millar, Kim Addonizio, and Jim Moore, among others. Receives about 1,500 poems/year, accepts about 20%. 50-100 word bio note is required.

HOW TO CONTACT Accepts e-mail submissions pasted into body of message; no postal, fax or disk submissions. Cover letter is unnecessary but 50-100 word bio note is required. Reads submissions during the months of November, April, and September. Submit seasonal poems anytime.

ADDITIONAL INFORMATION Editors: Oliver Lodge, Charles Morrison, Tony Walbran. Senior Editor: Lark Vernon. Publisher & Managing Editor: Ami Kaye.

TIPS "Please read submission guidelines carefully and send in at least 3 poems. We offer a poetry dis-

cussion group on Facebook, entitled Pirene's Fountain Poetry."

PLAINSONGS

Department of English, Hastings College, Hastings NE 68901. (402)461-7352. Fax: (402)461-7756. E-mail: plainsongs@hastings.edu. **Contact:** Laura Marvel Wunderlich, editor.

MAGAZINES NEEDS *Plainsongs*, published 3 times/year, considers poems "on any subject, in any style, but free verse predominates. Plains region poems encouraged." *Plainsongs*' title suggests not only its location on the Great Plains, but its preference for the living language, whether in free or formal verse. "*Plainsongs* is committed to poems only, to make space without visual graphics, bios, reviews, or critical positions." Has published poetry by Judith Tate O'Brien, Andrew H. Oerke, Lyn Lifshin, Larsen Bowker, and Louis Daniel Brodsky. *Plainsongs* is 40 pages, digest-sized, laser-set, printed on thin paper, saddle-stapled, with one-color matte card cover with generic black logo. "Published by the English department of Hastings College, the magazine is partially financed by subscriptions. Although editors respond to as many submissions with personal attention as they have time for, the editor offers specific observations to all contributors who also subscribe." Subscription: $15 for 3 issues. Sample: $5.

HOW TO CONTACT Submit up to 6 poems at a time, with name and address on each page. No fax, e-mail, or disk submissions; postal submissions only. Reads submissions according to the following deadlines: August 15 for Winter issue; November 15 for Spring issue; March 15 for Fall issue. Responds 7-8 weeks after deadline. Guidelines available for SASE. Pays 2 contributor's copies and one-year subscription. Acquires first rights.

CONTEST/AWARD OFFERINGS 3 poems in each issue receive a $25 prize. "A short essay in appreciation accompanies each award poem."

PLAIN SPOKE

Amsterdam Press, 6199 Steubenville Road SE, Amsterdam OH 43903. (740) 543-4333. E-mail: plainspoke@gmail.com. Website: www.plainspoke.net. Shaun M. Barcalow, fiction editor. **Contact:** Cindy Kelly, editor.

MAGAZINES NEEDS *Plain Spoke*, published quarterly, publishes "poetry heavy in sense images and with a clear, plain-spoken voice." Wants

"Americana, nostalgia, narrative." Does not want "esoteric, universal, clicheé." Has published poetry by Claudia Burbank, Deborah Bogen, Doug Ramspeck, Amy Sargent. *Plain Spoke* is 36-60 digest-sized, laser-printed, saddle-stitched, with a color art on cardstock cover. Receives about 2,500 poems/year, accepts about 5%. Press run is 300. Single copy: $8; subscription: $25. Make checks payable to Amsterdam Press.

HOW TO CONTACT Submit up to 6 poems at a time, preferably under 40 lines. Considers simultaneous submissions, no previously published poems (considers poetry posted on a public website/blog/forum). Accepts e-mail submissions (following guidelines on website at www.plainspoke.net. Cover letter is required. Paper submissions require an SASE. Submissions received without an SASE are recycled. No postcards. Reads submissions year round. Submit seasonal poems 3 months in advance. Time between acceptance and publication is 1-4 months. Poems are circulated to an editorial board. Sometimes comments on rejected poems. Never publishes theme issues. Guidelines available for SASE, by e-mail, and on website. Responds in 1 week. Pays 1 contributor's copy. Acquires first North American serial rights. Rights revert to poets upon publication. Reviews books and chapbooks of poetry in single-book format. Send cover letter and materials for review consideration to Reviews Editor, *Plain Spoke*.

TIPS "Work that surprises us stands out. We don't like the predictable. We don't want to feel like we're reading a story, pull us in. Make every word count and don't rely on adverbs."

🌑⬤🌓 PLANET-THE WELSH INTERNATIONALIST

P.O. Box 44, Aberystwyth Ceredigion SY23 3ZZ, United Kingdom. E-mail: planet.enquiries@planet-magazine.org.uk. Website: www.planetmagazine.org.uk. **Contact:** Jasmine Donahaye, Editor. P.O. Box 44, Aberystwyth, Ceredigion SY23 3ZZ, United Kingdom. E-mail: planet.enquiries@planetmagazine.org.uk. Website: www.planetmagazine.org.uk. *Planet: The Welsh Internationalist*, published quarterly, is a cultural magazine "centered on Wales, but with broader interests in arts, sociology, politics, history, and science." Wants "good poetry in a wide variety of styles. No limitations as to subject matter; length can be a problem." Has published poetry by Nigel Jenkins, Anne Stevenson, and Les Murray. *Planet* is 128 pages,

A5, professionally printed, perfect-bound, with glossy color card cover. Receives about 500 submissions/year, accepts about 5%. Press run is 1,550 (1,500 subscribers, about 10% libraries, 200 shelf sales). Single copy: £6.75; subscription: £22 (£38 overseas). Sample available. A literary/cultural/political journal centered on Welsh affairs but with a strong interest in minority cultures in Europe and elsewhere.

MAGAZINES NEEDS *Planet: The Welsh Internationalist*, published quarterly, is a cultural magazine "centered on Wales, but with broader interests in arts, sociology, politics, history, and science." Wants "good poetry in a wide variety of styles. No limitations as to subject matter; length can be a problem." Has published poetry by Nigel Jenkins, Anne Stevenson, and Les Murray. *Planet* is 128 pages, A5, professionally printed, perfect-bound, with glossy color card cover. Receives about 500 submissions/year, accepts about 5%. Press run is 1,550 (1,500 subscribers, about 10% libraries, 200 shelf sales). Single copy: £6.75; subscription: £22 (£38 overseas). Sample available.

HOW TO CONTACT Please submit 4-6 poems at a time. No previously published poems or simultaneous submissions. Accepts e-mail (as attachment) and disk submissions. SASE or SAE with IRCs essential for reply. Time between acceptance and publication is 4-6 months. Seldom comments on rejected poems. Guidelines available for SASE (or SAE/IRC). "We aim to respond within 3 months." Pays £30 minimum. Acquires first serial rights only. Reviews books of poetry in 700 words, single- or multi-book format.

TIPS "We do not look for fiction which necessarily has a 'Welsh' connection, which some writers assume from our title. We try to publish a broad range of fiction and our main criterion is quality. Try to read copies of any magazine you submit to. Don't write out of the blue to a magazine which might be completely inappropriate for your work. Recognize that you are likely to have a high rejection rate, as magazines tend to favor writers from their own countries."

⬤🗣️🌓 PLEIADES

Pleiades Press, Department of English, University of Central Missouri, Martin 336, Warrensburg MO 64093. (660)543-4425. Fax: (660)543-8544. E-mail: pleiades@ucmo.edu. Website: www.ucmo.edu/engl-phil/pleiades. **Contact:** G.B. Crump, Matthew Eck and Phong Nguyen, prose editors. "We publish contemporary fiction, poetry, interviews, literary essays, special-interest personal essays, reviews for a general and literary audience from authors from around the world."

○ "Also sponsors the Lena-Miles Wever Todd Poetry Series competition, a contest for the best book ms by an American poet. The winner receives $1,000, publication by Pleiades Press, and distribution by Louisiana State University Press. Deadline September 30. Send SASE for guidelines."

MAGAZINES NEEDS *Pleiades*, published semiannually in April and October, prints poetry, fiction, literary criticism, belles lettres (occasionally), and reviews. Open to all writers. Wants "avant-garde, free verse, and traditional poetry, and some quality light verse." Does not want anything "pretentious, didactic, or overly sentimental." Has published poetry by James Tate, Joyce Carol Oates, Brenda Hillman, Wislawa Szymborska, Carl Phillips, and Jean Valentine. *Pleiades* is 160 pages, digest-sized, perfect-bound, with heavy coated cover with color art. Receives about 9,000 poems/year, accepts fewer than 1%. Press run is 2,500-3,000; about 200 distributed free to educational institutions and libraries across the country. Single copy: $6; subscription: $12. Sample: $5. Make checks payable to Pleiades Press.

HOW TO CONTACT Submit 3-5 poems at a time. Considers simultaneous submissions with notification; no previously published poems. Cover letter is preferred. Include brief bio. Time between acceptance and publication "can be up to 1 year. Each poem published must be accepted by 2 readers and approved by the poetry editor." Seldom comments on rejected poems. Guidelines available for SASE or on website. Responds in up to 3 months. Payment varies. Acquires first and second serial rights.

TIPS "Submit only 1 genre at a time to appropriate editors. Show care for your material and your readers—submit quality work in a professional format. Include cover letter with brief bio and list of publications. Include SASE. Cover art is solicited directly from artists. We accept queries for book reviews. For summer submissions, the Poetry and Nonfiction Editors will no longer accept mss sent between June 1 & August 31. Any sent after May 31 will be held until the end of summer. Please do not send your only copy of anything."

PMS

(205)934-8578. E-mail: kmadden@uab.edu. Website: www.pms-journal.org/submissions-guidelines. **Contact:** Kerry Madden, Editor-in-Chief. "This is an all women's literary journal. The subject field is wide open." "Each issue of *PMS* includes a memoir written by a woman who has experienced a historically significant event. *PMS 10* features Masha Hamilton and her authors from the Afghan Women's Writing Project. Writer Donna Thomas's memoir, Kiddie Land, recalls Birmingham's segregated past when Kiddie Land opened to children of all colors. Look for excerpts of *PMS 10* to be online soon."

○ Work from PMS has been reprinted in a number of award anthologies: *New Stories from the South 2005, The Best Creative Nonfiction 200* and *2008, Best American Poetry 2003* and *2004*, and *Best American Essays 2005* and *2007*.

HOW TO CONTACT We will not acknowledge or return submissions not accompanied by SASE. Submissions should include a cover letter and a brief biographical statement of the writer. All manuscripts should be typed on one side only of 8 x 11 white paper with the author's name, address, phone number, and email address on the front of each submission. Prose should be double-spaced; poetry may be single-spaced. Poems of multiple pages should indicate whether or not stanza breaks accompany page breaks.

TIPS "We seek unpublished original work that we can recycle. Include cover letter, brief bio with SASE. All mss should be typed on 1-side of 8 X 11 white paper with author's name, address, phone no. and email address on front of each submission." Reading period runs from Jan. 1 - Mar. 31. Submissions received at other times of the year will be returned unread. Best way to make contact is through email.

POCKETS

Upper Room, P.O. Box 340004, 1908 Grand Ave., Nashville TN 37203-0004. (800)972-0433. Fax: (615)340-7275. E-mail: pockets@upperroom.org. Website: http://pockets.upperroom.org/. *Pockets*, published monthly (except February), is an interdenominational magazine for children ages 8-12. "Each issue is built around a specific theme, with material (including poetry) that can be used by children in a variety of ways. Submissions do not need to be overly religious;

they should help children experience a Christian lifestyle that is not always a neatly wrapped moral package but is open to the continuing revelation of God's will." Considers poetry by children. "We are a Christian, inter-denominational publication for children 8-12 years old. Each issue reflects a specific theme."

HOW TO CONTACT P.O. Box 34000, 41908 Grand Ave., Nashville, TN 37203-000. (800)972-0433. Fax: (615)340-7275. E-mail: pockets@upperroom.org. Website: http://pockets.upperroom.org/. Lines/poem: 20 maximum. Considers previously published poems (first reprint only). No fax or e-mail submissions. Submissions should be typed, double-spaced, on 8½x11 paper, accompanied by SASE for return. "Those who wish to save postage and are concerned about paper conservation may send a SASP for notification of accepted manuscripts. Please list the titles of the submissions on the postcards. We will recycle the paper the submission is printed on." Reads submissions year round. Publishes theme issues; themes are available each year the end of December. Guidelines available on website (under Adults/Writer's Corner). Pays $25 minimum for poems. Pays on acceptance. Places mss on long-term hold for specific issues. Acquires newspaper, periodical, and electronic rights.

TIPS "Theme stories, role models, and retold scripture stories are most open to freelancers. Poetry is also open. It is very helpful if writers read our writers' guidelines and themes on our website."

● POEM

Huntsville Literary Association, P.O. Box 2006, Huntsville AL 35804. E-mail: poem@hla-hsv.org. Website: www.hla-hsv.org. **Contact:** Rebecca Harbor, editor. Estab. 1967.

MAGAZINES NEEDS *Poem*, published twice/year in May and November, consists entirely of poetry. "We publish both traditional forms and free verse." Wants poems "characterized by compression, rich vocabulary, significant content, and evidence of 'a tuned ear and practiced pen.' We want coherent work that moves through the particulars of the poem to make a point. We equally welcome submissions from established poets as well as from less-known and beginning poets." Does not want translations. Has published poetry by Kathryn Kirkpatrick, Peter Serchuk, and Kim Bridgford. *Poem* is 90 pages, digest-sized, flat-spined, printed on good stock paper, with a clean design and a matte cover. Prints more than 60 poems/issue, generally featured 1 to a page. Press run is 500. Single copy: $10; subscription: $20. Sample: $7 (back issue). Member: CLMP.

HOW TO CONTACT Send 3-5 poems at a time. No previously published poems or simultaneous submissions. Include SASE. Reads submissions year-round. Guidelines available for SASE or on website. Responds in 1-2 months. Pays 2 contributor's copies. Acquires first serial rights.

●● POEMELEON: A JOURNAL OF POETRY

E-mail: editor@poemeleon.org. Website: www.poemeleon.org. **Contact:** Cati Porter, editor. Member: CLMP, Online Literary Association.d\fi720We are now accepting submissions for our next issue, Volume V Issue 2, The Open Issue, to be launched June 2011. Unlike past issues, The Open Issue is not focused on any one particular kind of poetry but instead will strive to include as wide a variety as possible. Please send only your best work; any length, any style. Deadline for this issue: March 31, 2011. Expect a response within 1 - 3 months after close of submissions. If you have not heard from us after 3 months please inquire. Please submit 1 to 5 poems, 1 craft essay, or 1 book review, using the forms online. Please include a brief third-person bio in your cover letter.

MAGAZINES NEEDS *Poemeleon: A Journal of Poetry*, published semiannually online, wants all forms and styles of poetry. "Does not want overly religious or sentimental, greeting card verse." Has published poetry by Tony Barnstone, Catherine Daly, Ann Fisher-Wirth, Richard Garcia, Eloise Klein Healy, Bob Hicok. Poemeleon receives about 1,000 poems/year, accepts about 150-200. Number of unique visitors: 25,000/year.

HOW TO CONTACT Submit 3-5 poems at a time. Considers previously published poems (as long as they have not appeared online) and simultaneous submissions as long as we are notified promptly if a poem is taken elsewhere). Considers poetry posted on a public website/blog/forum as published. All submissions must come through online submissions form located on the guidelines page of the website; no fax, paper, e-mail or disk submissions. Cover letter is preferred. Each issue is devoted to a particular type of poetry (past issues include poems of place, ekphrastic poems, poems in form, and the prose poem, The persona poem, humor, gender, and collaborative poetry). Please check the guidelines page for specifics before submitting. Reads submissions year round. Time between acceptance and publication is about 2 months. Poems are circulated to an editorial board. Sometimes comments on rejected poems. Regularly publishes theme issues. Upcoming themes and guidelines available on website. Responds in 2-4 months. Always sends prepublication galleys. Acquires one-time rights. Rights revert to poets upon publication. Reviews books and chapbooks of poetry.

ADDITIONAL INFORMATION Previously published is fine, as long as it was in print, not online, and as long as you as the author retain all copyright.

CONTEST/AWARD OFFERINGS Mystery Box Contest offers a prize of the Mystery Box and publication on the website. Submit 1 poem. Guidelines available on website. **Entry fee:** none. **Deadline:** none.

◑ POEMS & PLAYS

English Dept., Middle Tennessee State Univ., Murfreesboro TN 37132. E-mail: gbrewer@mtsu.edu. **Contact:** Gaylord Brewer, Editor. *Poems & Plays* is 88 pages, digest-sized, professionally printed, perfect-bound, with coated color card cover. Receives 1,500 poems per issue, publishes 30-35 "typically." Press run is 800. Subscription: $10 for 2 issues. Sample: $6.*Poems & Plays*, published annually in the spring, is an "eclectic publication for poems and short plays." No restrictions on style or content of poetry. Has published poetry by Naomi Wallace, Kate Gale, James Doyle, and Ron Koertge. *Poems & Plays* is 88 pages, digest-sized, professionally printed, perfect-bound, with coated color card cover. Receives 1,500 poems per issue, publishes 30-35 "typically." Press run is 800. Subscription: $10 for 2 issues. Sample: $6.

TIPS Considers chapbook mss (poems or short plays) of 20-24 pages for The Tennessee Chapbook Prize. "Any combination of poems or plays, or a single play, is eligible. The winning chapbook is printed within *Poems & Plays*." Winning author receives 50 copies of the issue. SASE required. **Entry fee:** $15 (includes 1 copy of the issue). **Deadline:** same as for the magazine (October-November). Past winners include Tammy Armstrong and Judith Sornberger. "The chapbook competition annually receives over 150 manuscripts from the U.S. and around the world."

◑ POESY MAGAZINE

P.O. Box 7823, Santa Cruz CA 95061. (831)239-4419. E-mail: info@poesy.org; submissions@poesy.org. Website: www.poesy.org. **Contact:** Brian Morrisey, editor/publisher. P.O. Box 7823, Santa Cruz CA, 95061. (831)239-4419. E-mail: info@poesy.org; submissions@poesy.org. Website: www.poesy.org. **Contact:** Brian Morrisey, editor/publisher. Estab. 1991. *POESY Magazine*, published biannually, is "an anthology of American poetry. POESY's main concentrations are Boston, Massachusetts and Santa Cruz, California, 2 thriving homesteads for poets, beats, and artists of nature. Our goal is to unite the 2 scenes, updating poets on what's happening across the country." Wants to see "original poems that express observational impacts with clear and concise imagery. Acceptence is based on creativity, composition, and relation to the format of POESY." Does not want "poetry with excessive profanity. We would like to endorse creativity beyond the likes of everyday babble." Has published poetry by Lawrence Ferlinghetti, Jack Hirschman, Edward Sanders, Todd Moore, Diane Di PrimAnd Julia Vinograd. POESY is 16 pages, magazine-sized, newsprint, glued/folded, includes ads. Receives about 1,000 poems/year, accepts about 10%. Press run is 1,000; most distributed free to local venues. Single copy: $1; subscription: $12/year. Sample: $2. Make checks payable to Brian Morrisey.*POESY Magazine*, published biannually, is "an anthology of American poetry. POESY's main concentrations are Boston, Massachusetts and Santa Cruz, California, 2 thriving homesteads for poets, beats, and artists of nature. Our goal is to unite the 2 scenes, updating poets on what's happening across the country." Wants to see "original poems that express observational impacts with clear and concise imagery. Acceptence is based on creativity, composition, and relation to the format of POESY." Does not want "poetry with excessive profanity. We would like to endorse creativity beyond the likes of everyday babble." Has published poetry by Lawrence Ferlinghetti, Jack Hirschman, Edward Sanders, Todd Moore, Diane Di PrimAnd Julia Vinograd. POESY is 16 pages, magazine-sized, newsprint, glued/folded, includes ads. Receives about 1,000 poems/year, accepts about 10%. Press run is 1,000; most distributed free to local venues. Single copy: $1; subscription: $12/year. Sample: $2. Make checks payable to Brian Morrisey.

HOW TO CONTACT Submit 3-5 poems at a time. Lines/poem: 32 maximum. No previously published poems or simultaneous submissions. Accepts e-mail (submissions@poesy.org) and disk submissions. "Snail mail submissions are preferred with a SASE." Cover letter is preferred. Reads submissions year round. Time between acceptance and publication is 1 month. "Poems are accepted by the Santa Cruz editor/publisher based on how well the poem stimulates our format." Guidelines available in magazine, for SASE, by e-mail, or on website. Responds in 1 month. Sometimes sends prepublication galleys. Pays 3 contributor's copies. Acquires one-time rights. Reviews books/chapbooks of poetry and other magazines/journals in 1,000 words, single-book format. Send materials for review consideration to *POESY*, c/o Brian Morrisey.

TIPS "Stay away from typical notions of love and romance. Become one with your surroundings and discover a true sense of natural perspective."

ⓘ POETALK

Bay Area Poets Coalition, P.O. Box 11435, Berkeley CA 94712-2435. E-mail: poetalk@aol.com. Website: www.bayareapoetscoalition.org. **Contact:** John Rowe (editorial board), Acquisitions. POETALK, currently published 1-2 issues/year, is the poetry journal of the Bay Area Poets Coalition (BAPC) and publishes 60+ poets in each issue. "POETALK is open to all. No particular genre. Rhyme must be well done." POETALK is 36 pages, digest-sized, photocopied, saddle-stapled, with heavy card cover. Press run is 400. Subscription: $5/2 issues. Sample: $2. **Deadline:** Submit September 1-November 15 (postmark).

> ⓘ Important note: As of year 2011, our longtime editor has retired. A new editorial board is in place. Please check website for up-to-date status on our submission policy. POETALK is also reemerging after a year-long hiatus.

CONTEST/AWARD OFFERINGS Sponsors yearly contest.

TIPS "If you don't want suggested revisions, you need to say so clearly in your cover letter or indicate on each poem submitted." Also Offers Bay Area Poets Coalition holds monthly open readers (in Berkeley, CA). BAPC has around 10 members which holds monthly readings (in Berkeley, CA). BAPC has 150 members. BAPC Membership: $15/year (includes subscription to POETALK and other privileges); extra outside U.S.

POETICA MAGAZINE, REFLECTIONS OF JEWISH THOUGHT

P.O. Box 11014, Norfolk VA 23517. Website: www.poeticamagazine.com. P.O. Box 11014, Norfolk VA 23517. Fax: (757)399-3936. E-mail: poeticamag@aol.com. Website: www.poeticamagazine.com. **Contact:** Michal Mahgerefteh, publisher/editor. Estab. 2002. *Poetica Magazine, Reflections of Jewish Thought*, published 3 times/year, offers "an outlet for the many writers who draw from their Jewish backgrounds and experiences to create poetry/prose/short stories, giving both emerging and recognized writers the opportunity to share their work with the larger community." Does not want long pieces, haiku, rhyming poetry. Considers poetry by children and teens, grades 6-12. *Poetica* is 70pages, perfect bound, full color cover, includes some ads. Receives about 500 poems/year, accepts about 60%. Press run is 350. Single copy: $10; subscription: $19.50.

MAGAZINES NEEDS *Poetica Magazine, Reflections of Jewish Thought*, published 3 times/year, offers "an outlet for the many writers who draw from their Jewish backgrounds and experiences to create poetry/prose/short stories, giving both emerging and recognized writers the opportunity to share their work with the larger community." Does not want long pieces, haiku, rhyming poetry. Considers poetry by children and teens, grades 6-12. *Poetica* is 70pages, perfect bound, full color cover, includes some ads. Receives about 500 poems/year, accepts about 60%. Press run is 350. Single copy: $10; subscription: $19.50.

HOW TO CONTACT Submit 3 poems at a time to submission@poeticamagazine.com. Lines/poem: 2 pages maximum. Considers simultaneous submissions. No e-mail or disk submissions. Cover letter is optional. Reads submissions year round. Time between acceptance and publication is 1 year. Seldom comments on rejected poems. Occasionally publishes theme issues. Guidelines available for SASE or on website. Responds in 1 month. Pays 1 contributor's copy. Poet retains all rights.

CONTEST/AWARD OFFERINGS Offers annual poetry contest with up to $50 awarded for First Prize; up to 5 Honorable Mentions. Selected poems will be published in future issues of *Poetica*. Accepts simultaneous submissions. No limit on number of entries (3 poems constitute an entry). Submit 2 copies of each poem, single-spaced, no more than 1 poem/page. Include poet's name on all pages. No e-mail submissions. Include SASE for results only; mss will not be returned. Guidelines available on website. **Entry fee:** $15 for up to 3 poems. **Deadline:** March 31 annually. Judge: Jane Ellen Glasser. Notifies winners by June. Other contests include the Poet of the Month Award, Annual Chapbook Award, and annual anthology centered on a theme.

◑◔ POETIC MATRIX, A PERIODIC LETTER

P.O. Box 1223, Madera CA 93639. E-mail: poeticmatrix@yahoo.com. Website: www.poeticmatrix.com. **Contact:** John Peterson, editor. P.O. Box 1223, Madera, CA 93639. E-mail: poeticmatrix@yahoo.com. Website: www.poeticmatrix.com. **Contact:** John Peterson, editor. Estab. 1997. *Poetic Matrix, a periodic letteR*, published 2 times/year online, seeks poetry that "creates a 'place in which we can live' rather than telling us about the place; poetry that draws from the imaginal mind and is rich in the poetic experience—hence the poetic matrix." Does not want poetry that talks about the experience. Has published poetry by Lyn Lifshin, Tony White, Gail Entrekin, James Downs, Joan Michelson, and Brandon Cesmat. *Poetic Matrix, a periodic letteR*, published 2 times/year online, seeks poetry that "creates a 'place in which we can live' rather than telling us about the place; poetry that draws from the imaginal mind and is rich in the poetic experience—hence the poetic matrix." Does not want poetry that talks about the experience. Has published poetry by Lyn Lifshin, Tony White, Gail Entrekin, James Downs, Joan Michelson, and Brandon Cesmat.

HOW TO CONTACT Accepts e-mail submissions (pasted into body of message, no attachments). Guidelines available by e-mail or on website. Acquires one-time rights. "*Poetic Matrix* has a call for manuscripts for the Slim Volume Series every 2 years. See website for when reading dates are set and for additional guidelines and awards. The Slim Volume Series is for manuscripts of 65-75 pages." **Charges reading fee of $17.**

TIPS "We seek writing of quality, with passion and intelligence."

◐ POET LORE

The Writer's Center, 4508 Walsh St., Bethesda MD 20815. E-mail: post.master@writer.org. Website: http://poetlore.com; www.writer.org. E. Ethelbert Miller, editor. **Contact:** Jody Bolz, editor. *Poet Lore*, published semiannually, is "dedicated to the best in American and world poetry as well as timely reviews and commentary." Wants "fresh uses of traditional forms and devices, but any kind of excellence is welcome." Has published poetry by Ai, Denise Duhamel, Jefferey Harrison, Eve Jones, Carl Phillips, and Ronald Wallace. *Poet Lore* is 144 pages, digest-sized, professionally printed, perfect-bound, with glossy card cover. Receives about 4,200 poems/year, accepts 125. Press run is at least 800. Single copy: $8; subscription: $18/nonmember, $12/member. "Add $1/single copy for shipping; add $5 postage for subscriptions outside U.S."

MAGAZINES NEEDS *Poet Lore*, published semiannually, is "dedicated to the best in American and world poetry as well as timely reviews and commentary." Wants "fresh uses of traditional forms and devices, but any kind of excellence is welcome." Has published poetry by Ai, Denise Duhamel, Jefferey Harrison, Eve Jones, Carl Phillips, and Ronald Wallace. *Poet Lore* is 144 pages, digest-sized, professionally printed, perfect-bound, with glossy card cover. Receives about 4,200 poems/year, accepts 125. Press run is at least 800. Single copy: $8; subscription: $18/nonmember, $12/member. "Add $1/single copy for shipping; add $5 postage for subscriptions outside U.S."

HOW TO CONTACT Considers simultaneous submissions "with notification in cover letter." No e-mail or disk submissions. "Submit typed poems (up to 5), with author's name and address on each page; SASE is required." Guidelines available for SASE or on website. Responds in 3 months. Pays 2 contributor's copies and a one-year subscription. Reviews books of poetry. Send materials for review consideration.

◑❸ POETRY

The Poetry Foundation, 444 N. Michigan Ave., Suite 1850, Chicago IL 60611-4034. (312)787-7070. Fax: (312)787-6650. E-mail: editors@poetrymagazine.org. Website: www.poetrymagazine.org. Christian Wiman, Editor. **Contact:** Helen Klaviter.

MAGAZINES NEEDS *Poetry*, published monthly by The Poetry Foundation (see separate listing in Organizations), "has no special manuscript needs and no special requirements as to form or genre: We examine in turn all work received and accept that which seems best." Has published poetry by the major voices of our time as well as new talent. *Poetry* is 5¹₂x9, elegantly printed, flat-spined. Receives 90,000 submissions/year, accepts about 300-350. Press run is 16,000. Single copy: $3.75; subscription: $35 ($38 for institutions). Sample: $5.50.

HOW TO CONTACT Submit no more than 4 poems at a time. No previously published poems or simultaneous submissions. Electronic submission preferred. When submitting by post put return address on outside of envelope; include SASE. Submissions must be typed, single-spaced, with poet's name and address on every page. Guidelines available for SASE. Responds in 1-2 months. Pays $10/line (with a minimum payment of $300). Reviews books of poetry in multi-book formats of varying lengths. Does not accept unsolicited reviews.

CONTEST/AWARD OFFERINGS 7 prizes (Bess Hokin Prize, Levinson Prize, Frederick Bock Prize, J. Howard and Barbara M.J. Wood Prize, John Frederick Nims Memorial Prize, Friends of Literature Prize, Union League Civic and Arts Poetry Prize) ranging from $300 to $5,000 are awarded annually to poets whose work has appeared in the magazine that year. Only verse already published in *Poetry* is eligible for consideration; no formal application is necessary.

ALSO OFFERS *Poetry*'s website offers featured poems, letters, reviews, interviews, essays, and web-exclusive features.

●◗ POETRYBAY

P.O. Box 114, Northport NY 11768. (631)427-1950. E-mail: poetrybay@aol.com; info@poetrybay.com. Website: www.poetrybay.com. **Contact:** George Wallace, editor. P.O. Box 114, Northport, NY 11768. (631)427-1950. E-mail:poetrybay@aol.com; info@poetrybay.com. Website: www.poetrybay.com. **Contact:** George Wallace, editor. *Poetrybay*, published semiannually online, seeks "to add to the body of great contemporary American poetry by presenting the work of established and emerging writers. Also, we consider essays and reviews." Has published poetry by Robert Bly, Yevgeny Yevtushenko, Marvin Bell, Diane Wakoski, Cornelius Eady, and William Heyen.

MAGAZINES NEEDS *Poetrybay*, published semiannually online, seeks "to add to the body of great contemporary American poetry by presenting the work of established and emerging writers. Also, we consider essays and reviews." Has published poetry by Robert Bly, Yevgeny Yevtushenko, Marvin Bell, Diane

Wakoski, Cornelius Eady, and William Heyen.

HOW TO CONTACT Submit 5 poems at a time. Considers simultaneous submissions; no previously published poems. Accepts e-mail submissions (pasted into body of message to info@poetrybay.com); no disk submissions. Time between acceptance and publication is 6-12 months. Seldom comments on rejected poems. Occasionally publishes theme issues. Guidelines available on website. Sometimes sends prepublication galleys. Acquires first-time electronic rights. Reviews books/chapbooks of poetry and other magazines/journals. Send materials for review consideration.

●◗ THE POETRY CHURCH MAGAZINE

Moorside Words and Music, Eldwick Crag Farm, High Eldwick, Bingley, W. Yorkshire BD16 3BB, England. E-mail: reavill@globalnet.co.uk. **Contact:** Tony Reavill, editor.

MAGAZINES NEEDS *The Poetry Church Magazine*, published quarterly, contains Christian poetry, prayers, and hymns. Wants "Christian or good religious poetry." Does not want "unreadable blasphemy." **Publishes subscribers' work only.** Considers poetry by children over age 10. Has published poetry by Laurie Bates, Joan Sheridan Smith, Idris Caffrey, Isabella Strachan, Walter Nash, and Susan Glyn. *The Poetry Church Magazine* is 40 pages, digest-sized, photocopied, saddle-stapled, with illustrated cover. Receives about 1,000 poems/year, accepts about 500. Press run is 1,000. Single copy: free; subscription: £12 for 4 issues ($20 USD). Make checks payable in sterling to Feather Books. Payment can also be made through website.

HOW TO CONTACT Submit 2 poems at a time. Lines/poem: usually around 20, "but will accept longer." Considers previously published poems and simultaneous submissions. Cover letter is preferred (with information about the poet). No e-mail submissions; postal submissions only. Include SASE, or SAE and IRC. Submissions must be typed. **Publishes "only subscribers' poems as they keep us solvent."** Time between acceptance and publication is 4 months. "The editor does a preliminary reading, then seeks the advice of colleagues about uncertain poems." Responds within 1 week. Poets retain copyright.

ADDITIONAL INFORMATION Feather Books publishes the Feather Books Poetry Series, collections of around 20 Christian poems and prayers. Has recently published the Glyn family, Walter Nash, David Grieve, and Rosie Morgan Barry. "We have now published 300 poetry collections by individual Christian poets." Books are usually photocopied, saddle-stapled, with illustrated covers. "We do not insist, but **most poets pay for their work. Enquire for current costs.** If they can't afford it, but are good poets, we stand the cost. We expect poets to read *The Poetry Church Magazine* to get some idea of our standards."

ALSO OFFERS Each winter and summer, selected poems appear in *The Poetry Church Collection*, the leading Christian poetry anthology used in churches and schools.

◑ POETRY INTERNATIONAL

San Diego State University, 5500 Campanile Dr., San Diego CA 92182-6020. (619)594-1522. Fax: (619)594-4998. E-mail: poetryinternational@yahoo.com. Website: http://poetryinternational.sdsu.edu. **Contact:** Fred Moramarco, Founding Editor. San Diego State University, 5500 Campanile Dr., San Diego, CA 92182-6020. (619)594-1522. Fax: (619)594-4998. E-mail: poetryinternational@yahoo.com. Website: http://poetryinternational.sdsu.edu. *Poetry International*, published annually in November, is "an eclectic poetry magazine intended to reflect a wide range of poetry being written today." Wants "a wide range of styles and subject matter. We're particularly interested in translations." Does not want "cliché-ridden, derivative, or obscure poetry." Has published poetry by Adrienne Rich, Robert Bly, Hayden Carruth, Kim Addonizio, Maxine Kumin, and Gary Soto. *Poetry International* is 200 pages, perfect-bound, with coated cardstock cover. Press run is 1,500. Subscription: $15/1 year."We intend to continue to publish poetry that makes a difference in people's lives, and startles us anew with the endless capacity of language to awaken our senses and expand our awareness."

○ Features the Poetry International Prize ($1,000) for best original poem. (Deadline April 15 for 2009.) Submit up to 3 poems with a $10 entry fee.

MAGAZINES NEEDS *Poetry International*, published annually in November, is "an eclectic poetry magazine intended to reflect a wide range of poetry being written today." Wants "a wide range of styles and subject matter. We're particularly interested

in translations." Does not want "clicheé-ridden, derivative, or obscure poetry." Has published poetry by Adrienne Rich, Robert Bly, Hayden Carruth, Kim Addonizio, Maxine Kumin, and Gary Soto. *Poetry International* is 200 pages, perfect-bound, with coated cardstock cover. Press run is 1,500. Subscription: $15/1 year.

HOW TO CONTACT Submit no more than 5 poems at a time. Considers simultaneous submissions, "but prefer not to"; no previously published poems. No fax or e-mail submissions. Reads submissions September 1 - Decemeber 1 only. Time between acceptance and publication is 8 months. Poems are circulated to an editorial board. Seldom comments on rejected poems. Responds in up to 4 months. Pays 1 contributor's copy. Acquires all rights. Returns rights "50/50," meaning they split with the author any payment for reprinting the poem elsewhere. "We review anthologies regularly."

TIPS "Seeks a wide range of styles and subject matter. We read unsolicited mss. only between Sept. 1st and Dec. 31st of each year. Mss. received any other time will be returned unread."

◐◑ POETRY KANTO

Kanto Poetry Center, 3-22-1 Kamariya-Minami Kanazawa-ku, Yokohama 236-8502, Japan. E-mail: alan@kanto-gakuin.ac.jp. Website: http://home.kanto-gakuin.ac.jp/~kg061001/. **Contact:** Alan Botsford, editor. Kanto Poetry Center, 3-22-1 Kamariya-Minami Kanazawa-ku, Yokohama 236-8502, Japan. E-mail: alan@kanto-gakuin.ac.jp. Website: http://home.kanto-gakuin.ac.jp/~kg061001/. **Contact:** Alan Botsford, editor.

MAGAZINES NEEDS *Poetry Kanto*, published annually in November by the Kanto Gakuin University, is a journal bridging east and west, featuring "outstanding poetry that navigates the divide of ocean and language from around the world. We seek exciting, well-crafted contemporary poetry in English, and also encourage and publish high-quality English translations of modern and emerging Japanese poets. All translations must be accompanied by the original poems." See website for sample poems. Has published poetry by Jane Hirschfield, Ilya Kaminsky, Beth Ann Fennelly, Vijay Seshadri, Michael S. Collins, Mari L'Esperance, Michael Sowder, and Sarah Arvio. *Poetry Kanto* is 120 pages, 6x9, professionally printed on coated stock, perfect-bound, with glossy cover. Press run is 1,000; many are distributed free worldwide to schools, poets, and presses. The magazine is unpriced. Sample: send SAE with IRCs.

HOW TO CONTACT Submit 5 poems at a time maximum. Queries welcome. No previously published poems or simultaneous submissions. Prefers e-mail submissions (as attachment in Word). Cover letter is required. Include brief bio. All postal submissions require SAE and IRCs. Reads submissions December - April. Guidelines available on website. Pays 3-5 contributor's copies.

POETRY NORTHWEST

Everett Community College, 2000 Tower Street, Everett WA 98103. (425)388-9395. E-mail: editors@poetrynw.org. Website: www.poetrynw.org. **Contact:** Kevin Craft, editor.

MAGAZINES NEEDS *Poetry Northwest* is published semiannually in April and October. "The mission of *Poetry Northwest* is to publish poetry with a vibrant snse of language at play in the world, and a strong presense of the physical world in language. We publish new, emerging, and established writers. In the words of founding editor Carolyn Kizer, we aim to 'encourage the young and the inexperienced, the neglected mature, and the rough major talents and the fragile minor ones.' All styles and aesthetics will find consideration." Has published poetry by Theodore Roethke, Czeslaw Milosz, Anne Sexton, Harold Pinter, Thom Gunn, and Philip Larkin, Heather McHugh, Richard Kenney. *Poetry Northwest* is 40+ pages, magazine-sized, Web press-printed, saddle-stapled, with 4-color cover, includes ads. Receives about 10,000 poems/year, accepts about 1%. Press run is 2,000. Single copy: $8. Sample: $9. Make checks payable to *Poetry Northwest*.

HOW TO CONTACT Submit 3-5 poems at a time once per submission period. No previously published poems; simultaneous submissions ok with notice. Regular mail or online submission form only. No e-mail or disk submissions. Cover letter is required. Time between acceptance and publication is 2-3 months. Sometimes comments on rejected poems. Sometimes publishes theme issues. Upcoming themes available in magazine or on website. Guidelines available on website. Responds in 8-12 weeks. Reading period September-April. Mss sent outside reading period will be returned unread. Always sends prepublication galleys. Pays 2 contributor's copies. Acquires all rights. Returns rights to poets upon request. Reviews books of poetry in single- and multi-book format.

POETRY NOW

1719 25th Street, Sacramento CA 95816. Richard Hansen, design/layout. **Contact:** Trina Drotar, Managing editor. *Poetry Now* is a literary review with additional online content, published bimonthly by the Sacramento Poetry Center. *Poetry Now* is available on SPC's website in a downloadable format and also at www.issuu.com. The publication includes a calendar of events, book reviews, interviews, and poetry from adults and from poets under 18 in a special column, Young Voices. Seeks submissions of all genres and forms of poetry. Has published poetry by Frank Andrick, James Benton, Martha Ann Blackman, Carol Claassen, Quinton Duval, Bill Gainer, Ann Menebroker, Joshua McKinney, Joyce Odam, and A.D. Winans. Receives over 300 poems/year, and accepts approximately 40%.

TIPS "Study the works of poets you love."

POETRY SALZBURG REVIEW

University of Salzburg, Department of English, Akademiestrasse 24, Salzburg A-5020, Austria. (43)(662)8044-4422. Fax: (43)(662)8044-167. E-mail: editor@poetrysalzburg.com. Website: www.poetrysalzburg.com. **Contact:** Dr. Wolfgang Goertschacher, editor. University of Salzburg, Department of English, Akademiestrasse 24, Salzburg A-5020, Austria. (43)(662)8044-4422. Fax: (43)(662)8044-167. Email: editor@poetrysalzburg.com. Website: www.poetrysalzburg.com. **Contact:** Dr. Wolfgang Goertschacher, editor. *Poetry Salzburg Review*, published twice/year, contains "articles on poetry, mainly contemporary, and 60 percent poetry. Also includes essays on poetics, review-essays, interviews, artwork, and translations. We tend to publish selections by authors who have not been taken up by the big poetry publishers. Nothing of poor quality." Has published poetry by Paul Muldoon, Alice Notley, Samuel Menashe, Jerome Rothenberg, Michael Heller. *Poetry Salzburg Review* is about 200 pages, A5, professionally printed, perfect-bound, with illustrated card cover. Receives about 5,000 poems/year, accepts 5%. Press run is 500. Single copy: $12; subscription: $22 (cash preferred; subscribers can also pay with PayPal). Make checks payable to Wolfgang Goertschacher.

"No requirements, but it's a good idea to subscribe to *Poetry Salzburg Review*."

MAGAZINES NEEDS *Poetry Salzburg Review*, published twice/year, contains "articles on poetry, mainly contemporary, and 60 percent poetry. Also includes essays on poetics, review-essays, interviews, artwork, and translations. We tend to publish selections by authors who have not been taken up by the big poetry publishers. Nothing of poor quality." Has published poetry by Paul Muldoon, Alice Notley, Samuel Menashe, Jerome Rothenberg, Michael Heller. *Poetry Salzburg Review* is about 200 pages, A5, professionally printed, perfect-bound, with illustrated card cover. Receives about 5,000 poems/year, accepts 5%. Press run is 500. Single copy: $12; subscription: $22 (cash preferred; subscribers can also pay with PayPal). Make checks payable to Wolfgang Goertschacher. "No requirements, but it's a good idea to subscribe to *Poetry Salzburg Review*."

HOW TO CONTACT No previously published poems or simultaneous submissions. Accepts e-mail submissions (as attachment). Time between acceptance and publication is 6 months. Seldom comments on rejected poems. Occasionally publishes theme issues. Responds in 2 months. No payment. Acquires first rights. Reviews books/chapbooks of poetry as well as books on poetics. Send materials for review consideration.

POETS AND ARTISTS (O&S)

E-mail: ospoetry@yahoo.com. Website: www.poetsandartists.com. **Contact:** Didi Menendez, publisher.

MAGAZINES NEEDS Reviews books of poetry, chapbooks of poetry, and other magazines/journals. Reads poetry submissions year round. Sometimes upcoming themes are available online at website. Prefers submissions from skilled, experienced poets; will consider work from beginning poets. Reviews books of poetry, chapbooks of poetry, and other magazines/journals. Reads poetry submissions year round. Sometimes upcoming themes are available online at website.

○ Prefers submissions from skilled, experienced poets; will consider work from beginning poets.

HOW TO CONTACT Buys 300 poems a year. Submit maximum 5 poems. Paste submissions into body of e-mail message. Cover letter is unnecessary. Does not like "weird" formats.

TIPS Publisher also publishes *MiPOesias Magazine*, which has been featured in Best American Poetry, and OCHO, which has received Pushcart Prize and has been featured in *Best American Poetry*.

◑ THE POET'S ART

171 Silverleaf Lane, Islandia, NY 11749. (631)439-0427. E-mail: davidirafox@yahoo.com. **Contact:** David Fox, editor.

MAGAZINES NEEDS *The Poet's Art*, published quarterly, is "a family-style journal, accepting work from the unpublished to the well known and all levels in between." Wants "family-friendly, positive poetry; any form considered. Topics include humor, nature, inspirational, children's poetry, or anything else that fits the family-friendly genre." Does not want "violent, vulgar, or overly depressing work. Work is read and accepted by the mentally-ill population, but they should keep in mind this is a family-friendly journal." Considers poetry by children and teens, "any age, as long as it's good quality; if under 18, get parents' permission." Has published poetry by Susan Marie Davniero, Ken Fisher, Dolores Patitz, James Webb Wilson, and Andy Roberts. *The Poet's Art* is 40 or more pages, magazine-sized, photocopied, paper-clipped or stapled, with computer cover, includes ads. Receives about 100 poems a year, accepts about 50%. Press run is 30+. "Due to limited supplies, only those who submit or whose review is accepted receive a copy; foreign contributors must pay for a copy. (There are no samples or subscriptions offered by this magazine.)"

HOW TO CONTACT Submit "as many poems that will fit on 1 page" at a time ("you can submit more, if compelled to do so; extra accepted pieces will be spread over a few issues"). Lines/poem: rarely accepts anything over 1 page. Considers simultaneous submissions ("list any other small press journals (if any) poems titles"). No e-mail or disk submissions; postal submissions only. Cover letter is preferred. "It's only polite. And include a SASE—a must! (I have been lax in this rule about SASEs, but I will now throw any submissions without a SASE away!)" Reads submissions year round, "but poets should be aware we are currently backlogged into June 2011, as of this listing. I review all poems submitted and then decide what I wish to publish." Always comments on rejected poems. Reviews chapbooks of poetry and other magazines/journals, "but editors and authors must write reviews themselves. After all, who knows your magazine/journal or chapbook better than you? (Little-known/newer journals sent in by editors or contributors get first consideration for reviews)." Send to David Fox.

⊙⊙ POETSESPRESSO

1426 Telegraph Ave. #4, Stockton CA 95204. E-mail: poetsexpresso@gmail.com. Website: www.poetsespresso.com. Donald R. Anderson, editor-in-chief. **Contact:** Patricia Mayorga, editor. Established 2005. Published bimonthly online and in print. "A small black and white publication of poetry, art, photography, recipes, and local events." Sponsored by the Writers' Guild, a club of San Joaquin Delta College.

MAGAZINES NEEDS "We value variety, appropriateness for most age groups, and poetry that goes well with the season of the issue, visual and bilingual poetry (side by side with translation), and of length that will fit on our Theet pages." Does not want "profanity, racially prejudiced, otherwise offensive material, porn, submissions that are excessively long, illegible writing, nor your only copy of the poem." Considers poetry by all ages. "Please include contact info of parent if from a minor." Has published poetry by David Humphreys, Nikki Quismondo, Susan Richardson Harvey, Marie J. Ross, Christine Stoddard, Michael C. Ford, and Allen Field Weitzel. *poetsespresso* (print edition) is 24-28 pages, digest-sized, printed "on College's industrial printers," stapled, with colored paper cover with b&w photograph/artwork, might include ads. Accepts about 100 poems/year. Number of unique visitors (online): "small count with rapid growth." Single copy: $2; subscription: $12/year (6 issues). Sample: free in return for review or swap for a desired publication. Make checks payable to Donald Anderson. *poetsespresso*, published bimonthly online and in print. "A small black and white publication of poetry, art, photography, recipes, and local events." Sponsored by the Writers' Guild, a club of San Joaquin Delta College. "We value variety, appropriateness for most age groups, and poetry that goes well with the season of the issue, visual and bilingual poetry (side by side with translation), and of length that will fit on our Theet pages." Does not want "profanity, racially prejudiced, otherwise offensive material, porn, submissions that are excessively long, illegible writing, nor your only copy of the poem." Considers poetry by all ages. "Please include contact info of parent if from

a minor." Has published poetry by David Humphreys, Nikki Quismondo, Susan Richardson Harvey, Marie J. Ross, Christine Stoddard, Michael C. Ford, and Allen Field Weitzel. *poetsespresso* (print edition) is 24-28 pages, digest-sized, printed "on College's industrial printers," stapled, with colored paper cover with b&w photograph/artwork, might include ads. Accepts about 100 poems/year. Number of unique visitors (online): "small count with rapid growth." Single copy: $2; subscription: $12/year (6 issues). Sample: free in return for review or swap for a desired publication. Make checks payable to Donald Anderson.

HOW TO CONTACT Submit "as many poems as you wish" at a time. Lines/poem: "from quote-size up to 80." Considers previously published poems and simultaneous submissions with notification. Accepts e-mail (as attachment in MS Word [.doc], MS Works [.wps], rich text [.rtf], InDesign Interchange [.inx], or notepad [.txt] formats) and disk submissions; no fax submissions. ."If postal submissions, submit copies, not originals of works, bio, optional photo. Pieces will not be returned, will respond if accepted with copy of publication. Text must be typed/printed without illegible markings. " "In any submission except ads, 2 to 4 line biography about the poet/artist is required, written in third person. Biography photo is optional. You may include info for readers to contact you, if you wish." Reads submissions year round. "Deadline for submissions are on or before the 25th of the month prior to the issue." Jan. 25 deadline for Feb-Mar, Mar. 25 for Apr-May, May 25 for Jun-Jul, Jul. 25 for Aug-Sep, Sep. 25 for Oct-Nov, Nov. 25 for Dec-Jan. Submit seasonal poems at least 1 week in advance. Time between acceptance and publication is 1 to 12 months. "Include SASE with cover requesting response if want release from publishing consideration of works after submission. Otherwise may publish up to 12 months after submission. The editor bases acceptance upon space available, interest and meeting the guidelines." Sometimes comments on rejected poems. Regularly publishes (seasonal) theme issues. Guidelines available for SASE with cover letter request, by e-mail, or on website. Responds in up to 2 months. Sometimes sends prepublication galleys (upon request). Pays 1 contributor's copy (extra copies at $2 postage per copy). Acquires one-time rights for print edition; acquires electronic rights "to keep an archived issue available online indefinitely in the future." "Rights remain with author to publish in any way; rights are given to *poetsespresso* for indefinite archive on website and 1 issue of the newsletter". Send materials for review consideration to Donald R. Anderson by e-mail (poetsespresso@gmail.com) or by postal mail with cover letter.

ADDITIONAL INFORMATION "We occasionally publish anthologies. For info on other works we have published, please visit the website for the book *Sun Shadow Mountain* and other projects linked on the project page at www.rainflowers.org ."

⭕◐ THE POET'S HAVEN

P.O. Box 1501, Massillon OH 44648. (330)844-0177. Website: www.PoetsHaven.com. **Contact:** Vertigo Xavier, publisher. (330)844-0177. Website: www.PoetsHaven.com. **Contact:** Vertigo Xavier, publisher. *The Poet's Haven* is a website "featuring poetry, artwork, stories, essays, and more." Wants work that's "emotional, personal, and intimate with the author or subject. Topics can cover just about anything." Does not publish religious material. Has published poetry by Robert O. Adair, Christopher Franke, T.M. Göttl, Mary I. Huang, and Anne McMillen. Work published on *The Poet's Haven* is left on the site permanently. Receives about 1,000 poems/year, accepts about 70%.

MAGAZINES NEEDS *The Poet's Haven* is a website "featuring poetry, artwork, stories, essays, and more." Wants work that's "emotional, personal, and intimate with the author or subject. Topics can cover just about anything." Does not publish religious material. Has published poetry by Robert O. Adair, Christopher Franke, T.M. Göttl, Mary I. Huang, and Anne McMillen. Work published on *The Poet's Haven* is left on the site permanently. Receives about 1,000 poems/ year, accepts about 70%.

HOW TO CONTACT Considers previously published poems and simultaneous submissions. Accepts submissions through online form only. Time between acceptance and publication is about 2 weeks. Never comments on rejected poems. Guidelines available on website. No payment for online publication. Acquires rights to publish on the website permanently and in any future print publications. Poet retains rights to have poems published elsewhere, "provided the other publishers do not require first-time or exclusive rights."

ADDITIONAL INFORMATION Publishes audio podcast as "Saturday Night With *The Poet's Haven.*"

Check website for submission information or to download sample episodes.

ALSO OFFERS Publisher's blog, and open-mic events.

⭕◐ POET'S INK

E-mail: poet_Kelly@yahoo.com. Website: www.PoetsInk.com. **Contact:** Kelly Morris, editor. E-mail: poet_Kelly@yahoo.com. Website: www.PoetsInk.com. **Contact:** Kelly Morris, editor. *Poet's Ink*, published monthly online, seeks "poetry of all kinds. Work by new poets is published alongside that of more experienced poets." Does not want "bad rhyme, clicheés, poetry riddled with abstractions." Considers poetry by teens. "Will be judged by the same standards as poetry by adults." Has published poetry by Alexandria Webb, David Waite, Colin Baker, Megan Arkenburg, and Robert Demaree. Receives about 500 poems/year, accepts about 10%.

MAGAZINES NEEDS *Poet's Ink*, published monthly online, seeks "poetry of all kinds. Work by new poets is published alongside that of more experienced poets." Does not want "bad rhyme, clicheés, poetry riddled with abstractions." Considers poetry by teens. "Will be judged by the same standards as poetry by adults." Has published poetry by Alexandria Webb, David Waite, Colin Baker, Megan Arkenburg, and Robert Demaree. Receives about 500 poems/year, accepts about 10%.

HOW TO CONTACT Submit 3-5 poems at a time. Lines/poem: 2 minimum, 100 maximum ("longer poems better not be long-winded!"). Considers previously published poems and simultaneous submissions. Accepts e-mail submissions (as attachment); no disk submissions. Cover letter is preferred. "No funky formatting of poems!" Reads submissions year round. Time between acceptance and publication is 2 months. Often comments on rejected poems. Sometimes publishes theme issues. Guidelines available by e-mail or on website. Responds in 1 month. Acquires one-time rights. Rights revert to poets upon publication.

◐ THE POET'S PEN

The Society of American Poets (SOAP), 6500 Clito Road, Statesboro GA 30461. 912-587-4400. Website: http://ihspub.com. **Contact:** Dr. Charles E. Cravey, editor. The Society of American Poets (SOAP), 6500 Clito Rd., Statesboro, GA 30461. (912) 587-4400. Website: http://ihspub.com. **Contact:** Dr. Charles E.

Cravey, editor. *The Poet's Pen*, published quarterly by The Society of American Poets, is "open to all styles of poetry and prose—both religious and secular." Does not want "gross or 'X-rated' poetry without taste or character." Has published poetry by Najwa Salam Brax, Henry Goldman, Henry W. Gurley, William Heffner, Linda Metcalf, and Charles Russ, among others. *The Poet's Pen* uses poetry **primarily by members and subscribers**, but outside submissions are also welcome. Subscription: included in membership, $30/year ($25 for students). Sample: $10.

MAGAZINES NEEDS *The Poet's Pen*, published quarterly by The Society of American Poets, is "open to all styles of poetry and prose—both religious and secular." Does not want "gross or 'X-rated' poetry without taste or character." Has published poetry by Najwa Salam Brax, Henry Goldman, Henry W. Gurley, William Heffner, Linda Metcalf, and Charles Russ, among others. *The Poet's Pen* uses poetry **primarily by members and subscribers**, but outside submissions are also welcome. Subscription: included in membership, $30/year ($25 for students). Sample: $10.

HOW TO CONTACT Submit 3 poems at a time/quarter. Considers simultaneous submissions and previously published poems, if permission from previous publisher is included. Include name and address on each page. "Submissions or inquiries will not be responded to without a #10 business-sized SASE. We do stress originality and have each new poet and/or subscriber sign a waiver form verifying originality." Publishes seasonal/theme issues. Guidelines available in magazine, for SASE, or by e-mail. Sometimes sends prepublication galleys. Always comments on rejected poems.

CONTEST/AWARD OFFERINGS Sponsors several contests each quarter, with prizes totaling $100-250. Also offers Editor's Choice Awards each quarter. The President's Award for Excellence is a prize of $50. **Deadline:** November 1. Also publishes a quarterly anthology from poetry competitions in several categories with prizes of $25-100. Guidelines available for SASE or by e-mail.

☉○ POETS' PODIUM

2-3265 Front Rd., E. Hawkesbury ON K6A 2R2, Canada. Ken Elliott, Catherine Heaney Barrowcliffe, Robert Piquette, or Ron Barrowcliffe, associate editors. **Contact:** Ken Elliot. 2-3265 Front Rd., E. Hawkes-

bury, ON K6A 2R2, Canada. **Contact:** Ken Elliott, Catherine Heaney Barrowcliffe, Robert Piquette, or Ron Barrowcliffe, associate editors. Estab. 1993. *Poets' Podium*, published quarterly, is a newsletter that aims "to promote the reading and writing of the poetic form, especially among those being published for the first time." Poetry specifications are open. "**Priority is given to valued subscribers.** Nevertheless, when there is room in an issue, we will publish nonsubscribers." Does not want poetry that is "gothic, erotic/sexual, gory, bloody, or that depicts violence." Subscription: $15 USD. Sample: $3 USD. *Poets' Podium*, published quarterly, is a newsletter that aims "to promote the reading and writing of the poetic form, especially among those being published for the first time." Poetry specifications are open. "**Priority is given to valued subscribers.** Nevertheless, when there is room in an issue, we will publish nonsubscribers." Does not want poetry that is "gothic, erotic/sexual, gory, bloody, or that depicts violence." Subscription: $15 USD. Sample: $3 USD.

HOW TO CONTACT Submit 3 poems at a time. Lines/poem: 4 minimum, 25 maximum. Considers previously published poems and simultaneous submissions. Cover letter is required. Include SASE (or SAE and IRC), name, address, and telephone number; e-mail address if applicable. Time between acceptance and publication varies. Guidelines available for SASE (or SAE and IRC), or by fax or by e-mail. Pays 3 contributor's copies. All rights remain with the author.

TIPS "Poetry is a wonderful literary form. Try your hand at it. Send us the fruit of your labours."

◑ POINTED CIRCLE

Portland Community College-Cascade, 705 N. Killing, Portland OR 97217. E-mail: lutgarda.cowan@pcc.edu. **Contact:** Lutgarda Cowan, English instructor, faculty advisor. Magazine: 80 pages; b&w illustrations; photos. "Anything of interest to educationally/culturally mixed audience." Annual. Ethnic/multicultural, literary, regional, contemporary, prose poem. "We will read whatever is sent, but encourage writers to remember we are a quality literary/arts magazine intended to promote the arts in the community. Be mindful of deadlines and length limits." Acquires one-time rights. Magazine: 80 pages; b&w illustrations; photos. "Anything of interest to educationally/culturally mixed audience." Annual. Ethnic/multicultural, literary, regional, contemporary, prose poem. "We will read whatever is sent, but encourage writers to remember we are a quality literary/arts magazine intended to promote the arts in the community. No pornography, nothing trite. Be mindful of deadlines and length limits." Accepts submissions only October 1-March 1, for July 1 issue. Accepts submissions by e-mail, mail. Prose up to 3,000 words; poetry up to 6 pages; artwork in high-resolution digital form. Submitted materials will not be returned; SASE for notification only. Accepts multiple submissions.

HOW TO CONTACT Accepts submissions only October 1-March 1, for July 1 issue. Accepts submissions by e-mail, mail. Prose up to 3,000 words; poetry up to 6 pages; artwork in high-resolution digital form. Submitted materials will not be returned; SASE for notification only. Accepts multiple submissions.

POLYPHONY H.S., AN INTERNATIONAL STUDENT-RUN LITERARY MAGAZINE FOR HIGH SCHOOL WRITERS AND EDITORS

E-mail: polyphonyhs@gmail.com. Website: www.polyphonyhs.com. **Contact:** Billy Lombarado, Managing Editor or Beth Keegan, Exec. Director. Literary magazine/journal: 9x6, 70-120 pages, silk finish 80 lb. white paper, silk finish 100 lb. cover. 501(c) 3 organization.Literary magazine/journal. "We are a 501(c) 3 organization. Our goal is to work directly with all of our submitting authors in an attempt to help them grow as writers, to publish the best of the year's submissions on our web edition, and to publish the best of those in our annual print edition. Deadline: April 15. Every submission sent in before our early deadline (March 15) is edited, commented upon, by at least 3 high school editors from around the country. Polyphony H.S. invites high school students to serve as readers and editors, and hosts summer workshops for National Editors. We manage the Claudia Ann Seaman Awards for Young Writers; cash awards for the best poem, best story, best work of creative nonfiction. See website for details." Annual. To be considered for CAS awards, entries must be accompanied by student name, address, email address, high school, high school address, and name and email address of your high school English teacher. Needs poetry, fiction, and creative nonfiction. Receives 1,500-2,000 mss/year. Accepts 50-75 mss/issue. Publishes new writers/year.

"We think this is the most important literary magazine in the world. Inherent in it is the collective value of every other magazine in circulation. If you're a high school teacher, you should have us in your classroom. If you teach in a university you should be paying attention to our writers."

HOW TO CONTACT Use online submission process.

ADDITIONAL INFORMATION "We think this is the most important literary magazine in the world. Inherent in it is the collective value of every other magazine in circulation. If you're a high school teacher, you should have us in your classroom. If you teach in a university you should be paying attention to our writers. They'll blow you away."

CONTEST/AWARD OFFERINGS "We manage the Claudia Ann Seaman Awards for Young Writers; cash awards for the best poem, best story, best work of creative nonfiction. See website for details."

THE PORTLAND REVIEW

Portland State University, P.O. Box 347, Portland OR 97207-0347. (503)725-4533. E-mail: theportlandreview@gmail.com. Website: http://portlandreview. tumblr.com. **Contact:** Jacqueline Treiber, Editor.

MAGAZINES NEEDS *The Portland Review*, published 3 times/year by Portland State University, seeks "submissions exhibiting a unique, compelling voice and content of substance. Experimental poetry welcomed." Has published poetry by Gaylord Brewer, Richard Bentley, Charles Jensen, Mary Biddinger, and Jerzy Gizella. *The Portland Review* is about 130 pages. Receives about 1,000 poems/year, accepts about 30. Press run is 1,000 for subscribers, libraries, and bookstores nationwide. Single copy: $9; subscription: $27/year, $54/2 years. Sample: $8.

HOW TO CONTACT Submit up to 5 poems at a time. No previously published poems. To submit, use submission manager on website. Include phone number, e-mail address, and other contact information. Reads submissions between September 1 and April 1. "Our website is a general introduction to our magazine, with samples of our poetry, fiction, and art. *The Portland Review*Â will only consider one submission per writer, per reading period. **If you would like to be considered for online publication, please specify this within your cover letter.** " Responds in up to 4 months. Pays 2 contributor's copies. Acquires first North American rights.

TIPS "View website for current samples and guidelines."

POST POEMS

Raw Dog Press, 151 S. West St., Doylestown PA 18901-4134. Website: http://rawdogpress.bravehost.com. **Contact:** R. Gerry Fabian, poetry editor. Estab. 1977.
MAGAZINES NEEDS Post Poems, published annually by Raw Dog Press, is a postcard series. Wants "short poetry (3-7 lines) on any subject. The positive poem or the poem of understated humor always has an inside track. No taboos, however. All styles considered. Anything with rhyme had better be immortal." Has published poetry by Don Ryan, John Grey, and the editor, R. Gerry Fabian. Send SASE for catalog to buy samples.
HOW TO CONTACT Submit 3-5 poems at a time. Lines/poem: 3-7. Cover letter is optional. SASE is required. Always comments on rejected poems. Guidelines available on website. Pays in contributor's copies. Acquires all rights. Returns rights on mention of first publication. Sometimes reviews books of poetry.
ADDITIONAL INFORMATION Raw Dog Press welcomes new poets and detests second-rate poems from "name" poets. "We exist because we are dumb like a fox, but even a fox takes care of its own." Send SASE for catalog to buy samples.
ALSO OFFERS Offers criticism for a fee; "if someone is desperate to publish and is willing to pay, we will use our vast knowledge to help steer the manuscript in the right direction. We will advise against it, but as P.T. Barnum said.."

THE POTOMAC

E-mail: Charles.Rammelkamp@ssa.gov. Website: http://thepotomacjournal.com. **Contact:** Charles Rammelkamp, editor. Estab. 2004. Member: Web del Sol.
MAGAZINES NEEDS The Potomac, published semi-annually online, features political commentary, cutting-edge poetry, flash fiction, and reviews. Open to all forms of poetry by new and established writers. Has published poetry and fiction by Robert Cooperman, Michael Salcman, Joanne Lowery, Roger Netzer, Pamela Painter, and L.D. Brodsky. Receives a "variable" number of poems/year, accepts about 50-60. Sample: free online.
HOW TO CONTACT Submit any number of poems at a time. Considers simultaneous submissions; no

previously published poems. Accepts e-mail submissions (as attachment) only; no postal or disk submissions. Cover letter is preferred. Reads submissions year round. Time between acceptance and publication is 3 months. Often comments on rejected poems. Guidelines available on website. Responds in 2 months. Sometimes sends prepublication galleys. No payment. Acquires one-time rights. Reviews books/chapbooks of poetry and other magazines/journals in up to 2,000 words, single- and multi-book format. Send materials for review consideration.

POTOMAC REVIEW: A JOURNAL OF ARTS & HUMANITIES

Montgomery College, 51 Mannakee St., MT/212, Rockville MD 20850. (240)567-4100. E-mail: zachary.benavidez@montgomerycollege.edu. Website: www.montgomerycollege.edu/potomacreview. **Contact:** Zachary Benavidez, editor-in-chief.
MAGAZINES NEEDS Potomac Review: A Journal of Arts & Humanities, published semiannually in November and May, "welcomes poetry, from across the spectrum, both traditional and nontraditional poetry, free verse and in-form (translations accepted). Essays and creative nonfiction are also welcome." Has published work by David Wagoner, Elizabeth Spires, Ramola D, Amy Holman, and Luke Johnson. Potomac Review is 150 pages, digest-sized, 50 lb paper; 65 lb cover stock. Receives about 2,500 poems/year, accepts 3%. Subscription: $18/year (includes 2 issues). Sample: $10.
HOW TO CONTACT Submit up to 3 poems (5 pages maximum) at a time. Considers simultaneous submissions; no previously published poems. Cover letter is preferred. Include brief bio; enclose SASE. Time between acceptance and publication is up to 1 year. Poems are read "in house," then sent to poetry editor for comments and dialogue. Often comments on rejected poems. Does not publish theme issues. Guidelines available on website. Responds within 3 months. Pays 2 contributor's copies and offers 40% discount on additional copies.
CONTEST/AWARD OFFERINGS Sponsors an annual poetry contest and annual fiction contest. Guidelines available in magazine (fall/winter issue), for SASE.

THE PRAIRIE JOURNAL

Prairie Journal Trust, P.O. Box 68073, 28 Crowfoot Terrace NW, Calgary AB Y3G 3N8, Canada. E-mail:

editor@prairiejournal.org (queries only); prairie-journal@yahoo.com. Website: prairiejournal.org. **Contact:** A.E. Burke, literary editor. "The audience is literary, university, library, scholarly, and creative readers/writers."

○ "Use our mailing address for submissions and queries with samples sor clippings."

MAGAZINES NEEDS *The Prairie Journal*, published twice/year, seeks poetry "of any length; free verse, contemporary themes (feminist, nature, urban, non-political), aesthetic value, a poet's poetry." Does not want to see "most rhymed verse, sentimentality, egotistical ravings. No cowboys or sage brush." Has published poetry by Liliane Welch, Cornelia Hoogland, Sheila Hyland, Zoe Lendale, and Chad Norman. *The Prairie Journal* is 40-60 pages, digest-sized, offset-printed, saddle-stapled, with card cover, includes ads. Receives about 1,000 poems/year, accepts 10%. Press run is 600; the rest are sold on newsstands. Subscription: $10 for individuals, $18 for libraries. Sample: $8 ("use postal money order"). No U.S. stamps.

HOW TO CONTACT No previously published poems or simultaneous submissions. No e-mail submissions. "We will not be reading submissions until such time as an issue is in preparation (twice yearly), so be patient and we will acknowledge, accept for publication, or return work at that time." Guidelines available for postage ("no U.S. stamps, please"; get IRCs from USPS) or on website. Sometimes sends prepublication galleys. Pays $10-50 and 1 contributor's copy. Acquires first North American serial rights. Reviews books of poetry, "but must be assigned by editor. Query first."

ADDITIONAL INFORMATION For chapbook publication by Prairie Journal Press, Canadian poets only (preferably from the plains region). Has published Voices From Earth, selected poems by Ronald Kurt and Mark McCawley, and In the Presence of Grace by McCandless Callaghan. "We also publish anthologies on themes when material is available." Query first, with 5 sample poems and cover letter with brief bio and publication credits. Responds to queries in 2 months; to mss in 6 months. Payment in modest honoraria. Publishes "Poems of the Month" online. Submit up to 4 poems with $1 reading fee by postal mail."Read recent poets! Experiment with line length, images, metaphors. Innovate."

TIPS "We publish many, many new writers and are always open to unsolicited submissions because we are 100% freelance. Do not send US stamps, always use IRCs. We have poems and reviews online (query first)."

○ ♡ PRAIRIE SCHOONER

The University of Nebraska Press, Prairie Schooner, 123 Andrews Hall, University of Nebraska, Lincoln NE 68588-0334. (402)472-7211, 1-800-715-2387. E-mail: jengelhardt2@unlnotes.unl.edu. Website: http://prairieschooner.unl.edu. 123 Andrews Hall, University of Nebraska, Lincoln, NE 68588-0334. (402)472-7211, 1-800-715-2387 . E-mail: jengelhardt2@unl-notes.unl.edu. Website: http://prairieschooner.unl.edu. Poetry published in Prairie Schooner has been selected for inclusion in *The Best American Poetry* and *The Pushcart Prize*. *Prairie Schooner*, published quarterly, prints poetry, fiction, personal essays, interviews, and reviews. Wants "poems that fulfill the expectations they set up." No specifications as to form, length, style, subject matter, or purpose. Has published poetry by Alicia Ostriker, Marilyn Hacker, D.A. Powell, Stephen Dunn, and David Ignatow. *Prairie Schooner* is about 200 pages, digest-sized, flat-spined. Receives about 5,500 submissions/year, uses about 300 pages of poetry. Press run is 2,500. Single copy: $9; subscription: $28/1 year. Sample: $6."We look for the best fiction, poetry, and nonfiction available to publish, and our readers expect to read stories, poems, and essays of extremely high quality. We try to publish a variety of styles, topics, themes, points of view, and writers with a variety of backgrounds in all stages of their careers. We like work that is compelling—intellectually or emotionally—either in form, language, or content."

○ Submissions must be received between September 1 and May 1.

MAGAZINES NEEDS Prairie Schooner, published quarterly, prints poetry, fiction, personal essays, interviews, and reviews. Wants "poems that fulfill the expectations they set up." No specifications as to form, length, style, subject matter, or purpose. Has published poetry by Alicia Ostriker, Marilyn Hacker, D.A. Powell, Stephen Dunn, and David Ignatow. *Prairie Schooner* is about 200 pages, digest-sized, flat-spined. Receives about 5,500 submissions/year, uses about 300 pages of poetry. Press run is 2,500. Single copy: $9; subscription: $28/1 year. Sample: $6.

HOW TO CONTACT Submit 5-7 poems at a time. No simultaneous submissions. No fax or e-mail submissions; postal submissions only. Reads submissions September 1-May 1 (mss must be received during that period). Guidelines available for SASE or on website. Responds in 3-4 months, "sooner if possible." Always sends prepublication galleys. Pays 3 contributor's copies. Acquires all rights. Returns rights upon request without fee. Reviews books of poetry. Send materials for review consideration.

CONTEST/AWARD OFFERINGS "All manuscripts published in *Prairie Schooner* automatically will be considered for our annual prizes." These include The Strousse Award for Poetry ($500), the Bernice Slote Prize for Beginning Writers ($500), the Hugh J. Luke Award ($250), the Edward Stanley Award for Poetry ($1,000), the Virginia Faulkner Award for Excellence in Writing ($1,000), the Glenna Luschei Prize for Excellence ($1,500), and the Jane Geske Award ($250). Also, each year 10 Glenna Luschei Awards ($250 each) are given for poetry, fiction, and nonfiction. All contests are open only to those writers whose work was published in the magazine the previous year. Editors serve as judges. Also sponsors The *Prairie Schooner* Book Prize (see separate listing Contests & Awards).

ALSO OFFERS Editor-in-Chief Hilda Raz also promotes poets whose work has appeared in her pages by listing their continued accomplishments in a special section (even when their work does not concurrently appear in the magazine).

TIPS "Send us your best, most carefully crafted work and be persistent. Submit again and again. Constantly work on improving your writing. Read widely in literary fiction, nonfiction, and poetry. Read *Prairie Schooner* to know what we publish."

⭕ PRAYERWORKS

P.O. Box 301363, Portland OR 97294-9363. (503)761-2072. E-mail: jay4prayer@aol.com. **Contact:** V. Ann Mandeville, editor. P.O. Box 301363, Portland, OR 97294-9363. (503)761-2072. E-mail: jay4prayer@aol.com. **Contact:** V. Ann Mandeville, editor. Estab. 1988. *PrayerWorks*, published weekly, is a newsletter "encouraging elderly people to recognize their value to God as prayer warriors." Established as a ministry to people living in retirement centers, *PrayerWorks* features "prayers, ways to pray, stories of answered prayers, teaching on a Scripture portion, articles that build faith, and poems." *PrayerWorks* is 4 pages, digest-sized, desktop-published, photocopied, folded. Receives about 50 poems/year, accepts about 25%. Press run is 1,100. Subscription: free. PrayerWorks is a ministry of THE MASTER'S WORK. Please send requests to: PO Box 301363, Portland OR 97294, Ph: (503)761-2072; Email: Jay4prayer@aol.com. *PrayerWorks*, published weekly, is a newsletter "encouraging elderly people to recognize their value to God as prayer warriors." Established as a ministry to people living in retirement centers, *PrayerWorks* features "prayers, ways to pray, stories of answered prayers, teaching on a Scripture portion, articles that build faith, and poems." *PrayerWorks* is 4 pages, digest-sized, desktop-published, photocopied, folded. Receives about 50 poems/year, accepts about 25%. Press run is 1,100. Subscription: free. PrayerWorks is a ministry of THE MASTER'S WORK. Please send requests to: PO Box 301363, Portland OR 97294, Ph: (503)761-2072; Email: Jay4prayer@aol.com. Website: www.prayerworksnw.org.

HOW TO CONTACT Submit 5 poems at a time. Considers previously published poems and simultaneous submissions. Accepts e-mail submissions (WordPerfect or Microsoft Word attachments). Cover letter is preferred. 1 poem/page. Time between acceptance and publication is usually within 1 month. Seldom comments on rejected poems. Publishes theme issues relating to the holidays (submit holiday poetry 2 months in advance). Guidelines available for SASE. Responds in 3 weeks. Pays 5 or more contributor's copies.

⭕🄳🗨️💲 PRISM INTERNATIONAL

Department of Creative Writing, Buch E462, 1866 Main Mall, University of British Columbia, Vancouver BC V6T 1Z1, Canada. (604)822-2514. Fax: (604)822-3616. Website: www.prismmagazine.ca. A quarterly international journal of contemporary writing—fiction, poetry, drama, creative nonfiction and translation. Readership: public and university libraries, individual subscriptions, bookstores—a world-wide audience concerned with the contemporary in literature.

MAGAZINES NEEDS *PRISM international*, published quarterly, prints poetry, drama, short fiction, creative nonfiction, and translation into English in all genres. "We have no thematic or stylistic allegiances: Excellence is our main criterion for acceptance of manuscripts." Wants "fresh, distinctive poetry that shows an awareness of traditions old and new. We read everything." Considers poetry by children and teens. "Excellence is the only criterion." Has published poetry by Margaret Avison, Elizabeth Bachinsky, John Pass, Warren Heiti, Don McKay, Bill Bissett, and Stephanie Bolster. *PRISM international* is 80 pages, digest-sized, elegantly printed, flat-spined, with original color artwork on a glossy card cover. Receives 1,000 submissions/year, accepts about 80. Circulation is for 1,200 subscribers. Subscription: $28/year, $46 for 2 years. Sample: $11. "Subscribers outside of Canada, please pay in U.S. dollars."

HOW TO CONTACT Submit up to 6 poems at a time. No previously published poems or simultaneous submissions. No e-mail submissions. Cover letter is required. Include brief introduction and list of previous publications. Poems must be typed or computer-generated (font and point size open). Include SASE (or SAE with IRCs). "Note: American stamps are not valid postage in Canada. No SASEs with U.S. postage will be returned. Translations must be accompanied by a copy of the original." Guidelines available for SASE (or SAE with IRCs), by e-mail, or on website. Responds in up to 6 months. Pays $40/printed page (for poetry) and one-year subscription; plus an additional $10/printed page to selected authors for publication online. Editors sometimes comment on rejected poems. Acquires first North American serial rights.

ADDITIONAL INFORMATION Sponsors annual Earle Birney Prize for Poetry. Prize awarded by the outgoing poetry editor to an outstanding poetry contributor published in PRISM *international*. Enter by regular submission only: no fee required. $500 prize.

CONTEST/AWARD OFFERINGS Annual Poetry Contest. First prize: $1,000; second prize: $300; third prize: $200. Entry fee: $28 for 3 poems; $7 per additional poem. Entry fee includes one-year subscription. Deadline: January 29. This year's poetry judge is **Brad Cran**, Vancouver poet laureate and author of *The Good Life* (2002; Nightwood Editions). He is a contributing editor at *Geist* magazine, and you can read some of his work on their site. The editorial board also awards an annual $500 prize to an outstanding poetry contributor in each volume. See below.

TIPS "We are looking for new and exciting fiction. Excellence is still our No. 1 criterion. As well as poetry, imaginative nonfiction and fiction, we are especially open to translations of all kinds, very short fiction pieces and drama which work well on the page. Translations must come with a copy of the original language work. We pay an additional $10/printed page to selected authors whose work we place on our online version of *Prism*."

⊙ PRISM QUARTERLY

3232 S. First St., Springfield IL 62703. (217)529-5933. E-mail: prism@daybreakpoetry.com. Website: http://www.pwlf.com/prism_quarterly.htm. **Contact:** Michelle Delheimer. 3232 S. First St., Springfield, IL 62703. (217)529-5933. E-mail:prism@daybreakpoetry.com. Website: www.pwlf.com/prism_quarterly.htm. Contact: Michelle Delheimer. *Quarterly*, published by Daybreak Press, a division of Pitch-Black LLC, considers "all styles and forms of poetry." Does not want poems over 100 lines long. Considers poetry by children and teens. Has published poetry by Marge Piercy, Marcellus Leonard, Barb Robinette, and Siobhan. *Prism Quarterly* is 128 pages, digest-sized, laser-printed, perfect-bound, with cardstock cover with original artwork, includes ads. Receives about 800 poems/year, accepts about 200. Press run is 200; 25 distributed free to contributors and reviewers. Single copy: $7.95; subscription: $29.95. Make checks payable to Pitch-Black LLC.*Prism Quarterly*, published by Daybreak Press, a division of Pitch-Black LLC, considers "all styles and forms of poetry." Does not want poems over 100 lines long. Considers poetry by children and teens. Has published poetry by Marge Piercy, Marcellus Leonard, Barb Robinette, and Siobhan. *Prism Quarterly* is 128 pages, digest-sized, laser-printed, perfect-bound, with cardstock cover with original artwork, includes ads. Receives about 800 poems/year, accepts about 200. Press run is 200; 25 distributed free to contributors and reviewers. Single copy: $7.95; subscription: $29.95. Make checks payable to Pitch-Black LLC.

HOW TO CONTACT Submit no more than 3 poems at a time. Lines/poem: 100 maximum. No previously published poems or simultaneous submissions. Accepts e-mail submissions (pasted into body of message or as attachment in Rich Text Format); no disk submissions. Cover letter is required. "Please include SASE and e-mail address (if available) if response is desired for any submission." Reads submissions year-round. Submit seasonal poems 3 months in advance. Time between acceptance and publication is 2-3 months. Poems are circulated to an editorial board. Always comments on rejected poems. Guidelines available on website. Responds in 1-3 months. Pays one contributor's copy. Acquires first rights. Rights revert to poet upon publication.

TIPS "Intermittent contests are announced at our website. Please see site for frequent updates.""*Prism Quarterly* is a superlative journal of eclectic literature. The publishers welcome poets and writers in all (publishable) stages of their careers and seek a variety of themes, forms, and styles."

PROVINCETOWN ARTS

(508)487-3167. E-mail: cbusa@comcast.net. Website: www.provincetownarts.org. (Specialized: Cape Cod & area art colony culture) 650 Commercial St., Provincetown MA 02657. (508)487-3167. E-mail: cbusa@comcast.net. Website: www.provincetownarts.org. Established 1985. **Contact:** Christopher Busa, editor. Published annually in July, prints quality poetry, focusing "broadly on the artists and writers who inhabit or visit the tip of Cape Cod." Seeks to "stimulate creative activity and enhance public awareness of the cultural life of the nation's oldest continuous art colony. Drawing upon a century-long tradition rich in visual art, literature, and theater, *Provincetown Arts* publishes material with a view towards demonstrating that the artists' colony, functioning outside the urban centers, is a utopian dream with an ongoing vitality." Has published poetry by Bruce Smith, Franz Wright, Sandra McPherson, and Cyrus Cassells. 170 pages, magazine-sized, perfect-bound, with full-color glossy cover. Press run is 10,000. Sample: $10. Reads submissions October-February. Guidelines available for SASE. Responds in 3 months. Usually sends prepublication galleys. Reviews books of poetry in 500-3,000 words, single- or multi-book format. Send materials for review consideration."*Provincetown Arts* focuses broadly on the artists and writers who inhabit or visit the Lower Cape, and seeks to stimulate creative activity and enhance public awareness of the cultural life of the nation's oldest continuous art colony. Drawing upon a 75-year tradition rich in visual art, literature, and theater, *Provincetown Arts* offers a unique blend of interviews, fiction, visual features, reviews, reporting, and poetry."

HOW TO CONTACT Submit up to 3 poems at a time. No e-mail submissions; "all queries and submissions should be sent via postal mail." Submissions must be typed.

ADDITIONAL INFORMATION The Provincetown Arts Press has published 8 volumes of poetry. The Provincetown Poets Series includes *At the Gate* by Martha Rhodes, *Euphorbia* by Anne-Marie Levine (a finalist in the 1995 Paterson Poetry Prize), and *1990* by Michael Klein (co-winner of the 1993 Lambda Literary Award).

⦿ PUDDING MAGAZINE: THE INTERNATIONAL JOURNAL OF APPLIED POETRY

(614)986-1881. Website: www.puddinghouse.com. 81 Shadymere Lane, Columbus OH 43213. (614)986-1881. Website: www.puddinghouse.com. E-mail (inquiries only): jen@puddinghouse.com **Contact:** Jennifer Bosveld, editor. Estab. 1979. *Pudding Magazine: The International Journal of Applied Poetry*, published "every several months," seeks "what hasn't been said before. Speak the unspeakable. Long poems okay as long as they aren't windy." *Pudding* also serves as "a forum for poems and articles by people who take poetry arts into the schools and the human services." Wants "poetry on popular culture, rich brief narratives, i.e. 'virtual journalism' (see website)." Does not want "preachments or sentimentality; obvious traditional forms without fresh approach." Has published poetry by Knute Skinner, David Chorlton, Mary Winters, and Robert Collins. *Pudding* is 70 pages, digest-sized, offset-composed on Microsoft Word PC. Press run is 1,500. Subscription: $29.95 for 4 issues. Sample: $8.95.

MAGAZINES NEEDS *Pudding Magazine: The International Journal of Applied Poetry*, published "every several months," seeks "what hasn't been said before. Speak the unspeakable. Long poems okay as long as they aren't windy." *Pudding* also serves as "a forum for poems and articles by people who take poetry arts into the schools and the human services." Wants "poetry on popular culture, rich brief narratives, i.e. 'virtual journalism' (see website)." Does not want "preachments or sentimentality; obvious traditional forms without fresh approach." Has published poetry by Knute Skinner, David Chorlton, Mary Winters, and Robert Collins. *Pudding* is 70 pages, digest-sized, offset-composed on Microsoft Word PC. Press run is 1,500. Subscription: $29.95 for 4 issues. Sample: $8.95.

HOW TO CONTACT Submit 3-10 poems at a time. Previously published submissions "respected, but include credits"; no simultaneous submissions. Cover letter is preferred ("cultivates great relationships with writers"). "Submissions without SASEs will be discarded. No postcards." Sometimes publishes theme issues. Guidelines available on website only. Responds on same day (unless traveling). Pays 1 contributor's copy; $10 and 4 contributor's copies to featured poets. Returns rights "with *Pudding* permitted to reprint." Send anthologies and books for review consideration or listing as recommended.

ALSO OFFERS "Our website is one of the greatest poetry websites in the country—calls, workshops, publication list/history, online essays, games, guest pages, calendars, poem of the month, poet of the week, much more." The website also links to the site for The Unitarian Universalist Poets Cooperative and American Poets Opposed to Executions, both national organizations.

○ PUERTO DEL SOL

New Mexico State University, English Department, New Mexico State Univ., Dept. of English, P.O. Box 30001, MSC 3E, Las Cruces NM 88003. (505)646-3931. E-mail: contact@puertodelsol.org. Website: www.puertodelsol.org. **Contact:** Carmen Giménez Smith, editor-in-chief. Wants "top-quality poetry, any style, from anywhere; excellent poetry of any kind, any form." Has published poetry by Richard Blanco, Maria Ercilla, Pamela Gemin, John Repp, and Lee Ann Roripaugh. *Puerto del Sol* is 150 pages, digest-sized, professionally printed, flat-spined, with matte card cover with art. Receives about 900 poetry submissions/year, accepts about 50. Press run is 1,250 (300 subscribers, 25-30 libraries). Subscription: $10/2 issues. Sample: $8.

HOW TO CONTACT Submit 3-6 poems at a time. Considers simultaneous submissions. No e-mail submissions. Brief cover letter is welcome. "Do not send publication vitae." One poem/page. Reads mss September 1-February 1 only. Offers editorial comments on most mss. Tries to respond within 6 months. Sometimes sends prepublication galleys. Pays 2 contributor's copies.

TIPS "We are especially pleased to publish emerging writers who work to push their art form or field of study in new directions."

●○ PULSAR POETRY MAGAZINE

Ligden Publishers, 34 Lineacre, Grange Park, Swindon, Wiltshire SN5 6DA, England. E-mail: pulsar.ed@btopenworld.com. Website: www.pulsarpoetry.com. **Contact:** David Pike, Editor. *Pulsar Poetry Magazine* changed and is now a web-zine only. We will publish poems on the Pulsar web on a quarterly basis, i.e. March, June, September and December. The selection process for poems will not alter and we will continue to publish on a merit basis only, be warned the editor is very picky! See poem submission guidelines online. We encourage the writing of poetry from all walks of life. Wants "hard-hitting, thought-provoking work; interesting and stimulating poetry." Does not want "racist material. Not keen on religious poetry." Has published poetry by A.C. Evans, Chris Hardy, Kate Edwards, Elizabeth Birchall, and Michael Newman.

○ Now is a web-zine only. "We will publish poems on the Pulsar web on a quarterly basis, i.e. March, June, September and December. The selection process for poems will not alter and we will continue to publish on a merit basis only, be warned the editor is very picky! See poem submission guidelines online. We encourage the writing of poetry from all walks of life. Wants 'hard-hitting, thought-provoking work; interesting and stimulating poetry.' Does not want 'racist material. Not keen on religious poetry.' Has published poetry by A.C. Evans, Chris Hardy, Kate Edwards, Elizabeth Birchall, and Michael Newman."

HOW TO CONTACT Submit 3 poems at a time. No previously published poems or simultaneous submissions. Accepts e-mail submissions (pasted into body of message). "Send no more than 2 poems via e-mail; file attachments will not be read." Cover letter is preferred. Include SAE with adequate IRCs for a reply only (mss not returned if non-UK). Manuscripts should be typed. Time between acceptance and publication is about 1 month. "Poems can be published in next edition if it is what we are looking for. The editor and assistant read all poems." Seldom comments on rejected poems. Guidelines available for SASE (or SAE and IRC) or on website. Responds within 1 month. Pays 1 contributor's copy.

Acquires first rights. "Originators retain copyright of their poems." Staff reviews poetry books and CDs (mainstream); word count varies. Send materials for review consideration.

ADDITIONAL INFORMATION "Give explanatory notes if poems are open to interpretation. Be patient and enjoy what you are doing. Check grammar, spelling, etc. (should be obvious). Note: we are a nonprofit-making society."

TIPS "Give explanatory notes if poems are open to interpretation. Be patient and enjoy what you are doing. Check grammar, spelling, etc. (should be obvious). Note: we are a nonprofit-making society."

⭘ PULSE ONLINE LITERARY JOURNAL

12 Center St., Rockland ME 04841. (760)243-8034. E-mail: mainepoet@mac.com. Website: www.heartsoundspressliterary.com. **Contact:** Carol Bachofner, poetry editor. 12 Center St., Rockland, ME 04841. (760)243-8034. E-mail: mainepoet@mac.com. Website: www.heartsoundspressliterary.com. **Contact:** Carol Bachofner, poetry editor. *Pulse Online Literary Journal* is open to formal poetry as well as free verse. Wants "your best. Send only work revised and revised again! Translations welcome with submitted original language piece." Does not want "predictable, sentimental, greeting card verse. No gratuitous sexuality or violence. No religious verse or predictable rhyme." Has published poetry by Walt McDonald and Lyn Lifshin. Receives about 400 poems/year, accepts about 30-45%.

MAGAZINES NEEDS *Pulse Online Literary Journal* is open to formal poetry as well as free verse. Wants "your best. Send only work revised and revised again! Translations welcome with submitted original language piece." Does not want "predictable, sentimental, greeting card verse. No gratuitous sexuality or violence. No religious verse or predictable rhyme." Has published poetry by Walt McDonald and Lyn Lifshin. Receives about 400 poems/year, accepts about 30-45%.

HOW TO CONTACT Submit 3-5 poems at a time. Lines/poem: up to 120. Considers previously published poems. Only accepts e-mail submissions (pasted into body of e-mail); no disk submissions. Cover letter is required. "Send bio of 50-100 words with submission." Reads submissions year round; publishes February, April, June, August, September, October, December. Submit seasonal poems 2 months in advance. Time between acceptance and publication is 3-4 weeks. Sometimes comments on rejected poems. Sometimes publishes theme issues. Themes for 2009 were April-September: Urban Landscape; September-December: Movements. Guidelines available on website. Responds in 3-4 weeks. Acquires first rights. Reviews books/chapbooks of poetry.

CONTEST/AWARD OFFERINGS Larry Kramer Memorial Chapbook Award; William Dunbar Book-length poetry contest. Submission ofr the contest is by USPS. See website for guidelines and deadlines. Entry fee: varies with contest (multiple entries okay with additional fee for each). Deadline: April 1.

⭘⭘ PURPLE PATCH

25 Griffiths Rd., West Bromwich B7I 2EH, England. E-mail: ppatch66@hotmail.com. Website: www.purplepatchpoetry.co.uk. **Contact:** Geoff Stevens, editor.

MAGAZINES NEEDS *Purple Patch*, published quarterly, is a poetry and short prose magazine with reviews, comments, and illustrations. "All good examples of poetry considered." Does not want "poor rhyming verse, non-contributory swear words or obscenities, hackneyed themes." Has published poetry by Raymond K. Avery, Bryn Fortey, Bob Mee, B.Z. Niditch, and Steve Sneyd. *Purple Patch* is 24 pages, digest-sized, photocopied, side-stapled, with cover on the same stock with b&w drawing. Receives about 2,500 poems/year, accepts about 8%. Circulation varies. Subscription: £7 UK/3 issues; £12 US/3 issues. Make checks (sterling only) payable to G. Stevens.

HOW TO CONTACT Submit 2 or more poems at a time. Lines/poem: 40 maximum. No e-mail submissions; postal submissions only. Cover letter is preferred. Include self-introduction. Submissions must be sent return postage-paid. Reads submissions year round. Time between acceptance and publication is 4 months. Comments on rejected poems. Occasionally publishes theme issues. Upcoming themes available for SASE (or SAE and IRCs). Guidelines available in magazine or on website. Responds in one month to Great Britain; can be longer to U.S. Pays one contributor's copy "to European writers only; overseas contributors must purchase a copy to see their work in print." Acquires first British serial rights. Staff reviews poetry chapbooks, short stories, and tapes in 30-300 words. Send materials for review consideration.

○ ⑤ PURPOSE

616 Walnut Ave., Scottdale PA 15683-1999. (724)887-8500. Fax: (724)887-3111. E-mail: purposeeditor@mpn.net. Website: www.mpn.net. **Contact:** Carol Duerksen, editor. *Purpose*, published monthly by Faith & Life Resources, an imprint of the Mennonite Publishing Network (the official publisher for the Mennonite Church in the U.S. and Canada), is a "religious young adult/adult monthly." Focuses on "action-oriented, discipleship living." *Purpose* is digest-sized with 4-color printing throughout. Press run is 8,000. Receives about 2,000 poems/year, accepts 150. Sample: (with guidelines) $2 and 9x12 SAE.

HOW TO CONTACT Lines/poem: up to 12. Considers simultaneous submissions. Prefers e-mail submissions. Postal submissions should be double-spaced, typed on one side of sheet only. Responds in 6 months. Guidelines available electronically or for SASE. Pays $7.50 to $20 per poem plus 2 contributor's copies.

TIPS "Many stories are situational, how to respond to dilemmas. Looking for first-person storylines. Write crisp, action moving, personal style, focused upon an individual, a group of people, or an organization. The story form is an excellent literary device to help readers explore discipleship issues. The first two paragraphs are crucial in establishing the mood/issue to be resolved in the story. Work hard on the development of these."

● ○ ⑤ QUANTUM LEAP

Website: www.qqpress.co.uk. Q.Q. Press, York House, 15 Argyle Terrace, Rothesay, Isle of Bute PA20 0BD Scotland. Website: www.qqpress.co.uk. **Contact:** Alan Carter, editor. Estab. 1997. *Quantum Leap*, published quarterly, uses "all kinds of poetry—free verse, rhyming, whatever—as long as it's well written and preferably well punctuated, too. We rarely use haiku." Has published poetry by Pamela Constantine, Ray Stebbing, Leigh Eduardo, Sky Higgins, Norman Bissett, and Gordon Scapens. *Quantum Leap* is 40 pages, digest-sized, desktop-published, saddle-stapled, with card cover. Receives about 2,000 poems/year, accepts 15%. Press run is 200. Single copy: $13; subscription: $40. Sample: $10. Make checks payable to Alan Carter. "All things being equal in terms of a poem's quality, **I will sometimes favor that of a subscriber (or someone who has at least bought an issue) over a nonsubscriber,** as it is they who keep us solvent."

MAGAZINES NEEDS *Quantum Leap*, published quarterly, uses "all kinds of poetry—free verse, rhyming, whatever—as long as it's well written and preferably well punctuated, too. We rarely use haiku." Has published poetry by Pamela Constantine, Ray Stebbing, Leigh Eduardo, Sky Higgins, Norman Bissett, and Gordon Scapens. *Quantum Leap* is 40 pages, digest-sized, desktop-published, saddle-stapled, with card cover. Receives about 2,000 poems/year, accepts about 15%. Press run is 200. Single copy: $13; subscription: $40. Sample: $10. Make checks payable to Alan Carter. "All things being equal in terms of a poem's quality, **I will sometimes favor that of a subscriber (or someone who has at least bought an issue) over a nonsubscriber,** as it is they who keep us solvent."

HOW TO CONTACT Submit 6 poems at a time. Lines/poem: 36 ("normally"). Considers previously published poems (indicate magazine and date of first publication) and simultaneous submissions. Cover letter is required. "Within the UK, send a SASE; outside it, send IRCs to the return postage value of what has been submitted." Time between acceptance and publication is usually 3 months "but can be longer now, due to magazine's increasing popularity." Sometimes comments on rejected poems. Guidelines available for SASE (or SAE and 2 IRCs). Responds in 3 weeks. Pays £2 sterling. Acquires first or second British serial rights.

ADDITIONAL INFORMATION Under the imprint "Collections," Q.Q. Press offers **subsidy arrangements** "to provide a cheap alternative to the 'vanity presses'—poetry only." Charges **£150 sterling ($300 USD) plus postage** for 50 32-page (A4) books. Write for details. Order sample books by sending $12 (postage included). Make checks payable to Alan Carter.

CONTEST/AWARD OFFERINGS Sponsors open poetry competitions as well as competitions for subscribers only. Send SAE and IRC for details.

○ ○ ⑤ QUARTERLY WEST

University of Utah, 255 S. Central Campus Dr., Room 3500, Salt Lake City UT 84112. E-mail: quarterlywest@gmail.com. Website: www.utah.edu/quarterlywest. **Contact:** Matt Kirkpatrick & Cami Nelson, editors. "We publish fiction, poetry, and nonfiction in long and short formats, and will consider experimental as well as traditional works."

○ *Quarterly West* was awarded First Place for Editorial Content from the American Literary Magazine Awards. Work published in the magazine has been selected for inclusion in the *Pushcart Prize* anthology and *The Best American Short Stories* anthology. *Quarterly West* was awarded First Place for Editorial Content from the American Literary Magazine Awards. Work published in the magazine has been selected for inclusion in the *Pushcart Prize* anthology and *The Best American Short Stories* anthology.

MAGAZINES NEEDS *Quarterly West*, published semiannually, seeks "original and accomplished literary verse—free or formal." Also considers translations (include originals with submissions). No greeting card or sentimental poetry. Has published poetry by Quan Barry, Medbh McGuckian, Alice Notley, Brenda Shaughnessy, Bob Hicok, David Kirby, and Linh Dinh. *Quarterly West* is 160 pages, digest-sized, offset-printed, with 4-color cover art. Receives 2,500 submissions/year, accepts less than 1%. Press run is 1,500 (500 subscribers, 300-400 libraries). Subscription: $14/year, $25 for 2 years. One issue: $8.50. Back issues: $6.

HOW TO CONTACT Submit 3-5 poems at a time. Only considers submissions through submission manager on website. Will not consider postal or e-mail submissions. Considers simultaneous submissions, with notification; no previously published poems. Reads submissions September 1-May 1. Seldom comments on rejected poems. Responds in up to 6 months. Pays 2 contributor's copies and money when possible. Acquires first North American serial rights. Returns rights with acknowledgment and right to reprint. Reviews books of poetry in 1,000-3,000 words.

TIPS We publish a special section of short shorts every issue, and we also sponsor a biennial novella contest. We are open to experimental work—potential contributors should read the magazine! Don't send more than 1 story/submission. Biennial novella competition guidelines available upon request with SASE. We prefer work with interesting language and detail—plot or narrative are less important. We don't do Western themes or religious work.

○○$ **QUEEN'S QUARTERLY**

144 Barrie St., Queen's University, Kingston ON K7L 3N6, Canada. (613)533-2667. Fax: (613)533-6822. E-mail: queens.quarterly@queensu.ca. Website: www.queensu.ca/quarterly. **Contact:** Joan Harcourt, editor. (Specialized: regional) Queen's University, Kingston ON K7L 3N6 Canada. (613)533-2667. Fax: (613)533-6822. E-mail:queens.quarterly@queensu.ca. Website: www.queensu.ca/quarterly. Established 1893. **Editor:** Boris Castel. *Queen's Quarterly* is "a general interest intellectual review featuring articles on science, politics, humanities, arts and letters, extensive book reviews, some poetry and fiction. We are especially interested in poetry by Canadian writers. Shorter poems preferred." Has published poetry by Evelyn Lau, Sue Nevill, and Raymond Souster. Each issue contains about 12 pages of poetry, digest-sized, 224 pages. Press run is 3,500. Receives about 400 submissions of poetry/year, accepts 40. Subscription: $20 Canadian, $25 US for US and foreign subscribers. Sample: $6.50 US.MSubmit up to 6 poems at a time. No simultaneous submissions. Submissions can be sent on hard copy with a SASE (no replies/returns for foreign submissions unless accompanied by an IRC) or by e-mail and will be responded to by same. Responds in 1 month. Pays usually $50 (Canadian)/poem, "but it varies," plus 2 copies."A general interest intellectual review, featuring articles, book reviews, poetry, and fiction."

○ Submissions can be sent as e-mail attachment or on hard copy with a S.A.S.E. (if submitting from the US or Int'l, the S.A.S.E. must have Canadian postage or be accompanied by an International Reply Coupon in order to receive a reply and will be responded to by same.) Payment will be determined at time of acceptance.

○ **QUEST**

Lynn University, 3601 N. Military Trail, Boca Raton FL 33431-5598. Website: www.lynn.edu. **Contact:** John Daily, editor. Lynn's Annual Literary and Arts Journal, Lynn University, 3601 N. Military Trail, Boca Raton, FL 33431-5598. Website: www.lynn.edu. **Contact:** John Daily, editor. *Quest*, published annually in autumn, is a literary and arts journal. Wants "poems with a clear voice that use careful diction to create poetry in which sound and sense work together, creating fresh perception." Does not want "poems that rely on profanity or shock value." Receives about 100 poems/year, accepts about 25. Press run is 1,000 (one library subscriber); 150 distributed free to Lynn University faculty, staff, and students. Single copy: $5. Make checks payable to Lynn University. Annual literary magazine publishes short fiction, poetry, one-act plays, and art created by and for students, faculty, staff, and friends of Lynn University. "We appreciate fresh voices as much as seasoned work."

MAGAZINES NEEDS *Quest*, published annually in autumn, is a literary and arts journal. Wants "poems with a clear voice that use careful diction to create poetry in which sound and sense work together, creating fresh perception." Does not want "poems that rely on profanity or shock value." Receives about 100 poems/year, accepts about 25. Press run is 1,000 (one library subscriber); 150 distributed free to Lynn University faculty, staff, and students. Single copy: $5. Make checks payable to Lynn University.

HOW TO CONTACT Submit up to 3 poems at a time. No previously published poems or simultaneous submissions. No e-mail or disk submissions. Cover letter is preferred. "Include adequate SASE if you want work returned." Reads submissions mid-September to April 30. Time between acceptance and publication is up to 7 months. "The Lynn English Department faculty and selected students form the Editorial Board to review submissions." Seldom comments on rejected poems. Responds in up to 4 months. Pays 1 contributor's copy. Acquires one-time rights.

◐ QUIDDITY INTERNATIONAL LITERARY JOURNAL AND PUBLIC-RADIO PROGRAM

Benedictine University at Springfield, 1500 N. 5th St., Springfield IL 62702. Website: www1.ben.edu/springfield/quiddity. **Contact:** Joanna Beth Tweedy, Founding editor. Benedictine University at Springfield, 1500 N. Fifth St., Springfield, IL 62702. Website: www1.ben.edu/springfield/quiddity. *Quiddity*, published semi-annually, is "a print journal and public-radio program featuring poetry, prose, and artwork by new, emerging, and established contributors from around the globe. Please visit the website for guidelines." Has published work by J.O.J. Nwachukwu-Agbada, Kevin Stein, Karen An-Hwei Lee, and Haider Al-Kabi. *Quiddity* is 176 pages, 7X9, perfect-bound, with 60 lb. full color cover. Receives about 3,500 poems/year, accepts

about 3%. Press run is 1,000. Single copy: $9; subscription: $15/year. Make checks payable to *Quiddity*. Member: CLMP, AWP." Each work selected is considered for public-radio program feature offered by NPR-member station (WUIS (PRI affiliate)."

◐ "International submissions are encouraged."
MAGAZINES NEEDS *Quiddity*, published semi-annually, is "a print journal and public-radio program featuring poetry, prose, and artwork by new, emerging, and established contributors from around the globe. Please visit the website for guidelines." Has published work by J.O.J. Nwachukwu-Agbada, Kevin Stein, Karen An-Hwei Lee, and Haider Al-Kabi. *Quiddity* is 176 pages, 7X9, perfect-bound, with 60 lb. full color cover. Receives about 3,500 poems/year, accepts about 3%. Press run is 1,000. Single copy: $9; subscription: $15/year. Make checks payable to *Quiddity*.

HOW TO CONTACT Submit up to 5 poems at a time, no more than 10 pages. Considers simultaneous submissions; no previously published poems (previously published includes work posted on a public website/blog/forum and on private, password-protected forums). Cover letter is preferred. "Address to poetry editor, SASE required (except international). See website for reading dates. Time between acceptance and publication is 6 months to 2 years. Poems are circulated to an editorial board. Never comments on rejected poems. Sometimes publishes theme issues. Upcoming themes and guidelines available on website. Responds in 6 months. Typically sends prepublication galleys. Pays 1 contributor's copy. Acquires first North American serial rights and may request broadcast rights. Print rights revert to poet on publication. Considers reviews for books of poetry only when sent from publisher. Send materials for review consideration to poetry editor.

CONTEST/AWARD OFFERINGS Sponsors the annual Teresa A. White Creative Writing Award and the Linda Bromberg Literary Award. **Entry fee:** $12. "See website for guidelines, deadline, and prize information. All entries are considered for publication."

◐ RADIX MAGAZINE

(510)548-5329. E-mail: radixmag@aol.com. Website: www.radixmagazine.com. **Contact:** Sharon Gallagher, editor. P.O. Box 4307, Berkeley, CA 94704. (510)548-5329. E-mail: radixmag@aol.com. Website: www.radixmagazine.com. Specialized: poetry that expresses a Christian world-view. *Radix Magazine*, published quarterly, is named for the Latin word for "root" and "has its roots both in the 'real world' and in the truth of Christ's teachings." Wants poems "that reflect a Christian world-view, but aren't preachy." Has published poetry by John Leax, Czeslaw Milosz, Madeleine L'Engle, and Luci Shaw. *Radix* is 32 pages, magazine-sized, offset-printed, saddle-stapled, with 60-lb. self cover. Receives about 120 poems/year, accepts about 10%. Press run varies. Subscription: $15. Sample: $5. Make checks payable to *Radix Magazine*."*Radix* is for thoughtful Christians who are interested in engaging the world around them."

○ "Needs poetry and book reviews. Email submissions only."

MAGAZINES NEEDS *Radix Magazine*, published quarterly, is named for the Latin word for "root" and "has its roots both in the 'real world' and in the truth of Christ's teachings." Wants poems "that reflect a Christian world-view, but aren't preachy." Has published poetry by John Leax, Czeslaw Milosz, Madeleine L'Engle, and Luci Shaw. *Radix* is 32 pages, magazine-sized, offset-printed, saddle-stapled, with 60-lb. self cover. Receives about 120 poems/year, accepts about 10%. Press run varies. Subscription: $15. Sample: $5. Make checks payable to *Radix Magazine*.

HOW TO CONTACT Submit 1-4 poems at a time. No previously published poems or simultaneous submissions. Accepts e-mail submissions only. Submit seasonal poems 6 months in advance. Time between acceptance and publication is 3 months to 3 years. "We have a serious backlog. The poetry editor accepts or rejects poems and sends the accepted poems to the editor. The editor then publishes poems in appropriate issues. If more than one poem is accepted from any poet, there will probably be a long wait before another is published, because of our backlog of accepted poems." Seldom comments on rejected poems. Occasionally publishes theme issues. Responds in 2 months. Pays 2 contributor's copies. Acquires first rights. Returns rights upon request. Reviews books of poetry.

TIPS "We accept very few unsolicited manuscripts. We do not accept fiction. All articles and poems should be based on a Christian world view. Freelancers should have some sense of the magazine's tone and purpose."

RAILROAD EVANGELIST

(360)699-7208. E-mail: rrjoe@comcast.net. Website: www.railroadevangelist.com. "The *Railroad Evangelist*'s purpose and intent is to reach people everywhere with the life-changing gospel of Jesus Christ. The railroad industry is our primary target, along with model railroad and rail fans."

○ All content must be railroad related.

❶ THE RAINTOWN REVIEW

Central Ave Press, 2132A Central SE #144, Albuquerque NM 87106. E-mail: theraintownreview@gmail.com. Website: www.theraintownreview.com. **Contact:** Anna Evans, Editor. We prefer poems that have NOT been previously published. *The Raintown Review*, published 2 times/year in Winter and Summer, contains poetry, reviews, and belletristic critical prose. Wants well-crafted poems. "We are primarily a venue for formal poetry." Has published poetry by Julie Kane, Alexandra Oliver, Rick Mullin, Annie Finch, Kevin Higgins, David Mason, A.E. Stallings, Richard Wilbur, and many others. The Raintown Review is 120 pages, perfect-bound. Receives about 2,500 poems/year, accepts roughly 5%. Press run is approximately 500. Subscription: $24/year, $45 for 2 years, $65 for 3 years. Sample: $12. Make checks/money orders payable to Central Ave Press.

❶❸ RATTAPALLAX

(212)560-7459. E-mail: info@rattapallax.com. Website: www.rattapallax.com. **Contact:** Alan Cheuse, fiction editor. *Rattapallax* is a literary magazine that focuses on issues dealing with globalization.

MAGAZINES NEEDS *Rattapallax*, published semiannually, is named for "Wallace Steven's word for the sound of thunder. The magazine includes a DVD featuring poetry films and audio files. *Rattapallax* is looking for the extraordinary in modern poetry and prose that reflect the diversity of world cultures. Our goals are to create international dialogue using literature and focus on what is relevant to our society." Has published poetry by Anthony Hecht, Sharon Olds, Lou Reed, Marilyn Hacker, Billy Collins, and Glyn Maxwell. *Rattapallax* is 112 pages, magazine-sized, offset-printed, perfect-bound, with 12-pt. CS1 cover. Receives about 5,000 poems/year, accepts 2%. Press run is 2,000 (100 subscribers, 50 libraries, 1,200 shelf sales); 200 distributed free to contributors, reviews, and promos. Single copy: $7.95; no subscriptions.

Make checks payable to *Rattapallax*.

HOW TO CONTACT Submit 3-5 poems at a time. Considers simultaneous submissions; no previously published poems. Accepts e-mail submissions (sent as simple text) from outside the U.S. and Canada; all other submissions must be sent via postal mail (SASE required). Cover letter is preferred. Reads submissions year round; issue deadlines are June 1 and December 1. Time between acceptance and publication is 6 months. "The editor-in-chief, senior editor, and associate editor review all the submissions and then decide on which to accept every week. Near publication time, all accepted work is narrowed, and unused work is kept for the next issue." Often comments on rejected poems. Guidelines available by e-mail or on website. Responds in 2 months. Always sends prepublication galleys. Pays 2 contributor's copies. Acquires first rights.

RATTLE

12411 Ventura Blvd., Studio City, CA 91604. (818)505-6777. E-mail: submissions@rattle.com; tim@rattle.com. Website: www.rattle.com. **Contact:** Timothy Green, editor.

MAGAZINES NEEDS *RATTLE*, published semiannually in June and December, includes poems, essays, reviews, interviews with poets, and a tribute section dedicated to a specific ethnic or vocational group. Wants "high-quality poetry of any form. Nothing unintelligible." Considers some poetry by children and teens (ages 10-18). Has published poetry by Lucille Clifton, Charles Simic, Mark Doty, Sharon Olds, Billy Collins, and Stephen Dunn. *RATTLE* is 196 pages, digest-sized, neatly printed, perfect-bound, with 4-color coated card cover. Receives about 8,000 submissions/year, accepts 200. Press run is 4,000. Subscription: $18/year, $30/2 years, $36/3 years. Sample: $10. Make checks payable to *RATTLE*.

HOW TO CONTACT Submit up to 5 poems at a time. Considers simultaneous submissions "if notified immediately by e-mail or phone should they be taken elsewhere." Accepts e-mail submissions (pasted into body of message). Cover letter is required (with e-mail address, if possible). Include bio. For postal submissions, put name, address, and phone number on each page in upper right corner; include SASE. Reads submissions year round. Seldom comments on rejected poems (unless requested by the author). Guidelines available in magazine, by e-mail, or on website. Responds in up to 2 months. Pays 2 contributor's copies. Rights revert to poet upon publication. Publishes reviews of books of poetry online. Send materials for review consideration.

ADDITIONAL INFORMATION Welcomes essays up to 2,000 words on poetry or the writing process. Publishes a biannual electronic issue in March and September, e-mailed as a PDF to 4,000 subscribers, featuring excerpts from poetry collections, chapbooks, reviews, and print issue previews.

CONTEST/AWARD OFFERINGS "All submissions are automatically considered for the Neil Postman Award for Metaphor, an annual $500 prize for the best use of metaphor as judged by the editors. No entry fee or special formatting is required, simply follow the regular guidelines." Also, the *RATTLE* Poetry Prize (see separate listing in Contests & Awards).

ⓝⓞ$ RAVING DOVE

P.O. Box 28, West Linn OR 97068. E-mail: editor@ravingdove.org. E-mail: ravingdog@gmail.com. Website: www.ravingdove.org/. **Contact:** Jo-Ann Moss, editor. Online literary journal published 4 times/year. "Our mission is to share thought-provoking poetry and prose that champions human rights and social justice, and opposes physical and psychological violence in all its forms, including war, discrimination against sexual orientation, and every shade of bigotry."

MAGAZINES NEEDS *Raving Dove*, published quarterly, "is an online literary journal that publishes original poetry, nonfiction, fiction, photography, and art with universal anti-violence, anti-hate, human rights, and social justice themes. We share sentiments that oppose physical and psychological violence in all its forms, including war, discrimination against sexual orientation, and every shade of bigotry." Wants free verse only, any length. Has published poetry by Howard Camner, Marguerite Bouvard, John Kay, Harry Youtt. Receives about 750 poems/year, accepts about 30. Number of visitors is "2,000/month and growing."

HOW TO CONTACT Considers simultaneous submissions. Accepts e-mail submissions only; allows attachments. No fax, disk, or postal submissions. Cover letter is unnecessary. "Poetry Submission" must appear as the subject of the e-mail; all submissions must include full name, general geographic location, and a third-person bio of 100 words or less. Weblinks are permitted. Reads submissions year round. Time between acceptance and publication is no more than 3 months. Sometimes comments on rejected poems. Guidelines available on website. Always sends prepublication galleys ("the link to the poet's Web page at *Raving Dove* is sent prior to publication"). Responds in 3 months. Payment is based on funding. Acquires first North American and Internet serial rights, exclusive for the duration of the edition in which the poetry appears (see submission guidelines on website for further information). Rights revert to poets at the end of the issue.

ADDITIONAL INFORMATION Nonprofit status granted by U.S. government.

REDHEADED STEPCHILD

E-mail: redheadedstepchildmag@gmail.com. Website:www.redheadedmag.com/poetry/. **Contact:** Malaika King Albrecht. Estab. 2008. "*The Redheaded Stepchild* only accepts poems that have been rejected by other magazines. We publish biannually, and we accept submissions in the months of August and February only. We do not accept previously published work. We do, however, accept simultaneous submissions, but please inform us immediately if your work is accepted somewhere else. We are open to a wide variety of poetry and hold no allegiance to any particular style or school. If your poem is currently displayed online on your blog or website or wherever, please do not send it to us before taking it down, at least temporarily. Submit 3-5 poems that have been rejected elsewhere with the names of the magazines that rejected the poems. We do not want multiple submissions, so please wait for a response to your first submission before you submit again. As is standard after publication, rights revert back to the author, but we request that you credit Redheaded Stepchild in subsequent republications. We do not accept e-mail attachments; therefore, in the body of your email, please include the following: a brief bio; 3-5 poems; the publication(s) that rejected the poems."

MAGAZINES NEEDS Wants a wide variety of poetic styles. Does not want previously published poems. Has published poetry by Kathryn Stripling Byer, Alex Grant, Amy King, Diane Lockward, Susan Yount, and Howie Good.

HOW TO CONTACT Submit 3-5 poems at a time. Considers simultaneous submissions. Accepts e-mail submissions pasted into body of e-mail message. Cover letter is preferred. Time between accep-

tance and publication is 3 months. Poems are circulated to an editorial board. Sometimes comments on rejected poems. Guidelines on website. Responds in 3 months. Acquires first rights. Rights revert to poets upon publication.

REDIVIDER

Department of Writing, Literature, and Publishing, Emerson College, 120 Boylston St., Boston MA 02116. E-mail: fiction@redividerjournal.com; poetry@redividerjournal.com. Website: www.redividerjournal.org.

MAGAZINES NEEDS *Redivider*, published semiannually, prints high-quality poetry, art, fiction, and creative nonfiction. Wants "all styles of poetry. Most of all, we look for language that seems fresh and alive on the page, that tries to do something new. Read a sample copy for a good idea." Does not want "greeting card verse or inspirational verse." Has published poetry by Bob Hicok, Billy Collins, Paul Muldoon, Tao Lin, Claudia Emerson, and Bobby Byrd. *Redivider* is 100+ pages, digest-sized, offset-printed, perfect-bound, with 4-color artwork on cover. Receives about 1,000 poems/year, accepts about 30%. Press run is 1,000. Single copy: $6; subscription: $10. Make checks payable to *Redivider* at Emerson College.

HOW TO CONTACT Submit 3-6 poems at a time through online submissions manager. Considers simultaneous submissions, but requires notification if your work is taken elsewhere; no previously published poems. Cover letter is required. Reads submissions year-round. Seldom comments on rejected poems. Guidelines available in magazine, for SASE, by e-mail, or on website. Responds in 5 months. Pays 2 contributor's copies. Acquires first North American serial rights. Reviews books of poetry in 500 words, single-book format. Send materials for review consideration, Attn: Review Copies. "Book reviews and interviews are internally generated." Our deadlines are July 1 for the Fall issue, and December 1 for the Spring issue.

TIPS "Our deadlines are July 1 for the Fall issue, and December 1 for the Spring issue."

RED LIGHTS

2740 Andrea Drive, Allentown PA 18103-4602. (212)875-9342. E-mail: mhazelton@rcn.com; marilynhazelton@rcn.com. **Contact:** Marilyn Hazelton, Editor.

MAGAZINES NEEDS *red lights*, published semiannually in January and June, is devoted to English-language tanka and tanka sequences. Wants "print-only tanka, mainly 'free-form' but also strictly syllabic 5-7-5-7-7; will consider tanka sequences and tan-renga." Considers poetry by children and teens. Has published poetry by Sanford Goldstein, Michael McClintock, Laura Maffei, Linda Jeannette Ward, Jane Reichhold, and Michael Dylan Welch. *red lights* is 36-40 pages, 8½x3¾, offset-printed, saddle-stapled, with Japanese textured paper cover; copies are numbered. Single copy: $8; subscription: $16 U.S., $18 USD Canada, $20 USD foreign. Make checks payable to "red lights" in the U.S.

HOW TO CONTACT Submit 10 tanka or 2 sequences at a time (maximum). No previously published poems or simultaneous submissions. Prefers e-mail submissions. Include SASE if mailing. Submissions are due in hand April 15th for the June issue and November 15th for the January issue. Reads submissions year-round. Time between acceptance and publication "depends on submission time." Guidelines available for SASE. Acquires first rights.

TIPS "Each issue features a '*red lights* featured tanka' on the theme of 'red lights.' Poet whose poem is selected receives 1 contributor's copy."

⊙⊙ THE RED MOON ANTHOLOGY OF ENGLISH LANGUAGE HAIKU

P.O. Box 2461, Winchester VA 22604-1661. E-mail: jim.kacian@redmoonpress.com. Website: www.redmoonpress.com. **Contact:** Jim Kacian, editor/publisher. Estab. 1996.

MAGAZINES NEEDS *The Red Moon Anthology of English Language Haiku*, published annually in February, is "a collection of the best haiku published in English around the world." Considers poetry by children and teens. Has published haiku and related forms by Carolyn Hall, Marcus Larsson, Yu Chang, and Harriot West. *The Red Moon Anthology of English Language Haiku* is 184 pages, digest-sized, offset-printed on quality paper, with 4-color heavy-stock cover. Receives several thousand submissions/year, accepts less than 2%. Print run is 1,000 for subscribers and commercial distribution. Subscription: $17 plus $5 p&h. Sample available for SASE or by e-mail.

HOW TO CONTACT "We do not accept direct submissions to the *Red Moon Anthology*. Rather, we employ an editorial board who are assigned journals and books from which they cull and nominate. Nominated poems are placed on a roster and judged anonymously by the entire editorial board twice a year." Guidelines available for SASE or by e-mail. Pays $1/page. Acquires North American serial rights.

ALSO OFFERS *contemporary haibun*, "an annual volume of the finest English-language haibun and haiga published anywhere in the world." (See separate listing in this section.)

⊙ RED ROCK REVIEW

College of Southern Nevada, CSN Department of English, J2A, 3200 E. Cheyenne Ave., North Las Vegas NV 89030. (702)651-4094. Fax: (702)651-4639. E-mail: redrockreview@csn.edu. Website: sites.csn.edu/english/redrockreview/. **Contact:** Rich Logsdon, Senior Editor. "We are dedicated to the publication of fine contemporary literature."

MAGAZINES NEEDS *Red Rock Review*, a nonprofit biannual journal, prints "the best poetry available," as well as fiction, creative nonfiction, and book reviews. Has published poetry by Dorianne Laux, Kim Addonizio, Ellen Bass, Cynthia Hogue, and Dianne di Prima. *Red Rock Review* is about 130 pages, magazine-sized, professionally printed, perfect-bound, with 10-pt. CS1 cover. Accepts about 15% of poems received/year. Press run is 2350. Subscriptions: $9.50/year. Sample: $5.50.

HOW TO CONTACT Submit 2-3 poems at a time by e-mail. Attach Word, RTF, or PDF file to redrockreview@csn.edu. Lines/poem: 80 maximum. Considers simultaneous submissions. No hard copy submissions will be accepted. "The e-mail to which the files are attached should serve as your cover letter clearly stating your contact information and the contents of your attachments. **We do not accept general submissions in June, July, August, or December.**" Time between acceptance and publication is 2-3 months. "Poems go to poetry editor, who then distributes them to 3 readers." Occasionally comments on rejected poems. Guidelines available on website. Responds in 2-3 months. Pays 2 contributor's copies. Acquires first North American serial rights. Reviews books/chapbooks of poetry in 500-1,000 words, multi-book format. Send materials for review consideration.

TIPS "Open to short fiction and poetry submissions from Sept. 1-May 31. Include SASE and include brief bio. No general submissions between June 1st and August 31st. See guidelines online."

REFERENTIAL MAGAZINE

E-mail: refermag@gmail.com. Website: referential-magazine.com. **Contact:** Jessie Carty, editor; Jenny Billings Beaver, managing editor. Estab. 2010. Submit up to 3 poems. "Please check out our guidelines page. We primarily use submishmash for submissions, but we are also open to queries for items not covered by submishmash."

🌀 RENDITIONS: A CHINESE-ENGLISH TRANSLATION MAGAZINE

Website: www.renditions.org. Research Centre for Translation, Chinese University of Hong Kong, Shatin, N.T., Hong Kong. (852)2609-7407. Fax: (852)2603-5110. E-mail: renditions@cuhk.edu.hk. Website: www.renditions.org. **Contact:** The Editor. *Renditions: A Chinese-English Translation Magazine*, published twice/year in May and November, uses "exclusively translations from Chinese, ancient and modern." Poems are printed with Chinese and English texts side by side. Has published translations of the poetry of Yang Lian, Gu Cheng, Shu Ting, Mang Ke, and Bei Dao. *Renditions* is about 150 pages, magazine-sized, elegantly printed, perfect-bound, with glossy card cover. Single copy: $19.90; subscription: $29.90/year, $49.90/2 years, $69.90/3 years.

MAGAZINES NEEDS *Renditions: A Chinese-English Translation Magazine*, published twice/year in May and November, uses "exclusively translations from Chinese, ancient and modern." Poems are printed with Chinese and English texts side by side. Has published translations of the poetry of Yang Lian, Gu Cheng, Shu Ting, Mang Ke, and Bei Dao. *Renditions* is about 150 pages, magazine-sized, elegantly printed, perfect-bound, with glossy card cover. Single copy: $19.90; subscription: $29.90/year, $49.90/2 years, $69.90/3 years.

HOW TO CONTACT Submissions should be accompanied by Chinese originals. Accepts e-mail and fax submissions. "Submissions by postal mail should include two copies. Use British spelling." Sometimes comments on rejected translations. Publishes theme issues. Guidelines available on website. Responds in 2 months. Manuscripts usually not returned.

ADDITIONAL INFORMATION Also publishes a hardback series (Renditions Books) and a paperback series (Renditions Paperbacks) of Chinese literature

in English translation. "Will consider" book mss; query with sample translations.

RHINO

The Poetry Forum, Inc., P.O. Box 591, Evanston IL 60204. E-mail: editors@rhinopoetry.org. Website: www.rhinopoetry.org. **Contact:** Ralph Hamilton, Sr., Editor; Helen Degen Cohen, Sr. Editor and Founder. *RHINO*, published annually in spring, prints poetry, short-shorts, and translations. Wants "work that reflects passion, originality, engagement with contemporary culture, and a love affair with language. We welcome free verse, formal poetry, innovation, and risk-taking." Has published poetry by Geoffrey Forsyth, Penelope Scambly Schott, F. Daniel Rzicznek, and Ricardo Pau-Llosa. *RHINO* is 150 pages, 7x10, printed on high-quality paper, with card cover with art. Receives 8,000-10,000 submissions/year, accepts 90-100, or 1%. Press run is 800. Single copy: $12. Sample: $5 (back issue). Submit 3-5 poems. Considers simultaneous submissions with notification; no previously published poems. Expects electronic copy upon acceptance. Reads submissions April 1-October 1. Guidelines available on website. Responds in up to 6 months. Pays 2 contributor's copies. Acquires first rights only." This eclectic annual journal of more than 30 years accepts poetry, flash fiction (1,000 words or less), and poetry-in-translation from around the world that experiments, provokes, compels. More than 80 poets are showcased. The regular call for poetry is from April 1 to October 1st, and the Founder's Contest submission period has been changed to July 1 to October 1st."

> 💬 "Founders' Contest submission period is from July 1 - October 1."

HOW TO CONTACT Submit online and by mail. Include SASE for USPS mail only.

TIPS "Please visit our website for further examples that will indicate the quality of poetry we look for, plus additional submission information, including updates on the Rhino Founders' Contest."

🚗🏠 RHODE ISLAND ROADS

2 Barber Ave., Warwick RI 02886. (401)480-9355. E-mail: editor@RIRoads.com; asurkont@local.net. Website: www.riroads.com. Paul Pence, managing editor. **Contact:** Amanda Surkont, poetry editor. Estab. 2000.

MAGAZINES NEEDS *Rhode Island Roads*, the online monthly magazine of travel, dining, life, and entertainment for people who love Rhode Island, features work with Rhode Island and New England themes. Open to all forms and styles, although "rhyme will have difficulty finding a home here." Considers poetry by children and teens. Has published poetry by Audrey Friedman, Barbara Schweitzer, Michele F. Cooper, Pat Hagneur, Lauri Burke, and Peggy Conti. Receives about 150 poems/year, accepts 12-16/year. Has about 70,000 readers/month. Sample: can view sample pages for free online.

HOW TO CONTACT Submit up to 5 poems at a time. Lines/poem: "We are flexible." Considers previously published poems and simultaneous submissions. Accepts e-mail submissions only (pasted into body of message). "We'll ask for a bio if we use your work." Reads submissions year round. Submit seasonal poems 3 months in advance. Time between acceptance and publication is 2 months "unless seasonal, then it could be several months." Sometimes comments on rejected poems. Sometimes publishes theme issues. Upcoming themes available by e-mail. Guidelines available by e-mail or on website. "I try to respond within a week or two." Pays free subscription. Acquires one-time rights and electronic rights. "We archive." Rights revert to poet upon publication. "Electronic rights returned to author if requested."

⊙❶⑤ THE RIALTO

P.O. Box 309, Alysham, Norwich NR11 6LN, England. Website: www.therialto.co.uk. **Contact:** Michael Mackmin, editor. P.O. Box 309, Alysham, Norwich NR11 6LN, England. Website: www.therialto.co.uk. **Contact:** Michael Mackmin, editor. Estab: 1984.

MAGAZINES NEEDS *The Rialto*, published 3 times/year, seeks "to publish the best new poems by established and beginning poets. We seek excellence and originality." Has published poetry by Alice Fulton, Jenny Joseph, Les Murray, George Szirtes, Philip Gross, and Ruth Padel. *The Rialto* is 64 pages, A4, with full-color cover. Receives about 12,000 poems/year, accepts about 1%. Press run is 1,500. Single copy: £7.50; subscription: £23 (prices listed are for U.S. and Canada). Make checks payable to *The Rialto*. "Checks in sterling only, please. Online payment also available on website." *The Rialto*, published 3 times/year, seeks "to publish the best new poems by established and beginning poets. We seek excellence and originality." Has published poetry by Alice Fulton, Jenny Joseph, Les Murray, George Szirtes, Philip Gross, and Ruth

Padel. *The Rialto* is 64 pages, A4, with full-color cover. Receives about 12,000 poems/year, accepts about 1%. Press run is 1,500. Single copy: £7.50; subscription: £23 (prices listed are for U.S. and Canada). Make checks payable to *The Rialto*. "Checks in sterling only, please. Online payment also available on website."

HOW TO CONTACT Submit up to 6 poems at a time. Considers simultaneous submissions; no previously published poems. Cover letter is preferred. "SASE or SAE with IRCs essential. U.S. readers please note that U.S. postage stamps are invalid in UK." No poetry submissions will be accepted by e-mail or online. Time between acceptance and publication is up to 4 months. Seldom comments on rejected poems. Responds in 5-6 months. Pays £20/poem. Poet retains rights.

TIPS "*The Rialto* has recently commenced publishing first collections by poets. Please do not send book-length manuscripts. Query first." Sponsors an annual young poets competition. Details available in magazine and on website. Before submitting, "you will probably have read many poems by many poets, both living and dead. You will probably have put aside each poem you write for at least 3 weeks before considering it afresh. You will have asked yourself, 'Does it work technically?'; checked the rhythm, the rhymes (if used), and checked that each word is fresh and meaningful in its context, not jaded and tired. You will hopefully have read *The Rialto*."

❶ RIBBONS: TANKA SOCIETY OF AMERICA JOURNAL

David Bacharach, TSA Editor, 5921 Cayutaville Rd., Alpine NY 14805. E-mail: davidb@htva.net. Website: www.tankasocietyofamerica.com. **Contact:** David Bacharach, Editor. Published quarterly, seeks and regularly prints "the best tanka poetry being written in English, together with reviews, critical and historical essays, commentaries, and translations." Wants "poetry that exemplifies the very best in English-language tanka, which we regard as 'the queen of short form poetry,' having a significant contribution to make to the short poem in English. All schools and approaches are welcome." Tanka should "reflect contemporary life, issues, values, and experience, in descriptive, narrative, and lyrical modes." Does not want "work that merely imitates the Japanese masters." Considers poetry by children and teens. "We have no age restrictions." Has published poetry by Cherie Hunter Day,

Marianne Bluger, Sanford Goldstein, Larry Kimmel, John Stevenson, and George Swede. *Ribbons* is 60-72 pages, 6x9 perfect-bound, with color cover and art. Receives about 2,000 poems/year, accepts about 20%. Press run is 275; 15 distributed free. Single copy: $10; subscription: $30. Make checks payable to Tanka Society of America and contact Carole MacRury, Secretary/Treasurer (e-mail: macrury@whidbey.com; 1636 Edwards Dr., Point Roberts, WA 98281).

TIPS "Work by beginning as well as established English-language tanka poets is welcome; first-time contributors are encouraged to study the tanka form and contemporary examples before submitting. No particular school or style of tanka is preferred over another; our publications seek to showcase the full range of English-language tanka expression and subject matter through the work of new and established poets in the genre from around the world."

RIO GRANDE REVIEW

University of Texas at El Paso, PMB 671, 500 W. University Ave., El Paso TX 79968-0622. E-mail: editors@riograndereview.com. Website: www.utep.edu/rgr. **Contact:** Poetry Editor. University of Texas at El Paso, PMB 671, 500 W. University Ave., El Paso, TX 79968-0622. E-mail:editors@riograndereview.com. Website: www.utep.edu/rgr. **Contact:** Poetry Editor.

MAGAZINES NEEDS *Rio Grande Review*, published in January and August, is a bilingual (English-Spanish) student publication from the University of Texas at El Paso. Contains poetry; flash, short, and nonfiction; short drama; photography and line art. *Rio Grande Review* is 168 pages, digest-sized, professionally printed, perfect-bound, with card cover with line art. Subscription: $8/year, $15/2 years.*Rio Grande Review*, published in January and August, is a bilingual (English-Spanish) student publication from the University of Texas at El Paso. Contains poetry; flash, short, and nonfiction; short drama; photography and line art. *Rio Grande Review* is 168 pages, digest-sized, professionally printed, perfect-bound, with card cover with line art. Subscription: $8/year, $15/2 years.

HOW TO CONTACT Poetry has a limit of 10 pages. No simultaneous submissions. Accepts e-mail submissions only (as attachment or pasted into body of message). Include short bio. Guidelines available for SASE, by e-mail, or on website. Check website for reception deadlines. Any submissions received after a reception deadline will automatically be considered for the following edition. Pays 2 contributor's copies. "Permission to reprint material remains the decision of the author. However, *Rio Grande Review* does request it be given mention."

RIVER OAK REVIEW

Elmhurst College, 190 Prospect Ave., Elmhurst IL 60126-3296. (630) 617-3137. Fax: (630) 617-3609. E-mail: riveroak@elmhurst.edu. Website: www.riveroakreview.org. Ann Frank Wake, poetry editor, annfw@elmhurst.edu.

MAGAZINES NEEDS *River Oak Review*, published annually, prints high-quality poetry, short fiction, and creative nonfiction. "We are a national journal striving to publish midwestern poets in each issue." Has published poetry by Wendy Bishop, Jim Elledge, James Doyle, Ken Meisel, Blair Beacom Deets, and Robin Becker. *River Oak Review* is at least 128 pages, digest-sized, neatly printed, perfect-bound, with glossy color cover with art. Publishes about 5% of poetry received. Press run is 500. Single copy: $10; subscription: $10/year, $20/2 years. Sample: $5. Make checks payable to *River Oak Review*.

HOW TO CONTACT Submit 4-6 poems at a time. No previously published poems. SASE required. Reads submissions year round. Sometimes comments on rejected poems. Guidelines available for SASE or on website. Tries to respond in 3 months. Pays 2 contributor's copies. Acquires first North American serial rights.

TIPS "The voice is what we notice first. Is the writer in command of the language? Secondly, does the story have anything to say? It's not that 'fluff' cannot be good, but we note our favorites stories tend to have meaning beyond the surface of the plot. Thirdly, the story must by populated by 'real' peoples who are also interesting, characters, in other words, who have lives underneath the storyline. Finally, look before you leap."

THE ROAD NOT TAKEN: THE JOURNAL OF FORMAL POETRY

E-mail: jimatshs@yahoo.com. Website: www.journalofformalpoetry.com. **Contact:** Dr. Jim Prothero, co-editor. Estab. 2007.

MAGAZINES NEEDS *The Road Not Taken: the Journal of Formal Poetry*, published quarterly online, prints formal poetry "in the tradition of Frost, Wordsworth, Tennyson, Hopkins, etc." Wants "formal poetry only. Nature and spiritual poetry always of interest but not required. Also essays/blogs on the topic of formal poetry would be of interest." Does not want free verse. Accepts poetry by children and teens; no age limitations, "it just has to be excellent."

HOW TO CONTACT Submit 5 poems at a time. Considers previously published poems; no simultaneous submissions. (Considers poetry posted on a public website/blog/forum as published.) Accepts e-mail submissions (pasted into body of message); no fax or disk submissions. Cover letter is unnecessary. Reads submissions year round. Submit seasonal poems 3 months in advance. Time between acceptance and publication is 2 months. Poems are circulated to an editorial board. "There are 2 editors, Dr. Jim Prothero and Dr. Don Williams. Poems must meet both of our approval." Sometimes comments on rejected poems. Never publishes theme issues. Guidelines available by e-mail and on website. Responds in 1 month. Acquires one-time rights. Rights revert to poets upon publication.

ROADRUNNER HAIKU JOURNAL

E-mail: scott@roadrunnerjournal.net;. Website: www.roadrunnerjournal.net. **Contact:** Scott Metz, editor. (Specialized: haiku, senryu, short haiku-like poetry)

MAGAZINES NEEDS *Roadrunner Haiku Journal*, published quarterly online, is "an international Web journal that publishes the most innovative modern haiku written today." Wants haiku, senryu, and short haiku-like poetry. Does not want tanka, haiga, or haibun. Considers poetry by children and teens. Best Haiku of previous issues have been selected by Rae Armantrout, Ron Silliman, Marjorie Perloff, Robert Grenier, Tom Raworth, Hiroaki Sato. Receives about 5,000 poems/year, accepts about 3%. Distributed free online. Number of unique visitors: 25,000/year.

HOW TO CONTACT Submit 5-25 poems at a time. Lines/poem: "less than 5 or so." No previously published poems or simultaneous submissions. Accepts e-mail submissions only (pasted into body of message, with "Roadrunner Submission" and poet's name in subject line); no disk submissions. Cover letter is unnecessary. Reads submissions year round. Time between acceptance and publication is less than 3 months. Sometimes comments on rejected poems. Guidelines available on website. Responds in 2 weeks. Sometimes sends prepublication galleys.

Acquires first rights. Rights revert to poets upon publication.

ROANOKE REVIEW

Roanoke College, 221 College Lane, Salem VA 24153-3794. E-mail: review@roanoke.edu. Website: http://roanokereview.wordpress.com. **Contact:** Paul Hanstedt, editor. "We're looking for fresh, thoughtful material that will appeal to a broader as well as literary audience. Humor encouraged." Annual. Estab. 1967. Circ. 500.

TIPS "Pay attention to sentence-level writing—verbs, metaphors, concrete images. Don't forget, though, that plot and character keep us reading. We're looking for stuff that breaks the MFA story style." "Be real. Know rhythm. Concentrate on strong images."

ROCKY MOUNTAIN RIDER MAGAZINE

P.O. Box 995, Hamilton MT 59840. (406)363-4085. E-mail: editor@rockymountainrider.com; info@rockymountainrider.com. Website: www.rockymountainrider.com. **Contact:** Natalie Riehl, editor. Cowboy poetry should be no more than 4-5 stanzas. Please submit articles typed and double-spaced on 8-1/2 x 11 paper. RMR buys first serial rights, one-time rights, as well as some reprint rights, if material has NOT been published in a competing publication in Montana, Idaho, Wyoming, Washington, Oregon, Colorado, or Utah.

MAGAZINES NEEDS *Rocky Mountain Rider Magazine*, published monthly, is a regional all-breed horse magazine. Wants "cowboy poetry; western or horse-themed poetry." *Rocky Mountain Rider Magazine* is 68+ pages, magazine-sized, Web offset-printed on SuperCal, stapled. Publishes 0-2 poems/issue. Press run is 16,500; distributed free through 500+ locations in 11 states.

HOW TO CONTACT Submit 1-10 poems at a time. Lines/poem: keep length to no more than 5 stanzas. Considers previously published poems and simultaneous submissions. No e-mail submissions; postal submissions only. Cover letter is preferred. Include SASE. Seldom comments on rejected poems. Occasionally publishes theme issues. Guidelines available for SASE. Pays $5/poem. Reviews books of poetry. Send materials for review consideration. Include SASE for returns.

TIPS "We aren't looking for 'how-to' or training articles, and are not currently looking at any fiction. Our geographical regions of interest is the U.S. West, especially the Rocky Mountain states."

☺🌑⑤ ROOM

P.O. Box 46160, Station D, Vancouver BC V6J 5G5, Canada. E-mail: contactus@roommagazine.com. Website: www.roommagazine.com. **Contact:** Growing Room Collective. "*Room* is Canada's oldest literary journal by, for, and about women. Published quarterly by a group of volunteers based in Vancouver, *Room* showcases fiction, poetry, reviews, art work, interviews and profiles about the female experience. Many of our contributors are at the beginning of their writing careers, looking for an opportunity to get published for the first time. Some later go on to great acclaim. *Room* is a space where women can speak, connect, and showcase their creativity. Each quarter we publish original, thought-provoking works that reflect women's strength, sensuality, vulnerability, and wit."

HOW TO CONTACT Send material for review consideration, attn. book review editor.

🌑💬⑤ ROSE & THORN JOURNAL

Website: www.roseandthornjournal.com. **Contact:** Barbara Quinn. "Adjective stacking doesn't make a poem better, but we do like strong, vivid images. Please avoid trite imagery like: 'Our hearts beat as one; our lips joined in passion.' While we prefer shorter poems, consideration is given to longer works if they meet the above criteria. Also, forms are welcome if they do not contain obtrusive rhyming.""We created this publication for readers and writers alike. Since 1998, the *R&T* has showcased the best of the Web with a unique blend of art and words. Visit this award-winning spot and find out for yourself why we are consistently rated a top spot for writers."

HOW TO CONTACT Copy and paste submission including a brief, third person bio into the body of an e-mail. Send to poetry@roseandthornjournal.com.

TIPS "Clarity, control of the language, evocative stories that tug at the heart and make their mark on the reader long after it's been read. We look for uniqueness in voice, style and characterization. New twists on old themes are always welcome. Use all aspects of good writing in your stories, including dynamic characters, strong narrative voice and a riveting original plot. We have eclectic tastes, so go ahead and give us a shot. Read the publication and other quality literary journals so you'll see what we look for. Always check your spelling and grammar before submitting. Reread your submission with a critical eye and ask yourself, 'Does it evoke an emotional response? Have I completely captured my reader?' Check your submission for 'it' and 'was' and see if you can come up with a better way to express yourself. Be unique."

🌑 ROSEBUD

N3310 Asje Rd., Cambridge WI 53523. (608)423-9780. E-mail: jrodclark@smallbytes.net. Website: www.rsbd.net. **Contact:** Roderick Clark, editor.

MAGAZINES NEEDS *Rosebud*, published 3 times/year in April, August, and December, has presented "many of the most prominent voices in the nation and has been listed as among the very best markets for writers." Wants poetry that avoids "excessive or well-worn abstractions, not to mention clicheés. Present a unique and convincing world (you can do this in a few words!) by means of fresh and exact imagery, and by interesting use of syntax. Explore the deep reaches of metaphor. But don't forget to be playful and have fun with words." *Rosebud* is "elegantly" printed with full-color cover. Press run is 10,000. Single copy: $7.95 U.S. Subscription: $20 for 3 issues, $35 for 6 issues.

HOW TO CONTACT Email up to 3 Poetry submissions to poetry editor John Smelcer at: jesmelcer@aol.com.

CONTEST/AWARD OFFERINGS Sponsors The William Stafford Poetry Award. Deadline: June 15, 2010. And the X.J. Kennedy Award for Creative Nonfiction. Deadline: January 15, 2011. Guidelines for both available on website.

TIPS "Each issue will have six or seven flexible departments (selected from a total of sixteen departments that will rotate). We are seeking stories; articles; profiles; and poems of: love, alienation, travel, humor, nostalgia and unexpected revelation. Something has to 'happen' in the pieces we choose, but what happens inside characters is much more interesting to us than plot manipulation. We like good storytelling, real emotion and authentic voice."

SALT HILL

E-mail: salthilljournal@gmail.com. Website: www.salthilljournal.com. **Contact:** "Please contact appropriate genre editor.". English Dept., Syracuse University, Syracuse, NY 13244.

MAGAZINES NEEDS *Salt Hill*, published semiannually, is "published by a group of writers affiliated with the Creative Writing Program at Syracuse University. Our eclectic taste ranges from traditional to experimental. All we ask is that it's good. Open to most themes. Accepting translations." Has published poetry by Denise Duhamel, Joe Wenderoth, Dorianne Laux, Campbell McGrath, Dean Young, Kim Addonizio, and James Tate. *Salt Hill* is 144-180 pages, digest-sized, includes ads. Receives about 3,000 poems/year, accepts about 2%. Press run is 1,000. Subscription: $15/year. Sample: $10 domestic.

HOW TO CONTACT Please send no more than five poems at a time to the poetry editor at salthillpoetry@gmail.com. "We do NOT accept unsolicited email submissions." Reads submissions between August 1 and April 1. Considers simultaneous submissions; no previously published poems. Send work, along with a cover letter including contact information addressed to correct genre editor. Include a brief bio. "Please enclose a SASE for a reply. We recycle manuscripts, and encourage you to use a "Forever" stamp on your SASE." Time between acceptance and publication is up to 8 months. Responds in up to 9 months. Pays 2 contributor's copies. Acquires one-time rights.

TIPS "*Salt Hill* seeks to publish writing that is exciting and necessary, regardless of aesthetic. Rather than trying to fit any subscribed style, send your best work. We recommend reading recent issues or samples on our website prior to submitting. Open submissions from Aug. 1-Apr. 1. Enclose SASE for reply. We recycle mss, and encourage you to use a 'Forever' stamp on your SASE. Clearly mark envelope to the appropriate genre editor's attention."

◑ THE SAME

P.O. Box 494, Mount Union PA 17066. E-mail: editors@thesamepress.com; submissions@thesamepress.com. Website: www.thesamepress.com. **Contact:** Philip Miller, editor. P.O. Box 494, Mount Union, PA 17066. E-mail: editors@thesamepress.com; submissions@thesamepress.com. Website: www.thesamepress.com. **Contact:** Philip Miller, editor. Estab. 2000. *The Same*, published semiannually, prints nonfiction (essays, reviews, literary criticism), poetry, and short fiction. Wants "eclectic poetry (formal to free verse,'mainstream' to experimental, all subject matter.)" Considers poetry by children and teens. Has published poetry by Phyllis Becker, Graham Duncan, Patricia Lawson, Holly Posner, Stephen Stepanchev,

and Robert Weaver. *The Same* is 50-100 pages, desktop-published, perfect-bound, with cardstock cover. Receives about 2,000 poems/year, accepts about 5%. Press run is 250 (125 subscribers/shelf sales). Single copy: $5; subscription: $10 for 2 issues, $18 for 4 issues. Make checks payable to Philip Miller.

MAGAZINES NEEDS *The Same*, published semiannually, prints nonfiction (essays, reviews, literary criticism), poetry, and short fiction. Wants "eclectic poetry (formal to free verse,'mainstream' to experimental, all subject matter.)" Considers poetry by children and teens. Has published poetry by Phyllis Becker, Graham Duncan, Patricia Lawson, Holly Posner, Stephen Stepanchev, and Robert Weaver. *The Same* is 50-100 pages, desktop-published, perfect-bound, with cardstock cover. Receives about 2,000 poems/year, accepts about 5%. Press run is 250 (125 subscribers/shelf sales). Single copy: $5; subscription: $10 for 2 issues, $18 for 4 issues. Make checks payable to Philip Miller.

HOW TO CONTACT Submit 1-7 poems at a time. Lines/poem: 120 maximum. No previously published poems or simultaneous submissions "without query." Prefers e-mail submissions (pasted into body of message). Cover letter is optional. "Include SASE if you want a snail mail response. If you don't want your manuscript returned, you may omit the SASE if we can respond by e-mail." Please query before submitting fiction and non-fiction. Reads submissions year round. Time between acceptance and publication can be up to 11 months. Sometimes comments on rejected poems. Guidelines available for SASE, by e-mail, or on website. Responds within 2 months. Pays one contributor's copy. Acquires first North American serial rights and online rights for up to 9 months; returns rights to poet.

ADDITIONAL INFORMATION Publishes 1-3 chapbooks/year. **Solicited mss only.** Chapbooks are 24-32 pages, desktop-published, saddle-stapled, with cardstock covers. Pays 25 author's copies (out of a press run of 100).

◯ SAMSARA: THE MAGAZINE OF SUFFERING

P.O. Box 467, Ashburn VA 20147. E-mail: rdfgoalie@gmail.com. Website: www.samsaramagazine.net. **Contact:** R. David Fulcher, editor. P.O. Box 467, Ashburn, VA 20147. E-mail:rdfgoalie@gmail.com. Website: www.samsaramagazine.net. **Contact:** R. David

Fulcher, editor. *Samsara, The Magazine of Suffering*, published biannually, prints poetry and fiction dealing with suffering and healing. "Both metered verse and free verse poetry are welcome if dealing with the theme of suffering/healing." Has published poetry by Michael Foster, Nicole Provencher, and Jeff Parsley. *Samsara* is 80 pages, magazine-sized, desktop-published, with color cardstock cover. Receives about 200 poems/year, accepts about 15%. Press run is 300 (200 subscribers). Single copy: $5.50; subscription: $10. Sample: $4.50. Make checks payable to R. David Fulcher.

MAGAZINES NEEDS *Samsara, The Magazine of Suffering*, published biannually, prints poetry and fiction dealing with suffering and healing. "Both metered verse and free verse poetry are welcome if dealing with the theme of suffering/healing." Has published poetry by Michael Foster, Nicole Provencher, and Jeff Parsley. *Samsara* is 80 pages, magazine-sized, desktop-published, with color cardstock cover. Receives about 200 poems/year, accepts about 15%. Press run is 300 (200 subscribers). Single copy: $5.50; subscription: $10. Sample: $4.50. Make checks payable to R. David Fulcher.

HOW TO CONTACT Submit up to 5 poems at a time. Lines/poem: 3 minimum, 100 maximum. Considers simultaneous submissions "if noted as such"; no previously published poems. Cover letter is preferred. No e-mail submissionis; accepts submissions by postal mail only. Time between acceptance and publication is 3 months. Seldom comments on rejected poems. Guidelines available for SASE or on website. Responds in 2 months. Pays 1 contributor's copy. Acquires first North American serial rights. Reviews books/chapbooks of poetry in 500 words, single-book format. Send material for review consideration.

➕ ◐ SANDY RIVER REVIEW

University of Maine at Farmington, 238 Main St., Farmington ME 04938. E-mail: srreview@gmail.com. Website: http://studentorgs.umf.maine.edu/~srreview. **Contact:** Emma Deans, editor (changes each semester); Kelsey Moore, assistant editor.

MAGAZINES NEEDS "*The Sandy River Review* seeks prose, poetry and art submissions twice a year for our Spring and Fall issues. Prose submissions may be either Fiction or Creative Non-Fiction and should be 15 pages or fewer in length, 12 pt., Times Roman

font, double-spaced. Most of our art is published in black & white, and must be submitted as 300 dpi quaity, CMYK color mode, and saved as a .TIF file. We publish a wide variety of work from students as well as professional, established writers. Your submission should be polished and imaginative with strongly drawn characters and an interesting, original narrative. The review is the face of the University of Maine at Farmington's venerable BFA Creative Writing program, and we strive for the highest quality prose and poetry standard.""*The Sandy River Review* seeks prose, poetry and art submissions twice a year for our Spring and Fall issues. Prose submissions may be either Fiction or Creative Non-Fiction and should be 15 pages or fewer in length, 12 pt., Times Roman font, double-spaced. Most of our art is published in black & white, and must be submitted as 300 dpi quaity, CMYK color mode, and saved as a .TIF file. We publish a wide variety of work from students as well as professional, established writers. Your submission should be polished and imaginative with strongly drawn characters and an interesting, original narrative. The review is the face of the University of Maine at Farmington's venerable BFA Creative Writing program, and we strive for the highest quality prose and poetry standard."

TIPS "We recommend that you take time with your piece. As with all submissions to a literary journal, submissions should be fully-completed, polished final drafts that require minimal to no revision once accepted. Double-check your prose pieces for basic grammatical errors before submitting."

◐ SANSKRIT LITERARY ARTS MAGAZINE

UNC Charlotte, 9201 University City Blvd., Student Union Rm 045, Charlotte NC 28223. (704)687-7141. E-mail: sanskrit@uncc.edu. Website: http://sanskrit.uncc.edu; http://www.facebook.com/group.php?gid=2201452053. **Contact:** Editor. *Sanskrit* is unc charlotte's nationally recognized, award-winning literary-arts magazine. It is published once a year, in April. Sanskrit is a collection of poems, short stories, and art from people all around the world and students, just like you. All of the work goes through a selection process that includes our staff and university professors. Finally, each year the magazine has a theme. This theme is completely independent from the work and is chosen by the editor as a design element to unify the magazine. The theme is kept secret until the return of the magazine in April when we have our annual gallery showing and poetry reading

THE SARANAC REVIEW

CVH, Department of English, SUNY Plattsburgh, 101 Broad St., Plattsburgh NY 12901. (518)564-2414. Fax: (518)564-2140. E-mail: saranacreview@plattsburgh. edu. Website: http://research.plattsburgh.edu/saranacreview. **Contact:** Fiction Editor. CVH, Plattsburgh State University, 101 Broad St., Plattsburgh NY 12901. (518)564-2241. E-mail: saranacreview@plattsburgh.edu. Website: http://research.plattsburgh.edu/saranacreview. **Contact:** Poetry Editor. Estab. 2004. *The Saranac Review*, published annually in the fall, wants poetry from both U.S. and Canadian writers. Does not want "amateurish or 'greeting card' poetry." Has published poetry by Donald Revell, Ricardo Pau-Llosa, Jim Daniels, Rustin Larson, Rane Arroyo, Ross Leckie, Diane Swan, T. Alan Broughton, Brian Bartlett, Barry Dempster. *The Saranac Review* is magazine-sized, with color photo or painting on cover, includes ads. Press run is 1,000. Single copy: $12/$14CA; subscription: $15/year, $20 for 2 years, $28 for 3 years, $45 for 5 years ($18/year for institutions—multi-year subscriptions receive 15% discount); all Canadian subscriptions add $3/year. Make checks payable to Subscriptions/*The Saranac Review*.

MAGAZINES NEEDS *The Saranac Review*, published annually in the fall, wants poetry from both U.S. and Canadian writers. Does not want "amateurish or 'greeting card' poetry." Has published poetry by Donald Revell, Ricardo Pau-Llosa, Jim Daniels, Rustin Larson, Rane Arroyo, Ross Leckie, Diane Swan, T. Alan Broughton, Brian Bartlett, Barry Dempster. *The Saranac Review* is magazine-sized, with color photo or painting on cover, includes ads. Press run is 1,000. Single copy: $12/$14CA; subscription: $15/year, $20 for 2 years, $28 for 3 years, $45 for 5 years ($18/year for institutions—multi-year subscriptions receive 15% discount); all Canadian subscriptions add $3/year. Make checks payable to Subscriptions/*The Saranac Review*.

HOW TO CONTACT Submit no more than 3 poems at a time. Considers simultaneous submissions if notified; no previously published poems. No e-mail or disk submissions. Cover letter is appreciated. Include phone and e-mail contact information (if possible) in cover letter. Manuscripts will not be returned without SASE. Reads submissions September 1-February 15 (firm). Poems are circulated to an editorial board. Sometimes comments on rejected poems. Guidelines available on website. Responds in 3-6 months. Pays 2 contributor's copies. Acquires first rights.

TIPS "We publish serious, generous fiction."

SCIENCE EDITOR

P.O. Box 4082, Alexandria VA 22303. (703)786-2272. Fax: (571)366-2089. E-mail: csescienceeditor@gmail. com. Website: www.CouncilScienceEditors.org. **Contact:** Rebecca S. Benner, editor. P.O. Box 4082, Alexandria, VA 22303. (703)786-2272. Fax:(571)366-2089. E-mail: csescienceeditor@gmail.com. Website:www. CouncilScienceEditors.org. **Contact:** Rebecca S. Benner, editor. Estab. 2000. Member: Council of Science Editors (CSE). *Science Editor*, published quarterly, is "a forum for the exchange of information and ideas among professionals concerned with publishing in the sciences." Wants "up to 90 typeset lines of poetry on the intersection of science (including but not limited to biomedicine) and communication. Geared toward adult scholars, writers, and editors in communication and the sciences." Has published poetry by Mary Knatterud, Judy Meiksin, David Goldblatt, Mary Donnelly, Nancy Overcott, Jyothirmai Gubili, Neil H. Segal, Michele Arduengo. *Science Editor* is approx. 32 pages, magazine-sized, 4-color process, saddle-stitched, with an 80 pd Dull Cover; includes ads. Press run is 1,500. Single copy: $12 US; $15 Int'l. "Journal is a membership benefit; dues are $164 per year; nonmember subscriptions: $55 US; $68 Int'l/ year." Make checks payable to Council of Science Editors (CSE).

MAGAZINES NEEDS *Science Editor*, published quarterly, is "a forum for the exchange of information and ideas among professionals concerned with publishing in the sciences." Wants "up to 90 typeset lines of poetry on the intersection of science (including but not limited to biomedicine) and communication. Geared toward adult scholars, writers, and editors in communication and the sciences." Has published poetry by Mary Knatterud, Judy Meiksin, David Goldblatt, Mary Donnelly, Nancy Overcott, Jyothirmai Gubili, Neil H. Segal, Michele Arduengo. *Science Editor* is approx. 32 pages, magazine-sized, 4-color process, saddle-stitched, with an 80 pd Dull Cover; includes ads. Press run is 1,500. Single copy: $12 US; $15 Int'l. "Journal is a membership benefit;

dues are $164 per year; nonmember subscriptions: $55 US; $68 Int'l/year." Make checks payable to Council of Science Editors (CSE).

HOW TO CONTACT Submit up to 3 poems at a time, maximum 90 lines. Does not consider previously published poems or simultaneous submissions. Accepts e-mail submissions (pasted into the body of message), no fax or disk. "Submit both cover letter and poetry by e-mail only in the body of the same e-mail message, with no attachments." Submit seasonal poems 9 months in advance. Time between acceptance and publication is 3-6 months. Sometimes comments on rejected poems. Guidelines available by e-mail. Responds in 3-6 weeks. Pays 3 contributor's copies. Acquires one-time rights, electronic rights. "*Science Editor* is posted online. Issues at least one year old are openly displayed accessible. Issues less than one year old can be accessed only by Council of Science Editors members." Rights revert to poet upon publication.

◐◑⊜ SCIFAIKUEST

P.O. Box 782, Cedar Rapids IA 52406-0782. E-mail: gatrix65@yahoo.com. Website: www.samsdotpublishing.com. **Contact:** Tyree Campbell, managing editor; Teri Santitoro, editor. P.O. Box 782, Cedar Rapids, IA 52406-0782. E-mail: gatrix65@yahoo.com. Website: www.samsdotpublishing.com. **Contact:** Teri Santitoro, editor. Estab. 2003. *Scifaikuest*, published quarterly both online and in print, features "science fiction/fantasy/horror minimalist poetry, especially scifaiku, and related forms. We also publish articles about various poetic forms and reviews of poetry collections. The online and print versions of *Scifaikuest* are different." Wants "artwork, scifaiku and speculative minimalist forms such as tanka, haibun, ghazals, senryu. No 'traditional' poetry." Has published poetry by Tom Brinck, Oino Sakai, Deborah P. Kolodji, Aurelio Rico Lopez III, Joanne Morcom, and John Dunphy. *Scifaikuest* (print edition) is 32 pages, digest-sized, offset-printed, perfect-bound, with color cardstock cover, includes ads. Receives about 500 poems/year, accepts about 160 (32%). Press run is 100/issue; 5 distributed free to reviewers. Single copy: $7; subscription: $20/year, $37 for 2 years. Make checks payable to Tyree Campbell/Sam's Dot Publishing. Member: The Speculative Literature Foundation. *Scifaikuest* was voted #1 poetry magazine in the 2004 Preditors & Editors poll.

MAGAZINES NEEDS *Scifaikuest*, published quarterly both online and in print, features "science fiction/fantasy/horror minimalist poetry, especially scifaiku, and related forms. We also publish articles about various poetic forms and reviews of poetry collections. The online and print versions of *Scifaikuest* are different." Wants "artwork, scifaiku and speculative minimalist forms such as tanka, haibun, ghazals, senryu. No 'traditional' poetry." Has published poetry by Tom Brinck, Oino Sakai, Deborah P. Kolodji, Aurelio Rico Lopez III, Joanne Morcom, and John Dunphy. *Scifaikuest* (print edition) is 32 pages, digest-sized, offset-printed, perfect-bound, with color cardstock cover, includes ads. Receives about 500 poems/year, accepts about 160 (32%). Press run is 100/issue; 5 distributed free to reviewers. Single copy: $7; subscription: $20/year, $37 for 2 years. Make checks payable to Tyree Campbell/Sam's Dot Publishing.

HOW TO CONTACT Submit 5 poems at a time. Lines/poem: varies, depending on poem type. No previously published poems or simultaneous submissions. Accepts e-mail submissions (pasted into body of message). No disk submissions; artwork as e-mail attachment or inserted body of e-mail. "Submission should include snail mail address and a short (1-2 lines) bio." Reads submissions year round. Submit seasonal poems 6 months in advance. Time between acceptance and publication is 1-2 months. "Editor Teri Santitoro makes all decisions regarding acceptances." Often comments on rejected poems. Guidelines available on website. Responds in 6-8 weeks. Pays $1/poem, $4/review or article, and 1 contributor's copy. Acquires first North American serial rights.

◑◑ SEAM

P.O. Box 1051, Sawston, Cambridge CB22 3WT, United Kingdom. Website: www.seampoetry.co.uk. P.O. Box 1051, Sawston, Cambridge CB22 3WT England. E-mail: seam.magazine@googlemail.com (inquiries only). Website: www.seampoetry.co.uk. **Contact:** Anne Berkeley, editor. Estab. 1994. *Seam*, published twice/year in spring and autumn, is "international in outlook and open to experimental work and authorized translations." Wants "good contemporary poetry and "high-quality poems that engage the reader." Has published poetry by Mike Barlow, Jane Holland, Sheenagh Pugh, Julian Stannard, George Szirtes, and Tamar Yoseloff. *Seam* is 72 pages, A5, perfect-bound, with b&w cover. Receives about 2,000 poems/year, accepts about 5%. Press run is 300. Subscription: £8/year (£12 or $18 overseas). Sample: £4.50 (£5.50 or $9 overseas). Payments accepted through PayPal.

MAGAZINES NEEDS *Seam*, published twice/year in spring and autumn, is "international in outlook and open to experimental work and authorized translations." Wants "good contemporary poetry and "high-quality poems that engage the reader." Has published poetry by Mike Barlow, Jane Holland, Sheenagh Pugh, Julian Stannard, George Szirtes, and Tamar Yoseloff. *Seam* is 72 pages, A5, perfect-bound, with b&w cover. Receives about 2,000 poems/year, accepts about 5%. Press run is 300. Subscription: £8/year (£12 or $18 overseas). Sample: £4.50 (£5.50 or $9 overseas). Payments accepted through PayPal.

HOW TO CONTACT Submit 5-6 poems at a time. No simultaneous submissions or previously published poems (if published in UK). No e-mail submissions. Type each poem on 1 sheet of paper (A4 size). Sometimes comments on rejected poems. Pays 1 contributor's copy. Can reply by e-mail to save postage and time standing in line at post office for International Reply Coupons.

THE SEATTLE REVIEW

(206)543-2302. E-mail: seaview@u.washington.edu. Website: www.seattlereview.org. Box 354330, University of Washington, Seattle, WA 98195. (206)543-2302. E-mail: seaview@u.washington.edu. Website: www. seattlereview.org. "We are looking for exceptional, risk-taking, intellectual and imaginative poems between ten and thirty pages in length." *The Seattle Review* will publish, and will only publish, long poems and novellas. The long poem can be: a single long poem in its entirety, a self-contained excerpt from a book-length poem, a unified sequence or series of poems. Subscriptions: $20/three issues, $32/five issues. Back issue: $4.Includes general fiction, poetry, craft essays on writing, and one interview per issue with a Northwest writer.

 Editors accept submissions only from October 1 through May 31.

HOW TO CONTACT Submit 3-5 poems via mail between October 1 and May 31, or use submission manager on website year round. Include SASE in mail. Submissions must be typed on white, 8 1/2x11 paper. The author's name and address should appear in the upper right hand corner. No simultaneous submissions.

TIPS "Beginners do well in our magazine if they send clean, well-written manuscripts. We've published a lot of 'first stories' from all over the country and take pleasure in discovery."

✪ THE SECRET PLACE

(610)768-2240. E-mail: thesecretplace@abc-usa.org.
TIPS "Prefers submissions via e-mail."

◑ SEEMS

P.O. Box 359, Lakeland College, Sheboygan WI 53082-0359. E-mail: elderk@lakeland.edu. E-mail: seems@lakeland.edu. Website: www.seems.lakeland.edu. P.O. Box 359, Lakeland College, Sheboygan WI 53082-0359. (920)565-1276 or (920)565-3871. Fax: (920)565-1206. E-mail: elderk@lakeland.edu. Website: www.seems.lakeland.edu. Established 1971. **Contact:** Karl Elder, editor. See submission guidelines online.

MAGAZINES NEEDS Has published poetry by Philip Dacey, William Hathaway, William Heyen, Sapphire, and Frank Stanford. *SEEMS* is handsomely printed, nearly square (7x8¼), saddle-stapled. Publishes less than .5% of submissions received. Press run is 500 (more than 250 subscribers, 20 libraries). Single copy: $4; subscription: $16 for 4 issues.

HOW TO CONTACT Lines/poem: open. No simultaneous submissions. No fax or e-mail submissions. Cover letter is optional. Include biographical information, SASE. Reads submissions year round. There is a 1- to 2-year backlog. "People may call or fax with virtually any question, understanding that the editor may have no answer." Guidelines available on website. Responds in up to 3 months (slower in summer). Pays 1 contributor's copy. Acquires first North American serial rights and permission to publish online. Returns rights upon publication.

ADDITIONAL INFORMATION *Word of Mouth* (alias Seems) — with focus on work that integrates economy of language, "the musical phrase," forms of resemblance, and the sentient — will consider unpublished poetry, fiction, and creative nonfiction.

CONTEST/AWARD OFFERINGS Subsequent issues may include themes and will alternate with chapbooks from Word of Mouth Books (query for the no-fee, any-genre, chapbook contest: elderk@lakeland.edu). See the editor's website at www.karlelder.com. "Links to my work and an interview may provide insight for the potential contributor."

⊕ SENECA REVIEW

Hobart and William Smith Colleges, Geneva NY 14456. (315)781-3392. E-mail: senecareview@hws.edu. Website: www.hws.edu/academics/senecareview/index.aspx. *Seneca Review*, Hobart and William Smith Colleges, Geneva, NY 14456. (315)781-3392. E-mail: senecareview@hws.edu. Website: www.hws.edu/academics/senecareview/index.aspx. Published semiannually, seeks "serious poetry of any form, including translations. Also essays on contemporary poetry and lyrical nonfiction. You'll find plenty of free verse here—some accessible and some leaning toward experimental—with emphasis on voice, image, and diction. All in all, poems and translations complement each other and create a distinct editorial mood in each issue." Does not want "light verse." Has published poetry by Seamus Heaney, Rita Dove, Denise Levertov, Stephen Dunn, and Hayden Carruth. *Seneca Review* is 100 pages, digest-sized, professionally printed on quality stock, perfect-bound, with matte card cover. Receives 3,000-4,000 poems/year, accepts about 100. Press run is 1,000. Subscription: $20/year, $30 for 2 years plus $4 s&h. Current issue: $10 plus $2.50 s&h. Back issues: $7 plus $2.50 s&h."The editors have special interest in translations of contemporary poetry from around the world. Publisher of numerous laureates and award-winning poets, we also publish emerging writers and are always open to new, innovative work. Poems from *SR* are regularly honored by inclusion in *The Best American Poetry* and *Pushcart Prize* anthologies. Distributed internationally."

MAGAZINES NEEDS *Seneca Review*, published semiannually, seeks "serious poetry of any form, including translations. Also essays on contemporary poetry and lyrical nonfiction. You'll find plenty of free verse here—some accessible and some leaning toward experimental—with emphasis on voice, image, and diction. All in all, poems and translations complement each other and create a distinct editorial mood in each issue." Does not want "light verse." Has published poetry by Seamus Heaney, Rita Dove, Denise Levertov, Stephen Dunn, and Hayden Carruth. *Seneca Review* is 100 pages, digest-sized, professionally printed on quality stock, perfect-bound, with matte card cover. Receives 3,000-4,000 poems/year, accepts about 100. Press run is 1,000. Subscription: $20/year, $30 for 2 years plus $4 s&h. Current issue: $10 plus $2.50 s&h. Back issues: $7 plus $2.50 s&h.

HOW TO CONTACT Submit 3-5 poems at a time. No previously published poems or simultaneous submissions. No e-mail submissions; postal submissions only. SASE required. Reads submissions September 1-May 1 only. "Submit only once during the annual reading period." Guidelines available on website. Responds in up to 3 months. Pays 2 contributor's copies and a 2-year subscription.

TIPS "One submission per reading period. Mss received during summer are returned."

THE SEWANEE REVIEW

(931)598-1000. Website: www.sewanee.edu/sewanee_review. 735 University Ave., Sewanee, TN 37383-1000. (931)598-1000. Fax: (931)598-1145. Website: www.sewanee.edu/sewanee_review. The *Sewanee Review* is America's oldest continuously published literary quarterly. Only erudite work representing depth of knowledge and skill of expression is published. Solicits brief, standard, and essay-reviews.Winners of the Allen Tate Prize and the Aiken Taylor Award for Modern American Poetry are determined by the editorial board and a prize committee; poets cannot apply for these awards. Subscriptions: $25/year. Samples: $8.50."A literary quarterly, publishing original fiction, poetry, essays on literary and related subjects, and book reviews for well-educated readers who appreciate good American and English literature."

◑ Does not read mss June 1 - August 31.

MAGAZINES NEEDS The *Sewanee Review* is America's oldest continuously published literary quarterly. Only erudite work representing depth of knowledge and skill of expression is published here.

HOW TO CONTACT Submit up to 6 poems at a time. Lines/poem: 40 maximum. No simultaneous submissions. No e-mail submissions; postal submissions only. "Unsolicited works should not be submitted between June 1 and August 31. A response to any submission received during that period will be greatly delayed." Guidelines available in magazine or on website. Responds in 2 months. Pays per line, plus 2 contributor's copies (and reduced price for additional copies).

TIPS "Please keep in mind that for each poem published in *The Sewanee Review*, approximately 250 poems are considered."

SHENANDOAH

(540)458-8765. Fax: (540)458-8461. E-mail: shenandoah@wlu.edu. Website: shenandoah.wlu.edu/faq.

html. **Contact:** R. T. Smith, editor. "Unsolicited manuscripts will not be read between January 1 and October 1, 2010. All manuscripts received during this period will be recycled unread."

CONTEST/AWARD OFFERINGS Sponsors the annual James Boatwright III Prize for Poetry, a $1,000 prize awarded to the author of the best poem published in *Shenandoah* during a volume year. The Shenandoah/Glasgow Prize for Emerging Writers $2,000 awarded for poetry on alternate years (see separate entry in Contests/Awards section of this book).

◑ THE SHEPHERD

1530 Seventh St., Rock Island IL 61201. (309)788-3980. **Contact:** Betty Mowery, poetry editor. 1530 Seventh St., Rock Island, IL 61201.(309)788-3980. **Contact:** Betty Mowery, poetry editor. *The Shepherd*, published quarterly, features inspirational poetry from all ages. Wants "something with a message but not preachy." Subscription: $12. Sample: $4. Make all checks payable to *The Oak.The Shepherd*, published quarterly, features inspirational poetry from all ages. Wants "something with a message but not preachy." Subscription: $12. Sample: $4. Make all checks payable to *The Oak*.

HOW TO CONTACT Submit up to 5 poems at a time. Lines/poem: 35 maximum. Considers previously published poems. Include SASE with all submissions. Responds in one week. "*The Shepherd* does not pay in dollars or copies, but you need not purchase to be published." Acquires first or second rights. All rights revert to poet upon publication.

TIPS Sponsors poetry contest. Guidelines available for SASE.

◑ SHIP OF FOOLS

Ship of Fools Press, University of Rio Grande, Box 1028, Rio Grande OH 45674-9989. (740)992-3333. Website: http://meadhall.homestead.com/Ship.html. Established 1983. **Contact:** Jack Hart, editor.

MAGAZINES NEEDS *Ship of Fools*, published "more or less quarterly," seeks "coherent, well-written, traditional or modern, myth, archetype, love—most types." Does not want "concrete, incoherent, or greeting card poetry." Considers poetry by children and teens. Has published poetry by Rhina Espaillat and Gale White. *Ship of Fools* is digest-sized, saddle-stapled, includes cover art and graphics. Press run is 200. Subscription: $8 for 4 issues. Sample: $2.

HOW TO CONTACT No previously published poems or simultaneous submissions. Cover letter is preferred. Often comments on rejected poems. Guidelines available for SASE. Responds in one month. "If longer than six weeks, write and ask why." Pays 1-2 contributor's copies. Reviews books of poetry.

ADDITIONAL INFORMATION Ship of Fools Press has "no plans to publish chapbooks in the next year due to time constraints."

◑ SIERRA NEVADA REVIEW

999 Tahoe Blvd., Incline Village NV 89451. E-mail: sncreview@sierranevada.edu. Website: www.sierranevada.edu/800. **Contact:** June Sylvester Saraceno, advisory editor. Estab. 1990. *Sierra Nevada Review*, published annually in May, features poetry and short fiction by new writers. Wants "image-oriented poems with a distinct, genuine voice. Although we don't tend to publish 'light verse,' we do appreciate, and often publish, poems that make us laugh. No limit on length, style, etc." Does not want "sentimental, clicheéd, or obscure poetry." Has published poetry by Virgil Suaárez, Simon Perchik, Carol Frith, and Marisella Veiga. *Sierra Nevada Review* is about 75 pages, with art on cover. Receives about 1,000 poems/year, accepts about 50. Press run is 500. Subscription: $10/year. Sample: $5.

MAGAZINES NEEDS *Sierra Nevada Review*, published annually in May, features poetry and short fiction by new writers. Wants "image-oriented poems with a distinct, genuine voice. Although we don't tend to publish 'light verse,' we do appreciate, and often publish, poems that make us laugh. No limit on length, style, etc." Does not want "sentimental, clicheéd, or obscure poetry." Has published poetry by Virgil Suaárez, Simon Perchik, Carol Frith, and Marisella Veiga. *Sierra Nevada Review* is about 75 pages, with art on cover. Receives about 1,000 poems/year, accepts about 50. Press run is 500. Subscription: $10/year. Sample: $5.

HOW TO CONTACT Submit up to 5 poems at a time. Considers simultaneous submissions; no previously published poems. Accepts e-mail submissions (pasted into body of message, no attachments). Reads submissions September 1-March 1 only. Sometimes comments on rejected poems. Guidelines available for SASE, by e-mail, or on website. Responds in about 3 months. Pays 2 contributor's copies.

● SKIDROW PENTHOUSE

68 E. Third St., Apt. 16, New York NY 10003. E-mail: info@skidrowpenthouse.com. Website: http://skidrowpenthouse.com. Stephanie Dickinson, co-editor. **Contact:** Rob Cook, editor. Estab. 1998. *Skidrow Penthouse* aims to "give emerging and idiosyncratic writers a new forum in which to publish their work. We are looking for deeply felt authentic voices, whether surreal, confessional, New York School, formal, or free verse. Work should be well crafted: attention to line-break and diction." Wants "poets who sound like themselves, not workshop professionals." Does not want "gutless posturing, technical precision with no subject matter, explicit sex and violence without craft, or abstract intellectualizing. We are not impressed by previous awards and publications." Has published poetry by Lisa Jarnot, Christopher Edgar, Aase Berg, Karl Tierney, James Grinwis, and Robyn Art. *Skidrow Penthouse* is 280 pages, 6×9, professionally printed, perfect-bound, with 4-color cover. Receives about 500 poems/year, accepts 3%. Press run is 300 (50 subscribers); 10% distributed free to journals for review consideration. Single copy: $12.50; subscription: $20. Make checks payable to Skidrow Penthouse. *Skidrow Penthouse* aims to "give emerging and idiosyncratic writers a new forum in which to publish their work. We are looking for deeply felt authentic voices, whether surreal, confessional, New York School, formal, or free verse. Work should be well crafted: attention to line-break and diction." Wants "poets who sound like themselves, not workshop professionals." Does not want "gutless posturing, technical precision with no subject matter, explicit sex and violence without craft, or abstract intellectualizing. We are not impressed by previous awards and publications." Has published poetry by Lisa Jarnot, Christopher Edgar, Aase Berg, Karl Tierney, James Grinwis, and Robyn Art. *Skidrow Penthouse* is 280 pages, 6×9, professionally printed, perfect-bound, with 4-color cover. Receives about 500 poems/year, accepts 3%. Press run is 300 (50 subscribers); 10% distributed free to journals for review consideration. Single copy: $12.50; subscription: $20. Make checks payable to Skidrow Penthouse. **HOW TO CONTACT** Submit 3-5 poems at a time. Considers previously published poems and simultaneous submissions. "Include a legal-sized SASE; name and address on every page of your submission. No handwritten submissions will be considered." Time between acceptance and publication is one year. Seldom comments on rejected poems. Responds in 2 months. Pays one contributor's copy. Acquires one-time rights. Reviews books and chapbooks of poetry and other magazines in 1,500 words, single-book format. Send materials for review consideration. "We're trying to showcase a poet in each issue by publishing up to 60-page collections within the magazine." Send query with SASE.

TIPS "We get way too many anecdotal fragments posing as poetry; too much of what we receive feels like this morning's inspiration mailed this afternoon. The majority of those who submit do not seem to have put in the sweat a good poem demands. Also, the ratio of submissions to sample copy purchases is 50:1. Just because our name is *Skidrow Penthouse* does not mean we are a repository for genre work or 'eat, shit, shower, and shave' poetry."

○ SKIPPING STONES: A MULTICULTURAL LITERARY MAGAZINE

P.O. Box 3939, Eugene OR 97403-0939. (541)342-4956. Fax: Call for number. E-mail: Editor@Skippingstones.org. Website: www.Skippingstones.org. **Contact:** Arun Toke, editor.

MAGAZINES NEEDS *Skipping Stones*, published bimonthly during the school year (5 issues), "encourages cooperation, creativity, and celebration of cultural and ecological richness." Wants "poetry by young writers under age 18, on multicultural and social issues, family, freedom—uplifting. No adult poetry, please." *Skipping Stones* is magazine-sized, saddle-stapled, printed on recycled paper. Receives about 500-1,000 poems/year, accepts 10%. Press run is 2,500. Subscription: $25. Sample: $6.

HOW TO CONTACT Submit up to 5 poems at a time. Lines/poem: 30 maximum. Considers simultaneous submissions; no previously published poems. Accepts e-mail submissions. Cover letter is preferred. "Include your cultural background, experiences, and the inspiration behind your creation." Time between acceptance and publication is 6-9 months. "A piece is chosen for publication when most of the editorial staff feel good about it." Seldom comments on rejected poems. Publishes multi-theme issues. Guidelines available for SASE. Responds in up to 4 months. Pays 1 contributor's copy, offers 40% discount for morecopies and subscription, if desired. Acquires first serial rights and non-exclusive reprint rights.

CONTEST/AWARD OFFERINGS Sponsors annual

youth honor awards for 7- to 17-year-olds. Theme is "multicultural, social, international, and nature awareness." Guidelines available for SASE or on website. Entry fee: $3 (entitles entrant to a free issue featuring the 10 winners). Deadline: June 25.

TIPS "Be original and innovative. Use multicultural, nature, or cross-cultural themes. Multilingual submissions are welcome."

ⓞ SLANT: A JOURNAL OF POETRY

University of Central Arkansas, P.O. Box 5063, 201 Donaghey Ave., Conway AR 72035-5000. (501)450-5107. Website: www.uca.edu/english/poetryjournal/. **Contact:** James Fowler, editor. University of Central Arkansas, P.O. Box 5063, 201 Donaghey Ave., Conway, AR 72035-5000. (501)450-5107. E-mail:jamesf@uca. edu. Website: www.uca.edu/english/poetryjournal/. **Contact:** James Fowler, editor. *Slant: A Journal of Poetry*, published annually in May, aims "to publish a journal of fine poetry from all regions of the United States and beyond." Wants "traditional and 'modern' poetry, even experimental; moderate length, any subject on approval of Board of Readers." Doesn't want "haiku, translations." Has published poetry by Richard Broderick, Susana H. Case, David Jordan, Timothy Martin, Barbara F. Lefcowitz, and Donna Pucciani. *Slant* is 120 pages, professionally printed on quality stock, flat-spined, with matte card cover. Receives about 1,200 poems/year, accepts 70-75. Press run is 175 (70-100 subscribers). Sample: $10.

MAGAZINES NEEDS *Slant: A Journal of Poetry*, published annually in May, aims "to publish a journal of fine poetry from all regions of the United States and beyond." Wants "traditional and 'modern' poetry, even experimental; moderate length, any subject on approval of Board of Readers." Doesn't want "haiku, translations." Has published poetry by Richard Broderick, Susana H. Case, David Jordan, Timothy Martin, Barbara F. Lefcowitz, and Donna Pucciani. *Slant* is 120 pages, professionally printed on quality stock, flat-spined, with matte card cover. Receives about 1,200 poems/year, accepts 70-75. Press run is 175 (70-100 subscribers). Sample: $10.

HOW TO CONTACT Submit up to 5 poems at a time. Lines/poem: poems should be of moderate length. No previously published poems or simultaneous submissions. Submissions should be typed; include SASE. "Put name, address (including e-mail if available), and phone number at the top of each page." Accepts submissions September 1-November 15. Comments on rejected poems "on occasion." Guidelines available in magazine, for SASE, or on website. Responds in 3-4 months from November 15 deadline. Pays 1 contributor's copy. Poet retains rights.

ⓞ SLATE & STYLE

2861 S. 93 Plaza APT 8, Omaha NE 68124. (402)350-1735. E-mail: bpollpeter@hotmail.com. Website: www. nfb-writers-division.org. **Contact:** Bridgit Pollpeter, editor.

MAGAZINES NEEDS *Slate & Style*, published quarterly, is the magazine of the Writers' Division of the National Federation of the Blind. Published for blind writers, *Slate & Style* is available in large print, in Braille, and by e-mail at: bpollpeter@hotmail.com, and includes resources and articles of interest to blind writers. "We prefer contributors be blind writers, or at least writers by profession or inclination. New writers welcome. No obscenities. Will consider all forms of poetry including haiku. Interested in new talent." Considers poetry by children and teens, "but please specify age." Has published poetry by Harriet Barrett, W. Burns Taylor, Chelsea Cook, Jennifer Shields, and David Thomas. *Slate & Style* (print format) is 28-32 pages, magazine-sized, stapled. Press run is 200 (160 subscribers, 4-5 libraries). Subscription/membership: $10/year (regardless of format). Sample: $3. Please specify format when subscribing, and make all checks out to the NFB writers' division.

HOW TO CONTACT Submit 3 poems at a time once or twice/year. Lines/poem: 5-36. No previously published poems or simultaneous submissions. Accepts submissions by e-mail at: bpollpeter@hotmail. com (pasted into body of message). "On occasion we receive poems in Braille. I prefer print, since Braille slows me down. Typed is best." Cover letter is preferred. Reads submissions according to the following deadlines: February 16, May 15, August 15, November 15; "do not submit manuscripts in July." Comments on rejected poems "if requested." Guidelines available in magazine, for SASE, by e-mail, or on website. Responds in 2 weeks "if I like it." Pays 1 contributor's copy. Reviews books of poetry. Send materials for review consideration.

CONTEST/AWARD OFFERINGS Sponsors an annual poetry contest, awarding 1st Prize: $100; 2nd Prize: $50; 3rd Prize: $25. Honorable mentions may also be awarded, and winning poems will be published in magazine. **Entry fee:** $5 for up to 3 poems. Make check or money order payable to NFB Writers' Division. "Include cover letter with title and your identifying information." Opens January 1st; **Deadline: June 1.** We are now sponsoring a poetry contest for blind students, K-12. Guidelines available for SASE, by e-mail, or on website.

TIPS "The best advice I can give is to send your work out; manuscripts left in a drawer have no chance at all."

○ SLEEPINGFISH

Via Titta Scarpetta #28, RM Rome 00153, Italy. E-mail: white@sleepingfish.net. Website: www.sleepingfish.net. **Contact:** Derek White, editor.

MAGAZINES NEEDS *SleepingFish*, published 1-2 times/year, is "a print or online magazine of innovative text and art. " Wants "art, visual poetry, prose poems, experimental texts, graffiti, collage, multi-cultural, cross-genre work—anything that defies categorization." Does not want "conventional 'lined' or rhyming poetry (anything that looks like a 'poem'), conventional stories, genre fiction or poetry, political, religious, New Age, anything with an agenda." Considers poetry by teens. Has published writings by Rick Moody, Diane Williams, Blake Butler, David Baptiste-Chirot, Miranada Mellis, Brian Evenson, Norman Lock, Peter Markus. *SleepingFish* print issues are 100-120 pages, magazine-sized, digitally printed, perfect-bound or with other binding, with 110 lb. cardstock cover in full color. Receives about 500 poems/year, accepts about 25 (5%). Press run is 400 (10 libraries, 300 shelf sales, 100 online sales); 50 distributed free to contributors. Single copy: $15.

HOW TO CONTACT Submit 1-5 prose or visual poems at a time. Lines/poem: 1-3 pages (prose less than 1,000 words). Considers simultaneous submissions; no previously published poems. Accepts e-mail submissions only (pasted into body of message or as small attachments (less than 2 MB) in DOC, RTF, JPG, GIF, or PDF format); no disk submissions. Cover letter is preferred. "Please send e-mail only. Reading period varies; see website for details." Time between acceptance and publication is 2-6 weeks. "Currently, an online operation based out of Rome. Tastes and whims vary and are subject to change. Sometimes there is a loose theme, and acceptance

may also be dependent on whether the admission fits in with other work in the issue." Sometimes comments on rejected poems." Poet should be familiar with *SleepingFish*. Online samples and work on site (www.sleepingfish.net) if you can't afford a copy. "Sometimes publishes theme issues. Guidelines available on website. Responds in 1-3 months. Sometimes sends prepublication galleys. Pays one contributor's copy, with additional contributor copies available at half price. "Payment depends on funds." Acquires first rights. Returns all rights "as long as *Sleeping-Fish* is acknowledged as first place of publication." Does not review books.

SLIPSTREAM

E-mail: editors@slipstream.org. Website: www.slipstreampress.org/index.html. **Contact:** Dan Sicoli, co-editor. "We prefer contemporary urban themes—writing from the grit that is not afraid to bark or bite. We shy away from pastoral, religious, and rhyming verse."

○ If you're unsure, the editors strongly recommend that you sample a current or back issue of *Slipstream*.

MAGAZINES NEEDS *Slipstream*, published annually in spring, is "about 95% poetry, with some artwork. We like new work with contemporary urban flavor. Writing must have a cutting edge to get our attention. Any length, subject, style. Best to see a sample to get a feel. Like city stuff as opposed to country." Wants "poetry that springs from the gut, screams from dark alleys, inspired by experience." Does not want "pastoral, religious, traditional, rhyming" poetry. Has published poetry by Terry Godbey, Gerald Locklin, David Chorlton, Patrick Carrington, Jim Daniels, Beth Royer, and Mofolasayo Ogundiran. *Slipstream* is 80-100 pages, 7x8$\frac{1}{2}$, professionally printed, perfect-bound. Receives more than 2,500 poetry submissions/year, accepts less than 10%. Press run is 500 (400 subscribers, 10 libraries). Subscription: $20 for 2 issues and 2 chapbooks. Sample: $10.

HOW TO CONTACT No e-mail submissions. Sometimes comments on rejected poems. Publishes theme issues. Guidelines available for SASE or on website. Responds in up to 2 months "if SASE included." Pays 1-2 contributor's copies.

CONTEST/AWARD OFFERINGS *Slipstream* Poetry Chapbook Contest (see separate listing in Contests & Awards).

TIPS "Slipstream is now accepting poetry submissions for its first theme issue in several years. We seek work exploring SEX-FOOD-DEATH. Your interpretation may include one, two, or all three of the subjects. No previous published work. All submissions must include a SASE for response. Originally examined back in Issue 14, the theme was so popular we have decided to revisit it. Deadline for submissions is: MARCH 1, 2011. Send copies of your poems, not originals. See Submission guidelines online."

SNOW MONKEY

E-mail: snowmonkey.editor@comcast.net. Website: www.ravennapress.com/snowmonkey/. Website covering original unpublished poems and micro-prose 10 times/year. Seeks writing "that's like footprints of the Langur monkeys left at 11,000 feet on Poon Hill, Nepal. Open to most themes." Accepts simultaneous submissions. Guidelines available online. Contact: John Burgess. Email: snowmonkey.editor@comcast. net. Website: www.ravennapress.com/snowmonkey/ John Burgess. Seeks writing "that's like footprints of the Langur monkeys left at 11,000 feet on Poon Hill, Nepal. Open to most themes."

HOW TO CONTACT E-mail. Responds to mss in 2 months.

ADDITIONAL INFORMATION Does not pay.

TIPS "Send submissions as text-only in the body of your email. Include your last name in the subject line. We do not currently use bios, but we love to read them."

🔵🌐 SNOWY EGRET

The Fair Press, P.O. Box 9265, Terre Haute IN 47808. Website: www.snowyegret.net. The Fair Press, P.O. Box 9265, Terre Haute IN 47808. Website: www. snowyegret.net. **Contact:** Editors. Guidelines available on website. Responds in 1 month. Always sends prepublication galleys. Pays $4/poem or $4/page plus 2 contributor's copies. Acquires first North American and one-time reprint rights. *Snowy Egret*, published in spring and autumn, specializes in work that is "nature-oriented: poetry that celebrates the abundance and beauty of nature or explores the interconnections between nature and the human psyche." Has published poetry by Conrad Hilberry, Lyn Lifshin, Gayle Eleanor, James Armstrong, and Patricia Hooper. *Snowy Egret* is 60 pages, magazine-sized, offset-printed, saddle-stapled. Receives about 500 poems/year, accepts about 30. Press run is 400. Sample: $8; subscription: $15/year, $25 for 2 years.

TIPS Looks for "honest, freshly detailed pieces with plenty of description and/or dialogue which will allow the reader to identify with the characters and step into the setting; fiction in which nature affects character development and the outcome of the story."

SOFA INK QUARTERLY

E-mail: publisher@sofaink.com. E-mail: acquisitions@sofaink.com. Website: www.sofaink.com; www.sofainkquarterly.com. **Contact:** David Cowsert. Submit 5 poems maximum at a time. Considers simultaneous submissions. Accepts e-mail submissions (as attachment in Word). Submit seasonal poems 4 months in advance. Time between acceptance and publication is about 3 months. Guidelines available for SASE or on website. Responds in 1-3 months. Pays $5 and 3 contributor's copies. Acquires first North American serial rights." Sofa Ink Quarterly offers wonderful original stories, poetry, and nonfiction that is entertaining yet wholesome. Sofa Ink Quarterly showcases original writing and art that avoids sensationalism. There is no swearing, profaning deity, excessive gore, gratuitous violence or gratuitous sex. You will find exceptional storytelling, delightful poetry, and beautiful art."

MAGAZINES NEEDS Submit 5 poems maximum at a time. Considers simultaneous submissions. Accepts e-mail submissions (as attachment in Word). Submit seasonal poems 4 months in advance. Time between acceptance and publication is about 3 months. Guidelines available for SASE or on website. Responds in 1-3 months. Pays $5 and 3 contributor's copies. Acquires first North American serial rights.

HOW TO CONTACT Sofa Ink Quarterly, P.O. Box 625, American Fork, UT 84003. (877)429-2396. E-mail: publisher@sofaink.com; acquisitions@ sofaink.com. Website: www.sofaink.com; www.sofainkquarterly.com.

TIPS Follow the content guidelines. Electronic submissions should be in a Word attachment rather than in the body of the message.

🔵 SONG OF THE SAN JOAQUIN

P.O. Box 1161, Modesto CA 95353-1161. E-mail: info@ ChaparralPoets.org. Website: www.ChaparralPoets. org/SSJ.html. **Contact:** The Editor. P.O. Box 1161, Modesto, CA 95353-1161. E-mail:info@Chaparral-Poets.org. Website: www.ChaparralPoets.org/SSJ.

html. **Contact:** The editor. Estab. 2003. *Song of the San Joaquin*, published quarterly, features "subjects about or pertinent to the San Joaquin Valley of Central California. This is defined geographically as the region from Fresno to Stockton, and from the foothills on the west to those on the east." Wants all forms and styles of poetry. "Keep subject in mind." Does not want "pornographic, demeaning, vague, or trite approaches." Considers poetry by children and teens. Has published poetry by Joyce Odam, Wilma Elizabeth McDaniel, Margarita Engle, Marnelle White, Frederick Zydek, and Nancy Haskett. *Song of the San Joaquin* is 60 pages, digest-sized, direct-copied, saddle-stapled, with cardstock cover with glossy color photo. Press run is 200 (25 copies to libraries); 40 distributed free to contributors.

MAGAZINES NEEDS *Song of the San Joaquin*, published quarterly, features "subjects about or pertinent to the San Joaquin Valley of Central California. This is defined geographically as the region from Fresno to Stockton, and from the foothills on the west to those on the east." Wants all forms and styles of poetry. "Keep subject in mind." Does not want "pornographic, demeaning, vague, or trite approaches." Considers poetry by children and teens. Has published poetry by Joyce Odam, Wilma Elizabeth McDaniel, Margarita Engle, Marnelle White, Frederick Zydek, and Nancy Haskett. *Song of the San Joaquin* is 60 pages, digest-sized, direct-copied, saddle-stapled, with cardstock cover with glossy color photo. Press run is 200 (25 copies to libraries); 40 distributed free to contributors.

HOW TO CONTACT Submit up to 3 poems at a time. Lines/poem: open ("however, poems under 40 lines have the best chance"). Considers previously published poems; no simultaneous submissions. E-mail submissions are preferred; no disk submissions. Cover letter is preferred. "SASE required. All submissions must be typed on 1 side of the page only. Proofread submissions carefully. Name, address, phone number, and e-mail address should appear on all pages. Cover letter should include any awards, honors, and previous publications for each poem, and a biographical sketch of 75 words or less." Reads submissions "periodically throughout the year." Submit seasonal poems at least 3 months in advance. Time between acceptance and publication is 3-6 months. "Poems are circulated to an editorial board of 7 who then decide on the final selections."

Seldom comments on rejected poems. Occasionally publishes theme issues. Upcoming themes available for SASE, by e-mail, or on website. Guidelines available in magazine, for SASE, by e-mail, or on website. Responds in up to 3 months. Pays 1 contributor's copy. Acquires one-time rights.

ADDITIONAL INFORMATION "Poets of the San Joaquin, which sponsors this publication, is a chapter of California Federation of Chaparral Poets, Inc., and publishes an annual anthology of members' works. Information available for SASE or by e-mail."

CONTEST/AWARD OFFERINGS Poets of the San Joaquin holds an annual local young poets' contest as well as regular poetry contests. Guidelines available for SASE or by e-mail.

SO TO SPEAK

4400 University Dr., MSN 2C5, Fairfax VA 22030-4444. E-mail: sts@gmu.edu. Website: http://sotospeakjournal.org. **Contact:** Jen Daniels, editor-in-chief. A Feminist Journal of Language and Art (Specialized: women/feminism), George Mason University, 4400 University Dr., MSN 2C5, Fairfax VA 22030-4444. (703)993-3625. E-mail: sts@gmu.edu (inquiries only). Website: http://sotospeakjournal.org. Established 1991. **Contact:** Eleanor Smith Tipton, poetry editor. *So to Speak*, published semiannually, prints "high-quality work relating to feminism, including poetry, fiction, nonfiction (including book reviews and interviews), photography, artwork, collaborations, lyrical essays, and other genre-questioning texts." Wants "work that addresses issues of significance to women's lives and movements for women's equality and are especially interested in pieces that explore issues of race, class, and sexuality in relation to gender." *So to Speak* is 100-128 pages, digest-sized, photo-offset-printed, perfect-bound, with glossy cover, includes ads. Receives about 800 poems/year, accepts 10%. Press run is 1,000 (75 subscribers, 100 shelf sales); 500 distributed free to students/contributors. Subscription: $12. Sample: $7.

MAGAZINES NEEDS *So to Speak*, published semiannually, prints "high-quality work relating to feminism, including poetry, fiction, nonfiction (including book reviews and interviews), photography, artwork, collaborations, lyrical essays, and other genre-questioning texts." Wants "work that addresses issues of significance to women's lives and movements for women's equality and are especially interested in pieces that explore issues of race, class, and sexuality in relation to gender." *So to Speak* is 100-128 pages, digest-sized, photo-offset-printed, perfect-bound, with glossy cover, includes ads. Receives about 800 poems/year, accepts 10%. Press run is 1,000 (75 subscribers, 100 shelf sales); 500 distributed free to students/contributors. Subscription: $12. Sample: $7.

HOW TO CONTACT Accepts submissions only via submissions manager on website. Submit 3-5 poems at a time. Considers simultaneous submissions; no previously published poems. No e-mail or paper submissions. "Please submit poems as you wish to see them in print. Be sure to include a cover letter with full contact info, publication credits, and awards received." Reads submissions August 15-October 15 and December 31-March 15. Time between acceptance and publication is 6-8 months. Seldom comments on rejected poems. Responds in 3 months if submissions are received during reading period. Pays 2 contributor's copies. Acquires one-time rights.

CONTEST/AWARD OFFERINGS *So to Speak* holds an annual poetry contest that awards $500. Guidelines available for SASE, by e-mail, or on website.

TIPS "We do not read between March 15 and August 15. Every writer has something they do exceptionally well; do that and it will shine through in the work. We look for quality prose with a definite appeal to a feminist audience. We are trying to move away from strict genre lines. We want high quality fiction, nonfiction, poetry, art, innovative and risk-taking work."

◐ SOUL FOUNTAIN

90-21 Springfield Blvd., Queens Village NY 11428. (718)479-2594. Fax: (718)479-2594. E-mail: davault@aol.com. Website: www.TheVault.org. **Contact:** Tone Bellizzi, editor. 90-21 Springfield Blvd., Queens Village, NY 11428. (718)479-2594. Fax: (718)479-2594. E-mail: davault@aol.com. Website: www.TheVault.org. **Contact:** Tone Bellizzi, editor. *Soul Fountain*, published 3 times/year, is produced by The Vault, a not-for-profit arts project of the Hope for the Children Foundation, "committed to empowering young and emerging artists of all disciplines at all levels to develop and share their talents through performance, collaboration, and networking." Prints poetry, art, photography, short fiction, and essays. Open to all. "We publish quality submitted work, and specialize in emerging voices. We favor visionary, challeng-

ing, and consciousness-expanding material." Does not want "poems about pets, nature, romantic love, or the occult. Sex and violence themes not welcome." Welcomes poetry by teens. *Soul Fountain* is 28 pages, magazine-sized, offset-printed, saddle-stapled. Subscription: $24. Sample: $7. Make checks payable to Hope for the Children Foundation.

MAGAZINES NEEDS *Soul Fountain*, published 3 times/year, is produced by The Vault, a not-for-profit arts project of the Hope for the Children Foundation, "committed to empowering young and emerging artists of all disciplines at all levels to develop and share their talents through performance, collaboration, and networking." Prints poetry, art, photography, short fiction, and essays. Open to all. "We publish quality submitted work, and specialize in emerging voices. We favor visionary, challenging, and consciousness-expanding material." Does not want "poems about pets, nature, romantic love, or the occult. Sex and violence themes not welcome." Welcomes poetry by teens. *Soul Fountain* is 28 pages, magazine-sized, offset-printed, saddle-stapled. Subscription: $24. Sample: $7. Make checks payable to Hope for the Children Foundation.

HOW TO CONTACT Submit 2-3 poems at a time. Lines/poem: 1 page maximum. Considers previously published poems and simultaneous submissions. Accepts e-mail submissions (pasted into body of message). Poems should be camera-ready. "When e-mailing a submission, it is necessary to include your mailing address. Cover letter not needed. SASE with postal mail submissions is not necessary, but $2 in postage is appreciated." Time between acceptance and publication is up to 1 year. Guidelines available for SASE or on website. Pays 1 contributor's copy.

◐ SOUTH CAROLINA REVIEW

Clemson University, Strode Tower Room 611, Box 340522, Clemson SC 29634-0522. (864) 656-5399. Fax: (864) 656-1345. E-mail: cwayne@clemson.edu. Website: www.clemson.edu/cedp/cudp/scr/scrintro.htm. **Contact:** Wayne Chapman, editor.

HOW TO CONTACT Submit 3-10 poems at a time. No previously published poems or simultaneous submissions. Cover letter is preferred. "Editor prefers a chatty, personal cover letter plus a list of publishing credits. Manuscript format should be according to new MLA Stylesheet." Submissions should be sent "in an 8x10 manila envelope so poems aren't creased." Do not submit during June, July, August, or December. Occasionally publishes theme issues. Responds in 2 months. Pays in 2 contributor's copies. Staff reviews books of poetry.

◑ SOUTH DAKOTA REVIEW

Univ. of South Dakota 414 E. Clark St., Vermillion SD 57069. (605)677-5184. Fax: (605)677-5298. E-mail: sdreview@usd.edu. Website: www.usd.edu/sdreview. **Contact:** Managing Editor. Univ. of South Dakota 414 E. Clark St., Vermillion, SD 57069. (605)677-5184. Fax: (605)677-5298. E-mail: sdreview@usd.edu. Website: www.usd.edu/sdreview. Specialized: American West subjects & work by Western authors. *South Dakota Review*, published quarterly, prints "poetry, fiction, criticism, and scholarly and personal essays. When material warrants, emphasis is on the American West; writers from the West; Western places or subjects. There are frequent issues with no geographical emphasis; periodic special issues on one theme, one place, or one writer." Wants "originality, sophistication, significance, craft—i.e., professional work." Has published poetry by Allan Safarik, Joanna Gardner, Nathaniel Hansen, and Jeanine Stevens. Press run is 500-600 (450 subscribers, half libraries). Single copy: $10; subscription: $30/year, $45/2 years. Sample: $8.

> ◒ *Pushcart* and *Best American Essays* nominees. *Pushcart* and *Best American Essays* nominees.

MAGAZINES NEEDS *South Dakota Review*, published quarterly, prints "poetry, fiction, criticism, and scholarly and personal essays. When material warrants, emphasis is on the American West; writers from the West; Western places or subjects. There are frequent issues with no geographical emphasis; periodic special issues on one theme, one place, or one writer." Wants "originality, sophistication, significance, craft—i.e., professional work." Has published poetry by Allan Safarik, Joanna Gardner, Nathaniel Hansen, and Jeanine Stevens. Press run is 500-600 (450 subscribers, half libraries). Single copy: $10; subscription: $30/year, $45/2 years. Sample: $8.

HOW TO CONTACT Submit up to 5 poems at a time. Postal submission or online submission using submission manager found on website. Cover letter is required. Must include SASE. Reads submissions year round. Time between acceptance and publication is up to 6 months. Sometimes comments on rejected poems. Publishes theme issues. Guide-

lines available for SASE or on website. Responds in 2-3 months ("sometimes longer if still considering manuscript for possible use in a forthcoming issue"). Pays 1 contributor's copy and a one-year subscription. Acquires first North American serial rights and reprint rights.

TIPS Rejects mss because of "careless writing; often careless typing; stories too personal ('I' confessional); aimlessness of plot; unclear or unresolved conflicts; subject matter that editor finds clicheéd, sensationalized, pretentious or trivial. We are trying to use more fiction and more variety."

● SOUTHERN CALIFORNIA REVIEW

3501 Trousdale Pkwy., Mark Taper Hall, THH 355J, University of Southern California, Los Angeles CA 90089-0355. E-mail: scr@college.usc.edu. Website: http://usc.edu/scr. **Contact:** Fiction Editor.

MAGAZINES NEEDS *Southern California Review (SCR)*, published semiannually in the fall and spring, "is the literary journal of the Master of Professional Writing program at the University of Southern California. It has been publishing fiction and poetry since 1982 and now also accepts submissions of creative nonfiction, plays, and screenplays." Accepts poetry in experimental and traditional styles. Features new, emerging, and established authors. Has published poetry by Yevgeny Yevtushenko, Philip Appleman, Tomaz Salamun, Joyce Carol Oates, Bei Ling, and Denise Levertov. *Southern California Review* is about 140 pages, digest-sized, perfect-bound, with a semi-glossy color cover with original artwork. Press run is 1,000. Sample: $10.

HOW TO CONTACT Submit up to 3 poems at a time. Considers simultaneous submissions, "but please note this in the cover letter and notify us immediately if your submission is accepted for publication elsewhere." No previously published poems. Reads submissions year round. Guidelines available for SASE or on website. Responds in 3-6 months. Pays 2 contributor's copies. Rights revert to poets upon publication; "author is asked to cite appearance in *Southern California Review* when the work is published elsewhere."

CONTEST/AWARD OFFERINGS The Ann Stanford Poetry Prize (see separate listing in Contests & Awards).

SOUTHERN HUMANITIES REVIEW

Auburn University, 9088 Haley Center, Auburn University AL 36849. (334)844-9088. E-mail: shrengl@auburn.edu. E-mail: shrsubmissions@auburn.edu. Website: www.auburn.edu/english/shr/home.htm. **Contact:** Karen Beckwith. 9088 Haley Center, Auburn University, AL 36849. (334)844-9088. Fax: (334)844-9027. E-mail: shrengl@auburn.edu; shrsubmissions@auburn.edu. Website: www.auburn.edu/english/shr/home.htm. *Southern Humanities Review*, published quarterly, is "interested in poems of any length, subject, genre. Space is limited, and brief poems are more likely to be accepted. Translations welcome, but also send written permission from the copyright holder." Has published poetry by Donald Hall, Andrew Hudgins, Margaret Gibson, Stephen Dunn, Walt McDonald, and R.T. Smith. *Southern Humanities Review* is 100 pages, digest-sized. Press run is 800. Subscription: $10/year for new subscriber, $18/year. Sample: $5. *Southern Humanities Review* publishes fiction, poetry, and critical essays on the arts, literature, philosophy, religion, and history for a well-read, scholarly audience.

MAGAZINES NEEDS *Southern Humanities Review*, published quarterly, is "interested in poems of any length, subject, genre. Space is limited, and brief poems are more likely to be accepted. Translations welcome, but also send written permission from the copyright holder." Has published poetry by Donald Hall, Andrew Hudgins, Margaret Gibson, Stephen Dunn, Walt McDonald, and R.T. Smith. *Southern Humanities Review* is 100 pages, digest-sized. Press run is 800. Subscription: $10/year for new subscriber, $18/year. Sample: $5.

HOW TO CONTACT Submit 3-5 poems at a time via postal or submissions e-mail. No previously published poems or simultaneous submissions. "Send poems in a business-sized envelope. Include SASE. Avoid sending faint computer printout." Responds in 2 months, "possibly longer in summer." Always sends prepublication galleys. Pays 2 contributor's copies and 2 offprints. Copyright reverts to author upon publication. Reviews books of poetry in approximately 750-1,000 words. Send materials for review consideration.

CONTEST/AWARD OFFERINGS Sponsors the Theodore Christian Hoepfner Award, a $50 prize for the best poem published in a given volume of *Southern Humanities Review*.

TIPS "Send us the ms with SASE. If we like it, we'll take it or we'll recommend changes. If we don't like it, we'll send it back as promptly as possible. Read the journal. Send typewritten, clean copy, carefully proofread. We also award the annual Hoepfner Prize of $100 for the best published essay or short story of the year. Let someone whose opinion you respect read your story and give you an honest appraisal. Rewrite, if necessary, to get the most from your story."

⊙ SOUTHERN POETRY REVIEW

Armstrong Atlantic State Univ., 11935 Abercorn St., Savannah GA 31419. (912)344-3196. E-mail: james.smith@armstrong.edu. Website: www.southernpoetryreview.org. James Smith, Associate Editor. **Contact:** Robert Parham, editor. Member: CLMP. Considers simultaneous submissions (with notification in cover letter); no previously published poems ("previously published" includes poems published or posted online). No e-mail or disk submissions. Cover letter is preferred. "Include SASE for reply; ms returned only if sufficient postage is included." Reads submissions year round. Poems are circulated to an editorial board ("multiple readers, lively discussion and decision-making"). Sometimes comments on rejected poems. Always sends prepublication galleys. Pays 2 contributor's copies. Sponsors annual Guy Owen Contest. See website for guidelines.

○ Work appearing in *Southern Poetry Review* received a 2005 Pushcart Prize and often has poems selected for VerseDaily.org.

MAGAZINES NEEDS *Southern Poetry Review*, published twice a year, is the second oldest poetry journal in the region. Wants "poetry eclectically representative of the genre; no restrictions on form, style, or content." Does not want fiction, essays, or reviews. Has published poetry by Cathy Smith Bowers, Carl Dennis, Robert Morgan, Linda Pastan, Margaret Gibson, and R. T. Smith. *Southern Poetry Review* is 80-88 pages, digest-sized, perfect-bound, with 80 lb. matte cardstock cover with b&w photography, includes ads. Receives about 8,000 poems/year, accepts about 2%. Press run is 1,200. Single copy: $7; subscription: $14 individuals, $18 institutions. Make checks payable to *Southern Poetry Review*.

HOW TO CONTACT Email: james.smith@armstrong.edu. Website: southernpoetryreview.org. Submit 5-7 poems at a time (10 pages maximum). Lines/poem: subject to limitations of space. Considers simultaneous submissions (with notification in cover letter); no previously published poems ("previously published" includes poems published or posted online). No e-mail or disk submissions. Cover letter is preferred. "Include SASE for reply; ms returned only if sufficient postage is included." Reads submissions year round. Time between acceptance and publication is 6 months. Poems are circulated to an editorial board ("multiple readers, lively discussion and decision-making"). Sometimes comments on rejected poems. Guidelines available in magazine, for SASE, by e-mail, or on website. Responds in 2 months. Always sends prepublication galleys. Pays 2 contributor's copies. Acquires one-time rights.

CONTEST/AWARD OFFERINGS Sponsors annual Guy Owen Contest. See website for guidelines.

THE SOUTHERN REVIEW

(225)578-5108. Fax: (225)578-5098. E-mail: southern-review@lsu.edu. Website: www.lsu.edu/tsr. **Contact:** Jeanne Leiby, Editor. Reading period: September1-June 1. All mss. submitted during summer months will be recycled.

MAGAZINES NEEDS *The Southern Review*, published quarterly, "has been committed to finding the next new voices in literature. In our pages were published the early works of Eudora Welty, John Berryman, Delmore Schwartz, Peter Taylor, Randall Jarrell, Mary McCarthy, and Nelson Algren, to name only a few. More recently, we can claim Robert Pinsky, Michael S. Harper, and David Kirby as being among those whom we helped "discover." Has published poetry by Aimee Baker, Wendy Barker, David Bottoms, Nick Courtright, Robert Dana, Oliver de la Paz, Ed Falco, Piotr Florczyk, Rigoberto Gonzalez, Ava Leavell Haymon, and Philip Schultz. *The Southern Review* is 200 pages, digest-sized, flat-spined, with full color cover. Receives about 10,000 poetry submissions/year. Press run is 3,200 (2,100 subscribers, 70% libraries). Subscription: $40. Sample: $12.

HOW TO CONTACT Submit up to 1-5 pages of poetry at a time. No previously published poems. No fax or e-mail submissions. "We do not require a cover letter, but we prefer one giving information about the author and previous publications." Reads submissions September-May. Guidelines available for SASE or on website. Responds in 1-2 months. Pays $25/printed page plus 2 contributor's copies. Acquires first North American serial rights. Staff

reviews books of poetry in 3,000 words, multi-book format. Send materials for review consideration.

TIPS "Careful attention to craftsmanship and technique combined with a developed sense of the creation of story will always make us pay attention."

SOUTH POETRY MAGAZINE

PO BOX 3744, Cookham Maidenhead SL6 9UY, England. E-mail: south@southpoetry.org. Website: www.southmagazine.org. *SOUTH Poetry Magazine*, published biannually in Spring and Autumn, is "for the southern counties of England. Poets from or poems about the South region are particularly welcome, but poets from all over the world are free to submit work on all subjects." Has published poetry by Ian Caws, Stella Davis, Lyn Moir, Elsa Corbluth, Paul Hyland, and Sean Street. *SOUTH* is 68 pages, digest-sized, litho-printed, saddle-stapled, with gloss-laminated duotone cover. Receives about 1,500 poems/year, accepts about 120. Press run is 350 (250 subscribers). Single copy: £5.60; subscription: £10/year, £18/2 years. Make checks (in sterling) payable to *SOUTH Poetry Magazine*.

"SOUTH is run by a management team. The current team is: Anne Clegg, Tim Harris, Peter Keeble, Patrick Osada, Tony Turner, and Chrissie Williams."

TIPS "Buy the magazine. Then it will still be there to consider and publish your work, and you'll get the idea of the sort of work we publish. These are basic steps, and both are essential."

SOUTHWESTERN AMERICAN LITERATURE

Center for the Study of the Southwest, Brazos Hall, Texas State University-San Marcos, San Marcos TX 78666-4616. (512)245-2224. Fax: (512)245-7462. E-mail: swpublications@txstate.edu. Website: http://swrhc.txstate.edu/cssw/. **Contact:** Twister Marquiss, assistant editor; Mark Busby, co-editor; Dick Maurice Heaberlin, co-editor. Center for the Study of the Southwest, Brazos Hall, Texas State University-San Marcos, San Marcos, TX. 78666-4616. (512)245-2224. Fax: (512)245-7462. E-mail:swpublications@txstate.edu. Website: http://swrhc.txstate.edu/cssw/. **Contact:** Twister Marquiss, assistant editor; Mark Busby, co-editor; Dick Maurice Heaberlin, co-editor. "We publish fiction, nonfiction, poetry, literary criticism and book reviews. Generally speaking, we want material covering the Greater Southwest or material written by Southwest writers. Ethnic/multicultural, literary, mainstream, regional. "No science fiction or romance." Receives 10-20 unsolicited poems/month. Accepts 5-10 poems/issue; 10-20 poems/year. Publishes 6 months after acceptance. Publishes 1-2 new writers/year. Recently published work by Sherwin Bitsui, Alison Hawthorne Deming, Keith Ekiss, Sara Marie Ortiz, Karla K. Morton, Jeffrey C. Alfier, Carol Hamilton, and Larry D. Thomas. Length: 100 lines max; average length: 15-25 lines. Also publishes fiction, literary essays, literary criticism. Sometimes comments on rejected mss.

MAGAZINES NEEDS "We publish fiction, nonfiction, poetry, literary criticism and book reviews. Generally speaking, we want material covering the Greater Southwest or material written by Southwest writers. Ethnic/multicultural, literary, mainstream, regional. "No science fiction or romance." Receives 10-20 unsolicited poems/month. Accepts 5-10 poems/issue; 10-20 poems/year. Publishes 6 months after acceptance. Publishes 1-2 new writers/year. Recently published work by Sherwin Bitsui, Alison Hawthorne Deming, Keith Ekiss, Sara Marie Ortiz, Karla K. Morton, Jeffrey C. Alfier, Carol Hamilton, and Larry D. Thomas. Length: 100 lines max; average length: 15-25 lines. Also publishes fiction, literary essays, literary criticism. Sometimes comments on rejected mss.

HOW TO CONTACT Include cover letter, estimated word count, 2-5 line bio and list of publications. Accepts email submissions as attachments. Include bio and list of publications in email. Responds in 3-6 months to mss. Sample copy for $10. Writer's guidelines free.

TIPS "We look for crisp language, an interesting approach to material; a regional approach is desired but not required. Read widely, write often, revise carefully. We are looking for stories that probe the relationship between the tradition of Southwestern American literature and the writer's own imagination in creative ways. We seek stories that move beyond stereotype and approach the larger defining elements and also ones that, as William Faulkner noted in his Nobel Prize acceptance speech, treat subjects central to good literature—the old verities of the human heart, such as honor and courage and pity and suffering, fear and humor, love and sorrow."

◑ SOUTHWEST REVIEW

P.O. Box 750374, Dallas TX 75275-0374. Website: www.smu.edu/southwestreview. P.O. Box 750374, Dallas TX 75275-0374. (214)768-1037. Fax: (214)768-1408. E-mail: swr@smu.edu. Website: www.smu.edu/southwestreview. **Contact:** Jennifer Cranfill, senior editor. Poetry published in *Southwest Review* has been included in The Best American Poetry and The Pushcart Prize. *Southwest Review*, published quarterly, prints fiction, essays, poetry, and occasional interviews. "We always suggest that potential contributors read several issues of the magazine to see for themselves what we like. We demand very high quality in our poems; we accept both traditional and experimental writing, but avoid unnecessary obscurity and private symbolism. We place no arbitrary limits on length but find shorter poems easier to fit into our format than longer ones. We have no specific limitations as to theme. Poems tend to be lyric and narrative free verse combining a strong voice with powerful topics or situations. Diction is accessible and content often conveys a strong sense of place." Has published poetry by Albert Goldbarth, John Hollander, Mary Jo Salter, James Hoggard, Dorothea Tanning, and Michael Rosen. *Southwest Review* is 144 pages, digest-sized, professionally printed, perfect-bound, with matte text stock cover. Receives about 1,000 poetry submissions/year, accepts about 32. Press run is 1,500. Subscription: $24. Sample: $6.

MAGAZINES NEEDS *Southwest Review*, published quarterly, prints fiction, essays, poetry, and occasional interviews. "We always suggest that potential contributors read several issues of the magazine to see for themselves what we like. We demand very high quality in our poems; we accept both traditional and experimental writing, but avoid unnecessary obscurity and private symbolism. We place no arbitrary limits on length but find shorter poems easier to fit into our format than longer ones. We have no specific limitations as to theme. Poems tend to be lyric and narrative free verse combining a strong voice with powerful topics or situations. Diction is accessible and content often conveys a strong sense of place." Has published poetry by Albert Goldbarth, John Hollander, Mary Jo Salter, James Hoggard, Dorothea Tanning, and Michael Rosen. *Southwest Review* is 144 pages, digest-sized, professionally printed, perfect-bound, with matte text stock cover. Receives about 1,000 poetry submissions/year, accepts about 32.

Press run is 1,500. Subscription: $24. Sample: $6.

HOW TO CONTACT No previously published poems or simultaneous submissions. Submit by mail or on website. Please note there is a $2 administrative fee for online submissions. Mailed manuscripts must be typed and should include SASE for a response. Guidelines available for SASE or on website. Responds within 1 month. Always sends prepublication galleys. Pays cash plus contributor's copies.

CONTEST/AWARD OFFERINGS The Elizabeth Matchett Stover Memorial Award presents $250 to the author of the best poem or groups of poems (chosen by editors) published in the preceding year. Also offers The Morton Marr Poetry Prize (see separate listing in Contests & Awards).

TIPS "Despite the title, we are not a regional magazine. Before you submit your work, it's a good idea to take a look at recent issues to familiarize yourself with the magazine. We strongly advise all writers to include a cover letter. Keep your cover letter professional and concise and don't include extraneous personal information, a story synopsis, or a resume. When authors ask what we look for in a strong story submission the answer is simple regardless of graduate degrees in creative writing, workshops, or whom you know. We look for good writing, period."

◑ SOU'WESTER

Box 1438, Dept. of English, Southern Illinois University, Edwardsville IL 62026-1438. (618)650-3190. Fax: (618)650-3509. E-mail: sw@siue.edu. Website: www.siue.edu/ENGLISH/SW. **Contact:** Adrian Matejka. Box 1438, Dept. of English, Southern Illinois University, Edwardsville IL 62026-1438. (618)650-3190. Fax: (618)650-3509. E-mail: sw@siue.edu. Website: www.siue.edu/ENGLISH/SW. Established 1960. **Contact:** Adrian Matejka, poetry editor.

MAGAZINES NEEDS *Sou'wester* appears biannually in spring and fall. "We lean toward poetry with strong imagery, successful association of images, and skillful use of figurative language." Has published poetry by Robert Wrigley, Beckian Fritz Goldberg, Eric Pankey, Betsy Sholl, and Angie Estes. *Sou'wester* has 30-40 pages of poetry in each digest-sized, 100-page issue. *Sou'wester* is professionally printed, flat-spined, with textured matte card cover, press run is 300 for 500 subscribers of which 50 are libraries. Receives 3,000 poems (from 600 poets) each year, accepts 36-40, has a 6-month backlog. Subscription: $18/2 issues.

Sample: $8.

HOW TO CONTACT Submit up to 5 poems via online journal manager. Accepts simultaneous submissions. No previously published poems. No e-mail submissions. Reads submissions from September 1 through May 1. Responds in 3 months. Pays 2 contributor's copies and one-year subscription. Acquires all rights. Returns rights. Editor comments on rejected poems "usually, in the case of those that we almost accept."

THE SOW'S EAR POETRY REVIEW

E-mail: sowsearpoetry@yahoo.com. Website: www.sows-ear.kitenet.net. **Contact:** Kristin Camitta Zimet. 217 Brookneill Dr., Winchester, VA 22602. E-mail: sowsearpoetry@yahoo.com. Website: www.sows-ear.kitenet.net. *The Sow's Ear* welcomes submissions of fine poetry of any style and length. Wants work that is carefully crafted, keenly felt, and freshly perceived, poems with voice, specificity, delight in language, and a meaning that unfolds. "We print occasional features that stretch our understanding of poetry- interviews with poets, essays, or reviews." Subscriptions: $27/1 year. Samples: $8."The Sow's Ear prints fine poetry of all styles and lengths, complemented by black and white art. We also welcome reviews, interviews, and essays related to poetry. We are open to group submissions. Our 'Crossover' section features poetry married to any other art form, including prose, music, and visual media."

HOW TO CONTACT Send up to five poems with a brief bio and SASE. Postal submissions only. Simultaneous submissions are allowed. "Poems are eligible if they have never appeared in a magazine, and you hold rights." Responds within 3 months.

TIPS "We like work that is carefully crafted, keenly felt, and freshly perceived. We respond to poems with voice, a sense of place, delight in language, and a meaning that unfolds. We look for prose that opens new dimensions to appreciating poetry."

◑Ⓢ SPACE AND TIME

458 Elizabeth Ave., Somerset NJ 08873. E-mail: nytebird45@aol.com. Website: www.spaceandtimemagazine.com. **Contact:** Linda D. Addison. (Specialized: science fiction/fantasy, horror)458 Elizabeth Ave., #5348, Somerset, NJ 08873. Website: www.spaceandtimemagazine.com. Established 1966. **Contact:** Linda D. Addison, poetry editor. *Space and Time* was about 100 pages, digest-sized, perfect-bound; however, the

magazine will be reformatted to 48 pages, magazine-sized, web press printed on 50 lb. stock and saddle-stapled with glossy card cover and interior b&w illustrations. Receives about 500 poems/year, accepts 5%. Press run is 2,000 (200 subscribers, 10 libraries, 1,200 shelf sales). Single copy: $5; subscription: $10. Sample: $6.50. Magazine. 8½x11, 48 pages, matte paper, glossy cover. Contains illustrations. "We love stories that blend elements—horror and science fiction, fantasy with SF elements, etc. We challenge writers to try something new and send us their unclassifiable works—what other publications reject because the work doesn't fit in their 'pigeonholes.'" Quarterly. Receives 250 mss/reading period. Accepts 8 mss/issue; 32 mss/year. Only open during announced reading periods. Check website to see if submissions are open. **Publishes 2-4 new writers/year.** Published PD Cacek, AR Morlan, Jeffrey Ford, Charles De Lint and Jack Ketchum. Length: 1,000-10,000 words. Average length: 6,500 words. Publishes short shorts. Average length of short shorts: 1,000 words. Also publishes poetry, occasional book reviews. Publication is copyrighted.

MAGAZINES NEEDS *Space and Time* is a quarterly magazine that publishes "primarily science fiction/fantasy/horror; some related poetry and articles. We do not want to see anything that doesn't fit science fiction/fantasy/weird genres." Has published poetry by G. O. Clark, Corinne de Winter, Bruce Boston and Ann K. Schwader.

HOW TO CONTACT Submit up to 4 poems at a time. No previously published poems or simultaneous submissions. Time between acceptance and publication is up to 9 months. Often comments on rejected poems. Guidelines available for SASE or on website. Responds in up to 6 weeks, "longer if recommended." Pays 1¢/word ($5 minimum) plus 2 contributor's copies. Acquires first North American serial rights.

⦿⦿⑤ SPACEPORTS & SPIDERSILK

Website: www.samsdotpublishing.com. P.O. Box 782, Cedar Rapids IA 52406-0782. E-mail: spacesilk@yahoo.com. Website: www.samsdotpublishing.com. Established 2002. **Contact:** Marcie Lynn Tentchoff, editor. Member: The Speculative Literature Foundation. *Spaceports & Spidersilk*, published quarterly online, prints "fantasy, science fiction, sword and sorcery, alternate history, myths/folktales, spooky short sto-

ries, poems, illustrations, puzzles, nonfiction articles, and movie and book reviews, all for a reading audience of 9-18 years old." Wants "fantasy, science fiction, spooky horror, and speculative poetry" appropriate to age group. Does not want "horror with excessive blood and gore." Considers poetry by children and teens. Has published poetry by Bruce Boston, Karen A. Romanko, Guy Belleranti, Aurelio Rico Lopez III, and Kristine Ong Muslim. Receives about 180 poems/year, accepts about 30 (16%).

MAGAZINES NEEDS *Spaceports & Spidersilk*, published quarterly online, prints "fantasy, science fiction, sword and sorcery, alternate history, myths/folktales, spooky short stories, poems, illustrations, puzzles, nonfiction articles, and movie and book reviews, all for a reading audience of 9-18 years old." Wants "fantasy, science fiction, spooky horror, and speculative poetry" appropriate to age group. Does not want "horror with excessive blood and gore." Considers poetry by children and teens. Has published poetry by Bruce Boston, Karen A. Romanko, Guy Belleranti, Aurelio Rico Lopez III, and Kristine Ong Muslim. Receives about 180 poems/year, accepts about 30 (16%).

HOW TO CONTACT Submit up to 5 poems at a time. Lines/poem: 25 maximum. Considers previously published poems; no simultaneous submissions. Accepts e-mail submissions only (pasted into body of message). "Submission should include snail mail address and a short (1-2 lines) bio." Reads submissions year round. Submit seasonal poems 6 months in advance. Time between acceptance and publication is 1-3 months. Often comments on rejected poems. Guidelines available on website. Responds in 4-6 weeks. Pays $2/original poem, $1/reprint. Acquires first, exclusive worldwide electronic rights for 90 days. Reviews books/chapbooks of poetry. Send materials for review consideration to Tyree Campbell.

⦿⦿ SPEEDPOETS ZINE

86 Hawkwood St., Brisbane QL 4122, Australia. (61)(7)3420-6092. E-mail: geenunn@yahoo.com.au. Website: http://speedpoets.com. **Contact:** Graham Nunn, editor. 86 Hawkwood St., Brisbane, QL4122, Australia. (61)(7)3420-6092. E-mail: geenunn@yahoo.com.au. Website: http://speedpoets.com. **Contact:** Graham Nunn, editor. *SpeedPoets Zine*, published monthly, showcases "the community of poets that perform at the monthly SpeedPoets readings in Bris-

bane, as well as showcasing poets from all around the world." Wants "shorter, experimental pieces." Does not want long submissions. Has published poetry by Robert Smith, Steve Kilbey, Brentley Frazer, Jayne Fenton Keane, Graham Nunn, and Marie Kazalia. *SpeedPoets Zine* is 28 pages, digest-sized, photocopied, folded and stapled, with color cover. Press run is 100. Single copy: $5 for overseas/interstate contributors. Payable to Graham Nunn via PayPal (in AUD only, or send well-concealed cash).

MAGAZINES NEEDS *SpeedPoets Zine*, published monthly, showcases "the community of poets that perform at the monthly SpeedPoets readings in Brisbane, as well as showcasing poets from all around the world." Wants "shorter, experimental pieces." Does not want long submissions. Has published poetry by Robert Smith, Steve Kilbey, Brentley Frazer, Jayne Fenton Keane, Graham Nunn, and Marie Kazalia. *SpeedPoets Zine* is 28 pages, digest-sized, photocopied, folded and stapled, with color cover. Press run is 100. Single copy: $5 for overseas/interstate contributors. Payable to Graham Nunn via PayPal (in AUD only, or send well-concealed cash).

HOW TO CONTACT Submit 2 poems at a time. Lines/poem: 25 maximum. Considers previously published poems. Accepts e-mail submissions (pasted into body of message—no attachments); no disk submissions. Cover letter is preferred. Reads submissions year round. Time between acceptance and publication is 2 weeks. Sometimes comments on rejected poems. Guidelines available by e-mail. Responds in 2 weeks. Rights revert to poet upon publication.

◑ ⊖ SPIDER

Carus Publishing, 70 E. Lake St., Suite 300, Chicago IL 60601. Website: www.cricketmag.com; www.spidermagkids.com. **Contact:** Alice Letvin, editorial director; Margaret Mincks, associate editor. Carus Publishing, 70 E. Lake St., Suite 300, Chicago, IL 60601. Website: www.cricketmag.com; www.spidermagkids.com. **Contacts:** Alice Letvin, editorial director; Margaret Mincks, associate editor. *SPIDER*, published monthly, is a reading and activity magazine for children ages 6-9. "It's specially written and edited for children who have reached that amazing age when they first get excited about reading on their own." Wants "serious and humorous poetry, nonsense rhymes." *SPIDER* is 38 pages, 8x10, staple-bound. Receives more than

1,200 submissions/month, accepts 25-30. Circulation is 70,000. Subscription: $35.97/year (12 issues). Sample: $5; sample pages available on website.

MAGAZINES NEEDS *SPIDER*, published monthly, is a reading and activity magazine for children ages 6-9. "It's specially written and edited for children who have reached that amazing age when they first get excited about reading on their own." Wants "serious and humorous poetry, nonsense rhymes." *SPIDER* is 38 pages, 8x10, staple-bound. Receives more than 1,200 submissions/month, accepts 25-30. Circulation is 70,000. Subscription: $35.97/year (12 issues). Sample: $5; sample pages available on website.

HOW TO CONTACT Submit no more than 5 poems at a time. Lines/poem: no more than 20. Considers previously published poems. Responds in 6 months. Guidelines available for SASE or on website. Pays up to $3/line on publications. Acquires North American publication rights for previously published poems; rights vary for unpublished poems.

TIPS "Before attempting to illustrate for *SPIDER*, be sure to familiarize yourself with this age group, and read several issues of the magazine. Please do not query first."

◑ SPILLWAY

P.O. Box 7887, Huntington Beach CA 92615-7887. (714)968-0905. E-mail: mifanwy.kaiser@gmail.com; spillway2@tebotbach.org. Website: www.tebotbach.org. **Contact:** Mifanwy Kaiswer, publisher; Susan Terris, editor. Published semi-annually in June and December, Spillway celebrates "writing's diversity and power to affect our lives." Open to all voices, schools, and tendencies. "We publish poetry, translations, reviews, essays, black-and-white photography, and color artwork and photography for the cover." Spillway is about 125 pages, digest-sized, attractively printed, perfect-bound, with 2-color or 4-color card cover. Press run is 2,000. Accepts simultaneous submissions. Single copy: $9; subscription plus $3 shipping and handling; one-year subscription $16 includes shipping and handling; two-year subscription $28. Make checks payable to Tebot Bach with Spillway in the notation line. Editorial Comments "We recommend ordering a sample copy before you submit, though acceptance does not depend upon purchasing a sample copy."

○ "We recommend ordering a sample copy before you submit, though acceptance does not depend upon purchasing a sample copy."

HOW TO CONTACT Submit 3-5 poems at a time (6 pages maximum total). Theme for June 2011 issue: 'My First Time'. Theme for December 2011 issue: 'Crossing Borders.' Theme for June 2012 issue: 'Games People Play.' For more complete information about upcoming themes and submission periods, check our website. E-mail submissions only to spillway2@tebotbach.org (Microsoft Word attachment); no disk or fax submissions. Cover letter is required. Include brief bio. Responds in up to 6 months. Pays 1 contributor's copy. Acquires one-time rights. Reviews books of poetry in 500-2,500 words. Accepts queries by e-mail. Send materials for review consideration. Email: mifanwy.kaiser@gmail.com; spillway2@tebotbach.org. Website: www.tebotbach.org. Contacts: Mifanwy Kaiser, publisher; Susan Terris, editor. Address: P.O. Box 7887, Huntington Beach CA 92615-7887.

◑ SPINNING JENNY

c/o Black Dress Press, P.O. Box 1067, New York NY 10014. E-mail: editor@spinning-jenny.com. Website: www.spinning-jenny.com. **Contact:** C.E. Harrison, editor. c/o Black Dress Press, P.O. Box 1067, New York, NY 10014. E-mail: editor@spinning-jenny.com. Website: www.spinning-jenny.com. **Contact:** C.E. Harrison, editor. *Spinning Jenny*, published once/year in the fall (usually September), has published poetry by Abraham Smith, Cynthia Cruz, Michael Morse, and Joyelle McSweeney. *Spinning Jenny* is 96 pages, digest-sized, perfect-bound, with heavy card cover. "We accept less than 5% of unsolicited submissions." Press run is 1,000. Single copy: $8; subscription: $15 for 2 issues.

MAGAZINES NEEDS *Spinning Jenny*, published once/year in the fall (usually September), has published poetry by Abraham Smith, Cynthia Cruz, Michael Morse, and Joyelle McSweeney. *Spinning Jenny* is 96 pages, digest-sized, perfect-bound, with heavy card cover. "We accept less than 5% of unsolicited submissions." Press run is 1,000. Single copy: $8; subscription: $15 for 2 issues.

HOW TO CONTACT Submit up to 6 poems at a time. No previously published poems or simultaneous submissions. Accepts submissions online only (see website for guidelines). Reads submissions

September 15-May 15 only. Seldom comments on rejected poems. Guidelines available on website. Responds within 4 months. Pays 3 contributor's copies. Authors retain rights.

◑ SPITBALL: THE LITERARY BASEBALL MAGAZINE

5560 Fox Rd., Cincinnati OH 45239. Website: www. spitballmag.com. **Contact:** Mike Shannon, editor-in-chief. 5560 Fox Rd., Cincinnati, OH 45239. Website: www.spitballmag.com. Contact: Mike Shannon, editor-in-chief. *Spitball: The Literary Baseball Magazine*, published semiannually, is "a unique magazine devoted to poetry, fiction, and book reviews exclusively about baseball. Newcomers are very welcome, but remember that you have to know the subject; we do, and our readers do. Perhaps a good place to start for beginners is one's personal reactions to the game, a game, a player, etc., and take it from there." Writers submitting to *Spitball* for the first time must buy a sample copy (waived for subscribers). "This is a one-time-only fee, which we regret, but economic reality dictates that we insist those who wish to be published in *Spitball* help support it, at least at this minimum level." *Spitball* is 96 pages, digest-sized, computer-typeset, perfect-bound. Receives about 1,000 submissions/year, accepts about 40. Press run is 1,000. Subscription: $12. Sample: $6. *Spitball: The Literary Baseball Magazine*, published semiannually, is "a unique magazine devoted to poetry, fiction, and book reviews exclusively about baseball. Newcomers are very welcome, but remember that you have to know the subject; we do, and our readers do. Perhaps a good place to start for beginners is one's personal reactions to the game, a game, a player, etc., and take it from there." Writers submitting to *Spitball* for the first time must buy a sample copy (waived for subscribers). "This is a one-time-only fee, which we regret, but economic reality dictates that we insist those who wish to be published in *Spitball* help support it, at least at this minimum level." *Spitball* is 96 pages, digest-sized, computer-typeset, perfect-bound. Receives about 1,000 submissions/year, accepts about 40. Press run is 1,000. Subscription: $12. Sample: $6.

HOW TO CONTACT Submit a "batch" of poems at a time ("we prefer to use several of same poet in an issue rather than a single poem"). Lines/poem: open. No previously published poems or simultaneous submissions. Cover letter is required. Include brief bio and SASE. "Many times we are able to publish accepted work almost immediately." Pays 2 contributor's copies."All material published in *Spitball* will be automatically considered for inclusion in the next *Best of Spitball* anthology."1) Poems submitted to *Spitball* will be considered automatically for Poem of the Month, to appear on the website. 2) "We sponsor the Casey Award (for best baseball book of the year) and hold the Casey Awards Banquet in late February or early March. Any chapbook of baseball poetry should be sent to us for consideration for the 'Casey' plaque that we award to the winner each year."

ADDITIONAL INFORMATION Tips: "Take the subject seriously. We do. In other words, get a clue (if you don't already have one) about the subject and about the poetry that has already been done and published about baseball. Learn from it—think about what you can add to the canon that is original and fresh—and don't assume that just anybody with the feeblest of efforts can write a baseball poem worthy of publication. And most importantly, stick with it. Genius seldom happens on the first try."

TIPS "Take the subject seriously. We do. In other words, get a clue (if you don't already have one) about the subject and about the poetry that has already been done and published about baseball. Learn from it— think about what you can add to the canon that is original and fresh—and don't assume that just anybody with the feeblest of efforts can write a baseball poem worthy of publication. And most importantly, stick with it. Genius seldom happens on the first try."

●O SPLIZZ

4 St. Marys Rise, Burry Port, Carms SA16 0SH, Wales. E-mail: splizz@tiscali.co.uk; splizzmag@yahoo.co.uk. **Contact:** Amanda Morgan, editor. 4 St. Marys Rise, Burry Port, Carms SA16 0SH, Wales. E-mail:splizzmag@yahoo.co.uk. **Contact:** Amanda Morgan, editor. *Splizz*, published quarterly, features poetry, prose, reviews of contemporary music, and background to poets. Wants "any kind of poetry. We have no restrictions regarding style, length, subjects." Does not want "anything racist or homophobic." Has published Colin Cross (UK), Anders Carson (Canada), Paul Truttman (U.S.), Jan Hansen (Portugal), and Gregory Arena (Italy). *Splizz* is 60-64 pages, A5, saddle-stapled, includes ads. Receives about 200-300 poems/year, accepts about 90%. Press run is 150 (35 subscribers). Single copy: £2 UK; subscription: £8 UK.

Email for current rates. Payments accepted in cash or paypal to splizz@tiscali.co.uk. No checks please.

MAGAZINES NEEDS *Splizz*, published quarterly, features poetry, prose, reviews of contemporary music, and background to poets. Wants "any kind of poetry. We have no restrictions regarding style, length, subjects." Does not want "anything racist or homophobic." Has published Colin Cross (UK), Anders Carson (Canada), Paul Truttman (U.S.), Jan Hansen (Portugal), and Gregory Arena (Italy). *Splizz* is 60-64 pages, A5, saddle-stapled, includes ads. Receives about 200-300 poems/year, accepts about 90%. Press run is 150 (35 subscribers). Single copy: £2 UK; subscription: £8 UK. Email for current rates. Payments accepted in cash or paypal to splizz@tiscali. co.uk. No checks please.

HOW TO CONTACT Submit 5 poems at a time. No previously published poems or simultaneous submissions. Accepts e-mail submissions (as attachment). Cover letter is required. Include short bio. Typed submissions preferred. Name and address must be included on each page of submitted work. Include SAE with IRCs. Time between acceptance and publication is 4 months. Often comments on rejected poems. **Charges criticism fee.** "Just enclose SAE/IRC for response, and allow 1-2 months for delivery. For those sending IRCs, please ensure that they have been correctly stamped by your post office." Guidelines available in magazine, for SASE (or SAE and IRC), or by e-mail. Responds in 2 months. Sometimes sends prepublication galleys. Reviews books/chapbooks of poetry or other magazines in 50-300 words. Send materials for review consideration. E-mail for further enquiries.

● THE SPOON RIVER POETRY REVIEW

4241 Department of English, Illinois State University, Normal IL 61790-4241. E-mail: krhotel@ilstu.edu. Website: www.litline.org/spoon. **Contact:** Kirstin Hotelling Zona, editor. 4241 Department of English, Illinois State University, Normal, IL 61790-4241. E-mail: krhotel@ilstu.edu. Website: www.litline.org/spoon. **Contact:** Kirstin Hotelling Zona, editor. *The Spoon River Poetry Review,* published biannually, is "one of the nation's oldest continuously published poetry journals. We seek to publish the best of all poetic genres, experimental as well as mainstream, and are proud of our commitment to regional as well as international poets and readers. *Spoon River* includes, alongside poems from emerging and established poets, original artwork and reviews solicited from poet-critics and translators. These essays situate selected books with regard to current poetic trends and conversations. In addition to poems across the United States and the world (in English translation), each issue publishes a *SRPR* Illinois poet feature (12-18 pages of unpublished poetry, an interview, and bio). The Summer/Fall issue also spotlights the winner and runners-up of our highly competitive editor's prize contest." *The Spoon River Poetry Review* is 128 pages, digest-sized, laser-set, with card cover. Receives about 3,000 poems/month, accepts 1%. Press run is 1,500. Subscription: $16. Sample: $10 (includes guidelines).

MAGAZINES NEEDS *The Spoon River Poetry Review*, published biannually, is "one of the nation's oldest continuously published poetry journals. We seek to publish the best of all poetic genres, experimental as well as mainstream, and are proud of our commitment to regional as well as international poets and readers. *Spoon River* includes, alongside poems from emerging and established poets, original artwork and reviews solicited from poet-critics and translators. These essays situate selected books with regard to current poetic trends and conversations. In addition to poems across the United States and the world (in English translation), each issue publishes a *SRPR* Illinois poet feature (12-18 pages of unpublished poetry, an interview, and bio).The Summer/Fall issue also spotlights the winner and runners-up of our highly competitive editor's prize contest." *The Spoon River Poetry Review* is 128 pages, digest-sized, laser-set, with card cover. Receives about 3,000 poems/month, accepts 1%. Press run is 1,500. Subscription: $16. Sample: $10 (includes guidelines).

HOW TO CONTACT Submit 3-5 poems at a time. Accepts simultaneous submissions "as long as you notify us immediately if a poem has been accepted elsewhere." Include name, e-mail, and address on every poem. Accepts submissions September 15-April 15. Comments on rejected poems "many times, if a poet is promising." Guidelines available in magazine or on website. Responds in 3 months. Pays a year's subscription. Acquires first North American serial rights. Reviews books of poetry. Send materials for review consideration.

CONTEST/AWARD OFFERINGS Sponsors *The Spoon River Poetry Review* Editor's Prize Contest (see separate listing in Contests & Awards).

SPOUT MAGAZINE

P.O. Box 581067, Minneapolis MN 55458-1067. E-mail: editors@spoutpress.org. Website: www.spout-press.com. **Contact:** Michelle Filkins, Poetry Editor. As the counterpart to Spout Press, Spout magazine features poetry, art, fiction, and thought pieces with diverse voices and styles.

> "We are currently accepting submissions of poetry, short stories, essays, opinion, art, and cartoons — *basically anything creative that can be affixed to an 8 1/2 x 11 page* — **for our latest magazine**. Follow our guidelines online."

MAGAZINES NEEDS *Spout*, published approximately 3 times/year, aims to provide "a paper community of unique expression." Wants "poetry of the imagination; poetry that surprises. We enjoy the surreal, the forceful, the political, the expression of confusion." No light verse, archaic forms or language. Has published poetry by Gillian McCain, Larissa Szporluk, Matt Hart, Joanna Fuhrman, Josie Rawson, and Richard Siken. *Spout* is 40-60 pages, saddle-stapled, with cardstock or glossy cover (different color each issue). Receives about 400-450 poems/year, accepts about 10%. Press run is 200-250 (35-40 subscribers, 100-150 shelf sales). Single copy: $5; subscription: $15.

HOW TO CONTACT Submit up to 5 poems at a time. Considers previously published poems and simultaneous submissions. Cover letter is preferred. Time between acceptance and publication is 2-3 months. "Poems are reviewed by 2 of 3 editors; those selected for final review are read again by all three." Seldom comments on rejected poems. Guidelines available for SASE or on website. Responds in 4 months. Pays 1 contributor's copy.

SPRING: THE JOURNAL OF THE E.E. CUMMINGS SOCIETY

129 Lake Huron Hall, Grand Valley State University, Allendale MI 49401-9403. E-mail: websterm@gvsu.edu. Website: www.gvsu.edu/english/cummings/In-dex.html. **Contact:** Michael Webster, editor. 129 Lake Huron Hall, Grand Valley State University, Allendale, MI 49401-9403. E-mail: websterm@gvsu.edu. Website: www.gvsu.edu/english/cummings/Index.html. **Contact:** Michael Webster, editor. *Spring: The Journal of the E.E. Cummings Society*, published annually (usually in the fall), is designed "to broaden the audience for

E.E. Cummings, and to explore various facets of his life and art." **Contributors are required to subscribe.** Wants poems in the spirit of Cummings, primarily poems of 1 page or less. Does not want "amateurish" work. Has published poetry by John Tagliabue, Jacqueline Vaught Brogan, and Gerald Locklin. *Spring* is about 180 pages, digest-sized, offset-printed, perfect-bound, with light cardstock cover. Press run is 400 (200 subscribers, 25 libraries, 200 shelf sales). Subscription or sample: $17.50.

MAGAZINES NEEDS *Spring: The Journal of the E.E. Cummings Society*, published annually (usually in the fall), is designed "to broaden the audience for E.E. Cummings, and to explore various facets of his life and art." **Contributors are required to subscribe.** Wants poems in the spirit of Cummings, primarily poems of 1 page or less. Does not want "amateurish" work. Has published poetry by John Tagliabue, Jacqueline Vaught Brogan, and Gerald Locklin. *Spring* is about 180 pages, digest-sized, offset-printed, perfect-bound, with light cardstock cover. Press run is 400 (200 subscribers, 25 libraries, 200 shelf sales). Subscription or sample: $17.50.

HOW TO CONTACT No previously published poems or simultaneous submissions. Accepts e-mail (as attachment) submissions. Cover letter is required. Reads submissions May-August only. Seldom comments on rejected poems. Guidelines available for SASE. Responds in 6 months.

● STAND MAGAZINE

School of English, University of Leeds, Leeds LS2 9JT, United Kingdom. (44)(113)343-4794. E-mail: stand@leeds.ac.uk. Website: www.standmagazine.org. School of English, University of Leeds, Leeds LS2 9JT England. 00 (44)(0)113 3434794. E-mail: stand@leeds. ac.uk. Website: www.standmagazine.org. Established 1952 (by Jon Silkin). **Contact:** Jon Glover and John Whale, editors. (U.S. Editor: David Latané, Dept. of English, Virginia Commonwealth University, Richmond VA 23284-2005; dlatane@vcu.edu.)"Quarterly literary magazine."

◌ "U.S. submissions can be made through the Virginia office (see separate listing)."

MAGAZINES NEEDS *Stand Magazine*, published quarterly, "seeks more subscriptions from U.S. readers and also hopes that the magazine will be seriously treated as an alternative platform to American literary journals." *Library Journal* calls *Stand* "one of England's best, liveliest, and truly imaginative little magazines." Has published poetry by John Ashbery, Mary Jo Bang, Brian Henry, and Michael Mott. *Stand* is about 64 pages, A5 (landscape), professionally printed on smooth stock, flat-spined, with matte color cover, includes ads. Press run is 2,000 (1,000+ subscribers, 600 libraries). Subscription: $49.50. Sample: $13.

HOW TO CONTACT No fax or e-mail submissions. Cover letter is required, "assuring us that work is not also being offered elsewhere." Publishes theme issues. Always sends prepublication galleys. Pays £20 for first poem and £5 for each subsequent poem over 6 lines, and one contributor's copy. Acquires first world serial rights for 3 months after publication. If work appears elsewhere, *Stand* must be credited. Reviews books of poetry in 3,000-4,000 words, multi-book format. Send materials for review consideration.

ST. ANTHONY MESSENGER

(Specialized: Catholic; spirituality/inspirational) 28 W. Liberty St., Cincinnati OH 45202-6498. Fax: (513)241-0399. Website: www.americancatholic.org. **Contact:** Christopher Heffron, poetry editor. We publish articles which report on a changing church and world, opinion pieces written from the perspective of Christian faith and values, personality profiles, and fiction which entertains and informs.

MAGAZINES NEEDS *St. Anthony Messenger*, published monthly, is a mgazine for Catholic families, mostly with children in grade school, high school, or college. Some issues feature a poetry page that uses poems appropriate for their readership. Poetry submissions are always welcome despite limited need. "We seek to publish accessible poetry of high quality. Spiritual/inspirational in nature a plus, but not required." Considers poetry by young writers, ages 14 and older. *St. Anthony Messenger* is 60 pages. Press run 280,000. Sample: free for 9x12 SASE.

HOW TO CONTACT Submit "a few" poems at a time. Lines/poem: under 25. No previously published poems. Accepts fax and e-mail submissions. "Please include your phone number and a SASE with your submission. Do not send us your entire collection of poetry. Poems must be original." Submit seasonal poems several months in advance. Guidelines available for SASE, by fax, or on website. Pays

$2/line on acceptance plus 2 contributor's copies. Acquires first worldwide serial rights.

TIPS "The freelancer should consider why his or her proposed article would be appropriate for us, rather than for *Redbook* or *Saturday Review*. We treat human problems of all kinds, but from a religious perspective. Articles should reflect Catholic theology, spirituality, and employ a Catholic terminology and vocabulary. We need more articles on prayer, scripture, Catholic worship. Get authoritative information (not merely library research); we want interviews with experts. Write in popular style; use lots of examples, stories, and personal quotes. Word length is an important consideration."

❾❶❸ STAPLE MAGAZINE

114-116 St. Stephen's Rd., Sneinton, Nottingham NG2 4FJ, England. Website: www.staplemagazine.com. **Contact:** Wayne Burrows, Editor. 114-116 St. Stephen's Rd., Sneinton, Nottingham NG2 4JS, England. E-mail: wayneburrows@ntlworld.com. Website:www. staplemagazine.co.uk. **Contact:** Wayne Burrows, editor. *Staple*, published 3 times/year, accepts "poetry, short fiction, and articles about the writing process and general culture in relation to writing, plus some artwork and photography." *Staple* is about 150 pages, perfect-bound. Press run is 500 (350 subscribers). Single copy: £10; subscription: £25/year, £35/year overseas. Sample: £5.00 (back issue).

MAGAZINES NEEDS *Staple*, published 3 times/year, accepts "poetry, short fiction, and articles about the writing process and general culture in relation to writing, plus some artwork and photography." *Staple* is about 150 pages, perfect-bound. Press run is 500 (350 subscribers). Single copy: £10; subscription: £25/year, £35/year overseas. Sample: £5.00 (back issue).

HOW TO CONTACT Submit 6 poems or 1-2 stories/essays at a time. No previously published poems or simultaneous submissions. Cover letter with author bio note is preferred. Include SAE and 2 IRCs. Issues are themed, contact for details. Reads submissions by the following deadlines: end of March, July, and November. Sometimes comments on rejected poems. Responds in up to 3 months. Pays £10/single poem, £25/group of poems; £25/story or essay.

❸ STAR*LINE

Science Fiction Poetry Association, 1412 NE 35th St., Ocala FL 34479. E-mail: SFPASL@aol.com. Web-site: www.sfpoetry.com. Established 1978. **Contact:** Marge Simon, editor.

MAGAZINES NEEDS *Star*Line*, published quarterly by the Science Fiction Poetry Association (see separate listing in Organizations), is a newsletter and poetry magazine. "Open to all forms—free verse, traditional forms, light verse—as long as your poetry shows skilled use of the language and makes a good use of science fiction, science, fantasy, horror, or speculative motifs." *Star*Line* is digest-sized, saddle-stapled. Receives about 300-400 submissions/year, accepts about 80. Has 250 subscribers. Subscription: $13 for 6 issues. Sample: $2. Send requests for copies/membership information to Samantha Henderson, SFPA Treasurer, P.O. Box 4846, Covina, CA 91723. Send submissions to *Star*Line* only.

HOW TO CONTACT Submit 3-5 poems at a time. Lines/poem: preferably under 50. No simultaneous submissions. Accepts e-mail submissions (preferred; pasted into body of message, no attachments). Cover letter is preferred (brief). Submissions must be typed. Responds in 1 month. Pays $3 for 10 lines or less; $5 for 11-50 lines; 10¢ per line rounded to the next dollar for 51+ lines. Buys first North American serial rights. Reviews books of poetry "within the science fiction/fantasy field" in 50-500 words. Open to unsolicited reviews. Send materials for review consideration.

ALSO OFFERS The Association also publishes *The Rhysling Anthology*, a yearly collection of nominations from the membership "for the best science fiction/fantasy long and short poetry of the preceding year and *Dwarf Stars*, an annual collection of poetry ten lines or fewer."

⊙ STEPPING STONES MAGAZINE: A LITERARY MAGAZINE FOR INNOVATIVE ART

First Step Press, P.O. Box 902, Norristown PA 19404-0902. E-mail: poetry@fspressonline.org. Website: www.fspressonline.org. **Contact:** Trinae A. Ross, publisher. First Step Press, P.O. Box 902, Norristown, PA 19404-0902. E-mail: poetry@fspressonline.org. Website: www.fspressonline.org. **Contact:** Trinae A. Ross, publisher. *Stepping Stones Magazine: A Literary Magazine for Innovative Art*, published 4 times/year online, delivered as a PDF document, seeks "poetry as diverse as are the authors themselves. Poems should have something to say other than, 'Hi, I'm a poem please publish me.'" Does not want "poems that promote intolerance for race, religion, gender, or sexual preference." Has published poetry by Clayton Vetter, Michael Hathaway, and Ivan Silverberg. Receives about 300 poems/year, accepts about 10-15%. Reviews chapbooks, Web sites, and other publications of interest to poets.

MAGAZINES NEEDS *Stepping Stones Magazine: A Literary Magazine for Innovative Art*, published 4 times/year online, delivered as a PDF document, seeks "poetry as diverse as are the authors themselves. Poems should have something to say other than, 'Hi, I'm a poem please publish me.'" Does not want "poems that promote intolerance for race, religion, gender, or sexual preference." Has published poetry by Clayton Vetter, Michael Hathaway, and Ivan Silverberg. Receives about 300 poems/year, accepts about 10-15%. Reviews chapbooks, Web sites, and other publications of interest to poets.

HOW TO CONTACT Submit no more than 5 poems at a time. Considers previously published poems and simultaneous submissions. Prefers e-mail submissions; should include cover letter and formatted with a simple font and saved as .doc, .rtf, or .odf. Attach submissions and cover letter to e-mail and send to poetry@fspressonline.org. Read submissions year round. Guidelines available for SASE, by sending an e-mail to guidelines @fspressonline.org, or on website. Responds within 2 months. Pays one contributor's copy and free advertising space, though will implement a pay schedule when funding permits. Acquires one-time print and electronic rights.

ALSO OFFERS "Free advertising space is available for those wishing to promote their website, book, or other literary venture. The continuing goal of First Step Press is to provide sanctuary for new and established writers, to hone their skills and commune with one another within the comfort of our electronic pages."

● THE WALLACE STEVENS JOURNAL

Clarkson University, Box 5750, 8 Clarkson Avenue, Potsdam NY 13699. (315)268-3987. Fax: (315)268-3983. E-mail: serio@clarkson.edu; jforjames@aol.com. Website: www.wallacestevens.com. **Contact:** James Finnegan, poetry editor. E-mail: jforjames@aol.com. Website: www.wallacestevens.com. **Contact:** James Finnegan, poetry editor. *The Wallace Stevens Journal*, published semiannually by the Wallace Stevens Society, uses "poems about or in the spirit of

Wallace Stevens or having some relation to his work. No bad parodies of Stevens's anthology pieces." Has published poetry by David Athey, Jacqueline Marcus, Charles Wright, X.J. Kennedy, A.M. Juster, and Robert Creeley. *The Wallace Stevens Journal* is 96-120 pages, digest-sized, typeset, flat-spined, with glossy cover with art. Receives 200-300 poems/year, accepts 15-20. Press run is 700. Subscription: $30 (includes membership in the Wallace Stevens Society). Sample: $10.

MAGAZINES NEEDS *The Wallace Stevens Journal*, published semiannually by the Wallace Stevens Society, uses "poems about or in the spirit of Wallace Stevens or having some relation to his work. No bad parodies of Stevens's anthology pieces." Has published poetry by David Athey, Jacqueline Marcus, Charles Wright, X.J. Kennedy, A.M. Juster, and Robert Creeley. *The Wallace Stevens Journal* is 96-120 pages, digest-sized, typeset, flat-spined, with glossy cover with art. Receives 200-300 poems/year, accepts 15-20. Press run is 700. Subscription: $30 (includes membership in the Wallace Stevens Society). Sample: $10.

HOW TO CONTACT Submit 1-4 poems at a time. No previously published poems, "though we have made a few exceptions to this rule." Manuscripts should be submitted electronically as attached documents, and saved either in .doc or .rtf format, not in .docx. "Please provide full contact information on a separate title page: name, address, phone, and e-mail." Cover letter is encouraged, but keep brief. Send clean, readable copy. Responds in up to 10 weeks. Always sends prepublication galleys. Pays 2 contributor's copies. Acquires all rights. Returns rights with permission and acknowledgment. Staff reviews books of poetry. Send materials for review consideration "only if there is some clear connection to Stevens."

● STIRRING: A LITERARY COLLECTION

Stirring: A Literary Collection, c/o Erin Elizabeth Smith, Department of English, 301 McClung Tower, University of Tennessee, Knoxville TN 37996-0430. E-mail: eesmith81@gmail.com. Website: www.sundresspublications.com/stirring/. **Contact:** Erin Elizabeth Smith, managing editor.

○ "*Stirring* is one of the oldest continually-published literary journals on the web. *Stirring* is a monthly literary magazine that publishes poetry, short fiction, creative nonfiction, and photography by established and emerging writers."

MAGAZINES NEEDS Wants free verse, formal poetry, etc. Doesn't want religious verse or children's verse. Has published poetry by Dorianne Laux, Sharon Olds, Patricia Smith, Chad Davidson. Receives about 1,500 poems/year, accepts 60.

HOW TO CONTACT Submit 1-7 poems at a time by e-mail. Considers previously published poems and simultaneous submissions. Past submissions into body of e-mail message. Reads submissions year round. Time between acceptance and publication is 1-2 weeks. Poems are circulated to an editorial board. Sometimes comments on rejected poems. Responds in 2-5 months. Acquires first North American serial rights.

STONE SOUP

(831)426-5557. Fax: (831)426-1161. E-mail: editor@stonesoup.com. Website: www.stonesoup.com. **Contact:** Ms. Gerry Mandel, editor. *Stone Soup* is 48 pages, 7x10, professionally printed in color on heavy stock, saddle-stapled, with coated cover with full-color illustration. Receives 5,000 poetry submissions/year, accepts about 12. Press run is 15,000 (14,000 subscribers, 3,000 shelf sales, 500 other). Subscription: membership in the Children's Art Foundation includes a subscription, $37/year."Audience is children, teachers, parents, writers, artists. We have a preference for writing and art based on real-life experiences; no formula stories or poems."

"Stories and poems from past issues are available online."

TIPS "All writing we publish is by young people ages 13 and under. We do not publish any writing by adults. We can't emphasize enough how important it is to read a couple of issues of the magazine. You can read stories and poems from past issues online. We have a strong preference for writing on subjects that mean a lot to the author. If you feel strongly about something that happened to you or something you observed, use that feeling as the basis for your story or poem. Stories should have good descriptions, realistic dialogue, and a point to make. In a poem, each word must be chosen carefully. Your poem should present a view of your subject, and a way of using words that are special and all your own."

STORYSOUTH

5603B W. Friendly Ave., Suite 282, Greensboro NC 27410. E-mail: terry@storysouth.com. Website: www.storysouth.com. **Contact:** Terry Kennedy, editor. "*storySouth* is interested in fiction, creative nonfiction, and poetry by writers from the New South. The exact definition of New South varies from person to person and we leave it up to the writer to define their own connection to the southern United States." Quarterly. Receives 70 unsolicited mss/month. Accepts 5 mss/issue; 20 mss/year. **Publishes 5-10 new writers/year.** Average length: 4,000 words. Publishes short shorts. Also publishes literary essays, literary criticism, poetry. Often comments on rejected mss. Send complete ms. Accepts online submissions only.

MAGAZINES NEEDS Experimental, literary, regional (south), translations.

TIPS "What really makes a story stand out is a strong voice and a sense of urgency—a need for the reader to keep reading the story and not put it down until it is finished."

THE STORYTELLER

2441 Washington Rd., Maynard, AR 72444. (870)647-2137. Fax: (870)647-2454. E-mail: storyteller1@hightowercom.com; storytellermag@@yahoo.com. Website: www.thestorytellermagazine.com; www.freewebs.com/fossilcreek/storyteller.html.

MAGAZINES NEEDS *The Storyteller*, published quarterly, "is geared to, but not limited to, new writers and poets." Wants "any form, any subject, any style, but must have a meaning. Do not throw words together and call it a poem." Does not want "explicit sex, violence, horror, or explicit language. I would like it to be understood that I have young readers, ages 9-18." Considers poetry by children and teens. Has published poetry by Patrick Lobrutto, Bryan Byrd, and Gerald Zipper. *The Storyteller* is 72 pages, magazine-sized, desktop-published, with slick cover black and white photography, includes ads. Receives about 300 poems/year, accepts about 40%. Press run is 700 (more than 600 subscribers). Single copy: $6 U.S., $8 Canada and foreign; subscription: $20 U.S., $24 Canada & foreign.

HOW TO CONTACT Submit 3 poems at a time, 1 poem per page. Lines/poem: up to 40. Considers previously published poems and simultaneous submissions, "but must state where and when poetry first appeared." No e-mail submissions; postal submissions only. "However, if accepted, you will be asked to send material by e-mail, if possible." Cover letter is preferred. Manuscripts must be typed and double-spaced. "Make sure name and address are on each page submitted. We are getting many submissions without names." Time between acceptance and publication is 9 months. "Poems are read and discussed by staff." Sometimes comments on rejected poems. Guidelines available for SASE or on website. Responds in 1-2 weeks. Does not provide contributor's copies. Acquires first or one-time rights. Reviews books/chapbooks of poetry by subscribers only.

CONTEST/AWARD OFFERINGS Sponsors a quarterly contest. "Readers vote on their favorite poems. Winners receive a copy of the magazine and a certificate. We also nominate for the Pushcart Prize." See website for yearly contest announcements and winners.

TIPS *The Storyteller* is one of the best places you will find to submit your work, especially new writers. Our best advice, be professional. You have one chance to make a good impression. Don't blow it by being unprofessional.

THE STRAY BRANCH

E-mail: thestraybranchlitmag@yahoo.com. Website: www.thestraybranch.org. **Contact:** Debbie Berk, editor/publisher.

MAGAZINES NEEDS *The Stray Branch*, published twice per year, is a journal "looking to publish well-crafted material from experienced writers who are serious about their craft. Looking for honest, personal, edgy, raw, real life material that is relatable to the human condition known as existence in all its dark, flawed, secret self..exposed in the wounds that bleed upon the page and leave a scar within the skull of the reader. Open to subject matter but prefers edgy, raw material written from the gut that reflects the heart and human experience. Wants poetry by real people that can be understood by all readers. *The Stray Branch* prefers works of a darker nature." Does not want "over-schooled, arrogant, self-righteous, religious, political, erotic poetry, or happy and light, pretty poetry. Not interested in rants, tantrums, and the use of profanity that is not fitting to the piece. Please, be tactful and respectful of the language." Has published poetry by Andy Robertson, Keith Estes, Kate Sjostrand, Lena Vanelslander, Michael Grover, and Justin Blackburn.

HOW TO CONTACT Submit 6 poems at a time. "Maximum length for poems is no longer than 1 page, shorter poems are preferred and stand a better chance." Considers previously published poems; no simultaneous submissions. (Considers poetry posted on a public website/blog/forum and poetry posted on a private, password-protected forum as published.) Accepts e-mail submissions (pasted into body of message); no fax or disk submissions. Cover letter is unnecessary. Reads submissions October-April. Sometimes comments on rejected poems. Guidelines available on website. Responds in 3 weeks. Acquires one-time rights ("includes material published on the web"). Rights revert to poets upon publication.

STRAYLIGHT

Website: www.straylightmag.com. English Department, University of Wisconsin-Parkside, 900 Wood Rd., Kenosha WI 53141. (262)595-2139. Fax: (262)595-2271. E-mail: straylight@litspot.net. Website: www.straylightmag.com. **Contact:** Poetry Editor.

MAGAZINES NEEDS *Straylight*, published biannually, seeks "poetry of almost any style as long as it's inventive." *Straylight* is digest-sized. Single copy: $10; subscription: $19. Make checks payable to *Straylight*.

HOW TO CONTACT Submit 3-6 poems at a time. No previously published poems or simultaneous submissions. Accepts e-mail submissions (preferred, as .rtf or .doc attachment); no fax or disk submissions. Cover letter is required. "Include contact information on all pages of submission." Reads submissions August 15-April 15. Submit seasonal poems 3 months in advance. Time between acceptance and publication is 6 months. Never comments on rejected poems. Sometimes publishes theme issues. Upcoming themes available on website. Guidelines available for SASE or on website. Responds in 2 months. Pays 2 contributor's copies. Additional payment when funding permits. Acquires first North American serial rights. Rights revert to poet upon publication.

TIPS "We tend to publish character-based and inventive fiction with cutting-edge prose. We are unimpressed with works based on strict plot twists or novelties. Read a sample copy to get a feel for what we publish."

◐◑◖ STRIDE MAGAZINE

E-mail: editor@stridemagazine.co.uk, submissions@ stridemagazine.co.uk. Website: www.stridemagazine.co.uk. **Contact:** Rupert Loydell, editor. E-mail: editor@stridemagazine.co.uk, submissions@stridemagazine.co.uk. Website: www.stridemagazine.co.uk. **Contact:** Rupert Loydell, editor. Estab. 1982. *Stride Magazine*, published online, is "a gathering of new poetry, short prose, articles, news, reviews, and whatever takes our fancy. *Stride* is regularly updated with new contributions."

MAGAZINES NEEDS *Stride Magazine*, published online, is "a gathering of new poetry, short prose, articles, news, reviews, and whatever takes our fancy. *Stride* is regularly updated with new contributions."

HOW TO CONTACT Submit 4-5 poems at a time. Accepts e-mail submissions (pasted into body of message; no attachments). "Attachments or snail mail without SAEs will not be considered or replied to."

◖ STRUGGLE: A MAGAZINE OF PROLETARIAN REVOLUTIONARY LITERATURE

P.O. Box 28536, Detroit MI 48228. (313)273-9039. E-mail: timhall11@yahoo.com. Website: www.strugglemagazine.net. **Contact:** Tim Hall, Editor. Publishes material related to "the struggle of the working class and all progressive people against the rule of the rich—including their war policies, repression, racism, exploitation of the workers, oppression of women and immigrants and general culture, etc." Quarterly. Recently published work by Billie Louise Jones, Tyler Plosia, Margaret Dimacou. Accepts multiple submissions. Magazine: 512×812; 36-72 pages; 20 lb. white bond paper; colored cover; illustrations; occasional photos.

MAGAZINES NEEDS *Struggle: A Magazine of Proletarian Revolutionary Literature*, published quarterly, focuses "on the struggle of the working people and all oppressed against the rich, dealing with such issues as racism, poverty, women's rights, full rights for immigrants, aggressive wars, workers' struggle for jobs and job security, the overall struggle for a non-exploitative society, a genuine socialism." The poetry and songs printed are "generally short, any style; subject matter must criticize or fight—explicitly or implicitly—against the rule of the billionaires. We welcome experimentation devoted to furthering such content. We are open to both subtlety and direct statement." Has published poetry by Christian Weaver, R. Nat Turner, Jose H. Villareal, Ly Doi, Tendai Mwanaka, Teresinka Pereira, Madeleine Michele Egger, Janine Fitzgerald, Nepthali De Leon. *Struggle* is 36 pages, digest-sized, photocopied. Subscription: $10/year (4 issues); $12 for institutions, $15 for foreign, $5 for prisoners. Sample: $5 (for the now-customary double-sized issue of 72 pages). Make checks payable to "Tim Hall—Special Account (not to *Struggle*)."

HOW TO CONTACT Submit up to 8 poems at a time or one story or plan up to 20 pages. Accepts e-mail submissions (pasted into body of message, no attachments), but prefers postal mail. "Writers must include SASE. Name and address must appear on the opening page of each poem."

ADDITIONAL INFORMATION Accepted work usually appears in the next or following issue. Comments on rejected poems "with every submission." Responds in 4 months, if possible, but often becomes backlogged. Pays one contributor's copy. "If you are unwilling to have your poetry published on our website, please inform us."

◐◑ STUDIO, A JOURNAL OF CHRISTIANS WRITING

727 Peel St., Albury NS 2640, Australia. (61)(2)6021-1135. Fax: (61)(2)6021-1135. E-mail: studio00@bigpond.net.au. E-mail: http://web.me.com/pdgrover/StudioJournal. **Contact:** Paul Grover, Publisher.

MAGAZINES NEEDS *Studio, A Journal of Christians Writing*, published quarterly, prints "poetry and prose of literary merit, offering a venue for previously published, new, and aspiring writers, and seeking to create a sense of community among Christians writing." Also publishes occasional articles as well as news and reviews of writing, writers, and events of interest to members. Wants "shorter pieces [[of poetry]] but with no specification as to form or length (necessarily less than 200 lines), subject matter, style, or purpose. People who send material should be comfortable being published under this banner: *Studio, A Journal of Christians Writing*." Has published poetry by John Foulcher, Les Murray, and other Australian poets. *Studio* is 36 pages, digest-sized, professionally printed on high-quality recycled paper, saddle-stapled, with matte card cover. Press run is 300 (all subscriptions). Subscription: $60 AUD for overseas members. Sample: $10 AUD (airmail to U.S.).

HOW TO CONTACT Lines/poem: less than 200. Considers simultaneous submissions. Cover letter is required. Include brief details of previous publishing history, if any. SAE with IRC required. "Submissions must be typed and double-spaced on one side of A4 white paper. Name and address must appear on the reverse side of each page submitted." Response time is 2 months. Time between acceptance and publication is 9 months. Pays 1 contributor's copy. Acquires first Australian rights. Reviews books of poetry in 250 words, single-book format. Send materials for review consideration.

CONTEST/AWARD OFFERINGS Conducts a biannual poetry and short story contest.

◑ STUDIO ONE

Mary Commons, College of St. Benedict, 37 S. College Ave., St. Joseph MN 56374. E-mail: studio1@csbsju. edu. Website: http://clubs.csbsju.edu/studio1. **Contact:** Poetry Editor. *Studio One*, published annually in May, is a "literary and visual arts magazine designed as a forum for local, regional, and national poets/writers. No specifications regarding form, subject matter, or style of poetry submitted." Considers poetry by children and teens. Has published poetry by Bill Meissner, Eva Hooker, and Larry Schug. *Studio One* is 50-80 pages, typeset, with soft cover. Receives 600-800 submissions/year. No subscriptions, but a sample copy can be obtained by sending a self-addressed, stamped manila envelope and $6 for p&h. Make checks payable to *Studio One*. Submissions are accepted August-December. The deadline is January 1 for spring publication. The reading/judging period between late November and February. Results will be sent by May. Submissions sent after the judging period concludes will be retained for consideration in the following year's publication. *Studio One*, published annually in May, is a "literary and visual arts magazine designed as a forum for local, regional, and national poets/writers. No specifications regarding form, subject matter, or style of poetry submitted." Considers poetry by children and teens. Has published poetry by Bill Meissner, Eva Hooker, and Larry Schug. *Studio One* is 50-80 pages, typeset, with soft cover. Receives 600-800 submissions/year. No subscriptions, but a sample copy can be obtained by sending a self-addressed, stamped manila envelope and $6 for p&h. Make checks payable to *Studio One*. Submissions are accepted August-December. The deadline is January 1 for spring publication. The reading/judging period between late November and February. Results will be sent by May. Submissions sent after the judging period concludes will be retained for consideration in the following year's publication.

SUBTROPICS

University of Florida, P.O. Box 112075, 4008 Turlington Hall, Gainesville FL 32611-2075. E-mail: dleavitt@ufl.edu; subtropics@english.ufl.edu. Website: www.english.ufl.edu/subtropics. **Contact:** David Leavitt. "Magazine published 3 times/year through the University of Florida's English department. *Subtropics* seeks to publish the best literary fiction, essays, and poetry being written today, both by established and emerging authors. We will consider works of fiction of any length, from short shorts to novellas and self-contained novel excerpts. We give the same latitude to essays. We appreciate work in translation and, from time to time, republish important and compelling stories, essays, and poems that have lapsed out of print by writers no longer living."

HOW TO CONTACT Submit in hard copy by mail. Please include cover letter with contact information included both on letter and on submission. Responds by e-mail. period from September 1-May 1. Does not return ms. Reading "We do not accept simultaneous submissions in poetry." Poets are paid $100 per poem.

TIPS "We publish longer works of fiction, including novellas and excerpts from forthcoming novels. Each issue will include a short-short story of about 250 words on the back cover. We are also interested in publishing works in translation for the magazine's English-speaking audience."

◑◐ SUNKEN LINES

E-mail: dogger@sunkenlines.com. Website: www.sunkenlines.com. **Contact:** Dogger Banks, poetry editor.

MAGAZINES NEEDS *Sunken Lines*, published biannually online, is a magazine of poetry, fiction, essays, and artwork "intended as a forum for talented writers looking for more exposure." Wants "poems that evoke a strong response in the reader, whether it be laughter, empathy, the conjuring of a strong image, or admiration of a witty line. Formal or (accessible) free verse." Does not want "poems that are excessively religious, offensive, or miserable." Has published poetry by Larry Rapant, Tony Gruenewald, Suzanne

Harvey, Anna Evans, Paul Lench, and Bruce Niedt. Receives about 500 poems/year, accepts about 10%.

HOW TO CONTACT Submit up to 5 poems at a time. Lines/poem: 40 maximum. Considers simultaneous submissions; no previously published poems. Accepts e-mail submissions (preferably pasted into body of message, or as attachment in MS Word or RTF format); no disk submissions. Cover letter is required. "Please be prepared to supply a short biography and optional photo upon notification of acceptance." Reads submissions year round. "We cannot consider or acknowledge unsolicited poetry or prose submissions received between July 1 and October 31." Time between acceptance and publication is up to 3 months. Poems are circulated to an editorial board. Sometimes comments on rejected poems. Guidelines available on website. Responds in 3 months. Acquires one-time rights. Rights revert to poet upon publication.

SUNSPINNER

E-mail: sunspinnermagazine@yahoo.com. Website: www.sunspinner.org. **Contact:** Ellen Lewis and Lisa Swanstrom, editors. Estab. 2004. *Sunspinner*, published biannually online, is based in southern California and features "fiction and poetry from writers everywhere. There are no restrictions on style or subject matter, and submissions are always welcome." Has published poetry by Ryan G. Van Cleave, Lyn Lifshin, Linda Mastrangelo, and Gary Lehman. *Sunspinner*, published biannually online, is based in southern California and features "fiction and poetry from writers everywhere. There are no restrictions on style or subject matter, and submissions are always welcome." Has published poetry by Ryan G. Van Cleave, Lyn Lifshin, Linda Mastrangelo, and Gary Lehman.

HOW TO CONTACT Submit 3-5 poems at a time. Considers previously published poems ("provided the author retains all rights") and simultaneous submissions. Accepts e-mail (pasted into body of message or as attachment in Microsoft Word) and disk submissions. Cover letter is preferred. "Please include a brief bio with each submission." Reads submissions year round. Time between acceptance and publication is 6 months to a year. Never comments on rejected poems. Guidelines available on website. Responds in 4-6 months. No payment. "Works accepted by *Sunspinner* will be archived for an indefinite period of time and removed at the author's request. Authors retain all rights to work featured in *Sunspinner*."

SUNSTONE

Website: www.sunstonemagazine.com. 343 N. Third W., Salt Lake City UT 84103-1215. (801)355-5926. E-mail: info@sunstonemagazine.com. Website: www.sunstonemagazine.com. Estab. 1974. **Contact:** Dixie Partridge, poetry editor. *Sunstone*, published 6 times/year, prints "scholarly articles of interest to an open, Mormon audience; personal essays; fiction and poetry." Wants "both lyric and narrative poetry that engages the reader with fresh, strong images, skillful use of language, and a strong sense of voice and/or place." Does not want "didactic poetry, sing-song rhymes, or in-process work." Has published poetry by Susan Howe, Anita Tanner, Robert Parham, Ryan G. Van Cleave, Robert Rees, and Virgil Suaárez. *Sunstone* is 64 pages, magazine-sized, professionally printed, saddle-stapled, with semi-glossy paper cover. Receives more than 500 poems/year, accepts 40-50. Press run is 3,000. Subscription: $45 for 6 issues. Sample: $10 postpaid.

MAGAZINES NEEDS *Sunstone*, published 6 times/year, prints "scholarly articles of interest to an open, Mormon audience; personal essays; fiction and poetry." Wants "both lyric and narrative poetry that engages the reader with fresh, strong images, skillful use of language, and a strong sense of voice and/or place." Does not want "didactic poetry, sing-song rhymes, or in-process work." Has published poetry by Susan Howe, Anita Tanner, Robert Parham, Ryan G. Van Cleave, Robert Rees, and Virgil Suaárez. *Sunstone* is 64 pages, magazine-sized, professionally printed, saddle-stapled, with semi-glossy paper cover. Receives more than 500 poems/year, accepts 40-50. Press run is 3,000. Subscription: $45 for 6 issues. Sample: $10 postpaid.

HOW TO CONTACT Submit up to 5 poems at a time. Lines/poem: 40 maximum. No previously published poems or simultaneous submissions. Include name and address on each poem. Time between acceptance and publication is 2 years or less. Seldom comments on rejected poems. Guidelines available for SASE. Responds in 3 months. Pays 5 contributor's copies. Acquires first North American serial rights.

SWELL

E-mail: swelleditor@yahoo.com. Website: www.swellzine.com. **Contact:** Jill Craig, editor. E-mail:

swelleditor@yahoo.com. Website: www.swellzine. com. **Contact:** Jill Craig, editor. Estab. 1980. "SWELL aims to reflect a spectrum of perspectives as diverse as the community from which it was born. Ideal publication candidates approach GLBT (gay/lesbian/bisexual/transgender) issues in a fresh way or present universal topics from a unique point of view. Pieces which avoid well-trodden areas of the GLBT canon are of particular interest. Fiction and non-fiction of all styles, as well as poetry and dramAre all acceptable forms for SWELL; aspiring contributors are also encouraged to experiment with the possibilities inherent in internet publication, such as multimedia compositions, creative hyperlinking, and works not easily categorized.""SWELL aims to reflect a spectrum of perspectives as diverse as the community from which it was born. Ideal publication candidates approach GLBT (gay/lesbian/bisexual/transgender) issues in a fresh way or present universal topics from a unique point of view. Pieces which avoid well-trodden areas of the GLBT canon are of particular interest. Fiction and non-fiction of all styles, as well as poetry and dramAre all acceptable forms for SWELL; aspiring contributors are also encouraged to experiment with the possibilities inherent in internet publication, such as multimedia compositions, creative hyperlinking, and works not easily categorized."

HOW TO CONTACT Lines/poem: no works over 3,000 words total. Welcomes multiple submissions as long as the total submitted is under the maximum word count. Accepts e-mail submissions only. Responds in 1-2 months. Rights revert to poet upon publication.

TIPS "SWELL is pleased to sponsor a fiction contest. Prizes Awarded: First Prize: $250; Second Prize: $100; Third Prize: $50. See our website for details."

SYCAMORE REVIEW

Purdue University Dept. of English, 500 Oval Dr., West Lafayette IN 47907. E-mail: sycamore@purdue.edu. Website: www.sycamorereview.com. Purdue University Dept. of English, 500 Oval Dr., West Lafayette, IN 47907. E-mail: sycamore@purdue.edu. Website: www.sycamorereview.com. *Sycamore Review*, published semiannually in January and June, uses "personal essays, short fiction, short shorts, drama, translations, and quality poetry in any form. We aim to publish many diverse styles of poetry from formalist to prose poems, narrative, and lyric." Has

published poetry by Denise Duhamel, Jonah Winter, Amy Gerstler, Mark Halliday, Dean Young, and Ed Hirsch. *Sycamore Review* is about 120 pages, 8x8, professionally printed, flat-spined, with matte color cover. Press run is 1,000 (200 subscribers, 50 libraries). Subscription: $14. Current issue: $7. Back Issue: $5. Make checks payable to Purdue University."Strives to publish the best writing by new and established writers. Looks for well crafted and engaging work, works that illuminate our lives in the collective human search for meaning. We would like to publish more work that takes a reflective look at our national identity and how we are perceived by the world. We look for diversity of voice, pluralistic worldviews, and political and social context."

> *Sycamore Review* is Purdue University's internationally acclaimed literary journal, affiliated with Purdue's College of Liberal Arts and the Dept. of English. Art should present politics in a language that can be felt.

MAGAZINES NEEDS *Sycamore Review*, published semiannually in January and June, uses "personal essays, short fiction, short shorts, drama, translations, and quality poetry in any form. We aim to publish many diverse styles of poetry from formalist to prose poems, narrative, and lyric." Has published poetry by Denise Duhamel, Jonah Winter, Amy Gerstler, Mark Halliday, Dean Young, and Ed Hirsch. *Sycamore Review* is about 120 pages, 8x8, professionally printed, flat-spined, with matte color cover. Press run is 1,000 (200 subscribers, 50 libraries). Subscription: $14. Current issue: $7. Back Issue: $5. Make checks payable to Purdue University.

HOW TO CONTACT Submit 3-6 poems at a time. with name and address on each page. Considers simultaneous submissions, if notified immediately of acceptance elsewhere; no previously published poems except translations. No fax or postal submissions. Only accepts submissions via submission manager on website. Cover letter is required. Poem should be typed single-spaced, one poem to a page. Please submit no more than twice per reading period. Reads submissions August 1-March 31 only. Responds in 4-5 months. Pays 2 contributor's copies. Acquires first North American rights. After publication, all rights revert to author. Staff reviews books of poetry. Send materials for review consideration to editor-in-chief.

TIPS "We look for originality, brevity, significance, strong dialogue, and vivid detail. We sponsor the Wabash Prize for Poetry (deadline: mid-October) and Fiction (deadline: March 1). $1,000 award for each. All contest submissions will be considered for regular inclusion in the *Sycamore Review*. No email submissions–no exception. Include SASE.

🌀💲 TAKAHE

Website: www.takahe.org.nz/index.php. P.O. Box 13-335, Christchurch 8141, New Zealand. (03)359-8133. E-mail: admin@takahe.org.nz. Website: http://takahe.org.nz. **Contact:** Poetry Editor. The Takahe 2010 Poetry Competition awards 1st Prize: $250 NZD; 2nd Prize: $100 NZD; plus one-year subscriptions to *Takahe* to 2 runners-up. Submit as many poems as you wish, but each much be named separately on the entry form. Submissions must be unpublished and may not be entered in other contests. Poems must be in English and typed on A4 paper, with no identifying information on the ms. Include SASE with entry for results and/or return of entries (or SAE with IRCs for overseas entrants; may also add $2 NZD to entry fee for handling and postage). All entries considered for publication in *Takahe*. Guidelines and entry form available on website. **Entry fee:** $5 NZD/poem. Deadline: September 30, 2010.

HOW TO CONTACT No simultaneous submissions. No e-mail submissions. "**Please note:** U.S. stamps should not be used on SAEs. They do not work in New Zealand. Please enclose IRCs or supply e-mail address." Cover letter is required. "

TIPS "We pay a flat rate to each writer/poet appearing in a particular issue regardless of the number/length of items. Editorials and literary commentaries are by invitation only."

➕⭕ TALENT DRIPS EROTIC PUBLISHING

(216)799-9775. E-mail: talent_drips_eroticpublishing@lycos.com. Website: http://ashygirlforgirls.tripod.com/talentdripseroticpublishings. **Contact:** Kimberly Steele, founder. *Talent Drips*, published bimonthly online, focuses solely on showcasing new erotic fiction.

MAGAZINES NEEDS Wants erotic poetry and short stories.

HOW TO CONTACT Submit 2-3 poems at a time, maximum 30 lines each by email to talent_drips_eroticpublishing@lycos.com. Considers previously published and simultaneous submissions. Accepts e-mail pasted into body of message. Reads submissions during publication months only. Time between acceptance and publication is 2 months. Guidelines available on website. Responds in 3 weeks. Pays $10 for each accepted poem. Acquires electronic rights only. Work to be archived on the site for a year.

CONTEST/AWARD OFFERINGS Talent Drips Erotic Publishings Poet of the Year Contest is held annually. Prizes: $75, $50, and certificate. Deadline: December 15. Guidelines on website.

TIPS "Does not want sci-fi/fantasy submissions; mythical creatures having pointless sex is not a turn-on; looking for more original plots than 'the beast takes the submissive maiden' stuff."

TALES OF THE TALISMAN

E-mail: hadrosaur@zianet.com. Website: www.talesofthetalisman.com. **Contact:** David Lee Summers, editor. "*Tales of the Talisman* is a literary science fiction and fantasy magazine. We publish short stories, poetry, and articles with themes related to science fiction and fantasy. Above all, we are looking for thought-provoking ideas and good writing. Speculative fiction set in the past, present, and future is welcome. Likewise, contemporary or historical fiction is welcome as long as it has a mythic or science fictional element. Our target audience includes adult fans of the science fiction and fantasy genres along with anyone else who enjoys thought-provoking and entertaining writing."

⭕ Fiction and poetry submissions are limited to reading periods of January 1-February 15 and July 1-August 15.

MAGAZINES NEEDS *Tales of the Talisman*, published quarterly, prints "well-written, thought-provoking science fiction and fantasy." Wants "strong visual imagery. Strong emotion from a sense of fun to more melancholy is good." Does not want "graphic/gory violence or poetry that strays too far from the science fiction/fantasy genre." Has published poetry by Mike Allen, Ian Watson, David Kopaska-Merkel, Terrie Leigh Relf, and Deborah P. Kolodji. *Tales of the Talisman* is 86 pages, $8\frac{1}{4}$x$10\frac{1}{2}$, printed on 60 lb. white paper, perfect-bound, with full-color cardstock cover. Receives about 500 poems/year, accepts up to 5%. Press run is 200 (100 subscribers). Single copy: $8; subscription: $20/year. Make checks payable to Hadrosaur Productions.

HOW TO CONTACT Submit 1-5 poems at a time. Considers previously published poems; no simultaneous submissions. Accepts e-mail submissions (pasted into body of message); no disk submissions. "For e-mail submissions, place the word 'Hadrosaur' in the subject line. Submissions that do not include this will be destroyed unread. Postal submissions will not be returned unless sufficient postage is provided." Accepts submissions from January 1-February 15 and July 1-August 15. Cover letter is preferred. Time between acceptance and publication is one year. Occasionally comments on rejected poems. Guidelines available for SASE or on website. Responds in 1 month. Sends prepublication galleys on request. Pays $4/poem plus 1 contributor's copy. Acquires one-time rights.

TIPS "Let your imagination soar to its greatest heights and write down the results. Above all, we are looking for thought-provoking ideas and good writing. Our emphasis is on character-oriented science fiction and fantasy. If we don't believe in the people living the story, we generally won't believe in the story itself."

⊙ TALKING RIVER

Division of Literature and Languages, 500 8th Ave., Lewiston ID 83501. (208)792-2189. Fax: (208)792-2324. E-mail: talkingriver@lcmail.lcsc.edu. Website: www. lcsc.edu/talkingriverreview. **Contact:** Kevin Goodan, editorial advisor. Magazine: 6×9; 150-200 pages; 60 lb. paper; coated, color cover; illustrations; photos. "We look for new voices with something to say to a discerning general audience." Semiannual. Circ. 250. Ethnic/multicultural, feminist, humor/satire, literary, regional. "Wants more well-written, character-driven stories that surprise and delight the reader with fresh, arresting yet unselfconscious language, imagery, metaphor, revelation." Nothing sexist, racist, homophobic, erotic for shock value; no genre fiction. Receives 400 unsolicited mss/month. Accepts 5-8 mss/issue; 10-15 mss/year. Reads mss September 1-May 1 only. Publishes ms 1-2 years after acceptance. **Publishes 10-15 new writers/year.** Length: 4,000 words; average length: 3,000 words. Sometimes comments on rejected mss. Responds in 3 months to mss. Does not accept simultaneous submissions. Sample copy for $6. Writer's guidelines for #10 SASE. Acquires one-time rights.

HOW TO CONTACT Send complete manuscript with cover letter. Include estimated word count, 2-sentence bio and list of publications. Send SASE for reply, return of ms or send disposable copy of ms.

TIPS "We look for the strong, the unique; we reject clichéd images and predictable climaxes."

⊙ TAPROOT LITERARY REVIEW

Box 204, Ambridge PA 15003. (724)266-8476. E-mail: taproot10@aol.com. **Contact:** Tikvah Feinstein, editor. Box 204 Ambridge, PA 15003. (724)266-8476. E-mail:taproot10@aol.com. **Contact:** Tikvah Feinstein, editor. *Taproot Literary Review*, published annually, is "a very respected anthology with increasing distribution. We publish some of the best poets in the U.S. We enjoy all types and styles of poetry from emerging writers to established writers to those who have become valuable and old friends who share their new works with us." Has published poetry by Shirley Barasch, Holly Day, Alena Horowitz, Chris Waters, Ellaraine Lockie, Craig Sipe, Greg Moglia, Elizabeth Swados, B.Z. Niditch and Robert Penick. *Taproot Literary Review* is about 95 pages, offset-printed on white stock, with one-color glossy cover. Circulation is 500. Single copy: $8.95; subscription: $7.50. Sample: $5.

MAGAZINES NEEDS *Taproot Literary Review*, published annually, is "a very respected anthology with increasing distribution. We publish some of the best poets in the U.S. We enjoy all types and styles of poetry from emerging writers to established writers to those who have become valuable and old friends who share their new works with us." Has published poetry by Shirley Barasch, Holly Day, Alena Horowitz, Chris Waters, Ellaraine Lockie, Craig Sipe, Greg Moglia, Elizabeth Swados, B.Z. Niditch and Robert Penick. *Taproot Literary Review* is about 95 pages, offset-printed on white stock, with one-color glossy cover. Circulation is 500. Single copy: $8.95; subscription: $7.50. Sample: $5.

HOW TO CONTACT Submit up to 5 poems at a time. Lines/poem: 35 maximum. No previously published poems or simultaneous submissions. Accepts submissions by e-mail (pasted into body of message), but "we would rather have a hard copy. Also, we cannot answer without a SASE." Cover letter is required (with general information). Reads submissions September 1-December 31 only. Guidelines available for SASE. Sometimes sends prepublication galleys. Pays 1 contributor's copy; additional copies are $6.50 each. Open to receiving books for review consideration. Send query first.

CONTEST/AWARD OFFERINGS Sponsors the annual Taproot Writer's Workshop Annual Writing

Contest. 1st Prize: $25 and publication in *Taproot Literary Review*; 2nd and 3rd Prizes: publication. Submit 5 poems of literary quality, in any form, on any subject except porn, religion, and politics. **Entry fee:** $12/5 poems (no longer than 35 lines each); fee includes copy of *Taproot*. **Deadline:** December 31. Winners announced the following March.

TIPS "*Taproot* is getting more fiction submissions, and every one is read entirely. This takes time, so response can be delayed at busy times of year. Our contest is a good way to start publishing. Send for a sample copy and read it through. Ask for a critique and follow suggestions. Don't be offended by any suggestions—just take them or leave them and keep writing. Looks for a story that speaks in its unique voice, told in a well-crafted and complete, memorable style, a style of signature to the author. Follow writer's guidelines. Research markets. Send cover letter. Don't give up."

◑◐ TARPAULIN SKY

P.O. Box 189, Grafton VT 05146. Website: www.tarpaulinsky.com. **Contact:** Poetry Editors. P.O. Box 189, Grafton, VT 05146. E-mail:editors@tarpaulinsky.com. Website: www.tarpaulinsky.com. **Contact:** Poetry Editors. Estab. 2002. *Tarpaulin Sky*, published biannually in print and online, features "highest-quality poetry, prose, cross-genre work, art, photography, interviews, and reviews. We are open to all styles and forms, providing the forms appear inevitable and/or inextricable from the poems. We are especially fond of inventive/experimental and cross-/trans-genre work. The best indication of our aesthetic is found in the journal we produce: Please read it before submitting your work. Also, hardcopy submissions may be received by different editors at different times; check guidelines before submitting." Has published poetry by Jenny Boully, Matthea Harvey, Bin Ramke, Eleni Sikelianos, Juliana Spahr, and Joshua Marie Wilkinson. Receives about 3,000 poems/year. *Tarpaulin Sky*, published biannually in print and online, features "highest-quality poetry, prose, cross-genre work, art, photography, interviews, and reviews. We are open to all styles and forms, providing the forms appear inevitable and/or inextricable from the poems. We are especially fond of inventive/experimental and cross-/trans-genre work. The best indication of our aesthetic is found in the journal we produce: Please read it before submitting your work. Also, hardcopy submissions may be received by different editors at different times; check

guidelines before submitting." Has published poetry by Jenny Boully, Matthea Harvey, Bin Ramke, Eleni Sikelianos, Juliana Spahr, and Joshua Marie Wilkinson. Receives about 3,000 poems/year.

HOW TO CONTACT Submit 4-6 poems at a time. Considers simultaneous submissions; no previously published poems. Accepts e-mail submissions ("best received as attachments in .rtf or .pdf formats"); no disk submissions. Cover letter is preferred. Reads submissions year round. Time between acceptance and publication is 2-6 months. "Poems are read by all editors. We aim for consensus." Rarely comments on rejected poems. Guidelines available for SASE, by e-mail, or on website. E-mail: editors@tarpaulinsky.com (inquiries) or submissions@tarpaulinsky.com (submissions). Responds in 1-4 months. Pays in contributor's copies and "by waiving readings fees for Tarpaulin Sky Press Open Reading Periods." Always sends prepublication galleys (electronic). Acquires first rights. Reviews books/chapbooks of poetry.

◑ TAR RIVER POETRY

13 Erwin Hall, East Carolina University, Greenville NC 27858-4353. E-mail: TarRiverPoetry@gmail.com. Website: www.tarriverpoetry.com. **Contact:** Luke Whisnant, Editor. *Tar River Poetry*, published twice/year, is an "'all-poetry' magazine that publishes 40-50 poems per issue, providing the talented beginner and experienced writer with a forum that features all styles and forms of verse." Wants "skillful use of figurative language; poems that appeal to the senses." Does not want "sentimental, flat-statement poetry." Has published poetry by William Stafford, Sharon Olds, Carolyn Kizer, A.R. Ammons, and Claudia Emerson. Has also published "many other well-known poets, as well as numerous new and emerging poets." *Tar River Poetry* is 64 pages, 9X5, professionally printed with color cover. Receives 6,000-8,000 submissions/year, accepts 60-80. Press run is 900 (500 subscribers, 125 libraries). Subscription: $12/year; $20/two years. Sample: $7.00 postpaid.

◗ "We only consider submissions during two six-week reading periods: one in the fall (usually Sept. 15-Nov. 1) and one in the spring (Feb. 1-Mar. 15); check our website for reading periods before submitting. Work submitted at other times will not be considered."

TIPS Familiarize yourself with the type of poetry we publish before submitting. Sample copies are available, or visit our website to read sample poems. "Writers of poetry should first be readers of poetry. Read and study traditional and contemporary poetry."

ⓘ TATTOO HIGHWAY

E-mail: submissions@tattoohighway.org. Website: www.tattoohighway.org. E-mail: submissions@tattoohighway.org. Website: www.tattoohighway.org. "Our tastes are eclectic. We like fresh, vivid language, and we like stories and poems that are actually about something- that acknowledge a world beyond the writer's own psyche. If they have an edge, if they provoke us to think or make us laugh, so much the better."

HOW TO CONTACT Submit up to 5 poems at a time. Considers previously published poems (if they've appeared in small-circulation print journals; unpublished work preferred) and simultaneous submissions ("but please let us know promptly if you place your piece elsewhere"). Accepts e-mail submissions (pasted into body of message) only. "For hypertext or New Media (Flash, etc.) submissions, please provide a URL where we may view the work." Reading periods vary; "typically last about three months. Blind readings by editorial board. Several rounds of 'triage' during the reading period, usually handled by e-mail. No payment.

TIPS "Look at past issues online, then bring us your best stuff."

⊕ⓘ THE TAYLOR TRUST: POETRY AND PROSE

P.O. Box 903456, Palmdale CA 93590-3456. E-mail: lavonne.taylor@sbcglobal.net. Website: http://thetaylortrust.wordpress.com. **Contact:** LaVonne Taylor, editor and publisher. P.O. Box 903456, Palmdale, CA 93590-3456. E-mail:lavonne.taylor@sbcglobal.net. Website: http://thetaylortrust.wordpress.com. **Contact:** LaVonne Taylor, editor and publisher. *The Taylor Trust*, published quarterly, "considers ourselves egalitarian in that we accept most poetry forms. We also accept flash fiction, short stories, nonfiction. We publish more than one poem per author in each issue." Wants "all styles and forms. Prefers uplifting subject matter. Humorous poetry also accepted." Does not want "profanity or sexually explicit material. No age restrictions. Child must state age and give a short bio. Parental permission also required." Has published poetry by Mary L. Ports, Trisha Nelson, J.F. Connolly, Fredrick Zydek, John Fitzpatrick, Michael Lee Johnson. *The Taylor Trust* is 60-100 pages, digest-sized,

press run, perfect bound with a heavy, clay-coated embossed stock full-bleed color photo background cover. Receives 800 poems/year; accepts 90%. Single copy: $10; subscription $40.

MAGAZINES NEEDS *The Taylor Trust*, published quarterly, "considers ourselves egalitarian in that we accept most poetry forms. We also accept flash fiction, short stories, nonfiction. We publish more than one poem per author in each issue." Wants "all styles and forms. Prefers uplifting subject matter. Humorous poetry also accepted." Does not want "profanity or sexually explicit material. No age restrictions. Child must state age and give a short bio. Parental permission also required." Has published poetry by Mary L. Ports, Trisha Nelson, J.F. Connolly, Fredrick Zydek, John Fitzpatrick, Michael Lee Johnson. *The Taylor Trust* is 60-100 pages, digest-sized, press run, perfect bound with a heavy, clay-coated embossed stock full-bleed color photo background cover. Receives 800 poems/year; accepts 90%. Single copy: $10; subscription $40.

HOW TO CONTACT Submit 6 poems at a time, between 4-100 lines. Considers previously published poems ("as long as the author owns the publication rights") and simultaneous submissions ("with the understanding that it is the author's duty to inform all concerned when a poem is accepted"). Accepts e-mail submissions pasted into body of e-mail message; disk submissions. Cover letter is required. "We require a bio of about 150-200 words with publication history adn any other information the author cares to provide. We prefer not to return declined hard copies, but if the author requests it, an SASE is required with postal submittals. SASEs are needed with requests for guidelines." Reads submissions year round. Submit seasonal poems 3 months in advance. Time between acceptance and publication is 3 months. Poems are circulated to an editorial board. Sometimes comments on rejected poems. Regularly published theme issues loosely based on the seasons. Upcoming themes available in magazine, by e-mail, and on website. Guidelines available for SASE, by e-mail, and on website. Responds in 1 week. Pays 1 contributor's copy. Acquires one-time rights, electronic rights, "selected poems from each print publication will be posted on the site." Rights revert to poet upon publication. Reviews poetry books, chapbooks, and other magazines and journals in 500-1,000 words.

ADDITIONAL INFORMATION "Fee-based publishing on demand is available on a limited basis."

THE TEACHER'S VOICE

P.O. Box 150384, Kew Gardens NY 11415. E-mail: editor@the-teachers-voice.org. Website: www.the-teachers-voice.org. **Contact:** Andres Castro, founding/managing editor. (Specialized: the American teacher experience, from pre-K to university professor)

MAGAZINES NEEDS *The Teacher's Voice*, was founded as an experimental hardcopy literary magazine and is now free and online. "We publish poetry, short stories, creative nonfiction, and essays that reflect the many different American teacher experiences." Wants "all styles and forms. We ask to see critical creative writing that takes risks without being overly self-indulgent or inaccessible. We welcome work that ranges from 'art for art's sake' to radically social/political. Writing that illuminates the most pressing/urgent issues in American education and the lives of teachers gets special attention." Has published poetry by Edward Francisco, Sapphire, Hal Sirowitz, and Antler. Receives about 1,000 poems/year, accepts about 10%.

HOW TO CONTACT Submit 3-5 poems at a time. Lines/poem: no limits. Considers previously published poems (if rights are held by the author) and simultaneous submissions (contact if submission has been accepted elsewhere). No e-mail or disk submissions. Send prose pieces under 2,000 words. Cover letter is preferred. "Are you a teacher, administrator, parent, student, librarian, custodian, coach, security officer, etc? We do not accept responsibility for submissions or queries not accompanied by a SASE with adequate postage." Reads submissions year round. Time between acceptance and publication is 4 months to 1 year. Poems are circulated to an editorial board. Guidelines available on website. Sometimes sends prepublication galleys "if requested." Acquires first rights and electronic reprint rights. Rights revert to poet "after work is first electronically published and archived on this site; no material on this site may be reproduced in any form without permission from their individual authors." No longer accepts online submissions.

ADDITIONAL INFORMATION "Since we publish open as well as theme issues (that require enough thematic pieces to be compiled) and do rely on readership financial support, our publishing schedule and format may vary from year to year. We publish hardcopy limited press collections when funds allow. Our production goal is to showcase strong cohesive collections that support our mission and satisfy the needs of particular issues. For the moment, our new focus on electronic publishing is a matter of survival that offers many new possibilities and opportunities in keeping with the changing times."

CONTEST/AWARD OFFERINGS Sponsors *The Teacher's Voice* Annual Chapbook Contest and *The Teacher's Voice* Annual Poetry Contest for Unpublished Poets. Final contest judges have included, Sapphire, Jack Hirschman, and Taylor Mali. Guidelines for both contests available for SASE, by e-mail, or on website.

TEARS IN THE FENCE

38 Hod View, Stourpaine, Nr. Blandford Forum, Dorset DT11 8TN England. (44)(1258)456803. Fax: (44)(1258)454026. E-mail: david@davidcaddy.wanadoo.co.uk. Website: www.myspace.com/tearsinthefence. Established 1984. **Contact:** David Caddy, general editor.

MAGAZINES NEEDS *Tears in the Fence*, published twice a year and is a "small press magazine of poetry, fiction, interviews, essays, and reviews. We are open to a wide variety of poetic styles. Work that shows social and poetic awareness whilst prompting close and divergent readings. However, we like to publish a variety of work." Has published poetry by John Hartley Williams, Sheila E Murphy, John Kinsella, Donna Hilbert, Anne Blonstein, Anthony Barnett, Glyn Hughes, Carrie Etter, Vahni Capildeo. *Tears in the Fence* is 168 pages, A5, docutech-printed on 110-gms. paper, perfect-bound, with matte card cover. Press run is 800 (522 subscribers). Subscription: $20/3 issues. Sample: $8.

HOW TO CONTACT Submit 6 poems at a time. Accepts e-mail (pasted into body of message) and disk submissions. Cover letter with brief bio is required. Poems must be typed; include SASE. Time between acceptance and publication is 3 months. Pays one contributor's copy. Reviews books of poetry in 2,000-4,000 words, single- or multi-book format. Send materials for review consideration.

ALSO OFFERS The magazine runs a regular series of readings in London, and an annual international literary festival.

⬤🔗 TERRAIN.ORG: A JOURNAL OF THE BUILT & NATURAL ENVIROMENTS

Terrain.org, P.O. Box 19161, Tucson AZ 19161. 520-241-7390. Website: www.terrain.org. **Contact:** Simmons Buntin, editor-in-chief. Terrain.org is based on and thus welcomes quality submissions from new and experienced authors and artists alike. Our online journal accepts only the finest poetry, essays, fiction, articles, artwork, and other contributions' material that reaches deep into the earth's fiery core, or humanity's incalculable core, and brings forth new insights and wisdom. Sponsors *Terrain.org 2nd Annual Contest in Poetry, Fiction, and Nonfiction!* Submissions due by August 1. How to Submit: Go to Submission Manager Online Tool. "Terrain.org is searching for that interface-the integration-among the built and natural environments, that might be called the soul of place. The works contained within Terrain.org ultimately examine the physical realm around us, and how those environments influence us and each other physically, mentally, emotionally and spiritually." Semiannual. All issues are theme-based. List of upcoming themes available on website. Receives 25 mss/month. Accepts 3-5 mss/issue; 6-10 mss/year. Agented fiction 5%. **Publishes 1-3 new writers/year.** Published Al Sim, Jacob MacAurthur Mooney, T.R. Healy, Deborah Fries, Andrew Wingfield, Braden Hepner, Chavawn Kelly, Tamara Kaye Sellman. Sometimes comments on/critiques rejected mss. Sends galleys to author. Publication is copyrighted.

◗ Awards: PLANetizen Top 50 Website 2002 & 2003. PLANetizen Top 50 Website 2002 & 2003. "Does not read August 1-September 30 and February 1-March 30."

HOW TO CONTACT Submit through online submission form.

ADDITIONAL INFORMATION Sponsors *Terrain.org 2nd Annual Contest in Poetry, Fiction, and Nonfiction!* Submissions due by August 1. See guidelines online.

TIPS "We have three primary criteria in reviewing fiction: 1) The story is compelling and well-crafted. 2) The story provides some element of surprise; i.e., whether in content, form or delivery we are unexpectedly delighted in what we've read. 3) The story meets an upcoming theme, even if only peripherally. Read fiction in the current issue and perhaps some archived work, and if you like what you read—and our overall enviromental slant—then send us your best work. Make sure you follow our submission guidelines (including cover note with bio), and that your manuscript is as error-free as possible."

⬤ TEXAS POETRY CALENDAR

Dos Gatos Press, 1310 Crestwood Rd., Austin TX 78722. (512)467-0678. E-mail: editors@dosgatospress.org. Website: www.dosgatospress.org. **Contact:** Scott Wiggerman or Cindy Huyser, Co-Editors; David Meischen, Managing Editor. (Specialized: poems with a TX connection)

MAGAZINES NEEDS *Texas Poetry* Calendar, published annually in August, features a "week-by-week calendar side-by-side with poems with a Texas connection." Wants "a wide variety of styles, voices, and forms, including rhyme—though a Texas connection is preferred. Humor is welcome! Poetry only!" Does not want "children's poetry, erotic poetry, profanity, obscure poems, previously published work, or poems over 35 lines." Texas Poetry Calendar is about 144 pages, digest-sized, offset-printed, spiral-bound, with full-color cardstock cover. Receives about 600 poems/year, accepts about 70-75. Press run is 1,200; 70 distributed free to contributors. Single copy: $13.95 plus $3 shipping. Make checks payable to Dos Gatos Press.

HOW TO CONTACT Submit 3 poems at a time. Lines/poem: 35 maximum, "including spaces and title." No simultaneous submissions; no previously published poems. No fax, e-mail, or disk submissions. Cover letter is required. "Include a short bio (100-200 words) and poem titles in cover letter. Also include e-mail address and phone number. Do not include poet's name on the poems themselves!" Reads submissions Jan-May. Time between acceptance and publication is 3-4 months. Poems are circulated to an editorial board. Never comments on rejected poems. Deadline: February 21 (postmark).

⬤ TEXAS REVIEW

Texas Review Press, Department of English, Sam Houston State University, Box 2146, Huntsville TX 77341-2146. (936)294-1992. Fax: (936)294-3070. E-mail: eng_pdr@shsu.edu; cww006@shsu.edu. Website: www.shsu.edu/~www_trp. Claude Wolley, assistant to director. **Contact:** Dr. Paul Ruffin, editor/director. Texas Review Press, c/o English Department, Box 2146, Sam Houston State University, Huntsville TX 77341-2146. (936)294-1992. Fax: (936)294-3070. E-mail: eng_pdr@shsu.edu. Website: www.shsu.edu/~www_trp. Established 1976. **Contact:** Robert

Phillips, poetry editor. *The Texas Review*, published semiannually, is a "scholarly journal publishing poetry, short fiction, essays and book reviews." Has published poetry by Donald Hall, X.J. Kennedy, and Richard Eberhart. *The Texas Review* is 152 pages, digest-sized, offset printed, perfect-bound, with 4-color cover, includes ads. Press run is 1,000. Single copy: $12; subscription: $24. Sample: $5. Make checks payable to Friends of Texas Review.

MAGAZINES NEEDS *The Texas Review*, published semiannually, is a "scholarly journal publishing poetry, short fiction, essays and book reviews." Has published poetry by Donald Hall, X.J. Kennedy, and Richard Eberhart. *The Texas Review* is 152 pages, digest-sized, offset printed, perfect-bound, with 4-color cover, includes ads. Press run is 1,000. Single copy: $12; subscription: $24. Sample: $5. Make checks payable to Friends of Texas Review.

HOW TO CONTACT No previously published poems or simultaneous submissions. Include SASE. Reads submissions September 1-April 30 only. Time between acceptance and publication is 6 months. Poems are circulated to an editorial board. Seldom comments on rejected poems. Responds in up to 6 months. Pays one-year subscription and one contributor's copy (may request more). Acquires first North American serial rights. Returns rights "for publication in anthology."

CONTEST/AWARD OFFERINGS Sponsors the X.J. Kennedy Poetry Prize (for best full-length book of poetry) and the Robert Phillips Poetry Chapbook Prize (for best poetry chapbook). Both competitions award $200 and publication for the winning mss. **Entry fee:** $20. Guidelines available for SASE (specifying "for poetry/fiction contest guidelines") or on website.

● THE AGUILAR EXPRESSION

1329 Gilmore Ave., Donora PA 15033. (724)379-8019. E-mail: xyz0@access995.com. Website: www.word-runner.com/xfaguilar. **Contact:** Xavier F. Aguilar, editor/publisher. 1329 Gilmore Ave., Donora PA 15033. (724)379-8019. E-mail: xyz0@access995.com (inquiries only). Website: www.wordrunner.com/xfaguilar. Established 1986. **Contact:** Xavier F. Aguilar, editor/publisher. *The Aguilar Expression*, published annually in October, encourages "poetics that deal with now, which our readers can relate to. Has published poetry by Martin Kich and Gail Ghai. *The Aguilar*

Expression is 4-20 pages, 8x11, typeset, printed on 20 lb. paper. Receives about 10-15 poems/month, accepts about 10-15/year. Circulation is 150. Sample: $5. Make checks payable to Xavier Aguilar. Submit up to 5 poems at a time. Lines/poem: 30 maximum. No e-mail submissions. Cover letter is required (include writing background). SASE (for contact purposes) is required. Manuscripts should be submitted in clear, camera-ready copy. Submit copies, not originals; mss will not be returned. "We encourage all writers to send a SASE for writer's guidelines before submitting." Responds in 2 months. Pays 2 contributor's copies.

○ "In publishing poetry, I try to exhibit the unique reality that we too often take for granted and acquaint as mediocre."

MAGAZINES NEEDS *The Aguilar Expression*, published annually in October, encourages "poetics that deal with now, which our readers can relate to. In publishing poetry, I try to exhibit the unique reality that we too often take for granted and acquaint as mediocre." Has published poetry by Martin Kich and Gail Ghai. *The Aguilar Expression* is 4-20 pages, 8x11, typeset, printed on 20 lb. paper. Receives about 10-15 poems/month, accepts about 10-15/year. Circulation is 150. Sample: $5. Make checks payable to Xavier Aguilar.

HOW TO CONTACT Submit up to 5 poems at a time. Lines/poem: 30 maximum. No e-mail submissions. Cover letter is required (include writing background). SASE (for contact purposes) is required. Manuscripts should be submitted in clear, camera-ready copy. Submit copies, not originals; mss will not be returned. "We encourage all writers to send a SASE for writer's guidelines before submitting." Responds in 2 months. Pays 2 contributor's copies.

● THE AUROREAN

Encircle Publications, P.O. Box 187, Farmington ME 04938. (207)778-0467. E-mail: Aurorean@encircle-pub.com (inquiries only). Website: www.encircle-pub.com. **Contact:** Devin McGuire, Assistant Editor. *The Aurorean*, published semiannually (spring/summer, fall/winter), uses "well crafted upbeat poetry. Seasonal/New England focus, but open to other subjects." Often in need of short poems (4-8 lines). Publishes haiku section each issue. "Mostly free verse and occasional rhyme. We publish newer poets alongside the biggest names in the small press." Does not want "anything hateful, overly religious." Has published poetry by Patricia Fargnoli, Thomas Griffin, Cleo Griffith, Connie Post, and Don Russ. *The Aurorean* since 1995, is digest-sized, professionally printed, perfect-bound. Press run is 550. Single copy: $11 U.S., $12 international; subscription: $21 U.S. (2 issues), $25 international. Sample: back issues from previous quarterly format, $3 each; back issues of current semiannual format, $7 each. Make checks payable to Encircle Publications, LLC. Submit 1-5 poems at a time in a #10 letter-sized envelope (larger envelopes discouraged due to space). Lines/poem: 36 maximum including stanza breaks. "Discourages simultaneous submissions "as we always reply in 3 months maximum. If you must submit simultaneously, be aware that none can be withdrawn once we have typeset/mailed a proof." Cover letter with brief introduction is preferred. "Fold cover letter separately and fold poems together. Poems folded individually cannot be reviewed." Include SASE with sufficient postage for return/reply; International submissions, include SAE and IRC. Manuscripts are acknowledged with a postcard or by e-mail upon receipt (e-mail address appreciated). Reads submissions August 16 - February 15 for spring/summer; February 16 - August 15 for fall/winter. Sends proofs with instructions for poets accepted each issue on how to submit bios. Pays 2 contributor's copies per poem published (maximum 4 copies/issue). Acquires one-time rights. Please credit if later published elsewhere. Two featured poets each issue (superb execution of poetic craft; in some way seasonally/New England reflective) receive publication of up to 3 poems with 100-word bio; 10 copies of magazine and 1-year subscription. You may submit to the Unrorean by e-mail: unrorean@encirclepub.com (Attn: Devin McGuire).

MAGAZINES NEEDS *The Aurorean*, published semiannually (spring/summer, fall/winter), uses "well crafted upbeat poetry. Seasonal/New England focus, but open to other subjects." Often in need of short poems (4-8 lines). Publishes haiku section each issue. "Mostly free verse and occasional rhyme. We publish newer poets alongside the biggest names in the small press." Does not want "anything hateful, overly religious." Has published poetry by Patricia Fargnoli, Thomas Griffin, Cleo Griffith, Connie Post, and Don Russ. *The Aurorean* since 1995, is digest-sized, professionally printed, perfect-bound. Press run is 550. Single copy: $11 U.S., $12 international; subscription: $21 U.S. (2 issues), $25 international. Sample: back

issues from previous quarterly format, $3 each; back issues of current semiannual format, $7 each. Make checks payable to Encircle Publications, LLC.

HOW TO CONTACT Submit 1-5 poems at a time in a #10 letter-sized envelope (larger envelopes discouraged due to space). Lines/poem: 36 maximum including stanza breaks. Does not consider previously published or simultaneous submissions. "Discourages simultaneous submissions "as we always reply in 3 months maximum. If you must submit simultaneously, be aware that none can be withdrawn once we have typeset/mailed a proof." Cover letter with brief introduction is preferred. "Fold cover letter separately and fold poems together. Poems folded individually cannot be reviewed." Include SASE with sufficient postage for return/reply; International submissions, include SAE and IRC. Manuscripts are acknowledged with a postcard or by e-mail upon receipt (e-mail address appreciated). Reads submissions August 16 - February 15 for spring/summer; February 16 - August 15 for fall/winter. Sends proofs with instructions for poets accepted each issue on how to submit bios. Pays 2 contributor's copies per poem published (maximum 4 copies/issue). Acquires one-time rights. Please credit if later published elsewhere. Two featured poets each issue (superb execution of poetic craft; in some way seasonally/New England reflective) receive publication of up to 3 poems with 100-word bio; 10 copies of magazine and 1-year subscription.

ALSO OFFERS *The Unrorean* broadsheet, appears twice/year mid-January and mid-July for poems too long, experimental, or dark for magazine. "Still, nothing hateful." 2-4 11x17 pages, laser-printed. Sample: $2 postpaid. Include SASE for return/reply. No proofs, bios; open submission dates. Pays 1 contributor's copy/poem, 1 "editor's pick" receives 2. You may submit to the unrorean by e-mail: unrorean@encirclepub.com (Attention Devin McGuire). Do not submit to the Aurorean by e-mail. "Poets may submit for the magazine or broadsheet individually (work submitted individually for broadsheet is not acknowledged by postcard or e-mail). Work sent to the magazine will also be considered for the broadsheet, unless otherwise requested in cover letter." Please see guidelines/announcements on website and be familiar with our journal when submitting.

◑◎ THE BEAR DELUXE MAGAZINE

Orlo, 810 SE Belmont #5, Portland OR 97214. (503)242-1047. E-mail: bear@orlo.org. Website: www.orlo.org. Kristin Rogers Brown, art director. **Contact:** Tom Webb, editor-in-chief. Submit 3-5 poems at a time. Lines/poem: 50 maximum. Considers previously published poems and simultaneous submissions "so long as noted." Poems are reviewed by a committee of 3-5 people. Publishes 1 theme issue/year. Guidelines available for SASE. Responds in 6 months. Acquires first or one-time rights." *The Bear Deluxe Magazine* is a national independent environmental arts magazine publishing significant works of reporting, creative nonfiction, literature, visual art and design. Based in the Pacific Northwest, it reaches across cultural and political divides to engage readers on vital issues effecting the environment. Published twice per year, *The Bear Deluxe* includes a wider array and a higher-percentage of visual art work and design than many other publications. Artwork is included both as editorial support and as stand alone or independent art. It has included nationally recognized artists as well as emerging artists. As with any publication, artists are encouraged to review a sample copy for a clearer understanding of the magazine's approach. Unsolicited submissions and samples are accepted and encouraged. *The Bear Deluxe* has been recognized for both its editorial and design excellence. Over the years, awards and positive reviews have been handed down from *Print* magazine, *Utne Reader, Literary Arts, Adbusters*, the Bumbershoot Arts Festival, *Orion, Fact Sheet 5*, the Regional Arts and Culture Council, *The Oregonian*, and the *Library Journal*, among others."

> ◒ "The magazine is moving away from using the term environmental writing. Quality writing which furthers the magazine's goal of engaging new and divergent readers will garner the most attention." The Orlo Office is open by appointment only.

HOW TO CONTACT Accepts e-mail submissions (pasted into body of message) but it is not as preferable as sending hard copy by mail. "We can't respond to e-mail submissions but do look at them."

TIPS "Offer to be a stringer for future ideas. Get a copy of the magazine and guidelines, and query us with specific nonfiction ideas and clips. We're looking for original, magazine-style stories, not fluff or PR. Fiction, essay, and poetry writers should know we have an open and blind review policy and should keep sending their best work even if rejected once. Be as specific as possible in queries."

◑◉ THE CHRISTIAN SCIENCE MONITOR

The Home Forum Page, 210 Massachussetts Ave., P02-30, Boston MA 02115. E-mail: homeforum@csmonitor.com. Website: www.csmonitor.com; http://www.csmonitor.com/About/Contributor-guidelines#homeforum. **Contact:** Editors: Susan Leach, Marjorie Kehe.

> ◒ *The Christian Science Monitor*, an international daily newspaper, regularly features poetry in The Home Forum section. Wants "finely crafted poems that explore and celebrate daily life; that provide a respite from daily news and from the bleakness that appears in so much contemporary verse." Considers free verse and fixed forms. Has published poetry by Diana Der-Hovanessian, Marilyn Krysl, and Michael Glaser. Publishes 1-2 poems/week.

◑ THE DERONDA REVIEW

P.O. Box 55164, Madison WI 53705. E-mail: derondareview@att.net. Website: www.derondareview.org; www.pointandcircumference.com. Mindy Aber Barad, co-editor for Israel, P.O.B. 1299, Efrat 90435, Israel. Email: maber4kids@yahoo.com. **Contact:** Esther Cameron, Editor-in-Chief. *The Deronda Review*, published semiannually, seeks to "promote a literature of introspection, dialogue, and social concern." Wants "poetry of beauty and integrity with emotional and intellectual depth, commitment to subject matter as well as language, and the courage to ignore fashion. Welcome: well-crafted formal verse, social comment (including satire), love poems, philosophical/religious poems. The website will also publish essays and fiction. *The Deronda Review* has a standing interest in work that sees Judaism as a source of values and/or reflects on the current situation of Israel and of Western civilization. Open, in principle, to writers of all ages." Has published poetry by Yakov Azriel, Ruth Blumert, Ida Fasel, Constance Rowell Mastores, Richard Moore, and Yaacov Dovid Shulman. *The Deronda Review* is 28-36 pages, magazine-sized, photocopied, saddle-stapled, with cardstock cover. Press run is 375. Single copy: $6; subscription: $12. Co-Editor for Israel: Mindy Aber Barad, P.O.B. 1299, Efrat 90435. *The Deronda Review*, published semiannually, seeks to "promote a literature of introspection, dialogue, and social concern." Wants "poetry of beauty and integrity with emotional and intellectual depth, commitment to subject matter as well as language, and the courage to ignore fashion. Welcome: well-crafted formal verse, social comment (including satire), love poems, philosophical/religious poems. The website will also publish essays and fiction. *The Deronda Review* has a standing interest in work that sees Judaism as a source of values and/or reflects on the current situation of Israel and of Western civilization. Open, in principle, to writers of all ages." *The Deronda Review* is 28-36 pages, magazine-sized, photocopied, saddle-stapled, with cardstock cover. Press run is 375. Single copy: $6; subscription: $12. Submit 3-5 poems at a time or, for the website, prose of any length. Longer works will be considered for installment publication. "The paper magazine rarely accepts reprints; the website invites submission of poems already published in paper format. All poems published for the first time on the website will be printed in the magazine." Cover letter is unnecessary. "Do include SASE with sufficient postage to return all mss or with 'Reply Only" clearly indicated. First-time contributors in the U.S. are requested to submit by surface mail. Poets whose work is accepted will be asked for titles of books available, to be published in the magazine." Often comments on rejected poems. Does not offer guidelines because "the tradition is the only 'guideline.'" Encourages contributors to obtain a sample." Pays 2 contributor's copies for magazine publication.

HOW TO CONTACT Submit 3-5 poems at a time or, for the website, prose of any length. Longer works will be considered for installment publication. Considers simultaneous submissions. "The paper magazine rarely accepts reprints; the website invites submission of poems already published in paper format. All poems published for the first time on the website will be printed in the magazine." Cover letter is unnecessary. "Do include SASE with sufficient postage to return all manuscripts or with 'Reply Only' clearly indicated. First-time contributors in the U.S. are requested to submit by surface mail. Poets whose work is accepted will be asked for titles of books available, to be published in the magazine." Time between acceptance and publication is up to 1 year. Often comments on rejected poems. Does not offer guidelines because "the tradition is the only 'guideline.' We do encourage contributors to write for a sample." Responds in up to 4 months; "if longer, please query by e-mail." Pays 2 contributor's copies for magazine

publication. Acquires first rights. Address: P.O. Box 55164, Madison WI 53705. Email: derondareview@att.net. Website: www.derondareview.org.

ADDITIONAL INFORMATION *The Deronda Review* publishes the addresses of poets who would welcome correspondence. Longer selections of poets frequently published in the magazine are posted on www.pointandcircumference.com.

THE JOURNAL

(614)292-4076. Fax: (614)292-7816. E-mail: thejournal@osu.edu; thejournalmag@gmail.com. Website: english.osu.edu/research/journals/thejournal/. "We're open to all forms; we tend to favor work that gives evidence of a mature and sophisticated sense of the language."

"We are interested in quality fiction, poetry, nonfiction, and reviews of new books of poetry. We impose no restrictions on category, type, or length of submission for Fiction, Poetry, and Nonfiction. We are happy to consider long stories and self-contained excerpts of novels. Please double-space all prose submissions. Address correspondence to the Editors. We will only respond to submissions accompanied by a SASE."

CONTEST/AWARD OFFERINGS Chooses the winning ms in the Ohio State University Press/*The Journal Award* (see separate listing in Contests & Awards)."However else poets train or educate themselves, they must do what they can to know our language. Too much of the writing we see indicates poets do not, in many cases, develop a feel for the possibilities of language, and do not pay attention to craft. Poets should not be in a rush to publish—until they are ready."

TIPS "Manuscripts are rejected because of lack of understanding of the short story form, shallow plots, undeveloped characters. Cure: Read as much well-written fiction as possible. Our readers prefer 'psychological' fiction rather than stories with intricate plots. Take care to present a clean, well-typed submission."

THE KERF

(707) 476-4370. E-mail: ken-letko@redwoods.edu. Website: http://www.redwoods.edu/Departments/english/poets&writers/clm.htm. **Contact:** Ken Letko, editor. *The Kerf*, published annually in fall, features "poetry that speaks to the environment and humanity." Wants "poetry that exhibits an environmental con-

sciousness." Considers poetry by children and teens. Has published poetry by Ruth Daigon, Alice D'Alessio, James Grabill, George Keithley, and Paul Willis. *The Kerf* is 54 pages, digest-sized, printed via Docutech, saddle-stapled, with CS2 coverstock. Receives about 1,000 poems/year, accepts up to 3%. Press run is 400 (150 shelf sales); 100 distributed free to contributors and writing centers. Sample: $5. Make checks payable to College of the Redwoods.

MAGAZINES NEEDS *The Kerf*, published annually in fall, features "poetry that speaks to the environment and humanity." Wants "poetry that exhibits an environmental consciousness." Considers poetry by children and teens. Has published poetry by Ruth Daigon, Alice D'Alessio, James Grabill, George Keithley, and Paul Willis. *The Kerf* is 54 pages, digest-sized, printed via Docutech, saddle-stapled, with CS2 coverstock. Receives about 1,000 poems/year, accepts up to 3%. Press run is 400 (150 shelf sales); 100 distributed free to contributors and writing centers. Sample: $5. Make checks payable to College of the Redwoods.

HOW TO CONTACT Submit up to 5 poems (7 pages maximum) at a time. No previously published poems or simultaneous submissions. Reads submissions January 15-March 31 only. Time between acceptance and publication is 3-4 months. "Our editors debate (argue for or against) the inclusion of each manuscript." Seldom comments on rejected poems. Guidelines available for SASE. Responds in 2 months. Sometimes sends prepublication galleys. Pays one contributor's copy. Acquires first North American serial rights.

❶ THE LYRIC

P.O. Box 110, Jericho Corners VT 05465. E-mail: themuse@thelyricmagazine.com. Website: www.thelyricmagazine.com. (Specialized: rhymed poetry, traditional) P.O. Box 110, Jericho Corners VT 05465. Phone/fax: (802)899-3993. E-mail: Lyric@sover.net. Established 1921. **Contact:** Jean Mellichamp-Milliken, editor. *The Lyric*, published quarterly, is "the oldest magazine in North America in continuous publication devoted to traditional poetry." Prints about 55 poems/issue. Wants "rhymed verse in traditional forms, for the most part, with an occasional piece of blank or free verse. Most of our poems are accessible on first or second reading. Frost wrote: 'Don't hide too far away.'" Has published poetry by Michael Burch,

Gail White, Joseph Awad, Ruth Harrison, Barbara Loots, and Glenna Holloway. *The Lyric* is 32 pages, digest-sized, professionally printed with varied typography, with matte card cover. Receives about 3,000 submissions/year, accepts 5%. Subscription: $15/year, $28/2 years, $38/3 years (U.S.), $17/year for Canada and other countries (in U.S. funds only). Sample: $4.

TIPS All contributors are eligible for quarterly and annual prizes totaling $650. Also offers the Lyric College Contest, open to undergraduate students. Awards prize of $400. **Deadline:** December 15. Send entries to Tanya Cimonetti, 1393 Spear St., S., Burlington VT 05403."Our *raison d'etre* has been the encouragement of form, music, rhyme, and accessibility in poetry. As we witness the growing tide of appreciation for traditional/lyric poetry, we are proud to have stayed the course for 89 years, helping keep the roots of poetry alive."

❶❸ THEMA

Thema Literary Society, P.O. Box 8747, Metairie LA 70011-8747. E-mail: thema@cox.net. Website: http://members.cox.net/thema. **Contact:** Gail Howard, poetry editor.

MAGAZINES NEEDS *THEMA*, published triannually, uses poetry related to specific themes. "Each issue is based on an unusual premise. Please, please send SASE for guidelines before submitting poetry to find out the upcoming themes." Does not want "scatologic language, alternate lifestyle, explicit love poetry." Has published poetry by Greg Tuleja, Max Gutmann, Chris Abernethy, James Penha, Rosalie Calabrese, Sharon Lask Munson, Robert Manaster, and Lori Williams. *THEMA* is 120 pages, digest-sized professionally printed, with glossy card cover. Receives about 400 poems/year, accepts about 8%. Press run is 400 (230 subscribers, 30 libraries). Subscription: $20 U.S./$30 foreign. Sample $10 U.S./$15 foreign.

HOW TO CONTACT Submit up to 3 poems at a time. Include SASE. "All submissions should be typewritten on standard 8½x11 paper. Submissions are accepted all year, but evaluated after specified deadlines." Specify target theme. Editor comments on submissions. Upcoming themes and guidelines available in magazine, for SASE, by e-mail, or on website. Pays $10/poem and 1 contributor's copy. Acquires one-time rights.

❶ THE MACGUFFIN

18600 Haggerty Rd., Livonia MI 48152-2696. (734)462-4400, ext 5327. E-mail: macguffin@schoolcraft.edu.

Website: www.macguffin.org. **Contact:** Steven A. Dolgin, editor; Nicholle Cormier, managing editor; Elizabeth Kircos, fiction editor. "Our purpose is to encourage, support and enhance the literary arts in the Schoolcraft College community, the region, the state, and the nation. We also sponsor annual literary events and give voice to deserving new writers as well as established writers."

MAGAZINES NEEDS *The MacGuffin*, published 3 times/year, prints "the best poetry, fiction, nonfiction, and artwork we receive. We have no thematic or stylistic biases. We look for well-crafted poetry." Does not want "pornography, triteness, and sloppy poetry. We do not publish haiku, concrete, or light verse." Has published poetry by Thomas Lynch, Gabriel Welsch, Linda Nemec Foster, Conrad Hilberry, and Laurence Lieberman. *The MacGuffin* is 160 pages, 6x9, perfect-bound, with color cover. Press run is 500. Subscription: $22/year. Sample: $6/copy.

HOW TO CONTACT Submit no more than 5 poems at a time. Lines/poem: 400 maximum. Considers simultaneous submissions if informed; no previously published poems. Accepts fax, e-mail (as Word attachment only), and hard copy submissions via mail (SASE for reply only). Cover letter is required. "List titles and brief bio in cover letter. Do not staple work." Poems should be typed, single-spaced, 1 per page. Poet's name, address, and e-mail should appear on each page. Include SASE. Guidelines available for SASE, by fax, e-mail, or on website. Responds in 2-6 months. Pays 2 contributor's copies plus discount on additional copies. Acquires first rights if published; rights revert to poets upon publication.

CONTEST/AWARD OFFERINGS "Also sponsors the National Poet Hunt Contest. See contest rules online. For mail submissions: do not staple work. Include name, email, address, and the page no. on each page. Include SASE for reply only. Submit each work (single story or five-poem submission) as a Word .doc attachment."

TIPS "We strive to give promising new writers the opportunity to publish alongside recognized writers. Follow the submission guidelines, proofread your work, and be persistent. When we reject a story, we may accept the next one you send. When we make suggestions for a rewrite, we may accept the revision. Make your characters come to life. Even the most ordinary people become fascinating if they live for your readers."

THE MAGAZINE OF FANTASY & SCIENCE FICTION

P.O. Box 3447, Hoboken NJ 07030. (201) 876-2551. E-mail: fandsf@aol.com. Website: www.fandsf.com. **Contact:** Gordon Van Gelder, editor. *The Magazine of Fantasy & Science Fiction* is 240 pages, digest-sized, offset-printed, perfect-bound, with glossy cover, includes ads. Receives about 20-40 poems/year, accepts about 1%. Press run is 35,000 (20,000 subscribers). Single copy: $7; subscription: $34.97. Sample: $6. Make checks payable to *The Magazine of Fantasy & Science Fiction.*"*The Magazine of Fantasy and Science Fiction* publishes various types of science fiction and fantasy short stories and novellas, making up about 80% of each issue. The balance of each issue is devoted to articles about science fiction, a science column, book and film reviews, cartoons, and competitions." Bimonthly."

> The *Magazine of Fantasy and Science Fiction* won a Nebula Award for Best Novelet for "The Merchant and the Alchemist's Gate" by Ted Chiang in in 2008. Also won the 2007 World Fantasy Award for Best Short Story for "Journey into the Kingdom" by M. Rickert. Editor Van Gelder won the Hugo Award for Best Editor (short form), 2007 and 2008.

HOW TO CONTACT Submit 1-3 poems at a time. No previously published poems or simultaneous submissions. No e-mail or disk submissions. Time between acceptance and publication is up to 2 years, but usually about 9 months.

TIPS "Good storytelling makes a submission stand out. Regarding manuscripts, a well-prepared manuscript (i.e., one that follows the traditional format, like that describted here: http://www.sfwa.org/writing/vonda/vonda.htm) stands out more than any gimmicks. Read an issue of the magazine before submitting. New writers should keep their submissions under 15,000 words—we rarely publish novellas by new writers."

THE MISSOURI REVIEW

(573)882-4474. Fax: (573)884-4671. E-mail: tmr@missourireview.com. Website: www.missourireview.com.

> "We publish contemporary fiction, poetry, interviews, personal essays, cartoons, special features—such as History as Literature series and Found Text series—for the literary and

the general reader interested in a wide range of subjects."

MAGAZINES NEEDS *The Missouri Review*, published 3 times/year, prints poetry "features" only—6-14 pages for each of 3-5 poets/issue. "By devoting more editorial space to each poet, *The Missouri Review* provides a fuller look at the work of some of the best writers composing today." Has published poetry by Ellen Bass, Anna Meek, Timothy Liu, Bob Hicok, George Bilgere, and Camille Dungy. Subscription: $24. Sample: $8.95.

HOW TO CONTACT Submit 6-12 poems at a time. Considers simultaneous submissions with notification; no previously published poems. No e-mail submissions; accepts postal and online submissions ($3 to download up to 20 pages of poetry at one time). Cover letter is preferred. Include SASE. Reads submissions year round. Responds in 10-12 weeks. Sometimes sends prepublication galleys. Pays $30/printed page and 3 contributor's copies. Acquires all rights. Returns rights "after publication, without charge, at the request of the authors." Staff reviews books of poetry.

ADDITIONAL INFORMATION The Tom McAfee Discovery Feature is awarded at least once/year to showcase an outstanding young poet who has not yet published a book; poets are selected from regular submissions at the discretion of the editors.

CONTEST/AWARD OFFERINGS The Jeffrey E. Smith Editors' Prize in Poetry (see separate listing in Contests & Awards).

TIPS "Send your best work." The Missouri Review holds two annual contests, the **Jeffrey E. Smith Editors' Prize** in Fiction, Essay and Poetry, and our recently instituted **Audio Competition**.

○○○ THE NEW ORPHIC REVIEW

706 Mill St., Nelson BC V1L 4S5, Canada. E-mail: dreamhorsepress@yahoo.com. Website: www.dreamhorsepress.com. "Unsolicited manuscripts ARE considered year round. Send a ten poem query first, with an SASE proper postage (keeping in mind postage rate changes), include a cover letter with biography, and a reading fee of $10 or for an additional 1 dollar save yourself the postage, paper and envelopes and submit online. Response times vary, but we will either respond with a request to review the manuscript in its entirety or with a simple rejection note. If you have submitted a full manuscript under the old system and

haven't received a response, please be patient, they are still being considered."

○ Margrith Schraner's story, "Dream Dig" was included in *The Journey Prize Anthology*, 2001. Margrith Schraner's story, "Dream Dig" was included in *The Journey Prize Anthology*, 2001.

ADDITIONAL INFORMATION New Orphic Publishers, 706 Mill St., Nelson BC V1L 4S5 Canada. (250)354-0494. Website: www.dreamhorsepress.com. Established 1995 (New Orphic Publishers), 1998 (New Orphic Review). **Contact:** Margrith Schraner, associate editor. Editor-in-Chief: Ernest Hekkanen. *New Orphic Review*, published in May and October, is run "by an opinionated visionary who is beholden to no one, least of all government agencies like the Canada Council or institutions of higher learning. He feels Canadian literature is stagnant, lacks daring, and is terribly incestuous." Publishes poetry, novel excerpts, mainstream and experimental short stories, and articles on a wide range of subjects. Each issue includes a Featured Poet section. "*New Orphic Review* publishes authors from around the world as long as the pieces are written in English and are accompanied by a SASE with proper Canadian postage and/or U.S. dollars to offset the cost of postage." Wants "tight, well-wrought poetry over leggy, prosaic poetry. No 'fuck you' poetry; no rambling pseudo Beat poetry." Has published poetry by Robert Cooperman, Step Elder, Louis E. Bourgeios, and Art Joyce. *New Orphic Review* is 120-140 pages, magazine-sized, laser-printed, perfect-bound, with color cover, includes ads. Receives about 400 poems/year, accepts about 10%. Press run is 500. Subscription: $30 CAD for individuals, $35 CAD for institutions. Sample: $20. Submit 6 poems at a time. Lines/poem: 5 minimum, 30 maximum. Considers simultaneous submissions; no previously published poems. Cover letter is preferred. "Make sure a SASE (or SAE and IRC) is included." Time between acceptance and publication is up to 8 months. "The managing editor and associate editor refer work to the editor-in-chief." Seldom comments on rejected poems. Occasionally publishes theme issues. Guidelines available for SASE (or SAE and IRC). Responds in 2 months. Pays 1 contributor's copy. Acquires first North American serial rights. New Orphic Publishers publishes 4 paperbacks/year. However, **all material is solicited**.

TIPS "I like fiction that deals with issues, accounts for every motive, has conflict, is well written and tackles something that is substantive. Don't be mundane; try for more, not less."

○ THE NOCTURNAL LYRIC

P.O. Box 542, Astoria OR 97103. E-mail: thenocturnallyric@rocketmail.com. Website: www.angelfire.com/ca/nocturnallyric. **Contact:** Susan Moon, editor.

HOW TO CONTACT Submit up to 4 poems at a time. Considers previously published poems and simultaneous submissions. No e-mail submissions. Seldom comments on rejected poems. Guidelines available in magazine, for SASE, or on website. Responds in up to 6 months. Pays 50¢ "discount on subscription" coupons. Acquires one-time rights.

TIPS "A manuscript stands out when the story has a very original theme and the ending is not predictable. Don't be afraid to be adventurous with your story. Mainstream horror can be boring. Surreal, satirical horror is what true nightmares are all about."

◑ THE PINCH

Dept. of English, The University of Memphis, Memphis TN 38152. (901)678-4591. E-mail: editor@thepinchjournal.com. Website: www.thepinchjournal.com. Laura Snider. **Contact:** Kristen Iverson, editor-in-chief. "Semiannual literary magazine. We publish fiction, creative nonfiction, poetry, and art of literary quality by both established and emerging artists." Give 2 copies of journal in which work appears on publication.

MAGAZINES NEEDS *The Pinch* (previously *River City*), published semiannually (fall and spring), prints fiction, poetry, interviews, creative nonfiction, and visual art. Has published poetry by Albert Goldbarth, Maxine Kumin, Jane Hirshfield, Terrance Hayes, S. Beth Bishop, and Naomi Shahib Nye. *The Pinch* is 160 pages, 7x10, professionally printed, perfect-bound, with colorful glossy cover and color art and photography. Press run is 2,500. Sample: $12.

HOW TO CONTACT Submit no more than 5 poems at a time. No e-mail submissions. Include SASE. "We do not read in the summer months." Reads submissions according to these deadlines only: August 15-November 1 (Spring issue) and January 15-March 15 (Fall issue). Guidelines available for SASE, by e-mail, or on website. Responds in up to 3 months. Pays 2 contributor's copies.

CONTEST/AWARD OFFERINGS Offers an annual award in poetry. 1st Prize: $1,000 and publication; 2nd- and 3rd-Prize poems may also be published. Any previously unpublished poem of up to 2 pages is eligible. No simultaneous submissions. Poems should be typed and accompanied by a cover letter. Author's name should not appear anywhere on ms. Manuscripts will not be returned. Guidelines available for SASE, by e-mail, or on website. **Entry fee:** $15 for up to 3 poems (includes one-year subscription). **Deadline:** January 15-March 15 (inclusive postmark dates). Winners will be notified in July; published in subsequent issue.

TIPS "We have a new look and a new edge. We're soliciting work from writers with a national or international reputation as well as strong, interesting work from emerging writers. The Pinch Literary Award (previously River City Writing Award) in Fiction offers a $1,500 prize and publication. Check our website for details."

THE PINK CHAMELEON

E-mail: dpfreda@juno.com. Website: www.thepinkchameleon.com. **Contact:** Mrs. Dorothy Paula Freda, editor/publisher. Needs fiction and nonfiction.

TIPS "Simple, honest, evocative emotion, upbeat fiction and nonfiction submissions that give hope for the future; well-paced plots; stories, poetry, articles, essays that speak from the heart. Read guidelines carefully. Use a good, but not ostentatious, opening hook. Stories should have a beginning, middle and end that make the reader feel the story was worth his or her time. This also applies to articles and essays. In the latter two, wrap your comments and conclusions in a neatly packaged final paragraph. Turnoffs include violence, bad language. Simple, genuine and sensitive work does not need to shock with vulgarity to be interesting and enjoyable."

○ THE PUCKERBRUSH REVIEW

English Dept., University of Maine, 413 Neville Hall, Orono ME 04469. E-mail: sanphip@aol.com. Website: http://puckerbrushreview.com. **Contact:** Sanford Phippen, Editor. *The Puckerbrush Review,* a print-only journal published twice/year, looks for "freshness and simplicity." Has published poetry by Wolly Swist and Muska Nagel. Submit 5 poems at a time. Guidelines available for SASE. Pays 2 contributor's copies.

○ "Please submit your poetry, short stories, literary essays and reviews through our website link. Hard-copy submissions will no longer be accepted."

TIPS "Just write the best and freshest poetry you can."

● THE SOUTHEAST REVIEW

Florida State University, Tallahassee FL 32306-1036. Website: southeastreview.org. **Contact:** Katie Cortese, editor. Established 1979. **Contact:** Rebecca Hazelton, poetry editor.

○ "The mission of *The Southeast Review* is to present emerging writers on the same stage as well-established ones. In each semi-annual issue, we publish literary fiction, creative nonfiction, poetry, interviews, book reviews and art. With nearly 60 members on our editorial staff who come from throughout the country and the world, we strive to publish work that is representative of our diverse interests and aesthetics, and we celebrate the eclectic mix this produces. We receive approximately 400 submissions per month and we accept less than 1-2% of them. We will comment briefly on rejected mss when time permits. Publishes ms 2-6 months after acceptance." **Publishes 4-6 new writers/year**. Recently published work by Elizabeth Hegwood, Anthony Varallo, B.J. Hollars, Tina Karelson, John Dufresne, and more.

MAGAZINES NEEDS *The Southeast Review*, published biannually, looks for "the very best poetry by new and established poets." *The Southeast Review* is 160 pages, digest-sized. Receives about 5,000 poems/year, accepts less than 4%. Press run is 1,000 (500 subscribers, 100 libraries, 200 shelf sales); 100 distributed free. Single copy: $8; subscription: $15/year. Sample: $6. Make checks payable to *The Southeast Review*.

HOW TO CONTACT Submit 3-5 poems at a time. Considers simultaneous submissions; no previously published poems. Accepts submissions by postal mail only; SASE required. Cover letter is preferred ("very brief"). Reads submissions year round. Time between acceptance and publication is up to 1 year. Seldom comments on rejected poems. Guidelines available for SASE, by e-mail, or on website. Responds in up to 3 months. Pays 2 contributor's copies. Acquires first North American serial rights. Reviews books and chapbooks of poetry. "Please query the

Book Review Editor (serbookreview@gmail.com) concerning reviews."

CONTEST/AWARD OFFERINGS Sponsors an annual poetry contest. Winner receives $500 and publication; 9 finalists will also be published. **Entry fee:** $15 for 3 poems. **Deadline:** March. Guidelines available on website.

TIPS The Southeast Review accepts regular submissions for publication consideration year-round exclusively through the **online Submission Manager**. Any breaks, hiatuses, or interruptions to the reading period will be announced online, and are more likely to occur during the summer months. *SER* does not, under any circumstances, accept work via email. **Except during contest season, paper submissions sent through regular postal mail will not be read or returned**. Please note that, during contest season, entries to our World's Best Short Short Story, Poetry, and Creative Nonfiction competitions must still be sent through regular postal mail. "Avoid trendy experimentation for its own sake (present-tense narration, observation that isn't also revelation). Fresh stories, moving, interesting characters and a sensitivity to language are still fiction mainstays. We also publish the winner and runners-up of the World's Best Short Story Contest, Poetry Contest, and Creative Nonfiction Contest."

THE SUN

The Sun Publishing Co., 107 N. Roberson St., Chapel Hill NC 27516. (919)942-5282. Fax: (919)932-3101. Website: www.thesunmagazine.org. Sy Safransky, editor. **Contact:** Luc Sanders, editorial associate. "We are open to all kinds of writing, though we favor work of a personal nature."

TIPS "Do not send queries except for interviews. We're looking for artful and sensitive photographs that aren't overly sentimental. We're open to unusual work. Read the magazine to get a sense of what we're about. Send the best possible prints of your work. Our submission rate is extremely high. Please be patient after sending us your work. Send return postage and secure return packaging."

◒ THE VIEW FROM HERE MAGAZINE

E-mail: editor@viewfromheremagazine.com; rear.view.poetry@gmail.com. Website: www.viewfromheremagazine.com. **Contact:** Sydney Nash, poetry editor; Claire King, fiction editor. "We are a print and online literary magazine designed and edited by an international team. We bring an entertaining mix of wit and insight all packaged in beautifully designed pages."

MAGAZINES NEEDS *The View From Here*, published monthly, "showcases new, emerging talent as well as the seasoned voice. Our poets are word wizards, prophets, mystics, and lyricists who are unafraid to demand attention by painting the world with their vision. Our poets will leave you yearning for more of the way they see the universe." Wants avant garde, free verse, haiku, light verse, traditional poetry. Has published Cyndi Dawson, Todd Heldt.

HOW TO CONTACT Submit up to 3 poems by e-mail, either as attachments or in the body of the message, plus a short bio and 3 most recent publishing credits with online links, if applicable. Does not accept previously published or simultaneous submissions. Please combine all poems into a single document.

TIPS "Due to the amount of submissions, work sent without a brief cover letter or introduction will be dismissed."

✚ THE VILLA

University of Wisconsin-Parkside, English Department, University of Wisconsin-Parkside, 900 Wood Rd., Box 2000, Kenosha WI 53414-2000. (262) 595-2139. Fax: (262) 595-2271. E-mail: villa@straylight-mag.com. Website: http://straylightmag.com. Dean Karpowicz, editor. **Contact:** Appropriate genre editor (revolving editors). English Department, University of Wisconsin-Parkside, 900 Wood Rd., Box 2000, Kenosha, WI 53414-2000. (262) 595-2139. Fax: (262) 595-2271. E-mail: villa@straylightmag.com. Website: http://straylightmag.com. **Contact:** Poetry Editor. "*The Villa* is the web counterpart to *Straylight Literary Arts Journal*. We publish some crossover print material, but the *Villa* is centered on publishing work suited to a biannual magazine." Acquires first North American serial rights. Copyrighted. Guidelines available on website."*The Villa* is the web counterpart to *Straylight Literary Arts Journal*. We publish some crossover print material, but the *Villa* is centered on publishing work suited to a biannual magazine."

MAGAZINES NEEDS Needs avant-garde, free verse, haiku, light verse, traditional.

HOW TO CONTACT Send 3-6 poems by using submission form on website or by e-mail. Include

a cover letter with a brief bio (25 words or so) with your submission.

TIPS "Please submit fiction and poetry through the website or by e-mail, and indicate you are submitting for the web magazine, and provide a short (25 word) bio with your submission. Query for reviews. We have publisher contacts and provide advanced copies."

○◑ THICK WITH CONVICTION

E-mail: twczine@yahoo.com. Website: www.angelfire.com/poetry/thickwithconviction. **Contact:** Arielle Lancaster-LaBrea and Kayla Middlebrook, co-editors. *Thick With Conviction*, published biannually online, is "run by a couple of twenty-something women who are looking for fresh and exciting voices in poetry. We don't want to take a nap while we're reading, so grab our attention, make us sit up and catch our breath." Wants all genres of poetry, "poems that make us exhale a deep sigh after reading them. Basically, if we can't feel the words in front of us, we're not going to be happy. We'd like to see new and cutting edge poets who think outside the box, but still know how to keep things from getting too strange and inaccessible." Does not want "teen angst poems, religious poems, or greeting card tripe." Has published poetry by Kendall A. Bell, April Michelle Bratten, Rachel Bunting, Kristina Marie Darling, James H. Duncan, and Kelsey Upward. Receives about 300 poems/year, accepts about 15%. Submit 3-5 poems at a time. Lines/poem: no limit. Considers previously published poems; no simultaneous submissions. Accepts e-mail submissions (pasted into body of message; "any attachments will be deleted"); no disk submissions. Cover letter and bio is required. Reads submissions year-round. Never comments on rejected poems.

THINK JOURNAL

E-mail: thinkjournal@yahoo.com. Website: http://web.me.com/christineyurick/Think_Journal/Home_Page.html. **Contact:** Christine Yurick, Editor. P.O. Box 454, Downingtown, PA 19335. (484)883-5806. E-mail: thinkjournal@yahoo.com. Website: http://web.me.com/christineyurick/Think_Journal/Home_Page.html. *Think Journal*, published quarterly, "focuses on words that have meaning, that are presented in a clear way, and that exhibit the skills demanded by craft. The journal prints work that achieves a balance between form and content. The most important traits that will be considered are form, structure, clarity, content, imagination, and style. *Think Journal* is

55 pages, digest-sized, desktop-printed, staple-bound with a cardstock cover containing original artwork. Single copy: $7; subscription: $20/year. Sample $6. Make checks payable to Christine Yurick."*Think Journal* focuses on words that have meaning, that are presented in a clear way, and that exhibit the skills demanded by craft. The Journal prints work that achieves a balance between form and content. The most important traits that will be considered are form, structure, clarity, content, imagination, and style."

MAGAZINES NEEDS *Think Journal*, published quarterly, "focuses on words that have meaning, that are presented in a clear way, and that exhibit the skills demanded by craft. The journal prints work that achieves a balance between form and content. The most important traits that will be considered are form, structure, clarity, content, imagination, and style. *Think Journal* is 55 pages, digest-sized, desktop-printed, staple-bound with a cardstock cover containing original artwork. Single copy: $7; subscription: $20/year. Sample $6. Make checks payable to Christine Yurick.

HOW TO CONTACT Submit 3-5 poems at a time, no restrictions in length. Accepts submissions by e-mail, mail. "Always include a SASE with submissions. Cover letter and brief biography preferred. Please include your e-mail address on the cover page for further communications. Include your name and address on each page of your submission." Reads submissions year round. Does not accept previously published or simultaneous submissions. Time between acceptance and publication is 6-12 months. Sometimes comments on rejected poems. Guidelines in magazine, for SASE, or on website. Responds in 2-3 months. Pays 1 contributor's copy. Acquires one-time rights. Rights revert to poet upon publication.

TIPS "Please visit the website to view samples of previously published work, or purchase a sample issue. Also looking for graphic design artwork for the cover."

◐◉ THIRD WEDNESDAY: A LITERARY ARTS MAGAZINE

174 Greenside Up, Ypsilanti MI 48197. (734) 434-2409. E-mail: submissions@thirdwednesday.org; Laurence-WT@aol.com. Website: http://thirdwednesday.org. Contact: Laurence Thomas, editor.

MAGAZINES NEEDS Wants "all styles and forms of poetry, from formal to experimental. Emphasis is placed on the ideas conveyed, craft and language, beauty of expression, and the picture that extends beyond the frame of the poem." Does not want "hate-filled diatribes, pornography (though eroticism is acceptable), prose masquerading as poetry, first drafts of anything." Has published poetry by Wanda Coleman, Philip Dacey, Richard Luftig, Simon Perchik, Marge Piercy, Charles Harper Webb. Receives 800 poems/year. Press run is 125. Single copy: $8; subscription: $30. Make checks payable to Third Wednesday.

HOW TO CONTACT Submit 1-5 poems at a time. Considers simultaneous submissions. Accepts submissions through e-mail, which is preferred to mail. Include SASE if submitting via postal mail. Reads submissions year round. Submit seasonal poems 3 months in advance. Time between acceptance and publication is 3 months. Poems are circulated to an editorial board. "Submissions are coded by executive editor and sent blind to members of editorial board; said members send up or down votes to executive editor who accepts pieces according to rule of majority." Sometimes comments on rejected poems. Guidelines available in magazine, by e-mail, and on website. Responds in 6-8 weeks. Pays $3-5 honorarium and 2 contributor's copies. Acquires first North American serial rights, electronic rights. "TW retains the right to reproduce accepted work as samples on our website." Rights revert to poet upon publication.

TIPS "Of course, originality is important along with skill in writing, deft handling of language and meaning which goes hand in hand with beauty, whatever that is. Short fiction is specialized and difficult, so the writer should read extensively in the field."

◐◉ TICKLED BY THUNDER

14076-86A Ave., Surrey BC V3W 0V9, Canada. (604)591-6095. E-mail: info@tickledbythunder.com. Website: www.tickledbythunder.com. **Contact:** Larry Lindner, publisher. 14076-86A Ave., Surrey, BC V3W 0V9, Canada. E-mail: info@tickledbythunder.com. Website: www.tickledbythunder.com. Established 1990. **Contact:** Larry Lindner, editor/publisher. *Tickled by Thunder*, published up to 2 times/year, uses poems "about fantasy particularly; writing or whatever. Require original images and thoughts. Welcome humor and creative inspirational verse." Does not want "anything pornographic, childish, unimaginative."

Has published poetry by Laleh Dadpour Jackson and Helen Michiko Singh. *Tickled by Thunder* is 24 pages, digest-sized, published on Macintosh. Has 1,000 readers/subscribers. Subscription: $12 CAD/4 issues. Sample: $2.50 CAD.

MAGAZINES NEEDS *Tickled by Thunder*, published up to 2 times/year, uses poems "about fantasy particularly; writing or whatever. Require original images and thoughts. Welcome humor and creative inspirational verse." Does not want "anything pornographic, childish, unimaginative." Has published poetry by Laleh Dadpour Jackson and Helen Michiko Singh. *Tickled by Thunder* is 24 pages, digest-sized, published on Macintosh. Has 1,000 readers/subscribers. Subscription: $12 CAD/4 issues. Sample: $2.50 CAD.

HOW TO CONTACT Submit 3-5 poems at a time. Lines/poem: up to 40 ("keep them short—not interested in long, long poems"). No e-mail submissions. Cover letter is required. Include "a few facts about yourself and brief list of publishing credits." Comments on rejected poems "80% of the time." Guidelines available for SASE or on website. Responds in up to 6 months. Pays 2¢/line, $2 CAD maximum. Acquires first rights. Reviews books of poetry in up to 300 words. Open to unsolicited reviews. Send materials for review consideration.

ADDITIONAL INFORMATION Publishes **author-subsidized chapbooks**. "We are also interested in student poetry and publish it in our center spread: *Expressions*." Send SASE (or SAE and IRC) for details.

CONTEST/AWARD OFFERINGS Offers a poetry contest 2 times/year. Prize: cash, publication, and subscription. **Entry fee:** $5 CAD for one poem; free for subscribers. **Deadlines:** the 15th of February, 15th of August.

TIPS "Allow your characters to breathe on their own. Use description with action."

⊙ TIGER'S EYE

Tiger's Eye Press, P.O. Box 2935, Eugene OR 97402. E-mail: tigerseyepoet@yahoo.com. Website: www.tigerseyejournal.com. **Contact:** Colette Jonopulos and JoAn Osborne, editors. Tiger's Eye Press, P.O. Box 2935, Eugene, OR 97402. E-mail:tigerseyepoet@yahoo.com. Website: www.tigerseyejournal.com. **Contacts:** Colette Jonopulos and JoAn Osborne, editors. *Tiger's Eye: A Journal of Poetry*, published semiannu-

ally, features both established and undiscovered poets. "Besides publishing the work of several exceptional poets in each issue, we feature two poets in interviews, giving the reader insight into their lives and writing habits." Wants "both free verse and traditional forms; no restrictions on subject or length. We welcome sonnets, haibun, haiku, ghazals, villenelles, etc. We pay special attention to unusual forms and longer poems that may have difficulty being placed elsewhere. Poems with distinct imagery and viewpoint are read and re-read by the editors and considered for publication." Has published poetry by Willis Barnstone, Kathy Kieth, Joyce Odam, Fiona Sze-Lorrain, and David Morse. *Tiger's Eye* is 64 pages, saddle-stitched. Receives 1,000 poems/year, accepts 100. Press run is 300. Single copy: $6; subscription: $11 for 2 issues. Make checks payable to Tiger's Eye Press.

MAGAZINES NEEDS *Tiger's Eye: A Journal of Poetry*, published semiannually, features both established and undiscovered poets. "Besides publishing the work of several exceptional poets in each issue, we feature two poets in interviews, giving the reader insight into their lives and writing habits." Wants "both free verse and traditional forms; no restrictions on subject or length. We welcome sonnets, haibun, haiku, ghazals, villenelles, etc. We pay special attention to unusual forms and longer poems that may have difficulty being placed elsewhere. Poems with distinct imagery and viewpoint are read and re-read by the editors and considered for publication." Has published poetry by Willis Barnstone, Kathy Kieth, Joyce Odam, Fiona Sze-Lorrain, and David Morse. *Tiger's Eye* is 64 pages, saddle-stitched. Receives 1,000 poems/year, accepts 100. Press run is 300. Single copy: $6; subscription: $11 for 2 issues. Make checks payable to Tiger's Eye Press.

HOW TO CONTACT Submit 3-5 poems at a time, no multiple submissions. Considers simultaneous submissions with notification if a poem is accepted elsewhere; no previously published poems. No e-mail submissions. Cover letter is required. Include brief bio. SASE for notification only; no submissions are returned. Reads submissions year-round; deadlines are February 28 and August 31. Time between acceptance and publication is 3 months. "All poems are read by the editors, then filed as poems we definitely want to publish, those we are still considering, and those we aren't publishing. Our two featured poets are chosen, then letters and e-mails are sent out." Seldom comments on rejected poems. Guidelines available in magazine or on website. Responds in 6 months. Always sends prepublication galleys. Pays one contributor's copy to each poet, 2 to featured poets. Acquires one-time rights.

ADDITIONAL INFORMATION *Tiger's Eye* nominates for *The Pushcart Prize.*

CONTEST/AWARD OFFERINGS Tiger's Eye Annual Poetry Contest (see separate listing in Contests & Awards) and Editor's Choice Chapbook Contest. "Our annual poetry contest awards $500, $100, $50. Send 3 pages of poetry, cover letter with poet's name and contact information (no identifying information on mss pages) SASE, and $10 entry fee. **Deadline: February 28.** Our chapbook contest awards $100 and 25 copies of the winning chapbook. Do not send entire mss, but 5 pages of poetry, cover letter with poet's name and contact information (no identifying contact information on mss pages), SASE, and $10 entry fee. **Deadline: August 31.**

⬤◉ TIME OF SINGING

E-mail: timesing@zoominternet.net. Website: www.timeofsinging.com. **Contact:** Lora Zill, Editor. *Time of Singing, A Magazine of Christian Poetry,* published 4 times/year, seeks "poems that 'show' rather than 'tell.' The viewpoint is unblushingly Christian—but in its widest and most inclusive meaning." Wants free verse and well-crafted rhyme; would like to see more forms. Does not want "collections of uneven lines, sermons that rhyme, unstructured 'prayers,' and trite sing-song rhymes." Has published poetry by John Grey, Luci Shaw, Bob Hostetler, Tony Cosier, Barbara Crooker, and Charles Waugaman. It is 44 pages, digest-sized, offset from typescript. Receives more than 800 submissions/year, accepts about 175. Press run is 250 (150 subscribers). Subscription: $17 USD, $21 USD Canada, $30 USD overseas. Sample: $4, or 2 for $7 (postage paid). Submit up to 5 poems at a time. Lines/poem: prefers less than 40, "but will publish up to 60 lines if exceptional." Considers previously published poems (indicate when/where appeared) and simultaneous submissions. Accepts e-mail submissions (pasted into body of message or as attachment). Poems should be single-spaced. Time between acceptance and publication is up to one year. Comments "with suggestions for improvement if close to publication." Guidelines available for SASE, by e-mail, or on website. Responds in 4 months. Pays 1 contributor's copy. "TOS has published poets from England, South Africa, Mexico, New Zealand, Scotland, RussiAustraliAnd Ireland."" *Time of Singing* publishes 'Christian' poetry in the widest sense, but prefers 'literary' type. Welcome forms, fresh rhyme, well-crafted free verse. Like writers who take chances, who don't feel the need to tie everything up neatly."

HOW TO CONTACT Submit or query by mail with SASE or email. timesing@zoominternet.net. "I will comment on work that has merit and is close to publication, and will clear major revisions with the poet."

ADDITIONAL INFORMATION "*Time of Singing* also welcomes general inspirational and nature poems. I prefer poems that don't preach, and "show" rather than "tell." Sermons and greeting card poetry have valid purposes, but aren't appropriate for this magazine. I suggest you obtain a sample back issue to help you ascertain TOS's style. I welcome fresh rhyme, beg for more forms, appreciate well-crafted free verse, and consider poems up to 60 lines in length. I try to respond within 3 months, and make every effort to publish poems within one year of acceptance." Lora Zill, editor. Mail submissions with SASE to: Time of Singing, P.O. Box 149, Conneaut Lake, PA 16316.

CONTEST/AWARD OFFERINGS Sponsors theme contests for specific issues. Guidelines available for SASE, by e-mail, or on website.

TIPS "Read widely and study the craft. You need more than feelings and religious jargon to make it into TOS. It's helpful to get honest critiques of your work. Cover letter not necessary. Your poems speak for themselves."

◉ TOASTED CHEESE

E-mail: editors@toasted-cheese.com. E-mail: submit@toasted-cheese.com. Website: www.toasted-cheese.com.

HOW TO CONTACT Send complete ms in body of e-mail; no attachments. Accepts submissions by e-mail. Responds in 4 months to mss. No simultaneous submissions. Sample copy online. Follow online submission guidelines. Acquires electronic rights.

CONTEST/AWARD OFFERINGS Sponsors awards/contests.

TIPS "We are looking for clean, professional writing from writers of any level. Accepted stories will be concise and compelling. We are looking for writers who are serious about the craft: tomorrow's literary stars before they're famous. Take your submission seriously, yet remember that levity is appreciated. You are submitting not to traditional 'editors' but to fellow writers who appreciate the efforts of those in the trenches." "Follow online submission guidelines."

⊙⊙ TORCH: POETRY, PROSE AND SHORT STORIES BY AFRICAN AMERICAN WOMEN

3720 Gattis School Rd., Suite 800, Round Rock TX 78664. E-mail: info@torchpoetry.org (inquiries), poetry@torchpoetry.org (submissions). Website: www.torchliteraryarts.com. **Contact:** Amanda Johnston, editor. *TORCH: Poetry, Prose, and Short Stories by African American Women*, published semiannually online, provides "a place to publish contemporary poetry, prose, and short stories by experienced and emerging writers alike. We prefer our contributors to take risks, and offer a diverse body of work that examines and challenges preconceived notions regarding race, ethnicity, gender roles, and identity." Has published poetry by Sharon Bridgforth, Patricia Smith, Crystal Wilkinson, Tayari Jones, and Natasha Trethewey. Receives about 250+ submissions/year, accepts about 20. Number of unique visitors: 600+/month. Submit 3 poems at a time. No previously published poems or simultaneous submissions. Accepts e-mail submissions only (as one MS Word attachment). Send to poetry@torchpoetry.org with "Poetry Submission" in subject line. Cover letter is preferred (in the body of the e-mail). Reads submissions April 15-August 31 only. Sometimes comments on rejected poems. Always sends prepublication galleys. No payment. "Within *TORCH*, we offer a special section called Flame that features an interview, biography, and work sample by an established writer as well as an introduction to their Spark—an emerging writer who inspires them and adds to the boundless voice of creative writing by Black women." A free online newsletter is available; see website.

MAGAZINES NEEDS *TORCH: Poetry, Prose, and Short Stories by African American Women*, published semiannually online, provides "a place to publish contemporary poetry, prose, and short stories by experienced and emerging writers alike. We prefer our contributors to take risks, and offer a diverse body of work that examines and challenges preconceived notions regarding race, ethnicity, gender roles, and identity." Has published poetry by Sharon Bridgforth,

Patricia Smith, Crystal Wilkinson, Tayari Jones, and Natasha Trethewey. Receives about 250+ submissions/year, accepts about 20. Number of unique visitors: 600+/month.

HOW TO CONTACT Submit 3 poems at a time. No previously published poems or simultaneous submissions. Accepts e-mail submissions only (as one MS Word attachment). Send to poetry@torchpoetry.org with "Poetry Submission" in subject line. Cover letter is preferred (in the body of the e-mail). Reads submissions April 15-August 31 only. Time between acceptance and publication is 2-7 months. Sometimes comments on rejected poems. Guidelines available on website. Always sends prepublication galleys. No payment. Acquires rights to publish accepted work in online issue and in archives. Rights revert to authors upon publication.

ALSO OFFERS "Within *TORCH*, we offer a special section called Flame that features an interview, biography, and work sample by an established writer as well as an introduction to their Spark—an emerging writer who inspires them and adds to the boundless voice of creative writing by Black women." A free online newsletter is available; see website.

⊙ TRESTLE CREEK REVIEW

English Dept., North Idaho College, 1000 W. Garden Ave., Coeur d'Alene ID 83814-2199. (208)769-3394. E-mail: tcr@nic.edu. Established 1982-83. **Contact:** Johnathan Frey, editorial advisor.

MAGAZINES NEEDS *Trestle Creek Review*, published annually by North Idaho College, accepts submissions of poetry, fiction, creative nonfiction, and b&w art from NIC students and residents of Idaho's five northern counties only. "We're very eclectic and favor the surprising and unconventional." Does not want "the romantic, the formulaic, and the clichéd." Has published poetry by Sean Brendan-Brown, E.G. Burrows, Ron McFarland, and Mary Winters. *Trestle Creek Review* varies in length and design. Receives 300 submissions/year, accepts about 30. Press run is 500. Single copy: $8.40. Sample: $5.25 (back issue).

HOW TO CONTACT Submit 3-5 poems at a time, or fiction/creative nonfiction mss of no more than 5,000 words. Multiple submissions by the same author will be returned without consideration as will work by authors who do not meet our regional criteria. No previously published work. Simultaneous submission is welcome. Accepts e-mail submissions only; no fax or mail submissions. Cover letter with "address, phone number, e-mail address, brief bio is required with all submissions." Accepts submissions to January 31 deadline (for May publication). Responds by May 30. Pays 3 contributor's copies.

➕ ⬤ TRIBECA POETRY REVIEW

25 Leonard Street, New York NY 10013. E-mail: editor@tribecareview.org. Website: www.tribecareview.org. **Contact:** Kenlynne Rini, editor.

MAGAZINES NEEDS *Tribeca Poetry Review*, published annually in December, is "a publication emerging out of the thick poetic history that is downtown New York. It seeks to expose its readers to the best smattering of poetry we can get our hands on. TPR will showcase new pieces by seasoned poets as well as illuminate the work of fresh voices." Wants "the kind of poetry that squirms in your head for days, hopefully longer, after reading it. Send us your best work. Will publish all forms (including traditional poesy, spoken word, or your experimental pieces) providing they translate well on the page, are intelligent, and well-crafted. New York City poets are always encouraged to submit their work, but this is NOT strictly a regional publication." Does not want "overly self-absorbed poems; pieces so abstract that all meaning and pleasure is lost on anyone but the poet; first drafts, goofy word play, trite nostalgia." Considers poetry by teens. "It's the poem itself that needs to resonate with readers, so the age of the poet means little. Occasionally, poetry by a 14 year old is more profound than the drivel generated by those adults who hang out unnecessarily in coffee shops and believe themselves 'poets.'" *Tribeca Poetry Review* is approximately 100 pages, digest-sized, professionally printed, flat-spine bound, with artwork cover. Press run is 1,000.

HOW TO CONTACT Submit no more than 5 poems at a time up to 10 pages in total. No previously published poems or simultaneous submissions. Cover letter is required. "Please do not use your cover letter as a place to explain your poems. The letter is a place to introduce yourself and your work but not sell or explain either. Your name, address, contact phone and e-mail should be on each page submitted." Reads submissions year round. Time between acceptance and publication is up to 1 year. Sometimes comments on rejected poems. Guidelines on website. Responds as soon as possible, can be up to

6 months. Pays 2 contributor's copies. Acquires first North American serial rights.

⬤ TULANE REVIEW

122 Norman Mayer, New Orleans LA 70118. E-mail: litsoc@tulane.edu. Website: www.review.tulane.edu. **Contact:** Abi Pollokoff, Poetry Editor. *Tulane Review*, published biannually, is a national literary journal seeking quality submissions of prose, poetry, and art. "We consider all types of poetry." Wants "imaginative poems with bold, inventive images." Has published poetry by Tom Chandler, Ace Boggess, Carol Hamilton, and Brady Rhoades. *Tulane Review* is 70 pages, 7×9, perfect-bound, with 100# cover with full-color artwork. Receives about 1,200 poems/year, accepts about 50 per issue. Single copy: $8; subscription: $15. Make checks payable to *Tulane Review*.

⬤ *Tulane Review* is the recipient of an AWP Literary Magazine Design Award.

⬤ THE TULE REVIEW

P.O. Box 160406, Sacramento CA 95816. (916)451-5569. E-mail: tulereview@sacramentopoetrycenter.org. Website: www.sacramentopoetrycenter.org. **Contact:** Theresa McCourt or Linda Collins. P.O. Box 160406, Sacramento, CA 95816. (916)451-5569. E-mail:tulereview@sacramentopoetrycenter.org. Website: www.sacramentopoetrycenter.org. **Contacts:** Theresa McCourt or Linda Collins. *The Tule Review*, published 1-2 times/year, uses "poetry, book reviews, and essays concerning contemporary poetry" Wants "all styles and forms of poetry." Primarily publishes poets living in the greater Sacramento area, but accepts work from anywhere. Has published poetry by Gary Snyder, Diane DiPrima, Jack Hirschman, Julia Connor, Joyce Odam, and Douglas Blazek. *The Tule Review* is 40-60 pages, digest-sized, perfect-bound, with cover artwork. Receives about 500 poems/year, accepts about 10-20%. Press run is 500; 50 distributed free to contributors and for review. Single copy: $10 ppd; subscription: $30/year (includes *Poetry Now*, a monthly publication). Make checks payable to Sacramento Poetry Center.

MAGAZINES NEEDS *The Tule Review*, published 1-2 times/year, uses "poetry, book reviews, and essays concerning contemporary poetry" Wants "all styles and forms of poetry." Primarily publishes poets living in the greater Sacramento area, but accepts work from anywhere. Has published poetry by Gary Snyder, Diane DiPrima, Jack Hirschman, Julia

Connor, Joyce Odam, and Douglas Blazek. *The Tule Review* is 40-60 pages, digest-sized, perfect-bound, with cover artwork. Receives about 500 poems/year, accepts about 10-20%. Press run is 500; 50 distributed free to contributors and for review. Single copy: $10 ppd; subscription: $30/year (includes *Poetry Now*, a monthly publication). Make checks payable to Sacramento Poetry Center.

HOW TO CONTACT Submit up to 6 poems at a time. Lines/poem: 96 maximum. Considers previously published poems; no simultaneous submissions. Prefers e-mail (include poems in a single attachment). Include name, street, and e-mail address on each page of submission. Provide short, 5 line bio. Reads submissions year round. Submit seasonal poems 6 months in advance. Time between acceptance and publication is 1-6 months. Poems are circulated to an editorial board. Sometimes comments on rejected poems. Sometimes publishes theme issues. Guidelines and upcoming themes available by e-mail, or on website. Responds in 3-4 months. Pays 1 contributor's copy. Acquires first North American serial rights. Rights revert to poet upon publication. See website for other publications and contests.

● TUNDRA: THE JOURNAL OF THE SHORT POEM

22230 NE 28th Place, Sammamish WA 98074-6408. E-mail: welchm@aol.com. Website: http://sites.google.com/site/tundrashortpoem/. **Contact:** Michael Dylan Welch, Editor.

TIPS "If your work centers on immediate and objective imagery, *Tundra* is interested. All poems must be 13 or fewer lines, with only very rare exceptions (where each line is very short). If you think that a haiku is merely 5-7-5 syllables, then I do not want to see your work (see 'Becoming a Haiku Poet' online at http://sites.google.com/site/graceguts/essays/becoming-a-haiku-poet for reasons why). Due to the excessive volume of inappropriate submissions for *Tundra* in the past, I now encourage only well-established poets to submit."

TURBULENCE

29 Finchley Close, Kingston-upon-Hull HU8 0NU United Kingdom. E-mail: turbulencemagazine@googlemail.com. Website: turbulencemagazine.webs.com. **Contact:** Ashley Fisher and Iain Walker, editors. Turbulence welcomes free verse poetry written in or

translated into English from around the world. Publishes 160 poems/year. Submit up to 6 poems.

⊘ TURTLE MAGAZINE FOR PRESCHOOL KIDS

Website: www.turtlemag.org. (Specialized: ages 3-5) *Turtle Magazine for Preschool Kids*, published by Children's Better Health Institute, is a magazine for children ages 3-5. "Colorful and entertaining..perfect for reading aloud." Wants light-hearted poetry appropriate for the age group. Reviews submissions for possible use in all Children's Better Health Institute publications.General interest, interactive magazine with the purpose of helping preschoolers develop healthy minds and bodies. Magazine of picture stories and articles for preschool children 3-5 years old. C Closed to submissions until further notice.

MAGAZINES NEEDS *Turtle Magazine for Preschool Kids*, published by Children's Better Health Institute, is a magazine for children ages 3-5. "Colorful and entertaining..perfect for reading aloud." Wants light-hearted poetry appropriate for the age group. Reviews submissions for possible use in all Children's Better Health Institute publications.

HOW TO CONTACT 1100 Waterway Blvd., Indianapolis, IN 46202. OR P.O. Box 567, Indianapolis, IN 46206. (317)634-1100. E-mail: editor@saturdayeveningpost.com. Website: www.turtlemag.org. Manuscripts must be typewritten with poet's contact information in upper right-hand corner of each poem's page. SASE required. Submit seasonal material at least 8 months in advance. Guidelines available for SASE or on website. Responds in about 3 months. Pays up to $35 for poetry. Acquires all rights.

TIPS We are looking for more short rebus stories, easy science experiments, and simple, nonfiction health articles. We are trying to include more material for our youngest readers. Material must be entertaining and written from a healthy lifestyle perspective.

● UNMUZZLED OX

105 Hudson St., New York NY 10013. (212)226-7170. Recent issues of this magazine have included art, poetry and essays only. Check before sending submissions. Recent issues of this magazine have included art, poetry and essays only. Check before sending submissions.

MAGAZINES NEEDS Unmuzzled Ox, published semi-annually, is a literary tabloid. Each edition is built around a theme or specific project. **"The chances of**

an unsolicited poem being accepted are slight since I always have specific ideas in mind." Has published poetry by Allen Ginsberg, Robert Creeley, and Denise Levertov. Subscription: $20. Sample copy: $15

HOW TO CONTACT Only unpublished work will be considered, but poems may be in French as well as English.

TIPS "You may want to check out a copy of the magazine before you submit."

UP AND UNDER: THE QND REVIEW

P.O. Box 115, Hainesport NJ 08036. E-mail: qndpoets@yahoo.com. Website: www.quickanddirtypoets.com. **Contact:** Kendall Bell, editor.

MAGAZINES NEEDS *Up and Under: The QND Review*, published annually in March, is "a journal with an eclectic mix of poetry: sex, death, politics, IKEA, Mars, food, and jug handles alongside a smorgasbord of other topics covered in such diverse forms as the sonnet, villanelle, haiku, and free verse. We are interested in excellent poetry with no bias between free verse or traditional forms." Does not want "greeting card verse, graphic pornography." Has published poetry by Dan Maguire, Gina Larkin, Leonard Gontarek, Autumn Konopka, John Grey and Taylor Graham. *Up and Under* is 50-60 pages, digest-sized, laser-printed, saddle-stapled, with card cover with photograph, includes ads. Receives about 300 poems/year, accepts about 30 (or 10%). Press run is 100. Single copy: $7. Chapbooks are available online or through U.S. Mail. Make checks payable to Kendall Bell.

HOW TO CONTACT Submit up to 5 poems at a time. Lines/poem: no limit. Considers simultaneous submissions (with notification); no previously published poems. Accepts e-mail submissions (pasted into body of message). Reads submissions September 1-December 30. Time between acceptance and publication is 3-6 months. Poems are circulated to an editorial board. Sometimes comments on rejected poems. Guidelines available in magazine, for SASE, or on website. Responds in 2-3 months. Pays 1 contributor's copy. Acquires one-time rights.

URTHONA MAGAZINE

Abbey House, Abbey Road, Cambridge CB5 8HQ, England. E-mail: urthonamag@onetel.com. Website: www.urthona.com. **Contact:** Poetry Editor.

MAGAZINES NEEDS *Urthona*, published biannually, explores the arts and Western culture from a Buddhist perspective. Wants "poetry rousing the imagination."

Does not want "undigested autobiography, political, or New Age-y poems." Has published poetry by Peter Abbs, Robert Bly, and Peter Redgrove. *Urthona* is 60 pages, A4, offset-printed, saddle-stapled, with 4-color glossy cover, includes ads. Receives about 300 poems/year, accepts about 40. Press run is 1,200 (200 subscribers, plus shelf sales in Australia and America). "See website for current subscription rates." Sample (including guidelines): $7.99 USD, $8.99 CAD.

HOW TO CONTACT Submit 6 poems at a time. No previously published poems or simultaneous submissions. Accepts e-mail submissions (as attachment). Cover letter is preferred. Time between acceptance and publication is up to 8 months. Poems are circulated to an editorial board and are read and selected by poetry editor. Other editors have right of veto. Responds within 6 months. Pays 1 contributor's copy. Acquires one-time rights. Reviews books/chapbooks of poetry and other magazines in 600 words. Send materials for review consideration.

U.S. 1 WORKSHEETS

Website: www.us1poets.com. U.S. 1 Worksheets, P.O. Box 127, Kingston, NJ 08528. E-mail: info@US1Poets.com. Website: www.us1poets.com. *U.S. 1 Worksheets*, published annually, uses high-quality poetry and, on occasion, short fiction. "We prefer complex, well-written work." Has published poetry by Alicia Ostriker, BJ Ward, James Richardson, Lois Marie Harrod, and Baron Wormser. *U.S. 1 Worksheets* is 112 pages, perfect-bound, with b&w cover art. Press run is 500. Subscription: 2 years for $15; sample copy $8. Back issues $5. "We are looking for well-crafted poetry with a focused point of view. Representative authors: Baron Wormser, Alicia Ostriker, Richard Jones, Bj Ward, Lois Harrod."

HOW TO CONTACT Submit up to 5 poems at a time. Considers simultaneous submissions if indicated; no previously published poems. "We use a rotating board of editors. We read April 15-June 30, and can no longer return manuscripts. Enclose SASE for reply." Pays 1 contributor's copy.

ALSO OFFERS The U.S. 1 Poets' Cooperative co-sponsors (with the Princeton Public Library) a series of monthly poetry readings (U.S. 1 Poets Invite) at the Princeton Public Library. "There is no formal membership, only the willingness of participants to share their work."

TIPS "Mss are accepted from April 15-June 30 and are read by rotating editors from the cooperative. Send us something unusual, something we haven't seen before, but make sure it's poetry. Proofread carefully."

U.S. CATHOLIC

(312)236-7782. Fax: (312)236-8207. E-mail: editors@ uscatholic.org. E-mail: submissions@uscatholic.org. Website: www.uscatholic.org. *U.S. Catholic* is dedicated to the belief that it makes a difference whether you're Catholic. We invite and help our readers explore the wisdom of their faith tradition and apply their faith to the challenges of the 21st century. C Please include SASE with written ms.

☯◑◉ VALLUM:
NEW INTERNATIONAL POETICS

P.O. Box 598, Victoria Station, Montreal QC H3Z 2Y6, Canada. (514)937-8946. Fax: (514)937-8946. E-mail: info@vallummag.com. Website: www.vallummag. com. **Contact:** Joshua Auerbach and Eleni Zisimatos, editors. Receives about 1,000 poems/year, accept about 85/year.

◑ "Poetry/fine arts magazine published twice/ year. Publishes exciting interplay of poets and artists. Sample copies available for $7 CAN/$8 US. Submission guidelines available on website. Content for magazine is selected according to themes listed on website. Material is not filed but is returned by SASE. Email response is preferred. Pays $30 honorarium for accepted poems and $65 for accepted reviews or essays on poetry. Buys first North American serial rights. Copyright remains with the author. Seeking exciting, unpublished, traditional or avant-garde poetry that reflects contemporary experience."

MAGAZINES NEEDS VALLUM: New International Poetics P.O. Box 598, Victoria Stn, Montreal QC H3Z 2Y6 Canada . E-mail: info@vallummag.com. Website: www.vallummag.com. Contacts: Joshua Auerbach and Eleni Zisimatos, editors. Estab. 2000. Poetry/fine arts magazine published twice/year. Publishes exciting interplay of poets and artists. Sample copies available for $7 CAN/$8 US. Submission guidelines available on website. Content for magazine is selected according to themes listed on website. Material is not filed but is returned by SASE. Email response is preferred. Pays $30 honorarium for accepted poems and $65 for accepted reviews or essays on poetry. Buys first North

American serial rights. Copyright remains with the author. Seeking exciting, unpublished, traditional or avant-garde poetry that reflects contemporary experience. *Vallum* is 100 pages, digest sized (7x8$\frac{1}{2}$), digitally printed, perfect-bound, with color images on coated stock cover. Includes ads. Press run is 1,800. Single copy: $10 CDN; subscription: $17/year CDN; $21 US (shipping included). Make checks payable to *Vallum*.

ADDITIONAL INFORMATION "The Vallum Chapbook Series publishes 2-3 chapbooks by both well-known and emerging poets. Past editions include *Gospel of X* by George Elliott Clarke, *The Art of Fugue* by Jan Zwicky and *Address* by Franz Wright. *Vallum* does not currently accept unsolicited mss for this project."

CONTEST/AWARD OFFERINGS "Sponsors annual contest. First Prize: $500, Second Prize: $250 and publication in an issue of *Vallum*. Honourable mentions may be selected but are not eligible for cash prizes. Submit 4-5 poems. Entry fee: $20 USD / CAD (includes subscription to *Vallum*). Deadline: June 30. Guidelines available in magazine, by e-mail, and on website. Poems may be submitted in any style or on any subject; max. 4-5 poems, up to 25-40 lines per poem. Entries should be labelled 'Vallum Contest' and submitted by regular mail. Submissions are not returned. In addition to cash prizes, winners will be announced on our website and published in the forthcoming issue."

◑◔ VALPARAISO POETRY REVIEW

Department of English, Valparaiso University, Valparaiso IN 46383-6493. (219)464-5278. Fax: (219)464-5511. E-mail: vpr@valpo.edu. Website: www.valpo. edu/vpr/. **Contact:** Edward Byrne, editor.

MAGAZINES NEEDS *Valparaiso Poetry Review: Contemporary Poetry and Poetics*, published semiannually online, accepts "submissions of unpublished poetry, book reviews, author interviews, and essays on poetry or poetics that have not yet appeared online and for which the rights belong to the author. Query for anything else." Wants poetry of any length or style, free verse or traditional forms. Has published poetry by Charles Wright, Cornelius Eady, Dorianne Laux, Dave Smith, Claudia Emerson, Billy Collins, Brian Turner, Daisy Fried, Stanley Plumly, and Annie Finch. Receives about 9,000 poems/year, accepts about 1%.

HOW TO CONTACT Submit 3-5 poems at a time (no more than 5). Considers previously published poems ("original publication must be identified to ensure proper credit") and simultaneous submissions. Accepts e-mail submissions (pasted into body of message, no attachments); no fax or disk submissions. **Postal submissions preferred.** Cover letter is preferred. Include SASE. Reads submissions year round. Time between acceptance and publication is 6-12 months. Seldom comments on rejected poems. Guidelines available on website. Responds in up to 6 weeks. Acquires one-time rights. "All rights remain with author." Reviews books of poetry in single- and multi-book format. Send materials for review consideration.

VEGETARIAN JOURNAL

P.O. Box 1463, Baltimore MD 21203-1463. (410)366-8343. E-mail: vrg@vrg.org. Website: www.vrg.org. (Specialized: poetry by children/teens only; vegetarianism) The Vegetarian Resource Group, P.O. Box 1463, Baltimore MD 21203. E-mail: vrg@vrg.org. Website: www.vrg.org. Established 1982.

MAGAZINES NEEDS *Vegetarian Journal*, published quarterly, considers poetry by children and teens only. *Vegetarian Journal* is 36 pages, magazine-sized, professionally printed, saddle-stapled, with glossy card cover. Press run is 20,000. Sample: $3. "Please, no submissions of poetry from adults; 18 and under only." The Vegetarian Resource Group offers an annual contest for ages 18 and under: $50 savings bond in 3 age categories for the best contribution on any aspect of vegetarianism. "Most entries are essay, but we would accept poetry with enthusiasm." **Deadline:** May 1 (postmark). Details available at website: http://www.vrg.org/essay/ *Vegetarian Journal* is 36 pages, magazine-sized, professionally printed, saddle-stapled, with glossy card cover. Press run is 20,000. Sample: $3. "Please, no submissions of poetry from adults; 18 and under only." The Vegetarian Resource Group offers an annual contest for ages 18 and under: $50 savings bond in 3 age categories for the best contribution on any aspect of vegetarianism. "Most entries are essay, but we would accept poetry with enthusiasm." **Deadline:** May 1 (postmark). Details available at website: http://www.vrg.org/essay/

TIPS Areas most open to freelancers are recipe section and feature articles. "Review magazine first to learn our style. Send query letter with photocopy sample of line drawings of food."

VERANDAH

Faculty of Arts, Deakin University, 221 Burwood Hwy., Burwood, Victoria 3125, Australia. (61)(3)9251-7134. E-mail: verandah@deakin.edu.au. Website: www.deakin.edu.au/verandah. **Contact:** Poetry Editor. Faculty of Arts, Deakin University, 221 Burwood Hwy., Burwood, Victoria 3125, Australia. E-mail:verandah@deakin.edu.au. Website: www.deakin.edu.au/verandah. Contact: Poetry Editor. *Verandah*, published annually in September, is "a high-quality literary journal edited by professional writing students. It aims to give voice to new and innovative writers and artists." Has published poetry by Christos Tsiolka, Dorothy Porter, Seamus Heaney, Les Murray, Ed Burger, and Joh Muk Muk Burke. *Verandah* is 120 pages, professionally printed on glossy stock, flat-spined, with full-color glossy card cover. Sample: $20 AUD.

MAGAZINES NEEDS *Verandah*, published annually in September, is "a high-quality literary journal edited by professional writing students. It aims to give voice to new and innovative writers and artists." Has published poetry by Christos Tsiolka, Dorothy Porter, Seamus Heaney, Les Murray, Ed Burger, and Joh Muk Muk Burke. *Verandah* is 120 pages, professionally printed on glossy stock, flat-spined, with full-color glossy card cover. Sample: $20 AUD.

HOW TO CONTACT Submit bt mail or e-mail. However, electronic version of work must be available if accepted by *Verandah*. **Do not submit work without the required submission form (available for download on website).** Reads submissions by June 1 deadline (postmark). Guidelines available on website. Some prizes awarded. Pays one contributor's copy, "with prizes awarded accordingly." Acquires first Australian publishing rights.

CONTEST/AWARD OFFERINGS Prizes awarded in each issue. Prize entry is automatic for Deakin students, no entry fee (student number is required). **Entry fee:** $10 AUD for first entry, $15 AUD for 3. Work submitted by non-Deakin students without an entry fee will not be considered for publication. **Deadline:** June 1. Guidelines available on website.

VERSAL

Postbus 3865, Amsterdam 1054 EJ , The Netherlands. +31 (0)63 433 8875. E-mail: Info@wordsinhere.com. Website: www.wordsinhere.com. Shayna Schapp, assistant art editor (artists); Megan Garr, editor (Designers). **Contact:** Megan M. Garr, editor. Annual print magazine. "*Versal*, published each May by *worsinhere*, is the only literary magazine of its kind in the Netherlands and publishes new poetry, prose and art from around the world. *Versal* and the writers behind it are also at the forefront of a growing translocal European literary scene, which includes exciting communities in Amsterdam, Paris and Berlin. *Versal* seeks work that is urgent, involved and unexpected."

MAGAZINES NEEDS *Versal*, published annually by wordsinhere, is the only English-language literary magazine in the Netherlands and publishes new poetry, prose, and art from around the world. "We publish writers with an instinct for language and line break, content and form that is urgent, involved, and unexpected." Has published poetry by Naomi Shihab Nye, Ben Doller, Marilyn Hacker, Emily Carr, Peter Shippy, William Doresky, Mary Miller, and Sawako Nakayasu. Receives about 1,000+ poems/year, accepts about 4%. Single copy: $15 USD. Ordering information available on website.

HOW TO CONTACT Submit 3-5 poems at a time. Considers simultaneous submissions; no previously published poems. Accepts submissions online only (online submission system can be found on website. Reads submissions September 15–January 15. Time between acceptance and publication is 4-7 months. Poems are circulated to an editorial board. Sometimes comments on rejected poems. Guidelines available on website. Responds in 2 months. Sends prepublication PDF galleys. Pays 1 contributor's copy. Acquires one-time rights. Rights revert to poet upon publication.

TIPS "We ask that all writers interested in submitting work first purchase a copy (available from our website) to get an idea of *Versal*'s personality. All unsolicited submissions must be submitted through our online submission system. The link to this system is live during the submission period, which is September 15–January 15 each year." "We like to see that a story is really a story, or, regardless of your definition of story, that the text has a shape. Often, we receive excellent ideas or anecdotes that have no real sense of development, evolution, or involution. Because we have a story limit of 3,000 words, the best stories have carefully considered their shape. A good shape for an 8,000 word story will rarely be successful in a two- or three thousand word story. We prefer work that has

really thought through and utilized detail/imagery which is both vivid and can carry some symbolic/metaphoric weight. While we like stories that test or challenge language and syntax, we do publish plenty of amazing stories that imply traditional syntax. Even in these stories, however, it is clear that the writers pay close attention to sound and language, which allows the stories to best display their power."

⊘ VERSE

English Department, University of Richmond, Richmond VA 23173. Website: http://versemag.blogspot.com. Andrew Zawacki, co-editor. **Contact:** Brian Henry. English Department, University of Richmond, Richmond, VA 23173. Website: http://versemag.blogspot.com. **Contact:** Brian Henry.

MAGAZINES NEEDS *Verse*, published 3 times/year, is "an international poetry journal which also publishes interviews with poets, essays on poetry, and book reviews." Wants "no specific kind; we look for high-quality, innovative poetry. Our focus is not only on American poetry, but on all poetry written in English, as well as translations." Has published poetry by James Tate, John Ashbery, Barbara Guest, Gustaf Sobin, and Rae Armantrout. *Verse* is 128-416 pages, digest-sized, professionally printed, perfect-bound, with card cover. Receives about 5,000 poems/year, accepts 1%. Press run is 1,000. Single copy: $10; subscription: $18 for individuals, $39 for institutions. Sample: $6. Everyone submitting work to the print magazine will receive a free copy of Verse (cover price $12-15). All contributors to the print magazine will receive at least $200 (possibly more) plus two copies and a one-year subscription. There is no reading fee for submissions to the *Verse* site and no payment for contributors to the *Verse* site. All submissions to the print magazine will also be considered for the VERSE site, so if a portfolio isn't selected for the print magazine, individual pieces still might be accepted for the VERSE site. *Verse*, published 3 times/year, is "an international poetry journal which also publishes interviews with poets, essays on poetry, and book reviews." Wants "no specific kind; we look for high-quality, innovative poetry. Our focus is not only on American poetry, but on all poetry written in English, as well as translations." Has published poetry by James Tate, John Ashbery, Barbara Guest, Gustaf Sobin, and Rae Armantrout. *Verse* is 128-416 pages, digest-sized, professionally printed, perfect-bound, with card cover.

Receives about 5,000 poems/year, accepts 1%. Press run is 1,000. Single copy: $10; subscription: $18 for individuals, $39 for institutions. Sample: $6. Everyone submitting work to the print magazine will receive a free copy of Verse (cover price $12-15). All contributors to the print magazine will receive at least $200 (possibly more) plus two copies and a one-year subscription. There is no reading fee for submissions to the *Verse* site and no payment for contributors to the *Verse* site. All submissions to the print magazine will also be considered for the VERSE site, so if a portfolio isn't selected for the print magazine, individual pieces still might be accepted for the VERSE site.

○ **NOTE:** *Verse is closed to unsolicited submissions until further notice; check website in Spring/Summer 2010 for any updates. Unsolicited submissions will be recycled.*

TIPS "Read widely and deeply. Avoid inundating a magazine with submissions; constant exposure will not increase your chances of getting accepted."

● ⑤ **THE VIRGINIA QUARTERLY REVIEW**
P.O. Box 400223, Charlottesville VA 22904-4223. (434)924-3124. Fax: (434)924-1397. E-mail: vqr@vqronline.org. Website: www.vqronline.org. Estab. 1925.

MAGAZINES NEEDS *The Virginia Quarterly Review* uses about 45-50 pages of poetry in each issue. No length or subject restrictions. Issues have largely included lyric and narrative free verse, most of which features a strong message or powerful voice. *The Virginia Quarterly Review* is 256 pages, digest-sized, flat-spined. Press run is 7,000.

HOW TO CONTACT Submit up to 5 poems at a time. No simultaneous submissions. Accepts online submissions only at http://vqronline.org/submission/. Responds in 1-3 months. Guidelines available on website; do not request by fax. Pays $5/line.

CONTEST/AWARD OFFERINGS Sponsors the Emily Clark Balch Prize for Poetry, an annual award of $1,000 given to the best poem or group of poems published in the *Review* during the year. 2007 winner was Peter Balakian.

● ◐ **VOICES ISRAEL**
P.O. Box 21, Metulla 10292, Israel. E-mail: hbarlev@netvision.net.il. Website: www.voicesisrael.com. **Contact:** Helen Barlev, editor-in-chief. Estab. 1972. *Voices Israel*, published annually by The Voices Israel Group of Poets, is "an anthology of poetry in English, with worldwide

contributions. We consider all kinds of poetry." Poems must be in English; translations must be accompanied by the original poem. *Voices Israel* is about 125 pages, digest-sized, offset from laser output on ordinary paper, flat-spined, with varying cover. Press run is 350. Single copy: $20 for nonmembers. Sample: $15 (back issue). "Members receive the anthology with annual dues ($35)." Visit website or e-mail millmanm@zahav.net.il for ordering information.

MAGAZINES NEEDS *Voices Israel*, published annually by The Voices Israel Group of Poets, is "an anthology of poetry in English, with worldwide contributions. We consider all kinds of poetry." Poems must be in English; translations must be accompanied by the original poem. *Voices Israel* is about 125 pages, digest-sized, offset from laser output on ordinary paper, flat-spined, with varying cover. Press run is 350. Single copy: $20 for nonmembers. Sample: $15 (back issue). "Members receive the anthology with annual dues ($35)." Visit website or e-mail millmanm@zahav.net.il for ordering information.

HOW TO CONTACT Submit up to 4 poems/year. Lines/poem: 40 maximum. Considers previously published poems, "but please include details and assurance that copyright problems do not exist." Accepts e-mail submissions (preferred, as a single Word.doc or Word.rtf attachment). Send 7 hard copies, for distribution to the Editorial Board. Reads submissions June 1-October 7. No reading fee, but **a contribution of $10 for up to 4 poems is requested**. "This is not mandatory and will not affect acceptance or rejection of poems. We reply to all submissions but do not return poems. We do not guarantee publication of any poem. In poems that we publish, we reserve the right to correct obviously unintentional errors in spelling, punctuation, etc."

CONTEST/AWARD OFFERINGS The annual International Reuben Rose Memorial Poetry Competition offers 1st Prize: $300; 2nd Prize $150; 3rd Prize: $100; 4th Prize: $50; and Honorable Mentions. Winning poems are published and distributed together with the *Voices Israel* anthology (as a separate booklet). Send poems of up to 40 lines each to John Dicks, P.O. Box 236, Kiriat Ata, 28101 Israel (john_d@netvision.net.il). Submit 2 copies of each poem: one with name and address; one with no identifying information. Enclose a cover letter providing the title(s) of the poem(s) submitted, your full name, address, and phone number. **Entry fee:**

$5/poem (unlimited entries). Make checks payable to *Voices Israel*. **Deadline:** October 7th. Guidelines available on website.

ALSO OFFERS *Monthly Poet's Voice*, edited by Ezra Ben-Meir, Herzl 45, Nahariya, 22406 Israel (ezrabm@gmail.com), is a newsletter sent only to members of the Voices Israel Group of Poets in English.

○ WATERWAYS: POETRY IN THE MAINSTREAM

Website: www.tenpennyplayers.org. (Specialized: thematic issues)Ten Penny Players, Inc., 393 Saint Pauls Ave., Staten Island NY 10304-2127. (718)442-7429. E-mail: tenpennyplayers@si.rr.com. Website: www.tenpennyplayers.org. Established 1977. **Contact:** Barbara Fisher and Richard Spiegel, poetry editors.

MAGAZINES NEEDS *Waterways: Poetry in the Mainstream*, published 11 times/year, prints work by adult poets. "We publish theme issues and are trying to increase an audience for poetry and the printed and performed word. While we do 'themes,' sometimes an idea for a future magazine is inspired by a submission, so we try to remain open to poets' inspirations. Poets should be guided, however, by the fact that we are children's and animal rights advocates and are a NYC press. We are open to reading material from people we have never published, writing in traditional and experimental poetry forms." Does not want "haiku or rhyming poetry; never use material of an explicit sexual nature." Has published poetry by Ida Fasel, Will Inman, and Richard Kostelanetz. *Waterways* is 40 pages, 4¹⁄₄x7, photocopied from various type styles, saddle-stapled, with matte card cover. Accepts 60% of poems submitted. Press run is 150. Subscription: $45. Sample: $5.

HOW TO CONTACT Submit less than 10 poems at a time (for first submission). Considers simultaneous submissions. Accepts e-mail submissions (pasted into body of message). "Since we've taken the time to be very specific in our response, writers should take seriously our comments and not waste their emotional energy and our time sending material that isn't within our area of interest. Sending for our theme sheet and a sample issue and then objectively thinking about the writer's own work is practical and wise. Manuscripts that arrive without a return envelope are not sent back." Sometimes comments on rejected poems. Guidelines available for SASE or on website. Responds in less than 1 month. Pays 1 contributor's copy. Acquires one-time publication rights.

ADDITIONAL INFORMATION Ten Penny Players publishes chapbooks "by children and young adults only—not by submission—they come through our workshops in the library and schools. Adult poets are published through our Bard Press imprint, **by invitation only**. Books evolve from the relationship we develop with writers we publish in *Waterways* and to whom we would like to give more exposure."

●⊙ WEBER: THE CONTEMPORARY WEST

Weber State University, 1405 University Circle, Ogden UT 84408-1405. Website: www.weber.edu/weberjournal. Weber State University, 1405 University Circle, Ogden UT 84408-1405. (801)626-6616. E-mail: weberjournal@weber.edu. Website: http://weberjournal.weber.edu. **Contact:** Michael Wutz, editor. Estab. 1983. *Weber: The Contemporary West*, published 3 times/year, is "an interdisciplinary journal interested in relevant works covering a wide range of topics." Wants "three or four poems; we publish multiple poems from a poet." Does not want "poems that are flippant, prurient, sing-song, or preachy." Has published poetry by Naomi Shihab Nye, Carolyn Forche, Stephen Dunn, Billy Collins, William Kloefkorn, David Lee, Gary Gildner, and Robert Dana. *Weber* is 150 pages, offset-printed on acid-free paper, perfect-bound, with color cover. Receives about 250-300 poems/year, accepts 30-40. Press run is 1,000; 90% libraries. Subscription: $20 ($30 for institutions); $40 for outside the US. Sample: $10 (back issue).

○ Poetry published in *Weber* has appeared in *The Best American Poetry*.

MAGAZINES NEEDS *Weber: The Contemporary West*, published 3 times/year, is "an interdisciplinary journal interested in relevant works covering a wide range of topics." Wants "three or four poems; we publish multiple poems from a poet." Does not want "poems that are flippant, prurient, sing-song, or preachy." Has published poetry by Naomi Shihab Nye, Carolyn Forche, Stephen Dunn, Billy Collins, William Kloefkorn, David Lee, Gary Gildner, and Robert Dana. *Weber* is 150 pages, offset-printed on acid-free paper, perfect-bound, with color cover. Receives about 250-300 poems/year, accepts 30-40. Press run is 1,000; 90% libraries. Subscription: $20 ($30 for institutions); $40 for outside the US. Sample:

$10 (back issue).

HOW TO CONTACT Submit 3-4 poems at a time, 2 copies of each (one without name). Considers simultaneous submissions; no previously published poems. Cover letter is preferred. Time between acceptance and publication is 15 months. Poems are selected by an anonymous (blind) evaluation. Themes and guidelines available in magazine, for SASE, by e-mail, or on website. Responds in up to 6 months. Always sends prepublication galleys. Pays 2 contributor's copies, a year's subscription, and a small honorarium ($100-300) depending on fluctuating grant monies. Acquires all rights. Copyright reverts to author after first printing.

CONTEST/AWARD OFFERINGS The Dr. Sherwin W. Howard Poetry Award, a $500 cash prize, is awarded annually to the author of the best set of poems published in *Weber* during the previous year. The competition is announced each year in the Spring/Summer issue.

ⓘ THE WELL TEMPERED SONNET

87 Petoskey St., Suite 120, New Hudson MI 48165. E-mail: thewelltemperedsonnet@yahoo.com. Website: http://thewelltemperedsonnet.com. **Contact:** James D. Taylor Jr., editor/publisher.

MAGAZINES NEEDS *The Well Tempered Sonnet*, published annually, features compositions in sonnet form only and "caters to those who love and appreciate the form Shakespeare made famous." Does not want "erotica, blasphemy, vulgarity, or racism." Considers poetry by children and teens. *The Well Tempered Sonnet* is magazine-sized, desktop-published, spiral-bound, with attractive heavy stock cover. Subscription: $25/year. Make checks payable to James Taylor. "We encourage submissions requesting subscriptions, details included in guidelines."

HOW TO CONTACT Submit up to 5 poems at a time. Considers previously published poems; no simultaneous submissions. Accepts submissions by mail or e-mail. Seldom comments on rejected poems. Occasionally publishes theme issues. Guidelines available for SASE or on website. Responds ASAP. Always sends prepublication galleys.

ALSO OFFERS "We encourage and try to provide the means for interaction between other sonneteers."

ⓢⓞⓈ WESTERLY

Westerly Centre (M202), The University of Western Australia, 35 Stirling Hwy, Crawley WA 6009, Aus-tralia. E-mail: westerly@uwa.edu.au. Website: http://westerly.uwa.edu.au. Westerly Centre (M202), The University of Western Australia, 35 Stirling Hwy, Crawley, WA 6009, Australia. E-mail: westerly@uwa.edu.au. Website: http://westerly.uwa.edu.au. Estab. 1956. *Westerly*, published annually in July and November, prints quality short fiction, poetry, literary critical, socio-historical articles, and book reviews with special attention given to AustraliAsiAnd the Indian Ocean region. "We don't dictate to writers on rhyme, style, experimentation, or anything else. We are willing to publish short or long poems. We do assume a reasonably well-read, intelligent audience. Past issues of *Westerly* provide the best guides. Not consciously an academic magazine." *Westerly* is about 200 pages, digest-sized, "electronically printed." Press run is 1,200. Subscription information available at website.

MAGAZINES NEEDS *Westerly*, published annually in July and November, prints quality short fiction, poetry, literary critical, socio-historical articles, and book reviews with special attention given to AustraliAsiAnd the Indian Ocean region. "We don't dictate to writers on rhyme, style, experimentation, or anything else. We are willing to publish short or long poems. We do assume a reasonably well-read, intelligent audience. Past issues of *Westerly* provide the best guides. Not consciously an academic magazine." *Westerly* is about 200 pages, digest-sized, "electronically printed." Press run is 1,200. Subscription information available at website.

HOW TO CONTACT Submit up to 3 poems or 1 short story (2 if quite short-suggested maximum length 5,000 words) at a time. No simultaneous submissions. Submit via post or e-mail. Cover letters should be brief and non-confessional. All manuscripts must show the name and address of the sender and should be single spaced in size 12 Times New Roman font. Deadline for July edition is March 31 and deadline for November edition is July 31. Time between acceptance and publication may be up to one year depending on when work is submitted. Please wait for a response before forwarding any additional submissions for consideration. Contributors receive payment plus one complimentary copy. Acquires first publication rights; requests acknowledgment on reprints. Reviews books of poetry in multi-book format in an annual review essay. Send materials for review consideration. For further information on contributing, please see website.

CONTEST/AWARD OFFERINGS The Patricia Hackett Prize (value approximately $750 AUD) is awarded annually for the best contribution published in the previous year's issue of *Westerly*.

WESTERN HUMANITIES REVIEW

University of Utah, English Department, 255 S. Central Campus Dr., Room 3500, Salt Lake City UT 84112-0494. (801)581-6070. Fax: (801)585-5167. E-mail: whr@mail.hum.utah.edu. Website: www.hum.utah.edu/whr. **Contact:** Dawn Lonsinger, Managing Editor.

> Reads mss September 1-April 1. Mss sent outside these dates will be returned unread.

MAGAZINES NEEDS *Western Humanities Review*, published semiannually in April and October, prints poetry, fiction, and a small selection of nonfiction. Wants "quality poetry of any form, including translations." Has published poetry by Charles Simic, Olena Kalytiak Davis, Ravi Shankar, Karen Volkman, Dan Beachy-Quick, Lucie Brock-Broido, Christine Hume, and Dan Chiasson. Innovative prose poems may be submitted as fiction or non-fiction to the appropriate editor. *Western Humanities Review* is 120-160 pages, digest-sized, professionally printed on quality stock, perfect-bound, with coated card cover. Receives about 1,500 submissions/year, accepts less than 5%. Press run is 1,000. Subscription: $16 to individuals in the U.S. Sample: $10.

HOW TO CONTACT Considers simultaneous submissions but no more than 5 poems or 25 pages per reading period. No fax or e-mail submissions. Reads submissions October 1-April 1 only. Time between acceptance and publication is 1-3 issues. Managing editor and assistant editors makes an initial cut, then the poetry editor makes the final selections. Seldom comments on rejected poems. "We do not publish writer's guidelines because we think the magazine itself conveys an accurate picture of our requirements." Responds in up to 6 months. Pays 2 contributor's copies. Acquires first serial rights then rights revert to author.

CONTEST/AWARD OFFERINGS Sponsors an annual contest for Utah writers.

TIPS "Because of changes in our editorial staff, we urge familiarity with recent issues of the magazine. We do not publish writer's guidelines because we think that the magazine itself conveys an accurate picture of our requirements. Please, no e-mail submissions."

◐ WESTVIEW: A JOURNAL OF WESTERN OKLAHOMA

Southwestern Oklahoma State University, 100 Campus Dr., Weatherford OK 73096. E-mail: james.silver@swosu.edu; westview@swosu.edu. Southwestern Oklahoma State University, 100 Campus Dr., Weatherford, OK 73096. E-mail: james.silver@swosu.edu; westview@swosu.edu. Contact: James Silver, editor. *Westview: A Journal of Western Oklahoma*, published semiannually, is "particularly interested in writers from the Southwest; however, we are open to quality work by poets from elsewhere. We publish free verse, prose poems, and formal poetry." Has published poetry by Carolynne Wright, Miller Williams, Walter McDonald, Robert Cooperman, Alicia Ostriker, and James Whitehead. *Westview* is 64 pages, magazine-sized, perfect-bound, with full-color glossy card cover. Receives about 500 poems/year, accepts 7%. Press run is 700 (300 subscribers, about 25 libraries). Subscription: $15/2 years. Sample: $6.*Westview: A Journal of Western Oklahoma*, published semiannually, is "particularly interested in writers from the Southwest; however, we are open to quality work by poets from elsewhere. We publish free verse, prose poems, and formal poetry." Has published poetry by Carolynne Wright, Miller Williams, Walter McDonald, Robert Cooperman, Alicia Ostriker, and James Whitehead. *Westview* is 64 pages, magazine-sized, perfect-bound, with full-color glossy card cover. Receives about 500 poems/year, accepts 7%. Press run is 700 (300 subscribers, about 25 libraries). Subscription: $15/2 years. Sample: $6.

HOW TO CONTACT Submit 5 poems at a time. Cover letter is required, including biographical data for contributor's note. Comments on submissions "when close." Manuscripts are circulated to an editorial board. Responds within 4-6 months. Pays 1 contributor's copy.

○ WESTWARD QUARTERLY: THE MAGAZINE OF FAMILY READING

Laudemont Press, P.O. Box 369, Hamilton IL 62341. (800)440-4043. E-mail: editor@wwquarterly.com. Website: www.wwquarterly.com. **Contact:** Shirley Anne Leonard, editor. Laudemont Press, P.O. Box 369, Hamilton, IL 62341. (800)440-4043. E-mail: editor@

wwquarterly.com. Website:www.wwquarterly.com. **Contact:** Shirley Anne Leonard, editor. *WestWard Quarterly: The Magazine of Family Reading* prints poetry. Wants "all forms, including rhyme—we welcome inspirational, positive, reflective, humorous material promoting nobility, compassion, and courage." Does not want "experimental or avant-garde forms, offensive language, depressing or negative poetry." Considers poetry by children and teens. Has published poetry by Jane Stuart, Brian Felder, Leland Jamieson, Joyce I. Johnson, Michael Keshigian, Arlene Mandell, J. Alvein Speers, Charles Waugaman. *WestWard Quarterly* is 32 pages, digest-sized, laser-printed, saddle-stapled, with inkjet color cover with scenic photos, includes ads. Receives about 1,500 poems/year, accepts about 10%. Press run is 150 (60 subscribers). Single copy: $4 ($6 foreign); subscription: $15/year ($18 foreign). Contributors to an issue may order extra copies at a discounted price. Make checks payable to Laudemont Press.

MAGAZINES NEEDS *WestWard Quarterly: The Magazine of Family Reading* prints poetry. Wants "all forms, including rhyme—we welcome inspirational, positive, reflective, humorous material promoting nobility, compassion, and courage." Does not want "experimental or avant-garde forms, offensive language, depressing or negative poetry." Considers poetry by children and teens. Has published poetry by Jane Stuart, Brian Felder, Leland Jamieson, Joyce I. Johnson, Michael Keshigian, Arlene Mandell, J. Alvein Speers, Charles Waugaman. *WestWard Quarterly* is 32 pages, digest-sized, laser-printed, saddle-stapled, with inkjet color cover with scenic photos, includes ads. Receives about 1,500 poems/year, accepts about 10%. Press run is 150 (60 subscribers). Single copy: $4 ($6 foreign); subscription: $15/year ($18 foreign). Contributors to an issue may order extra copies at a discounted price. Make checks payable to Laudemont Press.

HOW TO CONTACT Submit up to 5 poems at a time. Lines/poem: 40 maximum. Considers previously published poems and simultaneous submissions. Prefers e-mail submissions (pasted into body of message); no disk submissions. Reads submissions year round. Submit seasonal poems 3 months in advance. Time between acceptance and publication is "months." Often comments on rejected poems. Guidelines available for SASE, by e-mail, or on website. Responds in "weeks." Pays 1 contributor's copy. Acquires one-time rights.

ALSO OFFERS "Every issue includes a 'Featured Writer,' an article about 'Poets from the Past,' and a piece on improving writing skills or writing different forms of poetry."

WHISKEY ISLAND MAGAZINE

Cleveland State University, English Dept., 2121 Euclid Ave., Cleveland OH 44115-2214. (216)687-2000. E-mail: whiskeyisland@csuohio.edu. Website: www.csuohio.edu/class/english/whiskeyisland/.

MAGAZINES NEEDS *Whiskey Island Magazine*, published semiannually, prints poetry, fiction, creative nonfiction, and art. Wants "writing that engages the reader immediately. It's always good to be interesting early." Has published poetry by Denise Duhamel, H.L. Hix, James Allen Hall, Jay Hopler, and Wayne Miller. *Whiskey Island Magazine* is about 100 pages, digest-sized, professionally printed, perfect-bound, with glossy stock cover. Receives 1,000-1,500 poetry mss/year, accepts 6%. Press run is 1,000. Subscription: $12 domestic, $20 overseas. Sample: $6. Make checks payable to *Whiskey Island Magazine*."This is a nonprofit literary magazine that has been published (in one form or another) by students of Cleveland State University for over 30 years. Also features the Annual Student Creative Writing Contest ($5000-$400-$250)."

HOW TO CONTACT Submit up to 5 poems at a time. No previously published poems. Cover letter is required. Include brief bio and SASE for reply only, with name, address, e-mail, and phone number on each page of ms. Accepts e-mail submissions. "Please put cover letter and contact information in body of e-mail, send poems as a Word or .rtf attachment. By postal mail: please include cover letter and SASE. Name, address, e-mail and phone number on each page of ms." Reads submissions year round. Poems are circulated to an editorial committee. Guidelines available in magazine, for SASE, by e-mail, or on website. Responds within 6 months. Pays 2 contributor's copies.

TIPS "See submissions page. Include SASE. Wait at least a year before submitting again."

● WHITE PELICAN REVIEW

P.O. Box 7833, Lakeland FL 33813. **Contact:** Nancy Wiegel, editor. P.O. Box 7833, Lakeland, FL 33813. **Contact:** Nancy Wiegel, editor.

MAGAZINES NEEDS *White Pelican Review*, published semiannually in April and October, is dedicated to printing poetry of the highest quality. Wants "writing that goes beyond competency to exceptional acts of imagination and language." Has published poetry by Paul Hostovsky, Michael Hettich, Becky Sakellariou, Lyn Lifshin, and John Grey. *White Pelican Review* is about 48 pages, digest-sized, photocopied from typescript, saddle-stapled, with matte cardstock cover. Receives about 5,000 poems/year, accepts 3%. Circulation is 500. Single copy: $4; subscription: $8/year for individuals, $10/year for institutions. Make checks payable to *White Pelican Review.*

HOW TO CONTACT Submit 3-5 poems at a time. Lines/poem: "optimal length is 32 lines plus title, although longer poems are given full consideration." No previously published poems or simultaneous submissions. Cover letter is required. SASE is a must. "Please include name, address, telephone number, and (if available) e-mail address on each page. No handwritten poems." Reads submissions year round. Time between acceptance and publication is 1-6 months. Poems are circulated to an editorial board. Seldom comments on rejected poems. Guidelines available for SASE. Responds in 6 months. Pays 1 contributor's copy. Acquires one-time rights.

CONTEST/AWARD OFFERINGS The Hollingsworth Prize of $100 is offered to one distinguished poem published in each issue. No contest or fee is involved.

� ☽ WHITE WALL REVIEW

Department of English, Ryerson University, 10th Floor, Jorgenson Hall, 350 Victoria St., Toronto ON M5B 2K3, Canada. E-mail: wwr@ryerson.ca. Website: www.ryerson.ca/wwr/. **Contact:** The Editors. Department of English, Ryerson University, 10th Floor, Jorgenson Hall, 350 Victoria St., Toronto, ON M5B 2K3, Canada. E-mail: wwr@ryerson.ca. Website: www.ryerson.ca/wwr/. **Contact:** The Editors. *White Wall Review,* published annually in August, focuses on printing "clearly expressed, innovative poetry and prose. No style is unacceptable." Has published poetry by Vernon Mooers and David Sidjak. *White Wall Review* is 90-144 pages, digest-sized, professionally printed, perfect-bound, with glossy card cover. Press run is 500. Subscription: $10 plus GST.*White Wall Review,* published annually in August, focuses on printing "clearly expressed, innovative poetry and prose. No style is unacceptable." Has published poetry by Vernon Mooers and David Sidjak. *White Wall Review* is 90-144 pages, digest-sized, professionally printed, perfect-bound, with glossy card cover. Press run is 500. Subscription: $10 plus GST.

HOW TO CONTACT Submit up to 5 poems at a time by mail only. Length: 5 pages/piece maximum. Cover letter is required. Include short bio. Guidelines available in magazine, for SASE. Responds "as soon as possible." Pays one contributor's copy.

TIPS "Innovative work is especially appreciated."

➕◗ WICKED ALICE

dancing girl press, 410 S. Michigan #921, Chicago IL 60605. E-mail: wickedalicepoetry@yahoo.com. Website: www.sundresspublications.com/wickedalice. **Contact:** Kristy Bowen, editor.

MAGAZINES NEEDS "*Wicked Alice* is a women-centered poetry journal dedicated to publishing quality work by both sexes, depicting and exploring the female experience." Wants "work that has a strong sense of image and music. Work that is interesting and surprising, with innovative, sometimes unusual, use of language. We love humor when done well, strangenes, wackiness. Hybridity, collage, intertexuality." Does not want greeting card verse. Has published poetry by Daniela Olszewska, Rebecca Loudon, Robyn Art, Simone Muench, Brandi Homan, Karyna McGlynn. Receives about 500 poems/year, accepts about 8%.

HOW TO CONTACT Submit up to 5 poems at a time. Considers previously published poetry and simultaneous submissions. Accepts e-mail submissions pasted into body of message. Reads submissions March-September. Time between acceptance and publication is 1-6 months. Sometimes publishes theme issues. Guidelines and themes available on website. Sometimes sends prepublication galleys. Acquires one-time rights. Rights revert to poet upon publication. Review books and chapbooks of poetry in 300 words.

◗◐☽ WILD GOOSE POETRY REVIEW

E-mail: asowens1@yahoo.com. Website: www.wild-goosepoetryreview.com. E-mail: asowens1@yahoo.com. Website: www.wildgoosepoetryreview.com. Contact: Scott Owens, editor. *Wild Goose Poetry Review,* published quarterly online, is a poetry journal with essays, reviews, and interviews. Wants "poetry that exudes a sense of place, that is well-crafted, with an eye to imagery and an ear to music." Does not want "eroticAbstract stream-of-consciousness, or gratuitous obscenities." Has published poetry by Anthony Abbott. Receives about 1,000 poems/year, accepts about 12%.

MAGAZINES NEEDS *Wild Goose Poetry Review*, published quarterly online, is a poetry journal with essays, reviews, and interviews. Wants "poetry that exudes a sense of place, that is well-crafted, with an eye to imagery and an ear to music." Does not want "eroticAbstract stream-of-consciousness, or gratuitous obscenities." Has published poetry by Anthony Abbott. Receives about 1,000 poems/year, accepts about 12%.

HOW TO CONTACT Submit 3-5 poems at a time. Lines/poem: "no poems longer than two pages accepted." Considers simultaneous submissions; no previously published poems. Accepts e-mail submissions only as attachment; no disk submissions. Cover letter is preferred; include bio. Reads submissions year round. Time between acceptance and publication is up to 6 months. Poems are circulated to an editorial board. Guidelines available on website. Responds in 4-6 weeks. Rights revert to poet upon publication. Reviews books/chapbooks of poetry in 500 words. Send materials for review consideration to Patricia Bostian.

◐ WILD VIOLET

P.O. Box 39706, Philadelphia PA 19106-9706. E-mail: wildvioletmagazine@yahoo.com. Website: www.wild-violet.net. **Contact:** Alyce Wilson, editor. P.O. Box 39706, Philadelphia PA 19106-9706. E-mail: wildvi-oletmagazine@yahoo.com. Website: www.wildviolet. net. Established 2001. **Contact:** Alyce Wilson, editor.

MAGAZINES NEEDS *Wild Violet*, published quarterly online, aims "to make the arts more accessible, to make a place for the arts in modern life." Wants "poetry that is well crafted, that engages thought, that challenges or uplifts the reader. We have published free verse, haiku, blank verse, and other forms. If the form suits the poem, we will consider any form." Does not want "abstract, self-involved poetry; poorly managed form; excessive rhyming; self-referential poems that do not show why the speaker is sad, happy, or in love." Has published poetry by Lyn Lifshin, Andrew H. Oerke, Erik Kestler, Anselm Brocki, Carol Frith, Richard Fammereée, Joanna Weston and Graham Burchell. Accepts about 15% of

work submitted.

HOW TO CONTACT Submit 3-5 poems at a time. Considers simultaneous submissions (with notification); no previously published poems. Accepts e-mail submissions (pasted into body of message, or as text or Word attachment); no disk submissions. Cover letter is preferred. Reads submissions year round. Submit seasonal poems 3 months in advance. Time between acceptance and publication is 3 months. "Decisions on acceptance or rejection are made by the editor." Seldom comments on rejected poems, unless requested. Occasionally publishes theme issues. Guidelines available by e-mail or on website. Responds in up to 3 months. Pays by providing a bio and link on contributor's page. Requests electronic rights to publish and archive accepted works. Reviews books/chapbooks of poetry in 250 words, single-book format. Query for review consideration.

CONTEST/AWARD OFFERINGS Sponsors an annual poetry contest, offering 1st Prize: $100 and publication in *Wild Violet*; 2 Honorable Mentions will also be published. Guidelines available by e-mail or on website. **Entry fee:** $5/poem. Judged by independent judges.

TIPS "We look for stories that are well-paced and show character and plot development. Even short shorts should do more than simply paint a picture. Manuscripts stand out when the author's voice is fresh and engaging. Avoid muddying your story with too many characters and don't attempt to shock the reader with an ending you have not earned. Experiment with styles and structures, but don't resort to experimentation for its own sake."

◐ WILLARD & MAPLE

163 S. Willard St., Freeman 302, Box 34, Burlington VT 05401. (802)860-2700 ext. 2462. E-mail: willar-dandmaple@champlain.edu. **Contact:** Poetry Editor. *Willard & Maple*, published annually in spring, is "a student-run literary magazine from Champlain College's Professional Writing Program that publishes a wide array of poems, short stories, creative essays, short plays, pen & ink drawings, photographs, and computer graphics." Wants "creative work of the highest quality." Does not want any submissions over 10 typed pages in length; all submissions must be in English. Considers poetry by children and teens. Has published poetry by Frederick Zydek, Robert Cooperman,

Meghan Schardt, Patrick Willwerth, and N.B.Smith. Willard & Maple is 200 pages, digest-sized, digitally printed, perfect-bound. Receives about 500 poems/year, accepts about 20%. Press run is 600 (80 subscribers, 4 libraries); 200 are distributed free to the Champlain College writing community. Single copy: $12. Contact Lulu Press for Contributor's Copy.

MAGAZINES NEEDS *Willard & Maple*, published annually in spring, is "a student-run literary magazine from Champlain College's Professional Writing Program that publishes a wide array of poems, short stories, creative essays, short plays, pen & ink drawings, photographs, and computer graphics." Wants "creative work of the highest quality." Does not want any submissions over 10 typed pages in length; all submissions must be in English. Considers poetry by children and teens. Has published poetry by Frederick Zydek, Robert Cooperman, Meghan Schardt, Patrick Willwerth, and N.B.Smith. Willard & Maple is 200 pages, digest-sized, digitally printed, perfect-bound. Receives about 500 poems/year, accepts about 20%. Press run is 600 (80 subscribers, 4 libraries); 200 are distributed free to the Champlain College writing community. Single copy: $12. Contact Lulu Press for Contributor's Copy.

HOW TO CONTACT Submit up to 5 poems at a time. Lines/poem: 100 maximum. Considers simultaneous submissions; no previously published poems. Accepts e-mail and disk submissions. Cover letter is required. "Please provide current contact information including an e-mail address. Single-space submissions, one poem/page." Reads submissions September 1 -March 31. Time between acceptance and publication is less than 1 year. "All editors receive a blind copy to review. They meet weekly throughout the academic year. These meetings consist of the submissions being read aloud, discussed, and voted upon." Seldom comments on rejected poems. Occasionally publishes theme issues. Upcoming themes available by e-mail. Responds in less than 6 months. Pays 2 contributor's copies. Acquires one-time rights. Reviews books/chapbooks of poetry and other magazines/journals in 1,200 words. Send materials for review consideration to the poetry editor.

TIPS "The power of imagination makes us infinite."

◯◔ THE WILLOW

The Smithtown Poetry Society, P.O. Box 793, Nesconset NY 11767. (631)656-6690. Fax: (631)656-6690. E-mail: sherylmint@cs.com; editor@thesmithtownpoetrysociety.com. Website: www.thesmithtownpoetrysociety.com. **Contact:** Sheryl Minter, editor. The Smithtown Poetry Society, P.O. Box 793, Nesconset, NY 11767. (631)656-6690. Fax: (631)656-6690. E-mail: sherylmint@cs.com; editor@thesmithtownpoetrysociety.com. Website: www.thesmithtownpoetrysociety.com. **Contact:** Sheryl Minter, editor. *The Willow*, published quarterly online, features "new and upcoming poets alongside known poets. We also feature art, short stories, and poetry, regardless of length, that inspire intelligent thought and originality." Wants all forms of poetry. Does not want "poetry written without thought or in sing-song rhyme." Considers poetry by children and teens. Has published poetry by Marian Ford and Najwa Brax. Receives about 1,000 poems/year, accepts about 15%. Press run is 600; 300 distributed free to coffee shops. Single copy: $7; subscription: $20. Make checks payable to S. Minter.*The Willow*, published quarterly online, features "new and upcoming poets alongside known poets. We also feature art, short stories, and poetry, regardless of length, that inspire intelligent thought and originality." Wants all forms of poetry. Does not want "poetry written without thought or in sing-song rhyme." Considers poetry by children and teens. Has published poetry by Marian Ford and Najwa Brax. Receives about 1,000 poems/year, accepts about 15%. Press run is 600; 300 distributed free to coffee shops. Single copy: $7; subscription: $20. Make checks payable to S. Minter.

HOW TO CONTACT Submit up to 3 poems at a time. Lines/poem: 30 maximum (longer poems are considered but may take longer to publish, depending on magazine space; query before submitting). Considers previously published poems; no simultaneous submissions. Accepts disk submissions; no fax or e-mail submissions. Cover letter is preferred. "All submissions must be typed, double-spaced, with submitter's name and address clearly printed. Please include a SASE for all submissions if you would like your original work returned." Reads submissions year round. Submit seasonal poems 6 months in advance. **Charges $1 reading fee.** Time between acceptance and publication is up to one year. Poems are circulated to an editorial board. Sometimes comments on rejected poems. Guidelines available in magazine, for SASE, by e-mail, or on website. Responds in 1 month.

TIPS The Smithtown Poetry Society Yearly Contest is open to all poets and offers 50% of the contest proceeds as first prize; "the other half goes to the distribution of *The Willow*." Submit up to 3 poems, 20 lines maximum each. **Entry fee:** $5. **Deadline:** June 1. Guidelines available in magazine, for SASE, or on website. "All submissions may be edited for grammar and punctuation."

◑ WINDFALL: A JOURNAL OF POETRY OF PLACE

Website: www.hevanet.com/windfall. (Specialized: poetry of place, specifically in the Pacific Northwest) Windfall Press, P.O. Box 19007, Portland OR 97280-0007. E-mail: bsiverly@comcast.net. Website: www.hevanet.com/windfall. Established 2002. **Contact:** Bill Siverly and Michael McDowell, co-editors.

MAGAZINES NEEDS *Windfall: A Journal of Poetry of Place*, published semiannually in March and September, is "looking for poems of place, specifically places in the Pacific Northwest (the broad bioregion extending from the North Slope of Alaska to the San Francisco Bay AreAnd from the Rocky Mountains to the Pacific Coast). 'Place' can be named or unnamed; but if unnamed, then location should be clearly implied or suggested by observed detail. The poet does not have to be living in the Pacific Northwest, but the poem does. We favor poetry based on imagery derived from sensory observation. *Windfall* also favors poetry that occurs in lines and stanzas." Does not want "language poetry, metapoetry, surrealism, 'Internet poetry' (constructed from search engine information rather than experience), abstract, or self-centered poetry of any kind." Has published poetry by Judith Barrington, Gloria Bird, Barbara Drake, Clem Starck, Tom Wayman, and Robert Wrigley. *Windfall* is 52 pages, digest-sized, stapled, with art on covers ("all are drawings or prints by Portland artist Sharon Bronzan"). Receives about 160 poems/year, accepts about 60. Press run is 250. Single copy: $7; subscription: $14/year. Make checks payable to Windfall Press.

HOW TO CONTACT Submit 5 poems at a time. Lines/poem: up to 50. Considers simultaneous submissions; no previously published poems. Accepts e-mail submissions (as attachment). Cover letter is preferred. "SASE required for submissions by U.S. mail." Reads submissions "after the deadlines for each issue: February 1 for Spring, and August 1 for Fall." Time between acceptance and publication is 2 months. Never comments on rejected poems. Guidelines available in magazine or on website. Responds in 2 weeks to 6 months ("depends on when poems are submitted in the biannual cycle"). Pays 2 contributor's copies. Acquires first North American serial rights. "Poem may appear in sample pages on *Windfall* website." Rights revert to poet upon publication.

◑◐ WINDSOR REVIEW

(519)253-3000. Fax: (519)971-3676. E-mail: uwrevu@uwindsor.ca. Website: www.uwindsor.ca. Department of English, Windsor ON N9B 3P4 Canada. (519)253-4232, ext. 2290. Fax: (519)971-3676. E-mail: uwrevu@uwindsor.ca. **Art Editor:** Marty Gervais. Estab. 1966. Biannual 4-color literary magazine featuring poetry, short fiction and art. Circ. 400. Art guidelines free for #10 SASE with first-class postage."We try to offer a balance of fiction and poetry distinguished by excellence."

TIPS "Good writing, strong characters, and experimental fiction is appreciated."

◑ WISCONSIN REVIEW

University of Wisconsin Oshkosh, 800 Algoma Blvd., Oshkosh WI 54901. E-mail: wisconsinreview@uwosh.edu. Website: www.uwosh.edu/wisconsinreview. University of Wisconsin Oshkosh, 800 Algoma Blvd., Oshkosh, WI 54901. (920)424-2267. E-mail:wisconsinreview@uwosh.edu. Website: www.uwosh.edu/wisconsinreview. *Wisconsin Review*, published annually, is a "contemporary poetry, prose, and art magazine run by students at the University of Wisconsin Oshkosh." Wants all forms and styles of poetry. Does not want "poetry that is racist, sexist, or unnecessarily vulgar." Considers poetry by children and teens. "Minors may submit material by including a written letter of permission from a parent or guardian."*Wisconsin Review*, published annually, is a "contemporary poetry, prose, and art magazine run by students at the University of Wisconsin Oshkosh." Wants all forms and styles of poetry. Does not want "poetry that is racist, sexist, or unnecessarily vulgar." Considers poetry by children and teens. "Minors may submit material by including a written letter of permission from a parent or guardian." *Wisconsin Review* is 250 pages, digest-sized, perfect-bound, with 4-color glossy coverstock. Receives about 400 poetry submissions/year, accepts about 50;

Press run is 2,000. Single copy: $10; subscription: $10 plus $3 extra per issue for shipments outside the U.S. **HOW TO CONTACT** Send complete ms with cover letter and SASE. Sample copy and yearly subscription $10/year. Pays with 2 contributor copies. Acquires first rights. Simultaneous submissions are not accepted.

TIPS "We are open to any poetic form and style, and look for outstanding imagery, new themes, and fresh voices — poetry that induces emotions."

⊛ THE WOLF

April Heights, Fagnal Lane, Winchmore Hill, Amersham HP7 0PG, England. E-mail: editor@wolfmagazine.co.uk; thewolfpoetry@hotmail.com. Website: www.wolfmagazine.co.uk. **Contact:** James Byrne, editor. Estab. 2002. *The Wolf*, published 3 times per year, publishes "international translations, critical prose, and interviews with leading contemporary poets, which are frequently mentioned as distinguishing characteristics of the magazine. The poetry, however, comes purely through work submitted. There is no special treatment with regard to the consideration of any poet or poem. Since January 2008, *The Wolf* has benefited from Arts Council funding. Since receiving its grant the magazine has increased its content by a third and is perfect bound." $12 single isue, including postage and packing; $35 subscription. Accepts PayPal.

MAGAZINES NEEDS *The Wolf*, published 3 times per year, publishes "international translations, critical prose, and interviews with leading contemporary poets, which are frequently mentioned as distinguishing characteristics of the magazine. The poetry, however, comes purely through work submitted. There is no special treatment with regard to the consideration of any poet or poem. Since January 2008, *The Wolf* has benefited from Arts Council funding. Since receiving its grant the magazine has increased its content by a third and is perfect bound." $12 single isue, including postage and packing; $35 subscription. Accepts PayPal.

HOW TO CONTACT Submit up to 5 poems by e-mail to thewolfpoetry@hotmail.com. Reads submissions year round. Guidelines available on website. Responds in 6 months. Pays 1 contributor's copy. Accepts reviews of poetry books between 1,000-1,500 words.

ADDITIONAL INFORMATION Also accepts critical essays on any poetry subject between 2,000-3,000 words. Welcomes artwork or photographs.

⊙ THE WORCESTER REVIEW

1 Ekman St., Worcester MA 01607. (508)797-4770. E-mail: rodgerwriter@myfairpoint.net. Website: wreview.homestead.com. **Contact:** Rodger Martin, managing editor.

MAGAZINES NEEDS *The Worcester Review*, published annually by the Worcester County Poetry Association, encourages "critical work with a New England connection; no geographic limitation on poetry and fiction." Wants "work that is crafted, intuitively honest and empathetic." Has published poetry by Kurt Brown, Cleopatra Mathis, and Theodore Deppe. *The Worcester Review* is 160 pages, digest-sized, professionally printed in dark type on quality stock, perfect-bound, with matte card cover. Press run is 750. Subscription: $30 (includes membership in WCPA). Sample: $8.

HOW TO CONTACT Submit up to 5 poems at a time (recommend 3 or less receive the most favorable readings). Considers previously published poems "if they do not conflict with our readership" and simultaneous submissions "if notified." Cover letter is required. Include brief bio. Poems should be typed on $8\frac{1}{2}$x11 paper, with poet's name in upper left corner of each page. Include SASE for return of ms. Sometimes comments on rejected poems. Guidelines available for SASE or on website. Responds in up to 9 months. Pays 2 contributor's copies plus small honorarium. Acquires first rights.

TIPS "Send only one short story—reading editors do not like to read two by the same author at the same time. We will use only one. We generally look for creative work with a blend of craftsmanship, insight and empathy. This does not exclude humor. We won't print work that is shoddy in any of these areas."

⊙ WRITE ON!! POETRY MAGAZETTE

P.O. Box 901, Richfield UT 84701-0901. E-mail: jimnipoetry@yahoo.com. **Contact:** Jim Garman, editor. P.O. Box 901, Richfield, UT 84701-0901. E-mail:jimnipoetry@yahoo.com. **Contact:** Jim Garman, editor. *Write On!! Poetry Magazette*, published monthly, features "poetry from poets around the world." Wants poetry of "any style; all submissions must be suitable for all ages to read." Does not want "adult themes or vulgar material." Considers poetry by children and teens. Has published poetry by Cathy Porter, B.Z.

Niditch, Ron Koppelberger, and Betty Shelley. *Write On!!* is 24 pages, digest-sized, photostat-copied, saddle-stapled. Receives about 500 poems/year, accepts about 50%. Press run is 50. Single copy: $4. Sample: $3. Make checks payable to Jim Garman.

MAGAZINES NEEDS *Write On!! Poetry Magazette*, published monthly, features "poetry from poets around the world." Wants poetry of "any style; all submissions must be suitable for all ages to read." Does not want "adult themes or vulgar material." Considers poetry by children and teens. Has published poetry by Cathy Porter, B.Z. Niditch, Ron Koppelberger, and Betty Shelley. *Write On!!* is 24 pages, digest-sized, photostat-copied, saddle-stapled. Receives about 500 poems/year, accepts about 50%. Press run is 50. Single copy: $4. Sample: $3. Make checks payable to Jim Garman.

HOW TO CONTACT Submit 1-6 poems at a time. Lines/poem: 6 minimum, 28 maximum. Considers previously published poems and simultaneous submissions. Accepts e-mail submissions (pasted into body of message, no attachments). Reads submissions year round. Submit seasonal poems 2 months in advance. Time between acceptance and publication is one month. Never comments on rejected poems. Occasionally publishes theme issues. Guidelines available by e-mail. Responds in "approximately" 3 weeks. No payment or free copies provided. "*WRITE ON!!* contains no ads, no sponsors, all costs are covered out of pocket or by those desiring a copy." Acquires one-time rights, "which return to author upon publication."

◐ WRITER'S BLOC

Texas A&M University-Kingsville, Dept. of Language and Literature, MSC 162, Fore Hall 201B, Kingsville TX 78363. (361)593-2516. E-mail: c-downs@tamuk.edu. Website: www.tamuk.edu/langlit/writers-bloc.html. **Contact:** Dr. Cathy Downs. Texas A&M University-Kingsville, Dept. of Language and Literature MSC 162, Fore Hall 201B, Kingsville, TX 78363. (361)593-2516. Fax: (361)593-2116. E-mail: c-downs@tamuk.edu. Website: www.tamuk.edu/langlit/writers-bloc.html. *Writer's Bloc*, published annually, prints poetry, fiction, creative nonfiction, and graphic art. "About half of our pages are devoted to the works of Texas A&M University-Kingsville students and half to the works of writers and artists from all over the world." Wants quality poetry; no restrictions on con-

tent or form. *Writer's Bloc* is 96 pages, digest-sized. Press run is 300. Subscription: $7. Sample: $7.

MAGAZINES NEEDS *Writer's Bloc*, published annually, prints poetry, fiction, creative nonfiction, and graphic art. "About half of our pages are devoted to the works of Texas A&M University-Kingsville students and half to the works of writers and artists from all over the world." Wants quality poetry; no restrictions on content or form. *Writer's Bloc* is 96 pages, digest-sized. Press run is 300. Subscription: $7. Sample: $7.

HOW TO CONTACT Submit no more than 3 pages of poetry at a time ("prose poems okay"). Lines/poem: 50 maximum. No previously published poems or simultaneous submissions. No e-mail submissions; postal submissions only. "Submissions should be typed, double-spaced; SASE required for reply." Reads submissions September-February only. "Manuscripts are published upon recommendation by a staff of students and faculty." Seldom comments on rejected poems. Guidelines available in magazine or for SASE. "Acceptance letters are sent out in October." Pays 1 contributor's copy.

THE WRITER'S CHRONICLE

(703)993-4301. Fax: (703)993-4302. E-mail: chronicle@awpwriter.org. Website: www.awpwriter.org. "Writer's Chronicle strives to: present the best essays on the craft and art of writing poetry, fiction and nonfiction; help overcome the over-specialization of the literary arts by presenting a public forum for the appreciation, debate and analysis of contemporary literature; present the diversity of accomplishments and points of view within contemporary literature; provide serious and committed writers and students of writing the best advice on how to manage their professional lives; provide writers who teach with new pedagogical approaches for their classrooms; provide the members and subscribers with a literary community as a compensation for a devotion to a difficult and lonely art; provide information on publishing opportunities, grants and awards; promote the good works of AWP, its programs and its individual members. Published 6 times during the academic year/3 times a semester." *Writer's Chronicle* strives to: present the best essays on the craft and art of writing poetry, fiction and nonfiction; help overcome the over-specialization of the literary arts by presenting a public forum for the appreciation, debate and analysis of contemporary literature; present the diversity of accomplishments and points of view within contemporary literature; provide serious and committed writers and students of writing the best advice on how to manage their professional lives; provide writers who teach with new pedagogical approaches for their classrooms; provide the members and subscribers with a literary community as a compensation for a devotion to a difficult and lonely art; provide information on publishing opportunities, grants and awards; promote the good works of AWP, its programs and its individual members.

TIPS "In general, the editors look for articles that demonstrate an excellent working knowledge of literary issues and a generosity of spirit that esteems the arguments of other writers on similar topics. When writing essays on craft, do not use your own work as an example. Keep in mind that 18,000 of our readers are students or just-emerging writers. They must become good readers before they can become good writers, so we expect essays on craft to show exemmplary close readings of a variety of contemporary and older works. Essays must embody erudition, generosity, curiosity and discernment rather than self-involvement. Writers may refer to their own travails and successes if they do so modestly, in small proportion to the other examples.."

WRITERS' JOURNAL

Val-Tech Media, P.O. Box 394, Perham MN 56573-0394. (218)346-7921. Fax: (218)346-7924. E-mail: writersjournal@writersjournal.com. Website: www.writersjournal.com. **Contact:** Leon Ogroske, editor. *"Writers' Journal* is read by thousands of aspiring writers whose love of writing has taken them to the next step: writing for money. We are an instructional manual giving writers the tools and information necessary to get their work published. We also print works by authors who have won our writing contests."

MAGAZINES NEEDS *WRITERS" Journal*, published bimonthly, offers "advice and guidance, motivation, and inspiration to the more serious and published writers and poets." Features 2 columns for poets: "Esther Comments" offers critiques of poems sent in by readers, and "Every Day with Poetry" discusses a wide range of poetry topics, often—but not always—including readers' work. Wants "a variety of poetry: free verse, strict forms, concrete, Oriental. Since we appeal to those of different skill levels, some poems are more sophisticated than others, but those accepted must move, intrigue, or otherwise positively capture me. 'Esther Comments' is never used as a negative force to put a poem or a poet down. Indeed, I focus on the best part of a given work and seek to suggest means of improvement on weaker aspects." Does not want anything "vulgar, preachy, or sloppily written." Considers poetry by children (school-age). Has published poetry by Lawrence Schug, Diana Sutliff, and Eugene E. Grollmes. *WRITERS' Journal* is 64 pages, magazine-sized, professionally printed, with paper cover. Receives fewer than 900 submissions/year, accepts about 25 (including those used in columns). Press run is 20,000. Single copy: $5.99; subscription: $19.97/year U.S., add $15 for Canada/Mexico, $30 for Europe, all others add $35. Sample: $6.

HOW TO CONTACT May submit 3-4 poems at a time. Lines/poem: 25 maximum. No e-mail poetry submissions; postal submissions only. Responds in up to 5 months. Pays $5/poem plus 1 contributor's copy.

CONTEST/AWARD OFFERINGS Sponsors poetry contests for previously unpublished poetry. Submit serious verse only, on any subject or in any form, 25 lines maximum. "Submit in duplicate: one with name and address, one without." Receives fewer than 300 entries/contest. Winners announced in *The WRITERS' Journal* for SASE, and on website. **Entry fee:** $3/poem for each contest. **Deadline:** April 30, August 30, and December 30. Guidelines available for SASE or on website.

TIPS "Appearance must be professional with no grammatical or spelling errors, submitted on white paper, double spaced with easy-to-read font. We want articles that will help writers improve technique in writing, style, editing, publishing, and story construction. We are interested in how writers use new and fresh angles to break into the writing markets."

✛ ◑ THE WRITING DISORDER

P.O. Box 93613, Los Angeles CA 90093-0613. (323)336-5822. E-mail: submit@thewritingdisorder.com. Website: www.thewritingdisorder.com. **Contact:** C.E. Lukather, editor; Paul Garson, managing editor. Quarterly literary magazine featuring new and established writers. *"The Writing Disorder* is an online literary magazine devoted to literature, art, and culture. The mission of the magazine is to showcase new and emerging writers—particularly those in MFA writing programs—as well as established ones. The magazine also features original artwork, photography, and comic art. Although it strives to publish original and experimental work, *The Writing Disorder* remains rooted in the classic art of storytelling."

MAGAZINES NEEDS Quarterly literary magazine featuring new and established writers. "*The Writing Disorder* is an online literary magazine devoted to literature, art, and culture. The mission of the magazine is to showcase new and emerging writers—particularly those in MFA writing programs—as well as established ones. The magazine also features original artwork, photography, and comic art. Although it strives to publish original and experimental work, *The Writing Disorder* remains rooted in the classic art of storytelling." Wants avant garde, free verse, haiku, light verse, traditional.

HOW TO CONTACT Query by mail or e-mail. Publishes ms an average of 3-6 months after acceptance. Submit seasonal material 6 months in advance. Accepts simultaneous submissions. Responds in 6-12 weeks to queries; 3-6 months to ms. Sample copy and guidelines available online. Acquires first North American serial rights.

XAVIER REVIEW

Website: www.xula.edu/review. Xavier University, 1 Drexel Dr., New Orleans LA 70125-1098. (504)520-7805. Fax: (504)520-7917. Website: www.xula.edu/review. Estab. 1980 (review), 1988 (press). **Contact:** Dr. Nicole P. Greene, editor (review) or Katheryn K. Laborde, managing editor.

MAGAZINES NEEDS *Xavier Review*, published semiannually, is a journal of poetry, fiction, translations, essays, and reviews (contemporary literature) for professional writers, libraries, colleges, and universities. "Our content includes a focus on African American, Caribbean, and Southern literature, as well as works that touch on issues of religion and spirituality. We do, however, consider quality works on all themes." Has published poetry by Chris Waters, Lisa Sisk, Mark Taksa, Glenn Sheldon, Christine DeSimone, and Holly Pettit. Press run is 300. Subscription: $10/year for individuals, $15/year for institutions. Sample: $5.

HOW TO CONTACT Submit 3-5 poems at a time. Include SASE. "Overseas authors only may submit by e-mail attachment." Pays 2 contributor's copies; offers 40% discount on additional copies.

ADDITIONAL INFORMATION *Xavier Review* Press publishes book-length works of poetry and prose. Recent publications include *Turning Up the Volume* by Patrice Melnick and *Vespers at Mount Angel* by Stella Nesanovich. Books are available through website or by e-mailing klaborde@xula.edu. Query via e-mail: klaborde@xula.edu. **"Manuscripts should not be sent without permission of the editor."**

YEMASSEE

Department of English, University of South Carolina, Columbia SC 29208. (803)777-2085. Fax: (803)777-9064. E-mail: editor@yemasseejournalonline.org. Website: http://yemasseejournalonline.org. **Contact:** Editors. Magazine: $5^1_2 \times 8^1_2$; 70-90 pages; 60 lb. natural paper; 65 lb. cover; cover illustration. *Yemassee* publishes all genres and forms of writing, including poetry, fiction, drama, nonfiction, reviews, and interviews. Publishes in the fall and spring, printing three to five stories and twelve to fifteen poems per issue. "We tend to solicit reviews, essays, and interviews but welcome unsolicited queries. We do not favor any particular aesthetic or school of writing. Quality of writing is our only concern."" *Yemassee* is the University of South Carolina's literary journal. Our readers are interested in high quality fiction, poetry, dramAnd creative nonfiction. We have no editorial slant; quality of work is our only concern." "We publish in the fall and spring, printing three to five stories and 12-15 poems per issue. We tend to solicit reviews, essays, and interviews but welcome unsolicited queries. We do not favor any particular aesthetic or school of writing. Please limit any submission to 7,500 words. Simultaneous submissions are accepted, given that you identify them as such on your cover letter and immediately notify us if the submission is accepted elsewhere. We do not consider any work that has been previously published in any form, print or electronic. We do not accept electronic submissions (exceptions are made for overseas submissions and submissions from incarcerated persons). Address your manuscripts to the appropriate genre editor. Include a cover letter with your contact information (including email address) and a SASE with sufficient postage.

HOW TO CONTACT Postal or submission manager on website. Response time generally ranges from 1-4 months. Contributors receive 2 copies of the issue in which their work appears. *Yemassee* acquires first-time North American rights. Copyright reverts to authors upon publication. "Simultaneous submissions are accepted, given that you identify them as such on your cover letter and immediately notify us if the submission is accepted elsewhere." No previously published work in any form, print or electronic. Address manuscripts to the appropriate genre editor. Include cover letter with contact information (including email address) and a SASE with sufficient postage.

◐◖ ZEEK: A JEWISH JOURNAL OF THOUGHT AND CULTURE

Website: www.zeek.net. P.O. Box 1342, New York NY 10116. E-mail: zeek@zeek.net. Website: www.zeek.net. Established 2002. **Contact:** Richard Chess, poetry editor. Dan Friedman, associate editor.

MAGAZINES NEEDS *Zeek: A Jewish Journal of Thought and Culture*, published monthly online and in print, seeks poetry that is "poetically daring, with shades of the numinous as it manifests in moments non-poets would ignore." *Zeek* (print version) is 96 pages, digest-sized, perfect-bound, includes photography. Receives about 500 poems/year, accepts about 20. Press run (print) is 2,000 (200 subscribers); online version gets 60,000 hits/month. Single copy: $7; subscription: $14/year. Make checks payable to Zeek Media Inc.

HOW TO CONTACT Submit 3 poems at a time. Considers simultaneous submissions; no previously published poems. Accepts e-mail submissions only (pasted into body of message). Short cover letter is acceptable. Reads submissions year round. Time between acceptance and publication varies. "Poetry editor has final approval, but editorial board of four can propose or reject." Seldom comments on rejected poems. Occasionally publishes theme issues. Guidelines available on website. Responds anywhere from 1 month to 1 year. Pays 5 contributor's copies (to poets published in print edition). Acquires one-time rights. Reviews books of poetry.

➕◯ ZYLOPHONE POETRY JOURNAL

E-mail: faineugenia@yahoo.com. Website: poetezines.4mg.com. **Contact:** Eugenia Fain, editor.

MAGAZINES NEEDS *Zylophone* is published semiannually in print and online. Wants all common formats. Has published poetry by Edward W. Cousins, Daisy Whitmore, David Barger. *Zylophone* is 16 pages, tabloid-sized, staple-bound with line drawing artwork. Receives about 60 poems/year; accepts about 12. Press run is 20. Sample copy is $6.

HOW TO CONTACT Submit 3 poems at a time by e-mail. Lines/poem: 4-16 lines. Considers simultaneous submissions; no previously published work. Cover letter is preferred. Reads submissions year round. Time between acceptance and publication is 6 weeks. Guidelines available by e-mail. Pays one contributor copy. Acquires one-time rights.

BOOK/CHAPBOOK PUBLISHERS

//

Every poet dreams of publishing a collection of his or her work. However, it's surprising how many poets still envision putting out a thick, hardbound volume containing hundreds of poems. In reality, poetry books are usually slim, often paperback, with varying levels of production quality, depending on the publisher.

More common than full-length poetry books (i.e., 50-150 pages by modern standards) are poetry *chapbooks*, small editions of approximately 24-32 pages. They may be printed on quality paper with beautiful cover art on heavy stock; or they may be photocopied sheets of plain printer paper, folded and stapled or hand-sewn along the spine.

In this section you'll find a variety of presses and publishers of poetry books and chapbooks. However, it's a reflection of how poetry publishing works in the early 21st century that many book/chapbook publishing opportunities appear in the Contest & Awards section instead.

HOW LISTINGS ARE FORMATTED

Content of each listing was provided or verified by a representative of the press or publisher (poetry editor, managing editor, owner, etc.). Here is how that content is arranged in each listing:

ICONS. Icons at the beginning of each listing offer visual signposts to specific information about the book/chapbook publisher: ✛ this market is recently established and new to *Poet's Market*; ◐ this market publishes primarily online (some books and chapbooks are indeed published online, sometimes as a PDF that can be printed out); ✪ this market is located in Canada or ◕ outside the U.S. and Canada; ✸ this market pays a monetary amount (as opposed to a given number of author's copies); ○ this market welcomes submissions from beginning poets; ◑ this market prefers submissions from skilled, experienced poets, will consider work from beginning poets; ● this market prefers submissions from poets with a high degree of skill and experience; ◉ this market has a specialized focus (listed in parentheses after publisher/press name); ⊘ this market does not consider unsolicited submissions. (Keys to these icons are listed on the inside cover of this book.)

CONTACT INFORMATION. Next you'll find the information you need to contact the press or publisher, according to what was provided for each listing: name (in bold) of the publisher/press (with areas of specialization noted in parentheses where appropriate); regular mail address; telephone number; fax number; e-mail address; website address; year the publisher/press was established; the name of the person to contact (or an editorial title); and membership in small press/publishing organization(s). (Note: If a publisher or press wants electronic submissions exclusively, no street address may be given.)

NEEDS. This section provides an overview of the publisher/press, including such helpful information as editorial preferences; how manuscripts are considered; the number and kinds of books and/or chapbooks produced; a list of recently published titles; and production information about the titles (number of pages, printing/binding details, type of cover, press run).

HOW TO SUBMIT. This section states whether a poet should query with samples or send the complete manuscript; possible reading periods; reading fees, if applicable; response time; payment amount/terms; and how to order sample copies.

ADDITIONAL INFORMATION. Editors/publishers may use this section to explain other types of publishing activities (such as broadsides, postcards or anthologies), elaborate on some aspect of production—anything beyond the basic details of the submission process that readers may find of interest.

CONTEST/AWARD OFFERINGS. This section discusses prizes and competitions associated with the publisher, with either brief guidelines or a cross-reference to a separate listing in the Contests & Awards section.

ALSO OFFERS. Describes other offerings associated with this publisher (i.e., sponsored readings, website activities such as blogs and forums, related poetry groups, etc.).

TIPS. Provides direct quotes from the editor/publisher about everything from pet peeves to tips on writing to views on the state of poetry today.

GETTING STARTED, FINDING A PUBLISHER

If you don't have a publisher in mind, read randomly through the listings, making notes as you go. (Don't hesitate to write in the margins, underline, use highlighters; it also helps to flag markets that interest you with Post-It Notes). Browsing the listings is an effective way to familiarize yourself with the kind of information presented and the publishing opportunities that are available at various skill levels. If you're thinking of a specific publisher by name, however, begin with the General Index. Here all *Poet's Market* listings are alphabetized.

REFINE YOUR SEARCH

To supplement the General Index, we provide more specific indexes to help you refine your marketing plan for your manuscript. Not every listing appears in one of these indexes, so use them only to reinforce your other research efforts. The following indexes may be helpful:

Geographical Index sorts publishers/presses by state and by countries outside the U.S. Some publishers are more open to poets from their region, so use this index when you're pinpointing local opportunities.

Subject Index groups all markets into categories according to areas of special focus. These include all specialized markets as well as broader categories such as online markets, poetry for children, markets that consider translations, and others. Save time when looking for a specific type of publisher/press by checking this index first.

THE NEXT STEP

Once you know how to interpret the listings in this section and identify markets for your work, the next step is to start submitting your poetry collection. See "How to Use Poet's Market" and "Frequently Asked Questions" for advice, guidelines for preparing your manuscript and proper submissions procedures.

AHSAHTA PRESS

MFA Program in Creative Writing, Boise State University, 1910 University Dr., MS 1525, Boise ID 83725-1525. (208)426-4210. E-mail: ahsahta@boisestate.edu. E-mail: jholmes@boisestate.edu. Website: ahsahta-press.boisestate.edu. **Contact:** Janet Holmes, director. Ahsahta Press, which originally published contemporary poets of the American West, has since expanded its scope "to publish poets nationwide, seeking out and publishing the best new poetry from a wide range of aesthetics—poetry that is technically accomplished, distinctive in style, and thematically fresh." Has published *The True Keeps Calm Biding Its Story* by Rusty Morrison (James Laughlin Award, 2008), *Bone Pagoda* by Susan Tichy, *Case Sensitive* by Kate Greenstreet, *Quarantine* by Brian Henry, *Spell* by Dan Beachy-Quick, and *Saving the Appearances* by Liz Waldner.

"Our usual reading period is March 1-May 1, but because of a backlog of accepted manuscripts, *Ahsahta* cannot read unsolicited work until further notice. Please check our site periodically for announcements if you are interested. Ahsahta Press publishes chapbooks only occasionally and by invitation only. During the Sawtooth Poetry Prize Competition (January 1 through March 1) we are not able to consider manuscripts unless they are contest entries. However, we try to respond to submissions within 3 months. The press will continue to read manuscripts for the $1500 Sawtooth Poetry Prize Competition each year between January 1 and March 1. Please see the competition guidelines for more information."

HOW TO CONTACT Considers multiple and simultaneous submissions. Reading period is temporarily suspended due to backlog, but the press publishes runners-up as well as winners of the Sawtooth Poetry Prize. Forthcoming, new, and backlist titles available on website. Most backlist titles: $9.95; most current titles: $17.50.

CONTEST/AWARD OFFERINGS The Sawtooth Poetry Prize (see separate listing in Contests & Awards).

TIPS "Ahsahta's motto is that poetry is art, so our readers tend to come to us for the unexpected—poetry that makes them think, reflect, and even do something they haven't done before."

AMSTERDAM PRESS

6199 State Hwy 43, Amsterdam OH 43903. (740)543-4333. E-mail: editor@amsterdampress.net. Website: www.amsterdampress.net. **Contact:** Cindy Kelly, editor. 6199 Steubenville Rd. SE, Amsterdam, OH 43903. (740)543-4333. E-mail: editor@amsterdampress.net. Website:www.amsterdampress.net. **Contact:** Cindy Kelly, editor.

NEEDS Amsterdam Press, publishes chapbooks and broadsides, wants "poetry of place, poetry grounded in sense images, poetry that leaps, and has a clear voice." Does not want "esoteric poetry that focuses on the universal." Manuscripts are selected through open submission. Chapbooks are 36 pages, laser-printed, saddle-stitched, with card cover and black and white art/graphics.

HOW TO CONTACT Query first, with a few sample poems and a cover letter with brief bio and publication credits. Chapbook mss may include previously published poems. "Previously published poetry must be recognized on a separate page of mss." Responds to queries in 1-3 months; to mss in 1-3 months. Pays honorarium of $25-100 and 10 author's copies out of a press run of 100-300. Order sample books/chapbooks by sending $8 to Amsterdam Press, 6199 Steubenville Rd. SE, Amsterdam, OH 43903.

ANAPHORA LITERARY PRESS

104 Banff Dr., Apt. 101, Edinboro PA 16412. (814)273-0004. E-mail: pennsylvaniajournal@gmail.com. E-mail: pennsylvaniajournal@gmail.com. Website: www.anaphoraliterary.wordpress.com. **Contact:** Anna Faktorovich, editor-in-chief (general interest). "We are actively seeking submissions at this time. The genre is not as important as the quality of work. You should have a completed full-length ms ready to be emailed or mailed upon request. In the Winter of 2010, Anaphora began accepting book-length single-author submissions. We are actively seeking single and multiple-author books in fiction (poetry, novels, and short story collections) and non-fiction (academic, legal, business, journals, edited and un-edited dissertations, biographies, and memoirs). Email submissions to pennsylvaniajournal@gmail.com. Profits are split 50/50% with single-author writers. There are no costs to have a book produced by Anaphora. We do not offer any free contributor copies."

NEEDS Confession, contemporary, experimental, occult, picture books, plays, poetry, poetry in translation.

HOW TO CONTACT Contact by mail or email.

TIPS "Our audience is academics, college students and graduates, as well as anybody who loves literature. Regardless of profits, we love publishing great books and we enjoy reading submissions. So, if you are reading this book because you love writing and hope to publish as soon as possible, send a query letter or a submission to us. But, remember—proofread your work (most of our editors are English instructors)."

ANHINGA PRESS

P.O. Box 3665, Tallahassee FL 32315. (850)422-1408. Fax: (850)442-6323. E-mail: info@anhinga.org. Website: www.anhinga.org. **Contact:** Rick Campbell, editor. "Publishes only full-length collections of poetry (60-80 pages). No individual poems or chapbooks."

HOW TO CONTACT *"Anhinga Press is currently not accepting unsolicited manuscripts. (By "unsolicited" we mean manuscripts we haven't already accepted or requested.) Our publication calendar is filled through March, 2010."* Please check website for further updates. Submit query letter and 10-page sample by mail with SASE.

ARC PUBLICATIONS

Nanholme Mill, Shaw Wood Rd., Todmorden, Lancashire OL14 6DA, England. E-mail: info@arcpublications.co.uk. Website: www.arcpublications.co.uk. Angele Jarman, director of development. **Contact:** Tony Ward, managing editor,. Nanholme Mill, Shaw Wood Rd., Todmorden, Lancashire OL14 6DA, England. E-mail:info@arcpublications.co.uk. Website: www.arcpublications.co.uk. **Contact:** Tony Ward, managing editor; Angele Jarman, director of development. Publishes "contemporary poetry from new and established writers from the UK and abroad, specializing in the work of world poets writing in English, and the work of overseas poets in translation."

NEEDS Publishes "contemporary poetry from new and established writers from the UK and abroad, specializing in the work of world poets writing in English, and the work of overseas poets in translation."

HOW TO CONTACT *"At present we are not accepting submissions but keep updated by visiting the website."*

ARCTOS PRESS

P.O. Box 401, Sausalito, CA 94966-0401. (415)331-2503. E-mail:runes@aol.com. Website: www.arctospress.com. **Contact:** CB Follett, editor.

NEEDS Arctos Press, under the imprint HoBear Publications, publishes 1-2 paperbacks/year. "We publish quality, perfect-bound books and anthologies of poetry, usually theme-oriented, in runs of 1,500. as well as individual poetry collections such as *Prism*, poems by David St. John; *Fire Is Favorable to the Dreamer*, poems by Susan Terris; J.D. Whitney, Lowell Jaeger, and others.

HOW TO CONTACT "We do not accept unsolicited manuscripts. Accepts queries by e-mail."

AUTUMN HOUSE PRESS

(412)381-261. E-mail: info@autumnhouse.org. Website: www.autumnhouse.org. Sharon Dilworth, fiction editor. **Contact:** Michael Simms, editor-in-chief (fiction). "We are a non-profit literary press specializing in high-quality poetry and fiction. Our editions are beautifully designed and printed, and they are distributed nationally. Approximately one-third of our sales are to college literature and creative writing classes." **Published 2 new writers last year.** Plans 2 debut novels this year. Averages 6 total titles/year; 2 fiction titles/year. Member CLMP, AWP, Academy of American Poets. "We distribute our own titles. We do extensive national promotion through ads, web-marketing, reading tours, bookfairs and conferences. We are open to all genres. The quality of writing concerns us, not the genre." You can also learn about our annual Fiction Prize, Poetry Prize and Chapbook Award competitions, as well as our online journal, *Coal Hill Review*. (Please note that Autumn House accepts unsolicited manuscripts *only* through these competitions.)

"Extraordinary poetry and fiction."

NEEDS All full-length collections of poetry 50-80 pages in length are eligible.

CONTEST/AWARD OFFERINGS The winners will receive book publication, $1,000 advance against royalties, and a $1,500 travel grant to participate in the 2012 Autumn House Master Authors Series in Pittsburgh.

TIPS "The competition to publish with Autumn House is very tough. Submit only your best work."

THE BACKWATERS PRESS

3502 N. 52nd St., Omaha NE 68104-3506. (402)451-4052. E-mail: thebackwaterspress@gmail.com. Website: http://www.thebackwaterspress.org. **Contact:** Greg Kosmicki, editor.

NEEDS "The Backwaters Press continues to accept manuscripts for consideration for publication through the Open Submissions category. We're looking for manuscripts between 65 and 80 pages in length. **There is a $25 reading fee.**" The Backwaters Press is not currently seeking submissions in order that we may clear up our backlog. please watch the website for notice when the press will begin accepting new material.

HOW TO CONTACT "Please see the website for complete details, or send a self-addressed, stamped envelope to 'Guidelines' at the above address, or e-mail with a subject line of 'Open Submission Guidelines.'" Books available through Amazon.com, Barnes&Noble.com, and Small Press Distribution (SPD).

BEAR STAR PRESS

(530)891-0360. Website: www.bearstarpress.com. **Contact:** Beth Spencer, publisher/editor. "Bear Star is committed to publishing the best poetry it can attract. Each year it sponsors the Dorothy Brunsman contest, open to poets from Western and Pacific states. From time to time we add to our list other poets from our target area whose work we admire."

CONTEST/AWARD OFFERINGS The Dorothy Brunsman Poetry Prize awards $1,000 and publication by Bear Star Press to the best book-length ms by a poet who resides in the Western states (within Mountain or Pacific time zones, plus Alaska and Hawaii) and serves as their primary pool for finding new manuscripts. "You need not enter the contest to submit to us, but our first allegiance is to mss that come with a reading fee since they help to keep the press going."

TIPS "Send your best work, consider its arrangement. A 'wow' poem early keeps me reading."

BIRCH BOOK PRESS

P.O. Box 81, Delhi NY 13753. Fax: (607)746-7453. E-mail: birchbrook@copper.net. Website: www.birchbrookpress.info. **Contact:** Tom Tolnay, editor/publisher; Barbara dela Cuesta, assoc. editor. Member: American Academy of Poets, Small Press Center, Independent Book Publishers Association, American

Typefounders Fellowship.Birch Brook Press "is a letterpress book printer/typesetter/designer that uses monies from these activities to publish several titles of its own each year with cultural and literary interest." Specializes in literary work, flyfishing, baseball, outdoors, theme anthologies, occasional translations of classics, and books about books. Has published *Woodstoves & Ravens* by Robert Farmer, *Shadwell Hills*, by Rebecca Lilly, *Seasons of Defiance* by Lance Lee, *And This is What Happens Next*, by Marcus Rome, *Jack's Beans* by Tom Smith, and *Tony's World*, by Barry Wallenstein. Publishes 4 paperbacks and/or hardbacks/year. Specializes "mostly in anthologies with specific themes." Books are "handset letterpress editions printed in our own shop." **Offers occasional co-op contract.**

"No manuscripts, inquiries only."

TIPS "Write well on subjects of interest to BBP, such as outdoors, flyfishing, baseball, music, literary stories and occasional novellas, books about books."

BLACK LAWRENCE PRESS

115 Center Ave., Aspinwall PA 15215. E-mail: editors@blacklawrencepress.com. E-mail: submissions@blacklawrencepress.com. Website: www.blacklawrencepress.com. **Contact:** Diane Goettel, executive editor.

NEEDS Black Lawrence Press seeks "to publish intriguing books of literature: novels, short story collections, poetry. Will also publish the occasional translation (from the German and French)." Has published poetry by D.C. Berry, James Reidel, and Stefi Weisburd. Publishes 10-12 books/year, mostly poetry and fiction. Manuscripts are selected through open submission and competition (see below). Books are 48-400 pages, offset-printed or high-quality POD, perfectbound, with matte 4-color cover.

HOW TO CONTACT "Regular submissions are considered on a year-round basis. Please check the general submissions page on our website for the most up-to-date guidelines information before submitting." Responds in up to 4 months for mss, "sometimes longer depending on backlog." Pays royalties. Sample books available through website.

CONTEST/AWARD OFFERINGS The St. Lawrence Book Award, The Hudson Prize, and The Black River Chapbook Competition (see separate listings in Contests & Awards).

⊕● BLACK OCEAN

(617)304-9011. Fax: (617)849-5678. E-mail: carrie@
blackocean.org. Website: www.blackocean.org. **Contact:** Carrie Olivia Adams, poetry editor.

◑ BLUE LIGHT PRESS

1563-45th Ave., San Francisco CA 94122. E-mail:
bluelightpress@aol.com. Website: www.bluelight-
press.com. 1563-45th Ave., San Francisco, CA 94122.
E-mail:bluelightpress@aol.com. Website: www.blue-
lightpress.com. **Contact:** Diane Frank, chief editor.
NEEDS Blue Light Press publishes 3 paperbacks, 2
chapbooks/year. "We like poems that are imagistic,
emotionally honest, and push the edge—where the
writer pushes through the imagery to a deeper level of insight and understanding. No rhymed poetry."
Has published poetry by Alice Rogoff, Tom Centolel-
la, Rustin Larson, Tony Krunk, Lisha Adela Garcia,
Becky Sakellariou, and Christopher Buckley. "Books
are elegantly designed and artistic." Chapbooks are
30 pages, digest-sized, professionally printed, with
original cover art. Chapbooks available for $10 plus
$2 p books for $15.95 plus $3 p&h.
HOW TO CONTACT Submission guidelines available for SASE or by e-mail. Does not accept e-mail
submissions. **Deadlines:** January 30 full-sized ms.
and June 15 for chapbooks. "Read our guidelines
before sending your ms."
CONTEST/AWARD OFFERINGS The Blue Light
Poetry Prize and Chapbook Contest and Blue Light
Book Award for Full-Length Ms. (see separate listing
in Contests & Awards).
ALSO OFFERS "We have an online poetry
workshop with a wonderful group of American and
international poets—open to new members 3 times
per year. Send an e-mail for info. We work in person
with local poets, and will edit/critique poems by mail;
$40 for four poems."

●◉ BOA EDITIONS, LTD.

(585)546-3410. Fax: (585)546-3913. E-mail: conners@
boaeditions.org; hall@boaeditions.org. Website: www.
boaeditions.org. Melissa Hall, Development Director/
Office Manager. **Contact:** Peter Conners, editor. BOA
Editions, a Pulitzer Prize-winning, not-for-profit publishing house acclaimed for its work, reads poetry mss
for the American Poets Continuum Series (new poetry by distinguished poets in mid- and late career), the
Lannan Translations Selection Series (publication of 2
new collections of contemporary international poetry
annually, supported by The Lannan Foundation of
Santa Fe, NM), The A. Poulin, Jr. Poetry Prize (to hon-
or a poet's first book; mss considered through competition—see separate listing in Contests & Awards),
and The America Reader Series (short fiction and
prose on poetics). Has published poetry by Naomi
Shihab Nye, W.D. Snodgrass, Lucille Clifton, Brig-
it Pegeen Kelly, and Li-Young Lee. How to Contact:
Check website for reading periods for The American
Reader Series, The American Poets Continuum Series,
and The Lannan Translations Selection Series. "Please
adhere to the general submission guidelines for each
series. BOA Editions publishes distinguished collections of poetry, fiction and poetry in translation. Our
goal is to publish the finest American contemporary
poetry, fiction and poetry in translation."
HOW TO CONTACT Check website for reading periods for the American Poets Continuum Series and
The Lannan Translation Selection Series. "Please adhere to the general submission guidelines for each
series." Guidelines available for SASE or on website.
CONTEST/AWARD OFFERINGS The A. Poulin,
Jr. Poetry Prize (to honor a poet's first book; mss
considered through competition—see separate listing
in Contests & Awards).
ALSO OFFERS Pays advance plus 10 author's copies.
Available for download from website are reading
and teaching guides for selected titles; and Season
Sampler chapbooks, which provide introductions to
BOA poets and their work.

⊘ BOTTOM DOG PRESS, INC.

P.O. Box 425, Huron OH 44839. (419)433-5560. E-
mail: LsmithDog@smithdocs.net. Website: http://
smithdocs.net. Allen Frost and Laura Smith, associate editors. **Contact:** Larry Smith, director. Bottom
Dog Press, Inc., "is a nonprofit literary and educational organization dedicated to publishing the best
writing and art from the Midwest." Has published
poetry by Jeff Gundy, Jim Daniels, Maj Ragain, Diane
di Prima, and Sue Doro. Publishes the Midwest Series, Working Lives Series, and Harmony Series (105
books to date).
◗ Imprint: Bird Dog Publishing
NEEDS Bottom Dog Press, Inc., "is a nonprofit literary and educational organization dedicated to publishing the best writing and art from the Midwest."
Has published poetry by Jeff Gundy, Jim Daniels, Maj

Ragain, Diane di Prima, and Sue Doro. Publishes the Midwest Series, Working Lives Series, and Harmony Series (105 books to date).

HOW TO CONTACT Guidelines available on website.

⊕ ◐ BRICK ROAD POETRY PRESS, INC.

P.O. Box 751, Columbus GA 31902-0751. (706)649-3080. Fax: (706)649-3094. E-mail: editor@brickroadpoetrypress.com. Website: www.brickroadpoetrypress.com. **Contact:** Ron Self and Keith Badkowski, co-editors/founders.

NEEDS Publishes poetry only: books (single author collections), e-zine, and annual anthology. "We prefer poetry that offers a coherent human voice, a sense of humor, attentiveness to words and language, narratives with surprise twists, persona poems, and/or philosophical or spiritual themes explored through the concrete scenes and images." Does not want over-emphasis on rhyme, intentional obscurity or riddling, highfalutin vocabulary, greeting card verse, overt religious statements of faith and/or praise, and/or abstractions. Previous collections include *Dancing on the Rim*, by Clela Reed; *Possible Crocodiles*, by Barry Marks; *Damnatio Memoriae*, by Michael Meyerhofer; *Otherness*, by M. Ayodele Heath; *Etch and Blur*, by Jamie Thomas; and *Chosen*, by Toni Thomas. Publishes 10-12 poetry books/year and 1 anthology/year. Accepted poems meeting our theme requirements are published on our website. Mss accepted through open submission and competition. Books are 110 pages, print-on-demand, perfect-bound, paperback with full color art or photograph covers.

HOW TO CONTACT Book ms may include previously published poems. General submissions accepted February 1-August 1 annually. No reading fees for general submissions. Book-length poetry mss only. Simultaneous submissions accepted, provided notification if ms is accepted elsewhere. Original collection of 70-100 pages of poetry, excluding cover page, contents, acknowledgments, etc. Single sided, single spaced. "We prefer no more than one poem per page." Title page: include name, address, and phone number. No translations, unless the translations are your own poems. Electronic files accepted via online submission manager. Use the title of your collection for the file name. "We accept .doc, .rtf, or .pdf file formats. We prefer electronic submissions but will reluctantly consider hard copy submissions

by mail if USPS Flat Rate Mailing Envelope is used and with the stipulation that, should the author's work be chosen for publication, an electronic version (.doc or .rtf) must be prepared in a timely manner and at the poet's expense." Please include cover letter with poetry publication/recognition highlights and something intriguing about your life story or ongoing pursuits. "We would like to develop a connection with the poet as well as the poetry." Please include the collection title in the cover letter. "We want to publish poets who are engaged in the literary community, including regular submission of work to various publications and participation in poetry readings, workshops, and writers' groups. That said, we would never rule out an emerging poet who demonstrates ability and motivation to move in that direction." Pays royalties and 15 author copies. Initial print run of 150, print-on-demand thereafter.

CONTEST/AWARD OFFERINGS Brick Road Poetry Contest is an annual contest with a $1,000 prize. Entry fee: $25. Learn more online.

ALSO OFFERS "We seek individual poem submissions that relate to specified subjects. The submission period is February 1, 2012-December 31, 2012 for poems related to the subjects of nursery rhymes characters, fairy tales, folktales, myths, legends, and/or superheroes. Submit up to 5 poems per submission via our online submission manager. Poems accepted will be published on our website. Inclusion in a print anthology will be considered as well."

TIPS "The best way to discover all that poetry can be and to expand the limits of your own poetry is to read expansively. We recommend the following poets: Kim Addonizio, Ken Babstock, Coleman Barks, Billy Collins, Morri Creech, Alice Friman, Beth A. Gylys, Jane Hirshfield, Jane Kenyon, Ted Kooser, Stanley Kunitz, Thomas Lux, Barry Marks, Michael Meyerhofer, Linda Pastan, Mark Strand, and Natasha D. Trethewey."

BROOKS BOOKS

E-mail: brooksbooks@sbcglobal.net. Website: www.brooksbookshaiku.com. **Contact:** Randy Brooks, editor (haiku poetry, tanka poetry). "Brooks Books, formerly High/Coo Press, publishes English-language haiku books, chapbooks, magazines, and bibliographies."

NEEDS 15 haiku per issue.

TIPS "The best haiku capture human perception—moments of being alive conveyed through sensory images. They do not explain nor describe nor provide philosophical or political commentary. Haiku are gifts of the here and now, deliberately incomplete so that the reader can enter into the haiku moment to open the gift and experience the feelings and insights of that moment for his or her self. Our readership includes the haiku community, readers of contemporary poetry, teachers and students of Japanese literature and contemporary Japanese poetics."

⊘ CALAMARI PRESS

Via Titta Scarpetta #28, Rome 00153, Italy. E-mail: derek@calamaripress.net. Website: www.calamaripress.com. Helps to be published in *SleepingFish* first." See separate listing in magazines/journals. Order books through the website, Powell's, or SPD.

NEEDS Calamari Press publishes books of literary text and art. Publishes 1-2 books/year. Manuscripts are selected by invitation. Occasionally has open submission period— check website.

HOW TO CONTACT Helps to be published in *SleepingFish* first." See separate listing in magazines/journals. Order books through the website, Powell's, or SPD.

CAROLINA WREN PRESS

(919)560-2738. E-mail: carolinawrenpress@earthlink.net. Website: www.carolinawrenpress.org. **Contact:** Andrea Selch, president. Publishes 1 poetry book/year, "usually through our poetry series. Otherwise we primarily publish women, minorities, and North Carolina authors." Has published *"a half-red sea"* by Evie Shockley, as well as poetry by William Pitt Root, Karen Leona Anderson, Jaki Shelton Green, and Erica Hunt. Guidelines available for SASE, by e-mail, or on website. Carolina Wren Press Poetry Contest for a First of Second Book. Entry Deadline: February 15, 2011 (see separate listing in Contests & Awards)."We publish poetry, fiction, nonfiction, biography, autobiography, literary nonfiction work by, and/or about people of color, women, gay/lesbian issues, health and mental health topics in children's literature."

○ "We are no longer accepting general submissions of poetry and fiction. We welcome submissions to our two contests, which run in alternate years. Reads unsolicited mss of fiction and nonfiction from September 1 to December 1 and poetry and children's lit from February 1 to June 1, but prefers writers to wait and enter their contests—poetry contest in Fall 2012 and 2014; Doris Bawkin Award for Writing by a Woman - prose fiction (a collection of short stories or a novel) or memoir. Submissions are accepted in odd-numbered autumns, with a final deadline of December 1st, 2011, 2013, 2015, etc. There is a $20 reading fee for this contest. Full guidelines should be followed - check the website in late summer to see the current guidelines. See below for poetry contest.

HOW TO CONTACT Accepts e-mail queries, but send only letter and description of work; no large files. Reads unsolicited poetry submissions during the month of February. "Your best bet is to submit as part of our biennial poetry contest held in autumn of even-numbered years (e.g., 2010)."

CONTEST/AWARD OFFERINGS The Carolina Wren Press Poetry Series - full-length poetry manuscripts by authors who have not had more than one full-length book published. Submissions are accepted in even-numbered autums, with a final deadline of December 1st, 2010, 2012, 2014, etc. There is a $20 reading fee for this contest. Full guidelines should be followed - check the website in late summer to see the current guidelines.

TIPS Manuscripts are read year-round, but reply time is long unless submitting for a contest.

● CITY LIGHTS BOOKS

Website: www.citylights.com. 261 Columbus Ave., San Francisco CA 94133. (415)362-8193. Fax: (415)362-4921. E-mail: staff@citylights.com. Website: www.citylights.com. Established 1953.

NEEDS City Lights Books is the legendary paperback house that achieved prominence with the publication of Allen Ginsberg's *Howl* and other poetry of the "Beat" school. Publishes "poetry, fiction, philosophy, political and social history."

HOW TO CONTACT Does not accept unsolicited mss. No inquiries or submissions by e-mail. "Before sending a book proposal, we urge you to look at our catalog to familiarize yourself with our publication. If you feel certain that your work is appropriate to our list, then please send a query letter that includes your reésumeé (with a list of previous publications and a sample of no more than 10 pages." Include

SASE for response. Responds in 3 months. Guidelines available on website.

◐ CLEVELAND STATE UNIVERSITY POETRY CENTER

2121 Euclid Ave., RT 1841, Cleveland OH 44115-2214. (216)687-3986. Fax: (216)687-6943. E-mail: poetrycenter@csuohio.edu. Website: www.csuohio.edu/poetrycenter. **Contact:** Michael Dumanis or Rita Grabowski, Managers.

NEEDS The Cleveland State University Poetry Center publishes "full-length collections by established and emerging poets, through competition and solicitation, as well as occasional poetry anthologies, texts on poetics, and novellas. Eclectic in its taste and inclusive in its aesthetic, with particular interest in lyric poetry and innovative approaches to craft. Not interested in light verse, devotional verse, doggerel, or poems by poets who have not read much contemporary poetry." Recent CSU Poetry Center publications include *The Grief Performance*, by Emily Kendal Frey; *The Firestorm*, by Zach Savich; *Rust or Go Missing*, by Lily Brown; *Say So*, by Dora Malech; *Mule*, by Shane McCrae; *You Don't know What you Don't Know*, by John Bradley; *Clamor*, by Elyse Fenton; *Horse Dance Underwater*, by Helena Mesa; *Destruction Myth*, by Mathias Svalina; *Sum of Every Lost Ship*, by Allison Titus; *Trust*, by Liz Waldnere; and *Self-Portrait With Crayon*, by Allison Benis White.

CONTEST/AWARD OFFERINGS The Cleveland State University Poetry Center First Book Award and Open Competition (see separate listings in Contests & Awards).

ADDITIONAL INFORMATION "Most manuscripts we publish are accepted through the competitions. All manuscripts sent for competitions are considered for publication. Outside of competitions, manuscripts are accepted by solicitation only."

◑ COACH HOUSE BOOKS

(416)979-2217. Fax: (416)977-1158. E-mail: editor@chbooks.com. Website: www.chbooks.com. **Contact:** Alana Wilcox, editor.

TIPS "We are not a general publisher, and publish only Canadian poetry, fiction, artist books and drama. We are interested primarily in innovative or experimental writing."

◔ COPPER CANYON PRESS

P.O. Box 271, Port Townsend WA 98368. (360)385-4925. Fax: (360)385-4985. E-mail: poetry@coppercanyonpress.org. Website: www.coppercanyonpress.org. **Contact:** Editor. Copper Canyon publishes books of poetry. Has published collections by Lucille Clifton, Hayden Carruth, Carolyn Kizer, W.S. Merwin, Ruth Stone, and Jim Harrison. Currently accepts no unsolicited poetry. E-mail queries and submissions will go unanswered."Copper Canyon Press is dedicated to publishing poetry in a wide range of styles and from a full range of the world's cultures."

CONTEST/AWARD OFFERINGS Contest is no longer administered. We strongly encourage poets with first-book mss to consider submitting to 'The American Poetry Review'/Honickman First Book Award. More information can be found on our website under Opportunities.

TIPS "CCP publishes poetry exclusively and is the largest poetry publisher in the U.S. We will not review queries if guidelines are not followed. We will read queries from poets who have published a book. Please read our query guidelines."

◑ COTEAU BOOKS

(306)777-0170. Fax: (306)522-5152. E-mail: coteau@coteaubooks.com. Website: www.coteaubooks.com. **Contact:** Geoffrey Ursell, publisher. "Our mission is to publish the finest in Canadian fiction, nonfiction, poetry, drama, and children's literature, with an emphasis on Saskatchewan and prairie writers. De-emphasizing science fiction, picture books."

NEEDS Coteau Books is a "small literary press that publishes poetry, fiction, drama, anthologies, criticism, young adult novels—**by Canadian writers only**." Has published *The Crooked Good* by Louise Bernice Halfe, *Wolf Tree* by Alison Calder, and *Love of Mirrors* by Gary Hyland.

HOW TO CONTACT Submit mss (80-100 poems only) typed with at least 12-point font. No simultaneous or non-Canadian submissions. No e-mail or fax submissions. Cover letter is required. Include publishing credits and bio, and SASE for return of ms. Accepts poetry mss from September 1-December 31 only. Responds to queries and mss in 4 months. Always sends prepublication galleys. Author receives 10% royalties and 10 author's copies. Order samples by sending 9x12 SASE for catalog.

ADDITIONAL INFORMATION Website includes

title and ordering information, author interviews, awards, news and events, submission guidelines, and links.

TIPS "Look at past publications to get an idea of our editorial program. We do not publish romance, horror, or picture books but are interested in juvenile and teen fiction from Canadian authors. Submissions, even queries, must be made in hard copy only. We do not accept simultaneous/multiple submissions. Check our website for new submission timing guidelines."

⊙⊘ DESCRIBE ADONIS PRESS

297 Blake Boul. #4, Ottawa ON K1L 6L6, Canada. Website: http://vallance22.hpage.com. 297 Blake Boul. #4, Ottawa, ON K1L 6L6, Canada. E-mail: vallance22@gmail.com. Website: http://vallance22.hpage.com. **Contact:** Richard Vallance, editor-in-chief.

NEEDS Describe Adonis Press publishes Japanese form poetry only, "especially haiku, but also senryu, renga, tanka, etc." Does not want any other form or genre of poetry. Publishes one poetry book/year, 5 chapbooks/year on average.

HOW TO CONTACT Contact with up to 12 haikus via e-mail attachment in rtf form only. E-mail is through website form at http://vallance22.hpage.com. Format should be single-spaced with three blank lines between each haiku; subject line should read: "Submission of hiaku (or haikus) by [your name]." Must use Georgia Font 11 points, or, if absolutely unable to use that, in Times New Roman 11 point font. See website for complete guidelines and contact.

DIAL BOOKS FOR YOUNG READERS

(212)366-2000. Website: www.penguin.com/youngreaders. **Contact:** Submissions Editor. (Specialized: poetry for children/teens)345 Hudson St., New York NY 10014. Website: www.penguin.com. **Contact:** Submissions."Dial Books for Young Readers publishes quality picture books for ages 18 months-6 years; lively, believable novels for middle readers and young adults; and occasional nonfiction for middle readers and young adults."

HOW TO CONTACT "Submit entire picture book manuscripts, or the first 3 chapters of longer works. Please include a cover letter with brief bio and publication credits." Considers simultaneous submissions; no previously published poems. "Please note that, **unless interested in publishing them, Dial**

will not respond to unsolicited submissions. Please do not include a self-addressed, stamped envelope with your submission. If Dial is interested, you can expect a reply from us within 4 months." Payment varies.

TIPS "Our readers are anywhere from preschool age to teenage. Picture books must have strong plots, lots of action, unusual premises, or universal themes treated with freshness and originality. Humor works well in these books. A very well-thought-out and intelligently presented book has the best chance of being taken on. Genre isn't as much of a factor as presentation."

⊙●⑤ ÉCRITS DES FORGES

992-A, rue Royale, Trois-Rivières QC G9A 4H9, Canada. (819)840-8492. Website: www.ecritsdesforges.com. **Contact:** Stéphane Despatie, director. 992-A, rue Royale, Trois-Rivières, QC G9A 4H9, Canada. (819)840-8492. E-mail: ecrits.desforges@tr.cgocable.ca. Website: www.ecritsdesforges.com. Contact: Stéphane Despatie, director.

NEEDS Écrits des Forges publishes poetry only that is "authentic and original as a signature. We have published poetry from more than 1,000 poets coming from most of the francophone countries: Andreé Romus (Belgium), Amadou Lamine Sall (Seéneégal), Nicole Brossard, Claude Beausoleil, Jean-Marc Desgent, and Jean-Paul Daoust (Queébec)." Publishes 45-50 paperback books of poetry/year. Books are usually 80-88 pages, digest-sized, perfect-bound, with 2-color covers with art.

HOW TO CONTACT Query first with a few sample poems and a cover letter with brief bio and publication credits. Responds to queries in up to 6 months. Pays royalties of 10-20%, advance of 50% maximum, and 25 author's copies. Order sample books by writing or faxing.

● ENITHARMON PRESS

Website: www.enitharmon.co.uk. 26B Caversham Rd., London England NW5 2DU England. (44)(207)482-5967. Fax: (44)(207)284-1787. E-mail: info@enitharmon.co.uk. Website: www.enitharmon.co.uk. Established 1967. **Contact:** Stephen Stuart-Smith, poetry editor.

NEEDS Enitharmon is a publisher of fine editions of poetry and literary criticism in paperback, and some hardback, editions. "We publish about 15 volumes/year, averaging 100 pages each." Has published poetry by John Heath-Stubbs, Ted Hughes, David Gascoyne, Thom Gunn, Ruth Pitter, and Anthony Thwaite.

HOW TO CONTACT "Substantial backlog of titles to produce, so **no submissions possible before 2006**."

FARRAR, STRAUS & GIROUX/ BOOKS FOR YOUNG READERS

Books for Young Readers, 175 Fifth Ave., New York NY 10010. (646)307-5151. Website: www.fsgkidsbooks.com. **Contact:** Children's Editorial Department. (Specialized: children)"We publish original and well-written material for all ages."

NEEDS Publishes one book of children's poetry "every once in a while," in trade hardcover only. Open to book-length submissions of children's poetry only. Has published Valerie Worth's *Peacock and Other Poems*, Tony Johnston's *An Old Shell*, and Helen Frost's *Keesha's House* (a novel in poems).

HOW TO CONTACT Query first with sample poems and cover letter with brief bio and publication credits. Considers simultaneous submissions. Seldom comments on rejected poems. Send SASE for reply. Responds to queries in up to 2 months, to mss in up to 4 months. "We pay an advance against royalties; the amount depends on whether or not the poems are illustrated, etc." Also pays 10 author's copies.

TIPS Audience is full age range, preschool to young adult. Specializes in literary fiction.

FENCE BOOKS

(518)591-8162. E-mail: fence.fencebooks@gmail.com. E-mail: robfence@gmail.com. Website: www.fence-portal.org. **Contact:** Rob Arnold, Submissions Manager. "*Fence is closed to submissions right now.* We'll have another reading period in the Spring. Fence Books offers 2 book contests (in addition to the National Poetry Series) with 2 sets of guidelines and entry forms on our website."

TIPS "At present Fence Books is a self-selecting publisher; mss come to our attention through our contests and through editors' investigations. We hope to become open to submissions of poetry and fiction mss in the near future."

FINISHING LINE PRESS

P.O. Box 1626, Georgetown KY 40324. (859)514-8966. E-mail: FinishingBooks@aol.com. Website: www.finishinglinepress.com. **Contact:** Leah Maines, Poetry Editor. Submit up to 26 pages of poetry with cover letter, bio, acknowledgments, and **$12 reading fee**. Responds to queries and mss in up to 1 month. Pay varies; pays in author's copies. "Sales profits, if any, go to publish the next new poet." Sample chapbooks available by sending $6 to Finishing Line Press or through website. See The Finishing Line Press Open Chapbook Competition and the New Women's Voices Chapbook Competition (see separate listings in Contests & Awards).

Member of CLMP.

NEEDS Finishing Line Press seeks to "discover new talent" and hopes to publish chapbooks by both men and women poets who have not previously published a book or chapbook of poetry. Has published *Parables and Revelations* by T. Crunk, *Family Business* by Paula Sergi, *Putting in a Window* by John Brantingham, and *Dusting the Piano* by Abigail Gramig. Publishes 50-60 poetry chapbooks/year. Chapbooks are usually 25-30 pages, digest-sized, laser-printed, saddle-stapled, with card covers with textured matte wrappers.

HOW TO CONTACT Submit up to 26 pages of poetry with cover letter, bio, acknowledgments, and **$12 reading fee**. Responds to queries and mss in up to 1 month. Pay varies; pays in author's copies. "Sales profits, if any, go to publish the next new poet." Sample chapbooks available by sending $6 to Finishing Line Press or through website.

CONTEST/AWARD OFFERINGS The Finishing Line Press Open Chapbook Competition and the New Women's Voices Chapbook Competition (see separate listings in Contests & Awards).

FLARESTACK POETS

P.O. Box 14779, Birmingham, West Midlands B13 3GU, United Kingdom. E-mail: meria@btinternet.com; jacquierowe@hotmail.co.uk. Website: www.flarestackpoets.co.uk. **Contact:** Meredith Andrea and Jacqui Rowe. P.O. Box 14779, Birmingham, West Midlands B13 3GU.Estab. 2008. E-mail: meria@binternet.com; jacquierowe@hotmail.co.uk. Website: www.flarestackpoets.co.uk. Contact: Meredith Andrea. *Flarestack Poets is not currently accepting submissions.*

NEEDS Flarestack Poets wants "poems that dare outside current trends, even against the grain." Does not want "poems that fail to engage with either language or feeling." First chapbooks appearing in Autumn 2009. Publishes 8 chapbooks/year and 1 anthology.

Manuscripts are selected through open submission and competition. "Our first chapbooks are winners of the 2009 Flarestack Poets Pamphlet competition. Thereafter we will consider open submissions." Chapbooks are 20-30 pages, professional photocopy, saddle-stitched, card cover.

HOW TO CONTACT Query first with a few sample poems and a cover letter with brief bio and publication credits. Manuscript may include previously published poems. Responds in 6 weeks. Pays royalties of 25% and 6 author's copies (out of a press run of 200). See website to order sample copies.

● FLOATING BRIDGE PRESS

PO Box 18814, Seattle WA 98118. E-mail: floatingbridgepress@yahoo.com. Website: www.floatingbridgepress.org. (Specialized: WA poets)

NEEDS Floating Bridge Press publishes chapbooks and anthologies by Washington State poets, selected through an annual competition (see below). Has published *After* by Nancy Pagh, *In the Convent We Become Clouds* by Annette Spaulding-Convy, *Toccata & Fugue* by Timothy Kelly, and *The Former St. Christopher* by Michael Bonacci, among others. The press also publishes *Floating Bridge Review*, an annual anthology featuring the work of Washington State poets. *Floating Bridge Review* is 86-144 pages, digest-sized, offset-printed, perfect-bound, with glossy cardstock cover. For a sample chapbook or anthology, send $13 postpaid.

CONTEST/AWARD OFFERINGS For consideration, **Washington State poets only** should submit a chapbook ms of 20-24 pages of poetry. In addition to publication, the winner receives $500, 15 author's copies, and a reading in the Seattle area. All entrants receive a copy of the winning chapbook and will be considered for inclusion in *Floating Bridge Review*. Poet's name must not appear on the ms. Include a separate page with ms title, poet's name, address, phone number, and acknowledgments of any previous publications. Include SASE for results only; mss will not be returned. **Entry fee:** $12. **Deadline:** usual reading period is November 1-February 15 (postmark). Considers previously published individual poems and simultaneous submissions. Manuscripts are judged anonymously.

● FOUR WAY BOOKS

Box 535, Village Station, New York NY 10014. E-mail: fourwayeditors@fourwaybooks.com; editors@fourwaybooks.com. Website: www.fourwaybooks.com. Established 1993. **Contact:** Martha Rhodes, director.

NEEDS Four Way Books publishes poetry and short fiction. Considers full-length poetry mss only. Does not want individual poems or poetry intended for children/young readers. Has published poetry by D. Nurkse, Noelle Kocot, Susan Wheeler, Nancy Mitchell, Henry Israeli, and Paul Jenkins. Publishes 8-11 books a year. Manuscripts are selected through open submission and through competition. Books are about 70 pages, offset-printed digitally, perfect-bound, with paperback binding, art/graphics on covers.

HOW TO CONTACT See website for complete submission guidelines and open reading period. Book mss may include previously published poems. Responds to submissions in 4 months. Payment varies. Order sample books from Four Way Books online or through bookstores.

CONTEST/AWARD OFFERINGS The Intro Prize in Poetry and The Levis Poetry Prize (see separate listings in Contests & Awards).

⊕● FUTURECYCLE PRESS

313 Pan Will Rd., Mineral Bluff GA 30559. (706)622-4454. E-mail: submissions@futurecycle.org. Website: www.futurecycle.org. **Contact:** Robert S. King, director and editor-in-chief.

NEEDS Wants "poetry from highly skilled poets, whether well known or emerging. With a few exceptions, we are eclectic in our editorial tastes." Does not want concrete or visual poetry. Has published David Chorlton, John Laue, Temple Cone, Neil Carpathios, Tania Runyan, Timothy Martin, Joanne Lowery. Publishes 4 poetry books/year and 2 chapbooks/year. Ms. selected through open submission and competition. "We read unsolicited mss. but also conduct a yearly poetry book competition." Books are 60-90 pages; offset print, perfect-bound, with glossy, full color cover stock, b&w inside. Chapbooks are 20-40 pages, offset print, saddle-stitched.

HOW TO CONTACT Submit completes ms; no need to query. Read guidelines posted on website. May include previously published poems. Responds in 3 months. Pays royalties of 10% and 25 copies out of press run of 200.

◑ GERTRUDE PRESS

P.O. Box 83948, Portland OR 97283. (503)515-8252. E-mail: edelehoy@fc.edu. Website: www.gertrudepress.

org. **Contact:** Justus Ballard (all fiction). (Specialized: gay, lesbian, bisexual, transgendered, queer-identified & allied)

NEEDS Gertrude Press, a nonprofit 501(c)(3) organization, showcases and develops "the creative talents of lesbian, gay, bisexual, trans, queer-identified, and allied individuals." Has published *Bone Knowing* by Kate Grant. Gertrude Press publishes 2 chapbooks/year (1 fiction, 1 poetry) as well as *Gertrude*, a semi-annual literary journal (see separate listing in Magazines/Journals). Manuscripts are chosen through competition only (see below). Chapbooks are 20-24 pages, offset-printed, saddle-stapled, with cardstock cover with art. Submit up to 6 poems of any subject matter. There is no line limit; however, poems less than 60 lines are preferable.

HOW TO CONTACT Refer to guidelines for Gertrude Press Poetry Chapbook Contest (see separate listing in Contests & Awards). Order sample chapbooks for $10.

CONTEST/AWARD OFFERINGS The Gertrude Press Poetry Chapbook Contest (see separate listing in Contests & Awards).

TIPS Sponsors poetry and fiction chapbook contest. Prize is $50 and 50 contributor's copies. Submission guidelines and fee information on website. "Read the journal and sample published work. We are not impressed by pages of publications; your work should speak for itself."

⊘ GHOST PONY PRESS

P.O. Box 260113, Madison WI 53726-0113. E-mail: ghostponypress@hotmail.com. **Contact:** Ingrid Swanberg, editor/publisher. Estab. 1980. .

NEEDS Ghost Pony Press has published 3 books of poetry by proóspero saiíz, including *the bird of nothing & other poems* (168 pages, 7x10, with sewn and wrapped binding; paperback available for $20, signed and numbered edition for $35). Also published *zen concrete & etc.* by d.a. levy (268 pages, magazine-sized, perfect-bound, illustrated; paperback available for $27.50).

HOW TO CONTACT Query first, with a few sample poems (5-10) and cover letter with brief bio and publication credits. Include SASE. Considers previously published material for book publication. Accepts submissions by postal mail only; no e-mail submissions. Editor sometimes comments briefly on rejected poems. No promised response time. "We currently have a considerable backlog." Payment varies per project. Send SASE for catalog to buy samples.

⊕ GHOST ROAD PRESS

820 S. Monaco Pkwy #288, Denver CO 80224. (303)758-7623. E-mail: info@ghostroadpress.com; matt@ghostroadpress.com; evan@ghostroadpress.com. Website: ghostroadpress.com.

HOW TO CONTACT *Not currently accepting submissions.* Query via e-mail. "Send an attachment (word or.rtf only) that includes a complete synopsis, a description of your marketing plan and platform and samples. To view a complete list of our titles and changing submission guidelines, please visit website." Responds in 2-3 months. Accepts simultaneous submissions.

●⊘ GINNINDERRA PRESS

P.O. Box 3461, Port Adelaide 5015, Australia. (61)(2)6258-9060. Fax: (61)(2)6258-9069. E-mail: stephen@ginninderrapress.com.au. Website: www.ginninderrapress.com.au. P.O. Box 3461, Port Adelaide, 5015, Australia. (61)(2)6258-9060. Fax: (61)(2)6258-9069. E-mail:stephen@ginninderrapress.com.au. Website: www.ginninderrapress.com.au. **Contact:** Stephen Matthews, publisher. Estab. 1996. **Please note: Ginninderra Press no longer accepts mss from writers residing outside of Australia.**

 ◯ Please note: No longer accepting mss from writers residing outside of Australia.

NEEDS Ginninderra Press works "to give publishing opportunities to new writers." Has published poetry by Alan Gould and Geoff Page. Books are usually up to 72 pages, A5, laser-printed, saddle-stapled or thermal-bound, with board covers.

HOW TO CONTACT Query first, with a few sample poems and a cover letter with brief bio and publication credits. Considers previously published poems; no simultaneous submissions. No fax or e-mail submissions. Time between acceptance and publication is 6 months. Seldom comments on rejected poems. Responds to queries within 1 week; to mss in 2 months.

◍ GOOSE LANE EDITIONS

(506)450-4251. Fax: (506)459-4991. Website: www.gooselane.com/submissions.php. **Contact:** Angela Williams, publishing assistant. "Goose Lane publishes literary fiction and nonfiction from well-read and highly skilled Canadian authors."

NEEDS Goose Lane is a small literary press publishing Canadian fiction, poetry, and nonfiction. **Considers mss by Canadian poets only.** Receives about 400 mss/year, publishes 15-20 books/year, 4 of which are poetry collections. Has published *Beatitudes* by Herménégilde Chiasson and *I & I* by George Elliott Clarke.

HOW TO CONTACT "Call to inquire whether we are reading submissions." Accepts submissions by postal mail only. Guidelines available on website. Always sends prepublication galleys. Authors may receive royalties of up to 10% of retail price on all copies sold. Copies available to author at 40% discount.

TIPS "Writers should send us outlines and samples of books that show a very well-read author with highly developed literary skills. Our books are almost all by Canadians living in Canada; we seldom consider submissions from outside Canada. If I were a writer trying to market a book today, I would contact the targeted publisher with a query letter and synopsis, and request manuscript guidelines. Purchase a recent book from the publisher in a relevant area, if possible. Always send an SASE with IRCs or suffient return postage in Canadian stamps for reply to your query and for any material you'd like returned should it not suit our needs."

GOTHIC CHAPBOOK SERIES

2272 Quail Oak, Baton Rouge LA 70808. E-mail: gothicpt12@aol.com. Website: www.gwcgothicpress.com. Gothic Press publishes gothic, horror, and dark fantasy poetry in their Gothic Chapbook series. Wants poetry in "any form or style as long as gothic or horror elements are present." Does not want science fiction. Has published Bruce Boston, Joey Froehlich, Scott C. Hocstad. Manuscripts are selected through open submission. Chapbooks are 10-80 pages, offset, saddle-stapled, with cardstock cover or interior illustration by commission. Send samples of art.

HOW TO CONTACT *Gothic Press no longer accepts unsolicited submissions, and seeks chapbooks by invitation only.*

TIPS "Know gothic and horror literature well."

GRAYWOLF PRESS

E-mail: wolves@graywolfpress.org. Website: www.graywolfpress.org. **Contact:** Katie Dublinski, editorial manager (nonfiction, fiction). "Graywolf Press is an independent, nonprofit publisher dedicated to the creation and promotion of thoughtful and imaginative contemporary literature essential to a vital and diverse culture."

NEEDS Graywolf Press is considered one of the nation's leading nonprofit literary publishers. "Graywolf introduces and promotes some of the most exciting and creative writers of our times." Considers only mss by poets widely published in magazines and journals of merit; **does not generally consider unsolicited mss but considers queries**. Has published poetry by Elizabeth Alexander, Vijay Seshadri, Tess Gallagher, Tony Hoagland, Matthea Harvey, D.A. Powell, and many more. Publishes around 9 collections of poetry, 1-2 collections of poetry in translation, and 1-2 collections of essays on poetry/year.

HOW TO CONTACT *No unsolicited mss.* Query first, with 10 pages of poetry (as a sample from the ms) and cover letter with brief bio and publication credits through online submission form. See website for guidelines. SASE required for reply. No e-mail queries. Reads queries in January, May, and September. Responds to queries in 3-6 months. Order sample books through website, or request catalog through online submission form.

GUERNICA EDITIONS, INC.

489 Strathmore Blvd, Toronto ON M4C 1N8, Canada. Website: www.guernicaeditions.com. (Specialized: pluriculturalism; international translation)

NEEDS "We wish to bring together the different and often divergent voices that exist in Canada and the U.S. We are interested in translations. We are mostly interested in poetry and essays on pluriculturalism." Has published poetry by Pier Paolo Pasolini, Pasquale Verdichio, Carole David, Jean-Marc Desgent, Gilles Cyr, Claudine Bertrand, Paul Beélanger, Denise Desaulets.

HOW TO CONTACT Query with 1-2 pages of sample poems. Send SASE (Canadian stamps only) or SAE and IRCs for catalog.

TIPS "Look at what we do. Send some samples. If we like them, we'll write back."

HIPPOPOTAMUS PRESS

(44)(173)466-6653. E-mail: rjhippopress@aol.com. **Contact:** R. John, editor; M. Pargitter (poetry); Anna Martin (translation). "Hippopotamus Press publishes first, full collections of verse by those well represented in the mainstream poetry magazines of the English-speaking world."

TIPS "We publish books for a literate audience. We have a strong link to the Modernist tradition. Read what we publish."

HOLIDAY HOUSE, INC.

(212)688-0085. Fax: (212)421-6134. E-mail: info@holidayhouse.com. Website: holidayhouse.com. **Contact:** Mary Cash, editor-in-chief. (Specialized: poetry for children/teens)"Holiday House publishes children's and young adult books for the school and library markets. We have a commitment to publishing first-time authors and illustrators. We specialize in quality hardcovers from picture books to young adult, both fiction and nonfiction, primarily for the school and library market."

> "Holiday House is an independent publisher of children's books only. We specialize in quality hardcovers, from picture books to young adult, both fiction and nonfiction. We publish children's books for ages four and up. We do not publish mass-market books, including, but not limited to, pop-ups, activity books, sticker books, coloring books, or licensed books."

NEEDS A trade children's book house. Has published hardcover books for children by John Updike and Walter Dean Myers. Publishes one poetry book/year, averaging 32 pages.

HOW TO CONTACT "The acceptance of complete book mss of high-quality children's poetry is limited." Please send the entire manuscript, whether submitting a picture book or novel by mail. Does not accept submissions by e-mail or fax.

TIPS "We need manuscripts with strong stories and writing."

HOUSE OF ANANSI PRESS

110 Spadina Ave., Suite 801, Toronto ON M5V 2K4, Canada. (416)363-4343. Fax: (416)363-1017. Website: www.anansi.ca. **Contact:** Editors. 110 Spadina Ave., Suite 801, Toronto ON M5V 2K4 Canada. (416)363-4343. Fax: (416)363-1017. Website: www.anansi.ca. Estab. 1967.

NEEDS House of Anansi publishes literary fiction and poetry by Canadian and international writers. "We seek to balance the list between well-known and emerging writers, with an interest in writing by Canadians of all backgrounds. We publish Canadian poetry only, and poets must have a substantial publication record—if not in books, then definitely in journals and magazines of repute." Does not want "children's

poetry or poetry by previously unpublished poets." Has published *Power Politics* by Margaret Atwood and *Ruin & Beauty* by Patricia Young. Books are generally 96-144 pages, trade paperbacks with French sleeves, with matte covers.

HOW TO CONTACT Canadian poets should query first with 10 sample poems (typed double-spaced) and a cover letter with brief bio and publication credits. Considers simultaneous submissions. Poems are circulated to an editorial board. Often comments on rejected poems. Responds to queries within 1 year, to mss (if invited) within 4 months. Pays 8-10% royalties, a $750 advance, and 10 author's copies (out of a press run of 1,000).

ILIUM PRESS

2407 S. Sonora Dr., Spokane WA 99037-9011, United States. (509)928-7950. E-mail: contact@iliumpress.com. E-mail: submissions@iliumpress.com. Website: www.iliumpress.com. **Contact:** John Lemon, Owner/editor (literature, epic poetry, how-to).

TIPS "Read submission guidelines on my website."

ITALICA PRESS

595 Main St., Suite 605, New York NY 10044-0047. (212)935-4230. Fax: (212)838-7812. E-mail: inquiries@italicapress.com. Website: www.italicapress.com. **Contact:** Ronald G. Musto and Eileen Gardiner, publishers. "Italica Press publishes English translations of modern Italian fiction and medieval and Renaissance nonfiction."

NEEDS Italica is a small press publisher of English translations of Italian works in paperbacks, averaging 175 pages. Has published *Contemporary Italian Women Poets*, a dual-language (English/Italian) anthology edited and translated by Anzia Sartini Blum and Lara Trubowitz, and *Women Poets of the Italian Renaissance*, a dual-language anthology, edited by Laura Anna Stortoni, translated by Laura Anna Stortoni and Mary Prentice Lillie.

HOW TO CONTACT Query with 10 sample translations of medieval and Renaissance Italian poets. Include cover letter, bio, and list of publications. Accepts simultaneous submissions, but translation should not be "totally" previously published. Accepts e-mail submissions; no fax submissions. Responds to queries in 3 weeks, to mss in 3 months. Always sends prepublication galleys. Pays 7-15% royalties plus 10 author's copies. Acquires English language rights.

TIPS "We are interested in considering a wide variety of medieval and Renaissance topics (not historical fiction), and for modern works we are only interested in translations from Italian fiction by well-known Italian authors."*only* fiction that has been previously published in Italian. A *brief* call saves a lot of postage. 90% of proposals we receive are completely off base—but we are very interested in things that are right on target. Please send return postage if you want your*only* fiction that has been previously published in Italian. A *brief* call saves a lot of postage. 90% of proposals we receive are completely off base—but we are very interested in things that are right on target. Please send return postage if you want your manuscript back.""

❶ ALICE JAMES BOOKS

(207)778-7071. Fax: (207)778-7766. E-mail: info@alicejamesbooks.org. Website: www.alicejamesbooks.org. **Contact:** Carey Salerno, executive director. 238 Main St., Farmington, ME 04938. (207)778-7071. Fax:(207)778-7766. E-mail: info@alicejamesbooks.org. Website:www.alicejamesbooks.org. **Contact:** Carey Salerno, executive director. "Alice James Books is a nonprofit cooperative poetry press. The founders' objectives were to give women access to publishing and to involve authors in the publishing process. The cooperative selects mss for publication through both regional and national competitions." Seeks to publish the best contemporary poetry by both established and beginning poets, with particular emphasis on involving poets in the publishing process. Has published poetry by Jane Kenyon, Jean Valentine, B.H. Fairchild, and Matthea Harvey. Publishes flat-spined paperbacks of high quality, both in production and contents. Does not want children's poetry or light verse. Publishes 6 paperback books/year, 80 pages each, in editions of 1,500. Guidelines available on website."Alice James Books is a nonprofit cooperative poetry press. The founders' objectives were to give women access to publishing and to involve authors in the publishing process. The cooperative selects mss for publication through both regional and national competitions."

NEEDS "The mission of Alice James Books, a cooperative poetry press, is to seek out and publish the best contemporary poetry by both established and beginning poets, with particular emphasis on involving poets in the publishing process." Has published poetry by Jane Kenyon, Jean Valentine, B.H. Fairchild, and Matthea Harvey. Publishes flat-spined paperbacks of high quality, both in production and contents. Does not want children's poetry or light verse. Publishes 6 paperback books/year, 80 pages each, in editions of 1,500.

HOW TO CONTACT Manuscripts are selected through competitions (see below).

CONTEST/AWARD OFFERINGS The Kinereth Gensler Awards and The Beatrice Hawley Award (see separate listings in Contests & Awards).

TIPS "Send SASE for contest guidelines or check website. Do not send work without consulting current guidelines."

❷❷ LAPWING PUBLICATIONS

1 Ballysillan Dr., Belfast BT14 8HQ, Northern Ireland. +44 2890 500 796. Fax: +44 2890 295 800. E-mail: lapwing.poetry@ntlworld.com. Website: www.lapwing-poetry.com. **Contact:** Dennis Greig, editor.

Lapwing will produce work only if and when resources to do so are available.

NEEDS Lapwing publishes "emerging Irish poets and poets domiciled in Ireland, plus the new work of a suitable size by established Irish writers. Non-Irish poets are also published. Poets based in continental Europe have become a major feature. Emphasis on first collections preferrably not larger than 80 pages. Logistically, publishing beyond the British Isles is always difficult for 'hard copy' editions. PDF copies via e-mail are £3 or 3€ per copy. No fixed upperl limit to number of titles per year. Hard copy prices are £8 to £10 per copy. No e-reader required." Wants poetry of all kinds, but, "no crass political, racist, sexist propaganda, even of a positive or 'pc' tenor." Has published Alastair Thomson, Clifford Ireson, Colette Wittorski, Gilberte de Leger, Aubrey Malone, and Jane Shaw Holiday. Pamphlets up to 32 pages, chapbooks up to 44 pages, books 48-112 pages; New Belfast binding, simulated perfect binding for books, otherwise saddle stitching.

HOW TO CONTACT "Submit 6 poems in the first instance; depending on these, an invitation to submit more may follow." Considers simultaneous submissions. Accepts e-mail submissions in body of message or in DOC format. Cover letter is required. "All submissions receive a first reading. If these poems have minor errors or faults, the writer is advised. If poor quality, the poems are returned. Those 'passing' first reading are retained, and a letter of conditional offer is sent." Often comments on rejected poems. Responds to queries in 1 month; to mss in 2 months. Pays 20 author's copies; no royalties. "After initial publication, irrespective of the quantity, the work will be permanently available using 'print-on-demand' production; such publications will not always be printed exactly as the original, although the content will remain the same."

⊘ LETHE PRESS

118 Heritage Ave., Maple Shade NJ 08052. (609)410-7391. E-mail: editor@lethepressbooks.com. Website: www.lethepressbooks.com. **Contact:** Steve Berman, publisher. "Lethe Press is a small press seeking gay and lesbian themed poetry collections." Lethe Books are distributed by Ingram Publications and Bookazine, and are available at all major bookstores, as well as the major online retailers.

NEEDS "Lethe Press is an independent publishing house specializing in speculative fiction, books of gay interest, poetry, spirituality, as well as classic works of the occult & supernatural. Named after the Greek river of memory and forgetfulness (and pronounced Lee-Thee), Lethe Press is devoted to ideas that are often neglected or forgotten by mainstream publishers."

HOW TO CONTACT Send query letter. Accepts queries by e-mail. Rarely accepts unsolicited mss.

LOUISIANA STATE UNIVERSITY PRESS

(225)578-6294. Fax: (225)578-6461. E-mail: mkc@lsu.edu. Website: www.lsu.edu/lsupress. Exec. Editor: John Easterly (poetry, fiction, literary studies); Sr. Ed.: Rand Dotson (U.S. History & Southern Studies). **Contact:** MK Callaway, Director. Publishes in the fall and spring.

⊘ LUNA BISONTE PRODS

E-mail: bennett.23@osu.edu. Website: www.johnmbennett.net. **Contact:** John M. Bennett, editor/publisher. E-mail: bennett.23@osu.edu. Website: www.johnmbennett.net. Contact: John M. Bennett, editor/publisher.

NEEDS Luna Bisonte Prods considers book submissions. "Interested in avant-garde and highly experimental work only." Has published poetry by Jim Leftwich, Sheila E. Murphy, Al Ackerman, Richard Kostelanetz, Carla Bertola, Olchar Lindsann, and many others.

HOW TO CONTACT Query first, with a few sample poems and cover letter with brief bio and publication credits. "Keep it brief. Chapbook publishing usually depends on grants or other subsidies, and is usually by solicitation. **Will also consider subsidy arrangements on negotiable terms.**" A sampling of various Luna Bisonte Prods products is available for $20.

⊘ MAVERICK DUCK PRESS

E-mail: maverickduckpress@yahoo.com. Website: www.maverickduckpress.com. **Contact:** Kendall A. Bell, editor. E-mail: maverickduckpress@yahoo.com. Website:www.maverickduckpress.com. **Contact:** Kendall A. Bell, editor. Estab. 2005.

NEEDS Maverick Duck Press is a "publisher of chapbooks from undiscovered talent. We are looking for fresh and powerful work that shows a sense of innovation or a new take on passion or emotion. Previous publication in print or online journals will increase your chances of us accepting your manuscript." Does not want "unedited work." Has published *Devil's road Down*, by Adrienne Odasso; *Hemispheres*, by Jeanpaul Ferro; *Inside Bone There's Always Marrow*, by Rachel Mallino and *Big Time* by Don Kloss.Publishes 4-6 chapbooks/year. Manuscripts are selected through open submission. Chapbooks are 18-24 pages, photocopied, saddle-stapled, with cardstock covers (poet must provide desired cover art).

HOW TO CONTACT Send manuscript in Microsoft Word format with a cover letter with brief bio and publication credits. Chapbook mss may include previously published poems. "Previous publication is always a plus, as we may be more familiar with your work. Chapbook manuscripts should have at least 20 poems." Pays 20 author's copies (out of a press run of 50).

❶❸ MEADOWBROOK PRESS

5451 Smetana Dr., Minnetonka MN 55343. Fax: (952)930-1940. E-mail: info@meadowbrookpress.com. Website: www.meadowbrookpress.com. **Contact:** Art Director.

⬭ "We are not currently accepting unsolicited manuscripts or queries for the following genres: adult fiction, adult poetry, humor, and children's fiction. Also note that we do not currently publish picture books for children, travel titles, scholarly, or literary works. For children's poetry guidelines, please go to our website."

NEEDS Meadowbrook Press is "currently seeking poems to be considered for future funny poetry book anthologies for children." Wants humorous poems aimed at children ages 6-12. "Poems should be fun, punchy, and refreshing. We're looking for new, hilarious, contemporary voices in children's poetry that kids can relate to." Has published poetry by Shel Silverstein, Jack Prelutsky, Jeff Moss, Kenn Nesbitt, and Bruce Lansky. Published anthologies include *Kids Pick the Funniest Poems*, *A Bad Case of the Giggles*, and *Miles of Smiles*.

HOW TO CONTACT "Please take time to read our guidelines, and send your best work." Submit up to 10 poems at a time; 1 poem to a page with name and address on each; include SASE. Lines/poem: 25 maximum. Considers simultaneous submissions. Time between acceptance and publication is 1-2 years. Poems are tested in front of grade school students before being published. Guidelines available for SASE or on website. Responds only if interested. Pays $50-100/poem plus 1 contributor's copy.

TIPS "Always send for guidelines before submitting material. Always submit nonreturnable copies; we do not respond to queries or submissions unless interested."

MELLEN POETRY PRESS

P.O. Box 450, Lewiston NY 14092-0450. (716)754-2266. Fax: (716)754-4056. E-mail: jrupnow@mellen-press.com. Website: www.mellenpress.com. **Contact:** Dr. John Rupnow, acquisitions. Book length only, 50-64 pages. Poems must be thematically and metaphorically united. For a copy of our mission statement and submission guidelines e-mail: jrupnow@mellenpress.com, Dr. John Rupnow, acquisitions editor."We are a non-subsidy academic publisher of books in the humanities and social sciences. Our sole criterion for publication is that a manuscript makes a contribution to scholarship. We publish monographs, critical editions, collections, translations, revisionist studies, constructive essays, bibliographies, dictionaries, grammars and dissertations. We publish in English, French, German, Spanish, Italian, Portuguese, Welsh and Russian. Our books are well reviewed and acquired by research libraries worldwide. The *Press* also publishes over 100 continuing series, several academic journals, and the research generated by several scholarly institutes."

MIAMI UNIVERSITY PRESS

356 Bachelor Hall, Miami University, Oxford OH 45056. E-mail: tumakw@muohio.edu. Website: www.muohio.edu/mupress. **Contact:** Keith Tuma, Editor..

Currently closed to unsolicited mss, except for submissions to novella contest; see website for information on the contest.

NEEDS Publishes 1-2 books of poetry/year and one novella, in paperback editions. Recent poetry titles include *Virgil's Cow*, by Frederick Farryl Goodwin; *Between Cup and Lip*, by Peter Manson; and *Talk Poetry*, by Mairéad Byrne. Recent fiction titles include John Cotter, Under the Small Lights, Lee Upton, The Guide to the Flying Island, and Cary Holladay, A Fight in the Doctor's Office.

HOW TO CONTACT *Currently closed to unsolicited manuscripts, except for submissions to novella contest; see website for information on the contest.*

MIDMARCH ARTS PRESS

300 Riverside Dr., New York NY 10025. (212)666-6990. Fax: (212)865-5509. E-mail: info@midmarchartspress.org. Website: www.midmarchartspress.org. **Contact:** Editorial Director.

NEEDS Midmarch Arts Press publishes 4 paperbacks/year on the visual arts and one book of poetry. Has recently published *Rock Vein Sky*, by Charlotte Mandel; *Luminations*, art by Oriole F. feshbach for Wallace Stevens' poem "The Auroras of Autumn."

HOW TO CONTACT Query by letter or e-mail prior to submitting anything.

MILKWEED EDITIONS

(612)332-3192. E-mail: submissions@milkweed.org. Website: www.milkweed.org.

Please consider our previous publications when considering submissions.

NEEDS Milkweed Editions is "looking for poetry manuscripts of high quality that embody humane values and contribute to cultural understanding." Not limited in subject matter. Open to writers with previously published books of poetry or a minimum of 6 poems published in nationally distributed commercial or literary journals. Considers translations and bilingual mss. Has published *Fancy Beasts*, by Alex Lemon, *Reading Novalis in Montana*, by Melissa Kwasny, and *The Book of Props*, by Wayne Miller.

HOW TO CONTACT Submit through website. No fax or e-mail submissions. Do not send originals. Accepts and reads unsolicited mss all year. Guidelines available on website. Responds in up to 6 months. Order sample books through website.

TIPS "We are looking for excellent writing with the intent of making a humane impact on society. Please read submission guidelines before submitting and acquaint yourself with our books in terms of style and quality before submitting. Many factors influence our selection process, so don't get discouraged. Nonfiction is focused on literary writing about the natural world, including living well in urban environments."

⊘ MOVING PARTS PRESS

10699 Empire Grade, Santa Cruz CA 95060. (831)427-2271. E-mail: frice@movingpartspress.com. Website: www.movingpartspress.com. **Contact:** Felicia Rice, poetry editor.

NEEDS Moving Part Press publishes handsome, innovative books, broadsides, and prints that "explore the relationship of word and image, typography and the visual arts, the fine arts and popular culture." Published *Codex Espangliensis: from Columbus to the Border Patrol* (1998) with performance texts by Guillermo Goómez-Penña and collage imagery by Enrique Chagoya; *Cosmogonie Intime/An Intimate Cosmogony* (2005), a limited edition artists' book with poems by Yves Peyreé, translated by Elizabeth R. Jackson, and drawings by Ray Rice.

HOW TO CONTACT *Does not accept unsolicited mss.*

☺⊘ MULTICULTURAL BOOKS

307 Birchwood Court, 6311 Gilbert Rd., Richmond BC V7C 3V7, Canada. (60447-0979. E-mail: jrmbooks@hotmail.com. Website: www.mbooksofbc.com; www.thehypertexts.com. **Contact:** Joe M. Ruggier, publisher.

NEEDS "MBooks of BC is a small press. We publish poetry, prose and poetry leaflets, prose, translations, children's writing, sound recordings, fiction, and literary non-fiction. We also have a publishing services division. We belong to an international circle of poets and editors committed to reforming the prevailing order by bringing about a traditionalist revival in writing." Publishes 1-6 books/year "depending on availability and quality." Manuscripts are selected through open submission. Books are 120+ pages, digitally photocopied, perfect-bound, with heavy color cardstock cover.

HOW TO CONTACT Query first, with a few sample poems and a cover letter with brief bio and publica-

tion credits. Book mss may include previously published poems. "The only criteria is quality of work and excellence." Responds to queries in 2 months; to mss in 2 months. **Offers author-subsidy as well as publisher-subsidy options**; the selection process for the latter is extremely competitive and quality-conscious. "Authors who feel their work may be up to standard are welcome to query us with a sample or else submit an entire manuscript. All interested parties may consult our guidelines as well as our sample publication contract on website." Order sample books/chapbooks by contacting Joe M. Ruggier.

⊕ NEW ISSUES POETRY & PROSE

Western Michigan University, 1903 W. Michigan Ave., Kalamazoo MI 49008-5463. (269)387-8185. Fax: (269)387-2562. E-mail: new-issues@wmich.edu. Website: wmich.edu/newissues. **Contact:** Managing Editor. Established 1996. Contests: The Green Rose Prize in Poetry offers $2,000 and publication of a book of poems by an established poet who has published one or more full-length collections of poetry. New Issues may publish as many as 3 additional mss from this competition. Considers simultaneous submissions, but New Issues must be notified of acceptance elsewhere. Submit a ms of at least 48 pages, typed, single-spaced preferred. Clean photocopies acceptable. Do not bind; use manila folder or metal clasp. Include cover page with poet's name, address, phone number, and title of the ms. Also include brief bio, table of contents, and acknowledgments page. No e-mail or fax submissions. Include SASP for notification of receipt of ms and SASE for results only; mss will be recycled. Guidelines available for SASE, by fax, e-mail, or on website. Please visit the AWP website for guidelines to submit to the AWP Award Series in the Novel contest.

HOW TO CONTACT Query first. All unsolicited mss returned unopened. "The press considers for publication only manuscripts submitted during its competition reading periods and often accepts two or more manuscripts for publication in addition to the winner."

⊘ NEW NATIVE PRESS

P.O. Box 661, Cullowhee NC 28723. (828)293-9237. E-mail: newnativepress@hotmail.com. Website: www.newnativepress.com. **Contact:** Thomas Rain Crowe, publisher.

NEEDS New Native Press has "selectively narrowed its range of contemporary 20th- and 21st-century literature to become an exclusive publisher of writers in marginalized and endangered languages. All books published are bilingual translations from original languages into English." Publishes about 2 paperbacks/year. Has published *Kenneth Patchen: Rebel Poet in America* by Larry Smith; Gaelic, Welsh, Breton, Cornish, and Manx poets in an all-Celtic-language anthology of contemporary poets from Scotland, Ireland, Wales, Brittany, Cornwall, and Isle of Man, entitled *Writing The Wind: A Celtic Resurgence* (The New Celtic Poetry); and *Selected Poems* by Kusumagraj (poet from Bombay, India) in the Marathi language. Books are sold by distributors in 4 foreign countries, and in the U.S. by Baker & Taylor, Amazon.com, library vendors, and Small Press Distribution. Books are typically 80 pages, offset-printed on glossy 120 lb. stock, perfect-bound, with professionally designed color cover.

HOW TO CONTACT Query first, with 10 sample poems and cover letter with brief bio and publication credits. Considers previously published poems and simultaneous submissions. Time between acceptance and publication is up to 1 year. Always comments on rejected poems. Responds in 2 weeks. Pays in author's copies ("amount varies with author and title").

○ NEW RIVERS PRESS

MSU Moorhead, 1104 Seventh Ave. S., Moorhead MN 56563. E-mail: kelleysu@mnstate.edu. Website: www.newriverspress.com. **Contact:** Suzanne Kelley, managing editor.

NEEDS New Rivers Press publishes collections of poetry, novels or novellas, translations of contemporary literature, and collections of short fiction and nonfiction. "We continue to publish books regularly by new and emerging writers, but we also welcome the opportunity to read work of every character and to publish the best literature available nationwide. Each fall through the MVP competition (see below), we choose 2 books, 1 of them. Poetry and 1 of them Prose." Has published *The Pact* by Walter Roers, *Nice Girls* by Cezarija Abartis, *Mozart's Carriage* by Dan Bachhuber, *The Volunteer* by Candace Black, *The Hunger Bone* by Deb Marquart, and *Real Karaoke People* by Ed Bok-Lee, and *Terrain Tracks* by Purvi Shah.

HOW TO CONTACT Book-length mss of poetry, short fiction, novellas, or creative nonfiction are all considered. No fax or e-mail submissions. Guidelines available on website.

CONTEST/AWARD OFFERINGS The Many Voices Prize (MVP) awards $1,000, a standard book contract, and publication of a book-length ms by New Rivers Press. All previously published poems must be acknowledged. Considers simultaneous submissions "if noted as such. If your manuscript is accepted elsewhere during the judging, you must notify New Rivers Press immediately. If you do not give such notification and your manuscript is selected, your signature on the entry form gives New Rivers Press permission to go ahead with publication." Submit 50-80 pages of poetry. Entry form (required) and guidelines available on website. **Entry fee:** $20. **Deadline:** submit September 15-November 1 (postmark). 2010 Poetry winner was Robert Miltner (Hotel Utopia), Judge: Tim Seibles; 2010 Prose winner was Jacob Lampart (Muse of Ocean Parkway and other stories), Judge: John Dufresne.

⊘ NINETY-SIX PRESS

Furman University, 3300 Poinsett Hwy., Greenville SC 29613. (864)294-3152. Fax: (864)294-2224. E-mail: gil.allen@furman.edu. **Contact:** Gilbert Allen, editor.

◯ The normal first run is 500 paperback copies, and authors are compensated in copies.

NEEDS "The name of the press is derived from the old name for the area around Greenville, South Carolina—the Ninety-Six District. The name suggests our interest in the writers, readers, and culture of the region." Publishes 1-2 paperback books of poetry/year. Books are usually 45-70 pages, digest-sized, professionally printed, perfect-bound, with coated stock covers.

HOW TO CONTACT "We currently accept submissions by invitation only." For a sample, send $10.

OOLIGAN PRESS

(503)725-9410. E-mail: ooligan@ooliganpress.pdx.edu. Website: www.ooliganpress.pdx.edu. **Contact:** Acquisitions Committee.

NEEDS Ooligan is a general trade press that "specializes in publishing authors from the Pacific Northwest and/or works that have specific value to that community. We are limited in the number of poetry titles that we publish as poetry represents only a small percentage of our overall acquisitions. We are open to all forms of style and verse; however, we give special preference to translated poetry, prose poetry, and traditional verse. Although spoken word, slam, and rap poetry are of interest to the press, we will not consider such work if it does not translate well to the written page. Ooligan does not publish chapbooks." Has published *Deer Drink the Moon*, edited by Liz Nakazawa and *American Scream* and *Palindrome Apocalypse* by the Croatian poet Durbravaka Oraic-Tolid, translated by Julienne Eden Busic. Manuscripts are selected through open submissions. Books are most often offset-printed and perfect-bound with soft covers.

HOW TO CONTACT Query by postal mail, with 20 or more poems, a brief bio including poet's publication credits, and a SASE. May include previously published poems. Accepts simultaneous submissions. See website for explanation of acquisition process and complete submission guidelines. Responds to queries in 3 months. Payment varies, but generally 6-12% of retail price and 25 author's copies. Order sample books through website.

TIPS "For children's books, our audience will be middle grades and young adult, with marketing to general trade, libraries, and schools. Good marketing ideas increase the chances of a manuscript succeeding."

⊘ ORCHISES PRESS

(703)683-1243. E-mail: lathbury@gmu.edu. Website: mason.gmu.edu/~lathbury. **Contact:** Roger Lathbury, editor-in-chief. P.O. Box 320533, Alexandria, VA 22320-4533. (703)683-1243. E-mail: lathbury@gmu.edu. Website: mason.gmu.edu/~lathbury. **Contact:** Roger Lathbury, editor-in-chief. Orchises Press is a general literary publisher specializing in poetry with selected reprints and textbooks. *Orchises Press no longer reads unsolicited mss.* Poetry must have been published in respected literary journals. Publishes free verse, but has strong formalist preferences. Orchises Press is a general literary publisher specializing in poetry with selected reprints and textbooks. No new fiction or children's books.

○ Orchises Press no longer reads unsolicited mss.

✪ PALETTES & QUILLS

330 Knickerbocker Ave., Rochester NY 14615. (585)456-0217. E-mail: palettesnquills@gmail.com. Website: www.palettesnquills.com. **Contact:** Donna M. Marbach, publisher/owner. Palettes & Quills "is at this point, a poetry press only, and produces only a handful of publications each year, specializing in anthologies, individual chapbooks, and broadsides." Wants "work that should appeal to a wide audience." Has published Cornelius Eady (reprints with permission), M.J. Iuppa, Katharyn Howd Machan, Tom Holmes, Liz Rosenberg, Linda Allardt and Michael Meyerhofer. Published 1-2 chapbooks/year, occasional anthologies, and 3-5 broadsides. Query first with 3-5 poems and a cover letter with brief bio and publication credits for individual unsolicited chapbooks. May include previously published poems. Chapbook poets would get 20 copies of a run; broadside poets and artists get 5-10 copies and occasionally paid $10 for reproduction rights. Anthology poets get 1 copy of the anthology. All poets and artists get a discount on purchases that include their work. Palettes & Quills Biennial Chapbook Contest, held biennially. Prize: $200 plus 50 copies of chapbook and discount on purchase of others. Guidelines available for SASE or on website. Entry fee: $20. Next contest is planned for 2012, Past judges: Ellen Bass and Dorianne Laux." From time to time, Palettes & Quills will put out a special call for poems for themed anthologies (e.g. Women Celebrating Women). Specific directions for such calls are posted on the website when they are announced and our available for SASE."

NEEDS Palettes & Quills "is at this point, a poetry press only, and produces only a handful of publications each year, specializing in anthologies, individual chapbooks, and broadsides." Wants "work that should appeal to a wide audience." Does not want "poems that are sold blocks of text, long-lined and without stanza breaks. Wildly elaborate free-verse would be difficult and in all likelihood fight with art background, amateurish rhyming poem, overly sentimental poems, poems that use excessive profanity, or which denigrate other people, or political and religious diatribes." Has published Cornelius Eady (reprints with permission), M.J. Iuppa, Katharyn Howd Machan, Tom Holmes, Liz Rosenberg, Linda Allardt and Michael Meyerhofer. Published 1-2 chapbooks/year, occasional anthologies, and 3-5 broadsides.

HOW TO CONTACT Query first with 3-5 poems and a cover letter with brief bio and publication credits for individual unsolicited chapbooks. May include previously published poems. Chapbook poets would get 20 copies of a run; broadside poets and artists get 5-10 copies and occasionally paid $10 for reproduction rights. Anthology poets get 1 copy of the anthology. All poets and artists get a discount on purchases that include their work.

CONTEST/AWARD OFFERINGS Palettes & Quills Biennial Chapbook Contest, held biennually. Prize: $200 plus 50 copies of chapbook and discount on purchase of others. Guidelines available for SASE or on website. Entry fee: $20. Next contest is planned for 2012, Past judges: Ellen Bass and Dorianne Laux.

ALSO OFFERS "From time to time, Palettes & Quills will put out a special call for poems for themed anthologies (e.g. Women Celebrating Women). Specific directions for such calls are posted on the website when they are announced and our available for SASE."

⊘ PATH PRESS, INC.

1229 Emerson St., Evanston IL 60201. (847)492-0177. Fax: (773)651-0210. E-mail: pathpressinc@aol.com. **Contact:** Bennett J. Johnson, president.

NEEDS Path Press is a small publisher of books and poetry primarily "by, for, and about African American and Third World people." Open to all types of poetic forms; emphasis is on high quality. Books are "hardback and quality paperbacks."

HOW TO CONTACT Query first, with a few sample poems and cover letter with brief bio and publication credits. Submissions should be typewritten in ms format. Accepts submissions by e-mail (as attachment).

○ PECAN GROVE PRESS

Box AL, 1 Camino Santa Maria, San Antonio TX 78228. (210)436-3442. Fax: (210)436-3782. E-mail: phall@stmarytx.edu. Website: http://library.stmarytx.edu/pgpress. **Contact:** H. Palmer Hall, editor/director. Member, CLMP. Pecan Grove Press is a poetry-only press and conducts one national chapbook competition each year. Aside from that, the press publishes approximately 7-8 books and chapbooks each year outside of the competition.

NEEDS "PGP publishes a variety of 'types' of poetry (narrative, lyrical, formal, free, hetero, gay, male, female, etc.)." Has published *Small Songs of Pain*, by Patricia Fargnoli; *Like Li-Po Laughing at the Lonely Moon* by Chuck Taylor; *Oh Forbidden!* by Jill Alexander Essbaum; *The Heat of What Comes*, by Joel Peckham; *Visiting Home*, by Paul Willis; *Rio Vertabral/Vertabral River*, by Juan Arando Rojas. Publishes 5 poetry books/year, 3 chapbooks/year, and 1-2 anthologies/year. Manuscripts are selected through open submission. Books are 52-100 pages, off-set or laser print, perfect-bound with color index stock cover and full color art. Chapbooks are 32-45 pages, laser printed, perfect-bound, index stock cover with color in-house graphics.

HOW TO CONTACT Submit complete ms via submission manager on website only. Book/chapbook may include previously published poems. Prefers some record of publication in literary reviews prior to submission. Responds in 4 months. Pays poet 50% of proceeds after printing/binding costs are covered. Press run of 250 chapbooks and 500-1,000 for books. Pays 5 author's copies.

CONTEST/AWARD OFFERINGS Annual chapbook contest with prize of $250 and 25 copies of chapbook. Submit 32-42 pages. Guidelines are on website. Entry fee: $15; deadline: January 15.

ADDITIONAL INFORMATION "We are a non-profit, independent poetry press working under the umbrella of St. Mary's University in San Antonio, Texas."

● PELICAN PUBLISHING COMPANY

1000 Burmaster St., Gretna LA 70053. (504)368-1175. Fax: (504)368-1195. E-mail: editorial@pelicanpub.com. Website: www.pelicanpub.com. **Contact:** Nina Kooij, editor-in-chief. Has published *Alaskan Night Before Christmas* by Tricia Brown and *Hawaiian Night Before Christmas* by Carolyn Macy. Two of Pelican's popular series are prose books about Gaston the Green-Nosed Alligator by James Rice, and Clovis Crawfish by Mary Alice Fontenot. Books are 32 pages, magazine-sized, include illustrations. "We believe ideas have consequences. One of the consequences is that they lead to a best-selling book. We publish books to improve and uplift the reader. Currently emphasizing business and history titles."

HOW TO CONTACT Printout of ms with a cover letter including "work and writing backgrounds and promotional connections." No previously published poems or simultaneous submissions. Guidelines available on website. Responds to mss in 3 months. Always sends pre-publication galleys. Pays royalties. Acquires all rights. Returns rights upon termination of contract.

ADDITIONAL INFORMATION Typically, Pelican books sell for $16.99. Write for catalog or visit website to view catalog and/or buy samples.

TIPS "We do extremely well with cookbooks, popular histories, and business. We will continue to build in these areas. The writer must have a clear sense of the market and knowledge of the competition. A query letter should describe the project briefly, give the author's writing and professional credentials, and promotional ideas."

⊘ PLAN B PRESS

P.O. Box 4067, Alexandria VA 22303. (215)732-2663. E-mail: planbpress@gmail.com. Website: www.planbpress.com. **Contact:** Steven Allen May, president.

NEEDS Plan B Press is a "small publishing company with an international feel. Our intention is to have Plan B Press be part of the conversation about the direction and depth of literary movements and genres. Plan B Press's new direction is to seek out authors rarely-to-never published, sharing new voices that might not otherwise be heard. Plan B Press is determined to merge text with image, writing with art." Publishes poetry and short fiction. Wants "experimental poetry, concrete/visual work." Has published poetry by Lamont B. Steptoe, Michele Belluomini, Jim Mancinelli, Lyn Lifshin, Robert Miltner, and stevenallenmay. Publishes 1 poetry book/year and 5-10 chapbooks/year. Manuscripts are selected through open submission and through competition (see below). Books/chapbooks are 24-48 pages, with covers with art/graphics.

HOW TO CONTACT Query first, with a few sample poems and a cover letter with brief bio and publication credits. Book/chapbook mss may include previously published poems. Guidelines available on website. Responds to queries in 1 month; to mss in 3 months. Author keeps royalties. Pays varying number of author's copies; press run varies per book. Order sample books/chapbooks by writing to Plan B Press or through website.

CONTEST/AWARD OFFERINGS The annual Plan B Press Poetry Chapbook Contest (see separate listing in Contests & Awards).

⊜⊘ POETRY SALZBURG

University of Salzburg, Department of English, Akademiestrasse 24, Salzburg A-5020, Austria. (43)(662)8044-4422. Fax: (43)(662)8044-167. E-mail: editor@poetrysalzburg.com. Website: www.poetrysalzburg.com. **Contact:** Dr. Wolfgang Goertschacher, Andreas Schachermayr.

NEEDS Poetry Salzburg publishes "collections of at least 100 pages by mainly poets not taken up by big publishers." Publishes 6-8 paperbacks/year. Books are usually 100-350 pages, A5, professionally printed, perfect-bound, with card covers.

HOW TO CONTACT Query first, with a cover letter with brief bio and publication credits. Suggests authors publish in *Poetry Salzburg Review* (see separate listing in Magazines/Journals) first. Responds to queries in 4 weeks; to mss in about 3 months. Payment varies.

⬤ PRESA :S: PRESS

PO Box 792, 8590 Belding Rd NE, Rockford MI 49341. E-mail: presapress@aol.com. Website: www.presapress.com. **Contact:** Roseanne Ritzema, editor. Presa :S: Press publishes "perfect-bound paperbacks and saddle-stitched chapbooks of poetry." Wants " imagistic poetry where form is an extension of content, surreal, experimental, and personal poetry." Does not want "overtly political or didactic material." Has published poetry books by Kirby Congdon, John Amen, Hugh Fox, Eric Greinke, Donald Lev, Lyn Lifshin, Simon PerchikGlenna Luschei, and Harry Smith. Publishes 2-3 poetry books/year, 1-2 chapbooks/year, and an occasional anthology. Manuscripts are selected through open submission. Books are 64-144 pages, laser-printed on 24 lb. paper, perfect-bound paperback with a laminated, color art cover. Chapbooks are 28-48 pages, laser-printed on 20-24 lb. paper, saddle-stitched with a color art cover. Anthologies are 250-325 pages, laser-printed, perfect-bound paperback with a laminated color art cover. Press runs 500-1,000 copies. Wants "imagistic poetry where form is an extension of content, surreal, experimental, and personal poetry." Does not want "overtly political or didactic material." Has published poetry books by Kirby Congdon, John Amen, Hugh Fox, Eric Greinke, Donald Lev, Lyn Lifshin, Glenna Luschei, and Harry Smith. Publishes 2-3 poetry books/year, 1-2 chapbooks/year, and an occasional anthology. Manuscripts are selected through open submission. Books are 64-144 pages, laser-printed on 24 lb. paper, perfect-bound paperback with a laminated, color art cover. Chapbooks are 28-48 pages, laser-printed on 20-24 lb. paper, saddle-stitched with a color art cover. Anthologies are 250-325 pages, laser-printed, perfect-bound paperback with a laminated color art cover. Press runs 500-1,000 copies. Query first, with a few sample poems and a cover letter with brief bio and publication credits. Book/chapbook mss may include previously published poems.

NEEDS poems, reviews, essays, photos, criticism, and prose. Wants imagistic, surreal, experimental, and personal poetry. Dedicates 6-8 pages of each issue to a featured poet. Does not want political or didactic poetry. Considers previously published poems. (Considers poetry posted on a public website/blog/forum and poetry posted on a private, password-protected forum as published.) Accepts postal submissions only. Cover letter is preferred. Reads submissions year round. Poems are circulated to an editorial board. Never comments on rejected poems. Never publishes theme issues. Guidelines available in magazine, for SASE, and by e-mail. Responds in 4-8 weeks. Pays in contributor copies. Acquires first North American serial rights and the right to reprint in anthologies. Rights revert to poets upon publication. Reviews books and chapbooks of poetry. Send materials for review consideration to Roseanne Ritzema.

HOW TO CONTACT Query first, with a few sample poems and a cover letter with brief bio and publication credits. Book/chapbook mss may include previously published poems. Responds to queries in 2-4 weeks; to mss in 8-12 weeks. Pays 10-25 author\quotes copies.

PRINCETON UNIVERSITY PRESS

41 William St., Princeton NJ 08540. (609)258-4900. Fax: (609)258-6305. Website: www.pupress.princeton. edu. **Contact:** Hanne Winarsky, Editor. "The Lockert Library of Poetry in Translation embraces a wide geographic and temporal range, from Scandinavia to Latin America to the subcontinent of India, from the Tang Dynasty to Europe of the modern day. It especially emphasizes poets who are established in their native lands and who are being introduced to an English-speaking audience. The series, many of whose titles are bilingual editions, calls attention to some of the most widely-praised poetry available today. In the Lockert Library series, each book is given individual design treatment rather than stamped into a series mold. We have published a wide range of poets from other cultures, including well-known writers such as Hoölderlin and Cavafy, and those who have not yet had their due in English translation, such as Goöran Sonnevi. Manuscripts are judged with several criteria in mind: the ability of the translation to stand on its own as poetry in English; fidelity to the tone and spirit

of the original, rather than literal accuracy; and the importance of the translated poet to the literature of his or her time and country."

● PUDDING HOUSE PUBLICATIONS

81 Shadymere Lane, Columbus OH 43213. (614)986-1881. E-mail: jen@puddinghouse.com. Website: www. puddinghouse.com. **Contact:** Jennifer Bosveld, publisher. (Specialized: social issues; popular culture reflected in poetry arts)

NEEDS Pudding House Publications prints chapbooks, anthologies, and broadsides. Has over 1,200 titles in print. Provides "a sociological looking glass through poems that speak to the pop culture, struggle in a consumer and guardian society, and more—through 'felt experience.' Speaks for the difficulties and the solutions." Pudding House is also the publisher of the respected national archive, POETS' GREATEST HITS—an invitational which was sold to Sammy Greenspan at Kattywompus Press in 2010. Pudding Hosue has recently published *The Allegories* by Dan Sicoli, *Barb Quill Down* by Bill Griffin, *Sonnets to Hamlet* by David Rigsbee, *Mischief* by Charlene Fix, and over 700 others.

HOW TO CONTACT Chapbooks considered outside of competitions, no query. Send complete ms and a cover letter with publication credits and bio. Now accepts manuscripts by e-mail. **Reading fee:** $15. Sometimes comments; "no more critiquing, at any price, too busy now." See main page at puddinghouse.com for chapbook guidelines.

CONTEST/AWARD OFFERINGS Pudding House offers an annual chapbook competition. **Entry fee:** $15. **Deadline:** September 30. Strict guidelines available on website.

ALSO OFFERS "Our website is one of the greatest poetry websites in the country—calls, workshops, publication list/history, online essays, games, guest pages, calendars, poem of the month, poet of the week, much more." The website also links to the site for The Unitarian Universalist Poets Cooperative and American Poets Opposed to Executions, both national organizations.

● THE PUDDIN'HEAD PRESS

P.O. Box 477889, Chicago IL 60647. (708)656-4900. E-mail: phbooks@att.net. Website: www.puddinhead-press.com.

NEEDS The Puddin'head Press is interested in "well-rounded poets who can support their work with readings and appearances." Wants "quality poetry by active poets who read and lead interesting lives. We occasionally publish chapbook-style anthologies and let poets on our mailing lists know what type of work we're interested in for a particular project." Does not want experimental, overly political poetry, or poetry with overt sexual content; no shock or novelty poems. Has published poetry by Jared Smith, Carol Anderson, Larry Janowski, Sandy Goldsmith, and Norman Porter. Puddin'head Press publishes 2-3 books and 2-3 chapbooks per year. Books/chapbooks are 30-100 pages, perfect-bound or side-stapled ("we use various formats").

HOW TO CONTACT "Please visit our website for submission guidelines." Poets must include SASE with submission. Responds to queries in 2 months. Pays various royalty rates "depending on the publication. We usually have a press run of 500 books." **About 10% of books are author subsidy-published.** Terms vary. Order sample books/chapbooks by sending $10 (price plus postage) to The Puddin'head Press (also available through Amazon). "Please visit our website and see what we publish."

ADDITIONAL INFORMATION "In the last several years we have been increasingly active across the country. There are numerous readings and events that we sponsor. We do our own distribution, primarily in the Midwest, and also do distribution for other small presses. Please send a SASE for a list of our current publications and publication/distribution guidelines. We sell poetry books, not just print them. Submitted poetry is evaluated for its marketability and quality."

ALSO OFFERS "Extensive website with rare and used books, extensive links to who's who in poetry and online marketing."

⦸⑤ QED PRESS/CYPRESS HOUSE

Cypress House, 155 Cypress St., Fort Bragg CA 95437. (800)773-7782. Fax: (707)964-7531. E-mail: joeshaw@cypresshouse.com. Website: www.cypresshouse.com. **Contact:** Joe Shaw, Editor.

NEEDS QED Press publishes "clear, clean, intelligent, and moving work." Wants "concrete, personal, and spare writing. No florid rhymed verse." Has published poetry by Victoria Greenleaf, Luke Breit, Paula Tennant (Adams), Cynthia Frank, et al. Publishes no more than 1 poetry book/year. Books are usually about 96 pages (75-80 poems), digest-sized, offset-printed, perfect-bound, with full-color cover.

HOW TO CONTACT "We prefer to see 6 representative poems." Considers simultaneous submissions. Cover letter and SASE for return of materials are required. Time between acceptance and publication is up to 1 year. Poems are read by an editorial board. Responds to queries and mss in 1 month. Pays royalties of 7-12% and 25 author's copies (out of a press run of 500-1,000). Order sample books through website.

ALSO OFFERS Also offers book packaging, and promotion and marketing services to start-up publishers.

⦸⑤ RATTAPALLAX PRESS

Website: www.rattapallax.com. (Specialized: the diversity of world cultures) 217 Thomas St., Suite 353, New York NY 10012. E-mail: info@rattapallax.com. Website: www.rattapallax.com. Established 1998. **Contact:** Poetry Editor.

NEEDS Rattapallax Press publishes "contemporary poets and writers with unique, powerful voices." Publishes 5 paperbacks and 3 chapbooks/year. Books are usually 64 pages, digest-sized, offset-printed, perfect-bound, with 12-pt. CS1 covers.

HOW TO CONTACT Query first, with a few sample poems and cover letter with brief bio and publication credits. Include SASE. Requires authors to first be published in *Rattapallax* (see separate listing in Magazines/Journals). Responds to queries in 1 month; to mss in 2 months. Pays royalties of 10-25%. Order sample books from website.

⦸ RED DRAGON PRESS

P.O. Box 320301, Alexandria VA 22320-4301. Website: www.reddragonpress.com. P.O. Box 320301, Alexandria, VA 22320-4301. Website:www.reddragonpress.com.

NEEDS Red Dragon Press is a proponent "of works that represent the nature of man as androgynous, as in the fusing of male and female symbolism, and we support works that deal with psychological and parapsychological topics." Wants "innovative and experimental poetry and prose using literary symbolism and aspiring to the creation of meaningful new ideas, forms, and methods." Has published *The Distance of Ducks* by Louis Bourgeois, *Spectator Turns Witness* by George Karos, and *The Crown of Affinity* by Laura Qa. Publishes 3-4 chapbooks/year. Chapbooks are usually 64 pages, offset-printed on trade paper, perfect-bound.

HOW TO CONTACT Submit up to 5 poems at a time with SASE. Considers previously published poems and simultaneous submissions. Cover letter with brief bio is preferred. **Reading fee: $5 for poetry and short fiction, $10 for novels.** Make checks or money orders payable to Red Dragon Press. Time between acceptance and publication is 8 months. "Poems are selected for consideration by the publisher, then circulated to senior editor and/or poets previously published for comment. Poems are returned to the publisher for further action, i.e., rejection or acceptance for publication in an anthology or book by a single author. Frequently, submission of additional works is required before final offer is made, especially in the process for a book by a single author." Often comments on rejected poems. Responds to queries in 10 weeks, to mss in one year. Purchase sample books at bookstores, or mail-order direct from Red Dragon Press at the above address.

⊘ RED HEN PRESS

(818)831-0649. Fax: (818)831-6659. E-mail: redhenpressbooks.com. Website: www.redhen.org. **Contact:** Mark E. Cull, publisher/editor (fiction).

The mission of Red Hen Press is to discover, publish, and promote works of literary excellence that have been overlooked by mainstream presses, and to build audiences for literature in two ways: by fostering the literacy of youth and by bringing distinguished and emerging writers to the public stage.

HOW TO CONTACT *Red Hen Press is not currently accepting unsolicited material.* At this time, the best opportunity to be published by Red Hen is by entering one of our contests. Please find more information in our award submission guidelines.

CONTEST/AWARD OFFERINGS The Benjamin Saltman Award is awarded annually for the best poetry book collection. Submit 48 to 96 pages of poetry. Postmark deadline is August 31. $25 entry fee. SASE for notification only. Please include name, address, title, email address, and telephone number on cover sheet only. Award: $3,000 and publication of collection.

TIPS "Audience reads poetry, literary fiction, intelligent nonfiction. If you have an agent, we may be too small since we don't pay advances. Write well. Send queries first. Be willing to help promote your own book."

⊘ RED MOON PRESS

P.O. Box 2461, Winchester VA 22604-1661. (540)722-2156. E-mail: jim.kacian@redmoonpress.com. Website: www.redmoonpress.com. **Contact:** Jim Kacian, editor/publisher.

NEEDS Red Moon Press "is the largest and most prestigious publisher of English-language haiku and related work in the world." Publishes 6-8 volumes/year, usually 3-5 anthologies and individual collections of English-language haiku, as well as 1-3 books of essays, translations, or criticism of haiku. Under other imprints, the press also publishes chapbooks of various sizes and formats.

HOW TO CONTACT Query with book theme and information, and 30-40 poems or draft of first chapter. Responds to queries in 2 weeks, to mss (if invited) in 3 months. "Each contract separately negotiated."

○ RONSDALE PRESS

(604)738-4688. Fax: (604)731-4548. E-mail: ronsdale@shaw.ca. Website: http://ronsdalepress.com. **Contact:** Ronald B. Hatch, director (fiction, poetry, social commentary); Veronica Hatch, managing director (children's literature). Canadian authors only. Ronsdale publishes fiction, poetry, regional history, biography and autobiography, books of ideas about Canada, as well as young adult historical fiction.

NEEDS Publishes 3 flat-spined paperbacks of poetry per year—**by Canadian poets only**—classical to experimental. "Ronsdale looks for poetry manuscripts that show the writer reads and is familiar with the work of some of the major contemporary poets. It's also essential that you have published some poems in literary magazines. We have never published a book of poetry when the author has not already published a goodly number in magazines." Has published *Return to Open Water* by Harold Rhenisch, *Mother Time* by Joanne Arnott, *Cobalt 3* by Kevin Roberts, *Poems for a New World* by Connie Fife, *Steveston* by Daphne Marlatt, and *After Ted & Sylvia* by Crystal Hurdle.

HOW TO CONTACT Query first, with a few sample poems and cover letter with brief bio and publication credits. Considers previously published poems and simultaneous submissions. Often comments on rejected poems. Responds to queries in 2 weeks, to mss in 2 months. Pays 10% royalties and 10 author's copies. Write for catalog to purchase sample books.

TIPS "Ronsdale Press is a literary publishing house, based in Vancouver, and dedicated to publishing books from across Canada, books that give Canadians new insights into themselves and their country. We aim to publish the best Canadian writers."

ROSE ALLEY PRESS

4203 Brooklyn Ave. NE, #103A, Seattle WA 98105-5911. (206)633-2725. E-mail: rosealleypress@juno. com. Website: www.rosealleypress.com. **Contact:** David Horowitz. 4203 Brooklyn Ave. NE, #103A, Seattle, WA 98105-5911. (206)633-2725. E-mail: rosealleypress@juno.com. Website:www.rosealleypress. com. **Contact:** David Horowitz.

○ "Rose Alley Press does not consider unsolicited manuscripts."

HOW TO CONTACT "Rose Alley Press does not consider unsolicited manuscripts."

⊘⊗ SAM'S DOT PUBLISHING

P.O. Box 782, Cedar Rapids IA 52406-0782. E-mail: samsdot@samsdotpublishing.com. Website: www. samsdotpublishing.com. **Contact:** Tyree Campbell, managing editor.

NEEDS Sam's Dot Publishing prints collections of scifaiku, horror-ku, and minimalist poetry. Publishes 2-3 chapbooks/year and one anthology/year. Manuscripts are selected through open submission. Chapbooks are 32 pages, offset-printed, saddle-stapled, with cardstock covers.

HOW TO CONTACT Query first, with a few sample poems and a cover letter with brief bio and publication credits, up to 500 words. Chapbook mss may include previously published poems. Responds to queries in 2 weeks; to mss in 4-6 weeks. Pays royalties of 12.5% minimum and 1-2 author's copies (out of a press run of 50-100). Order sample chapbooks by sending $8 to Tyree Campbell/Sam's Dot Publishing.

⊘ SEAWEED SIDESHOW CIRCUS

P.O. Box 234, Jackson WI 53037. E-mail: sscircus@aol. com. Website: www.facebook.com/sscircus. **Contact:** Andrew Wright Milam, editor.

NEEDS Seaweed Sideshow Circus is "a place for young or new poets to publish a chapbook." Has published *Main Street* by Steven Paul Lansky and *The Moon Incident* by Amy McDonald. Publishes one chapbook/year. Chapbooks are usually 30 pages, digest-sized, photocopied, saddle-stapled, with card-stock covers.

HOW TO CONTACT Query first, with 5-10 sample poems and cover letter with brief bio and publications credits. Responds to queries in 6-9 weeks; to mss in 6-9 months. Pays 10 author's copies (out of a press run of 100). Order sample chapbooks by sending $6.

⊖⊘ SECOND AEON PUBLICATIONS

19 Southminster Rd., Roath, Cardiff CF23 5AT, Wales. +44(29)2049-3093. Fax: +44(29)2049-3093. E-mail: peter@peterfinch.co.uk. Website: www.peter-finch.co.uk. **Contact:** Peter Finch, poetry editor. 19 Southminster Rd., Roath, Cardiff CF23 5AT. Wales. +44(29)2049-3093. E-mail: peter@peterfinch.co.uk. Website: www.peterfinch.co.uk. Peter Finch, poetry editor.

○ Does not accept unsolicited mss.

HOW TO CONTACT Does not accept unsolicited mss.

⊕ SPOUT PRESS

P.O. Box 581067, Minneapolis MN 55458. (612) 782-9629. E-mail: spoutpress@hotmail.com; editors@spoutpress.org. Website: www.spoutpress.org. **Contact:** Carrie Eidem, fiction editor.

○ "Small independent publisher with a permanent staff of five—interested in experimental fiction for our magazine and books." Publishes paperback originals. Books: perfect bound; illustrations. Average print order: 1,000. Published 1 debut author within the last year. Distibutes and promotes books through the website, events and large Web-based stores such as Amazon.com. Runs annual. Accepts submissions all year around fall through spring. See website for specific dates and details. Does not accept unsolicited mss. Query with SASE. Accepts queries by mail. Include estimated word count, brief bio, list of publishing credits. Send SASE for return of ms or send a disposable ms and SASE for reply only. Rarely comments on rejected mss. Individual arrangement with author depending on the book.

HOW TO CONTACT Submit via mail with cover letter and SASE.

TIPS "We tend to publish writers after we know their work via publication in our journal, *Spout Maga-zine.*"

⦿⑤ SPS STUDIOS, INC.

P.O. Box 1007, Dept. PM, Boulder CO 80306-1007. E-mail: editorial@spsstudios.com. Website: www. sps.com. **Contact:** Editorial Staff. Publishers of Blue Mountain Arts [PIRg]. Dept. PM, P.O. Box 1007, Boulder CO 80306-1007. Phone/fax: (303)447-0939. E-mail: editorial@spsstudios.com. Website: www.sps. com. Established 1971. **Contact:** editorial staff.SPS Studios publishes greeting cards, books, calendars, prints, and other gift items. Looking for poems, prose, and lyrics ("usually non-rhyming") appropriate for publication on greeting cards and in poetry anthologies. Also actively seeking "book-length manuscripts that would be appropriate for book and gift stores. We are also very interested in receiving book and card ideas that would be appropriate for college stores, as well as younger buyers. Poems should reflect a message, feeling, or sentiment that one person would want to share with another. We'd like to receive creative, original submissions about love relationships, family members, friendships, philosophies, and any other aspect of life. Poems and writings for specific holidays (Christmas, Valentine's Day, etc.) and special occasions, such as graduation, anniversary, and get well are also considered. Only a small portion of the material we receive is selected each year and the review process can be lengthy, but be assured every ms is given serious consideration." Submissions must be typewritten, one poem/page or sent by e-mail (no attachments). Include SASE. Simultaneous submissions "discouraged but okay with notification." Accepts fax and e-mail (pasted into body of message) submissions. Submit seasonal material at least 4 months in advance.

NEEDS SPS Studios publishes greeting cards, books, calendars, prints, and other gift items. Looking for poems, prose, and lyrics ("usually non-rhyming") appropriate for publication on greeting cards and in poetry anthologies. Also actively seeking "book-length manuscripts that would be appropriate for book and gift stores. We are also very interested in receiving book and card ideas that would be appropriate for college stores, as well as younger buyers. Poems should reflect a message, feeling, or sentiment that one person would want to share with another. We'd like to receive creative, original submissions about love relationships, family members, friendships, philosophies, and any other aspect of life. Poems and writings for specific holidays (Christmas, Valentine's Day, etc.) and special occasions, such as graduation, anniversary, and get well are also considered. Only a small portion of the material we receive is selected each year and the review process can be lengthy, but be assured every manuscript is given serious consideration."

HOW TO CONTACT Submissions must be typewritten, one poem/page or sent by e-mail (no attachments). Include SASE. Simultaneous submissions "discouraged but okay with notification." Accepts fax and e-mail (pasted into body of message) submissions. Submit seasonal material at least 4 months in advance. Guidelines available for SASE or by e-mail. Responds in up to 6 months. Pays $300/poem, all rights for each of the first 2 submissions chosen for publication (after which payment scale escalates), for the worldwide, exclusive right, $50/poem for one-time use in an anthology.

CONTEST/AWARD OFFERINGS SPS Studios sponsors Biannual Poetry Card Contest.

⦿ STEEL TOE BOOKS

Department of English, Western Kentucky University, 1906 College Heights Blvd. #11086, Bowling Green KY 42101-1086. (270)745-5769. E-mail: tom.hunley@wku. edu. Website: www.steeltoebooks.com. **Contact:** Dr. Tom C. Hunley, director. Estab. 2003.

NEEDS Steel Toe Books publishes "full-length, single-author poetry collections. Our books are professionally designed and printed. We look for workmanship (economical use of language, high-energy verbs, precise literal descriptions, original figurative language, poems carefully arranged as a book); a unique style and/or a distinctive voice; clarity; emotional impact; humor (word plays, hyperbole, comic timing); performability (a Steel Toe poet is at home on the stage as well as on the page)." Does not want "dry verse, purposely obscure language, poetry by people who are so wary of being called 'sentimental' they steer away from any recognizable human emotions, poetry that takes itself so seriously that it's unintentionally funny." Has published poetry by Allison Joseph, Susan Browne, James Doyle, Martha Silano, Mary Biddinger, John Guzlowski, Jeannine Hall Gailey, and others. Publishes 1-3 poetry books/year. Manuscripts are normally selected through open submission.

HOW TO CONTACT "Check the website for news about our next open reading period." Book mss may include previously published poems. Responds to mss in 3 months. Pays $500 advance on 10% royalties and 10 author's copies. Order sample books by sending $12 to Steel Toe Books. *Must purchase a manuscript in order to submit*. See website for submission guidelines.

SWAN SCYTHE PRESS

515 P Street, #804, Sacramento CA 95814. E-mail: jimzbookz@yahoo.com. Website: www.swanscythe.com. **Contact:** James DenBoer, editor.

○ Swan Scythe Press has been awarded a California Arts Council Multicultural Entry Grant and a Fideicomiso para la Cultura Mexico-EUA/US-Mexico Fund for Culture Grant.

NEEDS "After publishing 25 chapbooks, a few full-sized poetry collections,and 1 anthology, then taking a short break from publishing, Swan Scythe Press is now re-launching its efforts with some new books, under a new editorship, in 2010. Our annual contest winner will be named in late June 2010. Our 2011 Chapbook contest is now underway; Deadline June 1, 2011. We have also begun a new series of books, called Poetas/Puentes, from emerging poets writing in Spanish, translated into English. We will also consider manuscripts in indigenous languages from North, Central and South America, translated into English. Has published poetry by Emmy Perez, Maria Melendez, John Olivares Espinoza, Karen An-hwei Lee, Pos Moua, and Walter Pavlich. Order books/chapbooks by using paypal at the Swan Scythe Press or order through website.

HOW TO CONTACT Query first before submitting a manuscript via email or through website.

◐ TARPAULIN SKY PRESS

P.O. Box 189, Grafton VT 05146. E-mail: editors@tarpaulinsky.com. Website: www.tarpaulinsky.com. **Contact:** Colie Collen, editor-in-chief.

NEEDS Tarpaulin Sky Press publishes cross- and trans-genre works as well as innovative poetry and prose. Produces full-length books and chapbooks, hand-bound books and trade paperbacks, and offers both hand-bound and perfect-bound paperback editions of full-length books. "We're a small, author-centered press endeavoring to create books that, as objects, please our authors as much their texts please us." Has published books and chapbooks by Jenny Boully, Danielle Dutton, Joyelle McSweeney, Chad Sweeney, Andrew Michael Roberts, and Max Winter, as well as a collaborative book by Noah Eli Gordon as Joshua Marie Wilkinson.

HOW TO CONTACT Writers whose work has appeared in or been accepted for publication in *Tarpaulin Sky* (see separate listing in Magazines/Journals) may submit chapbook or full-length manuscripts at any time, with no reading fee. Tarpaulin Sky Press also considers chapbook and full-length manuscripts from writers whose work has not appeared in the journal, but **asks for a $20 reading fee**. Make checks/money orders to Tarpaulin Sky Press. Cover letter is preferred. Reads periods may be found on the website.

∅ TEBOT BACH

P.O. Box 7887, Huntington Beach CA 92615-7887. (714)968-0905. E-mail: info@tebotbach.org. Website: www.tebotbach.org. **Contact:** Mifanwy Kaiser, editor/publisher. Tebot Bach (Welsh for "little teapot") publishes books of poetry. Has published *One Breath*, by Catharine Clark-Sayles, *Monkey Journal*, by Holly Prado; *Swagger and Remorse* by Richard Fox; *The Habit of Buenos Aires*, by Lorraine Healy; *In a Pasture With Palominos*, by Joan Stepp Smith; *Steady, My Gaze*, by Marie-Elizabeth Mali; *A Cafe in Boca*, by Sam Periera; *God, Seed*, by Rebecca Foust and Lorna Stevens.

○ Query first via e-mail, with a few sample poems and cover letter with brief bio. Include SASE. Write to order sample books. Sponsors The Patricia Bibby First Book Award (see separate listing in Contests & Awards). An anthology of California poets. Must be current or former resident of California in order to submit, but no focus or theme required for poetry. Query first. Submit up to 6 poems with "California Anthology" written on lower left corner of envelope. Accepts submissions by e-mail (pasted into body of message or as attachment in Word). Deadline for submission is in August of the year call for submissions is announced. Please check the website for calls for submissions. Also publishes *Spillway: A Literary Journal* (see separate listing in Magazines/Journals).

HOW TO CONTACT Query first via e-mail, with a few sample poems and cover letter with brief bio. Responds to queries and mss, if invited, in 3 months. Time between acceptance and publication is up to 2 years. We recommend that you order a sample copy from our online catalogue.

CONTEST/AWARD OFFERINGS The Patricia Bibby First Book Award.

⊘ TEXAS TECH UNIVERSITY PRESS

(Specialized: series), P.O. Box 41037, Lubbock TX 79409-1037. (806)742-2982. Fax: (806)742-2979. E-mail: ttup@ttu.edu. Website: www.ttupress.org. Established 1971. **Contact:** Judith Keeling, editor-in-chief. Director: Robert Mandel.

💬 Does not read unsolicited manuscripts.

● THE JOHNS HOPKINS UNIVERSITY PRESS

2715 N. Charles St., Baltimore MD 21218. (410)516-6900. Fax: (410)516-6968. E-mail: jmm@press.jhu.edu. Website: www.press.jhu.edu. **Contact:** Jacqueline C. Wehmueller, executive editor (consumer health, psychology and psychiatry, and history of medicine; jcw@press.jhu.edu); Matthew McAdam, editor (mxm@jhu@press.edu); Robert J. Brugger, senior acquisitions editor (American history; rjb@press.jhu.edu); Vincent J. Burke, exec. editor (biology; vjb@press.jhu.edu); Juliana McCarthy, acquisitions editor (humanities, classics, and ancient studies; jmm@press.jhu.edu); Ashleigh McKown, assistant editor (higher education, history of technology, history of science; aem@press.jhu.edu); Suzanne Flinchbaugh, Associate Editor (Political Science, Health Policy, and Co-Publishing Liaison; skf@press.jhu.edu; Greg Nicholl, Assistant Editor (Regional Books, Poetry and Fiction, and Anabaptist and Pietist Studies; gan@press.jhu.edu).

NEEDS "One of the largest American university presses, Johns Hopkins publishes primarily scholarly books and journals. We do, however, publish short fiction and poetry in the series Johns Hopkins: Poetry and Fiction, edited by John Irwin."

☯ TIGHTROPE BOOKS

602 Markham St., Toronto ON M6G 2L8, Canada. (647)348-4460. E-mail: shirarose@tightropebooks.com. Website: www.tightropebooks.com. **Contact:** Shirarose Wilensky, editor.

TIPS "Audience is young, urban, literary, educated, unconventional."

⊘⑤ TIMBERLINE PRESS

5710 S. Kimbark #3, Chicago IL 60637-1615. E-mail: steven_schroeder@earthlink.net. Website: http://vacpoetry.org/timberline/.

NEEDS "We publish limited letterpress editions with the goal of blending strong poetry with well-crafted and designed printing. We lean toward natural history or strongly imagistic nature poetry but will look at any good work. Also, good humorous poetry." Has published *Stark Beauty* by Larry D. Thomas, *Menagerie* by William Heyen, *Crossing Crocker Township* by Robert Tremmel, and *The Body of Water* by Walter Bargen. Sample copies may be obtained by sending $7.50, requesting sample copy, and noting you saw the listing in *Poet's Market*. Responds in less than one month. Pays "50-50 split with author after Timberline Press has recovered its expenses."

HOW TO CONTACT Query before submitting full ms.

TOKYO ROSE RECORDS/ CHAPULTEPEC PRESS

4222 Chambers, Cincinnati OH 45223. E-mail: chapultepecpress@hotmail.com. Website: www.TokyoRoseRecords.com. Established 2001. **Contact:** David Garza.

NEEDS Chapultepec Press publishes books of poetry/literature, essays, social/political issues, art, music, film, history, popular science; library/archive issues, and bilingual works. Wants "poetry that works as a unit, that is caustic, fun, open-ended, worldly, mature, relevant, stirring, evocative. Bilingual. Looking for authors who have a publishing history. No poetry collections without a purpose, that are mere collections. Also looking for broadsides/posters/illuminations." Publishes 1-2 books/year. Books are usually 1-100 pages.

HOW TO CONTACT Query first with a few sample poems, or a complete ms, and a cover letter with brief bio and publication credits. Pays 50% of profits and author's copies. Order sample books by sending $5 payable to David Garza.

TIPS Tokyo Rose Records/Chapultepec Press specializes in shorter-length publications (100 pages or less). Order sample books by sending $5 payable to David Garza.

TUPELO PRESS

P.O. Box 1767, North Adams MA 01247. (413)664-9611. E-mail: publisher@tupelopress.org. E-mail: www.tupelopress.org/submissions. Website: www.tupelopress.org. **Charges a $45 reading fee.** "We're an independent nonprofit literary press. Also sponsor these upcoming competitions: Dorset Prize: $10,000.

Entries must be postmarked between September 1 and December 31, 2011. Guidelines are online; Snowbound Series chapbook Award: $1,000 and 50 copies of chapbook. See website for submission period and guidelines. Every July we have Open Submissions. We accept book-length poetry, poetry collections (48 + pages), short story collections, novellas, literary non-fiction/memoirs and up to 80 pages of a novel. We're an independent nonprofit literary press. Also sponsor these upcoming competitions: Dorset Prize: $10,000. Entries must be postmarked between September 1 and December 31, 2011. Guidelines are online; Snowbound Series chapbook Award: $1,000 and 50 copies of chapbook. See website for submission period and guidelines. Every July we have Open Submissions. We accept book-length poetry, poetry collections (48 + pages), short story collections, novellas, literary non-fiction/memoirs and up to 80 pages of a novel."

○ **Charges a $45 reading fee.**

HOW TO CONTACT Submit complete ms of 48-90 pages through online submission or via mail during open submissions period in July. Please include the reading fee $25 and SASE for response.

⊕ THE UNIVERSITY OF AKRON PRESS

(330)972-5342. Fax: (330)972-8364. E-mail: uapress@uakron.edu. Website: www.uakron.edu/uapress. **Contact:** Thomas Bacher, Director and Acquisitions. "The University of Akron Press is the publishing arm of The University of Akron and is dedicated to the dissemination of scholarly, professional, and regional books and other content."

NEEDS "We publish two books of poetry annually, one of which is the winner of The Akron Poetry prize. We also are interested in literary collections based around one theme, especially collections of translated works."

HOW TO CONTACT If you are interested in publishing with The University of Akron Press, please fill out form online.

⊗ UNIVERSITY OF NEW MEXICO PRESS

(505)277-3324 or (800)249-7737. Fax: (505)277-3343. E-mail: clark@unm.edu. E-mail: wcwhiteh@unm.edu. Website: www.unmpress.com. **Contact:** W. Clark Whitehorn, Editor-in-Chief. "The Press is well known as a publisher in the fields of anthropology, archeology, Latin American studies, art and photography, architecture and the history and culture of the American West, fiction, some poetry, Chicano/a

studies and works by and about American Indians. We focus on American West, Southwest and Latin American regions."

⊕ VANHOOK HOUSE

925 Orchard St., Charleston WV 25302. E-mail: editor@vanhookhouse.com. E-mail: acquisitions@vanhookhouse.com. Website: www.vanhookhouse.com. **Contact:** Jim Whyte, acquisitions, all fiction/true crime/military/war.

○ "We employ the expertise of individuals qualified to review works falling within their field of study. Be sure of all sources and facts, as VanHook House *will* confirm any and all information. All editing is done in a way to ensure the author's voice remains unchanged."

NEEDS "VanHook House is a small press focused on the talents of new, unpublished authors. We are looking for works of fiction and non-fiction to add to our catalog. No erotica or sci-fi, please. Query via e-mail. Queries accepted ONLY during submissions periods."

HOW TO CONTACT "A collection MUST contain 200 individual poems to be considered." Query; submit 3 sample poems. Receives 20 mss/year. Pays authors 8-10% royalty on wholesale price. Advance negotiable. Time between acceptance and publication is 6 months. Responds in 1 month to queries; 2 months toproposals; 3 months to mss. Book catalog and guidelines free on request and available online at website.

TIPS "Visit our website."

◎ VÉHICULE PRESS

Box 125, Place du Parc Station, Montreal QC H2X 4A3, Canada. (514)844-6073. Fax: (514)844-7543. E-mail: vp@vehiculepress.com. Website: www.vehiculepress.com. **Contact:** Simon Dardick, president/publisher. (Specialized: work by Canadian poets only)"Montreal's Véhicule Press has published the best of Canadian and Quebec literature-fiction, poetry, essays, translations, and social history."

○ Mostly Canadian authors.

NEEDS Vehicule Press is a "literary press with a poetry series, Signal Editions, publishing the work of Canadian poets only." Publishes flat-spined paperbacks. Has published *The Empire's Missing Links* by Walid Bitar, *36 Cornelian Avenue* by Christopher Wiseman, and *Morning Gothic* by George Ellenbogen. Publishes

Canadian poetry that is "first-rate, original, content-conscious."

HOW TO CONTACT Query before submitting.

TIPS "Quality in almost any style is acceptable. We believe in the editing process."

⊘ ❸ WAKE FOREST UNIVERSITY PRESS

(Specialized: poetry by native Irish poets), P.O. Box 7333, Winston-Salem NC 27109. (336)758-5448. Fax: (336)758-5636. E-mail: wfupress@wfu.edu. Website: www.wfu.edu/wfupress. Established 1976. **Contact:** Jefferson Holdridge, director/poetry editor. Advisory Editor: Dillon Johnston.

NEEDS "We publish only poetry from Ireland. I am able to consider only poetry written by native Irish poets. I must return, unread, poetry from American poets." Has published *Collected Poems* by John Montague; *Ghost Orchid* by Michael Longley; *Selected Poems* by Medbh McGuckian; and *The Wake Forest Book of Irish Women's Poetry.*

HOW TO CONTACT Query with 4-5 samples and cover letter. No simultaneous submissions. Responds to queries in 1-2 weeks, to submissions (*if invited*) in 2-3 months. Sometimes sends prepublication galleys. Publishes on 10% royalty contract with negotiable advance, 6-8 author's copies. Buys North American or U.S. rights.

⊙ ❸ WASHINGTON WRITERS' PUBLISHING HOUSE

C/O Brandel France de Bravo, 3541 S. Street, NW, Washington DC 20007. E-mail: wwphpress@gmail.com. Website: www.washingtonwriters.org. **Contact:** Patrick Pepper, president.

 ○ Individual books by WWPH authors have been nominated for and/or won many awards, e.g. the Towson University Prize.

NEEDS Washington Writers' Publishing House publishes books by Washington, D.C.- and Baltimore-area poets through its annual book competition. "No specific criteria, except literary excellence." Has published books by Holly Karapetkova, Jehanne Dubrow, Brandel France de Bravo, Carly Sachs, Bruce MacKinnon, Piotr Gwiazda, Patric Pepper, Mary Ann Larkin, Moira Egan, Bernard jankowski, Kim Roberts, Sid Gold, Jane Satterfield, Ned Balbo, Jean Nordhaus, Grace Cavalieri, E.ethelbert Miller, and Gray Jacobik. Publishes 1-2 poetry books/year.

HOW TO CONTACT Washington Writers' Publishing House considers book-length mss for publication by poets living within 60 driving miles of the U.S. Capitol (Baltimore area included) through competition only (see below).

CONTEST/AWARD OFFERINGS Offers $500 and 50 copies of published book plus additional copies for publicity use. Manuscripts may include previously published poems. Submit 2 copies of a poetry ms of 50-60 pages, single-spaced (poet's name should not appear on ms pages). Include separate page of publication acknowledgments plus 2 cover sheets: one with ms title, poet's name, address, telephone number, and e-mail address, the other with ms title only. Include SASE for results only; mss will not be returned (will be recycled). Guidelines available for SASE or on website. "Author should indicate where they heard about WWPH." **Entry fee:** $20. **Deadline:** July 1-November 1 (postmark). Order sample books on website or by sending $12 plus $3 s&h to Washington Writers' Publishing House, P.O. Box 15271, Washington DC 20003.

⊘ WHITE EAGLE COFFEE STORE PRESS

P.O. Box 383, Fox River Grove IL 60021-0383. E-mail: WECSPress@aol.com. Website: whiteeagle-coffeestorepress.com. **Contact:** Frank Edmund Smith, Publisher. White Eagle is a small press publishing 2-3 chapbooks/year. "Alternate chapbooks are published by invitation and by competition. Author published by invitation becomes judge for next competition." Wants "any kind of poetry. No censorship at this press. Literary values are the only standard." Does not want "sentimental or didactic writing." Has published poetry by Timothy Russell, Connie Donovan, Scott Lumbard, Linda Lee Harper, Scott Beal, Katie Kingston, and Brian Brodeur. Sample: $6.95. *Regular submissions by invitation only.*

HOW TO CONTACT No e-mail submissions. Include SASE for results only; mss will not be returned. Guidelines available for SASE or on website.

TIPS "Poetry is about a passion for language. That's what we're about. We'd like to provide an opportunity for poets of any age who are fairly early in their careers to publish something substantial. We're excited by the enthusiasm shown for this press and by the extraordinary quality of the writing we've received."

WOODLEY MEMORIAL PRESS

English Dept., Washburn University, Topeka KS 66621. E-mail: karen.barron@washburn.edu. Web-

site: www.washburn.edu/reference/woodley-press.
Contact: Kevin Rabas, Acquisitions Editor.
NEEDS Woodley Memorial Press publishes 1-4 perfect-bound paperbacks/year, "most being collections from Kansas or with Kansas connections. Terms are individually arranged with author on acceptance of manuscript." Has published *Sunflower Sinner* by Cynthia Dennis, *Thailand Journal* by Denise Low, and *Kansas Poems of William Stafford.*

Sample books may be ordered from Woodley Memorial Press.
HOW TO CONTACT Guidelines available on website. Responds to queries in 2 weeks; to mss in 6 months. Time between acceptance and publication is 1 year.
TIPS "We only publish one to three works of fiction a year, on average, and those will definitely have a Kansas connection. We seek authors who are dedicated to promoting their works."

CONTESTS & AWARDS

This section contains a wide array of poetry competitions and literary awards. These range from state poetry society contests (with a number of modest monetary prizes) to prestigious honors bestowed by private foundations, elite publishers and renowned university programs. Because these listings reflect such a variety of skill levels and degrees of competitiveness, it's important to read each carefully and note its unique requirements. *Never* enter a contest without consulting the guidelines and following directions to the letter (including manuscript formatting, number of lines or pages of poetry accepted, amount of entry fee, entry forms needed and other details).

IMPORTANT NOTE: As we gathered information for this edition of *Poet's Market*, we found that some competitions hadn't yet established their 2012 fees and deadlines. In such cases, we list the most recent information available as a general guide. Always consult current guidelines for updates before entering any competition.

WHERE TO ENTER?

While it's perfectly okay to "think big," being realistic may improve your chances of winning a prize for your poetry. Many of the listings in the Contests & Awards section begin with symbols that reflect their level of difficulty:

CONTESTS IDEAL FOR BEGINNERS AND UNPUBLISHED POETS are coded with the **O** icon. That's not to say these contests won't be highly competitive—there may be a large number of entries. However, you may find these entries are more on a level with your own, increasing your chances of being "in the running" for a prize. Don't assume these contests reward low quality, though. If you submit less than your best work, you're wasting your time and money (in postage and entry fees).

CONTESTS FOR POETS WITH MORE EXPERIENCE are coded with the ◑ icon. Beginner/unpublished poets are usually still welcome to enter, but the competition is keener here. Your work may be judged against that of widely published, prize-winning poets, so consider carefully whether you're ready for this level of competition. (Of course, nothing ventured, nothing gained—but those entry fees do add up.)

CONTESTS FOR ACCOMPLISHED POETS are coded with the ● icon. These may have stricter entry requirements, higher entry fees and other conditions that signal these programs are not intended to be "wide open" to all poets.

SPECIALIZED CONTESTS are coded with the ◉ icon. These may include regional contests; awards for poetry written in a certain form or in the style of a certain poet; contests for women, gay/lesbian, ethnic, or age-specific poets (for instance, children or older adults); contests for translated poetry only; and many others.

There are also symbols that give additional information about contests. The ⊕ icon indicates the contest is newly established and new to *Poet's Market*; the ↻ icon identifies a Canadian contest or award and the ◑ icon an international listing. Sometimes Canadian and international contests require that entrants live in certain countries, so pay attention when you see these icons.

WHAT ABOUT ENTRY FEES?

Most contests charge entry fees, and these are usually quite legitimate. The funds are used to cover expenses such as paying the judges, putting up prize monies, printing prize editions of magazines and journals, and promoting the contest through mailings and ads. If you're concerned about a poetry contest or other publishing opportunity, see "Is It a 'Con'?" for advice on some of the more questionable practices in the poetry world.

OTHER RESOURCES Widen your search for contests beyond those listed in *Poet's Market*. Many Internet writer's sites have late-breaking announcements about competitions old and new. Often these sites offer free electronic newsletter subscriptions, sending valuable information right to your e-mail inbox.

The writer's magazines at your local bookstore regularly include listings for upcoming contests, as well as deadlines for artist's grants at the state and national level. The Association of Writers & Writing Programs (AWP) is a valuable resource, including its publication, *Writer's Chronicle*. State poetry societies are listed throughout this book; they offer many contests, as well as helpful information for poets (and mutual support). To find a specific group, search the General Index for listings under your state's name or look under "poetry society" or "society."

Don't overlook your local connections. City and community newspapers, radio and TV announcements, bookstore newsletters and bulletin boards, and your public library can be terrific resources for competition news, especially regarding regional contests.

◐ ⊖ THE 46ER PRIZE FOR POETRY

8405 Bay Parkway, C8, Brooklyn NY 11214. E-mail: editors@theadirondackreview.com; angela@black-lawrencepress.com. Website: www.theadirondack-review.com/46erPrize.html. With Black Lawrence Press, *The Adirondack Review* (see separate listing in Magazines/Journals) offers the 46er Prize for Poetry, to be awarded once each year for a previously unpublished poem. Winner receives $400 and publication in *The Adirondack Review*. Honorable Mention poems will also be published and receive an honorarium of $30. Considers simultaneous submissions if notified immediately of acceptance elsewhere. Submit up to 3 original poems, unpublished in either print or on-line publications. Submissions should be sent to angela@blacklawrencepress.com with poet's name, address, phone number, and e-mail address included. E-mail should be titled 46er PRIZE SUBMISSION in subject line; poems must be pasted into body of message. Guidelines available by e-mail or on website. **ENTRY FEE:** $5 for 1 poem, $8 for 2 poems, $10 for 3 poems. Make payment through website via PayPal. **DEADLINE:** December 31. Winners announced during the summer. Judges: The Adirondack Review editors.

ABZ PRESS FIRST BOOK POETRY PRIZE

P.O. Box 2746, Huntingon WV 25727-2746. E-mail: editorial@abzpress.com. Website: abzpress.com. There is no First Book Poetry Prize contest in 2011. The next contest will be in 2012. Wants poetry manuscripts between 48-80 pages. "Each manuscript must be bound only with a binder clip. Include a table of contents, acknowledgements, and two title pages. One title page should have only the title. The second title page should have the author's name, address, phone number with area code, and e-mail address. Please indicate any poetry books or chapbooks (with fewer than 48 pages) you may have published. Simultaneous submissions are OK with us. Include SASE to receive notice of contest winner. Let us know if you win another prize." Winner will receive $1000 and 50 free copies of the winning book. Guidelines available on website. Entry fee: $30; includes one copy of winning book.

ALLEN GINSBERG POETRY AWARDS

(973)684-6555. Fax: (973)523-6085. E-mail: mgillan@pccc.edu. Website: www.pccc.edu/poetry. **CONTACT:** Maria Mazziotti Gillan, exec. director. The Allen Ginsberg Poetry Awards offer annual prizes of 1st Prize: $1,000, 2nd Prize: $200, and 3rd Prize: $100. All winning poems, honorable mentions, and editor's choice poems will be published in Paterson Literary Review (see separate listing in Magazines/Journals). Winners will be asked to participate in a reading that will be held in the Paterson Historic District. Submissions must be unpublished. Submit up to 5 poems (no poem more than 2 pages long). Send 4 copies of each poem entered. Include cover sheet with poet's name, address, phone number, e-mail address and poem titles. Poet's name should not appear on poems. Include SASE for results only; poems will not be returned. Guidelines available for SASE or on website. **ENTRY FEE:** $18 (includes subscription to Paterson Literary Review). Write "poetry contest" in memo section of check and make payable to PCCC. **DEADLINE:** April 1 (postmark). Winners will be announced the following summer by mail and in newspaper announcements. 2010 winners Rafaella Del Bourgo and Kathleen Spivack (1st), Joyce Madelon Winslow and Francine Witte (2nd), and Kim Farrar (3rd).

◐ ⊖ ANABIOSIS PRESS CHAPBOOK CONTEST

(978)469-7085. E-mail: rsmyth@anabiosispress.org. Website: www.anabiosispress.org. **CONTACT:** Richard Smyth, editor. The Anabiosis Press Chapbook Contest offers $100 plus publication of the winning chapbook and 75 copies of the first run. Submit 16-20 pages of poetry on any subject. Include separate pages with a biography, table of contents, and acknowledgments for any previous publications. Include SASE with correct postage for return of ms. **ENTRY FEE:** $12 (all entrants receive a copy of the winning chapbook). Make checks payable to The Anabiosis Press. **DEADLINE:** June 30 (postmark). Winners announced by September 30. 2010 winner was Gaylord Brewer (Ghost).

ANNUAL BOOK COMPETITION

E-mail: wwphpress@gmail.com. Website: http://www.washingtonwriters.org. Poets living within 60 driving miles of the Capitol (Baltimore area included) are invited to submit 2 copies of a poetry ms (60-80 pages, single or 1-1/2 spaced), a reading fee of $20.00, and a SASE reply envelope. Mss will not be returned; rather they will be recycled. Guidelines: Author's name should not appear on the ms. The title page of each copy should contain the title only. Provide name, address, phone number, e-mail address, and title on a separate cover sheet accompanying the submission. A separate page for acknowledgments may be included for poems previously published in journals and anthologies. Mail poetry manuscripts to: Washington Writers' Publishing House C/O Brandel France de Bravo 3541 S Street, N.W. Washington, D.C. 20007.

ANNUAL VENTURA COUNTY WRITERS CLUB POETRY CONTEST WITH TWO DIVISIONS FOR YOUNG POETS

(805)524-6970. E-mail: kathleen@kathleenkaiser.com. E-mail: venturacountywriters@yahoo.com. **CONTACT:** Katherine Kaiser. Contest includes two youth categories for poets under 18. Division A is open to entrants ages 13 to 18. Division B is open to poets ages 12 and under. Poets 18 and older are invited to enter in the Adult category. The contest is open to poets throughout the country and does accept international entries. "This contest enriches the culture of our community and supports our poets," states Melissa Grossman, contest chair. "Poetry is alive in Ventura County! We must do all we can to nurture new poets and promote established writers." All winning poems will be published in the club's newsletter, *The Write Stuff,* and the winning poets will be invited to recite their works at the April club meeting. All winners and families will be honored at a reception following the readings. The winning poems will appear in the next volume of the club's anthology, to be published in 2012. There will be additional publicity for the winners to help promote their winning works. "Last year we divided the youth category into two parts and received an outstanding response from many area schools," commented club president Lee Wade. "Inspiring a new generation to embrace poetry and other forms of written communication goes to the core of VCWC's mission, to encourage the craft." Full details and rules are available for download from the club's website http://www.venturacountywriters. com Categories and Fees: Adult Category: $4.00 per poem for VCWC members, $5.00 per poem for others. Youth Categories - $3.00 per poem. Entry fees cannot be accepted online at this time. For both print and electronic entries, checks should be made payable to Ventura County Writers Club or VCWC and mail to: Ventura County Writers Club Poetry Contest, P. O. Box 3373 Thousand Oaks, CA 91362. Enter as many poems as you like. No poems that have been previously published in any form (including digital) are to be entered. Include a separate cover sheet with name, address, phone number, title(s) of submitted poem(s), with the category and division in which they are entered. Do not place your name or any other identification on the poem pages. This is to ensure authors are not identified during the judging process. Include a separate cover sheet with name, address, phone number, titles of submitted poems, with the category and division in which they are entered. For print submissions, submit one poem per page using Times New Roman 12 point type on white 8 1/2 X 11 inch paper. Send two copies of each poem. Submissions must be postmarked no later than February 28, 2011. For electronic submissions, email VenturaCountyWriters@ yahoo.com with 'Poetry Contest' in the subject line. Send one poem per attachment. Send cover sheet in separate attachment with information as shown above. Include a cover sheet copy with your entry fee(s). For more information, contact Kathleen Kaiser, 805-524-6970, Kathleen@KathleenKaiser.com.

A. POULIN, JR. POETRY PRIZE

BOA Editions, Ltd., 250 N. Goodman St., Suite 306, Rochester NY 14607. E-mail: conners@boaeditions. org. Website: www.boaeditions.org. Established 1976. **CONTACT:** Peter Conners, editor. BOA Editions, Ltd. (see separate listing in Book/Chapbook Publishers) sponsors the annual A. Poulin, Jr. Poetry Prize for a poet's first book. Awards $1,500 honorarium, paid in March 2012, and book publication in March, 2013 in the A. Poulin, Jr. New Poets of America Series. Entrants must be a citizen or legal resident of the US. Poets, who are at least 18 years of age, who have yet to publish a full length book collection of poetry. Translations are not eligible. Individual poems may have been previously published in magazines, journals, anthologies, chapbooks of 32 pages or less, or self-published books of 46 pages or less, but must be submitted in ms form. Considers simultaneous submissions. Submit 48-100 pages of poetry, paginated consecutively, typed or computer-generated in 11 pt. font. Bind with spring clip (no paperclips). Include cover/title page with poet's name, address, and telephone number. Also include table of contents; list of acknowledgments; and entry form (available for download on website). Multiple entries accepted with separate entry fee for each. No e-mail submissions.

Include SASP for notification of receipt and SASE for results. Mss will not be returned. Guidelines available on website in May. **ENTRY FEE:** $25. **DEADLINE:** submit August 1-November 30 annually. Published books in other genres do not disqualify contestants from entering this contest. Send by first class or priority mail (recommended).

⑤ ARIZONA LITERARY CONTEST & BOOK AWARDS

Website: www.azauthors.com. Arizona Authors Association, 6145 W. Echo Lane, Glendale, AZ 85302. (623)847-9343. E-mail: info@azauthors.com. Website: www.azauthors.com. **CONTACT:** Toby Heathcote, president. Arizona Authors Association sponsors annual literary contest in poetry, short story, essay, unpublished novels, and published books (fiction, nonfiction, and children's literature). Awards publication in *Arizona Literary Magazine*, prizes by Five Star Publications, Inc. and $100 1st Prize, $50 2nd Prize, and $25 3rd Prize in each category. Poetry submissions must be unpublished. Considers simultaneous submissions. Submit any number of poems on any subject up to 42 lines. Entry form and guidelines available on website or for SASE. **ENTRY FEE:** $15/poem. **DEADLINE:** reads submissions January 1-July 1. Competition receives 1,000 entries/year. Recent poetry winners include Dennis Schwesinger and Kelly Nelson. Judges: Arizona authors, editors, and reviewers. Winners announced at an award banquet by November 8.

➕ ART AFFAIR ANNUAL WRITING CONTEST

Art Affair, P.O. Box 54302, Oklahoma City OK 73154. E-mail: artaffair@aol.com. Website: www.shadetreecreations.com. **CONTACT:** Barbara Shepherd. Purpose of contest is to encourage new and established writers and to publicly recognize them for their efforts. Open to any writer or poet. Deadline: Oct. 1 (every year). "Fiction and poems must be unpublished. Multiple entries accepted and may be mailed in the same packet. For (general) Short Story, double-space in 12-point font (put page and word count in upper right-hand corner of first page—5,000 word limit. Include cover page with writer's name, address, phone number, and title of story. For Western Short Story, follow same directions but type 'Western' on cover page. For Poetry, submit original poems on any subject, in any style, no more than 60 lines (put line count in the upper right-hand corner of first page). Include cover page with poet's name, address, phone number, and title. Do not include SASE; mss will not be returned." $3/each poem. Make check payable to Art Affair. Poetry: 1st Prize: $40; 2nd Prize: $25; 3rd Prize: $15. (All winners also receive certificates. Additional certificates for Honorable Mentions will be awarded at discretion of the judges). Winners' list will be published on our website in Dec. Highly-qualified and professional judges—different each year (blind judging).

TIPS "Guidelines and entry forms available for SASE and on website."

◑⑤ ART AFFAIR POETRY CONTEST

P.O. Box 54302, Oklahoma City OK 73154. E-mail: okpoets@aol.com. Website: www.shadetreecreations.com. **CONTACT:** Barbara Shepherd, Acquisitions. The annual Art Affair Poetry Contest offers 1st Prize: $40 and certificate; 2nd Prize: $25 and certificate; and 3rd Prize: $15 and certificate. Honorable Mention certificates will be awarded at the discretion of the judges. Open to any poet. Poems must be unpublished. Multiple entries accepted with entry fee for each and may be mailed in the same packet. Submit original poems on any subject, in any style, no more than 60 lines (put line count in the upper right-hand corner of first page). Include cover page with poet's name, address, phone number, and title of poem. Do not include SASE; poems will not be returned. Guidelines available on website. **DEADLINE:** October 1, 2011 (postmark). **ENTRY FEE:** $3/poem. Make check payable to Art Affair. Winners' list will be published on the Art Affair website in December. 2010 winners were Sally Clark, Moriah Erickson, and Colleen Cleary.

◔ ATLANTIC WRITING COMPETITION FOR UNPUBLISHED MANUSCRIPTS

Writers' Federation of Nova Scotia, 1113 Marginal Rd., Halifax NS B3H 4P7. (902)423-8116. Fax: (902)422-0881. E-mail: director@writers.ns.ca; talk@writers.ns.ca. Website: www.writers.ns.ca. **CONTACT:** Nate Crawford, program coordinator. Full-length books of adult poetry written by Atlantic Canadians, and published as a whole for the first time in the previous calendar year, are eligible. Entrants must be native or resident Atlantic Canadians who have either been born in Newfoundland, Prince Edward Island,

Nova Scotia, or New Brunswick, and spent a substantial portion of their lives living there, or who have lived in one or a combination of these provinces for at least 24 consecutive months prior to entry deadline date. Publishers: Send 4 copies and a letter attesting to the author's status as an Atlantic Canadian and the author's current mailing address and telephone number.poetryDeadline: First Friday in December. Prize: $2,000.

◌ THE BAILEY PRIZE

The Chrysalis Reader, 1745 Gravel Hill Rd., Dillwyn VA 23936. (434)983-3021. Fax: (434)983-1074. E-mail: chrysalis@hovac.com. Website: www.swedenborg. com/chrysalis. **CONTACT:** The Editor. (Specialized: open to upper-level undergraduate & graduate-level writing students) Celebrating more than 25 years of publishing established and emerging writers, *The Chrysalis Reader* offers The Bailey Prize, an annual publishing prize for undergraduate and graduate-level students. *The Chrysalis Reader* published yearly in the fall, is an anthology of poetry, fiction, and nonfiction. Winners will be published in CR (see separate listing in Magazines/Journals), receive 3 copies of the issue, and have their work available online after print publication. The Bailey Prize is open to nominations by instructors of undergraduate and graduate-level courses. Instructors may submit a maximum of 3 nominations from their students' output within one academic year. Nominations may be any combination of previously unpublished poetry (100 lines maximum) or fiction or nonfiction (3,100 words maximum). "We welcome both traditional and experimental writing with an emphasis on insightful writing related to the *Chrysalis Reader's* annual theme. The 2012 theme is "The Marketplace." The 2013 Theme is "Patterns". Submit one copy of each entry with writer's contact information. Include a cover letter and SASE or send via e-mail to chrysalis@hovac.com. No nominated entries will be returned. Guidelines available on website. **ENTRY FEE:** none. **DEADLINE:** All entries must be dated on or before May 1 to be considered for that year's publishing cycle.

BARBARA BRADLEY PRIZE

E-mail: contests@nepoetryclub.org. Website: www. nepoetryclub.org/contests.htm. **CONTACT:** NEPC Contest Coordinator. Lyric poem under 21 lines written by a woman. Contest is free to all full time stu-

dents and paid up members of New England Poetry Club. Only one poem per contest. Annual. Entries should be original unpublished poems in English. Poem should not be entered in any other contest nor have won a previous contest. Poem should be typed and submitted in duplicate with author's name, address and email on one copy only. Label poem with contest name. No entries will be returned. NEPC will not engage in correspondence regarding poems or contest decisions. Entries should be sent by regular mail only. Special Delivery or signature required mail will be returned by the Post Office. Judges are well-known poets and sometimes winners of previous NEPC contests. Deadline is May 31 Submit only in April or May. Prize: $200.

TIPS "Send 2 copies of each entry with your name, address and e-mail on one copy."

⑤ THE BASKERVILLE PUBLISHERS POETRY AWARD & THE BETSY COLQUITT POETRY AWARD

(817)257-6537. Fax: (817)257-6239. E-mail: descant@ tcu.edu. Website: www.descant.tcu.edu. **CONTACT:** Dan Williams and Alex Lemon. "Annual award for an outstanding poem published in an issue of *descant*." Deadline: September - April. $250 for Baskerville Award; $500 for Betsy Colquitt Award. Publication retains copyright, but will transfer it to the author upon request.

●⑤ BINGHAMTON UNIVERSITY MILT KESSLER POETRY BOOK AWARD

Binghamton University Creative Writing Program, P.O. Box 6000, Binghamton NY 13902. (607)777-2713. Fax: (607)777-2408. E-mail: cwpro@binghamton. edu. Website: english.binghamton.edu/cwpro/bookawards/kesslerguidelines.htm. **CONTACT:** Maria Mazziotti Gillan, creative writing program director. Offers annual award of $1,000 for a book of poetry judged best of those published during the previous year. Submit books published that year; do not submit manuscripts." Entry form and guidelines available for SASE, by e-mail, or on website. **ENTRY FEE:** none; "just submit 3 copies of book." **DEADLINE:** March 1. Competition receives 500 books/year. 2010 winner was C.K. Williams. Winner will be announced in June in Poets & Writers and on website, or by SASE if provided. (**NOTE:** Not to be confused with the Milton Kessler Memorial Prize for Poetry sponsored by Harpur Palate).

BOSTON GLOBE-HORN BOOK AWARDS

(617)628-0225. Fax: (617)628-0882. E-mail: info@hbook.com; khedeen@hbook.com. Website: http://hbook.com/bghb/. **CONTACT:** Katrina Hedeen. The Boston Globe & The Horn Book, Inc.The Horn Book, 56 Roland St., Suite 200, Boston MA 02129. (617)628-0225. Fax: (617)628-0882. E-mail: info@hbook.com. Website: www.hbook.com/bghb/submissions_bghb. asp. Annual award. Estab. 1967. Purpose of award: To reward literary excellence in children's and young adult books. Awards are for picture books, nonfiction, fiction and poetry. Up to two honor books may be chosen for each category. Books must be published between June 1, 2010 and May 31, 2011. Deadline for entries: May 31, 2011. Textboks, e-books, and audiobooks will not be considered, nor will manuscripts. Books should be submitted by publishers, although the judges reserve the right to honor any eligible book. Award winners receive $500 and silver engraved bowl, honor book winners receive a silver engraved plate. Judging by 3 judges involved in children's book field. The book must have been published in the U.S. The Horn Book Magazine publishes speeches given at awards ceremonies.

THE BOSTON REVIEW ANNUAL POETRY CONTEST

Boston Review, P.O. Box 425786, Cambridge MA 02142. (617)324-1360. Fax: (617)452-3356. E-mail: review@bostonreview.net. Website: www.bostonreview.net. Offers $1,500 and publication in *Boston Review* (see separate listing in Magazines/Journals). "Any poet writing in English is eligible, unless he or she is a current student, former student, or close personal friend of the judge." Submissions must be unpublished. Submit up to 5 poems, no more than 10 pages total, in duplicate. Include cover sheet with poet's name, address, and phone number; no identifying information on the poems themselves. No mss will be returned. Guidelines available for SASE or on website. **ENTRY FEE:** $20 ($30 for international submissions); all entrants receive a one-year subscription to Boston Review . Make checks payable to Boston Review . **DEADLINE:** June 1 (postmark). Winner announced in early November on website. 2009 Winner: John Gallagher. 2010 judge: Peter Gizzi.

BOULEVARD EMERGING POETS CONTEST

PMB 325, 6614 Clayton Rd., Richmond Heights MO 63117. E-mail: kellyleavitt@boulevardmagazine.org. Website: www.boulevardmagazine.org. **CONTACT:** Kelly Leavitt, managing editor. Annual Emerging Poets Contest offers $1,000 and publication in *Boulevard* (see separate listing in Magazines/Journals) for the best group of 3 poems by a poet who has not yet published a book of poetry with a nationally distributed press. "All entries will be considered for publication and payment at our regular rates." Submissions must be unpublished. Considers simultaneous submissions. Submit 3 poems, typed; may be a sequence or unrelated. On page one of first poem type poet's name, address, phone number, and titles of the 3 poems. Include ASP for notification of receipt of ms; mss will not be returned. Guidelines available on website. **ENTRY FEE:** $15/group of 3 poems, $15 for each additional group of 3 poems; includes one-year subscription to *Boulevard*. Make checks payable to Boulevard . **DEADLINE:** June 1 (postmark). Judge: editors of *Boulevard* magazine. "No one editorially or financially affiliated with *Boulevard* may enter the contest."

THE BRIAR CLIFF REVIEW FICTION, POETRY, AND CREATIVE NONFICTION COMPETITION

E-mail: curranst@briarcliff.edu; jeanne.emmons@briarcliff.edu. Website: www.briarcliff.edu/bcreview. **CONTACT:** Tricia Currans-Sheehan, editor. The Briar Cliff Review (see separate listing in Magazines/Journals) sponsors an annual contest offering $1,000 and publication to each First Prize winner in fiction, poetry, and creative nonfiction. Previous year's winner and former students of editors ineligible. Winning pieces accepted for publication on the basis of First-Time Rights. Considers simultaneous submissions, "but notify us immediately upon acceptance elsewhere." Submit 3 poems, single-spaced on $8\frac{1}{2}$x11 paper, no more than 1 poem/page. Include separate cover sheet with author's name, address, e-mail, and poem title(s); no name on ms. Include SASE for results only; mss will not be returned. Guidelines available on website. **ENTRY FEE:** $20 for 3 poems. "All entrants receive a copy of the magazine (a $15 value) containing the winning entries." **DEADLINE:** November 1. Judge: the editors of The Briar Cliff Review.

○ "Send us your best work. We want stories with a plot."

➕ ◑ BRICK ROAD POETRY BOOK CONTEST

Brick Road Poetry Press, Inc., P.O. Box 751, Columbus GA 31902. (706)649-3080. Fax: (706)649-3094. E-mail: editor@brickroadpoetrypress.com. Website: www.brickroadpoetrypress.com. **CONTACT:** Ron Self and Keith Badowski, co-editors/founders. Offers annual award. The 1st Prize winner will receive a publication contract with Brick Road Poetry Press, $1,000, and 25 copies of the printed book. The winning book will be published in both print and e-book formats. "We may also offer publication contracts to the top finalists." Submissions must be unpublished as a collection, but individual poems may have been previously published elsewhere. Submit 70-100 pages of poetry. Guidelines available by e-mail or online. Entry fee is $25. Deadline is November 1. Competition receives 150 entries/year. Judged by Ron Self and Keith Badowski. Winners notified February 15. Copies of winning books available for $15.95. "The mission of Brick Road Poetry Press is to publish and promote poetry that entertains, amuses, edifies and surprises a wide audience of appreciative readers. We are not qualified to judge who deserves to be published, so we concentrate on publishing what we enjoy. Our preference is for poetry geared toward dramatizing the human experience in a langauge rich with sensory image and metaphor, recognizing that poetry can be, at one and the same time, both familiar as the perspiration of daily labor and outrageous as a carnival sideshow."

TIPS "The best way to discover all that poetry can be and to expand the limits of your own poetry is to read expansively."

◐ ⑤ CAA POETRY AWARD

Canadian Authors Association, 74 Mississaga Street E., Orillia ON L3V 1V5, Canada. Website: www.CanAuthors.org. (Specialized: Canadian Writers) The CAA Poetry Award offers $1,000 CAD and a silver medal to Canadian writers for a poetry collection (by a single poet) published during the previous year. Guidelines available on website. **ENTRY FEE:** $35 CAD/title. **DEADLINE:** December 15; except for works published after December 1, in which case the postmark deadline is January 15. Competition re-

ceives 100 entries/year. Shortlist usually announced early May, finalist announced by July. All awards are given at the annual CAA Awards Banquet.

◐ ⑤ GERALD CABLE BOOK AWARD

Silverfish Review Press, P.O. Box 3541, Eugene OR 97403. (541)344-5060. E-mail: sfrpress@earthlink.net. Website: www.silverfishreviewpress.com. **CONTACT:** Rodger Moody, Editor. Offers annual award of $1,000, publication by Silverfish Review Press, and 25 author copies to a book-length ms of original poetry by an author who has not yet published a full-length collection. No restrictions on the kind of poetry or subject matter; no translations. Individual poems may have been previously published elsewhere, but must be acknowledged. Considers simultaneous submissions (notify immediately of acceptance elsewhere). Submit at least 48 pages of poetry, no names or identification on ms pages. Include separate title sheet with poet's name, address, and phone number. Include SASP for notification of receipt and SASE for results; no mss will be returned. Accepts e-mail submissions in Word, plain text, or rich text; send entry fee and SASE by regular mail. Guidelines available for SASE, by e-mail, or on website. **ENTRY FEE:** $20. Make checks payable to Silverfish Review Press. **DEADLINE:** October 15 (postmark). Winner announced in March. Copies of winning books available through website. "All entrants who enclose a booksize envelope and $2.23 in postage will receive a free copy of a recent winner of the book award."

TIPS "Now accepting email submissions (save money on postage and photocopying); use Paypal for reading fee payment, see website for instructions."

CAKETRAIN CHAPBOOK COMPETITION

P.O. Box 82588, Pittsburgh PA 15218. E-mail: caketrainjournal@hotmail.com. Website: www.caketrain.org/competitions. Annual chapbook contest sponsored by Caketrain literary journal. Can submit by mail with SASE or by e-mail. See website for guidelines. Winner receives a $250 cash prize and 25 copies of their chapbook. **ENTRY FEE:** $15 for reading fee only or $20 for entry fee and copy of winning chapbook. **DEADLINE:** October 1. Past winners include Elizabeth Skurnick's *Check-In* (2005); Tom Whalen's *Dolls* (2007); Claire Hero's *afterpastures* (2008); Tina May Hall's *All the Day's Sad Stories* (2009); and Ben Mirov's *Ghost Machine* (2010).

JAMIE CAT CALLAN HUMOR PRIZE

National League of American Pen Women, The Webhallow House, 1544 Sweetwood Dr., Broadmoor Village CA 94015-2029. E-mail: pennobhill@aol.com. Website: www.soulmakingcontest.us. **CONTACT:** Eileen Malone.

○ ⑤ CIDER PRESS REVIEW BOOK AWARD

777 Braddock Lane, Halifax PA 17032. E-mail: editor@ciderpressreview.com. Website: http://ciderpressreview.com/bookaward/. **CONTACT:** Contest Director. The annual Cider Press Review Book Award offers $1,500, publication, and 25 author's copies. CPR acquires first publication rights. Initial print run is not less than 1,000 copies. Submissions must be unpublished as a collection, but individual poems may have been previously published elsewhere. Submit book-length ms of 48-80 pages. "Submissions can be made online using the submission form on the website or by mail. If sending by mail, include 2 cover sheets—1 with title, author's name, and complete contact information; and 1 with title only, all bound with a spring clip. Check website for change of address coming in the future. Include SASE for results only if no email address included; notification via email and on the website; manuscripts cannot be returned. Online submissions must be in Word for PC or PDF format, and should not include title page with author's name. The editors strongly urge contestants to use online delivery if possible." **ENTRY FEE:** $25. All entrants will receive a copy of the winning book and a one-issue subscription to *Cider Press Review*. 2010 winner was Liz Robbins. Deadline: submit September 1-November 30 (postmark). 2011 judge: Jeane Marie Beaumont. Acquisitions: Contest Director. Estab. 1999.

○ The annual Cider Press Review Book Award offers a $1,500 prize (as of 2010), publication, and 25 author's copies of a book length collection of poetry. Author receives a standard publishing contract. Initial print run is not less than 1,000 copies. Review the complete submission guidelines and learn more online at website.

⊕ ⑤ CLOCKWISE CHAPBOOK AWARD

(714)968-4677. Fax: (714)968-4677. E-mail: mifanwy@tebotbach.org. Website: www.tebotbach.org. **CONTACT:** Gail Wrongsky. Clockwise Chapbook Award.

Annual contest to honor winning entry. Must be previously unpublished poetry for the full collection; individual poems may have been published. Open to any writer. Address: 20592 Minerva Ln., Huntington Beach, CA 92646. Phone/Fax: (714) 968-4677. Email: mifanwy@tebotbach.org. Go to Website: www.tebotbach.org for guidelines. Deadline: April 15. Entry fee: $15. Guidelines online at website. Prize: $500 award, chapbook publication. Judged by Gail Wrongsky. Acquires First North American Rights for entire collection.

CLOUDBANK CONTEST

Website: www.cloudbankbooks.com. **CONTACT:** Michael Malan. Email: michael@cloudbankbooks.com. Website: www.cloudbankbooks.com. Contact: Michael Malan. A nominating process must be met before a writer's entry will be considered. Biannual poetry contest open to all. $200 1st place prize and publication. Also, author receives an extra copy of the issue in which their poem appears. Judged by Michael Malan (final) and Reading Board (initial). For contest submissions, the writer's name, address, e-mail address, and the titles of the poems being submitted should be typed on a cover sheet only, not on the pages of poems or short fiction. No electronic submissions. Please do not send more than five poems or short prose pieces (500 words or less) for the contest or regular submissions. The $15 entry fee covers up to 5 poems. The check should be made out to *Cloudbank*. All writers who enter the contest will receive a one-year (two-issue) subscription to *Cloudbank* magazine.

○ ⑤ THE COLORADO PRIZE FOR POETRY

(970)491-5449. E-mail: creview@colostate.edu. Website: http://coloradoprize.colostate.edu. **CONTACT:** Stephanie G'Schwind, editor. The annual Colorado Prize for Poetry awards an honorarium of $1,500 and publication of a book-length ms. Submission must be unpublished as a collection, but individual poems may have been published elsewhere. Submit mss of 48-100 pages of poetry (no set minimum or maximum) on any subject, in any form, double- or single-spaced. Include 2 titles pages: one with ms title only, the other with ms title and poet's name, address, and phone number. Enclosed SASP for notification of receipt and SASE for results; mss will not be returned. Guidelines available for SASE or by e-mail. **ENTRY FEE:** $25; includes one-year subscription to *Colorado Review* (see separate listing in Magazines/Journals). **DEADLINE:** submission period was October 1-January 14 for 2011. Winner was Eric Baus. 2011 judge was Cole Swensen.

COMMONWEALTH CLUB OF CALIFORNIA BOOK AWARDS

595 Market St., San Francisco CA 94105. (415)597-6724. Fax: (415)597-6729. E-mail: gdobbins@commonwealthclub.org. Website: www.commonwealthclub.org/bookawards. **CONTACT:** Wendy Wanderman, Associate Program Director. (Specialized: CA resident writers)595 Market St., San Francisco CA 94105. (415)597-6700. Fax: (415)597-6729. E-mail: cwc@sirius.com. Website: www.commonwealthclub.org. Annual awards "consisting of not more than two gold and eight silver medals" plus $2,000 cash prize to gold medal winners and $300 to silver medal winners. For books of "exceptional literary merit" in poetry, fiction, and nonfiction (including work related to California and work for children), plus 2 "outstanding" categories. Submissions must be previously published. Submit at least 3 copies of each book entered with an official entry form. (Books may be submitted by author or publisher.) Open to books, published during the year prior to the contest, whose author "must have been a legal resident of California at the time the manuscript was submitted for publication." Entry form and guidelines available for SASE or on website. **DEADLINE:** December 31. Competition receives approximately 50 poetry entries/year. Most recent award winners were Czeslaw Milosz and Carolyn Kizer. **TIPS** "Guidelines available on website."

○ ❸ CONCRETE WOLF POETRY CHAPBOOK CONTEST

P.O. Box 1808, Kingston WA 98346. E-mail: concretewolf@yahoo.com. Website: http://concretewolf.com. **CONTACT:** Contest Coordinator. (Specialized: theme-centric chapbooks) Member: CLMP. The Concrete Wolf Poetry Chapbook Contest offers publication and 100 author copies of a perfectly bound chapbook. Considers simultaneous submissions if notified of acceptance elsewhere. "We prefer chapbooks that have a theme, either obvious (i.e., chapbook about a divorce) or understated (i.e., all the poems mention the color blue). We like a collection that feels more like a whole than a sampling of work. We have no preference as to formal or free verse. We probably slight-ly favor lyric and narrative poetry to language and concrete, but excellent examples of any style get our attention." Submit up to 26 pages of poetry, paginated. Include table of contents and acknowledgments page. Include 2 cover sheets: one with ms title, poet's name, address, phone number, and e-mail; one without poet's identification. Include SASE for results; mss will not be returned. Guidelines available on website. **ENTRY FEE:** $20; include 10x12 envelope with $1.82 postage for a copy of the winning chapbook. Make checks payable to Concrete Wolf. **DEADLINE:** December 3 for 2011. Competition receives about 250 entries. Winner announced in February. Judge: editors and a final guest judge. Copies of winning chapbooks available through website and Amazon.com.

○ ❸ CRAB ORCHARD SERIES IN POETRY FIRST BOOK AWARD

Dept. of English, Mail Code 4503, Faner Hall 2380, Southern Illinois Univ. Carbondale, Carbondale IL 62901. E-mail: jtribble@siu.edu. Website: www.craborchardreview.siuc.edu. **CONTACT:** Jon Tribble, series editor. Established 1995. The Crab Orchard Series in Poetry First Book Award offers $2,500 ($1,000 prize plus $1,500 honorarium for a reading at Southern Illinois University Carbondale) and publication. "Manuscripts should be 50-75 pages of original poetry, in English, by a U.S. citizen or permanent resident who has neither published, nor committed to publish, a volume of poetry 40 pages or more in length (individual poems may have been previously published). Current students and employees of Southern Illinois University and authors published by Southern Illinois University Press are not eligible." See guidelines for complete formatting instructions. Guidelines available for SASE or on website. **ENTRY FEE:** $25/submission; includes a copy of the summer/fall Crab Orchard Review (see separate listing in Magazines/Journals). Make checks payable to Crab Orchard Series in Poetry. **DEADLINE:** see guidelines or check website. 2010 winner was Claire McQuerry (*Lacemakers*).

● ❸ CRAB ORCHARD SERIES IN POETRY OPEN COMPETITION AWARDS

Dept. of English, Mail Code 4503, Faner Hall 2380, Southern Illinois Univ. Carbondale, Carbondale IL 62901. E-mail: jtribble@siu.edu. Website: www.craborchardreview.siuc.edu. **CONTACT:** Jon Tribble, series editor. The Crab Orchard Series in Poetry

Open Competition Awards offer two winners $3,500 and publication of a book-length ms. "Cash prize totals reflect a $1,500 honorarium for each winner for a reading at Southern Illinois University Carbondale. Publication contract is with Southern Illinois University Press. Entrants must be U.S. citizens or permanent residents." Submissions must be unpublished as a collection, but individual poems may have been previously published elsewhere. Considers simultaneous submissions, but series editor must be informed immediately upon acceptance. Manuscripts should be typewritten or computer-generated (letter quality only, no dot matrix), single-spaced; clean photocopy is recommended as mss are not returned. See guidelines for complete formatting instructions. Guidelines available for SASE or on website. **ENTRY FEE:** $25/submission; includes a copy of the winning Crab Orchard Review (see separate listing in Magazines/Journals). Make checks payable to Crab Orchard Series in Poetry. **DEADLINE:** see guidelines or check website. 2010 winners were Brian Barker (*The Black Ocean*) and Camille Dungy (*Smith Blue*).

O CREATIVITY UNLIMITED PRESS® ANNUAL POETRY COMPETITION

30819 Casilina Dr., Rancho Palos Verdes CA 90275. E-mail: ihf@cox.net. Established 1978. **CONTACT:** Shelley Stockwell-Nicholas, PhD, editor. Annual invitation to submit offers possible widespread publication, with full credit to the author—Creativity Unlimited Press [PIRg] uses poetry submitted in published texts and newsletters. "We often use poems as chapter introductions in self-help books. Short, clever, quippy, humorous, and delightful language encouraged. No inaccessible, verbose, esoteric, obscure poetry." Enter no more than 2 pages/poem, double-spaced, 1 side of page. Submissions may be previously published "provided writer has maintained copyright and notifies us." Accepts e-mail submissions. **DEADLINE:** December 31.

●⑤ THE ROBERT DANA PRIZE FOR POETRY

Anhinga Press, Drawer W, P.O. Box 10595, Tallahassee FL 32302. (850)442-1408. Fax: (850)442-6323. E-mail: info@anhinga.org. Website: www.anhinga.org. **CONTACT:** Rick Campbell, poetry editor. The annual Anhinga Prize awards $2,000, a reading tour of Florida, and publication of a book-length poetry ms.

Guidelines available for SASE or on website. **ENTRY FEE:** $25. **DEADLINE:** submit February 15-May 1. Past judges include Donald Hall, Joy Harjo, Robert Dana, Mark Jarman, and Tony Hoagland. Past winners include Frank X. Gaspar, Julia Levine, Keith Ratzlaff, and Lynn Aarti Chandhok, and Rhett Iseman Trull.

O⑤ DANCING POETRY CONTEST

704 Brigham Ave., Santa Rosa CA 95404-5245. (707)528-0912. E-mail: jhcheung@comcast.net. Website: www.dancingpoetry.com. **CONTACT:** Judy Cheung, contest chair. 704 Brigham Ave., Santa Rosa CA 95404-5245. (707)528-0912. E-mail: jhcheung@comcast.net. Website: www.dancingpoetry.com. Annual contest offers three Grand Prizes of $100 each, six 1st Prizes of $50, twelve 2nd Prizes of $25, and thirty 3rd Prizes of $10. The 3 Grand Prize-winning poems will be choreographed, costumed, danced, and videotaped at the annual Dancing Poetry Festival at Palace of the Legion of Honor, San Francisco; Natica Angilly's Poetic Dance Theater Company will perform the 3 Grand Prize-winning poems. In addition, all prizes include an invitation to read your prize poem at the festival, and a certificate suitable for framing. Submissions must be unpublished or poet must own rights. Submit 2 copies of any number of poems, 40 lines maximum (each), with name, address, phone number on 1 copy only. Foreign language poems must include English translations. No entries by fax or e-mail. Entry form available for SASE. Entry fee: $5/poem or $10 for 3 poems. Deadline: May 15 annually. Competition receives about 500-800 entries. Winners will be announced by August 1; Ticket to festival will be given to all prize winners. Artist Embassy International has been a nonprofit educational arts organization since 1951, "Furthering intercultural understanding and peace through the universal language of the arts."

◎⑤ DANIEL VAROUJAN AWARD

E-mail: contests@nepoetryclub.org. Website: www.nepoetryclub.org/contests.htm. **CONTACT:** Contest Coordinator. For an unpublished poem (not a translation) to honor a poet killed by the Turks in the 1915 genocide destroying 3/4ths of the Armenian population. Funded by royalties from translations by Diana Der-Hovanessian. Send entries to contest coordinator, P.O. Box 190076 Boston, MA 02119. $10/up to 3 entries; made payable to New England Poetry

Club. Members free. Deadline: May 31. Prize: $1,000. Entries should be sent by regular mail only. Special Delivery or signature required mail will be returned by the Post Office. Entries should be original unpublished poems in English. No poem should be entered in more than one contest nor have won a previous contest. Poems should be typed and submitted in duplicate with author's name, address, and email on one copy only. Label poems with contest name. No entries will be returned. NEPC will not engage in correspondence regarding poems or contest decisions.

●○⑤ DAVID ST JOHN THOMAS CHARITABLE TRUST COMPETITIONS

David St. John Thomas Charitable Trust Competitions, P.O. Box 6055, Nairn IV12 4YB Scotland. (44)(1667)453351. Established 1990. **CONTACT:** Anne HIll, email dsjtcharitynairn@fsmail.net. We run two competitions jointly with Writers™ News, The Self-Publishing Awards with prizes totalling £2,250 plus two silver cups, and The Writers™ Circle Anthology Trophy with a prize of £100 plus a silver cup. The Self-Publishing Awards are divided into two categories, Self-Publisher of the Year and Self-Publishing for Charity. The Self-Publisher of the Year categories is divided into five sections: book of local interest, other non-fiction, poetry, fiction, and a book for children or younger people. All four shortlisted winners receive £250 each and the overall winner receives £750 and a silver cup. The winner of the Self-Publishing for Charity wins £500 for the charity plus a silver cup. These awards are open to anyone who has self-published a book during the preceding 18 months. For full details of these competitions please send a SAE to the above address.

DELAWARE DIVISION OF THE ARTS

820 N. French St., Wilmington DE 19801. (302)577-8278. Fax: (302)577-6561. E-mail: kristin.pleasanton@state.de.us. Website: www.artsdel.org. **CONTACT:** Kristin Pleasanton, coordinator. Award "to help further careers of emerging and established professional artists." For Delaware residents only. Prize: $10,000 for masters; $6,000 for established professionals; $3,000 for emerging professionals. Judged by out-of-state, nationally recognized professionals in each artistic discipline. No entry fee. Guidelines available after May 1 on website. Accepts inquiries by e-mail, phone. Expects to receive 25 fiction entries. Deadline: August 1. Open to any Delaware writer. Results announced in December. Winners notified by mail. Results available on website. "Follow all instructions and choose your best work sample."

●⑤ DIAGRAM/NEW MICHIGAN PRESS CHAPBOOK CONTEST

Dept. of English, P.O. Box 210067, University of Arizona, Tucson AZ 85721. E-mail: nmp@thediagram.com. Website: www.newmichiganpress.com/nmp. **CONTACT:** Ander Monson, Editor. The annual DIAGRAM /New Michigan Press Chapbook Contest offers $1,000 plus publication and author's copies, with discount on additional copies. Also publishes 2-4 finalist chapbooks each year. Submit 18-44 pages of poetry, fiction, mixed-genre, or genre-bending work (images okay if b/w and you have permissions). Include SASE. Guidelines available on website. **ENTRY FEE:** $16. **DEADLINE:** April 1, 2011. (In April each year).

DOBIE PAISANO PROJECT

Fax: (512)471-7620. E-mail: adameve@mail.utexas.edu. Website: www.utexas.edu/ogs/Paisano. **CONTACT:** Dr. Michael Adams.
TIPS "Guidelines and application forms are on the website or may be requested by sending a SASE (2 oz. postage) to the above address and attention of 'Dobie Paisano Fellowship Project.'"

●⑤ DREAM HORSE PRESS NATIONAL POETRY CHAPBOOK PRIZE

P.O. Box 2080, Felton CA 95001-2080. E-mail: dreamhorsepress@yahoo.com. Website: www.dreamhorsepress.com. **CONTACT:** J.P. Dancing Bear, Editor/Publisher. "The Dream Horse Press National Poetry Chapbook Prize offers an $500, publication, and 25 copies of a handsomely printed chapbook." All entries will be considered for publication. Submissions may be previously published in magazines/journals but not in books or chapbooks. Considers simultaneous submissions with notification. "Submit 20-28 pages of poetry in a readable font with table of contents, acknowledgments, bio, e-mail address for results, and entry fee. Poet's name should not appear anywhere on the manuscript." Accepts multiple submissions (with separate fee for each entry). Manuscripts will be recycled after judging. Guidelines available on website. **ENTRY FEE:** $15. Make checks/money orders made payable to Dream Horse Press. **DEADLINE:** June 30.

Recent previous winners include Amy Holman, Cyntha Arrieu-King, Charles Sweetman and Jason Bredle. 2010 judge: C.J. Sage.

⊕ ELINOR BENEDICT POETRY PRIZE

Contest sponsored by Passages North, Dept. of English, Northern Michigan University, 1401 Presque Isle Ave., Marquette MI 49855. (906)227-1203. Fax: (906)227-1096. E-mail: passages@nmu.edu. Website: myweb.nmu.edu/~passages. Acquisitions: Kate Myers Hanson. Contest. $1,000 first prize and publication. $10 for up to three poems entry fee ($3 for each additional poem after that). T. Johnston, Managing Editor, PN.

ERIKA MUMFORD PRIZE

E-mail: contests@nepoetryclub.org. Website: www. nepoetryclub.org/contests.htm. **CONTACT:** Contest Coordinator. $250 for a poem in any form about foreign culture or travel. Funded by Erika Mumford's family and friends.

⊕◖ FALL POETRY CHAPBOOK CONTEST

White Eagle Coffee Store Press, P.O. Box 383, Fox River Grove IL 60021-0383. (847)639-9200. E-mail: wecspress@aol.com. Website: whiteeaglecoffeestorepress. com. **CONTACT:** Frank Edmund Smith, publisher.

○◎❸ FAR HORIZONS AWARD FOR POETRY

The Malahat Review, University of Victoria, P.O. Box 1700, Stn CSC, Victoria BC V8W 2Y2, Canada. (250)721-8524. Fax: (250)472-5051. E-mail: malahat@ uvic.ca. Website: www.malahatreview.ca. **CONTACT:** John Barton, editor. The biennial Far Horizons Award for Poetry offers $1,000 CAD and publication in The Malahat Review (see separate listing in Magazines/ Journals). Open to "emerging poets from Canada, the United States, and elsewhere" who have not yet published a full-length book (48 pages or more). Submissions must be unpublished. No simultaneous submissions. Submit up to 3 poems per entry, each poem not to exceed 60 lines; no restrictions on subject matter or aesthetic approach. Include separate page with poet's name, address, e-mail, and poem title(s); no identifying information on mss pages. No e-mail submissions. Do not include SASE for results; mss will not be returned. Guidelines available on website. **ENTRY FEE:** $25 CAD for Canadian entries, $30 USD for US entries ($35 USD for entries from Mexico and outside North America); includes a one-year subscription to The Malahat Review. **DEADLINE:** May 1 (postmark) of alternate years (2010, 2012, etc.). 2010 winner: Darren Bifford. Winner and finalists contacted by e-mail. Winner published in fall in The Malahat Review and announced on website, Facebook page, and in quarterly e-newsletter, Malahat lite.

◐❸ THE FINISHING LINE PRESS OPEN CHAPBOOK COMPETITION

Finishing Line Press, P.O. Box 1626, Georgetown KY 40324. (859)514-8966. E-mail: FinishingBooks@aol. com. Website: www.finishinglinepress.com. **CONTACT:** Leah Maines, Poetry Editor. The Finishing Line Press Open Chapbook Competition offers a $1,000 cash award and publication. All entries will be considered for publication. Open to all poets regardless of past publications. Submit up to 26 pages of poetry. Include bio, acknowledgments, and cover letter. Guidelines available by e-mail or on website. **ENTRY FEE:** $15. **DEADLINE:** July 15 (postmark) for 2010.

●◎❸ FISH POETRY PRIZE

Website: www.fishpublishing.com. Fish Poetry Prize. Durrus, Bantry, Co. Cork, Ireland. Email: info@fishpublishing.com. Website: www.fishpublishing.com. "For poems up to 200 words. First Prize €1,000. Deadline 30 March 2011. Results 30 April 2011. Entry €14. Age Range: Adult. The best 10 will be published in the 2011 Fish Anthology, launched in July at the West Cork Literary Festival by Brian Turnr, the judge. Entries must not have been published before. Enter online or by post. Geographical area covered: Worldwide. See our website for full details of competitions, and information on the Fish Editorial and Critique Services, and the Fish Online Writing Courses." The 2011 Fish Short Story Prize will open on 1 June and close 30 Sept 2011.

TIPS The 2011 Fish Short Story Prize will open on 1 June and close 30 Sept 2011.

○❸ THE FLIP KELLY POETRY PRIZE

6199 Steubenville Road SE, Amsterdam OH 43903. (740)543-3345. E-mail: editor@amsterdampress.net. Website: www.amsterdampress.net. **CONTACT:** Cindy Kelly, editor. The Flip Kelly Poetry Prize offers a $200 honorarium for best chapbook and publication in Gob Pile Chapbook series, and 75 free copies of chapbook. Runners-up are considered for publication of chapbook in Gob Pile chapbook series. Chapbook submissions may include previously published works, with acknowledgment. Poems may be entered in other contests and/or under consideration elsewhere. Submit cover letter, brief biographical statement in 3rd person, and copy of manuscript of no more than 30 poems with poet's name, address, phone number. Very strict about submission guidelines. Current guidelines and entry forms available for SASE, by e-mail, and on website. Entry fee: $20. **DEADLINE: DECEMBER 31**. 2011 judge: TBA. Winners will be announced February 15 (or sooner). Entrants recieve copy of winning chapbook. Amsterdam Press was founded in 2007. **ADVICE** "We favor plain-spoken over esoteric, specificity over universality, strong sense of place, literal or reinterpreted." Contest est. 2008

❶ GEORGETOWN REVIEW

Georgetown Review, 400 East College St., Box 227, Georgetown KY 40324. (502) 863-8308. Fax: (502) 863-8888. E-mail: gtownreview@georgetowncollege.edu. Website: http://georgetownreview.georgetowncollege.edu. **CONTACT:** Steve Carter, editor. Annual. Contact: Steve Carter. Email: gtownreview@georgetowncollege.edu. Publishes short stories, poetry, and creative nonfiction. Reading period: September 1-December 31. Also sponsors yearly writing contest for short stories, poetry, and creative nonfiction." Prize: $1,000 and publication; runners-up receive publication. Receives about 300 entries for each category. Entries are judged by the editors. Entry fee: $10 for first entry, $5 for each one thereafter. Make checks payable to Georgetown College. Guidelines available in July. Accepts inquiries by e-mail. **ENTRY DEADLINE IS OCT. 15TH, 2011.** Entries should be unpublished. Contest open to anyone except family, friends of the editors. "We're just looking to publish quality work. Sometimes our contests are themed, so check the website for details." Results announced Feb. or March. Winners notified by e-mail. Results made available to entrants with SASE. Cover letter, ms should include name, address, phone, e-mail, novel/story title. Writers may submit own work.

GOLDEN ROSE AWARD

Website: www.nepoetryclub.org. **CONTACT:** N. Smith. "Given annually to the poet who has done the most for the art in the previous year or in a lifetime. Chosen by board." Contest open to members and non-members.

➕⟳ GOVERNOR GENERAL'S LITERARY AWARDS

Website: www.canadacouncil.ca/prizes/ggla. (Specialized: Canadian citizens/permanent residents; English- and French-language works) Established by Parliament, the Canada Council for the Arts "provides a wide range of grants and services to professional Canadian artists and art organizations in dance, media arts, music, theater, writing, publishing, and the visual arts." The Governor General's Literary Awards, valued at $25,000 CAD each, are given annually for the best English-language and best French-language work in each of 7 categories, including poetry. Non-winning finalists each receive $1,000 CAD. Books must be first edition trade books written, translated, or illustrated by Canadian citizens or permanent residents of Canada and published in Canada or abroad during the previous year (September 1 through the following September 30). Collections of poetry must be at least 48 pages long, and at least half the book must contain work not published previously in book form. In the case of translation, the original work must also be a Canadian-authored title. Books must be submitted by publishers with a Publisher's Submission Form, which is available on request from the Writing and Publishing Section of the Canada Council for the Arts. Guidelines and current deadlines on the website and available by mail, telephone, fax, or e-mail. 2009 winner for poetry in English was David Zieroth (*The Fly in Autumn*).

❶⑤ GRANDMOTHER EARTH NATIONAL AWARD

Grandmother Earth Creations, P.O. Box 2018, Cordova TN 38088. (901)309-3692. E-mail: gmoearth@gmail.com. Website: www.grandmotherearth.org. **CONTACT:** Frances Cowden, Award Director. **CONTACT:** Frances Cowden, award director. Offers annual award of $1,250 with varying distributions each year; separate contest for students ages 2-12; $1,250 minimum in awards for poetry and prose; $100 first, etc., plus publication in anthology; non-winning finalists considered for anthology if permission is given. Submissions may be published or unpublished. Considers simultaneous submissions. Submit at least 3 poems, any subject, in any form. See website for changes in the rules. Include SASE for winners list. Guidelines available for SASE or on website. **ENTRY FEE:** $10 for 3 works, $2 each additional work. Entry fee includes a copy of the anthology. **DEADLINE:** July 6. Winners will be announced in October at the Life Press Writers Conference in August in Cordova, TN. Copies of winning poems or books available from Grandmother Earth Creations.

● GRANTS FOR ARTIST'S PROJECTS

Artist Trust, 1835 12th Ave, Seattle WA 98122. (206) 467-8734, ext. 11. Fax: (206) 467-9633. E-mail: miguel@artisttrust.org. Website: www.artisttrust. org. **CONTACT:** Monica Miller, Director of Programs. "The GAP Program provides support for artist-generated projects, which can include (but are not limited to) the development, completion or presentation of new work." Annual. Prize: maximum of $1,500 for projects. Accepted are poetry, fiction, graphic novels, experimental works, creative non-fiction, screen plays, film scripts and teleplays. Entries are judged by work sample as specified in the guidelines. Winners are selected by a discipline-specific panel of artists and artist professionals. No entry fee. Guidelines available in March. Accepts inquiries by mail, phone. Submission period is March-May. **DEADLINE IS MAY 10.** Website should be consulted for exact date. Entries can be unpublished or previously published. Washington state residents only. Length: 8 pages max for poetry, fiction, graphic novels, experimental work and creative nonfiction; up to 12 pages for screen plays, film scripts and teleplays. All mss must be typed with a 12-point font size or larger and cannot be single-spaced (except for poetry). Include application with project proposal and budget, as well as resume with name, address, phone, e-mail, and novel/story title. "GAP awards are highly competitive. Please follow guidelines with care." Results announced in the fall. Winners notified by email. Results made available to entrants by email and on website.

●⑤ THE GREEN ROSE PRIZE IN POETRY

Website: www.wmich.edu/newissues. New Issues Poetry & Prose , Western Michigan University, 1903 W. Michigan Ave., Kalamazoo MI 49008-5463. (269)387-8185. Fax: (269)387-2562. Website: www.wmich.edu/newissues. Established 1996. The Green Rose Prize in Poetry offers $2,000 and publication of a book of poems by an established poet who has published one or more full-length collections of poetry. New Issues may publish as many as 3 additional mss from this competition. Considers simultaneous submissions, but New Issues must be notified of acceptance elsewhere. Submit a ms of at least 48 pages, typed, single-spaced preferred. Clean photocopies acceptable. Do not bind; use manila folder or metal clasp. Include cover page with poet's name, address, phone number, and title of the ms. Also include brief bio, table of contents, and acknowledgments page. No e-mail or fax submissions. Include SASP for notification of receipt of ms and SASE for results only; mss will be recycled. Guidelines available for SASE, by fax, e-mail, or on website. **ENTRY FEE:** $25. Make checks payable to New Issues Poetry & Prose. **DEADLINE:** submit May 1-September 30 (postmark). Winner is announced in January or February on website. 2010 winner was Corey Marks (The Radio Tree). Judge: New Issues editors. The winning manuscript will be published Spring 2012.

●⑤ THE DONALD HALL PRIZE IN POETRY

AWP, Carty House, Mail Stop 1E3, George Mason University, Fairfax VA 22030-4444. E-mail: chronicle@awpwriter.org. Website: www.awpwriter.org. The Association of Writers & Writing Programs (AWP) sponsors an annual competition for the publication of excellent new book-length works, the AWP Award Series, which includes The Donald Hall Prize in Poetry. Offers annual award of $5,000 and publication for the best book-length ms of poetry (book-length defined for poetry as 48 pages minimum of text). Open to published and unpublished poets alike. "Poems previously published in periodicals are eligible for inclusion in submissions, but mss previously published in their entirety, including self-published, are not eligible. As the series is judged anonymously, no list of acknowledgments should accompany your ms. You may submit your ms to other publishers while it is under consideration by the Award Series, but you must notify AWP immediately in writing if your ms is accepted elsewhere. Your ms must be submitted in accordance with the eligibility requirements, format guidelines, and entry requirements or it will be disqualified." Complete guidelines, including important formatting information, eligibility requirements, and required entry form available on website. **ENTRY**

FEE: $15 (AWP members) or $30 (nonmembers). Make checks/money orders payable in U.S. dollars only to AWP. **DEADLINE:** mss must be postmarked between January 1-February 28. 2010 winner was Quan Barry (*The Animals All Are Gathering*). 2011 judge: Dorianne Laux.

◐⑤ JAMES HEARST POETRY PRIZE

North American Review, University of Northern Iowa, 1222 W. 27th St., Cedar Falls IA 50614-0516. (319)273-6455. Fax: (319)273-4326. E-mail: nar@uni.edu. Website: www.northamericanreview.org. The James Hearst Poetry Prize offers 1st Prize: $1,000; 2nd Prize: $100; and 3rd Prize: $50. All winners and finalists will be published in North American Review (see separate listing in Magazines/Journals). Submissions must be unpublished. No simultaneous submissions. Submit up to 5 poems, 2 copies each; **NO NAMES** on ms pages. Cover sheet is required (MS Word or PDF). Include SASP for acknowledgment of receipt of ms and #10 SASE for results (or provide e-mail address on cover sheet); mss will not be returned. Guidelines available for SASE, by fax, e-mail, or on website. **ENTRY FEE:** $25 (includes one-year subscription). Make checks/money orders payable to North American Review. **DEADLINE:** October 31 (postmark).

◐⑤ THE LYNDA HULL MEMORIAL POETRY PRIZE

Crazyhorse, Dept. of English, College of Charleston, 66 George St., Charleston SC 29424. (843)953-7740. E-mail: crazyhorse@cofc.edu. Website: www.crazyhorsejournal.org. **CONTACT:** Prize Director. The annual Lynda Hull Memorial Poetry Prize offers $2,000 and publication in Crazyhorse (see separate listing in Contests & Awards). All entries will be considered for publication. Submissions must be unpublished. Submit online or by mail up to 3 original poems (no more than 10 pages). Include cover page (placed on top of ms) with poet's name, address, e-mail, and telephone number; no identifying information on mss (blind judging). Accepts multiple submissions with separate fee for each. Include SASP for notification of receipt of ms and SASE for results only; mss will not be returned. Guidelines available for SASE or on website. **ENTRY FEE:** $16/ms for new entrants. Fee includes a one-year/2 issue subscription to Crazyhorse; for each poetry ms entered and fee paid, subscription is extended by 1 year. Make checks payable to Crazyhorse

; credit card payments also accepted (see website for details). **DEADLINE:** January 15.

INDIANA REVIEW K (SHORT-SHORT/PROSE-POEM) CONTEST

BH 465/Indiana University, 1020 E. Kirkwood Ave., Bloomington IN 47405-7103. (812)855-3439. Fax: (812)855-4253. E-mail: inreview@indiana.edu. Website: www.indianareview.edu. **CONTACT:** Alessandra Simmons, editor. Competition for fiction and prose poems no longer than 500 words. Prize: $1,000 plus publication, contributor's copies and a year's subscription. All entries considered for publication. Judged by guest judges; 2010 prize judged by Alberto Rios. Entry fee: $15 fee for no more than 3 pieces (includes a year's subscription, two issues). Make checks payable to Indiana Review. **DEADLINE: JUNE.** Entries must be unpublished. Guidelines available in March for SASE, by phone, e-mail, on website, or in publication. Length: 500 words, 3 mss per entry. Open to any writer. Cover letter should include name, address, phone, e-mail, word count and title. No identifying information on ms. "We look for command of language and form." Results announced in August. Winners notified by mail. For contest results, send SASE or visit website. See website for detailed guidelines.

INDIANA REVIEW POETRY PRIZE

Indiana Review, Ballantine Hall 465, Indiana University, Bloomington IN 47405-7103. (812)855-3439. Fax: (812)855-9535. E-mail: inreview@indiana.edu. Website: www.indianareview.com. **CONTACT:** Alessandra Simmons, Editor. Offered annually for unpublished work. Judged by guest judges; 2011 prize will be judged by Marie Howe. Open to any writer. Send no more than 3 poems per entry. Guidelines on website and with SASE request. This year's deadline: March 25, 2011. Prize: $1,000. Costs: $15 fee (includes a 1-year subscription) Open to any writer.

◐⑤ INKWELL ANNUAL POETRY CONTEST

Manhattanville College, 2900 Purchase St., Purchase NY 10577. (914)323-7239. Fax: (914)323-3122. E-mail: inkwell@mville.edu. Website: www.inkwelljournal.org. **CONTACT:** Competition Poetry Editor. The Inkwell Annual Poetry Competition awards $1,000 grand prize and publication in *Inkwell* (see separate listing in Magazines/Journals) for best poem. Submissions must be unpublished. Submit up to 5 poems at a time, no more than 40 lines/poem, typed in 12 pt. font. Include cover sheet with poet's name, address, phone number, e-mail, and poems titles and line counts. No name or address should appear on mss. Also include Submission Checklist (download from website). Indicate "Poetry Competition" on envelope. Include SASE for results only; mss will not be returned. Guidelines available on website. **ENTRY FEE:** $10 for first poem, $5 for each additional poem (USD only). Make checks payable to Manhattanville—Inkwell . **DEADLINE:** August 1-October 30 (postmark). 2011 judge: Mark Doty.

IOWA POETRY PRIZES

(319)335-2000. Fax: (319)335-2055. E-mail: uipress@uiowa.edu. Website: www.uiowapress.org. The University of Iowa Press, 119 West Park Rd., 100 Kuhl House, Iowa City IA 52242-1000. (319)335-2000. E-mail: uipress@uiowa.edu. Website: www.uiowapress.org. The University of Iowa Press offers the annual Iowa Poetry Prizes for book-length mss (50-150 pages) originally in English by new or established poets. Winners will be published by the Press under a standard royalty contract. Poems from previously published books may be included only in mss of selected or collected poems, submissions of which are encouraged. Considers simultaneous submissions if Press is immediately notified if the book is accepted by another publisher. Guidelines available on website. **ENTRY FEE:** $20. **DEADLINE:** postmarked during April only.

◐ ⑤ THE IOWA REVIEW AWARD IN POETRY, FICTION, AND NONFICTION

308 EPB, University of Iowa, Iowa City IA 52242. E-mail: iowa-review@uiowa.edu. Website: www.iowareview.org. **CONTACT:** Contest Coordinator. The Iowa Review Award in Poetry, Fiction, and Nonfiction presents $1,000 to each winner in each genre, $500 to runners-up. Winners published in The Iowa Review (see separate listing in Magazines/Journals). Submissions must be unpublished. Considers simultaneous submissions (with notification of acceptance elsewhere). Submit up to 25 pages of prose, (double-spaced) or 10 pages of poetry (one poem or several, but no more than one poem per page). Include cover page with poet's name, address, e-mail and/or phone number, and title of each work submitted. Personal identification must not appear on ms pages. Label

mailing envelope as a contest entry, E.G., "Contest: Fiction." One entry per envelope. Include SASP for confirmation of receipt of entry, SASE for results. Guidelines available on website. **ENTRY FEE:** $20. Enclose additional $10 (optional) for yearlong subscription. Make checks payable to The Iowa Review. **DEADLINE:** submit January 1-31 (postmark). 2010 winners were Heather Winterer, Kathryn Scanlan, and Deborah Thompson. 2011 Judges: Claudia Rankine, Alan Gurganus, Patricia Hampl.

JANICE FARRELL POETRY PRIZE

E-mail: pennobhill@aol.com. Website: www.soulmakingcontest.us. **CONTACT:** Eileen Malone. Annual contest. "Poetry may be double- or single-spaced. One-page poems only, and only 1 poem/page. All poems must be titled. 3 poems/entry. Indicate category on each poem. Identify with 3X5 card only. Open to all writers." $5/entry (make checks payable to NLAPW, Nob Hill Branch). Deadline: November 30. Prizes: 1st Place: $100; 2nd Place: $50; 3rd Place: $25. Judged by a local San Francisco successfully published poet.

● JEAN PEDRICK PRIZE

CONTACT: N. Smith. Prize for a chapbook published in the last two years. Funded by club dues. Send to 2 Farrar St., Cambridge MA 02138. $5 handling fee for non-members. Deadline: May 31. Prize: $100. Contests are free to all full time students and paid up members of New England Poetry Club. Non-members pay $10 for three contests and $3 additional per additional entry. Only one poem per contest. "New England Poetry board members can enter only the Gretchen Warren competition."

⑤ JENNY McKEAN MOORE VISITING WRITER

English Dept. George Washington Univ., Rome Hall, 801 22nd St. NW, Suite 760, Washington DC 20052. (202)994-6180. Fax: (202)994-7915. E-mail: tvmallon@gwu.edu. Website: columbian.gwu.edu/departmentsprograms/english/creativewriting/activitiesevents. **CONTACT:** Thomas Mallon, Director of Creative Writing. Dept. of English, George Washington University, Rome Hall, Suite 760, 801 22nd St. NW, Washington DC 20052. (202)994-6515. Fax: (202)994-7915. E-mail: tvmallon@gwu.edu. Website: http://columbian.gwu.edu/departmentsprograms/english/creativewriting/activitiesevents . Offers fellowship for a visiting lecturer in creative writing, currently about

$55,000 for 2 semesters. Stipend varies slightly from year to year, depending on endowment payout. Teaching duties involve 2 workshops per semester—one for undergraduate students, the other free to the community. Apply with résumé and writing sample of 25 pages or less. Books may be submitted but will not be returned without SASE. Awarded to writers in different genres each year, typically alternating between poets and fiction writers. For the 2012-13 academic year we will be looking for a poet. (Check website for specific genre each year.) Deadline: November 11.

JOHN CIARDI PRIZE FOR POETRY

(816)235-2558. E-mail: bkmk@umkc.edu. Website: www.umkc.edu/bkmk. 5100 Rockhill Rd., Kansas City MO 02903-1803. Phone: (816)235-2558. Fax: (816)235-2611. Email: bkmk@umkc.edu. Website: www.umkc.edu/bkmk. Contact: Ben Furnish. "Offered annually for the best book-length collection (unpublished) of poetry in English by a living author. Translations are not eligible. Initial judging is done by a network of published writers. Final judging is done by a writer of national reputation. Guidelines for SASE, by e-mail, or on website." $25 fee. Deadline: January 15 (postmarked). Prize: $1,000, plus book publication by BkMk Press.

❶❸ JUDITH SIEGEL PEARSON AWARD

Wayne State Univ./Family of Judith Siegel Pearson, 5057 Woodward Ave., Suite 9408, Detroit MI 48202. (313)577-2450. Fax: (313)577-8618. E-mail: rhonda@wayne.edu. **CONTACT:** Rhonda Agnew, Contest Coordinator. Offers an annual award of up to $500 for the best creative or scholarly work on a subject concerning women. The type of work accepted rotates each year: fiction in 2011, drama in 2012, poetry in 2013 (poetry, 20 pages maximum), essays in 2014. Open to all interested writers and scholars. Submissions must be unpublished. Submit 4-10 poems (20 pages maximum). Guidelines available for SASE or by fax or e-mail.

❶❸ KATE TUFTS DISCOVERY AWARD

(909)621-8974. Fax: (909)607-8438. E-mail: tufts@cqu.edu. Website: www.cgu.edu/tufts. **CONTACT:** Wendy Martin, program director. The Kate Tufts Discovery Award ($10,000) is for a first book. 2011 winner is Atsuro Riley (Romey's Order). To be considered for the 2012 awards, books must have been published between September 1, 2010 and August 31,

2011. Entry form and guidelines available for SASE or on website. Check website for updated deadlines and award information.

❸ KATHLEEN MCCLUNG SONNETT COMPETITION

Category in the Soul-Making Literary Competition., National League of American Pen Women, The Webhallow House, 1544 Sweetwood Dr., Broadmoor Village CA 94015-2029. E-mail: pennobhill@aol.com. Website: www.soulmakingcontest.us. **CONTACT:** Eileen Malone. "Call for Shakespearean and Petrarchan sonnets on the theme of the 'beloved.' Previously published material is accepted. Indicate category on cover page and on identifying 3x5 card. Open annually to any writer." Deadline: November 30. Prize: 1st Place: $100; 2nd Place: $50; 3rd Place: $25.

KATHRYN HANDLEY PROSE POEM PRIZE

E-mail: pennobhill@aol.com. Website: www.soulmakingcontest.us. **CONTACT:** Eileen Malone. Kathryn Handley Prose Poem Prize open annually to all writers. $5/entry fee (make checks payable to NLAPW, Nob Hill Branch). Poetry may be double- or single-spaced. 1-page poems only, and only 1 prose poem/page. 3 poems/entry. Indicate category on each poem. Identify only with 3X5 card. Open annually to all writers. $5/entry fee (make checks payable to NLAPW, Nob Hill Branch). Deadline: November 30. Prizes: 1st Place: $100; 2nd Place: $50; 3rd Place: $25.

BARBARA MANDIGO KELLY PEACE POETRY AWARDS

(805)965-3443. Fax: (805)568-0466. E-mail: wagingpeace@napf.org. Website: www.wagingpeace.org. Offers an annual series of awards "to encourage poets to explore and illuminate positive visions of peace and the human spirit." Awards $1,000 to adult contestants, $200 to youth in each 2 categories (13-18 and 12 and under), plus Honorable Mentions in each category. Submissions must be unpublished. Submit up to 3 poems in any form, unpublished and in English; maximum 30 lines/poem. Send 2 copies; put name, address, e-mail, phone number, and age (for youth) in upper right-hand corner of 1 copy of each poem. Title each poem; do not staple individual poems together. "Any entry that does not adhere to ALL of the contest rules will not be considered for a prize. Poets should keep copies of all entries as we will be unable to return them." Guidelines available for SASE or on website. **ENTRY FEE:** Adult: $15 for up to 3 poems; 13-18: $5 for up to 3 poems; no fee for 12 and under. **DEADLINE:** July 1 (postmark). Judges: a committee of poets selected by the Nuclear Age Peace Foundation. Winners will be announced by October 1 by mail and on website. Winning poems from current and past contests are posted on the Foundation's website. "The Nuclear Age Peace Foundation reserves the right to publish and distribute the award-winning poems, including Honorable Mentions."

TIPS "Poets should keep copies of all entries as we will be unable to return them. Copies of the winning poems from the 2003 Awards will be posted on the Nuclear Age Peace Foundation website after October 1, 2009."

● ⑤ THE LAUREATE PRIZE FOR POETRY

The National Poetry Review, P.O. Box 2080, Aptos CA 95001-2080. E-mail: editor@nationalpoetryreview.com. Website: www.nationalpoetryreview.com. **CONTACT:** C.J. Sage, Editor. The National Poetry Review. Submit via email and paypal (see website for instructions: www.nationalpoetryreview.com) or via mail to P.O. Box 2080, Aptos CA 95001-2080. E-mail: editor@nationalpoetryreview.com. Acquisitions: C. J. Sage, editor. Poems must be uncommitted (not accepted for first publication elsewhere). Honors one new poem that The National Poetry Review believes has the greatest chance, of those entered, of standing the test of time and becoming part of the literary canon. Deadline: September 30. Prize $500, plus publication in *The National Poetry Review*. Costs $15 (personal checks only; no money orders).

TIPS Simultaneous submission acceptable, but if the work is selected by TNPR for the prize or for publication, it must be withdrawn from elsewhere unless you have withdrawn it from us 2 weeks before our acceptance. Multiple submissions are acceptable with a reading fee for each group of 3 poems. 10-page limit per group. [See separate listing in Magazines Journals.]

THE LEDGE ANNUAL POETRY CHAPBOOK CONTEST

E-mail: info@theledgemagazine.com. Website: www.theledgemagazine.com. **CONTACT:** Timothy Monaghan, Editor-in-Chief. The Ledge Press, 40 Maple Ave., Bellport NY 11713. Website: www.theledgemagazine.com. The Ledge Poetry Chapbook Contest offers an annual prize of $1,000, publication by The Ledge Press, and 25 chapbook copies. Considers simultaneous submissions. Accepts multiple submissions with separate entry fee for each. " No restrictions on form or content. Excellence is the only criterion." Submit 16-28 pages of poetry with bio and acknowledgements, if any. Include title page with poet's name, address, phone number, and e-mail address (if applicable). Include SASE for results or return of ms. Guidelines available on website. **ENTRY FEE:** $18; all entrants will receive a copy of the winning chapbook upon publication. **DEADLINE:** October 31. Sample chapbooks available for $8 postpaid. Winner announced in March.

● ⑤ THE MORTON MARR POETRY PRIZE

Southern Methodist University, P.O. Box 750374, Dallas TX 75275-0374. (214)768-1037. Fax: (214)768-1408. E-mail: swr@mail.smu.edu. Website: www.smu.edu/southwestreview. **CONTACT:** Prize coordinator. (Specialized: traditional poetry forms) The annual Morton Marr Poetry Prize awards 1st Prize: $1,000 and 2nd Prize: $500 to a poet who has not yet published a first book of poetry. Winners will be published in Southwest Review (see separate listing in Magazines/Journals). Submit 6 poems in a "traditional" form (e.g., sonnet, sestina, villanelle, rhymed stanzas, blank verse, et al). Include cover letter with poet's name, address, and other relevant information; no identifying information on entry pages. Manuscripts will not be returned. Guidelines available on website. **ENTRY FEE:** $5/poem. **DEADLINE:** September 30 (postmark). 2010 winners: Peter Kline (1st Place), Anne-Marie Thompson (2nd Place), Martha Miller (HM).

⊕ VASSAR MILLER PRIZE IN POETRY

University of North Texas Press, 1155 Union circle, #311336, Denton TX 76203-5017. (940)565-2142. Fax: (940)565-4590. Website: http://web3.unt.edu/untpress/. **CONTACT:** John Poch.

TIPS "No limitations to entrants. In years when the judge is announced, we ask that students of the judge not enter to avoid a perceived conflict. All entries should contain identifying material only on the one cover sheet. Entries are read anonymously."

O ⑤ MILTON DORFMAN NATIONAL POETRY PRIZE

c/o Rome Art & Community Center, 308 W. Bloomfield St., Rome NY 13440. (315)336-1040. Fax: (315)336-

1090. E-mail: supportstaff@romeart.org. Website: www.romeart.org. **CONTACT:** Sandra Coppage. c/o Rome Art & Community Center, 308 W. Bloomfield St., Rome NY 13440. (315)336-1040. Fax: (315)336-1090. E-mail: supportstaff@romeart.org. Website: www.romeart.org. **CONTACT:** Sandra Coppage. Annual award for unpublished poetry. First prize $100, Second prize $50, Third prize $25. Winners are published in center's newsletter. Poets must be 18 years of age to enter. Include name, address, e-mail, title and phone number on back of submission. **ENTRY FEE:** $5 per entry as many as one wishes. May enter online also, go to link. Make checks payable to Rome Art & Community Center. **DEADLINE:** July 29. May enter as of April 1. Awards ceremony TBA.

NAOMI LONG MADGETT POETRY AWARD

E-mail: lotuspress@comcast.net. Website: www.lotuspress.org. **CONTACT:** Constance Withers. "Naomi Long Madgett Poetry Award. Offered annually to recognize an unpublished poetry ms by an African American. Email: lotuspress@comcast.net. Wwebsite: www.lotuspress.org. Contact: Constance Withers. Guidelines for SASE, by e-mail, or online." Deadline: January 2 - March 31. $500 and publication by Lotus Press.

🌑🗿⑤ NATIONAL POETRY COMPETITION

Poetry Society, 22 Betterton Street, London WC2H 9BX, United Kingdom. E-mail: info@poetrysociety.org.uk. Website: www.poetrysociety.org.uk. **CONTACT:** Competition Organiser. Poetry Society, 22 Betterton Street, London WC2H 9BX United Kingdom. E-mail: info@poetrysociety.org.uk. Website: www.poetrysociety.org.uk. The National Poetry Competition offers 1st Prize: £5,000; 2nd Prize: £2,000; 3rd Prize: £1,000; plus 7 commendations of £100 each. Winners will be published in Poetry Review (see separate listing in Magazines/Journals), and on the Poetry Society website and the top three winners will receive a year's free membership in the Poetry Society (see separate listing in Organizations). Open to anyone aged 17 or over. Entries "received from all around the world. All entries are judged anonymously and past winners include both published and previously unknown poets." Submissions must be unpublished (poems posted on Web sites are considered published). Submit original poems in English, on any subject, no more than 40 lines/poem, typed on 1 side only of A4 paper, double- or single-spaced. Each poem must be titled. No identifying information on poems. Do not staple pages. Accepts online submissions; full details available on the National Poetry Competition pages on the Poetry Society website. Entry form (required) available for A5 SAE (1 entry form covers multiple entries, may be photocopied). Include SAE or SAP for notification of receipt of postal entries (confirmation of online entries will be e-mailed at time of submission); poems will not be returned. Guidelines available on website. Entry fee: £6 for first poem, £3 for each subsequent entry (Poetry Society members can enter a second poem free of charge). "Only sterling (checks, postal orders, money orders, or credit cards) will be accepted. All other payments will be returned. Checks must be drawn from UK banks." Make checks payable to the Poetry Society. Deadline: October 31. Acquisitions: Competition Organiser. Estab. 1978.

HOWARD NEMEROV SONNET AWARD

E-mail: mona.3773@yahoo.com. Website: theformalist.evansville.edu/contest.html. **CONTACT:** Mona Baer, contest coordinator. Although The Formalist has ceased publication, it continues to sponsor the annual Howard Nemerov Sonnet Award. Offers $1,000 prize; winner and 11 finalists will be published in Measure: A Review of Formal Poetry (see separate listing in Magazines/Journals). Submit original, unpublished sonnets, no translations; sonnet sequences acceptable, but each sonnet will be considered individually. Poets may enter as many sonnets as they wish. Poet's name, address, phone number, and e-mail address should be listed on the **back** of each entry. Enclose SASE for contest results; mss will not be returned. Guidelines available for SASE or on website. **ENTRY FEE:** $3/sonnet. Make all checks payable to The Formalist. Entry fees from outside U.S. must be paid in U.S dollars via check drawn on a U.S. bank or by cash. **DEADLINE:** November 15 (postmark). 2010 winner was Catherine Chandler. 2010 judge was A. E. Stallings.

🌑⑤ THE NEW ISSUES POETRY PRIZE

New Issues Poetry & Prose, New issues Poetry & Prose, Dept. of English, Western Michigan University, 1903 W. Michigan Ave., Kalamazoo MI 49008-5331. (269)387-8185. Fax: (269)387-2562. E-mail: new-issues@wmich.edu. Website: www.wmich.edu/newissues. The New Issues Poetry Prize offers $2,000 plus publication of a book-length ms. Open to "poets writing in English who have not previously published a full-length collection of poems." Additional mss will be considered from those submitted to the competition for publication. Considers simultaneous submissions, but New Issues must be notified of acceptance elsewhere. Submit ms of at least 48 pages, typed, single-spaced preferred. Clean photocopies acceptable. Do not bind; use manila folder or metal clasp. Include cover page with poet's name, address, phone number, and title of the ms. Also include brief bio and acknowledgments page. No e-mail or fax submissions. Include SASP for notification of receipt of ms and SASE for results only; no mss will be returned. Guidelines available for SASE, by fax, by e-mail, or on website. **ENTRY FEE:** $20. Make checks payable to New Issues Poetry & Prose. **DEADLINE:** November 30 (postmark). Winning manuscript will be named in May and published in the next spring. 2010 winner was Journal of American Foreign Policy, by Jeff Hoffman. "A national judge selects the prize winner and recommends other manuscripts. The editors decide on the other books considering the judge's recommendation, but are not bound by it." 2011 judge: David Wojahn.

❶❸ NEW LETTERS PRIZE FOR POETRY

New Letters Awards for Writers, UMKC, University House, 5101 Rockhill Road, Kansas City MO 64110-2499. Website: www.newletters.org. The annual New Letters Poetry Prize awards $1,500 and publication in *New Letters* (see separate listing in Magazines/Journals) to the best group of 3-6 poems. All entries will be considered for publication in *New Letters*. Submissions must be unpublished. Considers simultaneous submissions with notification upon acceptance elsewhere. Accepts multiple entries with separate fee for each. Submit up to 6 poems (need not be related). Include 2 cover sheets: 1 with poet's name, address, e-mail, phone number, prize category (poetry), and poem title(s); the second with category and poem title(s) only. No identifying information on ms pages. Accepts electronic submissions. Include SASE for notification of receipt of ms and entry number, and SASE for results only (send only 1 envelope if submitting multiple entries); mss will not be returned. Guidelines available for SASE or on website. **ENTRY FEE:** $15 for first entry, $10 for each subsequent entry; includes cost of a one-year subscription, renewal, or

gift subscription to *New Letters* (shipped to any address within the U.S.). Make checks payable to New Letters . **DEADLINE:** May 18 (postmark). 2009 winner was Heather Bell. 2009 judge was Kim Addonizio. "Current students and employees of the University of Missouri-Kansas City, and current volunteer members of the *New Letters* and BkMk Press staffs, are not eligible."

❶❸ NEW WOMEN'S VOICES CHAPBOOK COMPETITION

Finishing Line Press, P.O. Box 1626, Georgetown KY 40324. (859)514-8966. E-mail: FinishingBooks@aol. com. Website: www.finishinglinepress.com. **CONTACT:** Leah Maines, poetry editor.

❸ NORTH CAROLINA WRITERS' FELLOWSHIPS

(919)807-6500. Fax: (919)807-6532. E-mail: david-potorti@ncdcr.gov. Website: www.ncarts.org. **CONTACT:** David Potorti, literature director. North Carolina Arts Council, Dept. of Cultural Resources, Raleigh NC 27699-4632. (919)807-6500. Fax: (919)807-6532. E-mail: david.potorti@ncdcr.gov. Website: www.ncarts.org. Acquisitions: David Potorti, literature director and arts editor. Offered every even year to support writers of fiction, poetry, literary nonfiction, literary translation, and spoken word. See website for guidelines and other eligibility requirements. Writers must be current residents of North Carolina for at least 1 year, must remain in residence in North Carolina during the grant year, and may not pursue academic or professional degrees while receiving grant. Fellowships offered to support writers in the development and creation of their work. Deadline: Next offered in fall, 2012, see website for details. $10,000 grant. Reviewed by a panel of literature professionals (writers and editors).

NORTHERN CALIFORNIA BOOK AWARDS

Northern California Book Reviewers Association, c/o Poetry Flash, 1450 Fourth St. #4, Berkeley CA 94710. (510)525-5476. E-mail: editor@poetryflash.org. Website: www.poetryflash.org. **CONTACT:** Joyce Jenkins, exec. director. Northern California Book Awards, c/o Poetry Flash, 1450 Fourth St. #4, Berkeley CA 94710. (510) 525-5476. Fax: (510) 525-6752. E-mail: editor@ poetryflash.org. Website: www.poetryflash.org. "Offers annual awards to recognize "the best of Northern California (from Fresno north) fiction, poetry, nonfiction, and children's literature, as chosen by the Northern California Book Reviewers Association." NCBA translation award is selected by Center for the Art of Translation and the NCBR submissions must be published in the calendar year. Submit 3 copies of each book entered. The authors of the submitted books must live in Northern California. Guidelines on website. Deadline: December 1. NCBR also presents the Fred Cody Award for Lifetime Achievement for a body of work and service to the literary community. The Fred Cody Award does not accept applications. Estab. 1981.

ⓘⓢ OHIO STATE UNIVERSITY PRESS/ THE JOURNAL AWARD IN POETRY

Website: www.ohiostatepress.org. 180 Pressey Hall, 1070 Carmack Rd., Columbus OH 43210-1002. (614)292-6930. Fax: (614)292-2065. E-mail: ohiostatepress@osu.edu. Website: www.ohiostatepress.org. Each year The Journal selects one full-length book ms for publication by Ohio State University Press. Winner also receives the Charles B. Wheeler Prize of $3,000. Each entrant receives a one-year subscription (2 issues) to The Journal . Manuscript must be unpublished as a collection, but poems may have been published elsewhere and must be identified as such. Submit at least 48 pages of original poetry, typed; clear photocopies acceptable. Include cover page and contact information; poet's name or other identification must not appear on ms pages. Include SASP for notification of receipt of ms and SASE for results; no mss will be returned. Guidelines available for SASE, by e-mail, or on website. **ENTRY FEE:** $25. Make checks/money orders payable to The Ohio State University. **DEADLINE:** entry must be postmarked within the month of September. 2010 winner was Edward Hoeppner (Blood Prism).

⊕ OPEN SEASON AWARDS

The Malahat Review, University of Victoria, P.O. Box 1700, Stn CSC, Victoria BC V8V 2Y2, Canada. Fax: (250)472-5051. E-mail: malahat@uvic.ca. Website: www.malahatreview.ca. **CONTACT:** John Barton, editor. The annual Open Season Awards offers $1000 CAD and publication in *The Malahat Review* (see separate listing in Magazines/Journals). The Open Season Awards accepts entries of poetry, fiction, and creative non-fiction. Submissions must be unpublished. No simultaneous submissions. Submit up to 3 poems per entry, each poem not to exceed 100 lines; one piece of fiction (2500 words max.), or one piece of creative non-fiction (2500 words max.), no restrictions on subject matter or aesthetic approach. Include separate page with writer's name, address, e-mail, and title(s); no identifying information on mss pages. No e-mail submissions. Do not include SASE for results; mss will not be returned. Guidelines available on Web site. Entry fee: $35 CAD for Canadian entries, $40 USD for US entries, ($45 USD for entries from Mexico and outside North America); includes a one-year subscription to *The Malahat Review*. Deadline: November 1 (postmark) every year. 2010 winner in poetry category: Lorri Nielsen Glenn. Winner and finalists contacted by e-mail. Winners published in Spring issue of *Malahat Review* announced in winter on Web site, facebook page, and in quarterly e-newsletter, *Malahat lite*.

● OREGON BOOK AWARDS

224 NW 13th Ave., Ste. 306, #219, Portland OR 97209. E-mail: susan@literary-arts.org. Website: www.literary-arts.org. **CONTACT:** Susan Denning.

ⓘⓢ GUY OWEN PRIZE

Dept. of Languages, Literature and Philosophy, Armstrong Atlantic State Univ., 11935 Abercorn St., Savannah GA 31419-1997. (912)344-3123. E-mail: tonyraymorris@gmail.com (inquiries only). Website: www.southernpoetryreview.org. **CONTACT:** Tony Morris, managing editor.

ⓘⓢ PAUMANOK POETRY AWARD

English Department, Knapp Hall, Farmingdale State College of New York, 2350 Broadhollow Rd., Route 110, Farmingdale NY 11735. E-mail: brownml@farmingdale.edu. Website: www.farmingdale.edu. **CONTACT:** Margery L. Brown, director, Visiting Writers Program. Offers 1st Prize of $1,500 plus an all-expense-paid feature reading in their 2012-2013 visiting writers series. **(PLEASE NOTE: TRAVEL EXPENSES WITHIN THE CONTINENTAL U.S. ONLY.)** Also awards two 2nd Prizes of $750 plus expenses for a reading in the series. Submit cover letter, 1 paragraph literary bio, and 3-5 poems (no more than 10 pages total), published or unpublished. Include cover page with name, address, and phone number. Guidelines available for SASE or on website. **ENTRY FEE:** $25. Make checks payable to Farmingdale State University of New York, VWP. **DEADLINE:** by September 15 (postmark). Include SASE for results (to be mailed by late December); results also posted on website. Competition receives over 600 entries. 2010 winners were Mary Jo Bang (1st Prize) and Ellen Bass and Kathleen Spivack (runners-up).

PAVEMENT SAW PRESS CHAPBOOK AWARD

321 Empire Street, Montpelier OH 43543-1301. E-mail: info@pavementsaw.org. Website: www.pavementsaw.org. **CONTACT:** David Baratier, editor. Pavement Saw Press Chapbook Award is open to all poets regardless of previous publication history. SGuidelines available for SASE or on website. "Every entrant will receive the equivalent cost of the entry fee in Pavement Saw Press titles." Make checks payable to Pavement Saw Press. 2009 winner was Brian Teare.

PEARL POETRY PRIZE

Pearl Editions, 3030 E. Second St., Long Beach CA 90803. (562)434-4523. Fax: (562)434-4523. E-mail: pearlmag@aol.com. Website: www.pearlmag.com. **CONTACT:** Marilyn Johnson, editor/publisher. The annual Pearl Poetry Prize awards $1,000, publication, and 25 author's copies for a book-length ms. Guidelines available for SASE or on website. **ENTRY FEE:** $20. **DEADLINE:** submit May 1-June 30 only. 2009 winner was Kim roberts (*Animal Magnetism*). 2012 judge: Andrea Carter Brown.

PEN CENTER USA LITERARY AWARDS

(424)258-1180. E-mail: awards@penusa.org. Website: www.penusa.org. **CONTACT:** Literary Awards Coordinator. PEN Center USA Literary Awards. PEN Center USA. Offered for work published or produced in the previous calendar year. Open to writers living west of the Mississippi River. Award categories: fiction, poetry, research nonfiction, creative nonfiction, translation, children's/young adult, drama, screenplay, teleplay, journalism. Guidelines and submission form available on website. for SASE or download from website.Entry fee: $35 Entry fee. Deadline for book categories: 4 copies must be received by December 31. Deadline for non-book categories: 4 copies must be received by January 31.

PEN/VOELCKER AWARD FOR POETRY

(212)334-1600, ext. 108. E-mail: awards@pen.org. Website: www.pen.org. **CONTACT:** Nick Burd, Literary awards program manager. *Candidates may only be nominated by members of PEN.* Award given to an American poet whose distinguished and growing body of work to date represents a notable and accomplished presence in American literature. Offered in even-numbered years. Last year was in 2010; will be offered in 2012.

PERUGIA PRESS PRIZE

Perugia Press, P.O. Box 60364, Florence MA 01062. E-mail: info@perugiapress.com. Website: www.perugiapress.com. **CONTACT:** Susan Kan. The Perugia Press Prize for a first or second poetry book by a woman offers $1,000 and publication. Poet must be a living U.S. resident with no more than 1 previously published book of poems (chapbooks don't count). Submissions must be unpublished as a collection, but individual poems may have been previously published in journals, chapbooks, and anthologies. Considers simultaneous submissions if notified of acceptance elsewhere. Submit 48-72 pages (white paper) "with legible typeface, pagination, and fastened with a removable clip. No more than 1 poem per page." Two cover pages required: 1 with ms title, poet's name, address, telephone number, and e-mail address; and 1 with ms title only. Include table of contents and acknowledgments page. Electronic submissions available through our website. No translations or self-published books. Multiple submissions accepted if accompanied by separate entry fee for each. Include SASE for winner notification only; mss will be recycled. Guidelines available on website. **ENTRY FEE:** $25. Make checks payable to Perugia Press. **DEADLINE:** submit August 1-November 15 (postmark). "Use USPS or electronic submission, not FedEx or UPS." Winner announced by April 1 by e-mail or SASE (if included with entry). Judges: panel of Perugia authors, booksellers, scholars, etc.

THE RICHARD PETERSON POETRY PRIZE

Dept. of English, Mail Code 4503, Faner Hall 2380, Southern Illinois Univ Carbondale, Carbondale IL 62901. Website: www.craborchardreview.siuc.edu. **CONTACT:** Jon Tribble, managing editor. The Richard Peterson Poetry Prize offers $2,000 plus publication in the Winter/Spring issue of Crab Orchard Review (see separate listing in Magazines/Journals). "Submissions must be unpublished original work not under consideration elsewhere, written in English by a U.S. citizen or permanent resident. Name, address, telephone number, and/or e-mail address should appear only on the title page of manuscript; author's name should not appear on any subsequent pages. Mark 'poetry' on outside of envelope. Include #10 SASE for notification of winners." See guidelines for complete formatting instructions. Guidelines available for SASE or on website. **ENTRY FEE:** $20/entry (3 poems, 100 line limit per poem, no more than 1 poem per page; poet may submit up to 3 separate entries if not entering the fiction or nonfiction categories of the contest). Each fee entitles entrant to a one year subscription to Crab Orchard Review featuring the prize winner; include complete address. Make checks payable to Crab Orchard Review. **DEADLINE:** see guidelines or check website.

THE PINCH LITERARY AWARD IN FICTION AND POETRY

(901)678-4591. E-mail: editor@thepinchjournal.com. Website: www.thepinchjournal.com. Offered annually for unpublished short stories of 5,000 words maximum or up to three poems. Guidelines on website. Cost: $20/ which is put toward one issue of *The Pinch*. Deadline: March 15. Prize: 1st Place Fiction: $1,500 and publication; 1st Place Poetry: $1,000 and publication.

◑$ PLAN B PRESS POETRY CHAPBOOK CONTEST

P.O. Box 4067, Alexandria VA 22303. (215)732-2663. E-mail: planbpress@gmail.com. Website: www.planbpress.com. **CONTACT:** Contest Coordinator. The annual Plan B Press Poetry Chapbook Contest offers $225, publication by Plan B Press (see separate listing in Book/Chapbook Publishers), and 50 author's copies. Poems may be previously published individually. Accepts multiple submissions with separate fee for each. Submit up to 24 poems (48 pages total maximum) in English. Include table of contents and list of acknowledgments. Include e-mail address or SASE for notification of winner; mss will not be returned. Author retains copyright of poems, but Plan B reserves rights to layout and/or cover art and design. Guidelines available on website. **ENTRY FEE:** $15. **DEADLINE:** March 1.

PNWA LITERARY CONTEST

Pacific Northwest Writers Association, PMB 2717-1420 NW Gilman Blvd, Ste 2, Issaquah WA 98027. (425)673-2665. Fax: (206)824-4559. E-mail: staff@pnwa.org. Website: www.pnwa.org. **CONTACT:** Kelli Liddane.

◑$ POETR 2012 INTERNATIONAL POETRY COMPETITION

Atlanta Review, P.O. Box 8248, Atlanta GA 31106. E-mail: atlrev@yahoo.com. Website: www.atlantareview.com. **CONTACT:** Dan Veach, Editor/Publisher. *Atlanta Review* (see separate listing in Magazines/Journals) sponsors an annual international poetry competition, offering $2,010 Grand Prize, 20 International Publication Awards (winners will be published in *Atlanta Review*), and 30 International Merit Awards (includes certificate, Honorable Mention in *Atlanta Review*, and free issue). Poems must not have been published in a nationally distributed print publication. Online entry available at journal website. For mail entry: put your name and address on each page (e-mail and phone optional). Include SASE for results only; no entries will be returned. Guidelines available on website. **ENTRY FEE:** $5 for the first poem, $3 for each additional poem. Make checks payable to *Atlanta Review*. International entrants must use online entry. **DEADLINE:** March 1, 2011. Winners will be announced in August; Contest Issue published in October. Contest Issue available for $4, or free with $10 subscription to *Atlanta Review*.

⊕∅$ POETS & PATRONS ANNUAL CHICAGOLAND POETRY CONTEST

Sponsored by Poets & Patrons of Chicago, 416 Gierz St., Downers Grove IL 60515-3838. E-mail: eatonb1016@aol.com. Website: www.poetsandpatrons.org. **CONTACT:** Barbara Eaton, director.

PRAIRIE SCHOONER BOOK PRIZE

Prairie Schooner and the University of Nebraska Press, 123 Andrews Hall, University of Nebraska, Lincoln NE 68588-0334. (402)472-0911. E-mail: jengelhardt2@unlnotes.unl.edu; jengelhardt2@unl.edu. Website: prairieschooner.unl.edu. **CONTACT:** Kwame Dawes, editor. The annual Prairie Schooner Book Prize Series offers $3,000 and publication of a book-length collection of poetry by the University of Nebraska Press. Individual poems may have been previously published elsewhere. Considers simultaneous submissions if notified immediately of acceptance elsewhere. Submit at least 50 pages of poetry with acknowledgments page (if applicable). Poet's name should not appear on ms pages. Xeroxed copies are acceptable. Bind with rubber band or binder clip only. Include 2 cover pages: one with poet's name, address, phone number, and e-mail address; the other with ms title only. Include SASP for acknowledgment of receipt of ms and #10 SASE for results only; mss will not be returned. Guidelines available for SASE, by e-mail, or on website. **ENTRY FEE:** $25. Make checks payable to Prairie Schooner . **DEADLINE:** January 15-March 15 annually. 2008 winner was Kara Candito (*Taste of Cherry*). Winners announced on website in early July, with results mailed shortly thereafter. (See separate listing for Prairie Schooner in Magazines/Journals.)

RATTLE POETRY PRIZE

RATTLE, 12411 Ventura Blvd., Studio City CA 91604. (818) 505-6777. E-mail: tim@rattle.com. Website: www.rattle.com. **CONTACT:** Timothy Green, Editor. The RATTLE Poetry Prize awards 1st Prize of $5,000, plus fifteen $100 Finalists. Additional entries may be offered publication as well. Open to writers worldwide (see website for special international guidelines). Poems must be written in English (no translations). No previously published poems or works accepted for publication elsewhere. No simultaneous submissions. Submit no more than 4 poems/entry. Multiple entries by a single poet accepted; however, each 4-poem group must be treated as a separate entry with its own cover sheet and entry fee. Include cover sheet with poet's name, address, e-mail address, phone number, and poem titles. No contact information should appear on poems. Include SASE for results only; no poems will be returned. **NOTE:** Poems also may be entered through online submission on website. Guidelines available by e-mail or on website. **ENTRY FEE:** $18; includes one-year subscription to RATTLE (see separate listing in Magazines/Journals). Make checks/money orders payable to RATTLE (for credit card entries, see website). **DEADLINE:** August 1 (postmark). 2010 winner was Patricia Smith ("Tavern. Tavern. Church. Shuttered Tavern,"). Judge: Finalists selected by editors of RATTLE in blind review; winner voted on by subscribers/entrants after publication. Finalists announced in September; winner announced the following February.

MARGARET REID POETRY CONTEST FOR TRADITIONAL VERSE

c/o Winning Writers, 351 Pleasant St., PMB 222, Northampton MA 01060-3961. E-mail: johnreid@ mail.qango.com. Website: www.winningwriters. com. **CONTACT:** John Reid. Offers annual award of 1st Prize: $3,000; 2nd Prize: $1,000; 3rd Prize: $400; 4th Prize: $250; 5 High Distinction Awards of $200 each; and 6 Most Highly Commended Awards of $150 each. The top 10 entries will be published on the Winning Writers website. Submissions may be published or unpublished, may have won prizes elsewhere, and may be entered in other contests. Submit poems in traditional verse forms, such as sonnets, ballads, odes, blank verse, and haiku. No limit on number of lines or number of poems submitted. No name on ms pages; type or computer-print on letter-size white paper, single-sided. Guidelines available for SASE or on website. Submit online or by mail. **ENTRY FEE:** $8 USD for every 25 lines (exclude poem title and any blank lines from count). **DEADLINE:** November 15-June 30. 2010 winner was Philip Brown ("South Sea Odyssey"). 2010 judges: John H. Reid and Dee C. Konrad. Winners announced in December at WinningWriters. com; entrants who provide valid e-mail addresses also receive notification.

ROANOKE-CHOWAN POETRY AWARD

The North Carolina Literary & Historical Assoc., 4610 Mail Service Center, Raleigh NC 27699-4610. (919)807-7290. Fax: (919)733-8807. E-mail: michael. hill@ncdcr.gov. Website: http://www.history.ncdcr. gov/affiliates/lit-hist/awards/awards.htm. **CONTACT:** Michael Hill, awards coordinator. (Specialized: NC resident authors) Offers annual award for "an original volume of poetry published during the 12 months ending June 30 of the year for which the award is given." Open to "authors who have maintained legal or physical residence, or a combination of both, in North Carolina for the 3 years preceding the close of the contest period." Submit 3 copies of each entry. Guidelines available for SASE or by fax or e-mail. **DEADLINE:** July 15. Competition receives about 15 entries. 2010 winner was Joseph R. Bathanti , professor in Appalachian State University's Department of English and co-director of the creative writing program there for Bathantiâ's poetry collection *Restoring Sacred Art,* in which Bathanti shares rich ethnic associations, religious themes and vivid memories. The collectionwas published by Star Cloud Press.

●◐ ERNEST SANDEEN PRIZE IN POETRY

Dept. of English, University of Notre Dame, Notre Dame IN 46556-5639. (574)631-7526. Fax: (574)631-4795. E-mail: creativewriting@nd.edu. Website: www.nd.edu/~ndr/sandeen.html. **CONTACT:** Director of Creative Writing. The Sandeen Prize in Poetry offers $1,000 (a $500 award and a $500 advance against royalties from the Notre Dame Press) and publication of a book-length ms. Open to poets who have published at least 1 volume of poetry. "Please include a photocopy of the copyright and the title page of your previous volume. Vanity press publications do not fulfill this requirement. We will pay special attention to second volumes. Please include a vita and/or a biographical statement that includes your publishing history. We will be glad to see a selection of reviews of the earlier collection." Submit 2 copies of ms (inform if ms is available on computer disk). Include SASE for acknowledgment of receipt of ms and SASE for return of ms. **ENTRY FEE:** $15; includes one-year subscription to Notre Dame Review (see separate listing in Magazines/Journals). Make checks payable to University of Notre Dame. **DEADLINE:** submit May 1- September 1, 2012. 2009 winner was Luisa Igloria (*Juan Luna's Revolver*). Winners announced by the end of January.

THE MONA SCHREIBER PRIZE FOR HUMOROUS FICTION & NONFICTION

E-mail: brad.schreiber@att.net. Website: www.brashcyber.com. **CONTACT:** Brad Schreiber.
TIPS "No SASE's, Please."

SHEILA MOTTON BOOK AWARD

New England Poetry Club, 2 Farrar St., Cambridge MA 02138. Website: www.nepoetryclub.org. **CONTACT:** NEPC Contest Coordinator.
TIPS "For latest rules and rules for children's contests please check New England Poetry Club site."

◐◑◐ SHORT GRAIN CONTEST

Box 67, Saskatoon SK S7K 3K1, Canada. (306)244-2828. Fax: (306)244-0255. E-mail: grainmag@sasktel.net. Website: www.grainmagazine.ca. **CONTACT:** Mike Thompson, business administrator (inquiries only). The annual Short Grain Contest includes a category for poetry of any style up to 100 lines, offering 3 prizes with a first prize of $1,000 plus publication in Grain Magazine (see separate listing in Magazines/Journals). Each entry must be original, unpublished, not submitted elsewhere for publication or broadcast, nor accepted elsewhere for publication or broadcast, nor entered simultaneously in any other contest or competition for which it is also eligible to win a prize. Entries must be typed on 8- ½x 11 paper. It must be legible. Faxed and/or electronic entries not accepted. No simultaneous submissions. A separate covering page must be attached to the text of your entry, and must provide the following information: poet's name, complete mailing address, telephone number, e-mail address, entry title, category name, and line count. An absolutely accurate word or line count is required. No identifying information on the text pages. Entries will not be returned. Include SASE for results only. Entry fee: $35 CAD; $35 for US and international entrants, in US funds; includes 1 year subscription to Grain Magazine. Deadline: April 1. Winning entries will be posted on the Grain Magazine website in August.

SLIPSTREAM ANNUAL POETRY CHAPBOOK COMPETITION

E-mail: editors@slipstreampress.org. Website: www.slipstreampress.org. **CONTACT:** Dan Sicoli, co-editor. The annual Slipstream Poetry Chapbook Contest awards $1,000, publication of a chapbook ms, and 50 author's copies. All entrants receive copy of winning chapbook and an issue of Slipstream (see separate listing in Magazines/Journals). Considers simultaneous submissions if informed of status. Accepts previously published work with acknowledgments. Submit up to 40 pages of poetry, any style, format, or theme. Manuscripts will not be returned. Guidelines available for SASE or on website. **ENTRY FEE:** $20. **DEADLINE:** December 1. Latest winner is David Chorlton (*From the Age of Miracles*). Winner announced late spring/early summer.
TIPS "Winner announced in late spring/early summer."

HELEN C. SMITH MEMORIAL AWARD FOR POETRY

(512) 238-1871. E-mail: tilsecretary@yahoo.com. Website: http://texasinstituteofletters.org/. **CONTACT:** W.K. (Kip) Stratton, acquisitions. Offered annually for the best book of poems published January 1-December 31 of previous year. Poet must have been born in Texas, have lived in the state at some time for

at least 2 consecutive years, or the subject matter must be associated with the state. See website for guidelines. Deadline: Jan. 1. Prize: $1,200.

⊙⊙ KAY SNOW WRITERS' CONTEST

9045 SW Barbur Blvd. #5A, Portland OR 97219-4027. (503)452-1592. Fax: (503)452-0372. E-mail: wilwrite@teleport.com. Website: www.willamettewriters.com. **CONTACT:** Lizzy Shannon, contest director. Entry fee is $10 for Williamette Writers' members; $15, non-members; free for student writers grades 1-12. Submissions must be unpublished. Submit up to 2 poems (1 entry fee), maximum 5 pages total, on any subject, in any style or form, single-spaced, 1 side of paper only. Entry form and guidelines available for SASE or on website. **DEADLINE:** January 15-April 23 (postmarked) for 2011. Competition receives 150 entries. "Write and send in your very best poem. Read it aloud. If it still sounds like the best poem you've ever heard, send it in."

⊙⊙ SOUL-MAKING LITERARY COMPETITION

Nob Hill, San Francisco Bay Area Branch, 1544 Sweetwood Dr., Broadmoor Vlg CA 94015-1717. (650)756-5279. Fax: (650)756-5279. E-mail: PenNobHill@aol.com. Website: www.soulmakingcontest.us. **CONTACT:** Eileen Malone, Award Director. Annual open contest offers cash prizes in each of 11 literary categories, including poetry and prose poem. 1st Prize: $100; 2nd Prize: $50; 3rd Prize: $25. Submissions in some categories may be previously published. Submit 3 one-page poems on soul-making theme; any form for open poetry category. No names or other identifying information on mss; include 3x5 card with poet's name, address, phone, fax, e-mail, title(s) of work, and category entered. Include SASE for results only; mss will not be returned. Guidelines available on website. **ENTRY FEE:** $5/entry. **DEADLINE:** November 30. Competition receives 300 entries/year. Names of winners and judges are posted on website. Winners announced in January by SASE and on website. Winners are invited to read at the Koret Auditorium, San Francisco. Event is televised.

⊙⊙ THE SOW'S EAR POETRY COMPETITION

P.O. Box 127, Millwood VA 22646. E-mail: rglesman@gmail.com. Website: www.sows-ear.kitenet.net. **CONTACT:** Robert G. Lesman, Managing Editor. The Sow's Ear Poetry Review (see separate listing in Magazines/Journals) sponsors an annual contest for unpublished poems. Offers $1,000 and publication in The Sow's Ear Poetry Review. Submit up to 5 unpublished poems. Include separate sheet with poem titles, poet's name, address, phone number, and e-mail address (if available). "We will check with finalists regarding publication status of poems before sending to final judge." Poet's name should not appear on poems. Include SASE for results only; entries will not be returned. Guidelines available for SASE, by e-mail, or on website. **ENTRY FEE:** $27 for up to 5 poems. Contestants receive a year's subscription. Make checks payable to The Sow's Ear Poetry Review. Submit in September or October. **DEADLINE:** November 1 (postmark). Past judges include Gregory Orr and Marge Piercy. "Four criteria help us judge the quality of submissions: 1) Does the poem make the strange familiar or the familiar strange, or both? 2) Is the form of the poem vital to its meaning? 3) Do the sounds of the poem make sense in relation to the theme? 4) Does the little story of the poem open a window on the Big Story of the human situation?"

⊙⊙ SPIRE PRESS POETRY CHAPBOOK CONTEST

217 Thompson St., Suite 298, New York NY 10012. E-mail: editor@spirepress.org. Website: www.spirepress.org. Offers annual award of publication with royalty contract and promotion; author payment (see guidelines for each year). Submissions must be unpublished. Considers simultaneous submissions as long as Spire Press is informed. Submit a chapbook ms of 21-40 pages of poetry in any form (shorter poems preferred). Include SASE. Competition receives 400 entries/year. Past winners include Elizabeth Rees (*Now That We're Here*), Christina Olson (*Before I Came Home Naked*), Lori Romero (*The Emptiness That Makes Other Things Possible*), and Anthony Russell White (*Faith of Leaping*). Winners will be announced on website after contest deadline. Copies of winning chapbooks available through website, Amazon, selected bookstores, and Spire Press.

⊕ STAGE OF LIFE ESSAY WRITING CONTESTS

Stageoflife.com, P.O. Box 580950, Minneapolis MN 55458-0950. Fax: (717)650-3855. E-mail: contact@stageoflife.com. Website: www.stageoflife.com.

TIPS "Writer must be in the life stage for the contest they are entering."

◑ⓢ WALLACE E. STEGNER FELLOWSHIPS

Creative Writing Program, Stanford University, Stanford CA 94305-2087. (650)723-0011. Fax: (650)723-3679. E-mail: cablaza@stanford.edu. Website: www.creativewriting.stanford.edu. **CONTACT:** Christina Ablaza, Program Assistant. Offers 5 fellowships in poetry of $26,000 plus tuition of over $7,000/year for promising writers who can benefit from 2 years of instruction and criticism in the program. "We do not require a degree for admission. No school of writing is favored over any other. Chronological age is not a consideration." Accept applications between September 1 and December 1 (postmark). Applicants may apply online. Competition receives about 1,700 entries/year.

◐ STROKESTOWN INTERNATIONAL POETRY COMPETITION

Strokestown International Poetry Festival, Strokestown Poetry Festival Office, Strokestown, County Roscommon , Ireland. (+353) 71 9633759. E-mail: office@strokestownpoetry.org. Website: www.strokestownpoetry.org. **CONTACT:** Director.

●ⓢ MAY SWENSON POETRY AWARD

Utah State University Press, 7800 Old Main Hill, Logan UT 84322-7800. (435)797-1362. Fax: (435)797-0313. E-mail: michael.spooner@usu.edu. Website: www.usupress.org. **CONTACT:** Michael Spooner, director. The annual Swenson Award Competition offers a $1,000 prize plus publication for a full-length poetry collection. Must be original poetry in English, 50 to 100 pages. No restrictions on form or subject. $25 reading fee (includes copy of winning book). Postmark deadline September 30. Previous winners include Idris Anderson, Jason Whitmarsh, Elisabeth Murawski. Previous judges include Harold Bloom, Grace Schulman, Billy Collins, and Edward Field. See website for guidelines and the full series of Swenson volumes.

✚ⓢ TEXAS INSTITUTE OF LETTERS BOB BUSH MEMORIAL AWARD FOR FIRST BOOK OF POETRY

Website: http://texasinstituteofletters.org. **CONTACT:** W.K. (Kip) Stratton, acquisitions. Offered annually for best first book of poetry published in previous year. Writer must have been born in Texas, have lived in the state at least 2 consecutive years at some time, or the subject matter should be associated with the state. Deadline: Jan. 1. Prize: $1,000.

◑ⓢ THE AMERICAN POET PRIZE FOR POETRY

The American Poetry Journal, P.O. Box 2080, Aptos CA 95001-2080. E-mail: editor@americanpoetryjournal.com. Website: www.americanpoetryjournal.com. **CONTACT:** J.P. Dancing Bear, Editor. The American Poet Prize for Poetry offers $500 and publication in The American Poetry Journal (see separate listing in Magazines/Journals). All entries will be considered for publication, and all entrants receive a year's subscription. Submissions must be unpublished. Considers simultaneous submissions with notification. Accepts multiple submissions with separate fee for each entry (3 poems). Submit up to 3 original poems (10 pages maximum total). Include cover with poem titles, poet's name, contact information (including e-mail address), and bio. NO results will be posted on-line and in email. Guidelines available on website. **ENTRY FEE:** $16; all entrants receive a year's subscription to The American Poetry Journal . Make checks payable to Dream Horse Press. **DEADLINE:** July 1. Judge: all selections and winners made by the editor. Personal friends, relatives, and/or students of the editor are NOT eligible for the contest (their entry fees will be refunded).

◐● THE BOARDMAN TASKER AWARD FOR MOUNTAIN LITERATURE

The Boardman Tasker Charitable Trust, 8 Bank View Rd., Darley Abbey Derby DE22 1EJ, UK. Phone/fax: UK 01332342246. E-mail: steve@people-matter.co.uk. Website: www.boardmantasker.com. **CONTACT:** Steve Dean. "The award is to honor Peter Boardman and Joe Tasker, who disappeared on Everest in 1982." Offered annually to reward a work of nonfiction or fiction, in English or in translation, which has made an outstanding contribution to mountain literature. Books must be published in the UK between November 1 of previous year and October 31 of year of the prize. Writers may obtain information, but entry is by publishers only (includes self-publishing). "No restriction of nationality, but work must be published or distributed in the UK." Prize: £3,000. Judged by a panel of 3 judges elected by trustees. No entry fee. "May be fiction, nonfiction, poetry or drama. Not an anthology. Subject must be concerned with a mountain environment. Previous winners have been books on expeditions, climbing experiences, a biography of a mountaineer, novels." Guidelines available in January by e-mail or on website. Deadline: Midnight of August 17. Entries must be previously published. Publisher's entry only. Open to any writer. Results announced in November. Winners notified by phone or e-mail. For contest results, send e-mail or visit website. "The winning book needs to be well written to reflect a knowledge of and a respect and appreciation for the mountain environment."

❶❷❸❹ THE CENTER FOR BOOK ARTS POETRY CHAPBOOK COMPETITION

The Center for Book Arts, 28 W. 27th St., 3rd Floor, New York NY 10001. (212)481-0295. Fax: (866)708-8994. E-mail: info@centerforbookarts.org. Website: www.centerforbookarts.org. **CONTACT:** Sarah Nicholls. Competition offered annually for unpublished collections of poetry. Individual poems may have been previously published. Collection must not exceed 500 lines or 24 pages. Deadline: December 1 (postmarked). Prize: $500 award, $500 honorarium for a reading, publication, and 10 copies of letterpress printed, handbound chapbook. Cost: $25 fee. The Center for Book Arts, 28 W. 27th St., 3rd Floor, New York NY 10001. Phone: (212)481-0295. Fax: (866)708-8994. Email: info@centerforbookarts.org. Website: www.centerforbookarts.org.

> Contest needs poetry chapbooks. Offered annually for unpublished collections of poetry. Individual poems may have been previously published. Collection must not exceed 500 lines or 24 pages. Copies of winning chapbooks available through website.

❷❸ THE HODDER FELLOWSHIP

(609)258-4096. E-mail: jbraude@princeton.edu. Website: www.princeton.edu/arts/lewis_center/society_of_fellows. **CONTACT:** Janine Braude, program assistant-Creative Writing. "The Hodder Fellowship will be given to writers of exceptional promise to pursue independent projects at Princeton University during the 2011-2012 academic year. Typically the fellows are poets, playwrights, novelists, creative nonfiction writers and translators who have published one highly acclaimed work and are undertaking a significant new project that might not be possible without the "studious leisure" afforded by the fellowship. Preference is given to applicants outside academia. Candidates for the Ph.D. are not eligible. Submit a resumè, sample of previous work (10 pages maximum, not returnable), and a project proposal of 2-3 pages. Guidelines available on website. Princeton University is an equal opportunity employer and complies with applicable EEO and affirmative action regulations. Apply online at http://jobs.princeton.edu or for general application information and how to self-identify, see http://www.princeton.edu/dof/ApplicantsInfo.htm. We strongly recommend, however, that all interested candidates use the online application process. Deadline: November 1, 2010 (postmarked). Stipend: $63,900." Email: jbraude@princeton.edu. The current deadline has passed.

TIPS The current deadline has passed.

❶❸ THE LEAGUE OF MINNESOTA POETS CONTEST

Website: www.mnpoets.org. **CONTACT:** Susan Stevens Chambers. Website: www.mnpoets.org (see website for current contact information). **CONTACT:** Susan Stevens Chambers. Annual contest offers 18 different categories, with 3 prizes in each category ranging from $10-125. See guidelines for poem lengths, forms, and subjects. Guidelines available for #10 SASE, by e-mail, or on website. **ENTRY FEE:** (nonmembers) $1/poem per category; $2/poem (limit 6) for Grand Prize category; (members) $5 for 17 categories; $1/poem (limit 6) for Grand Prize category. Make checks payable to LOMP Contest. **DEADLINE:** July 31. Judged by nationally known, non-Minnesota judges. Winners will be announced at the October LOMP Conference and by mail. Additional information regarding LOMP membership available on website.

❶❸ THE LEVIS POETRY PRIZE

Four Way Books, Box 535, Village Station, New York NY 10014. (212)334-5430. Fax: (212)334-5435. E-mail: editors@fourwaybooks.com. Website: www.fourwaybooks.com. **CONTACT:** Martha Rhodes, director. The Levis Poetry Prize, offered biennially in odd-numbered years, offers publication by Four Way Books (see separate listing in Book/Chapbook Publishers), honorarium ($1,000), and a reading at one or more participating series. Open to any poet writing in English. Entry form and guidelines available on website. **ENTRY FEE:** $25. **DEADLINE:** March 31 (postmark). Winner announced by e-mail and on website. Copies of winning books available through Four Way Books online and at bookstores (to the trade through University Press of New England).

THE MACGUFFIN NATIONAL POET HUNT

The MacGuffin, 18600 Haggerty Rd., Livonia MI 48152. E-mail: macguffin@schoolcraft.edu. Website: www.macguffin.org. **CONTACT:** Nicholle Cormier, Managing Editor. Work is judged blindly by a renowned, published poet. Offered annually for unpublished work. Guidelines available by mail, e-mail, or on the website. Acquires first rights (if published). Once published, all rights revert to the author. Open to any writer. All non-winning poems will also be considered by staff for publication in an upcoming issue of *The MacGuffin*.$15 for a 5-poem entry. Check or MO payable to Schoolcraft College. Deadline: April 3-June 3 (postmarked)1st Place: $500; 2 Honorable Mentions will be published.2011 Judge: Terry Blackhawk. Past judges include Thomas Lynch, Vivian Shipley, Molly Peacock, Bob Hicok, Laurence Lieberman, Thomas Lux, and Conrad Hilberry.

☮☉ THE MALAHAT REVIEW LONG POEM PRIZE

E-mail: malahat@uvic.ca (queries only). Website: www.malahatreview.ca. **CONTACT:** John Barton, Editor. The biennial Long Poem Prize offers 2 awards of $1000 CAD each for a long poem or cycle (10-20 printed pages). Includes publication in The Malahat Review (see separate listing in Magazines/Journals). Open to "entries from Canadian, American, and overseas authors." Submissions must be unpublished. No simultaneous submissions. Submit a single poem or cycle of poems, 10-20 published pages (a published page equals 32 lines or less, including breaks between stanzas); no restrictions on subject matter or aesthetic approach. Include separate page with poet's name, address, e-mail, and title; no identifying information on mss pages. No e-mail submissions. Do not include SASE for results; mss will not be returned. Guidelines available on website. **ENTRY FEE:** $35 CAD for Canadian entries, $40 USD for US entries ($45 USD for entries from Mexico and outside North America); includes one-year subscription to *The Malahat Review.* **DEADLINE:** February 1 (postmark) of alternate years

(2011, 2013, etc.). 2009 winners: matt robinson, Marion Quednau. 2009 judges: Steve Noyes, Katia Grubisic, and Kathy Mac. Winners published in the June issue of *The Malahat Review,* announced in summer on website, Facebook page, and in quarterly e-newsletter *Malahat lite.*

❶☉ THE ORPHIC PRIZE FOR POETRY

Dream Horse Press, P.O. Box 2080, Aptos CA 95001-2080. E-mail: dreamhorsepress@yahoo.com. Website: www.dreamhorsepress.com. **CONTACT:** J.P. Dancing Bear, Editor/Publisher. The Orphic Prize for Poetry offers an annual award of $1,000 and publication of a book-length ms by Dream Horse Press. All entries will be considered for publication. Both free and formal verse styles are welcome. Submissions may be entered in other contests, "but if your manuscript is accepted for publication elsewhere, you must notify Dream Horse Press immediately." Submit 48-80 pages of poetry, paginated, with table of contents, acknowledgments, and bio. Include separate cover letter with poet's name, biographical information, and e-mail address (when available). Poet's name should not appear anywhere on the ms. Manuscripts will be recycled after judging. Guidelines available on website. **ENTRY FEE:** $25/ms entered. Entry fees are non-refundable. Make checks/money orders payable to Dream Horse Press. **DEADLINE:** August 31; check website for deadlines and details for subsequent years. Recent winners include: Kyle McCord, Gary L. McDowell and Juliana A. Gray. Judging will be anonymous.

⬤☉ THE PATERSON POETRY PRIZE

(973)684-6555. Fax: (973)523-6085. E-mail: mgillan@pccc.edu. Website: www.pccc.edu/poetry. **CONTACT:** Maria Mazziotti Gillan, Exec. Director. The Paterson Poetry Prize offers an annual award of $1,000 for the strongest book of poems (48 or more pages) published in the previous year. The winner will be asked to participate in an awards ceremony and to give a reading at The Poetry Center. Minimum press run: 500 copies. Publishers may submit more than 1 title for prize consideration; 3 copies of each book must be submitted. Include SASE for results; books will not be returned (all entries will be donated to the Poetry Center Library). Guidelines and application form (required) available for SASE or on website. **ENTRY FEE:** none. **DEADLINE:** February 1 (postmark). Winners will be announced in Poets & Writers Magazine and on website. 2010 winner was Sherman Alexie for the book *Face*.

●⊙ THE PATRICIA BIBBY FIRST BOOK AWARD

Tebot Bach, P.O. Box 7887, Huntington Beach CA 92615-7887. E-mail: mifanwy@tebotbach.org. Website: www.tebotbach.org. **CONTACT:** Mifanwy Kaiser. The Patricia Bibby First Book Award offers $1,000 and publication of a book-length poetry manuscript by Tebot Bach (see separate listing in Book/Chapbook Publishers). Open to "all poets writing in English who have not committed to publishing collections of poetry of 36 poems or more in editions of over 400 copies." Submissions must be unpublished as a collection, but individual poems may have been previously published elsewhere. Considers simultaneous submissions, but Tebot Bach must be notified immediately by e-mail if the collection is accepted for publication. Partial guidelines: Submit 60-84 pages of poetry, letter-quality, single-spaced; clear photocopies acceptable. Use binder clip; no staples, folders, or printer-bound copies. Include 2 title pages: 1 (not fastened to ms) with ms title, poet's name, address, phone number, and e-mail address; the second (fastened to ms) with ms title only. Also include table of contents. Include SASP for notification of receipt of entry and SASE for results only; mss will not be returned. Complete guidelines available by e-mail or on website. **READING FEE:** $25. Make checks/money orders payable to Tebot Bach with reading fee and title of ms. on the notation line. **DEADLINE:** October 31 (postmark) annually. Winner announced each year in April. Judges are selected annually. Email: mifanwy@tebotbach.org; Website: www.tebotbach.org.

❶⊙ THE RICHARD SNYDER MEMORIAL PUBLICATION PRIZE

Ashland Poetry Press, 401 College Ave., Ashland University, Ashland OH 44805. E-mail: app@ashland.edu. Website: www.ashland.edu/aupoetry. **CONTACT:** Sarah Wells, managing editor. Offers annual award of $1,000 plus book publication in a paper-only edition of 1,000 copies. Submissions must be unpublished in book form. Considers simultaneous submissions. Submit 50-80 pages of poetry. **ENTRY FEE:** $25. **DEADLINE:** April 30 annually. Competition receives 350 entries/year. 2009 Winner was Jason Schneiderman (*Striking Surface*). 2010 judge: David Wojahn.

Winners will be announced in Writer's Chronicle and Poets & Writers . Copies of winning books available from Small Press Distribution, Baker & Taylor, and directly from the Ashland University Bookstore online. The Ashland Poetry Press publishes 2-4 books of poetry/year.

THE ROBINSON JEFFERS TOR HOUSE 2011 PRIZE FOR POETRY

(831)624-1180. Fax: (831)624-1180. E-mail: thf@torhouse.org. Website: www.torhouse.org. **CONTACT:** Eliot Ruchowitz-Roberts, Poetry Prize Coordinator. "The annual Prize for Poetry is a living memorial to American poet Robinson Jeffers (1887-1962). Open to well-crafted poetry in all styles, ranging from experimental work to traditional forms, including short narrative poems. Each poem should be typed on 8 1/2" by 11" paper, and no longer than three pages. On a cover sheet only, include: name, mailing address, telephone number and email; titles of poems; bio optional. Multiple and simultaneous submissions welcome.$10 for first 3 poems, $15 for up to 6 poems; $2.50 for each additional poem. Checks and money orders should be made out to Tor House Foundation. Send poems, fee and SASE to Poetry Prize Coordinator, Tor House Foundation, P.O. Box 223240, Carmel, CA 93922. The annual Tor House Prize for Poetry is a living memorial to American poet Robinson Jeffers (1887-1962). Deadline: March 15. Prize: $1,000 honorarium for award-winning poem; $200 for up to 4 Honorable Mentions. Poems must be original and unpublished. Final judging by Ellen Bass."

❶⊙ TOM HOWARD/JOHN H. REID POETRY CONTEST

Tom Howard Books, c/o Winning Writers, 351 Pleasant St., PMB 222, Northampton MA 01060-3961. (866)946-9748. Fax: (413)280-0539. E-mail: johnreid@mail.qango.com. Website: www.winningwriters.com/poetry. **CONTACT:** John Reid, award director. Email: johnreid@mail.qango.com. Website: www.winningwriters.com/poetry. Contact: John Reid, award director Offers annual award of 1st Prize: $3,000; 2nd Prize: $1,000; 3rd Prize: $400; 4th Prize: $250; 5 High Distinction Awards of $200 each; and 6 Most Highly Commended Awards of $150 each. The top 10 entries will be published on the Winning Writers website. Submissions may be published or unpublished and may have won prizes elsewhere. Considers simultaneous submissions. Submit poems in any form, style, or genre. "There is no limit on the number of lines or poems you may submit." No name on ms pages; type or computer-print on letter-size white paper, single-sided. Submit online or by regular mail. Guidelines available for SASE or on website. **ENTRY FEE:** $7 USD for every 25 lines (exclude poem titles and any blank lines from line count). **DEADLINE:** December 15-September 30. Competition receives about 1,000 entries/year. 2010 winner was Carmine Dandrea ("On the Silk Road"). 2011 judges: John H. Reid and Dee C. Konrad. Winners announced in February at WinningWriters.com. Entrants who provide valid e-mail addresses will also receive notification.

TRANSCONTINENTAL POETRY AWARD

Pavement Saw Press, 321 Empire St., Montpelier OH 43543. (419)485-0524. E-mail: info@pavementsaw. org. Website: pavementsaw.org. **CONTACT:** David Baratier, editor. The Transcontinental Poetry Award offers $1,000, publication, and a percentage of the print run for a first or second book. "Each year, Pavement Saw Press will seek to publish at least 1 book of poetry and/or prose poems from manuscripts received during this competition, which is open to anyone who has not previously published a volume of poetry or prose. Poets who have not published a book, who have published 1collection, or who have published a second collection of fewer than 40 pages, or who have published a second full-length collection with a print run of no more than 500 copies are eligible. More than 1prize may be awarded." Submit 48-70 pages of poetry (1 poem/page), paginated and bound with a single clip. Include 2 cover sheets: 1 with ms title, poet's name, address, phone number, and e-mail, if available, the second with ms title only (this sheet should be clipped to ms). Also include one-page cover letter (a brief biography, ms title, poet's name, address, and telephone number, e-mail, and poet's signature) and acknowledgments page (journal, anthology, chapbook, etc., and poem published). Include SASP for acknowledgment of receipt; SASE unnecessary as result will be sent with free book and no mss will be returned. Guidelines available for SASE or on website. **ENTRY FEE:** $20; electronic submissions $27. "All U.S entrants will receive books, chapbooks, and journals equal to, or more than, the entry fee. Add $3 (USD) for other countries to cover the extra postal charge if sending by mail." Make checks payable to Pavement Saw Press. **DEADLINE:** reads submissions in June, July, and until August 15 (must have August 15 or earlier postmark).

◑◔ TUFTS POETRY AWARDS

Center for Arts & Humanities at Claremont Graduate, University, 160 E. 10th St., Harper East B7, Claremont CA 91711-6165. (909)621-8974. E-mail: tufts@ cgu.edu. Website: www.cgu.edu/tufts. **CONTACT:** Wendy Martin, Program Director. The annual Kingsley Tufts Poetry Award offers $100,000 for a work by an emerging poet, "one who is past the very beginning but has not yet reached the acknowledged pinnacle of his/her career." 2011 winner is Chase Twichell (*Horses Where the Answers Should Have Been*). The Kate Tufts Discovery Award ($10,000) is for a first book. 2011 winner is Atsuro Riley (*Romey's Order*). To be considered for the 2012 awards, books must have been published between September 1, 2010 and August 31, 2011. Entry form and guidelines available for SASE or on website. Check website for updated deadlines and award information.

◔ UTMOST CHRISTIAN POETRY CONTEST

Utmost Christian Writers Foundation, 121 Morin Maze, Edmonton AB T6K 1V1, Canada. E-mail: nnharms@telusplanet.net. Website: www.utmost-christianwriters.com. **CONTACT:** Nathan Harms, Exec. Director. The Novice Christian Poetry Contest opened for entries on April 1, 2011—For Christian poets only! $2,000 in cash prizes. Deadline: August 31, 2011. See rules and entry form online at website.

> ◔ Utmost sponsors at least four different contests each year. People occasionally confuse the contests. See the latest information on each contest on the website.

TIPS "Besides providing numerous resources for Christian writers and poets, Utmost also provides a market—a place where Christian writers and poets can sell their work. Please follow our guidelines. We receive numerous unsuitable submissions from writers. We encourage writers to submit suitable material. The best way to do this is to read the guidelines specific to your project—poetry, book reviews, articles—and then take time to look at the material we have already published in that area. The final step is to evaluate your proposed submission in comparison to the material we have used previously. If you complete these steps and strongly feel that your material is appropriate for us, we encourage you to submit it. Please use the submission link on the appropriate web page (links). For example, if you are submitting a poem, please click the "for Poetry Galley" guidelines (link) and use the submission link. If you fail to follow these instructions it's possible your submission will be lost."

○ Ⓢ MARICA AND JAN VILCEK PRIZE FOR POETRY

Bellevue Literary Review, New York University School of Medicine, OBV-A612, 550 First Ave., New York NY 10016. (212)263-3973. E-mail: info@BLReview.org. Website: www.BLReview.org. **CONTACT:** Stacy Bodziak. (Specialized: humanity, health, and healing.) The annual Marica and Jan Vilcek Prize for Poetry recognizes outstanding writing related to themes of health, healing, illness, the mind, and the body. Offers $1,000 for best poem and publication in Bellevue Literary Review (see separate listing in Magazines/Journals). All entries will be considered for publication. No previously published poems (including Internet publication). Submit up to 3 poems (5 pages maximum). Electronic (online) submissions only (as Word document with *.doc extension); combine all poems into one document and use first poem as document title. See guidelines for additional submission details. Guidelines available for SASE or on website. **ENTRY FEE:** $15/submission, limit of 2 submissions per person (one-year subscription available for additional $5). **DEADLINE:** July 1. Winner announced in December. 2012 judge: Cornelius Eady. Previous judges include Naomi Shihab Nye (2009), Tony Hoagland (2010).

WAR POETRY CONTEST

(866)946-9748. Fax: (413)280-0539. E-mail: adam@winningwriters.com. Website: www.winningwriters.com. **CONTACT:** Adam Cohen. Offers annual award of 1st Prize: $2,000; 2nd Prize: $1,200; 3rd Prize: $600; 12 Honorable Mentions of $100 each. All prizewinners receive online publication at WinningWriters.com; selected finalists may also receive online publication. Submissions must be unpublished. Considers simultaneous submissions. Submit 1-3 poems of up to 500 lines total on the theme of war, any form, style, or genre. No name on ms pages, typed or computer-printed on letter-size white paper, single-sided.

Submit online or by regular mail. Guidelines available for SASE or on website. **ENTRY FEE:** $15 for group of 1-3 poems. **DEADLINE:** November 15-May 31. Competition receives about 650 entries/year. 2010 winner was Gerardo Mena for *So I Was a Coffin*. 2010 final judge: Jendi Reiter. Winners announced on November 15 at WinningWriters.com and in free e-mail newsletter. Entrants who provided valid e-mail addresses will also receive notification. (See separate listing for the Wergle Flomp Humor Poetry Contest in this section and for Winning Writers in the Additional Resources section.)

WERGLE FLOMP HUMOR POETRY CONTEST

Winning Writers, 351 Pleasant St., PMB 222, Northampton MA 01060-3961. (866)946-9748. Fax: (413)280-0539. E-mail: adam@winningwriters.com. Website: www.winningwriters.com. **CONTACT:** Adam Cohen. Offers annual award of 1st Prize: $1,500; 2nd Prize: $800; 3rd Prize: $400; plus 12 Honorable Mentions of $75 each. Both published and unpublished poems are welcome. Final judge: Jendi Reiter. See the complete guidelines and past winners. All prizewinners receive online publication at WinningWriters.com. Submissions may be previously published. Considers simultaneous submissions. Submit 1 humorous poem of any length, in any form. See website for examples." Entries accepted only through website; no entries by regular mail. Guidelines available on website. **ENTRY FEE:** none. **DEADLINE:** April 1, 2012. Competition receives about 750 entries/year. Winners announced at WinningWriters.com and in free e-mail newsletter. "Please read the past winning entries and the judge's comments published at WinningWriters.com." Guidelines are a little unusual—please follow them closely. See separate listing for the War Poetry Contest in this section and for Winning Writers in the Additional Resources section.

TIPS "Submissions may be previously published and may be entered in other contests. Competition receives about 800 entries/year. Winners are announced on August 15 at WinningWriters.com. Entrants who provide a valid e-mail address will also receive notification.

WESTERN AUSTRALIAN PREMIER'S BOOK AWARDS

Website: www.slwa.wa.gov.au/pba.html. **CONTACT:** Doug George, awards manager. Offers annual poetry prize of $10,000 AUD for a published book of poetry. Winner also eligible for Premier's Prize of $25,000 AUD. Submissions must be previously published. Open to poets born in Western Australia, current residents of Western Australia, or poets who have resided in Western Australia for at least 10 years at some stage. Open to residents of Australia or Australian citizens. Entry form and guidelines available for SASE or on website. Online entry form and guidelines on website. **ENTRY FEE:** none. **DEADLINE:** January 31 each year. Competition receives about 10-15 entries in poetry category per year (350 overall). 2009 poetry winner was Kate Middleton for fire season. Winners announced in September each year at a presentation dinner given by the Premier of Western Australia. "The contest is organized by the State Library of Western Australia, with money provided by the Western Australian State Government to support literature."

WILLA LITERARY AWARD

(801)573-5309. E-mail: alicetrego@mac.com. Website: www.womenwritingthewest.org. **CONTACT:** Alice D. Trego, contest director.

WISCONSIN INSTITUTE FOR CREATIVE WRITING FELLOWSHIP

6195B H.C. White Hall, 600 N. Park St., Madison WI 53706. E-mail: rfkuka@wisc.edu. Website: www.wisc.edu/english/cw. **CONTACT:** Ron Kuka, Program Coordinator. Fellowship provides time, space and an intellectual community for writers working on first books. Receives approximately 300 applicants a year for each genre. Prize: $27,000 for a 9-month appointment. Judged by English Department faculty and current fellows. **ENTRY FEE:** $45, payable to the Department of English. Applicants should submit up to 10 pages of poetry and a résumé or vita directly to the program during February. An applicant's name must not appear on the writing sample (which must be in ms form) but rather on a separate sheet along with address, social security number, phone number, e-mail address and title(s) of submission(s). Candidates should also supply the names and phone numbers of two references. Accepts inquiries by e-mail and phone. **DEADLINE: FEBRUARY.** "Candidates must not yet have published, or had accepted for publication, a book by application deadline." Open to any writer with either an M.F.A. or Ph.D. in creative writing. Please enclose a SASE for notification of results. Results announced by May 1. "Send your best work."

WORKING PEOPLE'S POETRY COMPETITION

Blue Collar Review, P.O. Box 11417, Norfolk VA 23517. E-mail: red-ink@earthlink.net. Website: www.partisanpress.org. The Working People's Poetry Competition offers $100 and a one-year subscription to Blue Collar Review (see separate listing in Magazines/Journals) and "one year posting on of winning poem on our website. Poetry should be typed as you would like to see it published, with your name and address on each page. Include cover letter with entry." Guidelines available on website. **ENTRY FEE:** $15 per poem. Make checks payable to Partisan Press. **DEADLINE: MAY 1.** Previous winner was Luke Salazar.

WORLD'S BEST SHORT SHORT STORY FICTION CONTEST, NARRATIVE NONFICTION CONTEST & SOUTHEAST REVIEW POETRY CONTEST

E-mail: southeastreview@gmail.com. Website: www.southeastreview.org. **CONTACT:** Katie Cortese, acquisitions editor. English Department, Florida State University, Tallahassee FL 32306. Email: southeastreview@gmail.com. Website: www.southeastreview.org. Contact: Katie Cortese, acquisitions editor. "Annual award for unpublished short-short stories (500 words or less), poetry, and narrative nonfiction (6,000 words or less)." $15 reading fee for up to 3 stories or poems, $15 reading fee per nonfiction entry, fiction, nonfiction, poetry, short stories. Deadline: March 15. Prize: $500 per category. Winners and finalists will be published in *The Southeast Review*.

WRITER'S DIGEST WRITING COMPETITION

(513)531-2690, ext. 1328. E-mail: writing-competition@fwmedia.com; nicole.florence@fwmedia.com. Website: www.writersdigest.com. **CONTACT:** Nicki Florence.

WRITERS-EDITORS NETWORK ANNUAL INTERNATIONAL WRITING COMPETITION

E-mail: contest@writers-editors.com. Website: www. writers-editors.com. **CONTACT:** Dana K. Cassell, executive director. (formerly CNW/FFWA Florida State Writing Competition), Florida Freelance Writers Association, P.O. Box A, North Stratford NH 03590-0167. (603)922-8338. E-mail: contest@writers-editors.com. Website: www.writers-editors.com. Established 1978. Offers annual awards for nonfiction, fiction, children's literature, and poetry. Awards for each category are 1st Prize: $100 plus certificate; 2nd Prize: $75 plus certificate; 3rd Prize: $50 plus certificate; plus Honorable Mention certificates. Poetry submissions must be unpublished. Submit any number of poems on any subject in traditional forms, free verse, or children's. Entry form and guidelines available for SASE or on website. **EN-TRY FEE:** $3/poem (members), $5/poem (nonmembers). **DEADLINE:** March 15. Competition receives 350-400 entries/year. Competition is judged by writers, librarians, and teachers. Winners will be announced on May 31 by mail and on website.

WRITERS' JOURNAL POETRY CONTEST

Val-Tech Media, P.O. Box 394, Perham MN 56573. (218)346-7921. Fax: (218)346-7924. E-mail: writers-journal@writersjournal.com. Website: www.writers-journal.com. **CONTACT:** Esther M. Leiper-Estabrooks. "Contest offered for previously unpublished poetry. Receives fewer than 300 entries. Guidelines for SASE or online." $3/poem. Deadline: April 30, August 30, December 30. 1st Place: $50; 2nd Place: $25; 3rd Place: $15. First place, second place, third place, and selected honorable mention winners will be published in *WRITERS' Journal* magazine.

GRANTS:

State & Provincial

//

Arts councils in the United States and Canada provide assistance to artists (including poets) in the form of fellowships or grants. These grants can be substantial and confer prestige upon recipients; however, only state or province residents are eligible. Because deadlines and available support vary annually, query first (with a SASE) or check websites for guidelines.

UNITED STATES ARTS AGENCIES

ALABAMA STATE COUNCIL ON THE ARTS, 201 Monroe St., Montgomery AL 36130-1800. (334)242-4076. E-mail: staff@arts.alabama.gov. website: www.arts.state.al.us.

ALASKA STATE COUNCIL ON THE ARTS, 411 W. Fourth Ave., Suite 1-E, Anchorage AK 99501-2343. (907)269-6610 or (888)278-7424. E-mail: aksca_info@eed.state.ak.us. website: www.eed.state.ak.us/aksca.

ARIZONA COMMISSION ON THE ARTS, 417 W. Roosevelt St., Phoenix AZ 85003-1326. (602)771-6501. E-mail: info@azarts.gov. website: www.azarts.gov.

ARKANSAS ARTS COUNCIL, 1500 Tower Bldg., 323 Center St., Little Rock AR 72201. (501)324-9766. E-mail: info@arkansasarts.com. website: www.arkansasarts.com.

CALIFORNIA ARTS COUNCIL, 1300 I St., Suite 930, Sacramento CA 95814. (916)322-6555. E-mail: info@caartscouncil.com. website: www.cac.ca.gov.

COLORADO COUNCIL ON THE ARTS, 1625 Broadway, Suite 2700, Denver CO 80202. (303)892-3802. E-mail: online form. website: www.coloarts.state.co.us.

COMMONWEALTH COUNCIL FOR ARTS AND CULTURE (Northern Mariana Islands), P.O. Box 5553, CHRB, Saipan MP 96950. (670)322-9982 or (670)322-9983. E-mail: galaidi@vzpacifica.net. website: www.geocities.com/ccacarts/ccacwebsite.html.

CONNECTICUT COMMISSION ON CULTURE & TOURISM, Arts Division, One Financial Plaza, 755 Main St., Hartford CT 06103. (860)256-2800. website: www.cultureandtourism.org.

DELAWARE DIVISION OF THE ARTS, Carvel State Office Bldg., 4th Floor, 820 N. French St., Wilmington DE 19801. (302)577-8278 (New Castle Co.) or (302)739-5304 (Kent or Sussex Counties). E-mail: delarts@state.de.us. website: www.artsdel.org.

DISTRICT OF COLUMBIA COMMISSION ON THE ARTS & HUMANITIES, 410 Eighth St. NW, 5th Floor, Washington DC 20004. (202)724-5613. E-mail: cah@dc.gov. website: http://dcarts.dc.gov.

FLORIDA ARTS COUNCIL, Division of Cultural Affairs, R.A. Gray Building, Third Floor, 500 S. Bronough St., Tallahassee FL 32399-0250. (850)245-6470. E-mail: info@florida-arts.org. website: http://dcarts.dc.gov.

GEORGIA COUNCIL FOR THE ARTS, 260 14th St., Suite 401, Atlanta GA 30318. (404)685-2787. E-mail: gaarts@gaarts.org. website: www.gaarts.org.

GUAM COUNCIL ON THE ARTS & HUMANITIES AGENCY, P.O. Box 2950, Hagatna GU 96932. (671)646-2781. website: www.guam.net.

HAWAII STATE FOUNDATION ON CULTURE & THE ARTS, 2500 S. Hotel St., 2nd Floor, Honolulu HI 96813. (808)586-0300. E-mail: ken.hamilton@hawaii.gov. website: http.state.hi.us/sfca.

IDAHO COMMISSION ON THE ARTS, 2410 N. Old Penitentiary Rd., Boise ID 83712. (208)334-2119 or (800)278-3863. E-mail: info@arts.idaho.gov. website: www.arts.idaho.gov.

ILLINOIS ARTS COUNCIL, James R. Thompson Center, 100 W. Randolph, Suite 10-500, Chicago IL 60601. (312)814-6750. E-mail: iac.info@illinois.gov. website: www.state.il.us/agency/iac.

INDIANA ARTS COMMISSION, 150 W. Market St., Suite 618, Indianapolis IN 46204. (317)232-1268. E-mail: IndianaArtsCommission@iac.in.gov. website: www.in.gov/arts.

INSTITUTE OF PUERTO RICAN CULTURE, P.O. Box 9024184, San Juan PR 00902-4184. (787)724-0700. E-mail: www@icp.gobierno.pr. website: www.icp.gobierno.pr.

IOWA ARTS COUNCIL, 600 E. Locust, Des Moines IA 50319-0290. (515)281-6412. website: www.iowaartscouncil.org.

KANSAS ARTS COMMISSION, 700 SW Jackson, Suite 1004, Topeka KS 66603-3761. (785)296-3335. E-mail: KAC@arts.state.ks.us. website: http://arts.state.ks.us.

KENTUCKY ARTS COUNCIL, 21st Floor, Capital Plaza Tower, 500 Mero St., Frankfort KY 40601-1987. (502)564-3757 or (888)833-2787. E-mail: kyarts@ky.gov. website: http://artscouncil.ky.gov.

LOUISIANA DIVISION OF THE ARTS, Capitol Annex Bldg., 1051 N. 3rd St., 4th Floor, Room #420, Baton Rouge LA 70804. (225)342-8180. website: www.crt.state.la.us/arts.

MAINE ARTS COMMISSION, 193 State St., 25 State House Station, Augusta ME 04333-0025. (207)287-2724. E-mail: MaineArts.info@maine.gov. website: www.mainearts.com.

MARYLAND STATE ARTS COUNCIL, 175 W. Ostend St., Suite E, Baltimore MD 21230. (410)767-6555. E-mail: msac@msac.org. website: www.msac.org.

MASSACHUSETTS CULTURAL COUNCIL, 10 St. James Ave., 3rd Floor, Boston MA 02116-3803. (617)727-3668. E-mail: mcc@art.state.ma.us. website: www.massculturalcouncil.org.

MICHIGAN COUNCIL OF HISTORY, ARTS, AND LIBRARIES, 702 W. Kalamazoo St., P.O. Box 30705, Lansing MI 48909-8205. (517)241-4011. E-mail: artsinfo@michigan.gov. website: www.michigan.gov/hal/0,1607,7-160-17445_19272---,00.html.

MINNESOTA STATE ARTS BOARD, Park Square Court, 400 Sibley St., Suite 200, St. Paul MN 55101-1928. (651)215-1600 or (800)866-2787. E-mail: msab@arts.state.mn.us. website: www.arts.state.mn.us.

MISSISSIPPI ARTS COMMISSION, 501 N. West St., Suite 701B, Woolfolk Bldg., Jackson MS 39201. (601)359-6030. website: www.arts.state.ms.us.

MISSOURI ARTS COUNCIL, 815 Olive St., Suite 16, St. Louis MO 63101-1503. (314)340-6845 or (866)407-4752. E-mail: moarts@ded.mo.gov. website: www.missouriartscouncil.org.

MONTANA ARTS COUNCIL, 316 N. Park Ave., Suite 252, Helena MT 59620-2201. (406)444-6430. E-mail: mac@mt.gov. website: www.art.state.mt.us.

NATIONAL ASSEMBLY OF STATE ARTS AGENCIES, 1029 Vermont Ave. NW, 2nd Floor, Washington DC 20005. (202)347-6352. E-mail: nasaa@nasaa-arts.org. website: www.nasaa-arts.org.

NEBRASKA ARTS COUNCIL, 1004 Farnam St., Plaza Level, Omaha NE 68102. (402)595-2122 or (800)341-4067. website: www.nebraskaartscouncil.org.

NEVADA ARTS COUNCIL, 716 N. Carson St., Suite A, Carson City NV 89701. (775)687-6680. E-mail: online form. website: http://dmla.clan.lib.nv.us/docs/arts.

NEW HAMPSHIRE STATE COUNCIL ON THE ARTS, 21/2 Beacon St., 2nd Floor, Concord NH 03301-4974. (603)271-2789. website: www.nh.gov/nharts.

NEW JERSEY STATE COUNCIL ON THE ARTS, 225 W. State St., P.O. Box 306, Trenton NJ 08625. (609)292-6130. website: www.njartscouncil.org.

NEW MEXICO ARTS, DEPT. OF CULTURAL AFFAIRS, P.O. Box 1450, Santa Fe NM 87504-1450. (505)827-6490 or (800)879-4278. website: www.nmarts.org.

NEW YORK STATE COUNCIL ON THE ARTS, 175 Varick St., New York NY 10014. (212)627-4455. website: www.nysca.org.

NORTH CAROLINA ARTS COUNCIL, 109 East Jones St., Cultural Resources Building, Raleigh NC 27601. (919)807-6500. E-mail: ncarts@ncmail.net. website: www.ncarts.org.

NORTH DAKOTA COUNCIL ON THE ARTS, 1600 E. Century Ave., Suite 6, Bismarck ND 58503. (701)328-7590. E-mail: comserv@state.nd.us. website: www.state.nd.us/arts.

OHIO ARTS COUNCIL, 727 E. Main St., Columbus OH 43205-1796. (614)466-2613. website: www.oac.state.oh.us.

OKLAHOMA ARTS COUNCIL, Jim Thorpe Building, 2101 N. Lincoln Blvd., Suite 640, Oklahoma City OK 73105. (405)521-2931. E-mail: okarts@arts.ok.gov. website: www.arts.state.ok.us.

OREGON ARTS COMMISSION, 775 Summer St. NE, Suite 200, Salem OR 97301-1280. (503)986-0082. E-mail: oregon.artscomm@state.or.us. website: www.oregonartscommission.org.

PENNSYLVANIA COUNCIL ON THE ARTS, 216 Finance Bldg., Harrisburg PA 17120. (717)787-6883. website: www.pacouncilonthearts.org.

RHODE ISLAND STATE COUNCIL ON THE ARTS, One Capitol Hill, Third Floor, Providence RI 02908. (401)222-3880. E-mail: info@arts.ri.gov. website: www.arts.ri.gov.

SOUTH CAROLINA ARTS COMMISSION, 1800 Gervais St., Columbia SC 29201. (803)734-8696. E-mail: info@arts.state.sc.us. website: www.southcarolinaarts.com.

SOUTH DAKOTA ARTS COUNCIL, 711 E. Wells Ave., Pierre SD 57501-3369. (605)773-3301. E-mail: sdac@state.sd.us. website: www.artscouncil.sd.gov.

TENNESSEE ARTS COMMISSION, 401 Charlotte Ave., Nashville TN 37243-0780. (615)741-1701. website: www.arts.state.tn.us.

TEXAS COMMISSION ON THE ARTS, E.O. Thompson Office Building, 920 Colorado, Suite 501, Austin TX 78701. (512)463-5535. E-mail: front.desk@arts.state.tx.us. website: www. arts.state.tx.us.

UTAH ARTS COUNCIL, 617 E. South Temple, Salt Lake City UT 84102-1177. (801)236-7555. website: http://arts.utah.gov.

VERMONT ARTS COUNCIL, 136 State St., Drawer 33, Montpelier VT 05633-6001. (802)828-3291. E-mail: online form. website: www.vermontartscouncil.org.

VIRGIN ISLANDS COUNCIL ON THE ARTS, 5070 Norre Gade, St. Thomas VI 00802-6872. (340)774-5984. website: http://vicouncilonarts.org.

VIRGINIA COMMISSION FOR THE ARTS, Lewis House, 223 Governor St., 2nd Floor, Richmond VA 23219. (804)225-3132. E-mail: arts@arts.virginia.gov. website: www.arts.state.va.us.

WASHINGTON STATE ARTS COMMISSION, 711 Capitol Way S., Suite 600, P.O. Box 42675, Olympia WA 98504-2675. (360)753-3860. E-mail: info@arts.wa.gov. website: www.arts.wa.gov.

WEST VIRGINIA COMMISSION ON THE ARTS, The Cultural Center, Capitol Complex, 1900 Kanawha Blvd. E., Charleston WV 25305-0300. (304)558-0220. website: www.wvculture.org/arts.

WISCONSIN ARTS BOARD, 101 E. Wilson St., 1st Floor, Madison WI 53702. (608)266-0190. E-mail: artsboard@arts.state.wi.us. website: www.arts.state.wi.us.

WYOMING ARTS COUNCIL, 2320 Capitol Ave., Cheyenne WY 82002. (307)777-7742. E-mail: ebratt@state.wy.us. website: http://wyoarts.state.wy.us.

CANADIAN PROVINCES ARTS AGENCIES

ALBERTA FOUNDATION FOR THE ARTS, 10708-105 Ave., Edmonton AB T5H 0A1. (780)427-9968. website: www.affta.ab.ca/index.shtml.

BRITISH COLUMBIA ARTS COUNCIL, P.O. Box 9819, Stn. Prov. Govt., Victoria BC V8W 9W3. (250)356-1718. E-mail: BCArtsCouncil@gov.bc.ca. website: www.bcartscouncil.ca.

THE CANADA COUNCIL FOR THE ARTS, 350 Albert St., P.O. Box 1047, Ottawa ON K1P 5V8. (613)566-4414 or (800)263-5588 (within Canada). website: www.canadacouncil.ca.

MANITOBA ARTS COUNCIL, 525-93 Lombard Ave., Winnipeg MB R3B 3B1. (204)945-2237 or (866)994-2787 (in Manitoba). E-mail: info@artscouncil.mb.ca. website: www.artscouncil.mb.ca.

NEW BRUNSWICK ARTS BOARD (NBAB), 634 Queen St., Suite 300, Fredericton NB E3B 1C2. (506)444-4444 or (866)460-2787. website: www.artsnb.ca.

NEWFOUNDLAND & LABRADOR ARTS COUNCIL, P.O. Box 98, St. John's NL A1C 5H5. (709)726-2212 or (866)726-2212. E-mail: nlacmail@nfld.net. website: www.nlac.nf.ca.

NOVA SCOTIA DEPARTMENT OF TOURISM, CULTURE, AND HERITAGE, Culture Division, 1800 Argyle St., Suite 601, P.O. Box 456, Halifax NS B3J 2R5. (902)424-4510. E-mail: cultaffs@gov.ns.ca. website: www.gov.ns.ca/dtc/culture.

ONTARIO ARTS COUNCIL, 151 Bloor St. W., 5th Floor, Toronto ON M5S 1T6. (416)961-1660 or (800)387-0058 (in Ontario). E-mail: info@arts.on.ca. website: www.arts.on.ca.

PRINCE EDWARD ISLAND COUNCIL OF THE ARTS, 115 Richmond St., Charlottetown PE C1A 1H7. (902)368-4410 or (888)734-2784. E-mail: info@peiartscouncil.com. website: www.peiartscouncil.com.

QUÉBEC COUNCIL FOR ARTS & LITERATURE, 79 boul. René-Lévesque Est, 3e étage, Quebec QC G1R 5N5. (418)643-1707 or (800)897-1707. E-mail: info@calq.gouv.qc.ca. website: www.calq.gouv.qc.ca.

THE SASKATCHEWAN ARTS BOARD, 2135 Broad St., Regina SK S4P 1Y6. (306)787-4056 or (800)667-7526 (Saskatchewan only). E-mail: sab@artsboard.sk.ca. website: www.artsboard.sk.ca.

YUKON ARTS FUNDING PROGRAM, Cultural Services Branch, Dept. of Tourism & Culture, Government of Yukon, Box 2703 (L-3), Whitehorse YT Y1A 2C6. (867)667-8589 or (800)661-0408 (in Yukon). E-mail: arts@gov.yk.ca. website: www.tc.gov.yk.ca/216.html.

CONFERENCES, WORKSHOPS & FESTIVALS

//

There are times when we want to immerse ourselves in learning. Or perhaps we crave a change of scenery, the creative stimulation of being around other artists, or the uninterrupted productivity of time alone to work.

That's what this section of *Poet's Market* is all about, providing a selection of writing conferences and workshops, artist colonies and retreats, poetry festivals, and even a few opportunities to go traveling with your muse. These listings give the basics: contact information, a brief description of the event, lists of past presenters, and offerings of special interest to poets. Contact an event that interests you for additional information, including up-to-date costs and housing details. **(Please note that most directors had not finalized their 2012 plans when we contacted them for this edition of *Poet's Market*. However, where possible, they provided us with their 2011 dates, costs, faculty names or themes to give you a better idea of what each event has to offer.)**

Before you seriously consider a conference, workshop or other event, determine what you hope to get out of the experience. Would a general conference with one or two poetry workshops among many other types of sessions be acceptable? Or are you looking for something exclusively focused on poetry? Do you want to hear poets speak about poetry writing, or are you looking for a more participatory experience, such as a one-on-one critiquing session or a group workshop? Do you mind being one of hundreds of attendees, or do you prefer a more intimate setting? Are you willing to invest in the expense of traveling to a conference, or would something local better suit your budget? Keep these questions and others in mind as you read these listings, view Web sites and study conference brochures.

Some listings are coded with symbols to provide certain "information at a glance." The ✚ icon indicates a recently established conference/workshop; the ✺ icon denotes a Canadian event and the ✹ icon one located outside the U.S. and Canada.

ABROAD WRITERS CONFERENCES

17363 Sutter Creek Rd., Sutter Creek CA 95685. (209)296-4050. E-mail: abroadwriters@yahoo.com. Website: www.abroad-crwf.com/index.html. Conferences are held throughout the year in various places worldwide. See website for scheduling details. Conference duration: 7-10 days. "Instead of being lost in a crowd at a large conference, Abroad Writers' Conference prides itself on holding small group meetings where participants have personal contact with everyone. Stimulating talks, interviews, readings, Q&A's, writing workshops, film screenings, private consultations and social gatherings all take place within a week to ten days. Abroad Writers' Conference promises you true networking opportunities and full detailed feedback on your writing."

⊙ "Abroad Writers' Conference is proud to be holding Kolkata, India's first major literary conference in their historic City of Joy. This large literary conference and workshop will take place at the Victoria Memorial Museum and the Oberoi Hotel. We will have 40 authors including two Nobel Prize winners and literary agents. Workshops will be held in fiction, non-fiction, memoir, playwriting and poetry."

ADDITIONAL INFORMATION Agents participate in conference. Application is online at website.

AMERICAN CHRISTIAN WRITERS CONFERENCES

(800)219-7483. Fax: (615)834-7736. E-mail: acwriters@aol.com. Website: www.acwriters.com. **Contact:** Reg Forder, director.
COSTS/ACCOMMODATIONS Special rates are available at the host hotel (usually a major chain like Holiday Inn).
ADDITIONAL INFORMATION Send a SASE for conference brochures/guidelines.

● ANAM CARA WRITER'S AND ARTIST'S RETREAT

Eyeries, Beara, Co. Cork , Ireland. (353)(027)74441. Fax: (353)(027)74448. E-mail: anamcararetreat@gmail.com. Website: www.anamcararetreat.com. **Contact:** Sue Booth-Forbes, director. Offers up to one-month individual retreats as well as workshops on a variety of creative subjects for writers and artists. Length of workshops varies with subject and leader/facilitator. Location: "Beara is a rural and hauntingly beautiful part of Ireland that is kept temperate by the Gulf Stream. The retreat sits on a hill overlooking Coulagh Bay, the mountains of the Ring of Kerry, and the Slieve Mishkish Mountains of Beara. The village of Eyeries is a short walk away." Average attendance: 5 residents at the retreat when working individually; 12-18 workshop participants.
COSTS/ACCOMMODATIONS 2011 cost: residency fee ranges from 600-700 Euro per week for individual retreats, depending on room, and includes full room and board; editorial consulting; laundry; sauna; hot tub overlooking Coulagh Bay; 5 acres of gardens, meadows, riverbank and cascades, river island, swimming hole, and several unique working spots, such as the ruin of a stone mill and a sod-roofed beehive hut. Overflow from workshops stay in nearby B& Bs, a 10-minute walk or 2-minute drive away. Transportation provided if needed. Details regarding transporation to Anam Cara available on website.
ADDITIONAL INFORMATION Requests for specific information about rates and availability can be made through the website; also available by fax or e-mail.

● ART WORKSHOPS IN GUATEMALA

4758 Lyndale Ave. S, Minneapolis MN 55419-5304. (612)825-0747. E-mail: info@artguat.org. Website: www.artguat.org. **Contact:** Liza Fourre, director. Individual poetry critiques included. Call, write, e-mail, or check website. Annual 10-day creative writing courses, held in February, March, July, and October. Location: workshops held in Antigua, the old colonial capital of Guatemala. Average attendance: limit 10 students.
COSTS/ACCOMMODATIONS All transportation and accommodations included in price of conference.
ADDITIONAL INFORMATION Conference information available now. For brochure/guidelines visit website, e-mail, fax or call. Accepts inquiries by e-mail, phone.

ASPEN SUMMER WORDS LITERARY FESTIVAL & WRITING RETREAT

(970)925-3122. Fax: (970)925-5700. E-mail: info@aspenwriters.org. Website: www.aspenwriters.org. 110 E. Hallam St., Suite 116, Aspen CO 81611. (970)925-3122. Fax: (970)920-5700. E-mail: info@aspenwriters.org. Website: www.aspenwriters.org. Established

1976. Annual 5-day writing retreat and concurrent 5-day literary festival. 2009 dates: June 21-26. Location: Aspen, Colorado. Average attendance: 120 for the retreat, 300 for the festival.

COSTS/ACCOMMODATIONS Discount lodging at the conference site will be available. 2011 rates to be announced. Free shuttle around town.

ADDITIONAL INFORMATION Workshops admission deadline is April 15. Manuscripts for juried workshops must be submitted by April 15 for review and selection. 10 page limit for workshop application manuscript. A limited number of partial-tuition scholarships are available. Deadline for agent/editor meeting registration is May 27th. Brochures available for SASE, by e-mail and phone request, and on website.

AUSTIN INTERNATIONAL POETRY FESTIVAL

(512)777-1888. E-mail: aipfdirector@gmail.com. Website: www.aipf.org. **Contact:** Ashley S. Kim, festival director. Annual 4-day, city-wide 20th anniversary festival for all ages including over 100 poetry events. Adult and youth anthology contest. 2012 dates: April 26-29th. Location: Austin, TX. Average attendance: 300 poets, 2000 non-poets.

COSTS/ACCOMMODATIONS 2012 cost: $35; includes anthology submission fee, program bio, scheduled reading at one of AIPF's 15 venues, participation in all events, 1 catered meal, workshop participation, and more.

ADDITIONAL INFORMATION Offers multiple poetry contests as part of festival. Guidelines available on website. Registration form available on website. "Largest non-juried poetry festival in the U.S.!"

BREAD LOAF WRITERS' CONFERENCE

Middlebury College, Middlebury VT 05753. (802)443-5286. Fax: (802)443-2087. Email: blwc@middlebury.edu. Website: www.middlebury.edu/blwc. **Contact:** Noreen Cargill, administrative manager. Director: Michael Collier. Established 1926. Annual 10-day event. 2011 dates: August 10-20. Location: mountain campus of Middlebury College. Average attendance: 230.

COSTS/ACCOMMODATIONS Bread Loaf Campus in Ripton, Vermont.

ADDITIONAL INFORMATION 2011 Conference Dates: August 10-20. Location: mountain campus of Middlebury College. Average attendance: 230.

THE COLRAIN POETRY MANUSCRIPT CONFERENCE

Website: www.colrainpoetry.com. Concord Poetry Center, 40 Stow. St., Concord MA 01742. (978)897-0054. E-mail: conferences@colrainpoetry.com. Website: www.colrainpoetry.com. Established 2006. **Contact:** Joan Houlihan, founding director. Usually held 10 times/year in 3-day, weekend sessions. Location: Colrain, MA, Greenfield, MA, and others. Average attendance: 12 poets.

COSTS/ACCOMMODATIONS 2011 cost: $995-$1295, includes lodging, meals, and tuition.

ADDITIONAL INFORMATION Details, application, and registration form available on website.

FINE ARTS WORK CENTER

24 Pearl St., Provincetown MA 02657. (508)487-9960. Fax: (508)487-8873. E-mail: workshops@fawc.org. Website: www.fawc.org. **Contact:** Dorothy Antczak, summer program director. Offers more than 70 week-long and weekend workshops in poetry, fiction, and creative nonfiction. Location: The Fine Arts Work Center in Provincetown.

COSTS/ACCOMMODATIONS 2011 cost: Summer Workshop Program fees range $600-725. Accommodations available at the Work Center for $675 for 6 nights. Additional accommodations available locally.

ADDITIONAL INFORMATION See website for details and an application form.

FISHTRAP, INC.

400 Grant Street, P.O. Box 38, Enterprise OR 97828-0038. E-mail: director@fishtrap.org. Website: www.fishtrap.org. **Contact:** Barbara Dills, Interim Director. Writer workshops geared toward beginner, intermediate, advanced and professional levels. Not all poetry workshops. Open to students, scholarships available. A series of writing workshops and a writers' gathering is held each July. During the school year Fishtrap brings writers into local schools and offers workshops for teachers and writers of children's and young adult books. Other programs include writing and K-12 teaching residencies, writers' retreats, and lectures. College credit available for many workshops. See website for full program descriptions and to get on the e-mail and mail lists.

✚◗ FOOTHILL COLLEGE WRITERS' CONFERENCE

Website: www.foothill.edu/la/conference. 12345 El Monte Rd., Los Altos Hills CA 94022. (650)949-7924. Fax: (650)949-7695. E-mail: svetichkella@foothill.edu. Website: www.foothill.edu/la/conference. Established 1976. **Contact:** Kella de Castro Svetich, PhD/Director. Annually in July. Location: Los Altos, California. Average attendance: 150-250.

COSTS/ACCOMMODATIONS $53. Participants responsible for all meals. Accommodations available at area hotels. Information on overnight accommodations available in brochure, by e-mail, on website.

✚ HAIKU NORTH AMERICA CONFERENCE

1275 Fourth St. PMB #365, Santa Rosa CA 95404. E-mail: welchm@aol.com. Website: www.haikunorthamerica.com. **Contact:** Michael Dylan Welch. Five days, held every two years at varying locations throughout North America. Dates: August 3-7, 2011 (Eleventh) biennial conference. 2013 dates to be determined.

PURPOSE/FEATURES Seattle Center, Seattle, Washington.

COSTS/ACCOMMODATIONS Typically around $200, including a banquet and some additional meals. Accommodations at discounted hotels nearby are an additional cost. Information available on website as details are finalized closer to the conference date.

ADDITIONAL INFORMATION Past conferences have been held in San Francisco (twice), Toronto, Portland (Oregon), Chicago, Boston, New York City, Port Townsend (Washington), Winston-Salem (North Carolina), and Ottawa (Ontario). In the words of Jim Kacian, founder of the Haiku Foundation, "Haiku North America . . . is intellectually diverse, socially expansive, emotionally gratifying, and provides more than any other single experience the sense that haiku is a literary force to be reckoned with and capable of work that matters in the rest of the world."

HOFSTRA UNIVERSITY SUMMER WRITING WORKSHOPS

University College for Continuing Education, 250 Hofstra University, Hempstead NY 11549. (516)463-7600. E-mail: ce@hofstra.edu. Website: ce.hofstra.edu/summerwriters. **Contact:** Richard Pioreck, co-director. Established 1972. Annual 2-week event. Location: Hofstra University. Average attendance: 60-70.

COSTS/ACCOMMODATIONS Free bus operates between Hempstead Train Station and campus for those commuting from New York City on the Long Island Rail Road. Dormitory rooms are available.

ADDITIONAL INFORMATION Students entering grades 9-12 can now be part of the Summer Writers Program with a special section for high school students. Through exercises and readings, students will learn how to use their creative impulses to improve their fiction, poetry and plays and learn how to create cleaner and clearer essays. During this intensive 2-week course, students will experiment with memoir, poetry, oral history, dramatic form and the short story, and study how to use character, plot, point of view and language.

IOWA SUMMER WRITING FESTIVAL

(319)335-4160. Fax: (319)335-4743. E-mail: iswfestival@uiowa.edu. Website: www.uiowa.edu/~iswfest.

COSTS/ACCOMMODATIONS Accommodations available at area hotels. Information on overnight accommodations available by phone or on website.

ADDITIONAL INFORMATION Brochures are available in February. Inquire via e-mail or on website.

IWWG ANNUAL SUMMER CONFERENCE

International Women's Writing Guild "Remember the Magic" Annual Summer Conference, International Women's Writing Guild, P.O. Box 810, Gracie Station, New York NY 10028. (212)737-7536. Fax: (212)737-9469. E-mail: iwwg@iwwg.org. Website: www.iwwg.org. **Contact:** Hannelore Hahn, executive director. Held June 24-July 1, 2011.

PURPOSE/FEATURES Yale University, New Haven, CT.

ADDITIONAL INFORMATION "This workshop takes place at Yale University, New Haven, CT." Held June 24-July 1, 2011.

JACKSON HOLE WRITERS CONFERENCE

PO Box 1974, Jackson WY 83001. (307)413-3332. E-mail: nicole@jacksonholewritersconference.com. Website: www.jacksonholewritersconference.com.

ADDITIONAL INFORMATION Held at the Center for the Arts in Jackson, Wyoming and online.

KENYON REVIEW WRITERS WORKSHOP

Website: www.kenyonreview.org.

Annual 8-day workshop held in June. Participants apply in poetry, fiction, or creative nonfiction, and then participate in intensive daily workshops which focus on the generation and revision of significant new work. Held on the campus of Kenyon College in the rural village of Gambier, Ohio. Workshop leaders have included David Baker, Ron Carlson, Rebecca McClanahan, Meghan O'Rourke, Linda Gregorson, Dinty Moore, Tara Ison, Jane Hamilton, Lee K. Abbott, and Nancy Zafris.

COSTS/ACCOMMODATIONS The workshop operates a shuttle to and from Gambier and the airport in Columbus, Ohio. Offers overnight accommodations. Participants are housed in Kenyon College student housing. The cost is covered in the tuition.

ADDITIONAL INFORMATION Application includes a writing sample. Admission decisions are made on a rolling basis. Workshop information is available online at www.kenyonreview.org/workshops in November. For brochure send e-mail, visit website, call, fax. Accepts inquiries by SASE, e-mail, phone, fax.

KIMMEL HARDING NELSON CENTER FOR THE ARTS RESIDENCY PROGRAM

801 3rd Corso, Nebraska City NE 68410. 402-874-9600. Fax: 402-874-9600. E-mail: pfriedli@khncenterforthearts.org. Website: www.khncenterforthearts.org. **Contact:** Pat Friedli, Assistant Director. Residencies for visual artists, writers, or composers available consisting of 2-8 week stays with paid accommodations, studio space, and stipend. Residents responsible for all meals. Applicants must apply online.

PURPOSE/FEATURES Kimmel Harding Nelson Center for the Arts, Nebraska City NE. Average attendance: 50 residencies are awarded each year.

COSTS/ACCOMMODATIONS $35 application fee applies. Accommodations available on site.

LEDIG HOUSE INTERNATIONAL WRITERS RESIDENCY

Website: www.artomi.org. 55 Fifth Ave., 15th Floor, New York NY 10003.Fax: (212)206-6114. E-mail: writers@artomi.org. Website: www.artomi.org. Residency duration: 2 weeks to 2 months. Average attendance: Up to 20 writers per session. Residency. Site: "Up to 20 writers per session--10 at a given time--live and write on the stunning 300 acre grounds and sculpture park that overlooks the Catskill Mountains." Deadline: October 20.

COSTS/ACCOMMODATIONS Residents provide their own transportation. Offers overnight accommodations.

ADDITIONAL INFORMATION "Agents and editors from the New York publishing community are invited for dinner and discussion. Bicycles, a swimming pool, and nearby tennis court are available for use."

LIFE PRESS CHRISTIAN WRITERS' CONFERENCE

P.O. Box 2018, Cordova TN 38088. (901)309-3692. E-mail: gmoearth@gmail.com. Website: www.grandmotherearth.org. **Contact:** Frances Cowden, director. Annual one-day event. Location: Cordova, TN. Average attendance: 45.

COSTS/ACCOMMODATIONS 2011 cost: $30 registration fee (includes one contest entry), or $25 (includes food, no entries); $20 fee for spouses. Information on overnight accommodations available in brochure upon request.

ADDITIONAL INFORMATION Individual poetry critiques available. Poets should submit a limit of 6 works/category and $10 fee. "One payment for all entries--send with entries." Sponsors contest for "poetry and prose in general, open to all writers. Other contests require attendance." National Awards for poetry (open to everyone, 50-line limit) are $100, $50, $25, $15, and $10. Conference Awards for poetry (open to those who register for the conference, 30-line limit) are $100, $50, $15, and $10. and $10. . Entry fee: "$5 entitles you to one entry; Entry fee of $10 entitles you to up to 3 entries. $2 for each additional entry." Deadline: July 5. Critique from the judges is available for $10 for all entries. Guidelines available for SASE.

MARK TWAIN CREATIVE WRITERS WORKSHOPS

5101 Rockhill Rd., Kansas City MO 64110-2499. (816)235-1168. Fax: (816)235-2611. E-mail: BeasleyM@umkc.edu. Website: www.newletters.org. **Contact:** Betsy Beasley, admin. associate. Held first 3 weeks of June, from 9:30 to 12:30 each weekday morning. Conference duration: 3 weeks. Average attendance:

40. Focus is on fiction, poetry and literary nonfiction. University of Missouri-Kansas City Campus Panels planned for next conference include the full range of craft essentials. Staff includes Robert Stewart, editor-in-chief of newsletters and BkMk Press.Fees for regular and noncredit courses.Offers list of area hotels or lodging options. Submit for workshop 6 poems/one short story prior to arrival. Conference information is available in March by SASE, e-mail or on website. Editors participate in conference.

PURPOSE/FEATURES University of Missouri-Kansas City Campus.

COSTS/ACCOMMODATIONS Offers list of area hotels or lodging options.

ADDITIONAL INFORMATION Submit for workshop 6 poems/one short story prior to arrival. Conference information is available in March by SASE, e-mail or on website. Editors participate in conference.

MONTEVALLO LITERARY FESTIVAL

Sta. 6420, University of Montevallo, Montevallo AL 35115. (205)665-6420. Fax: (205)665-6422. E-mail: murphyj@montevallo.edu. Website: www.monte-vallo.edu/english. **Contact:** Dr. Jim Murphy, Director. Annual day-long event in April. Location: several sites on the bucolic University of Montevallo campus. Average attendance: 60-100.

COSTS/ACCOMMODATIONS Offers overnight accommodations at Ramsay Conference Center on campus; rooms $40/night. Call (205)665-6280 for reservations. Free on-campus parking. Additional information available at www.montevallo.edu/cont_ed/ramsay.shtm.

ADDITIONAL INFORMATION To enroll in a fiction workshop, contact Bryn Chancellor (bchancellor@montevallo.edu). Information for upcoming festival available in February For brochure, visit website. Accepts inquiries by mail (with SASE), e-mail, phone, and fax. Editors participate in conference. "This is a friendly, relaxed festival dedicated to bringing literary writers and readers together on a personal scale." Poetry workshop participants submit up to 5 pages of poetry; e-mail as Word doc to Jim Murphy (murphyj@montevallo.edu) at least 2 weeks prior to festival.

⊙ MOUNT HERMON CHRISTIAN WRITERS CONFERENCE

E-mail: info@mounthermon.org. Website: www.mounthermon.org/writers. Annual 5-day event held over Palm Sunday weekend. 2010 dates: March 26-30. Location: In heart of California redwoods near Santa Cruz, Mount Hermon Conference Center. Average attendance: 425-475.

COSTS/ACCOMMODATIONS Registrants stay in hotel-style accommodations. Meals are buffet style, with faculty joining registrants. See website Nov. 1 for cost updates.

ADDITIONAL INFORMATION "The residential nature of our conference makes this a unique setting for one-on-one interaction with faculty/staff. There is also a decided inspirational flavor to the conference, and general sessions with well-known speakers are a highlight. Registrants may submit 2 works for critique in advance of the conference, then have personal interviews with critiquers during the conference. All conference information is online by December 1 of each year. Send inquiries via e-mail. Tapes of past conferences are also available online."

PIMA WRITERS' WORKSHOP

Pima College, 2202 W. Anklam Rd., Tucson AZ 85709-0170. (520)206-6084. E-mail: mfiles@pima.edu. Established 1987. **Contact:** Meg Files, director. Annual 3-day event. 2011 dates: May 27-29. Features a dozen authors, editors, and agents talking about writing and publishing fiction, nonfiction, poetry, and stories for children. Average attendance: 300.

PURPOSE/FEATURES Pima College's Center for the Arts, "includes a proscenium theater, a black box theater, a recital hall, and conference rooms, as well as a courtyard with amphitheater."

COSTS/ACCOMMODATIONS Participants responsible for own meals. Information on overnight accommodations available.

ADDITIONAL INFORMATION Brochure and registration form available for SASE or by fax or e-mail.

POETRY WEEKEND INTENSIVES

40 Post Ave., Hawthorne NJ 07506. (973)423-2921. Fax: (973)523-6085. E-mail: mariagillan@verizon.net. Website: www.pccc.edu/poetry. **Contact:** Maria Mazziotti Gillan, executive director.

COSTS/ACCOMMODATIONS $375, including

meals. Offers a $25 early bird discount. Housing in on-site facilities included in the $375 price. Location: generally at Glastonbury Abbey, in Hingham, MA; also several other convents and monasteries.

ADDITIONAL INFORMATION Usually held 2 times/year in June and December. Average attendance: 26. Additional Information: Individual poetry critiques available. Poets should bring poems to weekend. Registration form available for SASE or by fax or email. Maria Mazziotti Gillan is the director of the Creative Writing Program of Binghamton University-State University of New York, exec. director of the Poetry Center at Passaic County Community College, and edits Paterson Literary Review. Laura Boss is the editor of *Lips* magazine. Fifteen professional development credits are available for each weekend.

SAN DIEGO STATE UNIVERSITY WRITERS' CONFERENCE

(619)594-2517. Fax: (619)594-8566. E-mail: sdsuwritersconference@mail.sdsu.edu. Website: www.ces. sdsu.edu/writers. 5250 Campanile Dr., San Diego CA 92182-1920. (619)594-2517. Fax: (619)594-8566. E-mail: rbrown2@mail.sdsu.edu. Website: www.ces. sdsu.edu. Established 1984. **Contact:** Rose Brown, program coordinator. Annual 3-day event. 2009 dates: February 6-8th. Location: Doubletree Hotel (Mission Valley), 7450 Hazard Center Dr., San Diego. Average attendance: 400.

COSTS/ACCOMMODATIONS Doubletree Hotel (800)222-TREE. Attendees must make their own travel arrangements.

SCHOOL OF THE ARTS AT RHINELANDER UW-MADISON CONTINUING STUDIES

Website: www.soawisconsin.org. 21 N Park St 7th Floor Madison WI 53715-1218 website:www.soawisconsin.org. Phone: (608)263-3494. Fax: (608)262-1694. E-mail:soa@dcs.wisc.edu. Website:www.soawisconsin.org Established 1964 **Contact:** Lynn Tarnoff, Director Email: ltarnoff@dcs.wisc.edu. Annual 5-day event with classes for adults in visual, performing and computer arts, writing, body-mind-spirit and more 2011 dates: July 24 - 29. Location: Crescent Elementary School Rhinelander, WI Average attendance: 250.

COSTS/ACCOMMODATIONS 2011 cost: registration costs range from $199-349. Informational available from Rhinelander Chamber of Commerce.

ADDITIONAL INFORMATION Catalog available

in mid-March. Additional information available by phone, e-mail, website.

SEACOAST WRITERS ASSOCIATION SPRING AND FALL CONFERENCES

59 River Rd., Stratham NH 03885-2358. (603)742-1030. E-mail: patparnell@comcast.net. Website: www. seacoastwritersassociation.org. **Contact:** Pat Parnell, conf. coordinator. Conferences held in May (May 14, 2011) and October. Conference duration: 1 day. Average attendance: 60. Our conferences offer workshops covering various aspects of fiction, nonfiction and poetry. Cost: Approx. $50. For further information, check the website www.seacoastwritersassociation. org, or visit us on Facebook: Seacoastwritersassociation.

PURPOSE/FEATURES McConnell Center, 61 Locust St., Dover NH. (603)742-1030.

ADDITIONAL INFORMATION "We sometimes include critiques. It is up to the workshop presenter." Spring meeting includes a contest. Categories are fiction, nonfiction (essays) and poetry. Judges vary from year to year. Conference and contest information available for SASE November 1, April 1, and September 1. Accepts inquiries by SASE, e-mail and phone. For further information, check the website www.seacoastwritersassociation.org, or visit us on Facebook: Seacoastwritersassociation.

SEWANEE WRITERS' CONFERENCE

735 University Ave., Sewanee TN 37383-1000. (931)598-1141. E-mail: cpeters@sewanee.edu. Website: www.sewaneewriters.org. Established 1990. **Contact:** Cheri B. Peters, creative writing programs manager. Annual 12-day event held the last 2 weeks in July. Location: the University of the South ("dormitories for housing, Women's Center for public events, classrooms for workshops, Sewanee Inn for dining, etc."). Attendance: about 120.

COSTS/ACCOMMODATIONS Participants are housed in single rooms in university dormitories. Bathrooms are shared by small groups. Motel or B&B housing is available, but not abundantly so.

ADDITIONAL INFORMATION "Complimentary chartered bus service is available from the Nashville Airport to Sewanee and back on the first and last days of the conference. We offer each participant (excepting auditors) the opportunity for a private manuscript conference with a member of the faculty.

These manuscripts are due 1 month before the conference begins. Brochures/guidelines are free. The conference provides a limited number of fellowships and scholarships; these are awarded on a competitive basis."

⊕ SOAPSTONE: A WRITING RETREAT FOR WOMEN

Website: www.soapstone.org. 622 S.E. 29th Ave., Portland OR 97214.(503)233-3936. E-mail: retreats@ soapstone.org. Website: www.soapstone.org. Duration: 1-4 weeks. Average attendance: 30 writers/year. Retreat/residency. "Soapstone provides women writers with a stretch of uninterrupted time for their work and the opportunity to live in semi-solitude close to the natural world. In addition to that rare but essential commodity for a writer-a quiet space away from jobs, children, and other responsibilities-Soapstone provides something less tangible but also invaluable: the validation and encouragement necessary to embark upon or sustain a long or difficult writing project." Located in Oregon\rquote s Coast Range, nine miles from the ocean, the retreat stands on twenty-two acres of densely forested land along the banks of Soapstone Creek and is home to much wildlife. The writers in residence enjoy a unique opportunity to learn about the natural world and join us in conscious stewardship of the land.

COSTS/ACCOMMODATIONS Residents must provide all of their own transportation. See website for more information. Offers overnight accommodations.

ADDITIONAL INFORMATION Application materials required include 3 copies of the completed application, a writing sample (no more than 3 pages of poetry or 5 pages, double-spaced, of prose), and application fee. Applications must be postmarked between July 1-August 1 each year. For brochure, visit website.

TAOS SUMMER WRITERS' CONFERENCE

(505)277-5572. Fax: (505)277-2950. E-mail: taosconf@ unm.edu. Website: www.unm.edu/~taosconf. University of New Mexico, Dept. of English Language and Literature, MSC03 2170, 1 University of New Mexico, Albuquerque NM 87131-0001. (505)277-5572. Fax: (505)277-2950. E-mail: taosconf@unm.edu. Website: www.unm.edu/~taosconf. Established 1999. **Contact:** Sharon Oard Warner, director. Annual 5-day (week-long) and 2-day (weekend) workshops usually held mid-July. Location: Sagebrush Inn in Taos. Average attendance: 180 total; 100 places available in each weekend, 180 places available in weeklong workshops. Class size limited to 12/class, usually smaller.

COSTS/ACCOMMODATIONS $69-109/night at the Sagebrush Inn; $89/night at Comfort Suites.

VERMONT STUDIO CENTER

P.O. Box 613, Johnson VT 05656. (802)635-2727. Fax: (802)635-2730. E-mail: info@vermontstudiocenter. org. Website: www.vermontstudiocenter.org.. **Contact:** Gary Clark, Writing Program Director. From 2-12 weeks, year-round; most residents stay for 4 weeks. Community size: 50+ writers and visual artists/month.

COSTS/ACCOMMODATIONS "The cost of a 4-week residency is $3,750. Generous fellowship and grant assistance available. "Accommodations available on site. "Residents live in single rooms in ten modest, comfortable houses adjacent to the Red Mill Building. Rooms are simply furnished and have shared baths. Complete linen service is provided. The Studio Center is unable to accommodate guests at meals, overnight guests, spouses, children or pets."

ADDITIONAL INFORMATION Fellowships application deadlines are February 15, June 15 and October 1. Writers encouraged to visit website for more information. May also e-mail, call, fax.

WESLEYAN WRITERS CONFERENCE

(860)685-3604. Fax: (860)685-2441. E-mail: agreene@ wesleyan.edu. Website: www.wesleyan.edu/writers. Wesleyan University, Middletown CT 06457. (860)685-3604. Fax: (860)685-2441. E-mail: agreene@wesleyan. edu. Website: www.wesleyan.edu/writers. Established 1956. **Contact:** Anne Greene, director. Annual 5-day event. 2010 dates: Thurs June 17- Mon, June 21. Location: the campus of Wesleyan University "in the hills overlooking the Connecticut River, a brief drive from the Connecticut shore. Wesleyan's outstanding library, poetry reading room, and other university facilities are open to participants." Average attendance: 100.

COSTS/ACCOMMODATIONS Meals are provided on campus. Lodging is available on campus or in town.

ADDITIONAL INFORMATION Ms critiques are available, but not required. Scholarships and teaching fellowships are available, including the Joan Jakobson Awards for fiction writers and poets; and the Jon Davidoff Scholarships for nonfiction writers and journalists. Inquire via e-mail, fax, or phone.

WINTER POETRY & PROSE GETAWAY IN CAPE MAY

(888)887-2105. E-mail: info@wintergetaway.com. Website: www.wintergetaway.com. **Contact:** Peter Murphy. Annual 4-day event. 2011 dates: January 14-17. Location: The Grand Hotel on the Oceanfront in Historic Cape May, NJ. Average attendance: 200 (10 or fewer participants in each poetry workshop).

COSTS/ACCOMMODATIONS Please see website or call for current fee information.

ADDITIONAL INFORMATION Previous faculty has included Julianna Baggott, Christian Bauman, Laure-Anne Bosselaar, Kurt Brown, Mark Doty (National Book Award Winner), Stephen Dunn (Pulitzer Prize Winner), Carol Plum-Ucci, James Richardson, Mimi Schwartz, Terese Svoboda, and more.

● WRITE IT OUT

P.O. Box 704, Sarasota FL 34230-0704. (941)359-3824. E-mail: rmillerwio@aol.com. Website: www.writeitout. com. **Contact:** Ronni Miller, director. Workshops held 2-3 times/year in March, June, July and August. Conference duration: 5-10 days. Average attendance: 4-10. Workshops retreats on "expressive writing and painting, fiction, poetry, memoirs. We also offer intimate, motivational, in-depth free private conferences with instructors." Past facilitators included Arturo Vivante, novelist. Estab. 1997. "Critiques on work are given at the workshops." Conference information available year round. For brochures/guidelines e-mail, call or visit website. Accepts inquiries by phone, e-mail. Workshops have "small groups, option to spend time writing and not attend classes, with personal appointments with instructors."

PURPOSE/FEATURES Workshops in Bermuda, Tuscany, Cape Cod & Woodstock, NY.

ADDITIONAL INFORMATION "Critiques on work are given at the workshops." Conference information available year round. For brochures/guidelines e-mail, call or visit website. Accepts inquiries by phone, e-mail. Workshops have "small groups, option to spend time writing and not attend classes, with personal appointments with instructors."

● WRITING WORKSHOP AT CASTLE HILL

1 Depot Rd., P.O. Box 756, Truro MA 02666-0756. E-mail: cherie@castlehill.org. Website: www.castlehill. org. 1 Depot Rd., P.O. Box 756, Truro MA 02666-0756. Phone: (508)349-7511. Fax: (508)349-7513. Email: cherie@castlehill.org. Website: www.castlehill.org. Contact: Cherie Mittenthal. Poetry, Fiction, Memoir workshops geared toward intermediate and advanced levels. **Open to students.** Workshops by Keith Althaus: Poetry; Anne Bernays: Elements of Fiction; Elizabeth Bradfield: Poetry in Plein Air & Broadsides and Beyond: Poetry as Public Art; Melanie Braverman: In Pursuit of Exactitude: Poetry; Josephine Del Deo: Preoccupation in Poetry; Martin Espada: Barbaric Yamp: A Poetry Workshop; Judy Huge: Finding the Me in Memoir; Justin Kaplan: Autobiography. See website under Summer 2011 Writers for dates and more information.

THE HELENE WURLITZER FOUNDATION

P.O. Box 1891, Taos NM 87571. (505)758-2413. Fax: (575)758-2559. E-mail: hwf@taosnet.com. Website: www.wurlitzerfoundation.org. **Contact:** Michael A. Knight, executive director. Three-month residencies. "The Foundation's purpose is to provide a quiet haven where artists may pursue their creative endeavors without pressure to produce while they are in residence."

COSTS/ACCOMMODATIONS "Provides individual housing in fully furnished studio/houses (casitas), rent and utility free. Artists are responsible for transportation to and from Taos, their meals, and the materials for their work. Bicycles are provided upon request."

ORGANIZATIONS

There are many organizations of value to poets. These groups may sponsor workshops and contests, stage readings, publish anthologies and chapbooks or spread the word about publishing opportunities. A few provide economic assistance or legal advice. The best thing organizations offer, though, is a support system to which poets can turn for a pep talk, a hard-nosed (but sympathetic) critique of a manuscript or simply the comfort of talking and sharing with others who understand the challenges, and joys, of writing poetry.

Whether national, regional or as local as your library or community center, each organization has something special to offer. The listings in this section reflect the membership opportunities available to poets with a variety of organizations. Some groups provide certain services to both members and nonmembers.

These symbols may appear at the beginning of some listings: The ⊕ icon indicates a recently established organization new to *Poet's Market*; the ☉ icon denotes a Canadian organization and the ◑ icon one headquartered outside the U.S. and Canada.

Since some organizations are included in listings in the other sections of this book, we've cross-referenced these listings under Additional Organizations at the end of this section. For further details about an organization associated with a market in this list, go to that market's page number.

To find out more about groups in your area (including those that may not be listed in *Poet's Market*), contact your YMCA, community center, local colleges and universities, public library and bookstores (and don't forget newspapers and the Internet). If you can't find a group that suits your needs, consider starting one yourself. You might be surprised to discover there are others in your locality who would welcome the encouragement, feedback and moral support of a writer's group.

THE ACADEMY OF AMERICAN POETS

75 Maiden Lane, Suite 901, New York NY 10038. (212)274-0343. Fax: (212)274-9427. E-mail: academy@poets.org. Website: www.poets.org. Executive Director: Tree Swenson. Established 1934. The Academy of American Poets was founded to support the nation's poets at all stages of their careers and to foster the appreciation of contemporary poetry. Levels of membership/dues: begin at $35/year (contributing member). Administers The Walt Whitman Award; The James Laughlin Award; The Harold Morton Landon Translation Award; The Lenore Marshall Poetry Prize; The Raiziss/de Palchi Translation Award; and The Wallace Stevens Award. (For further details, see individual listings in the Contests & Awards section.) Also awards The Fellowship of the Academy of American Poets ($25,000 to honor distinguished poetic achievement, no applications accepted) and The University & College Poetry Prizes. Publishes American Poet, an informative semiannual journal sent to all Academy members. The Academy's other programs include National Poetry Month (April), the largest literary celebration in the world; the Poetry Audio Archive, a 700-volume audio library capturing the voices of contemporary American poets for generations to come; an annual series of poetry readings and special events; and Poets.org, which includes thousands of poems, hundreds of essays and interviews, lesson plans for teachers, a National Poetry Almanac, a national Calendar of Events, and the National Poetry Map.

AMERICAN BOOKSELLERS FOUNDATION FOR FREE EXPRESSION

19 Fulton St., Suite 1504, New York NY 10038. (212)587-4025 ext. 15. Fax: (212)587-2436. E-mail: chris@abffe.com. Website: www.abffe.com. "The American Booksellers Foundation for Free Expression is the bookseller's voice in the fight against censorship. Founded by the American Booksellers Association, ABFFE's mission is to promote and protect the free exchange of ideas, particularly those contained in books, by opposing restrictions on the freedom of speech; issuing statements on significant free expression controversies; participating in legal cases involving First Amendment rights; collaborating with other groups with an interest in free speech; providing education about the importance of free expression to booksellers, other members of the book industry, politicians, the press and the public." Levels of membership/dues: $50. ABFFE is the bookseller's voice in all free speech controversies involving books and other written material. We alerted booksellers to the dangers posed by the USA Patriot Act and helped them communicate their concerns to Congress. We are also active on the local level. ABFFE opposes efforts to ban books in public schools and libraries and files amicus briefs in cases challenging school censorship. ABFFE is a sponsor of Banned Books Week. Additional information available on the website.

⊕ AMERICAN HAIKU ARCHIVES

California State Library, Library & Courts II Bldg, 900 N St., Sacramento CA 95814. E-mail: WelchM@aol.com. Website: www.americanhaikuarchives.org. **Contact:** Michael Dylan Welch. California State Library, Library & Courts II Bldg, Sacramento CA 95814. E-mail: WelchM@aol.com. Website: www.americanhaikuarchives.org. The American Haiku Archives, founded in 1996, is "the world's largest public collection of haiku and related poetry books and papers outside Japan." This repository is housed at the California State Library in Sacramento, California, and is dedicated to preserving the history of North American haiku. Materials are publicly available for research purposes through the library's California History Room. The American Haiku Archives actively seeks donations of books, journals, recordings, letters, ephemera, and personal papers relating to haiku poetry in all languages, but especially North American languages. The American Haiku Archives also appoints an honorary curator every July for a one-year term. The intent of this appointment is to honor leading haiku poets, translators, or scholars for their accomplishments or service in support of haiku poetry as a literary art. Past honorary curators have been Gary Snyder, Stephen Addiss, George Swede, H. F. Noyes, Hiroaki Sato, Francine Porad, Makoto Ueda, William J. Higginson, Leroy Kanterman, Lorraine Ellis Harr, Robert Spiess, Cor van den Heuvel, Jerry Kilbride, and Elizabeth Searle Lamb. Additional information about the archives is available on the website.

CALIFORNIA STATE POETRY SOCIETY

CSPS/CQ, P.O. Box 7126, Orange CA 92863. E-mail: pearlk@covad.net. Website: www.californiaquarterly.blogspot.com. **Contact:** The Membership Chair. The California State Poetry Society "is dedicated to the adventure of poetry and its dissemination. Although located in California, its members are from all over the U.S. and abroad." Levels of membership/dues: $30/year. Benefits include membership in the National Federation of State

Poetry Societies (NFSPS); 4 issues of California Quarterly (see separate listing in Magazines/Journals), *Newsbriefs*, and *The Poetry Letter*. Sponsors monthly and annual contests. Additional information available for SASE.

FURIOUS FLOWER POETRY CENTER

(Specialized: African American poetry), MSC 3802, James Madison University, Harrisonburg VA 22807. (540)568-8883. Fax: (540)568-8888. E-mail: gabbinjv@ jmu.edu. Website: www.jmu.edu/furiousflower. Established 1999. **Contact:** Joanne Gabbin, PhD, Executive Director. A non-membership-based organization. "The mission of the Furious Flower Poetry Center is to advance the genre of African American poetry by providing opportunities for education, research, and publication." Sponsors workshops and conferences related to African American poetry, including an annual poetry camp for children of the community. Sponsored national conferences in 1994 and 2004. Nationally known writers give readings that are open to the public. Sponsors open mic readings for the public; also sponsors the Central Shenandoah Valley Slam Team. Additional information available by e-mail or on website.

GEORGIA POETRY SOCIETY

P.O. Box 2184, Columbia GA 31902. E-mail: gps@georgiapoetrysociety.org. Website: www.georgiapoetrysociety.org. Statewide organization open to any person who is in accord with the objectives to secure fuller public recognition of the art of poetry, stimulate an appreciation of poetry, and enhance the writing and reading of poetry. Currently has 200 members. Levels of membership/dues: Active, $30 ($40 family), fully eligible for all aspects of membership; Student, $15, does not vote or hold office, and must be full-time enrolled student through college level; Lifetime, same as Active but pays a one-time membership fee of $500, receives free anthologies each year, and pays no contest entry fees. Membership includes affiliation with NFSPS. Holds at least one workshop annually. Contests are sponsored throughout the year, some for members only. "Our contests have specific general rules, which should be followed to avoid the disappointment of disqualification. See the website for details." Publishes Georgia Poetry Society Newsletter, a quarterly, and The Reach of Song, an annual anthology devoted to contest-winning poems and member works. Each quarterly meeting (open to the public) features at least one poet of regional prominence. Also sponsors a monthly open

mic at the Columbus Library (Macon Rd) in Columbus, GA (open to the public). Sponsors Poetry in the Schools project. Additional information available on website.

HAIKU SOCIETY OF AMERICA

P.O. Box 31, Nassau NY 12123. E-mail: hsa-9AT@comcast.net. Website: www.hsa-haiku.org. The Haiku Society of America is composed of haiku poets, editors, critics, publishers, and enthusiasts dedicated to "promoting the creation and appreciation of haiku and related forms (haibun, haiga, renku, senryu, sequences, and tanka) among its members and the public." Currently has over 800 members. Levels of membership/dues: $33 U.S.; $30 seniors or full-time students (in North America); $35 USD in Canada and Mexico; $45 USD for all other areas. Membership benefits include a year's subscription (3 issues in 2011) to the Society's journal, Frogpond (see separate listing in Magazines/Journals), and to the quarterly HSA Newsletter Ripples; the annual information sheet; an annual address/e-mail list of HSA members; and eligibility to submit work to the members' anthology. Administers the following annual awards: The Harold G. Henderson Awards for haiku, The Gerald Brady Awards for senryu, The Bernard Lionel Einbond Awards for renku, The Merit Book Awards, and The Nicholas Virgilio Haiku Awards for youth. For 2011, A Haibun contest is being offered as well. Guidelines available in the newsletter or on website. Meets quarterly at various locations throughout the U.S. Additional information available for SASE or on website.

INTERNATIONAL WOMEN'S WRITING GUILD

International Women's Writing Guild, P.O. Box 810, Gracie Station, New York NY 10028. (212)737-7536. Fax: (212)737-9469. E-mail: iwwg@iwwg.org; dirhahn@iwwg.org. Website: www.iwwg.org. **Contact:** Hannelore Hahn, Exec. Editor. A network for the personal and professional empowerment of women through writing. Levels of membership/dues: $55/year (domestic and overseas). The Guild publishes a quarterly 32-page journal, Network , which includes members' achievements, contests, calendar, and extensive publishing opportunities. IWWG is particularly known for its writing conferences; i.e. its week-long summer conference at Yale University; and its weekend conferences in New York City and California. Other benefits include regional/local writing groups and kitchen tables, agent list, and dental and vision insurance, health insurance in New York City. "We offer approximately 4 writing conferences throughout the U.S., including the weeklong summer conference held at Yale University in New Haven, CT. Poetry workshops are interspersed in the conference programs." Additional information available by fax, e-mail, or on website.

IOWA POETRY ASSOCIATION

(Specialized: IA residents only), 2325 61st St., Des Moines IA 50322. (515)279-1106. Website: www.iowapoetry.com. Established 1945. **Contact:** Lucille Morgan Wilson, editor. Statewide organization open to "anyone interested in poetry, with a residence or valid address in the state of Iowa." Currently has about 425 members. Levels of membership/dues: Regular ($8/year) and Patron ($15 or more/year; "same services, but patron members contribute to cost of running the association"). Offerings include "semiannual workshops to which a poem may be sent in advance for critique; annual contest—also open to nonmembers—with no entry fee; IPA Newsletter , published 5 or 6 times/year, including a quarterly national publication listing of contest opportunities; and an annual poetry anthology, Lyrical Iowa , containing prize-winning and high-ranking poems from contest entries, available for $10 postpaid. No requirement for purchase to ensure publication." Semiannual workshops "are the only 'meetings' of the association." Additional information available for SASE or on website.

⚫ LLENYDDIAETH CYMRU/ LITERATURE WALES

(44)(29)2047-2266. Fax: (44)(29)2049-2930. E-mail: post@academi.org. Website: www.academi.org. Academi is the Welsh National Literature Promotion Agency and Society of Writers and is open to "the population of Wales and those outside Wales with an interest in Welsh writing." Currently has 2,000 members.Levels of membership/dues: associate, full, and fellow; £15/year (waged) or £7.50/year (unwaged). Offerings include promotion of readings, events, conferences, exchanges, tours; employment of literature-development workers; publication of a quarterly events magazine; publication of a literary magazine in Welsh (Taliesin). Sponsors conferences/workshops and contests/awards. Publishes A470: What's On In Literary Wales , a magazine appearing quarterly containing information on literary events in Wales. Academi is also a resident company of the Wales Millenium Centre, where it runs the Glyn Jones Centre, a resource centre for writers and the pub-

lic. Additional information available for SASE (or SAE and IRC), by fax, e-mail, or on website.

THE LOFT LITERARY CENTER

Suite 200, Open Book, 1011 Washington Ave. S, Minneapolis MN 55414. (612)215-2575. E-mail: loft@loft.org. Website: www.loft.org. "The Loft is the largest and most comprehensive literary center in the country, serving both writers and readers with a variety of readings, Spoken Word performances, educational programs, contests and grants, and writing facilities." Supporting members (starting at $60/year - $25 for students/low income) receive benefits including discounted tuition, admission charges, and contest fees; check-out privileges at The Loft's Rachel Anne Gaschott Resource Library; rental access to the Book Club Meeting Room and writers' studios and more. Information on additional benefit levels, classes/workshops, contests and grants, and readings by local and national writers available at the website.

NEW HAMPSHIRE WRITERS' PROJECT

2500 North River Rd., Manchester NH 03106. (603)314-7980. Fax: (603)314-7981. E-mail: info@nhwritersproject.org. Website: www.nhwritersproject.org. **Contact:** Kathy Wurtz, Exec. Director. Statewide organization open to writers at all levels in all genres. Currently has 600+ members. Levels of membership/dues: $55/year; $25/year for seniors and students. Offerings include workshops, seminars, an annual conference, and a literary calendar. Sponsors daylong workshops and 4- to 6-week intensive courses. Also sponsors the biennial New Hampshire Literary Awards for outstanding literary achievement (including The Jane Kenyon Award for Outstanding Book of Poetry). Publishes NH Writer, a quarterly newsletter for and about New Hampshire writers. Members and nationally known writers give readings that are open to the public. Additional information available by fax, e-mail, or on website.

NORTH CAROLINA WRITERS' NETWORK

P.O. Box 21591, Winston-Salem NC 27120. (336)293-8844. E-mail: mail@ncwriters.org. Website: www.ncwriters.org. Supports the work of writers, writers' organizations, independent bookstores, little magazines and small presses, and literary programming statewide. Currently has 1,000 members. Levels of membership/dues: $75/year; seniors/students, $55/year. Membership benefits include The Writers' Network News , a 24-page quarterly newsletter containing organizational news, trend in writing and publishing, and other literary material of interest to writers; and access to the NCWN online resources, other writers, workshops, writer's residencies, conferences, readings and competitions, and NCWN's critiquing and editing service. Annual fall conference features nationally known writers, publishers, and editors, held in a different North Carolina location each November. Sponsors competitions in short fiction, nonfiction, and poetry for North Carolina residents and NCWN members. Guidelines available for SASE or on website.

PEN AMERICAN CENTER

588 Broadway Suit 303, New York NY 10012. (212)334-1660. Fax: (212)334-2181. E-mail: pen@pen.org. Website: www.pen.org. Established 1922. PEN American Center "is the largest of the 141 centers of International PEN, the world's oldest human rights organization and the oldest international literary association. PEN American Center works to advance literature, to defend free expression, and to foster international literary fellowship." The 2,900 members of the PEN American Center include poets, playwrights, essayists, editors, novelists (for the original letters in the acronym PEN), as well as translators and those editors and agents who have made a substantial contribution to the literary community. Levels of membership/dues: $100 Member (must meet standard qualifications to become a Member; see website); $40 Associate Member and $20 Student (both open to everyone). Membership benefits include subscription to PEN America Journal, discounts on admission to public programs, discounted access to Grants and Awards Available to American Writers (an online database), access to online bulletin board, and more (additional benefits at Member level, including reciprocal privileges in PEN American Center branches and in foreign centers for those traveling abroad). Sponsors public literary programs, forums on current issues, visits by prominent authors to inner-city schools, the promotion of international literature to U.S. readers, and grants and loans to writers with emergency financial need. Publishes PEN America Journal (available through website and selected bookstores, or by subscription at $18/year); and Grants and Awards Available to American Writers online (access available through membership or nonmember subscription of $12/year). Administers the PEN/Joyce Osterwell Award for Poetry for a new and emerging American poet of literary character ($5,000), and the PEN Award for Poetry in Translation ($3,000) for book-length translations of poetry into English from any language. Also sponsors the annual PEN World Voices: The New York Festival of International Literature. Additional information on membership and all programs and activities available on website.

POETRY SOCIETY OF NEW HAMPSHIRE

31 Reservoir, Farmington NH 03835. (603)332-0732. E-mail: poetrysocietyofnh@gmail.com. Website: www.poetrysocietyofnewhampshire.org. A statewide organization for anyone interested in poetry. Currently has 200 members. Levels of membership/dues: Junior ($10); Regular ($20). Offerings include annual subscription to quarterly magazine, The Poet's Touchstone; critiques, contests, and workshops; public readings; and quarterly meetings with featured poets. The Poet's Touchstone is available to nonmembers for $6 (single issue). Members and nationally known writers give readings that are open to the public. Sponsors open mic readings for members and the public. Additional information available for SASE or by e-mail. "We do sponsor a national contest four times a year with $100, $50, and $25 prizes paid out in each one. People from all over the country enter and win."

THE POETRY SOCIETY OF SOUTH CAROLINA

P.O. Box 1090, Charleston SC 29402. E-mail: flatbluesky@hotmail.com. Website: www.poetrysocietysc.org. The Poetry Society of South Carolina supports "the reading, writing, study, and enjoyment of poetry." Statewide organization open to anyone interested in poetry. Offers programs in Charleston that are free and open to the public September-May (except for members-only holiday party in December). Currently has 150 members. Levels of membership/dues: $15 student, $25 individual, $35 family, $50 patron, and $100 business or sponsor. Membership year runs July 1-June 30. Membership benefits include discounts to PSSC-sponsored seminars and workshops held in various SC locations; a copy of the annual Yearbook of contest-winning poems; eligibility to read at the open mic and to enter contests without a fee; and an invitation to the annual holiday party. Sponsors a monthly Writers' Group, a January open mic reading featuring PSSC members, a Charleston Poetry Walk during Piccolo Spoleto in June, and a May Forum leading to an audience-selected poetry prize. Sponsors two yearly contests, totaling 20-25 contest categories, some with themes; some are open to all poets, others open only to SC residents or PSSC members. Guidelines available on website. **Deadline:** November 15 (Fall round) and February 15 (Spring round). Also offers the Skylark Prize, a competition for SC high school students. Sometimes offers a chapbook competition. Members and nationally known writers give readings that are open to the public. Poets have included Billy Collins, Henry Taylor, Cathy Smith Bowers, and Richard Garcia, as well as emerging poets from the region. Additional information available by e-mail or on website.

THE AUTHORS GUILD, INC.

31 E. 32nd St., 7th Floor, New York NY 10016. E-mail: staff@authorsguild.org. Website: www.authorsguild.org. **Contact:** Paul Aiken, Exec. Director. Established in 1912, it "is the largest association of published writers in the United States. The Guild focuses its efforts on the legal and business concerns of published authors in the areas of publishing contract terms, copyright, taxation, and freedom of expression. The Guild services for members include free book and magazine contract reviews, exclusive website-building software, deeply discounted website hosting and domain name reservation, and BackIn-Print.com, a service that allows members to republish and sell their out-of-print books. The Guild also makes group health insurance available to members. Writers must be published by a recognized book publisher or periodical of general circulation to be eligible for membership. We do not work in the area of marketing mss to publishers nor do we sponsor or participate in awards or prize selections." Also publishes The Bulletin, a quarterly journal for professional writers. Additional information available by mail, phone, e-mail, or on website.

○ Purpose of organization: to offer services and materials intended to help authors with the business and legal aspects of their work, including contract problems, copyright matters, freedom of expression and taxation. Guild has 8,000 members. Qualifications for membership: Must be book author published by an established American publisher within 7 years or any author who has had 3 works (fiction or nonfiction) published by a magazine or magazines of general circulation in the last 18 months. Associate membership also available. Annual dues: $90. Different levels of membership include: associate membership with all rights except voting available to an author who has a firm contract offer or is currently negotiating a royalty contract from an established American publisher. "The Guild offers free contract reviews to its members. The Guild conducts several sympo-

sia each year at which experts provide information, offer advice and answer questions on subjects of interest and concern to authors. Typical subjects have been the rights of privacy and publicity, libel, wills and estates, taxation, copyright, editors and editing, the art of interviewing, standards of criticism and book reviewing. Transcripts of these symposia are published and circulated to members. The Authors Guild Bulletin, a quarterly journal, contains articles on matters of interest to writers, reports of Guild activities, contract surveys, advice on problem clauses in contracts, transcripts of Guild and League symposia and information on a variety of professional topics. Subscription included in the cost of the annual dues."

THE NORTH CAROLINA POETRY SOCIETY

NCPS, 3814 Hulon Dr., Durham NC 27705. E-mail: caren@windstream.net. Website: www.ncpoetrysociety. org. The North Carolina Poetry Society holds poetry-related contests and gives away several awards each year, for both Adults and Students (which includes 3rd Graders all the way to University Undergraduates). Contact through website: www.ncpoetrysociety.org or mail to: NCPS, 3814 Hulon Drive, Durham, NC 27705. Include SASE for reply. Established 1932. Statewide organization open to non-NC residents. Purpose: to encourage the reading, writing, study, and publication of poetry. NCPS brings poets together in meetings that feature workshops, presentations by noted poets and publishers, book and contest awards, and an annual anthology of award-winning poems. Currently has 350 members from NC and beyond. Levels of membership: Adult ($25/year) and Student ($10/year). NCPS conducts 6 general meetings and numerous statewide workshops/events each year. Sponsors annual Poetry Contest with categories for adults and students. Contests are open to anyone, with small fee for nonmembers. **Deadline** in January (verify date via Website or mail.) Winning poems are published in *Pinesong*, NCPS's annual anthology. A free copy is given to all winners, who are also invited to read at Awards Day. NCPS also sponsors the annual Brockman-Campbell Book Award for a book of poetry over 20 pages by a North Carolina poet (native-born or current resident for 3 years. Prize: $200 and a reading. Entry fee: none for members, $10 for nonmembers. Deadline: May 1.) NCPS also cosponsors the Gilbert-Chappell Distinguished Poet Series with

The North Carolina Center for the Book, for the purpose of mentoring young poets across the state. Please visit NCPS's Website for more information or to see additional benefits offered to members.

UNIVERSITY OF ARIZONA POETRY CENTER

1508 E. Helen St., P.O. Box 210129, Tucson AZ 85721. (520)626-3765. E-mail: poetry@email.arizona.edu. Website: www.poetrycenter.arizona.edu. **Contact:** Gail Browne, Exec. Director. 1508 E. Helen St., P.O. Box 210150, Tucson AZ 85721. (520)626-3765. Fax: (520)621-5566. E-mail: poetry@u.arizona.edu. Website: www.poetrycenter.arizona.edu. **Contact:** Gail Browne, executive director. Established 1960. "Open to the public, the University of Arizona Poetry Center is a contemporary poetry archive and a nationally acclaimed poetry collection that includes over 70,000 items. Programs and services include a library with a noncirculating poetry collection and space for small classes; online lesson plan library; High School Bilingual Corrido Contest; K-16 field trip program; summer camps; poetry-related meetings and activities; facilities, research support, and referral information about poetry and poets for local and national communities; Reading Series; community creative writing classes and workshops; a summer residency offered each year to two writers (one prose, one poetry) selected by jury; and poetry awards, readings, and special events for high school, undergraduate, and graduate students. Additional information available by phone, e-mail, or website. Become a 'Friend of the Poetry Center' by making an annual contribution."

✪☺ WORDS WITHOUT BORDERS

P.O. Box 1658, New York NY 10276. E-mail: info@wordswithoutborders.org. Website: www.wordswithoutborders.org. P.O. Box 1658, New York NY 10276.E-mail: info@wordswithoutborders.org. Website: www.wordswithoutborders.org. "Words Without Borders opens doors to international exchange through translation, publications, and promotion of the world's best writing. Our ultimate aim is to introduce exciting international writing to the general public—travelers, teachers, students, publishers, and a new generation of eclectic readers— by presenting international literature not as a static, elite phenomenon, but a portal through which to explore the world. The heart of WWB's work is its online magazine. Monthly issues feature new selections of contemporary world literature, most of which would never have been accessible to English-speaking readers without WWB." Members and international writers give readings that are open to the public. See website for additional information.

☾ WRITERS' FEDERATION OF NOVA SCOTIA

1113 Marginal Rd., Halifax NS B3H 4P7, Canada. (902)423-8116. Fax: (902)422-0881. E-mail: talk@writers.ns.ca. Website: www.writers.ns.ca. Purpose is "to foster creative writing and the profession of writing in Nova Scotia; to provide advice and assistance to writers at all stages of their careers; and to encourage greater public recognition of Nova Scotian writers and their achievements." Regional organization open to anybody who writes. Currently has 800+ members. Levels of membership/dues: $45 CAD annually ($20 CAD students). Offerings include resource library with over 2,500 titles, promotional services, workshop series, annual festivals, mentorship program. *Sponsors the Atlantic Writing Competition for unpublished works by beginning writers, and the annual Atlantic Poetry Prize for the best book of poetry by an Atlantic Canadian.* Publishes Eastword , a bimonthly newsletter containing "a plethora of information on who's doing what; markets and contests; and current writing events and issues." Members and nationally known writers give readings that are open to the public. Additional information available on website.

THE WRITERS ROOM

740 Broadway, 12th Floor, New York NY 10003. (212)254-6995. Fax: (212)533-6059. E-mail: writersroom@writersroom.org. Website: www.writersroom.org. Established 1978. Provides a "home away from home" for any writer who needs space to work. Open 24 hours a day, 7 days a week, **for members only**. Currently has about 350 members. Emerging and established writers may apply. Levels of membership/dues: vary from $$525 to $750/half year, plus one-time initiation fee of $75. Large loft provides desk space, Internet access, storage, and more. Call for application or download from website.

POETS IN EDUCATION

///

Whether known as PITS (Poets in the Schools), WITS (Writers in the Schools), or similar names, programs exist nationwide that coordinate residencies, classroom visits and other opportunities for experienced poets to share their craft with students. Many state arts agencies include such "arts in education" programs in their activities (see Grants on page 424 for contact information). Another good source is the National Assembly of State Arts Agencies (see below), which offers an online directory of contact names and addresses for arts education programs state-by-state. The following list is a mere sampling of programs and organizations that link poets with schools. Contact them for information about their requirements (some may insist poets have a strong publication history, others may prefer classroom experience) or check their websites where available.

THE ACADEMY OF AMERICAN POETS, 584 Broadway, Suite 604, New York NY 10012-5243. (212)274-0343. E-mail: academy@poets.org. website: www.poets.org (includes links to state arts in education programs).

ARKANSAS WRITERS IN THE SCHOOLS, WITS Director, 333 Kimpel Hall, University of Arkansas, Fayetteville AR 72701. (479)575-5991. E-mail: wits@cavern.uark.edu. website: www. uark.edu/~wits.

CALIFORNIA POETS IN THE SCHOOLS, 1333 Balboa St. #3, San Francisco CA 94118. (415)221-4201. E-mail: info@cpits.org. website: www.cpits.org.

E-POETS.NETWORK, a collective online cultural center that promotes education through videoconferencing (i.e., "distance learning"); also includes the *Voces y Lugares* project. website: http://learning.e-poets.net (includes online contact form).

IDAHO WRITERS IN THE SCHOOLS, Log Cabin Literary Center, 801 S. Capitol Blvd., Boise ID 83702. (208)331-8000. E-mail: info@thecabinidaho.org. website: www.thecabin idaho.org.

INDIANA WRITERS IN THE SCHOOLS, University of Evansville, Dept. of English, 1800 Lincoln Ave., Evansville IN 47722. (812)488-2962. E-mail: rg37@evansville.edu. website: http://english.evansville.edu/WritersintheSchools.htm.

MICHIGAN CREATIVE WRITERS IN THE SCHOOLS, ArtServe Michigan, 17515 W. Nine Mile Rd., Suite 1025, Southfield MI 48075. (248)557-8288 **OR** 1310 Turner St., Suite B, Lansing MI 48906. (517)371-1720 (toll free at (800)203-9633). E-mail: online form. website: www.artservemichigan.org.

NATIONAL ASSEMBLY OF STATE ARTS AGENCIES, 1029 Vermont Ave. NW, 2nd Floor, Washington DC 20005. (202)347-6352. E-mail: nasaa@nasaa-arts.org. website: www.nasaa-arts.org.

NATIONAL ASSOCIATION OF WRITERS IN EDUCATION (NAWE), P.O. Box 1, Sheriff Hutton, York YO60 7YU England. (44)(1653)618429. website: www.nawe.co.uk.

OREGON WRITERS IN THE SCHOOLS, Literary Arts, 224 NW 13th Ave., Suite 306, Portland OR 97209. (503)227-2583. E-mail: john@literary-arts.org. website: www.literary-arts.org/wits.

PEN IN THE CLASSROOM (PITC), Pen Center USA, Þco Antioch University, 400 Corporate Pointe, Culver City CA 90230. (310)862-1555. E-mail: pitc@penusa.org. website: www.penusa.org/go/classroom.

"PICK-A-POET," The Humanities Project, Arlington Public Schools, 1439 N. Quincy St., Arlington VA 22207. (703)228-6299. E-mail: online form. website: www.humanitiesproject.org.

POTATO HILL POETRY, 6 Pleasant St., Suite 2, South Natick MA 01760. (888)5-POETRY. E-mail: info@potatohill.com. website: www.potatohill.com (includes online contact form).

SEATTLE WRITERS IN THE SCHOOLS (WITS), Seattle Arts & Lectures, 105 S. Main St., Suite 201, Seattle WA 98104. (206)621-2230. website: www.lectures.org/wits.html.

TEACHERS & WRITERS COLLABORATIVE, 520 Eighth Ave., Suite 2020, New York NY 10018. (212)691-6590 or (888)BOOKS-TW (book orders). E-mail: info@twc.org. website: www.twc.org. "A catalog of T&W books is available online, or call toll-free to request a print copy.

TEXAS WRITERS IN THE SCHOOLS, 1523 W. Main, Houston TX 77006. (713)523-3877. E-mail: mail@witshouston.org. website: www.writersintheschools.org.

WRITERS & ARTISTS IN THE SCHOOLS (WAITS), COMPAS, Landmark Center, Suite 304, 75 Fifth St. West, St. Paul MN 55102-1496. (651)292-3254. E-mail: daniel@compas.org. website: www.compas.org.

YOUTH VOICES IN INK, Badgerdog Literary Publishing, Inc., P.O. Box 301209, Austin TX 78703-0021. (512)538-1305. E-mail: info@badgerdog.org. website: www.badgerdog.org.

GLOSSARY OF LISTING TERMS

A3, A4, A5. Metric equivalents of 11¾×16½, 8¼×11¾, and 5⅞×8¼ respectively.

ACKNOWLEDGMENTS PAGE. A page in a poetry book or chapbook that lists the publications where the poems in the collection were originally published; may be presented as part of the copyright page or as a separate page on its own.

ANTHOLOGY. A collection of selected writings by various authors.

ATTACHMENT. A computer file electronically "attached" to an e-mail message.

AUD. Abbreviation for Australian Dollar.

B&W. Black & white (photo or illustration).

BIO. A short biographical statement often requested with a submission.

CAD. Abbreviation for Canadian Dollar.

CAMERA-READY. Poems ready for copy camera platemaking; camera-ready poems usually appear in print exactly as submitted.

CHAPBOOK. A small book of about 24-50 pages.Circulation. The number of subscribers to a magazine/journal.

CLMP. Council of Literary Magazines and Presses; service organization for independent publishers of fiction, poetry, and prose.

CONTRIBUTOR'S COPY. Copy of book or magazine containing a poet's work, sometimes given as payment.

COVER LETTER. Brief introductory letter accompanying a poetry submission.

COVERSTOCK. Heavier paper used as the cover for a publication.

DIGEST-SIZED. About 5½×8½, the size of a folded sheet of conventional printer paper.

DOWNLOAD. To "copy" a file, such as a registration form, from a website.

ELECTRONIC MAGAZINE. See *online magazine.*E-mail. Mail sent electronically using computer and modem or similar means.

EURO. Currency unit for the 27 member countries of the European Union; designated by EUR or the INSERT EURO symbol.

FAQ. Frequently Asked Questions.

FONT. The style/design of type used in a publication; typeface.

GALLEYS. First typeset version of a poem, magazine, or book/chapbook.

GLBT. Gay/lesbian/bisexual/transgender (as in "GLBT themes").

HONORARIUM. A token payment for published work.Internet. A worldwide network of computers offering access to a variety of electronic resources.

IRC. International Reply Coupon; a publisher can exchange IRCs for postage to return a manuscript to another country.

JPEG. Short for *Joint Photographic Experts Group*; an image compression format that allows digital images to be stored in relatively small files for electronic mailing and viewing on the Internet.

MAGAZINE-SIZED. About 8½×11, the size of an unfolded sheet of conventional printer paper.

MS. Manuscript.

MSS. Manuscripts.

MULTI-BOOK REVIEW. Several books by the same author or by several authors reviewed in one piece.

OFFSET-PRINTED. Printing method in which ink is transferred from an image-bearing plate to a "blanket" and then from blanket to paper.

ONLINE MAGAZINE. Publication circulated through the Internet or e-mail.

P&H. Postage & handling.

P&P. Postage & packing.

"PAYS IN COPIES." See *contributor's copy*.

PDF. Short for *Portable Document Format*, developed by Adobe Systems, that captures all elements of a printed document as an electronic image, allowing it to be sent by e-mail, viewed online, and printed in its original format.

PERFECT-BOUND. Publication with glued, flat spine; also called "flat-spined."

POD. See *print-on-demand*.

PRESS RUN. The total number of copies of a publication printed at one time.

PREVIOUSLY PUBLISHED. Work that has appeared before in print, in any form, for public consumption.

PRINT-ON-DEMAND. Publishing method that allows copies of books to be published as they're requested, rather than all at once in a single press run.

PUBLISHING CREDITS. A poet's magazine publications and book/chapbook titles.

QUERY LETTER. Letter written to an editor to raise interest in a proposed project.

READING FEE. A monetary amount charged by an editor or publisher to consider a poetry submission without any obligation to accept the work.

RICH TEXT FORMAT. Carries the .rtf filename extension. A file format that allows an exchange of text files between different word processor operating systems with most of the formatting preserved.

RIGHTS. A poet's legal property interest in his/her literary work; an editor or publisher may acquire certain rights from the poet to reproduce that work.

ROW. "Rest of world."

ROYALTIES. A percentage of the retail price paid to the author for each copy of a book sold.

SADDLE-STAPLED. A publication folded, then stapled along that fold; also called "saddle-stitched."

SAE. Self-addressed envelope.

SASE. Self-addressed, stamped envelope.

SASP. Self-addressed, stamped postcard. Simultaneous submission. Submission of the same manuscript to more than one publisher at the same time.

SUBSIDY PRESS. Publisher who requires the poet to pay all costs, including typesetting, production, and printing; sometimes called a "vanity publisher."

TABLOID-SIZED. 11×15 or larger, the size of an ordinary newspaper folded and turned sideways.

TEXT FILE. A file containing only textual characters (i.e., no graphics or special formats).

UNSOLICITED MANUSCRIPT. A manuscript an editor did not ask specifically to receive.

URL. Stands for "Uniform Resource Locator," the address of an Internet resource (i.e., file).

USD. Abbreviation for United States Dollar. website. A specific address on the Internet that provides access to a set of documents (or "pages").

GLOSSARY OF POETRY TERMS

///

This glossary is provided as a quick-reference only, briefly covering poetic styles and terms that may turn up in articles and listings in *Poet's Market*. For a full understanding of the terms, forms, and styles listed here, as well as common literary terms not included, consult a solid textbook or handbook, such as John Drury's *The Poetry Dictionary* (Writer's Digest Books). (Ask your librarian or bookseller for recommendations).

ABSTRACT POEM: conveys emotion through sound, textures, and rhythm and rhyme rather than through the meanings of words.

ACROSTIC: initial letters of each line, read downward, form a word, phrase, or sentence.

ALLITERATION: close repetition of consonant sounds, especially initial consonant sounds. (Also known as *consonance*.)

ALPHABET POEM: arranges lines alphabetically according to initial letter.

AMERICAN CINQUAIN: derived from Japanese haiku and tanka by Adelaide Crapsey; counted syllabic poem of 5 lines of 2-4-6-8-2 syllables, frequently in iambic feet.

ANAPEST: foot consisting of 2 unstressed syllables followed by a stress (- - ').

ASSONANCE: close repetition of vowel sounds. Avant-garde: work at the forefront--cutting edge, unconventional, risk-taking.

BALLAD: narrative poem often in ballad stanza (4-line stanza with 4 stresses in lines 1 and 3, 3 stresses in lines 2 and 4, which also rhyme).

BALLADE: 3 stanzas rhymed *ababbcbC* (*C* indicates a refrain) with envoi rhymed *bcbC*.

BEAT POETRY: anti-academic school of poetry born in '50s San Francisco; fast-paced free verse resembling jazz.

BLANK VERSE: unrhymed iambic pentameter.

CAESURA: a deliberate rhetorical, grammatical, or rhythmic pause, break, cut, turn, division, or pivot in poetry.

CHANT: poem in which one or more lines are repeated over and over.

CINQUAIN: any 5-line poem or stanza; also called "quintain" or "quintet." (See also *American cinquain*.)

CONCRETE POETRY: see *emblematic poem*.

CONFESSIONAL POETRY: work that uses personal and private details from the poet's own life.

CONSONANCE: see *alliteration*.

COUPLET: stanza of 2 lines; pair of rhymed lines.

DACTYL: foot consisting of a stress followed by 2 unstressed syllables (' - -).

DIDACTIC POETRY: poetry written with the intention to instruct.

ECLECTIC: open to a variety of poetic styles (as in "eclectic taste").

EKPHRASTIC POEM: verbally presents something originally represented in visual art, though more than mere description.

ELEGY: lament in verse for someone who has died, or a reflection on the tragic nature of life.

EMBLEMATIC POEM: words or letters arranged to imitate a shape, often the subject of the poem.

ENJAMBMENT: continuation of sense and rhythmic movement from one line to the next; also called a "run-on" line.

ENVOI: a brief ending (usually to a ballade or sestina) no more than 4 lines long; summary.

EPIC POETRY: long narrative poem telling a story central to a society, culture, or nation.

EPIGRAM: short, witty, satirical poem or saying written to be remembered easily, like a punchline.

EPIGRAPH: a short verse, note, or quotation that appears at the beginning of a poem or section; usually presents an idea or theme on which the poem elaborates, or contributes background information not reflected in the poem itself.

EPITAPH: brief verse commemorating a person/group of people who died.

EXPERIMENTAL POETRY: work that challenges conventional ideas of poetry by exploring new techniques, form, language, and visual presentation.

FIBS: short form based on the mathematical progression known as the Fibonacci sequence; syllable counts for each line are 1/1/2/3/5/8/13 (count for each line is derived by adding the counts for the previous two lines).

FLARF: a malleable term that may refer to 1) poetic and creative text pieces by the Flarflist Collective; any poetry created from search engine (such as Google) results; any intentionally bad, zany, or trivial poetry.

FOOT: unit of measure in a metrical line of poetry. Found poem: text lifted from a non-poetic source such as an ad and presented as a poem.

FREE VERSE: unmetrical verse (lines not counted for accents, syllables, etc.).

GHAZAL: Persian poetic form of 5-15 unconnected, independent couplets; associative jumps may be made from couplet to couplet.

GREETING CARD POETRY: resembles verses in greeting cards; sing-song meter and rhyme.

HAIBUN: originally, a Japanese form in which elliptical, often autobiographical prose is interspersed with haiku.

HAIKAI NO RENGA: see *renku*.

HAY(NA)KY: a 3-line form, with 1 word in line 1, 2 words in line 2, and 3 words in line 3.

HAIKU: originally, a Japanese form of a single vertical line with 17 sound symbols in a 5-7-5 pattern. In English, typically a 3-line poem with fewer than 17 syllables in no set pattern, but exhibiting a 2-part juxtapositional structure, seasonal reference, imagistic immediacy, and a moment of keen perception of nature or human nature. The term is both singular and plural.

HOKKU: the starting verse of a renga or renku, in 5, 7, and then 5 sound symbols in Japanese; or in three lines, usually totaling fewer than 17 syllables, in English; the precursor for what is now called haiku. (See also *haiku*).

IAMB: foot consisting of an unstressed syllable followed by a stress (- ').Iambic pentameter: consists of 5 iambic feet per line.

IMAGIST POETRY: short, free verse lines that present images without comment or explanation; strongly influenced by haiku and other Oriental forms.

KYRIELLE: French form; 4-line stanza with 8-syllable lines, the final line a refrain.

LANGUAGE POETRY: attempts to detach words from traditional meanings to produce something new and unprecedented.Limerick: 5-line stanza rhyming *aabba*; pattern of stresses/ line is traditionally 3-3-2-2-3; often bawdy or scatalogical.

LINE: basic compositional unit of a poem; measured in feet if metrical.

LINKED POETRY: written through the collaboration of 2 or more poets creating a single poetic work.Long poem: exceeds length and scope of short lyric or narrative poem; defined arbitrarily, often as more than 2 pages or 100 lines.

LYRIC POETRY: expresses personal emotion; music predominates over narrative or drama.

METAPHOR: 2 different things are likened by identifying one as the other (A=B).Meter: the rhythmic measure of a line.

MINUTE: a 12-line poem consisting of 60 syllables, with a syllabic line count of 8,4,4,4,8,4,4,4, 8,4,4,4; often consists of rhyming couplets.

MODERNIST POETRY: work of the early 20th century literary movement that sought to break with the past, rejecting outmoded literary traditions, diction, and form while encouraging innovation and reinvention.

NARRATIVE POETRY: poem that tells a story.

NEW FORMALISM: contemporary literary movement to revive formal verse.

NONSENSE VERSE: playful, with language and/or logic that defies ordinary understanding.

OCTAVE: stanza of 8 lines.

ODE: a songlike, or lyric, poem; can be passionate, rhapsodic, and mystical, or a formal address to a person on a public or state occasion.

PANTOUM: Malayan poetic form of any length; consists of 4-line stanzas, with lines 2 and 4 of one quatrain repeated as lines 1 and 3 of the next; final stanza reverses lines 1 and 3 of the previous quatrain and uses them as lines 2 and 4; traditionally each stanza rhymes *abab*.

PETRARCHAN SONNET: octave rhymes *abbaabba*; sestet may rhyme *cdcdcd, cdedce, ccdccd, cddcdd, edecde,* or *cddcee.*

PROSE POEM: brief prose work with intensity, condensed language, poetic devices, and other poetic elements.

QUATRAIN: stanza of 4 lines.

REFRAIN: a repeated line within a poem, similar to the chorus of a song.

REGIONAL POETRY: work set in a particular locale, imbued with the look, feel, and culture of that place.

RENGA: originally, a Japanese collaborative form in which 2 or more poets alternate writing 3 lines, then 2 lines for a set number of verses (such as 12, 18, 36, 100, and 1,000). There are specific rules for seasonal progression, placement of moon and flower verses, and other requirements. (See also *linked poetry.*)

RENGAY: an American collaborative 6-verse, thematic linked poetry form, with 3-line and 2-line verses in the following set pattern for 2 or 3 writers (letters represent poets, numbers indicate the lines in each verse): A3-B2-A3-B3-A2-B3 or A3-B2-C3-A2-B3-C2. All verses, unlike renga or renku, must develop at least one common theme.

RENKU: the modern term for renga, and a more popular version of the traditionally more aristocratic renga. (See also *linked poetry.*)

RHYME: words that sound alike, especially words that end in the same sound.

RHYTHM: the beat and movement of language (rise and fall, repetition and variation, change of pitch, mix of syllables, melody of words).

RONDEAU: French form of usually 15 lines in 3 parts, rhyming *aabba aabR aabbaR* (*R* indicates a refrain repeating the first word or phrase of the opening line).

SENRYU: originally, a Japanese form, like haiku in form, but chiefly humorous, satirical, or ironic, and typically aimed at human foibles. (See also *haiku* and *zappai.*)

SEQUENCE: a group or progression of poems, often numbered as a series.

SESTET: stanza of 6 lines.

SESTINA: fixed form of 39 lines (6 unrhymed stanzas of 6 lines each, then an ending 3-line stanza), each stanza repeating the same 6 non-rhyming end-words in a different order; all 6 end-words appear in the final 3-line stanza.

SHAKESPEAREAN SONNET: rhymes *abab cdcd efef gg.*Sijo: originally a Korean narrative or thematic lyric form. The first line introduces a situation or problem that is countered or developed in line 2, and concluded with a twist in line 3. Lines average 14-16 syllables in length.

SIMILE: comparison that uses a linking word (*like, as, such as, how*) to clarify the similarities.

SONNET: 14-line poem (traditionally an octave and sestet) rhymed in iambic pentameter; often presents an argument but may also present a description, story, or meditation.Spondee: foot consisting of 2 stressed syllables (' ').

STANZA: group of lines making up a single unit; like a paragraph in prose.

STROPHE: often used to mean "stanza"; also a stanza of irregular line lengths.

SURREALISTIC POETRY: of the artistic movement stressing the importance of dreams and the subconscious, nonrational thought, free associations, and startling imagery/juxtapositions.

TANKA: originally, a Japanese form in one or 2 vertical lines with 31 sound symbols in a 5-7-5-7-7 pattern. In English, typically a 5-line lyrical poem with fewer than 31 syllables in no set syllable pattern, but exhibiting a caesura, turn, or pivot, and often more emotional and conversational than haiku.

TERCET: stanza or poem of 3 lines.

TERZA RIMA: series of 3-line stanzas with interwoven rhyme scheme (*aba, bcb, cdc . . .*).

TROCHEE: foot consisting of a stress followed by an unstressed syllable (' -).

VILLANELLE: French form of 19 lines (5 tercets and a quatrain); line 1 serves as one refrain (repeated in lines 6, 12, 18), line 3 as a second refrain (repeated in lines 9, 15, 19); traditionally, refrains rhyme with each other and with the opening line of each stanza.

VISUAL POEM: see *emblematic poem.*

WAKA: literally, "Japanese poem," the precursor for what is now called tanka. (See also *tanka.*)

WAR POETRY: poems written about warfare and military life; often written by past and current soldiers; may glorify war, recount exploits, or demonstrate the horrors of war.

ZAPPAI: originally Japanese; an unliterary, often superficial witticism masquerading as haiku or senryu; formal term for joke haiku or other pseudo-haiku.

ZEUGMA: a figure of speech in which a single word (or, occasionally, a phrase) is related in one way to words that precede it, and in another way to words that follow it.

GENERAL INDEX

X

Y

Z

EDITOR NAMES INDEX

M